WHAT ROMANCE DO I READ NEXT?

A Reader's Guide to
Recent Romance
Fiction

Explore your options!

Gale databases are offered in a variety of formats

 The information in this Gale publication is also available in some or all of the formats described here. Your Gale Representative will be happy to fill you in. Call toll-free 1-800-877-GALE.

GaleNet

A number of Gale databases are now available on GaleNet, our new online information resource accessible through the Internet. GaleNet features an easy-to-use end-user interface, the powerful search capabilities of BRS/SEARCH retrieval software and ease of access through the World Wide Web.

Diskette/Magnetic Tape

Many Gale databases are available on diskette or magnetic tape, allowing systemwide access to your most-used information sources through existing computer systems. Data can be delivered on a variety of mediums (DOS-formatted diskettes, 9-track tape, 8mm data tape) and in industry-standard formats (comma-delimited, tagged, fixed-field).

CD-ROM

A variety of Gale titles are available on CD-ROM, offering maximum flexibility and powerful search software.

Online

For your convenience, many Gale databases are available through popular online services, including DIALOG, NEXIS, DataStar, ORBIT, OCLC, Thomson Financial Network's I/Plus Direct, HRIN, Prodigy, Sandpoint's HOOVER, the Library Corporation's NLightN and Telebase Systems.

WHAT ROMANCE DO I READ NEXT?

A Reader's Guide to Recent Romance Fiction

GALE

Detroit
New York
Toronto
London

KRISTEN RAMSDELL

Kristen Ramsdell

Gale Research Staff:
Coordinating Editor: Charles B. Montney
Contributing Editors: Victoria A. Coughlin, Lydia Fink, Nancy Franklin, William Harmer,
Arlene Johnson, Debra M. Kirby, Rebecca Mansour, Dana Shonta
Managing Editor: Ann V. Evory

Production Director: MaryBeth Trimper
External Production Assistant: Shanna P. Heilveil
Product Design Manager: Cynthia Baldwin
Senior Art Director: Mary Krzewinski
Cover Photography: *The Kiss* from the Culver Collection/Superstock;
Woman Reading Book by Positive Images (model: Leslie Norback)

Manager, Technical Support Services: Theresa Rocklin
Programmer/Analyst: Joshua E. Cohen

∞™ This book is printed on acid-free paper that meets the minimum requirements of American National Standard for Information Sciences—Permanence Paper for Printed Library Materials, ANSI Z39.48-1984.

ISBN 0-7876-1867-5

Printed in the United States of America
10 9 8 7 6 5 4 3 2 1

Contents

Introduction

"Love is all around," goes the theme from *The Mary Tyler Moore* television show, and it's true. Love surrounds us in songs, in the movies, and especially in print. Romance fiction accounts for a huge share of total book sales, and claims a 48.6% chunk of mass market paperback sales, according to industry statistics ("True Romance," The Fresno Bee, July 7, 1995, Section B, page 41). Millions of people read romances, and they read a lot of them—up to 40 books per month, according to bookselling giant Barnes & Noble. This is no flash in the pan phenomenon either. Love stories have been popular for centuries, despite their detractors. Romance fiction is constantly expanding into new territories, exploring new issues, and responding to the wants of readers, ensuring that romances will be popular for many years to come.

What Romance Do I Read Next? brings together an impressive collection of some of the best romantic fiction of recent years. The 2,000 books profiled in this reference have been collected from the first seven editions of Gale's acclaimed series *What Do I Read Next?*, which has been published since 1989. An entry refers to up to five other titles, each selected for their quality as well as their similarity to the original title. Thus, *What Romance Do I Read Next?* unlocks the door to thousands of books and points the way to countless hours of reading pleasure for fans of romance fiction.

About the Author

The 2,000 romances that appear in *What Romance Do I Read Next?*, along with their recommended similar titles, were originally selected by Kristen Ramsdell, who is an associate librarian at California State University in Hayward.

She writes a romance review column for *Library Journal*, and is the author of *Happily Ever After: A Guide to Reading Interests in Romance Fiction* (published by Libraries Unlimited, 1987). She was also named Librarian of the Year by Romance Writers of America in 1996. Kristen and her assistants have spent countless hours over the years reading and researching romance fiction, bringing their expertise to romance readers via the *What Do I Read Next?* series.

Details on 2,000 Titles

What Romance Do I Read Next? describes 2,000 quality romance titles published between 1989 and 1996. The entries in the main section are listed alphabetically by author, so that an author's entries all appear together. Readers will find the following information:

- **Author or editor's name** and real name if a pseudonym is used. Co-authors and co-editors are also listed where applicable.
- **Book title.**
- **Date and place of publication; name of publisher.**
- **Series name.**
- **Story type:** Specific categories within the Romance genre, identified by the compiling expert. Definitions of these types are listed in the "Key to Story Types" section following the Introduction.
- **Major characters:** Names and brief descriptions of up to three characters featured in the title.
- **Time period:** Tells when the story takes place.
- **Locale**: Tells where the story takes place.

- **What the book is about:** A brief (usually two- or three-sentence) plot summary.

- **Other books you might like:** Titles by other authors written on a similar theme or in a similar style. These titles further the reader's exploration of the genre. The titles mentioned in this rubric range from contemporary books to classics in the genre, all sharing one or several components similar to the main title.

Indexes Answer Readers' Questions

The eight indexes in *What Romance Do I Read Next?*, used separately or in conjunction with each other, create many pathways to the featured titles, answering general questions or locating specific titles. For example:

"What are the recommended books in the Wind Dancer Trilogy?"

The SERIES INDEX lists entries by the name of the series of which they are a part. Note: not every title in a series is necessarily listed in *What Romance Do I Read Next?*

"I like books that take place during the British Regency period. Can you recommend any new ones?"

The STORY TYPE INDEX lists books by story type or "subgenre," for example, Historical/Regency, Contemporary, or Gothic. For the definitions of story types, see the "Key to Story Types" beginning on page xiii.

"Are there any romances set in New England?"

The GEOGRAPHIC INDEX lists titles by their locale. This can help readers pinpoint an area in which they may have a particular interest, such as their hometown, another country, or even Cyberspace.

"I'm looking for a romance novel set during prehistoric times."

The TIME PERIOD INDEX is a chronological listing of the time settings in which the main entry titles take place.

"What romances are available in which the heroine is a lawyer?"

The CHARACTER DESCRIPTION INDEX identifies the major characters by occupation (e.g. Accountant, Editor, Librarian) or persona (e.g. Historical Figure, Noblewoman).

"Has anyone written any new books in the last few years with Sherlock Holmes in them?"

The CHARACTER NAME INDEX lists the major characters named in the entries. This can help readers who remember some information about a book, but not an author or title.

"What has Amanda Quick written recently?"

The AUTHOR INDEX contains the names of all authors featured in the entries and those listed under "Other books

you might like." The Author Index contains both real names and pseudonyms. Entries listed in the main section under the author's pseudonym will appear in the Author Index under both the author's pseudonym and real name.

"What books are like *Outlander*?"

The TITLE INDEX includes all main entry titles and all titles recommended under the rubric and "Other books you might like" in one alphabetical listing. Thus a reader can find a specific title, new or old, then go to that entry to find out what new titles are similar.

The indexes can also be used together to narrow down or broaden choices. A reader interested in mysteries set in New York during the 19th century would consult the TIME PERIOD INDEX and GEOGRAPHIC INDEX to see which titles appear in both. With the AUTHOR and TITLE indexes, which include all books listed within entries under "Other books you might like," it is easy to compile an extensive list of recommended reading, beginning with a recently published title or a classic from the past.

Also Available in Electronic Format

The entries in *What Romance Do I Read Next?* can also be found in Gale's *What Do I Read Next? CD-ROM*. This electronic product encompasses over 55,000 books, including genre fiction, mainstream fiction, and nonfiction. All the books included in the *What Do I Read Next? CD-ROM* are recommended by librarians or other experts or appear on bestseller lists. The user-friendly software allows users to refine their searching by using several criteria, while making it easy to identify similar titles for further research and reading. An annual subscription includes four quarterly releases, each including new and updated information. For information or to order the *What Do I Read Next? CD-ROM*, contact Gale.

Suggestions Are Welcome

The editors welcome any comments and suggestions for enhancing and improving *What Romance Do I Read Next?*. Please address correspondence to:

Editors
What Romance Do I Read Next?
Gale Research
835 Penobscot Bldg.
Detroit, MI 48226-4094
Phone: 313-961-2242
Toll-free: 800-347-4253
Fax: 313-961-6083

Key to Story Types

Anthology - A collection of short stories by different authors, usually sharing a common theme.

Collection - A book of short stories by a single author.

Contemporary - A romance set in the present.

Contemporary/Exotic - Set in the present but with an especially unusual or exotic setting, e.g. the tent of a desert sheik, or a boat on the Amazon.

Contemporary/Fantasy - A contemporary romance that makes use of fantasy or supernatural elements.

Contemporary/Innocent - A romance set in the present that contains little or no sex. The Harlequin Romance lines and the romances published by Avalon Books are examples of this subgenre.

Contemporary/Mainstream - A romance set in the present that would be more properly categorized as fiction rather than romance. Often there is a strong love story line, but the primary emphasis is on other aspects of the plot.

Ethnic - A romance in which the ethnic background of the characters is integral to the story. Usually the focus is on an American ethnic minority group (e.g. African American, Asian American, Native American, Latino) and the two main characters are members of this group.

Fantasy - A romance that is not a Gothic or a Romantic Suspense but contains fantasy or supernatural elements.

Futuristic - A romance with a science fiction setting. Often these stories are set on other planets, aboard spaceships or space stations, or on Earth in an imaginary future or, in some cases, past.

Gothic - A romance with a strong mystery suspense plot that emphasizes mood, atmosphere, and/or supernatural or paranormal elements. Unexplained events, ancient family secrets, and a general feeling of impending doom often characterize these tales. These stories are most often set in the past, but several authors (e.g. Phyllis Whitney and Barbara Michaels) write gothics with contemporary settings.

Historical - A romance that takes place in the past that doesn't fall into one of the more specific Historical categories.

Historical/American Civil War - Set during the American Civil War (War Between the States), 1861-1865.

Historical/American Revolution - Set during the American Revolutionary period.

Historical/American West - Set in the Western portion of the United States, usually during the second half of the nineteenth century. Stories often involve the hardships of pioneer life (Indian raids, range wars, climatic disasters, etc.) and the main characters (most often the hero) can be of

Native American extraction.

Historical/American West Coast - Set in the American Far West (California, Oregon, Washington, or Alaska). Stories often focus on the Gold Rush and the tension between Spanish Land Grant families and immigrants from the Pacific Rim, usually China.

Historical/Antebellum American South - Set in the American Old South (prior to the Civil War).

Historical/Canadian West - Set in the Western or frontier portions of Canada, usually during the nineteenth century. Stories most often revolve around the hardships of frontier life.

Historical/Colonial America - Set in America before the American Revolution, 1620-1775. Stories featuring the Jamestown Colony, the Salem Witch Trials, and the French and Indian War are especially popular.

Historical/Edwardian - Set during the reign of Edward VII (1901-1910) and generally covers the period from Queen Victoria's death to the beginning of the First World War. Some of these stories are of the "Upstairs-Downstairs" variety.

Historical/Elizabethan - A romance set during the reign of Elizabeth I of England (1558-1603). There is some overlap with the last part of the Historical/Renaissance category but the emphasis is British.

Historical/Exotic - Historical romance set in an unusual or exotic place, e.g. a Middle Eastern harem or an archaeological dig in South America.

Historical/Fantasy - Historical romance that makes use of fantasy or supernatural elements.

Historical/French Revolution - Set during the French Revolution (1789-1795). Stories often focus on rescuing French nobility from the guillotine.

Historical/Georgian - Set during the reigns of the first three "Georges" of England. Roughly corresponds to the eighteenth century. Stories often focus on the Jacobite Rebellions and the escapades of Bonnie Prince Charlie.

Historical/Mainstream - Historical romance that would be more properly categorized as fiction rather than romance. Often there is a strong love story, but the primary emphasis is on other aspects of the plot.

Historical/Medieval - Set during the Middle Ages, approximately the fifth through the fifteenth centuries. Stories feature battles, raids, crusades, and court intrigues; plot-lines associated with the Battle of Hastings (1066) are especially popular.

Historical/Post-American Civil War - Set just following the American Civil War. These stories often deal with Reconstruction issues and the healing of wounds between North and South.

Historical/Post-American Revolution - Set mostly in America in the years following the American Revolution. Includes the last part of the eighteenth century.

Historical/Post-French Revolution - Set during the aftermath of the French Revolution, usually in France, but occasionally in England.

Historical/Pre-history - Set prior to the Middle Ages, but does not have a Classical Greek or Roman setting.

Historical/Regency - A romance that is set during the Regency period (1811-1820) but is not a "Regency Romance" (see below).

Historical/Renaissance - Set during the years of the Renaissance. This is a rather fuzzy category because the Renaissance took place over several centuries and began in Italy two hundred years before it finally reached England.

Historical/Roaring Twenties - Set in the 1920s, usually in America. Stories reflect the wild flamboyance of the period and often center on the ultimate crash of the stock market.

Historical/Russian Revolution - Set around and during the Russian Revolution (1917). Stories often feature disenfranchised Russian nobility and reflect the political and social unrest of the period.

Historical/Seventeenth Century - A romance set during the seventeenth century. Stories of this type often center around the clashes between the Royalists and the Cromwellians and the Restoration.

Historical/Victorian - Set during the reign of Queen Victoria, 1837-1901. This designation does not include works with a predominately American setting.

Historical/Victorian America - Set in America, usually the Eastern part, during the Victorian Period, 1837-1901.

Historical/War of 1812 - Set during the War of 1812 (1812-1815).

Historical/World War I - Set during the First World War (1914-1918).

Historical/World War II - Set during the Second World War (1939-1945).

Holiday Themes - A romance that focuses on or is set during a particular holiday or holiday season (e.g. Christmas, Valentine's Day, Mardi Gras).

Lesbian/Contemporary - A romance with lesbian protagonists set in the present.

Lesbian/Historical - A historical romance with lesbian ptotagonists.

Regency - A light romance involving the British upperclasses, set during the Regency Period, 1811-1820. During this time, the Prince of Wales acted as Prince Regent because of the incapacity of his father, George III. In 1820, "Prinny" became George IV. These stories, in the style of Jane Austen, are essentially comedies of manners and the emphasis is on language, wit, and style. Georgette Heyer set the standard for the modern version of this genre. This designation is also given to stories of similar type that may not fit precisely within the Regency time period.

Reincarnation - A romance in which one of the two main characters has been reincarnated as someone else. Often contains time travel elements.

Romantic Suspense - A romance with a strong mystery suspense plot. This is a broad category including works in the tradition of Mary Stewart as well as the newer women-in-jeopardy tales by writers such as Mary Higgins Clark. These stories usually have contemporary settings but some are also set in the past.

Saga- A multi-generational story that usually centers around one particular family and its trials, tribulations, successes, and loves.

Time Travel - A romance in which characters from one time are transported either literally or in spirit to another time period. The time shifts are usually between the present and another historical period. A period designation may sometimes be included (e.g. Time Change/American West) if it would seem to be particularly useful in more fully describing the story.

Young Adult - A romance written for the young adult or teenage reader. These can be sweet series romances or they can be more serious problem novels with a strong romance plotline.

Romance Awards

Affaire de Coeur Awards

1990

Classic Award--To recognize "All-Time Classics in the Romance marketplace." Designated as "keepers," these books should stand the test of time.

The Flame and the Flower by Kathleen Woodiwiss
Sweet Savage Love by Rosemary Rogers
Ballad in Blue by Linda Shaw
Now and Forever by Danielle Steel PB
Gypsy Lady by Shirlee Busbee
Love's Tender Fury by Jennifer Wilde
Fulfillment by LaVyrle Spencer
This Living Land by Dorothy Garlock
Love Cherish Me by Rebecca Brandewyne
Touch the Wind by Janet Dailey
Again the Magic by Lee Damon
Rainbow Season by Lisa Gregory
Roselynde Chronicles by Roberta Gellis
Adora by Bertrice Small
Whitney, My Love by Judith McNaught
Captive Bride by Johanna Lindsey
Black Lyon by Jude Deveraux
Devil's Embrace by Catherine Coulter
This Loving Torment by Valerie Sherwood
Caroline by Cynthia Wright

Golden Certificate Award--To recognize the best Foreign and American Historical Romance.

Historical
The Bride by Julie Garwood
Kingdom of Dreams by Judith McNaught
Hearts of Fire by Anita Mills
Love's Illusion by Katherine Sutcliffe
So Worthy My Love by Kathleen Woodiwiss
Seize the Fire by Laura Kinsale

American Historical
Fire's Lady by Barbara Bretton
Scarlet Ribbons by Judith French
Moon Flower by Shirl Henke
Savage Thunder by Johanna Lindsey
Bandit's Embrace by Lynne Murphy
San Antonio by Sara Orwig
Morning Glory by LaVyrle Spencer
Violet Fire by Catherine Coulter
Sweet Talkin' Stranger by Lori Copeland
Night Fire by Catherine Coulter
Touch of Fire by Emily Carmichael
This Time for Love by F. Rosanne Bittner
Shameless Ecstasy by Thea Devine

Silver Certificate Award--For the Best Contemporary Romances of 1989.

Mother Knows Best by Barbara Bretton
Mariah by Sandra Canfield

Miami Midnight by Maggie Davis
Family Fortunes by Sara Orwig
A Touch of Class by Rita Rainville
Best Kept Secrets by Sandra Brown
Best Laid Plans by Nora Roberts
Gift of Fire by Jayne Ann Krentz
Love This Stranger by Linda Shaw
Night of the Hunter by Jennifer Green
Midnight Blue by Nancy London

Golden Unicorn Award--For the Best Time and Travel and the Best Futuristic romances.

Time and Travel
Knight in Shining Armor by Jude Deveraux
Give Me Tonight by Lisa Kleypas
Time Was by Nora Roberts

Futuristic
Shield's Lady by Amanda Glass (Jayne Ann Krentz)

Silver Pen Award--"Represents the Shining Stars of today's romance market."

Kathleen Woodiwiss
Jude Deveraux
Dorothy Garlock
Shirl Henke
Judith McNaught
Anita Mills
LaVyrle Spencer
Silvie Sommerfield
Johanna Lindsey
Fern Michaels
Bertrice Small
Katherine Sutcliffe
Betina Krahn
Julie Garwood
Maggie Davis
Karen Robards
Nora Roberts
Catherine Coulter
Georgina Gentry
Linda Shaw
Virgina Henley
Barbara Britton
Sara Orwig
Janelle Taylor
Sandra Lee Smith
Marylyle Rogers

Golden Medallion Award--For the romance of the year.

So Worthy My Love by Kathleen Woodiwiss

Silver Quill Award--For "All Time '80s Best Contemporary" Romance.

Miami Midnight by Maggie Davis
Family Fortunes by Sara Orwig
Love This Stranger by Linda Shaw
Hot December by Deanna James

Golden Quill Award--For "All Time '80s Best Historical" Romance.

Whitney, My Love by Judith McNaught
Hummingbird by LaVyrle Spencer
When Love Awaits by Johanna Lindsey
Stormfire by Christine Monson
Love Cherish Me by Rebecca Brandewyne
Wind and the Sea by Marsha Canham
Blaze by Susan Johnson
Rose in Winter by Kathleen Woodiwiss
Windflower by Laura London

1991
Favorite Romantic Cover
Guardian Angel by Julie Garwood
Favorite Romance of the Year
Morning Glory by LaVyrle Spencer
Outstanding Achievement in Romance
Judith McNaught
Favorite Mainstream Historical Romance Author
Judith McNaught
Favorite Historical Romance Author
Catherine Coulter
Favorite Futuristic/Time Travel Romance
Time Spun Rapture by Thomasina Ring
Favorite American Historical Romance Novel
Night Flower by Shirl Henke

Persephone Awards
Presented in the area of popular fiction by WIN/WIN, a nonprofit organization in Fresno, California, whose goal is to promote literacy. Selection in most categories of the romance genre was made initially on the basis of *Affaire de Coeur's* Reader Writer Poll; final winners were chosen by WIN/WIN.

Contemporary Romance Author
Janet Dailey
Category Romance Author
Linda Howard
Historical Romance Author
Catherine Coulter
Mainstream Historical Romance Author
Judith McNaught

Mainstream Historical Fiction Author
LaVyrle Spencer
Outstanding Achievement in Romance Fiction
Judith McNaught
Up and Coming Romance Author
Jill Bartlett
Romance of the Year
Morning Glory by LaVyrle Spencer
Contemporary Romance Novel
Duncan's Bride by Linda Howard
Historical Romance Novel
Beyond the Savage Sea by JoAnn Wendt
American Historical Romance Novel
Night Flower by Shirl Henke
Foreign Historical Romance Novel
Almost Heaven by Judith McNaught
Futuristic/Time Travel Romance Novel
Time Spun Rapture by Thomasina Ring
Romantic Cover
Guardian Angel by Julie Garwood
Romantic Heroine
Gloria Summerfield in *Captain's Bride* by Kat Martin
Romantic Hero
Tyler in *A Wild Yearning* by Penelope Williamson

1991 Gold Certificate Awards
Presented by *Affaire de Coeur* as determined by its Reader-Writer Poll for romances.

Best Romance of the Year
Redeeming Love by Francine Rivers
Outstanding Hero
Khamed in *Fires in the Night* by Judith Hill; Joaquin Quinn in *Night Wind's Woman* by Shirl Henke
Outstanding Heroine
Eudora in *Fires in the Night* by Judith Hill
Best Cover
Night Wind's Woman by Shirl Henke
Best Foreign Historical
Fires in the Night by Judith Hill; *Highland Moon* by Judith E. French
Best American Historical
Promise Me Spring by Robin Lee Hatcher; *Night Wind's Woman* by Shirl Henke; *Western Winds* by Theresa Di Benedetto

1991 Golden Pen Award
Presented by *Affaire de Coeur* as determined by its Reader-Writer Poll to the favorite romance authors.

Amanda Quick, Julie Garwood, Robin Lee Hatcher, Betina Krahn, Shirl Henke, Anita Mills, Rosanne Bittner, Francine Rivers, and Karen Robards

1991 Outstanding Achievers Awards
Presented by *Affaire de Coeur* as determined by its Reader-Writer Poll in conjunction with a survey of booksellers for outstanding achievement in the sales of romance fiction

Sandra Brown, Johanna Lindsey, Judith McNaught, and LaVyrle Spencer

1991 Silver Pen Award
Presented by *Affaire de Coeur* as determined by its Reader-Writer Poll for the favorite contemporary romance authors.

Jayne Anne Krentz, Laura Paige, Deborah Smith, Linda Howard, Iris Johansen, Sandra Chastain, and Nora Roberts

1991 Best up-and-coming contemporary authors
Jane Bonander and Judith Hill

1994 Rom-Con Awards
Presented by *Affaire de Coeur* at its annual convention, Rom-Con. Awards are selected by popular vote. The following awards are for the 1993 calendar year and were presented in May 1994.

Romance of the Year
Cry Wolf by Tami Hoag
Best Contemporary-Category
Positive Proof by Sandra Canfield
Best Contemporary
Perfect by Judith McNaught
Cry Wolf by Tami Hoag
Best Overall Historical
Secrets by Brenda Joyce
Best Foreign Historical
The Viking by Margaret Moore
Lord of the Night by Cara Miles
Best American Historical
Across a Rebel Sea by Cheryl Biggs
Best Regency
The Highwayman by Catherine Reynolds
Awakening Heart by Dorothy Mack
Best Futuristic
A Distant Star by Anne Avery
Heart of the Wolf by Saranne Dawson
Best Time Travel
Fire and Rain by Kathleen Eagle
Time Remembered by Elizabeth Crane
A Time To Love Again by Flora Speer
Best Up-and-Coming Author
Linda Hughes for *Outside Rules*
Best Cover
Zebra for *Across a Rebel Sea*

Outstanding Heroine
Elora Simmon in *From a Silver Heart* by Elizabeth Ann Michaels
Outstanding Hero
Bruce Warfield in *From a Silver Heart* by Elizabeth Ann Michaels
Outstanding Achiever (Presented for contributions to the romance industry—imagery, promotion, articles or activities that reflect positively on the romance market)
    Brenda Joyce
    Virginia Henley
    Nora Roberts
Top Ten Favorite Historical Romance Authors
(in descending order)
    Judith McNaught
    Elizabeth Lowell
    Laura Kinsale
    Amanda Quick
    Arnette Lamb
    Cheryl Biggs
    Jude Deveraux
    Heather Graham
    Elizabeth Ann Michaels
    Bonnie K. Winn
Top Ten Favorite Contemporary Romance Authors
(in descending order)
    Nora Roberts
    Ann Maxwell
    Debbie Macomber
    Jayne Ann Krentz
    Linda Howard
    Sandra Brown
    Jude Deveraux
    Tami Hoag
    Sandra Canfield
    Linda Lael Miller
Reviewers' Award of Excellence
(in descending order)
    Hearts Enslaved by Judith Hill
    Half Way to Paradise by Emily Carmichael
    Forever His by Shelly Thacker

1995 Affaire de Coeur Awards

Best Cover
Apache Legacy
Best Inspirational
Iditarod Dream by Janelle Jamison
Best Regency
Dark Angel by Mary Balogh
Best Futuristic
All's Fair by Anne Avery
Best Time Travel
When Lightning Strikes by Kristin Hannah

Up and Coming Writers
    Paranormal: Susan Krinard
    Historical: Karen Lockwood
    Contemporary: Sharon Sala
Best American Historical
Pure Sin by Susan Johnson
Best Foreign Historical
Sweet Madness Mine by Elizabeth Michaels
Best Overall Historical
Forbidden Fires by Bonnie Winn
Best Contemporary
It Had to Be You by Susan Elizabeth Phillips
Romance of the Year
It Had to Be You by Susan Elizabeth Phillips
Top Favorite Authors
Jill Barnett, Madeline Baker, Janet Dailey, Barbara Delinsky, Julie Garwood, Georgina Gentry, Kristin Hannah, Tami Hoag, Linda Howard, Susan Johnson, Jayne Ann Krentz, Elizabeth Lowell, Judith McNaught, Nora Roberts
Outstanding Achiever
Linda Howard
***Affaire de Coeur* Hall of Fame**
Jennifer Blake, Janet Dailey, Patricia Hagan, Kathleen Woodiwiss
Reviewers' Award for Excellence
    Inspirational: *An Echo in the Darkness* by Francine Rivers
    Ethnic/Multicultural: *No Ordinary Love* by Monique Gilmore
    Category: *Luck of the Irish* by Sharon Brandos
    Regency: *Elizabeth's Gift* by Donna Davidson
    Western/Americana: *Wildest Dreams* by Rosanne Bittner
    Supernatural: *For All Eternity* by Linda Lael Miller
    Futuristic: *Stardust Dreams* by Marilyn Campbell
    Contemporary: *Dark Paradise* by Tami Hoag and *Shameless* by Jennifer Blake
    Historical: *Heartstrings* by Rebecca Paisley
    Medieval: *Chieftain* by Arnette Lamb

1996 Affaire de Coeur Awards

Best Contemporary Novel
Gotta Have It by Faye Hughes
Contemporary Ethnic
Body and Soul by Felicia Mason
Overall Historical
Dark Warrior by Iris Johansen
Foreign Historical
The Promise by Nessa Hart
American Historical
Wild Hearts by Jane Bonander
Regency
Improper Widow by Kate Moore

Futuristic
Naked in Death by J.D. Robb
Time Travel
Waiting for the Moon by Kristin Hannah
Science Fiction
Sorcerer's Lady by Debra Dier
Supernatural
Prince of Dreams by Sue Krinard
Inspirational
As Sure as the Dawn by Francine Rivers
Outstanding Achiever
Judith Krentz
Best Up and Coming Author
Nessa Hart
Top Ten Favorite Romance Authors
(in alphabetical order)
    Sandra Brown
    Jane Bonander
    Jude Devereaux
    Tami Hoag
    Linda Howard
    Faye Hughes
    Jayne Ann Krentz
    Judith McNaught
    Laurie Page
    Susan Elizabeth Phillips
    Nora Roberts
Best Cover
Wild Heart by Jane Bonander
Outstanding Heroine
Angela de Grae in *Brazen* by Susan Johnson
Outstanding Hero
Kit Braddock in *Brazen* by Susan Johnson
Romance of the Year
(tie) *Night Sins* by Tami Hoag and *The Red Head and the Preacher* by Sandra Chastain
1996 Affaire de Coeur Hall of Fame
    Shirlee Busbee
    Johanna Lindsey
    Rosemary Rogers
    Valerie Sherwood

Waldenbooks Bestselling Romance Awards

Presented by Waldenbooks for the bestselling romances of the preceding year.

1993
Original Series Romance
Falling for Rachel by Nora Roberts

Series Romance by a New Author
His Other Mother by Suzette Vann
Short Historical or Regency Romance
A Precious Jewel by Mary Balogh
Original Long Contemporary Romance
Wildest Hearts by Jayne Ann Krentz
Long Historical Romance
The Magic of You by Johanna Lindsey
Hardcover Debut Romance
Saving Grace by Julie Garwood
Special Achievement Award
Elizabeth Lowell (Ann Maxwell)
Lifetime Achievement Award
Catherine Coulter

1994
Long Contemporary Romance
November of the Heart by LaVyrle Spencer
Long Historical Romance
Seduced by Virginia Henley
Regency Romance
Tempting Harriet by Mary Balogh
Multicultural Romance
Night Song by Beverly Jenkins
Hardcover Debut Romance
For My Daughters by Barbara Delinsky
Sales Growth
The Last Bachelor by Betina Krahn
Special Achievement Award
Judith McNaught

1995
Long Historical Romance
Seduce by Virginia Henley
Long Contemporary Romance
Suddenly by Barbara Delinsky
Regency Romance
Tempting Harriet by Mary Balogh
Hardcover Debut Romance
For My Daughters by Barbara Delinsky
Multicultural Romance Romance
Night Song by Beverly Jenkins
Sales Growth
The Last Bachelor by Bettina Krahn
Special Achievement Award
Judith MacNaught

RRA-L Awards

Selected by the members of the Romance Readers Anonymous (RRA-L) electronic mailing list. First awarded in 1994.

1994

Best Short Series Romance
Cinderman by Anne Stuart
Best Long Series Romance
A Soldier's Heart by Kathleen Korbel
Best Contemporary Single Title Romance
It Had to Be You by Susan Elizabeth Phillips
Best Historical Single Title Romance
Lord of Scoundrels by Loretta Chase
Best Regency Romance
Deidre and Don Juan by Jo Beverley
Best Romantic Suspense/Mystery/Adventure
Night Smoke by Nora Roberts
Best Alternative Realities Romance
Lord of the Storm by Justine Davis
Best Time Travel Romance
Voyager by Diana Gabaldon
Best Love and Laughter Romance
It Had to Be You by Susan Elizabeth Phillips
Best All-Around 1994 Romance
It Had to Be You by Susan Elizabeth Phillips
Author Awards
> **Best Contemporary Author:** Nora Roberts and Rachel Lee
> **Best Historical Romance Author:** Jo Beverley
> **Best Series/Category Author:** Rachel Lee
> **Best All-Around Romance Author:** Elizabeth Lowell

Best Classic Romances
> **Best Classic Historical Romance:** *The Windflower* by Sharon and Tom Curtis and *Whitney, My Love* by Judith McNaught
> **Best Classic Contemporary Romance:** *Tell Me No Lies* by Elizabeth Lowell
> **Best Classic All-Around Favorite Romance:** *Pride and Predjudice* by Jane Austin
> **Best Classic Regency/Romance:** *Emily and the Dark Angel* by Jo Beverley
> **Best Classic Series/Category Romance:** *MacKenzie's Mountain* by Linda Howard
> **Best All-Around Classsic Romance Author:** Jo Beverley

1995

Best Short Series Romance
Surrender the Dark by Donna Kaufman
Best Long Series Romance
The Morning Side of Dawn by Justine Davis

Best Contemporary Single Title Romance
Heaven, Texas by Susan Elizabeth Phillips
Best Historical Single Title Romance
Only Love by Elizabeth Lowell
Best Regency Romance
The Vampire Viscount by Karen Harbaugh
Best Romantic Suspense/Mystery/Adventure
Dream Man by Linda Howard
Best Alternative Realities Romance
Knight of a Trillion Stars by Dara Joy
Best Time Travel Romance
Until Forever by Johanna Lindsey
Best Love and Laughter Romance
Basket of Wishes by Rebecca Paisley
Best All-Around 1995 Romance
Waiting for the Moon by Kristin Hannah
Author Awards
> **Best Contemporary Author:** Nora Roberts
> **Best Historical Romance Author**: Judith McNaught
> **Best Series/Category Author:** Jennifer Crusie
> **Best All-Around Romance Author**: Nora Roberts

Best Classic Romances
> **Best Classic Historical Romance:** *Pride and Prejudice* by Jane Austen
> **Best Classic Contemporary Romance:** *Sarah's Child* by Linda Howard
> **Best Classic All-Around Favorite Romance:** *Outlander* by Diana Gabaldon
> **Best Classic Regency Romance:** *Devil's Cub* by Georgette Heyer
> **Best Classic Series Romance:** *MacKenzie's Mountain* by Linda Howard
> **Best All-Around Classic Romance Author:** Nora Roberts
> **Best Romance Cover:** *Dream Man* by Linda Howard

Romance Writers Association Awards

Favorite Book of the Year (formerly Golden Choice Award)

Presented by the Romance Writers Association for the best romance of the year as determined by the membership at large. Selection is made by ballot from a slate of nominees. This and all the other RITA Awards are named after Rita Clay Estrada, RWA's first president.

1990 *Morning Glory* by LaVyrle Spencer
1991 *The Prince of Midnight* by Laura Kinsale
1992 *Outlander* by Diana Gabaldon
1993 *Come Spring* by Jill Marie Landis

1994 *Lord of the Night* by Susan Wiggs
1995 *It Had to Be You* by Susan Elizabeth Phillips

Lifetime Achievement in Romantic Fiction
Presented by the Romance Writers of America for lifetime achievement in romance fiction as determined by a vote of the RWA membership. First awarded in 1983

1991 Barbara Mertz
1992 Mary Stewart
1993 Janet Dailey
1994 Ann Maxwell
1995 Jayne Ann Krentz

Janet Dailey Award
Presented by the Romance Writers of America for the romance novel which best raises public consciousness about an important social issue. First awarded in 1994 for the previous year.

1993 *My Wild Rose* by Deborah Camp
1994 *Coming Up Roses* by Catherine Anderson
1995 *The Trouble with Joe* by Emilie Richards

Golden Heart RITA Awards
Presented by the Romance Writers of America for the best romance novel by an unpublished writer. Golden Hearts are given in a number of categories, some of which have changed over the years.

1989
Traditional Romance
Heaven Sent by Jackie Radoumis
Short Contemporary Romance
Merrie for Love by Donna Lynn Deeb
Long Contemporary Romance
Nothing Could Be Finer by Gloria Alvarez
Young Adult
The Odd Couple by Janie Locke Begeman
Single Title Release-Contemporary
Ultimate Glory by Ann Linderman
Historical Series Romance
A Handful of Heaven by Kristin Hannah
Single Title Release-Historical
Candle in the Window by Christina Dodd
Regency
The Monthaven Legacy by Thomasina Robinson
Romantic Suspense
Secrets to Share by Julia Brinegar

1990
Traditional Romance
By the Book by Sandra Novy Chvostal

Short Contemporary Romance
Red Hawk's Return by Deborah Vargas
Long Contemporary Romance
No Limit to Love by Kate Freiman
Young Adult
A Summer Nanny by Donna Jean Tennis
Single Title Contemporary
Dream Givers, Dream Robbers by Crystal Stovall
Historical Series Romance
Night Singer by Michele Wyan
Single Title Historical
Wings of the Storm by Susan Sizemore
Regency
Town Bronze by Barbara A. Yirka
Romantic Suspense
Beloved Wife, Mother and Mistress by Sarah Wolford

1991
Best Traditional Romance
Redeeming Love by Francine Rivers
Short Contemporary Romance
Beauty and the Beastmaster by Carol Rusley
Long Contemporary Romance
Yesterday's Hero by Karen Muir
Young Adult Romance
Tug of War by Barbara A. Scott
Regency Romance
A Delicate Condition by Angie Ray
Romantic Suspense
Hard Evidence by Laurie Gilbert
Futuristic/Fantasy/Paranormal Romance
The Beckoning Ghost by Catherine Kohman
Series Historical Romance
A Journey Home by Susan Kay Law
Single Title Contemporary Romance
The Killing Hour by Lynn Miller

1992
Traditional Romance
Wee-Care by Elizabeth Eliot
Short Contemporary Series
Deja Vu by Metsy Gravois Hingle
Long Contemporary Series
Explosive Attraction by Gay Thornton
Young Adult
Video Magic by Victoria Simmons
Regency
Baron and the Bookseller by June Lea Calvin
Romantic Suspense/Gothic
The Rivers Run Free by Laurie Creasy
Futuristic/Fantasy/Paranormal
A Margin in Time by Laura Hayden

Series Historical
The Raven's Lady by Kate Welsh
Single Title Contemporary
Secrets That Free by Tina Ritter Wainscott
Single Title Historical
A Touch of Camelot by Donna Grove

1994
Traditional Romance
Nothing Ventured by Betty Monthei
Short Contemporary Series
Hale's Point by Patricia Burford Ryan
Long Contemporary Series
Gideon's Promise
Young Adult
Ghostly Acts by Melinda Rucker Haynes
Regency
Lord of St. Leger's Find by Jennifer Zorger
Romantic Suspense/Gothic
Heavenly Bodies by Lori L. Harris
Futuristic/Fantasy/Paranormal
The Crystal Prophecy by Janice M. Tarantino
Series Historical
Heart's Keep by Kayla Westra
Single Title Contemporary
The Gospel Truth by Rachel Gibson
Single Title Historical
Lord of Misrule by Stephanie Maynard

1995
Traditional Romance
Strong, Silent Type by Leanna Wilson
Short Contemporary Series
Tornado Ali by Robin Rouse Wells
Long Contemporary
Deceived by Rexanne Rustand
Young Adult
Junkyard Annie by Rita Herron
Regency
A Bargain with Fate by Annemarie Hasnain
Romantic Suspense/Gothic
Wrong Time, Wrong Place by Kathleen S. Nance
Paranormal/Fantasy/Time Travel Romance
Time Was by Linda G. Harmon
Long Historical
Bradenholm's Bride by Linda S. Needham
Single Title Contemporary
Child of Hope by Sharon C. Mignerey
Historical
Blackthorne's Revenge by Melitta Kit Dee
Inspirational
Consider Her Ways by Vince Brach

ARTemis Awards
Presented by the Romance Writers of America for best published romance novel cover. Determined by popular vote at the annual conference.

1993
Young adult
The Dream Horse by Virginia Campbell Scott
Regency
A Reluctant Heart by Lois Stewart
Paranormal
Whispers in Time by Becky Lee Weyrich
Contemporary Single Title
Cry Wolf by Tami Hoag
Contemporary Series
Two for the Road by Mary Anne Wilson
Historical
The Mist and the Magic by Susan Wiggs

1995
Young Adult
Paradise by Cheryl Zack. Broeck Steadman, Artist
Regency
Regency Diamonds by Brenda Hiatt (Barber). Robert Sabin, Artist
Paranormal
Prince of Wolves by Susan Krinard. Steve Assel, Artist
Contemporary Single Title
Sins by Jillian Grey (Donna Julian). Edwin Herder, Artist
Contemporary Series
Snow Bride by Dallas Schulze. Derek James, Artist
Historical
Mistress by Amanda Quick (Jayne Ann Krentz). Alan Ayers, Artist

RITA Awards
Presented by the Romance Writers of America for the best romance novel published during the year. Golden Medallions are given in a number of categories, some of which have changed over the year.

1990
Best Traditional Romance
Rhapsody in Bloom by Mona Van Wieren
Best Short Contemporary Series Romance
Night of the Hunter by Jennifer Greene
Best Long Contemporary Series Romance
The Ice Cream Man by Kathleen Korbel
Best Young Adult
Renee by Vivian Schurfranz
Best Contemporary Single Title Release
Private Relations by Diane Chamberlain

Best Historical Series Romance
Silver Noose by Patricia Gardner Evans
Best Historical Single Title Release
The Bride by Julie Garwood
Best Regency Romance
The Rake and the Reformer by Mary Jo Putney
Best Romantic Suspense
Perchance to Dream by Kathleen Korbel
Best First Book
Out of the Blue by Alaina Hawthorne

1991
Best Traditional Romance
Song of the Lorelei by Christine Fiorotto (writing as Lucy Gordon)
Best Short Contemporary Series Romance
Step Into My Parlor by Janece Hudson (writing as Jan Hudson)
Best Long Contemporary Series Romance
Patrick Gallagher's Widow by Cheryl Reavis
Best Contemporary Single Title Release
Public Secrets by Nora Roberts
Best Historical Series Romance
A Wild Yearning by Penelope Williamson
Best Historical Single Title Release
Where Love Dwells by Elizabeth Awbrey Beach (writing as Elizabeth Stuart)
Best Regency
The Sandalwood Princess by Loretta Chokani (writing as Loretta Chase)
Best Romance Suspense
Night Spice by Sandra Canfield (writing as Karen Keast)
Best First Novel
Black Horse Island by Nancy Harwood Bulk (writing as Dee Holmes)

1992
Best Traditional Romance
Every Kind of Heaven by Bethany Campbell (Sally McCluskey)
Best Short Contemporary Series Romance
A Human Touch by Glenda Sanders (Glenda Kachelmeier)
Best Long Contemporary Series Romance
A Rose for Maggie by Kathleen Korbel (Eileen Dreyer)
Best Young Adult
Now I Lay Me Down to Sleep by Lurlene McDaniel
Best Contemporary Single Title
A Man to Die For by Kathleen Korbel (Eileen Dreyer)
Best Historical Series Romance
The Tender Texan by Jodi Thomas (Jodi Koumalats)
Best Historical Single Title
Courting Miss Hattie by Pamela Ann Morsi

Best Regency Romance
Emily and the Dark Angel by Jo Beverley
Best Romantic Suspense
Night Shift by Nora Roberts
Best Futuristic/Fantasy/Paranormal
Angel for Hire by Justine Davis (Janice Davis Smith)
Best First Novel
Candle in the Wind by Christina Dodd

1993
Best First Book
Trust Me by Joane Renick
Best Traditional
Father Goose by Maria Ferrarella
Best Short Contemporary
Navarrone by Helen R. Myers
Best Long Contemporary
The Silence of Midnight by Karen Young/Karen Young Stone
Best Young Adult
Song of the Buffalo Boy by Sherry Garland
Best Regency Romance
An Unwilling Bride by Jo Beverley
Best Romantic Suspense/Gothic
Divine Evil by Nora Roberts
Best Futuristic/Fantasy/Paranormal
Emily's Ghost by Antoinette Stockenberg
Best Series Historical
The Prisoner by Cheryl Reavis
Best Single Title Contemporary
This Time Forever by Kathleen Eagle
Best Single Title Historical
Keeper of the Dream by Penelope Williamson

1994
Best First Book
A Candle in the Dark by Megan Chance
Best Traditional
Annie and the Wise Men by Lindsay Longford (Jimmie Morel)
Best Short Contemporary
Avenging Angel by Glenna McReynolds
Best Long Contemporary
Dragonslayer by Emilie Richards (Emilie Richards McGee)
Best Young Adult
Summer Lightning by Wendy Corsi Staub
Best Regency Romance
Deirdre and Don Juan by Jo Beverley
Best Romantic Suspense/Gothic
Nightshade by Nora Roberts
Best Futuristic/Fantasy/Paranormal
Falling Angel by Anne Stuart (Anne Stuart Ohlrogge)

Best Series Historical
Untamed by Elizabeth Lowell (Ann Maxwell)
Best Single Title Contemporary
Private Scandals by Nora Roberts
Best Single Title Historical
My Lady Notorious by Jo Beverley

1995
Best First Book
Ghostly Enchantment by Angie Ray
Best Traditional
Oh, Baby! by Lauryn Chandler (Wendy Warren)
Best Short Contemporary
Getting Rid of Bradley by Jennifer Crusie (Jennifer Crusie Smith)
Best Long Contemporary
A Soldier's Heart by Kathleen Korbel (Eileen Dreyer)
Best Young Adult
Second to None by Arlynn Presser
Best Regency Romance
Mrs. Drew Plays Her Hand by Carla Kelly
Best Romantic Suspense/Gothic
Hidden Riches by Nora Roberts
Best Paranormal/Fantasy/Time Travel
Lord of the Storm by Justine Davis (Janice Davis Smith)
Best Historical
To Tame a Texan's Heart by Jodi Thomas
Best Single Title Contemporary
Again by Kathleen Gilles Seidel
Best Long Historical
Dancing on the Wind by Mary Jo Putney
Best Inspirational
An Echo in the Darkness by Francine Rivers

1996
Best Traditional
Stranger in Her Arms by Elizabeth Sites
Best Short Contemporary
Single Dad by Jennifer Greene
Best Long Contemporary
The Morning Side of Dawn by Justine Davis
Best Contemporary Single Title
Born in Ice by Nora Roberts
Best Young Adult
Runaway by Cheryl Zach
Best Short Historical
Lord of Scoundrels by Loretta Chase
Best Long Historical
Something Shady by Pamela Morsi
Best Regency
Gwen's Christmas Ghost by Lynn Kerstan & Alicia Rasley
Best Romantic Suspense/Gothic
Winter's Edge by Anne Stuart

Best Paranormal
The Covenant by Modean Moon
Best Inspirational
As Sure as the Dawn by Francine Rivers
Best First Book
The Warlord by Elizabeth Elliott

Romantic Times Awards

Romantic Times Reviewer's Choice Awards
Presented by *Romantic Times* for outstanding series romances. Selection is done by the *RT* series romance reviewer and a committee.

1989
Best All-Around Series Author
Sara Chance
Best New Series Author
Courtney Henke
Series Love & Laughter
Judith McWilliams
Best Second Chance
Foul Play by Steffie Hall
Best Loveswept
Mismatch by Tami Hoag
Best Silhouette Romance
Confidentially Yours by Helen R. Myers
Best Silhouette Special Edition
Phoenix Rising by Mary Kirk
Best Silhouette Desire
Irresistible by Annette Broadrick
Best Silhouette Intimate Moments
Desperate Measures by Paula Detmer Riggs
Best Harlequin American
Together Always by Dallas Schulze
Best Harlequin Intrigue
Roses of Constant by Bethany Campbell
Best Harlequin Superromance
The Honey Trap by Pamela Bauer
Best Harlequin Temptation
A Novel Approach by Emma Jane Spenser
Special Achievement Awards:
    Contemporary Novel
    Beginnings by Eileen Nauman
    Contemporary Romance
    Love's Miracles by Sandra Lee Smith
    Romantic Adventure
    A Tender Silence by Karen Keast
    Romantic Suspense
    Sweet Revenge by Nora Roberts
    Gothic Romace
    Secrets of Tyrone by Regan Forest

Series Book of the Year
Somebody's Baby by Marilyn Pappano
Series W.I.S.H. Hero
Cmdr. Scott Sanders from *Kissed by an Angel* by Kathy Clark
Best Regency Author
MarleneSusan
Best New Regency Author
Jo Beverley
Best Regency Romance
The Devilish Marquis by Karla Hocker
Best Historical Regency Romance
Fallen Angel by Elizabeth Thornton
Best Regency Farce
Brighton Road by Susan Carroll
Best Regency Adventure
Bewitching Minz by Janis Laden
Best Regency Intrigue
Brighton Intrigue by Emma Lange

1990

Best All-Around Series Author
Gina Wilkins
Best New Series Author
Lois Faye Dyer
Best Series Book of the Year
Miracles by Mary Kirk
Best Series Love & Laughter
Marcia Evanick
Best Loveswept
The Devil and Ms. Moody by Suzanne Forster
Best Silhouette Romance
Her Special Angel by Marie Ferrarella
Best Silhouette Special Edition
The Spirit is Willing by Pat Coughlin
Best Silhouette Desire
Hotshot by Kathleen Korbel
Best Silhouette Intimate Moments
Tender Offer by Paula Detmer Riggs
Best Harlequin American
Angel of Mercy by Kathy Clark
Best Harlequin Intrigue
Shadowplay by Linda Stevens
Best Harlequin Superromance
Streets of Fire by Judith Duncan
Best Harlequin Temptation
I Do, Again by Carin Rafferty
Best Kismet
Prodigal Lover by Margo Gregg
Best Regency Author
Irene Saunders
Best New Regency Author
Margaret Evans Porter

Best Regency Romance
A Natural Attachment by Katherine Kingsley
Best Regency Novel
Marian's Christmas Wish by Carla Kelly
Best Regency Comedy
Cupboard Kisses by Barbara Metzger
Special Achievement Awards:
  Contemporary Romance
  White Lies and Alibis by Tracy Hughes
  Romantic Mystery
  Scarlet Scandals by Carol Budd
  Romantic Adventure
  Never Say Goodbye by Suzanne Carey
  Romantic Suspense
  Heart of the Night by Barbara Delinsky
  Innovative Series
  The Runaway Trilogy by Emilie Richards
  Time Travel
  West of the Sun by Lynn Erickson & *Blue Moon* by Dawn Stewardson
  Storyteller
  Diana Palmer
  Best First Series Book
  Jake's Child by Lindsay Longford
  Series W.I.S.H. Hero
  Diablo from *The Devil and Ms. Moody* by Suzanne Forster
  Regency Rake
  Edward, Marquess of Seaton in *A Natural Attachment* by Katherine Kingsley

1991

Best Series Romance
An Officer and a Gentleman by Rachel Lee
Best First Series Romance
Hunter's Way by Justine Davis
Best Loveswept
Guardian Spirit by Marcia Evanick
Best Silhouette Romance
Pictures of Emily by Theresa Weir
Best Silhouette Special Edition
Accompanying Alice by Teresa Ramin
Best Silhouette Desire
Red Hot Satin by Carole Buck
Best Silhouette Intimate Moments
Echoes of the Garden by Marilyn Tracy
Best Harlequin American
Bundle of Joy by Barbara Bretton
Best Harlequin Intrigue
Dead Ringer by M.J. Rodgers
Best Harlequin Superromance
Thy Heart in Mine Cara West
Best Harlequin Temptation
Making It by Elise Title

Best Kismet
Foster Love by Jani Reams Hudson
Best Contemporary Novel
Hot Shot by Susan Elizabeth Phillips
Best Contemporary Romantic Novel
A Marriage of Convenience by Georgia Bockoven
Best Contemporary Suspense
A Man to Die For by Kathleen Korbel
Best Contemporary Romantic Suspense
Silver Linings by Jayne Ann Krentz
Best Contemporary Romantic Mystery
Money Burns by A.E. Maxwell
Best Regency Romance
The Luck of the Devil by Barbara Metzger
Best First Regency Romance
The Duke's Daughter by Melinda McRae
Best Regency Novel
The Secret Pearl by Mary Balogh
Best Regency Intrigue
A Midsummer Night's Kiss by Cleo Chadwick
Best Regency Farce
Miss Gordon's Mistake by Anita Mills
Series W.I.S.H. Hero
Zach Stone in *Maybe This Time* by Dee Holmes
Regency Rake
Piers Verderan, the Dark Angel in *Emily and the Dark Angel* by Jo Beverley

1992

Best Series Romance
From a Distance by Emilie Richards
Best First Series Romance
Kidnapped! By Kate Carlton
Best Series Love and Laughter
Arc of the Arrow by Rita Rainville
Best Series Romantic Adventure
The Child Bride by Suzanne Forster
Best Series Romantic Fantasy
Angel for Hire by Justine Davis
Best Series Romantic Novel
The Woman Downstairs by Judith Arnold
Best Bantam Loveswept
Desert Rose by Laura Taylor
Best Silhouette Romance
Pete's Dragon by Lindsay Longford
Best Silhouette Special Edition
Beyond the Night by Christine Flynn
Best Silhouette Desire
Untouched by Man by Laura Leone
Best Silhouette Intimate Moments
Song of the Mourning Dove by Lee Magner
Best Harlequin American
Happy New Year, Darling by Margaret St. George

Best Harlequin Intrigue
Never Say Die by Tess Gerritsen
Best Harlequin Presents
Deal of a Lifetime by Susan Napier
Best Harlequin Romance
The Marriage Bracelet by Rebecca Winters
Best Harlequin Superromance
The Silence of Midnight by Karen Young
Best Harlequin Temptation
The Last Honest Man by Leandra Logan
Best Harlequin Tyler
Wisconsin Wedding by Carla Neggers
Best Meteor Kismet
Travelin' Man by Lois Faye Dyer
Best Contemporary Fantasy
The Legacy by Patricia Simpson
Best Contemporary Glitz
Glass by Christiane Heggan
Best Contemporary Novel
Fortune's Child by Pamela Simpson
Best Contemporary Romance
Lucky's Lady by Tami Hoag
Best Contemporary Romantic Suspense
The Diamond Tiger by Ann Maxwell
Best Contemporary Suspense
Divine Evil by Nora Roberts
Best Series Romantic Suspense
Exile's End by Rachel Lee
Best Regency Romance
A Counterfeit Betrothal by Mary Balogh
Best First Regency Romance
A Talent for Trouble by Anne Barbour
Best Regency Novel
A Highly Respectable Widow by Melinda McRae
Best Regency Intrigue
The Black Widow by Charlotte Dolan
Best Regency Comedy
Mad Maria's Daughter by Patricia Rice
Best W.I.S.H. Heroes
Dean Cornell in *Sometimes A Lady* by Linda Randall
Wisdom and Joe MacKenzie in *MacKenzie's Mission* by Linda Howard
Regency Rake
Edward Beauchamp, Earl of Knowlton, in *A Highly Respectable Widow* by Melinda McRae
Best Futuristic Romance
Pyramid of Dreams by Marilyn Campbell
Best Historical Romance
Through a Dark Mist by Marsha Canham
Best First Historical Romance
Pirate in My Arms by Danelle Harmon
Best Historical Novel
The Legacy of the Rose by Kasey Michaels

Best Western Romance
Only Forever by Kimberly Cates
Best First Western Romance
More Than Just a Night by Connie Rinehold
Best Indian Romance
Apache Magic by Janis Reams Hudson
Best Americana Historical Romance
Heirloom by Candace Camp
Best Historical Romance Sequel
Silk and Secrets by Mary Jo Putney
Best Fictionalized Biography
The Dragon and the Jewel by Virginia Henley
Best Historical Romance Adventure
The Enchantment by Kristin Hannah
Best Historical Romance Suspense
Dance of Deception by Suzannah Davis
Best Medieval Romance
Keeper of the Dream by Penelope Williamson
Best First Medieval Romance
My Cherished Enemy by Samantha James
Best Bristish Isles Historical Romance
No Greater Love by Katherine Kingsley
Best Colonial Historical Romance
Nobody's Angel by Karen Robards
Best Regency Historical Romance
The Lion's Daughter
Best Southern Historical Romance
A Jewel So Rare by Elizabeth Ann Michaels
Best Civil War Historical Romance
A Corner of Heaven by Theresa Michaels
Best Historical Fantasy
My Warrior's Heart by Betina Krahn
Best Victorian Romance
The Ruby by Christina Skye
Best Sensual Historical Romance
A Touch of Fire by Linda Howard
Best Historical Time Travel Romance
Somewhere in Time by Barbara Bretton
Best New Age Historical Romance
Moonshadow by Laura Parker
Best Historical Love and Laughter
Just a Kiss Away by Jill Barnett
Best K.I.S.S. Hero
Christian de Rivers in *Lady Gallant* by Suzanne Robinson

1993

Best Series Romance
A Walk on the Wild Side by Kathleen Korbel
Best First Series Romance
Wild Card Wedding by Julie McBride
Best Bantam Loveswept
Shameless by Glenna McReynolds
Best Silhouette Romance
Man Trap by Liz Ireland

Best Silhouette Special Edition
The Awakening by Patricia Coughlin
Best Silhouette Desire
Dangerous by Caroline Cross
Best Silhouette Intimate Moments
Obsessed! By Amanda Stevens
Best Silhouette Shadows
Imminent Thunder by Rachel Lee
Best Harlequin American
One More Valentine by Anne Stuart
Best Harlequin Intrigue
Bittersweet Legacy Jenna Ryan
Best Harlequin Presents
Two-Faced Woman by Roberta Leigh
Best Harlequin Presents Plus
The Widow's Mite by Emma Goldrick
Best Harlequin Romance
Hero on the Loose by Rebecca Winters
Best Harlequin Superromance
Daniel and the Lion by Margaret Dalton
Best Harlequin Temptation
Rafe's Island by Gina Wilkins
Best Harlequin Crystal Creek
Deep in the Heart by Barbara Kaye
Best Meteor Kismet
Bits and Pieces by Merline Lovelace
Best Contemporary Fantasy
Raven in Amber by Patricia Simpson
Best Contemporary Glitz
Prime Time by Barbara Cummings and JoAnn Power
Best Contemporary Novel
Forever by Judith Gould
Best Contemporary Romance
Tempting Fate by Carla Neggers
Best Contemporary Romantic Suspense
Cry Wolf by Tami Hoag
Best Contemporary Suspense
Midnight Baby by Wendy Hornsby
Best Futuristic Romance
The Wizard of Seattle by Kay Hooper
Best Regency Romance
Elizabeth's Rake by Emily Hendrickson
Best First Regency Romance
The Scandalous Wager by Olivia Fontayne
Best Regency Novel
The Duke's Mistress by Lois Stewart
Best W.I.S.H. Hero
Alden in *Somewhere Out There* by Emilie Richards
Best Regency Rake
Ross Montclaire, Earl of Gardiner in *Lady in Green* by Barbara Metzger
Best Historical Romance
No Sweeter Heaven by Katherine Kingsley

Best First Historical Romance
Candle in the Dark by Megan Chance
Best Historical Novel
The Courtesan by Diane Haeger
Best Western Historical Romance
Wyoming Ecstasy by Carol Finch
Best Americana Historical Romance
Sweet Everlasting by Patricia Gaffney
Best Historical Romance Adventure
Phantom Lover by Millie Criswell
Best North American Historical Romance
Legacy by Leigh Bristol
Best Medieval Romance
The Pagan's Prize by Miriam Minger
Best British Isles Historical Romance
The Mist and the Magic by Susan Wiggs
Best Regency Historical Romance
The Lily and the Hawk by Marlene Suson
Best Historical Romance Fantasy
Splendor by Catherine Hart
Best Victorian Historical Romance
My Only Love by Katherine Sutcliffe
Best Sensual Historical Romance
The Last Highwayman by Katherine O'Neal
Best Historical Time Travel Romance
Whispers in Time by Becky Lee Weyrich
Best Historical Love & Laughter
Wild Western Desire by Kathy Jones
Best K.I.S.S. Hero
Reynard Parks in *Santana Rose* by Olga Bicos

1994
Series Romance Book of the Year
Lost Warriors by Rachel Lee
Best First Series Romance
Suspect by Jo Leigh
Best Bantam Loveswept
Starwalker by Billie Green
Best Silhouette Romance
Jilted! By Joleen Daniels
Best Silhouette Special Edition
Convincing Alex by Nora Roberts
Best Silhouette Desire
Carolina on My Mind by Anne Marie Winston
Best Silhouette Intimate Moments
Annie and the Outlaw by Sharon Sala
Best Silhouette Shadows
Kiss of Darkness by Sharon Brondos
Best Harlequin American
Eight-Second Wedding by Anne McAllister
Best Harlequin Intrigue
Who Is Jane Williams? By M.J. Rodgers
Best Harlequin Presents
A Wedding to Remember by Emma Darcy

Best Harlequin Presents Plus
House of Glass by Michelle Reid
Best Harlequin Romance
Expectations by Shannon Waverly
Best Harlequin Superromance
Roses and Rain by Karen Young
Best Harlequin Temptation
Dangerous at Heart by Elise Title
Best Harlequin Crystal Creek
Gentle on My Mind by Bethany Campbell
Regency Romance
    Best Regency Romance
    Lord Glenraven's Return by Anne Barbour
    Best First Regency Romance
    Elizabeth's Rake by Donna Davidson
    Best Regency Novel
    The Fortescue Diamond by Monica Ellis
    Best Regency Comedy
    The Dutiful Duke by Joan Overfield
Mainstream and New Reality Romance
    Best Contemporary Fantasy
    This Dark Paradise by Wendy Haley
    Best Contemporary Glitz
    Star-Crossed by Jillian Grey
    Best Contemporary Novel
    Fire and Rain by Kathleen Eagle
    Best Contemporary Romance
    It Had to Be You by Susan Elizabeth Phillips
    Best Contemporary Romantic Suspense
    Silent Sonata by Deborah Nicholas
    Best Contemporary Suspense
    One for the Money by Janet Evanovich
    Best Futuristic Romance
    Lord of the Storm by Justine Davis
    Best Fantasy Romance
    The Demon Prince by Kathleen Morgan
    Best to Love Again
    Tangled Hearts by Phoebe Conn
Historical Romance
    Historical Romance Book of the Year
    Until You by Judith McNaught
    Best First Historical Romance
    Winter Heat by Denise Domning
    Best Historical Novel
    Mrs. De Winter by Susan Hill
    Best Western Romance
    The Law and Miss Penny by Sharon Ihle
    Best Americana Historical Romance
    If You Believe by Kristin Hannah
    Best Medieval Historical Romance
    In the Shadow of Midnight by Marsha Canham
    Best British Isles Historical Romance
    Outrageous by Christna Dodd

Best Victorian Historical Romance
A Deeper Magic by Jillian Hunter
Best Regency Historical Romance
Vixen by Jane Feather
Best North American Historical Romance
Tarnished Hearts by Raine Cantrell
Best Historical Romance Fantasy
Swan Witch by Betina Lindsey
Best Historical Time Travel Romance
Destined to Love by Suzanne Elizabeth
Best Historical Love and Laughter
Rebel in Silk by Sandra Chastain

Romantic Times Reviewer's Choice Awards for Historical Romances

Historical romance fiction awards for years 1992 through 1995 appear in the listing for *Romantic Times* Review's Choice Awards above.

1990
Best Historical Romance
Seduction by Amanda Quick
Best Historical Romance by a New Author
Masques of Enchantment by Charlene Cash
Best Historical Fiction
Paint the Wind by Cathy Cash Spellman
Best Historical Fiction by a New Author
The Last Disciple by Leslie H. Whitten Jr.
Best Western Romance
Escape Not My Love by Elaine Coffman
Best Western Adventure Romance
Midnight Rider by Colleen Shannon
Most Sensual Western Romance
The Darkest Heart by Brenda Joyce
Western Love & Laughter
Compromised Hearts by Hannah Howell
Best Western
Red River Story by Alfred Silver
Best Western by a New Author
Passion's Prize by Barbara Ankrum
Best Romantic Western Saga
Nightrose by Dorothy Garlock
Best Western Series
The Texas Series by Deana James
Best Indian Romance
Heaven and Earth by Kathleen Eagle
Best Sequel
My Darling Melissa by Linda Lael Miller
Outstanding Cross-Over Author
The Forever Rose by Curtiss Ann Matlock
Best Fictionalized Biography
Panther in the Sky by James Alexander Thom

Best Saga
Diamond Heart by Jeanne Montague
Best Saga by a New Author
A Taste of Heaven by Laura Simon
Best Swashbuckling Romance
A Heart's Disguise by Lisa Ann Verge
Best Historical Adventure Romance
Destiny's Dream by Joanna Jordan
Best Historical Romantic Suspense
Dreamspinner by Barbara Dawson Smith
Best Historical Romance Set Before 1066
Viking's Woman by Heather Graham
Best Historical Novel Set Before 1066
The Red Branch by Morgan Llywelyn
Best Medieval Romance
Where Love Dwells by Elizabeth Stuart
Best Medieval Historical
Castle of the Heart by Flora Speer
Best Medieval Romance by a New Author
My Gallant Enemy by Rexanne Bechel
Best Tudor Romance
The Spitfire by Bertrice Small
Best Restoration Romance
Beyond the Savage Sea by Jo Ann Wendt
Best Colonial Romance
A Promise of Fire by Veronica Sattler
Best Colonial Adventure Romance
A Wild Yearning by Penelope Williamson
Best Romance Set During the French and Indian War
Follow the Heart by Anita Mills
Best Romance Set During the Revolutionary War
The Firelands by Karen Harper
Best Frontier Romance
Northern Fire, Northern Star by Scotney St. James
Best Romance Set During the War of 1812
Visions of the Heart by Emily Carmichael
Best Regency-Set Historical Romance
Guardian Angel by Julie Garwood
Best Antebellum Romance
The Captain's Bride by Kat Martin
Best Civil War Romance
Freedom Angel by Robin LeAnne Wiete
Best Post-Civil War Romance
Embers of the Heart by F. Rosanne Bittner
Best Victorian Romance
When Angels Fall by Meagan McKinney
Best Turn-of-the-Century Romance
A Woman's Own by Robyn Carr
Most Sensual Romance
A Fire in the Heart by Katherine Sutcliffe
Most Exotic Historical Romance
Swept Away by Julie Tetel
Best Historical Love & Laughter
Victoria's Ecstasy by Gwen Cleary

Best Historical Fantasy
Wishes by Jude Deveraux
Storyteller
Connie Mason
Most Exciting Cover
Sweet Fury by Catherine Hart
Special Achievement
Christina Skye
K.I.S.S. (Knight In Shining Silver) Award
Prince Baraitinsky in *Golden Promise* by Susan Johnson

1991

Best Historical Romance
The Prince of Midnight by Laura Kinsale
Best First Historical Romance
Heaven Sent by Pamela Morsi
Best Historical Novel
October Winds by Susan Wiggs
Best Western Romance
Yesterday's Shadows by Marianne Willman
Best First Western Romance
Rough and Tender by Selena MacPherson
Best Western Saga
Follow the Wind by Janelle Taylor
Best Indian Romance
Night Wind's Woman by Shirl Henke
Best First Indian Romance
Comanche Moon by Catherine Anderson
Best Americana Historical Romance
Homeplace by Dorothy Garlock
Best Sequel
Emma and the Outlaw by Linda Lael Miller
Best Cross-over Author
Surrender in Scarlet by Patricia Camden
Best Fictionalized Biography
The Raven's Bride by Elizabeth Crook
Best Romantic Saga
Tattered Silk by Elaine Barbieri
Best Historical Adventure
Till Dawn Tames the Night by Meagan McKinney
Best Historical Romantic Suspense
Midnight Magic by Betina M. Krahn
Best Medieval Romance
The Conquest by Jude Deveraux
Best First Medieval Romance
Candle in the Window by Christina Dodd
Best Medieval Novel
Blood Red Roses by Katherine Deauxville
Best English Historical Romance
The Pirate and the Pagan by Virginia Henley
Best Scottish Historical Romance
Highland Rogue by Arnette Lamb
Best Colonial Historical Romance
This Side of Heaven by Karen Robards

Best Regency Historical Romance
Scandal by Amanda Quick
Best Southern Historical Romance
Thief of Hearts by Rexanne Becnel
Best Civil War Historical Romance
One Wore Blue by Heather Graham
Best Historical Fantasy
Across a Wine Dark Sea by Jessica Bryan
Best Victorian Romance
Speak to Me of Love by Deana James
Best Sensual Historical Romance
Only His by Elizabeth Lowell
Best Medieval Fantasy
Chanting the Dawn by Marylyle Rogers
Best New Age Novel
Outlander by Diana Gabaldon
Best Historical Romantic Mystery
Good Night, Mr. Holmes by Carole Nelson Douglas
K.I.S.S. (Knight in Shining Silver) Award
Lachlan MacKenzie in *Highland Rogue* by Arnette Lamb

Romantic Times Career Achievement Awards

Presented by *Romantic Times* to authors for outstanding career achievement

1991

Series Romance
    Series Romance: Kathleen Korbel
    Innovative Romance: Judith Duncan
    Romantic Suspense: Deborah Smith
    Romantic Fantasy: Nora Roberts
    Most Sensual Romance: Suzanne Forster
    Love and Laughter: Cait London
    Romantic Mystery: Amanda Stevens
    Romantic Adventure: Anne Stuart
    Storyteller of the Year: Dallas Schulze
Contemporary Fiction
    Contemporary Romance: Judith McNaught
    Contemporary Novel: Sara Orwig
    Contemporary Romantic Suspense: Iris Johansen
    Contemporary Suspense: Barbara Michaels
Regency Romance
    Regency Romance: Jo Beverley
Futuristic Romance
    Futuristic Romance: Rebecca Brandewyne
Historical Romance:
    Historical Romance: Julie Garwood
    Historical Adventure: Jillian Hunter
    Love and Laughter: Lori Copeland
    Historical Fantasy: Bertrice Small
    Indian Romance: Jessica Douglas
    Western Romance: Georgina Gentry
    Most Sensual Romance: Susan Johnson

Innovative Romance: Katherine Sutcliffe
Storyteller of the Year: Penelope Neri
Historical Romantic Mystery: Elizabeth Peters

1992

Series Romance
Series Romance: Anne Stuart
Innovative Romance: Mary Kirk
Romantic Suspense: Paula Detmer Riggs
Romantic Fantasy: Annette Broadrick
Sensual Romance: Olivia Rupprecht
Love and Laughter: Lacey Dancer
Romantic Mystery: M.J. Rodgers
Romantic Adventure: Ginna Gray
Storyteller of the Year: Cathie Linz
Contemporary Fiction
Contemporary Romance: Jayne Ann Krentz
Contemporary Novel: Barbara Delinsky
Contemporary Romantic Suspense: Laura Hastings
Contemporary Suspense: Eileen Dreyer
Contemporary Fantasy: Diana Gabaldon
Regency Romance
Regency Romance: Barbara Metzger
Regency Short Story: Edith Layton
Futuristic Romance
Futuristic Romance: Jackie Casto
Historical Romance
Historical Romance: Heather Graham
Historical Adventure: Susan Wiggs
Love and Laughter: Jill Marie Landis
Historical Fantasy: Kathleen Morgan
Western Romance: Catherine Hart
Sensual Romance: Johanna Lindsey
Innovative Romance: Francine Rivers
Storyteller of the Year: Patricia Potter

1993

Series Romance
Series Romance: Emilie Richards
Innovative Romance: Marilyn Pappano
Romantic Suspense: Patricia Gardner Evans
Romantic Fantasy: Margaret St. George
Sensual Romance: Leanne Banks
Love and Laughter: Theresa Gladden
Romantic Mystery: Rebecca York
Romantic Adventure: Laura Taylor
Storyteller of the Year: Diana Palmer
Contemporary Fiction
Contemporary Romance: Debbie Macomber
Contemporary Novel: Diane Chamberlain
Contemporary Romantic Suspense: Meryl Sawyer
Contemporary Suspense: Faye Kellerman
Contemporary Fantasy: Constance O'Day-Flannery

Regency Romance
Regency Romance: Emma Lange
Regency Short Story: Mary Balogh
Futuristic Romance
Futuristic Romance: Marilyn Campbell
Historic Romance
Historical Romance: Amanda Quick
Historical Novel: Karen Harper
Historical Adventure: Kimberly Cates
Love and Laughter: Rebecca Paisley
Historical Fantasy: Jessica Bryan
Western Romance: Catherine Anderson
Regency Historical Romance: Jane Feather
Sensual Romance: Brenda Joyce
Innovative Romance: Iris Johansen
Storyteller of the Year: Patricia Rice

1994

Series Romance
Series Romance: Karen Young
Innovative Series Romance: Cheryl Reavis
Series Romantic Suspense: Mary Anne Wilson
Series Romantic Fantasy: Rebecca Flanders
Series Love and Laughter: Muriel Jensen
Series Romantic Mystery: Jenna Ryan
Series Romantic Adventure: Glenna McReynolds
Storyteller of the Year: Barbara Bretton
Contemporary Fiction
Contemporary Romance: Deborah Smith
Contemporary Novel: Kathleen Gilles Seidel
Contemporary Romantic Suspense: Sherryl Woods
Contemporary Suspense: Elizabeth George
Contemporary Fantasy: Cheri Scotch
Regency Romance
Regency Romance: Carla Kelly
Futuristic Romance
Futuristic Romance: Johanna Lindsey
Historical Romance
Historical Romance: Elizabeth Lowell
Historical Novel: Susan Wiggs
Historical Adventure: Katherine Kingsley
Historical Fantasy: Jill Barnett
Western Historical Romance: Connie Mason
Americana Historical Romance: Robin Lee Hatcher
Regency Historical Romance: Veronica Sattler
Sensual Historical Romance: Arnette Lamb
Innovative Historical Romance: Deanna James
Historical Storyteller of the Year: Bobbi Smith

WHAT ROMANCE DO I READ NEXT?

A Reader's Guide to Recent Romance Fiction

Romance Titles

1

ALINA ADAMS

The Fictitious Marquis
(New York: Avon, 1995)

Story type: Regency
Major character(s): Lady Julia Highsmith, Heiress—Dispossessed, Noblewoman; Jamie Lowell, Convict
Time period(s): 1810s
Locale(s): London, England

Summary: Lady Julia Highsmith has a plan to save her family from a life or death situation. She just has to find a husband her uncle will approve of—and fast. Jamie Lowell is a convict headed for the gallows when Julia arrives with a proposition that will save his life. Together they find the means to save Julia's family and discover love along the way.

Other books you might like:
Gail Eastwood, *The Captain's Dilemma*, 1995
    another pair of mismatched lovers
Suzanne Enoch, *Angel's Devil*, 1995
    more matrimonial subterfuge
Margaret Evans Porter, *Road to Ruin*, 1992
    another marriage of convenience
Kathleen E. Woodiwiss, *Shanna*, 1977
    another hero intended for death/very different setting and treatment

2

JOANNE Z. ADAMS

Intimate Connections
(New York: Popular Library, 1991 PB)

Story type: Contemporary/Mainstream
Major character(s): Serita Smith, Television Personality (talk show host), Adoptee; Rick Finney, Journalist (newspaper investigative report)
Time period(s): 1990s (1991)
Locale(s): Chicago, Illinois

Summary: When beautiful, exotic Scrita Smith unexpectedly rockets to fame as a sympathetic TV talkshow host, she discovers that personal privacy is a thing of the past as she becomes the target of a vengeful writer for a scandal sheet bent on uncovering the secrets of her past. Hoping to protect her, hard-hitting investigative reporter Rick Finney decides to look into her past himself — but when he finds potentially explosive information, he is forced to come to terms with his real feelings for Serita. A fast-paced, passionate story that touches on a number of sensitive contemporary issues.

Other books you might like:
Sally Beauman, *Destiny*, 1987
Jennifer Blake, *Love and Smoke*, 1989
Rebecca Forster, *A Delicate Matter*, 1989
Velda Johnston, *Flight to Yesterday*, 1990
Judith Michael, *Deceptions*, 1982

3

YVONNE ADAMSON (Pseudonym of Mary Jo Adamson and Yvonne Montgomery)

Bridey's Mountain
(New York: Delacorte, 1993)

Story type: Historical/American West; Saga
Major character(s): Ariana MacAllister, Heiress; Morna Gregory, Singer; Bridey Gregory, Rancher
Time period(s): 19th century; 20th century
Locale(s): Telluride, Colorado

Summary: A passionate story of love, strength, and survival that chronicles the lives of four women, the men they love, and the land they will sacrifice anything to keep.

Other books you might like:
Elaine Barbieri, *More Precious than Gold*, 1992
Rosanne Bittner, *In the Shadow of the Mountains*, 1991
Barbara Faith, *Gamblin' Man*, 1993
Linda Howard, *A Lady of the West*, 1990
Catherine Lanigan, *A Promise Made*, 1991

3

4

ELIZABETH ADLER

Fortune Is a Woman
(New York: Delacorte, 1992)

Story type: Saga
Major character(s): Francesca "Francie" Harrison, Business-woman
Time period(s): 1890s (1895-1963); 20th century (1895-1963)
Locale(s): San Francisco, California; Hong Kong; Yorkshire, England

Summary: Francie Harrison, unwanted daughter of a San Francisco multi-millonaire, becomes a highly successful businesswoman through the mentoring of financial mandarin Lai Tsin. She survives earthquake, fire, gossip, her treacherous brother, and finally is privy to the mandarin's triumphant and surprising story. A sweeping story of achievement against incredible odds.

Other books you might like:
Barbara Taylor Bradford, *A Woman of Substance*, 1979
Sandra Bregman, *Reach for the Dream*, 1990
Beverly Byrne, *The Firebirds*, 1992
Barbara Delinsky, *Facets*, 1990
Danielle Steel, *No Greater Love*, 1992

5

JENNY AIKEN

Love Evergreen
(New York: Jove, 1993)

Story type: Historical/American West
Major character(s): Cecelia Scanlon, Young Woman; Matthew of the Strong People, Indian (Klallam)
Time period(s): 1880s (1888)
Locale(s): Port Gamble, Washington

Summary: When the lonely, convent-bred Cece encounters Matthew in the forest, their mutual attraction wreaks havoc on his "spirit quest" and throws both their futures into disarray. Cece must deal with her father and his marriage plans for her, and Matthew must choose between Cece and his tribe.

Other books you might like:
Kathryn Lynn Davis, *Sing to Me of Dreams*, 1990
Cassie Edwards, *Savage Promise*, 1991
Kathleen Harrington, *Cherish the Dream*, 1990
Catherine Palmer, *Gunman's Lady*, 1993

6

SARAH ALDRIDGE

Keep to Me, Stranger
(Tallahassee: Naiad, 1989)

Major character(s): Helena Worrall, Businesswoman (Company manager), Lesbian; Billie Rosenstein, Businesswoman, Lesbian (Jewish)
Time period(s): 1980s
Locale(s): New York, New York

Summary: As the first woman on the executive board since the legendary matriarch of the Rosenstein empire, Helena faces a series of new challenges, including her growing love for the daughter of the family, Billie. The fact that Helena is a gentile and Billie is a Jew further complicates their romance.

Other books you might like:
Karin Kallmaker, *In Every Port*, 1989
Evelyn Kennedy, *Of Love and Glory*, 1989
   World War II Setting
Elisabeth Newbold, *The City Within*, 1973
Valerie Taylor, *Love Images*, 1977

7

SARAH ALDRIDGE

Michaela
(Tallahassee, Florida: Naiad, 1994)

Story type: Lesbian/Contemporary
Major character(s): Laura Houghton, Widow(er), Lesbian; Julia, Professor, Lesbian
Time period(s): 1990s
Locale(s): Paris, France; Sutford, Virginia; New York, New York

Summary: While vacationing in Paris, Julia and Laura discover Michaela, an unusual teenager with a gift for ballet. However, she cannot afford the necessary training, so Julia and Laura take Michaela and her mother back to America to arrange for Michaela to begin her studies. Complications of a personal nature arise, however, in the form of Laura's late husband's ex-mistress, Catharine. Catharine's anger and unbalanced behavior puts everything, even Michaela's future, in jeopardy. AIDS, betrayal, abuse, and jealousy are all part of this innocent lesbian romance.

Other books you might like:
Catherine Ennis, *Up, Up and Away*, 1994
   sensual
Katherine V. Forrest, *The Romantic Naiad*, 1993
   anthology of lesbian short fiction
Melissa Hartman, *The Sure Thing*, 1994
   sensual
Karin Kallmaker, *Painted Moon*, 1994
Molleen Zanger, *Gardenias Where There Are None*, 1994
   paranormal elements

8

ROCHELLE ALERS
SHIRLEY HAILSTOCK, Co-Author
ANGELA BENSON, Co-Author

Holiday Cheer
(New York: Pinnacle, 1995)

Story type: Ethnic; Holiday Themes
Time period(s): 1990s
Locale(s): United States

Summary: This trilogy of contemporary novellas highlights the Winter Holiday season and is part of the Arabesque multicultural series which currently features African American protagonists. "Invitation to Love" by Shirley Hailstock focuses on Christmas, "First Fruits" by Rochelle Alers is a story of Kwanzaa, and Angela Benson's "Friend and Lover" deals with New Year's.

Other books you might like:
Janet Dailey, *Santa's Little Helpers*, 1995
    contemporary Christmas anthology/not multicultural
Monica Harris, *Spirit of the Season*, 1994
    Arabesque's first holiday anthology (Harris is editor.)
Virginia Henley, *A Gift of Joy*, 1995
    Christmas anthology/not multicultural
Muriel Jensen, *Merry Christmas, Mommy*, 1995
    contemporary Christmas romance/not multicultural
Mary Anne Wilson, *The Christmas Husband*, 1995
    contemporary Christmas romance/not multicultural

9

JO ANN ALGERMISSEN

Golden Bird
(Toronto: Harlequin, 1990)

Story type: Historical/Post-American Civil War
Major character(s): Laura Lee Shannon, Southern Belle; Jack Winthrop, Rancher
Time period(s): 1860s (1867)
Locale(s): Louisiana; Texas

Summary: Independent, feisty Laura Lee Shannon intends to do anything she has to to save the family plantation—anything, that is, except marry a man she doesn't even know, let alone love. But that is just what she is expected to do according to an old agreement between her father and the father of her intended. Predictably, Laura Lee rebels; and unpredictably she falls in love with her fiance's brother, creating a dilemma that takes the rest of the story to set straight.

Other books you might like:
Brenna Braxton-Barshon, *Southern Oaks*, 1991
Gwen Bristow, *Deep Summer*, 1937
    first in Plantation Trilogy
Thea Devine, *Southern Seduction*, 1991
Carla Simpson, *Always, My Love*, 1990
Leta Tegler, *Gabrielle*, 1990

10

ROSALYN ALSOBROOK

Elusive Caress
(New York: Zebra, 1990)

Story type: Historical/Victorian America
Major character(s): Audrey Stoane, Servant, Businesswoman (Would-be); Landon Steed, Heir (son of Audrey's employer)
Time period(s): 1870s
Locale(s): New York, New York

Summary: Audrey's aim is to become rich and independent, but she must avoid being seduced by Landon, the handsome son of the man for whom she works. An unusual heroine sparkles her way through this fast-paced historical.

Other books you might like:
Barbara Taylor Bradford, *A Woman of Substance*, 1979
Rosalind Laker, *Banners of Silk*, 1981
    English Setting/Similar plot
Victoria Morrow, *Jenny's Dream*, 1990
Catherine M. Rae, *Julia's Story*, 1989
    Great Depression setting
Victoria Thompson, *Fortune's Lady*, 1990
    American West setting/Strong heroine

11

ROSALYN ALSOBROOK

Endless Seduction
(New York: Zebra, 1992)

Story type: Historical/American West
Major character(s): Leona Stagnall, Businesswoman (store owner); Lathe Caldwell, Doctor
Time period(s): 1870s (1875)
Locale(s): West

Summary: When Leona gets involved in a gunfight, she also becomes involved with Lathe Caldwell and his search for some mysterious murderers. A number of things complicate their relationship, including a lawyer who wants Leona's store, but in the end, the villains are unmasked, old wrongs are righted, and Leona and Lathe can look happily toward the future. Complex, witty, and sensual.

Other books you might like:
Gwen Cleary, *Nevada Temptation*, 1992
Carol Finch, *Montana Mistress*, 1990
Lindsey Hanks, *Nevada Ecstasy*, 1992
Pamela Litton, *Stardust and Whirlwinds*, 1991

12

ROSALYN ALSOBROOK

Passion's Bold Fire
(New York: Zebra, 1993)

Story type: Historical/Victorian America
Major character(s): Karissa Caine, Mine Owner, Saloon Hostess (in disguise); Shawn McGowan, Detective—Private, Miner (disguised as a coal miner)
Time period(s): 1870s (1873)
Locale(s): Black Wall, Pennsylvania

Summary: Determined to find her father's murderer, mine owner Karissa Caine takes a job as a barmaid in the hope of gathering information about her chief suspects, the infamous and murderous Molly Maguires. Her efforts put her into contact with undercover private investigator, Shawn McGowan, but since neither knows of the other's true identity, suspicion and mistrust get in the way of their growing attraction for each other. Interesting historical detail.

Other books you might like:
Elaine Barbieri, *Wishes on the Wind*, 1991
Sonya Birmingham, *Spitfire*, 1991
Rebecca Brandewyne, *Rainbow's End*, 1991
Doreen Owens Malek, *Torchlight*, 1991

13

GLORIA ALVAREZ

Heart Waves

(Bensalem, Pennsylvania: Meteor, 1992)

Story type: Contemporary
Major character(s): Peyton Adair, Radio (program director); Cassidy Sloane, Radio (general station manager)
Time period(s): 1990s
Locale(s): Columbus, Ohio

Summary: When smooth-talking, ambitious radio announcer Cass Sloane takes a job at an Ohio radio station, his hot shot New York ideas put him at immediate odds with the fiery station program director, Peyton Adair. However, as they work together, they begin to develop a mutual respect — a respect that eventually evolves into an unexpected love.

Other books you might like:
Joanne Z. Adams, *Intimate Connections*, 1991
Sally Falcon, *Stolen Kisses*, 1992
Ellen Fletcher, *Pure Instinct*, 1992
Iris Johansen, *Winter Bride*, 1992

14

SUSAN AMARILLAS

Snow Angel

(Toronto: Harlequin, 1993)

Story type: Historical/American West
Major character(s): Katherine Thorn, Rancher (sheep); Logan McCloud, Rancher (cattle)
Time period(s): 1880s
Locale(s): Wyoming

Summary: When Katherine's father decides to run sheep right in the middle of cattle country, to avoid bloodshed cattleman Logan McCloud generously offers to buy them out. Katherine, however, refuses, in spite of the fact that she finds Logan incredibly attractive. She plans to keep her distance, but when they are trapped together during a blizzard, things take a romantic turn with far-reaching results. Filled with historical detail of 1880s winter ranch life.

Other books you might like:
Linda Howard, *Angel Creek*, 1991
DiAnna June, *Yesterday's Promise*, 1991
Connie Mason, *Wild Land, Wild Love*, 1992
    Australian setting
Bonnie K. Winn, *Summer Rose*, 1992

15

BLAINE ANDERSON

Heartspell

(New York: Warner, 1991)

Story type: Historical/Medieval; Historical/Fantasy
Major character(s): Grania, Sorceress (Druid); Niall, Royalty (Christian prince)
Time period(s): 7th century (628)
Locale(s): Ireland

Summary: To bring peace to her people, Druid sorceress Grania marries the Christian High Prince Niall in exchange for a magical sword for her foster father, the high king; but Grania's sorcery and Druidic beliefs and Niall's Christianity are at odds with each other and even love may not be enough to save their relationship. Mystical, magical, and thoroughly grounded in ancient lore.

Other books you might like:
Marion Zimmer Bradley, *The Mists of Avalon*, 1988
Rebecca Brandewyne, *Beyond the Starlit Frost*, 1991
Rebecca Brandewyne, *Passion Moon Rising*, 1988
Flora M. Speer, *Castle of Dreams*, 1990
Joan Wolf, *Born of the Sun*, 1991

16

CATHERINE ANDERSON

Cheyenne Amber

(New York: Harper, 1994)

Story type: Historical/American West
Major character(s): Laura Cheney, Widow(er) (wealthy), Abuse Victim; Deke Sheridan, Hunter, Frontiersman
Time period(s): 1860s (1864)
Locale(s): Denver, Colorado; Mexico

Summary: Deke Sheridan has no reason to help her, but desperate and cruelly abused Laura Cheney needs him to rescue her infant son who has been kidnapped by the Comancheros. Raised by the Cheyenne, Deke thinks he knows what has happened to the baby, but in order to get possession of him, Deke and Laura must be married according to Cheyenne tradition. A well-done "issues" romance that features a compassionate and caring her.

Other books you might like:
Kathleen Eagle, *Heaven and Earth*, 1990
    another caring hero
Cait Logan, *Wild Dawn*, 1992
    an abused and abandoned heroine
Lindsay McKenna, *Brave Heart*, 1993
    another story of abuse
Amanda Scott, *Dangerous Illusions*, 1994
    abuse victim/Regency period

17

CATHERINE ANDERSON

Comanche Heart

(New York: Harper, 1992)

Story type: Historical/American West
Major character(s): Amy Masters, Teacher; Swift "Swift Antelope" Lopez, Gunfighter, Indian (Comanche)
Time period(s): 1870s (1879)
Locale(s): Oregon

Summary: When Comanche brave Swift Lopez, finds that his betrothed of 15 years ago is not dead but very much alive, he wants to begin anew—but Amy, abused by both the Comanches and her stepfather, isn't so sure. Swift sets out to win her (even going to school in the process), and as she slowly works through her fears, they both put aside their personal demons and begin to build a relationship. A sensual rape-recovery story.

Other books you might like:
Madeline Baker, *Comanche Flame*, 1992
Lisa Bingham, *Distant Thunder*, 1992
Catherine Hart, *Tempest*, 1991
Constance O'Banyon, *Cheyenne Sunrise*, 1990

18

CATHERINE ANDERSON

Comanche Moon
(New York: Harper Collins, 1991)

Story type: Historical/American West
Major character(s): Loretta Simpson, Handicapped (mute); Hunter of the Wolf, Indian (Half Comanche), Warrior
Time period(s): 1860s
Locale(s): Texas

Summary: Hunter of the Wolf has known since childhood that his destiny lies with a golden-haired, blue-eyed silent woman. Loretta Simpson, mute since the massacre of her parents, is that woman. Both Loretta and Hunter must confront their own fears and prejudices, as well as those of the outside world, before they can fulfill their love. First of a projected trilogy.

Other books you might like:
Madeline Baker, *A Whisper on the Wind*, 1991
    Time change elements
Jessie Ford, *A Different Breed*, 1988
Catherine Hart, *Silken Savage*, 1985
Lindsay McKenna, *Sun Woman*, 1991
Constance O'Banyon, *Cheyenne Sunrise*, 1990

19

CATHERINE ANDERSON

Indigo Blue
(New York: Harper, 1992)

Story type: Historical/American West
Series: Wolf Family
Major character(s): Indigo Wolf, Indian (half-Comanche), Mine Owner (daughter of owner); Jake Rand, Businessman, Imposter
Time period(s): 1880s (1885)
Locale(s): Wolf's Landing, Oregon

Summary: To discover the truth about his father's suspect business practices, Jake Rand goes to Wolf's Landing and ends up temporarily running a local family mine while the owner recovers from an accident. This puts him into direct conflict with the owner's spirited, but gentle, daughter, Indigo, who had hoped to run the mine herself. The situation becomes truly interesting when a series of mishaps and a compromising situation result in the marriage of Indigo and Jake, but it isn't until Jake can win his wife's trust and love that the marriage becomes real. Follows *Comanche Moon* and *Comanche Heart*.

Other books you might like:
Rebecca Brandewyne, *Rainbow's End*, 1991
Gwen Cleary, *Victoria's Ecstasy*, 1990
Joan Hohl, *Silver Thunder*, 1992
Charlotte Simms, *Silver Caress*, 1990

20

CATHERINE ANDERSON
CHRISTINA DODD, Co-Author
SUSAN SIZEMORE, Co-Author

Tall, Dark, and Dangerous
(New York: Harper, 1994)

Story type: Anthology; Historical/American West
Time period(s): 19th century
Locale(s): West

Summary: This collection of three novellas features "dangerous" western-type heroes and includes: Shotgun Bride by Catherine Anderson, Wild Texas Rose by Christina Dodd, and One Riot, One Ranger by Susan Sizemore.

Other books you might like:
Catherine Anderson, *Cheyenne Amber*, 1994
Catherine Anderson, *Coming Up Roses*, 1993
    Janet Dailey Award winner
Christina Dodd, *Treasure of the Sun*, 1991
    historical California setting
Susan Sizemore, *My First Duchess*, 1991
    a "dangerous" English hero

21

LEE ANDERSON

Dangerous Bequest
(New York: Avalon, 1992)

Story type: Contemporary/Innocent; Romantic Suspense
Major character(s): Jill Champion, Heiress (newspaper); Adrian Kingman, Businessman (factory owner)
Time period(s): 1990s
Locale(s): Cameron

Summary: Jill inherits not only her outspoken Aunt Agatha's small-town newspaper, but some of her problems, as well — including becoming the target of the same person who did away with Aunt Agatha in the first place! Old-flame Adrian joins forces with Jill to solve the mystery and ends up coming back into Jill's life on a permanent basis.

Other books you might like:
Alma Blair, *The Unwitting Witness*, 1990
S.R. Hawley, *Formula for Murder*, 1992
Tami Hoag, *Still Waters*, 1992
    sensual
Phyllis A. Whitney, *The Glass Flame*, 1978

22

BARBARA ANKRUM

Chase the Fire

(New York: Zebra, 1991)

Story type: Historical/American West
Major character(s): Elizabeth "Libby" Honeycutt, Rancher, Widow(er); Chase Whitlaw, Military Personnel (Union officer)
Time period(s): 1860s (1866)
Locale(s): New Mexico

Summary: Honoring the dying wish of the rebel soldier he shot, Union officer Chase Whitlaw goes to New Mexico to return a locket and bring a final message to the rebel's wife, Libby Honeycutt—and finds himself staying to help the young widow and her son with their horse ranch. Of course, problems arise when Libby learns that Chase shot her husband, but love and understanding win out in the end. Strong, well-defined characters.

Other books you might like:
Theresa DiBenedetto, *Wildflower*, 1989
Elizabeth Lowell, *Reckless Love*, 1990
JoAnne Redd, *Chasing a Dream*, 1988
Jodi Thomas, *The Tender Texan*, 1991

23

BARBARA ANKRUM

Renegade Bride

(New York: Zebra, 1992)

Story type: Historical/American West
Major character(s): Mariah Parkins, Young Woman, Fiance(e); Creed Devereaux, Bounty Hunter
Time period(s): 1860s (1864)
Locale(s): Montana; Virginia City, Nevada

Summary: While escorting beautiful Mariah Parkins to his best friend and her fiance, Seth, bounty hunter Creed Devereaux and Mariah fall in love with each other. Problems arise, of course, because neither wants to betray Seth. Their wildly differing personalities don't help matters either. Nevertheless, there is plenty of action, passion, and adventure in this non-stop story.

Other books you might like:
Madeline Baker, *Prairie Heat*, 1991
Jill Gregory, *Cherished*, 1992
Rebecca Sinclair, *Forbidden Desires*, 1992
Rochelle Wayne, *Nevada Flame*, 1992

24

BARBARA ANKRUM

Renegade's Kiss

(New York: Zebra, 1993)

Story type: Historical/Post-American Civil War
Major character(s): Andrea Winslow, Widow(er), Farmer; Jesse Winslow, Landowner, Farmer (reluctant)
Time period(s): 1860s
Locale(s): United States

Summary: Widowed by the Civil War, Andrea Winslow vows to make a success of Willow Bank Farm for herself and her infant son, even though her renegade brother-in-law wants to sell it and head back to Montana. However, things become complicated when Andi and Jesse fall in love and he realizes he can't leave her. Nicely done characterizations—the neighbors are particularly interesting.

Other books you might like:
Leigh Bristol, *Legacy*, 1993
Heather Graham, *And One Rode West*, 1992
Jill Metcalf, *Autumn Leaves*, 1993
Cheryl Reavis, *The Prisoner*, 1992

25

EVELYN ANTHONY

The Doll's House

(New York: Harper/Collins, 1992)

Story type: Romantic Suspense
Major character(s): Rosa Bennett, Diplomat, Spy; Harry Oakham, Spy (retired)
Time period(s): 1990s
Locale(s): England

Summary: Assigned to discover whether or not former intelligence officer Harry Oakham is into something illegal since his retirement, Rosa Bennett investigates his fancy resort and his strange assorted associates. She isn't looking for romance, particularly not with someone who is twenty years her senior, but there is an attraction — plus the added aphrodesiac, DANGER. Complex.

Other books you might like:
Helen MacInnes, *Message From Malaga*, 1971
Elizabeth Peters, *Summer of the Dragon*, 1979
Patricia Potter, *Island of Dreams*, 1991
Anne Stevenson, *A Game of Shadows*, 1972
Anne Armstrong Thompson, *Message From Absalom*, 1975

26

EVELYN ANTHONY (Pseudonym of Evelyn Ward-Thomas)

The Scarlet Thread

(New York: Harper and Row, 1990)

Story type: Romantic Suspense
Major character(s): Angela Drummond, Nurse; Stephen Falconi, Accountant (for his Mafioso family)
Time period(s): 20th century
Locale(s): England; United States; Europe

Summary: Thinking his wife, Angela Drummond, was killed in a bombing raid in England, Stephen Falconi returns home to America to pick up the pieces of his life. However, soon after he marries again, he rediscovers Angela and his son whom he has never seen and realizes his future is with Angela and not his current wife, Clara. While Stephen and Angela make plans, Clara is plotting murder—and the resulting adventure is suspenseful and satisfying.

Other books you might like:
Mary Higgins Clark, *Stillwatch*, 1984
Helen MacInnes, *Message From Malaga*, 1971
Elizabeth Peters, *Naked Once More*, 1989
Sidney Sheldon, *If Tomorrow Comes*, 1985
Mary Stewart, *The Ivy Tree*, 1961

27

CATHERINE ARCHER

Rose Among Thorns

(Toronto: Harlequin, 1992)

Story type: Historical/Medieval
Major character(s): Lady Rose of Carlyle, Noblewoman (Saxon); Hubert de Thorne, Knight (Norman); Gaston de Thorne, Knight (Norman)
Time period(s): 11th century (1067)
Locale(s): England

Summary: Having lost her brother and father in battle, Lady Rose determines to care for her land and people, even though William the Conqueror sends the overbearing Hubert de Thorne to be in charge -and to marry the noble Lady Rose. Matters are complicated when Rose and Hubert's brother, Gaston de Thorne, fall in love; further entanglements arise when Hubert becomes attracted to Rose's cousin, Elspeth. Loyalty, honor, and cultural differences all work to keep the lovers apart, but in true romance fashion, all the right people eventually end up together.

Other books you might like:
Jude Deveraux, *Highland Velvet*, 1982
Jude Deveraux, *The Taming*, 1989
Samantha James, *My Cherished Enemy*, 1992
Flora M. Speer, *Castle of Dreams*, 1990
Libby Sydes, *The Lion's Angel*, 1992

28

ELLEN ARCHER
STEPHANIE BARTLETT, Co-Author
CHRISTINE DORSEY, Co-Author
LISA ANN VERGE, Co-Author

Under His Spell

(New York: Zebra, 1995)

Story type: Anthology; Historical/Fantasy
Locale(s): United States; Ireland

Summary: This quartet of magical and mystical historical novellas ranges from the American Gay Nineties to medieval Ireland and contains a wide variety of characters in an equally diverse set of romantic predicaments. Included are "Wishes" by Ellen Archer, "Smoke and Mirrors" by Stephanie Bartlett, "Deja Vu" by Christine Dorsey, and "The O'Madden" by Lisa Ann Verge.

Other books you might like:
Cheryl Biggs, *My Spellbound Heart*, 1994
  anthology

Shannon Drake, *Avon Books Presents: Haunting Love Stories*, 1991
  anthology
Cathie Linz, *A Wife in Time*, 1995
Angie Ray, *Ghostly Enchantment*, 1994
Maura Seger, *The Lady and the Laird*, 1992

29

JANE ARCHER

Bayou Passion

(New York: Zebra, 1991)

Story type: Historical/American West
Major character(s): Selene Morgan, Apothecary; Drake Dalton, Cowboy
Time period(s): 1880s
Locale(s): New Orleans, Louisiana; Martinique; Texas

Summary: Apothecary owner and occasional love potion-maker Selene Gordan and rancher Drake Dalton team up to solve the mystery of their vanishing friends and relatives and end up finding love in the process. A fast-paced story that sweeps the characters from exotic New Orleans to lush, but sometimes sinister, Martinique and finally on to the wilds of the Texas range.

Other books you might like:
Rebecca Paisley, *Moonlight and Magic*, 1990
Diane Gates Robinson, *Delta Desire*, 1991
Bobbi Smith, *Bayou Bride*, 1991
Jane Toombs, *Riverboat Rogue*, 1990

30

JANE ARCHER

Rebel Seduction

(New York: Zebra, 1990)

Story type: Historical/Post-American Civil War
Major character(s): Lacey Whitmore, Southern Belle, Nurse; Clint McCullough, Military Personnel, Spy
Time period(s): 1860s (1865)
Locale(s): Georgia

Summary: When Southerner Lacey Whitmore's haven for wounded soldiers is destroyed by a group of renegade Yankees, she joins forces with Clint McCullough, a Yankee in Rebel's clothing, to catch the raiders. They prove to be quite a team, tracking down their man and falling in love in the process. Action, deception, and passion in this novel of the Reconstruction Era.

Other books you might like:
Norah Hess, *Wildfire*, 1990
Linda Ladd, *Frostfire*, 1990
Linda Madl, *Sunny*, 1990
Maura Seger, *Perchance to Dream*, 1989
  South wins the War
Terri Valentine, *Yankee's Caress*, 1989

JANE ARCHER

Wild Wind

(New York: Pinnacle, 1993)

Story type: Historical/American West
Major character(s): Deirdre Clarke-Jargon, Suffragette, Businesswoman (family-owned shipping business); Hunter, Bodyguard
Time period(s): 19th century
Locale(s): Texas; Bahamas; Arizona

Summary: Intrepid suffragette Deirdre Clarke-Jargon goes to the Bahamas to rescue the family shipping business and falls in love with Hunter, the man who was hired to protect her. However, the devastating news that Hunter is in the employ of her family's old nemesis, Lady Caroline, changes her plans—and it takes a change of scene, and of life-style, before Hunter and Deirdre's dreams can come true.

Other books you might like:
Rosanne Bittner, *Shameless*, 1993
Martha Hix, *Lone Star Loving*, 1993
Kathy Jones, *Wild Western Desire*, 1993
Mary Martin, *Wild Texas Angel*, 1993
Patricia Watters, *Come Be My Love*, 1993

32

MELLYORA ASHLEY

A Lady in Disguise

(New York: Zebra 1990)

Story type: Regency
Major character(s): Briana Rosewynn, Noblewoman (impoverished); Darnier, Nobleman (Duke of Brocco)
Time period(s): 1810s
Locale(s): Shipton, England (Milburn Place)

Summary: To earn some money and to help her cousin get to know the highly eligible Duke of Brocco, penniless Lady Briana Rosewynn takes a job redecorating the future Duchess of Brocco's bedchamber—and finds herself strangely attracted to the Duke's unusual secretary, Darnier. Of course, Darnier is the Duke is disguise, and he will stop at nothing to win Briana. A somewhat unorthodox Regency.

Other books you might like:
Clare Darcy, *Georgina*, 1971
Carola Dunn, *Angel*, 1984
Leigh Haskell, *The Vengeful Viscount*, 1990
Georgette Heyer, *The Nonesuch*, 1962
Eva Rutland, *Enterprising Lady*, 1990

33

MOLLIE ASHTON

Terms of Surrender

(Toronto: Harlequin, 1990 PB)

Story type: Historical/French Revolution

Major character(s): Julie Farroux, Gentlewoman; Sebastian Ramlin, Gentleman
Time period(s): 1790s
Locale(s): France

Summary: When Julie Farroux finds herself married to an old man who wants only her fortune—and an heir, she wonders if death at the guillotine (from which she was earlier rescued) might not have been preferable; and when she falls in love with the man she learns her husband had hired to seduce her, she is sure of it. Passion, treachery, and romance in a Reign of Terror setting.

Other books you might like:
Brian Cleeve, *Hester*, 1979
Charles Dickens, *A Tale of Two Cities*, 1959
classic novel of the French Revolution
Jane Feather, *Reckless Angel*, 1989
Ellen Tanner Marsh, *If This Be Magic*, 1990
Rafael Sabatini, *Scaramouche*, 1921
another classic tale of the French Revolution

34

KATHRYN ATTALLA

Homeward Bound

(Bensalem, Pennsylvania: Meteor, 1993)

Story type: Contemporary
Major character(s): Kate "Leather" Costello, Musician (rock star), Entertainer; Jake Callahan, Rancher, Twin; Trevor Callahan, Rancher, Twin
Time period(s): 1990s
Locale(s): New Mexico

Summary: Jake and Trevor Callahan's New Mexican ranch is just the place for rock star Kate Costello to find a bit of peace and quiet and relief from her high pressure world; however, she doesn't count on a couple of matchmakers and she doesn't count on falling in love. Nightmares, scandals, and long-kept secrets keep the road from being too smooth, but love does win out in the end.

Other books you might like:
Carole Dean, *California Man*, 1992
Judith Duncan, *Beyond All Reason*, 1993
Lynette Kent, *No Illusion*, 1993
Danielle Steel, *Palomino*, 1981

35

ELIZABETH AUGUST

Pirate's Bride

(Toronto: Harlequin, 1992)

Story type: Historical/Colonial America
Major character(s): Kathleen James, Captive, Bride; Jonathan Ashford, Plantation Owner
Time period(s): 17th century (1673)
Locale(s): American Colonies; At Sea

Summary: For eleven years Kathleen has tried to escape from a pirate ship, and when her chance finally comes, she takes it — even though it means marrying Virginia planter Jonathan

Ashford. His difficult mother makes her pirate ship experience seem pleasant by contrast, but their love eventually wins out — despite family problems, Indian attacks, and a host of other obstacles. Sensual, gripping, and dramatic.

Other books you might like:
Christine Dorsey, *Sea Fires*, 1992
Shannon Drake, *Bride of the Wind*, 1992
Catherine Lanigan, *Jewel of the Nile*, 1985
Catherine Lanigan, *Romancing the Stone*, 1984
Connie Mason, *Tempt the Devil*, 1990

36
ELIZABETH AUGUST
The Virgin Wife
(New York: Silhouette, 1993)

Story type: Contemporary
Major character(s): Madaline MacGregor-Smythe, Architect, Spouse (virgin); Colin Darnell, Contractor; Devin Smythe, Spouse
Time period(s): 1990s
Locale(s): Smythshire, Massachusetts

Summary: Madaline is stunned to learn the owner of her new home is an old lover, Colin Darnell—and the fact that she still has feelings for him doesn't help matters. Neither does the fact that her marriage is a romantic sham. Her husband, Devin, protects and cares for her, but her contacts with Colin make him suspicious—and the more he tries to hold on to her, the more she is drawn to Colin. A suspenseful story with interestingly drawn characters.

Other books you might like:
Blythe Bradley, *To Love a Stranger*, 1993
Christina Dodd, *Lady in Black*, 1993
Deborah Nicholas, *Night Vision*, 1993
Rebecca York, *What Child Is This?*, 1993

37
ANNE AVERY
All's Fair
(New York: Love Spell, 1994)

Story type: Futuristic
Major character(s): Calista York, Trader; Rhys Fairdane, Trader
Time period(s): Indeterminate Future
Locale(s): Karta, Planet—Imaginary; Outer Space

Summary: Over the years, space traders Calista and Rhys have been partners, lovers, and competitors. Now, however, they find they both need the same lucrative business and they must work together to win. Learning to compromise isn't easy for either of them, but love helps them sort it all out.

Other books you might like:
Marilyn Campbell, *Stardust Dreams*, 1993
Justine Davis, *Lord of the Storm*, 1994
Justine Davis, *The Skypirate*, 1995
Amanda Glass, *Shield's Lady*, 1989
Patricia Roenbuck, *Golden Temptress*, 1991

38
ANNE AVERY
Far Star
(New York: Love Spell, 1995)

Story type: Futuristic
Major character(s): Dayra Smith, Fugitive, Settler; Coil Larren, Wanderer
Time period(s): Indeterminate Future
Locale(s): Far Star Colony, Planet—Imaginary

Summary: Dayra Smith and her siblings hide from her ruthless and powerful step-father on the harsh Far Star Colony world. Coil Larren, an embittered wanderer with nothing to live for, becomes Dayra's protector, fights her pursuer, and eventually realizes he has a new life—and a new love—to live for. Well-developed characters, poignant, and emotionally involving.

Other books you might like:
Lois McMaster Bujold, *Shards of Honor*, 1986
Justine Davis, *Lord of the Storm*, 1994
Justine Davis, *The Sky Pirate*, 1995
Susan Krinard, *Star-Crossed*, 1995
Anne McCaffrey, *Restoree*, 1967

39
SUSAN AYLWORTH
Ride the Rainbow Home
(New York: Avalon, 1995)

Story type: Contemporary/Innocent
Major character(s): Meg Taylor, Consultant (management trainer); Jim McAllister, Art Dealer (Native American art objects)
Time period(s): 1990s
Locale(s): Rainbow Rock, Arizona

Summary: When Meg Taylor returns home to the Arizona high desert for her high school reunion, she is stunned to find that her childhood friend ''little Jimmy McAllister'' has suddenly turned into the most eligible bachelor in town. But despite their mutual attraction, Meg's career plans are centered in California and don't include Rainbow Rock—or at least they don't until love changes things. Short, sweet, and peopled with appealing characters. Well-handled sexual tension.

Other books you might like:
Kathryn E. Coulter, *Does Cupid Do Take-Out?*, 1995
Faith E.W. Garner, *When Someday Comes*, 1995
Debbie Macomber, *Morning Comes Softly*, 1993
Debbie Macomber, *Someday Soon*, 1995

40
MADELINE BAKER
Cheyenne Surrender
(New York: Leisure, 1994)

Story type: Historical/American West

Major character(s): Callie McGuire, Housekeeper, Ward; Caleb Stryker, Bounty Hunter, Guardian
Time period(s): 19th century
Locale(s): Wyoming

Summary: Returning to Cheyenne to claim his inheritance, half-breed bounty hunter Caleb Stryker, finds that he is also the guardian of young Callie McGuire, the daugher of his father's mistress. He gives her a job as his housekeeper, they fall in love, and then they learn that she is the true heir to his father's estate. Attempted murder and all kinds of dastardly deeds plague the pair; but the culprits are eventually caught and Callie and Caleb are finally free to be happy together.

Other books you might like:
JoAnn De Lazzari, *Scoundrel's Captive*, 1991
    action in rowdy Wyoming
Theresa DiBenedetto, *Western Winds*, 1991
    passionate and violent
Norah Hess, *Mountain Rose*, 1993
    unlikely guardian plot/gentler, funnier treatment
Johanna Lindsey, *Savage Thunder*, 1989

MADELINE BAKER

Comanche Flame

(New York: Leisure, 1992)

Story type: Historical/American West
Major character(s): Jessica Landry, Governess; Dancer, Indian (half-Comanche), Gunfighter
Time period(s): 19th century
Locale(s): West

Summary: The infamous Dancer rescues governess Jessica Landry and takes her along as he outruns a posse. Along the way she learns survival skills and a lot of Indian lore—and she realizes that Dancer is gentle beneath his violent exterior. He tries to protect her by returning to his village, but is betrayed, tortured, and sent to a slave gang. However, Jessica, with the help of the Judge, is able to save Dancer; and together they avenge his past as they learn to love. Fast-paced and sensual.

Other books you might like:
Catherine Anderson, *Comanche Heart*, 1992
Kathleen Eagle, *Heaven and Earth*, 1990
Kathleen Harrington, *Cherish the Dream*, 1990
Johanna Lindsey, *Savage Thunder*, 1989

MADELINE BAKER
ANNE AVERY, Co-Author
KATHLEEN MORGAN, Co-Author

Enchanted Crossings

(New York: Love Spell, 1994)

Story type: Anthology; Fantasy
Summary: A varied collection of three novellas that use time and space in unusual ways. Included are: *Heart of the Hunter* by Madeline Baker, a fantasy with a Native American hero,

and *Dream Seeker* by Anne Avery and *The Last Gatekeeper* by Kathleen Morgan, both futuristic romances.

Other books you might like:
Marilyn Campbell, *Stolen Dreams*, 1994
Joan Hohl, *Love Beyond Time*, 1994
    anthology
Susan Sizemore, *Wings of the Storm*, 1994
Marilyn Tracy, *Memory's Lamp*, 1994

43
MADELINE BAKER

Forbidden Fires

(New York: Leisure, 1990)

Story type: Historical/American West
Major character(s): Caitlyn Carmichael, Rancher; Rafe Gallagher, Indian (half), Cowboy
Time period(s): 19th century
Locale(s): West

Summary: An Indian-hating heroine and a half-Indian hero make for a lively and sensitive story as Caitlyn and Rafe overcome treachery, jealousy, and prejudice to make their love a lasting reality.

Other books you might like:
Elaine Barbieri, *Wishes on the Wind*, 1991
    similar theme (prejudice)/different setting
Kathleen Harrington, *Cherish the Dream*, 1990
Stef Ann Holm, *Firefly*, 1990
Jill Marie Landis, *Rose*, 1990
Jill Marie Landis, *Wild Flower*, 1989

44
MADELINE BAKER

Lacey's Way

(New York: Leisure, 1990)

Story type: Historical/American West
Major character(s): Matt Drago, Indian (Half); Lacey Montana, Young Woman
Time period(s): 19th century
Locale(s): Arizona

Summary: After surviving an attack on their wagon train, Lacey Montana and Matt Drago search for Lacey's father who was captured by the Indians. Adventure and romance are the order of the day as they not only look for Lacey's father but seek to clear him of the murder of which he had been convicted.

Other books you might like:
Cassie Edwards, *When Passion Calls*, 1990
Rene J. Garrod, *Temptation's Wild Embrace*, 1990
Christine Monson, *Golden Nights*, 1990
Bobbi Smith, *Arizona Caress*, 1989
Victoria Thompson, *Fortune's Lady*, 1990

45

MADELINE BAKER

Midnight Fire
(New York: Leisure, 1992)

Story type: Historical/American West
Major character(s): Carolyn Chandler, Runaway; Morgan Slade, Indian, Alcoholic
Time period(s): 19th century
Locale(s): Texas; Nebraska

Summary: Carolyn Chandler literally trips over drunken Morgan Slade as she escapes from her home and an arranged marriage. She saves his life, and in return he takes her to Nebraska where their adoption by an Indian tribe results in a complete change of life for Morgan — and Carolyn. Pregnancy, a return to ''civilization,'' and an ex-fiance all complicate matters, but love does win out in the end. Poignant, heart-warming, and sensual.

Other books you might like:
Rosanne Bittner, *Sioux Splendor*, 1990
Cassie Edwards, *When Passion Calls*, 1990
Johanna Lindsey, *Savage Thunder*, 1989
Janelle Taylor, *Savage Conquest*, 1985

46

MADELINE BAKER

Prairie Heat
(New York: Leisure, 1991)

Story type: Historical/American West
Major character(s): Matilda Thornton, Mail Order Bride; Jesse McCord, Bounty Hunter, Indian (half-Apache)
Time period(s): 19th century
Locale(s): Southwest

Summary: Married by proxy to a husband she has never seen, Matilda Thornton is headed west to join him when she is caught in an Indian raid and ends up in the company of a disturbingly attractive bounty hunter, Jesse McCord. Although they are unsuccessful in fighting their attraction for each other, they eventually go their separate ways—Mattie to her husband and Jesse to find his wife's killer; but fate brings them together again with violent and passionate results. Well-drawn characters and good historical detail.

Other books you might like:
Rosanne Bittner, *Arizona Ecstasy*, 1989
Rosanne Bittner, *Song of the Wolf*, 1992
Johanna Lindsey, *Savage Thunder*, 1989
Penelope Williamson, *A Wild Yearning*, 1990

47

MADELINE BAKER

The Spirit Path
(New York: Leisure, 1993)

Story type: Time Travel

Major character(s): Maggie St. Claire, Writer (romance novels), Handicapped (wheelchair-bound); Shadow Hawk, Shaman, Indian (Sioux)
Time period(s): 1990s; 19th century
Locale(s): Black Hills, South Dakota; Canada

Summary: Modern day Maggie St. Claire, a paraplegic writer of Indian romance novels, encounters 19th century Sioux shaman, Shadow Hawk, when he comes through time to find his Spirit Woman. As she teaches him about the present world, he teaches her about love and healing; but it isn't until she goes with him to his time, that she truly learns about the people who have been the subjects of her novels all these years. Interesting historical detail.

Other books you might like:
Beverly Bird, *Comes the Rain*, 1990
    no time travel elements
Rosanne Bittner, *Sioux Splendor*, 1990
    no time travel elements
Michael Blake, *Dances with Wolves*, 1988
    no time travel elements
Penelope Neri, *Forever and Beyond*, 1990
Becky Lee Weyrich, *Forever, for Love*, 1989

48

MADELINE BAKER

Warrior's Lady
(New York: Leisure, 1993)

Story type: Fantasy
Major character(s): Leyla, Healer; Jarrett, Captive, Nobleman
Time period(s): Indeterminate Past
Locale(s): Fictional Country

Summary: Jarrett, imprisoned and blindfolded as a traitor, is healed by ''She,'' the one he cannot see. ''She'', Leyla helps him escape, and they head for her home, encountering fire-breathing dragons and giants along the way. Although already betrothed, Leyla defies tradition and faces the loss of her powers by loving Jarrett. Mystical creatures and mad killers add to the adventure.

Other books you might like:
Rebecca Brandewyne, *Passion Moon Rising*, 1988
Kay Hooper, *The Wizard of Seattle*, 1993
Johanna Lindsey, *Keeper of the Heart*, 1993
Johanna Lindsey, *Warrior's Woman*, 1990

49

MADELINE BAKER

A Whisper on the Wind
(New York: Leisure, 1991)

Story type: Time Travel
Major character(s): Elayna O'Brien, Young Woman; Michael Wolf, Indian (Cheyenne), Time Traveller
Time period(s): 1950s (1955); 1870s (1875)
Locale(s): South Dakota

Summary: Miraculously whisked from the 1950s into the past century, Michael Wolf learns first-hand what it meant to be a

Cheyenne in 1875. His experiences in the past result in a changed life for him in the present—and with his new-found purpose, he also is given a chance at a love that lasts throughout time. Good historical detail—interesting ending(s).

Other books you might like:
Johanna Lindsey, *Savage Thunder*, 1989
Penelope Neri, *Forever and Beyond*, 1990
Constance O'Day-Flannery, *A Time for Love*, 1991
Pamela Simpson, *Partners in Time*, 1990
Becky Lee Weyrich, *Forever, for Love*, 1989

50

KAREN BALE

Bold Montana Bride
(New York: Zebra, 1991)

Story type: Historical/American West
Major character(s): Maddie Broderick, Young Woman; Flint McCormick, Friend
Time period(s): 19th century
Locale(s): Montana

Summary: When Maddie Broderick tells her childhood friend Flint McCormick that her father is going to literally sell her into marriage, he offers for her himself. A delightful story of two people who discover that love is closer to home that they ever imagined.

Other books you might like:
Rosanne Bittner, *Montana Woman*, 1990
Dorothy Garlock, *Nightrose*, 1990
Kristin James, *The Yankee*, 1990
Jill Marie Landis, *Sunflower*, 1989
Pamela Morsi, *Heaven Sent*, 1990

51

RITA BALKEY

Midnight Ecstasy
(New York: Zebra, 1990)

Story type: Historical/American West
Major character(s): Clover Sinclair, Animal Lover (Lion owner); Luke Emerson, Animal Lover
Time period(s): 1870s (1876)

Summary: Clover is looking for the lion she raised from a cub. She finds him in the care of Luke and is overjoyed to have her lion back. However, Clover blames Luke for her father's death, while Luke blames her father for framing him earlier. Love flourishes despite these difficulties.

Other books you might like:
Elizabeth Lowell, *Reckless Love*, 1990
   Horse-lover/Western setting
Rebecca Paisley, *Barefoot Bride*, 1990
Cynthia Wright, *Brighter than Gold*, 1990

52

RITA BALKEY

Passion's Fury
(New York: Zebra, 1989)

Story type: Historical/Victorian America
Major character(s): Hester Vail, Writer (Popular novels); Jack Wilmot, Sports Figure (Boxer)
Time period(s): 1880s (1881)
Locale(s): Ohio

Summary: When revealed as the writer of popular novels that Boston society found unacceptable, Hester Vail is sent to stay with her aunt in Ohio. But Ohio is far more interesting than Hester had expected. Robbery, witchcraft, and love all play a part.

Other books you might like:
Gwen Cleary, *Ecstasy's Masquerade*, 1989
Phyllis Herrmann, *Hidden Fire*, 1989
Norah Hess, *Wildfire*, 1989
Elizabeth Lane, *Wind River*, 1989
Rebecca Sinclair, *California Caress*, 1989

53

MARY BALOGH
MARILYN CAMPBELL, Co-Author
CAROLE NELSON DOUGLAS, Co-Author
EMMA MERRITT, Co-Author
PATRICIA RICE, Co-Author

Angel Christmas
(New York: Topaz, 1994)

Story type: Anthology; Holiday Themes
Time period(s): Indeterminate Past; 1990s
Locale(s): United States; England

Summary: This well-done collection of Christmas stories includes British and American settings and past and present time periods; however, the stories all have a common focus—angels who meddle in the love lives of the characters. Included are "Guarded by Angels" by Mary Balogh, "The Trouble with Angelina" by Marilyn Campbell, "Catch a Falling Star" by Carole Nelson Douglas, "Brush of Angel Wings" by Emma Merritt, and "Tin Angel" by Patricia Rice.

Other books you might like:
Mary Balogh, *A Regency Christmas VII*, 1995
   anthology
Mary Chase Comstock, *A Christmas Wish*, 1994
   anthology
Sandra Heath, *Lucy's Christmas Angel*, 1995
   Regency period
Lynn Kerstan, *Gwen's Christmas Ghost*, 1995
   Alicia Rasley, co-author
Heather Graham Pozzessere, *An Angel's Touch*, 1995
   contemporary

54

MARY BALOGH

Beyond the Sunrise

(New York: NAL, 1992)

Story type: Historical/Regency
Major character(s): Jeanne Morisette, Spy; Robert Blake, Spy
Time period(s): 1810s
Locale(s): England; Spain; Portugal

Summary: Brutally and deviously separated in their youth, Robert Blake and Jeanne Morisette encounter each other years later while engaged in undercover work for the British during the Napoleonic Wars -and realize that their future still lies together. Political intrigue and fast-paced action highlight this romantic story of rekindled love.

Other books you might like:
Shirl Henke, *Paradise and More*, 1992
Amanda Quick, *Reckless*, 1992
Irene Saunders, *Lady Lucinde's Locket*, 1990
  Regency treatment
Elizabeth Thornton, *Scarlet Angel*, 1990

55

MARY BALOGH

Christmas Beau

(New York: Signet, 1992)

Story type: Regency; Holiday Themes
Major character(s): Judith Easton, Widow(er), Gentlewoman; Max Denbigh, Nobleman (Marquess)
Time period(s): 1810s
Locale(s): England

Summary: When young widow Judith Easton attends her first party since her debut, she is shocked to be re-introduced to the Marques of Denbigh, the very man she had jilted years earlier to elope with another man! A witty, charming tale of revenge and love.

Other books you might like:
Jo Beverley, *An Unwilling Bride*, 1992
Sandra Heath, *A Christmas Courtship*, 1990
Michelle Kasey, *The Somerville Farce*, 1991
Carla Kelly, *Marian's Christmas Wish*, 1989

56

MARY BALOGH

Christmas Belle

(New York: Signet, 1994)

Story type: Regency; Holiday Themes
Major character(s): Isabella Gellee de Vacheron, Actress, Noblewoman (comtesse); Jack Frazer, Gentleman, Rake
Time period(s): 1810s
Locale(s): England

Summary: Summoned from town life to his grandparent's estate for a family Holiday gathering, elegant rake Jack Frazer

suspects his grandmother has decided his single days are about to come to an end—and when the charming, innocent, and highly suitable Juliana Beckworth appears on the scene, he's sure of it. However, what he doesn't expect is the arrival of another holiday guest, the acclaimed actress, Isabella Gellee, Comtesse de Vacheron, the woman who was his mistress years ago—the one woman he could never forget—or forgive. A typical Balogh Regency that pushes the boundaries of the subgenre right to the edge.

Other books you might like:
Jo Beverley, *The Christmas Angel*, 1992
Susan Carroll, *Christmas Belles*, 1992
Gail Eastwood, *The Persistent Earl*, 1995
Carla Kelly, *Marian's Christmas Wish*, 1989
Carla Kelly, *Mrs. Drew Plays Her Hand*, 1994

57

MARY BALOGH

Dancing with Clara

(New York: Signet, 1994)

Story type: Regency
Major character(s): Clara Danford, Heiress, Handicapped (invalid); Frederick Sullivan, Rake
Time period(s): 1810s
Locale(s): Bath, England; London, England

Summary: Knowing that men are only interested in her for her money, invalid Clara Danford decides that the rakish Frederick Sullivan is her only chance to marry—and so they do. The honeymoon goes well, but eventually pride causes problems and Frederick leaves—for a "better" life. However, he finds that the dissolute life now seems strangely wrong—and he realizes that what he left behind is really what he wants.

Other books you might like:
Elisabeth Fairchild, *The Silent Suitor*, 1994
  blind heroine
Emma Lange, *A Heart in Peril*, 1994
  marriage of convenience
Mary Jo Putney, *The Diabolical Baron*, 1987
Mary Jo Putney, *The Rake and the Reformer*, 1989

58

MARY BALOGH

Deceived

(New York: Onyx, 1993)

Story type: Historical/Regency
Major character(s): Elizabeth Ward, Noblewoman, Amnesiac; Christopher Bouchard, Nobleman (Earl of Trevelyan)
Time period(s): 1810s
Locale(s): England

Summary: Returning to England after an absence of seven years, Christopher Bouchard, Earl of Trevelyan, is appalled that his ex-wife, Elizabeth, is about to remarry; so he does the only thing he can—he kidnaps the bride. A bout of temporary amnesia allows the pair to have several passionate weeks together, but when Elizabeth's memory returns, Christopher

15

must not only clear his name of earlier accusations, but he must also regain Elizabeth's love and trust, as well. A realistic historical that touches on some darker issues, including divorce and rape-recovery.

Other books you might like:
Catherine Coulter, *The Heiress Bride*, 1993
Kasey Michaels, *Legacy of the Rose*, 1992
  dark and sensual
Mary Jo Putney, *Uncommon Vows*, 1991
  medieval time period
Anne Stuart, *A Rose at Midnight*, 1993
  dark and sensual
Marlene Suson, *The Errant Earl*, 1989
  sweet and innocent

59

MARY BALOGH

Heartless
(New York: Berkely, 1995)

Story type: Historical/Georgian
Major character(s): Lady Anna Marlowe, Noblewoman, Spinster; Lucas Kendrick, Nobleman (Duke of Harndon)
Time period(s): 18th century
Locale(s): England

Summary: Resigned to being a spinster, Lady Anna Marlowe is amazed to find herself falling in love with Lucas Kendrick, a man who had never thought to marry. By the same token, Lucas is enchanted by Lady Anna. As a result, their marriage begins as one of hope, but misunderstandings soon turn it into one of resignation. Past secrets return to haunt them and present villains plot against them. Well-done, somewhat dark, and sensual.

Other books you might like:
Kasey Michaels, *The Illusion of Love*, 1991
Anita Mills, *Secret Nights*, 1994
Mary Jo Putney, *Thunder and Roses*, 1993
Anne Stuart, *To Love a Dark Lord*, 1994

60

MARY BALOGH

Lord Carew's Bride
(New York: Signet, 1995)

Story type: Regency
Major character(s): Samantha Newman, Spinster; Lord Hartley Wade, Nobleman (Marquess of Carew)
Time period(s): 1810s
Locale(s): London, England; Yorkshire, England

Summary: Samantha Newman is no young schoolroom miss, and at the advanced age of five and twenty, she is definitely not looking for a husband. What she really wants is a companion—someone like Mr. Wade. But Mr. Wade is not all that he seems and the two discover their dark pasts are connected by the same ruthless man. A typical Balogh Regency that pushes at the boundaries of the subgenre.

Other books you might like:
Emma Lange, *A Second Match*, 1993
Mary Jo Putney, *The Diabolical Baron*, 1987
Catherine Reynolds, *The Highwayman*, 1993
Sheila Simonson, *The Bar Sinister*, 1986

61

MARY BALOGH

The Notorious Rake
(New York: Signet, 1992)

Story type: Regency
Major character(s): Mary Gregg, Noblewoman (Lady Mornington); Edmond Waite, Nobleman, Rake
Time period(s): 1810s
Locale(s): London, England

Summary: Lady Mary has no intentions toward the notorious Lord Waite, but a chance thunderstorm during an innocent stroll in the garden changes all that. She is frightened, he takes advantage, she avoids him, but he pursues. Eventually, the pair are united, but not before a number of passionate discussions and some remarkable changes occur.

Other books you might like:
Loretta Chase, *The Lion's Daughter*, 1992
Charlene Cross, *A Heart So Innocent*, 1990
Mary Kingsley, *A Gentleman's Desire*, 1991
Judith McNaught, *Almost Heaven*, 1990
Amanda Quick, *Seduction*, 1990

62

MARY BALOGH

Promise of Spring
(New York: Signet, 1990)

Story type: Regency
Major character(s): Grace Howard, Gentlewoman (Impoverished); JSir Peregrine Lampman, Gentleman
Time period(s): 1810s

Summary: When Sir Perry Lampman and Grace Howard agree to a marriage of convenience to save Grace from poverty, love isn't part of the bargain. Nevertheless, they fall in love in spite of the fact that Grace is older than Perry and has a "past" that returns to haunt her. A different Regency.

Other books you might like:
Joan Aiken, *The Five-Minute Marriage*, 1977
Georgette Heyer, *The Convenient Marriage*, 1934
Leslie Lynn, *The Rake's Redemption*, 1989
Sheila Simonson, *The Bar Sinister*, 1986
Marlene Suson, *The Errant Earl*, 1989

63

MARY BALOGH

A Regency Christmas II
(New York: New American Library/Signet, 1990)

Story type: Regency; Holiday Themes

Time period(s): 1810s
Locale(s): England

Summary: Holiday romance Regency-style in this collection of five stories by top Regency writers Mary Balogh, Carla Kelly, Anita Mills, Mary Jo Putney, and Sheila Walsh.

Other books you might like:
Sandra Heath, *A Christmas Courtship*, 1990
Carla Kelly, *Marian's Christmas Wish*, 1989

64

MARY BALOGH

A Regency Christmas VI

(New York: Signet, 1994)

Story type: Holiday Themes; Anthology
Time period(s): 1810s
Locale(s): England

Summary: A diverse collection of Christmas romances set during the Regency Period. Includes "The Best Gift" by Mary Balogh, "Dinner at Grillion's" by Sandra Heath, "The Christmas Knight" by Emily Hendrickson, "Christmas Magic" by Emma Lange, and "It Came upon a Midnight Clear" by Sheila Walsh. Signet's sixth annual Regency Christmas Anthology.

Other books you might like:
Mary Balogh, *Christmas Belle*, 1994
Mary Chase Comstock, *A Christmas Wish*, 1994
   anthology
Carla Kelly, *Marian's Christmas Wish*, 1989
Meg-Lynn Roberts, *Christmas Escapade*, 1994
Jeanne Savery, *A Christmas Treasure*, 1994

65

MARY BALOGH
SANDRA HEATH, Co-Author
EDITH LAYTON, Co-Author
LAURA MATTHEWS, Co-Author
JO BEVERLEY, Co-Author

A Regency Christmas VII

(New York: Signet, 1995)

Story type: Anthology; Holiday Themes
Time period(s): 1810s
Locale(s): England

Summary: Signet's seventh annual collection of love stories set in Regency England during the Christmas Holiday season. Included are "The Christmas Ghost" by Sandra Heath, "The Rake's Christmas" by Edith Layton, "Lady Bountiful" by Laura Matthews, "A Mummer's Play" by Jo Beverley, and "A Surprise Party" by Mary Balogh.

Other books you might like:
Mary Balogh, *Christmas Belle*, 1994
Mary Chase Comstock, *A Christmas Wish*, 1994
Carla Kelly, *Mrs. Drew Plays Her Hand*, 1994
Lynn Kerstan, *Gwen's Christmas Ghost*, 1995
   Alicia Rasley, co-author

Barbara Metzger, *Father Christmas*, 1995

66

MARY BALOGH

A Regency Valentine

(New York: New American Library/Signet, 1991)

Story type: Regency; Holiday Themes
Time period(s): 1810s
Locale(s): England

Summary: A Valentine confection consisting of five short Regency romances by noted Regency authors. Includes: "The Golden Rose" by Mary Balogh, "The Secret Benefactor" by Katherine Kingsley, "Lady Valentine's Scheme" by Emma Lange, "Fathers and Daughters" by Patricia Rice, and "The Antogonists" by Joan Wolf.

Other books you might like:
Donna Bell, *The Valentine's Day Ball*, 1991
Marion Chesney, *My Lords, Ladies, and Marjorie*, 1983
Clare Darcy, *Georgina*, 1971
Georgette Heyer, *Black Sheep*, 1967

67

MARY BALOGH

The Secret Pearl

(New York: New American Library, 1991)

Story type: Regency
Major character(s): Isabelle Fleur Bradshaw, Governess, Prostitute; Adam Kent, Nobleman (Duke of Rideway)
Time period(s): 1810s
Locale(s): London, England

Summary: Forced to leave her home, penniless Isabelle Fleur arrives in London with two choices—starve, or become a woman of the streets. Fortunately, her first client is a man of conscience, and when Adam Kent, the Duke of Rideway, finds he cannot forget Fleur, he hires her as governess to his daughter. Their proximity to each other results in a growing bond between them, but since the Duke is already married, albeit unhappily, their own dreams of love and happiness seem out of reach. Well-drawn characters in an unusual Regency.

Other books you might like:
Catherine Coulter, *Night Shadow*, 1990
Edith Layton, *Fireflower*, 1989
Mary Jo Putney, *Dearly Beloved*, 1990
Mary Jo Putney, *The Rake and the Reformer*, 1989
Amanda Quick, *Seduction*, 1990

68

MARY BALOGH

The Snow Angel

(New York: New American Library, 1991)

Story type: Regency

Major character(s): Rosamund Hunter, Widow(er), Runaway; Justin Halliday, Nobleman (Earl of Wetherby)
Time period(s): 1810s
Locale(s): England
Summary: Young widow Rosamund Hunter rebels against her brother's controlling ways and escapes into a snow storm only to be rescued by the Earl of Wetherby en route to a shooting box for a final bachelorhood fling. The pair, of course, end up snowbound together, and in non-traditional Regency fashion have an affair. All is well for the lovers by the end of the book, but this is an atypical Regency with Balough rather successfully breaking a number of long-standing Regency rules.

Other books you might like:
Jo Beverley, *An Arranged Marriage*, 1991
Clare Darcy, *Letty*, 1980
Sarah Eagle, *The Reluctant Suitor*, 1991
Katherine Kingsley, *A Natural Attachment*, 1990
Amanda Quick, *Surrender*, 1990
    sensual

69

MARY BALOGH

Tangled

(New York: Topaz, 1994)

Story type: Historical/Victorian
Major character(s): Rebecca Cardwell, Noblewoman; Lord David Tavistock, Nobleman (viscount), Military Personnel (major); Sir Julian Cardwell, Nobleman (baronet), Military Personnel (captain)
Time period(s): 1850s
Locale(s): England
Summary: Upon learning her husband, Julian, has been killed in the Crimean War, Rebecca Cardwell reluctantly agrees to marry Lord David Tavistock, her late husband's foster brother. Then, just as she is learning to love David, Julian returns from captivity and Rebecca is duty-bound to honor her first marriage. Revenge, secrets, and murder are all part of a well-written but truly tangled romance that explores the darker side of Victorian society.

Other books you might like:
Judy Cuevas, *Black Silk*, 1991
    dark and Victorian
Barbara Keller, *The Heart's Legacy*, 1993
Pierre Choderlos de Laclos, *Les Liaisons Dangereuses*, 1782
    a classic from an earlier time period
Kasey Michaels, *Legacy of the Rose*, 1992
Mary Jo Putney, *Petals in the Storm*, 1993

70

ELAINE BARBIERI

Midnight Rogue

(New York: Zebra, 1995)

Story type: Historical/Antebellum American South
Major character(s): Gabrielle Dubay, Debutante, Captive; Rogan Whitney, Military Personnel, Pirate (''Rapace'')

Time period(s): 1810s
Locale(s): New Orleans, Louisiana; Grand Terre, Louisiana
Summary: In a plan to avenge the destruction of his ship and murder of his crew, Captain Rogan Whitney turns pirate, kidnaps the daughter of the man he considers responsible, and takes her to the legendary Grand Terre. This captive-in-love-with-captor story features intricate plotting and a plethora of well-developed characters. The villain is especially intriguing.

Other books you might like:
Christine Dorsey, *Sea of Dreams*, 1993
    more pirates/faster pacing
Robin Lee Hatcher, *The Magic*, 1993
    pirates, vengeance, and exotic settings
Lisa Kleypas, *Only with Your Love*, 1992
Meagan McKinney, *Till Dawn Tames the Night*, 1991
    more pirates
Becky Lee Weyrich, *Sweet Forever*, 1992
    pirates and time travel elements

71

ELAINE BARBIERI
KATHLEEN EAGLE, Co-Author
MARGARET MOORE, Co-Author
PATRICIA GARDNER, Co-Author

Mistletoe Marriages

(Toronto: Harlequin, 1994)

Story type: Anthology; Holiday Themes
Summary: A collection of four heartwarming Christmas novels focusing on the themes of love and marriage. Included are ''Rendezvous'' by Elaine Barbieri, ''The Wolf and the Lamb'' by Kathleen Eagle, ''Christmas in the Valley'' by Margaret Moore, and ''Keeping Christmas'' by Patricia Gardner Evans.

Other books you might like:
Rexanne Becnel, *Christmas Journey*, 1992
Kathleen Creighton, *A Christmas Love*, 1992
Maggie Daniels, *Moonlight and Mistletoe*, 1993
Ann LaFarge, *The Joy of Christmas*, 1994
Ellen Tanner Marsh, *A Christmas Embrace*, 1994

72

ELAINE BARBIERI

More Precious than Gold

(New York: Zebra, 1992)

Story type: Historical/American West; Saga
Major character(s): Rosie, Saloon Keeper/Owner (partner); Tag Willis, Saloon Keeper/Owner (partner); Drake McNeil, Mountain Man
Time period(s): 19th century
Locale(s): Deadwood, South Dakota
Summary: In this multi-story romantic saga, Rosie eventually discovers that love is ofte n where one least expects to find it. Fast-paced, yet tender, tale of the Olf West filled with unusual and likeable characters.

Other books you might like:
Stephanie Bartlett, *Highland Flame*, 1992
Rosanne Bittner, *In the Shadow of the Mountains*, 1991
Linda Howard, *A Lady of the West*, 1990
Jill Marie Landis, *Come Spring*, 1992
Catherine Lanigan, *A Promise Made*, 1991

73

ELAINE BARBIERI

Only for Love
(New York: Zebra, 1994)

Story type: Historical/Exotic
Major character(s): Gillian Haige, Servant (indentured); Derek Andrews, Sea Captain
Locale(s): At Sea; Caribbean

Summary: Captain Derek Andrews agrees to transport indentured servants, Gillian Haige and her ailing twin sister to the islands on one condition—that Gillian share his bed. Eventually, the sister recovers and Derek buys their papers, but their problems are not over. Dangerous and vindictive enemies, jealousy, and Gillian's pride and need for freedom continue to cause trouble. A passionate and loving story in an exotic setting.

Other books you might like:
Elizabeth DeLancey, *Sea of Dreams*, 1992
   adventurous, daring heroine
Stef Ann Holm, *King of the Pirates*, 1994
   tropical setting
Teresa Medeiros, *Once an Angel*, 1993
Laura Simon, *A Taste of Heaven*, 1989
   Caribbean setting
Kathleen E. Woodiwiss, *Shanna*, 1977
   1970s-type historical/Caribbean setting

74

ELAINE BARBIERI
EVELYN ROGERS, Co-Author
KAREN LOCKWOOD, Co-Author
LORI COPELAND, Co-Author

Seasons of Love
(New York: Harper, 1995)

Story type: Anthology
Time period(s): 19th century
Locale(s): United States

Summary: Billed as "A Year's Worth of Romance," this quartet of historical novellas by four popular writers focuses on romance during the four seasons of the year. Included are "Winter Moon" by Elaine Barbieri, "Gentle Rain" by Evelyn Rogers, "Summer Storm" by Karen Lockwood, and "Golden Harvest" by Lori Copeland.

Other books you might like:
Jill Barnett, *Midsummer Night's Madness*, 1995
   midsummer anthology
Edith Layton, *A Love for All Seasons*, 1992
   five seasonal Regency short stories

Anita Mills, *Cherished Moments*, 1994
   Mother's Day anthology
Kathleen E. Woodiwiss, *Three Weddings and a Kiss*, 1995
   wedding anthology

75

ELAINE BARBIERI

Tattered Silk
(New York: Zebra, 1991)

Story type: Historical/Mainstream; Saga
Major character(s): Sophia Marone, Designer (aspiring dress designer), Worker (in a silk mill); Lyle Kingston, Manager (of silk mill); Aaron Weiss, Businessman (son of mill owner)
Locale(s): Patterson, New Jersey

Summary: Determined to realize her dreams of being a dress designer, beautiful Italian immigrant Sophia Marone gives up her love for ambition and false promises—and almost loses her life in the process.

Other books you might like:
Barbara Taylor Bradford, *A Woman of Substance*, 1979
Sandra Bregman, *Reach for the Dream*, 1990
Jill Marie Landis, *Rose*, 1990
Belva Plain, *Evergreen*, 1978
Lucy Taylor, *Avenue of Dreams*, 1990

76

ELAINE BARBIERI

Wings of a Dove
(New York: Jove, 1990)

Story type: Historical/Victorian America
Major character(s): Allie Pierce, Orphan; Delaney Marsh, Orphan
Time period(s): 1850s
Locale(s): Midwest

Summary: Fast friends from their journey West on the orphan train, Allie and Delaney face jealousy, separation, marriage to others, lies, and deception before they can both be truly happy.

Other books you might like:
Sally Beauman, *Destiny*, 1987
Rebecca George, *Call Home the Heart*, 1989
Lisa Gregory, *The Rainbow Promise*, 1989
Jill Marie Landis, *Sunflower*, 1988
Jack McGowan, *Flame in the Night*, 1990

77

ELAINE BARBIERI

Wishes on the Wind
(New York: Berkley, 1991)

Story type: Historical/Victorian America
Major character(s): Meghan O'Connor, Servant; David Lang, Mine Owner (nephew and heir of owner)

Time period(s): 1870s (1869-1875)
Locale(s): Pennsylvania

Summary: Irish spitfire and miner's daughter Meghan O'Connor and David Lang, wealthy nephew of the mine owner, clash from the day they meet; but despite their social and political differences, they grow close—and eventually fall in love. A poignant, moving story of love that endures against all odds. Set during the tumultuous years of the activities of the Mollie Maguires.

Other books you might like:
Sally Beauman, *Destiny*, 1987
Olga Bicos, *By My Heart Betrayed*, 1991
Taylor Caldwell, *Ceremony of the Innocent*, 1976
    serious look at inter-class relationships
Rebecca George, *Call Home the Heart*, 1989
Lisa Gregory, *The Rainbow Promise*, 1989

78

ANNE BARBOUR

A Dangerous Charade

(New York: Signet, 1995)

Story type: Regency
Major character(s): Alison Fox, Companion; Anthony Brent, Nobleman (Earl of Marchford)
Time period(s): 1810s
Locale(s): London, England

Summary: Fearing his dear aunt is being fleeced, Lord Anthony Brent must check out her young companion—and in fact, Alison Fox does have a hidden identity that could land her in jail. However, Anthony is soon enamored of her, but he knows there's a mystery that he can't uncover. Her name isn't Fox and her talent isn't as a lady's companion. Intrigue builds as her past threatens her security and her love for him.

Other books you might like:
Rita Boucher, *A Misbegotten Match*, 1994
April Kihlstrom, *Dangerous Masquerade*, 1992
Barbara Metzger, *Lady in Green*, 1993
Diana Palmer, *Noelle*, 1995
    Edwardian companion

79

ANNE BARBOUR

Kate and the Soldier

(New York: Signet, 1993)

Story type: Regency
Major character(s): Kate, Gentlewoman, Cousin; David Merritt, Heir, Military Personnel (major)
Time period(s): 1810s
Locale(s): England

Summary: When wounded David Merritt returns to his childhood home to his father's deathbed, he meets with hostility on the part of his stepmother, joy on the part of his cousin Kate, and a surprising posthumous revelation from his father. Engaging characters in a warm and realistic Regency love story.

Other books you might like:
Rosemary Edghill, *Fleeting Fancy*, 1993
Barbara Metzger, *The Luck of the Devil*, 1991
Irene Saunders, *Talk of the Town*, 1991
Sheila Simonson, *A Cousinly Connexion*, 1984
Marlene Suson, *The Errant Earl*, 1989

80

ANNE BARBOUR

Lord Glenraven's Return

(New York: Signet, 1994)

Story type: Regency
Major character(s): Claudia Carstairs, Widow(er); Jeremy Standish, Nobleman (Lord Glenraven), Imposter ("Jem January")
Time period(s): 1810s
Locale(s): Ravencroft, England (an estate)

Summary: When Lord Glenraven returns in disguise to reclaim the estate his father had been cheated out of, he finds Ravencroft in decline and his plans totally confused by the lovely young widow of the former owner—a woman as committed to the estate as he is and just as determined to see it restored. Likable characters and witty dialogue in a charmingly told tale.

Other books you might like:
Mary Chase Comstock, *A Midsummer's Magic*, 1994
Sarah Eagle, *The Bedeviled Baron*, 1994
Barbara Metzger, *The Luck of the Devil*, 1991
Evelyn Richardson, *Lady Alex's Gamble*, 1995
Sheila Simonson, *A Cousinly Connexion*, 1984

81

ANNE BARBOUR (Pseudonym of Barbara Yirka)

My Cousin Jane

(New York: Signet, 1995)

Story type: Regency
Major character(s): Jane Burch, Companion, Imposter; Lord Simon Talent, Nobleman, Guardian
Time period(s): 1810s (1817)
Locale(s): London, England

Summary: When Jane Burch agrees to masquerade as a respectable, and not particularly attractive, chaperone so her cousin Winnifred can have a Season, she ends up attracted to Winnifred's new guardian, Lord Simon Talent. But Simon has made a deathbed promise to Winnifred's brother to see her safely married, something that is proving difficult because the willful Winnifred is determined to be an actress! Eventually, of course, Simon discovers Jane's secret and together they try to deal with Winnifred's thespian aspirations—and their feelings for each other. Well-crafted, humorous, and filled with appealing characters.

Other books you might like:
Clare Darcy, *Caroline and Julia*, 1982
Marian Devon, *Lord Harlequin*, 1994
    more thespians

Carla Kelly, *Miss Billings Treads the Boards*, 1993
　more thespians
Barbara Metzger, *Lady in Green*, 1993
　another masquerading heroine

82

ANNE BARBOUR

A Talent for Trouble
(New York: Signet, 1992)

Story type: Regency
Major character(s): Lady Talitha Burnside, Noblewoman, Artist; Viscount Chelmsford, Nobleman, Writer
Time period(s): 1810s
Locale(s): London, England

Summary: Lady Talitha, no ordinary debutante, is poor but talented. As an artist, she collaborates with author Lord Chelmsford on a scandalous satire of town life, and in the process, they are drawn to each other, even though Lord Chelmsford is already engaged. Spies, politics, and blackmail figure in this intriguing Regency as Tally risks everything for the man she loves.

Other books you might like:
Mary Balogh, *The Secret Pearl*, 1991
Cleo Chadwick, *A Midsummer Night's Kiss*, 1991
Emily Hendrickson, *Miss Wyndham's Escapade*, 1990
Georgette Heyer, *Sylvester, or the Wicked Uncle*, 1957
Carla Kelly, *Miss Grimsley's Oxford Career*, 1992

83

SUZANNE BARCLAY

Knight's Lady
(Toronto: Harlequin, 1993)

Story type: Historical/Medieval
Major character(s): Ariana de Clerc, Artisan (goldsmith); Lord Gareth Sommerville, Nobleman, Widow(er)
Time period(s): 14th century (1325)
Locale(s): England

Summary: Lord Gareth Somerville's late wife was treacherous and dangerous; as a result, his opinion of women is low. However, he changes his mind when he is wounded and lovingly cared for by Ariana de Clerc, a goldsmith with a somewhat "diverse" family. He worries about clearing his family's name, she worries about their class differences. Eventually, of course, they see that love is really the answer to their dilemma. A beautifully researched sequel to *Knight Dreams*.

Other books you might like:
Christina Dodd, *Candle in the Window*, 1991
Roberta Gellis, *Roselynde*, 1984
　first of the Roselynde Chronicles
Joanna McGauran, *A Love So Fierce*, 1993
Flora M. Speer, *Castle of the Heart*, 1990

84

JILL BARKIN (Pseudonym of Susan Johnson)

Hot Streak
(New York: Berkley, 1990)

Story type: Contemporary/Mainstream
Major character(s): Molly Darian, Businesswoman; Cary Fersten, Producer (Movie)
Time period(s): 1980s
Locale(s): Minneapolis, Minnesota

Summary: This mainstream contemporary romance reunites former lovers Molly and Cary against a background of murder, kidnapping, and international terrorism. Fast-paced and passionate.

Other books you might like:
Judith Michael, *Deceptions*, 1982
Nora Roberts, *Public Secrets*, 1990
Sidney Sheldon, *If Tomorrow Comes*, 1985
Sherryl Woods, *Stolen Moments*, 1990
　Sequel to *Body & Soul* and *Reckless*

85

LINDA BARLOW

Intimate Betrayal
(New York: Warner, 1995)

Story type: Contemporary; Romantic Suspense
Major character(s): Annie Jefferson, Architect (Architectural Designer), Businesswoman (company owner); Matt Carlyle, Businessman (CEO of Powerdyme)
Time period(s): 1990s
Locale(s): San Francisco, California

Summary: Widow and architectural designer Annie Jefferson is determined to rebuild her life. When wealthy Matt Carlyle backs her current building project, things become more interesting—and more dangerous. Murder, sabotage, and treachery are part of this intriguing, emotionally involving story.

Other books you might like:
Tami Hoag, *Dark Paradise*, 1994
Linda Howard, *After the Night*, 1995
Nora Roberts, *Hidden Riches*, 1995
Meryl Sawyer, *Kiss in the Dark*, 1995
Katherine Stone, *Pearl Moon*, 1994
　mysteries and buildings, Hong Kong style

86

ELIZABETH BARNES

In Spite of Themselves
(Toronto: Harlequin, 1991)

Story type: Contemporary
Major character(s): Anne Chaplin, Art Dealer, Imposter; Nicholas Thayer, Businessman
Time period(s): 1990s
Locale(s): New York, New York

Summary: In order to raise the money necessary to expand the art gallery where she works, Anne Chaplin reluctantly agrees to pose as Nick Thayer's mistress during a visit to St. Denis. Naturally, they don't plan to fall in love, but of course they do—"in spite of themselves." Well-developed characters.

Other books you might like:
Jean Barrett, *Heat*, 1991
Emma Darcy, *The Falcon's Mistress*, 1990
Jayne Ann Krentz, *Silver Linings*, 1991
Valerie Parv, *Tasmanian Devil*, 1990
Laura Taylor, *Jade's Passion*, 1990

87

JILL BARNETT

Dreaming

(New York: Pocket, 1994)

Story type: Historical/Regency
Major character(s): Letitia "Letty" Hornsby, Debutante; Richard Lennox, Nobleman (Earl of Downe)
Time period(s): 1810s
Locale(s): England

Summary: In love with Richard Lennox, Earl of Downe since childhood, Letitia Hornsby considers him her destiny and pursues him determinedly. Unfortunately, to Richard, she is simply an annoying hellion. Eventually, of course, all works out, but the road to true love is filled with various disasters, most of which are caused by Letty's "dreaminess." Funny, witty, and magical.

Other books you might like:
Connie Brockway, *Promise Me Heaven*, 1994
Virginia Brown, *Hidden Touch*, 1992
Marion Chesney, *The Dreadful Debutante*, 1994
Julie Garwood, *The Gift*, 1991
Betina M. Krahn, *Midnight Magic*, 1990

88

JILL BARNETT

Imagine

(New York: Pocket, 1995)

Story type: Historical/Exotic; Historical/Fantasy
Major character(s): Margaret Huntington Smith, Lawyer, Castaway; Hank Wyatt, Fugitive (escaped convict), Castaway; Muhdula Ali "Muddy", Mythical Creature (genii)
Time period(s): 1890s
Locale(s): Pacific Islands

Summary: Muhdula Ali, or "Muddy" for short, has his magical hands full when his bottle ends up on a tropical island and is uncorked by a young castaway. Three lively children, a hero with an attitude, and a city-bred heroine learn they must work together to survive—and in the process, they become a family. Generally briskly-paced and occasionally hilarious.

Other books you might like:
Michelle Brandon, *Heaven on Earth*, 1993
  islands and angels

Jude Deveraux, *Wishes*, 1989
  an angel with a mission
Kasey Michaels, *Timely Matrimony*, 1994
  contemporary fantasy/funny and fast-paced
Rebecca Paisley, *Moonlight and Magic*, 1990
  children, comedy, and "magic"

89

JILL BARNETT

Just a Kiss Away

(New York: Pocket, 1992)

Story type: Historical/Victorian
Major character(s): Eulalia Grace "Lollie" LaRue, Southern Belle; Sam Forester, Adventurer (freedom fighter)
Time period(s): 1890s (1896)
Locale(s): Philippines

Summary: Thrown together and then captured by his enemies, freedom fighter Sam Forester and inept southern belle Lollie LaRue struggle to escape through the steamy Philippine jungles—and fall in love along the way. Funny, sensual, and filled with non-stop action.

Other books you might like:
Katherine Compton, *Eden's Angel*, 1990
Laura Kinsale, *Seize the Fire*, 1989
Katherine Sutcliffe, *Shadow Play*, 1991
Marianne Willman, *Tilly and the Tiger*, 1990

90

JILL BARNETT
ELAINE COFFMAN, Co-Author
ALEXIS HARRINGTON, Co-Author
SONIA SIMONE, Co-Author

Midsummer Night's Madness

(New York: St. Martin's, 1995)

Story type: Anthology; Historical/Fantasy
Locale(s): England; United States

Summary: This quartet of historical novellas focuses on the romance and magic of Midsummer. Included are "A Knight in Tarnished Armor" by Jill Barnett, "A Ribbon of Moonlight" by Elaine Coffman, "Enchanted" by Alexis Harrington, and "Golden Mermaid" by Sonia Simone. Light, charming, and magical.

Other books you might like:
Ellen Archer, *Under His Spell*, 1995
  another magical historical anthology
Jill Barnett, *Bewitching*, 1993
Gayle Buck, *Full Moon Magic*, 1992
  another magical anthology
Mary Chase Comstock, *A Midsummer's Magic*, 1994
  magic and wit, Regency-style

91

JILL BARNETT

Surrender a Dream
(New York: Pocket, 1991)

Story type: Historical/American West Coast
Major character(s): Adelaide Pinkney, Farmer, Heiress; Montana Creed, Heir, Farmer
Time period(s): 1890s
Locale(s): California

Summary: When former librarian Adelaide Pinkney and drifter Montana Creed inherit the same California farm, the battle lines are drawn. They both want the farm and will stop at nothing to get it—not even a marriage of convenience. Funny, fast-paced, and passionate.

Other books you might like:
Barbara Bretton, *Midnight Lover*, 1989
Dorothy Garlock, *Midnight Blue*, 1989
Barbara Hargis, *Heart Song*, 1990
Kathy Lawrence, *Tin Angel*, 1989
Rebecca Sinclair, *California Caress*, 1989

92

LINDA LANG BARTELL

Caressa
(New York: Onyx, 1990)

Story type: Historical/Renaissance
Major character(s): Caressa Rugger, Widow(er), Noble-woman; Dante de Allesandro, Nobleman
Time period(s): 15th century (1475)
Locale(s): Tuscany, Italy

Summary: To avenge the death of her brother, Caressa kidnaps the supposed murderer, Dante de Allesandro, and suddenly finds herself forced to marry him in an effort to end the longstanding family feud. Renaissance Italy at its treacherous and intriguing best.

Other books you might like:
Pamela Belle, *The Lodestar*, 1989
    English court intrigue
Roberta Gellis, *The Silver Mirror*, 1989
    French/English court intrigue
Mary Ellen Gronau, *Passionate Warriors*, 1989
    Irish conflict and intrigue
Samuel Shellabarger, *Prince of Foxes*, 1947
    Classic of Renaissance romantic intrigue
Bertrice Small, *Skye O'Malley*, 1980

93

LINDA LANG BARTELL

Tender Warrior
(New York: Zebra, 1992)

Story type: Historical/Medieval
Major character(s): Merlyn, Widow(er) (Saxon), Imposter; Rolf de Valmont, Nobleman (Norman)

Time period(s): 11th century (1075)
Locale(s): Renford, England

Summary: When Norman Baron Rolf is sent to rebuild Renford in England, he finds it has been practically destroyed by Scots and Vikings and is now presided over by a bitter old hag who detests Normans. Merlyn, the old lady, is change-able, sharp-tongued, and surprisingly energetic — and it doesn't take Rolf long to discover her secret. Fast-paced and sensual.

Other books you might like:
Shannon Drake, *Princess of Fire*, 1989
Julie Garwood, *The Prize*, 1991
Rebecca Sinclair, *Wild Scottish Embrace*, 1991
    different period
Bertrice Small, *A Moment in Time*, 1991
Kathleen E. Woodiwiss, *The Wolf and the Dove*, 1974

94

STEPHANIE BARTLETT

Dearest Enemy
(New York: Zebra, 1995)

Story type: Historical/American West
Major character(s): Victoria Pruitt, Settler (homesteader), Farmer; Stephen Beaumont, Veteran, Farmer
Time period(s): 1860s (1869)
Locale(s): Jacksonville, Oregon

Summary: Struggling to work her homestead and care for her son and war-incapacitated husband, Victoria Pruitt nurses a deep hatred for anyone who fought for the South. It is no surprise, then, when she threatens a trespassing returning Rebel soldier and holds him at gun point while she sends for the sheriff. The surprise comes when her trespasser turns out to be one of the former owners of her homestead who is well-known and liked by everyone in town and who has no place to go! Love and understanding come, but so do more problems. Tender, realistic, and emotionally involving.

Other books you might like:
Barbara Ankrum, *Renegade's Kiss*, 1993
    Civil War aftermath
Micki Brown, *Because of You*, 1993
    Civil War aftermath
Candace Camp, *Flame Lily*, 1994
    Civil War aftermath
Jill Marie Landis, *Until Tomorrow*, 1994
    Civil War aftermath

95

STEPHANIE BARTLETT

Highland Flame
(New York: Doubleday, 1992)

Story type: Historical/American West; Saga
Major character(s): Catriona McLeod, Widow(er), Rancher; Will Bascom, Doctor
Time period(s): 19th century
Locale(s): New Arlington, Texas

Summary: When a Texas landowner leaves Scottish Catriona McLeod a widow, she determines to build a new life for herself and her daughter — just as her husband would have wanted. Physical hardships, land battles, and the adjustment to a new country test Cat's strength and will to the limit, but with her independent spirit and eventually the love of a long time friend, Will Bascom, she succeeds in realizing her dreams. Realistic and filled with good historical detail. Sequel to *Highland Rebel*.

Other books you might like:
Linda Howard, *A Lady of the West*, 1990
Catherine Lanigan, *A Promise Made*, 1991
Jeanne Williams, *Home Mountain*, 1990
Jeanne Williams, *No Roof but Heaven*, 1990
Jeanne Williams, *The Valiant Woman*, 1980

96

STEPHANIE BARTLETT

Highland Rebel
(New York: Bantam, 1992)

Story type: Historical/Victorian
Major character(s): Catriona Galbraith, Landowner; Ian Mc-Leod, Rancher
Time period(s): 1880s (1881)
Locale(s): Isle of Skye, Scotland

Summary: Lovely Catriona's homeland and heritage are threatened by her tyrannical father's greed. Texas rancher Ian McLeod comes to bury his grandfather and stays to be part of the solution to Cats' problems and ends up becoming a part of Cat's life. Authentic and historically accurate detail.

Other books you might like:
Ruth Langan, *Highland Fire*, 1991
Ruth Langan, *Highland Heart*, 1992
Judith McNaught, *Almost Heaven*, 1990
Deborah Smith, *Legends*, 1990
   contemporary

97

LOIS BATTLE

The Past Is Another Country
(New York: Fawcett, 1992)

Story type: Contemporary/Mainstream
Major character(s): Megan Hanlon, Actress; Greta Papandreou, Farmer; Sister Mary Magdalene, Religious (nun)
Time period(s): 1990s
Locale(s): Australia

Summary: Three young women build a lifetime friendship at the convent school, and it sees them through individual trials. Megan has to face her ex-husband and her love—and choose; Greta lives in the bush and her loneliness is magnified by her husband's betrayal; and Sister Mary Magdalene must choose between her order and her love. Warm, witty, entertaining, and realistic.

Other books you might like:
Leigh Bristol, *Sunswept*, 1990
Connie Mason, *Wild Land, Wild Love*, 1992
Colleen McCullough, *The Thorn Birds*, 1977
Charlotte Simms, *Silver Caress*, 1990
Katherine Sinclair, *Far Horizons*, 1991

98

LOIS BATTLE

Storyville
(New York: Viking, 1993)

Story type: Historical/Mainstream; Saga
Major character(s): Julia Randsome, Feminist, Gentlewoman (bluestocking); Kate Cavanaugh, Feminist, Prostitute
Time period(s): 19th century (late)
Locale(s): New Orleans, Louisiana

Summary: Gently-bred Julia Randsome and prostitute Kate Cavanaugh would seem to have little in common—except for a passion for feminist ideals and a child. A poignant, powerful story of two determined women and the diverse worlds in which they live. Excellent depiction of New Orleans society of the period, genteel and otherwise.

Other books you might like:
Gwen Bristow, *The Handsome Road*, 1938
   second in the Plantation Trilogy
Karen Harper, *The Wings of Morning*, 1993
Katherine Sinclair, *A Distant Dawn*, 1991
Katherine Sinclair, *Far Horizons*, 1991
   Australian setting

99

MARSHA BAUER

Pirate's Angel
(New York: Zebra, 1991)

Story type: Historical/Colonial America
Major character(s): Ivy Woodruff, Gentlewoman; Drake Jordan, Plantation Owner, Pirate
Time period(s): 18th century
Locale(s): American Colonies; England; At Sea

Summary: When parsonage-raised Ivy Woodruff finds herself aboard her pirate father's ship, she presents herself to him as his daughter and demands protection. He obliges her by putting her in the care of dashing Drake Jordan, which is a bit like putting the fox among the chickens; but as they travel the seas searching for spies and the killer of her father's son, she and Drake fall in love. Passionate, adventurous, and peopled with caring, gentle characters.

Other books you might like:
Pamela K. Forrest, *Autumn Ecstasy*, 1990
Meagan McKinney, *Till Dawn Tames the Night*, 1991
Anita Mills, *Follow the Heart*, 1990
Joan Van Nuys, *Beloved Avenger*, 1989
Lynette Vinet, *Pirate's Bride*, 1989

100
MARSHA BAUER
Sweet Conquest
(New York: Zebra, 1990)

Story type: Historical/American West Coast
Major character(s): Melody Grayum, Businesswoman (bordello owner), Wealthy; Clay "Barclay" Weston, Gunfighter
Time period(s): 1870s (1875)
Locale(s): California

Summary: Wealthy, independent, and unconventional, young Melody Grayum has already acquired a certain notoriety, as well as the attention of someone who means to destroy her. She needs help and seeks it in the form of bodyguards. But when she is kidnapped in spite of all her precautions, it takes hired gun Clay Weston to rescue her—and eventually win her love.

Other books you might like:
Gwen Bristow, *Calico Palace*, 1970
Jude Deveraux, *Mountain Laurel*, 1990
Kathy Lawrence, *Tin Angel*, 1989
Betina Lindsey, *Waltz with the Lady*, 1990
Rebecca Sinclair, *California Caress*, 1989

101
PAMELA BAUER
Swinging on a Star
(Toronto: Harlequin, 1992)

Story type: Contemporary
Major character(s): Meridee Osborn, Businesswoman; Zeb Farrell, Consultant (efficiency expert)
Time period(s): 1990s

Summary: Serious-minded Meridee is concerned about her company's merger, but her meeting with the efficiency expert turns into play instead of work when he shows up at her sister's wedding. She ends up passing out in his room and later thinks she's pregnant! They obviously have more problems to solve than mere business-related ones.

Other books you might like:
Linda Jenkins, *Maverick's Lady*, 1992
Pamela Litton, *Stardust and Whirlwinds*, 1991
  historical setting
Debbie Macomber, *Rainy Day Kisses*, 1990
Noelle Berry McCue, *Look Beyond the Dream*, 1990

102
MARY LYNN BAXTER
Priceless
(New York: Warner, 1995)

Story type: Contemporary/Mainstream
Major character(s): Leah Frazier, Widow(er), Architect; Dalton Montgomery, Businessman (riverboat casino owner), Gambler
Time period(s): 1990s
Locale(s): Belusa, Louisiana; Biloxi, Mississippi

Summary: When young profligate Dalton Montgomery donates his sperm in return for quick cash, he has no idea that years later his forced search for the child he may have fathered will lead him to the child—and to love. Deception, intrigue, and greed abound in this fast-paced, emotionally involving story of love, sacrifice, and choices.

Other books you might like:
Rebecca Brandewyne, *Dust Devil*, 1995
Barbara Delinsky, *The Passions of Chelsea Kane*, 1992
  reversal of theme/child seeks mother
Lisa Jackson, *Wishes*, 1995
Karen Robards, *Maggy's Child*, 1994

103
MARY LYNN BAXTER
Sweet Justice
(New York: Warner, 1994)

Story type: Contemporary/Mainstream; Romantic Suspense
Major character(s): Kate Colson, Judge; Sawyer Brock, Detective
Time period(s): 1990s
Locale(s): United States

Summary: Twenty years ago, Kate Colson gave up her baby to her teenage boyfriend, Tom. Now she wants to locate her child, but Tom cruelly taunts her with the fact that he actually abandoned the baby instead. The action escalates when Kate hires private investigator Sawyer Brock and Tom reacts by hiring a hit man.

Other books you might like:
Rexanne Becnel, *The Christmas Wish*, 1993
  long-lost child theme/different treatment
Barbara Delinsky, *The Passions of Chelsea Kane*, 1992
  reversal of theme
Belva Plain, *Blessings*, 1988
  reversal of theme
Karen Robards, *Maggy's Child*, 1994
Katherine Stone, *Pearl Moon*, 1995
  search for identity and self/more lyrical treatment

104
MARY LYNN BAXTER
Winter Heat
(New York: Silhouette, 1990)

Story type: Contemporary
Major character(s): Allison Young, Widow(er) (Wealthy), Businesswoman (Silkflower Shop); Rafe Beaumont, Convict (Ex-con), Artisan (Woodworker)
Time period(s): 1980s

Summary: Wealthy socialite widow Allison Young goes into the silkflower business, much to the amazement and disapproval of her friends, and asks her neighbor, ex-con Rafe Beaumont, to help her remodel her shop. In spite of their differences, love blossoms between the two.

Other books you might like:
Dixie Browning, *Ships in the Night*, 1989
Kathleen Creighton, *Love and Other Surprises*, 1990
Elizabeth Lowell, *Fire and Rain*, 1989
Courtney Ryan, *Ten to Midnight*, 1989
Sherryl Woods, *One Touch of Moondust*, 1989

105

JULIE BEARD

The Lady and the Wolf
(New York: Diamond, 1994)

Story type: Historical/Medieval
Major character(s): Lady Katherine Gilbert, Fiance(e), Noblewoman; Stephen Bartingham, Knight (''The Wolf'')
Time period(s): 14th century (1350)
Locale(s): England

Summary: Although she wants to enter a convent to keep her vow to pray forever for her dying brother, Lady Katherine honors her father's command and marries Sir Stephen. Her new family situation is less than desirable with an evil brother, a dying father, and a peculiar mother; nevertheless, she has her duty to do—and she does come to love Stephen. Treachery and murder are all part of this detailed and somewhat realistic romance.

Other books you might like:
Jude Deveraux, *The Taming*, 1989
 another reluctant, but capable, bride
Julie Garwood, *Saving Grace*, 1994
 another reluctant bride/lighter and more humorous
Roberta Gellis, *Roselynde*, 1978
 1st of the Roselynde Chronicles
Roberta Gellis, *Rhiannon*, 1982
 4th of the Roselynde Chronicles
Laura Kinsale, *For My Lady's Heart*, 1993
 detailed/realistic/more challenging and complex

106

NINA BEAUMONT

Across Time
(Toronto: Harlequin, 1994)

Story type: Time Travel
Major character(s): Adrienne de Beaufort, Time Traveller, Reincarnated Person (as Isabella di Montefiore); Alexandro de Montefiori, Nobleman
Time period(s): 1790s (1794); 15th century (1494)
Locale(s): France; Italy

Summary: Swept through time from the Reign of Terror in France to Renaissance Italy, Adrienne de Beaufort ''becomes'' her ancestress, Isabella di Montefiore, and ends up using her knowledge of the future to save her husband from the machinations of both the Borgias and her own brother. A dark romance filled with treachery, court intrigue, and all the requisite Renaissance pageantry.

Other books you might like:
Linda Lang Bartell, *Caressa*, 1990
 Italian Renaissance intrigue/ no time travel elements
Laura Gilmour Bennett, *By All That Is Sacred*, 1991
Jasmine Cresswell, *To Catch the Wind*, 1993
Diana Gabaldon, *Outlander*, 1991
Iris Johansen, *The Wind Dancer*, 1991
 first of a trilogy/no time travel elements

107

NINA BEAUMONT

Promises to Keep
(Toronto: Harlequin, 1992)

Story type: Historical/Victorian
Major character(s): Felicity Allen, Singer; Maximilian Von Berg, Military Personnel, Spy (double agent)
Time period(s): 1840s (1847)
Locale(s): Vienna, Austria

Summary: American singer Felicity Allen is intrigued by Count Maximilian Von Berg who, in his efforts to protect her from the dangers of the Viennese political situation, whisks her away to an isolated estate. They proceed to fall in love, but revolution and reality interfere with their idyll and it is some time before they can be together on a permanent and peaceful basis.

Other books you might like:
Charlene Cross, *Masque of Enchantment*, 1990
Serena Richards, *Rendezvous*, 1991
Suzanne Robinson, *Lady Gallant*, 1992
 Renaissance Setting
Susan Wiggs, *The Raven and the Rose*, 1992

108

NINA BEAUMONT

Sapphire Magic
(Toronto: Harlequin, 1991)

Story type: Historical/Georgian
Major character(s): Arabella Douglas, Gentlewoman; Fernando ''Nando'' Berg, Military Personnel (Austrian army officer), Nobleman
Time period(s): 19th century (early)
Locale(s): Vienna, Austria

Summary: Treachery and deceit abound as Nando and Arabella struggle to find happiness and outwit their enemies in this fast-paced story of passion and intrigue set in the glittering world of early 19th century Vienna.

Other books you might like:
Jill Gregory, *Moonlit Obsession*, 1986
Patricia Matthews, *Dancer of Dreams*, 1984
Claudette Williams, *Fire and Desire*, 1984

109

REXANNE BECNEL

Christmas Journey
(New York: Dell, 1992)

Story type: Contemporary; Holiday Themes
Major character(s): Judith Montgomery, Spouse; Charles Montgomery, Businessman
Time period(s): 1990s
Locale(s): New York

Summary: A heartwarming story of love rekindled and values reassessed as Judith and Charles Montgomery learn what is really important to them as a family. Set during the Christmas season in upstate New York.

Other books you might like:
Janice Bennett, *A Christmas Keepsake*, 1991
    time travel elements
Bethany Campbell, *The Snow Garden*, 1989
Kathleen Creighton, *A Christmas Love*, 1992
Ruth Langan, *Christmas Miracle*, 1992
LaVyrle Spencer, *Bygones*, 1992

110

REXANNE BECNEL

The Christmas Wish
(New York: Dell, 1993)

Story type: Contemporary
Major character(s): Lucy Ann Vargas, Model; Gil Cooper, Principal (school); Erin Fielding, Student
Time period(s): 1990s
Locale(s): Waverly, Rhode Island

Summary: When Lucy decides to reclaim the daughter she gave up 16 years ago, she meets with strong opposition from both her parents and the school principal, Gil Cooper. A painful, sensitive, and beautiful story of loss, reconciliation, and love.

Other books you might like:
Kathleen Creighton, *A Christmas Love*, 1992
Maggie Daniels, *Moonlight and Mistletoe*, 1993
Debbie Macomber, *A Season of Angels*, 1993
    light and humorous
Belva Plain, *Blessings*, 1988

111

REXANNE BECNEL

A Dove at Midnight
(New York: Jove, 1993)

Story type: Historical/Medieval
Major character(s): Lady Joanna Preston, Noblewoman; Sir Rylan, Knight, Warrior
Time period(s): 13th century
Locale(s): England

Summary: Fleeing from a life of brutality and grief, Lady Joanna takes refuge in a convent rather than continuing to fight for what is rightfully hers. Her respite, however, is short, and she is soon forced by the warrior knight Sir Rylan to return to her home and, for political reasons, to marry him. Struggles, compromises, and love are all part of this realistic look at medieval life.

Other books you might like:
Catherine Coulter, *Earth Song*, 1990
Julie Garwood, *Saving Grace*, 1993
    light
Marylyle Rogers, *Hidden Hearts*, 1989
Marylyle Rogers, *Proud Hearts*, 1990

112

REXANNE BECNEL

My Gallant Enemy
(New York: Dell, 1990)

Story type: Historical/Medieval
Major character(s): Lady Lilliane of Orrick, Noblewoman; Corbett of Colchester, Nobleman
Time period(s): 13th century (1273)
Locale(s): England

Summary: When independent, fiery Lady Lilliane of Orrick refuses to marry returning crusader Corbett of Colchester, he kidnaps her in an effort to change her mind. He is surprisingly successful, and they enter into a marriage that proves to be both passionate and combative. Outside forces (political intrigue, treachery, and old lovers) also threaten the pair, but these difficulties only serve to strengthen their love. Nicely medieval.

Other books you might like:
Jude Deveraux, *The Taming*, 1989
Roberta Gellis, *The Roselynde Chronicles Series*, 1978-1983
Virginia Henley, *The Falcon and the Flower*, 1989
Virginia Henley, *The Raven and the Rose*, 1989
Kathleen E. Woodiwiss, *The Wolf and the Dove*, 1974

113

REXANNE BECNEL

The Rose of Blacksword
(New York: Dell, 1992)

Story type: Historical/Medieval
Major character(s): Rosalynde, Noblewoman; Aric of Wycliffe, Knight, Outlaw (Blacksword)
Time period(s): 12th century (1156)
Locale(s): England

Summary: Needing protection, Lady Rosalynde rescues the notorious outlaw, Blacksword, from hanging by claiming him as a handfast husband. However, she certainly doesn't expect him to turn out to be a knight — and neither of them expects to fall in love. Fast-paced and passionate.

Other books you might like:
Julie Garwood, *The Prize*, 1991
Judith Hill, *Knight's Desire*, 1992

Hannah Howell, *Silver Flame*, 1992
Anita Mills, *The Fire and the Fury*, 1991
Shelly Thacker, *Midnight Raider*, 1992

114

REXANNE BECNEL

Thief of My Heart
(New York: Dell, 1991)

Story type: Historical/American West; Historical/Post-American Civil War
Major character(s): Lacie Montgomery, Teacher, Imposter; Dillon Lockwood, Heir
Time period(s): 1870s (1872)
Locale(s): Louisiana; Colorado

Summary: To keep the Sparrow Hill School open, Lacie Montgomery resorts to deception, pretending to be the widow of the former schoolmaster. Then trouble arrives in the form of Dillon Lockwood, the brother of Lacie's supposed husband, who is intent on gaining his inheritance and proving Lacie a liar. But love interferes; and when he tricks her into following him to Denver, the sparks really fly.

Other books you might like:
Virginia Brown, *Renegade Embrace*, 1990
Elaine Coffman, *Escape Not My Love*, 1990
Linda Ladd, *Frostfire*, 1990
Mayo Lucas, *Camelot Jones*, 1989
Jane Toombs, *Riverboat Rogue*, 1990

115

REXANNE BECNEL

When Lightning Strikes
(New York: Dell, 1995)

Story type: Historical/American West
Major character(s): Abigail Bliss, Frontierswoman, Writer; Tanner McKnight, Bounty Hunter
Time period(s): 1850s (1855)
Locale(s): St. Joseph, Missouri; Oregon Trail; Chicago, Illinois

Summary: When Abigail Bliss's staid father takes her to Oregon (via the Oregon Trail) under an assumed name, she is obeys, but her life is totally disrupted and she is unhappy and confused. Bounty-hunter Tanner McKnight's mission is to join the wagon train and find the missing Abigail for her wealthy grandfather. It isn't easy to fool the suspicious father and win the daughter over, but he succeeds with appropriately romantic results. The "villainous" grandfather is a true surprise. Suspenseful and filled with lively banter.

Other books you might like:
Julie Garwood, *For the Roses*, 1995
Robin Lee Hatcher, *Liberty Blue*, 1995
Susan Kay Law, *Home Fires*, 1995
Gina Robins, *Forbidden Kiss*, 1995

116

REXANNE BECNEL

Where Magic Dwells
(New York: Dell, 1994)

Story type: Historical/Medieval; Historical/Fantasy
Major character(s): Wynne ab Gruffydd, Witch ("Seeress of Radnor"), Guardian (of five homeless children); Cleve Fitzwarin, Knight
Time period(s): 12th century (1172)
Locale(s): Radnor Forest, Wales; England

Summary: Wynn ab Gruffydd, Seeress of Radnor, will do anything for her five adopted children; but when an English knight comes to Wales in search of his lord's wartime bastard, she ends up relinquishing—and gaining—more than she had ever dreamed. Gentle and passionate.

Other books you might like:
Kathryn Lynn Davis, *Child of Awe*, 1990
Iris Johansen, *Midnight Warrior*, 1994
Judith Merkle Riley, *In Pursuit of the Green Lion*, 1990
Coral Smith Saxe, *Enchantment*, 1994
Penelope Williamson, *Keeper of the Dream*, 1992

117

DEBORAH BEDFORD

A Child's Promise
(New York: Harper, 1995)

Story type: Contemporary
Major character(s): Lisa Jo Jensen, Abuse Victim, Parent; John Owen, Military Personnel (former Marine), Farmer (dairy)
Time period(s): 1990s
Locale(s): Star Valley, Wyoming

Summary: Returning Marine Johnny Owen has his life planned: he will own a dairy farm and marry the girl he fell in love with after four years of intimate correspondence. But Lisa Jo's letters have been pure fiction, portraying a wonderful life she doesn't have; and when Lisa arrives, complete with baby, John is stunned and feels deeply betrayed. His protective family and Lisa's abused past almost make marriage impossible, but John's unwillingness to retract his proposal and the deep bond they had forged through letters help them put their past behind them and make their marriage work. Heartwarming with definite inspirational and religious elements.

Other books you might like:
Elaine Coffman, *Angel in Marble*, 1991
    another unwed mother/historical
Dorothy Garlock, *Sins of Summer*, 1994
    another unwed mother/historical/realistic
Debbie Macomber, *Morning Comes Softly*, 1993
Francine Rivers, *Redeeming Love*, 1991
    heroine with an unsavory past
LaVyrle Spencer, *Morning Glory*, 1989

118

PAMELA BELLE

The Lodestar
(New York: St. Martin's, 1989)

Story type: Historical/Medieval
Major character(s): Julian Bray, Noblewoman (Wealthy and spoiled); Christopher "Christie" Heron, Courtier (Aide to Richard, Duke of Glouc)
Time period(s): 15th century (1470s - 1480s (Wars of the Roses))

Summary: Totally self-oriented and ambitious for power, Christie Heron attaches himself to Richard, Duke of Gloucester and rises with him. Only when he is given a feisty, spoiled bride as selfish as he is does he come to understand the nature and value of love. Filled with violence, intrigue, and rich historical detail.

Other books you might like:
Margaret Campbell Barnes, *The King's Bed*, 1961
    Richard III from a child's viewpoint
Rebecca Brandewyne, *Forever My Love*, 1982
    Scotland/Similar time period
Roberta Gellis, *The Silver Mirror*, 1989
    Earlier time period (Henry III)/Political intrigue
Gail Link, *Wolf's Embrace*, 1989
    Similar time period
Sharon Kay Penman, *The Sunne in Splendour*, 1982
    Richard III

119

CLARE BENEDICT

The Brides of Eden
(New York: Robert Hale, 1995)

Story type: Contemporary/Innocent; Gothic
Major character(s): Alison Blair-Coupland, Noblewoman, Actress (aspiring); Mark Jarman, Producer
Time period(s): 1990s
Locale(s): England

Summary: Socialite and aspiring actress Lady Alison Blair-Coupland has her much-needed peaceful retreat shattered when Mark Jarman and his crew arrive to do some filming at her family estate. Romance soon follows and although family curses and "the other woman" threaten to cause problems, Mark and Alison are happily together by the book's end. This British category romance is typically sweet, slightly gothic, and predictable.

Other books you might like:
Liz Fielding, *Dangerous Flirtation*, 1995
Mary Stewart, *Nine Coaches Waiting*, 1958
    classic contemporary Gothic
Mary Stewart, *Touch Not the Cat*, 1976
Patricia Wilson, *Dark Illusion*, 1995

120

CONSTANCE BENNETT

Blossom
(New York: Diamond, 1991)

Story type: Historical/American West
Major character(s): Libby Ashford, Gentlewoman (from the East); Case Longstreet, Indian (Apache), Military Personnel (army scout)
Time period(s): 1840s (1847); 1860s (1863)
Locale(s): Arizona

Summary: After Case's Indian parents are massacred by bounty hunters, he becomes an Army scout and falls in love with Libby, the sister of the Army doctor.

Other books you might like:
Kathleen Eagle, *Heaven and Earth*, 1990
Kathleen Harrington, *Cherish the Dream*, 1990
Shirl Henke, *Night Wind's Woman*, 1991
Lindsay McKenna, *Sun Woman*, 1991

121

CONSTANCE BENNETT

Morning Sky
(New York: Berkley, 1991)

Story type: Historical/American West
Major character(s): Allyce "Lacey" Spencer, Widow(er), Journalist (newspaper owner); Justice Morgan, Gunfighter
Time period(s): 1880s (1886)
Locale(s): Willow Springs, Wyoming

Summary: Fiery newspaperwoman Laccy Spencer and the mysterious gunslinger Justic Morgan join forces to fight the local cattle baron and bring peace to a small Wyoming town. An involving story, a consummate heroine, and a hero worthy of her.

Other books you might like:
Sonya Birmingham, *Spitfire*, 1991
Kat Martin, *Lover's Gold*, 1991
Rebecca Sinclair, *California Caress*, 1989
Lass Small, *A Nothing Town in Texas*, 1991
Janelle Taylor, *Follow the Wind*, 1990

122

ELIZABETH BENNETT

Changes of Heart
(New York: Jove, 1992)

Story type: Contemporary
Major character(s): Jane Millicent Penrod, Artist; Zachary Dorn, Advertising; Alain Chanson, Businessman (French)
Time period(s): 1990s
Locale(s): New York, New York; France

Summary: Although chunky Jane Penrod finds life difficult trying to live up to her family's expectations, she eventually discovers her artistic talent and finds both a wonderful career and a great boss. However, when she falls for a dashing Frenchman, she is faced with some difficult choices and must decide what she really wants from life. Well-drawn characters.

Other books you might like:
Sally Beauman, *Destiny*, 1987
Catherine Coulter, *Beyond Eden*, 1991
Barbara Delinsky, *Facets*, 1990
Lass Small, *A Nothing Town in Texas*, 1991

123
JANICE BENNETT

A Christmas Keepsake
(New York: Zebra, 1991)

Story type: Regency; Time Travel
Major character(s): Christy Campbell, Businesswoman (book dealer); James Holborn, Writer
Time period(s): 1990s; 1810s
Locale(s): London, England

Summary: Intrigued by a book written by James Holborn in 1811, book dealer Christy Campbell suddenly finds herself transported, courtesy of an antique snow globe, back to Regency London where whom should she meet but Holborn himself. She quickly realizes that there is a purpose for her being there, but as she struggles to find out what it is, she and James become more and more attracted to each other. Social and political unrest, an identity search, and romance are all part of this intriguing tale that takes the Regency just one step beyond.

Other books you might like:
Mary Balogh, *The Snow Angel*, 1991
    Regency
Jude Deveraux, *A Knight in Shining Armor*, 1989
Constance O'Day-Flannery, *Once in a Lifetime*, 1992
Becky Lee Weyrich, *Forever, for Love*, 1989

124
JANICE BENNETT

Forever in Time
(New York: Zebra, 1990)

Story type: Regency; Time Travel
Major character(s): Erica ''Riki'' Von Hamel, Heiress, Time Traveller; Gilbert Randall, Nobleman (Viscount Bedford), Time Traveller
Time period(s): 1990s; 1810s
Locale(s): England

Summary: When a 19th century nobleman is washed up on Erica's 20th century beach claiming to be on a mission to Wellington, Erica has her doubts. However, a series of events, including an altered present reality, convice her that he is telling the truth and that he needs her help—in the past. Together they return to Regency England, unravel an intriguing mystery, set history to rights, and fall in love—thereby creating an obvious dilemma.

Other books you might like:
Joan Aiken, *The Five-Minute Marriage*, 1977
    Regency/not time change
Jude Deveraux, *A Knight in Shining Armor*, 1989
    Time change/different period
Heather Graham, *Every Time I Love You*, 1988
    Time change/different period
Leslie Lynn, *Scandal's Child*, 1990
    Regency/not time change
Becky Lee Weyrich, *Forever, for Love*, 1989
    Time change/different period

125
JANICE BENNETT

A Tempting Miss
(New York: Zebra, 1989)

Story type: Regency
Series: Carstairs Quartet
Major character(s): Augusta Carstairs, Gentlewoman, Actress (Amateur); Major MacKennoch, Military Personnel, Detective
Time period(s): 1810s (Napoleonic Wars)
Locale(s): London; Brussels

Summary: Everyone in Augusta Carstairs' amateur theatre group is a suspect in a murder being investigated by Scotsman Major MacKennoch. Suspense, adventure, and espionage abound in a romance set against the background of the Napoleonic Wars.

Other books you might like:
Gail Clark, *The Baroness of Bow Street*, 1979
Annabel Laine, *The Reluctant Heiress*, 1978
    Regency Romantic Suspense
Jane Lovelace, *Rolissa*, 1985
    Regency with a murder
Joan Smith, *Lovers' Vows*, 1981
    More theatrics
Linda Walker, *My Lady's Deception*, 1990

126
JANICE BENNETT

A Touch of Forever
(New York: Zebra, 1992)

Story type: Regency; Time Travel
Major character(s): Alexandra Anderson, Student, Time Traveller; Earl of Wyndham, Nobleman
Time period(s): 1800s (1805); 1990s
Locale(s): England

Summary: When a jewelled dagger transports history student Lexie Anderson back to 1805, she finds herself rescued by the dashing Earl of Wyndham — and is torn between wanting to retrieve the dagger from a band of smugglers so she can return to her own time and staying with the man she has come to love.

Other books you might like:
Jo Beverley, *An Arranged Marriage*, 1991

Barbara Bretton, *Somewhere in Time*, 1992
Jude Deveraux, *A Knight in Shining Armor*, 1989
Kasey Michaels, *Out of the Blue*, 1992
Amanda Quick, *Surrender*, 1990

127

LAURA GILMOUR BENNETT (Pseudonym of Justine Harlow)

By All That Is Sacred
(New York: Avon, 1991)

Story type: Contemporary/Fantasy; Time Travel
Major character(s): Louise (Sancha) Carey, Businesswoman (shop owner), Orphan; Owen (Hugo) Morgan, Businessman, Knight; Rex (Gaucelm) Monckton, Demon (devil reincarnated)
Time period(s): 1990s; 13th century (1244)
Locale(s): London, England; Puivaillon, France

Summary: Louise and Owen are caught in an intrigue over a golden chalice that links them to the Spanish Inquisition in 1244. Their love and search for this treasure is 800 years old. A fascinating story of good and evil and a love that lasts throughout time.

Other books you might like:
Jude Deveraux, *A Knight in Shining Armor*, 1989
Diana Gabaldon, *Outlander*, 1991
Laurie Grant, *Emerald Fire*, 1990
Teresa Medeiros, *Shadows and Lace*, 1990
Penelope Neri, *Forever and Beyond*, 1990
　　reincarnation Native American-style

128

GILA BERKOWITZ

The Brides
(New York.: St. Martin, 1992)

Story type: Contemporary/Mainstream
Major character(s): Erica Vanenta, Businesswoman (corporate executive); Melissa John, Model, Actress (aspiring); Cindy Prewitt, Prostitute
Time period(s): 1990s
Locale(s): New York, New York

Summary: Three young women meet at a bridal salon, share their dreams, and eventually become fast friends. Erica, an immigrant, marries a Brahmin, quits school and later succeeds in a chemical corporation. Cindy leaves Arkansas and comes to New York to find an old boyfriend; instead, she becomes a hooker. Melissa models as she strives to become an actress. A story of friendship, adventure, and surprises. First novel.

Other books you might like:
Lois Battle, *The Past Is Another Country*, 1992
Lois Battle, *War Brides*, 1982
Leigh Bristol, *Sunswept*, 1990
Katherine Sinclair, *Far Horizons*, 1991
Jacqueline Susann, *Valley of the Dolls*, 1966

129

VIRGINIA BERNHARD

A Durable Fire
(New York: Morrow, 1990)

Story type: Historical/Colonial America
Major character(s): Temperance Yardley, Settler (Jamestown colonist); Will Sterling, Settler (Jamestown colonist)
Time period(s): 17th century (1609)
Locale(s): United States; Jamestown, Virginia; At Sea

Summary: Aboard different ships headed toward Jamestown, Temperance and George Yardley are separated by a storm. He is stranded on the Bermuda Islands and she, along with George's friend Will Sterling, ends up in Jamestown. Based on fact and filled with excellent historical detail.

Other books you might like:
Gwen Bristow, *Celia Garth*, 1959
　　Revolutionary America
Jane Aiken Hodge, *Judas Flowering*, 1976
　　Revolutionary America
Adrienne Jones, *Another Place, Another Spring*, 1971
　　A trek across Siberia ends at Ft. Bragg
Anya Seton, *My Theodosia*, 1941
　　The story of the daughter of Aaron Burr
Anya Seton, *The Winthrop Woman*, 1958
　　Colonial setting

130

DIANE GONZALES BERTRAND

Touchdown for Love
(New York: Avalon, 1991)

Story type: Contemporary/Innocent
Major character(s): Kaylene Morales, Teacher (student); Alex Garrison, Teacher, Coach
Time period(s): 1990s
Locale(s): San Antonio, Texas

Summary: In addition to learning to handle a classroom full of undisciplined high school students and teach them English at the same time, student teacher Kaylene Morales must also deal with her feelings for her old friend, now the JV football coach, Alex Garrison. Campus gossip, failing football players, and Alex's one-track mind (on football) all add to her romantic dilemma.

Other books you might like:
Lynn Bulock, *Roses for Caroline*, 1989
Donna Clayton, *Take Love in Stride*, 1991
Patricia Ellis, *Champagne and Wildflowers*, 1991
Emma Goldrick, *The Girl He Left Behind*, 1991
Moyra Tarling, *All About Adam*, 1991

131

JO BEVERLEY

An Arranged Marriage

(New York: Zebra, 1991)

Story type: Regency
Major character(s): Eleanor Chivenham, Debutante; Nicholas Delaney, Nobleman
Time period(s): 1810s
Locale(s): England

Summary: Although this lively story begins with the rape of the heroine (indeed, a dubious beginning for a Regency), the characters and plot do develop nicely as Eleanor struggles to make the best of her hastily arranged marriage. Of course, her husband's undercover assignment to keep tabs on his former mistress doesn't help, but there is a happy ending in sight and a lot of fun along the way. Good period detail.

Other books you might like:
Mary Balogh, *The Snow Angel*, 1991
Gayle Buck, *Mutual Consent*, 1991
Teresa DesJardien, *A June Bride*, 1991
Mary Kingsley, *A Gentleman's Desire*, 1991
Judith McNaught, *Whitney, My Love*, 1985

132

JO BEVERLEY

The Christmas Angel

(New York: Zebra, 1992)

Story type: Regency; Holiday Themes
Major character(s): Judith Rossiter, Widow(er); Leander Knollis, Nobleman (Earl of Charrington)
Time period(s): 1810s
Locale(s): England

Summary: When hero and adventurer Leander Knollis, Earl of Charrington, decides to settle down, he thinks widowed Judith Rossiter and her young children would make a perfect family — but Judith is not so sure she wants to give up her hard-won independence. Love, however, has a way of creeping in and changing people's minds when they least expect it, and Leander and Judith find happiness where neither had thought to find it. Warm, witty, and complex

Other books you might like:
Mary Balogh, *Christmas Beau*, 1992
Mary Balogh, *The Snow Angel*, 1991
Janice Bennett, *A Christmas Keepsake*, 1991
Susan Carroll, *Christmas Belles*, 1992
Carla Kelly, *Marian's Christmas Wish*, 1989

133

JO BEVERLEY

Dangerous Joy

(New York: Zebra, 1995)

Story type: Historical/Regency
Series: Company of Rogues

Major character(s): Felicity Monahan, Heiress, Ward; Miles Cavanagh, Guardian, Nobleman (heir to the Earl of Kilgoran)
Time period(s): 1810s (1816)
Locale(s): Ireland; England

Summary: When foot-loose Miles Cavanaugh is named guardian of a 20-year-old heiress, he thinks his primary concern will be keeping her out of the clutches of fortune hunters. When he finds himself attracted to this irrepressible hellion, he quickly realizes he should be more concerned for his heart—and his future. Passionate, fast-paced, and witty.

Other books you might like:
Virginia Brown, *Hidden Touch*, 1993
 ward-guardian theme/humor and lively action
Jane Feather, *Vixen*, 1994
 lively, sensual
Amanda Quick, *Seduction*, 1990
 lively, sensual
Amanda Quick, *Surrender*, 1990
 lively, sensual
Susan Sizemore, *My First Duchess*, 1993

134

JO BEVERLEY

Deirdre and Don Juan

(New York: Avon, 1993)

Story type: Regency
Major character(s): Deirdre Stowe, Noblewoman, Artist (needlework); Mark Juan Carlos Renfrew, Nobleman (Earl of Everdon), Widow(er) (rake)
Time period(s): 1810s
Locale(s): London, England

Summary: ''Don Juan'' Everdon's runaway wife has died, and he needs a new one to provide him with an heir. Plain, young Deirdre is the choice of their parents, but she will have none of him. After all, she is in love with a rather dull man who ''needs'' her, and really can't imagine anyone (especially an infamous rake) ''wanting'' her. Everdon sets out to change her mind and, through wit and a lot of creativity, succeeds admirably. Funny and charming.

Other books you might like:
Georgette Heyer, *A Civil Contract*, 1961
 classic Regency
Dorothy Mack, *The Mock Marriage*, 1991
Kasey Michaels, *Bride of the Unicorn*, 1993
 sensual
Amanda Quick, *Seduction*, 1990
 sensual

135

JO BEVERLEY

Forbidden

(New York: Zebra, 1994)

Story type: Historical
Series: Company of Rogues

Major character(s): Lady Serena Riverton, Widow(er), Noblewoman; Lord Frances Middlethorpe, Rake, Nobleman

Locale(s): England

Summary: Lady Serena, widow of a despicable rake, is desperate to escape from her brothers who will "sell" her off. So she runs away, and ends up meeting, and eventually marrying, Lord Frances Middlethorpe, a rake who is in need of an heir. Passion, humor, and strong, well-done characters are hallmarks of this fast-paced romance.

Other books you might like:
Jane Feather, *Virtue*, 1993
Judith McNaught, *Almost Heaven*, 1990
Amanda Quick, *Seduction*, 1990
Amanda Quick, *Surrender*, 1990
Susan Sizemore, *My First Duchess*, 1993

136

JO BEVERLEY

My Lady Notorious
(New York: Avon, 1993)

Story type: Historical/Georgian

Major character(s): Chastity Ware, Noblewoman, Highwayman; Cynric Malloren, Nobleman, Military Personnel

Time period(s): 18th century

Locale(s): England

Summary: Determined to find a way to help her sister and young nephew escape their cruel father, the disgraced Lady Chastity Ware dons her brother's clothes, hold up a coach, and ends up capturing the attractive, arrogant, and extremely bored Lord Cynric Malloren. Cyn, however, is more than intrigued by his charming captor, and he joins Chastity in a daring adventure that not only exposes an old treason, but binds them in an impossible love, as well. A realistic, highly sensual, and sometimes bawdy tale of Georgian England. Interesting historical and political detail.

Other books you might like:
Kat Martin, *Gypsy Lord*, 1992
Amanda Quick, *Ravished*, 1992
Susan Sizemore, *My First Duchess*, 1993
Marlene Suson, *Devil's Bargain*, 1992

137

JO BEVERLEY

The Stanforth Secrets: A Regency Romantic Intrigue
(New York: Walker, 1989)

Story type: Regency

Major character(s): Chloe, Widow(er); Justin Delamere, Nobleman (Heir to Stanforth Manor)

Time period(s): 1810s (Regency period)

Summary: To Chloe, the imminent arrival of the new Lord Stanforth means one thing: escape from the isolated manor house and the strange things that have been happening there recently. That, however, is before they fall in love with each other. Mystery, humor, and apples are all part of this Regency that atypically has a hint of the gothic about it.

Other books you might like:
Joan Aiken, *The Five-Minute Marriage*, 1977
Clare Darcy, *Lady Pamela*, 1975
June Drummond, *The Bluestocking*, 1986
Annabel Laine, *The Reluctant Heiress*, 1978
Alice Chetwynd Ley, *A Reputation Dies*, 1982

138

JO BEVERLEY

Tempting Fortune
(New York: Zebra, 1995)

Story type: Historical/Georgian

Major character(s): Portia St. Clair, Gentlewoman; Arcenbryght Malloren, Nobleman, Rake

Time period(s): 18th century

Locale(s): England

Summary: Accosted at gunpoint one night by the fiery Portia St. Claire, Lord Arcenbryght Malloren finds his somewhat jaded existence has suddenly become more interesting. Filled with passion, gambling, and a lot of bawdy action, this nicely crafted adventure is second in the Malloren series and follows the award-winning *My Lady Notorious*. Beverley is a member of the RWA Hall of Fame.

Other books you might like:
Catherine Coulter, *The Valentine Legacy*, 1995
Jane Feather, *Valentine*, 1995
Amanda Quick, *Dangerous*, 1993
  light and fast-paced
Amanda Scott, *The Bawdy Bride*, 1995
Anne Stuart, *To Love a Dark Lord*, 1994
  darker

139

JO BEVERLEY

An Unwilling Bride
(New York: Zebra, 1992)

Story type: Regency

Major character(s): Elizabeth Armitage, Teacher, Spinster; Lucien DeVaux, Nobleman ("son" of the Duke of Belcraven), Heir

Time period(s): 1810s

Locale(s): London, England

Summary: Lucien de Vaux is suddenly confronted with the necessity to marry by his "father." The Duke of Belcraven has passed him off as his son, and circumstances now make him a true heir! The Duke coerces school-mistress Beth Armitage into a marriage of convenience; but both Lucien and Beth find it very *inconvenient*—and their emotional bonding takes some time.

Other books you might like:
Joan Aiken, *The Five-Minute Marriage*, 1977
Mary Balogh, *Christmas Beau*, 1992
Janis Laden, *Moonlight Veil*, 1991

Annabel Laine, *The Reluctant Heiress*, 1989

140
OLGA BICOS

By My Heart Betrayed
(New York: Dell, 1991)

Story type: Historical/Victorian America; Historical/Victorian
Major character(s): Esmeralda MacClure, Seamstress, Heiress—Dispossessed; Molly Egan, Servant, Seamstress; Keane Marshall, Nobleman (Viscount Eldridge)
Time period(s): 19th century
Locale(s): England; Cincinnati, Ohio

Summary: Cheated out of her inheritance as a child by a greedy and murderous cousin and rescued from certain death by Molly Egan, Esmeralda MacClure plans for the day when she can leave Ohio and return to England and claim her family estate. However, she needs money to do this. Together she and Molly conceive an audacious plan that unintentionally nets Esme a husband, not just a bankroll. But she and Keane Marshall are in love and he will do anything to help her, including returning to England to help her regain her home.

Other books you might like:
Elaine Barbieri, *Wishes on the Wind*, 1991
Laura Black, *Albany*, 1984
Cordia Byers, *Lady Fortune*, 1989
Victoria Morrow, *Jenny's Dream*, 1990
Catherine Palmer, *The Wild Winds*, 1990
    exotic setting

141
OLGA BICOS

Santana Rose
(New York: Dell, 1992)

Story type: Historical/Post-American Civil War
Major character(s): Mercedes De Dreux, Imposter (Santana Rose), Thief; Reynard Parks, Detective
Time period(s): 19th century
Locale(s): Louisiana

Summary: Madame de Dreux's secret life as Santana Rose, a Robin Hood-type bandit, is jeopardized when she not only robs the wrong man, but then must relate to him as her real self, the genteel wife of plantation owner Benart de Dreux. Complex and sensual.

Other books you might like:
Virginia Brown, *Renegade Embrace*, 1990
Deborah Martin, *Creole Nights*, 1992
Diane Gates Robinson, *The Falcon and the Swan*, 1992
Evelyn Rogers, *A Love So Wild*, 1991
DeLoras Scott, *Rogue's Honor*, 1992

142
OLGA BICOS

White Tiger
(New York: Dell, 1991)

Story type: Historical/Victorian; Historical/Exotic
Major character(s): Katherine Nicole "Nicky" Marshall, Royalty (grandchild of Rajput princess), Gentlewoman; Holt Atley, Scientist (naturalist)
Time period(s): 1860s (1860-1863)
Locale(s): England; India

Summary: Nicole's search for her Rajput heritage and the legendary white tiger leads her into the Indian jungles and straight into the arms of naturalist Holt Atley when he saves her life. But their missions are at cross-purposes—Nicole's party intends to hunt the tiger down; Holt wants to save it. Nevertheless, they are attracted to each other, and when Nicole is sold into slavery by her treacherous fiance, Holt once again comes to her rescue. Nicole, however, is still searching for her royal heritage, and it isn't until she goes to the village where her grandmother was raised that she is free to convince Holt that she loves him unconditionally. High adventure in an exotic setting.

Other books you might like:
E.M. Forster, *A Passage to India*, 1924
H. Rider Haggard, *King Solomon's Mines*, 1885
    a classic action-adventure story
Victoria Holt, *The India Fan*, 1988
Christine Monson, *This Fiery Splendor*, 1991
Janelle Taylor, *Whispered Kisses*, 1990

143
CHERYL BIGGS

Mississippi Flame
(New York: Zebra, 1993)

Story type: Historical/American West
Major character(s): Elizabeth Devlin, Fugitive (from an unwanted marriage); Grayson Cantrell, Gunfighter, Gambler
Time period(s): 19th century
Locale(s): Mississippi River; West; Louisiana

Summary: Running from a disastrous engagement, Elizabeth leaves Louisiana for Texas and ends up on the Mississippi River with a charming gambler for company. Together they head for safety, fighting all the way; but no matter how many times they try to go their separate ways, they keep ending up with each other. Lots of sparks, spice, and humor.

Other books you might like:
Rebecca George, *A Wild Desire*, 1989
Teresa Hart, *Hearts Are Wild*, 1993
Linda Lael Miller, *Angelfire*, 1989
Linda Lael Miller, *My Darling Melissa*, 1990

144
CHERYL BIGGS
AMY J. FETZER, Co-Author
AMBER KAYE, Co-Author
SARA ORWIG, Co-Author

My Spellbound Heart
(New York: Zebra, 1994)

Story type: Anthology; Historical/Fantasy

Summary: A diverse collection of unusual time travel and fantasy romances just right for Halloween. Included are "Love's Darkness" by Cheryl Biggs, "Rescued By Time" by Amy J. Fetzer, "Faery Magic" by Amber Kaye, and "Nightspell" by Sara Orwig.

Other books you might like:
Madeline Baker, *Enchanted Crossings*, 1994
    time and space fantasy anthology
Shannon Drake, *Avon Books Presents: Haunting Love Stories*, 1991
    fantasy anthology
Joan Hohl, *Love Beyond Time*, 1994
    time travel anthology

145
LISA BINGHAM

Distant Thunder
(New York: Pocket, 1992)

Story type: Historical/American West
Major character(s): Susan Hurst, Religious (novice), Orphan; Daniel Crocker, Detective (Pinkerton agent), Orphan
Time period(s): 1860s (1865); 1880s (1885)
Locale(s): West

Summary: When Pinkerton agent David Crocker learns that his childhood friend from the orphanage intends to become a nun, he hurries to persuade her to marry him instead, vowing to give up his colorful life and help Susan come to terms with her tragic past. Fear, passion, and more tragedy await the pair before they can put the past behind them and build a future together.

Other books you might like:
Madeline Baker, *Lacey's Way*, 1990
Elaine Barbieri, *Wings of a Dove*, 1990
Kathleen Eagle, *Heaven and Earth*, 1990
Charlotte Hubbard, *Gambler's Tempting Kisses*, 1991

146
LISA BINGHAM

Eden Creek
(New York: Pocket, 1991)

Story type: Historical/American West
Major character(s): Ginny Parker, Mail Order Bride; Orrin Ghant, Businessman, Widow(er)
Time period(s): 1870s
Locale(s): Eden Creek, Utah

Summary: Ginny Parker is pregnant, abandoned, and desperate. Orrin Ghant is in dire need of a wife. The resulting marriage of convenience brings surprises to them both as they struggle to put the past behind them and make their dreams reality. Funny, passionate, and involving.

Other books you might like:
Stef Ann Holm, *Firefly*, 1990
Catherine Lanigan, *A Promise Made*, 1991
Victoria Pade, *The Doubletree*, 1990
LaVyrle Spencer, *Morning Glory*, 1989
Jodi Thomas, *The Tender Texan*, 1991

147
LISA BINGHAM

Silken Dreams
(New York: Pocket, 1991)

Story type: Historical/American West; Historical/Victorian America
Major character(s): Lettie Grey, Young Woman (daughter of boarding house own); Ethan McGuire, Criminal (former bank robber), Fugitive
Time period(s): 1880s
Locale(s): Illinois

Summary: Young Lettie Grey is sure that Ethan McGuire has given up his former life of crime as "The Gentleman." Now if only she could convince her lawman brother of that fact. The best approach seems to be to help Ethan unmask the murderer who is posing as "The Gentleman," a task that proves more dangerous to her life and her heart than she would have thought possible. Action packed and passionate.

Other books you might like:
Rosanne Bittner, *Embers of the Heart*, 1990
Virginia Brown, *Wildfire*, 1990
Rebecca Paisley, *Moonlight and Magic*, 1990
Judith Steel, *Seduction's Raging Flame*, 1989

148
LISA BINGHAM

Silken Promises
(New York: Pocket, 1994)

Story type: Historical/American West
Major character(s): Fiona McFee, Gambler (card sharp), Con Artist; Jacob Grey, Lawman (U. S. Marshal)
Time period(s): 1870s (1875); 1880s (1885)
Locale(s): Chicago, Illinois

Summary: Lawman Jacob Grey has neither forgotten nor forgiven the lovely con artist who left him lying naked in a field. When he finds he needs her help years later to catch a counterfeiter, he finds that Fiona McFee hasn't forgotten him either—she's still gunning for him. However, working together would have its advantages, but neither counts on falling in love. Funny and fast-paced.

Other books you might like:
Lori Copeland, *Promise Me Forever*, 1994
Teresa Hart, *Hearts Are Wild*, 1993

Lisa Hendrix, *Hostage Heart*, 1994
Kathryn Hockett, *Outlaw Seduction*, 1993
Dana Ransom, *Dakota Destiny*, 1993

149

BEVERLY BIRD

Comes the Rain
(New York: Avon, 1990)

Story type: Historical/American West
Major character(s): Gray Eyes, Indian (Navaho), Shaman (healer); Hawk, Indian (Navaho), Warrior
Time period(s): 19th century (1857-1868)
Locale(s): New Mexico

Summary: Destined from birth to be a powerful healer for her people, young Gray Eyes understands many mysteries—except her conflicting feelings for the warrior Hawk. However, with maturity comes the knowledge that she and Hawk are not only meant to be together, but that they are to help their people in their tragic, inevitably futile struggle against the encroaching white world. Passionate, eloquent, and poignant.

Other books you might like:
Rosanne Bittner, *Arizona Ecstasy*, 1989
Michael Blake, *Dances with Wolves*, 1988
Kathryn Lynn Davis, *Sing to Me of Dreams*, 1990
Lucia St. Clair Robson, *Ride the Wind*, 1982
Anna Lee Waldo, *Sacajawea*, 1979

150

BEVERLY BIRD

A Man Without a Wife
(New York: Silhouette, 1995)

Story type: Contemporary; Ethnic
Major character(s): Ellen Lonetree, Nurse; Dallas Lazo, Parent (adoptive)
Time period(s): 1990s
Locale(s): New Mexico

Summary: When nurse Ellen Lonetree decides to locate the son she gave up years ago for adoption, using a government study as an excuse, she angers Dallas Lazo, the boy's adoptive father, and sets events in motion that produce dangerous, as well as romantic, results. Mystery, intrigue, and Navajo lore are part of this fast-paced romance.

Other books you might like:
Kathleen Eagle, *Reason to Believe*, 1995
Kathleen Eagle, *This Time Forever*, 1992
Rachel Lee, *Thunder Mountain*, 1994
  somewhat mystical
Deborah Smith, *Beloved Woman*, 1991
Peggy Webb, *Witch Dance*, 1994
  suspenseful

151

SONYA BIRMINGHAM

Spitfire
(New York: Avon, 1991)

Story type: Historical/American West
Major character(s): Carrie O'Leary, Journalist, Activist; Matt Worthington, Journalist, Editor (newspaper)
Time period(s): 19th century
Locale(s): Crested Butte, Colorado

Summary: Furious that Matt Worthington, editor of the local newspaper, refuses to print her articles criticizing the conditions in his uncle's mine, Carrie O'Leary kidnaps him in an effort to change his mind. Their encounter results in a job for Carrie on Matt's paper; but when Carrie's hard-hitting articles begin to draw blood, Matt's uncle sues her. Lively and funny.

Other books you might like:
Linda Benjamin, *Midnight Chase*, 1989
Constance Bennett, *Morning Sky*, 1991
Catherine Hart, *Sweet Fury*, 1990
Colleen Quinn, *Colorado Flame*, 1989
Cynthia Wright, *Brighter than Gold*, 1990

152

ROSANNE BITTNER

Arizona Ecstasy
(New York: Zebra, 1989)

Story type: Historical/American West
Major character(s): Lisa Powers, Captive (Captured by Apaches); Chaco, Indian (Half-Apache)
Time period(s): 19th century
Locale(s): Southwest

Summary: Feeling rejected by the white world, Chaco returns to the Apache way of life to find peace and acceptance. What he finds, however, is a star-crossed love and a doomed way of life. Depicts final days of the free Apache nation and the injustices done to the Native Americans—a recurring theme in Bittner's novels.

Other books you might like:
Cheryl Black, *Comanche Love Song*, 1989
Betty Brooks, *Warrior's Embrace*, 1989
Johanna Lindsey, *Savage Thunder*, 1989
Sonya T. Pelton, *Dakota Flame*, 1989
Janelle Taylor, *Savage Conquest*, 1985

153

ROSANNE BITTNER

Caress
(New York: Zebra, 1992)

Story type: Historical/American West; Historical/Antebellum American South
Major character(s): Samantha Walters, Activist (Abolitionist); Blake Hastings, Activist (Abolitionist)
Time period(s): 1850s

Locale(s): Lawrence, Kansas; Missouri

Summary: When Blake Hastings rescues abolitionist Samantha Walters from a group of pro-slavers, the two join forces in more ways than one. Love, murder, marriage, and revenge are all part of this accurate and sensual tale of the anti-slavery movement in the days just before the Civil War.

Other books you might like:
Emily Bradshaw, *The Heart's Journey*, 1992
Christine Dorsey, *Kansas Kiss*, 1992
Charlotte Hubbard, *Gambler's Tempting Kisses*, 1991
Betina Lindsey, *Waltz with the Lady*, 1990

154

ROSANNE BITTNER

Embers of the Heart
(New York: Bantam, 1990)

Story type: Historical/American West
Major character(s): Anna Kelly, Restauranteur; Nate Foster, Lawman (U.S. Marshall)
Time period(s): 1860s
Locale(s): Abilene, Kansas

Summary: Believing her husband killed in the War, Anna moves to Kansas, opens a restaurant, and tries to begin a new life. Love arrives in the form of Marshall Nate Foster; but their love, and Anna's new life, is threatened by the reappearance of her husband—a man who was once a gentle, caring doctor but has been changed by the War into a vicious, violent member of Quantrill's Raiders. A spinoff from *Montana Woman*.

Other books you might like:
Jessie Ford, *A Different Breed*, 1988
Ann Gabriel, *South Texas*, 1989
Norah Hess, *Wildfire*, 1989
Linda Howard, *A Lady of the West*, 1990
Leta Tegler, *Gabrielle*, 1990

155

ROSANNE BITTNER

The Forever Tree
(New York: Bantam, 1995)

Story type: Historical/American West Coast; Saga
Major character(s): Santana Maria Chavez Lopez, Noblewoman (California Spanish aristocrat); Will Lassater, Businessman (lumberman)
Time period(s): 1850s
Locale(s): San Francisco, California

Summary: Intent on building a logging empire, Will Lassater is side-tracked by the lovely Spanish aristocrat Santana. They eventually marry, earning the everlasting hatred of her fiance, Don Hugo. Despite the Civil War, tragedy, and a series of other complications, they eventually succeed in carving out a successful life for themselves and their family. An intense, emotional saga.

Other books you might like:
Yvonne Adamson, *Bridey's Mountain*, 1993
　　Colorado Saga
Elaine Barbieri, *More Precious than Gold*, 1992
Stephanie Bartlett, *Highland Flame*, 1992
Catherine Lanigan, *A Promise Made*, 1992
Penelope Williamson, *Heart of the West*, 1995

156

ROSANNE BITTNER

In the Shadow of the Mountains
(New York: Bantam, 1991)

Story type: Historical/American West; Saga
Major character(s): Beatrice Ritter, Spouse, Orphan; David Kirkland, Miner (gold); Irene Kirkland, Indian (half-Cheyenne)
Time period(s): 19th century
Locale(s): Colorado

Summary: Married to each other essentially for mutual convenience, Bea and Kirk overcome many obstacles and carve out a life for themselves and their children in gold rush Colorado. A saga in both scope and timespan, this insightful story chronicles the growth of a city, the evolution of a family, and the painful, triumphant coming of age of a determined woman.

Other books you might like:
Ann Gabriel, *South Texas*, 1990
Jill Gregory, *Lone Star Lady*, 1990
Catherine Lanigan, *A Promise Made*, 1991
Sara Orwig, *Denver*, 1990
　　follows *San Antonio* and *Albuquerque*

157

ROSANNE BITTNER

Montana Woman
(New York: Bantam, 1990)

Story type: Historical/American West
Major character(s): Joline Masters, Widow(er), Settler; Clint Reeves, Settler
Time period(s): 1860s
Locale(s): Montana

Summary: Following the death of her father and husband in the War Between the States, Joline Masters and another person seeking a new start, Clint Reeves, head for the Montana Territory and a new life.

Other books you might like:
Jessie Ford, *A Different Breed*, 1988
Ann Gabriel, *South Texas*, 1990
　　Strong heroine/Mainstream elements
Norah Hess, *Wildfire*, 1989
Betina Lindsey, *Waltz with the Lady*, 1990
Gina Robins, *Texas Temptation*, 1989

158

ROSANNE BITTNER

Oregon Bride

(New York: Popular Library, 1990)

Story type: Historical/American West
Major character(s): Marybeth MacKinder, Widow(er), Settler; Josh Rivers, Guide (Trailguide)
Time period(s): 1850s (1851)

Summary: With the death of her abusive husband, young Marybeth MacKinder is fair game for her even more abusive brother-in-law, John, and the entire MacKinder clan. When they join a westward-bound wagon train, Mary finds love and a champion in trailguide Josh Rivers; but before they can be happy, they must deal with Indians, snakes, tornados, and the MacKinders.

Other books you might like:
Sandra Brown, *Sunset Embrace*, 1985
Janet Dailey, *The Pride of Hannah Wade*, 1985
Norah Hess, *Wildfire*, 1989
Jill Marie Landis, *Sunflower*, 1988
Jill Marie Landis, *Wild Flower*, 1989

159

ROSANNE BITTNER

Outlaw Hearts

(New York: Bantam, 1993)

Story type: Historical/American West
Major character(s): Miranda Hayes, Widow(er); Jake Harkner, Outlaw
Time period(s): 1880s
Locale(s): Kansas; West

Summary: On her way west to find her only living relative, Miranda Hayes accidentally shoots outlaw Jake Harkner—and then ends up nursing him back to health. They continue on their separate ways West, but fate has a way of bringing them together—and tearing them apart—until they eventually can come to terms with not only their pasts, but their feelings for each other. A novel of adversity, challenges, love, and trust.

Other books you might like:
Kit Gardner, *The Stolen Heart*, 1993
Terri Herrington, *Silena*, 1993
Martha Hix, *Lone Star Loving*, 1993
Johanna Lindsey, *Angel*, 1992
Rebecca Paisley, *Midnight and Magnolias*, 1992
    funny and off-beat

160

ROSANNE BITTNER

Shameless

(New York: Zebra, 1993)

Story type: Historical/American West

Major character(s): Nina Juarez, Outlaw (horse thief); Lt. Clay Youngblood, Military Personnel (U.S. Camel Corps)
Time period(s): 1850s
Locale(s): Texas

Summary: When Lt. Clay Youngblood captures "horse trader" (read horse thief) Nina Juarez, he ends up with more than just a charming outlaw on his hands. Her brothers want her back—and will stop at nothing to accomplish this; and Nina, herself, has a way of landing them in more scrapes than Clay would have thought possible. And on top of it all, he loves her! The camels add a bit of interest to this romantic western adventure.

Other books you might like:
Suzanne Ellison, *Sunburst*, 1993
Carol Finch, *Promise Me Moonlight*, 1993
Phoebe Fitzjames, *Oklahoma Angel*, 1993
Kit Gardner, *The Stolen Heart*, 1993

161

ROSANNE BITTNER

Sioux Splendor

(New York: Zebra, 1990)

Story type: Historical/American West
Major character(s): Cynthia Ann Wells, Captive, Gentlewoman; Red Wolf, Indian (Sioux), Warrior
Time period(s): 1860s (1865)
Locale(s): South Dakota; Washington, District of Columbia

Summary: When Cynthia Ann Wells is "rescued" from Red Wolf, the Sioux warrior she loves, she agrees to return East for the sake of her unborn child—certain that Red Wolf will eventually come for her. Circumstances, however, conspire to keep them apart; and by the time they meet again Red Wolf has become a teacher and Cynthia has married to provide a home for their son. Love does win out, but "eventually" is the operative word. Sensitive descriptions of Sioux life and culture.

Other books you might like:
Cassie Edwards, *When Passion Calls*, 1990
Jessie Ford, *A Different Breed*, 1988
Judith E. French, *Lovestorm*, 1990
Judith E. French, *Moonfeather*, 1990
Constance O'Banyon, *Cheyenne Sunrise*, 1990

162

ROSANNE BITTNER

Sweet Mountain Magic

(New York: Zebra, 1990)

Story type: Historical/American West
Major character(s): Venado, Amnesiac; Sage MacKenzie, Mountain Man
Time period(s): 1840s (1846)
Locale(s): Rocky Mountains

Summary: When Sage finds "Venado" near a burnt wagon, she has no memory and will not speak. As he cares for her, they fall in love; but when her memory returns, they must face a number of difficulties, including an already existing husband.

Other books you might like:
Cheryl Black, *Comanche Love Song*, 1989
Lori Copeland, *Fool Me Once*, 1990
Genell Dellin, *Cherokee Dawn*, 1990
Cassie Edwards, *When Passion Calls*, 1990
Jill Marie Landis, *Wild Flower*, 1989

163
ROSANNE BITTNER

Unforgettable
(New York: Zebra, 1994)

Story type: Historical/American West
Major character(s): Allyson Mills, Pioneer, Settler; Ethan Temple, Military Personnel (Army scout), Indian (half Cheyenne)
Time period(s): 1880s (1889)
Locale(s): Oklahoma; Cripple Creek, Colorado

Summary: Self-sufficient and tough, but in need of money and security, Allyson Mills joins the Oklahoma Land Rush. However, when her brother is killed, Cheyenne army scout Ethan Temple agrees to help her, even though it is against his principles. Love slowly blooms, but land grabbers, prejudice, and ghosts from the past drive them apart. It is only when they meet again that their relationship has a chance of becoming a permanent reality. Realistic depiction of the Old West.

Other books you might like:
Yvonne Adamson, *Bridey's Mountain*, 1993
Ann Gabriel, *South Texas*, 1989
Linda Howard, *A Lady of the West*, 1990
Catherine Lanigan, *A Promise Made*, 1991
Patricia Potter, *Renegade*, 1993

164
ROSANNE BITTNER

Wildest Dreams
(New York: Bantam, 1994)

Story type: Historical/American West; Saga
Major character(s): Lettie MacBride, Single Parent (unwed mother); Luke Fontaine, Rancher (cattle)
Time period(s): 1860s; 1870s
Locale(s): Montana

Summary: Luke Fontaine is on his way to Montana to run his ranch. Lettie MacBride is trying to escape the disgrace of being raped and made destitute. Their marriage is the beginning of an empire that, despite numerous obstacles, endures. A saga of the Old West.

Other books you might like:
Yvonne Adamson, *Bridey's Mountain*, 1993
    Colorado saga/4 generations
Elaine Barbieri, *More Precious than Gold*, 1992
    Colorado saga
Catherine Lanigan, *A Promise Made*, 1991
    strong heroine

Larry McMurtry, *Lonesome Dove*, 1985
    saga
Larry McMurtry, *Streets of Laredo*, 1993
    Sequel to *Lonesome Dove*

165
CHERYL BLACK

Comanche Love Song
(New York: Zebra, 1989)

Story type: Historical/American West
Major character(s): Silver Dawn, Captive, Indian; Walker Grayson, Military Personnel (U.S. Cavalry; Major)
Time period(s): 19th century (Mid-to-Late)
Locale(s): Texas; Louisiana

Summary: Angry and confused at being rescued by the cavalry from the only life she has ever known, Silver Dawn struggles to reconcile her Comanche upbringing with the strange ways of civilization. Not the least of her confusion concerns Walker Grayson, the man she loves and who seems to care for her, but who is planning to marry someone else.

Other books you might like:
Janet Dailey, *The Pride of Hannah Wade*, 1985
De Wanna Pace, *Surrender Sweet Stranger*, 1988
Maureen Reynolds, *One Golden Hour*, 1988
Bobbi Smith, *Arizona Caress*, 1989
Sylvie Sommerfield, *Wild Wyoming Heart*, 1988

166
ALMA BLAIR

The Dark Side of Paradise
(New York: Avalon, 1990)

Story type: Contemporary/Innocent; Romantic Suspense
Major character(s): Jessica Holland, Accountant (CPA); Clint Wheeler, Businessman (investments)
Time period(s): 1990s
Locale(s): Hawaii

Summary: Jessica Holland has been living dangerously! Since she's been in Hawaii on vaction she's been shoved in front of a car, assaulted by poisonous sea snakes, and is being pursued by two attractive men. But when things move from sheer coincidence to deliberate intent, she suddenly realizes her life is really at risk.

Other books you might like:
Joan Aiken, *A Cluster of Separate Sparks*, 1972
Marion Smith Collins, *Home to Stay*, 1991
Lucy Keane, *False Impressions*, 1991
Alice Sharpe, *The Vanishing Bridegroom*, 1990
Mary Stewart, *This Rough Magic*, 1972

167

ALMA BLAIR

The Unwitting Witness

(New York: Avalon Books, 1990)

Story type: Romantic Suspense
Major character(s): Karen Whitaker, Photographer; Mitch Logan, Writer (Mystery)
Time period(s): 1980s
Locale(s): St. Andrew, Florida

Summary: When Karen's photography studio is ransacked and she is pursued by people shooting at her, to avoid returning home, she runs to a friend's house only to find mystery writer Mitch Logan there instead. Intrigued, Mitch helps Karen try to solve the mystery—and in the process they fall in love.

Other books you might like:
Loretta Jackson, *Nightmare in Morocco*, 1989
    Moroccan setting
Karen G. McCullough, *The Night Prowlers*, 1990
Mary Stewart, *Madam, Will You Talk?*, 1955
    Classic romantic suspense/French setting
Anne Armstrong Thompson, *Message From Absalom*, 1975
Constance Walker, *One Perfect Springtime*, 1989

168

LEONA BLAIR

A World of Difference

(New York: Bantam, 1989)

Story type: Saga
Major character(s): Georgia Brandon, Heiress, Businesswoman; Connor MacKenzie, Businessman
Time period(s): 20th century (First half of century)
Locale(s): New York, New York; London

Summary: Following the fortunes of the wealthy, industrial Brandon family, this sweeping tale focuses on the relationship between Georgia, daughter of Rhys Brandon, and Connor MacKenzie, the dynamic son of a labor leader. Set against the dramatic backdrop of two world wars, financial speculation and chaos, and a world-wide depression.

Other books you might like:
Jackie Collins, *Chances*, 1981
Catherine Gavin, *Possessions*, 1984
Susan Howatch, *The Rich Are Different*, 1977
Jayne Ann Krentz, *The Golden Chance*, 1989
Erica Spindler, *Chances Are*, 1989

169

JENNIFER BLAKE

Arrow to the Heart

(New York: Fawcett, 1993)

Story type: Historical/Antebellum American South
Major character(s): Katrine Castlereagh, Gentlewoman; Rowan de Blanc, Gentleman
Time period(s): 19th century

Locale(s): New Orleans, Louisiana

Summary: Unable to father a child, Giles Castlereagh holds a "medieval" tournament with the private intention of having the winner act as his proxy and impregnate his young wife, Katrine. However, the two principals in this endeavor, Katrine and the tournament winner, Rowan de Blanc, are highly uncooperative—until they are locked in a tower together. Mystery, treachery, and passion combine in this tale with an unusual twist from a classic writer in the romance genre.

Other books you might like:
Charla Cameron, *Sultry Nights*, 1992
Shirl Henke, *Moonflower*, 1989
Lisa Kleypas, *Only in Your Arms*, 1992
Karen Robards, *Morning Song*, 1989

170

JENNIFER BLAKE
RUTH JEAN DALE, Co-Author
MARGARET BROWNLEY, Co-Author
SHERYL LYNN, Co-Author

Honeymoon Suite

(New York: St. Martin's, 1995)

Story type: Anthology; Contemporary
Time period(s): 1990s
Locale(s): Dallas, Texas

Summary: This sensual, funny collection of contemporary novellas is linked by setting (a Dallas luxury hotel honeymoon suite) and by pace and style (lively and upbeat). Included are "Wake-up Call" by Ruth Jean Dale, "Check-out Time" by Margaret Brownley, "Reservations" by Jennifer Blake, and "Lost and Found" by Sheryl Lynn.

Other books you might like:
Sandra Brown, *Texas! Sage*, 1991
    fast-paced
Carole Buck, *Love Goddesses*, 1996
    anthology
Jayne Ann Krentz, *Grand Passion*, 1994
    fast-paced
Ellen Tanner Marsh, *A Christmas Embrace*, 1994
    marriage renewal theme
Susan Elizabeth Phillips, *It Had to Be You*, 1994
    lively and funny

171

JENNIFER BLAKE

Joy and Anger

(New York: Fawcett, 1991)

Story type: Contemporary/Mainstream; Romantic Suspense
Major character(s): Julie Bullard, Director (Film); Ray Tabary, Consultant (Cajun)
Time period(s): 1990s
Locale(s): Louisiana

Summary: When film director Julie Bullard enlists the aid of reluctant "bayou expert" Ray Tabary as technical consultant to her latest project, she finds herself plagued by a growing attraction for Ray as well as an increasingly serious series of accidents that threaten to ruin the film. Passion, sabatoge, and revenge combine in this powerful story of treachery and greed.

Other books you might like:
Jill Barkin, *Hot Streak*, 1990
Janet Dailey, *Aspen Gold*, 1991
Mollie Gregory, *Birthstone*, 1991
Susan Kyle, *Night Fever*, 1990
Sandra Marton, *Night Fires*, 1991

172

JENNIFER BLAKE (Pseudonym of Patricia Maxwell)

Love and Smoke
(New York: Ballantine, 1989)

Story type: Contemporary
Major character(s): Riva Staulet, Socialite (Accomplished and wealthy), Widow(er) (Noel's stepmother); Noel Staulet, Heir (of Riva's late husband)
Locale(s): New Orleans, Louisiana (Bonnie Vie, family estate)

Summary: Recently widowed after a long marriage to a much older man, Riva Staulet has a few old scores to settle, the major one being how to ruin the political career of the man who left her pregnant at 15. She also needs to come to terms with her feelings for her stepson, Noel (and his for her), with whom she had a brief, impulsive affair years ago.

Other books you might like:
Janet Dailey, *The Glory Game*, 1985
Julie Ellis, *The Hampton Heritage*, 1978
Susan Howatch, *Sins of the Fathers*, 1980
Judith Michael, *The Sunset Dream*, 1984
Belva Plain, *Evergreen*, 1978

173

JENNIFER BLAKE

Shameless
(New York: Fawcett Columbine, 1994)

Story type: Contemporary; Romantic Suspense
Major character(s): Camilla Greenley, Young Woman; Reid Sayers, Hero
Time period(s): 1990s
Locale(s): South

Summary: When Reid Sayers returns to his small hometown, the last thing he wants to do is become involved in other people's problems, especially those of Camilla Greenley, the one woman he could never forget. Nevertheless, her problems become his, and together they fight their feelings and the town, eventually arriving at a most satisfactory solution. A fast-paced, highly sensual story—rife with steamy Southern atmosphere.

Other books you might like:
Sandra Brown, *Breath of Scandal*, 1991
Tami Hoag, *Lucky's Lady*, 1992
Karen Robards, *One Summer*, 1993

Nora Roberts, *Divine Evil*, 1992
Alexandra Thorne, *Lawless*, 1994
  Texas setting

174

SARA BLAYNE (Pseudonym of Marcia Howl)

A Noble Deception
(New York: Zebra, 1995)

Story type: Regency
Major character(s): Lady Lucy Powell, Debutante, Writer (aspiring); Phillip Carmichael, Imposter (posing as the duke's agent), Nobleman (Duke of Lathrop)
Time period(s): 1810s
Locale(s): England

Summary: Vowing only to marry for love, red-haired, green-eyed Lucy Powell refuses a proposed arranged marriage with the Duke of Lathrop, a man she has never met, preferring instead to devote herself to spinsterhood and the writing of gothic novels. Her attitude changes, however, when she meets the Duke's agent, Phillip Carmichael, a man who is every bit as mysterious and romantic as the heroes she writes about. But Phillip is not what he seems, and there is much that needs to be sorted be sorted out before the pair can make their way happily to the altar. A group of delightful sisters add to this passionate, funny, warm, and well-written story.

Other books you might like:
Gail Eastwood, *The Captain's Dilemma*, 1995
  appealing characters/well-done sexual tension
Jean R. Ewing, *Rogue's Reward*, 1995
  another deceptive hero/witty
Jean R. Ewing, *Virtue's Reward*, 1995
  warm/well-handled sexual tension
Carla Kelly, *Mrs. Drew Plays Her Hand*, 1994
  warm, passionate, and laced with humor
April Kihlstrom, *The Wicked Groom*, 1996
  another deceptive hero

175

SARA BLAYNE

Sweet Abandon
(New York: Zebra, 1990)

Story type: Historical/Georgian
Major character(s): Angelique, Runaway; Wesley Locke, Sea Captain
Time period(s): 18th century (Mid-Century)
Locale(s): St. Dominique, Caribbean; At Sea

Summary: In the process of trying to return to St. Dominique, Angelique, posing as a woman of the streets, ends up injured, feverish, and on her way to the West Indies aboard Wesley Locke's ship. Romance and adventure laced with political unrest and voodoo.

Other books you might like:
Heather Graham, *A Pirate's Pleasure*, 1989
Betina M. Krahn, *Passion's Ransom*, 1987
Laurie McBain, *Moonstruck Madness*, 1977

Deborah Simmons, *Heart's Masquerade*, 1989
Kathleen E. Woodiwiss, *Shanna*, 1977

176

CLAIRE BOCARDO

Lovers and Friends
(New York: Zebra, 1995)

Story type: Contemporary
Major character(s): Florence Huckabee, Cook, Baker; Ivy Grimes, Divorced Person
Time period(s): 1990s
Locale(s): Cedar Grove, Texas

Summary: Florence Huckabee and Ivy Grimes are girlhood friends who grow up to have very different lives. Flo settles down in their hometown to raise a family and Ivy goes to the big city to escape her life of poverty. Twenty years later, now widowed and divorced, they resume their friendship and each becomes determined to help the other find the perfect mate— whether she wants one or not! When they are able to conquer their long-denied fears, they find love in the most unexpected place.

Other books you might like:
Betty Cothran, *Over the Moon*, 1994
Garda Parker, *Out of the Blue*, 1992
Marilyn Pappano, *Operation Homefront*, 1992
Kristine Rolofson, *I'll Be Seeing You*, 1993
Ray Sipherd, *The Courtship of Peggy McCoy*, 1990

177

GEORGIA BOCKOVEN

A Marriage of Convenience
(New York: Harper Collins, 1991)

Story type: Contemporary
Major character(s): Christine Taylor, Businesswoman, Parent (Adoptive); Mason Winter, Businessman (developer)
Time period(s): 1990s
Locale(s): United States

Summary: Five years earlier, Christine Taylor gave up her career to become guardian and fulltime mother to her orphaned nephew, Kevin. Now, Mason Winter, Kevin's natural father, is on the scene demanding his parental rights! Legal battles ensue; but a wise judge makes a suggestion they can't refuse and what begins as a marriage of convenience for the sake of a child, eventually becomes one of love.

Other books you might like:
Janet Dailey, *Terms of Surrender*, 1982
Judy Gill, *Golden Swan*, 1990
Shirl Henke, *Summer Has No Name*, 1990
  mainstream
LaVyrle Spencer, *Bittersweet*, 1990
LaVyrle Spencer, *Morning Glory*, 1989

178

GEORGIA BOCKOVEN

Moments
(New York: Harper, 1994)

Story type: Contemporary
Major character(s): Jenny Cavanaugh, Advertising, Imposter (aka Elizabeth Preston); Amado Montoya, Businessman, Vintner; Mike Logan, Vintner
Time period(s): 1990s
Locale(s): New York; California

Summary: Successful advertising executive Jenny Cavanaugh is hired by Amado Montoya, the owner of a prestigious winery, and ends up accepting his proposal of marriage— hoping she will come to love him. However, problems arise when she falls in love with the winemaster, Mike Logan, and realizes that she actually loves two men. Hidden identities and well-kept secrets add to the intriguing flavor of this romance.

Other books you might like:
Shirl Henke, *Bouquet*, 1994
  winery environment
Shirl Henke, *Summer Has No Name*, 1990
  wine industry tie-ins
Marcia Martin, *Southern Secrets*, 1991
LaVyrle Spencer, *Loved*, 1984
  historical triangle
Lisa Ann Verge, *Sweet Harvest*, 1992
  winery environment

179

JANE BONANDER
TANYA ANNE CROSBY, Co-Author
JENNIFER HORSMAN, Co-Author
JOAN JOHNSTON, Co-Author

Avon Books Presents: A Christmas Together
(New York: Avon, 1994)

Story type: Anthology; Holiday Themes

Summary: A Christmas anthology consisting of four historical novellas. Included are: Angel Face by Jane Bonander, a romantic story of love amid a snowstorm in 19th century Minnesota; Heaven's Gate by Tanya Ann Crosby, a spritely story of love among the British elite; The Ice Queen by Jennifer Horsman, a Victorian tale in which a young widow and a dashing doctor are brought together by a sick child; and The Christmas Baby by Joan Johnston, a humorous story of feuds, weddings, and babies—Texas-style.

Other books you might like:
Jo Beverley, *The Christmas Angel*, 1992
  a Regency-style Christmas
Stella Cameron, *Avon Books Presents: A Christmas Collection*, 1992
  historical Christmas anthology
Ruth Langan, *Christmas Miracle*, 1992
  Christmas in the American West

Judith McNaught, *A Holiday of Love*, 1994
  historical Christmas anthology; Jude Deveraux, Jill
  Barnett, Arnette Lamb, co-authors

180
JANE BONANDER

Dancing on Snowflakes
(New York: Pocket, 1995)

Story type: Historical/American West
Major character(s): Susannah Walker, Abuse Victim, Fugitive; Nathan Wolf, Bounty Hunter
Time period(s): 1860s (1867)
Locale(s): Nevada

Summary: In an effort to protect her son, Susannah Walker is forced to kill her abusive husband and flee her home in rural Missouri and head west. Once settled in the Nevada Foothills, Susannah believes she will be able to start a new life. But then Nathan Wolf, a bounty hunter in search of her, arrives in town. A wounded hero and a strong, but also wounded, heroine combine in a moving story of growing love and trust.

Other books you might like:
Catherine Anderson, *Cheyenne Amber*, 1994
  abused heroine
Dorothy Garlock, *Homeplace*, 1991
Robin Lee Hatcher, *Liberty Blue*, 1995
  tender
Maggie Osborne, *The Wives of Bowie Stone*, 1994
  wounded heroine
Patricia Potter, *Defiant*, 1995
  wounded hero

181
JANE BONANDER

Secrets of a Midnight Moon
(New York: St. Martin's, 1991)

Story type: Historical/American West
Major character(s): Anna Jensen, Teacher; Nicholas ''Bear'' Gaspard, Indian
Time period(s): 1850s (1858)
Locale(s): California

Summary: Beautiful, naive, and enthusiastic, Anna Jensen comes to California for her first teaching position and finds herself kidnapped, taken to the mountains, and compelled to teach a group of Indian children that her abductor has rescued from virtual slavery. Anna battles her fears, her prejudices, and her passions as she learns to love the children and their determined, vengeful champion, as well. Tender, sensual, and sensitive. Interesting and unusual historical detail.

Other books you might like:
Madeline Baker, *Forbidden Fires*, 1990
Kathleen Eagle, *Heaven and Earth*, 1990
Joan Johnston, *Sweetwater Seduction*, 1991
Jill Marie Landis, *Rose*, 1990
Jan McKee, *Sweet Justice*, 1991

182
PARIS AFTON BONDS

Dream Time
(New York: Harper, 1993)

Story type: Historical/Mainstream; Saga
Major character(s): Nan Briscoll, Convict, Businesswoman (shipping company entrepreneuer); Captain Tom Livingston, Spouse; Miles Randolph, Villain
Time period(s): 19th century
Locale(s): Australia

Summary: Pregnant and betrayed by her lover, Miles, Nan Briscoll is sent to Australia for political crimes. She marries Captain Tom Livingston, has two daughters (one of which she gives away), and develops a trading company. Although her daughters grow along very different lines, the lives of the three remain intertwined; and when Miles Randolph reappears on the scene, Nan's thoughts turn to revenge. A complex story steeped in the Australian history of the period.

Other books you might like:
Leigh Bristol, *Stormswept*, 1990
Dorothy Eden, *The Vines of Yarabee*, 1969
Colleen McCullough, *The Thorn Birds*, 1977
Katherine Sinclair, *Far Horizons*, 1991

183
ELIZABETH BONNER

A Vow to Keep
(New York: Diamond, 1993)

Story type: Historical/Medieval
Major character(s): Adrienne, Captive, Royalty (princess); Hugh de Clairmont, Nobleman
Time period(s): 13th century

Summary: Hugh vows to reclaim his ancient family land and abducts Henry II's illegitimate daughter, the Princess Adrienne, to do so. As she has already been commanded to marry the evil Duke Wilhelm, much against her wishes, Adrienne actually doesn't mind being kidnapped—certainly not by someone as attractive as Hugh. Enchanted by Adrienne, Hugh ends up the captive and he begins to question his desire for vengeance. A passionate story set during a volatile era.

Other books you might like:
Catherine Coulter, *Earth Song*, 1990
Susan Johnson, *Outlaw*, 1993
Marylyle Rogers, *Dark Whispers*, 1991
  Gothic elements
Lynette Vinet, *Knight's Caress*, 1993

184
ALICE BORCHARDT

Devoted
(New York: Dutton, 1995)

Story type: Historical/Medieval

Major character(s): Elin, Young Woman (pagan); Owen, Religious (Bishop of Chatalon)
Time period(s): 10th century (c. 900)
Locale(s): France

Summary: As a reward for warning him of his imminent capture, Owen, Bishop of Chatalon, rescues Elin from the Vikings and marries her. More Viking raids, treachery, and betrayal add complications. A classic story of the conflict between the old and new ways, set in the France of Charlemagne and featuring humor, action, and well-done, historically accurate characters. First novel.

Other books you might like:
Rexanne Becnel, *Where Magic Dwells*, 19944
Iris Johansen, *Lion's Bride*, 1996
    well-rounded characters, humor, mystical elements
Laura Kinsale, *For My Lady's Heart*, 1993
    complex characters
Judith Merkle Riley, *In Pursuit of the Green Lion*, 1990
    well-rounded characters, paranormal elements
Judith Merkle Riley, *A Vision of Light*, 1989

185

BARBARA BOSWELL

Red Velvet
(New York: Jove, 1995)

Story type: Contemporary
Major character(s): Sierra Everly, Vintner (winery owner); Nicholas Nicholai, Businessman (security investigation expert), Heir (half-ownership in the winery)
Time period(s): 1990s
Locale(s): New York

Summary: When an eccentric uncle sells his shares in the family winery to a virtual stranger (and then dies), Sierra Everly finds herself in partnership with attractive Nicholas Nicholai, a man with no knowledge of wineries, but with definite ideas as to how to run them. Suspicions of embezzlement plague their growing relationship, as do their divergent ideas for running the winery. Well-handled sexual tension and good characterizations keep things interesting.

Other books you might like:
Georgia Bockoven, *Moments*, 1994
    winery environment
Shirl Henke, *Bouquet*, 1994
    mystery elements/good winery detail
Shirl Henke, *Summer Has No Name*, 1990
    winery environment
Jayne Ann Krentz, *Perfect Partners*, 1992
    forced business partnership
Nora Roberts, *Born in Fire*, 1995
    two strong-willed protagonists

186

RITA BOUCHER

A Misbegotten Match
(New York: Avon, 1994)

Story type: Regency
Major character(s): Amanda Metcalfe, Companion, Heiress; Sebastian Armitage, Orphan, Plantation Owner (in Jamaica)
Time period(s): 1820s (1821)
Locale(s): England

Summary: When her employer and benefactor falls ill, Amanda Metcalfe becomes seriously concerned and reluctantly sends to Jamaica for Sebastian Armitage, the rakehell godson that Lady Claire adores. However, both Amanda and Sebastian have secrets that they will guard at all costs, and despite their mutual attraction, their deep suspicions of each other keep getting in the way. Features traditional Regency wit and ambience in combination with non-traditional Regency characters.

Other books you might like:
Mary Balogh, *The Snow Angel*, 1991
Marion Chesney, *The Desirable Duchess*, 1993
Carla Kelly, *Libby's London Merchant*, 1991
Mary Jo Putney, *The Rake and the Reformer*, 1989
Sheila Simonson, *The Bar Sinister*, 1986

187

RITA BOUCHER

Miss Gabriel's Gambit
(New York: Avon, 1993)

Story type: Regency
Major character(s): Sylvia Gabriel, Debutante, Sports Figure (chess player); David Rutherford, Nobleman (Lord Dornhill), Sports Figure (chess player)
Time period(s): 1810s
Locale(s): England

Summary: When, in a state of inebriation, the new Lord Dornhill, chess-master David Rutherford, bets that he will only marry a woman who can beat him at chess, he has no idea that the person he has been playing mail chess with for months—and who has just beaten him—is none other than Miss Sylvia Gabriel! A delightfully convoluted story of love and deception, peopled with charmingly different characters.

Other books you might like:
Sarah Eagle, *The Marriage Gamble*, 1992
Georgette Heyer, *Sylvester, or the Wicked Uncle*, 1957
Kasey Michaels, *The Anonymous Miss Addams*, 1989
Amanda Quick, *Seduction*, 1990
    sensual
Sheila Simonson, *Lady Elizabeth's Comet*, 1985

188

RITA BOUCHER

The Scandalous Schoolmistress
(New York: Avon, 1992)

Story type: Regency
Major character(s): Guinivere Courtney, Teacher; Daniel Corvin, Nobleman
Time period(s): 1810s
Locale(s): London, England

Summary: Guinivere Courtney runs a school for the ton 's most unmanageable young hellions, and has great success in turning them into young ladies. However, when Lord Corvin entrusts his sister into Guin's care, he soon realizes that the capable Miss Courtney has tamed not only his sister, but his heart as well.

Other books you might like:
Jo Beverley, *An Unwilling Bride*, 1992
Cathleen Clare, *The Mistress of Mishap*, 1992
Michelle Kasey, *The Somerville Farce*, 1991
Amanda Quick, *Scandal*, 1991
　　sensual
Meg-Lynn Roberts, *An Alluring Lady*, 1992

189

CAROLINE BOURNE

Allegheny Captive
(New York. Zebra, 1990)

Story type: Historical
Major character(s): Charissa Sherwood, Noblewoman, Heiress; Andrew Donovan, Sea Captain (Riverboat)
Time period(s): 1820s
Locale(s): Mississippi River; New Orleans, Louisiana; Allegheny Mountains, Pennsylvania

Summary: Lady Charissa Sherwood's romantic opinion of adventure changes drastically when she is kidnapped, sold into white slavery, and forced to become "one of the girls" at a New Orleans brothel. However, never one to give up easily, Charissa plans her own escape and stows away aboard Andrew Donovan's riverboat. Trouble follows, as well as romance, as they go up the Mississippi and then head east toward Andrew's Pennsylvania home. A passionate, fast-paced sequel To *Allegheny Ecstasy.*

Other books you might like:
Elane Osborn, *Skylark*, 1990
Rebecca Paisley, *Barefoot Bride*, 1990
Michalann Perry, *Love's Windswept Embrace*, 1990
Gina Robins, *Mississippi Mistress*, 1990
Jane Toombs, *Riverboat Rogue*, 1990

190

CAROLINE BOURNE

Allegheny Ecstasy
(New York: Zebra, 1990)

Story type: Historical/Post-American Revolution
Major character(s): Diana Rourke, Psychic, Heiress; Cole Donovan, Murderer (accused)
Time period(s): 1780s (1786)
Locale(s): Allegheny Mountains, Pennsylvania; Philadelphia, Pennsylvania

Summary: Naive, clairvoyant Diana Rourke's father has been killed and her unscrupulous uncle wants her inheritance. When hero Cole Donovan is accused of the murder and seems to join in the plot against her, things seem hopeless. But all is not what it seems, and by the end of the story, most problems are solved and the lovers are finally united.

Other books you might like:
Jill Marie Landis, *Wild Flower*, 1989
Rebecca Paisley, *Barefoot Bride*, 1990
　　Backwoods setting
Victoria Thompson, *Fortune's Lady*, 1990
Phyllis A. Whitney, *Rainbow in the Mist*, 1989
　　Contemporary setting/Psychic heroine

191

CAROLINE BOURNE

Love's Perfect Dream
(New York: Zebra, 1993)

Story type: Historical/American West
Major character(s): Isobel Emerson, Heiress, Socialite; Shadoe McCain, Gambler, Fugitive
Time period(s): 1870s (1878)
Locale(s): New Orleans, Louisiana; Oklahoma

Summary: When Isobel meets gambler Shadoe McCain, it is instant love for both. Shadoe, however, has had his fill of rich, spoiled women and tries to reject her, but Isobel convinces him to go to Montana with her to seek her long-lost brother. The long, arduous trip tests all their resolve, but they slowly come to love and trust each other. Treachery, gold caches, and ghosts add delightful complications to this passionate romance.

Other books you might like:
Jude Deveraux, *Mountain Laurel*, 1990
Kathleen Harrington, *Cherish the Dream*, 1990
Elizabeth Lowell, *Only Mine*, 1992
Meagan McKinney, *Fair Is the Rose*, 1993

192

CAROLINE BOURNE

Riverboat Seduction
(New York: Zebra, 1992)

Story type: Historical/American Civil War

Major character(s): Delilah Wickley, Orphan, Southern Belle; Grant Emerson, Gambler (riverboat)
Time period(s): 1860s
Locale(s): New Orleans, Louisiana

Summary: Delilah will do anything to regain her plantation — even marry the Yankee riverboat gambler who bought it! Gambler Grant Emerson sees through Delilah's schemes, and while he can't trust her, he does love her — even when she just can't tell him the truth. Lies, dangers, and passion combine in this intricately plotted and lavishly presented story of the old South.

Other books you might like:
Olga Bicos, *By My Heart Betrayed*, 1991
Kathleen Kane, *Mountain Dawn*, 1992
Ana Leigh, *Angel Hunter*, 1992
Gina Robins, *Mississippi Mistress*, 1990
Sylvie Sommerfield, *Love's Stolen Promise*, 1992

193

BARBARA TAYLOR BRADFORD

Remember

(New York: Random, 1992)

Story type: Contemporary/Mainstream
Major character(s): Nicky Wells, Television Personality (newscaster); Clee Donovan, Photojournalist; Charles Devereaux, Television Personality (newscaster)
Time period(s): 1990s
Locale(s): New York, New York; Europe

Summary: Slowly recovering from the death of her beloved Charles, Nicky, a strong and daring newscaster, finally meets Clee Donovan, someone she is willing to risk loving. However, Charles' shocking reappearance sends her on a dangerous and difficult quest to track him down. In the process she learns some truths about Charles, Clee, and most of all, herself.

Other books you might like:
Joanne Z. Adams, *Intimate Connections*, 1991
Catherine Coulter, *Beyond Eden*, 1992
Janet Dailey, *Masquerade*, 1990
Marie Ferrarella, *Sapphire and Shadow*, 1991
Judith Michael, *Deceptions*, 1982

194

BLYTHE BRADLEY

To Love a Stranger

(Bensalem, Pennsylvania: Meteor, 1993)

Story type: Contemporary
Major character(s): Diana Foster, Teacher (former high school teacher); Trevor Sinclair, Businessman; Crystal Sinclair, Young Woman
Time period(s): 1990s
Locale(s): Bellington Cay, Caribbean

Summary: Diana Foster has fire in her eye as she sets out to confront her niece's father and make him own up to being a deserting, "dead-beat dad." A storm and a chance meeting bring them face to face, and Trevor is surprised to find himself dredging up fatherly emotions for Crystal he thought long dead. As Diana begins to understand his feelings, she knows that Crystal will at last have her father's love; she, however, is not so sure about her own future. A believable love story.

Other books you might like:
Elizabeth August, *The Virgin Wife*, 1993
Christina Dodd, *Lady in Black*, 1993
Merline Lovelace, *Bits and Pieces*, 1993
Ann Howard White, *All but Love*, 1993

195

EMILY BRADSHAW

Cactus Blossom

(New York: Dell, 1992)

Story type: Historical/American West
Major character(s): Maxie Maxwell, Frontierswoman, Outlaw (daughter of an outlaw); Aaron Fletcher, Lawman, Outlaw (former)
Time period(s): 1860s (1868)
Locale(s): Texas; Mexico

Summary: Maxie Maxwell, the carelessly raised, fiesty, prickly daughter of an infamous outlaw, is "rescued" from her situation by outlaw-turned-lawman Aaron Fletcher, who hopes to turn Cactus Maxie into a lady. Of course, Maxie resists his efforts—however, she cannot resist him, and Maxie eventually has to choose between Aaron and her family.

Other books you might like:
Catherine Hart, *Sweet Fury*, 1990
Norah Hess, *Devil in Spurs*, 1990
Robin Leigh, *Rugged Splendor*, 1991
Elizabeth Lowell, *Reckless Love*, 1990

196

EMILY BRADSHAW

Halfway to Paradise

(New York: Dell, 1993)

Story type: Historical/Seventeenth Century
Major character(s): Jane Alexander, Widow(er) (Puritan); Matthew Hawkins, Thief, Nobleman (Earl of Chester)
Time period(s): 17th century
Locale(s): England

Summary: Jane, desperate to "buy" a son, takes in the child of the notorious thief and traitor, Hawk. However, Hawk escapes from prison and is determined to keep the prim Puritan Jane from caring for his son. Both, however, truly care about young Gideon, and their love for him brings them together in spite of their vast differences.

Other books you might like:
Diane Wicker Davis, *Heart of the Falcon*, 1990
    later time period
Laura Kinsale, *Flowers From the Storm*, 1992
    dark and serious/later time period

Maura Seger, *Light on the Mountain*, 1992
later time period
Maura Seger, *Tapestry*, 1993
Medieval setting

197

EMILY BRADSHAW

The Heart's Journey
(New York: Dell, 1992)

Story type: Historical/American West
Major character(s): Harriet Foster, Activist (feminist reformer); Jake Carradine, Drifter, Gunfighter
Time period(s): 19th century
Locale(s): West

Summary: Determined to reach California, activist reformer Harriet Foster hires disreputable, embittered Jake Carradine as an escort. Danger, hardship, and plenty of sparks accompany them on their journey — and as they come to understand each other, they also learn about love.

Other books you might like:
Rosanne Bittner, *Caress*, 1992
Rebecca Brandewyne, *Desperado*, 1993
Christine Dorsey, *Kansas Kiss*, 1992
Betina Lindsey, *Waltz with the Lady*, 1990

198

REBECCA BRANDEWYNE

Across a Starlit Sea
(New York: Warner, 1989)

Story type: Gothic
Major character(s): Laura Prescott, Fiance(c) (Sea Captain's Daughter); Jarrett Chandler, Landowner (Master of Stormswept Heights)
Time period(s): 1830s (1832); 1980s (1989)

Summary: This continues the stories of the Chandler/Sheffield/Prescott families begun in *Upon a Moon-Dark Moor*.

Other books you might like:
Daphne Du Maurier, *Rebecca*, 1938
The modern gothic prototype
Philippa Gregory, *Wideacre*, 1987
First of a trilogy with some gothic elements
Victoria Holt, *Mistress of Mellyn*, 1960
Pure gothic
Lee Karr, *Dark Cries of Gray Oaks*, 1989
Mary Stewart, *Nine Coaches Waiting*, 1958
A classic gothic

199

REBECCA BRANDEWYNE

Beyond the Starlit Frost
(New York: Pocket, 1991)

Story type: Futuristic

Major character(s): Rhiannon, Hunter; Iskander, Royalty (Prince of Iglacia)
Time period(s): Indeterminate Future
Locale(s): Tintagel, Planet—Imaginary

Summary: Sent to seek and destroy the source of power of the Darkness, Iskander, Prince of Iglacia is rescued from a storm by the maid Rhiannon who then joins him in his quest. As they journey Iskander helps Rhiannon develop her incipient powers; and by the time they reach their destination, Rhiannon has come to terms with her abilities and has also discovered love. Sequel to *Passion Moon Rising*.

Other books you might like:
Jessica Bryan, *Across a Wine-Dark Sea*, 1991
Saranne Dawson, *From the Mist*, 1991
Nancy Harding, *Wind Child*, 1990
Tanith Lee, *A Heroine of the World*, 1989
Lindsay Randall, *Silversword*, 1990

200

REBECCA BRANDEWYNE

Desperado
(New York: Warner, 1993)

Story type: Historical/American West
Major character(s): Araminta Winthrop, Journalist, Artist; Rigo de Castillo, Military Personnel (Mexican General), Revolutionary
Time period(s): 1910s (1912-1913)
Locale(s): Texas; Mexico

Summary: Kidnapped on her wedding night by the infamous General Rigo de Castillo, Araminta Winthrop endures the hardships of a journey through Mexico during the turbulent pre-Revolutionary era. Her feelings go from panic to love as she comes to understand her captor and sympathize with his cause. Stormy and passionate.

Other books you might like:
Emily Bradshaw, *The Heart's Journey*, 1992
Suzanne Ellison, *Eagle Knight*, 1991
earlier period
Nicole Jordan, *Wild Star*, 1992
Linda Ladd, *Midnight Fire*, 1991
Linda Ladd, *Dragon Fire*, 1992

201

REBECCA BRANDEWYNE

Heartland
(New York: Warner, 1990)

Story type: Historical/American West
Major character(s): Rachel Wilder, Guardian (of 7 children); Slade Maverick, Gunfighter, Bounty Hunter
Time period(s): 1870s (1874)
Locale(s): Kansas

Summary: When Rachel Wilder assumes the guardianship of her late best friend's seven children, she has to deal with both their drunken father, who doesn't want his life disturbed, and their mother's gunslinging half-brother Slade, who wants the children, too. The romantic results between Rachel and Slade are inevitable in this action-packed story that dishes up a healthy does of historical detail along with the romance.

Other books you might like:
Deborah Camp, *Black-Eyed Susan*, 1990
Ann Gabriel, *South Texas*, 1990
Charlotte Hinger, *Come Spring*, 1986
Victoria Thompson, *Fortune's Lady*, 1990

202
REBECCA BRANDEWYNE
The Jacaranda Tree
(New York: Warner, 1995)

Story type: Historical/Victorian
Major character(s): Arabella Darracott, Gentlewoman, Castaway; Lucien Sinclair, Convict (former), Rescuer
Time period(s): 1840s (1845); 1850s (1855)
Locale(s): Yorkshire, England; New South Wales, Australia

Summary: Arabella plans to join her guardian in Australia but is shipwrecked on a deserted beach and rescued by the wealthy ex-convict "Demon" Lucien Sinclair. He takes her to civilization, but in the process, they become passionately involved. Although they go their separate ways, they move in the same social circles and so they meet again, eventually with permanent results. A fast-paced, passionate romance, laced with Jack-the-Ripper murders and Brandewyne's typical intensity.

Other books you might like:
Linda Ladd, *White Rose*, 1994
  similar setting
Connie Mason, *Brave Land, Brave Love*, 1992
  similar setting
Katherine Sutcliffe, *Dream Fever*, 1991
Katherine Sutcliffe, *Once a Hero*, 1994
Katherine Sutcliffe, *Shadow Play*, 1991

203
REBECCA BRANDEWYNE
Rainbow's End
(New York: Warner, 1991)

Story type: Historical/American West
Major character(s): Josselyn O'Rourke, Religious (novice), Mine Owner; Durango de Navarro, Mine Owner, Gambler; Wylie Gresham, Mine Owner, Businessman
Time period(s): 1870s (1877)
Locale(s): Central City, Colorado

Summary: Summoned to Colorado upon the death of her father, Ursuline novice Josselyn O'Rourke is stunned to discover that according to her father's will, she must marry one of his partners in order to claim her inheritance. Courted by both men, Jossie is confused by her feelings, especially those for the disreputable Durango. Nicely done secondary characters in this passionate, action-filled, and intriguing story.

Other books you might like:
Georgina Gentry, *Quicksilver Passion*, 1990

Colleen Quinn, *Colorado Flame*, 1989
Charlotte Simms, *Silver Caress*, 1990
Lynda Trent, *Heaven's Embrace*, 1990

204
REBECCA BRANDEWYNE
Swan Road
(New York: Warner, 1994)

Story type: Historical/Fantasy
Major character(s): Rhowenna, Royalty (princess), Captive; Wulfgar Bloodaxe, Warrior (Viking)
Time period(s): 9th century (865)
Locale(s): England; Scandinavia

Summary: When Princess Rhowenna is captured by Northmen, she fully expects to spend the rest of her days as a slave. However, Wulfgar proves to be more her protector than her master; and as they gradually fall in love, she joins him in his fight against his father and half-brother to save the land from invasion. Action and passion in a classic captive-in-love-with-captor tale.

Other books you might like:
Saranne Dawson, *Awakenings*, 1994
Betina M. Krahn, *My Warrior's Heart*, 1992
Betina Lindsey, *Swan Star*, 1994
Susan Sizemore, *In My Dreams*, 1994
  time travel
Flora M. Speer, *A Love Beyond Time*, 1994
  time travel

205
MICHELLE BRANDON
Heaven on Earth
(New York: Berkley, 1993)

Story type: Historical/Fantasy
Major character(s): Elizabeth Lee, Feminist; Kincaide MacKay, Nobleman; Tabitha, Angel (guardian angel)
Time period(s): 1870s (1877-1880)
Locale(s): Atlantic Ocean; Florida Keys, Florida; West

Summary: Kincaide, running for his life, and Elizabeth, a temperance worker, are cast away on an island. Guardian angels protect them and try to help them reconcile their widely differing interests. Kincaide and Elizabeth might have a chance, but dark forces keep interfering and the guardian angels have their work cut out for them.

Other books you might like:
Annette Broadrick, *A Loving Spirit*, 1990
  contemporary guardian angels
Evelyn A. Crowe, *Reunited*, 1993
Jude Deveraux, *Wishes*, 1989
Debbie Macomber, *A Season of Angels*, 1993
Julie Tetel, *Swept Away*, 1989
  no fantasy elements

206

MICHELLE BRANDON

Touch of Heaven

(New York: Berkley/Diamond, 1992)

Story type: Historical/American West; Historical/Fantasy
Major character(s): Susan Whitten, Rancher; Hunter Carson, Banker; Tabitha, Spirit
Time period(s): 1870s (1876)
Locale(s): Texas

Summary: Tabitha is dead, but she still finds a way to meddle in other people's affairs. This time she is out to help distant relative Susan Whitten. Even though all Susan wants from banker Hunter Carson is an extension of her credit to keep her ranch working, Tabitha makes sure that Susan not only gets the loan but Hunter's heart, as well. Sensual, funny, and simply enchanting.

Other books you might like:
Jude Deveraux, *Wishes*, 1989
Betina M. Krahn, *Midnight Magic*, 1990
Kasey Michaels, *The Haunted Miss Hampshire*, 1992
    meddling ghost, Regency style
Laura Parker, *For Love's Sake Only*, 1991
    more historical ghosts
Judith Merkle Riley, *In Pursuit of the Green Lion*, 1990
    helpful ghost in a 14th century setting

207

PAIGE BRANTLEY

Captive to His Kiss

(New York: Zebra, 1992)

Story type: Historical/Medieval
Major character(s): Madeleine de Moncclet, Noblewoman, Orphan; Wulf of Rugen, Nobleman
Time period(s): 14th century (1348)
Locale(s): France

Summary: Orphaned by the plague, young Madeleine refuses to agree to her Uncle Heribert's plans for her future and finds herself guarded by Baron Wulf of Rugen, her uncle's soldier. He sleeps in her chamber and ultimately in her bed. However, Wulf is loyal to Heribert, and Madeleine has sworn to fight her uncle to the end. Unique and historically accurate.

Other books you might like:
Catherine Coulter, *Secret Song*, 1991
Hannah Howell, *Conqueror's Kiss*, 1991
Johanna Lindsey, *Prisoner of My Desire*, 1991
Mary Jo Putney, *Uncommon Vows*, 1991
Shelly Thacker, *Falcon on the Wind*, 1991

208

PAIGE BRANTLEY

Heart's Awakening

(New York: Zebra, 1995)

Story type: Historical/Medieval

Major character(s): Dominique ''Sancha'' de Severies, Noblewoman (lady-in-waiting to the queen); Hugh Loxton, Bastard Son (of William Canby), Nobleman (Earl of Evistone)
Time period(s): 15th century (1400)
Locale(s): England

Summary: Abducted, drugged, and forced to marry a man she has never met—all because she overhears a plot to kill the king—Lady Dominique de Severies is pleased to find her new husband is not the ogre she expects. He is gentle and caring, and as they come to know each other, they fall in love. But intrigue abounds threatening their lives and their new-found happiness. A well-written, richly detailed story of intrigue, treachery, and love set against the colorful backdrop of the late Medieval era. Sensual.

Other books you might like:
Marsha Canham, *In the Shadow of Midnight*, 1994
    slightly earlier time period/good historical detail
Katherine Deauville, *Daggers of Gold*, 1993
    earlier time period/plots, conspiracies
Roberta Gellis, *The Silver Mirror*, 1989
    court intrigue/good historical detail
Laura Kinsale, *For My Lady's Heart*, 1993
    slightly earlier time period/good historical detail

209

BRENNA BRAXTON-BARSHON

Southern Oaks

(New York: Harper, 1991)

Story type: Historical/Antebellum American South
Major character(s): Brandelene Barnett, Southern Belle, Plantation Owner; Armand Kordell ''Kord'' Bouclair, Servant (indentured), Gentleman
Time period(s): 19th century
Locale(s): South

Summary: When Brandelene needs a husband to save her plantation, she decides to buy one. However, what she gets is not quite what she bargained for; and Brandy soon finds herself in a real marriage with Kord Bouclair rather than the marriage in name only she had planned. Filled with lively action and likeable characters, redolent of jasmine and magnolias, and laced with Southern charm.

Other books you might like:
Thea Devine, *Southern Seduction*, 1991
Wendy Garrett, *Sweet Southern Caress*, 1991
Patricia Hagan, *Midnight Rose*, 1991
Kat Martin, *The Captain's Bride*, 1990
Alexandra Ripley, *Charleston*, 1982

210

BRENNA BRAXTON-BARSHON

Through All Eternity

(New York: Harper, 1992)

Story type: Historical/French Revolution; Historical/Georgian

Major character(s): Shawnalese Grenville, Ward; Gayhawke Carrington, Nobleman (Earl of Foxridge), Guardian
Time period(s): 1770s
Locale(s): England; France

Summary: When Gayhawke Carrington rescues young Shawnalese Grenville from the streets of New Orleans and takes her to England as his ward, he has no idea that his guttersnipe will soon turn into a lovely, sensuous, and highly attractive woman — one that he must send to France so she will be safe — from him! Shawnalese vows revenge, and her escapades lead her guardian a merry chase with passionate and, sometimes dangerous, results. A romantic coming-of-age story and an adventurous romance that shifts from England to France during the time of the French Revolution.

Other books you might like:
Laurie McBain, *Moonstruck Madness*, 1977
Laurie McBain, *Wild Bells to the Wild Sky*, 1983
Shirlee Busbee, *Gypsy Lady*, 1977
Shirlee Busbee, *Whisper to Me of Love*, 1991
Iris Johansen, *Storm Winds*, 1991

211

SANDRA BREGMAN

Reach for the Dream

(New York: Dell, 1990)

Story type: Saga
Major character(s): Anna Dunay, Immigrant
Time period(s): 20th century (1910s to the present)

Summary: The story of Anna, who comes to America from Russia, and her struggles to make a life for herself, her children, and eventually her grandchildren. Family saga.

Other books you might like:
Barbara Taylor Bradford, *A Woman of Substance*, 1979
Followed by *Hold the Dream*
Virginia Coffman, *The Gaynor Women*, 1978
American South
Susan Howatch, *The Rich Are Different*, 1977
Followed by *Sins of the Fathers*
Belva Plain, *Evergreen*, 1978

212

BARBARA BRETTON

The Invisible Groom

(Toronto: Harlequin, 1994)

Story type: Contemporary/Fantasy
Major character(s): Jenna Grey, Businesswoman (wedding chapel owner); Chase Quinn, Magician (illusionist; invisible person)
Time period(s): 1990s
Locale(s): Las Vegas, Nevada

Summary: Informed by the powers-that-be that his only option for removing an ancient curse and regaining his "visibility" is to face the thing he fears the most, magician Chase Quinn reluctantly sets out to do just that—get married. Unfortunately, his intended bride, Jenna Grey, has been jilted one time too many and has absolutely no use for men, especially invisible ones. There is plenty of lively, fast-paced action as they work toward an appropriately romantic solution.

Other books you might like:
Jude Deveraux, *Wishes*, 1989
more "divine" intervention, this time from an angel/historical
Kristin Hannah, *When Lightning Strikes*, 1994
time travel fantasy
Constance O'Day-Flannery, *Second Chances*, 1992
contemporary fantasy with a gentle, "angelic" touch.
Sharon Sala, *Annie and the Outlaw*, 1994
another brash hero in need of redemption
Patricia Simpson, *Whisper of Midnight*, 1991
a contemporary ghost

213

BARBARA BRETTON

Maybe This Time

(New York: Berkley, 1995)

Story type: Contemporary
Major character(s): Christine Cannon, Television Personality, Divorced Person (Joe's ex-wife); Joe McMurphy, Journalist, Divorced Person (Christine's ex-husband)
Time period(s): 1990s
Locale(s): New York; New Jersey; Nevada

Summary: A bizarre turn of events forces television superstar Christine Cannon and noted journalist Joe McMurphy into dealing with their feelings as they are thrown together in a fast-paced, sometimes hilarious, jaunt across the country. A well-match hero and heroine are complemented by several well-done secondary characters and the sexual tension between the protagonists is nicely handled.

Other books you might like:
Joan Hohl, *Compromises*, 1995
Jayne Ann Krentz, *Absolutely, Positively*, 1996
Jayne Ann Krentz, *Wildest Hearts*, 1993
Susan Elizabeth Phillips, *Heaven, Texas*, 1995
Susan Elizabeth Phillips, *Kiss an Angel*, 1996

214

BARBARA BRETTON

Midnight Lover

(New York: Pocket, 1989)

Story type: Historical/American West
Major character(s): Caroline Bennett, Heiress (Would-be), Businesswoman (Saloon and mine owner (joint)); Jessie Reardon, Businessman (Saloon and mine owner (joint))
Time period(s): 1870s (1876)
Locale(s): Silver Spurs, Nevada (A mining town)

Summary: Caroline Bennett comes West to take over a saloon and silver mine left to her by her father but is surprised to discover that he had lost it to Jessie Reardon. Neither wants to give up the prize, and when they are told by a judge that the only solution is to marry each other, they reluctantly do so.

Love, of course, eventually follows, but only after a somewhat unusual courtship.

Other books you might like:
Sandra Brown, *Sunset Embrace*, 1985
LaRee Bryant, *Arizona Captive*, 1989
LaRee Bryant, *Arizona Vixen*, 1989
Dorothy Garlock, *Midnight Blue*, 1989
Georgina Gentry, *Nevada Nights*, 1989

`215`

BARBARA BRETTON

One and Only
(New York: Berkley, 1994)

Story type: Romantic Suspense; Contemporary
Major character(s): Isabelle, Royalty (princess), Businesswoman (Fashion); Daniel Bronson, Businessman
Time period(s): 1990s
Locale(s): New York, New York; Perreault, Fictional Country

Summary: When her father dies and her jealous elder sister assumes the throne of tiny Perreault, Princess Isabelle ends up in New York, destitute and forced to make her own way—which she does with style, flair, and a resourcefulness that surprises all concerned. But just when she has it all, the past returns and threatens everything she holds dear. Engaging main characters and a couple of slimy villains you won't soon forget. Fast-paced and involving.

Other books you might like:
Barbara Delinsky, *Facets*, 1990
Jude Deveraux, *Sweet Liar*, 1992
Susan Kyle, *After Midnight*, 1993
Susan Elizabeth Phillips, *Hot Shot*, 1991
Meryl Sawyer, *Promise Me Anything*, 1994
  intense

`216`

BARBARA BRETTON

Somewhere in Time
(Toronto: Harlequin, 1992)

Story type: Time Travel; Historical/American Revolution
Major character(s): Zane Grey Rutledge, Adventurer, Time Traveller; Emilie Crosse, Appraiser (antique expert), Time Traveller; Andrew McVie, Military Personnel, Hero (Revolutionary war hero)
Time period(s): 1990s; 1770s
Locale(s): American Colonies; United States

Summary: Zane and Emilie divorce because she needs security and he needs adventure, but when he inherits a Revolutionary War uniform, he knows she is the expert to evaluate it. A balloon stunt sends them crashing into the 1770s and suddenly Zane is involved in more adventure than he has ever imagined — and he finds himself fighting for both his country and the affections of his ex-wife. Sensual, funny, and filled with wonderful characters.

Other books you might like:
Lori Copeland, *Forever Ashley*, 1992

Diana Gabaldon, *Outlander*, 1991
Thomasina Ring, *Time-Spun Rapture*, 1990
Thomasina Ring, *Time-Spun Treasure*, 1992
Bertrice Small, *A Moment in Time*, 1991

`217`

LEIGH BRISTOL

Legacy
(New York: Warner, 1933)

Story type: Historical/American Civil War
Major character(s): Laurel Sinclair Laughton, Widow(er); Seth ''Peach Brady'' Tait, Outlaw
Time period(s): 1860s
Locale(s): Charleston, South Carolina

Summary: Laurel Laughton will do just about anything to save her family home, even strike a bargain with a wanted criminal bent on recovering a cache of Yankee gold. However, their growing love for each other changes their strictly business arrangement into one of lasting commitment, one that neither Pinkerton agents nor natural disasters can destroy. Memorable characters.

Other books you might like:
Barbara Ankrum, *Renegade's Kiss*, 1933
Micki Brown, *Once a Rebel*, 1992
Heather Graham, *And One Rode West*, 1992
Heather Graham, *One Wore Blue*, 1991

`218`

LEIGH BRISTOL

Sunswept
(New York: Warner, 1990)

Story type: Historical
Major character(s): Maddie Burns, Imposter (Original name: Gladys Whistlew), Businesswoman (Tavernkeeper); Ashton Kitteridge, Artist, Nobleman (Third son of an earl)
Time period(s): 1810s
Locale(s): Sydney

Summary: A shipboard friendship and a twist of fate give Gladys (now Maddie) a family, a future, and a love she never thought she'd have. But her past catches up with her, and before she and Ashton can be happy, they must settle some old accounts.

Other books you might like:
Catherine Coulter, *Night Storm*, 1990
  Third in a trilogy
Dorothy Eden, *The American Heiress*, 1980
  Identity-switch theme
Dorothy Eden, *The Vines of Yarabee*, 1969
  Australian Setting/Strong heroine
Richard Peck, *Amanda/Miranda*, 1981
  Identity-switch theme

219

LEIGH BRISTOL

Twice Blessed

(New York: Warner, 1991)

Story type: Historical/American West
Major character(s): Victoria "Tori" Meredith, Heiress; Ethan Cantrell, Lawman (undercover)
Time period(s): 1870s (1878)
Locale(s): Texas; Mexico

Summary: Victoria's father is furious when she runs off to Mexico to marry his arch rival, Don Diego—so furious that he hires Ethan Cantrell to kidnap her and return her to Texas. A forced marriage and dark secrets enliven this complex and sensual story.

Other books you might like:
Elaine Coffman, *Escape Not My Love*, 1990
Catherine Coulter, *Night Storm*, 1990
    third in a series
Carol Finch, *Montana Moonfire*, 1990
Linda Ladd, *Midnight Fire*, 1991

220

ANNETTE BROADRICK

A Loving Spirit

(New York: Silhouette, 1990)

Story type: Contemporary/Fantasy
Major character(s): Sabrina Sheldon, Businesswoman (Gift shop owner); Michael Donovan, Police Officer (Highway Patrol Sergeant)
Time period(s): 1980s
Locale(s): Lake of the Ozarks, Missouri

Summary: Two angels take a hand in bringing two independent people together.

Other books you might like:
Jude Deveraux, *Wishes*, 1989
    A "heavenly" fairy godmother assists in a Cinderella romance
Janet Evanovich, *Ivan Takes a Wife*, 1989
Madeline Harper, *This Time Forever*, 1990
Elda Minger, *Spike Is Missing*, 1990
Sarah Temple, *Kindred Spirits*, 1980

221

CONNIE BROCKWAY

Promise Me Heaven

(New York: Avon, 1994)

Story type: Historical/Regency
Major character(s): Catherine "Cat" Sinclair, Noblewoman; Thomas Montrose, Rake, Spy (retired)
Time period(s): 1810s (1814)
Locale(s): Paris, France; London, England

Summary: In order to catch the husband of her choice, Lady Catherine seeks the help of notorious rake and former spy Thomas Montrose, who has retired to a more peaceful existence. Although disgusted with his past, he still agrees to teach Cat the art of seduction. However, her innocence and quick mind intrigue him; and as he instructs her in the finer points of "man hunting," he ends up ensnared himself. Charming and heartwarming.

Other books you might like:
Jo Beverley, *Tempting Fortune*, 1995
Anita Mills, *Secret Nights*, 1994
Amanda Quick, *Surrender*, 1990
Suzanne Simmons, *Diamond in the Rough*, 1994
Elizabeth Thornton, *Highland Fire*, 1994

222

ELIZABETH BRODNAX

The Marquis of Carabas

(New York: Walker, 1991)

Story type: Regency
Major character(s): Cat Brown, Imposter (Marchesa di Carabas); Alexander Carrock, Nobleman
Time period(s): 1810s
Locale(s): London, England

Summary: When the mysterious and beautiful Marchesa di Carabas takes the town by storm and becomes the protege of the influential Dowager Duchess of Tyne, the only person who suspects she may not be what she seems is her mentor's grandson, Alexander Carrock. Drawn to each other, they at first resist the attraction; but as they begin to fall in love, Cat must deal with the inevitable consequences of her deception.

Other books you might like:
Joan Aiken, *If I Were You*, 1987
Melinda McRae, *The Duke's Daughter*, 1991
Joan Smith, *Madcap Miss*, 1989
Lois Stewart, *Romantic Masquerade*, 1990
Daisy Vivian, *Counterfeit Lady*, 1987

223

BETTY BROOKS

Love's Endless Flame

(New York: Zebra, 1992)

Story type: Historical/American West
Major character(s): Miranda Hartford, Young Woman (Spelunker); Rogue McClaren, Rancher
Time period(s): 1890s (1897)
Locale(s): Texas

Summary: When Miranda's cave-loving, archaeologist father wanders off, she enlists the reluctant aid of rancher Rogue McClaren to find him. A rock slide strands them in a cave, and as they explore the wonders of the underground world they have discovered, Rogue and Miranda also fall in love. Good descriptions and characterizations in a well-researched story that is unusual in that most of the action takes place underground.

Other books you might like:
Rebecca Brandewyne, *Rainbow's End*, 1991
Nicole Jordan, *Wild Star*, 1992
Amanda Quick, *Ravished*, 1992
    Regency period
Colleen Quinn, *Colorado Flame*, 1989

224
BETTY BROOKS

Wild Magnolia
(New York: Zebra, 1990)

Story type: Historical/American West
Major character(s): Michelle De Leroy, Twin, Fiance(e) (Reluctant); Judd McCord, Fiance(e)
Time period(s): 1880s (1882)
Locale(s): Texas

Summary: Engaged, sight-unseen to a Texan who has a most unromantic view of marriage, Michelle decides to teach him a lesson. A lively story in which Michelle's pretending to be other people, including her twin brother, Michael, leads to some interesting adventures.

Other books you might like:
Deborah Camp, *Black-Eyed Susan*, 1990
Julie Garwood, *The Bride*, 1989
    Medieval setting
Norah Hess, *Devil in Spurs*, 1990
Gina Robins, *Deception's Sweet Kiss*, 1990
Vivian Vaughn, *Texas Gamble*, 1990

225
MICKI BROWN

Because of You
(New York: St. Martin's, 1993)

Story type: Historical/American Civil War
Major character(s): Amber Jenn, Young Woman, Wealthy; Nick Windsor, Prisoner (former)
Time period(s): 1860s (1865)
Locale(s): Memphis, Tennessee

Summary: When Amber agrees to help Jessamy find her brother, she has no idea he is a bitter ex-prisoner who can't forgive Jessamy for marrying a Yankee. Amber is relentless, Nicholas is elusive; but their mutual attraction finally wins out and his bitterness and loneliness fade as he comes to understand the power of love. A story of loss, love, and hope set during the turbulent aftermath of the Civil War.

Other books you might like:
Christine Dorsey, *Kansas Kiss*, 1992
Heather Graham, *And One Wore Gray*, 1992
Heather Graham, *One Wore Blue*, 1992
Margaret Mitchell, *Gone with the Wind*, 1936
    classic Civil War story
Diane Gates Robinson, *The Falcon and the Swan*, 1993

226
MICKI BROWN

Once a Rebel
(New York: St. Martin, 1992)

Story type: Historical/American Civil War
Major character(s): Jessamyn Windsor, Southern Belle; Alex Steele, Military Personnel (Union soldier)
Time period(s): 1850s (1856-1861); 1860s
Locale(s): Tennessee

Summary: Spirited Jessamyn isn't happy to have Alex, her eighteen-year-old step-cousin visit the plantation. She plans one of her practical jokes, but it backfires, leaving her confused and unsettled by his kiss. Later, Jessamyn finds that her "southern" cousin has joined the Union Army and the playful days come to an end, replaced by hatred and war. Stormy and passionate.

Other books you might like:
Christine Dorsey, *Kansas Kiss*, 1992
Heather Graham, *And One Wore Gray*, 1992
Heather Graham, *One Wore Blue*, 1992
Diane Gates Robinson, *The Falcon and the Swan*, 1992

227
SANDRA BROWN

Breath of Scandal
(New York: Warner, 1991)

Story type: Contemporary/Mainstream
Major character(s): Jade Sperry, Businesswoman (textiles); Dillon Burke, Engineer
Time period(s): 1990s; 20th century
Locale(s): Palmetto, South

Summary: When popular Jade Sperry is gang-raped by three local boys and then denied the means to prosecute them, she leaves the company town of Palmetto, vowing vengeance. Years later, armed with both the will and the means, she returns to exact retribution—and finds that revenge can be bitter as well as sweet as she is forced to deal with her feelings for the man she loves. Sizzling passion, Southern-style.

Other books you might like:
Sally Beauman, *Destiny*, 1987
Jennifer Blake, *Love and Smoke*, 1989
Lisa Gregory, *Seasons*, 1990
Susan Kyle, *True Colors*, 1991
Judith McNaught, *Paradise*, 1991

228
SANDRA BROWN

French Silk
(New York: Warner, 1992)

Story type: Contemporary/Mainstream
Major character(s): Claire Laurent, Businesswoman (Mail order lingerie company); Robert Cassidy, Lawyer (district attorney)

Time period(s): 1990s
Locale(s): New Orleans, Louisiana; New York, New York

Summary: When the TV evangelist who has been threatening to destroy her budding mail-order lingerie business by calling her catalog pornographic is brutally murdered, Claire Laurent immediately becomes the prime suspect. Unfortunately, her past contains secrets she must protect — and her actions seem to incriminate her, even in the eyes of the district attorney, Robert Cassidy, who is gradually falling in love with her. Fast-paced, suspenseful, and well-written.

Other books you might like:
Joanne Z. Adams, *Intimate Connections*, 1991
Marsha Bauer, *Sweet Conquest*, 1990
Jessica Gregory, *Once Innocent*, 1991
Iris Johansen, *Winter Bride*, 1992
Sara Orwig, *Sweeter than Sin*, 1992

229

SANDRA BROWN

Mirror Image

(New York: Warner, 1990)

Story type: Contemporary/Mainstream
Major character(s): Avery Daniels, Journalist (television news reporter); Tate Rutledge, Political Figure (senatorial candidate)
Time period(s): 1990s
Locale(s): United States

Summary: When TV news reporter Avery Daniels is disfigured in a plane crash, she is mistakenly identified as senatorial hopeful Tate Rutledge's wife, Carole, and is given Carole's lovely face via plastic surgery. However, in addition to Carole's beauty, she also "inherits" dangerous information that could cost her her life, as well as that of Tate, the man she has come to love. Fast-paced, passionate, and suspenseful.

Other books you might like:
Jill Barkin, *Hot Streak*, 1990
Judith Michael, *Deceptions*, 1982
Nora Roberts, *Public Secrets*, 1990

230

SANDRA BROWN

Texas! Chase

(New York: Doubleday, 1991)

Story type: Contemporary
Series: Texas Trilogy
Major character(s): Chase Tyler, Businessman (oil company owner), Rodeo Rider; Marcie Johns, Real Estate Agent
Time period(s): 1990s
Locale(s): Texas

Summary: Although Chase is the title character of this, the second volume of Brown's Texas Trilogy, it is as much, if not more Marcie's story. She is the one who has loved him for years, went on to become a success in her own right, and is now back in his life helping him pick up the pieces after the accidental death of his wife.

Other books you might like:
Jennifer Blake, *Love and Smoke*, 1989
Susan Kyle, *Night Fever*, 1990
Fern Michaels, *Texas Rich*, 1985
    sudsy Texas glitz
Susan Elizabeth Phillips, *Fancy Pants*, 1989
Danielle Steel, *Palomino*, 1981

231

SANDRA BROWN

Texas! Lucky

(New York: Doubleday, 1990)

Story type: Contemporary
Series: Texas Trilogy
Major character(s): Lucky Tyler, Businessman (oilman)
Time period(s): 1990s
Locale(s): Texas

Summary: The first book in Brown's Texas Trilogy deals with independent oilman Lucky Tyler who rescues and then spends the night with a beautiful woman; but when she vanishes without a trace and Lucky suddenly needs an alibi for that night, he sets out to find her. He is aided in his search by sister Sage and brother Chase, the focal characters of the two remaining books in the series.

Other books you might like:
Lori Copeland, *Tall Cotton*, 1990
Emma Darcy, *The Falcon's Mistress*, 1990
Susan Kyle, *Night Fever*, 1990
Mayo Lucas, *Camelot Jones*, 1989
Jane Toombs, *Riverboat Rogue*, 1990

232

SANDRA BROWN

Texas! Sage

(New York: Doubleday, 1991)

Story type: Contemporary
Series: Texas Trilogy
Major character(s): Sage Tyler, Businesswoman (family oil business); Harlan Boyd, Drifter, Engineer
Time period(s): 1990s
Locale(s): Texas

Summary: Jilted and humiliated, willful Sage Tyler ends up at home for the Christmas holidays bleakly contemplating her future—and finds it, in spite of herself, in the arms of strong, perceptive, and highly sensual Harlan Boyd, a man who is everything her ex-fiance was not. Passionate and lively. Final volume in the Texas Trilogy.

Other books you might like:
Terri Herrington, *Her Father's Daughter*, 1991
Judith Michael, *Possessions*, 1984
Susan Elizabeth Phillips, *Fancy Pants*, 1989
Danielle Steel, *Palomino*, 1981
Leta Tegler, *Gabrielle*, 1990
    different time period

233

VIRGINIA BROWN

Emerald Nights
(New York: Zebra, 1991)

Story type: Historical/Exotic
Major character(s): Bethany Brasfield, Gentlewoman, Archaeologist; Trace Taylor, Guide
Time period(s): 1880s (1889)
Locale(s): Peru (in the jungle)

Summary: Love blooms in the Peruvian jungle as Bethany Brasfield and guide Trace Taylor accompany Bethany's archaeologist father on his search for the lost city of gold. Murder, deception, and greed abound in this romantic adventure that is as steamy and exotic as the setting.

Other books you might like:
Leslie O'Grady, *Seek the Wild Shore*, 1989
Maggie Osborne, *Emerald Rain*, 1991
Susan Sackett, *Passion's Golden Fire*, 1989
Katherine Sutcliffe, *Shadow Play*, 1991
Janelle Taylor, *Whispered Kisses*, 1990

234

VIRGINIA BROWN

Hidden Touch
(New York.: Zebra, 1992)

Story type: Historical/Regency
Major character(s): Alyssa Trenton, Twin, Noblewoman; Nicholas Trenton, Twin, Nobleman; Blake Crandell, Nobleman (Duke of Deverill)
Time period(s): 1810s (1816)
Locale(s): Virginia; England

Summary: When defiant and adventuresome Alyssa Trenton goes off to England impersonating her twin brother so he can go to sea, she proves to be a puzzling challenge to her guardian, the Duke of Deverill — until he decides to see to the "manly" education of his young ward and, in the process, discovers her secret. Sparks fly and passion soon follows as the Duke tries to turn an unwilling termagant into a lady and ends up falling in love with her instead. A funny, passionate Pygmalion-type story.

Other books you might like:
Catherine Coulter, *The Sherbrooke Bride*, 1992
Julie Garwood, *Guardian Angel*, 1990
Betina M. Krahn, *Midnight Magic*, 1990
Kathryn Kramer, *Lady Rogue*, 1991
Johanna Lindsey, *Gentle Rogue*, 1990

235

VIRGINIA BROWN

Renegade Embrace
(New York: Zebra, 1990)

Story type: Historical/American West Coast

Major character(s): Laurette Allen, Imposter (El Vengador), Gentlewoman; Nicolas Cade, Criminal (accused)
Time period(s): 1840s
Locale(s): California; Texas; Louisiana

Summary: When Laurie Allen, the ambassador's independent daughter, learns how the California peons are being treated, she becomes the Robin Hood-like "El Vengador" and robs from the rich and gives to the poor. However, Nicolas Cade is blamed, and Laurie sets out to prove him innocent. This fast-paced tale moves from California to Texas and Louisiana and back again as Laurie and Nicolas fight for their love and the people they care about.

Other books you might like:
Rexanne Becnel, *Thief of My Heart*, 1991
Julie Garwood, *Guardian Angel*, 1990
Donna Fletcher, *San Francisco Surrender*, 1990
Marylyle Rogers, *Hidden Hearts*, 1989
    medieval Robin Hood
Cynthia Wright, *Brighter than Gold*, 1990

236

VIRGINIA BROWN

Wildfire
(New York: Warner, 1990)

Story type: Historical/American West
Major character(s): Jennifer "Jenny" Allison, Heroine (sister of Dawson Gang member); Kane Ransom, Lawman (Texas Ranger), Imposter (photographer)
Time period(s): 1880s (1881)
Locale(s): Texas; Kansas; Colorado

Summary: Determined to capture the infamous Dawson Gang, Texas Ranger Kane Ransom coerces Jenny Allison, the sister of one of the gang members, into helping him. Antagonists, and eventually lovers, Kane and Jenny chase the gang across the West with adventure, passion, and humor aplenty.

Other books you might like:
Rosanne Bittner, *Embers of the Heart*, 1990
Elaine Coffman, *Escape Not My Love*, 1990
Kathleen Harrington, *Cherish the Dream*, 1990
Norah Hess, *Wildfire*, 1989
Christine Monson, *Golden Nights*, 1990

237

LYDIA BROWNE

Heart Strings
(New York: Diamond, 1993)

Story type: Historical/Mainstream
Major character(s): Antonia Castle, Feminist; Jake Faraday, Lawman (marshal)
Time period(s): 19th century (late)
Locale(s): Culverton, Missouri

Summary: When Antonia outrages people with her lecture tour on Enlightened Sex, she is sentenced to spend a month with a single man and remain virtuous. Lucky Marshal Jake

Faraday gets the job and they both have quite a time trying to keep their relationship platonic! Funny and lively.

Other books you might like:
Sonya Birmingham, *Spitfire*, 1991
Emily Bradshaw, *The Heart's Journey*, 1992
Joan Johnston, *Sweetwater Seduction*, 1991
Pamela Morsi, *Wild Oats*, 1993

238
MARGARET BROWNLEY
Rawhide and Lace
(New York: Topaz, 1994)

Story type: Historical/American West Coast
Major character(s): Libby Summerfield, Widow(er); Logan St. John, Miner, Mountain Man
Time period(s): 19th century (late)
Locale(s): Deadman's Gulch, California

Summary: Libby, pregnant and widowed, stranded and cold, is rescued by mountain man Logan St. John. Although Libby is frightened by men like Logan, they are able to develop a compassionate and caring relationship. It is not easy for a loner like Logan to give up his old ways, but he can't stand the thought of Libby's leaving—and he does eventually make a few changes. Interestingly, their relationship transforms not only Libby and Logan, but the town, as well.

Other books you might like:
Pamela K. Forrest, *Autumn Ecstasy*, 1991
Pamela K. Forrest, *Wild Savage Heart*, 1993
  a strong, gentle hero to the rescue; warm and romantic.
Norah Hess, *Mountain Rose*, 1993
  another trapper to the rescue.
Cait Logan, *Wild Dawn*, 1992
  another rescuing trapper.

239
JESSICA BRYAN
Across a Wine-Dark Sea
(New York: Bantam, 1991)

Story type: Historical/Fantasy; Historical/Pre-history
Major character(s): Thalassa, Warrior (Amazon); Dorian, Royalty (King of Atlantis)
Time period(s): 13th century B.C. (1260)
Locale(s): Amazonia, Mythical Place; Atlantis, Mythical Place

Summary: Just as she comes of age, Amazon warrior Thalassa is abducted by Dorian, King of Atlantis, and taken to his watery home to become his bride. Thalassa resists, but her feelings for Dorian grow into a relationship of love and trust—one that is severely tested by Thalassa's strong commitment to her war-like people. Marvelous combination of myth, history, and romance.

Other books you might like:
Rebecca Brandewyne, *Passion Moon Rising*, 1988
Saranne Dawson, *From the Mist*, 1991
Nancy Harding, *Wind Child*, 1990

Lindsay Randall, *Silversword*, 1990
Jane Yolen, *Sister Light, Sister Dark*, 1989

240
JESSICA BRYAN
Dawn on a Jade Sea
(New York: Bantam, 1992)

Story type: Historical/Fantasy
Major character(s): Rhea, Mythical Creature (merwoman); Zhao Tamudj, Healer (Buddhist)
Time period(s): 9th century (841)
Locale(s): China

Summary: When merwoman Rhea takes part in a scientific observation of the people of Chin a during the T'ang Dynasty, she ends up becoming involved with a renegade Buddh ist healer who is headed for a violent confrontation with the man who killed hi s family. Magical and unique.

Other books you might like:
Saranne Dawson, *The Enchanted Land*, 1992
Saranne Dawson, *From the Mist*, 1991
Betina Lindsey, *Swan Bride*, 1990
Marylyle Rogers, *Chanting the Dawn*, 1991

241
LAREE BRYANT
Arizona Captive
(New York: Zebra, 1989)

Story type: Historical/American West
Major character(s): Callie Nolan, Governess (For Claymore family); Logan Powers, Bodyguard (For Mr. Claymore)
Time period(s): 1890s (1891)
Locale(s): Bisbee, Arizona

Summary: In the beginning, governess Callie Nolan thought her biggest problem was going to be the Claymore family's bodyguard, Logan Powers. She quickly learned that there were more serious—and dangerous—problems within the Claymore family itself. Joining forces, Callie and Logan eventually make things right—and fall in love in the process.

Other books you might like:
Gwen Cleary, *Ecstasy's Masquerade*, 1989
Dorothy Garlock, *Midnight Blue*, 1989
Georgina Gentry, *Nevada Nights*, 1989
Mayo Lucas, *Camelot Jones*, 1989
Bobbi Smith, *Arizona Caress*, 1989

242
LAREE BRYANT
Sweet Texas Fury
(New York: Zebra, 1990)

Story type: Historical/American West
Major character(s): Lydia Upton, Rancher; Morgan Hunter, Government Official (assistant treasury agent)
Time period(s): 1860s (1867)

Locale(s): Prairie Grove, Texas

Summary: Lydia Upton will do anything to save her ranch, Prairie Grove, including holding Morgan Hunter, the new assistant tax collector at gunpoint until he agrees to give her more time to raise money for her taxes. Intrigued, Morgan grants the extension; and as Lydia struggles against sinister odds to meet the payments, Morgan joins in her battle. KKK burnings, cattle drives, and buried treasure add to this gentle and passionate story.

Other books you might like:
Dorothy Garlock, *Midnight Blue*, 1989
Martha Hix, *Wild Texas Rose*, 1990
Stef Ann Holm, *Firefly*, 1990
Jill Marie Landis, *Sunflower*, 1989
Victoria Pade, *The Doubletree*, 1990

243
PATT BUCHEISTER

Once Burned, Twice as Hot
(New York: Bantam, 1990)

Story type: Contemporary
Major character(s): Lani ''Kapiolani'' Makena, Banker (Foreign Currency Exchange); Rhys Jones, Lawyer (Solicitor)
Time period(s): 1980s
Locale(s): Hawaii

Summary: When Rhys Jones comes to Hawaii in search of the daughter of a client, he doesn't expect her to be a beautiful Hawaiian and he doesn't expect to fall in love with her. Passion tinged with a hint of mystery set in a tropical paradise.

Other books you might like:
Emma Darcy, *The Falcon's Mistress*, 1990
Kay Hooper, *Enemy Mine*, 1989
Valerie Parv, *Tasmanian Devil*, 1990
Susan Sackett, *Passion's Golden Fire*, 1989
    Historical/Chitzen Itza setting
Phyllis A. Whitney, *Silversword*, 1987
    Classic contemporary gothic writer

244
CAROLE BUCK

Knight and Day
(New York: Silhouette, 1992)

Story type: Contemporary
Major character(s): Donna Day, Psychologist (child psychologist); Marty Knight, Entertainer (star comedian)
Time period(s): 1990s
Locale(s): United States

Summary: Donna Day, counselor for abused children, and Marty Knight, TV comic, both have bitter secrets about their tragic pasts, but they are brought together and healed through the magic of amusement and laughter. Nicely done characters in a funny, well-plotted story.

Other books you might like:
Marcia Evanick, *Midnight Kiss*, 1992

Cindy Gerard, *Temptation From the Past*, 1991
Theresa Gladden, *Just Desserts*, 1991
Diana Palmer, *The Case of the Mesmerizing Boss*, 1992

245
CAROLE BUCK

Love and Laughter
(New York: Berkley, 1989)

Story type: Contemporary
Major character(s): Kelsey Howard, Entertainer (Stand-up comic; dyslexic); Elias Fletcher, Scientist (Physicist), Genius
Time period(s): 1980s
Locale(s): San Francisco, California; Berkeley, California

Summary: When Kelsey Howard hits Elias Fletcher squarely in the face with a pie, she has no idea that it will result in a dinner invitation, let alone romance. Their new-found love, however, is threatened by insecurities on both sides—hers because of dyslexia and his because of a genius IQ—and it takes a lot of understanding to resolve their differences.

Other books you might like:
Bevlyn Marshall, *Radio Daze*, 1989
Victoria Pade, *Twice Shy*, 1989
    Silhouette Special Edition
Lynda Trent, *Repeat Performance*, 1989
Jamisan Whitney, *The Wilde Kingdom*, 1989
    Second Chance at Love (Berkley)
Gina Wilkins, *A Stroke of Genius*, 1989
    Harlequin Temptation

246
GAYLE BUCK

Full Moon Magic
(New York: Signet, 1992)

Story type: Historical; Holiday Themes

Summary: A quintet of magical love stories — includes: ''The Dark Rider'' by Mary Balogh, ''Black Magic'' by Anita Mills, ''The Ghost of Castle Ravenswych'' by Charlotte Louise Dolan, ''The Holybrook Curse'' by Gayle Buck, and ''Deceiving Appearances'' by Patricia Rice.

Other books you might like:
Shannon Drake, *Avon Books Presents: Haunting Love Stories*, 1991
Lori Herter, *Confession*, 1992
Lori Herter, *Obsession*, 1991
Anne Rice, *The Witching Hour*, 1990
Anne Stuart, *Night of the Phantom*, 1991

247
GAYLE BUCK

Mutual Consent
(New York: New American Library/Signet, 1991)

Story type: Regency

Major character(s): Barbara Cribbage, Young Woman; Marcus, Nobleman (Earl of Chatsworth)
Time period(s): 1810s
Locale(s): England

Summary: When the Earl of Chatsworth gambles himself into near ruin, the banker who holds his notes offers him a solution—marry his daughter and the debts will be forgiven. The resulting marriage of convenience achieves solvency for the Earl and freedom from her father for Barbara—but then the unexpected happens, they fall in love. A delightfully fresh look at a classic plot.

Other books you might like:
Charlotte Louise Dolan, *The Substitute Bridegroom*, 1991
Rosemary Edghill, *The Ill-Bred Bride*, 1990
Georgette Heyer, *The Convenient Marriage*, 1934
Mary Kingsley, *A Gentleman's Desire*, 1991
Annabel Laine, *The Reluctant Heiress*, 1978

248

GAYLE BUCK

The Waltzing Widow
(New York: New American Library/Signet, 1991)

Story type: Regency
Major character(s): Mary Spence, Noblewoman, Widow(er); Robert, Nobleman (Earl of Kenmore), Widow(er)
Time period(s): 1810s
Locale(s): England; Brussels, Belgium

Summary: In order to give her seventeen-year-old daughter an appropriate debut, young widow Lady Mary Spence takes her household to join the rest of the *ton* in Brussels and ends up attracting the attentions of the aloof, widowed Earl of Kenmore. Lady Mary is a delightful change from the typical Regency "marriageable miss" heroine, and the social scene in Brussels during the time of Napoleon's escape from Elba and the Battle of Waterloo is effectively portrayed.

Other books you might like:
Georgette Heyer, *An Infamous Army*, 1937
Georgette Heyer, *Lady of Quality*, 1972
Carla Kelly, *Libby's London Merchant*, 1991
Irene Saunders, *Lady Lucinde's Locket*, 1990

249

CAROL BUDD

Scarlet Scandals
(New York: Pocket, 1990)

Story type: Contemporary; Romantic Suspense
Major character(s): Georgette Richards, Socialite, Heiress; Adam Lawrence, Gardener
Time period(s): 1990s
Locale(s): San Francisco, California

Summary: When handsome and mysterious Adam Lawrence collapses "tranquilly" on Georgette Richards' hall rug and is then accused of murdering one of Scarlet Street's eccentric residents, Georgette sets out to find the real killer. Funny, offbeat, and peopled with wonderfully wacky characters.

Other books you might like:
Carole Nelson Douglas, *Crystal Days*, 1990
Kay Hooper, *Crime of Passion*, 1991
Elizabeth Peters, *Crocodile on the Sandbank*, 1975 first in the Amelia Peabody Series
Elizabeth Peters, *Summer of the Dragon*, 1979
Sherryl Woods, *Body and Soul*, 1990

250

LYNN BULOCK

In Your Dreams
(Bensalem, Pennsylvania: Meteor, 1992)

Story type: Contemporary
Major character(s): Meg Shepherd, Public Relations (for a hospital); Alex Langdon, Journalist (sports columnist)
Time period(s): 1990s
Locale(s): St. Louis, Missouri

Summary: Their college friendship was shattered by a misunderstanding, and six years later Meg wants as little as possible to do with brash Alex Langdon. However, Alex has other ideas — and so does Meg's heart.

Other books you might like:
Dixie Dubois, *Home Fires*, 1992
Peggy Morse, *The Stillman Curse*, 1992
Kathleen Gilles Seidel, *Maybe This Time*, 1990
Judith Yoder, *A Matter of Compromise*, 1992

251

LYNN BULOCK

The Promise of Summer
(New York: Avalon Books, 1990)

Story type: Contemporary/Innocent
Major character(s): Skye Cameron, Agent (Literary); Bob Harris, Writer (Romance), Teacher (Elementary School)
Time period(s): 1980s
Locale(s): St. Louis, Missouri

Summary: Love blossoms as literary agent Skye Cameron helps teacher Bob Harris sell his romance novel. Characters from *Roses for Caroline* reappear in this sweet, humorous love story.

Other books you might like:
Debbie Macomber, *Country Bride*, 1990
Laura Parrish, *Love's Quiet Corner*, 1989
Constance Walker, *One Perfect Springtime*, 1989
Peggy Webb, *Harvey's Missing*, 1990

252

LYNN BULOCK

Roses for Caroline
(New York: Avalon Books, 1989)

Story type: Contemporary/Innocent
Major character(s): Caroline Blake, Teacher (Elementary); Derek James, Writer (of romances)

Time period(s): 1980s
Locale(s): St. Charles, Missouri

Summary: When closet-romantic Caroline Blake wins dinner with one of her favorite romance writers, Derek James, she is surprised to discover that he is one of the most unromantic men she has ever met. Despite all odds, they fall in love; and with the help of Lynn's second grade class, Derek even manages to stage a very romantic proposal.

Other books you might like:
Lindsay Armstrong, *The Marrying Game*, 1989
Lynda Stowe Landers, *A Season to Remember*, 1989
Jan McDaniel, *This Fragile Heart*, 1989
Laura Parrish, *Love's Quiet Corner*, 1989
Peggy Webb, *A Gift for Tenderness*, 1989

253

ROBIN BURCELL

When Midnight Comes

(New York: Harper, 1995)

Story type: Time Travel
Major character(s): Kendra Browning, Detective—Homicide, Time Traveller; Captain Brice Montgomery, Sea Captain, Nobleman (Duke of Blackmoor)
Time period(s): 1990s; 1830s
Locale(s): England; At Sea

Summary: While sailing off the coast of Florida, homicide detective Kendra Browning is thrown overboard and finds herself rescued by Captain Brice Montgomery, Duke of Blackmoor, and aboard a ship bound for England—more than a century earlier, in the middle of the 19th century! She is incredulous and unbelieving until they reach London and she is forced to recognize the truth. Plots, gypsies, wicked villains, and more time travel add spice to this fast-paced, often humorous story. The anachronistic heroine is especially interesting.

Other books you might like:
Suzanne Elizabeth, *When Destiny Calls*, 1993
　　another detective time traveller
Diana Gabaldon, *Outlander*, 1991
　　modern classic time travel/set in Scotland
Kasey Michaels, *Out of the Blue*, 1992
　　time travelling heroine
Kasey Michaels, *Timely Matrimony*, 1994
　　time travelling hero from the past/humorous
Susan Sizemore, *My Own True Love*, 1994
　　another time travelling heroine

254

JUSTINA BURGESS

Winds of Eden

(New York: Jove, 1991)

Story type: Historical/Georgian; Historical/Mainstream
Major character(s): Desiree MacKenzie, Young Woman; Athelstan Kirby, Military Personnel (captain in the Highland Guard); Hector McLeod, Trader, Gambler

Time period(s): 1800s
Locale(s): India; Scotland

Summary: Forced to leave her small Indian village, Desiree is escorted by dashing Captain Athelstan Kirby to her uncle's care in Calcutta. Her treacherous uncle, however, has plans to gamble Desiree away, and it is only through Athelstan's intervention that she is saved by trader Hector MacLeod. However, unknown to her, her salvation has a price—Athelstan must leave, breaking off their growing relationship. Eventually, Desiree marries Hector, but she never forgets Athelstan—and as fate will have it, they are eventually reunited. A sweeping, highly descriptive tale of the India of the early 19th century as seen through the eyes of a valiant Scottish woman.

Other books you might like:
E.M. Forster, *A Passage to India*, 1924
Victoria Holt, *The India Fan*, 1988
M.M. Kaye, *The Far Pavilions*, 1978
Christine Monson, *This Fiery Splendor*, 1991

255

MALLORY BURGESS

Ballenrose

(New York: Onyx, 1991)

Story type: Historical/Seventeenth Century
Major character(s): Molly Flowers, Young Woman (flower vendor); Ballenrose, Gentleman
Time period(s): 17th century
Locale(s): London, England

Summary: When flowergirl Molly Flowers is suddenly identified by Buckingham as his long lost niece, Lady Mary Catherine Villers, she is taken abruptly from prison and poverty and thrust into the glittering society world of the wealthy. There is, of course, a devious purpose to all this; but Mary and Ballenrose, the man with whom she falls in love (and the man Buckingham had hoped to bring down with his ploy) are a winning team in every sense of the word.

Other books you might like:
Shirlee Busbee, *Whisper to Me of Love*, 1991
Georgette Heyer, *These Old Shades*, 1926
　　classic Regency
Louisa Rawlings, *Promise of Summer*, 1989
Julie Tetel, *And Heaven Too*, 1990

256

MARY BURKHARDT

Highland Ecstasy

(New York: Zebra, 1993)

Story type: Historical/Georgian
Major character(s): Myrtle Prescott, Noblewoman, Heiress; Ian Sinclair, Laird (dispossessed), Imposter (ghost/"dimwitted" servant)
Time period(s): 1740s
Locale(s): Scotland

Summary: When the King vengefully strips Laird Ian Sinclair of his title and lands and orders him out of Scotland, the only way he can continue to protect his clan is to "die"—and become the castle ghost. However, strong-willed Lady Myrtle Prescott puts a crimp in his plans; and as she struggles to "save the clan," she also manages to win the respect—and the heart—of her ghostly tenant. A passionate, humerous tale with more than a dash of suspense.

Other books you might like:
Julie Garwood, *The Bride*, 1989
Julie Garwood, *The Secret*, 1992
Arnette Lamb, *The Border Lord*, 1993
Amanda Scott, *Border Bride*, 1990

257

MARY BURKHARDT

The Panther and the Rose
(New York: Zebra, 1993)

Story type: Historical
Major character(s): Amy Stockwell, Heiress, Businesswoman (shipping); Toshiro Valerius, Nobleman, Businessman (importer)
Locale(s): England; Japan

Summary: Amy, wheelchair-bound and seeking a partner for her new business venture, is saved from disaster by Toshiro Valerius, who is determined to become Amy's partner and champion. However, Amy's aunt is just as intent on keeping Amy helpless and goes to great lengths to foil Amy and Toshiro's growing relationship. Gothic touches.

Other books you might like:
Elizabeth Adler, *Fortune Is a Woman*, 1992
   saga
Laurel Collins, *The Jade Garden*, 1992
Victoria Holt, *Snare of Serpents*, 1991
Maggie Osborne, *Emerald Rain*, 1991

258

SHIRLEE BUSBEE

Love a Dark Rider
(New York: Avon, 1994)

Story type: Historical/American West; Saga
Major character(s): Sara Rawlings, Young Woman, Ward; Yancy Cantrell, Rancher
Time period(s): 1860s (1860-1868)
Locale(s): Texas

Summary: Destitute, Sara becomes the ward of an older cousin who takes her home. When his vicious, much hated wife is murdered, everyone is suspect. Son Yancy, absent for a number of years, returns home to find Sara married to his father; but when his father dies, Sara inherits Yancy's land. A convenient marriage seems to be in order, but this marriage eventually becomes one in fact, as well. Passionate and sex-filled. Reminiscent of the historicals of the seventies. (Busbee is one of the original Avon Ladies.)

Other books you might like:
Dorothy Garlock, *Homeplace*, 1991
   dark and realistic
Brenda Joyce, *Secrets*, 1993
   dark, sensual, occasionally brutal
Rosemary Rogers, *The Wildest Heart*, 1974
   classic sweet-savage romance, with a mystery
Nan Ryan, *The Legend of Love*, 1991
   passion and action/ different plot

259

SHIRLEE BUSBEE

Whisper to Me of Love
(New York: Avon, 1991)

Story type: Historical/Regency
Major character(s): Morgana "Pip" Fowler, Thief (pickpocket), Heiress—Lost; Royce Manchester, Plantation Owner
Time period(s): 1810s
Locale(s): England

Summary: Given away at birth to avoid being killed by a greedy uncle, heiress and noblewoman Morganna Fowler grows up in the streets of London, becoming a pickpocket in the process. But when American Royce Manchester catches her stealing his watch, her fortune changes and he not only makes her a servant in his house, but he proceeds to fall in love with her. Lots of tension and romance as they solve the mystery of her birth and elude those who are out to kill them. Vintage 1970s style historical romance from a classic writer.

Other books you might like:
Laura Black, *Glendraco*, 1977
Mallory Burgess, *Ballenrose*, 1991
Georgette Heyer, *These Old Shades*, 1926
   classic Regency treatment
Louisa Rawlings, *Promise of Summer*, 1989

260

NANCY BUSH

Jesse's Renegade
(New York: Pocket, 1991)

Story type: Historical/American West
Major character(s): Kelsey "Orchid Simpson" Garrett, Spinster; Jesse Danner, Rogue
Time period(s): 1890s (1897)
Locale(s): Portland, Oregon

Summary: Bent on revenge, Jesse Danner returns to Oregon and ends up "temporarily married" to feisty Kelsey Garrett, a member of the family he has been fighting with for years. But vengeance can be dangerous and unpredictable, and Kelsey and Jesse almost lose everything before love eventually wins out. Follows *Lady Sundown* and *Danner's Lady*.

Other books you might like:
Jill Barnett, *Surrender a Dream*, 1991
Jude Deveraux, *The Enchanted Land*, 1978
Kathy Lawrence, *Tin Angel*, 1989

Amanda Quick, *Scandal*, 1991
   revenge Regency-style

261
CORDIA BYERS

The Black Angel
(New York: Fawcett, 1993)

Story type: Historical/Exotic
Major character(s): Brianna McClure, Fugitive; Roarke O'Connor, Privateer
Time period(s): 1770s
Locale(s): England; West Indies
Summary: Thinking she's killed her lecherous step-father, Brianna takes her maid and flees England for the West Indies only to end up shipwrecked and rescued by privateer Roarke O'Connor. Roarke's basic mistrust of women, the war in the colonies, a would-be lover, and a jealous mistress add complexity to a familiar plot.
Other books you might like:
Danelle Harmon, *Master of My Dreams*, 1993
Barbara Hazard, *The Heart Remembers*, 1990
Patricia Rice, *Moon Dreams*, 1991
JoAnn Wendt, *Beyond the Savage Sea*, 1990

262
CORDIA BYERS

Desire and Deceive
(New York: Ballantine, 1990)

Story type: Historical/Medieval
Major character(s): Megan Wakefield, Noblewoman (Estate owner), Thief (Highwayman); Richard St. Clare, Nobleman, Thief (Highwayman)
Time period(s): 14th century (1337)
Summary: To save her estate, Megan begins robbing travelers along the King's wool routes; and to avoid marrying against her will, she disguises herself and repulses the would-be suitor, Richard. Circumstances change, however, and when Richard (now "Royce") joins Megan in her larcenous escapades, love blooms in spite of their resistance. Filled with adventure, humor, and passion.
Other books you might like:
Jude Deveraux, *The Taming*, 1989
Julie Garwood, *The Bride*, 1989
Roberta Gellis, *The Silver Mirror*, 1989
Kathleen E. Woodiwiss, *The Wolf and the Dove*, 1964

263
CORDIA BYERS

Lady Fortune
(New York: Fawcett, 1989)

Story type: Historical/Georgian
Series: Gold Medal
Major character(s): Fortune, Heiress; Kane, Hero

Time period(s): 1790s
Locale(s): North Carolina
Summary: Raised by three mountain men, orphaned Fortune is surprised to learn that she is not only the granddaughter of a wealthy English peer, but that she stands to inherit his entire fortune. Loved by Kane and hated by her jealous cousin, Fortune stops at nothing to "have it all"—her inheritance and love, too.
Other books you might like:
Laura Black, *Albany*, 1984
Catherine Coulter, *Midnight Star*, 1986
Jude Deveraux, *The Taming*, 1989
   Earlier time period; strong heroine
Sarah Edwards, *Crystal Rapture*, 1989
   Americans Abroad (St. Martin's)
Roberta Gellis, *Roselynde*, 1978
   First of six—all have strong heroines; earlier time period

264
BEVERLY BYRNE

The Firebirds
(New York: Bantam, 1992)

Story type: Saga
Series: Mendoza Trilogy
Major character(s): Lillian "Lili" Cramer, Businesswoman, Researcher (family); Andrew Mendoza, Writer
Time period(s): 1950s (1955-1963); 1960s
Locale(s): London, England; Spain
Summary: In the process of trying to find her roots, Lili Cramer meets, falls in love with, and is deserted by struggling writer Andrew Mendoza. With the help of a friend, Lili gets her life back on track—and then Andy comes back into her life and wants to resume their romance and her search for her family. Slowly they reunite as strange strings draw them back to Spain and the Mendoza story. Third in the Mendoza Trilogy.
Other books you might like:
Elizabeth Adler, *Fortune Is a Woman*, 1992
Barbara Delinsky, *A Woman Betrayed*, 1991
Iris Johansen, *Reap the Wind*, 1991
   third in the Wind Dancer Trilogy
Judith McNaught, *Paradise*, 1991
Nora Roberts, *Public Secrets*, 1990

265
BEVERLY BYRNE

The Flames of Vengeance
(New York: Bantam, 1991)

Story type: Saga
Series: Mendoza Trilogy
Major character(s): Lila Curran, Gentlewoman; Fergus Kelly, Nobleman (Lord Sharrick)
Time period(s): 1860s; 1890s (1895)
Locale(s): Cordoba, Spain; London, England; San Juan, Puerto Rico

Summary: Lila Curran vows revenge on the Mendoza family for the vile treatment she received during her marriage by grooming her son, Michael, for an elaborate scheme aimed at bringing down the powerful Mendoza banking empire. Sweeping, mysterious action in London, Spain and Puerto Rico. Second in the Mendoza Trilogy.

Other books you might like:
Leona Blair, *A World of Difference*, 1989
Jennifer Blake, *Love and Smoke*, 1989
Susan Howatch, *Sins of the Fathers*, 1980
Iris Johansen, *Storm Winds*, 1991
 second in Wind Dancer Trilogy

266

BEVERLY BYRNE

A Lasting Fire

(New York: Bantam, 1991)

Story type: Saga; Historical/Georgian
Major character(s): Sofia Valon, Singer (La Gitiana); Robert Mendoza, Financier
Time period(s): 18th century; 19th century
Locale(s): Spain

Summary: The first book in a proposed trilogy, this volume chronicles the events in the life of Sofia Valon, gypsy-raised, Jewish orphan and renowned singer, and her interactions with the powerful and wealthy Mendoza family. An intricately plotted, passionate story set against the background of the Napoleonic Wars.

Other books you might like:
Brian Cleeve, *Hester*, 1979
Madeline Hale, *Pirouette*, 1990
Iris Johansen, *Storm Winds*, 1991
 second in Wind Dancer Trilogy
Louisa Rawlings, *Stranger in My Arms*, 1990

267

JULIE CAILLE

An Impetuous Bride

(New York: Zebra, 1991)

Story type: Regency
Major character(s): Stacia Ashcroft, Heiress; Derek Devereaux, Rake
Time period(s): 1810s
Locale(s): London, England

Summary: To avoid the numerous restrictions placed on young, single women in Regency society, country-bred heiress Stacia Ashcroft decides to enjoy the London season by claiming to be a widow—and finds herself the object of a devastatingly dangerous rake's attentions! Likeable characters and a somewhat unusual plot add interest to this witty Regency.

Other books you might like:
Mary Balogh, *Christmas Beau*, 1992
Georgette Heyer, *The Grand Sophy*, 1950
Georgette Heyer, *The Reluctant Widow*, 1946

Jeanne Savery, *The Last of the Winter Roses*, 1991

268

JULIE CAILLE

A Mother's Heart

(New York: Zebra, 1992)

Story type: Regency; Holiday Themes
Summary: This set of six Regency short romances on the theme of motherhood includes the following: Journey's End by Julie Caille, Midnight Lady by Georgina Devon, Matters of the Heart by Karla Hocker, The Perfect Mother by Anthea Malcolm, A Breath of Scandal by Cyntian Richey, and A Mischievous Matchmaker by Olivia Sumner.

Other books you might like:
Anne Caldwell, *Scandal's Darling*, 1991
Emily Hendrickson, *A Scandalous Suggestion*, 1991
Katherine Kingsley, *A Natural Attachment*, 1990
Elizabeth Peters, *The Curse of the Pharoahs*, 1981
 romantic suspense — Victorian setting
Sheila Simonson, *The Bar Sinister*, 1986

269

JULIE CAILLE

The Rake and His Lady

(New York: Zebra, 1993)

Story type: Historical/Regency
Major character(s): Linnea Leyton, Noblewoman; Anthony Stanton, Nobleman (Viscount Carrock), Rake
Time period(s): 1810s
Locale(s): England

Summary: A marriage of convenience seems just the thing to solve Linnea and Anthony's difficulties—she needs to escape from an abusive father; he needs to marry in order to inherit his estate. However, their vastly different lifestyles make things difficult, to say the least—until, of course, love sets everything to rights. Warm and passionate.

Other books you might like:
Sarah Eagle, *The Marriage Gamble*, 1992
Georgette Heyer, *A Civil Contract*, 1962
 classic Regency
Georgette Heyer, *The Convenient Marriage*, 1934
 Another classic Regency
Karla Hocker, *Lady Maryann's Dilemma*, 1990
Eva Rutland, *Gretna Bride*, 1993

270

JULIE CAILLE

A Valentine's Day Fancy

(New York: Zebra, 1992)

Story type: Regency
Major character(s): Valentina Jardine, Companion; Gerard Marchant, Nobleman (Viscount Laverstoke)
Time period(s): 1810s

Locale(s): England

Summary: Compelled by her overbearing aunt and employer, Valentina Jardine takes her lovely young cousin to visit an elderly relative on the estate where her former fiance lives, and ends up attracting the attentions of Viscount Laverstoke, the man who caused her to be jilted. Nicely plotted and filled with lively banter and three-dimensional characters.

Other books you might like:
Georgette Heyer, *Sylvester, or the Wicked Uncle*, 1957
Carla Kelly, *Libby's London Merchant*, 1991
Mary Kingsley, *A Maddening Minx*, 1992
Joan Smith, *Madcap Miss*, 1989

271
BARBARA CAITLIN

Shotgun Wedding
(New York: Silhouette, 1992)

Story type: Contemporary
Major character(s): Maggie Howard, Parent (adoptive mother); Nick, Inventor (toy)
Time period(s): 1990s

Summary: Maggie couldn't produce evidence of a stable home in order to adopt orphan, B.J., so she asks her neighbor to pretend to be her husband—and he surprises her with his take-charge attitude. Nick falls in love with both B.J. and Maggie and then looks for ways to convince Maggie to make their marriage real.

Other books you might like:
Elizabeth Krueger, *For the Children*, 1992
Debbie Macomber, *Marriage of Inconvenience*, 1992
Kim Stanley Robinson, *Pacific Edge*, 1990
LaVyrle Spencer, *Morning Glory*, 1989

272
KIMBERLEIGH CAITLIN

Wildwitch
(New York: Berkley, 1991)

Story type: Historical/Elizabethan
Major character(s): Tessa Ravenscroft, Foundling, Witch (accused); Rafael "Rafe" Santador, Sea Captain (Spanish Armada), Nobleman (long-lost English Earl)
Time period(s): 16th century (1580s)
Locale(s): England

Summary: The object of a fanatic witch hunt, beautiful Tessa Ravenscroft outwits her pursuers and goes over the sea cliffs—straight into the arms of startled, shipwrecked sea captain, Rafe Santador. Love follows, but so does deceit, jealousy, and evil as Rafe and Tessa are enmeshed in the snares of a court intrigue that reaches from Elizabeth's court to Spain and the Inquisition. Interesting historical detail in a nicely plotted and passionate tale of good, evil, and long-kept secrets.

Other books you might like:
Philippa Carr, *The Lion Triumphant*, 1974

Victoria Holt, *My Enemy the Queen*, 1978
Catherine Linden, *Highland Flame*, 1991
Bertrice Small, *Skye O'Malley*, 1980
Becky Lee Weyrich, *Silver Tears*, 1990
　later period/Salem witch trials

273
LINDA CAJIO

Desperate Measures
(New York: Bantam, 1989)

Story type: Contemporary
Major character(s): Ellen Kitteridge, Socialite; Joe Carlini, Businessman
Time period(s): 1980s

Summary: Ellen thinks that Joe Carlini is just another fortune-hunter. However, she soon realizes that he is serious when he says he loves her and that he needs her help in catching whoever it is who is trying to ruin his business.

Other books you might like:
Sara Chance, *Fire in the Night*, 1989
Marilyn Cunningham, *Someone To Turn To*, 1990
Joan Elliott Pickart, *Mixed Signals*, 1990
Ann Williams, *Loving Lies*, 1990

274
ANNE CALDWELL

Pirates and Promises
(New York: Diamond, 1994)

Story type: Historical
Series: Tea Rose
Major character(s): Sabrina "Bree" Smythe, Noblewoman, Runaway; Justin Tyler St. Clair, Nobleman, Highwayman (in disguise)
Time period(s): 19th century
Locale(s): England; Virginia

Summary: Although Bree remembers her childhood promise to marry Justin, he seems to have forgotten all about it. Nevertheless, disguised as a highwayman, he saves her from his wicked brother and hires her as a maid in payment for her passage to America. The journey to America proves both educational and passionate, although he still is reluctant to share his real identity with her. A fast-paced story filled with humor, escapades, and numerous complications.

Other books you might like:
Jill Barnett, *Dreaming*, 1994
Jo Beverley, *My Lady Notorious*, 1993
Elizabeth DeLancey, *Touch of Fire*, 1993
Christine Dorsey, *Sea of Dreams*, 1993
Amanda Quick, *Dangerous*, 1993

275

ANNE CALDWELL

Scandal's Darling
(New York: Avon, 1991)

Story type: Regency

Major character(s): Danielle "Danni" Wakefield, Gentlewoman; Devon Alexander Stanton, Nobleman (Duke of Burnshire)

Time period(s): 1810s

Locale(s): England

Summary: Newly returned to England to assume the responsibilities of his estate, Lord Devon Stanton encounters lovely, young Danielle Wakefield in the process of "stealing" an orphan from his own orphanage (currently run by his cousin, the unscrupulous vicar Nathan Holmes). Needing a wife to claim his inheritance and not averse to a little blackmail, Devon determines to convince Danni to marry him. However, things are not to be so peacefully resolved—the nefarious vicar has a few ideas of his own and so does Danni in this witty, delightful Regency romp.

Other books you might like:

Joan Aiken, *The Five-Minute Marriage*, 1977
Annabel Laine, *The Reluctant Heiress*, 1978
Leslie Lynn, *The Rake's Redemption*, 1989
Stephanie Stevens, *Defiant Angel*, 1991
    sensual
Marlene Suson, *The Errant Earl*, 1989

276

PAMELA CALDWELL

Scandalous
(New York: Zebra, 1993)

Story type: Historical/Regency

Major character(s): Jane Oxenby, Noblewoman; George Aubrey Tate, Nobleman (Earl of Sefton)

Time period(s): 1810s

Locale(s): England

Summary: Determined to marry off his sister Portia, but not to Jane Oxenby's foppish cousin, Jonas, confirmed bachelor George Aubrey Tate, Earl of Sefton, is totally unprepared for his attraction to the lovely Jane. However, the elopement of Portia and Jonas throws the situation into chaos—with some romantically interesting results. Likeable characters with real problems, including unpleasant relatives and past difficulties, in a nicely plotted romance.

Other books you might like:

Jo Beverley, *An Arranged Marriage*, 1991
Jane Feather, *Virtue*, 1993
Kit Gardner, *The Dream*, 1992
    later time period
Georgette Heyer, *Black Sheep*, 1967
    classic Regency
Amanda Quick, *Scandal*, 1991

277

PATRICIA CAMDEN

Scarlet Kisses
(New York: Avon, 1992)

Story type: Historical/Georgian

Major character(s): Eleanora Batthyny, Noblewoman (Hungarian countess); Achille d'Agenais, Nobleman (French count)

Time period(s): 1740s (1741)

Locale(s): France

Summary: In France for the sole purpose of luring the arrogant and seemingly decadent Achille d'Agenais to his doom at the hands of her vengeful brothers, lovely Eleanora Batthyny is unprepared for the intense attraction that develops between them. Her deception, however, causes problems and it takes revelations from both their mothers to set things straight. Fiery, intricate, and unusual. Sequel to *Surrender in Scarlet*.

Other books you might like:

Nina Beaumont, *Sapphire Magic*, 1991
Patricia Potter, *The Abduction*, 1991
Veronica Sattler, *A Dangerous Longing*, 1990
Valerie Sherwood, *Lisbon*, 1989

278

PATRICIA CAMDEN

Surrender in Scarlet
(New York: Avon, 1991)

Story type: Historical/Exotic; Historical/Georgian

Major character(s): Kaatje de St. Benoit, Widow(er); Becket Thorne, Military Personnel (British Colonel)

Time period(s): 18th century (1708)

Locale(s): Europe

Summary: Beautiful widow Kaatje and revenge-driven Becket find passion, adventure, and a solution to their problems as they travel throughout Europe looking for the diabolical El Muzier.

Other books you might like:

Laura Kinsale, *The Prince of Midnight*, 1990
Connie Mason, *Tempt the Devil*, 1990
Veronica Sattler, *A Dangerous Longing*, 1990
Valerie Sherwood, *Lisbon*, 1989

279

CARYN CAMERON (Pseudonym of Karen Harper)

Freedom Flame
(Toronto: Harlequin, 1990)

Story type: Historical/American Revolution

Major character(s): Meredith "Merry" Morgan, Spy ("Freedom Flame"); Darcy Mont, Spy ("Torch"), Nobleman (Comte de Belfort)

Time period(s): 1770s (1776)

Locale(s): American Colonies

Summary: Romantic Merry and embittered Darcy join forces in helping America win its independence—and win each other's love in the process. A fast-paced tale that combines good historical detail with romantic intrigue. Sequel to *Liberty's Lady*.

Other books you might like:
Colleen Faulkner, *Temptation's Tender Kiss*, 1990
Judith E. French, *Scarlet Ribbons*, 1989
Heather Graham, *Love Not a Rebel*, 1989
Robin Maderich, *Faith and Honor*, 1989
Maura Seger, *Fortune's Tide*, 1990
    England wins the American Revolution!

280
CARYN CAMERON
Liberty's Lady
(Toronto: Harlequin, 1990)

Story type: Historical/American Revolution
Major character(s): Libby Morgan, Publisher (Newspaper owner), Revolutionary; Cameron Grant, Loyalist
Time period(s): 1770s (1775)
Locale(s): New York, New York

Summary: Revolutionary Libby Morgan and Loyalist Cameron Grant clash politically and romantically as Libby tries to keep her family's newspaper in business.

Other books you might like:
Christine Dorsey, *Traitor's Embrace*, 1990
Judith E. French, *Scarlet Ribbons*, 1989
Robin Maderich, *Faith and Honor*, 1989
Christina Savage, *Hearts of Fire*, 1984
Maura Seger, *Fortune's Tide*, 1990
    England wins the American Revolution!

281
CHARLA CAMERON (Pseudonym of Gloria Dale Skinner)
Sultry Nights
(New York: Zebra, 1992)

Story type: Historical/Antebellum American South
Series: Magnolia Road
Major character(s): Caramarena Cantrell, Plantation Owner, Southern Belle; Asher Worthy, Businessman, Shipowner
Time period(s): 1840s (1848)
Locale(s): Florida

Summary: Intent on fulfilling a promise to his father, Asher Worthy goes to Florida to seek vengeance on John Cantrell and his daughters and finds himself dealing with the attractive and capable Caramarena Cantrell, who sees in Asher the answer to the problem of providing an heir for the family. The resulting marriage is filled with passion, sparks, and plenty of deception, but love does survive in this sultry and sensuous tale of the Old South.

Other books you might like:
Brenna Braxton-Barshon, *Southern Oaks*, 1991
Thea Devine, *Southern Seduction*, 1991
Shirl Henke, *Moonflower*, 1989

Miriam Minger, *Defiant Imposter*, 1992

282
KATE CAMERON
Orenda
(New York: Ballantine, 1991)

Story type: Historical/Mainstream
Major character(s): Morning Song, Orphan, Indian (Iroquois)
Locale(s): Iroquois Nation

Summary: An enthralling story of the Iroquois Nation told through the life and love of Morning Song. Lyrical, passionate, and filled with memorable characters and much historical detail.

Other books you might like:
Beverly Bird, *Comes the Rain*, 1991
Michael Blake, *Dances with Wolves*, 1988
Cassie Edwards, *When Passion Calls*, 1990
Judith E. French, *Moonfeather*, 1990

283
STELLA CAMERON
Avon Books Presents: A Christmas Collection
(New York: Avon, 1992)

Story type: Historical; Holiday Themes
Summary: A diverse quartet of heartwarming, historical romances set during the Christmas holidays. Includes: ''The Greatest Gift'' by Stella Cameron, ''Falling Stars'' by Loretta Chase, ''The Scent of Snow'' by Linda Lael Miller, and ''Footsteps in the Snow'' by Joan Hohl.

Other books you might like:
Janice Bennett, *A Christmas Keepsake*, 1992
Sandra Heath, *A Christmas Courtship*, 1990
Carla Kelly, *Marian's Christmas Wish*, 1989

284
STELLA CAMERON
Breathless
(New York: Avon, 1994)

Story type: Contemporary/Exotic
Major character(s): Angelica Dean, Writer; Sinjin Breaker, Businessman (island owner)
Time period(s): 1990s
Locale(s): Hell, Pacific Islands

Summary: Sinjin Breaker, the wealthy owner of the island Hell, knows that someone is out to kill him; and when writer Angelica Dean shows up claiming she is doing a story on his life, she becomes a suspect. In reality, she *is* there under false pretenses; she wants to expose Sinjin for the part he played in her mother's death. But the more she learns, the more danger she is in; and it isn't until the old mysteries are solved that love can take its intended course.

Other books you might like:
Emma Darcy, *The Sheikh's Revenge*, 1993
   unusual exotic contemporary
Nora Roberts, *Divine Evil*, 1992
Nora Roberts, *Genuine Lies*, 1991
Katherine Sutcliffe, *Shadow Play*, 1991
Jane Toombs, *Traitor's Kiss*, 1992

285

STELLA CAMERON

Charmed

(New York: Avon, 1995)

Story type: Historical/Regency
Major character(s): Lady Philipa Chauncey, Noblewoman, Fiance(e); Calum Innes, Nobleman (Duke of Franchot), Heir—Dispossessed
Time period(s): 1820s (1823)
Locale(s): London, England; Cornwall, England

Summary: Calum Innes knows that he is the rightful Duke of Franchot and he has returned to London to prove it. Determined to discover who has been plotting against him since birth, he will do almost anything to learn the truth and regain all that is rightfully his—including the imposter's promised bride! Duty-bound to marry the man who calls himself the Duke of Franchot, Lady Philipa Chauncey is resigned to her fate—until Calum comes into her life and changes it forever. Fast-paced, dark, intriguing action.

Other books you might like:
Catherine Coulter, *The Wyndham Legacy*, 1994
Jane Feather, *Valentine*, 1995
Jane Feather, *Virtue*, 1994
Christina Skye, *Come the Dawn*, 1995

286

STELLA CAMERON

Fascination

(New York: Avon, 1993)

Story type: Historical; Gothic
Major character(s): Grace Wren, Noblewoman, Spinster; Arran Rossmara, Widow(er) (reclusive), Nobleman
Time period(s): 1820s (1822)
Locale(s): Scotland

Summary: Grace, seeking an elderly, ailing husband to secure her and her mother's future, is chosen by the arrogant Lord Arran to bear him a child. Both are surprised by the other—he sees her as attractive, she finds him to be young and virile. He disguises himself and, in an attempt to discredit her, seduces her—and in the process becomes emotionally involved. Greedy relatives, less than honorable motivations, and passion are part of this dark, and somewhat gothic, romance.

Other books you might like:
Rebecca Brandewyne, *Upon a Moon-Dark Moor*, 1988
Brenda Joyce, *Dark Fires*, 1991
Brenda Joyce, *Scandalous Love*, 1992
Andrea Kane, *Dream Castle*, 1992

287

STELLA CAMERON

His Magic Touch

(New York: Avon, 1993)

Story type: Historical
Major character(s): Celine Godwin, Debutante, Fiance(e) (reluctant); James St. Giles, Heir—Dispossessed, Imposter ("James Eagleton")
Locale(s): England

Summary: Celine will do just about anything to avoid marriage to the unsavory Bertram Letchwith, even ruin her reputation. However, when she innocently asks dashing James Eagleton to compromise her, she little suspects that she is playing right into his hands, both romantically and politically. Evil, intrigue, and passion are part of this tale of revenge and retribution.

Other books you might like:
Judith Hill, *Knight's Desire*, 1992
   medieval setting
Susan Johnson, *Sinful*, 1993
Andrea Kane, *Dream Castle*, 1993
Katherine Kingsley, *No Greater Love*, 1992
Meagan McKinney, *Lions and Lace*, 1992

288

STELLA CAMERON
JUDITH E. FRENCH, Co-Author
LINDA LAEL MILLER, Co-Author
ANNE STUART, Co-Author

To Love and to Honor

(New York: Avon, 1993)

Story type: Anthology; Historical

Summary: Four historical novellas focusing on the subject of marriage. Included are: "Bargain Bride" by Stella Cameron, "The Bride of Wildcat Purchase" by Judith E. French, "Store-bought Woman" by Linda Lael Miller, and "The High Sheriff of Huntingdon" by Anne Stuart.

Other books you might like:
Robin Lee Hatcher, *Promise Me Spring*, 1991
Georgette Heyer, *The Convenient Marriage*, 1934
Theresa Michaels, *Gifts of Love*, 1992
Linda Lael Miller, *Daniel's Bride*, 1992
Victoria Pade, *The Doubletree*, 1990

289

CANDACE CAMP

Flame Lily

(New York: Monogram, 1994)

Story type: Historical/Post-American Civil War
Major character(s): Linette Sanders, Young Woman; Hunter Tyrell, Military Personnel (former)
Time period(s): 1860s
Locale(s): United States

Summary: Home from the Civil War, embittered Hunter Tyrell has no use for Linette, his childhood sweetheart, who married when she thought he had been killed. But when Linette discovers her husband's true nature, she needs Hunter—and they are both forced to realize that their feelings for each other never did die and they are still very much in love. They have much to overcome and resolve in this warm and tender love story—and they succeed. Follows *Rain Lily*.

Other books you might like:
Barbara Ankrum, *Renegade's Kiss*, 1993
Robin Lee Hatcher, *Where the Heart Is*, 1993
Jill Marie Landis, *Until Tomorrow*, 1994
Sylvie Sommerfield, *Love's Stolen Promise*, 1992

290
CANDACE CAMP
Heirloom
(New York: Harper 1992)

Story type: Historical/American West
Major character(s): Juliet Drake, Actress, Singer; Amos Morgan, Farmer
Time period(s): 1900s (early)
Locale(s): Nebraska

Summary: Desperately needing a job, stranded actress Juliet Drake lies about her skills and goes to work for taciturn, rude farmer Amos Morgan. Fortunately, Amos's sister takes pity on the disastrously inept Juliet and teaches her some of what she needs to know. Love develops slowly in this realistic, warm romance.

Other books you might like:
Stef Ann Holm, *Firefly*, 1990
Jill Marie Landis, *Sunflower*, 1988
Pamela Morsi, *Courting Miss Hattie*, 1991
Rebecca Paisley, *Barefoot Bride*, 1990

291
CANDACE CAMP
Rosewood
(New York: Harper, 1991)

Story type: Historical/American West
Major character(s): Millicent Hayes, Spinster, Gentlewoman; Jonathan Lawrence, Widow(er), Journalist (newspaper owner)
Time period(s): 19th century
Locale(s): Emmetsville, Texas

Summary: The life of starchy, respectable Millicent Hayes changes drastically when unconventional newspaperman Jon Lawrence and his young daughter move in next door. A warm and funny story with an added bonus—a secondary love story between Millie's handicapped brother and an impoverished and pregnant servant girl.

Other books you might like:
Gwen Cleary, *Colorado Temptation*, 1991
Jude Deveraux, *Wishes*, 1989
    fantasy elements

Theresa DiBenedetto, *Silver Mist*, 1990
Joan Johnston, *Sweetwater Seduction*, 1991
Victoria Thompson, *Playing with Fire*, 1990

292
DEBORAH CAMP
Black-Eyed Susan
(New York: Avon, 1990)

Story type: Historical/American West
Major character(s): Susan Armitage, Child-Care Giver (to Logan's two children); Logan Vance, Journalist, Publisher (newspaper owner)
Time period(s): 1890s
Locale(s): St. Louis, Missouri; Tulsa, Oklahoma

Summary: Susan accompanies her recently widowed brother-in-law to the Oklahoma Territory to care for his two children. Town censure forces the two to marry for propriety's sake; however, love has a way of complicating things and the two must deal with their true feelings for each other as well as a variety of frontier problems.

Other books you might like:
Barbara Bretton, *Midnight Lover*, 1989
Barbara Hargis, *Heart Song*, 1990
Victoria Thompson, *Fortune's Lady*, 1990
Vivian Vaughn, *Texas Gamble*, 1990

293
DEBORAH CAMP
Cheyenne's Shadow
(New York: Avon, 1994)

Story type: Historical/American West
Major character(s): Henrietta Hollister, Rancher; Jonnie Cheyenne, Gunfighter, Indian (half Cheyenne)
Time period(s): 19th century
Locale(s): West

Summary: Henrietta has not managed her ranch well at all—and she needs cattle to save it. Hiring gunslinger Jonnie Cheyenne to do the job sounds ideal, but she is so taken with him that it is hard to concentrate on all the problems that come along. Stampedes, fires, and injuries all add to the excitement of this fast-paced romance.

Other books you might like:
Dorothy Garlock, *Midnight Blue*, 1989
Shirl Henke, *A Fire in the Blood*, 1994
    more rustlers and ranch life/different treatment
Johanna Lindsey, *Angel*, 1992
    another gunslinging hero/humorous and fast-paced
Victoria Thompson, *Wild Texas Promise*, 1990

294

DEBORAH CAMP

Fallen Angel

(New York: Avon, 1989)

Story type: Historical/American West
Major character(s): Justine Drussard, Actress (robbed, deserted, and wounded), Prostitute; York Master, Detective—Private (Pinkerton agent)
Time period(s): 1800s
Locale(s): Tombstone, Arizona

Summary: Deserted by her fellow actors and wounded in a gunfight, Justine Drussard decides she has no choice but to join the world's oldest profession. Her scheme to render her customers unconscious fails when she encounters Pinkerton agent, York Masters, who forces her into working with him to locate his missing sister. An action-filled historical romance with a definite touch of the Old West.

Other books you might like:
Barbara Bretton, *Midnight Lover*, 1989
Sandra Brown, *Sunset Embrace*, 1985
Gwen Cleary, *Ecstasy's Masquerade*, 1989
Johanna Lindsey, *Savage Thunder*, 1989
Mayo Lucas, *Camelot Jones*, 1989

295

DEBORAH CAMP

Fire Lily

(New York: Avon, 1991)

Story type: Historical/Victorian America
Major character(s): Lily Meeker, Psychic (reluctant); Griffin Goforth, Psychic (Gypsy)
Time period(s): 19th century
Locale(s): New England

Summary: Highly suspicious of the purported psychic abilities of gypsy Griffin Goforth, Lily Meeker accompanies him as he searches for her missing cousin—and ends up finding not only her cousin, but love and passion as well. A sensual, intriguing story of growing love and trust—unusual in that *both* the hero and heroine are clairvoyant.

Other books you might like:
Caroline Bourne, *Allegheny Ecstasy*, 1990
  clairvoyant heroine
Johanna Lindsey, *Once a Princess*, 1991
Nancy Moulton, *Defiant Heart*, 1989
Patricia Rice, *Moon Dreams*, 1991
  clairvoyant heroine

296

DEBORAH CAMP

Lady Legend

(New York: Avon, 1992)

Story type: Historical/American West

Major character(s): Copper-Headed Woman, Healer, Adoptee (by the Crow Indians); Tucker Jones, Military Personnel (Union soldier)
Time period(s): 1860s
Locale(s): Crow Territory, Wyoming

Summary: Copper Headed Woman, the legendary white healer of the Crow Indians, finds and heals Union Army officer Tucker Jones following a vicious Indian attack and ends up spending the winter with him. In spite of, or perhaps because of, Indian attacks, injuries, jealousy, and childbirth, their relationship grows into love and they learn to understand and respect each other and their cultures.

Other books you might like:
Fela Dawson Scott, *Ghost Dancer*, 1992
Ruth Langan, *Texas Healer*, 1992
Pamela Litton, *Dance with the Devil*, 1992
Constance O'Banyon, *Cheyenne Sunrise*, 1990

297

DEBORAH CAMP

My Wild Rose

(New York: Avon, 1992)

Story type: Historical/American West
Major character(s): Regina Rose, Activist (temperance), Innkeeper (boarding house owner); Theodore Dane, Lawyer
Time period(s): 1890s (1895)
Locale(s): Eureka Springs, Arkansas

Summary: When temperance activist Regina Rose fervently supports Carrie Nation's actions in the small Arkansas town of Eureka Springs, she clashes head-on with the entire town, including Theodore Dane, the lawyer who is prosecuting Ms. Nation for destroying a local saloon. Eventually, Theo and Regina work out their differences, but not before a lot of long-standing problems are addressed. Fast-paced and sensual, with a bit of a message.

Other books you might like:
Joan Johnston, *Sweetwater Seduction*, 1991
Kathleen Kane, *Mountain Dawn*, 1992
Betina Lindsey, *Waltz with the Lady*, 1990
DeLoras Scott, *Rogue's Honor*, 1992

298

DELAYNE CAMP (Pseudonym of Deborah Camp)

Newsworthy Affair

(Toronto: Harlequin, 1990)

Story type: Contemporary
Major character(s): Tess Maxwell, Journalist (Newspaper Entertainment Editor); Asher Ames, Journalist (Newspaper Entertainment Editor)
Time period(s): 1980s
Locale(s): Kansas City, Missouri

Summary: Fierce competitors since college, Tess and Asher are rivals once again—this time in the Kansas City newspaper world. Asher wants Tess; Tess wants to get even. Vibrant.

Other books you might like:
Billie Green, *Bad for Each Other*, 1990
Carol Jerina, *Flirting with Danger*, 1990
Kathleen Gilles Seidel, *Maybe This Time*, 1990
Vickie Lewis Thompson, *Full Coverage*, 1990

299

BETHANY CAMPBELL

The Man Who Came for Christmas
(Toronto: Harlequin, 1993)

Story type: Contemporary; Holiday Themes
Major character(s): Abbie Hale, Young Woman; Yates Connley, Police Officer (undercover), Appraiser
Time period(s): 1990s
Locale(s): Nebraska

Summary: Young Abbie, missing her grandfather, goes once more to his beloved ranch before it is sold. When an appraiser appears to check things out, Abbie resents and mistrusts him, wishing her rodeo-rider fiance, Lucky, would come home. However, Yates Connley isn't really an insurance adjuster, he is an undercover police investigator—and he suspects Lucky. Confusion reigns; but Abbie eventually sorts it all out with a little help from Yates.

Other books you might like:
Rexanne Becnel, *Christmas Journey*, 1992
Kathleen Creighton, *A Christmas Love*, 1992
Janet Dailey, *Mistletoe and Holly*, 1983
Maggie Daniels, *Moonlight and Mistletoe*, 1993
Debbie Macomber, *A Season of Angels*, 1993

300

BETHANY CAMPBELL

The Snow Garden
(Toronto: Harlequin, 1989)

Story type: Contemporary/Innocent
Major character(s): Hedy Hansen, Orphan; Ty Marek, Writer (Columnist)
Time period(s): 1980s
Locale(s): Chicago, Illinois

Summary: Fleeing from unhappy memories of Christmas, Hedy buys a house in Chicago sight unseen—and then learns that the entire neighborhood decorates extravagantly for Christmas. Friends and the love of Ty Marek eventually turn things around, and Christmas takes on a new meaning for Hedy.

Other books you might like:
Mary Blaynay, *Father Christmas*, 1989
Janet Dailey, *Mistletoe and Holly*, 1983
    Christmas in Vermont
Carla Kelly, *Marian's Christmas Wish*, 1989
    Regency period Christmas story
Jan McDaniel, *This Fragile Heart*, 1989

301

MARILYN CAMPBELL

Pretty Maids in a Row
(New York: Villard, 1994)

Story type: Romantic Suspense
Major character(s): Holly Kaufman, Lobbyist (environmentalist), Crime Victim (rape victim); David Wells, Journalist
Time period(s): 1990s
Locale(s): United States

Summary: Years ago, a group of fraternity brothers brutally raped five young women. Now the women are seeking retribution and Holly, one of the victims, is asked to join the vengeance-oriented "Little Sister's Society." The men are being gruesomely murdered and the women are suspects. David wants to help Holly, but hc actually suspects that she might have done it. Nevertheless, together David and Holly solve the crime—and find time to fall in love.

Other books you might like:
Sandra Brown, *Breath of Scandal*, 1991
    rape/revenge theme — Southern style
Mary Higgins Clark, *All around the Town*, 1992
Tami Hoag, *Still Waters*, 1992
Nora Roberts, *Carnal Innocence*, 1992
Nora Roberts, *Divine Evil*, 1992

302

MARILYN CAMPBELL

Stardust Dreams
(New York: Topaz, 1993)

Story type: Futuristic
Major character(s): Cherry Cochran, Actress; Gallant Voyager, Space Explorer
Time period(s): Indeterminate Future
Locale(s): Spaceship; Interstellar Empire/Federation

Summary: Cherry, a content actress in fantasy films, is surprised to find herself a space traveller with the mysterious Gallant Voyager and an interesting assortment of magical characters on a mission to save the universe! Warlike, exiled aliens cause problems for the pair, but their partnership is unique and they are determined to accomplish their goal. Suspenseful and humorous.

Other books you might like:
Amanda Glass, *Shield's Lady*, 1989
Johanna Lindsey, *Keeper of the Heart*, 1993
Anne McCaffrey, *Killashandra*, 1985
Patricia Roenbuck, *The Golden Conquest*, 1992
Patricia Roenbuck, *Golden Temptress*, 1991

303
MARILYN CAMPBELL
Stolen Dreams
(New York: Topaz, 1994)

Story type: Futuristic
Series: Innerworld
Major character(s): Shara Locke, Scientist (Geneticist), Time Traveller; Gabriel Drumayne, Teacher (history professor), Time Traveller
Time period(s): Indeterminate Future
Locale(s): Innerworld, Fictional Country

Summary: Going back in time to try to prevent the birth of a future political radical, geneticist Shara Locke and historian Gabriel Drumayne find passion, love, and adventure in a setting that features numerous classical characters—and an entirely new way of interpreting ancient mythology. Fast paced. Another addition to Campbell's Innerworld Series.

Other books you might like:
Jessica Bryan, *Across a Wine-Dark Sea*, 1991
Amanda Glass, *Shield's Lady*, 1989
Jayne Ann Krentz, *Sweet Starfire*, 1986 reissued 1994
Flora M. Speer, *No Other Love*, 1993
Marilyn Tracy, *Memory's Lamp*, 1994

304
SANDRA CANFIELD
Dark Journey
(New York: Bantam, 1994)

Story type: Romantic Suspense; Contemporary
Major character(s): Anna Ramey, Widow(er); Sloan Marshall, Military Personnel (war hero)
Time period(s): 1990s
Locale(s): Cook's Bay, Maine

Summary: Swept up in a tumult of betrayal, pain, and passion, newly widowed Anna Ramey finds herself the object of gossip and suspicion in the small Maine resort town of Cook's Bay. Eventually she is put on trial for the murder of her husband—all because she fell in love with the mysterious stranger, Sloan Winslow. Strong in internal conflict and intensely emotional.

Other books you might like:
Barbara Delinsky, *The Passions of Chelsea Kane*, 1992
Maggie Shayne, *Forgotten Vows*, 1994
Maggie Shayne, *Kiss of the Shadow Man*, 1994
LaVyrle Spencer, *Bittersweet*, 1990
LaVyrle Spencer, *Morning Glory*, 1990

305
SANDRA CANFIELD
The Loving
(New York: Harper Collins, 1992)

Story type: Time Travel; Historical

Major character(s): Engelina Lamartine, Gentlewoman; Roan Jacobs, Doctor (heart surgeon), Time Traveller
Time period(s): 1990s; 19th century
Locale(s): Houston, Texas; New Orleans, Louisiana

Summary: While in New Orleans recuperating from a near-fatal accident, Dr. Roan Jacobs is transported to the 19th century in order to help the abused and lovely Engelina. An evil and vindictive husband complicates matters, but Roan tries, nevertheless. Memorable characters, fast-paced action, and an interesting premise.

Other books you might like:
Barbara Bretton, *Somewhere in Time*, 1992
Lori Copeland, *Forever Ashley*, 1992
Jude Deveraux, *A Knight in Shining Armor*, 1992
Diana Gabaldon, *Dragonfly in Amber*, 1992
Vivian Knight-Jenkins, *Passion's Timeless Hour*, 1992

306
MARSHA CANHAM
In the Shadow of Midnight
(New York: Dell, 1994)

Story type: Historical/Medieval
Major character(s): Lady Ariel de Claire, Noblewoman; Eduard FitzRandewulf d'Ambroise, Knight, Nobleman
Time period(s): 13th century (1203)
Locale(s): England; Wales; Normandy, France

Summary: Doomed to marry a common lout, Lady Ariel plots to escape King John's plan. Her brother and Lord Randewulf agree to conduct her to safety; but in the meantime, they set off to rescue the imprisoned Princess Eleanor, taking a somewhat reluctant Ariel along. During the adventure-filled journey, Ariel falls in love with Randewulf; however, because of his promise to protect the princess, she determines that he is unavailable. A well-plotted, richly detailed historical featuring all the violence, intrigue, and grandeur of the 13th Century—plus some actual historical characters.

Other books you might like:
Marion Zimmer Bradley, *The Mists of Avalon*, 1988
Katherine Deauville, *Daggers of Gold*, 1993
Roberta Gellis, *The Silver Mirror*, 1989
Elizabeth Lowell, *Enchanted*, 1994
Caryl Wilson, *Firebrand's Lady*, 1992

307
MARSHA CANHAM
Through a Dark Mist
(New York: Dell, 1992)

Story type: Historical/Medieval
Major character(s): Servanne de Briscourt, Noblewoman; Black Wolf, Nobleman (Lord Lucien Wardieu), Outlaw; Lucien "The Dragon" de Gourney, Nobleman
Time period(s): 12th century (1180)
Locale(s): England

Summary: Lady Servanne is attracted to the outlaw Black Wolf, even though she is engaged to his mortal enemy, Lucien de Gourney, The Dragon. After she surrenders to Black Wolf, he heartlessly turns her over to her betrothed; nevertheless, she finds ways to help Black Wolf in his fight to defeat The Dragon and regain his heritage. A sensual, action-adventure, with Robin Hood elements.

Other books you might like:
Laura Kinsale, *The Prince of Midnight*, 1990
Mary Lide, *Ann of Cambray*, 1984
Mary Jo Putney, *Uncommon Vows*, 1991
Marylyle Rogers, *Hidden Hearts*, 1989
Marylyle Rogers, *Wary Hearts*, 1988

308
MARSHA CANHAM
Under the Desert Moon
(New York: Dell, 1992)

Story type: Historical/American West
Major character(s): Aubrey Blue, Young Woman (sharpshooter), Teacher; Christian McBride, Convict (former)
Time period(s): 19th century
Locale(s): New Mexico

Summary: Unaware that they are both out for vengeance on the same man, Aubrey Blue and Christian McBride struggle to survive a stagecoach attack, the Comanches, and the hostile environment as they head toward civilization. In addition, of course, Aubrey has to survive her growing feelings for Christian. Dramatic gunfights, fast-paced adventure, and plenty of passion.

Other books you might like:
Elaine Coffman, *Escape Not My Love*, 1991
Linda Howard, *The Touch of Fire*, 1992
Susannah Leigh, *The Turquoise Trail*, 1991
Evelyn Rogers, *Desert Fire*, 1992

309
RAINE CANTRELL (Pseudonym of Theresa DiBenedetto)
Calico
(New York: Diamond, 1993)

Story type: Historical/American West
Major character(s): Mary Margaret O'Rourke, Mine Owner, Captive; C.V. McCready, Saloon Keeper/Owner
Time period(s): 19th century
Locale(s): West

Summary: When fiery, independent Mary Margaret's groom is kidnapped just before their wedding, she accuses local saloon owner C.V. McCready of the deed—and ends up abducted and confined to a cabin with just McCready for company. Proxy marriages, gold claims, and double dealing add spice to this fast-paced, funny, sensual romance.

Other books you might like:
Lori Copeland, *Promise Me Forever*, 1994
Norah Hess, *Kentucky Bride*, 1992
Sharon Ihle, *Wild Rose*, 1993
Rebecca Paisley, *Barefoot Bride*, 1990

310
RAINE CANTRELL (Pseudonym of Theresa DiBenedetto)
Desert Sunrise
(New York: Diamond, 1992)

Story type: Historical/American West
Major character(s): Faith Ann Becket, Frontierswoman (settler's daughter); Delany Carmichael, Scout, Adoptee (by Apache)
Time period(s): 19th century
Locale(s): Prescott, Arizona; Dragoon Mountains, Arizona

Summary: Faith Becket hires Delaney Carmichael to guide her, along with her entire family, to their Arizona claim. Delaney's behavior and less-than-pristine reputation make his acceptance by Faith's father difficult, but the attraction between Delaney and Faith persists -with the predictable results. Lost mines, murder, and old conflicts add to the adventure.

Other books you might like:
Norah Hess, *Wildfire*, 1989
Joanna Jordan, *Destiny's Dream*, 1990
Connie Mason, *Beyond the Horizon*, 1990
Bobbi Smith, *Arizona Caress*, 1989

311
RAINE CANTRELL
Tarnished Hearts
(New York: Topaz, 1994)

Story type: Historical/Antebellum American South
Major character(s): Leah Reese, Young Woman (overseer's daughter); Trevor Shelby, Landowner, Military Personnel (Confederate Soldier)
Time period(s): 1850s
Locale(s): Georgia; Wyoming

Summary: Trevor Shelby temporarily leaves Leah Reese, the woman he loves, to rescue his sister from their cruel father and returns to find Leah has been forced to marry another. Wild with anger and grief, Trevor suffers betrayal, near destruction, years of war, and prison before he is finally reunited with Leah. Dark and sensual.

Other books you might like:
Rosanne Bittner, *Unforgettable*, 1994
  realistic
Linda Howard, *A Lady of the West*, 1990
  dark and hard-hitting
Linda Howard, *The Touch of Fire*, 1992
  another wounded hero
Dana Ransom, *Texas Destiny*, 1994
Patricia Rice, *Texas Lily*, 1994

312
RAINE CANTRELL
Whisper My Name
(New York: Topaz, 1995)

Story type: Historical/American West

Major character(s): Dominica Kirkland, Orphan; Luke, Teacher
Time period(s): 1870s (1877)
Locale(s): Florence, Idaho

Summary: Dominica Kirkland has no money and can't prove who she is, but she is determined to uncover the mystery surrounding her father's death and discover why she was summoned to the wilds of Idaho. Luke is a hard man and used to being on his own, but a debt to Dominica's father and an unexplainable attraction draws him to her. They set out on a journey that will either bind them together or rip them apart forever.

Other books you might like:
Rebecca Brandewyne, *Rainbow's End*, 1991
   another heroine looking for answers
Lori Copeland, *Promise Me Forever*, 1994
   humorous
Garda Parker, *Arizona Temptation*, 1992
   humorous and fast-paced
Linda Sandifer, *Mountain Ecstasy*, 1992
   Idaho setting

313

DONNA CARLISLE

Matchmaker, Matchmaker
(New York: Silhouette, 1990)

Story type: Contemporary
Major character(s): Cassie Averil, Businesswoman (Matchmaker); Shane Bartlett, Businessman (Millionaire)
Time period(s): 1980s
Locale(s): Dallas, Texas

Summary: When wealthy Shane Bartlett walks into Cassie Averil's matchmaking service and "orders" a young, home-loving blonde, Cassie almost refuses; but she needs the money to save her business. Cassie eventually helps Shane "make a match," but it isn't the one either of them originally expected.

Other books you might like:
Gail Douglas, *The Dreamweavers: Bewitching Lady*, 1990
Naomi Horton, *The Ideal Man*, 1989
Jayne Ann Krentz, *Lady's Choice*, 1989
Diana Palmer, *His Girl Friday*, 1989

314

TENA CARLYLE (Pseudonym of Ellen Lyle Tabor)

Captive Treasure
(New York.: Zebra, 1992)

Story type: Historical/Exotic; Historical/Victorian
Major character(s): Constance Meriweather, Gentlewoman; Hale Wyndham, Archaeologist
Time period(s): 1860s (1866)
Locale(s): Mexico City, Mexico

Summary: When archaeologist Hale Wyndham answers an expedition advertisement, he is appalled to discover he will be working with Constance Meriweather and not her well-known father. Nevertheless, in spite of their mutual dislike,

Hale and Constance head to Mexico, determined to locate her father's Aztec treasure, unaware that both danger and love are waiting in the ruins. Natural disasters, banditos, and a glass-eyed parrot provide adventure and humor in this swiftly-moving historical.

Other books you might like:
Katherine Compton, *Eden's Angel*, 1990
Nancy Moulton, *Defiant Heart*, 1989
Rebecca Paisley, *Midnight and Magnolias*, 1992
Susan Sackett, *Passion's Golden Fire*, 1989
Katherine Sutcliffe, *Shadow Play*, 1991
   similar premise, but intense and dark.

315

TENA CARLYLE (Pseudonym of Ellen Lyle Tabor)

Runaway Heart
(New York: Zebra, 1993)

Story type: Historical/Victorian America
Major character(s): Jonquil Rose Trevain, Musician (carnival singer); Adam Coulter, Avenger (Seeking his brother's killers)
Time period(s): 1880s (1882)
Locale(s): Eureka Springs, Arkansas

Summary: Adam Coulter's search for his lawman brother's killers leads him to carnival singer Jonquil Rose and her companions, but the truth is not quite what he expects. Property, money, and greed are all part of this romance with a somewhat unusual setting.

Other books you might like:
Lori Copeland, *Promise Me Today*, 1992
Charlotte Hubbard, *Gambler's Tempting Kisses*, 1991
Pamela Morsi, *Wild Oats*, 1993
Rebecca Paisley, *Rainbows and Rapture*, 1992
Shirley Parenteau, *Golden Prospect*, 1991

316

EMILY CARMICHAEL

Outcast
(New York: Warner, 1995)

Story type: Historical/American West
Major character(s): Olivia Baron, Doctor; Gabriel William Danaher O'Connell, Miner, Fugitive (accused murderer)
Time period(s): 1880s (1887-1889)
Locale(s): Elkhorn, Montana

Summary: Gabe lives for two reasons: to provide his two daughters with a future and to avenge the murder of his wife. When his daughters fall prey to a deadly fever, he will stop at nothing to save them, including kidnapping Dr. Olivia Baron. Olivia proves to be not only a competent doctor, but a desirable woman as well. When Gabe finds himself falling in love with her, he ends up protecting her as well as his family from his wife's killer. Heartwarming and humorous.

Other books you might like:
Linda Howard, *The Touch of Fire*, 1992
   another abducted woman doctor/different treatment

Jill Marie Landis, *Come Spring*, 1992
   another abducted heroine/heartwarming and humorous
Ruth Langan, *Texas Healer*, 1992
   another woman doctor/Native American themes
Debbie Macomber, *Morning Comes Softly*, 1993
   heartwarming

317

EMILY CARMICHAEL (Pseudonym of Emily Krokosz)

Visions of the Heart
(New York: Warner, 1990)

Story type: Historical/War of 1812
Major character(s): Miriam "Miri" Sutcliffe, Gentlewoman, Fugitive; Jordan Scott, Indian (White—Chippewa), Frontiersman
Time period(s): 1810s
Locale(s): Michilimackinac Island, Michigan; Ontario, Canada

Summary: Forced to leave England to avoid prosecution for treason, proper Miriam Sutcliffe flees to America in search of her duplicitous fiance. Instead, she finds Jordan Scott, a refugee from the Boston social scene, who is living the life he prefers among the Chippewas and has little use for a prim English miss who threatens to upset his life. Funny and highly romantic.

Other books you might like:
Judith E. French, *Lovestorm*, 1990
Patricia Gaffney, *Thief of Hearts*, 1990
Brenda Joyce, *Darkest Heart*, 1989
Jill Marie Landis, *Rose*, 1990
Leta Tegler, *Gabrielle*, 1990

318

JEANNE CARMICHAEL

Madcap Johnny
(Toronto: Harlequin, 1993)

Story type: Regency
Major character(s): Diana Talbot, Debutante; Lord John Drayton, Spy, Imposter ("Black Domino")
Time period(s): 1810s
Locale(s): England; France

Summary: Diana doesn't think much of wimpish dandy Lord John Drayton, or any of his kind. She only has eyes for and fantasies of the infamous Black Domino, who has been spying against the French for years. Once she meets her hero, she knows he is the love of her life—and she already knows his true identity, or so she thinks. Of course, she is wrong—and that creates a problem for Lord John that only love can solve. Appealing characters and plot.

Other books you might like:
Mary Chase Comstock, *An Impetuous Miss*, 1993
Mary Kingsley, *The Rake's Reward*, 1991
Melinda McRae, *An Unlikely Attraction*, 1991
Baroness Orczy, *The Scarlet Pimpernel*, 1905
   classic double identity story

Amanda Quick, *Seduction*, 1990

319

LENORE CARROLL

The Heart Remembers
(New York: Harper, 1993)

Story type: Contemporary
Major character(s): Jessica Shelby, Scientist (hydrologist); Kip Kilpatrick, Photojournalist
Time period(s): 1960s; 1990s
Locale(s): New Mexico; Wyoming

Summary: When Jess and Kip first meet in the Sixties, each has a career to pursue. So despite being in love, they each go their separate ways. The years bring happiness and pain to each of them, but eventually they come full circle and are together once more.

Other books you might like:
Marilyn Cunningham, *Seasons of the Heart*, 1992
Susan Kyle, *Escapade*, 1992
Kathleen Gilles Seidel, *Maybe This Time*, 1990
Deborah Smith, *Miracle*, 1991
LaVyrle Spencer, *Bittersweet*, 1990

320

MARISSA CARROLL

Loveknot
(Toronto: Harlequin, 1993)

Story type: Contemporary
Series: Tyler
Major character(s): Alyssa Barron, Widow(er); Ed Wochek, Widow(er), Businessman
Time period(s): 1990s
Locale(s): Tyler, Wisconsin

Summary: Alyssa Barron and Ed Wochek's love story provides the central focus for this, the concluding volume in the Tyler series. In a story that ties up a number of loose ends, Ed's stepson tracks down the "missing man," and everyone learns what happened on the night that changed so many lives. The Timberlake Lodge is restored, and a murderer is identified. Heartwarming.

Other books you might like:
Kathy Clark, *Stand by Your Man*, 1993
Nancy Martin, *Monkey Wrench*, 1992
Karren Radko, *Dreams and Wishes*, 1993
Lass Small, *A Nothing Town in Texas*, 1991

321

SUSAN CARROLL (Pseudonym of Susan Coppula)

The Bishop's Daughter
(New York: Fawcett, 1990)

Story type: Regency

Major character(s): Kathryn Towers, Gentlewoman; Harcourt "Harry" Arundel, Nobleman, Military Personnel (supposedly deceased)
Time period(s): 1810s
Locale(s): England

Summary: When Lord Harry Arundel shows up at his own funeral, he shocks his family and discovers, much to his delight, that the object of his true affections, the appropriately proper bishop's daughter Kathryn Towers, cares for him after all. This is all the motivation Hellfire Harry needs to reform his profligate ways. Aided by Kathryn's grandmother, he begins a campaign to win Kathryn's approval and her heart as well.

Other books you might like:
Jo Beverley, *The Stanforth Secrets: A Regency Romantic Intrigue*, 1989
Anne Caldwell, *Scandal's Darling*, 1991
Georgette Heyer, *Powder and Patch*, 1930
Georgette Heyer, *The Unknown Ajax*, 1960
Stephanie Stevens, *Defiant Angel*, 1989
    sensual

322

SUSAN CARROLL (Pseudonym of Susan Coppula)

Christmas Belles

(New York: Fawcett, 1992)

Story type: Regency; Holiday Themes
Major character(s): Chloe Waverly, Debutante, Ward; William Trent, Military Personnel (navy captain), Guardian
Time period(s): 1810s
Locale(s): England

Summary: When Captain William Trent, the man who has inherited their family estate, gallantly proposes a marriage of convenience to the eldest of the four Waverly sisters, young Chloe decides she can't let her sister sacrifice herself that way, so she sets out to stop the marriage — and ends up a bride herself. Christmas warmth and magic in a Regency setting.

Other books you might like:
Mary Balogh, *Christmas Beau*, 1992
Sandra Heath, *A Christmas Courtship*, 1990
Georgette Heyer, *The Convenient Marriage*, 1934
Carla Kelly, *Marian's Christmas Wish*, 1989

323

SUSAN CARROLL (Pseudonym of Susan Coppula)

Mistress of Mischief

(New York: Fawcett, 1992)

Story type: Regency
Major character(s): Frederica Raincliff, Widow(er) (impoverished), Noblewoman; Max Warfield, Nobleman
Time period(s): 1810s
Locale(s): London, England

Summary: Homeless and penniless, beautiful Frederica decides she can become rich at London's gaming tables. Unfortunately, the cards say otherwise. But when she decides to become a rich man's mistress and sets her sights on her distant cousin Max, she has much better results. Witty, charming, and just plain fun.

Other books you might like:
Carla Kelly, *Miss Billings Treads the Boards*, 1992

324

SUSAN CARROLL

The Painted Veil

(New York: Fawcett Gold Medal, 1995)

Story type: Historical/Regency
Major character(s): Lady Anne Fairhaven, Noblewoman, Widow(er); Mandell, Nobleman (Marquis of Mandell)
Time period(s): 1810s
Locale(s): London, England

Summary: Anne Fairhaven will do just about anything to regain custody of her young daughter, even accept help from the infamous libertine, the Marquis of Mandell. A vicious killer and shocking secrets add interest to this somewhat dark and dangerous historical set in Regency England. Passionate and nicely written.

Other books you might like:
Mary Balogh, *Deceived*, 1993
Christina Dodd, *Move Heaven and Earth*, 1995
    wounded hero
Sarah Eagle, *Lady Vengeance*, 1995
Anita Mills, *Secret Nights*, 1993
Mary Jo Putney, *Petals in the Storm*, 1993

325

ANGELA CARSON

Sweet Illusion

(Toronto: Harlequin, 1990)

Story type: Contemporary/Innocent
Major character(s): Marion Rowley, Nurse, Widow(er); Luke Challoner, Doctor (Surgeon)
Time period(s): 1980s
Locale(s): England

Summary: Marion Rowley, single parent and nurse, thinks surgeon Luke Challoner is rigid and unsympathetic until he helps treat her young son who was injured in an accident. Love grows in spite of a multitude of misunderstandings.

Other books you might like:
Kasey Michaels, *His Chariot Awaits*, 1990
Alice Sharpe, *A Garland of Love*, 1990
Marcine Smith, *Just Neighbors*, 1990
Lee Stafford, *A Song in the Wilderness*, 1990
Diana Whitney, *A Liberated Man*, 1990

326

ANNEE CARTIER

Tradewinds

(New York: Pinnacle, 1995)

Story type: Historical/Exotic
Major character(s): Golden Gaverly, Orphan; Mast Iverson, Sea Captain
Time period(s): 18th century (1782)
Locale(s): Grand Abaco Island, Bahamas

Summary: Captain Mast Iverson has vowed that no woman will ever board his ship; but in order to rescue the daughter of an old friend, he is forced to break his own rule. Unprepared for the untamed and beautiful Golden Graverly, Mast begins to wonder if he is losing his mind or just his heart.

Other books you might like:
Elaine Barbieri, *Only for Love*, 1994
Elizabeth DeLancey, *Sea of Dreams*, 1992
Stef Ann Holm, *King of the Pirates*, 1994
Meagan McKinney, *Till Dawn Tames the Night*, 1991
Kathleen E. Woodiwiss, *Shanna*, 1977
　　1970s-type historical

327

JACKIE CASTO

Daughter of Destiny

(New York: Leisure, 1990)

Story type: Futuristic
Major character(s): Esme, Telepath; Captain Raul, Spaceship Captain
Time period(s): Indeterminate Future
Locale(s): Earth; Planet—Imaginary

Summary: Telepathic, Earth-born Esme must help fulfill the Master's Prophecy in which two remnants of mankind (one on Earth, one scattered among the stars) come together to fight an ultimate evil. Love blossoms between Esme and spaceship Captain Raul in spite of their wariness and suspicions of each other. Follows *Dreams of Destiny*.

Other books you might like:
Amanda Glass, *Shield's Lady*, 1989
Johanna Lindsey, *Warrior's Woman*, 1990
Kathleen Morgan, *The Knowing Crystal*, 1991
Patricia Roenbuck, *Golden Temptation*, 1991
Janelle Taylor, *Moondust and Madness*, 1986

328

KIMBERLY CATES (Pseudonym of Kim Ostrum Bush)

Crown of Dreams

(New York: Pocket, 1993)

Story type: Historical/Georgian
Major character(s): Devlin Chastain, Noblewoman; Myles Farrington, Nobleman (defender of Prince Charles)
Time period(s): 1740s (1745)
Locale(s): England

Summary: Devlin and Myles have been raised as siblings and have been close all their lives—so when Myles is branded as a traitor and forced to flee, Devlin ends up going with him. Naturally, she expects her fiance, politically oriented Braden Tracey, to rescue her; and just as naturally, Myles knows he won't—because Braden can't "afford" to marry a compromised woman. The old bond between Devlin and Myles eventually develops into something more, and as they battle their common enemies, they strengthen their love at the same time. High adventure.

Other books you might like:
Catherine Coulter, *Night Shadow*, 1989
Catherine Linden, *Highland Flame*, 1991
　　Renaissance political intrigue
Kat Martin, *Gypsy Lord*, 1992
Casey Stuart, *Highland Rogue*, 1991

329

KIMBERLY CATES
CHRISTINA DODD, Co-Author
DEBORAH MARTIN, Co-Author
ANNE STUART, Co-Author

One Night with a Rogue

(New York: St. Martin's, 1995)

Story type: Anthology; Historical
Time period(s): 18th century; 19th century
Locale(s): England; United States

Summary: This wide-ranging collection of sensual historical novellas features stories in which the protagonists spend one night together—and their lives are changed as a result. Included are "Wild Enchantment" by Kimberly Cates, "The Lady and the Tiger" by Christina Dodd, "Too Wicked for Heaven" by Deborah Martin, and "Dangerous Touch" by Anne Stuart.

Other books you might like:
Jo Beverley, *Tempting Fortune*, 1995
Patricia Potter, *Diablo*, 1996
Anne Stuart, *Highland Fling*, 1993
　　anthology/four tales of Scotland
Anne Stuart, *To Love a Dark Lord*, 1994
Kathleen E. Woodiwiss, *Three Weddings and a Kiss*, 1995
　　anthology

330

KIMBERLY CATES (Pseudonym of Kim Ostrum Bush)

Only Forever

(New York: Pocket, 1992)

Story type: Historical/American West
Major character(s): Ashleen O'Shea, Religious (novice), Heiress; Garret MacQuade, Guide
Time period(s): 1840s (1847)
Locale(s): Ireland; Texas

Summary: When renegade novice Ashleen O'Shea steals the convent chalice in order to save the children from the workhouse, she begins a journey that will take her, together with four orphans, from Ireland to America and into the Texas west in search of a home for them all. Guided by revenge-driven Garret MacQuade, Ashleen perseveres and wins not only the home she seeks, but the love of her life, as well. Emotional, passionate, and funny.

Other books you might like:
Rebecca Brandewyne, *Heartland*, 1990
Deborah Camp, *Black-Eyed Susan*, 1990
Rebecca Paisley, *Moonlight and Magic*, 1990
Lynda Trent, *Heaven's Embrace*, 1990

331

KIMBERLY CATES (Pseudonym of Kim Ostrum Bush)

The Raider's Bride
(New York: Pocket, 1994)

Story type: Historical/Colonial America
Major character(s): Emily Rose d'Autrecourt, Spy (British), Seamstress; Ian Blackheath, Spy, Rake
Time period(s): 18th century
Locale(s): Virginia, American Colonies
Summary: Believing Ian to be her Patriot counterpart, British spy Emily d'Autrecourt becomes a caregiver to a young foundling left on Ian's doorstep—and finds herself falling in love with her enemy. Secrets, surprises, and transformations are part of this warm and tender story.

Other books you might like:
Barbara Cummings, *Rebel Wildfire*, 1992
Lucy Elliot, *The Claim*, 1992
Judith E. French, *Scarlet Ribbons*, 1991
Gretchen Genet, *Winds of Glory*, 1993
Robin Maderich, *Faith and Honor*, 1989

332

KIMBERLY CATES (Pseudonym of Kim Ostrum Bush)

To Catch the Flame
(New York: Pocket, 1991)

Story type: Historical/Georgian
Major character(s): Isabeau "Beau" De Burgh, Highwayman (Devil's Flame), Noblewoman; Griffin Stone, Nobleman
Time period(s): 1760s (1768)
Locale(s): England
Summary: Lord Griffin Stone gains more than is taken when he is robbed by the infamous highwayman, Devil's Flame, and then proceeds to take the Flame (Isabeau De Burgh) home with him. But when he tries to turn the termagant into the lady she actually is, he finds the Flame can burn as well as warm his heart. A funny, heartwarming tale reminiscent of Pygmalion.

Other books you might like:
Mallory Burgess, *Ballenrose*, 1991
Shirlee Busbee, *Whisper to Me of Love*, 1991
Georgette Heyer, *The Black Moth*, 1921
  Regency treatment
Louisa Rawlings, *Promise of Summer*, 1989
Myra Rowe, *Cypress Moon*, 1990

333

CLEO CHADWICK

A Midsummer Night's Kiss
(New York: Zebra, 1991)

Story type: Regency
Major character(s): Aurelia "Lia" Maudsley, Gentlewoman; Breverton Dayne, Nobleman, Government Official
Time period(s): 1800s (1803)
Locale(s): Brighton, England
Summary: Dashing Lord Dayne comes to Brighton to investigate the possible treason of a deceased government agent and ends up falling in love with the quite extraordinary Miss Aurelia Maudsley, the daughter of his suspect. Accidental midnight swims, secret documents, and highly unorthodox relatives are all part of this intriguing and somewhat unusual Regency.

Other books you might like:
Sarah Eagle, *The Reluctant Suitor*, 1991
Emily Hendrickson, *Miss Wyndham's Escapade*, 1990
Mary Kingsley, *The Rake's Reward*, 1991
Joan Overfield, *Bride's Leap*, 1991
Patricia Veryan, *Logic of the Heart*, 1991

334

ELIZABETH CHADWICK

Virgin Fire
(New York: Leisure, 1991)

Story type: Historical/American West
Major character(s): Jessica Harte, Scholar; Travis Parnell, Businessman (oil man), Rancher
Time period(s): 1900s
Locale(s): Texas
Summary: Travis Parnell seeks to avenge the suicide of his father by marrying the daughter of the woman he considers responsible, but his plans are complicated by a greedy, vindictive woman—and the fact that he has fallen in love with his new wife. Good historical detail about the beginnings of the oil industry in Texas.

Other books you might like:
Nancy Bush, *Jesse's Renegade*, 1991
Edna Ferber, *Giant*, 1952
  Texas classic
Catherine Hart, *Forever Gold*, 1990
Sara Orwig, *Favors of the Rich*, 1991
  contemporary oil industry

335

DANETTE CHARTIER

Stolen Fire
(New York: Zebra, 1993)

Story type: Historical/Victorian
Major character(s): Cianda d'Rouchert, Thief (jewel); Drake Weston, Sea Captain; Godfrey Thorne, Thief

Time period(s): 1850s
Locale(s): England
Summary: Forced into stealing by the villainous Godfrey Thorne who holds her brother hostage, Cianda literally collapses into the arms of Drake Weston, a man in pursuit of the thieving ring. Frightened, she escapes, but he continues the pursuit and eventually convinces her to help him get Godfrey. Trust doesn't come easily to Cianda, but Drake eventually manages to prove both his trust and his love.

Other books you might like:
Patricia Gaffney, *Thief of Hearts*, 1990
Meagan McKinney, *Till Dawn Tames the Night*, 1991
Kay McMahon, *Betray the Night*, 1991
Linda Lael Miller, *Angelfire*, 1989

336

LINDSAY CHASE

Honor

(New York: Diamond, 1994)

Story type: Historical/Mainstream
Major character(s): Honor Davis, Lawyer; Nevada LaRouche, Businessman
Time period(s): 1890s (1894-1897)
Locale(s): New York, New York

Summary: Although she knows how difficult becoming a lawyer will be, Honor Elliot perseveres, aided by fellow student and eventual husband, Robert. Once they are married, however, Robert's career comes first and Honor's practice just limps along. However, all that changes dramatically when the infamous Nevada LaRouche comes into her life and she is forced to decide how important integrity and excellence really are to her.

Other books you might like:
Elaine Barbieri, *Tattered Silk*, 1991
Sandra Bregman, *Reach for the Dream*, 1990
Karen Harper, *The Wings of Morning*, 1993
    another honorable woman
Belva Plain, *Evergreen*, 1992
Laura Simon, *Dreams of Paradise*, 1991

337

LINDSAY CHASE

The Vow

(New York: Diamond, 1992)

Story type: Historical/Victorian America; Saga
Major character(s): Hannah Whitby Shaw, Spouse (reluctant); Reiver Shaw, Businessman (silk manufacturer); Samuel Shaw, Artist
Time period(s): 1840s
Locale(s): Coldwater, Connecticut

Summary: Forced by circumstances into a marriage of convenience to a wealthy silk merchant who is devoted to his work — and his mistress, Hannah sets out to find happiness on her own terms — and she eventually does — with her husband's brother. A story of passion, ambition, and enduring love.

Other books you might like:
Elaine Barbieri, *Tattered Silk*, 1991
Sandra Bregman, *Reach for the Dream*, 1990
Rosalind Laker, *Banners of Silk*, 1981
Rosalind Laker, *The Silver Touch*, 1987
Lucy Taylor, *Avenue of Dreams*, 1990

338

LORETTA CHASE (Pseudonym of Loretta Chekani)

Captives of the Night

(New York: Avon, 1994)

Story type: Historical
Major character(s): Leila Beaumont, Artist (painter); Ismal Delvina, Royalty (prince), Nobleman (Comte d'Esmond); Francis Beaumont, Crime Victim (murder victim)
Time period(s): 1810s; 1820s (1819-1829)
Locale(s): England; Italy; France

Summary: After her father's murder, Leila is saved by Francis Beaumont. She marries him, only to see him murdered 10 years later. Determined to find the killer, she seeks the help of the enigmatic Comte d'Esmond—and ends up finding more mysteries and secrets than she had bargained for. Passionate and intriguing.

Other books you might like:
Mary Balogh, *The Notorious Rake*, 1992
Jane Feather, *Valentine*, 1994
Ruth Langan, *Deception*, 1993
Amanda Quick, *Reckless*, 1992
Amanda Quick, *Rendezvous*, 1992

339

LORETTA CHASE (Pseudonym of Loretta Chekani)

The Lion's Daughter

(New York: Avon, 1992)

Story type: Historical/Regency
Major character(s): Esme Brentmor, Noblewoman; Varian St. George, Nobleman, Rake
Time period(s): 1810s (1818)
Locale(s): Italy; Albania

Summary: An arrogant, decadent rake and a fiery, independent hoyden join forces in locating her missing father and rescuing her young cousin from kidnappers — and end up finding love amid political turmoil and diverse family expectations. Intriguing characters, fast-paced action, and charming dialogue.

Other books you might like:
Mary Balogh, *The Notorious Rake*, 1992
Charlene Cross, *A Heart So Innocent*, 1990
Kathryn Kramer, *Lady Rogue*, 1991
Amanda Quick, *Reckless*, 1992

340

LORETTA CHASE

Lord of Scoundrels

(New York: Avon, 1995)

Story type: Historical
Major character(s): Jessica Trent, Spinster; Sebastian de Ath Ballister, Nobleman (Marquess of Dain), Rake
Time period(s): 1820s (1828)
Locale(s): London, England; Paris, France

Summary: Jessica, distraught that her brother has taken up with the infamous Sebastian, Lord Dain, determines to rescue him from debauchery. Her reaction to the self-proclaimed ''Devil,'' and his to this prim spinster cause sparks and a battle of wits. Malevolent outsiders add to the suspenseful, emotional mix. Unusual, well-done, and laced with lively wit.

Other books you might like:
Mary Balogh, *The Notorious Rake*, 1992
Arnette Lamb, *The Betrothal*, 1992
   witty battle of opposites
Mary Jo Putney, *Thunder and Roses*, 1993
   darker treatment/another self-sacrificing heroine
Amanda Quick, *Mistress*, 1994
   another lively heroine

341

SANDRA CHASTAIN

Jasmine and Silk

(Toronto: Harlequin, 1993)

Story type: Historical/Antebellum American South
Major character(s): Amanda Caden, Plantation Owner; Rush Randolph, Businessman
Time period(s): 1790s
Locale(s): Georgia

Summary: After the Revolution, Amanda fights for her Georgia home, but her greedy uncle holds all the cards and will try arson, sabotage, and fraud to get both Amanda and her land. She tries being a highwayman but when that fails, she looks around for a rich man to marry. Her hero turns out to be her uncle's business partner, Rush Randolph: but it takes Amanda a long time to come to the realization that all men aren't like her uncle and that Rush really is the man of her dreams. Fast-paced, good dialogue.

Other books you might like:
Thea Devine, *Southern Seduction*, 1991
Nicole Jordan, *Moonwitch*, 1991
Karen Robards, *Morning Song*, 1989
Kathleen E. Woodiwiss, *The Flame and the Flower*, 1972

342

SANDRA CHASTAIN

Penthouse Suite

(New York: Bantam, 1990)

Story type: Contemporary

Major character(s): Kate Weston, Maintenance Worker (Free spirit); Max Sorrenson, Hotel Owner
Time period(s): 1980s
Locale(s): Florida (Gulf Coast)

Summary: Kate Weston is a free-spirited maintenance person intent on living an adventurous life. Max Sorrenson is a wealthy hotel owner determined to live a life relatively devoid of risk. But when Kate arrives to fix the shower in his suite and finds him clad only in a towel, the attraction is instantaneous and they must both reassess their goals and feelings.

Other books you might like:
Dixie Browning, *Beginner's Luck*, 1989
Anne Caviliere, *Squeeze Play*, 1989
Sara Chance, *With a Little Spice*, 1989
Sherryl Woods, *One Touch of Moondust*, 1989

343

SANDRA CHASTAIN

Rebel in Silk

(New York: Bantam, 1994)

Story type: Historical/American West
Series: Once upon a Time
Major character(s): Dallas Banning, Editor (newspaper), Detective (former); Jake Silver, Rancher
Time period(s): 1870s
Locale(s): Willow Creek, Wyoming

Summary: After Dallas Banning's brother is murdered, she tries, using his newspaper, to keep peace between the immigrants and the ranchers. At the same time, keeping her former detective status and abilities a secret, she is searching for his killers. Rancher Jake Silver is both dangerous and desirable; and when she really needs him, he comes through. Highly sensual.

Other books you might like:
Phoebe Fitzjames, *Oklahoma Angel*, 1993
   highly sensual/fast paced
Jane Kidder, *Passion's Bargain*, 1994
   another assertive heroine/sexy
Linda Lael Miller, *Emma and the Outlaw*, 1991
Patricia Potter, *Renegade*, 1993

344

SANDRA CHASTAIN

The Redhead and the Preacher

(New York: Bantam, 1995)

Story type: Historical/American West
Major character(s): McKenzie Kathryn ''Macky'' Calhoun, Fugitive, Imposter (preacher's wife); John Lee Brandon, Imposter (preacher), Avenger
Time period(s): 1860s
Locale(s): West; Heaven, Kansas

Summary: When Macky Calhoun accidentally robs the local bank, she takes the money and runs—right into the life of ''Preacher Adams,'' a man who is set on avenging the deaths of his family. But things become even more interesting when they are taken for the new minister and his wife by the townspeople of Heaven, Kansas and then they must act the part. A pair of likable protagonists on the run, a situation just made for laughter, and lively dialogue produce a delightful, fast-paced, warm romance.

Other books you might like:
Katherine Compton, *Outlaw Bride*, 1991
Lori Copeland, *Sweet Hannah Rose*, 1991
Linda Lael Miller, *Daniel's Bride*, 1992
Pamela Morsi, *Heaven Sent*, 1990
Maggie Osborne, *The Seduction of Samantha Kincade*, 1995

345

SANDRA CHASTAIN

Summer of the Soldiers
(New York: Pinnacle, 1993)

Story type: Contemporary/Mainstream; Saga
Major character(s): Margie Raines, Young Woman; Glory Winslow, Young Woman; Jo Ellen Dixon, Young Woman
Time period(s): 1950s; 1980s (1954-1980)
Locale(s): Winslow, Georgia; Galilee, Georgia

Summary: In 1954 when three busloads of soldiers from the Korean War are invited to Galilee, Georgia, for a picnic, four girls make decisions about sexual experiences that forever shape their lives. Novel of life, death, love, and hurt among women whose lives are forever intertwined.

Other books you might like:
Lois Battle, *The Past Is Another Country*, 1992
Lois Battle, *War Brides*, 1982
Gila Berkowitz, *The Brides*, 1992
Katherine Sinclair, *Far Horizons*, 1991
   historical
Jacqueline Susann, *Valley of the Dolls*, 1966

346

SANDRA CHASTAIN

Sweetwater
(New York: Warner, 1990)

Story type: Historical/Victorian America
Major character(s): Portia MacIntosh, Actress (in Shakespearean troupe); Daniel Logan, Detective—Private (Pinkerton agent)
Time period(s): 1890s (1890)
Locale(s): Sweetwater, Georgia

Summary: When Portia's father loses their Shakespearean theatre company in a card game to wealthy Pinkerton agent Daniel Logan, it takes drastic measures on Portia's part to get the troupe back. With situations and plot twists reminiscent of Shakespeare's comedies, this funny and charming tale leads the lovers on a merry and convoluted chase before allowing them all to be happily in love with the right people.

Other books you might like:
Rita Balkey, *Passion's Fury*, 1989
Janice Bennett, *A Tempting Miss*, 1989
   Regency

Betty Brooks, *Wild Magnolia*, 1990
Elizabeth Kary, *Midnight Lace*, 1990
   English setting
Joan Smith, *Lovers' Vows*, 1981
   Regency

347

MARION CHESNEY

The Desirable Duchess
(New York: Fawcett, 1993)

Story type: Regency
Major character(s): Alice Lacey, Noblewoman, Debutante; Sir Gerald Warby, Nobleman; Duke of Farrant, Nobleman
Time period(s): 1810s
Locale(s): England

Summary: Kept apart by illness, "grand tours," and uncooperative parents, Alice Lacey tries to wait for her love, Gerald Warby, but eventually succumbs to the attentions of the Duke of Ferrant. A marriage of convenience soon follows; but when Gerald returns—and the Duke strays—Alice is faced with some difficult choices. Witty and fast-paced.

Other books you might like:
Emily Hendrickson, *A Scandalous Suggestion*, 1991
Georgette Heyer, *The Convenient Marriage*, 1934
Barbara Metzger, *The Luck of the Devil*, 1991
Eva Rutland, *Gretna Bride*, 1993

348

MARION CHESNEY

The Dreadful Debutante
(New York: Fawcett Crest, 1995)

Story type: Regency
Major character(s): Mirabelle "Mira" Markham, Debutante; Marquess Rupert of Grantley, Nobleman; Charles Devere, Nobleman
Time period(s): 1810s
Locale(s): England

Summary: Considered a failure by her father (primarily because she was born a girl rather than a boy), spirited Mira heads for London and her debut. Despite jealousy, treachery, and a few scandalous social disasters, she ends up making the match of the Season. Light and frothy.

Other books you might like:
Mary Chase Comstock, *An Impetuous Miss*, 1993
Suzanne Enoch, *Angel's Devil*, 1995
Sandra Heath, *Lucy's Christmas Angel*, 1995
Georgette Heyer, *Cotillion*, 1953
Emily Hendrickson, *The Rake and the Redhead*, 1994

349

MARION CHESNEY

The First Rebellion

(New York: Fawcett, 1989)

Story type: Regency
Series: Maria Waverly's Family Accounts
Major character(s): Fanny Waverly, Foundling (Adopted; marriageable young la); Earl of Tredair, Nobleman (Earl; bachelor)
Time period(s): 1810s (Regency period)
Locale(s): England

Summary: Raised by their adopted mother to be ardent feminists, the three Waverly sisters knew little about men—until the Earl of Tredair came into their lives and swept Fanny off her feet. Witty and typically "regency."

Other books you might like:
Clare Darcy, *Lydia: Or, Love in Town*, 1973
Georgette Heyer, *Arabella*, 1949
Georgette Heyer, *Friday's Child*, 1944
Eva Rutland, *The Vicar's Daughter*, 1989
Amanda Scott, *The Dauntless Miss Wingrave*, 1989

350

MARION CHESNEY

Silken Bonds

(New York: Fawcett, 1989)

Story type: Regency
Series: Maria Waverly's Family Accounts
Major character(s): Frederica Waverly, Foundling (Adopted; marriageable young la); Lord Harry Danger, Nobleman
Time period(s): 1810s (Regency period)

Summary: The middle adopted daughter of a wealthy, well-educated family, Frederica thinks Lord Harry Danger is not serious about her—but when he takes her to meet his mother, she begins to wonder. A witty romp.

Other books you might like:
Marian Devon, *Fortunes of the Heart*, 1989
Georgette Heyer, *Faro's Daughter*, 1942
Georgette Heyer, *The Unknown Ajax*, 1959
Marian Lorraine, *The Mischievous Spinster*, 1983
Phyllis Taylor Pianka, *The Tart Shoppe*, 1989

351

JANE MCBRIDE CHOATE

Badge of Love

(New York: Avalon Books, 1989)

Story type: Contemporary/Innocent
Major character(s): Kathleen O'Rourke, Police Officer (Sheriff); Kyle Hobart, Government Official (State Crime Commissioner)
Time period(s): 1980s
Locale(s): Hennessey, Colorado

Summary: Ever since Kathleen O'Rourke's brother was killed by a drunk driver and she assumed his duties as sheriff in the small town of Hennessey, she has made it a point to keep drunk drivers off the road. But when the handsome brother of an exceptionally unrepentant drunk driver asks her to dinner, she has to fight her attraction to him and face the possiblity that he may be using her to win his brother's release.

Other books you might like:
Arlene James, *Dream of a Lifetime*, 1989
Jan McDaniel, *Angels in the Sand*, 1989
Kasey Michaels, *His Chariot Awaits*, 1990
Alice Sharpe, *Just One More Secret*, 1990
Constance Walker, *One Perfect Springtime*, 1989

352

JANE MCBRIDE CHOATE

Blessings of the Heart

(New York: Avalon, 1994)

Story type: Contemporary/Innocent
Major character(s): Carla Stevens, Religious (pastor), Activist (for the homeless); Sam Hastings, Architect, Political Figure
Time period(s): 1990s
Locale(s): Saratoga, New York

Summary: When young, activist pastor Carla Stevens decides to help the homeless, no one, not even architect and city council candidate Sam Hastings, can stand in her way. Eventually, of course, the two do come to an agreement—and they fall in love in the process. Light and innocent.

Other books you might like:
Marjorie Everitt, *Somewhere Near Paradise*, 1992
Debbie Macomber, *Rainy Day Kisses*, 1990
Debbie Macomber, *A Season of Angels*, 1993
 fantasy aspects
Marcia Martin, *Southern Storms*, 1992
 another heroine with a cause/sensual
Audrey McConachie, *No Blueprint for Love*, 1992

353

JUDY CHRISTENBERRY

Moonlight Charade

(New York: Jove, 1991)

Story type: Regency
Major character(s): Katherine St. Cloud, Gentlewoman (impoverished); Daniel, Hero (stranger from Montreal)
Time period(s): 1810s
Locale(s): England

Summary: To avoid having her estate revert to the Crown for want of a male heir, Katherine St. Cloud decides to claim a stranger from Canada as her long lost cousin, Daniel. Love, of course, has a way of interfering in this nicely conceived plan (as do certain mysterious events); but Katherine and Daniel prove equal to the challenge. Intriguing and lively.

Other books you might like:
Rosemary Edghill, *The Ill-Bred Bride*, 1990

Carla Kelly, *Libby's London Merchant*, 1991
Leslie Lynn, *The Rake's Redemption*, 1989
Margaret Sebastian, *The Poor Relation*, 1978
Patricia Veryan, *Logic of the Heart*, 1991

354

JUDY CHRISTENBERRY

Susannah's Secret

(New York: Jove, 1993)

Story type: Regency
Major character(s): Susannah Brown, Governess, Widow(er) (Lady Craven in disguise); Lord Nicholas Danvers, Nobleman, Widow(er)
Time period(s): 1810s
Locale(s): England

Summary: In an attempt to hide from her murderous brother-in-law, widow and mother Lady Craven ''becomes'' Susannah Brown, governess, and takes a position in Lord Nicholas Danvers' household. However, when Lord Nicholas wants to marry her, things become complicated. Warm and witty.

Other books you might like:
Jo Beverley, *My Lady Notorious*, 1993
    sensual
Sarah Eagle, *The Marriage Gamble*, 1992
Emily Hendrickson, *Elizabeth's Rake*, 1993
Sheila Simonson, *The Bar Sinister*, 1986
Susan Sizemore, *My First Duchess*, 1993

355

AMY CHRISTOPHER

Captive Kiss

(New York: Zebra, 1992)

Story type: Historical/Colonial America
Major character(s): Rachel Linton, Captive, Spinster; White Wolf, Indian (half-French)
Time period(s): 1700s (1704)
Locale(s): Deerfield, Massachusetts; New England; Quebec, Canada

Summary: Not only is young spinster Rachel Linton taken from her Massachusetts village by Indians, but now she has two brothers fighting over her—one wants her *scalp*, the other simply wants *her*. The journey to Mont Real, complete with wolves, bears, and forest idylls, brings White Wolf and Rachel together—but the dangers and pain they faced in the wild can't begin to compare with what they will have to endure first in White Wolf's village and then in Quebec. Exciting, nicely-plotted, and filled with interesting historical detail.

Other books you might like:
Emily Carmichael, *Visions of the Heart*, 1990
Judith E. French, *Lovestorm*, 1990
Judith E. French, *Moonfeather*, 1990
Dana Ransom, *Wild Savage Love*, 1990
Lynette Vinet, *Savage Deception*, 1989

356

AMY CHRISTOPHER

Rebel's Captive

(New York: Zebra, 1991)

Story type: Historical/American Revolution
Major character(s): Laura Hadley, Captive; Colby Roth, Military Personnel (captain in American Army)
Time period(s): 1770s (1775)
Locale(s): Boston, Massachusetts, American Colonies; Nassau, Bahamas

Summary: Won by rebel Captain Colby Roth in a card game, Laura Hadley runs away—only to end up headed for Nassau with the same man she had been trying to elude. The starlit nights and balmy breezes work their magic and the pair become lovers; but when treachery and suspicion rear their ugly heads, Laura and Colby's growing love is put to the test.

Other books you might like:
Caryn Cameron, *Liberty's Lady*, 1990
Christine Dorsey, *Traitor's Embrace*, 1990
Judith E. French, *Scarlet Ribbons*, 1989
Maura Seger, *Fortune's Tide*, 1990
    England wins the war
Lynette Vinet, *Pirate's Bride*, 1989

357

CATHLEEN CLARE (Pseudonym of Catherine Toothman)

Felicia

(New York: Avon, 1993)

Story type: Regency
Major character(s): Lady Felicia Harding, Noblewoman (Daughter of duke), Debutante; Lord Shannon Carlington, Nobleman (Earl of Carlington), Rake (somewhat reformed)
Time period(s): 1810s (1816)
Locale(s): London, England

Summary: Blaming the interference of the very proper Earl of Carlington for the abrupt curtailment of her reckless escapades, Lady Felicia Harding goes to watch the fun when the Earl's friends play a prank on him by advertising for a wife. Naturally, neither realizes that the Earl really will end up with a wife — and that wife will be Felicia! Quick-witted Regency fun.

Other books you might like:
Georgette Heyer, *These Old Shades*, 1926
Sheila O'Hallion, *The Captured Heart*, 1991
Amanda Quick, *Surrender*, 1990
    sensual
Irene Saunders, *The Reluctant Bride*, 1986
Joan Smith, *Madcap Miss*, 1990

358

CATHLEEN CLARE (Pseudonym of Catherine Toothman)

The Mistress of Mishap
(New York: Avon, 1992)

Story type: Regency
Major character(s): Ellen Trevanye, Spinster; Harry Singleton, Nobleman (Marquess of Singleton)
Time period(s): 1810s
Locale(s): England

Summary: Ellen Trevayne's beauty is surpassed only by her clumsiness; so when she sets her sights on the Marquess of Singleton, the mishaps only worsen. Not only is she clumsy, but her malady seems to be catching! Everytime she is around, the Marquess seems to make a misstep. Is he losing his mind or merely his heart? Light Regency fun.

Other books you might like:
Rita Boucher, *The Scandalous Schoolmistress*, 1992
Julie Caille, *A Valentine's Day Fancy*, 1992
Emily Hendrickson, *A Scandalous Suggestion*, 1991
Melinda McRae, *A Highly Respected Widow*, 1992
Joan Overfield, *Bride's Leap*, 1991

359

KATHY CLARK

Sight Unseen
(New York: Toronto: Harlequin, 1990)

Story type: Contemporary
Major character(s): Nicki Chandler, Businesswoman (Boarding stables owner), Psychic; Jake Kelly, Police Officer (Investigator)
Time period(s): 1980s
Locale(s): United States

Summary: Nicki Chandler becomes the chief suspect in the murder of her husband, a murder about which she had a psychic premonition. Investigator Jake Kelly is too realistic to place much stock in extrasensory phenomena; but when he begins to fall in love with Nicki, he is forced to re-evaluate his opinions.

Other books you might like:
Caroline Bourne, *Allegheny Ecstasy*, 1990
    Historical setting/Psychic heroine
Lori Copeland, *Tall Cotton*, 1990
Susan Kyle, *Night Fever*, 1990
Anne Maybury, *Whisper in the Dark*, 1966
Phyllis A. Whitney, *Rainbow in the Mist*, 1989
    Psychic and gothic elements

360

KATHY CLARK

Stand by Your Man
(Toronto: Harlequin, 1993)

Story type: Contemporary
Series: Crystal Creek

Major character(s): Tracey Cotter, Businesswoman; Manny Hernandez, Veterinarian
Time period(s): 1990s
Locale(s): Crystal Creek, Texas

Summary: When Tracey accidentally hits a deer and seeks the help of veterinarian Manny Hernandez, she finds friendship but also encounters prejudice and criminal activity. This small town story brings back series characters in a warm and pleasant situation.

Other books you might like:
Marissa Carroll, *Loveknot*, 1993
Anne Marie Duquette, *On the Line*, 1993
Wendy Martin, *Love on Trial*, 1990
Miriam Pace, *Warm Creature Comforts*, 1991
Thelma Zirkelbach, *A Man of Few Words*, 1993

361

NORMA LEE CLARK

The Infamous Rake
(New York: Signet, 1990)

Story type: Regency
Major character(s): Dilys Bryn, Debutante; Travis Gallant Lord, Nobleman
Time period(s): 1810s
Locale(s): England

Summary: Dilys whirls through her first season pursued by two men—one highly eligible, the other a notorious rake. Well-plotted, witty, and peopled with interesting characters.

Other books you might like:
Clare Darcy, *Georgina*, 1971
Georgette Heyer, *Black Sheep*, 1967
Georgette Heyer, *Sylvester, or the Wicked Uncle*, 1957
Leslie Lynn, *The Rake's Redemption*, 1989
Marlene Suson, *The Errant Earl*, 1989

362

GWEN CLEARY

Colorado Temptation
(New York: Zebra, 1991)

Story type: Historical/American West
Major character(s): Cornelia Lloyd Talbot, Divorced Person; Locke Breckenridge, Neighbor
Time period(s): 1880s (1885)
Locale(s): Denver, Colorado

Summary: Escaping to the Colorado mountains to mend her broken heart and help her brother recover his health, divorcee Cornelia Talbot finds healing and freedom in the arms of her audacious neighbor, Locke Breckenridge. A funny, passionate romance that addresses some rather contemporary topics.

Other books you might like:
Candace Camp, *Rosewood*, 1991
Jude Deveraux, *Mountain Laurel*, 1990
Jill Marie Landis, *Wild Flower*, 1989
Victoria Thompson, *Playing with Fire*, 1990

`363`
GWEN CLEARY

Ecstasy's Masquerade
(New York: Zebra, 1989)

Story type: Historical/American West
Major character(s): Elizabeth "Libby" Hollis, Runaway, Imposter; Cordell Chandler, Rancher (Wealthy)
Time period(s): 1840s
Locale(s): St. Louis, Missouri; Montana

Summary: In order to escape from her lecherous, hypocritical stepfather, Libby agrees to take Katherine Rutcliffe's place and go to Montana to marry wealthy rancher, Cordell Chandler. But deception is not easy, and before long things get very complicated for Libby.

Other books you might like:
Linda Benjamin, *Midnight Chase*, 1989
Mayo Lucas, *Matters of the Heart*, 1988
Louisa Rawlings, *Promise of Summer*, 1989
   Deception in 18th century France
Gina Robins, *Captive Enchantress*, 1989
Janelle Taylor, *Kiss of the Night Wind*, 1989
   Deception in Arizona

`364`
GWEN CLEARY

Nevada Temptation
(New York: Zebra, 1992)

Story type: Historical/American West
Major character(s): Carson Mueller, Businesswoman (former Brewery owner); Kohl Baron, Businessman, Gunfighter (former)
Time period(s): 1880s
Locale(s): Carson City, Nevada

Summary: Convent-bred Carson does wild things to make ends meet after her brewery is stolen from her. Ex-gunfighter Kohl Baron saves her a number of times from kidnappers and other assorted villains, and in the process they fall in love. Sharp dialogue, lots of humor and surprises.

Other books you might like:
Martha Hix, *Wild Texas Rose*, 1990
Robin Leigh, *Rugged Splendor*, 1991
Patricia Rice, *Cheyenne's Lady*, 1989
Ashley Snow, *Dangerous Desire*, 1990

`365`
GWEN CLEARY

Riverboat Temptation
(New York: Zebra, 1992)

Story type: Historical/American West Coast
Major character(s): Columbia Saranoff, Pilot (river pilot), Imposter; Nick Foster, Businessman
Time period(s): 1850s (1857)
Locale(s): Willamette River, Oregon

Summary: When aspiring river pilot Columbia Saranoff disguises herself as a cabin boy to spy on her enemies, she ends up falling in love with the very man who is trying to keep her from her dreams. Storms, Indian attacks, and sabotage serve to keep the action lively in this passionate and intricately plotted romance.

Other books you might like:
Kathleen Kane, *Mountain Dawn*, 1992
Miriam Minger, *Defiant Imposter*, 1992
Patricia Potter, *Rainbow*, 1991
Gina Robins, *Mississippi Mistress*, 1990
   lots of humor

`366`
GWEN CLEARY

Tender Heart
(New York: Zebra, 1994)

Story type: Historical/American West
Major character(s): Hannah Turner, Divorced Person, Imposter (seamstress); Max Garat, Widow(er), Settler
Time period(s): 19th century (late)
Locale(s): West

Summary: Fleeing from an abusive marriage, Hannah Turner is mistaken for a seamstress hired by Max Garat to sew for his children; unfortunately, she knows next to nothing about sewing. She does, however, need a home, and when a snowstorm keeps her from leaving, she and Max have the time to get to know one another and develop a relationship. Max's children and her ex-husband add a few complications, but gentle Hannah is stronger than she seems—and love and family win out in the end. Loving and tender.

Other books you might like:
Kristin Hannah, *Once in Every Life*, 1993
   fantasy elements/"new beginnings"
Robin Lee Hatcher, *Where the Heart Is*, 1993
Victoria Pade, *The Doubletree*, 1990
Libby Sydes, *Until Spring*, 1993
Lynda Trent, *Beloved Wife*, 1992

`367`
GWEN CLEARY

Victoria's Ecstasy
(New York: Zebra, 1990)

Story type: Historical/American West
Major character(s): Victoria Elizabeth Torrington, Rancher; Judge Colston, Rancher
Time period(s): 1880s (1883)
Locale(s): Wyoming; New York, New York

Summary: Headstrong and iron-willed, Victoria intends to claim her half of a Wyoming ranch in spite of the fact that the joint owner, Judge, doesn't think she owns it. Things get off to an interesting start when Judge pretends to be his own foreman, and the pace doesn't let up. Fun, witty, and nicely done characterizations.

Other books you might like:
Dorothy Garlock, *Midnight Blue*, 1989
Martha Hix, *Wild Texas Rose*, 1990
Kathy Lawrence, *Tin Angel*, 1989
Betina Lindsey, *Waltz with the Lady*, 1990
Patricia Rice, *Cheyenne's Lady*, 1989

368
ELAINE COFFMAN

Angel in Marble
(New York: Dell, 1991)

Story type: Historical/American West
Major character(s): Tibbie Buchanan, Health Care Professional (doctor's assistant), Single Parent (unwed mother); Nicholas MacKinnon, Businessman (shipbuilder)
Time period(s): 1840s (1849-1850)
Locale(s): Indianola, Texas

Summary: Loved and left pregnant six years ago, Tibbie Buchanan raises her daughter Beth, helps her physician father care for the ailments of the townspeople, and shuns the company of men—until virile and handsome Nick MacKinnon arrives in town and sets out to win Tibbie's love. Trust doesn't come easily to Tibbie and misunderstandings and the eventual return of Tibbie's first love (and Beth's father) complicate things a bit.

Other books you might like:
Celeste DeBlasis, *The Proud Breed*, 1978
Jude Deveraux, *Mountain Laurel*, 1990
Catherine Lanigan, *A Promise Made*, 1991
LaVyrle Spencer, *Forgiving*, 1990
Jane Toombs, *Midnight Whispers*, 1989

369
ELAINE COFFMAN

Escape Not My Love
(New York: Dell, 1990)

Story type: Historical/American West
Major character(s): Jennifer Baxter, Teacher; Jay Culhane, Lawman (Sheriff)
Time period(s): 1880s (1882)
Locale(s): Texas; Mexico

Summary: Determined to make a difference, Jennifer goes to teach school in Mexico. However, her father is appalled and sends Sheriff Jay Culhane to bring her home. Sparks fly between the two from the very beginning, but love eventually wins out.

Other books you might like:
Lori Copeland, *Fool Me Once*, 1990
JoAnne Jordan, *Destiny's Dream*, 1990
Betina Lindsey, *Waltz with the Lady*, 1990
    Another woman-with-a-cause
Johanna Lindsey, *Savage Thunder*, 1989
JoAnne Redd, *Apache Bride*, 1990

370
ELAINE COFFMAN

For All the Right Reasons
(New York: Dell, 1991)

Story type: Historical/American West
Series: MacKinnon Clan
Major character(s): Katherine Simon, Rancher; Alex MacKinnon, Rancher, Prospector
Time period(s): 1840s (1848-1849)
Locale(s): Brownsville, Texas; California (logging camps)

Summary: Katherine has loved Alex since childhood, even though he loves her sister. This strong, independent woman faces many problems because of her love for a man she believes doesn't love her. Follows *Angel in Marble* in the MacKinnon Brothers Series.

Other books you might like:
Deborah Camp, *Black-Eyed Susan*, 1990
Ann Gabriel, *South Texas*, 1990
Ginna Gray, *Quiet Fires*, 1991
Catherine Lanigan, *A Promise Made*, 1991

371
ELAINE COFFMAN

Heaven Knows
(New York: Fawcett, 1994)

Story type: Historical/Victorian America
Series: MacKinnon Clan
Major character(s): Elizabeth "Lizzie" Robinson, Gentlewoman; Tavis MacKinnon, Artisan (ship designer)
Time period(s): 1850s
Locale(s): Nantucket, Massachusetts; Boston, Massachusetts

Summary: By the time Lizzie Robinson is 11, she knows that Tavis MacKinnon will be hers one day; but for now, all she does is irritate him. Eventually, her wild behavior causes her to be sent to Aunt Phoebe for "refining," and over the next few years she develops a finesse and style that makes Tavis look at her in a new light. However, his first loyalty is to his ship design and a wedding definitely isn't in his plans—until Elizabeth lends a hand. Fast-paced and highly sensual.

Other books you might like:
Emily Bradshaw, *Cactus Blossom*, 1991
    "transformation" story/funny and fast-paced
Virginia Lynn, *River's Dream*, 1991
    another "transformation" story
Pamela Morsi, *Runabout*, 1994
    funny and fast-paced
Rebecca Paisley, *Barefoot Bride*, 1990
    funny and fast-paced
Garda Parker, *Arizona Temptation*, 1992
    funny and fast-paced

372

ELAINE COFFMAN

Somewhere Along the Way
(New York: Dell, 1992)

Story type: Historical/American West
Major character(s): Annabella Stewart, Noblewoman; Ross MacKinnon, Nobleman (Duke of Dunford), Rake
Time period(s): 1840s (1848)
Locale(s): Scotland; Texas

Summary: Hell-raiser Ross MacKinnon needs to escape some angry fathers, so he decides to leave Texas and go to Scotland and to take his rightful place as the Duke of Dunford. However, the transition is not particularly easy — and it is made even less so when he finds himself attracted to the aloof, and engaged, Lady Annabella. However, never one to give up, Ross sets out to win her — and he does, despite family opposition and violence.

Other books you might like:
Stephanie Bartlett, *Highland Rebel*, 1992
Shannon Drake, *Emerald Embrace*, 1991
    Gothic overtones
Patricia Gaffney, *Thief of Hearts*, 1990
Dawn Lindsey, *The Barbarous Scot*, 1992
    Regency treatment

373

ELAINE COFFMAN

A Time for Roses
(New York: Fawcett, 1995)

Story type: Historical/Regency
Major character(s): Natasha Simonov, Orphan, Ward; Lord Trevor Hamilton, Nobleman, Sea Captain
Time period(s): 1810s
Locale(s): England; St. Petersburg, Russia

Summary: Lord Trevor Hamilton arrives from his world travels to find his brother, Tony, on the brink of throwing away his life to marry their young Russian ward, Natasha, instead of his lovely, wealthy fiancee. So in order to give Tony time to come to his senses, Trevor kidnaps Natasha— and proceeds to fall in love with her. But reality intervenes and Natasha is lured home to Russia—and it takes some doing before the lovers can be reunited. A poetic, tragic, and funny rendition of the star-crossed lovers theme.

Other books you might like:
Mary Balogh, *Deceived*, 1993
    similar theme/darker treatment
Susan Johnson, *Golden Paradise*, 1990
    highly sensual/Russian setting
Kasey Michaels, *Legacy of the Rose*, 1992
Anita Mills, *Falling Stars*, 1993
    Russian setting

374

VIRGINIA COFFMAN

The Princess Royal
(New York: Severn House, 1994)

Story type: Historical/Mainstream
Series: Royals
Major character(s): Alexia Kuragin, Royalty (princess); Stefan Elsbach, Diplomat
Time period(s): 1940s (1941)
Locale(s): Lichtenbourg, Fictional Country (fictional European country); Austria

Summary: Europe is in turmoil and Princess-to-be Alexia has fallen in love with the mysterious Stefan. However, Stefan's mother is a friend to the hated Nazis who are in the process of taking over the tiny country of Lichtenbourg. Alexia's concerns are many—Is her marriage only a political tool? Will her father be killed? Will her mother continue in her adultery? A complex, intriguing, and suspenseful romance.

Other books you might like:
Evelyn Anthony, *The Scarlet Thread*, 1990
Taylor Caldwell, *The Final Hour*, 1944
    3rd in the Bouchard/Barber Families Trilogy
Antony Lambton, *Elizabeth and Alexandra*, 1986
Helen MacInnes, *Message From Malaga*, 1971
Evelyn Wilde Meyerson, *Princess in Amber*, 1985
    story of Beatrice, Queen Victoria's daughter

375

CLARE COLEMAN (Pseudonym of Clare Bell)

Daughter of the Reef
(New York: Jove, 1992)

Story type: Historical/Exotic
Major character(s): Tepua, Royalty (chieftain's daughter)
Time period(s): Indeterminate Past
Locale(s): Tahiti, French Polynesia

Summary: Caught in a fierce storm on her way to be married, chieftain's daughter, Tepau, manages to reach the shore of Tahiti, where she must learn to deal with a new people and a new culture, and build a new life. A unique tale in a lush and exotic setting.

Other books you might like:
Jean M. Auel, *Clan of the Cave Bear*, 1980
Sue Harrison, *Mother Earth, Father Sky*, 1990
Betina Lindsey, *The Serpent Beguiled*, 1992
Lynn Armistead McKee, *Woman of the Mists*, 1991
Linda Lay Shuler, *She Who Remembers*, 1990

376

CLARE COLEMAN (Pseudonym of Clare Bell)

Sister of the Sun
(New York: Jove, 1993)

Story type: Historical/Exotic
Major character(s): Tepua, Chieftain; Kiore, Sailor

Time period(s): Indeterminate Past
Locale(s): Pacific Islands

Summary: Returning to her homeland after being held in Tahiti, Tepua finds herself the chief of her tribe. However, a shipwreck brings outside influences to her island paradise and she realizes that things will never be the same again. An authentic, realistic story of love and change. Sequel to *Daughter of the Reef*.

Other books you might like:
Jean M. Auel, *Clan of the Cave Bear*, 1980
Sue Harrison, *Mother Earth, Father Sky*, 1990
Betina Lindsey, *The Serpent Beguiled*, 1992
Lynn Armistead McKee, *Woman of the Mists*, 1991
Linda Lay Shuler, *She Who Remembers*, 1990

377
JACKIE COLLINS

American Star
(New York: Pocket, 1993)

Story type: Contemporary/Mainstream; Saga
Major character(s): Lauren Roberts, Model; Nick Angelo, Actor (film star)
Time period(s): 1960s; 1990s (1969-1992)
Locale(s): Kansas; Hollywood, California; New York, New York

Summary: Nick Angelo, misfit, and Lauren, nice girl, begin their love in high school. However, eventually they are separated by fate, poverty, ambition, and prejudice. They each achieve their dreams in their own way, helped and hurt by the powerful forces that inhabit the fast-paced Hollywood world; but the one thing that endures, is their love for each other. Fast moving, glitzy, and sexy.

Other books you might like:
Julia Fenton, *Blue Orchids*, 1992
Mollie Gregory, *Birthstone*, 1991
Catherine Mann, *Tinsel Town*, 1985
JoAnn Ross, *Secret Sins*, 1990
Candace Schuler, *The Right Direction*, 1993
  short and fast-paced

378
LAUREL COLLINS

The Jade Garden
(New York: Diamond, 1992)

Story type: Historical/Exotic; Gothic
Major character(s): Claire Pennington, Gentlewoman; Jordan Sharpe, Military Personnel (naval officer)
Time period(s): 1860s (1865)
Locale(s): Sag Harbor, New York; Japan; Sri Lanka

Summary: Summoned to Japan by her long-missing father, Claire Pennington escapes a stifling life of genteel spinsterhood and ends up embroiled in a mystery as adventurous and exotic as it is dangerous. Deception, greed, murder, and romance are all part of this fast-paced, finely-detailed historical mystery.

Other books you might like:
Victoria Holt, *The House of a Thousand Lanterns*, 1974
Victoria Holt, *Snare of Serpents*, 1991
Jill Marie Landis, *Jade*, 1991
Maggie Osborne, *Emerald Rain*, 1991
Patricia Potter, *Dragonfire*, 1990

379
KATHERINE COMPTON

Eden's Angel
(New York: Avon, 1990)

Story type: Historical/Exotic
Major character(s): Alena Sutton, Teacher; Zachariah Summerfield, Museum Curator, Adventurer
Time period(s): 1890s (1898)
Locale(s): Amazon Jungle, South America

Summary: Proper teacher Alena Sutton and dashing museum curator Zach Summerfield combine their separate halves of a treasure map and go off to the Amazon jungle to look for wealth—and Alena's lost father (who sent them the maps in the first place). Mystery, passion, and adventure a la Indiana Jones.

Other books you might like:
Nancy Moulton, *Defiant Heart*, 1989
  lost treasure
Leslie O'Grady, *Seek the Wild Shore*, 1989
  Amazon setting
Susan Sackett, *Passion's Golden Fire*, 1989
  Chichen Itza
Janelle Taylor, *Whispered Kisses*, 1990
  African safari
Julie Tetel, *Swept Away*, 1989
  tropical island

380
KATHERINE COMPTON

The Lady and the Outlaw
(New York: Avon, 1994)

Story type: Historical/American West
Major character(s): Kate O'Donovan, Mail Order Bride (Irish), Captive; Caddo, Indian (half Apache), Outlaw; Thorin Delaney, Fiance(e)
Time period(s): 1870s (1877)
Locale(s): New Mexico

Summary: Irish mail-order bride Kate O'Donovan arrives to wed Thorin Delaney only to find the wedding postponed and her dreams of the "romantic West" somewhat altered when she is captured by renegades. Thorin bargains with the outlaw Caddo to return her; but true villain that he is, Thorin then locks up Caddo and attacks Kate. By now Caddo knows that he wants Kate for himself, and he pursues her, fighting off anyone in his way. A fast-paced and sensual story with elements of "the chase."

Other books you might like:
Madeline Baker, *Comanche Flame*, 1992

Madeline Baker, *Prairie Heat*, 1991
   similar plot
Elaine Crawford, *Love So Wild*, 1994
   captor-captive/highly sensual
Johanna Lindsey, *Savage Thunder*, 1989
   passionate action

381

KATHERINE COMPTON

Outlaw Bride
(New York: Avon, 1991)

Story type: Historical/American West
Major character(s): Annie Calhoun, Outlaw (Bank robber); Eli Larson, Lawman (Sheriff)
Time period(s): 1880s
Locale(s): Oklahoma

Summary: When Sheriff Eli Larson marries bank robber Annie Calhoun to save her from hanging, he doesn't expect his urchin to turn into a beautiful woman—and he certainly doesn't expect to fall in love with her. A gentle, sensual, funny story of love and transformation.

Other books you might like:
Emily Bradshaw, *Cactus Blossom*, 1991
Catherine Hart, *Sweet Fury*, 1990
Virginia Lynn, *River's Dream*, 1991
Pamela Morsi, *Heaven Sent*, 1990
Rebecca Paisley, *Barefoot Bride*, 1990

382

MARY CHASE COMSTOCK
TERESA DESJARDIEN, Co-Author
KARLA HOCKER, Co-Author

A Christmas Wish
(New York: Zebra, 1994)

Story type: Holiday Themes; Anthology
Time period(s): 1810s
Locale(s): England

Summary: A trio of Regency Christmas romances featuring family, children, and traditional holiday entertainments and traditions and centering on the idea that wishes sometimes do come true—especially at Christmas. Includes *A Christmas Conspiracy* by Mary Chase Comstock, *Wish upon An Angel* by Teresa DesJardien, and *A Wish for Christmas* by Karla Hocker.

Other books you might like:
Mary Balogh, *A Regency Christmas VI*, 1994
   anthology (See also anthologies from earlier years)
Mary Balogh, *Christmas Belle*, 1994
Carla Kelly, *Marian's Christmas Wish*, 1989
Carla Kelly, *Mrs. Drew Plays Her Hand*, 1994
Joan Smith, *The Kissing Bough*, 1994

383

MARY CHASE COMSTOCK

An Impetuous Miss
(New York: Zebra, 1993)

Story type: Regency
Major character(s): Catherine Mansard, Heiress, Debutante; Charles Hazelford, Gentleman (confirmed bachelor)
Time period(s): 1810s
Locale(s): London, England

Summary: Appalled that she must spend every season in London looking for a husband so she can claim her inheritance, fiery and independent Catherine Mansard enlists the aid of longtime friend Charles Hazelford in making her choice. Of course, their collaboration develops into something more; and, suddenly, marriage doesn't seem to be such a bad thing, after all!

Other books you might like:
Jeanne Carmichael, *Madcap Johnny*, 1993
Georgette Heyer, *Bath Tangle*, 1955
Arnette Lamb, *The Betrothal*, 1992
   sensual
Judith Nelson, *Lady's Choice*, 1990
Melinda Pryce, *The Last Lord*, 1993

384

MARY CHASE COMSTOCK

A Midsummer's Magic
(New York: Zebra, 1994)

Story type: Regency; Historical/Fantasy
Major character(s): Hyppolyta, Noblewoman (Countess of Trevalyn), Witch; Julian St. Ives, Gentleman
Time period(s): 1810s
Locale(s): Rookeshaven, England (an estate)

Summary: According to Hyppolyta, she merely seeks "the hidden wisdom in the world" to use it for good; according to everyone else, she is a witch. She is also the Countess of Trevalyn, the mistress of the mysterious and enchanted Rookeshaven, and intent on continuing her own magical studies. However, relatives, danger, and love all arrive to complicate things—and Hyppolyta, with the help of the charming Julian St. Ives, must set everything to rights. Magical, witty, and funny.

Other books you might like:
Anne Barbour, *Lord Glenraven's Return*, 1994
Sandra Heath, *The Halloween Husband*, 1994
Mary Kingsley, *A Maddening Minx*, 1992
Kasey Michaels, *The Haunted Miss Hampshire*, 1994
Joan Overfield, *The Spirited Bluestocking*, 1992

385
PHOEBE CONN

By Love Enslaved
(New York: Warner, 1989)

Story type: Historical/Medieval
Major character(s): Dana, Householder (In her father's absence; Danis); Brendan, Slave (Celt)
Time period(s): 9th century (886)
Locale(s): Isle of Fyn, Denmark

Summary: In charge of the household in her father's absence, Dana is faced with solving the problem of Brendan, the handsome, insolent Celtic slave belonging to her aunt's household. The solution, however, brings love—and more problems to Dana.

Other books you might like:
Blaine Anderson, *Love's Sweet Captive*, 1989
Julie Garwood, *The Bride*, 1989
Mary Ellen Gronau, *Passionate Warriors*, 1989
   Early Irish setting
Mary Ellen Gronau, *Gentle Conqueror*, 1989
   Sequel to *Passionate Warriors*
Linda Madl, *Sweet Ransom*, 1989
   Different period/similar ambiance

386
PHOEBE CONN

Desire
(New York: Zebra, 1993)

Story type: Historical/Exotic
Major character(s): Michelle Minoux, Young Woman; Luis Augustin Aragon y Bourbon, Heir (shipping firm), Gypsy (disguised as)
Time period(s): 19th century (late)
Locale(s): Madrid, Spain; At Sea; Mediterranean

Summary: When Michelle Minoux falls in love with a roving gypsy, she has no idea he is really Luis Aragon y Bourbon, the heir to a large shipping empire. Nevertheless, a duel precipitates their marriage and subsequent flight to the Mediterranean. Treasure and shipwreck add spice to the adventure, but things really become difficult when they return to Spain and must deal with serious problems.

Other books you might like:
Shirl Henke, *Paradise and More*, 1992
Valerie Sherwood, *Lisbon*, 1989
Katherine Sutcliffe, *My Only Love*, 1993
Julie Tetel, *Swept Away*, 1989

387
PHOEBE CONN

Tempt Me with Kisses
(New York: Zebra, 1991)

Story type: Historical/American West Coast

Major character(s): Harmony Russell, Gentlewoman; Daniel Aragon, Doctor
Time period(s): 1850s (1851)
Locale(s): California

Summary: Spunky Harmony Russell accompanies her land commissioner uncle to California and proceeds to fall in love with, seduce, and marry California doctor Daniel Aragon. Their struggle to build a solid marriage, however, takes a backseat to their fight to save their land and their tradition. Lots of Old California history. Continues the story of the Aragons begun in *No Sweeter Ecstasy*.

Other books you might like:
Marsha Bauer, *Sweet Conquest*, 1990
Rebecca Brandewyne, *Heartland*, 1990
Gwen Bristow, *Calico Palace*, 1970
Ann Gabriel, *South Texas*, 1990
Dana Fuller Ross, *California!*, 1981

388
PHOEBE CONN
COLLEEN FAULKNER, Co-Author
DEBRA HAMILTON, Co-Author
VICTORIA THOMPSON, Co-Author

To Love and to Honor
(New York: Zebra, 1995)

Story type: Anthology; Historical
Time period(s): 18th century; 19th century
Locale(s): United States; England

Summary: This historical anthology features four novellas focusing on love, marriage, brides, and weddings. Included are "A Groom for Holly" by Phoebe Conn, "Man of My Dreams" by Colleen Faulkner, "Daisies" by Debra Hamilton, and "The Wrong Man" by Victoria Thompson.

Other books you might like:
Stella Cameron, *To Love and to Honor*, 1993
   historical anthology
Kimberly Cates, *The Raider's Bride*, 1994
Catherine Coulter, *The Sherbrooke Bride*, 1992
Lynda Trent, *Beloved Wife*, 1992
Bronwyn Williams, *The Warfield Bride*, 1994

389
JAN CONSTANT

The Only Hope
(New York: Signet, 1994)

Story type: Regency
Major character(s): Amy Standish, Spinster, Companion; Hugo Dysart, Nobleman
Time period(s): 1810s
Locale(s): England

Summary: When Amy Standish saves young Clarissa Dysart from an unwanted elopement, she ends up as a companion to the charming debutante and in direct conflict with—and eventually in love with—Clarissa's dashing, aristocratic brother, Sir Hugo. Witty, detailed, and classic.

Other books you might like:
Georgette Heyer, *Bath Tangle*, 1955
Georgette Heyer, *Lady of Quality*, 1972
Elizabeth Jackson, *A Brilliant Alliance*, 1993
Barbara Metzger, *An Affair of Interest*, 1992
Meg-Lynn Roberts, *Christmas Escapade*, 1994

390
LORI COPELAND

Darling Deceiver
(New York: Bantam, 1990)

Story type: Contemporary
Major character(s): Harriet "Harri" Whitlock, Zoo Keeper (assistant director); Shae Malone, Writer (mystery)
Time period(s): 1980s
Locale(s): Cloverdale

Summary: Shae Malone (who writes as Perry Beal) returns to the small town where he grew up to finish his latest mystery novel and finds himself living next door to Harri Whitlock, the detestable girl who'd had a crush on him in junior high. Only Harri has grown up and Shae can hardly believe what a knockout she has become. A nosy python reintroduces them to each other; and in spite of other animal interventions and Shae's reluctance to tell Harri he's a best-selling author, they proceed to fall in love.

Other books you might like:
Ruth Jean Dale, *Together Again*, 1990
Mary Tate Engels, *Best-Laid Plans*, 1989
Kate Jenkins, *The Reluctant Bachelor*,
Laura Leone, *Guilty Secrets*, 1990

391
LORI COPELAND

Fool Me Once
(New York: Dell, 1990)

Story type: Historical/American West
Major character(s): Gideon Wakefield, Heiress, Amnesiac; Tom Flannigan, Lumberjack
Time period(s): 1870s
Locale(s): Michigan

Summary: Tom will do anything to stop Philadelphia heiress Gideon Wakefield from selling her lumber company—including telling her that she is the new school teacher when she loses her memory in a train wreck. As Gideon adapts to her "new life," she and Tom fall in love; but the real test of their love will come when Gideon learns the truth.

Other books you might like:
Elaine Coffman, *Escape Not My Love*, 1990
Shirl Henke, *Moonflower*, 1989
Linda Lael Miller, *My Darling Melissa*, 1990
Rebecca Paisley, *Barefoot Bride*, 1990
Robin LeAnne Wiete, *Fortune's Lady*, 1990

392
LORI COPELAND

Forever Ashley
(New York: Dell, 1992)

Story type: Time Travel; Historical/American Revolution
Major character(s): Ashley Wheeler, Tour Guide, Time Traveller; Aaron Kenneman, Doctor
Time period(s): 1990s; 1770s
Locale(s): Boston, Massachusetts

Summary: Her dislike of history makes it doubly difficult for Ashley Wheeler when she suddenly finds herself dragged through time and literally dropped into the middle of a secret meeting of notable American patriots just prior to Paul Revere's famous ride. Confusion and suspicion reign, but she eventually gains their trust and becomes part of the "Midnight Ride." She even manages to influence history — just a bit! Likeable and highly memorable characters are central to this funny and colorful adventure.

Other books you might like:
Barbara Bretton, *Somewhere in Time*, 1992
Sandra Canfield, *The Loving*, 1992
Diana Gabaldon, *Dragonfly in Amber*, 1992
Thomasina Ring, *Time-Spun Rapture*, 1990
Thomasina Ring, *Time-Spun Treasure*, 1992

393
LORI COPELAND

Promise Me Forever
(New York: Fawcett Gold Medal, 1994)

Story type: Historical/American West
Series: Sisters of Mercy Flats
Major character(s): Amelia McDougal, Outlaw, Orphan; Morgan Kane, Rescuer
Time period(s): 19th century
Locale(s): Texas; Mississippi River

Summary: Dressed as nuns, the infamous McDougal sisters are being taken to jail when their wagon is attacked by Comanches and the women end up being rescued by different men. Amelia can't believe her good luck at having the dashing Captain Morgan Kane carry her off to safety—until, that is, she ends up on a riverboat headed toward prostitution in New Orleans! Lots of sparks and adventure before all works out in this fast-paced, funny story. Third in the trilogy.

Other books you might like:
Lisa Bingham, *Silken Promises*, 1994
Lisa Hendrix, *Hostage Heart*, 1994
Sharon Ihle, *Wild Rose*, 1993
Pamela Morsi, *Wild Oats*, 1993
Rebecca Paisley, *Rainbows and Rapture*, 1992

394

LORI COPELAND

Promise Me Today

(New York: Fawcett, 1992)

Story type: Historical/American West
Major character(s): Abigail McDougal, Orphan, Outlaw; Barrett Drake, Imposter, Spy
Time period(s): 19th century
Locale(s): Texas

Summary: Caught in one of their scams, the three McDougal sisters are on their way to jail when they are attacked by Comanches. Two of the sisters are rescued by brave, bold heroes; it is Abby's luck to be rescued by a wimp. It doesn't take her long, however, to discover that her "hero" is not a wimp at all, but a master of disguise. Adventurous, funny, and charming.

Other books you might like:
Pamela Morsi, *Garters*, 1992
Pamela Morsi, *Heaven Sent*, 1990
Rebecca Paisley, *Midnight and Magnolias*, 1992
Rebecca Paisley, *Moonlight and Magic*, 1990

395

LORI COPELAND

Sweet Hannah Rose

(New York: Dell, 1991)

Story type: Historical/American West
Major character(s): Hannah Rose Brewster, Rancher (daughter of); Luke Kincaid, Rancher
Time period(s): 19th century
Locale(s): Texas

Summary: When Hannah Rose and Luke end up in bed—and in love—it takes all their ingenuity and determination to settle the 90 year old feud between their two families so they can live happily ever after. A kind of Texas-style Romeo and Juliet with lots of humor and action.

Other books you might like:
Rosanne Bittner, *Texas Bride*, 1988
Kay Hooper, *Star-Crossed Lovers*, 1990
    contemporary setting
Alison Irving, *No Greater Love*, 1991
Rebecca Paisley, *Barefoot Bride*, 1990
Rebecca Paisley, *Moonlight and Magic*, 1990

396

LORI COPELAND

Tall Cotton

(Toronto: Harlequin, 1990)

Story type: Contemporary
Major character(s): Kelly Smith, Horse Trainer; Tanner McCrey, Businessman (Racing stable owner)
Time period(s): 1980s
Locale(s): Arkansas

Summary: Kelly takes a job as a horse trainer at Tanner McCrey's stable to try to discover who framed her late father in a horse theft. Her attraction to Tanner doesn't make her job any easier, especially when she thinks he may have been involved with ruining her father's reputation.

Other books you might like:
Kathy Clark, *Sight Unseen*, 1990
Lee Magner, *The Mistress of Foxgrove*, 1989
Vella Munn, *White Moon*, 1989
Eleanor Woods, *Above Suspicion*, 1990

397

MICHAEL CORDA

Curtain

(New York: Warner, 1992)

Story type: Contemporary/Mainstream
Major character(s): Felicia Lyle, Actress; Robert Vane, Actor
Time period(s): 20th century
Locale(s): London, England; Hollywood, California

Summary: When renowned Shakespearean actor Robert Vane performs with Felicia Lyle, they fall madly in love, leave their spouses, and tour together. Their fragile, though enduring, relationship is almost torn apart by secrets, rivalries, snubs and gossip. A glitzy, sensual story sprinkled with Hollywood personalities, allegedly based on the real-life relationship of Laurence Olivier and Vivian Leigh.

Other books you might like:
Sandra Chastain, *Sweetwater*, 1990
    historical setting
Jackie Collins, *Hollywood Wives*, 1985
Madeline Hale, *Pirouette*, 1990
Eva Ibbotson, *A Company of Swans*, 1985
JoAnn Ross, *Secret Sins*, 1990

398

CHRISTINA CORDAIRE

Daring Illusion

(New York: Jove, 1994)

Story type: Regency
Major character(s): Rosalind Winston, Imposter (posing as a housekeeper), Gentlewoman (impoverished); Viscount Moreland, Nobleman (Earl of Moreland), Spy (for the government)
Time period(s): 1810s
Locale(s): England

Summary: The destitute Winston family has a plan to keep their castle: They will rent the estate to Viscount Moreland and pretend to be the staff. But Moreland has a secret of his own. He is there to spy out a traitor and he keeps being distracted by the lovely "housekeeper," Rosalind Winston. Delightful children, suspenseful action, and charming romance are part of this lively Regency.

Other books you might like:
April Kihlstrom, *Dangerous Masquerade*, 1992
Mary Kingsley, *Scandal's Lady*, 1994

Barbara Metzger, *Lady in Green*, 1993
Marlene Suson, *The Fair Imposter*, 1992

399
DIANE CORY

High Society
(New York: Pocket, 1990)

Story type: Historical/Mainstream
Major character(s): Trudi Groves, Socialite; Phillip Gates, Lawyer
Time period(s): 1920s
Locale(s): St. Louis, Illinois

Summary: When socialite Trudi Groves falls in love with struggling young lawyer Phillip Gates, they find themselves not only defying the existing social order, but becoming involved in a dangerous and treacherous situation that threatens their happiness and their future, as well. Set against the colorful, flamboyant background of the Roaring Twenties.

Other books you might like:
Barbara Taylor Bradford, *Voice of the Heart*, 1983
Sandra Bregman, *Reach for the Dream*, 1990
Jackie Collins, *Chances*, 1981
Janet Dailey, *Masquerade*, 1990
Catherine Lanigan, *All or Nothing*, 1989

400
DIANE CORY

A Token of Jewels
(New York: Pocket, 1989)

Story type: Historical/World War I
Major character(s): Annastatia Brassova, Socialite (Russian; Wealthy); Joseph Sutherland, Military Personnel (British officer)
Time period(s): 1910s (1914)
Locale(s): St. Petersburg, Russia; Milwaukee, Wisconsin; England

Summary: As the political situation in Russia deteriorates, Anna leaves, aided by Joseph, the man she loves. Her troubles are not over, however, as war breaks out and she is pursued by her nemesis, Felix. Serious reading; evocative of the period.

Other books you might like:
Alan Fisher, *The Three Passions of Countess Natalya*, 1985
Constance Heaven, *The House of Kuragin*, 1972
    First of three novels about Tsarist Russia
Eva Ibbotson, *A Countess Below Stairs*, 1981
    Similar situation/light treatment

401
BETTY COTHRAN

Over the Moon
(New York: Zebra,.1994)

Story type: Contemporary

Major character(s): Rebecca Roswell, Businesswoman (hot air balloons), Widow(er); Steve Jordan, Widow(er), Grandparent
Time period(s): 1990s
Locale(s): Willow Ridge

Summary: Rebecca and Steve, both widowed, are enjoying their older years in different ways—she by being active and adventurous; he by being a grandparent—and different though they are, their relationship fulfills and complements their lives. Steve's jealous daughter tries to cause problems, but Rebecca and Steve are both mature enough to know what a good thing their love is and won't let anyone spoil things for them.

Other books you might like:
Diane E. Lock, *True Love*, 1994
Marilyn Pappano, *Operation Homefront*, 1992
Garda Parker, *Out of the Blue*, 1992
Ray Sipherd, *The Courtship of Peggy McCoy*, 1990
LaVyrle Spencer, *Bittersweet*, 1990

402
CATHERINE COULTER

Beyond Eden
(New York: Dutton, 1991)

Story type: Contemporary
Major character(s): Lindsay ''Eden'' Foxe, Model, Heiress; S.C. Taylor, Police Officer (former)
Time period(s): 1990s; 1980s
Locale(s): San Francisco, California; Paris, France; New York, New York

Summary: Rejected as a child by the father she adores and raised in the shadow of her beautiful and talented older sister, shy, awkward Lindsay Foxe stuns her family by becoming the successful model, Eden. However, the tragic and scandalous events of her past haunt her present in a real and terrifying sense, and it is only when ex-cop S.C. Taylor comes into her life that she can learn to trust and love again. A combination rape-recovery/ugly duckling-swan story set against the glittering backdrop of New York's modeling scene.

Other books you might like:
Joanne Z. Adams, *Intimate Connections*, 1990
Elizabeth Bennett, *Changes of Heart*, 1992
Janet Dailey, *Heiress*, 1987
Linda Renee De Jong, *Shattered Illusions*, 1992
Jessica Gregory, *Once Innocent*, 1991

403
CATHERINE COULTER

Earth Song
(New York: Onyx, 1990)

Story type: Historical/Medieval
Series: Song Trilogy
Major character(s): Philippa de Beauchamp, Noblewoman; Dienwald de Fortenberry, Nobleman
Time period(s): 13th century (1275)

Locale(s): England

Summary: In order to avoid her father's marriage plans for her, Philippa de Beauchamp escapes in a wool wagon dressed as a peasant—and ends up at St. Erth Castle being held for ransom by Dienwald de Fortenberry. Philippa, however, takes charge and before long St. Erth is a very different place. Conflict and humor are hallmarks of this lively historical.

Other books you might like:
Jude Deveraux, *The Taming*, 1989
Julie Garwood, *The Bride*, 1989
Virginia Henley, *The Falcon and the Flower*, 1989
Marylyle Rogers, *Hidden Hearts*, 1989
Kathleen E. Woodiwiss, *The Wolf and the Dove*, 1974

404
CATHERINE COULTER

The Heiress Bride
(New York: Putnam, 1993)

Story type: Historical/Regency; Historical/Fantasy
Series: Bride Trilogy
Major character(s): Sinjin Sherbrooke, Heiress; Colin Kinross, Widow(er), Nobleman (Earl of Ashburnham)
Time period(s): 1810s
Locale(s): England; Scotland

Summary: When Colin Kinross, the seventh Earl of Ashburnham, sets out to marry an heiress, young Sinjin Sherbrooke decides that she will be that heiress—even though her brothers forbid her even to see the Earl. Naturally, Sinjin gets what she wants—but not before she is almost killed in the process. Family ghosts and a murder plot add to this fast-paced tale. Third in the "Bride Trilogy."

Other books you might like:
Mary Balogh, *Deceived*, 1993
Susan Johnson, *Sinful*, 1992
Brenda Joyce, *Scandalous Love*, 1992
    later period
Laura Parker, *For Love's Sake Only*, 1991
Amanda Quick, *Surrender*, 1990

405
CATHERINE COULTER

Lord of Hawkfell Island
(New York: Jove, 1993)

Story type: Historical/Medieval
Major character(s): Mirana, Captive, Noblewoman; Rorik Haraldsson, Warrior (viking)
Time period(s): 10th century (910)
Locale(s): Ireland

Summary: Furious at being kidnapped by the Viking warrior, Rorik, Mirana changes her mind and marries him when she learns that her self-serving brother had planned to sell her into marriage against her wishes. She is kidnapped again, this time by her brother's men, and is rescued by Rorik just as she is about to be married to someone else! More action follows in this fast-paced medieval Viking adventure.

Other books you might like:
Shannon Drake, *Knight of Fire*, 1993
Anita Gordon, *The Defiant Heart*, 1993
Heather Graham, *The Viking's Woman*, 1990
Julie Tetel, *The Viking's Bride*, 1987

406
CATHERINE COULTER

Night Shadow
(New York: Avon, 1989)

Story type: Historical/Regency
Series: Night Trilogy
Major character(s): Lily Tremaine, Governess; Knight Winthrop, Nobleman (Viscount Castlerosse), Rake
Time period(s): 1810s (Regency Period, 1814)
Locale(s): London, England

Summary: After her fiance is murdered, Lily Tremaine takes his three children and seeks help from her fiance's cousin, Knight Winthrop. A confirmed bachelor and notorious rake, Knight has no desire to have his life disrupted; but he reckons without falling in love with both the children and their governess. Romance with some mystery and suspense thrown in. Sequel to *Night Fire*; prequel to *Night Storm*.

Other books you might like:
Julie Garwood, *Guardian Angel*, 1990
Judith McNaught, *Almost Heaven*, 1990
Amanda Quick, *Seduction*, 1990
Georgette Heyer, *Frederica*, 1965
Sheila Simonson, *The Bar Sinister*, 1986

407
CATHERINE COULTER

Night Storm
(New York: Avon, 1990)

Story type: Historical/Regency
Series: Night Trilogy
Major character(s): Eugenia Paxton, Businesswoman (Shipyard owner), Imposter (Disguised as a man); Alec Carrick, Sea Captain, Nobleman (Baron Sherard)
Time period(s): 1810s (1819)
Locale(s): Chesapeake Bay, Maryland; England

Summary: In order to save her shipyard, Eugenia becomes partners with sea captain Alec Carrick; but when partners are attracted to each other, things get complicated. Murder, amnesia, passion, and revenge spice up this sensual romance.

Other books you might like:
Heather Graham, *A Pirate's Pleasure*, 1989
Jean Innes, *Buccaneer's Bride*, 1989
Betina M. Krahn, *Passion's Ransom*, 1989
    Another woman shipyard owner; witty and humorous
Joan Van Nuys, *Beloved Avenger*, 1989
Lisa Ann Verge, *The Heart's Disguise*, 1990
    Heroine pretends to be a boy

408

CATHERINE COULTER

Secret Song

(New York: Onyx, 1991)

Story type: Historical/Medieval
Series: Song Trilogy
Major character(s): Daria de Fortesque, Noblewoman, Heiress; Roland de Tourneay, Adventurer, Knight
Time period(s): 13th century (1275)
Locale(s): England

Summary: Hired by her greedy uncle to rescue Daria de Fortesque when she is captured by a local madman, adventurer Roland de Tourneay saves the lady in question, takes her virtue, and then comes down with a fever that robs him of that particular part of his memory. Naturally, when Daria becomes pregnant, he doesn't believe the baby is his. Nevertheless, they marry. Love, and Daria's wise persistence, result in a happy ending for them both. Sensual, funny, and warm. Final volume of Song Trilogy (*Fire Song, Earth Song*).

Other books you might like:
Christina Dodd, *Candle in the Window*, 1991
Mary Jo Putney, *Uncommon Vows*, 1991
Marylyle Rogers, *Proud Hearts*, 1990
Bertrice Small, *The Spitfire*, 1990
Shelly Thacker, *Falcon on the Wind*, 1991

409

CATHERINE COULTER

The Sherbrooke Bride

(New York.: Jove, 1992)

Story type: Historical/Regency; Historical/Georgian
Series: Bride Trilogy
Major character(s): Alexandra Chambers, Noblewoman, Bride (reluctant); Douglas Sherbrooke, Nobleman (Earl of Northcliffe), Bridegroom (reluctant)
Time period(s): 1800s (1807)
Locale(s): England

Summary: Confronted by the necessity of doing his duty and finally wedding, Douglas Sherbrooke, Earl of Northcliffe, selects the reigning beauty, Melissande Chambers, to be his bride — and ends up married to Alexandra, Melissande's intelligent, independent sister instead. Funny and highly sensual. First in a trilogy.

Other books you might like:
Virginia Brown, *Hidden Touch*, 1992
Diane Wicker Davis, *Heart of the Falcon*, 1990
Georgette Heyer, *A Civil Contract*, 1961
    traditional Regency
Amanda Quick, *Surrender*, 1990
Stephanie Stevens, *Defiant Angel*, 1991

410

CATHERINE COULTER

The Valentine Legacy

(New York: Putnam, 1995)

Story type: Historical/Regency
Series: Legacy Trilogy
Major character(s): Jessie Warfield, Gentlewoman, Child-Care Giver (nanny); James Wyndham, Nobleman, Equestrian
Time period(s): 1820s (1822)
Locale(s): Maryland; England

Summary: Just because they were caught in a compromising situation, Jessie Warfield sees no need to be forced into marriage with James Wyndham. She flees to England and life as a nanny to the children of James' cousins. James, however, is not one to give up so easily and when he comes to England to claim Jessie and take her home, things become more interesting and more passionate. Filled with humor and action, this story concludes the Legacy Trilogy.

Other books you might like:
Jo Beverley, *My Lady Notorious*, 1993
Jo Beverley, *Tempting Fortune*, 1995
Susan Carroll, *The Painted Veil*, 1995
Jane Feather, *Virtue*, 1993
Amanda Quick, *Deception*, 1993

411

CATHERINE COULTER

The Wyndham Legacy

(New York: Putnam, 1994)

Story type: Historical/Regency
Series: Legacy Trilogy
Major character(s): Josephina Cochrane, Noblewoman; Marcus Wyndham, Nobleman (earl)
Time period(s): 1810s (1813)
Locale(s): England

Summary: All her life Josephina Cochrane has submerged her emotions and hidden her feelings. On the other hand, her cousin, Marcus Wyndham, has no control at all. When Josephina tricks him into marriage to keep his estate from being stolen, his continuing abuse and violence causes her to rebel and she leaves. Eventually, of course, he comes to realize and appreciate what she has done for him. A dark, violent romance filled with greed and avarice as well as passion.

Other books you might like:
Stella Cameron, *Fascination*, 1993
    dark and gothic with a less than honorable hero
Brenda Joyce, *Dark Fires*, 1991
    cruel hero/dark and violent
Brenda Joyce, *Scandalous Love*, 1992
Connie Mason, *Brave Land, Brave Love*, 1992
    Australian setting/sweet-savage elements

412

KATHRYN E. COULTER

Does Cupid Do Take-Out?

(New York: Avalon, 1995)

Story type: Contemporary/Innocent
Major character(s): Mallory Devon, Restauranteur (pizza parlor), Cook; Jake Cutter, Military Personnel (Navy captain (SEAL team))
Time period(s): 1990s
Locale(s): Balboa Island, California

Summary: Mallory Devon's peaceful existence is shattered when recuperating Navy Captain Jake Cutter moves into the rooftop apartment just across from hers. He is simply too attractive to be that close—and Mallory isn't interested in a fling. Nice pacing, zingy dialogue, and surprisingly good sexual tension for a sweet romance.

Other books you might like:
Sally Carleen, *An Improbable Wife*, 1995
Kay Gregory, *Roses in the Night*, 1995
Vanessa Hale, *Sweet Deception*, 1995
Debbie Macomber, *Rainy Day Kisses*, 1990
Elizabeth Sites, *Stranger in Her Arms*, 1995
    another wounded hero

413

LINDA COVINGTON

Wild Tory Rose

(New York: Pinnacle, 1992)

Story type: Historical/American Revolution
Major character(s): Meg Shahan, Spouse (unwilling wife); Conner Donovan, Plantation Owner, Smuggler
Time period(s): 1780s
Locale(s): Ireland; United States

Summary: When Meg's childhood friend Conner returns to Ireland, they are instantly in love—but Conner goes to the Colonies and Meg is forced into a cruel marriage. Eventually Meg and her husband, Charles, go to America where Charles is obsessed with searching for the mysterious smuggler, Damien, who is actually Conner. Meg cannot forget her passion for Conner and they fight numerous obstacles to be together—and they finally succeed. Good characterizations.

Other books you might like:
Heather Graham, *Love Not a Rebel*, 1989
Katherine Kincaid, *Stormswept*, 1991
Robin Maderich, *Faith and Honor*, 1989
Lois Wolfe, *The Schemers*, 1991
    Civil War setting

414

DEBRA COWAN

Almost Home

(New York: Diamond, 1994)

Story type: Historical/American West

Major character(s): Leah Becker, Widow(er), Businesswoman; Cabot Montgomery, Wealthy
Time period(s): 1870s
Locale(s): Missouri

Summary: Desperate for the money to save her late husband's business, Leah Becker agrees to marry wealthy Cabot Montgomery, who is desperate for an heir. Their marriage of convenience eventually becomes one of love, but not before they uncover some truly horrible secrets and are forced to come to terms with the past.

Other books you might like:
Candace Camp, *Heirloom*, 1992
Lindsay Chase, *The Vow*, 1992
Elizabeth DeLancey, *Meant to Be*, 1994
Elizabeth DeLancey, *Touch of Lace*, 1993
Stef Ann Holm, *Firefly*, 1990

415

ELAINE CRAWFORD

Love So Wild

(New York: Jove, 1994)

Story type: Historical/American West
Major character(s): Carrie Jackson, Captive, Abuse Victim; Chama Campbell, Outlaw (Comanchero), Indian (half-Kiowa)
Time period(s): 1870s (1876)
Locale(s): Texas

Summary: When Carrie Jackson, the abused daughter of the local sheriff, is kidnapped and taken to a Comanchero hideout, she is afraid of them—but she is even more frightened of her father. One of the outlaws, Chama, protects her and takes her to his people where she experiences the peace of the Kiowa life and learns to love Chama. A realistic depiction of the difficulties of Native American life and the brutal Comancheros. Highly sensual.

Other books you might like:
Catherine Anderson, *Comanche Heart*, 1992
    abused heroine/different treatment
Deborah Camp, *Lady Legend*, 1992
    culture differences/gentler treatment
Georgina Gentry, *Sioux Slave*, 1992
    captor-captive theme/highly sensual
Nan Ryan, *Sun God*, 1990
    highly sensual
Nan Ryan, *Written in the Stars*, 1993
    captor-captive theme/realistic and highly sensual

416

KATHLEEN CREIGHTON

A Christmas Love

(New York: St. Martin, 1992)

Story type: Contemporary; Holiday Themes
Major character(s): Carolyn Robards, Divorced Person, Counselor (family); Clay Traynor, Police Officer (former), Farmer

Time period(s): 1990s
Locale(s): United States

Summary: Carolyn Robards moves with her teen-aged daughter to the country in an effort to put her life back together following a difficult divorce — and ends up with a small runaway (and his dog) in the basement and an attractive farmer next door. Romance follows, but so do complications, in this warm and loving story set during the Holiday Season.

Other books you might like:
Rexanne Becnel, *Christmas Journey*, 1992
Janice Bennett, *A Christmas Keepsake*, 1991
Mary Blaynay, *Father Christmas*, 1989
Bethany Campbell, *The Snow Garden*, 1989
Janet Dailey, *Mistletoe and Holly*, 1983

417

KATHLEEN CREIGHTON

Love and Other Surprises
(New York: Silhouette, 1990)

Story type: Contemporary
Major character(s): Toby Thomas, Widow(er) (Sorority housemother); Stony Brank, Businessman (Marine salvage company owner)
Time period(s): 1980s
Locale(s): United States

Summary: Newly widowed, back in school, and housemother for a sorority at the University, Toby is attracted to the father of one of her girls. As their relationship deepens, they find they must deal with their very real fears and doubts before they can be happy. Realistic and sensitive.

Other books you might like:
Joanna McClelland Glass, *Woman Wanted*, 1985
LaVyrle Spencer, *Bittersweet*, 1990
LaVyrle Spencer, *Morning Glory*, 1989
Patricia Wilson, *Guardian Angel*, 1990

418

KATHLEEN CREIGHTON
LINDSAY MCKENNA, Co-Author
ANN MAJOR, Co-Author
RITA RAINVILLE, Co-Author

Silhouette Christmas Stories 1990
(New York: Silhouette, 1990)

Story type: Anthology; Holiday Themes
Time period(s): 1990s
Locale(s): United States

Summary: Four Christmas romances by major Sihouette authors Kathleen Creighton, Lindsay McKenna, Ann Major, and Rita Rainville.

Other books you might like:
Mary Blaynay, *Father Christmas*, 1989
Bethany Campbell, *The Snow Garden*, 1989
Janet Dailey, *Mistletoe and Holly*, 1983
Jan McDaniel, *This Fragile Heart*, 1989

419

KATHLEEN CREIGHTON

Wolf and the Angel
(New York: Silhouette, 1992)

Story type: Contemporary
Major character(s): Terry Duncan, Doctor; Jack Wolf, Pilot
Time period(s): 1990s
Locale(s): Baja California, Mexico

Summary: Although Dr. Terry Duncan badly needs medical supplies flown into Mexico, she suspects that pilot Jack Wolf has sinister, vengeful motives—and she is right. He finds the men who slaughtered his parents, Terry finds a tiny baby, and they both find love. Steamy and adventurous.

Other books you might like:
Paula Detmer Riggs, *Rough Passage*, 1991
Alice Sharpe, *Yesterday's Dream*, 1990
  innocent
Nancy Sheehan, *Harvest of Love*, 1990
  innocent
Scotney St. James, *Northern Fire, Northern Star*, 1990
  historical

420

JASMINE CRESSWELL

Prince of the Night
(New York: Topaz, 1995)

Story type: Historical/Fantasy; Gothic
Major character(s): Cordelia Hope, Gentlewoman; Dakon, Vampire, Nobleman (Count of Albion)
Time period(s): 1850s (1859)
Locale(s): Modena, Italy

Summary: Arriving at the Villa of Three Fountains, an estate that has been given to her by her uncle, with her cousin and her maid in tow, Cordelia is dismayed to find that it is already occupied by the mysterious Count of Albion—and has been held by his family for years. But there is something strange about the household, and Cordelia, with her uncanny ability to read people's feelings, senses it—yet the Count continues to fascinate and attract her. An elegant, almost lyrical, dark and gothic vampire romance.

Other books you might like:
Wendy Haley, *This Dark Paradise*, 1994
  first in the Danilov Family Saga/vampires
Lori Herter, *Obsession*, 1991
  first of Herter's Vampire Series
Sabine Kells, *A Deeper Hunger*, 1994
  more vampires
Susan Krinard, *Prince of Dreams*, 1995
  an unusual vampire/interesting use of dreams
Linda Lael Miller, *Forever and the Night*, 1993
  more vampires

421

JASMINE CRESSWELL

Timeless

(New York: Topaz Dreamspun, 1994)

Story type: Time Travel
Major character(s): Robyn Delany, Antiques Dealer; Zack Bowleigh, Antiques Dealer
Time period(s): 1990s; 1740s (1747)
Locale(s): England

Summary: Antiques expert Robyn Delany and her boss, Zach Bowleigh, have it all—a successful business and a perfect love. However, when Robyn ends up in a coma, and is zapped back to 1746 as the wife of Zach's ancestor, she wonders if she will spend her life with Baron William Bowleigh or if she can return to Zach. Loving two men does complicate things a bit.

Other books you might like:
Diana Gabaldon, *Outlander*, 1991
    classic time travel/different time and place
Thomasina Ring, *Time-Spun Rapture*, 1990
    time travel
Thomasina Ring, *Time-Spun Treasure*, 1992
    time travel
Becky Lee Weyrich, *Forever, for Love*, 1989
    time travel/different time, place, and feel

422

JASMINE CRESSWELL

To Catch the Wind

(New York: Topaz, 1993)

Story type: Contemporary/Fantasy; Historical/Fantasy
Major character(s): Noelle Van Bredin, Historian, Reincarnated Person; Andrew MacDonald, Lawyer
Time period(s): 1990s; 17th century (1660s)
Locale(s): England

Summary: Skeptical, historian Noelle agrees to a reincarnation seance and suddenly finds herself in the 1660s as Catherine, wife of King Charles II. Tragedy and sorrow are hers, and she can't break away. However, she's still entwined with her 20th century lover, Andrew, and their mutual search for truth finally results in an understanding of their combined destiny.

Other books you might like:
Laura Gilmour Bennett, *By All That Is Sacred*, 1991
Jude Deveraux, *A Knight in Shining Armor*, 1989
Diana Gabaldon, *Dragonfly in Amber*, 1992
Diana Gabaldon, *Outlander*, 1991
Diana Gabaldon, *Voyager*, 1994

423

MILLIE CRISWELL

Brazen Virginia Bride

(New York: Zebra, 1990)

Story type: Historical/Colonial America; Historical/American Revolution
Major character(s): Alexandra Courtland, Revolutionary (American); Nicholas Fortune, Nobleman (British)
Time period(s): 1770s (1774)
Locale(s): Virginia, American Colonies

Summary: Secretly betrothed to each other as children by their parents, British aristocrat Nicholas and American Colonial Alexandra meet for the first time as adults and hate each other on sight. Obviously, this does not bode well for their future marriage—a marriage which must take place or Nicholas will lose his inheritance. An ex-mistress, a murder attempt, and treachery all play their parts in this passionate story set during the turbulence of Revolutionary America.

Other books you might like:
Caryn Cameron, *Freedom Flame*, 1990
Amy Christopher, *Rebel's Captive*, 1991
Barbara Cummings, *Frontier Fire*, 1991
Colleen Faulkner, *Temptation's Tender Kiss*, 1990
Christina Savage, *Hearts of Fire*, 1984

424

MILLIE CRISWELL

California Temptress

(New York: Zebra, 1991)

Story type: Historical/American West Coast
Major character(s): Elizabeth Forrester, Amnesiac, Gentlewoman; Cole MacAlister, Lawyer
Time period(s): 1870s (1870)
Locale(s): San Francisco, California

Summary: Arriving in California to be reunited with her father after a twenty year forced separation, Elizabeth Forrester is surprised by the suspicion and hostility of Cole MacAlister, her father's law partner—but she is intrigued by the man himself. A vindictive grandfather, a kidnapping, and amnesia are all elements of this fast-paced, funny historical.

Other books you might like:
Rene J. Garrod, *Temptation's Wild Embrace*, 1990
Barbara Hargis, *Heart Song*, 1990
Kathy Lawrence, *Tin Angel*, 1989
Cynthia Wright, *Brighter than Gold*, 1990

425

MILLIE CRISWELL

Desire's Endless Kiss

(New York: Zebra, 1991)

Story type: Historical/War of 1812
Series: Fortune Family

Major character(s): Samantha Wilder, Gentlewoman, Socialite; Daniel Fortune, Patriot
Time period(s): 1810s (1813)
Locale(s): Washington, District of Columbia

Summary: When Boston socialite Samantha Wilder reluctantly goes to Washington to find her missing brother, she ends up embroiled in politics and intrigue—and in love with a man who thinks she might be a spy! A fascinating story of love and trust set against the tumultuous background of the War of 1812. Second in the Fortune Family series.

Other books you might like:
Caryn Cameron, *Freedom Flame*, 1990
Heather Graham, *Love Not a Rebel*, 1989
Deana James, *Masque of Sapphire*, 1990
Emma Merritt, *Masque of Jade*, 1990

426

MILLIE CRISWELL

Diamond in the Rough
(New York: Harper, 1994)

Story type: Historical/American West
Major character(s): Prudence Daniels, Care Giver (hospice), Spinster; Brock Peters, Drifter
Time period(s): 19th century
Locale(s): West

Summary: When drifter Brock Peters delivers an unwed mother to Prudence Daniel's hospice, he ends up being hired as ranch foreman. Straight-laced Prudence is not at all impressed by the exceedingly masculine Brock. She does, however, need his help in dealing with the local ranchers, and as she comes to know him, respect and love soon follow.

Other books you might like:
Candace Camp, *Rosewood*, 1991
Lori Copeland, *Promise Me Today*, 1992
Johanna Lindsey, *Angel*, 1992
Elizabeth Lowell, *Lover in the Rough*, 1994
Linda Sandifer, *Mountain Ecstasy*, 1992

427

MILLIE CRISWELL

Mail Order Outlaw
(New York: Harper, 1994)

Story type: Historical/Victorian America; Historical/American West
Major character(s): Cassandra Templeton, Socialite; Jake Steele, Outlaw (Accused), Bridegroom (mail order)
Time period(s): 1890s
Locale(s): New York; Waco, Texas

Summary: Socialite Cassandra Templetom advertises for a husband and outlaw Jake Steele is only too glad to comply. However, he wants more than just a name-only marriage. Different though they are, they do fall in love; but when her behavior sends him away, she follows him -all the way to Texas. Pride, treachery, ''bad guys,'' and lots of adventure combine in this fast-paced, funny story of the attraction of two opposites.

Other books you might like:
Lori Copeland, *Promise Me Forever*, 1994
Jude Deveraux, *Eternity*, 1991
    different kind of marrige of convenience
Pamela Morsi, *Garters*, 1992
Maggie Osborne, *The Wives of Bowie Stone*, 1994
    another outlaw husband
Rebecca Paisley, *Barefoot Bride*, 1990

428

MILLIE CRISWELL

Phantom Lover
(New York: Harper, 1993)

Story type: Historical/American Revolution
Major character(s): Danielle Sheridan, Saloon Hostess; Phillip Cameron, Patriot, Imposter (''James Ashland III'')
Time period(s): 18th century
Locale(s): Fredericksburg, Virginia, American Colonies

Summary: To elude the British but still continue his patriotic role as ''The Phantom,'' privateer Phillip Cameron assumes a new identity, that of foppish and slightly boring James Ashland III. He then proceeds to take a wife, the sharp tongued, patriotic Danielle Sheridan, who will do anything to escape working in her parents tavern. Their relationship proves most interesting, but when she finally discovers the truth of her husband's double identity, suddenly things take a dangerous turn. Witty and lively.

Other books you might like:
Linda Covington, *Wild Tory Rose*, 1992
Robin Maderich, *Faith and Honor*, 1989
Baroness Orczy, *The Scarlet Pimpernel*, 1905
    a classic double identity tale
Sue Rich, *The Scarlet Temptress*, 1991

429

MILLIE CRISWELL

Temptation's Fire
(New York: Zebra, 1992)

Story type: Historical/American West
Major character(s): Margaret Parker, Spinster (care-giver); Chase Gallagher, Lawman (U. S. Marshal)
Time period(s): 19th century
Locale(s): Purgatory, Arizona

Summary: At 26, Margaret has put aside all thoughts of romance and is dedicated to caring for her mother, never dreaming that Marshall Gallagher will enter her life searching for a man who may be her father. His attention to her, at first, may be because of his quest; but when he takes a second look, he's hooked. After they marry, Margaret is torn between father and husband, and it takes a murder to make things right.

Other books you might like:
Elaine Coffman, *Angel in Marble*, 1991
Lori Copeland, *Sweet Hannah Rose*, 1991

Jude Deveraux, *Wishes*, 1989
Pamela Morsi, *Courting Miss Hattie*, 1991

430
MILLIE CRISWELL

Wild Heather
(New York: Warner, 1995)

Story type: Historical/American West Coast; Historical/Victorian America
Series: Flowers of the West
Major character(s): Heather Martin, Artist (aspiring), Governess; Brandon Montgomery, Publisher (newspaper owner)
Time period(s): 1880s (1883)
Locale(s): San Francisco, California

Summary: Filled with dreams of becoming an artist and possessing the talent to acomplish them, Heather Martin leaves the Kansas farm where she was raised and heads for San Francisco — and ends up unable to find an illustrating job simply because she is a woman. Desperate, she takes a job as governess to the two young children of Brandon Montgomery, the rigid owner of one of San Francisco's newspapers and proceeds, Mary Poppins style, to turn their lives upside down. Warm and light-hearted.

Other books you might like:
Kimberly Cates, *Only Forever*, 1992
  children and another determined heroine
Patricia Gaffney, *Crooked Hearts*, 1994
  a humorous San Francisco romp
Julie Garwood, *Prince Charming*, 1994
  lively humor
Pamela Morsi, *Garters*, 1992
  another determined heroine/humorous
Pamela Morsi, *Something Shady*, 1995
  another independent heroine

431
TANYA ANNE CROSBY

Angel of Fire
(New York: Avon, 1992)

Story type: Historical/Medieval
Major character(s): Chrestien de Lontaine, Twin, Noblewoman (Norman); Adelaine de Lontaine, Twin, Noblewoman (Norman); Weston "the Silver Wolf" Fitzstephens, Knight (English)
Time period(s): 12th century
Locale(s): England; France

Summary: Upon the death of their father, resourceful Chrestien disguises herself as a knight and escorts her twin sister to marriage and safety, and ends up the prisoner of Weston Fitzstephens, a man she has hated for years. A funny, passionate, and action-filled adventure, peopled with captivating characters. First novel.

Other books you might like:
Catherine Coulter, *Earth Song*, 1990
Catherine Coulter, *Secret Song*, 1991

Jude Deveraux, *The Taming*, 1989
Julie Garwood, *The Bride*, 1989
Julie Garwood, *The Secret*, 1992

432
TANYA ANNE CROSBY

Kissed
(New York: Avon, 1995)

Story type: Historical/Georgian; Historical/Colonial America
Major character(s): Jessamine Stone, Young Woman; Lord Christian Haukinge, Nobleman (dispossessed), Smuggler ("Hawk")
Time period(s): 1760s (1763)
Locale(s): England; Charlestown, American Colonies

Summary: When Jessamine Stone's father breaks off her engagement to Lord Christian Haukinge because his elder brother took his fortune, Christian vows vengeance against the Stone family—and his chance comes when Jessie's brother, in an effort to convince Jessie to marry the rich Lord St. John, solicits Christian to break her heart. The problem comes, of course, when Jessie and Christian realize they are still in love. But all does not run smoothly and they are separated again, only to meet once more in the colonies where Christian has a secret life as a rebel smuggler. Fast-paced, highly sensual, involving.

Other books you might like:
Robin Lee Hatcher, *The Magic*, 1993
Arnette Lamb, *Border Bride*, 1993
  revenge theme/different setting/appealing characters
Amanda Quick, *Reckless*, 1992
  vengeance gone awry/lighter treatment
Sue Rich, *Shadowed Vows*, 1992
  another trans-Atlantic romance

433
TANYA ANNE CROSBY

Once upon a Kiss
(New York: Avon, 1995)

Story type: Historical/Medieval
Major character(s): Lady Dominique Beauchamp, Noblewoman; Sir Blaec d'Lucy, Nobleman, Knight
Time period(s): 12th century (during the reign of King Stephen)
Locale(s): England

Summary: Dominique Beauchamp is prepared to marry the Lord of Drakewich to end the feuding of their two families. However, she isn't ready for the undeniable attraction she feels for the lord's brother, the fierce Blaec d'Lucy, the Black Dragon.

Other books you might like:
Marsha Canham, *In the Shadow of Midnight*, 1994
Roberta Gellis, *Roselynde*, 1978
  first of the Roselynde Chronicles
Sandra Hill, *The Tarnished Lady*, 1994
Ruth Langan, *The Highlander*, 1994

Emma Merritt, *Lord of Fire*, 1994

434

TANYA ANNE CROSBY

Sagebrush Bride
(New York: Avon, 1993)

Story type: Historical/American West
Major character(s): Elizabeth Bowcock, Doctor; Cutter McKenzie, Indian (half-Cheyenne); Katie Boss, Orphan
Time period(s): 1860s (1865)
Locale(s): Dakota Territory
Summary: Doctor Elizabeth Bowcock needs a husband so she can be considered a fit guardian for her orphaned niece, and she doesn't much care who it is—just so long as it is platonic. Cutter McKenzie decides he is the one, so he gets Elizabeth drunk and spirits her away to be married. She is furious and sets about causing Cutter no end of grief. Prejudice, old army enemies, and a host of other problems combine in this fast-paced, suspenseful romance.

Other books you might like:
Deborah Camp, *Black-Eyed Susan*, 1990
Jill Marie Landis, *Come Spring*, 1992
Theresa Michaels, *Gifts of Love*, 1992
LaVyrle Spencer, *The Endearment*, 1992

435

TANYA ANNE CROSBY

Viking's Prize
(New York: Avon, 1994)

Story type: Historical/Medieval
Major character(s): Elienor of Baume-les-Nonnes, Captive, Noblewoman; Alarik Trygvason, Warrior (Viking)
Time period(s): 14th century
Locale(s): France; Norway
Summary: Seeking French Count Phillipe's death, Viking Alarik Trygvason has to settle for kidnapping his betrothed, Elienor. She hates Alarik with a passion, even "dreaming" that he will die in battle, but he chooses to keep her for his own. As they come to care for each other, they are torn by loyalties to their countries and passion for each other. Betrayal and loss are part of this sensual and fiery story.

Other books you might like:
Shannon Drake, *Princess of Fire*, 1989
Heather Graham, *The Viking's Woman*, 1990
Brenda Joyce, *The Conqueror*, 1990
Brenda Joyce, *Promise of the Rose*, 1993
Johanna Lindsey, *Surrender My Love*, 1994

436

CHARLENE CROSS

Almost a Whisper
(New York: Pocket, 1994)

Story type: Historical/Victorian

Major character(s): Leah Balfour Dalton, Imposter (posing as Ian Sinclair s niece); Ian Sinclair, Lawyer
Time period(s): 1840s (1841)
Locale(s): England
Summary: In order to save her orphaned siblings, destitute Leah pretends to be the niece of wealthy solicitor Ian Sinclair. As she becomes more and more involved in Lord Sinclair's life, she discovers her bigamous father's "other" family living in wealth and determines to get some of the money. Although suspicious and a bit wary, Ian is drawn to Leah; but when he discovers her deception, it takes a near disaster to make him swallow his pride and anger and realize that he loves her. Sequel of *Masque of Enchantment*.

Other books you might like:
Kimberly Cates, *Only Forever*, 1992
   saving the children theme/American West setting
Laura Parker, *Caprice*, 1994
   deception plot/ lighter treatment
Amanda Quick, *Deception*, 1993
   more deception/different period
Colleen Quinn, *Unveiled*, 1993
   a different type of deception/American setting

437

CHARLENE CROSS

Deeper than Roses
(New York: Pocket, 1992)

Story type: Historical/Renaissance
Major character(s): Kristiana Harcourt, Noblewoman; Balo, Nobleman (Gypsy)
Time period(s): 16th century (1540s)
Locale(s): Scotland
Summary: Kristiana and Balo are unlikely lovers, but the gypsy life and Balo's rescue and protection of Kristiana save their love. Cruel Edward McHugh kills Kristiana's father, forces her into marriage, nearly hacks Balo to death, and eventually is brought to justice by Balo. Sensual, colorful portrait of gypsy life.

Other books you might like:
Patricia Grasso, *Emerald Enchantment*, 1992
Patricia Grasso, *Highland Belle*, 1991
Iris Johansen, *The Wind Dancer*, 1991
Kathryn Kramer, *Highland Bride*, 1991
Amanda Scott, *Border Bride*, 1990

438

CHARLENE CROSS

A Heart So Innocent
(New York: Pocket, 1990)

Story type: Historical/Victorian
Major character(s): Aiden Prescott, Noblewoman; Justin Warfield, Nobleman (Duke of Westover), Rake
Time period(s): 1840s (1840)
Locale(s): London, England

Summary: When Lady Aiden Prescott plans to elope with one suitor to avoid marriage to another, she accidentally ends up marrying another man entirely—Justin Warfield, Duke of Westover, one of the most notorious rakes in town. Angered by what he considers a plot by Aiden to gain his title, Justin plans to continue his life as usual, mistress and all; but he reckons without feisty, audacious Aiden. Passion, old mysteries, false accusations, and murder are part of this fast-paced, well-conceived, and highly intriguing tale.

Other books you might like:
Julie Garwood, *Guardian Angel*, 1990
Judith McNaught, *Almost Heaven*, 1990
Amanda Quick, *Seduction*, 1990
Amanda Quick, *Surrender*, 1990
Claudette Williams, *Heart of Fancy*, 1990

439
CHARLENE CROSS

Masque of Enchantment
(New York: Pocket, 1990)

Story type: Historical/Victorian
Major character(s): Alissa Ashford, Imposter (Alias Miss Pembroke), Governess (Really is an actress); Jared Braxton, Gentleman
Time period(s): 1840s
Locale(s): Hawkstone, Scotland; England

Summary: To avoid being arrested as a murderer, actress Alissa Ashford leaves London posing as the new governess to the mute daughter of Jared Braxton. However, instead of peace and safety she finds secrets, intrigue, real danger, and love awaiting her at Hawkstone.

Other books you might like:
Blaine Anderson, *Destiny's Kiss*, 1989
    Mystery and suspense
Lee Karr, *Dark Cries of Gray Oaks*, 1989
    Gothic
Louisa Rawlings, *Promise of Summer*, 1989
Barbara Dawson Smith, *Silver Splendor*, 1989

440
CHARLENE CROSS

Splendor
(New York: Pocket, 1995)

Story type: Historical/Medieval
Major character(s): Lady Catherine de Mortain, Noblewoman, Captive; Rolphe de Mont St. Michel, Knight, Kidnapper
Time period(s): 12th century (1153)
Locale(s): Normandy, France; England

Summary: Lady Catherine loves the man she is going to marry; but the king assigns his Sir Rolfe St. Michel to kidnap her and prevent the marriage which would align two powerful families against the king. Desperately trying to escape and failing time and again, Catherine begins to appreciate her gentle captor; and although she prays her father will rescue her, part of her doesn't really want to leave. A passionate,

fast-paced story set during a particularly interesting and violent time.

Other books you might like:
Elizabeth Bonner, *A Vow to Keep*, 1993
Julie Garwood, *Saving Grace*, 1993
    lighter
Mary Jo Putney, *Uncommon Vows*, 1991
Elizabeth Stuart, *Where Love Dwells*, 1990
Lynette Vinet, *Knight's Caress*, 1993

441
EVELYN A. CROWE

Reunited
(Toronto: Harlequin, 1993)

Story type: Contemporary/Fantasy
Major character(s): Sydney Tanner, Journalist (reporter); Andrew Wallace, Spirit (ghost)
Time period(s): 1990s
Locale(s): Wallace, Texas

Summary: When reporter Sydney Tanner is knocked out in an accident while in Texas for an interview, she is rescued by an attractive man who proceeds to disappear. When she inquires, the townspeople say he no longer exists, but she meets him later alive and well! The mystery has everyone on edge and the past holds the secrets.

Other books you might like:
Michelle Brandon, *Heaven on Earth*, 1993
Constance O'Day-Flannery, *Once in a Lifetime*, 1992
Patricia Simpson, *The Legacy*, 1992
Patricia Simpson, *Whisper of Midnight*, 1991

442
JENNIFER CRUSIE

What the Lady Wants
(Toronto: Harlequin, 1995)

Story type: Contemporary
Major character(s): Mae Belle Sullivan, Heiress, Volunteer (Riverbend Art Institute); Mitchell Kincaid, Detective—Private (aka Mitchell Peatwick), Stock Broker
Time period(s): 1990s
Locale(s): Riverbend, Midwest

Summary: Mae Sullivan hires Mitch to find a diary and a killer. They end up involved in a steamy, funny, fast-paced romp that nearly gets them killed. A sexy, off-beat story filled with unconventional characters, humor, and zingy dialogue.

Other books you might like:
Justine Davis, *Errant Angel*, 1995
Debra Dixon, *Hot as Sin*, 1995
Kristin James, *Once in a Blue Moon*, 1995
Jayne Ann Krentz, *Silver Linings*, 1991
    longer
Susan Elizabeth Phillips, *Kiss an Angel*, 1996
    longer

443

JUDY CUEVAS

Black Silk

(New York: Berkley, 1991)

Story type: Historical/Victorian

Major character(s): Submit Channing-Downes, Widow(er), Noblewoman (Marchioness of Montmarche); Graham Wessit, Rake

Time period(s): 1850s (1858)

Locale(s): England

Summary: When newly-widowed Submit Channing-Downes is compelled by her late husband's will to deliver a pornographic work of art to his cousin, the disreputable rake Graham Wessit, she is drawn into a world of passion and intrigue as she struggles to resist falling in love with this totally unacceptable man. A darkly different romance that elegantly explores the shadowy side of Victorian society.

Other books you might like:

Dorothy Eden, *Melbury Square*, 1970

Pierre Choderlos de Laclos, *Les Liaisons Dangereuses*, 1782
   a classic, inspired the film *Dangerous Liaisons*

Laura Parker, *Rebellious Angels*, 1985

Laura Parker, *A Wilder Love*, 1990

444

JUDY CUEVAS

Bliss

(New York: Jove, 1995)

Story type: Historical/Edwardian

Major character(s): Hannah Van Evans, Companion; Nardi de Saint Vallier, Artist, Nobleman

Time period(s): 1900s (1903)

Locale(s): Miami, Florida; France

Summary: Hannah Van Evans, a young American determined to see the world, embarks on a journey that will change her life forever. While traveling as a lady's companion, she meets Nardi de Saint Vallier, a French artist of noble blood who has given up his passion for sculpting and is in the process of destroying himself. Hannah's freshness of spirit slowly reopens his heart to life and beauty—and the bliss of true love.

Other books you might like:

Elaine Barbieri, *Tattered Silk*, 1991
   American setting

Elizabeth, *The Enchanted April*, 1922

Georgia Hampton, *Desire*, 1989
   1950-1960s setting

Karen Harper, *The Wings of the Morning*, 1993
   earlier time period/saga

Katherine Sinclair, *Through the Years*, 1994
   American setting

445

BARBARA CUMMINGS

Blazing Passion

(New York: Zebra, 1991)

Story type: Historical/Colonial America

Series: Fire

Major character(s): Emily Gorton, Doctor, Spinster; Robert Sears, Privateer, Sea Captain

Time period(s): 1770s (1772)

Locale(s): Block Island, American Colonies; At Sea

Summary: Dr. Emily Gorton is so singleminded when it comes to her patients and so convinced that her destiny is not to marry, that it takes all of Captain Robert Sears' determination to convince her that she can (and should) do both. A fast-paced, highly romantic read. Second in the Fire series.

Other books you might like:

Caryn Cameron, *Dawn's Early Light*, 1988

Caryn Cameron, *Freedom Flame*, 1990

Caryn Cameron, *Liberty's Lady*, 1990

Judith E. French, *Scarlet Ribbons*, 1989

Robin Maderich, *Faith and Honor*, 1989

446

BARBARA CUMMINGS

Frontier Fire

(New York: Zebra, 1991)

Story type: Historical/Colonial America

Major character(s): Constance Proctor, Widow(er); Jean Louis D'Epier, Spy, Trapper

Time period(s): 1760s (1766)

Locale(s): New Hampshire, American Colonies

Summary: When the snobbish English family of her late husband refuses to recognize their marriage, Constance takes her son and moves to a small remote farm. Several years later Constance is rescued from a bear by trapper Jean Louis (who turns out to be her first love who left to fight the French and Indian War and never returned) and they revive their romance. All is well until Constance's nefarious in-laws arrive to cause trouble—but Jean Louis and the Sons of Liberty save the day. Well-plotted with interesting characters.

Other books you might like:

Emily Carmichael, *Visions of the Heart*, 1990

Millie Criswell, *Brazen Virginia Bride*, 1990

Pamela K. Forrest, *Autumn Ecstasy*, 1990

Anita Mills, *Follow the Heart*, 1990

Robin LeAnne Wiete, *Freedom Angel*, 1990

447

BARBARA CUMMINGS

Rebel Wildfire

(New York: Zebra, 1992)

Story type: Historical/American Revolution

Series: Revolutionary Fire Trilogy

Major character(s): Savannah Stewart, Artist, Spy (patriot); David Montgomery, Nobleman (Tory)
Time period(s): 1770s
Locale(s): Georgia, American Colonies; Williamsburg, Virginia, American Colonies; England

Summary: David Montgomery and Savannah Stewart are attracted to each other; unfortunately, their political loyalties are to opposite sides of the Revolutionary conflict! Susannah's spying activities take her throughout the Colonies, with David in pursuit; but it isn't until they are together in England that their differences can be reconciled in favor of love. Third in the Fire Trilogy.

Other books you might like:
Caryn Cameron, *Freedom Flame*, 1990
Charles Durham, *Walk in the Light*, 1992
Colleen Faulkner, *Temptation's Tender Kiss*, 1990
Judith E. French, *Scarlet Ribbons*, 1991
Robin Maderich, *Faith and Honor*, 1989

448
BARBARA CUMMINGS
Wilderness Flame
(New York: Zebra, 1993)

Story type: Historical/Colonial America
Major character(s): Hannah Yost, Orphan (reluctant Mennonite); Vincent Scott, Military Personnel (British officer)
Time period(s): 1770s (1772)
Locale(s): Pennsylvania, American Colonies

Summary: Fulfilling her mother's deathbed wish, orphaned Hannah Yost leaves Holland and accompanies a party of Mennonites to a new life in the American Colonies. However, instead of the peaceful existence she expects, she finds shipwreck, massacre, and bloodshed—and, eventually, love in the arms of a British soldier. A story of new beginnings, told from an unusual historical perspective.

Other books you might like:
Pamela K. Forrest, *Wild Savage Heart*, 1993
Judith E. French, *Lovestorm*, 1990
Jill Marie Landis, *Sunflower*, 1989
    later time period
Maura Seger, *The Taming of Amelia*, 1993

449
MARILYN CUNNINGHAM
Seasons of the Heart
(New York: Harper, 1992)

Story type: Historical/Mainstream; Saga
Major character(s): Jessica Whittaker, Teacher; Mark Hardy, Rebel; Clinton Carter, Rancher
Time period(s): 1930s
Locale(s): Hope, Idaho

Summary: Pregnant and deserted, school teacher Jessica Whittaker waits patiently for her love, Mark Hardy, to return. However, after several years, she eventually relents and marries rancher Clinton Carter, establishes a home, and settles into a contented marriage. Years later, Mark's return reignites long-suppressed emotions, and Jessica must deal with the fact that she has never stopped loving Mark.

Other books you might like:
Dorothy Garlock, *Ribbon in the Sky*, 1991
Lisa Gregory, *The Rainbow Promise*, 1989
Deborah Smith, *Miracle*, 1991
LaVyrle Spencer, *Bittersweet*, 1990
LaVyrle Spencer, *The Fulfillment*, 1979

450
JILLIAN DAGG
Sungold
(New York: Avalon, 1992)

Story type: Contemporary/Innocent
Major character(s): Danny Murphy, Writer; Andrew Drake, Farmer
Time period(s): 1990s
Locale(s): Pinedale, Minnesota

Summary: In rural Minnesota to research an article on midwestern farming, writer Danny Murphy falls in love with farmer Andrew Drake and then must decide what she really wants in her future. Good depiction of midwestern farm life.

Other books you might like:
Anne Ladley, *Moriah's Magic*, 1992
Debbie Macomber, *A Little Bit of Country*, 1990
Audrey McConachie, *No Blueprint for Love*, 1992
Carolyn Monroe, *Kiss of Bliss*, 1992
Laura Parrish, *Love's Quiet Corner*, 1989

451
MARY DAHEIM
Gypsy Baron
(Toronto: Harlequin, 1992)

Story type: Historical/Seventeenth Century
Major character(s): Katherine de Vere, Noblewoman, Courtier (lady-in-waiting); Stefan Dvorak, Nobleman, Gypsy
Time period(s): 17th century (1612)
Locale(s): London, England

Summary: When Katherine is blamed for the death of her fiance and thrown in prison, she is rescued by Stefan Dvorak, the bold Gypsy Baron of Bohemia, who takes it upon himself to become her protector. Political turmoil, treachery, and court intrigue abound in this fast-paced, sweet romantic adventure set during the turbulent days of the early 17th century.

Other books you might like:
Charlene Cross, *Deeper than Roses*, 1992
Betina M. Krahn, *Behind Closed Doors*, 1991
Kat Martin, *Gypsy Lord*, 1992
Lindsay McKenna, *King of Swords*, 1992
Maura Seger, *Beloved Enemy*, 1992

`452`

BETTY DAHLIN

Roman Butterfly

(New York: Avalon Books, 1989)

Story type: Contemporary/Innocent
Major character(s): Julie Cramer, Student, Tour Guide; Stephen Kerns, Tour Guide, Professor (Art)
Time period(s): 1980s
Locale(s): Florence, Italy; Rome, Italy

Summary: When art student Julie Cramer takes a temporary job in Rome as an assistant to the director of the Elderhostel in order to earn money for art school, she doesn't expect to find one of the instructors at the art school working as a tour guide, let alone fall in love with him.

Other books you might like:
Jane Edwards, *Dangerous Odyssey*, 1990
    Mystery in Greece
Loretta Jackson, *Nightmare in Morocco*, 1989
    Mystery in Morocco
Leigh Michaels, *Let Me Count the Ways*, 1989
Lee Stafford, *A Song in the Wilderness*, 1990
Mary Stewart, *Madam, Will You Talk?*, 1955
    Romantic Suspense in southern France

`453`

JANET DAILEY

Aspen Gold

(New York: Little, Brown, 1991)

Story type: Contemporary/Mainstream
Major character(s): Kit Masters, Actress; John Travis, Actor (has been); Tom Bannon, Rancher, Lawyer
Time period(s): 1990s
Locale(s): Aspen, Colorado

Summary: When Kit Masters returns home to Aspen to film a picture, she must deal with a former love, a present suitor, and jealousy that almost results in murder.

Other books you might like:
Sally Beauman, *Destiny*, 1987
Barbara Delinsky, *Facets*, 1990
Shirl Henke, *Summer Has No Name*, 1990
Meryl Sawyer, *Blind Chance*, 1989
Danielle Steel, *Passion's Promise*, 1976

`454`

JANET DAILEY

Masquerade

(New York: Little Brown, 1990)

Story type: Contemporary/Mainstream
Major character(s): Remy Jardin, Socialite (Wealthy), Amnesiac; Cole Buchanan, Businessman (President of a shipping compan)
Time period(s): 1980s
Locale(s): New Orleans, Louisiana; France

Summary: Someone wants to kill her, but Remy has lost her memory and can't remember who it is. Cole Buchanan, the CEO of her family's shipping company, is a prime suspect; but Remy is confused about other emotions she senses concerning him. A second story set earlier parallels the love story of Remy and Cole, but has different results. Mystery and romance in a Mardi Gras setting. Typically solid Dailey.

Other books you might like:
Judith Michael, *Deceptions*, 1982
Penelope Neri, *Bold Breathless Nights*, 1989
    Historical/Heroine has amnesia and is in love with her enemy
Nora Roberts, *Public Secrets*, 1990
Becky Lee Weyrich, *Forever, for Love*, 1989
    Time change/historical

`455`

JANET DAILEY
JENNIFER GREENE, Co-Author
PATRICIA GARDNER EVANS, Co-Author

Santa's Little Helpers

(New York: Silhouette, 1995)

Story type: Anthology; Holiday Themes
Time period(s): 1990s
Locale(s): United States

Summary: A diverse trio of contemporary Holiday stories with widely varying styles, sensuality levels, and treatments. Included are the sweet and traditional "The Healing Touch" by Janet Dailey, the funny, modern "Twelfth Night" by Jennifer Greene, and the heartwarming "Comfort and Joy" by Patricia Gardner Evans.

Other books you might like:
Monica Harris, *Spirit of the Season*, 1994
    African American holiday anthology
Virginia Henley, *A Gift of Joy*, 1995
    Christmas anthology
Ann LaFarge, *The Joy of Christmas*, 1994
    holiday anthology
Ellen Tanner Marsh, *A Christmas Embrace*, 1994
    contemporary Christmas romance
Mary Anne Wilson, *The Christmas Husband*, 1995
    contempory Christmas story

`456`

MARGOT DALTON

Angels in the Light

(Toronto: Harlequin, 1993)

Story type: Contemporary
Major character(s): Abby Malone, Journalist (reporter); Brad Carmichael, Survivor
Time period(s): 1990s
Locale(s): United States

Summary: Reporter Abby Malone doesn't believe in near-death experiences, and is surprised to find her insensitive ex-lover Brad Carmichael at a meeting of survivors. Still bitter about his lack of understanding of her grief over losing her son, she is amazed at his radical change to a compassionate, caring person. A mystical experience and Brad's loving hope convince her of a few difficult truths and allows her to change and rebuild her life.

Other books you might like:
Patricia Simpson, *Whisper of Midnight*, 1991
Antoinette Stockenberg, *Emily's Ghost*, 1992
Phyllis A. Whitney, *Rainbow in the Mist*, 1989
Phyllis A. Whitney, *The Singing Stones*, 1990

457

LACEY DANCER

Baby Makes Five
(Bensalem, Pennsylvania: Meteor, 1992)

Story type: Contemporary
Major character(s): Caitland Fox, Recluse, Computer Expert; Robert Thornton, Businessman (CEO of Thornton Enterprises); Baby, Computer
Time period(s): 1990s
Locale(s): New York, New York; Smoky Mountains

Summary: Unaccustomed to being refused, Robert Thornton, the charming and persuasive CEO of Thornton Enterprises, takes matters into his own hands and beards computer expert Caitland Fox in her remote, luxurious, and highly-computerized Smoky Mountain "den," intent on convincing her to take on a project for his company. Her refusal simply makes him more determined, and when the weather conspires to keep them together in relative isolation for a few days, the resulting battle of wills takes on some interesting and romantic aspects. An unusual, passionate love story with a marvelous computer as a character.

Other books you might like:
Jayne Ann Krentz, *Family Man*, 1993
Karen G. McCullough, *Programmed for Danger*, 1990
   innocent
Peggy Morse, *The Stillman Curse*, 1992
Susan Elizabeth Phillips, *Hot Shot*, 1992

458

LACEY DANCER

Forever Joy
(Bensalem, Pennsylvania: Meteor, 1993)

Story type: Contemporary
Major character(s): Joy Clarebridge, Detective (Hunter of kidnapped children); Slater McGuire, Security Officer
Time period(s): 1990s
Locale(s): Florida

Summary: Joy and Slater join forces to find a kidnapped child and discover that they are a good team professionally, and eventually, romantically. Secondary characters add depth to this one.

Other books you might like:
Kay Hooper, *Crime of Passion*, 1991
Liana Laverentz, *Ashton's Secret*, 1993

Merline Lovelace, *Bits and Pieces*, 1993
Sherryl Woods, *Hot Property*, 1992
Sherryl Woods, *Hot Secret*, 1992

459

LACEY DANCER

Lightning Strikes Twice
(Bensalem, Pennsylvania: Meteor, 1993)

Story type: Contemporary
Major character(s): Tempest Whitney-King, Adventurer; Stryker McGuire, Hero
Time period(s): 1990s
Locale(s): Central America

Summary: Tempest has lived up to her name all her life, and since she was 15 she has routinely been rescued and saved by Stryker McGuire, who can't help loving her. One last time he goes after her in Central America and finds her in deep trouble, trouble so deep that he has to marry her to get her out! He doesn't mind, of course, until he thinks about trying to curb her adventuring streak and then they realize they really do have problems.

Other books you might like:
Leslie O'Grady, *Seek the Wild Shore*, 1989
Jeane Renick, *Trust Me*, 1992
Susan Sackett, *Passion's Golden Fire*, 1989
Anne Marie Winston, *Unlikely Eden*, 1993

460

ELIZABETH DANIELS (Pseudonym of Elizabeth Daniels Henderson)

Paradise in His Arms
(New York: Leisure, 1992)

Story type: Historical/Victorian America; Historical/American West Coast
Series: Paradise Family Saga
Major character(s): Kate Paradise, Singer, Heiress; Caleb Innes, Sea Captain
Time period(s): 1870s (1873)
Locale(s): San Francisco, California

Summary: In love with Caleb Innes from childhood, Kate Paradise will stop at nothing to convince him that she is all grown up — and that they belong together in spite of their 20 year age difference. Her various schemes eventually result in marriage, but Kate has made a number of enemies along the way and she and Caleb must deal with some serious issues before they can be truly happy. Follows *Bird of Paradise*, continuing the Paradise Family Saga.

Other books you might like:
Elizabeth Adler, *Fortune Is a Woman*, 1992
Georgette Heyer, *These Old Shades*, 1926
   classic May/December love story
Jill Marie Landis, *Jade*, 1991
Constance O'Banyon, *Forever My Love*, 1991
Jean Webster, *Daddy-Long-Legs*, 1912
   Classic May/December love story

461

KRISTY DANIELS

Gilded Dreams
(New York: Fawcett, 1993)

Story type: Historical/Victorian; Historical/Mainstream
Major character(s): Cendrine Le Clerc, Dancer (ballerina); Jonathan Caras, Journalist (reporter); Alexander Profitt, Journalist (newspaper owner)
Time period(s): 1890s
Locale(s): New York, New York; Paris, France; London, England

Summary: When journalist Jonathan Caras is given a Paris assignment by wealthy newspaper owner, Alexander Profitt, he meets and falls in love with the lovely ballerina, Cendrine. But Cendrine's career comes first and she says no, setting the stage for some devastating conflicts to come. An interesting triangular relationship develops among the three—Cendrine who wants her ballet career, Jonathan who loves her, and Alex who wants Cendrine as his mistress in exchange for his help.

Other books you might like:
Madeline Hale, *Pirouette*, 1990
    later time period
Eva Ibbotson, *A Company of Swans*, 1985
Edith Layton, *The Gilded Cage*, 1991

462

MAGGIE DANIELS

Moonlight and Mistletoe
(New York: St. Martin's)

Story type: Contemporary; Holiday Themes
Major character(s): Scarlet O'Hara Scaggs, Runaway; Buck Grissom, Lawman (sheriff)
Time period(s): 1990s
Locale(s): Blue Ridge Mountains, Georgia

Summary: Sheriff Buck Grissom isn't prepared for two ragtag girls who have run away from an abusive grandfather—especially girls from a well-known poverty stricken, bootlegging family. Nevertheless, in the spirit of the Christmas season he takes them home—and some miraculous changes begin to take place.

Other books you might like:
Bethany Campbell, *The Man Who Came for Christmas*, 1993
Kathleen Creighton, *A Christmas Love*, 1992
Janet Dailey, *Mistletoe and Holly*, 1983
Heather Graham, *Spirit of the Season*, 1993
Debbie Macomber, *A Season of Angels*, 1993

463

EMMA DARCY

The Falcon's Mistress
(Toronto: Harlequin, 1990)

Story type: Contemporary/Exotic

Major character(s): Bethany McGregor, Traveller; Zakr Tahnun Sadiq, Royalty (Sheik of Bayrar)
Time period(s): 1980s
Locale(s): Rhafhar, Fictional Country

Summary: Feisty, independent Bethany McGregor goes to Rhafhar in search of her missing father—and falls in love with the local Sheik.

Other books you might like:
Madeleine Brent, *Stormswift*, 1986
Sarah Edwards, *Fire and Sand*, 1989
Jane Feather, *Bold Destiny*, 1990
Mary Lide, *Isobelle*, 1988
Joanne Redd, *Desert Bride*, 1989

464

EMMA DARCY

The Sheikh's Revenge
(Toronto: Harlequin, 1993)

Story type: Contemporary/Exotic
Major character(s): Leah Marlow, Young Woman, Captive; Sharif Al Kader, Royalty (sheikh)
Time period(s): 1990s
Locale(s): Middle East

Summary: Leah is abducted by the Sheikh as revenge for her brother's taking the Sheikh's intended. Although initially frightened by his fierceness, she comes to appreciate his gentleness, and their relationship takes on some interesting aspects.

Other books you might like:
Sarah Edwards, *Fire and Sand*, 1989
Jane Feather, *Bold Destiny*, 1990
Mary Lide, *Isobelle*, 1988
Diana Palmer, *King's Ransom*, 1993
Mary Stewart, *The Gabriel Hounds*, 1967
    classic romantic suspense

465

PEGGY DARTY

The Crimson Roses of Fountain Court
(New York: Zebra, 1991)

Story type: Gothic
Major character(s): Margaret Morgan, Artist; Jordan La Marsh, Artist, Widow(er)
Locale(s): New Orleans, Louisiana

Summary: In spite of the rumors surrounding the disappearance of master artist Jordan La Marsh's wife, Angelique, aspiring artist Margaret Morgan blithely moves into his carriage house—and finds she has put both her life and her heart in danger. Curses, superstitions, and a very real threat are all part of this sensual gothic.

Other books you might like:
Victoria Holt, *The King of the Castle*, 1967
Susan Howatch, *The Dark Shore*, 1972
Carola Salisbury, *An Autumn in Araby*, 1983

Anne Stuart, *Night of the Phantom*, 1991
Clara Wimberly, *The Emerald Tears of Foxfire Manor*, 1990

466

PEGGY DARTY

The Wailing Winds of Juneau Abbey

(New York: Zebra, 1990)

Story type: Gothic
Major character(s): Abigail Martin, Heiress, Journalist (newspaper reporter)
Time period(s): 1900s
Locale(s): Juneau, Alaska

Summary: When spunky newspaper heiress Abigail Martin goes to Alaska to settle her uncle's affairs, she finds an unsolved murder, a ghost, a series of mysterious happenings, and two attractive men to choose between. A classic gothic with bits of local history thrown in for good measure.

Other books you might like:
Dorothy Eden, *Darkwater*, 1964
Victoria Holt, *The King of the Castle*, 1967
Elsie Lee, *Dark Moon, Lost Lady*, 1976
Carola Salisbury, *The Winter Bride*, 1970
Jill Tattersall, *Lyonesse Abbey*, 1968

467

CAY DAVID (Pseudonym of Carla Cameron Luan)

Swept Away

(Bensalem, Pennsylvania: Meteor, 1992)

Story type: Contemporary
Major character(s): Charlotte Huntington, Banker (loan officer); Sam Gibson, Landowner (beach bum)
Time period(s): 1990s
Locale(s): Florida

Summary: In Florida to arrange for the renovation and quick sale of a complex of condos she had suggested her Colorado bank buy, loan officer Charlotte Huntington runs into problems in the form of Sam Gibson, owner of the other half of the condos. He firmly intends to relax, and repairing buildings isn't at all on his agenda. Charlotte, however, is — and the inevitable conflict is right in keeping with the sultry Florida climate.

Other books you might like:
Suzanne Ellison, *Shifting Sands*, 1992
Jayne Ann Krentz, *Sweet Fortune*, 1991
Laura Phillips, *Beginnings*, 1992
Karen Rose Smith, *Garden of Fantasy*, 1992

468

DONNA DAVIDSON

Elizabeth's Gift

(New York: Signet, 1994)

Story type: Regency; Historical/Fantasy

Major character(s): Elizabeth Wydner, Psychic; Nathan Hawksley, Nobleman
Time period(s): 1810s
Locale(s): Scotland; London, England

Summary: Although Elizabeth's psychic gift allows her to "see" things, she can't quite read all of Lord Hawksley's future; and when she tells him of her gift, he feels that she is in danger. Actually, he is the one who is most at risk, but it takes both of them to confront their enemy and resolve the problem. Lots of political intrigue and romantic adventure.

Other books you might like:
Mary Chase Comstock, *A Midsummer's Magic*, 1994
    paranormal elements
Teresa DesJardien, *Haunted Hearts*, 1992
Teresa DesJardien, *Love's Magic*, 1995
    Druidic magic
Barbara Metzger, *An Angel for the Earl*, 1994
    paranormal elements

469

SANDRA DAVIDSON

The Heart Remembers

(New York: Zebra, 1995)

Story type: Time Travel
Major character(s): Destiny Davidson, Writer (romance), Time Traveller; Colt Mandrell, Rancher (stud farm owner)
Time period(s): 1870s
Locale(s): St. Augustine, Florida

Summary: When a combination of an old diary and a Celtic cross zaps best-selling romance writer Destiny Davidson back to 1870 Florida and into the bed of one of the sexiest men she has ever encountered, nothing makes sense—until she begins to encounter people who know the characters in her latest novel, and she suddenly realizes that they were real! Of course it doesn't help that she is falling in love with a man in another time, but a truly creative twist eventually sets everything right. Sexy and warm, but occasionally violent.

Other books you might like:
Madeline Baker, *The Spirit Path*, 1993
    another time-travelling romance writer/Native American theme
Sandra Canfield, *The Loving*, 1992
Kristin Hannah, *When Lightning Strikes*, 1994
    another time-travelling romance writer
Nelle McFather, *Tears of Fire*, 1994
Judith O'Brien, *Ashton's Bride*, 1995
    Rita-winning Civil War era time travel

470

SANDRA DAVIDSON

A Love for All Time

(New York: Zebra, 1993)

Story type: Historical/Colonial America; Time Travel
Major character(s): Summer Winslow, Historian, Time Traveller; John Hawke, Military Personnel (Colonel), Rogue

Time period(s): 1990s; 1740s (1744)
Locale(s): Massachusetts; Massachusetts, American Colonies

Summary: Historian Summer Winslow is obsessed by 18th century Col. John Hawke's life, career, and love life. When her fixation on touching his sword results in instant travel into the past—and into his arms—she finds herself facing more difficulties than she had imagined—including pregnancy and some interesting love triangles.

Other books you might like:
Shannon Drake, *Avon Books Presents: Haunting Love Stories*, 1991
Kristin Hannah, *Once in Every Life*, 1993
Eugenia Riley, *Tempest in Time*, 1993
Antoinette Stockenberg, *Emily's Ghost*, 1992
Becky Lee Weyrich, *Sweet Forever*, 1992

471

SANDRA DAVIDSON

Rosefire
(New York: Zebra, 1992)

Story type: Historical/Elizabethan
Major character(s): Arianne, Noblewoman; Robert Warwick, Nobleman
Time period(s): 16th century (1583)
Locale(s): England

Summary: Arianne, daughter of Queen Mary and the Earl of Leicester, is hidden and raised as a peasant. However, when she falls in love with Sir Robert Warwick and eventually learns of her true parentage, serious problems arise — in the form of a jealous and deadly Queen Elizabeth. Intrigue, chivalry, and romance set during a particularly colorful historical era.

Other books you might like:
Karen Harper, *Passion's Reign*, 1992
Virginia Henley, *The Dragon and the Jewel*, 1991
Betina M. Krahn, *Behind Closed Doors*, 1991
Rebecca Sinclair, *Wild Scottish Embrace*, 1991

472

DIANE WICKER DAVIS

Heart of the Falcon
(New York: Avon, 1990)

Story type: Historical/Regency
Major character(s): Tabitha Fell, Governess (Quaker); Robert Ransome, Nobleman (Viscount Langley), Rake
Time period(s): 1820s (1825)
Locale(s): England

Summary: Forced into marriage when they are compromised by Robert's heroic rescue of her, Quaker Tabitha Fell and rakehell Robert Ransome, Viscount Langley, are about as opposite as they can be. But Tabitha's gentle ways intrigue and attract Robert and their love grows in spite of their differences. Funny, poignant, and unusual. Sequel to *Heart of the Raven*.

Other books you might like:
Julie Garwood, *The Bride*, 1989
Julie Garwood, *The Gift*, 1991
Judith McNaught, *Almost Heaven*, 1990
Ashland Price, *Wild Irish Heather*, 1991
Lynda Trent, *The Black Hawk*, 1991

473

JUSTINE DAVIS

Lord of the Storm
(New York: Topaz, 1994)

Story type: Futuristic
Major character(s): Captain Shaylah Graymist, Pilot (starship fighter pilot), Military Personnel; Wolf, Slave
Time period(s): Indeterminate Future
Locale(s): *Sunbird*, Spaceship; Trios, Planet—Imaginary; Arellia, Planet—Imaginary

Summary: On leave from duty, Spaceship Captain Shaylah Graymist is given Wolf, a Troitian love slave, to fulfill her sexual wishes. However, when she refuses to use him, he is punished for failing; and rather than allow him to die, she rescues him, risking her own life in the process. With the removal of his brain controller, Wolf regains command of his true identity, and together he and Shaylah return to his home planet. Highly sensual, fast-paced, and filled with detail.

Other books you might like:
Anne Avery, *All's Fair*, 1994
Lois McMaster Bujold, *Shards of Honor*, 1986
Marilyn Campbell, *Stardust Dreams*, 1993
Marilyn Campbell, *Stolen Dreams*, 1994
Anne McCaffrey, *Restoree*, 1967

474

JUSTINE DAVIS

The Sky Pirate
(New York: Topaz, 1995)

Story type: Futuristic
Major character(s): Dax Silverbrake, Pirate; Califa Claxton, Pilot, Slave
Time period(s): Indeterminate Future
Locale(s): Spaceship

Summary: Sky pirate and one of the last surviving Triosans, Dax is intent on avenging the destruction of his small planet by the cruel Coalition. However, in the process of rescuing one of of his crew members from a Coalition prison, he ends up capturing a valuable Coalition slave, little knowing that she is also a former Coalition officer. Passion, intrigue, and distrust are all part of this fast paced story of interstellar conflict and revenge.

Other books you might like:
Lois McMaster Bujold, *Shards of Honor*, 1986
Marilyn Campbell, *Stolen Dreams*, 1994
Amanda Glass, *Shield's Lady*, 1989
Susan Krinard, *Star-Crossed*, 1995
Anne McCaffrey, *Restoree*, 1967

475

JUSTINE DAVIS

Suspicion's Gate

(New York: Silhouette, 1992)

Story type: Contemporary
Major character(s): Nicki Lockwood, Businesswoman; Travis Halloran, Businessman
Time period(s): 1990s
Locale(s): United States

Summary: Travis and Nicki were separated fifteen years ago but are now reunited in a joint-ownership struggle for their property. Travis' cynicism and Nicki's blind love for her brother provide barriers to their growing relationship. A novel of renewed trust and love featuring a thoroughly wonderful hero.

Other books you might like:

Delayne Camp, *Newsworthy Affair*, 1990
Phyllis Houseman, *Call Back Yesterday*, 1992
Debbie Macomber, *First Comes Marriage*, 1991
Patricia Potter, *Island of Dreams*, 1991

476

KATHRYN LYNN DAVIS

All We Hold Dear

(New York: Pocket, 1995)

Story type: Historical/Fantasy; Contemporary/Fantasy
Major character(s): Eva Crawford, Adoptee
Time period(s): 1980s (1988); 1880s (1882)
Locale(s): Eader Island, Scotland (one of the Inner Hebrides); Glen Affric, Scotland (in the Highlands); Glasgow, Scotland

Summary: Raised in the relative isolation of a remote island off the Scottish coast, intuitive and somewhat fey Eva Crawford has always known she is different, but it isn't until her 18th birthday that she finally learns why—and goes in search of her heritage. Mystical and compelling. Sequel to *Too Deep for Tears*.

Other books you might like:

Rexanne Becnel, *If This Be Magic*, 1994
   magical and mystical/medieval
Jillian Hunter, *A Deeper Magic*, 1994
Meagan McKinney, *The Ground She Walks Upon*, 1994
   mystical
Maggie Shayne, *Fairy Tale*, 1996
   contemporary fantasy/another heroine searching for her destiny
Penelope Williamson, *Keeper of the Dream*, 1992
   lyrical and mystical/earlier time period

477

KATHRYN LYNN DAVIS

Sing to Me of Dreams

(New York: Pocket, 1990)

Story type: Historical/Mainstream
Major character(s): Saylah "Tanu", Shaman (Salish), Servant; Julian Ivy, Rancher
Time period(s): 1870s (1876-1879)
Locale(s): Vancouver Island, British Columbia, Canada

Summary: Raised from birth to be her tribe's revered shaman, Tanu, the daughter of a Salish woman and a Scottish trapper, is devastated when she cannot save her people from an epidemic. Feeling her usefulness to the tribe is over, she leaves her village for the white world. After a stay in the missionary school, she goes to work on the Ivy's farm and uses her skills to bring peace and love to a troubled family. Her own journey to fulfillment and peace, however, will not be completed until she returns to her Indian roots once more. Eloquent, thoughtful, and involving.

Other books you might like:

Beverly Bird, *Comes the Rain*, 1990
Susan Donnell, *Pocahantas*, 1991
Kathleen Herbert, *Bride of the Spear*, 1990
   another mystical healer/different setting
Lucia St. Clair Robson, *Ride the Wind*, 1982
Anna Lee Waldo, *Sacajawea*, 1978

478

SUZANNAH DAVIS

Angel Eyes

(New York: Avon, 1993)

Story type: Historical/American West
Major character(s): Beth Ann Linder, Young Woman, Outcast ("scarlet woman"); Zach Madison, Rogue, Imposter (disguised as a preacher)
Time period(s): 1870s (1871)
Locale(s): Arizona

Summary: Kept a veritable prisoner by her father so she can help with his hotel, fiesty and fearless Beth Lindner shoots the trespassing Zach, and then takes him in to heal. His preacher disguise doesn't stop his designs on Beth, but she can fend for herself. A sadistic father, cruel, judgmental townspeople, exlovers, and Apaches all add to the chaos in this action-filled adventure

Other books you might like:

Patricia Hagan, *Orchids in Moonlight*, 1992
Norah Hess, *Kentucky Bride*, 1992
Johanna Lindsey, *Angel*, 1992
Katherine O'Neal, *Princess of Thieves*, 1993
Catherine Reynolds, *The Highwayman*, 1993
   different time period/Regency treatment

479

SUZANNAH DAVIS

Dance of Deception
(New York: Avon, 1992)

Story type: Historical/Regency; Romantic Suspense
Major character(s): Genevieve Maples, Actress, Designer (costume); Bryce Darcy Cormick, Spy, Actor
Time period(s): 1800s
Locale(s): London, England; Paris, France

Summary: Genevieve tries to keep her acting troupe alive, but in protecting her aged grandfather, she gets involved in an intriguing deception with fellow actor Bryce. They weather danger and mutual suspicion before they do the inevitable and fall in love.

Other books you might like:
Gail Clark, *The Baroness of Bow Street*, 1979
Elizabeth Kary, *Midnight Lace*, 1990
Jane Lovelace, *Rolissa*, 1985
Amanda Quick, *Scandal*, 1991
Joan Smith, *Lovers' Vows*, 1981

480

SUZANNAH DAVIS

Devil's Deception
(New York: Avon, 1990)

Story type: Historical/American Revolution
Major character(s): Mary Alexandra "Lexa" Howard, Noblewoman (impoverished), Imposter (indentured Servant); Christopher "The Dandy" Ryan, Pirate
Time period(s): 1770s (1779)
Locale(s): United States (Carolina); At Sea

Summary: To escape an arranged marriage, Lexa poses as an indentured servant and goes to America. She ends up in jail, is rescued by a privateer, and then the adventure begins. Lively tale filled with revenge, hate, and love.

Other books you might like:
Heather Graham, *A Pirate's Pleasure*, 1989
Jean Innes, *Buccaneer's Bride*, 1989
Allison Knight, *Captive Innocent*, 1989
Betina M. Krahn, *Passion's Ransom*, 1989
Lynette Vinet, *Pirate's Bride*, 1987

481

SUZANNAH DAVIS

The Master's Bride
(New York: Avon, 1993)

Story type: Historical/Victorian America
Major character(s): Lili Latham, Young Woman; Lock McKin, Businessman (shipyard owner and shipbuilder)
Time period(s): 1850s (1859-1860)
Locale(s): Boston, Massachusetts; Hawaii

Summary: When Lili Lathan shows up in Boston on a ship from Hawaii claiming to be the long-lost granddaughter of shipping mogul Alex Latham, she finds herself in the middle of an old and dangerous rivalry between Alex's family and shipyard owner Lock McKin—to whom she quickly becomes attracted. Fires and accidents mar their relationship, but eventually love wins out. A ruthless tale of greed, envy, power—and evil.

Other books you might like:
Catherine Coulter, *Beyond Eden*, 1991
  contemporary time period
Elizabeth Daniels, *Paradise in His Arms*, 1992
Deborah Martin, *Creole Nights*, 1992

482

GERALYN DAWSON

Capture the Night
(New York: Bantam, 1993)

Story type: Historical/American West; Historical/Exotic
Major character(s): Madeline Christophe, Thief; Brazo Sinclair, Drifter
Time period(s): 1850s
Locale(s): Texas; France; Mexico

Summary: Madeline's scheme to marry nearly mad Brazo simply to obtain passage for both of them to Texas isn't simple. His tortured, vengeful soul and her need to hide keeps them both fearful, no matter where they run; their love is the only place where they are truly safe and secure. Their love is tested all along the way, but their journey to Mexico proves to be the ultimate test. Extremely dark with Beauty and the Beast elements.

Other books you might like:
Rebecca Brandewyne, *Desperado*, 1993
Brenda Joyce, *Darkest Heart*, 1989
Brenda Joyce, *The Fires of Paradise*, 1991

483

SARANNE DAWSON

Awakenings
(New York: Love Spell, 1994)

Story type: Futuristic
Major character(s): Rozlynd, Healer (apprentice), Sorceress; Justan, Nobleman, Ruler (lord of the land)
Time period(s): Indeterminate Future
Locale(s): Llantis, Fictional Country; Katandi, Fictional Country

Summary: The last of the sorcerers of Dammai, Rozlynd and her brother seek to begin a new life in the land of their ancestors; but Lord Justan needs Rozlynd's powers to rule his kingdom and he determines to wed her. Her powers, however, are just awakening, and the wild magic she wields is a bit more than Justan had expected. Mythical and romantic.

Other books you might like:
Rebecca Brandewyne, *Across a Starlit Sea*, 1991
Rebecca Brandewyne, *Swan Road*, 1994

Betina Lindsey, *Swan Star*, 1994
   3rd in a trilogy
Kathleen Morgan, *Fire Queen*, 1994
Susan Sizemore, *In My Dreams*, 1994

484

SARANNE DAWSON

The Enchanted Land
(New York: Leisure, 1992)

Story type: Contemporary/Fantasy
Major character(s): Emily Carr, Teacher (professor of folklore); Alyeka, Sorcerer
Time period(s): 1990s
Locale(s): New York; Scotland

Summary: Fascinated with the story of Azonyee and Nevoshee, magical people in an enchanted valley in New York, Professor Emily Carr is obsessed with the desire to visit it. Meanwhile, Sorcerer Aleyka has been sent to discover if Emily is the child of a forbidden union between her people and the Nevoshee. As Aleyka works with Emily, she discovers powers of her own and they discover love. A sensual, romantic, fairytale-like fantasy.

Other books you might like:
Laura Gilmour Bennett, *By All That Is Sacred*, 1991
Jessica Bryan, *Across a Wine-Dark Sea*, 1991
Barbara Erskine, *Kingdom of Shadows*, 1988
Bertrice Small, *A Moment in Time*, 1991

485

SARANNE DAWSON

From the Mist
(New York: Leisure, 1991)

Story type: Futuristic
Time period(s): Indeterminate
Locale(s): Volas, Fictional Country

Summary: Separated for years, the men and women of Volas have developed life-styles that leave no room for each other. Now, however, when climactic events force them together, they must face their ingrained prejudices and come to terms with reality—which includes some very pleasant and passionate discoveries.

Other books you might like:
Rebecca Brandewyne, *Beyond the Starlit Frost*, 1991
Rebecca Brandewyne, *Passion Moon Rising*, 1988
Jessica Bryan, *Across a Wine-Dark Sea*, 1991
Anne McCaffrey, *Dragonflight*, 1986
   first in the Dragonriders of Pern series
Judith Tarr, *Alamut*, 1989

486

ADRIENNE DAY

A Gentle Taming
(New York: Avon, 1994)

Story type: Historical/American West
Major character(s): Lauren Cooper, Rancher; Alec MacKenzie, Rancher
Time period(s): 1890s
Locale(s): Arizona

Summary: Feisty, tough Lauren slaves away on her alcoholic father's ranch, barely making ends meet. So it is small wonder that when the new neighbor puts up fences and blocks off the best pastures, Lauren takes revenge and rustles his prize steer. Naturally, this does not get their relationship off to a good start, but when Alec saves the day by rescuing Lauren from a particularly vicious man, things take a turn for the better—and peace and love soon follow.

Other books you might like:
Jude Deveraux, *Wishes*, 1989
Linda Howard, *A Lady of the West*, 1990
Pamela Litton, *Stardust and Whirlwinds*, 1991
Jill Metcalf, *Spring Blossom*, 1992
Victoria Thompson, *Sweet Texas Surrender*, 1991

487

LINDA RENEE DE JONG

Shattered Illusions
(New York: St. Martin's, 1992)

Story type: Contemporary/Mainstream
Major character(s): Amanda Farraday, Amnesiac; Brent Farraday, Doctor
Time period(s): 1990s
Locale(s): United States

Summary: Waking up in the hospital with no memory of her past, Amanda Farraday is stunned to discover that not only has she been missing for four years, but that she has a husband and two children who want her back. As she struggles to put together the pieces of her past, she is appalled to learn what she had been like in her former life, and is determined to make the most of her second chance. However, her chance for happiness is threatened when secrets from those missing years begin to come to light.

Other books you might like:
Catherine Coulter, *Beyond Eden*, 1991
Janet Dailey, *The Glory Game*, 1985
Janet Dailey, *Masquerade*, 1990
Jessica Gregory, *Once Innocent*, 1991

488

JOANN DE LAZZARI

Scoundrel's Captive
(New York: Avon, 1991)

Story type: Historical/American West

Major character(s): Jessica Morgan, Rancher; Steven Kincaid, Rancher
Time period(s): 1880s
Locale(s): Wyoming

Summary: Feisty, independent Jessica Morgan resists wealthy Steven Morgan's high-handed attempts to marry her—even though she eventually comes to love him. A story of pride, blackmail, and misunderstandings set in the rowdy and somewhat wild Wyoming West.

Other books you might like:
Constance Bennett, *Morning Sky*, 1991
Hannah Howell, *Stolen Ecstasy*, 1991
Joan Elliott Pickart, *The Bonnie Blue*, 1991
Victoria Thompson, *Wild Texas Promise*, 1990

489
JOANN DE LAZZARI
Scoundrel's Desire
(New York: Avon, 1993)

Story type: Historical/American West Coast
Major character(s): Breanna Sullivan, Young Woman, Activist; Alexander King, Activist (freedom fighter)
Time period(s): 1840s (1845)
Locale(s): Boston, Massachusetts; Monterey, California

Summary: Breanna hurries from Boston to Monterey to find her missing father—and finds infamous Alexander King, whom she strongly suspects of having something to do with her father's ''disappearance.'' King is working to free California from Mexican rule, so Breanna sets out to thwart his plans—with dangerous and passionate results. Good historical detail in a fast-paced story told from a somewhat unusual perspective.

Other books you might like:
Diane Austell, *Lights Along the Shore*, 1991
Virginia Brown, *Renegade Embrace*, 1990
Christina Dodd, *Treasure of the Sun*, 1991
Robin Lee Hatcher, *Midnight Rose*, 1992

490
CAROLE DEAN (Pseudonym of Edna Sheedy)
California Man
(Bensalem, Pennsylvania: Meteor, 1992)

Story type: Contemporary
Major character(s): Emily Welland, Businesswoman (bookstore owner); Quinn Ramsay, Businessman (entrepeneur)
Time period(s): 1990s
Locale(s): Salt Spring Island, British Columbia, Canada

Summary: Quinn Ramsay goes to a remote Canadian island to escape the California rat-race and ends up in love with a quiet, yet passionate, bookstore owner. A story of awakening and re-evaluation set in the majestic Pacific Northwest.

Other books you might like:
Muriel Jensen, *Valentine Hearts and Flowers*, 1992
Judi Lind, *Heart Song*, 1992

Nancy Sheehan, *The Heart's Journey*, 1992
   innocent
Chloe Summers, *No Easy Task*, 1991

491
CAROLE DEAN (Pseudonym of Edna Sheedy)
One Tough Cookie
(Bensalem, Pennsylvania: Meteor, 1993)

Story type: Contemporary
Major character(s): Willy Desmond, Writer (cookbooks/freelance); Taylor Monroe, Businessman; Dan Monroe, Photographer
Time period(s): 1990s
Locale(s): Costa del Sol, Spain

Summary: Willy Desmond, determined to remain aloof from romantic or emotional ties, is perfectly happy being an independent, wandering writer for Dan's photos. She is rudely surprised by strong-minded, business-like Taylor who wants brother Dan to settle down in New York and give up his rather Bohemian life-style. Although they fight it, Taylor and Willy are strongly attracted to each other; but their differences keep getting in the way. Likable characters.

Other books you might like:
Jeane Gilbert-Lewis, *Common Ground*, 1993
Emma Goldrick, *Summer Storm*, 1993
Jayne Ann Krentz, *Family Man*, 1993
Vella Munn, *Midnight Sun*, 1993
Karen Robards, *One Summer*, 1993
   steamy

492
KATHERINE DEAUVILLE (Pseudonym of Maggie Davis)
The Amethyst Crown
(New York: Zebra, 1994)

Story type: Historical/Medieval
Major character(s): Constance de Jobourg, Noblewoman; Cenred, Entertainer (juggler)
Time period(s): 12th century
Locale(s): England

Summary: Running from his past and his birthright, Cenred feigns insanity and becomes a travelling juggler. However, when Constance rescues him from captivity—and makes him her prisoner instead—he learns that he can't run away from either life or love. Interesting twist on the captive-in-love-with-captor pattern.

Other books you might like:
Rexanne Becnel, *The Rose of Blacksword*, 1992
Roberta Gellis, *The Rope Dancer*, 1986
Samantha James, *My Cherished Enemy*, 1992
Miriam Minger, *Wild Angel*, 1994
Judith Merkle Riley, *In Pursuit of the Green Lion*, 1990

KATHERINE DEAUVILLE (Pseudonym of Maggie Davis)

Blood Red Roses

(New York: St. Martins, 1991)

Story type: Historical/Medieval
Major character(s): Alwyn Lesneven, Noblewoman; Fulk De Jobourg, Nobleman (Knight)
Time period(s): 11th century (1078)
Locale(s): Wales

Summary: When William the Conqueror gives his loyal knight Fulk de Jobourg Lady Alwyn's castle—and the lady along with it—she rebels—and ends up tied and gagged at the altar, but wed, nonetheless. With Alwyn's fiery independence and Fulk's suspicions, their relationship is not an easy one, but love does have a way of changing things. A realistic, passionate, and not always romantic portrayal of a violent, dangerous period in history.

Other books you might like:
Julie Garwood, *The Prize*, 1991
Roberta Gellis, *Roselynde*, 1978
    first of the Roselynde Chronicles
Virginia Henley, *The Falcon and the Flower*, 1989
Anita Mills, *The Fire and the Fury*, 1991
Sharon Kay Penman, *Here Be Dragons*, 1985

KATHERINE DEAUVILLE (Pseudonym of Maggie Davis)

Daggers of Gold

(New York: St. Martin's, 1993)

Story type: Historical/Medieval
Major character(s): Ingrith, Young Woman (Saxon); Simon de Borge, Knight (crusader)
Time period(s): 11th century
Locale(s): England

Summary: Ingrith is given as a gift to old Prince Henry, and Simon de Borge is charged with taking her to the Prince. Neither suspects that they are being used as pawns in a conspiracy to overthrow the King and destroy London's greatest leaders. Naturally, they are attracted to each other, but circumstance keeps them apart, until Ingrith surmises that she won't have to marry Henry if she loses her virtue and the seduction begins. Treachery, intrigue, and a host of villains keep things interesting.

Other books you might like:
Julie Garwood, *The Prize*, 1991
    light and funny
Roberta Gellis, *The Silver Mirror*, 1989
Marylyle Rogers, *Dark Whispers*, 1991
Katherine Vickery, *Desire of the Heart*, 1990

CLAIRE DELACROIX

The Sorceress

(Toronto: Harlequin, 1994)

Story type: Historical/Medieval; Historical/Fantasy
Major character(s): Sophie Maucelerc, Adoptee (illegitimate child), Witch; Sir Hugues de Pontesse, Knight, Diplomat
Time period(s): 13th century (1226)
Locale(s): Bordeaux, France

Summary: Driven to discover the meaning of her dreams, Sophie leaves her adopted family and sets out after Hugues de Pontesse, the knight she has seen in her dreams. Shipwreck, hardship, an enchanted forest, and the witch Melusine await them on their journey—and Sophie is eventually forced to choose between her magical heritage and love.

Other books you might like:
Rexanne Becnel, *Where Magic Dwells*, 1994
Linda Madl, *A Tender Magic*, 1993
Maura Seger, *Tapestry*, 1993
Flora M. Speer, *A Love Beyond Time*, 1994
    time travel
Penelope Williamson, *Keeper of the Dream*, 1992

ELIZABETH DELANCEY

Meant to Be

(New York: Diamond, 1994)

Story type: Historical/American West
Major character(s): Julia Metcalf, Widow(er), Healer; Gib Booth, Con Artist, Drifter
Time period(s): 1880s (1883)
Locale(s): Stiles, Montana; Butte, Montana

Summary: Drifter and outcast Gib Booth returns to Stiles intending to con Julia Metcalf's husband out of his fortune. Instead, he finds that his quarry is dead and Julia has taken over the money and the medical practice; so he decides to win Julia. The hostile townsfolk and another suitor initially deter him, but as his attitude slowly changes, Julia begins to trust him. But circumstances and crooks intervene and it takes a bit of doing to restore Julia's trust and convince her that he is truly a changed person. Mainstream feel. Good research.

Other books you might like:
Elaine Barbieri, *More Precious than Gold*, 1992
    mainstream elements
Paris Afton Bonds, *Dream Time*, 1993
    another Bad-boy-returns story/Australian setting/ mainstream
Jill Gregory, *Lone Star Lady*, 1990
    another return-of-the-villain story/mainstream/strong heroine
Catherine Lanigan, *A Promise Made*, 1991
    strong heroine
Penelope Williamson, *Heart of the West*, 1995
    mainstream

497

ELIZABETH DELANCEY

Sea of Dreams
(New York: Diamond, 1992)

Story type: Historical/Exotic
Major character(s): Norah Paige, Gentlewoman, Orphan; Rob MacKenzie, Sea Captain
Time period(s): 19th century (first half)
Locale(s): United States; England; At Sea

Summary: Orphaned and gently raised, independent Norah Paige dreams of the sea and adventure. Sea captain Rob MacKenzie values his freedom and love for the sea above all things — until he meets Norah. A passionate, far-reaching adventure tale that sweeps from Boston and England to the Orient. Norah and Rob come to terms with their feelings for each other and then must confront secrets from their pasts. Strong characters, burning passion, and intriguing action.

Other books you might like:
Christine Dorsey, *Captain's Captive*, 1991
Meagan McKinney, *Till Dawn Tames the Night*, 1991
Karen Robards, *Green Eyes*, 1991
Karen Stratford, *Lavender Flame*, 1991
Jennifer West, *Passion's Legacy*, 1991

498

ELIZABETH DELANCEY

Touch of Lace
(New York: Diamond, 1993)

Story type: Historical/Victorian; Historical/Victorian America
Major character(s): Anna Massie, Seamstress (lace-maker), Immigrant; Stephen Flynn, Sports Figure (prize fighter)
Time period(s): 19th century
Locale(s): Ireland; New York, New York

Summary: Anna thinks she has left pain and fear behind her in Ireland when she heads for America, but when she attracts some unwanted attention and ends up involved in a murder, she realizes that fresh starts aren't so easy to come by. Stephen Flynn saves her by marrying her, but their differing ideas as to their vows cause some problems. Anna's dark past eventually causes her to flee once more, and Stephen once again saves her. An interesting picture of Irish immigrant life in the United States.

Other books you might like:
Elaine Barbieri, *Tattered Silk*, 1991
Sonja Massie, *Far and Away*, 1992
Victoria Morrow, *Jenny's Dream*, 1990
Laura Simon, *Garden of Dreams*, 1992
Lucy Taylor, *Avenue of Dreams*, 1990

499

BARBARA DELINSKY

Facets
(New York: Warner, 1990)

Story type: Contemporary/Mainstream
Major character(s): Pamela St. George, Artist (jewelry designer), Businesswoman (company owner); Hillary Cox, Writer; John St. George, Businessman (company owner)
Time period(s): 20th century
Locale(s): Maine; Boston, Massachusetts

Summary: Over the years, manager of the family gem (tourmaline) company, Facets, John St. George has cruelly manipulated the lives of those around him in order to get what he wants. But when he announces on national television that he is going to be married to a prominent socialite, his long-time lover, Hillary Cox, vows vengeance. John's younger half-sister, Pam, also has revenge in mind; and together Pam, Hillary and Cutter Reid (another victim) set in motion a plan that will right a number of old wrongs and ensure the future of the family and Facets, as well.

Other books you might like:
Sally Beauman, *Destiny*, 1987
Jacqueline Briskin, *Dreams Are Not Enough*, 1986
Janet Dailey, *Heiress*, 1987
Rebecca Forster, *A Delicate Matter*, 1989
Danielle Steel, *Daddy*, 1989

500

BARBARA DELINSKY

More than Friends
(New York: Harper, 1993)

Story type: Contemporary/Mainstream
Major character(s): Annie Pope, Professor (of literature); Sam Pope, Lawyer; Teke Maxwell, Housewife
Time period(s): 1990s
Locale(s): United States

Summary: The long-time close relationship between two families is shattered when an affair between Sam Pope and Teke Maxwell abruptly comes to light. Trust, forgiveness, and the true meaning of love are all issues explored in this perceptive and complex story of contemporary relationships.

Other books you might like:
Rexanne Becnel, *Christmas Journey*, 1992
Jillian Karr, *Something Borrowed, Something Blue*, 1993
Garda Parker, *Out of the Blue*, 1992
LaVyrle Spencer, *Bygones*, 1992
Helen Van Slyke, *No Love Lost*, 1980

501

BARBARA DELINSKY

The Passions of Chelsea Kane
(New York: Harper, 1992)

Story type: Contemporary/Mainstream; Romantic Suspense

Major character(s): Chelsea Kane, Architect, Adoptee; Judd Streeter, Foreman (of a quarry); Hunter Love, Bastard Son (of quarry owner)
Time period(s): 1990s
Locale(s): Norwich Notch, New England

Summary: When architect Chelsea Kane goes to the isolated New England mining town of Norwich Notch to learn more about her birth mother, she sets the town on its conservative ear and stirs up controversies and long-kept secrets that threaten her happiness and her life, as well. Fast-paced, suspenseful, and filled with interesting characters.

Other books you might like:
Janet Dailey, *Heiress*, 1987
Jayne Ann Krentz, *The Golden Chance*, 1990
Susan Kyle, *Night Fever*, 1990
Marcia Martin, *Southern Nights*, 1990
Nora Roberts, *Genuine Lies*, 1991

502

BARBARA DELINSKY

Suddenly

(New York: Harper, 1994)

Story type: Contemporary/Mainstream
Major character(s): Paige Pfeiffer, Doctor (pediatrician); Noah Perrine, Administrator
Time period(s): 1990s
Locale(s): Tucker, Vermont

Summary: Devastated by her best friend Mara's suicide, Dr. Paige Pfeiffer takes responsibility for Mara's East Indian foster baby, fully intending not to become emotionally attached. But Mara's death changes many people's lives in unexpected ways, and Paige suddenly finds herself in conflict with Noah Perrine, the local school headmaster. The situation eventually leads to love, and forces Paige to reassess her feelings about Mara's death and the baby. Good character development.

Other books you might like:
Barbara Taylor Bradford, *Remember*, 1992
Marie Ferrarella, *Sapphire and Shadow*, 1991
good characterizations/personal growth
Deborah Smith, *Miracle*, 1991
well done characters
Katherine Stone, *Pearl Moon*, 1995
self-discovery aspects/vastly different setting

503

BARBARA DELINSKY

A Woman Betrayed

(New York: Harper, 1991)

Story type: Contemporary/Mainstream
Major character(s): Laura Frye, Businesswoman (restaurant/catering), Spouse (abandoned); Christian Frye, Relative (Laura's brother-in-law); Jeffrey Frye, Spouse (vanished), Accountant
Time period(s): 1990s

Locale(s): United States

Summary: When Laura's husband of 20 years suddenly disappears, she is thrown into a nightmare of doubt and disillusionment as she is forced to deal with one devastating revelation after another. It is only when her husband's younger brother, Christian, returns and helps her begin to sort things out that Laura can get her life back on track once more. Powerful, well-drawn characters in a fascinating story of betrayal and rebirth.

Other books you might like:
Janet Dailey, *Masquerade*, 1990
Catherine Lanigan, *A Promise Made*, 1991
betrayal and determination in the Old West
Judith Michael, *Possessions*, 1984
Danielle Steel, *Palomino*, 1981
Helen Van Slyke, *No Love Lost*, 1980

504

GENELL DELLIN

Cherokee Dawn

(New York: Avon, 1990)

Story type: Historical/American West
Major character(s): Lacey Longbaugh, Orphan; Ridge Chekote, Indian (Part-Cherokee)
Time period(s): 1860s
Locale(s): Oklahoma

Summary: When her parents are killed young Lacey Longbaugh runs into the wilderness only to end up saving Ridge's life. Although passionately attracted to each other, they are eventually separated with Ridge in jail and Lacey returned to civilization. A story of passion and hardship set in the American West against the background of the Civil War.

Other books you might like:
Rosanne Bittner, *Arizona Ecstasy*, 1989
Rosanne Bittner, *Sweet Mountain Magic*, 1990
Cheryl Black, *Comanche Love Song*, 1989
Georgina Gentry, *Nevada Nights*, 1989
Jill Marie Landis, *Wild Flower*, 1989

505

GENELL DELLIN

Cherokee Nights

(New York: Avon, 1991)

Story type: Historical/American West
Major character(s): Celina Hawthorne, Lawyer, Indian (Cherokee); Kingfisher Chekote, Indian (Cherokee), Businessman (developer)
Time period(s): 1880s (1887)
Locale(s): California; Cherokee Nation

Summary: Fledgling attorney Celina Hawthorne accepts King Chekote as her first client and wins his land grant case for him but loses her heart in the process. A delightful, passionate story filled with Indian lore and legend that takes Celina and King from California to the Cherokee Nation on a search for her heritage. Second in a trilogy that began with *Cherokee Dawn*.

Other books you might like:
Madeline Baker, *A Whisper on the Wind*, 1991
Rosanne Bittner, *Sioux Splendor*, 1990
Cheryl Black, *Comanche Love Song*, 1989
Kathleen Harrington, *Cherish the Dream*, 1990
Shirl Henke, *Night Wind's Woman*, 1991

506
GENELL DELLIN

Cherokee Sundown
(New York: Avon, 1992)

Story type: Historical/American West
Series: Cherokee Nation
Major character(s): Tiana Tenkiller, Indian (Cherokee), Businessman (plantation manager); Standing Deer Chekote, Indian (Cherokee)
Time period(s): 1820s (1823); 1830s (1833)
Locale(s): Cherokee Nation, Georgia

Summary: Standing Deer and Tiana must deal with intertribal conflicts as well and external pressures as they struggle to realize their love and help their people fight for their land. Poignant, warm, and uplifting. Follows *Cherokee Nights* and *Cherokee Dawn*.

Other books you might like:
Beverly Bird, *Comes the Rain*, 1990
Michael Blake, *Dances with Wolves*, 1988
Deborah Smith, *Beloved Woman*, 1991
Patricia Werner, *Cherokee Bride*, 1992

507
GENELL DELLIN

Comanche Flame
(New York: Avon, 1994)

Story type: Historical/American West
Major character(s): Ysidora Pretty Sky, Indian, Royalty (Indian princess); Don Rafael Montoya, Rancher; High Wolf, Shaman
Time period(s): 1850s (1858)
Locale(s): New Mexico

Summary: The search to recover some lost gold joins the Spanish Don Rafael Montoya, Native American Princess Ysidora Pretty Sky, and Shaman High Wolf in a fast-paced, sensual adventure that involves murder, outlaws, land-grabbers, and Native American mysticism.

Other books you might like:
Madeline Baker, *Prairie Heat*, 1991
    fast-paced and passionate
Shirl Henke, *Night Wind's Woman*, 1990
Lindsay McKenna, *Sun Woman*, 1991
Nan Ryan, *Sun God*, 1990
    highly sensual

508
GENELL DELLIN

Comanche Wind
(New York: Avon, 1992)

Story type: Historical/American West
Major character(s): Jennie "Fire Flower" O'Bannion, Fugitive; Windrider, Chieftain, Indian (Comanche)
Time period(s): 1830s (1838)
Locale(s): Texas

Summary: Running from an abusive marriage, Jennie O'Bannion is taken captive by Comanche war chief Windrider, who defies tradition and keeps her himself instead of giving her away. Their wary respect for each other grows into love, but outside forces constantly seek to tear them apart. Passionate and fast-paced.

Other books you might like:
Cassie Edwards, *Wild Splendor*, 1993
Kathleen Harrington, *Cherish the Dream*, 1990
Catherine Hart, *Silken Savage*, 1985
Meagan McKinney, *Fair Is the Rose*, 1993
Bobbi Smith, *Dream Warrior*, 1993

509
TERESA DESJARDIEN

A June Bride
(New York: Zebra, 1991)

Story type: Regency
Major character(s): Alessandra, Noblewoman; Jeffrey, Nobleman
Time period(s): 1810s
Locale(s): England

Summary: When Lessie and her cousin Jeffrey are rushed into marriage to save their reputations (her dress fell apart in the park when they were together), Jeffrey's "intended" strives to keep the newlyweds from having a real marriage—with predictably Regency results.

Other books you might like:
Jo Beverley, *An Arranged Marriage*, 1991
Jo Beverley, *Lord Wraybourne's Betrothed*, 1988
Mary Kingsley, *A Gentleman's Desire*, 1991
Judith Nelson, *Lady's Choice*, 1990
Irene Saunders, *Talk of the Town*, 1991

510
TERESA DESJARDIEN

The Marriage Mart
(New York: Zebra, 1992)

Story type: Regency
Major character(s): Mary, Noblewoman, Spinster; Godfrey, Nobleman (Duke of Rothayne)
Time period(s): 1810s
Locale(s): England

Summary: Mary, an attractively plain spinster, gives up all hope for love and goes to the "Marriage Mart," where she meets very handsome Godfrey, who is friendly but definitely not marriage-minded. He changes his mind—almost too late to save her from another man. Wonderful characterizations and delightful wit.

Other books you might like:
Julie Caille, *An Impetuous Bride*, 1991
Marion Chesney, *Finessing Clarissa*, 1989
Jude Deveraux, *Wishes*, 1989
Carola Dunn, *Two Corinthians*, 1989

511

JUDE DEVERAUX (Pseudonym of Jude Gilliam White)

The Conquest
(New York: Pocket, 1991)

Story type: Historical/Medieval
Major character(s): Zared Peregrine, Noblewoman; Tearle Howard, Nobleman
Time period(s): 15th century
Locale(s): England

Summary: Determined to win her love at all costs, gentle Tearle pursues and woos the fiesty Zared in this fast-paced story of family feuds and long-held prejudices that gracefully drives home the message that love can, indeed, conquer hate. Ghosts, ancient mysteries, and plenty of medieval action in this the sequel the *The Taming*.

Other books you might like:
Rexanne Becnel, *My Gallant Enemy*, 1990
Julie Garwood, *The Bride*, 1989
Johanna Lindsey, *Defy Not the Heart*, 1989
Susan Wiggs, *The Lily and the Leopard*, 1991
Kathleen E. Woodiwiss, *The Wolf and the Dove*, 1971

512

JUDE DEVERAUX (Pseudonym of Jude Gilliam White)

Eternity
(New York: Pocket, 1991)

Story type: Historical/American West
Major character(s): Carrie Montgomery, Bride, Matchmaker; Joshua Greene, Farmer
Time period(s): 19th century (late)
Locale(s): Eternity, Colorado

Summary: Carrie arranges to marry Josh by proxy and travels west to meet him. Although she can't cook or plow, she loves his children, makes a difference in his home, and eventually wins him over by rising to challenges with her superb talent for organizing. Lively and heartwarming.

Other books you might like:
Rexanne Becnel, *Thief of My Heart*, 1990
Dorothy Garlock, *Homeplace*, 1991
Linda Howard, *A Lady of the West*, 1990
Kristin James, *The Yankee*, 1990

513

JUDE DEVERAUX

The Heiress
(New York: Pocket, 1995)

Story type: Historical/Elizabethan
Major character(s): Axia Maidenhall, Heiress, Imposter (pretends not to be the heiress); Jamie Montgomery, Nobleman (Earl of Dalkeith), Knight
Time period(s): 16th century (1572)
Locale(s): Dalkeith, England

Summary: Shocked to find his father and brother dead of a fever, his family's holdings and income gone, and his two sisters living in poverty, Jamie Montgomery knows he must marry an heiress. His opportunity comes when he is hired to escort the renowned Maidenhall heiress to the home of her fiance—and Jamie acquiesces to the suggestion of his sisters that he try to get the heiress to fall in love with him instead. Mistaken identity lends a lively twist and appealing secondary characters add to this story that is lighter and more of a romp than some of Deveraux's romances. Latest in the Montgomery family saga.

Other books you might like:
Christina Dodd, *The Greatest Lover in All England*, 1994
    similar time period/enchanting heroine/humorous
Christina Dodd, *Outrageous*, 1994
    similar time period/another "escort" plot/humorous
Julie Garwood, *The Bride*, 1989
    earlier time period/funny and lively
Betina M. Krahn, *Caught in the Act*, 1990
    similar time period/witty with a bit of a mystery
Suzanne Robinson, *Lord of Enchantment*, 1995
    similar time period/humorous/hidden identity

514

JUDE DEVERAUX (Pseudonym of Jude Gilliam White)

The Invitation
(New York: Pocket, 1994)

Story type: Collection
Time period(s): 1890s; 20th century (1930s and 1990s)
Locale(s): Colorado

Summary: Members of Deveraux's Montgomery clan are featured in three novellas set during the 1890s, 1930s, and the 1990s, which tell the stories of three unusual couples who receive invitations that change their lives.

Other books you might like:
Yvonne Adamson, *Bridey's Mountain*, 1993
    saga
Elaine Barbieri, *More Precious than Gold*, 1992
Stephanie Bartlett, *Highland Flame*, 1992
Rosanne Bittner, *In the Shadow of the Mountains*, 1991

JUDE DEVERAUX (Pseudonym of Jude Gilliam White)

A Knight in Shining Armor
(New York: Pocket, 1989)

Story type: Time Travel
Major character(s): Dougless Montgomery, Teacher (Elementary); Nicholas Stafford, Nobleman (Earl of Thornwyck)
Time period(s): 1980s; 16th century (1560s)
Locale(s): England

Summary: Stranded in England near the tomb of an Elizabethan nobleman, heroine Dougless Montgomery is stunned to see the very same knight materialize and come to rescue her. Their adventures take them from the present to the past and back again. Unusual historical romance with fantasy elements.

Other books you might like:
Johanna Lindsey, *A Gentle Feuding*, 1984
    Similar time period but no fantasy elements
Laurie McBain, *Moonstruck Madness*, 1977
    First of a romantic, action-packed trilogy—no fantasy elements
Lynda Trent, *The Tryst*, 1986
    Set in Elizabethan England with no fantasy elements
Kathleen Winsor, *Forever Amber*, 1944
    Classic historical with similar setting but no fantasy elements
Kathleen E. Woodiwiss, *The Wolf and the Dove*, 1974
    Sensual historical with no fantasy elements

JUDE DEVERAUX (Pseudonym of Jude Gilliam White)

Mountain Laurel
(New York: Pocket, 1990)

Story type: Historical/American West
Major character(s): Maddie "La Reina" Worth, Singer (opera); Ring Montgomery, Military Personnel (army captain)
Time period(s): 1850s (1859)
Locale(s): Rocky Mountains

Summary: To rescue her little sister Laurel from the men who have kidnapped her, opera singer Maddie Worth, billed as La Reina, follows instructions and performs at a series of mining towns in the Rockies. Captain Ring Montgomery has been assigned the task of protecting her, but in the process of keeping her safe, he falls in love. Funny, fast-paced, and peopled with interesting characters.

Other books you might like:
Marsha Bauer, *Sweet Conquest*, 1990
Jill Marie Landis, *Wild Flower*, 1989
Sara Orwig, *Albuquerque*, 1990
Rebecca Sinclair, *California Caress*, 1989
Jane Toombs, *Riverboat Rogue*, 1990

JUDE DEVERAUX (Pseudonym of Jude Gilliam White)

Remembrance
(New York: Pocket, 1994)

Story type: Reincarnation; Time Travel
Major character(s): Hayden Lane, Writer (of romance novels), Reincarnated Person; Jamie Tavistock, Nobleman, Reincarnated Person
Time period(s): 1910s; 16th century
Locale(s): New York, New York; England

Summary: When a psychic tells romance writer Hayden Lane that the reason she can't truly fall in love (i.e., can't connect with her soul mate) is that she is "blocked" because of something that happened in one of her past lives, she is intrigued. And when she ends up in the body of Lady de Grey during Edwardian times, and then in Callie's during the Elizabethan period, she knows she is on the right track. Eventually, all connections are made and all "blocks" are undone as Hayden finds her soul mate in this rather dark, yet occasionally funny, story of reincarnation and a love that lasts through time.

Other books you might like:
Nina Beaumont, *Across Time*, 1994
Laura Gilmour Bennett, *By All That Is Sacred*, 1991
Jasmine Cresswell, *Timeless*, 1994
Kristin Hannah, *Once in Every Life*, 1993
Eugenia Riley, *Tempest in Time*, 1993

JUDE DEVERAUX (Pseudonym of Jude Gilliam White)

Sweet Liar
(New York: Pocket, 1992)

Story type: Contemporary; Romantic Suspense
Major character(s): Samantha Elliott, Young Woman; Michael Taggert, Landlord
Time period(s): 1990s
Locale(s): New York, New York

Summary: Samantha is willing to do what her father's will asks — go to New York to try to find out what happened to her grandmother Maxie, a blues singer in the Twenties. She runs into problems, however, in the form of a charming and sexy landlord, who ends up helping in her search. Gangsters, murders, and vengeance are all part of this fast-paced mystery.

Other books you might like:
Carol Budd, *Scarlet Scandals*, 1990
Laura Hastings, *The Turtledove's Secret*, 1992
Jayne Ann Krentz, *Silver Linings*, 1991
Nora Roberts, *Genuine Lies*, 1991
Patricia Simpson, *Whisper of Midnight*, 1991
    supernatural elements

519

JUDE DEVERAUX (Pseudonym of Jude Gilliam White)

The Taming
(New York: Pocket, 1989)

Story type: Historical/Medieval
Major character(s): Liana Neville, Heiress; Rogan Peregrine, Landowner
Time period(s): 15th century (1440s)
Locale(s): England

Summary: When revenge-driven Rogan Peregrine marries wealthy Liana Neville as a means of gaining money to further his feud with the Howards, he does not bargain on also gaining a fiery woman who will not only organize his chaotic household and unproductive estates, but who will win his heart as well.

Other books you might like:
Rebecca Brandewyne, *Forever My Love*, 1982
Rebecca Brandewyne, *No Gentle Love*, 1980
Roberta Gellis, *Roselynde*, 1978
   First of the six Roselynde Chronicles
Johanna Lindsey, *A Gentle Feuding*, 1984
Johanna Lindsey, *When Love Awaits*, 1986

520

JUDE DEVERAUX (Pseudonym of Jude Gilliam White)

Wishes
(New York: Pocket, 1989)

Story type: Historical/Fantasy
Major character(s): Nellie Grayson, Spinster (overweight), Housekeeper (for her family); Jocelyn "Jace" Montgomery, Businessman (heir to a shipping concern)
Time period(s): 1890s (1896); Indeterminate Future
Locale(s): Chandler, Colorado

Summary: When shallow, self-centered Bernie suddenly dies, she finds herself in the novel position of having to help someone in order to get to heaven. Through wishes and personal intervention she succeeds in extricating sweet Nellie Grayson from her selfish sister and father and sends her off in the arms of wealthy Jace Montgomery. A real Cinderella story.

Other books you might like:
Marion Chesney, *Finessing Clarissa*, 1989
   School for Manners Series/All heroines need help to "make a match"
Lisa Gregory, *The Rainbow Promise*, 1989
Marie Joseph, *A Leaf in the Wind*, 1982
   Another "Cinderella" story
Jill Marie Landis, *Wild Flower*, 1989
Colleen McCullough, *The Ladies of Missalonghi*, 1987

521

THEA DEVINE

Montana Mistress
(New York: Zebra, 1990)

Story type: Historical/American West
Major character(s): Julienne Montgomery, Orphan; Sam Garrison, Mine Owner
Time period(s): 19th century (late)
Locale(s): New York; Montana

Summary: When beautiful Rosalind Montgomery doesn't show up at her own wedding, her penniless cousin Julienne marries the astonished groom instead. Together, Sam and Julienne head for the copper mines of Montana and into passionate and intriguing adventure.

Other books you might like:
Rosanne Bittner, *Montana Woman*, 1990
Deborah Camp, *Black-Eyed Susan*, 1990
Dorothy Garlock, *Nightrose*, 1990
Norah Hess, *Wildfire*, 1989
Charlotte Simms, *Silver Caress*, 1990

522

THEA DEVINE

Southern Seduction
(New York: Zebra, 1991)

Story type: Historical/Antebellum American South
Major character(s): Cassandra Taggart, Widow(er), Plantation Owner; Coltrane "Trane" Taggart, Young Man (stepson of Cassandra)
Time period(s): 1850s (1859)
Locale(s): Georgia; Texas

Summary: To retain control of her plantation and her life, Cassandra Taggart invents a long-lost son from her late husband's first marriage; but when the real Coltrane Taggart shows up, events take an interesting and passionate turn. A battle of wills in the Antebellum South.

Other books you might like:
Brenna Braxton-Barshon, *Southern Oaks*, 1991
Wendy Garrett, *Sweet Southern Caress*, 1991
Shirl Henke, *Moonflower*, 1989
Bobbi Smith, *Bayou Bride*, 1991
Kathleen E. Woodiwiss, *The Flame and the Flower*, 1972

523

THEA DEVINE

Tempted by Fire
(New York: Zebra, 1992)

Story type: Historical/Regency
Major character(s): Jaine Beaumont, Gambler; Nicholas Carradine, Nobleman (Lord Southam)
Time period(s): 1800s (1807)
Locale(s): England

Summary: When young Jaine Beaumont loses 10,000 pounds to Nicholas Carradine, the only way she thinks she can pay her debt is by becoming his mistress. Nicholas tries to arrange things respectably, but when scandal starts, they end up getting married — and Jaine goes off to the country. The country, however, proves to be a dangerous place and Nicholas returns just in time to save her life. Mystery, murder, and surprises are all part of this highly sensual romance.

Other books you might like:
Nicole Jordan, *Touch Me with Fire*, 1993
Brenda Joyce, *Scandalous Love*, 1992
DeLoras Scott, *Rogue's Honor*, 1992
Carla Simpson, *Seductive Caress*, 1992

524

MARIAN DEVON

Deck the Halls

(New York: Fawcett Crest, 1995)

Story type: Regency; Holiday Themes
Major character(s): Lady Audrey Hunt, Widow(er), Noblewoman; Lord Edwin Elliot, Nobleman; Sir Jervis Brougham, Nobleman
Time period(s): 1810s
Locale(s): England

Summary: A supposed death bed summons by Sir Jervis Brougham brings his far-flung family to his country estate for the holidays and a bit of matchmaking. The results are appropiately romantic, although somewhat different from what Sir Jervis had planned. A light-hearted, traditional Regency romp with good period detail and dialogue.

Other books you might like:
Mary Balogh, *Christmas Belle*, 1994
　a bit more serious than some/holiday theme
Sandra Heath, *A Christmas Courtship*, 1990
　holiday theme
Carla Kelly, *Marian's Christmas Wish*, 1995
　holiday theme
Barbara Metzger, *Father Christmas*, 1995
　light and lively
Joan Smith, *The Kissing Bough*, 1994

525

MARIAN DEVON

Lord Harlequin

(New York: Fawcett Crest, 1994)

Story type: Regency
Major character(s): Persephone "Persey" McCall, Actress; Jonathan Forsythe, Nobleman (Lord Worth), Fugitive
Time period(s): 1810s
Locale(s): England

Summary: When Lord Worth is falsely accused of shooting an acquaintance in the back, he takes refuge among his uncle's pantomime troupe — and ends up playing harlequin to Persey McCall's Columbine, both on stage and in real life. Light and predictable—with a touch of mystery.

Other books you might like:
Mary Balogh, *Christmas Belle*, 1994
Clare Darcy, *Caroline and Julia*, 1982
Emily Hendrickson, *Miss Wyndham's Escapade*, 1990
Carla Kelly, *Miss Billings Treads the Boards*, 1993
Mary Kingsley, *The Rake's Reward*, 1991

526

MARIAN DEVON

Miss Osborne Misbehaves

(New York: Fawcett Crest, 1990)

Story type: Regency
Major character(s): Eliza Osborn, Debutante; Garrick Slaughter, Nobleman (Bastard Son), Convict
Time period(s): 1810s
Locale(s): Cornwall, England

Summary: While her father is honeymooning with his new bride, Eliza takes a public coach to visit her aunt in Cornwall and meets Garrick Slaughter, a gentleman just out of Newgate. Eliza thinks he was accused of theft unjustly and sets out to prove it. A spirited Regency mystery.

Other books you might like:
Janice Bennett, *A Tempting Miss*, 1989
Gail Clark, *The Baroness of Bow Street*, 1979
Annabel Laine, *The Reluctant Heiress*, 1978
Jane Lovelace, *Rolissa*, 1985
Linda Walker, *My Lady's Deception*, 1990

527

THERESA DIBENEDETTO

Silver Mist

(New York: Charter/Diamond)

Story type: Historical/Victorian America
Major character(s): Dara Owens, Businesswoman (daughter of store owner); Eden "Silver" McQuade, Miner (of phosphate)
Time period(s): 19th century
Locale(s): Rainy, Florida

Summary: When sexy miner Eden "Silver" McQuade comes to town as part of the "phosphate rush," prim Dara Owens' peaceful and proper world is turned upside down. Old enemies, turf fights, and divided families are all part of this sensual historical with an unusual setting.

Other books you might like:
Emily Carmichael, *Visions of the Heart*, 1990
Dorothy Garlock, *Midnight Blue*, 1989
Jill Marie Landis, *Rose*, 1990
Victoria Thompson, *Playing with Fire*, 1990

528

THERESA DIBENEDETTO

Western Winds

(New York: Diamond, 1991)

Story type: Historical/American West
Major character(s): Lacey Garrett, Heiress, Rancher; Rafe Parrish, Heir, Rancher
Time period(s): 19th century
Locale(s): Texas

Summary: Upon the death of Sy Garrett, Lacey is shocked to discover that not only is she *not* Sy's natural daughter, but that she must share the ownership of her Texas ranch with Sy's long-lost, illegitimate son. Antagonism eventually turns into love in this fast-paced, violent, and highly passionate romance.

Other books you might like:
Rebecca Brandewyne, *Heartland*, 1990
Martha Hix, *Wild Texas Rose*, 1990
Linda Lael Miller, *Caroline and the Raider*, 1992
Penelope Neri, *Cherish the Night*, 1992

529

DEBRA DIER
EUGENIA RILEY, Co-Author
AMY ELIZABETH SAUNDERS, Co-Author
TRANA MAE SIMMONS, Co-Author

Christmas Angels

(New York: Love Spell, 1995)

Story type: Anthology; Holiday Themes
Time period(s): 1990s; 19th century
Locale(s): United States; England

Summary: This angel-filled quartet of Christmas novellas takes the reader from a 19th century English estate to a trendy contemporary Seattle boutique, with side trips to the Old West and an English country village. Included are "The Trouble with Hannah" by Debra Dier, "Tryst with an Angel" by Eugenia Riley, "A Time for Joy" by Amy Elizabeth Saunders, and "Chrissy's Wish" by Trana Mae Simmons.

Other books you might like:
Mary Balogh, *Angel Christmas*, 1995
  paranormal Christmas anthology
Mary Chase Comstock, *A Christmas Wish*, 1994
  Christmas anthology
Sandra Heath, *Lucy's Christmas Angel*, 1995
  Regency period
Debbie Macomber, *A Season of Angels*, 1993
Heather Graham Pozzessere, *An Angel's Touch*, 1995

530

DEBRA DIER

A Quest of Dreams

(New York: Love Spell, 1994)

Story type: Historical/Exotic

Major character(s): Katherine Whitmore, Archaeologist; Devlin McCain, Guide (reluctant)
Time period(s): 1880s (1886)
Locale(s): Rio de Janiero, Brazil

Summary: Determined to join her father on a search for the lost city of Atlantis, archaeologist Kate Whitmore hires the reluctant Devlin McCain as her guide. Constant battles over her presence only add to the other problems—natives, wild animals, killers, and the jungle in general—but love comes to the fore when Devlin must save Kate from disaster. Sensual jungle adventure with the added bonus of a new theory concerning Atlantis.

Other books you might like:
Kristin Hannah, *The Enchantment*, 1992
  quests and mystical adventure
James Hilton, *Lost Horizon*, 1933
Iris Johansen, *Tiger Prince*, 1993
  quests and adventure
Laura Kinsale, *The Dream Hunter*, 1994
  a desert quest/complex characters

531

DEBRA DIER

Surrender the Dream

(New York: Leisure, 1993)

Story type: Historical/American West Coast
Major character(s): Victoria Granger, Heiress, Activist; Spence Kincaid, Shipowner
Time period(s): 1850s
Locale(s): San Francisco, California

Summary: Jilted and embittered, wealthy Victoria Granger secretly devotes herself to saving young girls from the brothels, all the while rejecting her father's demands that she marry and settle down—until, that is, she meets shipowner Spence Kincaid. However, his "marital condition" and a series of kidnappings and murders keep things in turmoil in this somewhat sordid, realistic, suspense-filled story of old San Francisco.

Other books you might like:
Gwen Bristow, *Calico Palace*, 1970
Deborah Camp, *My Wild Rose*, 1992
Donna Fletcher, *San Francisco Surrender*, 1990
Robin Lee Hatcher, *Midnight Rose*, 1992
Patricia Watters, *Come Be My Love*, 1993

532

DEBRA DIXON

Hot as Sin

(New York: Bantam, 1995)

Story type: Contemporary
Major character(s): Emily Quinn, Fugitive (in witness program), Imposter (nun); Christian Gabriel, Saloon Keeper/Owner (bartender), Military Personnel (former SEAL team member)
Time period(s): 1990s

Locale(s): Rock Falls, Washington

Summary: When her protector is suddenly killed, material witness and ice-skating champion Emily Quinn "takes the veil" and heads in search of the man she was told could make her "disappear." Funny, fast-paced, and sexy with likable characters.

Other books you might like:
Jennifer Crusie, *What the Lady Wants*, 1995
　　fast-paced/good dialogue
Justine Davis, *Errant Angel*, 1995
Jennifer Greene, *Arizona Heat*, 1995
B.J. James, *The Heart of the Hunter*, 1995
Paula Detmer Riggs, *Hiding Jessica*, 1995

533

DEBRA DIXON

Mountain Mystic

(New York: Bantam, 1994)

Story type: Contemporary/Fantasy
Major character(s): Victoria Bennett, Midwife; Joshua Logan, Archaeologist, Psychic
Time period(s): 1990s
Locale(s): Appalachian Mountains, Tennessee

Summary: Psychic archaeologist Joshua Logan and nurse midwife Victoria Bennett are both running—he from fame, fortune, and notoriety; she from rigid societal expectations and an empty life. But when they meet in the mountains of Tennessee, they are forced to face the fact that no matter how hard they try, they can't run away from either life or love. Good characterization and interesting secondary characters.

Other books you might like:
Maggie Daniels, *Moonlight and Mistletoe*, 1993
　　Christmas theme/rural setting
Patricia Gaffney, *Sweet Everlasting*, 1993
　　historical setting
Coral Smith Saxe, *Enchantment*, 1994
　　historical healer
Deborah Smith, *Sara's Surprise*, 1990

534

CHRISTINA DODD

Candle in the Window

(New York: Harper, 1991)

Story type: Historical/Medieval
Major character(s): William of Miraval, Nobleman, Handicapped (blind); Saura of Roget, Noblewoman, Handicapped (blind)
Time period(s): 12th century (1153)
Locale(s): England

Summary: When Sir William loses his sight in battle, Lady Saura, blind since childhood, comes to teach him her skills and helps him deal with his blindness. Unaware that Saura is blind herself, William teases her, learns from her, and falls in love with her—only to be forced to deal with her refusal to marry him when he suddenly regains his sight. Tender, gentle, and romantic.

Other books you might like:
Jude Deveraux, *The Taming*, 1989
Laura Kinsale, *The Prince of Midnight*, 1990
　　different period
Teresa Medeiros, *Shadows and Lace*, 1990
Mary Jo Putney, *Uncommon Vows*, 1991
Kathleen E. Woodiwiss, *The Wolf and the Dove*, 1971

535

CHRISTINA DODD

Castles in the Air

(New York: Harper, 1993)

Story type: Historical/Medieval
Major character(s): Julianna of Lofts, Noblewoman (castle owner), Widow(er); Raymond of Avrache, Nobleman, Imposter (disguised as a castle builder)
Time period(s): 12th century
Locale(s): England

Summary: Thrown together by fate, deception, and decree, Julianna and Raymond work to overcome mistrust and outside interference, eventually discovering a love they thought they would never have. Gentle, humorous, and well-crafted.

Other books you might like:
Rexanne Becnel, *The Rose of Blacksword*, 1992
Julie Garwood, *The Bride*, 1989
Jennifer Horsman, *Awaken My Fire*, 1992
Hannah Howell, *Beauty and the Beast*, 1992

536

CHRISTINA DODD

The Greatest Lover in All England

(New York: Harper, 1994)

Story type: Historical/Elizabethan
Major character(s): Rosencrantz "Rosie", Actress, Heiress—Lost; Anthony "Tody" Rycliffe, Nobleman, Bastard Son
Time period(s): 17th century (1600)
Locale(s): England

Summary: When the leader of a travelling theatre company decides to pass his ward, Rosie, off as the missing heiress to an estate, the results are funny, romantic, and occasionally, dangerous—particularly when Rosie turns out actually to be the heiress in question. Old secrets, wicked schemes, and historical characters (Shakespeare, for one) pepper the scene in this fast-paced story set during the bawdy and colorful reign of Elizabeth I.

Other books you might like:
Jo Beverley, *My Lady Notorious*, 1993
　　bawdy, witty and fast-paced/later period
Carla Kelly, *Miss Billings Treads the Boards*, 1993
　　more theatrics, Regency-style
Betina M. Krahn, *Behind Closed Doors*, 1991
Betina M. Krahn, *Caught in the Act*, 1990

Erin Yorke, *Heaven's Gate*, 1992
  Elizabethan intrigue

537

CHRISTINA DODD

Lady in Black

(Bensalem, Pennsylvania: Meteor, 1993)

Story type: Contemporary
Major character(s): Margaret Guarneri, Servant (butler), Widow(er); Reid Donovan, Businessman (retired), Handicapped
Time period(s): 1990s
Locale(s): Houston, Texas

Summary: Margaret Guarneri, butler par excellence, thinks she has found the perfect job to support herself and her daughter when she comes to work for 92 year old Jim Donovan—that is, until his grandson, Reid, moves in. He challenges her at every turn and their mutual distrust—and attraction—get in the way of coping with threats of kidnapping wealthy Mr. Donovan. Suspicions and very real danger are the order of the day.

Other books you might like:
Elizabeth August, *The Virgin Wife*, 1993
Blythe Bradley, *To Love a Stranger*, 1993
Pam Hart, *Lies and Shadows*, 1993
Jeane Gilbert Lewis, *Common Ground*, 1993

538

CHRISTINA DODD

Move Heaven and Earth

(New York: Harper, 1995)

Story type: Historical/Regency; Gothic
Major character(s): Sylvan Miles, Nurse, Gentlewoman; Lord Randolf Malkin, Nobleman, Handicapped (paralyzed from a war wound)
Time period(s): 1810s (1816)
Locale(s): Somerset, England; England

Summary: Plagued by memories of the war and needing a change, Sylvan Miles comes to Clairmont Court to nurse the angry, reclusive, and paralyzed Randolf Malkin. What she finds, however, is a vulnerable (if somewhat obnoxious) wounded hero, a few family ghosts, and a passionate love. Well-written, with plenty of gothic atmosphere.

Other books you might like:
Susan Carroll, *The Painted Veil*, 1995
  an emotionally wounded hero
Laura Kinsale, *Flowers From the Storm*, 1992
  brain-damaged hero
Mary Jo Putney, *Thunder and Roses*, 1993
Amanda Scott, *The Bawdy Bride*, 1995
  Gothic tendencies
Anne Stuart, *To Love a Dark Lord*, 1994
  dark and dangerous

539

CHRISTINA DODD

Outrageous

(New York: Harper, 1994)

Story type: Historical/Renaissance
Major character(s): Lady Marian Wenthaven, Noblewoman, Warrior; Griffith ap Powel, Mercenary
Time period(s): 16th century
Locale(s): England

Summary: When Welsh mercenary Griffith is sent by the king to deliver gold to Lady Marian, he gets more than he bargains for. Schooled as a warrior and and excellent swordswoman, Marian needs no protection. However, royal intrigue, treachery, and Marian's dangerous secret puts Griffith to the test—both to defend the honor of his king and to claim Marian for his own. Fast-paced, exciting, and humorous.

Other books you might like:
Rexanne Becnel, *The Rose of Blacksword*, 1992
  earlier period/determined heroine
Julie Garwood, *The Prize*, 1991
  lively humor
Julie Garwood, *Saving Grace*, 1993
  more lively humor
Hannah Howell, *Silver Flame*, 1992
  intrigue and humor from a different viewpoint
Judith Merkle Riley, *In Pursuit of the Green Lion*, 1990
  wit and charm — and a helpful ghost

540

CHRISTINA DODD

Priceless

(New York: Harper, 1992)

Story type: Historical/Georgian
Major character(s): Bronwyn Edana, Gentlewoman; Adam Keane, Nobleman (Viscount Rawson)
Time period(s): 1720s
Locale(s): England

Summary: Intelligent, adventurous, ugly-duckling Bronwyn Edana is betrothed to a haunted, scandal-plagued nobleman — and he needs her help! Someone is framing him in a financial scheme! Bronwyn has her own problems to solve, but together they find the answers — and love in the process. Nice mixture of mystery, murder, and romance.

Other books you might like:
Jude Deveraux, *Wishes*, 1989
Amanda Quick, *Scandal*, 1991
Amanda Quick, *Ravished*, 1992

541

CHRISTINA DODD

Treasure of the Sun

(New York: Harper, 1991)

Story type: Historical/American West

Major character(s): Katherine Maxwell, Widow(er), House-keeper; Damian de la Sol, Landowner (Californio)
Time period(s): 1840s (1846)
Locale(s): California
Summary: Widowed within days of her wedding, independent Easterner Katherine Maxwell suddenly finds herself under the protection and in the employ of her late husband's best friend, the arrogant and aristocratic Californio Damian de la Sol. Driven by passion, pride, and independence, Katherine and Damian battle each other and the settlers who would take the de la Sol land and gold. Excellent historical detail and realistic portrayal of Mexican-held, pre-Gold Rush California.

Other books you might like:
Diane Austell, *Lights Along the Shore*, 1991
Jill Barnett, *Surrender a Dream*, 1991
Gwen Bristow, *Calico Palace*, 1970
Virginia Brown, *Renegade Embrace*, 1990

542
CHARLOTTE LOUISE DOLAN
The Black Widow
(New York: Signet, 1992)

Story type: Regency
Major character(s): Meribe Prestwich, Debutante; Demetrius Thorverton, Nobleman
Time period(s): 1810s
Locale(s): England
Summary: In spite of the lovely Meribe Prestwich's "Black Widow" reputation (all her suitors die), Lord Thorverton is determined to befriend her. However, when he is physically attacked, he begins to wonder who and why someone wants to keep Meribe from marrying. A witty and intriguing Regency with a touch of mystery and suspense.

Other books you might like.
Cathleen Clare, *The Mistress of Mishap*, 1992
Jennifer Horsman, *Awaken My Fire*, 1992
    different time period/sensual
Melinda McRae, *A Highly Respected Widow*, 1992
Amanda Quick, *Ravished*, 1992

543
CHARLOTTE LOUISE DOLAN
The Counterfeit Gentleman
(New York: Signet, 1994)

Story type: Regency
Major character(s): Bethia Pepperell, Heiress; Digory Rendel, Smuggler (former)
Time period(s): 1810s
Locale(s): London, England
Summary: Heiress Bethia Pepperell is in the process of being drowned by kidnappers when former smuggler Digory Rendel reluctantly comes to her rescue. It was, after all, the right thing to do. Nevertheless, he is through with smuggling and he simply doesn't want to get involved in the mysteries and intrigue that surround Bethia. Eventually, of course, his

adventurous spirit and his attraction to Bethia win out and the fun begins.

Other books you might like:
Rita Boucher, *Miss Gabriel's Gambit*, 1993
Jean R. Ewing, *Rogue's Reward*, 1995
Carla Kelly, *Libby's London Merchant*, 1991
Michelle Martin, *Queen of Hearts*, 1995
Kate Moore, *Sweet Bargain*, 1993

544
CHARLOTTE LOUISE DOLAN
Fallen Angel
(New York: Signet, 1993)

Story type: Regency
Major character(s): Verity Jolliffe, Spinster; Lord Gabriel Rainsford, Nobleman (Lord Sherington)
Time period(s): 1810s
Locale(s): England
Summary: Arrogant Gabriel Rainsford and plain Verity Jolliffe are both possessed of exceedingly obnoxious and offensive families—families that cause an incredible amount of trouble when Verity and Gabriel decide that they just might "suit." A witty regency with interesting characters.

Other books you might like:
Sarah Eagle, *The Marriage Gamble*, 1992
Georgette Heyer, *Friday's Child*, 1946
Sheila O'Hallion, *The Captured Heart*, 1991
Marlene Suson, *Devil's Bargain*, 1992
Sheila Walsh, *The Arrogant Lord Alistair*, 1990

545
CHARLOTTE LOUISE DOLAN
The Substitute Bridegroom
(New York: New American Library/Signet, 1991)

Story type: Regency
Major character(s): Elizabeth Goldsborough, Gentlewoman; Darius St. John, Nobleman, Military Personnel (army captain)
Time period(s): 1810s
Locale(s): England
Summary: When her fiance cries off after Elizabeth is disfigured in a carriage accident, the cause of the accident, reckless Captain Darius St. John, is coerced into marrying Elizabeth as recompense. Events conspire to keep the newlyweds apart, but in spite of a series of misunderstandings, the situation resolves itself happily—in true Regency style.

Other books you might like:
Gayle Buck, *Mutual Consent*, 1991
Rosemary Edghill, *The Ill-Bred Bride*, 1990
Georgette Heyer, *The Convenient Marriage*, 1934
Mary Kingsley, *A Gentleman's Desire*, 1991
Marlene Suson, *The Errant Earl*, 1989

546

DENISE DOMNING

Autumn's Flame

(New York: Topaz, 1995)

Story type: Historical/Medieval
Major character(s): Lady Elyssa of Freyne, Widow(er), Noblewoman; Geoffrey FitzHenry, Government Official (sheriff), Guardian
Time period(s): 12th century (1194)
Locale(s): England

Summary: Although widowed and in danger, Lady Elyssa is incensed that she has been placed in the ''care'' of the sheriff of the shire, Geoffrey FitzHenry. Sparks fly as they try to come to terms with their situation and their growing feelings for each other. Treachery and passion in a ruthless age.

Other books you might like:
Linda Lang Bartell, *Tender Warrior*, 1992
Rebecca Brandewyne, *Forever My Love*, 1982
Jude Deveraux, *The Taming*, 1989
Julie Garwood, *Saving Grace*, 1993
Arnette Lamb, *Chieftain*, 1994

547

DENISE DOMNING

Summer Storm

(New York: Topaz, 1994)

Story type: Historical/Medieval
Major character(s): Lady Phillipa Lindhurst, Noblewoman, Abuse Victim; Temric Graiston, Knight (reluctant), Bastard Son
Time period(s): 12th century
Locale(s): England; England

Summary: Although Temric refuses knighthood because of his illegitimacy, nevertheless he often acts as a knight. When he kidnaps the unhappy, frightened Phillipa so she can visit her sister, he makes a dangerous enemy of her abusive husband. Phillipa and Temric's growing love for each other doesn't help the situation and in the face of no other alternatives, eventually they become fugitives and outcasts. An intense, emotional, unusual love story.

Other books you might like:
Kathryn Lynn Davis, *Child of Awe*, 1990
Julie Garwood, *Saving Grace*, 1993
  humorous touches
Roberta Gellis, *The Silver Mirror*, 1989
Iris Johansen, *Midnight Warrior*, 1994
Laura Kinsale, *For My Lady's Heart*, 1993

548

DENISE DOMNING

Winter's Heat

(New York: Topaz, 1994)

Story type: Historical/Medieval

Major character(s): Rowena of Benfield, Religious (novice); Rannulf Fitzhenry, Nobleman (Lord of Graistan), Widow(er)
Time period(s): 12th century (1194)
Locale(s): Graistan, England

Summary: Forced to leave the convent where she was raised, Lady Rowena reluctantly marries wealthy and influential Lord Rannulf. Being of a practical nature, Rowena decides to make the best of things and so she takes matters in hand. Unfortunately, she doesn't count on family treachery and deceit. Rannulf is surprised and confused—all he wants is a good, dutiful wife. Nevertheless, he does defend her when she is threatened—and they do eventually fall in love.

Other books you might like:
Roberta Gellis, *Roselynde*, 1978
  1st in the Roselynde Chronicles
Johanna Lindsey, *Defy Not the Heart*, 1989
Elizabeth Lowell, *Untamed*, 1993
  lyrical
Anita Mills, *The Fire and the Fury*, 1991
Anita Mills, *Winter Roses*, 1992

549

CHRISTINE DORSEY

Captain's Captive

(New York: Zebra, 1991)

Story type: Historical/War of 1812
Major character(s): Charlotte Winston, Fiance(e) (reluctant), Gentlewoman; Jonathan Knox, Sea Captain, Plantation Owner
Time period(s): 1810s
Locale(s): At Sea; Montreal, Quebec, Canada; United States

Summary: Although English Miss Charlotte Winston had romantically dreamt of being swept away in the arms of a handsome pirate, when the American Captain Jonathan Knox does just that, the reality is a bit different from the fantasy. A swiftly paced, neatly plotted adventure filled with passion and romance set against the political and military background of the War of 1812.

Other books you might like:
Deana James, *Masque of Sapphire*, 1990
Betina M. Krahn, *Passion's Ransom*, 1989
Cara Miles, *Promise Me Forever*, 1992
Maura Seger, *Into the Storm*, 1990

550

CHRISTINE DORSEY

Kansas Kiss

(New York: Zebra, 1992)

Story type: Historical/Post-American Civil War
Major character(s): Samantha Lowery, Activist (abolitionist), Farmer; Jacob Morgan, Military Personnel (Confederate Captain), Doctor
Time period(s): 1860s
Locale(s): Kansas

Summary: When abolitionist and farmer Samantha Lowery mistakenly shoots Confederate Captain Jacob Morgan, she reluctantly nurses him back to health—only to find the recovered and virile doctor is very much a threat to her heart. Pride, conflicting values, and the War in general keep their relationship in turmoil until they can come to terms with their true feelings for each other.

Other books you might like:
Micki Brown, *Once a Rebel*, 1992
Elizabeth Kary, *Let No Man Divide*, 1987
Diane Gates Robinson, *The Falcon and the Swan*, 1992
Kathleen E. Woodiwiss, *Ashes in the Wind*, 1979

551
CHRISTINE DORSEY
Sea Fires
(New York: Zebra, 1992)

Story type: Historical/Colonial America
Series: Charleston Trilogy
Major character(s): Miranda Chadwick, Scientist; Jack Blackstone, Pirate, Sea Captain
Time period(s): 17th century (1699); 18th century
Locale(s): Barbary Coast, Africa; Carolinas, American Colonies

Summary: When lovely and fiesty Miranda Chadwick is kidnapped by pirate captain Jack Blackstone, she ends up charming his entire crew and Jack, as well. Fast-paced, sensual action.

Other books you might like:
Marsha Bauer, *Pirate's Angel*, 1991
Shannon Drake, *Bride of the Wind*, 1992
Connie Mason, *Tempt the Devil*, 1990
Meagan McKinney, *Till Dawn Tames the Night*, 1991
Kathleen E. Woodiwiss, *Shanna*, 1977

552
CHRISTINE DORSEY
Sea of Dreams
(New York: Zebra, 1993)

Story type: Historical/American Revolution; Historical/Georgian
Major character(s): Merideth Baxter, Noblewoman; Jared Blackstone, Privateer, Sea Captain
Time period(s): 1770s (1777)
Locale(s): England; France; At Sea

Summary: While in England in search of a traitor, dashing American privateer Jared Blackstone suddenly finds his "almost informant" dead and himself in jail accused of the murder. His only hope to avoid hanging and to clear his name is to take the dead man's beautiful daughter, Merideth, hostage and sail for France. Passion, adventure, and intrigue await.

Other books you might like:
Barbara Cummings, *Rebel Wildfire*, 1992
Gretchen Genet, *Winds of Glory*, 1993

Karen Harper, *The Firelands*, 1990
Maura Seger, *Fortune's Tide*, 1990
    England wins the War

553
CHRISTINE DORSEY
Traitor's Embrace
(New York: Zebra, 1990)

Story type: Historical/American Revolution
Major character(s): Elizabeth, Loyalist; Alexander Kent, Spy (Revolutionary)
Time period(s): 1770s (1777)
Locale(s): Maryland; Philadelphia, Pennsylvania

Summary: Although she recognizes Alexander Kent as a revolutionary, loyalist Elizabeth surprises herself and covers for him as he spies on loyalist activities. When he is eventually caught, it is she who must figure out how to save him.

Other books you might like:
Caryn Cameron, *Liberty's Lady*, 1990
Judith E. French, *Scarlet Ribbons*, 1989
Heather Graham, *Love Not a Rebel*, 1989
Robin Maderich, *Faith and Honor*, 1989
Maura Seger, *Fortune's Tide*, 1990
    England wins the American Revolution!

554
CAROLE NELSON DOUGLAS
Crystal Days
(New York: Bantam, 1990)

Story type: Romantic Suspense
Major character(s): Midnight Louie, Animal (Cat), Detective—Private
Time period(s): 1990s
Locale(s): Las Vegas, Nevada

Summary: As the "official" private detective for the new Crystal Phoenix Casino, Midnight Louie, an irrepressible, arrogant cat, makes it his business to know everything that goes on in his domain. Nothing escapes his notice; and as a result, he is in a good position to keep watch over his favorite people and ensure the happy endings. The two stories in this volume revolve around the manager of the Crystal Phoenix and the mob-related owner—and a professor and a writing student who supports herself as a showgirl. Midnight Louie, of course, sees to it that all ends happily. *Crystal Nights* is next in series.

Other books you might like:
Carol Budd, *Scarlet Scandals*, 1990
Claire Martin, *Best Man*, 1983

555

CAROLE NELSON DOUGLAS

Crystal Nights

(New York: Bantam, 1990)

Story type: Romantic Suspense
Major character(s): Midnight Louie, Animal (cat), Detective—Private
Time period(s): 1990s
Locale(s): Las Vegas, Nevada

Summary: Midnight Louie, the private-eye cat at the posh Las Vegas casino, the Crystal Phoenix, once again oversees the lives of all within his purview, arranging all the necessary happy endings. In the two stories included, love and misunderstanding blossoms between a singer and a poker player, and a baccarat night supervisor and a tourist flee from hit men and end up in the desert. Preceded by *Crystal Days*.

Other books you might like:
Carol Budd, *Scarlet Scandals*, 1990
Claire Martin, *Best Man*, 1983

556

GAIL DOUGLAS

After Hours

(New York: Bantam, 1991)

Story type: Contemporary
Major character(s): Casey McIntyre, Journalist (aspiring newspaperwoman); Alex McLean, Publisher (newspaper)
Time period(s): 1990s
Locale(s): Vancouver, British Columbia, Canada

Summary: Casey McIntyre, ambitious, independent, and relatively innocent, cannot appreciate Alex McLean's concern for her safety. He also questions her loyalty until she helps him save his publishing house.

Other books you might like:
Suzanne Ellison, *Shifting Sands*, 1992
Theresa Gladden, *Just Desserts*, 1991
Elizabeth Krueger, *For the Children*, 1992
La Verne St. George, *A Private Proposal*, 1990
   innocent

557

GAIL DOUGLAS

The Dreamweavers: Bewitching Lady

(New York: Bantam, 1990)

Story type: Contemporary
Series: Dreamweavers
Major character(s): Heather Sinclair, Travel Agent; Josh Campbell, Businessman (Former Deep sea diver)
Time period(s): 1980s
Locale(s): Scotland

Summary: Independent, yet vulnerable, Heather Sinclair just knows her "one and only" isn't strong, determined Josh Campbell; and Josh doesn't want to become involved with a woman as innocent as Heather. Both change their opinons in this sensual romance set in contemporary Scotland.

Other books you might like:
Anne McCaffrey, *Stitch-in-Snow*, 1984
Judith McNaught, *Almost Heaven*, 1990
   Historical setting
Deborah Smith, *Legends*, 1990
Pat Tracy, *Tiger by the Tail*, 1990
   Sweet Contemporary

558

GAIL DOUGLAS

The Dreamweavers: Sophisticated Lady

(New York: Bantam, 1990)

Story type: Contemporary
Series: Dreamweavers
Major character(s): Lisa Sinclair, Travel Agent; Pete Cochrane, Musician (Jazz Pianist)
Time period(s): 1980s
Locale(s): New Orleans, Louisiana; Nice, France

Summary: The attraction between Lisa and Pete is instantaneous, but the road to true love is not smooth. Lisa doesn't want a wandering jazz musician in her life; Pete thinks she's a touch above him. Both are proved wrong in this sensual contemporary.

Other books you might like:
Barbara Boswell, *Rule Breaker*, 1990
Candace Schuler, *Sophisticated Lady*, 1989
Lass Small, *Contact*, 1990
Elise Title, *MacNamara and Hall*, 1989

559

JESSICA DOUGLASS

All My Heart Can Hold

(New York: Dell, 1991)

Story type: Historical/American West
Major character(s): Jenna Riordan, Southern Belle; Caleb Harper, Indian (half-Comanche), Scout (Army)
Time period(s): 1860s (1867)
Locale(s): New Mexico

Summary: Stranded in Kansas on the way to California, Southerner Jenna Riordan and her brother and sister are aided by army scout Caleb Harper, who agrees to escort them—and he does, right into disaster. Treachery, violence, prejudice, and passion are all part of this stormy love story as two people fight against all odds to keep their love.

Other books you might like:
Madeline Baker, *Lacey's Way*, 1990
Virginia Brown, *Wildfire*, 1990
Kathleen Harrington, *Cherish the Dream*, 1990
Gina Robins, *Whispers of Love*, 1991

560

JESSICA DOUGLASS

Angel of Fire
(New York: Dell, 1994)

Story type: Historical/American West
Major character(s): Victoria Landsford, Bounty Hunter, Imposter (disguised as Vic Langley); Noah Killian, Military Personnel (former)
Time period(s): 19th century
Locale(s): Kansas

Summary: Desperate to find the outlaws who killed her family, Victoria Lansford "becomes" bounty hunter Vic Langley. Her masquerade, however, is suspected by Noah Killian, who helps her in her search. As they encounter killers, rugged terrain, and other western difficulties, they learn to respect each other, come to terms with their own pasts, and fall in love in the process.

Other books you might like:
Rosalyn Alsobrook, *Passion's Bold Fire*, 1993
Linda Madl, *Sunny*, 1990
Alisa McBride, *Love's Bounty*, 1993
    audio tape
Kasey Michaels, *Masquerade in Moonlight*, 1994
Andrea Parnell, *My Only Desire*, 1993
    another female bounty hunter

561

JESSICA DOUGLASS

Wish Me a Rainbow
(New York: Dell, 1992)

Story type: Historical/American West
Major character(s): Amelia O'Rourke, Young Woman (tomboy); Matt Grayson, Rancher
Time period(s): 1880s
Locale(s): Texas

Summary: In love with Matt from childhood, Amelia is determined that Matt see her as more than just a good friend. Unfortunately, his father, Zachary, has other ideas—and when Matt's late brother's widow, the lovely Lysette, comes to town, Zachary makes plans. Amelia, however, does not give up—and eventually proves that hope and love can overcome even the most difficult of obstacles. Fast-moving story.

Other books you might like:
Elaine Barbieri, *Wings of a Dove*, 1990
Lisa Gregory, *The Rainbow Promise*, 1989
Pamela Morsi, *Courting Miss Hattie*, 1991
LaVyrle Spencer, *Bittersweet*, 1990
    contemporary

562

SHANNON DRAKE
BETINA M. KRAHN, Co-Author
LINDA LAEL MILLER, Co-Author
CHRISTINA SKYE, Co-Author
KATHERINE SUTCLIFFE, Co-Author

Avon Books Presents: Haunting Love Stories
(New York: Avon, 1991)

Story type: Historical; Holiday Themes

Summary: An appropriately chilling collection of romantic tales by noted historical writers. Includes "And I Will Love You Forever" by Shannon Drake, "A Certain Magic" by Betina Krahn, "That Other Katherine" by Linda Lael Miller, "Enchantment" by Christina Skye, and "Forever Yours" by Katherine Sutcliffe.

Other books you might like:
Lori Herter, *Obsession*, 1991
Lori Herter, *Possession*, 1991
Susan Kay, *Phantom*, 1991
Anne Rice, *The Witching Hour*, 1990
Anne Stuart, *Night of the Phantom*, 1991

563

SHANNON DRAKE (Pseudonym of Heather Graham Pozzessere)

Bride of the Wind
(New York: Avon, 1992)

Story type: Historical/Colonial America; Historical/Seventeenth Century
Major character(s): Rose Woodbine, Heiress; Pierce de Forte, Pirate ("Dragonslayer"), Nobleman
Time period(s): 17th century (1670s)
Locale(s): Virginia, American Colonies; England

Summary: In love with one woman but forced to wed another, Lord Pierce de Forte finds himself accused of murdering his former love and he flees for his life. In the process, he takes over a ship, becomes a pirate captain, and then sets about dealing with his wife, whom he suspects of treachery. Rose, however, loves him and eventually overcomes his suspicion and pride and wins his love. A fast-paced, highly sensual tale.

Other books you might like:
Christine Dorsey, *Captain's Captive*, 1991
Christine Dorsey, *Sea Fires*, 1992
Heather Graham, *A Pirate's Pleasure*, 1989
    Same author/different pseudonym
Cara Miles, *Promise Me Forever*, 1992
Kathleen E. Woodiwiss, *Shanna*, 1977

564

SHANNON DRAKE (Pseudonym of Heather Graham Pozzessere)

Damsel in Distress
(New York: Avon, 1992)

Story type: Historical/Medieval
Major character(s): Katherine de Montrain, Noblewoman, Outlaw ("Lady Greensleeves"); Damian Mountjoy, Nobleman (knight), Outlaw ("Silver Sword")
Time period(s): 12th century
Locale(s): England

Summary: Working with Robin Hood's people as the Lady Greensleeves, Lady Katherine de Montrain is rescued from one arranged marriage only to find herself ordered into another. Her problem? She has fallen in love with her gallant rescuer, the legendary knight Silver Sword. His problem? Silversword is really Katherine's betrothed in disguise, and now that they are married he wonders whom she really loves. Lots of 12th century action, political intrigue, and excitement.

Other books you might like:
Linda Lang Bartell, *Caressa*, 1990
Jude Deveraux, *The Taming*, 1989
Laura Kinsale, *The Prince of Midnight*, 1990
Marylyle Rogers, *Hidden Hearts*, 1989

565

SHANNON DRAKE (Pseudonym of Heather Graham Pozzessere)

Emerald Embrace
(New York: Berkley, 1991)

Story type: Historical/Victorian; Gothic
Major character(s): Martise St. James, Imposter, Plantation Owner; Bruce Creeghan, Nobleman
Time period(s): 1860s (1865)
Locale(s): Scotland

Summary: When her cousin dies under mysterious circumstances, Martise heads to Scotland to investigate the cause and to recover a valuable emerald; but what she finds is not quite what she expects. A gloomy castle perched on windswept cliffs, a series of strange and ominous occurrences, and a dark and brooding hero all combine in this chillingly well-done tale that is in the classic tradition of *Rebecca* and *Mistress of Mellyn*, but is also highly sensual.

Other books you might like:
Rebecca Brandewyne, *Upon a Moon-Dark Moor*, 1988
Daphne Du Maurier, *Rebecca*, 1938
    classic Gothic
Roberta Gellis, *Sing Witch, Sing Death*, 1975
Pamela Hill, *Witton's Folly*, 1975
Victoria Holt, *Mistress of Mellyn*, 1970

566

SHANNON DRAKE (Pseudonym of Heather Graham Pozzessere)

Knight of Fire
(New York: Avon, 1993)

Story type: Historical/Medieval
Major character(s): Allora Canadys, Royalty (Scottish princess); Bret d'Anlou, Nobleman (Norman)
Time period(s): 11th century (1088)
Locale(s): England; Scotland

Summary: Allora's marriage to Bret, the dreaded Norman knight, is battle-filled and passionate as she fights to save her family and her country. Filled with action, suspense, and historical detail.

Other books you might like:
Linda Lang Bartell, *Tender Warrior*, 1992
Julie Garwood, *The Bride*, 1989
Brenda Joyce, *Promise of the Rose*, 1993
Sir Walter Scott, *Ivanhoe*, 1819
Kathleen E. Woodiwiss, *The Wolf and the Dove*, 1974

567

SHANNON DRAKE (Pseudonym of Heather Graham Pozzessere)

Princess of Fire
(New York: Berkley Jove, 1989)

Story type: Historical/Medieval
Major character(s): Fallon Godwinson, Royalty (Saxon princess); Alaric of Anion, Nobleman (Norman Count)
Time period(s): 11th century (1066)
Locale(s): England

Summary: Saxon warrior princess Fallon Godwinson wins the notice of Alaric of Anion, William the Conqueror's right hand man, for her fierce fighting during the Battle of Hastings. Their involuntary attraction for each other eventually draws them together, but not before their stubbornness and determination make sparks fly in unexpected directions.

Other books you might like:
Linda Lang Bartell, *Brianna*, 1986
Julie Garwood, *The Bride*, 1989
Mary Ellen Gronau, *Passionate Warriors*, 1989
Johanna Lindsey, *When Love Awaits*, 1986
Kathleen E. Woodiwiss, *The Wolf and the Dove*, 1974

568

SANDRA DUBAY

Nightrider
(New York: Leisure, 1991)

Story type: Historical/Seventeenth Century
Major character(s): Bliss Paynter, Noblewoman, Ward; Christopher de Wylde, Nobleman (impoverished), Highwayman
Time period(s): 17th century (1660s)

Locale(s): England

Summary: When nobleman-turned-highwayman Christopher de Wylde stops Lady Bliss Paynter's carriage one night, both of their lives change irrevocably. A fast-moving, lively tale with a touch of Robin Hood set during the Restoration period. Interesting in that the hero and heroine, although they are noble, are fighting the king, among others.

Other books you might like:
Jane Feather, *Reckless Angel*, 1989
Laura Kinsale, *The Prince of Midnight*, 1990
Patricia Potter, *The Abduction*, 1991
Marylyle Rogers, *Hidden Hearts*, 1989
Jennifer West, *Passion's Legacy*, 1991

569

DIXIE DUBOIS (Pseudonym of Dixie L. Gaspard)

Home Fires
(Bensalem, Pennsylvania: Meteor, 1992)

Story type: Contemporary
Major character(s): Leara James Lockwood, Child-Care Giver (day-care center owner); Gareth Conroe, Architect
Time period(s): 1990s
Locale(s): Columbus, Ohio

Summary: Leara Lockwood returns to her hometown to settle her father's estate and comes face to face with the one man she never stopped loving. A story of renewed love with all its attendant joys and problems.

Other books you might like:
Lynn Bulock, *In Your Dreams*, 1992
Georgia Helm, *Mad Hatter*, 1992
Nancy Martin, *Monkey Wrench*, 1992
LaVyrle Spencer, *Bittersweet*, 1990

570

ELIZABETH DUKE

Outback Legacy
(Toronto: Harlequin, 1993)

Story type: Contemporary
Major character(s): Kate Ramsey, Widow(er), Rancher; Nick Ramsey, Relative (brother-in-law)
Time period(s): 1990s
Locale(s): Australia

Summary: Kate, struggling to keep her late husband's ranch, has been taught to believe that her brother-in-law, Nick, is despicable. However, she does owe him for saving her life, and as he stays on, her feelings for him change, and she begins to wonder if everything her husband had told her about Nick was true. Classic internal dilemma for the heroine.

Other books you might like:
Dorothy Eden, *The Vines of Yarabee*, 1969
Connie Mason, *Wild Land, Wild Love*, 1992
   historical setting
Ann Maxwell, *The Diamond Tiger*, 1992

Ann Victoria Roberts, *Morning's Gate*, 1991
   historical setting
Barbara Wood, *The Dreaming*, 1992
   historical setting

571

ALICE DUNCAN

One Bright Morning
(New York: Harper, 1995)

Story type: Historical/American West
Major character(s): Maggie Bright, Widow(er), Farmer; Jubal Green, Cowboy
Time period(s): 19th century (late)
Locale(s): New Mexico

Summary: Maggie Bright, a widowed young mother, is doing all right on her bleak homestead, but when wounded cowboy Jubal Green rides into the yard, he brings more than his handsome self. His Indian foster brothers move into her life and a feud with a crazed man brings terror to all of them. As Jubal heals, so does her broken heart. Suspense and tender moments draw readers in.

Other books you might like:
Jane Bonander, *Dancing on Snowflakes*, 1995
   similar premise
Robin Lee Hatcher, *Promise Me Spring*, 1991
Linda Howard, *The Touch of Fire*, 1992
   darker
Patricia Potter, *Defiant*, 1995
   another widow and wounded hero
Libby Sydes, *Until Spring*, 1993

572

JUDITH DUNCAN

Better than Before
(New York: Silhouette, 1992)

Story type: Contemporary
Major character(s): Carlie Pearson, Spouse; Derek Pearson, Farmer
Time period(s): 1990s
Locale(s): Canada

Summary: Carlie and Derek's marriage is shaken at a high school reunion when ghosts from their past make unspoken doubts surface. They learn, at last, to see beyond their fears.

Other books you might like:
Lisa Gregory, *The Rainbow Promise*, 1989
Elizabeth Quinn, *Any Day Now*, 1989
Kathleen Gilles Seidel, *Maybe This Time*, 1990
LaVyrle Spencer, *Bittersweet*, 1990

573

JUDITH DUNCAN

Beyond All Reason

(New York: Silhouette, 1993)

Story type: Contemporary
Major character(s): Kate Quinn, Runaway (mother), Abuse Victim (battered wife); Tanner McCall, Rancher, Indian
Time period(s): 1990s
Locale(s): Alberta, Canada

Summary: Kate and her boys find refuge in a home where she will take care of a bed-ridden man. Having escaped an abusive husband, she feels safe at last. Lonely Tanner McCall isn't the romantic type, but Kate finds true joy as she falls in love with him in an emotion packed love story.

Other books you might like:
Kathryn Attalla, *Homeward Bound*, 1993
Lindsay McKenna, *Point of Departure*, 1993
Sharon Sala, *Always a Lady*, 1993
LaVyrle Spencer, *Morning Glory*, 1989
  historical

574

CAROLA DUNN

The Lady and the Rake

(New York: Zebra, 1995)

Story type: Regency
Major character(s): Nerissa Wingate, Seamstress (theatrical); Miles Courtenay, Rake, Gambler
Time period(s): 1810s
Locale(s): Dorset, England

Summary: The only things standing in the way of Miles Courtenay and Nerissa Wingate inheriting a fortune are their less-than-exemplary pasts and one mischievous ghost. For six months they must be the very models of decorum—and the ghost is there to see that his wishes are carried out. Lively, Regency fun with a touch of the paranormal.

Other books you might like:
Elisabeth Fairchild, *The Love Knot*, 1995
Sandra Heath, *The Halloween Husband*, 1994
  more ghostly interferance
Candice Hern, *A Change of Heart*, 1995
Barbara Metzger, *An Angel for the Earl*, 1994
  paranormal elements
Kasey Michaels, *The Haunted Miss Hampshire*, 1992

575

CAROLA DUNN

Two Corinthians

(New York: Walker, 1989)

Story type: Regency
Major character(s): Claire Sutton, Spinster, Gentlewoman; Lizzie Sutton, Debutante, Gentlewoman
Time period(s): 1810s

Locale(s): London, England

Summary: After seeing to it that her sister Lizzie is successfully launched into society during the Season, Claire Sutton plans to retire to a peaceful life away from society and her family. But love—and her sister—change her plans. Witty, fun, and typically Regency. Spin off of *Miss Hartwell's Dilemma*.

Other books you might like:
Georgette Heyer, *Frederica*, 1965
Georgette Heyer, *Lady of Quality*, 1972
Dawn Lindsey, *Dunraven's Folly*, 1989
Evelyn Richardson, *Education of Lady Frances*, 1989
Sheila Simonson, *Love and Folly*, 1988

576

ANNE MARIE DUQUETTE

On the Line

(Toronto: Harlequin, 1993)

Story type: Contemporary
Major character(s): Deanna Leighton, Veterinarian; J.D. Vaughn, Rancher
Time period(s): 1990s
Locale(s): United States

Summary: Deanna has paid her parents debts incurred by a bad deal with rancher, J.D. Now he wants to buy her prized stallion! However, she really needs the money, and believing that he sincerely wants to help her, Deanna and her mother consider it. Attraction between Deanna and J.D. develops in due time, and she is forced to reconsider her original opinion of him.

Other books you might like:
Kathy Clark, *Stand by Your Man*, 1993
Joey Light, *High Riding Heroes*, 1993
Lass Small, *A Nothing Town in Texas*, 1991
Thelma Zirkelbach, *A Man of Few Words*, 1993

577

CHARLES DURHAM

Walk in the Light

(New York: Ballantine, 1992)

Story type: Historical/American Revolution; Historical/Mainstream
Major character(s): Rachel Calhoun, Doctor; Andrew Wolfe, Doctor
Time period(s): 18th century (1753-1781)
Locale(s): Scotland; Philadelphia, Pennsylvania

Summary: A sweeping tale of the American Revolutionary period as experienced through the lives of Doctors Rachel Calhoun and Drew Wolf. Complex and detailed.

Other books you might like:
Gwen Bristow, *Celia Garth*, 1959
James Fenimore Cooper, *The Spy*, 1821
  classic Revolutionary War novel
Barbara Cummings, *Blazing Passion*, 1991

Robin Maderich, *Faith and Honor*, 1989
Joan Van Nuys, *Beloved Intruder*, 1992
    frontier doctor

578
SANDRA DUSTIN

Highland Hearts
(New York: Diamond, 1992)

Story type: Historical/Renaissance
Major character(s): Comyn "Tess" Delgado, Noblewoman (contessa), Heiress; Revan Halyard, Knight
Time period(s): 15th century (1455)
Locale(s): Scotland

Summary: When Tess rescues Revan Halyard from prison, she thinks he has been imprisoned for romantic, not political, reasons. She also has no idea that her life is in as much danger as his; but when she realizes that there are those who would kill her for her fortune, she joins forces with Revan, and in the process of outwitting their foes, they fall in love. Highly sensual, witty, and action-filled.

Other books you might like:
Katherine Deauville, *Blood Red Roses*, 1991
Roberta Gellis, *Roselynde*, 1978
Virginia Henley, *The Falcon and the Flower*, 1989
Sharon Kay Penman, *Here Be Dragons*, 1985

579
LOIS FAYE DYER

Travelin' Man
(Bensalem, Pennsylvania: Meteor, 1992)

Story type: Contemporary
Major character(s): Katherine Bennington, Heiress; Josh McFadden, Hero
Time period(s): 1990s
Locale(s): Mexico; Iowa

Summary: Josh McFadden agrees to rescue beautiful, sophisticated Katherine Bennington from village locals and a possible stay in a Mexican jail, on one condition — that she marry him, in name only, of course. Their marriage of convenience presents the expected problems to them both — and when they go to Iowa for a family wedding, things take an interesting turn.

Other books you might like:
Debbie Macomber, *First Comes Marriage*, 1991
Debbie Macomber, *Marriage of Inconvenience*, 1992
Kristin Morgan, *First Comes Baby*, 1992
Fayrene Preston, *Magnificent Affair*, 1992

580
KATHLEEN EAGLE

Fire and Rain
(New York: Avon, 1994)

Story type: Contemporary

Major character(s): Priscilla Twiss, Teacher (Quaker); Cecily Metcalf, Volunteer
Time period(s): 1870s (1871); 1970s (1971)
Locale(s): Lakota Reservation, South Dakota

Summary: When Cecily Metcalf, volunteer at the Lakota reservation, finds the story of Priscilla, who 100 years ago had the same deep love for a Lakota brave in her time that Cecily has for a Lakota man today, she realizes she has found a kindred spirit. Both women, in their own time, change their lives completely, casting their lots with the Lakota's struggle to live in dignity and peace. Powerful, realistic, and well-written. Not a time-travel; simply two parallel, merging stories.

Other books you might like:
Beverly Bird, *Comes the Rain*, 1990
Michael Blake, *Dances with Wolves*, 1988
Rachel Lee, *Thunder Mountain*, 1994
Deborah Smith, *Beloved Woman*, 1991
Peggy Webb, *Witch Dance*, 1994

581
KATHLEEN EAGLE

Heaven and Earth
(Toronto: Harlequin, 1990)

Story type: Historical/American West
Major character(s): Katherine Fairchild, Religious (missionary); Jed West, Trapper, Indian
Time period(s): 1840s
Locale(s): Oregon

Summary: Saved from certain death by trapper Jed West when she is abandoned by the rest of her party along the Oregon Trail, widowed missionary Katherine Fairchild regains her health and falls in love with Jed in the process. However, she will not give up her religious calling and for a time they go their separate ways. Fate intervenes and they are reunited — but their happiness will not be complete until Jed deals with his past and comes to terms with his feelings and beliefs.

Other books you might like:
Janet Dailey, *The Pride of Hannah Wade*, 1985
Jessie Ford, *A Different Breed*, 1988
Jill Marie Landis, *Rose*, 1990
Jill Marie Landis, *Sunflower*, 1988
Johanna Lindsey, *Savage Thunder*, 1989

582
KATHLEEN EAGLE

Reason to Believe
(New York: Avon, 1995)

Story type: Contemporary
Major character(s): Clara Pipestone, Historian; Ben Pipestone, Cowboy, Indian
Time period(s): 1990s
Locale(s): Bismarck, North Dakota; South Dakota

Summary: After two years of separation, Ben Pipestone, a Lakota Indian, has begun to wonder if Clara Pipestone will ever forgive him for his deception and betrayal. It isn't until their daughter reunites them for a sacred winter journey that they rediscover the passion and love they have tried to live without. Sensitive treatment of Native American issues.

Other books you might like:
Beverly Bird, *Comes the Rain*, 1990
Janet Dailey, *Night Way*, 1981
Rachel Lee, *Thunder Mountain*, 1994
Deborah Smith, *Beloved Woman*, 1991
Peggy Webb, *Witch Dance*, 1994

583

KATHLEEN EAGLE

This Time Forever
(New York: Avon, 1992)

Story type: Contemporary/Mainstream
Major character(s): Susan Ellison, Nurse; Cleve Black Horse, Indian, Prisoner
Time period(s): 1990s
Locale(s): United States

Summary: Tried, convicted, and imprisoned for a murder he didn't commit, rodeo champion Cleve Black Horse is wary when nurse Susan Ellison (who was also on his jury) comes to visit him in an effort to make arrangements for the adoption of a child she believes to be his. Unique, realistic, and memorable with strong mainstream tendencies.

Other books you might like:
Madeline Baker, *A Whisper on the Wind*, 1991
   time change elements
Janet Dailey, *Night Way*, 1981
Janis Reams Hudson, *For the Thrill*, 1992
Johanna Lindsey, *Savage Thunder*, 1989
   historical
Deborah Smith, *Beloved Woman*, 1991

584

SARAH EAGLE (Pseudonym of Sally Falcon and Sarah Hawkes)

The Bedeviled Baron
(New York: Jove, 1994)

Story type: Regency
Major character(s): Lady Hillary, Debutante; Bramwell Dempster, Nobleman (Baron Teale), Military Personnel (Navy)
Time period(s): 1810s
Locale(s): England

Summary: Determined not to give in to his mother's plans to get him safely wed, Bramwell Dempster scorns all the eligible women she sends his way; but when he meets the woman of his dreams on the street one day, and then discovers that she is one of his mother's choices—life suddenly becomes much more complex. A feigned courtship seems to solve their problem—and then it becomes the real thing. Diverting.

Other books you might like:
Mary Balogh, *Christmas Belle*, 1994

Anne Barbour, *Lord Glenraven's Return*, 1994
Cathleen Clare, *Felicia*, 1993
Mary Chase Comstock, *An Impetuous Miss*, 1993
Georgette Heyer, *The Unknown Ajax*, 1959

585

SARAH EAGLE (Pseudonym of Sarah Hawkes)

Lady Vengeance
(New York: Harper, 1995)

Story type: Historical/Regency
Major character(s): Celia Tregaron, Widow(er), Heiress (American); Marcus Knowles, Nobleman (Earl of Ashmore)
Time period(s): 1810s
Locale(s): England

Summary: Determined to avenge her brother's reported death, Celia Tregaron leaves America and heads for England to murder the man she considers responsible, the Earl of Ashmore and ends up falling in love with him instead. Elegant, witty, and sensual, this well-researched historical features likable protagonists, numerous secondary characters, and a large dose of suspense, murder, and intrigue.

Other books you might like:
Jo Beverley, *My Lady Notorious*, 1993
Carla Kelly, *Miss Billings Treads the Boards*, 1993
Judith McNaught, *Almost Heaven*, 1990
Laura Parker, *Caprice*, 1991
Amanda Quick, *Mistress*, 1994

586

SARAH EAGLE (Pseudonym of Sally Falcon and Sarah Hawkes)

The Marriage Gamble
(New York: Jove, 1992)

Story type: Regency
Major character(s): Damara Tarrant, Noblewoman, Fiance(e); Simon Hilliard Alton, Nobleman (Marquess of Emsley), Fiance(e)
Time period(s): 1810s
Locale(s): England

Summary: When the betrothal of Lady Damara Tarrant and Simon, the Marquess of Emsley appears in the papers, it takes everyone by surprise—even the parties involved. Never having heard of each other before, let alone met, Damara and Simon are wary and suspicious of each other—but they are attracted to each other nevertheless. A rather dangerous mystery lies at the heart of this delightful Regency and it must be solved before Damara and Simon can find the happiness they both want. Engaging characters in an unusual story.

Other books you might like:
Joan Aiken, *The Five-Minute Marriage*, 1977
Mary Balogh, *Promise of Spring*, 1990
Georgette Heyer, *Bath Tangle*, 1955
Kasey Michaels, *The Anonymous Miss Addams*, 1989

587

SARAH EAGLE (Pseudonym of Sally Falcon and Sarah Hawkes)

The Reluctant Suitor
(New York: Berkley, 1991)

Story type: Regency
Major character(s): Joslyn Penderton, Fiance(e) (reluctant); Captain Farraday, Imposter
Time period(s): 1810s
Locale(s): England

Summary: Furious upon discovering that her father's will decrees that she marry the unknown Captain Farraday, Joslyn Penderton runs away—and practically trips on the unconscious body of a stranger lying in the road. Smuggling, treason, and deception are part of this fast-paced sparkling Regency.

Other books you might like:
Mary Balogh, *The Snow Angel*, 1991
Cleo Chadwick, *A Midsummer Night's Kiss*, 1991
Emily Hendrickson, *Miss Wyndham's Escapade*, 1990
Georgette Heyer, *Bath Tangle*, 1955
Judith McNaught, *Whitney, My Love*, 1985

588

GAIL EASTWOOD

The Captain's Dilemma
(New York: Signet, 1995)

Story type: Regency
Major character(s): Merissa Pritchard, Gentlewoman; Alexandre Valmont, Military Personnel (French captain), Fugitive (prisoner of war)
Time period(s): 1810s
Locale(s): England

Summary: Despite the fact that independent, free-spirited Merissa Pritchard knows she should be thinking of marriage—probably to her quite eligible, but increasingly obnoxious, neighbor Harlan Gatesby—she wants something more. When she finds a wounded French prisoner of war hiding in an abandoned mill, she realizes that she has found it. Well-done characters, interesting historical detail, and a high degree of sexual tension add to this somewhat unusual Regency.

Other books you might like:
Sarah Eagle, *The Bedeviled Baron*, 1994
Suzanne Enoch, *Angel's Devil*, 1995
Jean R. Ewing, *Rogue's Reward*, 1995
Elisabeth Fairchild, *The Love Knot*, 1995
Carla Kelly, *Miss Whittier Makes a List*, 1994

589

GAIL EASTWOOD

The Persistent Earl
(New York: Signet, 1995)

Story type: Regency
Major character(s): Lady Phoebe Brodfield, Widow(er), Noblewoman; John Jameson, Nobleman (Earl of Devenham), Military Personnel
Time period(s): 1810s
Locale(s): England

Summary: Resigned to a quiet and uneventful life as a widow and "favorite aunt" to her sister's charming children, young Phoebe Brodfield is forced out of seclusion when the dashing war hero, the Earl of Devenham, ends up wounded, delirious, and in her care. Wonderfully done characters, a high degree of sexual tension, and a truly depraved villain add to the mix.

Other books you might like:
Jean R. Ewing, *Rogue's Reward*, 1995
Jean R. Ewing, *Virtue's Reward*, 1995
Carla Kelly, *Mrs. Drew Plays Her Hand*, 1994
Kate Moore, *An Improper Widow*, 1995
Evelyn Richardson, *The Willful Widow*, 1994

590

ROBERTA ECKERT

Heir to Vengeance
(New York: Signet, 1990)

Story type: Regency
Major character(s): Anne Marshall, Gentlewoman, Equestrian; Seth Blakewell, Indian (Half)
Time period(s): 1810s
Locale(s): England

Summary: Seth Blakewell comes to England to avenge the loss of his father's fortune and is attracted to spirited Anne Marshall in the process. Typical Regency fun, but unusual in that it is viewed through the eyes of someone from the American West.

Other books you might like:
Norma Lee Clark, *The Infamous Rake*, 1990
Gladys McGorian, *The Prince Regent's Silver Bell*, 1987
Carol Proctor, *Unlikely Guardian*, 1990
Mary Jo Putney, *The Rake and the Reformer*, 1989
Amanda Scott, *The Dauntless Miss Wingrave*, 1989

591

ROSEMARY EDGHILL

Fleeting Fancy
(New York: Fawcett, 1993)

Story type: Regency
Major character(s): Primula Greetwell, Gentlewoman, Bride; Severn, Nobleman (Viscount Severn), Rake
Time period(s): 1810s
Locale(s): England

Summary: Allowed to return to England after a 10 year exile in India—if he marries the woman of his father's choice—Lord Severn is shocked to discover that his bride is the women he cruelly compromised years before, but she doesn't seem to remember! Charming, witty, and unusual.

Other books you might like:
Anne Barbour, *Kate and the Soldier*, 1993
Julie Caille, *An Impetuous Bride*, 1991
Sheila Simonson, *A Cousinly Connexion*, 1984
Marlene Suson, *Devil's Bargain*, 1992
Marlene Suson, *The Errant Earl*, 1989

592

ROSEMARY EDGHILL

The Ill-Bred Bride

(New York: St. Martin's, 1990)

Story type: Regency
Major character(s): Susannah Potter, Heiress, Orphan; Hanford, Nobleman (Lord Hanford of Laceby)
Time period(s): 1810s
Locale(s): England

Summary: Wealthy, but not gently bred, Susannah Potter needs a husband (preferably noble) to foil her greedy relatives. Excessively noble Lord Hanford of Laceby needs a rich wife to support his estate, family, and lifestyle. The resulting marriage of convenience is a surprise to them both as they find that love can solve some seemingly insurmountable problems.

Other books you might like:
Gayle Buck, *Mutual Consent*, 1991
Georgette Heyer, *A Civil Contract*, 1962
Annabel Laine, *The Reluctant Heiress*, 1978
Judith McNaught, *Almost Heaven*, 1990
Amanda Quick, *Seduction*, 1990
    sensual

593

CASSIE EDWARDS

Savage Promise

(New York: Leisure, 1991)

Story type: Historical/American West
Major character(s): Letitia Wilson, Frontierswoman; Kanuga, Indian (Tlingit), Chieftain
Time period(s): 19th century
Locale(s): Alaska

Summary: Letitia Wilson is lost in the snow, attacked by a polar bear, kidnapped by trappers, and rescued by the virile Tlingit Chief, Kanuga—all on her first day in Alaska! Kanuga insists that she remain with him and while Letitia resists becoming a true Tlingit, she cannot resist the chief of the tribe. Lots of action, passion, and Indian lore.

Other books you might like:
Madeline Baker, *Lacey's Way*, 1990
Cheryl Black, *Comanche Love Song*, 1989
Cordia Byers, *Lady Fortune*, 1989
Janet Dailey, *The Pride of Hannah Wade*, 1985
Kathryn Lynn Davis, *Sing to Me of Dreams*, 1990

594

CASSIE EDWARDS

When Passion Calls

(New York: Leisure, 1990)

Story type: Historical/American West
Major character(s): Melanie Stanton, Debutante; Shane Brennan, Captive (Raised by Indians)
Time period(s): 1850s
Locale(s): West

Summary: Rescued and raised by Indians after his mother was brutally murdered, Shane Brennan returns to the white world, upsetting a number of plans including those of his twin brother to marry the beautiful Melanie Stanton. Shane finds love and rights some old wrongs in this action-filled romance.

Other books you might like:
Madeline Baker, *Lacey's Way*, 1990
Cheryl Black, *Comanche Love Song*, 1989
    Woman captive returns to "civilization"
Cordia Byers, *Lady Fortune*, 1989
    Earlier time period/"Long lost" heroine returns
Janet Dailey, *The Pride of Hannah Wade*, 1985
    Another returning woman captive
Bobbi Smith, *Arizona Caress*, 1989

595

CASSIE EDWARDS

Wild Splendor

(New York: Topaz, 1993)

Story type: Historical/American West
Major character(s): Leonida Branson, Young Woman; Sage, Chieftain, Indian (Navaho)
Time period(s): 1880s
Locale(s): Arizona

Summary: Although engaged to a general, when Leonida meets Navajo chief Sage, the attraction is instantaneous. During hostilities, she tries to escape but is captured by Sage; on the way to his mountain home, they marry. Prejudice and hatred make their life together hazardous, but the historically accurate treatment of the Navajo merely serves to test and reinforce their love.

Other books you might like:
Michael Blake, *Dances with Wolves*, 1990
Genell Dellin, *Comanche Wind*, 1993
Kathleen Eagle, *Heaven and Earth*, 1990
Kathleen Harrington, *Cherish the Dream*, 1990
Bobbi Smith, *Dream Warrior*, 1993

596

COLLEEN EDWARDS

Puzzle Mansion

(Aurora, Colorado: Audio Entertainment, 1993)

Story type: Contemporary; Romantic Suspense

Major character(s): Susan Eliot, Lawyer, Heiress; Alex Martin, Architect, Heir
Time period(s): 1990s
Locale(s): Maine

Summary: When childhood sweethearts Susan and Alex are called back to an isolated island off the Maine coast for the reading of the will of their old friend and puzzle enthusiast Zeke Pelz, they find themselves confronted with Zeke's final puzzle for them to solve and their growing feelings for each other. An original romance in audio format.

Other books you might like:
Lee Anderson, *Dangerous Bequest*, 1992
S.R. Hawley, *Formula for Murder*, 1992
Patricia Simpson, *Whisper of Midnight*, 1991
    supernatural elements
Phyllis A. Whitney, *Spindrift*, 1975

597

JANE EDWARDS

Dangerous Odyssey

(New York: Avalon Books, 1990)

Story type: Romantic Suspense
Major character(s): Kelsey Anderson, Teacher (Of gifted children); Michael Devos, Businessman (Air Taxi Service Owner)
Time period(s): 1980s
Locale(s): Seattle, Washington; Greece

Summary: When Kelsey agrees to care for Zoe while her Uncle Michael goes to Greece in search of her parents, she doesn't plan to get caught up in an international intrigue. But when she takes Zoe to Greece, her life is suddenly in danger—and so is her heart. A real treasure hunt.

Other books you might like:
Joan Aiken, *A Cluster of Separate Sparks*, 1972
Alma Blair, *The Unwitting Witness*, 1990
Loretta Jackson, *Nightmare in Morocco*, 1989
Mary Stewart, *The Moon-Spinners*, 1962
    Set on Crete
Mary Stewart, *My Brother Michael*, 1959
    Greek setting/Classic Romantic Suspense

598

JANE EDWARDS

Terror by Design

(New York: Avalon Books, 1990)

Story type: Romantic Suspense
Major character(s): Rae ''Rachel'' Travis, Engineer (Airplane Safety); Simon Kirk, Police Officer
Time period(s): 1980s
Locale(s): Shell Bay, Florida

Summary: Rae works on a secret government project to protect airplanes from terrorists; Simon has been sent to Florida to find out who has been aiding terrorists in their escape efforts. However, Rae doesn't see a connection until she learns that a colleague is not who she pretends to be and the

discovery of a radio transmitter puts her life in danger. Sweet romance laced with mystery.

Other books you might like:
Evelyn Anthony, *The Tamarind Seed*, 1971
Alma Blair, *The Unwitting Witness*, 1990
Mary Stewart, *Airs Above the Ground*, 1965
    Intrigue in Austria
Mary Stewart, *The Moon-Spinners*, 1962
    Set on Crete
Anne Armstrong Thompson, *Message From Absalom*, 1975

599

SUZANNE ELIZABETH

Kiley's Storm

(New York: Harper, 1994)

Story type: Historical/American West
Major character(s): Daniella Storm, Frontierswoman; Jake Kiley, Lawman (marshall)
Time period(s): 1850s (1859)
Locale(s): Shady Gulch, Colorado

Summary: When Daniella's rancher father finds gold in the creek which divides their property from the Potter's, a feud erupts. Marshall Kiley settles things by throwing everyone in jail—and to get them out, Daniella sets out to seduce the marshall. Lots of humor, sensuality, and fast-paced action.

Other books you might like:
Lori Copeland, *Sweet Hannah Rose*, 1991
Joan Johnston, *Sweetwater Seduction*, 1991
Johanna Lindsey, *Angel*, 1992
Pamela Morsi, *Garters*, 1992

600

SUZANNE ELIZABETH

When Destiny Calls

(New York: Harper, 1993)

Story type: Time Travel
Major character(s): Kristen Ford, Police Officer; Jake Parriah, Outlaw
Time period(s): 1990s; 1890s
Locale(s): Nevada

Summary: Modern-day police officer Kristen Ford is surprised by a guardian angel who informs her that she is in the 20th Century by mistake and that she really belongs in 1890 Nevada protecting outlaw Hank Parriah. Once there, however, she discovers that her real ''destiny'' is Hank's brother, Jake, who must eventually decide between a life of crime with Hank and a life of love with Kristen. Original and funny.

Other books you might like:
Michelle Brandon, *Touch of Heaven*, 1992
Dorothy Garlock, *Nightrose*, 1990
Betina M. Krahn, *Midnight Magic*, 1990
Constance O'Day-Flannery, *A Time for Love*, 1991
Pamela Simpson, *Partners in Time*, 1990

601

LUCY ELLIOT (Pseudonym of Nancy A. Greenman)

The Claim
(Toronto: Harlequin, 1992)

Story type: Historical/American Revolution
Major character(s): Sarah "S. J." Meade, Landowner; Zeke Brownell, Vigilante
Time period(s): 1770s (1773)
Locale(s): New York, American Colonies

Summary: When Sarah Meade decides to sell the land her father willed her, Zeke Brownell and his Green Mountain Boys arrest her, try her, and challenge her to stay on the barren land for one week — all in an effort to keep her from selling "their" land. In the process, Sarah and Zeke fall in love — and then, it really doesn't matter who owns the land, just so long as they are together. Gentle and realistic.

Other books you might like:
Barbara Cummings, *Frontier Fire*, 1991
Pamela K. Forrest, *Autumn Ecstasy*, 1990
Jill Marie Landis, *Come Spring*, 1992
    later time period/American West
Victoria Pade, *The Doubletree*, 1990
Jodi Thomas, *The Tender Texan*, 1991

602

LUCY ELLIOT (Pseudonym of Nancy A. Greenman)

The Conquest
(Toronto: Harlequin, 1992)

Story type: Historical/American Revolution
Major character(s): Anne-Marie Doucet, Spy; Eli Brownell, Military Personnel (Green Mountain Boys)
Time period(s): 1770s
Locale(s): Quebec, Canada; American Colonies

Summary: Determined to avenge her family's treatment by the British, Anne-Marie Doucet joins forces with rebel Eli Brownell in an adventurous trek from Canada to the American Colonies in their search for peace, freedom, and love. A sweet love story with realistic, historically accurate detail. Sequel to *The Claim*.

Other books you might like:
Gwen Bristow, *Celia Garth*, 1959
Caryn Cameron, *Liberty's Lady*, 1990
Caryn Cameron, *Freedom Flame*, 1990
Robin Maderich, *Faith and Honor*, 1989

603

LUCY ELLIOT (Pseudonym of Nancy A. Greenman)

Private Paradise
(Toronto: Harlequin, 1991)

Story type: Historical/Victorian America
Major character(s): Lena Tabor, Seamstress, Immigrant; Gilbert Brigham, Doctor
Time period(s): 1880s (1883)

Locale(s): New York, New York; Hudson River Valley, New York

Summary: When wealthy, young Doctor Gilbert Brigham, spends a day visiting impoverished immigrant patients in crowded Manhattan, he is intrigued and impressed with feisty Lena Tabor's devotion to her family and her determination to make a better life for them. Aided by his mother's philanthropic bent, Gil arranges for a "summer in the country" (on his estate) for some of the children—with Lena as chaperone. In spite of their intentions to the contrary, Lena and Gil fall in love—and then must face the inevitable social class problems that arise. Warm and witty.

Other books you might like:
Rosalyn Alsobrook, *Elusive Caress*, 1990
Elaine Barbieri, *Wishes on the Wind*, 1991
Doreen Owens Malek, *Torchlight*, 1991
Victoria Morrow, *Jenny's Dream*, 1989

604

KATHLEEN ELLIOTT

A Special License
(New York: Harper, 1995)

Story type: Regency
Major character(s): Linnea Ashley, Young Woman (impoverished), Bride (reluctant); William Staynes, Nobleman (Earl of Rothwick), Bridegroom (reluctant)
Time period(s): 1810s
Locale(s): London, England

Summary: Thinking he is saving his nephew from making a disastrous marriage, the Earl of Rothwick abducts Miss Linnea Ashley; however, when he realizes his mistake, he does the only honorable thing he can—he marries her. This marriage of convenience is anything but convenient until the earl and Linnea finally acknowledge their love for one another.

Other books you might like:
Jo Beverley, *An Arranged Marriage*, 1991
Jo Beverley, *An Unwilling Bride*, 1992
Theresa DesJardien, *A June Bride*, 1991
Sarah Eagle, *The Marriage Gamble*, 1992
Georgette Heyer, *The Convenient Marriage*, 1934
    classic Regency

605

JULIE ELLIS

Trespassing Hearts
(New York: Putnam, 1992)

Story type: Contemporary/World War II; Contemporary/Mainstream
Major character(s): Betsy Bernstein, Interior Decorator; Paul Forrest, Student (law student)
Time period(s): 1940s (1941)
Locale(s): New York, New York; Long Island, New York

Summary: The love of Betsy Bernstein and Paul Forrest endures despite parental efforts to separate them, but when Paul is killed during the War, it takes all of Betsy's courage and determination to raise her son as she sees fit — and carve out a new and meaningful life for herself.

Other books you might like:
Elizabeth Adler, *Fortune Is a Woman*, 1992
Sandra Bregman, *Reach for the Dream*, 1990
Lisa Gregory, *Seasons*, 1990
   contemporary
Belva Plain, *Evergreen*, 1978

606
MONIQUE ELLIS
Delacey's Angel
(New York: Zebra, 1995)

Story type: Regency
Major character(s): Elizabeth Driscoll, Young Woman; Richard Delacey, Nobleman (Baron Monfort)
Time period(s): 1810s (1816)
Locale(s): London, England

Summary: Richard Delacey is at death's door when he is rescued by an unknown "angel." He vows to find her and after searching for over a year, he meets her by chance in his own home. Richard is determined to make Elizabeth his wife, and he is willing to challenge anyone who thinks to stop him.

Other books you might like:
Judy Christenberry, *Susannah's Secret*, 1993
Barbara Metzger, *Lady in Green*, 1993
Margaret Evans Porter, *Dangerous Diversions*, 1994
Catherine Reynolds, *The Highwayman*, 1993

607
SUZANNE ELLISON
Arrowpoint
(Toronto: Harlequin, 1992)

Story type: Contemporary
Series: Tyler
Major character(s): Renata Meyer, Artist (free-lance); Michael Youngthunder, Businessman (computer store manager), Indian (Winnebago)
Time period(s): 1990s
Locale(s): Tyler, Wisconsin; Milwaukee, Wisconsin

Summary: Renata Meyer owns land which Michael Youngthunder believes is a sacred Winnebago burial ground. However, even though they are obviously attracted to each other, Michael refuses to become involved with a white woman, something that confuses Renata because he has no problem using computers or driving expensive cars — all of which are symbols of "white" success. A loving story of choices, heartbreak, and acceptance.

Other books you might like:
Madeline Baker, *A Whisper on the Wind*, 1991
   time change elements
Allison Hayes, *Storm Dancers*, 1991
   historical setting
Johanna Lindsey, *Savage Thunder*, 1989
   historical setting

Lynda Trent, *Follow Your Heart*, 1992

608
SUZANNE ELLISON
Eagle Knight
(New York: Harper, 1991)

Story type: Historical/Exotic
Major character(s): Elena de la Rosa, Gentlewoman; Tizoc Santiago, Royalty (prince (Eagle Knight)), Indian (Aztec)
Time period(s): 16th century
Locale(s): Mexico

Summary: Fleeing to Mexico with her family to avoid the long arm of the Spanish Inquisition, Elena falls in love with the exotic land—and one of its Aztec princes. Cultural differences, the Church, illness, and relatives work to keep the lovers apart, but Elena and Tizoc's love proves stronger in the end. Lots of historical detail.

Other books you might like:
Kathryn Lynn Davis, *Sing to Me of Dreams*, 1990
Nan Ryan, *Sun God*, 1990
   later period
Susan Sackett, *Passion's Golden Fire*, 1989
   later period
Julie Tetel, *Swept Away*, 1989

609
SUZANNE ELLISON
Shifting Sands
(New York: Harlequin, 1992)

Story type: Contemporary
Major character(s): Ellen Anderson, Surveyor, Divorced Person; Reed Campbell, Planner (county)
Time period(s): 1990s

Summary: Ellen's discovery of a "time capsule" and its odd collection of items leads her into danger—and into love as she battles for her independence with county planner Reed Campbell. Intriguing.

Other books you might like:
Gail Douglas, *After Hours*, 1991
Jayne Ann Krentz, *Silver Linings*, 1991
Chloe Summers, *No Easy Task*, 1991
Theresa Weir, *Iguana Bay*, 1990

610
SUZANNE ELLISON
Sunburst
(New York: Harper, 1993)

Story type: Historical/American West
Major character(s): Mandy Henderson, Young Woman; Drew Robelard, Military Personnel (Army captain)
Time period(s): 19th century (late)
Locale(s): Fort Tejon, California; Sierra Nevadas, California

Summary: Seeking her missing fiance, Mandy heads for California and is surprised to encounter camels and a devastatingly handsome officer, Captain Drew Robelard. She enlists his aid, and though they disagree about a number of things, her feelings for him gradually change, and when they find the remains of Mandy's fiance's party, she can finally let her true feelings for Drew come to the surface. Funny, historically accurate, and slightly mysterious.

Other books you might like:
Rosanne Bittner, *Shameless*, 1993
Catriona Flynt, *Lost Treasure*, 1993
Robin Lee Hatcher, *Midnight Rose*, 1992
Terri Herrington, *Silena*, 1993

611

CATHERINE ENNIS

South of the Line

(Tallahassee: Naiad Press, 1989)

Story type: Lesbian/Historical
Major character(s): Faith O'Neal, Governess; Dominique LeCompte, Plantation Owner
Time period(s): 1860s
Locale(s): Tennessee; Mississippi River; Louisiana

Summary: Faith travels to Nashville to become a governess to the children of her widowed di nt cousin Dominique. They find love and adventure on their perilous journey down the Mississippi River to meet the children in New Orleans.

Other books you might like:
Penny Hayes, *The Long Trail*, 1986
   American West
Evelyn Kennedy, *Of Love and Glory*, 1989
   World War II
Michelle Martin, *Pembroke Park*, 1986
   Regency
Victoria Ramstetter, *The Marquise and the Novice*, 1981
   Gothic

612

CATHERINE ENNIS

Up, Up and Away

(Tallahassee, Florida: Naiad, 1994)

Story type: Lesbian/Contemporary
Major character(s): Sarah Bodman, Businesswoman (video specialist), Lesbian; Margaret Paige, Lawyer, Lesbian
Time period(s): 1990s
Locale(s): New Orleans, Louisiana; Manchac Swamp, Louisiana

Summary: When Sarah Bodman is assigned to videotape the deposition of a witness that will incriminate the infamous crime boss, Vinnie Scalio, she had no idea that she will eventually become a target for murder herself. But when the witness and a lawyer are murdered, suddenly she and attorney Margaret Paige become the only two people alive who heard the deposition—and the mob is hot on their trail. Taking to the skies in a balloon, Sarah and Margaret make their escape

only to crash land in the Manchac swamp—and the situation becomes even more treacherous—and passionate.

Other books you might like:
Sarah Aldridge, *Keep to Me, Stranger*, 1989
Katherine V. Forrest, *The Romantic Naiad*, 1993
   anthology of lesbian short fiction
Melissa Hartman, *The Sure Thing*, 1994
Karin Kallmaker, *Car Pool*, 1993
Molleen Zanger, *Gardenias Where There Are None*, 1994
   lesbian ghost story

613

SUZANNE ENOCH

Angel's Devil

(New York: Avon, 1995)

Story type: Regency
Major character(s): Angelique Graham, Noblewoman, Fiance(e); James Faring, Nobleman (Marquis of Abbonley), Rake; Simon Talbot, Nobleman, Fiance(e)
Time period(s): 1810s
Locale(s): England

Summary: When Simon Talbot talks his rakehell cousin, the Marquis of Abbonley, into pretending to be interested in his fiancee in a last ditch effort to convince Angelique's parents to allow an early wedding, the last thing he expects is that his cousin and Angelique will actually fall in love. Some interesting secondary characters, a dash to Gretna Green, and a heroic rescue enhance this witty, engaging Regency. Traditional, lively, and predictable.

Other books you might like:
Marion Chesney, *The Dreadful Debutante*, 1995
Marian Devon, *Deck the Halls*, 1995
   holiday theme
Gail Eastwood, *The Captain's Dilemma*, 1995
Elisabeth Fairchild, *The Love Knot*, 1995
Sandra Heath, *Lucy's Christmas Angel*, 1995

614

BARBARA ERSKINE

Kingdom of Shadows

(New York: Dell, 1988)

Story type: Time Travel
Major character(s): Clare Royland, Landowner, Psychic; Paul Royland, Spouse (Clare's spouse)
Time period(s): 20th century; 14th century
Locale(s): Scotland (Duncairn Castle)

Summary: Receiving vivid visions of her long-dead ancestor Isobel, Clare struggles against her husband Paul's wish to sell the castle as he plots to convince everyone that Clare is mad. Time change elements, gaslight feeling, and lots of Scottish history. Not your typical romance.

Other books you might like:
Jude Deveraux, *A Knight in Shining Armor*, 1989
   Time change elements

Chloe Gartner, *Mistress of the Highlands*, 1976
  Historical Scotland/17th century
Chloe Gartner, *Woman from the Glen*, 1973
  Historical Scotland/Bonnie Prince Charlie
Anya Seton, *Dragonwyck*, 1944
Becky Lee Weyrich, *Forever, for Love*, 1989
  Time change elements

615
MARCIA EVANICK

Midnight Kiss
(New York: Bantam, 1992)

Story type: Contemporary
Major character(s): Autumn O'Neil, Administrator (recreation director); Thane Clayborne, Doctor, Administrator (nursing home director)
Time period(s): 1990s
Locale(s): New York, New York

Summary: Autumn O'Neil plans exciting activities for her grandfather and the other patients at the nursing home even though stuffy Dr. Clayborne tries to interfere. She playfully teases him into her arms, and then both of their secret problems are solved.

Other books you might like:
Angela Carson, *Sweet Illusion*, 1990
Nancy Sheehan, *Harvest of Love*, 1990
  innocent
Jeanne Stephens, *At Risk*, 1989
Jeanne Stephens, *Broken Dreams*, 1987
Diana Whitney, *A Liberated Man*, 1990

616
MARJORIE EVERITT

Somewhere Near Paradise
(New York: Avalon, 1992)

Story type: Contemporary/Innocent
Major character(s): Marcie Newberry, Teacher, Landowner; Jim Wolverton, Restauranteur (cafe owner)
Time period(s): 1990s
Locale(s): Chennowah Grove, Illinois

Summary: A warm, sweet romance in which big city teacher Marcie and small town cafeowner Jim find love and romance in spite of their real estate conflicts.

Other books you might like:
Lori Copeland, *Darling Deceiver*, 1990
Leigh Michaels, *Let Me Count the Ways*, 1989
Laura Parrish, *Love's Quiet Corner*, 1989
Nancy Sheehan, *The Heart's Journey*, 1992

617
JEAN R. EWING

Rogue's Reward
(New York: Zebra, 1995)

Story type: Regency
Major character(s): Lady Eleanor Acton, Debutante, Noblewoman; Leander Campbell, Bastard Son, Rake
Time period(s): 1810s (1815)
Locale(s): England

Summary: Scandal, adventure, and blackmail are all part of this nicely-paced Regency that takes a beautiful, intelligent heroine, pairs her with a noted rake (who is not quite what he seems), adds equal measures of suspicion and love—and lets human nature take its course. Charming dialogue, accurate period detail, and a well-done mystery add enjoyment.

Other books you might like:
Jo Beverley, *Dierdre and Don Juan*, 1993
Charlotte Louise Dolan, *The Counterfeit Gentleman*, 1995
Gail Eastwood, *The Captain's Dilemma*, 1995
Gail Eastwood, *The Persistent Earl*, 1995
Carla Kelly, *Miss Grimsley's Oxford Career*, 1992

618
JEAN R. EWING

Virtue's Reward
(New York: Zebra, 1995)

Story type: Regency
Major character(s): Helena Trethaerin, Gentlewoman (impoverished); Richard Acton, Nobleman (Viscount Lenwood), Military Personnel (captain)
Time period(s): 1810s
Locale(s): England

Summary: When Captain Richard Acton arrives in Cornwall, he simply intends to fulfill the dying request of one of his men and check up on his cousin, Helena Trethaerin. However, when he finds her on the verge of agreeing to a disastrous marriage, he does the only thing he can think of, he marries her himself. An intriguing plot, a dash of mystery, and good sexual tension add spice to this warm and lively Regency.

Other books you might like:
Julie Caille, *The Rake and His Lady*, 1993
Gail Eastwood, *The Persistent Earl*, 1994
Carla Kelly, *Mrs. Drew Plays Her Hand*, 1994
Katherine Kingsley, *King of Hearts*, 1993
Kate Moore, *An Improper Widow*, 1995

619
ELISABETH FAIRCHILD

The Love Knot
(New York: Signet, 1995)

Story type: Regency

Major character(s): Aurora Ramsay, Gentlewoman, Steward (estate manager); Miles Fletcher, Gentleman, Art Dealer (also an art collector)
Time period(s): 1810s
Locale(s): England

Summary: Realizing that she must find a wealthy husband or lose her home because of her brothers' profligate ways, Aurora Ramsay agrees to teach art expert Miles Fletcher how to manage his new estate in return for his help in learning to attract a suitable husband. Remarkably, the plan succeeds—and then Aurora and Miles must decide what they both really want. Appealing characters and well-researched detail are highlights.

Other books you might like:
Gail Eastwood, *The Captain's Dilemma*, 1995
Suzanne Enoch, *Angel's Devil*, 1995
Candice Hern, *A Change of Heart*, 1995
April Kihlstrom, *The Wicked Groom*, 1996
Evelyn Richardson, *Lady Alex's Gamble*, 1995

620

ELISABETH FAIRCHILD

The Silent Suitor

(New York: Signet, 1994)

Story type: Regency
Major character(s): Sarah Lyndle, Handicapped (blind), Noblewoman; Ashley Hawkes, Nobleman (Earl of Henley)
Time period(s): 1810s
Locale(s): London, England

Summary: Although she is blind, Sarah Lyndle loves and enjoys life, and the Castleford family protects her and has great plans for her. However, Ashley Hawkes, Earl of Henley and "the Beast," has other ideas—and his actions stir up family anger and make Sarah wonder how she really feels. Eventually, she must make her choice, but will it be for safety or for love?

Other books you might like:
Mary Balogh, *Dancing with Clara*, 1994
   invalid heroine
Marjorie Farrell, *Lady Barbara's Dilemma*, 1993
Carla Kelly, *Marian's Christmas Wish*, 1989
Carla Kelly, *Mrs. Drew Plays Her Hand*, 1994
Deborah Simmons, *Fortune Hunter*, 1992

621

BARBARA FAITH

Gamblin' Man

(Toronto: Harlequin, 1993)

Story type: Historical/American West
Major character(s): Carrie McLellan, Teacher (aspiring), Saloon Hostess; Matthew Craddock, Saloon Keeper/Owner
Time period(s): 19th century
Locale(s): Cripple Creek, Colorado

Summary: When prim and proper Carrie McLellan arrives in Cripple Creek to find her sister and niece, she is appalled by the raucous iniquity of the town. However, her plans to become a teacher and save her actress sister fall into disarray when she becomes ill and is cared for by the local madam—in the local brothel! As a result, no respectable jobs are open to her so she takes a job in Matt Craddock's saloon and casino—and in the process learns a lot about tolerance and even more about love.

Other books you might like:
Yvonne Adamson, *Bridey's Mountain*, 1993
   saga
Paula Paul, *Sweet Ivy's Gold*, 1993
LaVyrle Spencer, *Forgiving*, 1990
Isabel Whitfield, *Bodie Bride*, 1992

622

SALLY FALCON

Stolen Kisses

(Bensalem, Pennsylvania: Meteor, 1992)

Story type: Contemporary
Major character(s): Jessie DeLord, Businesswoman, Interior Decorator (corporate); Trevor Planchet, Television Personality (sportscaster)
Time period(s): 1990s
Locale(s): Little Rock, Arkansas

Summary: Thirty-eight year-old corporate interior decorator Jessica DeLord's idea of a marriageable male is anything but smooth-talking, skirt-chasing Trevor Planchet. But when the TV sportscaster sets his sights on Jessie, it takes all her skills and determination to resist his incredible charms.

Other books you might like:
Gloria Alvarez, *Heart Waves*, 1992
Sandra Brown, *Texas! Sage*, 1991
Nora Roberts, *Courting Catherine*, 1991
Lisa Ann Verge, *Sweet Harvest*, 1992

623

MARJORIE FARRELL

Lady Barbara's Dilemma

(New York: Signet, 1993)

Story type: Regency
Major character(s): Lady Barbara Stanley, Noblewoman, Musician (pianist); Alec Gower, Musician (violinist), Nobleman (Lord Alec McLeod); Peter Rushcliffe, Nobleman
Time period(s): 1810s
Locale(s): London, England

Summary: Twenty-six and long on the shelf, pianist Lady Barbara Stanley feels incredibly lucky to be engaged to Peter. However, as the plans proceed, Peter is shown up for the bigot and snob that he is, and Barbara is increasingly drawn to violinist Alec, even though he appears not to be of her class. As it happens, Alec is a nobleman, so everything works out in true regency fashion.

Other books you might like:
Marion Chesney, *Finessing Clarissa*, 1989
Teresa DesJardien, *The Marriage Mart*, 1992
Georgette Heyer, *Bath Tangle*, 1955
Karla Hocker, *Lady Maryann's Dilemma*, 1990

624
COLLEEN FAULKNER

Flames of Love
(New York: Zebra, 1993)

Story type: Historical/Colonial America
Major character(s): Mary Alexandra Lambert, Noblewoman, Captive; Geoffrey Rordan, Nobleman, Hunter
Locale(s): Maryland, American Colonies; England

Summary: Outspoken, independent, and jilted, Lady Mary Alexandra Lambert heads for the American Colonies, only to be captured by Indians and then rescued by the very man who had left her standing at the altar! But that is just the beginning. A quest for vengeance, a marriage of convenience, and unexpected passion all add to this fast-paced adventure.

Other books you might like:
Emily Carmichael, *Visions of the Heart*, 1990
Shannon Drake, *Bride of the Wind*, 1992
Robin Lee Hatcher, *The Magic*, 1993
Anita Mills, *Follow the Heart*, 1990
Karen Robards, *Nobody's Angel*, 1992

625
COLLEEN FAULKNER

Love's Sweet Bounty
(New York: Zebra, 1991)

Story type: Historical/American West
Major character(s): Jessica Landon, Orphan (sharpshooter); Adam Stern, Indian (half), Detective (for railroad)
Time period(s): 1880s (1881)
Locale(s): Utah; Alaska; West

Summary: When her brother is killed in a train robbery, strong-willed Jessica Landon is forced reluctantly to team up with railroad detective Adam Stern to find the killers. Passion and plenty of action accompany this fascinating pair as they track their quarry from Utah to Alaska—and fall in love along the way. Funny and lively.

Other books you might like:
Virginia Brown, *Wildfire*, 1990
Carol Finch, *Thunder's Tender Touch*, 1989
Catherine Hart, *Tempest*, 1991
Kathy Jones, *Sweet Obsession*, 1990
Robin Leigh, *Rugged Splendor*, 1991

626
COLLEEN FAULKNER

Sweet Deception
(New York: Zebra, 1992)

Story type: Historical/Seventeenth Century
Major character(s): Thomasina Waxton, Noblewoman, Actress; Gavin Waxton, Landowner (colonial)
Time period(s): 17th century (1664)
Locale(s): London, England; Maryland, American Colonies

Summary: Freed from a mockery of a marriage by her husband's accidental death, Thomasina Waxton seeks safety and annonymity on the London stage as Ellen Scarlett. But two men are in hot pursuit — the Duke of Hunt wants to kill her, and Gavin Waxton wants to win her. Of course, he's her late husband's brother bent on seeing Thomasina brought to justice, but neither of them knows who the other is, yet! Fast-paced action that sweeps its characters from Restoration England to the American Colonies in a dangerous game of intrigue, power, and passion.

Other books you might like:
Sandra DuBay, *Nightrider*, 1991
Jean Plaidy, *The Pleasure of Love*, 1992
Karen Robards, *This Side of Heaven*, 1991
Ciji Ware, *Wicked Company*, 1992
JoAnn Wendt, *The Golden Dove*, 1989

627
COLLEEN FAULKNER

Temptation's Tender Kiss
(New York: Zebra, 1990)

Story type: Historical/American Revolution
Major character(s): Reagan Llewellyn, Revolutionary (American); Sterling Grayson, Spy (Colonial), Imposter (impersonates his twin brother)
Time period(s): 1770s (1777)
Locale(s): American Colonies

Summary: American revolutionary Reagan Llewellyn finds her pro-indenpendence publishing activities somewhat hampered by the arrival of lodger Sterling Grayson, a supposed Tory. Sterling, however, is not what he seems, and before long, Reagan and Sterling are involved in a battle to save their own lives and win America's independence as well. Murder, treachery, and deception during the turbulent American Revolutionary Era.

Other books you might like:
Gwen Bristow, *Celia Garth*, 1959
Judith E. French, *Scarlet Ribbons*, 1989
Heather Graham, *Love Not a Rebel*, 1989
Robin Maderich, *Faith and Honor*, 1989
Ashley Snow, *Dangerous Desire*, 1990

628
JANE FEATHER

Bold Destiny
(New York: Avon, 1990)

Story type: Historical/Exotic
Major character(s): Annabel Spencer, Captive (Member of a harem), Orphan; Kit Ralston, Military Personnel (Lieutenant)
Time period(s): 1840s
Locale(s): Afghanistan

Summary: Captured as a child and placed in the harem of an Afghan chieftain, Ayesha is given to Lieutenant Kit Ralston for a night of love. Their intense mutual attraction surprises them both and together they fight for their love and their lives.

Other books you might like:
Madeleine Brent, *Stormswift*, 1986
    Gothic overtones
Victoria Holt, *The India Fan*, 1988
    Gothic overtones
Mary Lide, *Isobelle*, 1988
    Exceptionally lyrical and well-written
Joanne Redd, *Desert Bride*, 1989
Bertrice Small, *Skye O'Malley*, 1980

629
JANE FEATHER

Brazen Whispers
(New York: Avon, 1990)

Story type: Historical/Medieval
Major character(s): Magdalen de Brese, Noblewoman; Guy de Gervais, Nobleman
Time period(s): 14th century (1370s)
Locale(s): England; France

Summary: As a child Magdalen was in love with Guy de Gervais; as a young woman she was soon wed to another. Used as a pawn by both England and France, it would take all her strength and courage to regain the man she loved.

Other books you might like:
Pamela Belle, *The Lodestar*, 1989
Cordia Byers, *Desire and Deceive*, 1990
Roberta Gellis, *Roselynde*, 1978
    1st of the Roselynde Chronicles
Roberta Gellis, *The Silver Mirror*, 1989
Johanna Lindsey, *Defy Not the Heart*, 1989
    earlier time period, same spirit

630
JANE FEATHER

The Eagle and the Dove
(New York: Avon, 1991)

Story type: Historical/Exotic
Major character(s): Sarita, Captive (of Caliph); Muley Abdul Hassan, Royalty (Caliph)

Time period(s): 15th century
Locale(s): Spain (Moorish-held Granada)

Summary: Beautiful Sarita, trying to avoid a forced marriage, is taken to the palace of a Moorish lord. She is held captive and her presence enrages the first wife and causes trouble in the empire.

Other books you might like:
Sarah Edwards, *Fire and Sand*, 1989
Victoria Holt, *The Captive*, 1989
Laura Kinsale, *Seize the Fire*, 1989
Mary Lide, *Isobelle*, 1988
Joanne Redd, *Desert Bride*, 1989

631
JANE FEATHER

Reckless Angel
(New York: Avon, 1989)

Story type: Historical/Seventeenth Century
Major character(s): Henrietta "Harry" Ashby, Runaway (From an unwanted marriage); Daniel Drummond, Gentleman (Royalist), Widow(er)
Time period(s): 17th century (1648)
Locale(s): England; Netherlands

Summary: Having rescued Henrietta Ashby from the battlefield, Sir Daniel Drummond finds he doesn't want to let her go—instead he marries her and is swept up in passion and political intrigue as they fight for the Royalist cause. Plenty of Royalist/Roundhead action and adventure.

Other books you might like:
Philippa Carr, *Saraband for Two Sisters*, 1976
    England of Charles I
Kimberly Cates, *Crown of Mist*, 1988
Chloe Gartner, *Mistress of the Highlands*, 1976
    Scotland during time of Charles I and Cromwell
Kathryn Kramer, *Desire's Deception*, 1989
JoAnn Wendt, *The Golden Dove*, 1989
    Restoration England

632
JANE FEATHER

Valentine
(New York: Bantam, 1995)

Story type: Historical/Regency
Major character(s): Theodora Belmont, Noblewoman; Sylvester Gilbraith, Nobleman (Earl of Stoneridge), Heir
Time period(s): 1810s
Locale(s): London, England; England

Summary: Faced with the unacceptable prospect of inheriting a title and estate but with no income to support it—unless he complies with the secret conditions of the will and marries one of the late earl's granddaughters—the Earl of Stoneridge bows to the inevitible and marries the independent, outspoken Theodora Belmont. And then, of course, Theo finds out—with predictably fiery results. This fast-paced, passionate story features a strong, likable heroine and a tormented, somewhat domineering hero.

Other books you might like:
Jo Beverley, *My Lady Notorious*, 1993
Jo Beverley, *Tempting Fortune*, 1995
Catherine Coulter, *The Valentine Legacy*, 1995
Amanda Quick, *Rendezvous*, 1992
Christina Skye, *Come the Dawn*, 1995

633

JANE FEATHER

Velvet

(New York: Bantam, 1994)

Story type: Historical/Regency
Major character(s): Gabrielle de Beaucaire, Spy (French); Nathaniel Praed, Spy (English)
Time period(s): 1810s
Locale(s): France; England

Summary: With her experience and French/English background, Gabrielle is an excellent spy; but when she tries to join Nathaniel Praed's spy network, he refuses to have a woman working for him, however talented. Nevertheless, the angry sparks between them soon blaze into something else, throwing passion into the mix of intrigue and confusion. Sensual and fast-paced.

Other books you might like:
Mary Balogh, *Beyond the Sunrise*, 1992
 Regency spies/darker than some
Baroness Orczy, *The Scarlet Pimpernel*, 1905
 classic intrigue during the French Revolution
Serena Richards, *Rendezvous*, 1991
 more spies
Suzanne Robinson, *Lady Gallant*, 1992
 spies and intrigues in 16th century England
Elizabeth Thornton, *Scarlet Angel*, 1990

634

JANE FEATHER

Violet

(New York: Bantam, 1995)

Story type: Historical/Regency
Major character(s): Tamsyn ''La Violette'' Baron, Mercenary (Bandit), Noblewoman; Lord Julian St. Simon, Military Personnel (colonel), Nobleman
Time period(s): 1810s (1812)
Locale(s): Portugal; England

Summary: When the noted outlaw leader Tamsyn, nicknamed ''La Violette,'' is captured by the French, it becomes the duty of Wellington's officer, Colonel Julian St. Simon, to rescue her, despite his contempt for her mercenary ways. But her beauty and spirit captivates him and as the tale unfolds, he ends up taking her to England, charged with the responsibility of turning her into a lady—a challenging, but immensely rewarding task. Fast-paced, sensual, and descriptive.

Other books you might like:
Mary Balogh, *Beyond the Sunrise*, 1992
Jo Beverley, *Tempting Fortune*, 1995
 fiery heroine
Susan Johnson, *Forbidden*, 1991
 creatively sensual
Amanda Quick, *Rendezvous*, 1992
 another intrepid heroine

635

JANE FEATHER

Virtue

(New York: Doubleday, 1993)

Story type: Historical/Regency
Major character(s): Judith Davenport, Gambler; Marcus Devlin, Nobleman (Marquis of Carrington)
Time period(s): 1810s
Locale(s): England; Belgium

Summary: When the Marquis of Carrington, Marcus Devlin, saves his young ward from the gambling skills of the charming brother and sister team of Sebastian and Judith Davenport, he finds himself intrigued, attracted, and eventually married to the intelligent and uncompromising Judith. Revenge, deception, and desire all complicate matters, but love does win out in the end; and all, good and bad alike, are appropriately rewarded.

Other books you might like:
Pamela Caldwell, *Scandalous*, 1993
Georgette Heyer, *Faro's Daughter*, 1942
 classic Regency
Mary Jo Putney, *The Rake and the Reformer*, 1989
Amanda Quick, *Seduction*, 1990
Amanda Quick, *Surrender*, 1990

636

JANE FEATHER

Vixen

(New York: Bantam, 1994)

Story type: Historical/Regency
Major character(s): Chloe Gresham, Heiress, Orphan; Sir Hugo Lattimer, Nobleman, Guardian
Time period(s): 1810s (1819)
Locale(s): England

Summary: Sir Hugo Lattimer is sharply reminded of his drunken past when young Chloe Gresham arrives and announces that he is her guardian. She needs protection from her half-brother and his step-son, but Hugo can't forget the shameful circumstances surrounding his relationship with her parents. Nevertheless, their relationship develops along passionate lines and love is not far behind. Reformed rake theme.

Other books you might like:
Deana James, *Speak Only Love*, 1991
 Gothic elements
Brenda Joyce, *Dark Fires*, 1991
 darker and more violent than some

Mary Jo Putney, *The Rake and the Reformer*, 1989
Anne Stuart, *To Love a Dark Lord*, 1994

637

JULIA FENTON

Blue Orchids
(New York: Berkley, 1992)

Story type: Contemporary/Mainstream
Major character(s): Orchid Lederer, Writer, Actress; Keith Leonard, Producer; Valentina Lederer, Actress, Adoptee (adopted sister)
Time period(s): 1990s
Locale(s): United States

Summary: A new show for Keith, Orchid, and Valentina offers a new beginning for all. Keith can prove he has not lost his talent, Orchid can show she is more than a bit-player, and Valentine can make a comeback after personal tragedy. However, the assassination of a Senator, plus some truly malevolent forces, conspire to destroy their hopes and dreams. A story of the ruthless need to win, and the high price of success.

Other books you might like:
Lois Battle, *The Past Is Another Country*, 1992
Jennifer Blake, *Joy and Anger*, 1991
Nora Roberts, *Genuine Lies*, 1991
Meryl Sawyer, *Blind Chance*, 1989

638

KELLY FERJUTZ

Windsong
(New York: Jove, 1994)

Story type: Historical/American West
Major character(s): Windsong, Indian, Widow(er); Etienne Nicolet, Trapper
Time period(s): 1830s (1837)
Locale(s): Mackinac Island, Michigan

Summary: Etienne, French trapper and Indian scout, is fascinated by Windsong, the lovely Indian widow and mother he shelters from a blizzard. As they grow to love each other, they are faced with the fact that she cannot marry him because she is the mother of a future chief and must marry within the tribe. Nevertheless, they defy tradition, agree to a short-term marriage, and then set out to convince the chief to let them make it permanent.

Other books you might like:
Michael Blake, *Dances with Wolves*, 1988
Pamela K. Forrest, *Autumn Ecstasy*, 1991
    another rescuing trapper
Ruth Langan, *Texas Healer*, 1992
    love and culture clashes
Dana Ransom, *Dakota Dawn*, 1991
    love and prejudice

639

MARIE FERRARELLA

Sapphire and Shadow
(New York: Harper, 1991)

Story type: Contemporary/Mainstream
Major character(s): Johanna Whitney, Spouse, Artist; Joshua MacKenzie, Art Dealer
Time period(s): 1990s
Locale(s): United States; England

Summary: Married to a film director who is slowly ruining his life with drugs, Johanna Whitney finally escapes, and with the help of an old friend, begins to build a new life for her daughter and herself. Exceptionally well-done characterizations in this insightful story of coming-of-age, growth, and healing.

Other books you might like:
Sally Beauman, *Destiny*, 1987
Barbara Taylor Bradford, *Remember*, 1992
Janet Dailey, *The Glory Game*, 1985
Madeline Hale, *Pirouette*, 1990
Marcia Martin, *Southern Secrets*, 1991

640

AMY J. FETZER

Lion Heart
(New York: Zebra, 1995)

Story type: Historical/Exotic; Historical/Georgian
Major character(s): Aurora Lassiter, Healer, Witch; Ransom Montgomery, Pirate
Time period(s): 1750s (1756)
Locale(s): Ottoman Empire

Summary: In the heat of battle pirate captain Ran Montgomery saves Scotswoman Aurora Lassiter and her Japanese protector. She is a Wiccan healer barred from her homeland, and when she is captured by a sheik, Ran bargains for her and takes her away with him. She heals her protector and wins over Ran's pirate crew as he tries to resist his growing feelings for her. Time and again Ran saves her life until they finally realize it is their destiny to be together.

Other books you might like:
Judith E. French, *Fortune's Mistress*, 1993
Robin Lee Hatcher, *The Magic*, 1993
    another pirate/witch combination
Iris Johansen, *Midnight Warrior*, 1994
    a medieval healer
Kathleen Morgan, *Fire Queen*, 1994
    another healer

641

GAYLE FEYRER

The Prince of Cups
(New York: Dell, 1995)

Story type: Historical/Renaissance

Major character(s): Veronica Danti, Gypsy, Healer; Antonio di Fabiani, Nobleman
Time period(s): 15th century (1490s)
Locale(s): Florence, Italy

Summary: Although wed for political reasons to a man with the mind of a child, beautiful Veronica Danti knows, through the Tarot, that her future lies with the Prince of Cups; and when she meets Antonio de Fabiani, she knows he is that man. Filled with intrigue, betrayal, and treachery, this passionate story of two star-crossed lovers is set against the colorful and violent backdrop of Renaisance Italy. Fast-paced, intricate, and richly detailed. First novel.

Other books you might like:
Linda Lang Bartell, *Caressa*, 1990
    passion and violence in Italy
Diana Gabaldon, *Outlander*,
    excellent historical detail/Scottish setting/time travel elements
Iris Johansen, *The Wind Dancer*, 1991
    passion and violence in Italy
Samuel Shellabarger, *Prince of Foxes*, 1947
    classic tale of the Renaissance
Susan Wiggs, *Circle in the Water*, 1994
    intrigue in Renaissance England

642

SANDRA FIELD

Goodbye Forever

(Toronto: Harlequin, 1990)

Story type: Contemporary
Major character(s): Roslin Hebb, Musician (concert pianist), Runaway; Tyson McCully, Hero
Time period(s): 1990s

Summary: Lost and soaking wet, runaway concert pianist Roslin Hebb is rescued by camper Tyson McCully and given shelter in his van. After an innocent night, they part company and Roslin goes to find the property and house her great aunt left her. But Roslin hasn't seen the last of Tyson. He wants her property—and so does a developer. However, Roslin not only wants her own property, she also wants Tyson! Lyrical.

Other books you might like:
Lori Copeland, *Darling Deceiver*, 1990
Kathleen Creighton, *Love and Other Surprises*, 1990
Vanessa Grant, *Awakening Dreams*, 1990
Debbie Macomber, *A Little Bit of Country*, 1990
Valerie Parv, *Tasmanian Devil*, 1990

643

CAROL FINCH (Pseudonym of Connie Feddersen)

Apache Wind

(New York: Zebra, 1993)

Story type: Historical/American West
Major character(s): Tempest Litchfield, Lawyer; Cord McIntosh, Criminal (accused), Indian
Time period(s): 19th century

Locale(s): El Paso, Texas

Summary: Cord, in jail for rustling, is down on life and women. In his escape, he kidnaps the woman he thinks is his enemy's fiancee. Instead he gets attorney Tempest Litchfield, who doesn't bother to tell him he is wrong. As they travel together to find the real rustlers (she even marries him), their relationship turns to love. But when she finally tells him who she really is, he returns her to her father and then no one is happy! A scrappy, fast-moving tale.

Other books you might like:
Lori Copeland, *Promise Me Forever*, 1994
Sharon Ihle, *Wild Rose*, 1993
Rebecca Paisley, *Rainbows and Rapture*, 1992
Evelyn Rogers, *Sweet Texas Magic*, 1992

644

CAROL FINCH

Montana Mistress

(New York: Zebra, 1990)

Story type: Historical/American West
Major character(s): Victoria Flemming Cassidy, Captive; Dru Sullivan, Rancher
Time period(s): 1860s (1865)
Locale(s): Montana

Summary: Literally kidnapped from the church on her wedding day, Victoria Cassidy finds herself on the way to Montana in the company of a highly attractive rancher. Dru Sullivan, her father's partner, was delighted to have the opportunity to pay Victoria's sleazy intended groom back for cheating him in a business deal—and to return Victoria to her father in the process. He didn't, however, plan to fall in love with her. Family complications and old secrets add intrigue and interest to this sensual western romance.

Other books you might like:
Leigh Bristol, *Twice Blessed*, 1991
Carol Finch, *Thunder's Tender Touch*, 1989
Lindsey Hanks, *Outlaw Lover*, 1990
Catherine Hart, *Forever Gold*, 1988

645

CAROL FINCH

Moonlight Enchantment

(New York: Zebra, 1992)

Story type: Historical/American West
Major character(s): Darcey O'Rourke, Accountant; Kane Callahan, Detective—Private
Time period(s): 1860s (1866)
Locale(s): Colorado

Summary: Hired by stagecoach line owner Patrick O'Rourke to see that his independent daughter Darcey returns to St. Louis from Denver for her own safety, private investigator Kane Callahan meets his match in the fiery, fearless woman who is determined not only to prove she can handle her father's company, but catch a band of robbers as well. Funny, action-filled, and sensual.

Other books you might like:
Constance Bennett, *Morning Sky*, 1991
Sonya Birmingham, *Spitfire*, 1991
Charlotte Hubbard, *Colorado Moonfire*, 1992
Eugenia Riley, *Taming Kate*, 1992
DeLoras Scott, *Devil's Delight*, 1992

646

CAROL FINCH (Pseudonym of Connie Feddersen)

Promise Me Moonlight
(New York: Zebra, 1993)

Story type: Historical/American West
Major character(s): Cairo Calhoun, Outlaw (suspected); Lawton Stone, Lawman (U.S. Marshal)
Time period(s): 1880s
Locale(s): Oklahoma; Arkansas

Summary: When Marshal Lawton Stone is assigned to escort Cairo Calhoun, he has mixed emotions—he's reluctant to have anything to do with this hot-headed woman, but he doesn't mind getting away from searching for a gang of outlaws. Problems arise when he notices a strong resemblance between Cairo and the outlaws. He's falling for her fast, he can't trust her, and he certainly can't out talk her! Charming banter ends in steamy romance.

Other books you might like:
Rosanne Bittner, *Outlaw Hearts*, 1993
Rosanne Bittner, *Shameless*, 1992
Kit Gardner, *The Stolen Heart*, 1993
Martha Hix, *Lone Star Loving*, 1993
Rebecca Paisley, *Rainbows and Rapture*, 1992

647

CAROL FINCH

Thunder's Tender Touch
(New York: Zebra, 1989)

Story type: Historical/American West
Major character(s): Piper Malone, Heiress—Dispossessed; Vince Logan, Gunfighter (Bounty hunter), Rancher
Time period(s): 1850s (1857)
Locale(s): Arkansas

Summary: In tracking down her stepbrother who has stolen her inheritance, feisty Piper Malone enlists the aid of hired gun Vince Logan. At first sparks fly between these two opposites, but love wins out in the end.

Other books you might like:
Jessie Ford, *A Different Breed*, 1988
    Unusual
Norah Hess, *Wildfire*, 1989
Betina Lindsey, *Waltz with the Lady*, 1990
Johanna Lindsey, *Savage Thunder*, 1989
Gina Robins, *Texas Temptation*, 1989

648

CAROL FINCH

Wild Mountain Honey
(New York: Zebra, 1991)

Story type: Historical/American West
Major character(s): Mariah Laverty, Heiress—Dispossessed, Handicapped (temporarily blind); Devlin "White Shadow" Granger, Indian (half-Apache)
Time period(s): 1860s (1865)
Locale(s): Southwest

Summary: Desired by her stepfather (and most of the other men on the wagon train) and hated by her greedy, murderous stepmother, it is not surprising that after an attempt on her life, beautiful Mariah Laverty disappears into the New Mexico mountains. On her flight toward civilization she is first observed and then aided by Apache warrior White Shadow who has a vendetta against all whites, in general, and one army officer, in particular. However, before they find love, the pair must face numerous obstacles, including blindness, murder, treachery, and their own volatile tempers. Fast-paced, funny, and sensual.

Other books you might like:
Kathleen Eagle, *Heaven and Earth*, 1991
Joanna Jordan, *Destiny's Dream*, 1990
Rebecca Paisley, *Moonlight and Magic*, 1990
DeLoras Scott, *The Miss and the Maverick*, 1990

649

PHOEBE FITZJAMES

Oklahoma Angel
(New York: Zebra, 1993)

Story type: Historical/American West
Major character(s): Charity Caine, Young Woman; Jake Turlow, Lawman
Time period(s): 19th century
Locale(s): Oklahoma

Summary: Charity Caine's family is notorious and the law is their sworn enemy; but when she saves lawman Jake Turlow's life, she is drawn to him in spite of herself. However, their romance is interrupted by Charity's capture by the very outlaws that Jake has been chasing. Naturally, he rescues her—and later she returns the favor! Fast-paced, highly sensual western romance.

Other books you might like:
Rosanne Bittner, *Shameless*, 1993
Katherine Compton, *Outlaw Bride*, 1991
Kit Gardner, *The Stolen Heart*, 1993
Martha Hix, *Lone Star Loving*, 1993
Linda Lael Miller, *Daniel's Bride*, 1992

650

PHOEBE FITZJAMES

Renegade Angel
(New York: Zebra, 1992)

Story type: Historical/American West
Major character(s): Jenny Templeton, Servant (bordello kitchen worker); Ace Denton, Murderer (suspected)
Time period(s): 1870s
Locale(s): Missouri; Kansas

Summary: Unskilled and penniless, naive Jenny Templeton goes to work in the kitchens of a bordello. Her one aim in life is to find her father's murderer. She knows Ace Denton was involved, but when he enters her life, they end up falling in love and she realizes she needs to find the truth before she can be truly content. Passion, adventure, and romance.

Other books you might like:
Norah Hess, *Devil in Spurs*, 1990
Jill Marie Landis, *Wild Flower*, 1989
Linda Lael Miller, *Emma and the Outlaw*, 1991
Victoria Thompson, *Fortune's Lady*, 1990

651

REBECCA FLANDERS (Pseudonym of Donna Ball)

The Sensation
(Toronto: Harlequin, 1990)

Story type: Historical/Roaring Twenties
Major character(s): Alice Fontaine, Actress (Aspiring), Imposter; Nick Crawford, Bachelor (eligible)
Time period(s): 1920s
Locale(s): New York, New York

Summary: When aspiring actress Alice Fontaine crashes wealthy Nick Crawford's posh party in the hopes of meeting a potential Broadway backer, she ends up piquing Nick's curiosity and winning his heart as well. A charming romance that touches on some serious issues.

Other books you might like:
Diane Cory, *High Society*, 1990
　　mainstream/20s setting
Janet Dailey, *Masquerade*, 1990
Elizabeth Kary, *Midnight Lace*, 1990
　　another aspiring actress/different setting
Catherine M. Rae, *Julia's Story*, 1989

652

DONNA FLETCHER

San Francisco Surrender
(New York: Zebra, 1990)

Story type: Historical/American West Coast
Major character(s): Victoria Chambers, Thief (pickpocket—"The Serpent"); Sebastian Blood, Detective ("The Dragon")
Time period(s): 1870s (1873)
Locale(s): San Francisco, California

Summary: Victoria Chambers masquerades as a boy and becomes a pickpocket, the infamous "Serpent," in order to provide for her dying sister. Sebastian Blood, "The Dragon," is hired to stop the slippery thief; but when they meet, the results are unexpected; and when the two end up married to each other, the action increases dramatically. Deception, murder, and passion are all part of this fast-paced love story.

Other books you might like:
Virginia Brown, *Renegade Embrace*, 1990
Barbara Hargis, *Heart Song*, 1990
Kathy Lawrence, *Tin Angel*, 1989
Cynthia Wright, *Brighter than Gold*, 1990

653

ELLEN FLETCHER

Pure Instinct
(Bensalem, Pennsylvania: Meteor, 1992)

Story type: Contemporary
Major character(s): Amie Phillips, Activist (homeless advocate); Buck Cameron, Businessman, Hunter
Time period(s): 1990s
Locale(s): Charlotte, North Carolina

Summary: Fascinated by wealthy, unconventional, big-game hunter Buck Cameron, Amie Phillips rather enjoys soliciting money from him for her shelter for the homeless. However, Buck has some secrets in his life that must be solved before the two can find happiness together.

Other books you might like:
Gloria Alvarez, *Heart Waves*, 1992
Judy Gill, *Bad Billy Culver*, 1991
Susan Kyle, *Escapade*, 1992
Anne Ladley, *Moriah's Magic*, 1992

654

CHRISTINE FLYNN

Renegade
(New York: Silhouette, 1989)

Story type: Contemporary
Major character(s): Ellie Bennett, Businesswoman (florist); Cain Whitlow, Businessman (successful)
Time period(s): 1980s
Locale(s): Aubrey, Oklahoma

Summary: When Cain Whitlow returns to his hometown to take care of his mother's estate, he has bitter memories and an old reputation to contend with. He doesn't count on being attracted to Ellie, someone who can only remind him of a past he wants to forget.

Other books you might like:
Lisa Gregory, *The Rainbow Promise*, 1989
Debbie Macomber, *Denim and Diamonds*, 1989
Jan Matthews, *Class Reunion*, 1989
Elizabeth Quinn, *Any Day Now*, 1990
LaVyrle Spencer, *Bittersweet*, 1990

655

CATRIONA FLYNT

Lost Treasure

(New York: Harper, 1993)

Story type: Historical/American West
Major character(s): Mollene Kennedy, Teacher, Actress (former); Winslow Fortune, Businessman (logging company owner)
Time period(s): 1890s (1896)
Locale(s): Summit, California

Summary: Winslow has enough trouble with avaricious cousins without Mollene's causing problems just by her very presence in his logging town. Her beauty, talents, and secrets keep things in an uproar; but Mollene and Winslow work everything out eventually. Then, of course, outside forces try to intervene—but all in all, a sweet and funny love story.

Other books you might like:
Candace Camp, *Rosewood*, 1991
Suzanne Ellison, *Sunburst*, 1993
Joan Johnston, *Sweetwater Seduction*, 1991
Victoria Thompson, *Playing with Fire*, 1990

656

BETTE FORD

For Always

(New York: Pinnacle, 1995)

Story type: Contemporary; Ethnic
Major character(s): Heather Gregory, Counselor (high school); Quinn Montgomery, Lawyer; Cynthia Montgomery, Teenager
Time period(s): 1990s
Locale(s): Detroit, Michigan

Summary: High school counselor Heather Gregory is disgusted with attorney Quinn Montgomery, father of teenage Cynthia. His busy, grief-filled life can't emotionally support his troubled daughter, and Heather's interference only angers and confuses him. Sparks fly as they fight over how to save Cynthia—pregnant and a runaway—and as they learn to deal with their intense attraction for each other. A sensual, realistic love story with an emotionally wounded hero and a heroine who cares.

Other books you might like:
Angela Benson, *Between the Lines*, 1996
 ethnic
Sandra Brown, *Eloquent Silence*, 1995
 emotionally compelling/father-daughter aspect
Patricia Potter, *Lawless*, 1991
 wounded hero/Western setting/not ethnic
Francis Ray, *Forever Yours*, 1994
 ethnic
Amberlina Wicker, *Private Matters*, 1995
 father/daughter sub-plot

657

BETTE FORD

Forever After

(New York: Pinnacle, 1995)

Story type: Contemporary; Ethnic
Major character(s): Diane Rivers, Teacher (business/computer classes); Charles Alexander Randol III, Businessman (pharmaceutical company vp), Coach (former)
Time period(s): 1990s
Locale(s): At Sea; Detroit, Michigan

Summary: In a bold effort to win the only man she has ever loved, Diane Rivers books passage on the same cruise ship as Charles Randol, the man who broke off their budding relationship a year earlier because she offered only friendship. This time their relationship is different, and before the cruise is over they are married. But Diane has hides a large—and important—part of her past from Charles, a past that returns to haunt her and may even threaten their marriage. This involving story features well-drawn characters, good sexual tension, and vivid description.

Other books you might like:
Angela Benson, *For All Time*, 1995
Sandra Kitt, *The Color of Love*, 1995
Sandra Kitt, *Serenade*, 1994
Francis Ray, *Undeniable*, 1995
Margie Walker, *Breathless*, 1995

658

KATHERINE V. FORREST, Editor

The Romantic Naiad

(Tallahassee, Florida: Naiad, 1993)

Story type: Lesbian/Contemporary; Anthology
Time period(s): 1990s
Locale(s): United States

Summary: A diverse anthology of 27 short love stories by lesbian writers.

Other books you might like:
Sarah Aldridge, *Michaela*, 1994
Catherine Ennis, *Up, Up and Away*, 1994
Karin Kallmaker, *Painted Moon*, 1994
Molleen Zanger, *Gardenias Where There Are None*, 1994

659

PAMELA K. FORREST

Autumn Ecstasy

(New York: Zebra, 1990)

Story type: Historical/Post-American Revolution
Major character(s): Linsey MacAdams, Gentlewoman; Luc ''Bear'' LeClerc, Trapper
Time period(s): 1780s (1784)
Locale(s): Ohio

Summary: Kidnapped, auctioned off, and given to a trapper as payment for a debt, gently bred Linsey MacAdams struggles to make the best of an impossible situation—and in the process she learns to survive in the wilderness, overcomes her fear of Indians, and falls in love with Bear (Luc LeClerc), the trapper to whom she was "given." A gentle, sensitive, sensual Beauty-and-the-Beast-type story.

Other books you might like:
Madeline Baker, *Forbidden Fires*, 1990
Peggy Hanchar, *Tomorrow's Dream*, 1989
Kathleen Harrington, *Cherish the Dream*, 1990
Jill Marie Landis, *Wild Flower*, 1989
Robin McKinley, *Beauty*, 1978
  classic retelling of Beauty and the Beast

660
PAMELA K. FORREST

Desert Angel
(New York: Zebra, 1994)

Story type: Historical/American West
Major character(s): March Evans, Abuse Victim, Housekeeper; Jim Travis, Rancher, Widow(er) (father)
Time period(s): 19th century
Locale(s): Arizona

Summary: March Evans is the answer to widower Jim Travis' prayer for someone to take care of his infant son. In turn, he is her escape from an abusive father. Both have a lot to learn and much healing to do, as she learns that men can be tender and gentle and he learns that women can be strong and survive. Warm and satisfying.

Other books you might like:
Catherine Anderson, *Cheyenne Amber*, 1994
  caring hero
Robin Lee Hatcher, *Promise Me Spring*, 1991
Lorraine Heath, *Sweet Lullaby*, 1992
  gentle and tender
Jill Marie Landis, *Until Tomorrow*, 1994
Libby Sydes, *Until Spring*, 1993

661
PAMELA K. FORREST

Wild Savage Heart
(New York: Zebra, 1993)

Story type: Historical/Colonial America
Major character(s): Molly Gallager, Widow(er); Nathan Morning Hawk, Indian (Shawnee)
Locale(s): South Carolina, American Colonies

Summary: When Molly's husband Adam is killed, Shawnee warrior Nathan Morning Hawk comes to her aid, helping her set up her homestead and gather supplies for the winter. As they work together, their friendship develops into something more; and when Molly discovers she is carrying Adam's child, Hawk knows he must take action. A warm, romantic, and humorous tale of the Carolina Frontier.

Other books you might like:
Barbara Cummings, *Wilderness Flame*, 1993
Judith E. French, *Lovestorm*, 1990
Judith E. French, *Moon Dancer*, 1991
Maura Seger, *The Taming of Amelia*, 1993
Penelope Williamson, *A Wild Yearning*, 1990

662
REBECCA FORSTER

A Delicate Matter
(New York: Pocket Books, 1989)

Story type: Contemporary/Mainstream
Major character(s): Calla Oaks, Orphan, Spouse (Doctor's); Jonathan Drake, Doctor
Time period(s): 1940s; 1970s
Locale(s): California (southern)

Summary: When a man from her past threatens to destroy her happiness, Calla is faced with a choice—will she be a victim once again or will she fight?

Other books you might like:
Sally Beauman, *Destiny*, 1987
Eileen Goudge, *Garden of Lies*, 1989
Meryl Sawyer, *Blind Chance*, 1989

663
SUZANNE FORSTER

Come Midnight
(New York: Berkley, 1995)

Story type: Contemporary; Romantic Suspense
Major character(s): Leigh Rappaport, Psychologist; Nick Montera, Photographer
Time period(s): 1990s
Locale(s): Los Angeles, California

Summary: Psychologist Leigh Rappaport can't explain her fascination with photographer and accused murderer Nick Montera, but there's no denying the attraction she has to this complicated, mysterious man. Although he sometimes frightens her in his intensity, she isn't convinced that he used his legendary seductive powers in a crime of passion. Her job is to probe the mind of a possible killer; what she finds is a passion she has never known.

Other books you might like:
Tami Hoag, *Guilty as Sin*, 1996
  follows *Night Sins*
Tami Hoag, *Night Sins*, 1995
Linda Howard, *Dream Man*, 1995
Meagan McKinney, *A Man to Slay Dragons*, 1996
Nora Roberts, *Genuine Lies*, 1991

664

SUZANNE FORSTER

Shameless

(New York: Berkley, 1994)

Story type: Contemporary/Mainstream
Major character(s): Jessie Flood-Warnecke, Widow(er), Step-Parent; Luc Warnecke, Relative (Jessie s stepson)
Time period(s): 1990s
Locale(s): California

Summary: Forced apart by murder, an illegitimate child, and an ugly affair, childhood sweethearts Jessie and Luc come together again when Luc returns home to settle some unfinished business. The fact that Jessie had married Luc's late father doesn't help their relationship. Suspicion and even hate are the order of the day. A powerful, passionate story with a surprising ending.

Other books you might like:

Sandra Canfield, *Dark Journey*, 1994
Christiane Heggan, *Passions*, 1993
Mary-Ben Lorris, *Sing Me to Sleep*, 1994
Doris Parmett, *Risk*, 1994
Nora Roberts, *Genuine Lies*, 1991

665

EMILY FRENCH

Capture

(Toronto: Harlequin, 1994)

Story type: Historical
Major character(s): Jeanne Marie De La Rocques, Captive, Orphan; Black Eagle, Indian (Algonquin), Warrior
Time period(s): 17th century (1637-1640)
Locale(s): Quebec, Canada

Summary: Alone in the New World, Jeanne is captured by Black Eagle, who decides that she is a moondaughter of his people, the Algonquins. She fights for freedom; but as she lives with the tribe, she slowly learns both women's work and men's warfare strategies. She marries Black Eagle and although a few hateful people still threaten them, eventually their combined wisdom and skills bring peace and prosperity to the people.

Other books you might like:

Michael Blake, *Dances with Wolves*, 1988
    much later period/Sioux life
Kate Cameron, *Orenda*, 1992
    story of Iroquois life
Judith E. French, *Highland Moon*, 1991
    Shawnee life
Judith E. French, *Moonfeather*, 1990
    Shawnee life
Joan Van Nuys, *Beloved Intruder*, 1992
    later period

666

JUDITH E. FRENCH

Fortune's Bride

(New York: Avon, 1994)

Story type: Historical/American Revolution
Major character(s): Caroline Steele, Plantation Owner; Garrett Faulkner, Sea Captain, Privateer
Time period(s): 1770s (1777)
Locale(s): Maryland; South Carolina; Arawak Island, Caribbean

Summary: Caroline, a widowed patriot, struggles to save her plantation by letting British forces (and her lecherous cousin) occupy her home, all the while pretending to be loyal to the Crown. Salvation, of a sort, comes in the form of privateer Garrett Faulkner, who ends up in her bed and ruins her reputation. He agrees to marry her in return for the family fortune which is hidden somewhere in the Caribbean, which, of course, they set out to find. Ancient curses, pirates, intrigue, and passion are all part of this fast-paced rather exotic adventure.

Other books you might like:

Wendy Garrett, *Sweet Southern Caress*, 1991
    later time period
Katherine Kincaid, *Midnight Treasure*, 1992
Meagan McKinney, *Till Dawn Tames the Night*, 1991
    later period/sea-faring action and island intrigue
JoAnn Wendt, *Beyond the Savage Sea*, 1990
    another determined heroine/exotic setting

667

JUDITH E. FRENCH

Fortune's Mistress

(New York: Avon, 1993)

Story type: Historical/Exotic
Major character(s): Lacy Burnett, Witch, Psychic; James Black, Pirate, Bastard Son (of Charles II)
Time period(s): 17th century (1672-1703)
Locale(s): England; Caribbean; New England, American Colonies

Summary: Lacy Bennett, witch, and James Black, pirate, are chained together on their way to the gallows. However, when Lacy's brother frees them, James unceremoniously throws him in the Thames, steals his ship, and, with Lacy, heads for the Caribbean and a sunken treasure. An Incan prince, Spanish gold, psychic visions, and plenty of passion add to this fast-paced adventure.

Other books you might like:

Shannon Drake, *Bride of the Wind*, 1992
Heather Graham, *A Pirate's Pleasure*, 1992
Diana Haviland, *Pirate's Kiss*, 1992
Kathleen Morgan, *Child of the Mist*, 1993
Kathleen E. Woodiwiss, *Shanna*, 1977

668

JUDITH E. FRENCH

Lovestorm

(New York: Avon, 1990)

Story type: Historical/Colonial America
Major character(s): Elizabeth Sommersett, Noblewoman (daughter of an Earl); Cain Dare, Indian (Lenni Lappe)
Time period(s): 17th century (second half of century)
Locale(s): Virginia, American Colonies (the coast and Jamestown)

Summary: Rescued from a shipwreck by an unusual, English-speaking Indian named Cain Dare, Lady Elizabeth struggles with her growing feelings for Cain and her desire to return to civilization. However, when she does return, things are not as she expected and it takes all her courage and resolve to set things straight again.

Other books you might like:
Colleen Faulkner, *Passion's Savage Moon*, 1989
  American Colonial Setting
Veronica Sattler, *A Promise of Fire*, 1989
  American Colonial setting
Lynette Vinet, *Savage Deception*, 1989

669

JUDITH E. FRENCH

Moon Dancer

(New York: Avon, 1991)

Story type: Historical/Colonial America
Series: Indian Moon Trilogy
Major character(s): Fiona O'Neal, Healer, Servant (indentured); Wolf Shadow, Shaman, Indian (Shawnee)
Time period(s): 1730s
Locale(s): Maryland, American Colonies

Summary: When Wolf Shadow, an educated shaman of the Shawnee, rescues Fiona O'Neal from a lustful backwoodsman, Wolf Shadow is torn by his duty to bring peace to his people and his love for a white woman. Third in the Indian Moon Trilogy.

Other books you might like:
Cheryl Black, *Comanche Love Song*, 1989
Kate Cameron, *Orenda*, 1992
Genell Dellin, *Cherokee Dawn*, 1990
Jessie Ford, *A Different Breed*, 1988
Janelle Taylor, *Savage Conquest*, 1985

670

JUDITH E. FRENCH

Moonfeather

(New York: Avon, 1990)

Story type: Historical/Colonial America
Series: Indian Moon Trilogy

Major character(s): Moonfeather "Leah" Stewart, Indian (half Shawnee), Noblewoman (daughter of Scottish Earl); Brandon, Nobleman (Viscount)
Time period(s): 1700s (1706)
Locale(s): England; American Colonies

Summary: Deserted by her Scots nobleman father and raised by her mother's people, the Shawnee, Moonfeather has enjoyed a relatively peaceful existence until it is shattered when a spoiled arrogant Englishman is captured by her people and in order to save his life, she must marry him. But marriage brings changes; and eventually Moonfeather finds herself in England dealing not only with prejudice and suspicion but real evil as well. A passionate, action-filled story laced with intrigue and some mysticism.

Other books you might like:
Emily Carmichael, *Visions of the Heart*, 1990
Cassie Edwards, *When Passion Calls*, 1990
Colleen Faulkner, *Passion's Savage Moon*, 1989
Constance O'Banyon, *Cheyenne Sunrise*, 1990
Janelle Taylor, *Bittersweet Ecstasy*, 1987

671

JUDITH E. FRENCH

Scarlet Ribbons

(New York: Avon, 1989)

Story type: Historical/American Revolution
Major character(s): Sarah Turner, Innkeeper; Forest Irons, Spy, Revolutionary
Time period(s): 1770s (1777)
Locale(s): Maryland

Summary: When Sarah's Tory husband disappears, the inn she runs, always an easy target for thievery by the hungry Americans, becomes even more vulnerable. Aided by a spy for the Americans, Forest, Sarah manages to endure and in the process learns about love, the American cause, and the man who rescued her.

Other books you might like:
Heather Graham, *Love Not a Rebel*, 1989
  Third in a trilogy
Karen Harper, *Eden's Gate*, 1989
  French and Indian War
Robin Maderich, *Faith and Honor*, 1989
Christina Savage, *Hearts of Fire*, 1984
Lynette Vinet, *Pirate's Bride*, 1989

672

SHEILA FYFE

Appointment with Love

(New York: Avalon, 1990)

Story type: Contemporary/Innocent
Major character(s): Sandy Booker, Government Official (presidential advisor); Rick Aragon, Lawyer (immigration expert), Government Official (presidential appointee)
Time period(s): 1980s
Locale(s): Washington, District of Columbia

Summary: Sandy and Rick are attracted to each other, but when she overhears news of a possible scandal in his past, she is torn between her feelings and her sense of duty. Interesting insights into the political scene.

Other books you might like:
Jane Edwards, *Terror by Design*, 1990
Dana James, *Dark Moon Rising*, 1990
Lynda Stowe Landers, *A Season to Remember*, 1989
Jane Shore, *The Cinderella Game*, 1990
Constance Walker, *One Perfect Springtime*, 1989

673

DIANA GABALDON

Dragonfly in Amber
(New York: Delacorte, 1992)

Story type: Time Travel; Historical/Georgian
Series: Outlander
Major character(s): Claire Beauchamp Randall, Time Traveller, Doctor; Jamie Fraser, Nobleman, Military Personnel
Time period(s): 1740s (1743); 1960s (1968)
Locale(s): France; Scotland

Summary: Claire, a 20th century doctor, tries to convince her daughter, Brianna, that her true father has been missing for 200 years. Claire relates a time-travel tale of passion, intrigue, and drama which includes a stay in Charles Stuart's racy French court, a stint of hospital work (aided by her modern knowledge), and an attempt to stop a battle that must continue. Through it all, Jamie Fraser (Brianna's father) helps her and loves her. Good historical detail in this highly sensual, non-traditional time travel story. Follows *Outlander*.

Other books you might like:
Laura Gilmour Bennett, *By All That Is Sacred*, 1991
Jude Deveraux, *A Knight in Shining Armor*, 1989
R. Garcia y Robertson, *The Spiral Dance*, 1991
Judith Merkle Riley, *In Pursuit of the Green Lion*, 1990
Bertrice Small, *A Moment in Time*, 1991

674

DIANA GABALDON

Outlander
(New York: Delacorte, 1991)

Story type: Time Travel
Series: Outlander
Major character(s): Claire Beauchamp Randall, Nurse, Time Traveller; Jamie Fraser, Nobleman, Military Personnel
Time period(s): 1940s (1945); 1740s (1743)
Locale(s): Scotland

Summary: Abruptly transported from 1945 to 1743, Claire Randall finds herself in the midst of the violent political battle raging between the English and the Scots. Her innate courage and adaptability allow her to survive; but when she falls in love with valiant James Fraser, she truly becomes caught between two worlds. This is the author's first novel and the first of a trilogy.

Other books you might like:
Laura Gilmour Bennett, *By All That Is Sacred*, 1991
Jude Deveraux, *A Knight in Shining Armor*, 1989
Eugenia Riley, *A Tryst in Time*, 1992
Thomasina Ring, *Time-Spun Rapture*, 1990
Bertrice Small, *A Moment in Time*, 1991

675

DIANA GABALDON

Voyager
(New York: Delacorte, 1994)

Story type: Time Travel
Series: Outlander
Major character(s): Claire Beauchamp Randall, Doctor, Time Traveller; Jamie Fraser, Military Personnel, Smuggler; Brianna Randall, Child (Daughter of Claire)
Time period(s): 20th century (1945 and 1968); 1750s (1752)
Locale(s): Scotland

Summary: Concludes the powerful and involving love story of 20th century Claire and 18th century Jamie begun with *Outlander*. Excellent characterizations and historical detail.

Other books you might like:
Laura Gilmour Bennett, *By All That Is Sacred*, 1991
Jasmine Cresswell, *To Catch the Wind*, 1993
Susan Sizemore, *Wings of the Storm*, 1992
Susan Sizemore, *My Own True Love*, 1994
Anne Stuart, *Highland Fling*, 1993
    anthology

676

PATRICIA GAFFNEY

Crooked Hearts
(New York: Topaz, 1994)

Story type: Historical/American West Coast
Major character(s): Grace Russell, Con Artist, Imposter (posing as a nun); Reuben Jones, Con Artist, Imposter (posing as a blind count)
Time period(s): 1890s
Locale(s): San Francisco, California

Summary: "Blind" Reuben Jones and "Sister" Grace Russell meet and recognize each other for the scam artists that they are. As they work their way to San Francisco, eventually invading the treacherous Chinese underworld, they confront not only danger, but their growing feelings for each other as well. Intricately plotted schemes and humorous escapades add to the charm of this fast-paced romance.

Other books you might like:
Lori Copeland, *Promise Me Today*, 1992
    fun and deception in the Old West
Donna Fletcher, *San Francisco Surrender*, 1990
    danger and deception in San Francisco
Robin Lee Hatcher, *Midnight Rose*, 1992
    fun and deception in Gold Rush California
Dana Ransom, *Dakota Destiny*, 1993
    Dakota con games/different treatment

677

PATRICIA GAFFNEY

Lily

(New York: Leisure, 1991)

Story type: Historical; Gothic
Major character(s): Lily Trehearne, Servant (maid), Runaway; Devon Darkwell, Nobleman
Locale(s): Cornwall, England

Summary: When Lily runs away from her guardian to avoid an unwanted marriage, she ends up in the employ of the dark and brooding master of Darkstone Hall, Lord Devon Darkstone. When he is injured, Lily cares for him and as he regains his health, he gains a new appreciation for Lily. Their unusual friendship turns into love, but old hatreds interfere, forcing Lily and Devon apart, and it is only when they can learn to trust each other that they can begin to have a future together. Dark and sensual.

Other books you might like:
Laura Kinsale, *The Prince of Midnight*, 1991
Laura Kinsale, *The Shadow and the Star*, 1990
Meagan McKinney, *Till Dawn Tames the Night*, 1991
Katherine Sutcliffe, *A Heart Possessed*, 1988

678

PATRICIA GAFFNEY

Sweet Everlasting

(New York: Topaz, 1993)

Story type: Historical/Victorian America
Major character(s): Carrie Wiggins, Handicapped (mute), Healer; Tyler Wilkes, Doctor
Time period(s): 1890s (1897)
Locale(s): Wayne's Crossing, Pennsylvania

Summary: Dr. Tyler Wilkes goes to rural Pennsylvania to find peace and recovery following a military stint in Cuba and finds himself drawn to a shy mountain girl who is a skilled healer and who is also mute. Despite vast differences in class and education, their love blossoms; but outside forces and Carrie's inner insecurity challenge them every step of the way. Tender, passionate, and heartwarming.

Other books you might like:
Sharon Harlow, *Country Kiss*, 1993
Stef Ann Holm, *Firefly*, 1990
Deana James, *Speak Only Love*, 1991
    mute heroine/different ambience
Jill Marie Landis, *Wild Flower*, 1989
Karen Lockwood, *Harvest Song*, 1993

679

PATRICIA GAFFNEY

Thief of Hearts

(New York: Leisure, 1990)

Story type: Historical/Victorian

Major character(s): Anna Jourdaine, Spinster, Businesswoman (shipping company owner); John Brody, Sailor, Imposter (twin of dead brother)
Time period(s): 1860s (1862)
Locale(s): England

Summary: Widowed by the murder of her husband Nick within hours of their marriage, Anna is forced into a mockery of a marriage with Nick's twin brother John in order to trap a traitor. Anna's prim ways and John's brashness make for lively conflict as they solve the mystery of Nick's death and fall in love at the same time. Passion and political intrigue.

Other books you might like:
Catherine Coulter, *Night Storm*, 1990
    3rd in Night Trilogy
Shirl Henke, *Moonflower*, 1989
    American setting
Teresa Medeiros, *Shadows and Lace*, 1990
    earlier time period
Charlotte Simms, *Silver Caress*, 1990
    American setting
JoAnn Wendt, *Beyond the Savage Sea*, 1990

680

PATRICIA GAFFNEY

To Love and to Cherish

(New York: Topaz, 1995)

Story type: Historical/Victorian
Major character(s): Ann Verlaine, Noblewoman (lady of the manor); Christian Morrell, Religious (vicar)
Time period(s): 19th century
Locale(s): Wycherley, England

Summary: After her disastrous marriage to Lord D'Aubrey, Anne Verlaine is sure she will never love again. However, when her friendship with Christian Morrell, the local village vicar, turns passionate, neither she nor Christian can deny the love that threatens to complicate their small world. Tender and sensual with dashes of humor.

Other books you might like:
Stef Ann Holm, *Liberty Rose*, 1993
    tender, similar setting
Carla Kelly, *Mrs. Drew Plays Her Hand*, 1994
    small town ambience/well-done characters/earlier time period
Pamela Morsi, *Courting Miss Hattie*, 1991
    tender, funny/American west setting/appealing characters
Pamela Morsi, *Runabout*, 1994
    tender, funny/small town ambience/appealing characters

681

ELIZABETH GAGE

Taboo

(New York: Pocket, 1993)

Story type: Historical/Mainstream
Major character(s): Kate Hamilton, Actress; Joseph Knight, Filmmaker; Eve Sinclair, Actress

Time period(s): 1930s; 1940s
Locale(s): Hollywood, California

Summary: Kate, survivor of an abusive childhood and marriage and Eve, survivor of an ambitious mother and a corrupt system, both love Joseph Knight, miracle man of the movies. Both become stars, one by accident, the other by design, and both influence Joseph as he battles the greed and corruption of the industry. An engrossing love story set during Hollywood's Golden Decades.

Other books you might like:
Jackie Collins, *American Star*, 1993
Michael Corda, *Curtain*, 1992
Catherine Coulter, *Beyond Eden*, 1993
Julia Fenton, *Blue Orchids*, 1992
Doris Parmett, *Lies*, 1993

682

JENNIE GALLANT (Pseudonym of Joan Smith)

Thick as Thieves
(New York: Fawcett, 1993)

Story type: Regency
Major character(s): Eve Denver, Heiress; Richard Dalton, Gentleman
Time period(s): 1810s
Locale(s): London, England

Summary: Eccentric heiress Eve Denver meets Richard Dalton during a visit to the pawnbroker. Intrigued with his situation, she offers to help him capture a cat burglar by setting herself up as bait for the thief. The trap, however, nets more than they had expected in this witty and lively Regency adventure.

Other books you might like:
Julie Caille, *The Rake and His Lady*, 1993
Emily Hendrickson, *Miss Wyndham's Escapade*, 1990
Barbara Metzger, *An Affair of Interest*, 1992
Amanda Quick, *Surrender*, 1990
Amanda Scott, *The Battling Bluestocking*, 1985

683

KIT GARDNER (Pseudonym of Katherine Manning Garland)

The Dream
(Toronto: Harlequin, 1992)

Story type: Historical/Victorian
Major character(s): Elizabeth Burbridge, Spinster, Teacher; Alec Sinclair, Nobleman, Rake
Time period(s): 1870s (1872)
Locale(s): London, England

Summary: When straight-laced spinster school teacher Elizabeth Burbridge is invited to spend the holidays at the home of one of her "young ladies," she is totally unprepared for the devastating effect her student's father, the dashing Alec Sinclair, has on her. In her confusion, she makes a number of blunders and mistakes, including becoming engaged to the wrong man. Despite this and assorted problems, including ex-

wives and old family secrets, things do work out for Elizabeth and Alec in this sweet, action-filled romance.

Other books you might like:
Jo Beverley, *An Unwilling Bride*, 1992
    Regency
Theresa DiBenedetto, *Silver Mist*, 1991
    sensual
Patricia Gaffney, *Thief of Hearts*, 1990
Pamela Morsi, *Courting Miss Hattie*, 1991
    sensual
Jeanne Savery, *The Last of the Winter Roses*, 1991
    Regency

684

KIT GARDNER (Pseudonym of Katherine Manning Garland)

Island Star
(Toronto: Harlequin, 1994)

Story type: Historical/Exotic
Major character(s): Alexa Fairfield, Plantation Owner, Heiress; Oliver Keane, Businessman
Time period(s): 1890s
Locale(s): Chicago, Illinois; Barbados

Summary: When his father's will is read in Barbados, Oliver Keane discovers that Alexa, the daughter of his father's mistress, gets half interest in the family plantation. In addition, Alexa doesn't believe that her mother murdered his father and she sets out to prove it. Meantime, Oliver decides to win Alexa. Engagements, pregnancy, and the real murderer add to the adventure in this steamy story with an exotic setting.

Other books you might like:
Laura Simon, *A Taste of Heaven*, 1989
    island setting/reluctant partners
Lynette Vinet, *Wild, Wicked Eden*, 1990
    reluctant partners
JoAnn Wendt, *Beyond the Savage Sea*, 1990
    island plantation setting
Kathleen E. Woodiwiss, *Shanna*, 1977
    classic Seventies-type pirate/island romance

685

KIT GARDNER (Pseudonym of Katherine Manning Garland)

The Stolen Heart
(Toronto: Harlequin, 1993)

Story type: Historical/American West
Major character(s): Phoebe Sinclair, Heiress, Runaway; Jace McAllister, Detective—Private (undercover)
Time period(s): 1870s (1876)
Locale(s): Laramie, Wyoming

Summary: Lawman Jace McAllister finally nabs the lucious jewel thief, Peaches, only to have her claim that she is a runaway English heiress! Naturally, he doesn't believe her; but when the real thief and her partner appear, things take a drastically different turn and Jace must deal with his job, the thieves, and his growing love for Phoebe all at the same time.

Other books you might like:
Rosanne Bittner, *Shameless*, 1993
Carol Finch, *Promise Me Moonlight*, 1993
Phoebe Fitzjames, *Oklahoma Angel*, 1993
Terri Herrington, *Silena*, 1993
Martha Hix, *Lone Star Loving*, 1993

686

DOROTHY GARLOCK

Homeplace
(New York: Warner, 1991)

Story type: Historical/American West
Major character(s): Ana Fairfax, Widow(er); Owen Jamison, Farmer
Time period(s): 1880s (1885)
Locale(s): Iowa

Summary: When Ana Fairfax hurries to the bedside of her young, runaway stepdaughter, Harriet, to be with her during childbirth, she finds an appalling family situation and her stepdaughter near death. When Harriet dies, Ana intends to honor her request that she raise her son, but Owen insists that the boy is a Jamison and should be raised by him. The solution is, of course, to marry; but Ana would be forced to deal not only with Owen's jealous, vindictive, and dangerous sister, but with her growing feelings for him as well. A realistic story with dark secrets, including incest and child abuse, and peopled with interesting, unique characters.

Other books you might like:
Rosanne Bittner, *Oregon Bride*, 1990
Deborah Camp, *Black-Eyed Susan*, 1990
Ginna Gray, *Quiet Fires*, 1991
Norah Hess, *Hawke's Pride*, 1991
Kristin James, *The Yankee*, 1990

687

DOROTHY GARLOCK

Midnight Blue
(New York: Warner, 1989)

Story type: Historical/American West
Major character(s): Mara Shannon McCall, Rancher; Pack Gallagher, Hero
Time period(s): 1860s
Locale(s): Wyoming

Summary: When Mara Shannon McCall decides to return home and take over the running of her family ranch, she finds it inhabited by her drunken cousin and a group of crooked gunslingers who want her gone—by whatever means. Naturally, she stays—and, with the help of Pack Gallagher, she reclaims her land and finds love in the bargain.

Other books you might like:
Barbara Bretton, *Midnight Lover*, 1989
Thea Devine, *Relentless Passion*, 1989
Kathryn Hockett, *Endless Ecstasy*, 1989
Elizabeth Lane, *Wind River*, 1989
Johanna Lindsey, *Savage Thunder*, 1989

688

DOROTHY GARLOCK

Nightrose
(New York: Warner, 1990)

Story type: Historical/American West
Major character(s): Katy Burns, Spinster; Garrick Rowe, Frontiersman
Time period(s): 1870s
Locale(s): Montana

Summary: Stranded in a deserted mining town, Katy and her sister and niece are terrified when a stranger shows up. However, Garrick Rowe soon inspires other emotions in Katy as he tries to convince her that they have loved each other in another life and are destined to fall in love again.

Other books you might like:
Rosanne Bittner, *Montana Woman*, 1990
Elaine Coffman, *Escape Not My Love*, 1990
Genell Dellin, *Cherokee Dawn*, 1990
Victoria Thompson, *Fortune's Lady*, 1990
　　Similar ambiance
Jane Toombs, *Midnight Whispers*, 1989

689

DOROTHY GARLOCK

Ribbon in the Sky
(New York: Warner, 1991)

Story type: Historical/World War I
Major character(s): Letty Pringle, Single Parent; Mike Dolan, Military Personnel
Time period(s): 1910s
Locale(s): Nebraska

Summary: Pregnant, condemned, and beaten by her ultra-conservative preacher father, 16-year-old Letty seeks refuge with her grandparents and begins to make a life for herself and her son. Five years and a war later, Mike Dolan returns to find that Letty is not dead, as he had been told, but very much alive and also the mother of his son. It takes a lot of love and understanding to set things right in this earthy, realistic, and "typically Garlock" western romance.

Other books you might like:
Rosanne Bittner, *Embers of the Heart*, 1990
Elaine Coffman, *Angel in Marble*, 1991
Lisa Gregory, *Seasons*, 1990
　　contemporary setting
Catherine Lanigan, *A Promise Made*, 1991
Katherine Sinclair, *A Distant Dream*, 1991

690

DOROTHY GARLOCK

Sins of Summer
(New York: Warner, 1994)

Story type: Historical/American West

Major character(s): Dory Callahan, Single Parent (unwed mother); Benton Waller, Mechanic
Time period(s): 19th century (late)
Locale(s): Idaho

Summary: Dory's illegitimate daughter is enough to condemn her for life in the eyes of her brothers; but Benton Waller has another opinion. Gentle, lonely, and hardworking, Ben grows to respect and love her as he watches Dory care for his deaf daughter, as well as her own. Harsh realities intrude—brutality, murder, and other evils, but together they withstand them and make a life together. Realistic with gentle and caring protagonists.

Other books you might like:
Rosanne Bittner, *Wildest Dreams*, 1994
  similar theme
Elaine Coffman, *Angel in Marble*, 1991
  similar plot
Jill Marie Landis, *Sunflower*, 1988
Catherine Lanigan, *A Promise Made*, 1991
  another abandoned heroine
LaVyrle Spencer, *Forgiving*, 1990

691
FAITH E.W. GARNER

When Someday Comes
(New York: Avalon, 1995)

Story type: Contemporary/Innocent
Major character(s): Carin Mitchell, Teacher, Artist; Robert Neillson, Businessman (paper company partner)
Time period(s): 1990s
Locale(s): Smith Springs, Georgia

Summary: When Carin Mitchell comes to a small Georgia town to teach art classes at the request of her former teacher, she only plans to help a friend and mentor, not fall in love with her son! Sweet and gentle.

Other books you might like:
Susan Aylworth, *Ride the Rainbow Home*, 1995
Vanessa Hale, *Sweet Deception*, 1995
Debbie Macomber, *First Comes Marriage*, 1990
Debbie Macomber, *A Little Bit of Country*, 1990
Laura Parrish, *Love's Quiet Corner*, 1989

692
JULIANA GARNETT

The Quest
(New York: Bantam, 1995)

Story type: Historical/Medieval
Major character(s): Lady Annice d'Arcy, Noblewoman, Captive; Rolf of Dragonwyck, Nobleman (Lord of Dragonwyck)
Time period(s): 13th century (1214)
Locale(s): England

Summary: When his attempt to regain custody of his young son from the treacherous Earl of Seabrook fails, Rolf, Lord of Dragonwyck kidnaps the Lady Annice instead, intending to

trade her for his son. But a forced marriage changes his plans—and eventually his life. Political intrigue, betrayal, and passion abound in this well-done story set amid the turmoil and conflict during the reign of King John.

Other books you might like:
Katherine Deauville, *Blood Red Roses*, 1991
Roberta Gellis, *Roselynde*, 1978
  1st of the Roselynde Chronicles
Anita Mills, *The Fire and the Fury*, 1991
Anita Mills, *Winter Roses*, 1992
Sharon Kay Penman, *Here Be Dragons*, 1985

693
WENDY GARRETT

Arizona Lovestorm
(New York: Zebra, 1991)

Story type: Historical/American West
Major character(s): Billie Meyrick, Rancher; Nick Larabee, Cowboy
Time period(s): 19th century
Locale(s): Arizona

Summary: Billie Meyrick is bothered by rustlers; Nick Larabee is seeking revenge. Together they solve both their problems and find love in spite of misunderstandings. A traditional Western romance with plenty of passion and non-stop action.

Other books you might like:
Catherine Hart, *Forever Gold*, 1990
Kathy Jones, *Sweet Obsession*, 1990
Robin Leigh, *Rugged Splendor*, 1991
Janelle Taylor, *Kiss of the Night Wind*, 1989

694
WENDY GARRETT

Carolina Dawn
(New York: Zebra, 1994)

Story type: Historical/Antebellum American South
Major character(s): Jenna Llewellyn, Healer, Witch (perceived as); Alan Langston, Plantation Owner, Nobleman
Time period(s): 1800s (1809)
Locale(s): Dismal Swamp, North Carolina; Heronsgate, North Carolina (plantation)

Summary: When lovely Jenna Llewellyn, the elusive healer of the Dismal Swamp, saves the life of English nobleman Alan Langston, the attraction between them is instantaneous—and then Jenna learns he is the new master of Heronsgate, placing him squarely under the curse of the Llewellyn witches and making her his blood enemy. Fast-paced, passionate, and occasionally violent.

Other books you might like:
Rexanne Becnel, *Where Magic Dwells*, 1994
  Medieval setting
Catherine Coulter, *The Hellion Bride*, 1992
Nicole Jordan, *Moonwitch*, 1991
Coral Smith Saxe, *Enchantment*, 1994

Penelope Williamson, *Keeper of the Dream*, 1992
  Medieval setting

695
WENDY GARRETT

Love's Magic Spell
(New York: Zebra, 1992)

Story type: Historical/Victorian; Historical/Victorian America
Major character(s): Lauren Stanton, Spinster; Stephen Hawkes, Detective; Portia Danforth, Widow(er)
Time period(s): 1870s (1872)
Locale(s): London, England; New York, New York

Summary: Needing a way out of London, Lauren accepts the widow Portia Danforth's offer to be her companion—and finds unlooked for excitement, love, and missing relatives! Lots of interesting characters, lots of action, lots of fun.

Other books you might like:
Kimberly Cates, *To Catch the Flame*, 1991
  different setting
Jude Deveraux, *Wishes*, 1989
Amanda Quick, *Seduction*, 1990
Colleen Quinn, *Defiant Rose*, 1992

696
WENDY GARRETT

Sweet Southern Caress
(New York: Zebra, 1991)

Story type: Historical/Antebellum American South
Major character(s): Alisha Frobisher, Plantation Owner, Activist (abolitionist); Hugh Barrett, Sea Captain, Shipowner
Time period(s): 1810s (1817)
Locale(s): Windlea, Georgia; At Sea

Summary: When Hugh Barrett is rescued from a shipwreck by beautiful plantation owner and secret abolitionist Alisha Frobisher, he is smitten from the start and determines to marry her. Alisha, however, wants to control her own life; and when her guardian consents to the marriage in spite of her wishes, she boards a ship bound for Jamaica. The only problem is that Hugh is on board, too, and he owns the ship. Passion, mystery, and adventure in the Antebellum South.

Other books you might like:
Brenna Braxton-Barshon, *Southern Oaks*, 1991
Thea Devine, *Southern Seduction*, 1991
Jeanne E. Hansen, *Midnight Enchantment*, 1990
Shirl Henke, *Moonflower*, 1989
Sonya T. Pelton, *Love Hear My Heart*, 1990

697
WENDY GARRETT

Western Enchantress
(New York: Zebra, 1993)

Story type: Historical/Canadian West

Major character(s): Rianne Kierney, Musician (saloon singer); Pagan Roark, Saloon Keeper/Owner
Time period(s): 19th century
Locale(s): Yukon Territory, Canada

Summary: Rianne goes to the Yukon to locate her father and ends up blackmailed and singing in Pagan Roark's saloon to pay off her father's debts. Rianne plans revenge but finds love, and gold, instead. Then Roark's wife shows up! Passionate and fast-paced.

Other books you might like:
Peggy Hanchar, *Tomorrow's Dream*, 1989
Kristin Hannah, *A Handful of Heaven*, 1991
Samantha James, *Outlaw Heart*, 1993
Annalise Sun, *The Golden Mountain*, 1990

698
RENE J. GARROD

Temptation's Wild Embrace
(New York: Zebra, 1990)

Story type: Historical/American West Coast
Major character(s): Sarah Williams, Widow(er); Tyler Bennett, Lawyer
Time period(s): 1870s (1873)
Locale(s): San Francisco, California

Summary: In the process of helping Sarah locate her long-lost father, Tyler falls for Sarah but can't convince her to marry him. (She refuses because she thinks she is barren and has sworn never to marry.) Sarah's pregnancy turns the tables and now she must convince Tyler of her love.

Other books you might like:
Madeline Baker, *Lacey's Way*, 1990
Gwen Bristow, *Calico Palace*, 1970
  Gold Rush San Francisco
Rebecca Sinclair, *California Caress*, 1989
Jane Toombs, *Riverboat Rogue*, 1990
Cynthia Wright, *Brighter than Gold*, 1990

699
JULIE GARWOOD

The Bride
(New York: Pocket, 1989)

Story type: Historical/Medieval
Major character(s): Jamie Jamison, Noblewoman (English); Alec Kincaid, Laird
Time period(s): 12th century (1102)
Locale(s): Scotland; England

Summary: When macho Alec marries spirited Jamie on the command of the king, both discover they have some adjusting to do. Humor, sensuality, and an old mystery just add to the fun.

Other books you might like:
Jude Deveraux, *Highland Velvet*, 1982
Shannon Drake, *Princess of Fire*, 1989
Johanna Lindsey, *A Gentle Feuding*, 1984

Penelope Neri, *Bold Breathless Nights*, 1989
Kathleen E. Woodiwiss, *The Wolf and the Dove*, 1974

700

JULIE GARWOOD

Castles

(New York: Pocket, 1993)

Story type: Historical/Regency
Major character(s): Princess Alesandra, Royalty, Orphan; Colin Hallbrook, Nobleman
Time period(s): 1810s
Locale(s): England

Summary: Brought to England by her guardian to avoid kidnapping and an unwanted political marriage, Princess Alesandra must marry—and soon—before her would-be abductor makes good his threat. Her only problem is Colin, the arrogant son of her guardian; he keeps rejecting every suitor on her list! Eventually, of course, there is only one left—himself. Funny, witty, and peopled with interesting and likable characters. Tie-ins to several earlier novels, including *The Gift* and *Guardian Angel*.

Other books you might like:
Brenna Braxton-Barshon, *Through All Eternity*, 1992
Johanna Lindsey, *Once a Princess*, 1991
Sheila O'Hallion, *Ravished Bride*, 1992
Amanda Quick, *Mistress*, 1994
Amanda Quick, *Scandal*, 1992

701

JULIE GARWOOD

For the Roses

(New York: Pocket, 1995)

Story type: Historical/American West; Historical/Victorian America
Major character(s): Mary Rose Clayborne, Heiress, Orphan; Harrison Stanford MacDonald, Nobleman
Time period(s): 1870s (1879)
Locale(s): Mountain Valley, Montana

Summary: Rescued from a trash bin on the streets of New York, "adopted" by a gang of homeless boys, and whisked off to a more appropriate life in Montana, Mary Rose grows up in a totally unorthodox, but loving and successful, household. Things change, however, when Harrison MacDonald arrives on the scene, intent on returning Mary Rose to her rightful life as an English lady. Charming, humorous, and filled with appealing characters.

Other books you might like:
Elaine Barbieri, *Wings of a Dove*, 1990
Jude Deveraux, *Eternity*, 1991
Jill Marie Landis, *Come Spring*, 1992
Pamela Morsi, *Courting Miss Hattie*, 1991
Rebecca Paisley, *Moonlight and Magic*, 1990

702

JULIE GARWOOD

The Gift

(New York: Pocket, 1991)

Story type: Historical/Regency
Major character(s): Sara Winchester, Noblewoman; Nathan St. James, Nobleman (Marques St. James)
Time period(s): 1810s
Locale(s): England

Summary: Wed as a child, ignored for years, and finally kidnapped by her own husband and ensconced aboard his pirate ship, Sara blithely sets out to make her marriage work. Surprisingly, she succeeds, but not before she almost destroys the ship. Charming, funny, and passionately romantic. A spinoff of *Guardian Angel*.

Other books you might like:
Diane Wicker Davis, *Heart of the Falcon*, 1990
Laurie McBain, *Moonstruck Madness*, 1977
Amanda Quick, *Scandal*, 1991
Amanda Quick, *Surrender*, 1990
Julie Tetel, *And Heaven Too*, 1990

703

JULIE GARWOOD

Guardian Angel

(New York: Pocket, 1990)

Story type: Historical/Regency
Major character(s): Jade "Pagan", Pirate; Caine, Nobleman (Marquess of Cainewood), Spy
Time period(s): 1810s (1815)
Locale(s): London, England

Summary: Caine is determined to trap the mysterious pirate rogue Pagan, whom he blames for his brother's death; however, his plans are put on hold when the beautiful Jade comes to him for protection and he agrees to help her. But he soon learns things aren't always what they seem in this passionate story of deception and adventure.

Other books you might like:
Judith McNaught, *Almost Heaven*, 1990
Amanda Quick, *Seduction*, 1990
Louisa Rawlings, *Promise of Summer*, 1989
    Deception in France
Lynette Vinet, *Pirate's Bride*, 1989
    Deception on the High Seas

704

JULIE GARWOOD

Prince Charming

(New York: Pocket, 1994)

Story type: Historical/Victorian; Historical/Victorian America
Major character(s): Taylor Baker, Noblewoman, Fugitive; Lucas Ross, Nobleman, Mountain Man
Time period(s): 1860s (1868)

Locale(s): London, England; Boston, Massachusetts; Montana

Summary: In order to please her dying grandmother and save her late sister's children from their dissolute uncle, Lady Taylor Baker marries Lucas Ross and heads for America, little guessing that she has just married the man of her dreams—a true "mountain man," straight from the wilds of Montana. Fast-paced, witty, and filled with typical Garwood humor.

Other books you might like:
Elizabeth DeLancey, *Touch of Lace*, 1993
Betina M. Krahn, *The Last Bachelor*, 1994
Elizabeth Lowell, *Only Mine*, 1992
Pamela Morsi, *Garters*, 1992
Amanda Quick, *Deception*, 1993

705

JULIE GARWOOD

The Prize
(New York: Pocket, 1991)

Story type: Historical/Medieval
Major character(s): Lady Nichola, Noblewoman; Baron Royce, Nobleman (Norman)
Time period(s): 11th century (1066)
Locale(s): England

Summary: Feisty, proud, and a demon with a slingshot, Saxon Lady Nichola vows to keep both her castle and her person out of the hands of the hated Normans; but clever though she is, she reckons without the patience and determination of Baron Royce, the man charged with her acquisition and safe delivery to William the Conqueror's court in London. Fast-paced, witty, and just plain fun, this sensual historical is vintage Garwood.

Other books you might like:
Linda Lang Bartell, *Brianna*, 1986
Jude Deveraux, *The Taming*, 1989
Shannon Drake, *Princess of Fire*, 1989
Anita Mills, *The Fire and the Fury*, 1991
Penelope Neri, *Bold Breathless Nights*, 1989

706

JULIE GARWOOD

Saving Grace
(New York: Pocket, 1993)

Story type: Historical/Medieval
Major character(s): Lady Johanna, Noblewoman, Bride (reluctant); Gabriel McBain, Laird
Time period(s): 13th century (1206-1207)
Locale(s): Highlands, Scotland; England

Summary: Forced to marry Scottish laird Gabriel McBain for political reasons, young widow Lady Johanna is terrified that McBain will be as cruel and condescending as her first husband, Raulf—and she is determined to hold her own. Misunderstandings and suspicions give way to trust and respect; but just as they are falling in love, politics—and a "resurrected"

husband—interfere once again. Good characterizations and a nicely handled hero/heroine relationship.

Other books you might like:
Rexanne Becnel, *A Dove at Midnight*, 1993
Kathryn Lynn Davis, *Child of Awe*, 1990
Arnette Lamb, *Chieftain*, 1994
Miriam Minger, *Wild Angel*, 1994
Amanda Quick, *Desire*, 1994

707

JULIE GARWOOD

The Secret
(New York: Pocket, 1992)

Story type: Historical
Major character(s): Judith Elizabeth Hampton, Young Woman (English), Midwife; Frances Catherine Kirkcaldy, Young Woman (Scottish); Iain Maitland, Laird
Locale(s): Scotland; England

Summary: When English Lady Judith agrees to assist her best friend, Frances Catherine in childbirth, it doesn't matter one bit that Frances is Scottish and that the English and the Scots are enemies. Strong-willed and determined, Judith accompanies Laird Iain Maitland to Scotland, fascinating and frustrating him in the process. Their bond grows with each clash; but as it does, Judith is faced with the knowledge that she carries a secret that could keep them apart forever. A story of friendship, love, and passion filled with memorable characters and heartwarming relationships.

Other books you might like:
Tanya Anne Crosby, *Angel of Fire*, 1992
Jude Deveraux, *Highland Velvet*, 1982
Patricia Potter, *The Abduction*, 1991
Amanda Scott, *Border Bride*, 1990
Elizabeth Stuart, *Where Love Dwells*, 1990

708

ROBERTA GELLIS

A Delicate Balance
(New York: Leisure, 1993)

Story type: Contemporary; Romantic Suspense
Major character(s): Linda Hepler, Heiress, Companion; Peter Tattershall, Gentleman
Time period(s): 1990s
Locale(s): London, England

Summary: Wealthy, but bored, Linda takes a job as travelling companion to an older lady. She would enjoy it tremendously if it weren't for her employer's attractive nephew, Peter. He definitely is distracting. However, Linda has more on her mind that that; strange things are happening to her her employer and Linda is determined to keep her safe. A tale of suspense with romantic complications.

Other books you might like:
Alma Blair, *The Dark Side of Paradise*, 1990
Mary Stewart, *My Brother Michael*, 1959
Mary Stewart, *The Stormy Petrel*, 1991

Mary Stewart, *Wildfire at Midnight*, 1956
Phyllis A. Whitney, *Silverhill*, 1967

709

ROBERTA GELLIS
MORGAN LLYWELYN, Co-Author
BARBARA SAMUEL, Co-Author
SUSAN WIGGS, Co-Author

Irish Magic
(New York: Kensington, 1995)

Story type: Anthology; Historical/Fantasy
Time period(s): Indeterminate Past
Locale(s): Ireland

Summary: These four novellas by popular historical writers focus on the magic and mysticism surrounding the legends and lore of Ireland. Included are "Rarer than a White Crow" by Roberta Gellis, "Galway Bay" by Morgan Llywelyn, "The Harper's Daughter" by Barbara Samuel, and "The Trysting Hour" by Susan Wiggs.

Other books you might like:
Rexanne Becnel, *Where Magic Dwells*, 1994
Kathryn Lynn Davis, *All We Hold Dear*, 1995
    later time period/mystical
Meagan McKinney, *The Ground She Walks Upon*, 1994
    later time period/mystical
Kathleen Morgan, *Enchant the Heavens*, 1995
    Celtic lore
Marylyle Rogers, *Emerald Enchantment*, 1995
    Irish anthology

710

ROBERTA GELLIS

The Silver Mirror
(New York: Jove, 1989)

Story type: Historical/Medieval
Major character(s): Lady Barbara Bigod, Noblewoman, Bastard Daughter (of an English lord); Sir Alphonse D'Aix, Nobleman, Bastard Son (of a French lord)
Time period(s): 13th century (1260s, time of Henry III)
Locale(s): England; France

Summary: Caught up amid the turbulence and violence of the 13th century and King Henry III's divisive war that pitted the French against the English, Lady Barbara and Sir Alphonse renew an old, youthful love—one that must now survive intrigue, war, and divided loyalties.

Other books you might like:
Pamela Belle, *The Lodestar*, 1989
    Different period (Richard III)/Court intrigues
Virginia Henley, *The Falcon and the Flower*, 1989
    Similar time period
Marylyle Rogers, *Hidden Hearts*, 1989
    Similar time period
Marylyle Rogers, *Wary Hearts*, 1988

711

GRETCHEN GENET

Winds of Glory
(New York: Pinnacle, 1993)

Story type: Historical/American Revolution
Major character(s): Alexandra Pennington, Widow(er); Dalton "Jack Flash" Phillips, Patriot (and sometime thief), Horse Trainer
Time period(s): 1770s
Locale(s): American Colonies

Summary: As wealthy Tory widow Alexandra Pennington makes plans to wed the charming Charles Villard, Dalton Phillips, an "undercover" patriot, tries his best to show Charles to Alex as the slimy person he really is. His efforts eventually begin to pay off; and when Alex nurses Dalton after he is wounded during one of his "patriotic endeavors," they both realize that they have fallen in love—with the enemy! Fast-paced, passionate action.

Other books you might like:
Christine Dorsey, *Sea of Desire*, 1993
Lucy Elliot, *The Conquest*, 1992
Colleen Faulkner, *Temptation's Tender Kiss*, 1990
Robin Maderich, *Faith and Honor*, 1989

712

GEORGINA GENTRY

Apache Caress
(New York: Zebra, 1991)

Story type: Historical/American West
Major character(s): Sierra Forester, Widow(er); Cholla, Scout, Indian (Apache)
Time period(s): 1880s
Locale(s): West

Summary: Taken as a hostage by the Apache scout Cholla when he escapes forced relocation in Florida, young widow Sierra Forester helps him, first out of fear and then out of love, as they make their was across the west to Arizona. Outlaws, moonshiners, and a host of other problems confront them in this passionate, fast-paced captive-in-love-with-captor romance.

Other books you might like:
Rosanne Bittner, *Arizona Ecstasy*, 1989
Shirl Henke, *Night Wind's Woman*, 1990
Janis Reams Hudson, *Apache Magic*, 1991
Susan Johnson, *Blaze*, 1986
Susan Johnson, *Forbidden*, 1991

713

GEORGINA GENTRY

Nevada Nights
(New York: Zebra, 1989)

Story type: Historical/American West

Major character(s): Dallas Durango, Runaway (from boarding school), Imposter (posing as a boy); Quint Randolph, Cowboy (supplies horses)
Time period(s): 1860s
Locale(s): St. Joseph, Missouri; West

Summary: In classic sweet/savage fashion, Dallas and Quint are repeatedly united and torn apart by various circumstances. They survive separation, deception, and Indian raids, and eventually fulfill an old Indian prophecy when they are united once more. One of Gentry's Old West series.

Other books you might like:
Deborah Camp, *Fallen Angel*, 1989
Rebecca George, *A Wild Desire*, 1989
Brenda Joyce, *Violet Fire*, 1989
Nora Roberts, *Lawless*, 1989
Janelle Taylor, *Kiss of the Night Wind*, 1989

714
GEORGINA GENTRY
Quicksilver Passion
(New York: Zebra, 1990)

Story type: Historical/American West
Major character(s): Silver Jones, Saloon Keeper/Owner, Abuse Victim; Cherokee Evans, Miner
Time period(s): 1860s
Locale(s): Buckskin Joe, Colorado

Summary: Badly abused as a young girl, beautiful saloon owner Silver Jones has no use for men—until she meets Cherokee Evans, a man who has the patience and determination to help her deal with her past, sort out her feelings, and win her love and trust. Compassionate and realistic.

Other books you might like:
Barbara Bretton, *Midnight Lover*, 1989
Deborah Camp, *Fallen Angel*, 1989
Dorothy Garlock, *Nightrose*, 1990
Victoria Thompson, *Fortune's Lady*, 1990
Jane Toombs, *Midnight Whispers*, 1989

715
GEORGINA GENTRY
MADELINE BAKER, Co-Author
SHIRL HENKE, Co-Author
PATRICIA RICE, Co-Author
JENNIFER BLAKE, Co-Author
Secrets of the Heart
(New York: Topaz, 1994)

Story type: Anthology

Summary: This collection of stories from five well-known romance writers has a little bit of something for everyone—historicals, fantasy, and timetravel. Included are: "Gambler's Delight" by Georgina Gentry, "Masquerade" by Madeline Baker, "Falling in Love" by Shirl Henke, "Keeping in Love" by Patricia Rice, and "Besieged Heart" by Jennifer Blake.

Other books you might like:
Catherine Anderson, *Tall, Dark, and Dangerous*, 1994
Western anthology
Madeline Baker, *Enchanted Crossings*, 1994
time and space fantasy anthology
Stella Cameron, *To Love and to Honor*, 1993
historical anthology focusing on marriage
Joan Hohl, *Love Beyond Time*, 1994
time travel anthology
Anita Mills, *Cherished Moments*, 1994
anthology focusing on motherhood

716
GEORGINA GENTRY
Sioux Slave
(New York: Zebra, 1992)

Story type: Historical/American West
Major character(s): Kimimila, Indian (Sioux); Rand Erickson, Military Personnel (Indian fighter)
Time period(s): 19th century
Locale(s): Kentucky; Dakota Territory

Summary: Wounded in battle and cared for by Sioux maiden Kimi, Rand Erickson decides to become more than a slave and sets about learning the Sioux language and culture. In the process he and Kimi fall in love and marry. Their real problems begin when they return to the white world where difficult adjustments, prejudice, and a vindictive ex-fiancee all work to complicate things. Sweet/savage elements.

Other books you might like:
Genell Dellin, *Cherokee Sundown*, 1992
Brenda Joyce, *Darkest Heart*, 1989
Constance O'Banyon, *Cheyenne Sunrise*, 1990
Nan Ryan, *The Legend of Love*, 1991

717
GEORGINA GENTRY
Song of the Warrior
(New York: Zebra, 1995)

Story type: Historical/American West
Major character(s): Willow, Teacher, Indian (Nez Perce); Bear, Warrior, Indian (Nez Perce)
Time period(s): 1870s (1877)
Locale(s): Pacific Northwest

Summary: Willow, part Nez Perce, returns to her people to teach them the "white man's ways." However, she soon finds herself falling in love with Bear, a warrior who has no use for a "white Indian," and in the middle of a conflict between the US government and her people. Tensions run high as the Nez Perce fight for their survival and Willow and Bear test their new-found love.

Other books you might like:
Madeline Baker, *Comanche Flame*, 1992
Madeline Baker, *Midnight Fire*, 1992
Rosanne Bittner, *Sioux Splendor*, 1990
Genell Dellin, *Comanche Wind*, 1992

718

REBECCA GEORGE

Call Home the Heart

(New York: New American Library, 1989)

Story type: Historical
Major character(s): Cassandra "Cassie" Harding, Young Woman; Diccon, Nobleman (son of Earl of Stratford)
Time period(s): 19th century (early)
Locale(s): Stratford, England; United States

Summary: To thwart a growing romance between Diccon, her son, and Cassie, the Dowager Duchess of Stratford has Cassie kidnapped and sent to America. When Cassie returns years later and financially independent, it takes a lot of understanding before she and Diccon can love and trust each other again.

Other books you might like:
Sally Beauman, *Destiny*, 1987
Lisa Gregory, *The Rainbow Promise*, 1989
Heidi Strasser, *Love's Memories*, 1988
    Old love rekindled
Patricia Strothers, *Silvermore*, 1989
    Old love rekindled

719

REBECCA GEORGE

A Wild Desire

(New York: Pocket, 1989)

Story type: Historical/American West
Major character(s): Brier Morgan, Runaway (from fiance); Matt Cavanaugh, Gambler
Time period(s): 19th century
Locale(s): Ogden, Utah

Summary: Running away to avoid becoming the third wife of Johnny Anderson, Brier Morgan is rescued outside an Ogden saloon by professional gambler Matt Cavanaugh. Intrigue, mystery, and adventure are part of this fast-paced love story.

Other books you might like:
Deborah Camp, *Fallen Angel*, 1989
Dorothy Garlock, *Midnight Blue*, 1989
Norah Hess, *Wildfire*, 1989
Colleen Quinn, *Colorado Flame*, 1989
Janelle Taylor, *Kiss of the Night Wind*, 1989

720

CINDY GERARD

Temptation From the Past

(New York: Bantam, 1991)

Story type: Contemporary
Major character(s): January Stewart, Lawyer; Michael Hayward, Journalist
Time period(s): 1990s
Locale(s): Boulder, Colorado

Summary: Cool, collected January Stewart, intense defender of abused children, spars with Mike Hayward, a brash journalist and childhood friend, as he tries to break through her reserve and help her come to terms with her past.

Other books you might like:
Harrison Arnston, *Trade-Off*, 1992
Tracy Hughes, *White Lies and Alibis*, 1990
Carol Jerina, *Flirting with Danger*, 1990
Kathleen Gilles Seidel, *Maybe This Time*, 1990

721

CAROL BLAKE GERROND

Shadows and Secrets

(New York: Avalon, 1992)

Story type: Romantic Suspense; Contemporary/Innocent
Major character(s): Mindi Carle, Teacher; Michael J. McCain, Principal (school)
Time period(s): 1990s
Locale(s): United States

Summary: Mortified when she mistakes the new school principal for an intruder, art teacher Mindi Carle plans to stay out of his way—and then she learns that they will be living in the same house, both as "paying guests" of Miss Kellor. Love soon follows, but there are dark secrets that must be dealt with before Michael and Mindi can find happiness.

Other books you might like:
Diane Gonzales Bertrand, *Touchdown for Love*, 1991
Lynn Bulock, *Roses for Caroline*, 1989
Lynn Bulock, *The Promise of Summer*, 1990
Kathleen Gilles Seidel, *Maybe This Time*, 1990
    sensual
Phyllis A. Whitney, *Flaming Tree*, 1986

722

JILL GIENCKE

Secrets of Echo Moon

(New York: Avalon, 1991)

Story type: Contemporary/Innocent; Romantic Suspense
Major character(s): Sarah Holmes, Librarian (rare book specialist); Andrew Clayton, Heir
Time period(s): 1990s
Locale(s): Echo Moon Island, Wisconsin

Summary: When Sarah comes to isolated Echo Moon Island to catalog the rare book collection of the late Roland Clayton, she finds not only a library in need of organization, but a devastatingly attractive man and a potentially deadly mystery to unravel.

Other books you might like:
Loretta Jackson, *Nightmare in Morocco*, 1989
Barbara Michaels, *Into the Darkness*, 1990
Mary Stewart, *The Gabriel Hounds*, 1967
Mary Stewart, *The Moon-Spinners*, 1962
Phyllis A. Whitney, *Rainbow in the Mist*, 1989

723

JEANE GILBERT-LEWIS

Common Ground

(Bensalem, Pennsylvania: Meteor, 1993)

Story type: Contemporary
Major character(s): Leslie Braddock, Mechanic, Plantation Owner; Blaise Hollander, Businessman (developer)
Time period(s): 1990s
Locale(s): Virginia

Summary: Blaise is surprised and entranced when gorgeous Leslie rescues him and his broken-down car; she is likewise smitten, but trouble brews when she finds that he is trying to buy her property. Their relationship is tarnished by mistrust, but they eventually they work things out—with a little outside help. Sexy.

Other books you might like:
Carol Deane, *One Tough Cookie*, 1993
Christina Dodd, *Lady in Black*, 1993
Pam Hart, *Lies and Shadows*, 1993
Karen Robards, *One Summer*, 1993

724

JUDY GILL

Bad Billy Culver

(New York: Doubleday, 1991)

Story type: Contemporary
Major character(s): Arlene Lambert, Single Parent; Billy Culver, Businessman (entrepreneur)
Time period(s): 1990s
Locale(s): Puget Sound, Washington

Summary: When wild and rebellious Billy Culver returns to his hometown a wealthy and sophisticated man, he fully intends to exact revenge from the island elitists for the cruel treatment he endured as a boy. But circumstances and his growing feelings for his teenage love cause some revision of his plans. Touching and heartwarming.

Other books you might like:
Georgia Bockoven, *A Marriage of Convenience*, 1991
Jude Deveraux, *Wishes*, 1989
Lisa Gregory, *The Rainbow Promise*, 1989
  historical setting
Shirl Henke, *Summer Has No Name*, 1990
Susan Kyle, *True Colors*, 1991

725

JUDY GILL

Golden Swan

(New York: Bantam, 1990)

Story type: Contemporary
Major character(s): B.J. Gray, Teacher; Cal Mixall, Hotel Owner (resort), Artist (painter)
Time period(s): 1980s
Locale(s): Kinikinik Lake, Canada

Summary: B.J. literally crashes into Cal's life when her motorcycle slams into his greenhouse at his lodge on Kinikinik Lake as she arrives to help him care for his (and her) two nieces for the summer. B.J. remembers Cal as the insensitive boy who had ridiculed her teenage "ugliness," but Cal sees her only as a beautiful, desirable woman. Passion, maturity, and matchmaking relatives help love win out.

Other books you might like:
Muriel Jensen, *Everything*, 1990
Penny Jordan, *Equal Opportunities*, 1990
Jackie Merritt, *Babe in the Woods*, 1990
Kay Wilding, *Rainbow's End*, 1990

726

SHARON GILLENWATER

Highland Whispers

(New York: Leisure Books, 1989)

Story type: Historical/Georgian
Major character(s): Sheridan Sinclair, Noblewoman (Countess); Jeremy MacKenzie, Privateer (American)
Time period(s): 1790s
Locale(s): Loch Earn, Scotland; England; France

Summary: Accosted on her way home to the Scottish Highlands, Lady Sheridan Sinclair is rescued by a dashing American, Jeremy MacKenzie. Jeremy and his partner escort Sheridan and her friend to Loch Earn where a deranged former lover of her long-dead mother focuses his attentions on Sheridan. Jeremy continually saves the day, and love and romance with a gothic tinge bloom amid the heather.

Other books you might like:
Catherine Coulter, *Night Shadow*, 1989
Jude Deveraux, *Highland Velvet*, 1982
Lee Karr, *Dark Cries of Gray Oaks*, 1989
  Quite Gothic
Johanna Lindsey, *A Gentle Feuding*, 1984
Penelope Williamson, *Beloved Rogue*, 1988

727

MONIQUE GILMORE

Hearts Afire

(New York: Pinnacle, 1995)

Story type: Contemporary; Ethnic
Major character(s): Celeste Dunbar, Dentist (dental student); Dante Lattimore, Coach (basketball)
Time period(s): 1990s
Locale(s): Washington, District of Columbia

Summary: Dental student Celeste Dunbar and college basketball coach Dante Lattimore are well on their way to a wonderful relationship, but people and secrets from their pasts cause problems. Mystery, suspense, and romance keep readers involved.

Other books you might like:
Bette Ford, *Forever After*, 1995
  ethnic emphasis

Felicia Mason, *Body and Soul*, 1995
  ethnic emphasis
Francis Ray, *Undeniable*, 1995
Margie Walker, *Breathless*, 1995
  ethnic emphasis/some suspense
Amberlina Wicker, *Private Matters*, 1996
  suspense/ethnic emphasis

728

THERESA GLADDEN

Just Desserts

(New York: Bantam, 1991)

Story type: Contemporary
Major character(s): Caitlin MacKenzie, Doctor (OB/GYN); Drew Daniels, Doctor (pediatrician)
Time period(s): 1990s
Locale(s): New Orleans, Louisiana

Summary: Doctors Drew Daniels and Caitlin MacKenzie share a house and work together, but Drew's marvelous sense of humor is totally lost on serious, ambitious Caitlin. However, in spite of differing plans for the future and their diverse personalities, it seems that opposites do attract.

Other books you might like:
Carole Buck, *Knight and Day*, 1992
Gail Douglas, *After Hours*, 1991
Linda Jenkins, *Maverick's Lady*, 1992
Debbie Macomber, *Rainy Day Kisses*, 1990

729

AMANDA GLASS (Pseudonym of Jayne Ann Krentz)

Shield's Lady

(New York: Popular Library, 1989)

Story type: Futuristic
Major character(s): Sariana Dayne, Businesswoman; Gryph Chassyn, Psychic (psychic mercenary)
Time period(s): Indeterminate Future
Locale(s): Windarra, Planet—Imaginary

Summary: When Sariana Dayne, daughter of a prominent banking clan, decides to hire a "shield" in order to retrieve a stolen gem cutter, she does more than just hire Gryph Chassyn—she unintentionally ends up marrying him. Fiery clashes of will, cultural misunderstandings, and eventually, love, follow.

Other books you might like:
Barbara Erskine, *Kingdom of Shadows*, 1989
  Science fiction/time change—Scotland
Anne McCaffrey, *Crystal Singer*, 1985
  More SF than romance
Anne McCaffrey, *Dragonflight*, 1986
  Science fiction with a fantasy flavor. First in a trilogy.
Anne McCaffrey, *Killashandra*, 1985
Janelle Taylor, *Moondust and Madness*, 1986

730

JO GOODMAN

Always in My Dreams

(New York: Zebra, 1995)

Story type: Historical/Victorian America
Major character(s): Mary Schuyler "Skye" Dennehy, Heiress, Adventurer; Walker Cain, Bodyguard
Time period(s): 1880s (1881)
Locale(s): New York, New York

Summary: Skye Dennehy is not quite sure why her father has sent her to spy on a peculiar inventor or what role Walker Cain plays in the inventor's mysterious life. Walker doesn't know who Skye is, but he knows he can't trust her. Sparks fly when the two find passion and love as they are drawn deeply into a plot of deception and greed.

Other books you might like:
Rosalyn Alsobrook, *Passion's Bold Fire*, 1993
  another spying heroine
Kimberly Cates, *The Raider's Bride*, 1994
  more spies/earlier setting
Jane Feather, *Velvet*, 1994
  Regency heroine spy
Erin Yorke, *Dangerous Deceptions*, 1992
  Victorian spy

731

JO GOODMAN

Wild Sweet Ecstasy

(New York: Zebra, 1992)

Story type: Historical/American West
Major character(s): Mary Michael Dennekey, Journalist (news reporter); Ethan Stone, Imposter (spy), Thief (train robber)
Time period(s): 1870s (1875)
Locale(s): West

Summary: When aspiring journalist Mary Michael Dennekey recognizes fine, upstanding, businessman Ethan Stone during a train holdup as one of the robbers, he is faced with a major decision — kill her or keep her. He keeps her, much to her initial frustration — and eventual delight. His need to keep his "double agent" identity hidden is at odds with her "nosy reporter" personality and the resulting conflicts are lively, funny, and passionate.

Other books you might like:
Sonya Birmingham, *Spitfire*, 1991
Hannah Howell, *Stolen Ecstasy*, 1991
Rebecca Paisley, *Midnight and Magnolias*, 1992
DeLoras Scott, *The Miss and the Maverick*, 1990

732

ANITA GORDON

The Defiant Heart

(New York: Jove, 1993)

Story type: Historical/Medieval; Historical/Exotic

Major character(s): Ailinn of Briann, Captive; Lyting Althson, Nobleman

Time period(s): 10th century (950)

Locale(s): Ireland; Denmark; Byzantium

Summary: Captured by Vikings and taken to Denmark as a slave, Irish Ailinn is saved from her obvious fate by the sympathetic Norman lord, Lyting, a man intent on the priesthood and supposedly immune to feminine wiles. However, he cannot deny his attraction to Ailinn; and as the action sweeps from the Baltic to Byzantium, their love for each other grows and they are both faced with some irrevocable choices. Emotional and sensual.

Other books you might like:

Catherine Coulter, *Lord of Hawkfell Island*, 1993

Heather Graham, *The Viking's Woman*, 1992

Brenda Joyce, *Promise of the Rose*, 1993

Bertrice Small, *To Love Again*, 1993

733

ANITA GORDON

The Valiant Heart

(New York: Jove, 1991)

Story type: Historical/Medieval

Major character(s): Brienne, Noblewoman (Frankish); Rurik, Nobleman (Norseman)

Time period(s): 10th century (912)

Locale(s): England

Summary: Attracted to the son, but promised to the father for political reasons, Frankish noblewoman Brienne accepts her fate and marries the older man—who quite conveniently dies immediately following the wedding! However, the path to true love is anything but smooth and Brienne and Rurik must deal with court intrigue, jealous lovers, and murderous plots before they are free to seek their own happiness. Interesting historical detail.

Other books you might like:

Katherine Deauville, *Blood Red Roses*, 1991

Heather Graham, *The Viking's Woman*, 1990

Mary Ellen Gronau, *Passionate Warriors*, 1989

Anita Mills, *The Fire and the Fury*, 1991

Kathleen E. Woodiwiss, *The Wolf and the Dove*, 1974

734

DEBORAH GORDON

Beating the Odds

(New York: Harper, 1992)

Story type: Romantic Suspense

Major character(s): Laura Miller, Businesswoman; Michael Clemente, Organized Crime Figure (Mafioso)

Time period(s): 1990s

Locale(s): United States

Summary: When Laura Miller helps her tipsy boss by driving him to a client's funeral — and ends up charitably removing the dead man's mistress from the scene — she finds herself in the middle of a money laundering scheme that involves both the Mafia and the FBI. Fast-paced and filled with intriguingly different characters.

Other books you might like:

Jennifer Blake, *Joy and Anger*, 1991

Janet Dailey, *Masquerade*, 1990

Jayne Ann Krentz, *Silver Linings*, 1991

Nora Roberts, *Genuine Lies*, 1991

Meryl Sawyer, *Midnight in Marrakesh*, 1991

735

EMMA GORDON

Crossing Eden

(New York: Warner, 1992)

Story type: Saga

Major character(s): Sara Ashford, Young Woman (granddaughter of London); London Kirkland, Grandparent

Time period(s): 20th century (1937); 19th century (1879)

Locale(s): Sahara Desert, Algeria; London, England

Summary: Sara Ashford comes from America to visit London Kirkland, her grandmother, who recently has given over her magnificent estate to her brother. Interestingly, Sara's visit causes memories of London's lost loves to surface and they affect the entire family. Only London remains serene as she lives through jealousy, sadness, and family disintegration. However, Sara is inspired by her grandmother's somewhat exotic past to seek her own life and reclaim her heritage. Detailed, complex, and engrossing.

Other books you might like:

Sandra Bregman, *Reach for the Dream*, 1990

Philippa Gregory, *Meridon*, 1992

　　third in the Wideacre Trilogy

Iris Johansen, *The Wind Dancer*, 1991

Belva Plain, *Evergreen*, 1979

Danielle Steel, *No Greater Love*, 1992

736

HEATHER GRAHAM (Pseudonym of Heather Graham Pozzessere)

And One Rode West

(New York: Dell, 1992)

Story type: Historical/Post-American Civil War

Major character(s): Christa Cameron, Plantation Owner; Jeremy McCauley, Military Personnel

Time period(s): 1860s (1865)

Locale(s): Harper's Ferry, Virginia; West

Summary: To save her plantation, Christa Cameron convinces a visiting Army friend to marry her — in name only of course — and then he can go West as he had planned. However, Jeremy has other ideas, and instead of rebuilding her Virginia home, Christa ends up an Army wife, pregnant, and on her way West, battling with Jeremy all the way. Love does win out, but not before a lot of prejudices and anger are worked out.

Other books you might like:

Christine Dorsey, *Kansas Kiss*, 1992

Norah Hess, *Wildfire*, 1989
Linda Howard, *A Lady of the West*, 1990
Deborah Satinwood, *Angel Fire*, 1992
Leta Tegler, *Gabrielle*, 1990

Lynette Vinet, *Pirate's Bride*, 1989

737

HEATHER GRAHAM (Pseudonym of Heather Graham
Pozzessere)

And One Wore Gray
(New York.: Dell, 1992)

Story type: Historical/American Civil War
Major character(s): Callie Michaelson, Widow(er), Yankee;
Daniel Cameron, Military Personnel (Confederate Army
Colonel)
Time period(s): 1860s
Locale(s): Sharpsburg, Maryland; Washington, District of Columbia

Summary: When Yankee widow Callie Michaelson saves the
life of Confederate officer Daniel Cameron and then nurses
him back to health, she fully intends to return him unharmed
to the south; however, the Union Army intervenes and Callie
is forced to surrender Daniel to the North in order to save his
life. Angry and betrayed, Daniel plots revenge, and when he is
freed from prison, he goes in search of Callie — and finds he
has a son! A sensual, poignant, and emotionally involving
look at the personal side of the War Between the States.
Sequel to *One Wore Blue*.

Other books you might like:
Micki Brown, *Once a Rebel*, 1992
Christine Dorsey, *Kansas Kiss*, 1992
Dorothy Garlock, *Ribbon in the Sky*, 1991
    WWI setting
Elizabeth Kary, *Let No Man Divide*, 1987
Kathleen E. Woodiwiss, *Ashes in the Wind*, 1979

738

HEATHER GRAHAM (Pseudonym of Heather Graham
Pozzessere)

Love Not a Rebel
(New York: Dell, 1989)

Story type: Historical/American Revolution
Series: American Woman
Major character(s): Amanda Sterling, Noblewoman (English),
Spy (Unwilling); Eric Cameron, Patriot (American)
Time period(s): 1770s (Revolutionary period)
Locale(s): United States

Summary: A reluctant spy, Lady Amanda Sterling finds
herself quickly captured and wed to Eric Cameron, the American traitor on whom she was to spy. Passionate, patriotic, and
adventurous.

Other books you might like:
Karen Harper, *Eden's Gate*, 1989
    French & Indian War
Robin Maderich, *Faith and Honor*, 1989
Christina Savage, *Hearts of Fire*, 1984

739

HEATHER GRAHAM (Pseudonym of Heather Graham
Pozzessere)

One Wore Blue
(New York: Dell, 1991)

Story type: Historical/American Civil War
Major character(s): Kiernan MacKay, Southern Belle,
Widow(er); Jesse Cameron, Doctor, Military Personnel
(Union officer)
Time period(s): 1860s (1859-1861)
Locale(s): Harper's Ferry, Virginia

Summary: When physician Jesse Cameron chooses to fight for
the Union instead of his native South, Kiernan MacKay can
hardly believe that the man she has known and loved since
childhood is deserting the Southern Cause. Lots of sparks fly
before these two stubborn, highly principled people can reconcile their feelings, both political and personal, and begin to
see things from the other's point of view. Interesting historical
detail—partly centered around the Harper's Ferry Incident.
Companion novel to *And One Wore Gray*.

Other books you might like:
Patricia Hagan, *The Daring*, 1991
Patricia Matthews, *Flames of Glory*, 1982
    Spanish-American War setting
Alexandra Ripley, *Scarlett*, 1991
    sequel to *Gone With the Wind*
Terri Valentine, *Yankee's Caress*, 1989
Kathleen E. Woodiwiss, *Ashes in the Wind*, 1979

740

HEATHER GRAHAM (Pseudonym of Heather Graham
Pozzessere)

A Pirate's Pleasure
(New York: Dell, 1989)

Story type: Historical/Colonial America
Series: North American Woman
Major character(s): Skye Kinsdale, Runaway (Reluctant
bride); Roc "Silver Hawk" Cameron, Pirate
Time period(s): 1710s
Locale(s): American Colonies

Summary: Betrothed against her will, Skye Kinsdale sets sail
for America determined to fight her fate. Then pirates step in
and the fun begins. Filled with humor, romance, and
swashbuckling action.

Other books you might like:
Kathryn Davenport, *Pirate's Mistress*, 1989
Jean Innes, *Buccaneer's Bride*, 1989
Valerie Sherwood, *Lovesong*, 1985
    First in a trilogy
Joan Van Nuys, *Beloved Avenger*, 1989
Kathleen E. Woodiwiss, *Shanna*, 1977

741

HEATHER GRAHAM (Pseudonym of Heather Graham Pozzessere)

Spirit of the Season
(New York: Delacorte, 1993)

Story type: Contemporary; Holiday Themes
Major character(s): Becky Wexham, Widow(er); Tim Yeager, Sports Figure (baseball player); Davey Larson, Orphan
Time period(s): 1990s
Locale(s): United States

Summary: Davey Larson, newly added to Becky's household, wants only two things for Christmas, a Babe Ruth baseball card and a spot on the Little League team, but prospects for both are slim. Ex-pro Tim Yeager wants Davey to have a chance and befriends him. Becky and Tim find they have a lot in common and pursue a family merger. Meanwhile Davey gets some surprising help from a rather magical source and his dreams do come true.

Other books you might like:
Bethany Campbell, *The Snow Garden*, 1989
Kathleen Creighton, *A Christmas Love*, 1992
Debbie Macomber, *A Season of Angels*, 1993
Peg Sutherland, *Yes, Virginia*, 1993

742

HEATHER GRAHAM (Pseudonym of Heather Graham Pozzessere)

The Viking's Woman
(New York: Dell, 1990)

Story type: Historical/Medieval
Major character(s): Rhiannon, Noblewoman; Eric of Dubhlain, Royalty (prince), Warrior
Time period(s): 9th century (878)
Locale(s): Ireland

Summary: Assuming the dragonships sailing into the harbor are the enemy, Rhiannon leads the attack against the invaders herself, wounding the blond Viking leader in the process. The invaders, however, turn out to be friends here at the King's invitation. In order to make amends, Rhiannon is ordered to marry Eric of Dubhlain—the warrior she wounded earlier. Passion and intrigue with plenty of fire in a medieval setting.

Other books you might like:
Linda Lang Bartell, *Brianna*, 1986
Phoebe Conn, *By Love Enslaved*, 1989
Shannon Drake, *Princess of Fire*, 1989
Johanna Lindsey, *Fires of Winter*, 1980
Kathleen E. Woodiwiss, *The Wolf and the Dove*, 1984

743

DEBORAH GRAMBIEN

Fire Queen
(New York: Bantam, 1990)

Story type: Historical/Pre-history

Major character(s): Maeve, Ruler (Queen), Warrior; Connal, Ruler (Chieftain), Warrior
Time period(s): Indeterminate Past
Locale(s): Ireland

Summary: As enemies Maeve and Connal fight each other with skill; as lovers they inflame each other with passion; and as companions they hunt down the man who could destroy them both.

Other books you might like:
Shannon Drake, *Princess of Fire*, 1989
Mary Ellen Gronau, *Gentle Conqueror*, 1987
Mary Ellen Gronau, *Passionate Warriors*, 1989
Johanna Lindsey, *Fires of Winter*, 1980
Teresa Medeiros, *Lady of Conquest*, 1989

744

LAURIE GRANT

Beloved Deceiver
(Toronto: Harlequin, 1993)

Story type: Historical/Medieval
Major character(s): Elise de Vire, Widow(er), Spy; Adam Saker, Knight, Spy
Time period(s): 15th century (1413)
Locale(s): France

Summary: Forced by King Henry to wed a Frenchwoman, Sir Adam Saker choses the lovely widow, Elise de Vire, and finds himself falling love with a woman who is not only the enemy, but a spy, as well. Elise is not immune to Adam either, but their happiness is short-lived and is threatened from within by deceptions and revenge, as well as from without by politics and social conditions. Adventurous and intriguing.

Other books you might like:
Pamela Belle, *The Lodestar*, 1989
  mainstream historical
Jane Feather, *Brazen Whispers*, 1990
Roberta Gellis, *The Silver Mirror*, 1989
Jennifer Horsman, *Awaken My Fire*, 1992
Amanda Scott, *The Rose at Twilight*, 1993

745

LAURIE GRANT

Emerald Fire
(New York: Warner, 1990)

Story type: Historical/Medieval
Major character(s): Joan of Hawkingham, Noblewoman; Richard of Kingsclere, Knight (Crusader)
Time period(s): 12th century
Locale(s): England

Summary: A pilgrimage to save her sister's soul puts Lady Joan in the company of Sir Richard, the man reputed to be responsible for her sister's mysterious death. As she tries to learn the truth, Joan and Richard first fight and finally acknowledge their growing attraction to each other. Murder, kidnapping, duels, and a villainous fiance all complicate things before the truth is learned and the lovers can be happy.

Other books you might like:
Rexanne Becnel, *My Gallant Enemy*, 1990
Roberta Gellis, *The Silver Mirror*, 1989
Heather Graham, *The Viking's Woman*, 1990
Penelope Neri, *Bold Breathless Nights*, 1989
Kathleen E. Woodiwiss, *The Wolf and the Dove*, 1974

746
VANESSA GRANT

Awakening Dreams
(Toronto: Harlequin, 1990)

Story type: Contemporary
Major character(s): Crystal Selwyn, Auditor (tax); Jesse Campbell, Pilot
Time period(s): 1980s
Locale(s): British Columbia, Canada

Summary: On the way to Queen Charlotte City, Jesse's small plane crashes into the Pacific, stranding Crystal and Jesse along the British Columbian coast. A classic story of love and survival.

Other books you might like:
Donna Carlisle, *Interlude*, 1989
Anne Lacey, *Light for Another Night*, 1989
Anne McCaffrey, *Stitch in Snow*, 1984
Tracy Sinclair, *Sky High*, 1989

747
PATRICIA GRASSO

Desert Eden
(New York: Dell, 1993)

Story type: Historical/Renaissance; Historical/Exotic
Major character(s): Heather Elizabeth Devereux, Noblewoman, Captive; Prince Khalid Beg, Royalty
Time period(s): 16th century (1588)
Locale(s): At Sea; Turkey

Summary: Although wishing for adventure and excitement rather than an arranged marriage, Heather Devereux gets a bit more than she bargained for when she is kidnapped by pirates and ends up in a Turkish harem, a gift to handsome, arrogant Prince Khalid. Naturally, Heather doesn't take this lying down, but the more she resists, the more fascinated Khalid becomes. A passionate, exotic tale of love and vengeance filled with interesting period detail of the Turkish culture.

Other books you might like:
Jane Feather, *Bold Destiny*, 1990
Jane Feather, *The Eagle and the Dove*, 1991
Victoria Holt, *The Captive*, 1989
Miriam Minger, *Captive Rose*, 1991
Bobbi Smith, *Capture My Heart*, 1992

748
PATRICIA GRASSO

Emerald Enchantment
(New York: Dell, 1992)

Story type: Historical/Elizabethan
Major character(s): Katherine Devereux, Noblewoman, Widow(er); Hugh O'Neill, Nobleman
Time period(s): 16th century
Locale(s): Ireland; England

Summary: Kathryn, pregnant with her dead husband's child, is willing to marry Queen Elizabeth's choice for her, but she won't consummate the marriage until the child is born. This, of course, complicates the relationship, as do the plans of Kathryn's greedy, brutal step-son Turlough. Violence, kidnapping, intrigue, and misunderstandings abound in this realistic, authentically detailed tale of the Elizabethan Era.

Other books you might like:
Jude Deveraux, *Highland Velvet*, 1982
Betina M. Krahn, *Behind Closed Doors*, 1991
Jennifer O'Green, *Royal Captive*, 1987
Bertrice Small, *Skye O'Malley*, 1980
Casey Stuart, *Highland Rogue*, 1991

749
PATRICIA GRASSO

Highland Belle
(New York: Dell, 1991)

Story type: Historical/Renaissance
Major character(s): Brigitte Devereux, Bride (reluctant), Noblewoman; Ian MacArthur, Laird
Time period(s): 16th century
Locale(s): Scotland; England

Summary: Angered that her new husband didn't even have the decency to show up at his own wedding, Brigitte heads home to England and ends up in the arms of a devastatingly handsome Scotsman who turns out to be none other than Lord Ian MacArthur, the man she has just married by proxy. Humor, intrigue, and a spiteful sister-in-law add spice to this lively historical.

Other books you might like:
Jude Deveraux, *Highland Velvet*, 1982
Johanna Lindsey, *A Gentle Feuding*, 1984
Penelope Neri, *Bold Breathless Nights*, 1989
Amanda Scott, *Border Bride*, 1990
Casey Stuart, *Highland Rogue*, 1991

750
GINNA GRAY

For The Love of Grace
(New York: Pinnacle, 1995)

Story type: Contemporary; Romantic Suspense
Major character(s): Grace Somerset-Ames, Widow(er); Jake Paxton, Drifter, Abuse Victim

Time period(s): 1990s
Locale(s): Cedar Grove, Texas

Summary: When Jake Paxton left town 12 years ago, everyone thought he was a murderer—everyone except the local pastor's daughter, Grace Somerset. But now Jake is back, determined to find out who really killed Carla Mae Sheffield and to clear his name once and for all. Murder, mystery, and unlooked-for love are all part of this warm romance that makes good use of a wounded hero and the ''return of the bad boy'' plot pattern.

Other books you might like:
Jennifer Blake, *Love and Smoke*, 1989
Rebecca Brandewyne, *Dust Devil*, 1996
Kay Hooper, *Amanda*, 1995
Marilyn Pappano, *In Sinful Harmony*, 1995
Karen Robards, *One Summer*, 1994

751

GINNA GRAY

Quiet Fires

(New York: Harper, 1991)

Story type: Historical/American West
Major character(s): Elizabeth Stanton, Settler, Young Woman; Conn Cavanaugh, Trapper, Settler
Time period(s): 1830s (1834)
Locale(s): West; Texas

Summary: In love with her flirtatious, shallow cousin's trapper husband, Elizabeth Stanton has resigned herself to her hopeless situation—until her cousin dies in a tragic accident on their way west. Forced to marry for the sake of propriety, Elizabeth and Conn develop a new, passionate and supportive relationship as they begin their new life together during the tumultuous days of Texas' fierce fight for independence.

Other books you might like:
Rebecca Brandewyne, *Heartland*, 1990
Ann Gabriel, *South Texas*, 1990
Dorothy Garlock, *Homeplace*, 1991
Alison Irving, *No Greater Love*, 1991
Kristin James, *The Yankee*, 1990

752

VANESSA GRAY

Best-Laid Plans

(New York: New American Library/Signet, 1990)

Story type: Regency
Major character(s): Melpomene ''Pommy'' Fiske, Heiress; Justin Rutledge, Nobleman
Time period(s): 1810s
Locale(s): England

Summary: Determined to avoid marriage to moist-handed, greedy Cousin Freddie, heiress Melpomene Fiske escapes down the trellis—right into Lord Justin Rutledge's arms, a man who also is in possession of an unwanted fiancee. Justin ''rescues'' Pommy, takes her to his sister's house and then, in Pommy's eyes, continues to interfere with her life as she

seeks to evade the determined Freddie. They lead each other a merry chase before all the strands of this light-hearted tale are untangled and the lovers are appropriately united.

Other books you might like:
Norma Lee Clark, *The Infamous Rake*, 1990
Clare Darcy, *Letty*, 1980
Emily Hendrickson, *The Gallant Lord Ives*, 1989
Georgette Heyer, *Cotillion*, 1953
Georgette Heyer, *Sylvester, or the Wicked Uncle*, 1957

753

ELIZABETH GRAYSON

Bride of the Wilderness

(New York: Jove, 1995)

Story type: Historical/American Revolution
Major character(s): Celene Peugeot Bernard, Widow(er); Burke Cardwell, Trapper, Nobleman (Earl of Hammondsford)
Time period(s): 18th century (1774)
Locale(s): Midwest; London, England

Summary: Freed by the death of her abusive husband, Celene is determined to make a new life for herself and her son. When her father wants her to marry a young English trapper, she understandably resists, preferring to remain single instead. But Burke Caldwell has a reason for wanting to marry Celene and so he persists. A series of near disasters and the surprising news that Burke is now an earl keep things lively, and it takes a trip to England before the pair can sort out what is really important and get on with their lives. Rich details of both frontier life and English high society. Sensual.

Other books you might like:
Rosanne Bittner, *Unforgettable*, 1994
  western setting/good historical detail
Charles Durham, *Walk in the Light*, 1992
  mainstream/similar period
Karen Harper, *Eden's Gate*, 1989
  similar period/good historical detail
Joan Van Nuys, *Beloved Intruder*, 1992
  similar setting
Robin LeAnne Wiete, *When Morning Comes*, 1993
  similar setting/realistic/good historical detail

754

BILLIE GREEN

Bad for Each Other

(New York: Bantam, 1990)

Story type: Contemporary
Major character(s): Keely Durant, Journalist (magazine); Dylan Tate, Actor, Musician (saxophone player)
Time period(s): 1980s
Locale(s): Dallas, Texas

Summary: When journalist Keely Durant is sent by her editor to interview successful actor/musician Dylan Tate, she knows it's a journalist's dream—and it would be if she and Dylan hadn't had a flaming secret affair five years ago. Now she must deal with old passions that threaten to become new ones, and Dylan must come to terms with his real feelings for Keely.

Other books you might like:
Delayne Camp, *Newsworthy Affair*, 1990
Janet Dailey, *Terms of Surrender*, 1982
Tracy Hughes, *White Lies and Alibis*, 1990
Carol Jerina, *Flirting with Danger*, 1990

755

JENNIFER GREENE

Pink Topaz

(New York: Silhouette, 1992)

Story type: Contemporary
Major character(s): Regan Thorne, Appraiser (gem); Cole Shepard, Pilot
Time period(s): 1990s
Locale(s): Arizona

Summary: Needing to recuperate after the loss of her grandfather and the ransacking of her house, gem appraiser Regan Thorne hires carefree pilot Cole Shepherd to fly her to her Arizona hideaway. Regan's need for a protector becomes apparent, and in spite of himself, Cole turns into a wonderful, it somewhat reluctant, hero. Well-done characterizations.

Other books you might like:
Barbara Delinsky, *Facets*, 1990
Vanessa Grant, *Awakening Dreams*, 1990
Laura Kinsale, *The Prince of Midnight*, 1990
 another reluctant hero/historical setting
Elizabeth Lambert, *Wings of Desire*, 1990
Doreen Roberts, *Broken Wings*, 1992

756

MARIA GREENE

Winter's Flame

(New York: Avon, 1990)

Story type: Historical/Victorian
Major character(s): Maggie Hartwell, Widow(er); Thaddeus Webb, Detective—Private, Antiques Dealer
Time period(s): 1890s (1895)
Locale(s): London, England

Summary: When Maggie hires Thaddeus West to help her find her sister, she has no idea how dangerous the search will prove, both to her life and to her emotions. Love and adventure in London.

Other books you might like:
Carol Finch, *Thunder's Tender Touch*, 1989
 American West setting
Victoria Holt, *The Judas Kiss*, 1981
Christine Monson, *Golden Nights*, 1990
 American West setting
Katherine Sutcliffe, *A Fire in the Heart*, 1990

757

LEIGH GREENWOOD

Fern

(New York: Leisure, 1994)

Story type: Historical/American West
Series: Seven Brides
Major character(s): Fern Sproull, Cowboy; Madison Randolph, Lawyer
Time period(s): 1870s (1871)
Locale(s): Abilene, Kansas

Summary: Back in Kansas to defend his brother, sophisticated attorney Madison Randolph is confronted by fiery, hoydenish, and determined Fern Sproull who thinks Madison's brother is guilty. She's almost a match for them, and her attack forces them to join ranks and deal with the long-standing problems between them. Fern also does some self-reassessment, and eventually, she and Madison settle their differences in a highly romantic way.

Other books you might like:
Carol Finch, *Promise Me Moonlight*, 1993
 hot-headed heroine
Johanna Lindsey, *Angel*, 1992
 strong-minded heroine
Connie Mason, *Ice and Rapture*, 1993
 independent, hot-tempered heroine/Alaska
Maggie Osborne, *The Wives of Bowie Stone*, 1994
 independent heroine

758

LEIGH GREENWOOD (Pseudonym of Harold Lowry)

Laurel

(New York: Leisure, 1995)

Story type: Historical/American West
Series: Seven Brides
Major character(s): Laurel Blackthorne, Widow(er), Outcast; Henry Randolph, Lawman (sheriff)
Time period(s): 1890s
Locale(s): Sycamore Flats, Arizona

Summary: Social outcast and widowed mother Laurel Blackthorne doesn't need to be rescued by Sheriff Hen Randolph; she doesn't like his guns and she can take care of herself. Unfortunately, when her despicable in-laws show up to take her son, she needs his help. He helps willingly, intrigued by her determination, courage, and her apparent dislike of him. Love and danger are part of this warm, lively novel that deals with some rather serious issues. Fourth in the Seven Brides series

Other books you might like:
Lydia Browne, *Heart Strings*, 1993
Lori Copeland, *Sweet Hannah Rose*, 1991
Jill Marie Landis, *Sunflower*, 1988
Pamela Morsi, *Wild Oats*, 1993
Libby Sydes, *Until Spring*, 1993

759

LEIGH GREENWOOD

Scarlet Sunset, Silver Nights

(New York: Zebra, 1992)

Story type: Historical/American West
Major character(s): Penelope White, Rancher; Slade Morgan, Drifter, Cowboy
Time period(s): 1880s
Locale(s): Arizona

Summary: When Penelope helps wounded drifter Slade Morgan by offering him a job, she gains a champion and he takes on a cause as he fights to help Penelope save her ranch. Passionate, realistic, and interesting in that the story is told from Slade's point of view.

Other books you might like:
Catherine Lanigan, *A Promise Made*, 1991
Janelle Taylor, *Follow the Wind*, 1990
Janelle Taylor, *Kiss of the Night Wind*, 1989
Victoria Thompson, *Wild Texas Promise*, 1990

760

LEIGH GREENWOOD
BOBBY HUTCHINSON, Co-Author
THERESA SCOTT, Co-Author
CONNIE MASON, Co-Author

Their First Noel

(New York: Leisure, 1995)

Story type: Anthology; Holiday Themes
Time period(s): 19th century
Locale(s): United States

Summary: This quartet of historical Christmas novellas focuses on the protagonists first Christmases together. "Father Christmas" by Leigh Greenwood, "Lantern in the Window" by Bobby Hutchinson, and "The Treasure" by Theresa Scott all have a definite Western flavor; "A Christmas Miracle" by Connie Mason has an urban setting and a more Victorian feel.

Other books you might like:
Mary Balogh, *Angel Christmas*, 1995
 angelic Christmas anthology
Jane Bonander, *Avon Books Presents: A Christmas Together*, 1994
 historical Christmas anthology
Ruth Langan, *Christmas Miracle*, 1992
Judith McNaught, *A Holiday of Love*, 1994
 historical Christmas anthology

761

JESSICA GREGORY

Once Innocent

(New York: Pocket, 1991)

Story type: Romantic Suspense
Major character(s): Robyn Prescott, Amnesiac, Model; Scott Kendall, Businessman
Time period(s): 1990s
Locale(s): New York, New York

Summary: When Robyn Prescott loses her memory as a result of a hit and run accident, she moves to New York and begins a new life as a model for a cosmetics firm, attracting the attention of the company's president, Scott Kendall, in the process. But her past has not been forgotten by everyone; and Robyn is soon caught up in a tangle of revenge, jealousy, and murder that threatens her life and that of Scott as well. Fast-paced, gripping, and glitzy.

Other books you might like:
Joanne Z. Adams, *Intimate Connections*, 1990
Jill Barkin, *Hot Streak*, 1990
Janet Dailey, *Masquerade*, 1990
Sidney Sheldon, *If Tomorrow Comes*, 1985

762

JILL GREGORY

Cherished

(New York: Dell, 1992)

Story type: Historical/American West
Major character(s): Juliana Montgomery, Orphan; Cole Rawdon, Bounty Hunter
Time period(s): 1870s (1873)
Locale(s): New Mexico; Colorado

Summary: While searching for her long-lost family, Juliana steals a horse to escape and her ruthless fiance puts a price on her head—turning her into a hunted outlaw. She is captured by a bitter bounty hunter, Cole Rawdon, who doesn't believe her. Eventually, he comes to respect her courage and determination and together they confront demons from their separate pasts. Full of action and humor.

Other books you might like:
Rosanne Bittner, *Montana Woman*, 1990
Ann Gabriel, *South Texas*, 1990
Sara Orwig, *Albuquerque*, 1989
Sara Orwig, *San Antonio*, 1989
Victoria Thompson, *Fortune's Lady*, 1990

763

JILL GREGORY

Forever After

(New York: Dell, 1993)

Story type: Historical/Regency
Major character(s): Camilla Brent, Orphan, Saloon Hostess; Phillip Audley, Nobleman (Earl of Westcott)
Time period(s): 1810s
Locale(s): England

Summary: A murder, a necklace, and a quest for her true identity propel orphaned Camilla Brent straight into the arms of Philip Audley, the Earl of Westcott, and eventually into a counterfeit betrothal, with predictably passionate results. Danger, however, stalks Camilla; and the pair must unmask a killer and find answers to old questions before they are free to find their own happiness. A colorful, engaging Cinderella mystery.

Other books you might like:
Jo Beverley, *An Unwilling Bride*, 1992
Annabel Laine, *The Reluctant Heiress*, 1978
Amanda Quick, *Ravished*, 1992
Louisa Rawlings, *Wicked Stranger*, 1993
Marlene Suson, *Devil's Bargain*, 1992

764

JILL GREGORY

Lone Star Lady

(New York: Jove, 1990)

Story type: Historical/American West
Major character(s): Maggie Clay, Orphan, Rancher
Time period(s): 1860s; 1870s
Locale(s): Texas

Summary: Abandoned and pregnant at 16, Maggie determines to survive; and she succeeds in making a good life for herself. Then the father of her son returns and her problems begin. Treachery, murder, greed, and eventually love are all part of this story of one woman's struggle to overcome the obstacles life presents. Mainstream elements.

Other books you might like:
Rosanne Bittner, *Montana Woman*, 1990
Ann Gabriel, *South Texas*, 1990
  Mainstream elements
Sara Orwig, *Albuquerque*, 1989
Sara Orwig, *San Antonio*, 1989
Victoria Thompson, *Fortune's Lady*, 1990

765

LISA GREGORY (Pseudonym of Candace Camp)

The Rainbow Promise

(New York: Warner, 1989)

Story type: Historical/American West
Major character(s): Julia Turner Dobson, Widow(er) (2 children); James Banks, Doctor
Time period(s): 19th century
Locale(s): Texas

Summary: When Julia returns to her home town, she is once again faced with her old feelings of inferiority—the same feelings that years ago kept her from the man she loved. Now she must face both him and her feelings if she is to find happiness.

Other books you might like:
Jude Deveraux, *Wishes*, 1989
  Hero overcomes heroine's feelings of inferiority
Rebecca George, *Call Home the Heart*, 1989
  Old love rekindled
Jill Marie Landis, *Sunflower*, 1988
Johanna Lindsey, *Savage Thunder*, 1989
Patricia Strothers, *Silvermore*, 1989
  Fulfillment of an old love

766

LISA GREGORY (Pseudonym of Candace Camp)

Seasons

(New York: Warner, 1990)

Story type: Contemporary/Mainstream
Major character(s): Sharon Thompson, Single Parent, Artist (stained glass); Reid Maitland, Political Figure (congressional representative)
Time period(s): 1990s
Locale(s): Texas; Washington, District of Columbia

Summary: When young, pregnant college student Sharon Thompson seeks aid from the family of her now-dead lover, she is rudely turned away by Reid Maitland, her boyfriend's brother. Vowing never to ask the Maitlands for anything again, she proceeds to raise her daughter alone—until a twist of fate thirteen years later sends her knocking at Reid's door once again.

Other books you might like:
Sally Beauman, *Destiny*, 1987
Rebecca Forster, *A Delicate Matter*, 1989
Eileen Goudge, *Garden of Lies*, 1989
Jill Gregory, *Lone Star Lady*, 1990
LaVyrle Spencer, *Bittersweet*, 1990

767

MOLLIE GREGORY

Birthstone

(New York: Jove, 1991)

Story type: Contemporary/Mainstream
Major character(s): Belinda Oliver, Socialite
Time period(s): 1980s (1985-1990)
Locale(s): Beverly Hills, California; San Francisco, California; Hollywood, California

Summary: The Wyman family is torn by Belinda's return after crime and tragedy. Her success in film-making doesn't let her forget her secret life and she fights to keep the world from knowing.

Other books you might like:
Jennifer Blake, *Joy and Anger*, 1991
Barbara Delinsky, *Facets*, 1990
Nora Roberts, *Genuine Lies*, 1991
Meryl Sawyer, *Blind Chance*, 1989
Danielle Steel, *Secrets*, 1985

768

PHILIPPA GREGORY

Meridon

(New York: Pocket, 1992)

Story type: Historical/Georgian; Gothic
Series: Wideacre Trilogy
Major character(s): Sarah ''Meridon'' Lacey, Heiress—Lost; Will Tyake, Foreman; Peregrine Havering, Nobleman
Time period(s): 18th century

Locale(s): England

Summary: Somehow Meridon knows that she doesn't belong with her adopted gypsy tribe; but although she does nothing about her feelings, eventually, and somewhat miraculously, she comes "home" to Wideacre carrying the necklace that proves she is the missing heiress, Sarah Lacey. Her struggles, however, are just beginning as she must come to terms with her feelings for the earthy Will Tyake and her desire for the kind of life that marriage to aristocratic Peregrine Havering would provide. Final volume in the Wideacre trilogy.

Other books you might like:
Rebecca Brandewyne, *Upon a Moon-Dark Moor*, 1988
Susan Howatch, *Penmarric*, 1971
Mary Lide, *The Legacy of Tregaran*, 1991
Mary Lide, *Tregaran*, 1989
Thomas Tryon, *The Wings of the Morning*, 1992

769
LOIS GREIMAN
Highland Jewel
(New York: Avon, 1994)

Story type: Historical/Renaissance
Major character(s): Rose Gunther, Healer, Religious (novice); Leith Forbes, Laird, Warrior
Time period(s): 15th century (1491)
Locale(s): Scotland

Summary: Laird Leith's hope to end his clan's feud hinges on his marriage to the daughter of old Laird Ian MacAuley. Unfortunately, the daughter has died, so Leith convinces young novice and healer Rose Gunther to go to the ill Laird MacAuley and pose as his daughter and Leith's wife. Rose and Leith are a highly unlikely pair, but as they work to bring the feuds to an end, they develop a turbulent relationship that eventually evolves into love.

Other books you might like:
Sandra Dustin, *Highland Hearts*, 1993
Julie Garwood, *Saving Grace*, 1994
　another feud-averting marriage/some humor
Anna Jennet, *Reckless*, 1993
　realistic
Arnette Lamb, *The Border Lord*, 1993
　later time period/some humor
Anne Stuart, *Highland Fling*, 1993
　anthology

770
LOIS GREIMAN
Surrender My Heart
(New York: Avon, 1993)

Story type: Historical/Antebellum American South
Major character(s): Megan O'Rourke, Con Artist, Captive; Justin Stearns, Gentleman, Plantation Owner
Time period(s): 1850s
Locale(s): Charleston, South Carolina

Summary: When con-man Michael O'Rourke tries to get $700 for a scam that involves his sister, she is rescued by gentleman Justin Stearns. However, when he learns that she was a part of the game, he decides to keep her as his "slave." But he reckons without Megan's charm and kindness, and it isn't long before he has fallen under her spell. Warm and witty with memorable characters.

Other books you might like:
Deborah Martin, *Creole Nights*, 1992
Kat Martin, *Creole Fires*, 1992
Alexandra Ripley, *Charleston*, 1982
Bobbi Smith, *Bayou Bride*, 1991
Lois Wolfe, *Mask of Night*, 1993

771
ROSLYNN GRIFFITH
The Wind Casts No Shadow
(New York: Harper, 1994)

Story type: Historical/American West
Major character(s): Frances MacDonnell, Teacher (former), Saloon Keeper/Owner; Chaco Jones, Gunfighter, Indian (half-Apache)
Time period(s): 1880s
Locale(s): Boston, Massachusetts; Santa Fe, New Mexico

Summary: After she loses her teaching job, Frances marries and goes to New Mexico, where her husband is accidentally killed by the gunfighter, Chaco. Naturally, Frances doesn't think much of Chaco, but he keeps coming into her life, even to the point of getting a job in the saloon she has inherited. Plagued by strange dreams that seem connected to a series of murders in their small town, Chaco needs help—and Frances, now threatened, too, helps him solve the crimes. As they work together, they discover friendship—and something they had never thought possible—love.

Other books you might like:
Rosanne Bittner, *Outlaw Hearts*, 1993
　good character development
Barbara Faith, *Gamblin' Man*, 1993
　another prim and proper heroine/different treatment
Terri Herrington, *Silena*, 1993

772
MARY ELLEN GRONAU
Gentle Conqueror
(New York: Bantam, 1989)

Story type: Historical/Medieval
Major character(s): Lady Claudia, Captive (British); Angus McMahon, Warrior (Irish)
Time period(s): 10th century (987)
Locale(s): Brittany, France; England

Summary: When Angus McMahon wins Lady Claudia as a prize of war, he not only gets a beautiful woman but an extended family as well. Friendship and love follow in short order.

Other books you might like:
Blaine Anderson, *Love's Sweet Captive*, 1989
Phoebe Conn, *By Love Enslaved*, 1989
　　9th century Denmark
Julie Garwood, *The Bride*, 1989
　　Pre-Norman England/Scotland
Johanna Lindsey, *Fires of Winter*, 1980
　　Vikings
Kathleen E. Woodiwiss, *The Wolf and the Dove*, 1974

773

MARY ELLEN GRONAU

Passionate Warriors
(New York: Bantam, 1989)

Story type: Historical/Medieval
Major character(s): Dorcas McMahon, Warrior (Irish); Neil McNeil, Warrior (Viking descent)
Time period(s): 10th century (987)
Locale(s): Ireland

Summary: When Dorcas and Neil marry to bring peace to their warring clans, the sparks fly instead. Pride keeps getting in the way, but love and passion win in the end.

Other books you might like:
Linda Lang Bartell, *Brianna*, 1986
　　Norman/English
Shannon Drake, *Princess of Fire*, 1989
　　Norman/English marriage
Julie Garwood, *The Bride*, 1989
　　Pre-Norman England/Scotland
Johanna Lindsey, *Fires of Winter*, 1980
　　Viking captive tale
Teresa Medeiros, *Lady of Conquest*, 1989
　　Early Erin (Ireland)

774

JANE HADDAM (Pseudonym of Orania Papazoglou)

Bleeding Hearts
(New York: Bantam, 1994)

Story type: Romantic Suspense; Contemporary
Major character(s): Hannah Krikorian, Widow(er); Gregor Demarkian, FBI Agent (former)
Time period(s): 1990s
Locale(s): United States

Summary: When Hannah's new love is found murdered, she is shocked to find herself as a prime suspect. However, her neighbor, ex-FBI agent Gregor Demarkian, keeps the police at bay and eventually unmasks a clever killer. Romance blooms between the two as they work together to solve the mystery.

Other books you might like:
Sandra Canfield, *Dark Journey*, 1994
Roberta Gellis, *A Delicate Balance*, 1993
Maggie Shayne, *Forgotten Vows*, 1994
Anne Stevenson, *A Game of Statues*, 1972

Antoinette Stockenberg, *Embers*, 1994
　　fantasy elements

775

DIANE HAEGER

Courtesan
(New York: Pocket, 1993)

Story type: Historical/Mainstream
Major character(s): Diane De Poitiers, Historical Figure (mistress of Henri II), Noblewoman (Duchess of Valentinois); Henri II, Royalty (King of France), Historical Figure; Catherine de Medici, Royalty (Queen of France), Historical Figure
Time period(s): 16th century (1547-1569)
Locale(s): France

Summary: Long before Henri II becomes king, he and Diane are lovers. Henri feels that he has been a pawn all his life, but he knows that Diane has no designs or ambitions except to love him, so with her, he is secure. Henri's miserable marriage to Catherine de Medici and the political intrigues surrounding him almost undo him, but his and Diane's love remains the only stable thing in his life. A finely woven tapestry of rich historical detail, fascinating characters, and human emotion.

Other books you might like:
Susan Kay, *Legacy*, 1986
Jean Plaidy, *The Pleasure of Love*, 1992
Suzanne Robinson, *Lady Defiant*, 1992
Anya Seton, *Katherine*, 1954

776

DIANE HAEGER

The Return
(New York: Pocket, 1993)

Story type: Historical/Victorian; Historical/Exotic
Major character(s): Charlotte Langston, Noblewoman; Edward Langston, Military Personnel (Army captain)
Time period(s): 1860s (1867)
Locale(s): India; England

Summary: Scarred beyond recognition during the Sepoy uprising, Charlotte discovers, after ten years of "widowhood", that her husband is not only alive, but that he has a wife and family! Unwilling to hurt them, but still in love with Edward, she chooses to remain unmarried. Unforseen events eventually turn things around.

Other books you might like:
Marilyn Cunningham, *Seasons of the Heart*, 1992
　　American 1930s setting
Lisa Gregory, *The Rainbow Promise*, 1989
Victoria Holt, *The India Fan*, 1988
Mary Jo Putney, *Veils of Silk*, 1992

777

PATRICIA HAGAN

The Daring
(Toronto: Harlequin, 1991)

Story type: Historical/American Civil War
Major character(s): Jessica Coulter, Teacher; Derek Stanton, Religious (pastor); Belinda Coulter, Singer
Time period(s): 1860s
Locale(s): Blue Ridge Mountains, Tennessee

Summary: When Jessica falls in love with Derek Stanton, the new pastor, her obnoxious fiance causes problems for everyone. Rape, prejudice, and violence are part of this intricately crafted tale of Southern mountain life that demonstrates once again that love can triumph over all hardships.

Other books you might like:
Jill Marie Landis, *Wild Flower*, 1989
Catherine Marshall, *Christy*, 1967
    inspirational elements
Catherine Marshall, *Julie*, 1984
    inspirational elements
Penelope Neri, *Forever in His Arms*, 1991
    sensual
Rebecca Paisley, *Barefoot Bride*, 1990
    sensual

778

PATRICIA HAGAN

A Forever Kind of Love
(New York: Harper, 1992)

Story type: Historical/Post-American Civil War
Major character(s): Dancy O'Neal, Orphan; Clint McCabe, Landowner
Time period(s): 1850s; 1860s (1854-1866)
Locale(s): Tennessee; Ireland

Summary: When Dancy's grandfather sells her to the town bully, she flees Ireland for America to claim the refuge promised by her Uncle Dooley. However, when she arrives in Tennessee, she learns that her childhood adversary, Clint McCabe, has bought Uncle Dooley's estate — and then the conflict begins. Their distrust of each other, the Klan, and other suitors all add to the danger and excitement of this fast-paced romance.

Other books you might like:
Rosanne Bittner, *Embers of the Heart*, 1990
Micki Brown, *Once a Rebel*, 1992
Linda Howard, *A Lady of the West*, 1990
Jill Marie Landis, *Rose*, 1990
Penelope Neri, *Forever in His Arms*, 1991

779

PATRICIA HAGAN

Love and Triumph
(New York: Avon, 1991)

Story type: Historical/Russian Revolution
Series: Coltrane Saga
Major character(s): Marilee Coltrane Mikhailonov, Young Woman; Cord Brant, Spy
Time period(s): 1910s (1917)
Locale(s): Russia; Spain

Summary: Determined to clear her father's name, Marilee sets out to track him down and ends up being kidnapped by Bolshevik revolutionaries and held for ransom. She is rescued by, and subsequently falls in love with, enigmatic Cord Brant. With his help, she finds the answers to her questions and the solutions to her problems. Final novel in the Coltrane Saga.

Other books you might like:
Jennifer Blake, *Prisoner of Desire*, 1986
Diane Cory, *A Token of Jewels*, 1989
Alan Fisher, *The Three Passions of Countess Natalya*, 1985
Susan Johnson, *Golden Paradise*, 1990
    Tsarist Russia
Boris Pasternak, *Doctor Zhivago*, 1957
    classic of the Russian Revolution

780

PATRICIA HAGAN

Midnight Rose
(New York: Harper, 1991)

Story type: Historical/Antebellum American South
Major character(s): Erin Sterling, Activist (abolitionist); Ryan Youngblood, Plantation Owner
Time period(s): 1810s (1819)
Locale(s): Virginia

Summary: Ryan Youngblood "allows" himself to be blackmailed into marrying the spirited Erin Sterling by her well-meaning mother. Erin fights the union until she realizes that marrying Ryan will allow her to continue her work with the "free soldiers," a group that helps free slaves. However, just as the couple begins to work out their differences, Ryan's mother discovers a secret about Erin that can remove her from his life forever.

Other books you might like:
Brenna Braxton-Barshon, *Southern Oaks*, 1991
Jeanne E. Hansen, *Midnight Enchantment*, 1990
Leona Karr, *Nightfire*, 1990
Kat Martin, *The Captain's Bride*, 1990
Sonya T. Pelton, *Love Hear My Heart*, 1990

781
PATRICIA HAGAN

Orchids in Moonlight
(New York: Harper, 1993)

Story type: Historical/American West
Major character(s): Jamie Chandler, Traveller; Cord Austin, Wagonmaster
Time period(s): 1840s (1849)
Locale(s): West; California

Summary: Determined to get to California to catch a husband, Jamie stows away in wagonmaster Cord's wagon, and ends up with a passionate love instead. Once in California, they go their separate ways; but fate keeps them connected, and eventually they realize their true feelings for each other.

Other books you might like:
Rosanne Bittner, *Montana Woman*, 1990
Suzannah Davis, *Angel Eyes*, 1993
Norah Hess, *Wildfire*, 1989
Elizabeth Lowell, *Only His*, 1991
Carla Simpson, *Seduced*, 1993

782
MADELINE HALE

Pirouette
(New York: Pocket, 1990)

Story type: Saga
Major character(s): Nicole Varonne, Dancer (Ballerina); Carlo Domenici, Dancer
Time period(s): 20th century
Locale(s): England; United States

Summary: The daughter of two of the ballet world's greats, Nicole Varonne has dancing in her blood; but although she achieves stellar success in the dance arena, her personal life is another story. She must experience estranged parental relations, a lost love, and an abusive, broken marriage before she can find true happiness.

Other books you might like:
Sally Beauman, *Destiny*, 1987
Janet Dailey, *The Glory Game*, 1985
Eileen Goudge, *Garden of Lies*, 1989
Eva Ibbotson, *A Company of Swans*, 1985
Rosalind Laker, *Tree of Gold*, 1986

783
VANESSA HALE

Sweet Deception
(New York: Avalon, 1995)

Story type: Contemporary/Innocent
Major character(s): Belinda Brooks, Artist, Student; Gannon Roarke, Businessman (snack food company owner)
Time period(s): 1990s
Locale(s): Los Angeles, California

Summary: When a fight with her roommate and a street purse-snatching render art student Belinda Brooks both apartmentless and penniless in unfamiliar Los Angeles, fate lands her in the home of a delightfully eccentric woman—who just happens to be the mother of the devastatingly handsome man Belinda met earlier under somewhat embarrassing circumstances. Light, sweet, and predictable.

Other books you might like:
Kathryn E. Coulter, *Does Cupid Do Take-Out?*, 1995
Faith E.W. Garner, *When Someday Comes*, 1995
Kay Gregory, *Roses in the Night*, 1995
Mary Leask, *Sing Carols with the Angels*, 1995
La Verne St. George, *A Private Proposal*, 1990

784
WENDY HALEY

Dead Heat
(New York: Zebra, 1994)

Story type: Contemporary; Romantic Suspense
Major character(s): Louise Malotti, Inspector (ship welding); Bob Whitaker, Police Officer (arson investigator)
Time period(s): 1990s
Locale(s): Portsmouth, Virginia

Summary: Louise Malotti witnesses a fire at the shipyard where she works, and Lt. Bob Whitaker is in charge of the arson investigation. As they compare notes—and get to know each other and their families—they soon become aware of a pyromaniac who for some reason has it in for both of them. Suspense and terror draw the two families together and the results are appropriately frightening, romantic, and satisfying as the mystery is solved and the two families become one.

Other books you might like:
Tami Hoag, *Still Waters*, 1992
Susan Kyle, *Night Fever*, 1990
Sandra Marton, *Night Fires*, 1991
Nora Roberts, *Carnal Innocence*, 1994
Nora Roberts, *Night Smoke*, 1992

785
WENDY HALEY

Shadow Whispers
(New York: Zebra, 1992)

Story type: Romantic Suspense
Major character(s): Garland Ross, Store Owner (bookstore)
Time period(s): 1990s
Locale(s): United States

Summary: A crazed serial killer wreaks havoc in the up until now peaceful life of bookstore owner Garland Ross as she tries to solve the mystery of her beautiful sister's murder and escape being killed herself. Suspenseful, frightening, and peopled with well-drawn characters.

Other books you might like:
Jennifer Blake, *Joy and Anger*, 1991
Sandra Marton, *Night Fires*, 1991
Nora Roberts, *Carnal Innocence*, 1992

Sherryl Woods, *Hot Property*, 1992
Sherryl Woods, *Stolen Moments*, 1990

786

WENDY HALEY

White Light
(New York: Zebra, 1995)

Story type: Contemporary; Romantic Suspense
Major character(s): Connie Matthias, Accountant, Divorced Person; John Bruycker, Psychic; Derek Valle, Fire Fighter, Parent
Time period(s): 1990s
Locale(s): Virginia Beach, Virginia

Summary: In a desperate effort to turn her teenage son's behavior around, Connie Matthias sends him to live with his father in Virginia Beach, only to have him end up the prime suspect in the bizarre killing of her twin brother. Channeling, satanism, and firewalking add a twist to this hard-hitting, gritty tale of suspense.

Other books you might like:
Tami Hoag, *Still Waters*, 1992
Heather Graham Pozzessere, *Slow Burn*, 1994
Karen Robards, *One Summer*, 1993
Nora Roberts, *Divine Evil*, 1992

787

VIOLET HAMILTON

A Traitorous Heart
(New York: Zebra, 1990)

Story type: Regency
Major character(s): Katherine Wilde, Debutante; Simon Stafford, Nobleman (Marquis of Staines)
Time period(s): 1810s
Locale(s): England

Summary: Aristocratic Simon Stafford sets out to uncover a French spy and ends up falling in love with Katherine Wilde, the daughter of the man he suspects. A witty, lively, Regency mystery. Spinoff of *The Hidden Heart*.

Other books you might like:
Janice Bennett, *A Tempting Miss*, 1989
Clare Darcy, *Lady Pamela*, 1975
Emily Hendrickson, *Queen of the May*, 1989
Annabel Laine, *The Reluctant Heiress*, 1978
Linda Walker, *My Lady's Deception*, 1990

788

CHRISTINA HAMLETT

Charade
(New York: Harper, 1993)

Story type: Contemporary; Romantic Suspense
Major character(s): Maggie Price, Businesswoman; Troy McCormick, Detective, Police Officer; Derek Channing, Businessman (developer)
Time period(s): 1990s
Locale(s): Seattle, Washington

Summary: Maggie's search for the reason behind her father's death leads to her working with and falling for a multimillionaire developer, Derek Channing. Detective Troy McCormick, however, has serious doubts about Channing and originally Maggie agrees with him. However, as her romance with Derek grows, her faith in Troy diminishes and she is soon in serious trouble. Suspenseful action.

Other books you might like:
Jude Deveraux, *Sweet Liar*, 1992
Liana Laverentz, *Ashton's Secret*, 1993
Barbara Michaels, *Vanish with the Rose*, 1992
Tracey Tillis, *Deadly Deception*, 1994

789

GEORGIA HAMPTON

Desire
(New York: Jove, 1989)

Story type: Contemporary/Mainstream
Major character(s): Emma Blackstone, Socialite; Ivan St. Peters, Artist (Sculptor)
Time period(s): 1950s; 1960s
Locale(s): New York, New York

Summary: Emma Blackstone leaves behind Bostonian society to follow her heart and live with Ivan St. Peters, the brooding Russian sculptor who will fill her life with passion, beauty, and pain.

Other books you might like:
Sally Beauman, *Destiny*, 1987
Rebecca Forster, *A Delicate Matter*, 1989
Anne Harrell, *Betrayals*, 1990
Meryl Sawyer, *Blind Chance*, 1989

790

PEGGY HANCHAR (Pseudonym of Peggy Henshar)

Cheyenne Dreams
(New York: Fawcett, 1993)

Story type: Historical/American West
Major character(s): Colly "Spotted Woman" Mead, Orphan, Frontierswoman; Lone Wolf, Indian (Cheyenne), Warrior
Time period(s): 1840s (1848)
Locale(s): Dakota Territory

Summary: Orphaned on the way west by a cholera epidemic, Colly Mead struggles valiantly against overwhelming odds to survive. Her eventual salvation comes in the form of the gentle Cheyenne warrior, Lone Wolf, who finds the freckled, red-headed young woman both brave and beautiful. Their journey toward understanding—and eventually love—is threatened by treachery and misunderstanding; but Colly and Lone Wolf eventually succeed in establishing a relationship that no outside forces can destroy. A bittersweet romance with good cultural detail.

Other books you might like:
Rosanne Bittner, *Sioux Splendor*, 1990
Deborah Camp, *Lady Legend*, 1992
Kathleen Harrington, *Cherish the Dream*, 1991
Ruth Langan, *Texas Healer*, 1992
Janelle Taylor, *Bittersweet Ecstasy*, 1989

791

PEGGY HANCHAR

Fancy Lady
(New York: Fawcett, 1994)

Story type: Historical/American West
Major character(s): Fancy Bourne, Actress, Mail Order Bride; Coop Fletcher, Businessman, Indian (half)
Time period(s): 19th century
Locale(s): Elizabethtown, Colorado

Summary: Coop Fletcher has overcome his tawdry origins to build a vast business empire—now he needs a respectable wife. Destitute actress Fancy Bourne isn't exactly ''respectable'' but she does need a future, so she invents an appropriately genteel background and becomes Coop's mail order bride. Unfortunately, when Coop finds out he explodes, and it isn't until he takes a whole new look at the situation that he realizes that Fancy is really his kind of lady after all.

Other books you might like:
Teresa Hart, *Hearts Are Wild*, 1993
    another less-than-perfect heroine
Norah Hess, *Fancy*, 1995
Samantha James, *Outlaw Heart*, 1993
Catherine Palmer, *Gunman's Lady*, 1993
Patricia Potter, *Notorious*, 1993

792

PEGGY HANCHAR (Pseudonym of Peggy Henshar)

Tomorrow's Dream
(New York: New American Library, 1989)

Story type: Historical/American West
Major character(s): Kathleen ''Kate'' Moira O'Riley, Prospector (Gold); Hogan O'Shea, Prospector (Gold)
Time period(s): 1890s (Klondike Gold Rush)
Locale(s): Alaska; Canada

Summary: When her father is killed in an avalanche, Kate is forced to marry his partner, Hogan O'Shea, for protection. A romance with all the action and violence of the Klondike Gold Rush days.

Other books you might like:
Barbara Bretton, *Midnight Lover*, 1989
Jo Ann Ferguson, *At the Rainbow's End*, 1989
    Yukon setting
Julie Garwood, *The Bride*, 1989
    Different period and setting/Arranged marriage
Sara Orwig, *Albuquerque*, 1989

793

LINDSEY HANKS (Pseudonym of Georgia Pierce and Linda Chestnut)

Long Texas Nights
(New York: Zebra, 1991)

Story type: Historical/American West
Major character(s): Sarah Hogan, Widow(er) (preacher's), Heiress; Coleman ''Cole'' Blade, Lawman (sheriff)
Time period(s): 1880s (1885)
Locale(s): Hazard, Texas

Summary: When the highly respectable and proper preacher's widow Sarah Hogan goes to Texas to run a saloon in order to claim her inheritance, she attracts not only trouble but the handsome sheriff, as well. Lots of classic Western action along with a blossoming heroine and a sensitive, caring hero in this sensual romance.

Other books you might like:
Charlotte Hubbard, *Gambler's Tempting Kisses*, 1991
Kathy Lawrence, *Tin Angel*, 1989
Charlotte Simms, *Silver Caress*, 1990
Jodi Thomas, *The Tender Texan*, 1991

794

LINDSEY HANKS (Pseudonym of Georgia Pierce and Linda Chestnut)

Nevada Ecstasy
(New York: Zebra, 1992)

Story type: Historical/American West
Major character(s): Reilly Reynolds, Photographer; Sam Chandler, Gambler
Time period(s): 1880s (1881)
Locale(s): Castletown, Nevada

Summary: Hired by the local sheriff to take a picture of the dead leader of a gang of bank robbers, photographer Reilly Reynolds is shocked when the body speaks! Realizing that Sam Chandler, the ''dead man,'' is not really the bank robber (that honor belongs to the sheriff), she impulsively hides the fact that he is alive and takes him to her cabin to recover. Passion soon follows and so do the murdering sheriff and his henchmen, who have caught on to the fact that Reilly has figured out the truth. A fast-paced, sensual romance.

Other books you might like:
Rosalyn Alsobrook, *Endless Seduction*, 1992
Caroline Bourne, *Allegheny Captive*, 1990
Barbara Bretton, *Midnight Lover*, 1989
Elizabeth Lowell, *Only His*, 1991
Catherine Palmer, *Outlaw Heart*, 1992

795

LINDSEY HANKS (Pseudonym of Georgia Pierce and Linda Chestnut)

Outlaw Lover
(New York: Zebra, 1990)

Story type: Historical/American West
Major character(s): Samantha Savage, Journalist (newspaper); Tyler Dalton, Fugitive (murder suspect)
Time period(s): 1890s (1897)
Locale(s): Collins, Wyoming

Summary: Desperate for a good story, reporter Samantha Savage agrees to help accused murderer Tyler Dalton escape and become his hostage—if he will let her write the story. Thus begins a lively, funny adventure with action that doesn't stop. Interesting characters including Butch Cassidy and the Sundance Kid.

Other books you might like:
Linda Benjamin, *Midnight Chase*, 1989
Sonya Birmingham, *Spitfire*, 1991
Carol Finch, *Montana Moonfire*, 1990
Robin Leigh, *Rugged Splendor*, 1991
Rebecca Sinclair, *California Caress*, 1989

796

KRISTIN HANNAH

The Enchantment
(New York: Fawcett, 1992)

Story type: Historical/Exotic
Major character(s): Emmaline Hatter, Businesswoman; Lorence Digby, Explorer, Professor
Time period(s): 1890s (1893)
Locale(s): Cibola, Mythical Place

Summary: In order to protect her investment, arrogant and worldly Emmaline Hatter accompanies Lorence Digby in a search for the legendary Cibola and its gold. Their journey and their stay in the magical kingdom changes them both — in ways they could never have foreseen. Sensual, magical, and peopled with unique and memorable characters.

Other books you might like:
Virginia Brown, *Emerald Nights*, 1991
Jessica Bryan, *Across a Wine-Dark Sea*, 1991
fantasy elements
Laura Kinsale, *Seize the Fire*, 1989
Mary Jo Putney, *Silk and Secrets*, 1992
Susan Sackett, *Passion's Golden Fire*, 1989

797

KRISTIN HANNAH

A Handful of Heaven
(New York: Fawcett, 1991)

Story type: Historical/Canadian West
Major character(s): Devon O'Shea, Store Owner; Stone Man McKenna, Store Owner, Photographer

Time period(s): 1890s (1896)
Locale(s): Dawson, Yukon Territory, Canada

Summary: Independent and adventuresome, Devon O'Shea goes to Dawson City to become a part-owner in the local mercantile and discovers her new partner not only expected a man, but he also didn't want a partner at all—only someone to watch his "store" (really a tent) while he goes off to take pictures! Sparks fly, passions rise, and hearts melt in this funny and delightfully heartwarming story of two people who finally learn to love and trust each other.

Other books you might like:
Lisa Gregory, *The Rainbow Season*, 1979
Peggy Hanchar, *Tomorrow's Dream*, 1989
Jill Marie Landis, *Wild Flower*, 1989
LaVyrle Spencer, *Forgiving*, 1990
LaVyrle Spencer, *Morning Glory*, 1989

798

KRISTIN HANNAH

If You Believe
(New York: Fawcett, 1994)

Story type: Historical/American West Coast
Major character(s): Mariah Throckmorton, Spinster (reclusive), Farmer; Mad Dog Stone, Drifter, Handyman
Time period(s): 19th century
Locale(s): Washington

Summary: Reclusive Mariah Throckmorton isn't at all anxious to have drifter Mad Dog Stone working on her apple farm, but he's there, nonetheless, making her life strangely uncomfortable. Neither realizes that the other is hiding deep pain and loneliness, and it isn't until an orphan comes into their lives that they are able to share their true feelings with each other. A story of two lonely people discovering the powerful combination of hope and love.

Other books you might like:
Jude Deveraux, *Wishes*, 1989
fantasy elements
Joan Johnston, *The Barefoot Bride*, 1992
Colleen McCullough, *The Ladies of Missalonghi*, 1987
Pamela Morsi, *Courting Miss Hattie*, 1991
LaVyrle Spencer, *Morning Glory*, 1989

799

KRISTIN HANNAH

Once in Every Life
(New York: Fawcett, 1993)

Story type: Historical/American West Coast; Time Travel
Major character(s): Tess "Amarylis" Gregory, Handicapped (deaf), Time Traveller; Jack Rafferty, Rancher (sheep rancher)
Time period(s): 1990s; 1870s (1873)
Locale(s): Seattle, Washington; San Juan Island, Washington

Summary: Despite being deaf and orphaned since childhood—and never quite "belonging" anywhere—Tess Gregory is warm, loving, and optimistic with a firm belief that love makes everything else possible. It is these qualities that she takes back through time with her when she suddenly finds herself in the body of a woman with a family, a new baby, a dour husband, and a reputation for slothful mothering and self-centeredness. Tess, however, is *not* the lazy Amarylis; and as she works to care for and heal her dysfunctional family, she brings love to her own life, as well. Warm, funny, emotionally wrenching, and poignant.

Other books you might like:
Sandra Davidson, *A Love for All Time*, 1993
Robin Lee Hatcher, *Promise Me Spring*, 1991
    no time travel elements
Constance O'Day-Flannery, *A Time for Love*, 1991
Constance O'Day-Flannery, *Timeless Passion*, 1986
Eugenia Riley, *Tempest in Time*, 1993

800

KRISTIN HANNAH

Waiting for the Moon

(New York: Fawcett Gold Medal, 1995)

Story type: Historical/Victorian America; Historical/Fantasy
Major character(s): Selena ''Agnes'', Amnesiac, Handicapped (brain-damaged); Ian Carrick, Doctor, Telepath
Time period(s): 1880s (1882)
Locale(s): Maine

Summary: When a bruised and bleeding woman with severe head trauma is brought to the isolated Lethe House for healing, the reclusive Dr. Ian Carrick reluctantly takes her in, never realizing she will be the means of his own healing as well. A lyrical, sensitive tale that confronts the issues of brain damage and mental illness and overlays them with the miraculous power of love. Emotionally involving and well written.

Other books you might like:
Christina Dodd, *Candle in the Window*, 1991
    blind heroine
Hannah Howell, *Beauty and the Beast*, 1992
Laura Kinsale, *Flowers From the Storm*, 1992
    brain-damaged hero
Laura Kinsale, *The Prince of Midnight*, 1990
    another wounded hero
LaVyrle Spencer, *Morning Glory*, 1989
    empathetic, wounded characters

801

KRISTIN HANNAH

When Lightning Strikes

(New York: Fawcett, 1994)

Story type: Time Travel
Major character(s): Alaina ''Lainie'' Costanza, Writer (romance), Time Traveller; John Killian, Outlaw
Time period(s): 1990s; 1880s
Locale(s): Bainbridge Island, Washington; Fortune Flats, West

Summary: When a bolt of lightning sends romance novelist Lainie Costanza back through time and into the Western set-

ting of her current book, she decides to relax and enjoy the story—after all, she wrote it. But when she ends up kidnapped by the villain—and falls in love with him rather than the hero, she begins to realize that something is very wrong—or very right! Funny, fast-paced, and involving.

Other books you might like:
Sandra Canfield, *The Loving*, 1992
Sandra Hill, *The Reluctant Viking*, 1994
Merline Lovelace, *Somewhere in Time*, 1994
Sharon Sala, *Annie and the Outlaw*, 1994
Susan Sizemore, *My Own True Love*, 1994

802

JEANNE E. HANSEN

Midnight Enchantment

(New York: Zebra, 1990)

Story type: Historical/Antebellum American South
Major character(s): Emily Harcourt, Runaway; Seneca Prescott, Sea Captain (Cargo Ship)
Time period(s): 19th century (Antebellum Period)
Locale(s): Washington, District of Columbia

Summary: When Emily seeks safety aboard Seneca Prescott's ship, she fears she may have made a dreadful mistake, because what Seneca is involved in may be far more dangerous to her than merely being chased by someone who wants to kill her. Slavery, murder, intrigue, and romance are here in full measure.

Other books you might like:
Jean Innes, *Buccaneer's Bride*, 1989
Deborah Simmons, *Heart's Masquerade*, 1989
Lynette Vinet, *Pirate's Bride*, 1989
Linda Windsor, *Pirate's Wild Embrace*, 1990
Kathleen E. Woodiwiss, *Shanna*, 1977

803

KAREN HARBAUGH

The Vampire Viscount

(New York: Signet, 1995)

Story type: Regency; Historical/Fantasy
Major character(s): Leonore Farleigh, Gentlewoman (impoverished); Nicholas St. Vire, Vampire, Nobleman (Viscount St. Vire)
Time period(s): 1810s
Locale(s): London, England

Summary: When the dissolute vampire and rake Nicholas St. Vire inadvertently wins the hand of the innocent Leonore Farleigh in a game of cards, he suddenly realizes that she may hold the key to his desire to become human once again. Well-handled sexual tension and intriguing protagonists combine in an interesting, occasionally dark example of genreblending.

Other books you might like:
Mary Chase Comstock, *A Midsummer's Magic*, 1994
    fantasy elements/lighter
Sandra Heath, *The Halloween Husband*, 1994
    fantasy elements

Carla Kelly, *Libby's London Merchant*, 1991
Carla Kelly, *Mrs. Drew Plays Her Hand*, 1994
Lynn Kerstan, *Gwen's Christmas Ghost*, 1995
    Alicia Rasley, co-author; paranormal elements

804
BARBARA HARGIS

Heart Song
(New York: Avon, 1990)

Story type: Historical/American West
Major character(s): Eliza Nolenberg, Worker, Guardian (aunt); Nate Truesdale, Businessman (shipping company owner), Parent (father)
Time period(s): 1890s (1893)
Locale(s): San Francisco, California

Summary: In order to become the legal guardian of her illegitimate niece Daisy, Eliza must first have the consent of Daisy's father, Nate Truesdale—and he refuses to give it. But Eliza is determined and eventually she wins not only Daisy but Daisy's father as well.

Other books you might like:
Deborah Camp, *Black-Eyed Susan*, 1990
Ann Gabriel, *South Texas*, 1990
    Mainstream elements
Kathy Lawrence, *Tin Angel*, 1989
Jane Toombs, *Midnight Whispers*, 1989

805
SHARON HARLOW

Country Kiss
(New York: Diamond, 1993)

Story type: Historical/Victorian America
Major character(s): Rebecca Stephens, Widow(er); Luke Northcutt, Neighbor (newcomer)
Time period(s): 19th century
Locale(s): Midwest

Summary: Rebecca invites newcomer Luke to dinner, and although he prefers to be alone, he accepts and finds her friendliness warms him. They enjoy being together, and when they find three homeless children to care for, their lonely and loveless lives take on a new purpose. However, it takes a tornado to jolt them into acknowledging their feelings for each other. Gentle and warm.

Other books you might like:
Patricia Gaffney, *Sweet Everlasting*, 1993
Robin Lee Hatcher, *Promise Me Spring*, 1991
Terri Herrington, *Silena*, 1993
Karen Lockwood, *Harvest Song*, 1993
Isabel Whitfield, *Bodie Bride*, 1992

806
ANNE HARMON

Desert Flame
(New York: Diamond, 1992)

Story type: Historical/American West
Major character(s): Emily Crabtree, Widow(er), Rancher (Ostrich); Zach Hollis, Foreman
Locale(s): Arizona

Summary: When widowed Emily Crabtree heads to Uncle Billy's Arizona ostrich ranch to make a new start, she is surprised to find that a foreman has been hired and is well on his way to planning the ranch's future! The attraction between the two is immediate, but Zach's quest for vengeance, Emily's ardent suitor, and their own stubborn personalities keep them at odds, until love finally wins out. A sweetly sensual romance with a dash of mystery.

Other books you might like:
Rosanne Bittner, *Embers of the Heart*, 1990
Candace Camp, *Rosewood*, 1991
Jill Marie Landis, *Rose*, 1990
Isabel Whitfield, *Bodie Bride*, 1992

807
ANNE HARMON

Wyoming Wildfire
(New York: Diamond, 1993)

Story type: Historical/American West
Major character(s): Lily Avenil, Equestrian, Entertainer (circus performer); Grayson Benedict, Rancher
Time period(s): 19th century
Locale(s): Cheyenne, Wyoming

Summary: When rancher Grayson Benedict saves circus performer Lily Avenil from some unwanted cowpoke attentions, he finds himself both attracted to her and concerned by her unsettling influence on his teenage daughter. Rustlers, vigilantes, and a jealous widow all add to the excitement as Gray and Lily struggle to reconcile their lives and their feelings for each other.

Other books you might like:
Linda Hilton, *Secret Fires*, 1991
Jill Marie Landis, *Come Spring*, 1992
Susan Macias, *Tender Victory*, 1993
Jodi Thomas, *The Tender Texan*, 1991

808
DANELLE HARMON

Captain of My Heart
(New York: Avon, 1992)

Story type: Historical/Georgian
Major character(s): Mira Ashton, Imposter, Stowaway; Brendan Jay Merrick, Privateer
Time period(s): 1770s
Locale(s): Mississippi

Summary: Told by her boat-building father to marry or else, adventuresome Mira Ashton decides that dashing privateer Brendan Jay Merrick is The One —and she sets out to make it happen! Lots of passion and high seas action as Mira, disguised as a ship's gunner, leads the Captain a merry and seductive chase.

Other books you might like:
Julie Garwood, *The Gift*, 1991
Heather Graham, *A Pirate's Pleasure*, 1989
Virginia Henley, *The Pirate and the Pagan*, 1990
Connie Mason, *Tempt the Devil*, 1990
Kathleen E. Woodiwiss, *Shanna*, 1977

809

DANELLE HARMON

Master of My Dreams

(New York: Avon, 1993)

Story type: Historical/American Revolution; Historical/Colonial America
Major character(s): Deirdre O'Devir, Stowaway; Christian Lord, Sea Captain
Time period(s): 1770s (1775)
Locale(s): Ireland; England; American Colonies

Summary: Seeking passage to America to find her brother who had been pressed into service 13 years earlier, Deirdre takes the ship of the man she blames for her brother's abduction. She vows to kill him, but he has his own demons to contend with, the ghost of his dead wife and a crew of malcontents. A fiery and passionate tale.

Other books you might like:
Cordia Byers, *The Black Angel*, 1993
Christine Dorsey, *Sea Fires*, 1992
Shannon Drake, *Bride of the Wind*, 1992
Lynette Vinet, *Pirate's Bride*, 1989

810

KAREN HARPER

Eden's Gate

(New York: Berkley, 1989)

Story type: Historical/Colonial America
Major character(s): Claire Chandon, Gentlewoman (French), Servant (laundress); Ethan Trent, Patriot (American)
Time period(s): 1750s (1755-56)
Locale(s): Mohawk Valley, New York, American Colonies

Summary: Because she is French, keeps a journal, and is always where the action is, Ethan suspects Claire of being a spy. He vows to see that she doesn't succeed, but ends up falling in love with her. A story of love and adventure laced with real historical characters and events.

Other books you might like:
Gwen Bristow, *Celia Garth*, 1959
    American Revolution
Judith E. French, *Scarlet Ribbons*, 1989
    American Revolution

Heather Graham, *Love Not a Rebel*, 1989
    Dell's American Woman Series a3
Robin Maderich, *Faith and Honor*, 1989
    American Revolution
Christina Savage, *Hearts of Fire*, 1984

811

KAREN HARPER

The Firelands

(New York: Charter, 1990)

Story type: Historical/American Revolution
Major character(s): Althea Arnold, Young Woman (cousin of Benedict Arnold), Apothecary; Morgan Glenn, Military Personnel (aide to Benedict Arnold)
Time period(s): 1770s (1776)
Locale(s): Connecticut

Summary: Lies and treachery pervade the personal as well as the political plotlines of this action-oriented historical. Attracted to her cousin Benedict Arnold's aide-de-camp, Morgan Glenn, Althea must deal with both her best friend's jealousy and the public reaction to her cousin's treachery.

Other books you might like:
Judith E. French, *Scarlet Ribbons*, 1989
Heather Graham, *Love Not a Rebel*, 1989
Robin Maderich, *Faith and Honor*, 1989
Veronica Sattler, *A Promise of Fire*, 1989
Terri Valentine, *Yankee's Caress*, 1989
    American Civil War

812

KAREN HARPER

The Wings of Morning

(New York: Dutton, 1993)

Story type: Historical/Mainstream; Saga
Major character(s): Abby Adair, Widow(er); Morgan West, Shipowner, Sea Captain
Time period(s): 1850s; 1860s
Locale(s): Scotland; England; United States

Summary: Although when Abby Adair loses her husband and child she is shunned as an outsider by the St. Kilda townspeople, she is determined to discover why the children are dying, so she goes to London to research the problem. Her determination costs her dearly, and her life is filled with short-term happiness, but she is determined and eventually she finds peace and joy.

Other books you might like:
Stephanie Bartlett, *Highland Flame*, 1992
Lois Battle, *Storyville*, 1993
Sandra Bregman, *Reach for the Dream*, 1990
Katherine Sinclair, *Visions of Tomorrow*, 1989
Lucy Taylor, *Avenue of Dreams*, 1990

WHAT ROMANCE DO I READ NEXT?

Harris **817**

813

MADELINE HARPER

Dangerous Charade
(Toronto.: Harlequin, 1992)

Story type: Historical/American West
Major character(s): Maggie Hanson, Resistance Fighter, Imposter; Steven Payton, Rancher, Heir
Time period(s): 1870s (1874)
Locale(s): Wyoming; Mendorra, Fictional Country

Summary: Mysterious Maggie Hanson fraudently tries to get into Steven Payton's life by any means whatever. She lies, finagles, and searches his home. It seems that the Wyoming rancher might just possibly be the rightful heir to the throne of her homeland, Mendorra, which is now under the control of a repressive dictator. Naturally, Steven has a hard time believing the less-than-honest Maggie, even though he is strongly attracted to her. Nevertheless, he relents and accompanies her to Mendorra, paving the way for even more difficult decisions in the future.

Other books you might like:
Rexanne Becnel, *Thief of My Heart*, 1991
Constance Bennett, *Morning Sky*, 1991
Johanna Lindsey, *Once a Princess*, 1991
Miriam Minger, *Defiant Imposter*, 1992
Dana Ransom, *Wild Wyoming Love*, 1991

814

ALEXIS HARRINGTON

A Light for My Love
(New York: Topaz, 1995)

Story type: Historical/American West Coast
Major character(s): China Sullivan, Young Woman; Jake Chastaine, Sea Captain
Time period(s): 1880s (1888)
Locale(s): Astoria, Oregon

Summary: Handsome Captain Jake Chastaine returns to Astoria for one reason—to to show the town's people and the woman he has secretly loved since childhood that he is no longer the rag tag boy he once was. But people have long memories; and though China Sullivan finds Jake alarmingly attractive, she can't forget his wild, womanizing youth or the fact that her brother left to go to sea with him and never returned. Only trust and outside forces will bring these two together.

Other books you might like:
Paris Afton Bonds, *Dream Time*, 1994
   another bad-boy-returns story/Australian setting
Elizabeth DeLancey, *Meant to Be*, 1994
Joan Johnston, *Maverick Heart*, 1995
Patricia Rice, *Shelter From the Storm*, 1993
   mainstream feel
Terri Valentine, *Master of Her Heart*, 1990
   more social issues

815

KATHLEEN HARRINGTON

Cherish the Dream
(New York: Avon, 1990)

Story type: Historical/American West
Major character(s): Theodora Gordon, Cartographer; Blade Roberts, Military Personnel (army captain), Indian (half-Cheyenne)
Time period(s): 1830s (1836)
Locale(s): West (Kansas to California)

Summary: Expecting the arrival of the two Gordon brothers, Thomas and Theo, to complete the U.S. Geological mapmaking expedition team, Captain Blade Roberts is shocked to learn that Theo is a woman—and she is insistant on going with the team. She goes, of course; and as Blade continually rescues her, they fall in love. Witty, funny, and passionate.

Other books you might like:
Norah Hess, *Wildfire*, 1989
Johanna Jordan, *Destiny's Dream*, 1990
Betina Lindsey, *Waltz with the Lady*, 1990
Johanna Lindsey, *Savage Thunder*, 1989
Christine Monson, *Golden Nights*, 1990

816

KATHLEEN HARRINGTON

Sunshine and Shadow
(New York: Avon, 1993)

Story type: Historical/Georgian
Major character(s): Christina Berringer, Noblewoman; Roderick Fielding, Nobleman (Earl of Rugden), Military Personnel (colonel)
Time period(s): 18th century
Locale(s): England; France

Summary: When wealthy lute collector Lady Christina Berringer is accidentally compromised by Roderick Fielding, the Earl of Rugden, he does the honorable thing and marries her to save her reputation. Christina, however, thinks he has married her for her money and goes to great lengths to protect her virtue so she can seek an annulment. Fast-paced, funny, and laced with a bit of suspense and true danger.

Other books you might like:
Julie Garwood, *Castles*, 1993
Julie Garwood, *The Gift*, 1991
Lisa Kleypas, *Then Came You*, 1993
Mary Jo Putney, *Thunder and Roses*, 1993
Amanda Quick, *Mistress*, 1994

817

MONICA HARRIS, Editor

Spirit of the Season
(New York: Pinnacle, 1994)

Story type: Ethnic; Holiday Themes

Time period(s): 1990s
Locale(s): United States

Summary: This trio of romantic novellas set during the Winter Holidays features African American heroes and heroines and is part of the Arabesque multicultural line. ''The Choice'' by Donna Hill focuses on Christmas, ''Harvest the Fruits'' by Margie Walker highlights the tradition of Kwanzaa, and ''Sarah's Miracle'' by Francis Ray centers on New Year's.

Other books you might like:
Kathleen Creighton, *Silhouette Christmas Stories*, 1990
    contemporary holiday anthology/not multicultural
Donna Hill, *Temptation*, 1994
Ellen Tanner Marsh, *A Christmas Embrace*, 1994
    contemporary holiday theme/not multicultural
Francis Ray, *Forever Yours*, 1994
Margie Walker, *Sweet Refrain*, 1994

818

CATHERINE HART
BETINA M. KRAHN, Co-Author
LINDA LADD, Co-Author
BARBARA DAWSON SMITH, Co-Author
KATHERINE SUTCLIFFE, Co-Author

Avon Books Presents: Christmas Romance
(New York: Avon, 1991)

Story type: Anthology; Holiday Themes

Summary: A collection of five romances for the holidays by noted historical writers. Includes ''A Christmas Melodie'' by Catherine Hart, ''Six Little Angels'' by Betina Krahn, ''A Match Made in Heaven'' by Linda Ladd, ''Candle in the Snow'' by Barbara Dawson Smith, and ''Silent Night, Starry Night'' by Katherine Sutcliffe.

Other books you might like:
Janice Bennett, *A Christmas Keepsake*, 1992
Sandra Heath, *A Christmas Courtship*, 1990

819

CATHERINE HART

Forever Gold
(New York: Leisure, 1990)

Story type: Historical/American West
Major character(s): Megan Coulson, Captive; Blake Montgomery, Gunfighter
Time period(s): 19th century
Locale(s): West

Summary: When Blake Montgomery kidnaps his cousin's fiancee in an effort to regain his ranch, he doesn't plan on falling in love with his captive; but he does, and together Megan and Blake surmount a number of obstacles as they seek the proof necessary for Blake to claim his heritage. Passion and wild western adventure.

Other books you might like:
Virginia Brown, *Wildfire*, 1990
LaRee Bryant, *Sweet Texas Fury*, 1990

Carol Finch, *Montana Moonfire*, 1990
Judith Steel, *Wild Colorado Passion*, 1991

820

CATHERINE HART

Irresistible
(New York: Avon, 1994)

Story type: Historical/American West
Major character(s): Jade Donovan, Singer; Matt Richards, Religious (pastor)
Time period(s): 1860s (late)
Locale(s): Oregon Trail

Summary: Jade is befriended by a madam and her ''girls'' and ends up with a reputation as a prostitute as the wagon train sets out for Oregon. In addition, her past, in the form of unscrupulous Sean O'Neill, comes back to haunt her—even after she marries a widowed minister and becomes a loving mother to an assortment of orphans. Tragedy, prejudice, and the daily difficulties of a wagon trip west add depth to this sensitive and historically detailed novel.

Other books you might like:
Yvonne Adamson, *Bridey's Mountain*, 1993
Elaine Barbieri, *More Precious than Gold*, 1992
Elaine Barbieri, *Wings of a Dove*, 1990
Rosanne Bittner, *Oregon Bride*, 1990
Pamela Morsi, *Wild Oats*, 1993
    humorous and light

821

CATHERINE HART

Sweet Fury
(New York: Leisure, 1990)

Story type: Historical/American West
Major character(s): Sam Downing, Outlaw (Female); Travis Kincaid, Lawman (Marshall)
Time period(s): 1880s
Locale(s): Tumbleweed, Texas

Summary: Raised in a family of train-robbing bandits, Sam Downing grows up to be a very unusual young woman—one who presents a number of problems to the marshall of Tumbleweed, Texas. Charming, funny, and romantic.

Other books you might like:
Cheryl Black, *Comanche Love Song*, 1989
Jill Marie Landis, *Wild Flower*, 1989
Bobbi Smith, *Arizona Caress*, 1989
Judith Steel, *Seduction's Raging Flame*, 1989
Lisa Ann Verge, *The Heart's Disguise*, 1990

822

CATHERINE HART

Tempest
(New York: Avon, 1991)

Story type: Historical/American West

Major character(s): Charity Prindle, Widow(er); Luke Sterling, Gunfighter
Time period(s): 1880s
Locale(s): Kansas; Texas

Summary: Bitter and angry, young Charity Prindle hires gunfighter Luke Sterling to teach her his skills so she can take revenge on the party of men who killed her husband and brutally raped her, killing their unborn child. Through Luke and an Indian shaman she learns to come to terms with her past and discovers room for love in her future. Brutal, realistic, and funny.

Other books you might like:
Caroline Bourne, *Allegheny Captive*, 1990
LaRee Bryant, *Sweet Texas Fury*, 1990
Colleen Faulkner, *Love's Sweet Bounty*, 1991
Kathy Jones, *Sweet Obsession*, 1990
LaVyrle Spencer, *Forgiving*, 1990

823

CATHERINE HART

Temptation
(New York: Avon, 1992)

Story type: Historical/Victorian America
Major character(s): Amanda Sites, Gambler (riverboat), Farmer (horse farm owner); Grant Gardner, Farmer (horse farm owner)
Time period(s): 1870s (1877)
Locale(s): Lexington, Kentucky

Summary: When Amanda Sites wins half of a Kentucky horse farm in a riverboat poker game, she is delighted to have her own home at last — and then she discovers she must share it with attractive Grant Gardner! As she struggles to learn about horses, racing, and becoming a "lady," she and Grant spar constantly. A difficult fiancee, unhappy employees, and a series of near disasters don't help the situation, but a marriage of convenience has a surprising effect. Passionate, funny, and filled with interesting people and appealing horses.

Other books you might like:
Pamela Litton, *Stardust and Whirlwinds*, 1991
Marcia Martin, *Southern Storms*, 1992
   contemporary horse story
Carolyn Monroe, *Kiss of Bliss*, 1992
   contemporary horse story
Charlotte Simms, *Silver Caress*, 1990
Pat Tracy, *The Flaming*, 1992

824

TERESA HART

Hearts Are Wild
(New York: Jove, 1993)

Story type: Historical/American West
Series: Brides of the West
Major character(s): DeLacey Honeycutt, Mail Order Bride, Gambler; Joss McRae, Rancher
Time period(s): 1880s (1888)

Locale(s): West

Summary: Desperately in need of money to continue her gambling career, DeLacey Honeycutt finances her way West by agreeing to become a mail-order bride. Her plans, however, change abruptly when Joss McRae catches her cheating and blackmails her into helping him prove that her husband-to-be is really a murderer and a thief. Love and all its attendant complications soon follow in this fast-paced tale of the Old West. First in the Brides of the West series.

Other books you might like:
Cheryl Biggs, *Mississippi Flame*, 1993
Danette Chartier, *Stolen Fire*, 1993
   English setting
Kathryn Hockett, *Outlaw Seduction*, 1993
Dana Ransom, *Dakota Destiny*, 1993

825

DUFF HART-DAVIS

Horses of War
(New York: St. Martin's, 1992)

Story type: Historical/Mainstream
Major character(s): Katya Mironov, Nurse, Prisoner; Joseph Clements, Horse Trainer
Time period(s): 1910s (1918)
Locale(s): Kharkov, Russia

Summary: When one of his prize mares is killed by the Bolsheviks, English Czarist horse trainer Joseph Clements decides to flee, but he wants his lover, Katya, to come with him. She refuses, remaining to care for the war victims and ends up the sex-prisoner of a Red Army General who has taken over the hospital. A harrowing journey, murder, and imprisonment make life difficult for Joseph and Katya in this sweeping tale that graphically depicts the horror and brutality of war and at the same time shows the saving and healing powers of love.

Other books you might like:
Diane Cory, *A Token of Jewels*, 1989
Alan Fisher, *The Three Passions of Countess Natalya*, 1985
Patricia Hagan, *Love and Triumph*, 1991
Boris Pasternak, *Doctor Zhivago*, 1957
   classic tale of Revolutionary Russia

826

MELISSA HARTMAN

The Sure Thing
(Tallahassee, Florida: Naiad, 1994)

Story type: Lesbian/Contemporary
Major character(s): Christine Kennedy, Scientist (seismologist), Lesbian; Dory Moraga, Journalist (television), Lesbian
Time period(s): 1990s
Locale(s): Los Angeles, California

Summary: When earthquake scientist Christine Kennedy and TV reporter Dory Moraga meet following a correctly predicted southern California earthquake, their relationship is passionate and seems ideal. However, Dory's compulsion to succeed pushes her to extremes and puts her at odds with Chris's more measured ways, driving the pair apart. Love and risk in contemporary Los Angeles setting.

Other books you might like:
Sarah Aldridge, *Michaela*, 1994
Katherine V. Forrest, *The Romantic Naiad*, 1993
  anthology of lesbian short fiction
Katherine V. Forrest, *Curious Wine*, 1983
  classic popular lesbian romance
Karin Kallmaker, *Painted Moon*, 1994
Karin Kallmaker, *Car Pool*, 1993

827

LAURA HASTINGS

The Turtledove's Secret

(New York: Dell, 1992)

Story type: Romantic Suspense; Contemporary/Mainstream
Major character(s): Joselyn Merriman, Museum Curator (antiquities); Riordan Nolan, Archaeologist
Time period(s): 1990s
Locale(s): Vatican City; New York, New York (Queens); Italy

Summary: When the possessor of the famed Magdalene scroll is found dead, antiquities curator Joselyn Merriman contacts her old flame, archaeologist Riordan Nolan, for advice. Together they locate the scroll, only to become targets of the murderers themselves. Fast-paced action laced with romance.

Other books you might like:
Janet Dailey, *Aspen Gold*, 1991
Jude Deveraux, *Sweet Liar*, 1992
Elizabeth Peters, *Borrower of the Night*, 1973
Elizabeth Peters, *The Dead Sea Cypher*, 1970
Patricia Simpson, *Whisper of Midnight*, 1991

828

ROBIN LEE HATCHER

Liberty Blue

(New York: Harper, 1995)

Story type: Historical/American West
Major character(s): Liberty ''Libby'' Blue, Rancher, Fugitive (aka Olivia Vanderhoof); Remington Walker, Detective—Private
Time period(s): 1890s
Locale(s): Blue Springs Ranch, Idaho

Summary: Libby's new-found existence, far away from her controlling, aristocratic father, is threatened by the arrival of a stranger at Libby's isolated Idaho sheep ranch—a stranger Libby shoots for trespassing and then ends up nursing back to health. But what she doesn't know is that he has been sent by her father to find her; and what Libby's father doesn't know is that Remington Walker is out for revenge—on him! A warm, gentle, but somewhat complex story.

Other books you might like:
Jill Marie Landis, *Rose*, 1990

Maggie Osborne, *The Brides of Bowie Stone*, 1994
  another independent heroine/more hard-hitting
Victoria Pade, *The Doubletree*, 1990
Patricia Potter, *Defiant*, 1995
  more sensual and hard-hitting
Jodi Thomas, *The Texan and the Lady*, 1994

829

ROBIN LEE HATCHER

The Magic

(New York: Leisure, 1993)

Story type: Historical/Colonial America; Historical/Exotic
Major character(s): Cassandra Jamison, Fiance(e) (reluctant), Captive; Damien Tate, Sea Captain, Pirate
Time period(s): 1710s (1714)
Locale(s): At Sea

Summary: Vowing vengeance on the man who stole his title and ruined her family business, pirate captain Damien Tate kidnaps the villain's niece, Cassandra, and ends up falling love with her. An action-filled adventure that sweeps Cassandra and Damien from one exotic setting to another in their search for retribution and love. Nicely drawn characters.

Other books you might like:
Marsha Bauer, *Pirate's Angel*, 1991
Colleen Faulkner, *Flames of Love*, 1993
Meagan McKinney, *Till Dawn Tames the Night*, 1991
Diane Gates Robinson, *The Eagle and the Rose*, 1993
Joan Van Nuys, *Beloved Avenger*, 1989

830

ROBIN LEE HATCHER

Midnight Rose

(New York: Leisure, 1992)

Story type: Historical/American West Coast
Major character(s): Leona Washington, Fiance(e), Outlaw (La Rosa); Diego Salazar, Fiance(e)
Time period(s): 1850s
Locale(s): California

Summary: When Diego Salazar comes to California from Texas to end his engagement to Leona Washington, a woman he has never met, he ends up falling in love with her—but, Leona doesn't want to get married! Her secret life as ''La Rosa'' is too important to her—and anyway, independence is too much fun! Naturally, they do eventually get together, but not before they overcome a number of rather large obstacles. Funny, fiery, and adventurous.

Other books you might like:
Virginia Brown, *Renegade Embrace*, 1990
Christina Dodd, *Treasure of the Sun*, 1991
Eugenia Riley, *Taming Kate*, 1992
Cynthia Wright, *Brighter than Gold*, 1990

831

ROBIN LEE HATCHER

Promise Me Spring

(New York: Leisure, 1991)

Story type: Historical/American West
Series: Women of the West
Major character(s): Rachel Harris, Governess; Gavin Blake, Rancher
Time period(s): 1880s (1883)
Locale(s): Idaho

Summary: When she answers an ad for a governess on Gavin and Drucilla Blake's Idaho ranch, Rachel Harris finds herself in a bizarre situation—in charge of the two daughters of the slowly dying Drucilla and falling in love with Drucilla's husband, Gavin—all with Drucilla's blessing. Heart warming, passionate, and thought-provoking. Continues Women of the West Series.

Other books you might like:
LaRee Bryant, *Arizona Captive*, 1989
Deborah Camp, *Black-Eyed Susan*, 1990
Victoria Pade, *The Doubletree*, 1990
LaVyrle Spencer, *Morning Glory*, 1989

832

ROBIN LEE HATCHER

Promised Sunrise

(New York: Leisure, 1990)

Story type: Historical/American West
Major character(s): Maggie, Orphan; Tucker Branigan, Settler
Time period(s): 1860s
Locale(s): Oregon Trail; Boise, Idaho

Summary: Determined to make a fresh start after losing the family plantation to taxes, Tucker Branigan takes his mother and younger siblings and heads west to Idaho. Along the way they acquire the beautiful and resourceful Maggie, who captures Tucker's attention and finally his heart as well as they battle the danger and adversity of the frontier. To be continued by *Beyond the Horizon* by Connie Mason.

Other books you might like:
Rosanne Bittner, *Montana Woman*, 1990
Thea Devine, *Montana Mistress*, 1990
Kathleen Harrington, *Cherish the Dream*, 1990
Norah Hess, *Wildfire*, 1989
DeLoras Scott, *The Miss and the Maverick*, 1990

833

ROBIN LEE HATCHER

Where the Heart Is

(New York: Leisure, 1993)

Story type: Historical/American West
Series: Americana
Major character(s): Addie Sherwood, Teacher; Will Rider, Landlord
Time period(s): 1880s
Locale(s): Homestead, Idaho

Summary: When Addie goes to Idaho to teach school, she ends up living close to Will Rider and his needy niece, Lark, and gradually finds herself drawn into their lives. Will, of course, says marriage isn't for him, but when others begin to show an interest in Addie, his jealousy comes to the fore and matters take a different turn. Outside forces also have a part to play, but happiness doesn't elude them forever.

Other books you might like:
Deborah Camp, *Black-Eyed Susan*, 1990
Norah Hess, *Kentucky Bride*, 1992
Rebecca Hagan Lee, *Golden Chances*, 1992
Jodi Thomas, *The Tender Texan*, 1992

834

DIANA HAVILAND

Pirate's Kiss

(New York: Pinnacle, 1992)

Story type: Historical/Seventeenth Century
Major character(s): Sybilla Thornton, Young Woman; Gavin Broderick, Pirate, Sea Captain
Time period(s): 17th century
Locale(s): Caribbean

Summary: Intending to live with her brother in Montego Bay, Sybilla Thornton finds him destitute and working for the despicable Nicholas Hobart. When Sybilla discovers there is a plan in the works to marry her off to Nicholas, she turns to Captain Gavin Broderick and together they devise a scheme of their own — and end up sailing blissfully away across the Caribbean. Problems, however, do appear, but none that the pair can't handle. Fast-paced, passionate, and adventurous.

Other books you might like:
Marsha Bauer, *Pirate's Angel*, 1991
Wendy Garrett, *Sweet Southern Caress*, 1991
Jean Innes, *Buccaneer's Bride*, 1989
Meagan McKinney, *Till Dawn Tames the Night*, 1991
Lynette Vinet, *Pirate's Bride*, 1989

835

S.R. HAWLEY

Deadly Secrets

(New York: Avalon, 1990)

Story type: Contemporary/Innocent; Romantic Suspense
Major character(s): Marissa Meade, Radio (assistant promotions director); Riley Hertz, Radio (manager)
Time period(s): 1990s
Locale(s): Phoenix, Arizona

Summary: When Marissa Meade takes a job as promotions assistant at a small Phoenix radio station, she must contend with jealousy, rudeness, and very real danger as she struggles to begin her career, solve a puzzling mystery, and handle her feelings for her station manager—all at the same time.

Other books you might like:
Alma Blair, *The Unwitting Witness*, 1990
Mignon Eberhart, *Alpine Condo Crossfire*, 1984
Jane Edwards, *Terror by Design*, 1990
Phyllis Halldorson, *Lady Diamond*, 1991
Mary Stewart, *Thunder on the Right*, 1957

836

S.R. HAWLEY

Formula for Murder
(New York: Avalon, 1992)

Story type: Contemporary/Innocent; Romantic Suspense
Major character(s): Jessica Chambers, Researcher, Scientist; Dan Hollinger, Pilot (test pilot)
Time period(s): 1990s
Locale(s): Arizona

Summary: With all the evidence indicating that researcher Jessica Chambers is not only a corporate spy but a murderer as well, handsome Dan Hollinger joins forces with Jessica and together they find the killers — and love.

Other books you might like:
Lee Anderson, *Dangerous Bequest*, 1992
Jane Edwards, *Terror by Design*, 1990
Karen G. McCullough, *Programmed for Danger*, 1990
Phyllis A. Whitney, *Vermilion*, 1981

837

LAURA HAYDEN

A Margin in Time
(New York: Pinnacle, 1995)

Story type: Time Travel
Major character(s): Emma Nolan, Teacher; J. Barrett Callan V, Businessman (Executive), Lawman
Time period(s): 1990s; 1890s
Locale(s): Margin, Colorado

Summary: Barrett Callan's future is grim. He's about to be accused of embezzlement and doesn't know which way to turn. Suddenly his great-great grandfather's face appears in the washroom mirror and invites him to change places. Impulsively, he agrees and ends up as Margin, Colorado's, sheriff in the 1890s. Learning the ropes causes him a few problems, and his attraction to the prim schoolmistress, Emma Nolan, only adds to his predicament. Lively action, humor, and engaging characters add to this nicely-done time travel.

Other books you might like:
Robin Burcell, *When Midnight Comes*, 1995
    modern homicide detective in Victorian England
Suzanne Elizabeth, *When Destiny Calls*, 1993
    humorous time travel
Kasey Michaels, *Timely Matrimony*, 1994
    funny and fast-paced/hero comes from the past
Pamela Simpson, *Partners in Time*, 1990
    more detective time travellers

838

ALLISON HAYES

Storm Dancers
(New York: Avon, 1991)

Story type: Historical/American West
Major character(s): Genny Stone, Gentlewoman; Gus Renard, Indian (half Lakota/Sioux)
Time period(s): 1860s (1864)
Locale(s): Chadds Ford, Pennsylvania; Nebraska

Summary: Genny's year of adventure in Nebraska involves her with Gus's tribal customs and the explosive dangers of the early west. Plenty of passion and fast-paced action.

Other books you might like:
Genell Dellin, *Cherokee Nights*, 1991
Kathleen Harrington, *Cherish the Dream*, 1990
Penelope Neri, *Forever and Beyond*, 1990
    time change elements
Constance O'Banyon, *Cheyenne Sunrise*, 1990

839

PENNY HAYES

Kathleen O'Donald
(Tallahassee, Florida: Naiad, 1994)

Story type: Lesbian/Contemporary
Major character(s): Kathleen Anne Mary O'Donald, Immigrant (Irish), Worker (in a factory); Rose Stewart, Immigrant (English), Worker (in a factory)
Time period(s): 1900s; 1910s (1909-1911)
Locale(s): New York, New York

Summary: Kathleen O'Donald leaves Ireland for America filled with dreams for a better future. However, what she finds is hardship, pain, and, ultimately, hope and love as she and English immigrant Rose Stewart become involved in the struggle for better working conditions and a better life for everyone.

Other books you might like:
Catherine Ennis, *South of the Line*, 1989
    the historical South
Katherine V. Forrest, *The Romantic Naiad*, 1993
    anthology of lesbian short fiction
Evelyn Kennedy, *Of Love and Glory*, 1989
    World War II setting
Michelle Martin, *Pembroke Park*, 1986
    lesbian romance/Regency period
Victoria Ramstetter, *The Marquise and the Novice*, 1981
    A lesbian gothic

840

BARBARA HAZARD

Call Back the Dream
(New York: New American Library, 1990)

Story type: Historical/Victorian

Major character(s): Camille Talbot, Gentlewoman (Clergyman's daughter); Alexander Maxwell, Nobleman (Viscount Styne)
Time period(s): 18th century (1740-1761)
Locale(s): England

Summary: Horrified that his son Alexander is in love with a poor clergyman's daughter, the Earl of Granbourne uses treachery to separate the lovers. Years later, Alexander and Camille meet, but she is now married. True love, aided by favorable circumstances, does win out in the end.

Other books you might like:
Elaine Barbieri, *Wings of a Dove*, 1990
Rebecca George, *Call Home the Heart*, 1989
Lisa Gregory, *The Rainbow Promise*, 1989
Jack McGowan, *Flame in the Night*, 1990

841
BARBARA HAZARD
A Handful of Dreams
(New York: Onyx, 1992)

Story type: Historical/Renaissance
Major character(s): Sally Desmond, Young Woman, Runaway; Harry Tredman, Nobleman (Earl of Darlington)
Time period(s): 16th century
Locale(s): England; Ireland

Summary: When fifteen-year-old Sally Desmond runs away from a disastrous marriage, she is befriended and taken to England to be a companion to Colonel Peter Jenkin's daughter. She is seen, however, by the dark and dour Earl of Darlington, who "pays" for her and takes her to London, intending to marry her once her husband is dead. Sally brightens up his life considerably, but it takes some doing on both their parts before they can be truly happy. Fast-paced, sensual, Renaissance romance.

Other books you might like:
Shirl Henke, *Paradise and More*, 1992
Laura Parker, *For Love's Sake Only*, 1991
    Regency period
Amanda Quick, *Seduction*, 1990
    Regency period
Patricia Potter, *The Abduction*, 1991

842
BARBARA HAZARD
The Heart Remembers
(New York: Onyx, 1990)

Story type: Historical/Georgian
Major character(s): Kate Hathaway, Debutante; John "Jack" Reade, Bastard Son, Nobleman
Time period(s): 1770s (1772)
Locale(s): London, England; Bermuda

Summary: It is love at first sight for Kate Hathaway when she meets Sir John Reade during the London Season; but she knows it is hopeless. He is a highly eligible bachelor and she is an innocent miss from the Colonies. Years later, however,

an old scandal sends John to make a new life for himself in Bermuda where he re-encounters Kate—this time with very different results. Sequel to *Call Back the Dream*.

Other books you might like:
Sara Blayne, *Sweet Abandon*, 1990
Laura Simon, *A Taste of Heaven*, 1990
Julie Tetel, *Swept Away*, 1989
Kathleen E. Woodiwiss, *Shanna*, 1977

843
LORRAINE HEATH
Sweet Lullaby
(New York: Diamond, 1994)

Story type: Historical/American West
Major character(s): Rebecca Anderson, Young Woman (pregnant); Jake Burnett, Heir (to ranch), Cowboy
Time period(s): 1880s (1883)
Locale(s): Kentucky; Texas

Summary: Jake Burnett will inherit half of a successful ranch—if he agrees to marry the owner's pregnant daughter, Rebecca Anderson. They are both willing to start a new life, but the the road is not easy. But through it all—dangers, hardships, and Rebecca's feelings for her baby's father—Jake is patient, kind, and understanding. Eventually, they both come to learn what real love is. Gentle and tender.

Other books you might like:
Pamela K. Forrest, *Desert Angel*, 1994
    caring hero
Robin Lee Hatcher, *Promise Me Spring*, 1991
LaVyrle Spencer, *Morning Glory*, 1989
Jodi Thomas, *The Tender Texan*, 1991

844
SANDRA HEATH
The Halloween Husband
(New York: Signet, 1994)

Story type: Regency; Historical/Fantasy
Major character(s): Rowena Melcombe, Debutante, Noblewoman; Justin Alderney, Nobleman, Rake; Lady Margaret Melcombe, Noblewoman, Spirit
Time period(s): 1810s
Locale(s): England

Summary: When the financially incompetent William Melcombe dies leaving his family destitute, the spirit of Lady Margaret decides to rectify the situation. She will marry off Rowena! Granted permission by the Powers-that-Be to leave her portrait each year on Halloween and look after family interests, Lady Margaret sets about doing just that—but she quickly discovers that a match between the innocent Rowena and the worldly Lord Justin Alderney, the only available choice at the moment, will not be easy to arrange. Magical, charming, and well-written.

Other books you might like:
Mary Chase Comstock, *A Midsummer's Magic*, 1994
Karla Hocker, *A Deceitful Heart*, 1993

Mary Kingsley, *A Maddening Minx*, 1992
Kasey Michaels, *The Haunted Miss Hampshire*, 1992
Joan Overfield, *The Spirited Bluestocking*, 1992

845
SANDRA HEATH

Lucy's Christmas Angel
(New York: Signet, 1995)

Story type: Regency; Holiday Themes
Major character(s): Lucy Trevallion, Companion, Heiress; Geoffrey St. Athan, Nobleman; Emily Trevallion, Spirit
Time period(s): 1810s (1816)
Locale(s): England; Switzerland

Summary: Before she can become a true angel, youg Emily Trevallion has one last thing to do—save her cousin Lucy from being murdered by her greedy relatives and bring her home safely to the family she has never known. However, complications arise when it turns out that Emily is only visible to the attractive Geoffrey St. Athan and Lucy stubbornly refuses to believe anything he says.

Other books you might like:
Marion Chesney, *The Dreadful Debutante*, 1995
Suzanne Enoch, *Angel's Devil*, 1995
Carla Kelly, *Marian's Christmas Wish*, 1989
Lynn Kerstan, *Gwen's Christmas Ghost*, 1995
   Alicia Rasley, co-author; paranormal elements
Meg-Lynn Roberts, *Christmas Escapade*, 1994

846
SANDRA HEATH

Magic at Midnight
(New York: Signet, 1995)

Story type: Regency; Time Travel
Major character(s): Kathryn Vansomeren, Journalist, Time Traveller; Sir Dane Marchwood, Nobleman
Time period(s): 1990s; 1810s (1815)
Locale(s): Gloucestershire, England

Summary: Kathryn Vansomeren's journalistic career and marriage are in a shambles and a trip to England seems just what she needs to clear her head. However, she is totally unprepared for a journey that takes her back in time to Regency England and she is equally unprepared to fall passionately in love with Sir Dane Marchwood, a man who died years before she was born! Kathryn must have faith to see this strange tale through to its conclusion.

Other books you might like:
Janice Bennett, *Christmas Keepsake*, 1991
Janice Bennett, *A Touch of Forever*, 1992
Lynn Kerstan, *Gwen's Christmas Ghost*, 1995
   Alicia Rasley, co-author
Kasey Michaels, *The Haunted Miss Hampshire*, 1992
   no time travel elements
Kasey Michaels, *Out of the Blue*, 1992

847
CHRISTIANE HEGGAN

Passions
(New York: New American Library, 1993)

Story type: Contemporary; Romantic Suspense
Major character(s): Paige Granger McKenzie, Collector (art); Matt McKenzie, Detective; Jeremy Newman, Fiance(e)
Time period(s): 1990s

Summary: Paige McKenzie becomes implicated in a smuggling scheme and only her ex-husband, Matt, can help her. His jealousy of Paige's current fiance, wealthy Jeremy Newman, spurs him on in his desire to find Paige innocent and Jeremy guilty of it all. Love, hate, and money all combine in this suspenseful story.

Other books you might like:
Jennifer Blake, *Joy and Anger*, 1991
Velda Johnston, *Flight to Yesterday*, 1990
Judith McNaught, *Perfect*, 1993
Rebecca York, *What Child Is This?*, 1993

848
GEORGIA HELM

Mad Hatter
(Bensalem, Pennsylvania: Meteor, 1992)

Story type: Contemporary
Major character(s): Sara Dugan, Secretary, Apprentice (hat maker); Owen Dixon, Businessman (Western hat maker)
Time period(s): 1990s
Locale(s): Arizona

Summary: When grown-up Sara Dugan walks back into "bad boy" Owen Dixon's life, boldly asking for a job, against his better judgment, he hires her — and then he realizes she means more to him than he had thought and he must find a way to protect her — from himself! Old secrets, new revelations, and rekindled love.

Other books you might like:
Lori Copeland, *Darling Deceiver*, 1990
Dixie Dubois, *Home Fires*, 1992
Judy Gill, *Bad Billy Culver*, 1991
Susan Kyle, *Escapade*, 1992

849
VENITA HELTON

Sapphire
(New York: Harper, 1993)

Story type: Historical/American Civil War
Major character(s): Arienne Lloyd, Southern Belle; Joshua Langdon, Military Personnel (Union major), Spy (intelligence officer)
Time period(s): 1860s
Locale(s): Florida; New Orleans, Louisiana

Summary: When Arienne's father conspires to help the Confederacy, his ship is destroyed in battle and Arienne is rescued by Union Major Joshua Langdon. Mistrust and intrigue are the order of the day in this this romantic sea adventure. Good view of Civil War Naval history.

Other books you might like:
Katherine Kincaid, *Stormswept*, 1991
Patricia Potter, *Lightning*, 1992
Maura Seger, *Perchance to Dream*, 1989
   South wins the War
Lois Wolfe, *The Schemers*, 1991

850

EMILY HENDRICKSON

The Contrary Corinthian
(New York: Signet, 1995)

Story type: Regency
Major character(s): Phoebe Thorpe, Gentlewoman, Governess (of two children); Val Latham, Nobleman (baron), Rake
Time period(s): 1810s
Locale(s): London, England

Summary: Baron Val Latham is rumored to be the father of twins who are seen in the company of the lovely governess, Phoebe Thorpe; and Val has to admit that they do look like him. Nevertheless, he is convinced that Phoebe is out to bilk his elderly aunt and he is determined to find out why. Convoluted coincidences, clashes of wills, and clever characters add spice to this subtle, well-done romance.

Other books you might like:
Rita Boucher, *A Misbegotten Match*, 1994
Rita Boucher, *Miss Gabriel's Gambit*, 1993
   more deception
Charlotte Louise Dolan, *The Black Widow*, 1992
Margaret Evans Porter, *Road to Ruin*, 1992
   excellent characterization
Barbara Metzger, *Lady in Green*, 1993
   more deception

851

EMILY HENDRICKSON

Elizabeth's Rake
(New York, Signet, 1993)

Story type: Regency; Holiday Themes
Major character(s): Lady Elizabeth Dancy, Noblewoman; Lord David Leighton, Nobleman, Rake
Time period(s): 1810s
Locale(s): England

Summary: Heading for Surrey to relax and escape the too-attractive, rakish David Leighton, Elizabeth is appalled to find that David is also in Surrey to care for his ill father. Fate throws them together in a number of delightful ways; and as they search for a would-be murderer, they also fall in love. Valentine's Day tie-in.

Other books you might like:
Julie Caille, *A Valentine's Day Fancy*, 1992

Judy Christenberry, *Susannah's Secret*, 1993
Georgette Heyer, *Venetia*, 1959
Mary Kingsley, *A Maddening Minx*, 1992
Joan Overfield, *Bride's Leap*, 1991

852

EMILY HENDRICKSON

The Gallant Lord Ives
(New York: Signet, 1989)

Story type: Regency
Major character(s): Alissa Ffolkes, Gentlewoman, Animal Trainer (Falconer); Christopher Ivesleigh, Nobleman (Earl of Ives)
Time period(s): 1810s
Locale(s): England

Summary: When Alissa is temporarily paralyzed in an accident, Lord Ives feels responsible for her. What he doesn't realize is that he is also falling in love with her. Finely-drawn characters, interesting information on falconry during the Regency period.

Other books you might like:
Mary Balogh, *Promise of Spring*, 1990
Carola Dunn, *Lavender Lady*, 1983
Georgette Heyer, *Venetia*, 1959
Dawn Lindsey, *Dunraven's Folly*, 1989
Judith Nelson, *Patience Is a Virtue*, 1989

853

EMILY HENDRICKSON

Miss Cheney's Charade
(New York: Signet, 1994)

Story type: Regency
Major character(s): Emma Cheney, Debutante, Imposter (dresses as a boy); Peter Dancy, Nobleman, Historian
Time period(s): 1810s
Locale(s): London, England

Summary: Using her brother's clothing and invitation, debutante Emma Cheney goes to an all-male party to view the unwrapping of a mummy—and as a "boy," gets to know historian Sir Peter Dancy. He, of course, soon catches on, but plays along and enjoys the whole thing—even to the point of meeting Emma (as herself) at a party. Eventually, everything gets straightened out, even though it takes thieves to help things along. Witty and delightful.

Other books you might like:
Jo Beverley, *My Lady Notorious*, 1993
   heroine as highwayman, Georgian-style/sensual
Rita Boucher, *Miss Gabriel's Gambit*, 1993
   hidden identity
Georgette Heyer, *These Old Shades*, 1926
   heroine as boy
Evelyn Richardson, *Lady Alex's Gamble*, 995
   another cross-dressing heroine

854

EMILY HENDRICKSON

Miss Wyndham's Escapade

(New York: New American Library/Signet, 1990)

Story type: Regency
Major character(s): Marianna Wyndham, Teacher; George Mayne, Nobleman (Lord Barringer), Scientist
Time period(s): 1810s
Locale(s): England

Summary: The somewhat eccentric George Mayne comes to the rescue of Marianna Wyndham when she is accused of stealing a sapphire necklace and summarily dismissed from her teaching position in a small girls' school. Together they solve the nicely plotted mystery and find love in the process. A highly unusual hero and a winning heroine are featured in this spinoff of Hendrickson's *Queen of May*.

Other books you might like:
Georgette Heyer, *The Toll-Gate*, 1954
Annabel Laine, *The Reluctant Heiress*, 1978
Amanda Scott, *The Battling Bluestocking*, 1985
Sheila Simonson, *Lady Elizabeth's Comet*, 1985

855

EMILY HENDRICKSON

Queen of the May

(New York: New American Library, 1989)

Story type: Regency
Major character(s): Samantha "Sam" Mayne, Noblewoman; Charles Winford, Nobleman (Marquess of Laverstock), Spy
Time period(s): 1810s
Locale(s): England (Mayne Court)

Summary: A madcap heroine and a marquess who is secretly conducting a miltary investigation run headlong into excitement, danger, and love in the English countryside. More complex than the average Regency; contains several subplots.

Other books you might like:
Joan Aiken, *The Five-Minute Marriage*, 1977
Janice Bennett, *A Tempting Miss*, 1989
Annabel Laine, *The Reluctant Heiress*, 1978
Alice Chetwynd Ley, *A Reputation Dies*, 1982
Jane Lovelace, *Rolissa*, 1985

856

EMILY HENDRICKSON

The Rake and the Redhead

(New York: Signet, 1994)

Story type: Regency
Major character(s): Hyacinthe Dancy, Noblewoman; Blase Montague, Nobleman (Lord Norwood)
Time period(s): 1810s
Locale(s): England

Summary: Angered by arrogant Lord Norwood's plan to destroy her cousin's small village, as well as by his past snubs, Hyacinthe takes matters into her own hands—with disastrous, but eventually satisfyingly romantic, results.

Other books you might like:
Marion Chesney, *The Dreadful Debutante*, 1994
Cathleen Clare, *The Mistress of Mishap*, 1992
Georgette Heyer, *Faro's Daughter*, 1941
Katherine Kingsley, *King of Hearts*, 1993
Betina M. Krahn, *Midnight Magic*, 1990
   sensual

857

EMILY HENDRICKSON

A Scandalous Suggestion

(New York: Fawcett, 1991)

Story type: Regency
Major character(s): Sibyl Eagleton, Debutante; Robert Medland, Gentleman
Time period(s): 1810s
Locale(s): London, England

Summary: When shy, retiring Robert Medland saves a lovely young woman from throwing herself into the river because her debut was unsuccessful, he resigns himself to the fact that he will never see her again. However, fate takes a hand in the form of two determined mothers, and when the pair are once again united, the results are surprising—and all their mothers could want. Likeable characters and excellent Regency flavor.

Other books you might like:
Carola Dunn, *Two Corinthians*, 1989
Georgette Heyer, *The Quiet Gentleman*, 1951
Kasey Michaels, *The Anonymous Miss Addams*, 1989
Sheila Simonson, *Lady Elizabeth's Comet*, 1985

858

EMILY HENDRICKSON

The Scoundrel's Bride

(New York: Signet, 1994)

Story type: Regency
Major character(s): Chloe Maitland, Noblewoman, Heiress; Julian St. Aubyn, Rake
Time period(s): 1810s
Locale(s): London, England

Summary: Proper, inexperienced, and naive, Lady Chloe is being groomed for old Lord Twisdale; however, in the process she attracts the attention of the notorious rake Julian St. Aubyn who takes on the task of teaching her how to dress and how to flirt. At first he considers her a sweet child, but she is a quick study and soon becomes the darling of the town—causing Julian to see her in a new light.

Other books you might like:
Connie Brockway, *Promise Me Heaven*, 1994
   historical/similar plot
Mary Chase Comstock, *An Impetuous Miss*, 1994
Georgette Heyer, *These Old Shades*, 1926

Lynn Kerstan, *A Spirited Affair*, 1993
Carol Proctor, *Unlikely Guardian*, 1990

859
LISA HENDRIX

Hostage Heart
(New York: Diamond, 1994)

Story type: Historical/American West
Major character(s): Abigail Morgan, Captive, Fiance(e); Cam Garrett, Outlaw
Time period(s): 19th century
Locale(s): West

Summary: Kidnapped en route to marry a wealthy cattle baron, Abigail is an ideal hostage for Cam Garrett. Abigail's fiance is Cam's long-time enemy and this is his chance for revenge. Unfortunately, his plans are complicated by the fact that he falls in love with his captive—and she with him. Lots of funny, hot action.

Other books you might like:
Lisa Bingham, *Silken Promises*, 1994
Lori Copeland, *Promise Me Forever*, 1994
Lori Copeland, *Promise Me Today*, 1992
Carol Finch, *Montana Mistress*, 1990
Rebecca Paisley, *Rainbows and Rapture*, 1992

860
SHIRL HENKE

Bouquet
(New York: Onyx, 1994)

Story type: Contemporary/Mainstream
Major character(s): Marti Beaumont, Vintner; Adam Moreland, Drifter, Businessman (corporate tycoon)
Time period(s): 1990s
Locale(s): Napa, California; New Orleans, Louisiana

Summary: Enamored of drifter Adam Wade, Marci Beaumont, the plain daughter of the owner of a local winery, is left devastated and pregnant when Adam suddenly disappears—not knowing that he has fallen victim to thugs and been left for dead. When he reappears months later as Adam Moreland, heir to a vast winery corporation, things become more interesting—with a possessive father, killers, a beautiful sister, and a baby adding to the mix. Good winery and Napa Valley detail.

Other books you might like:
Georgia Bockoven, *Moments*, 1994
    winery environment
Catherine Coulter, *Beyond Eden*, 1991
Lisa Jackson, *Treasures*, 1994
Danielle Steel, *Thurston House*, 1983
    historical saga/Napa Valley connections
Lisa Ann Verge, *Sweet Harvest*, 1992
    winery environment

861
SHIRL HENKE

A Fire in the Blood
(New York: Leisure, 1994)

Story type: Historical/American West
Major character(s): Melissa Jacobson, Frontierswoman, Rancher; Jesse Robbins, Gunfighter
Time period(s): 1880s (1881)
Locale(s): Cheyenne, Wyoming; Texas

Summary: Hired by a cattle baron to get rid of rustlers, gunfighter Jesse meets and seduces the baron's spoiled daughter, Melissa. After their passionate affair ends in pregnancy, Melissa is sent back east and Jesse plans to disappear. However, when Melissa inherits the ranch, she returns and discovers she needs Jesse to help her rid the ranch of rustlers—and to be a father to the baby. It's not easy, but love and commitment do win out.

Other books you might like:
Deborah Camp, *Cheyenne's Shadow*, 1994
    more rustlers and ranch life/different treatment
Joan Hohl, *Silver Thunder*, 1992
Johanna Lindsey, *Angel*, 1992
    another gunslinging hero/different treatment
Dallas Schulze, *Temptation's Price*, 1992

862
SHIRL HENKE

Moonflower
(New York: Warner, 1989)

Story type: Historical/Antebellum American South
Series: Gone to Texas Trilogy
Major character(s): Deborah Manchester, Heiress (Bostonian); Rafael Flamenco, Gentleman (Creole)
Time period(s): 1830s (1836)
Locale(s): Boston, Massachusetts; Louisiana; Texas

Summary: When Rafael gallantly saves Deborah from being ravished by her own angry fiance, he accidentally compromises her—and then must marry her. Their conflicting opinions and personalities make for a fiery but passionate marriage.

Other books you might like:
Julie Garwood, *The Bride*, 1989
    Different period/Forced marriage of opposites
Linda Lael Miller, *My Darling Melissa*, 1990
Kathleen E. Woodiwiss, *Come Love a Stranger*, 1984
Kathleen E. Woodiwiss, *The Flame and the Flower*, 1972

863
SHIRL HENKE

Night Flower
(New York: Warner, 1990)

Story type: Historical/American West

Major character(s): Melanie Fleming, Suffragette, Activist (Abolitionist); Lee Velazquez, Outlaw
Time period(s): 1840s
Locale(s): Texas

Summary: A forced marriage between two opposites that attract results in the inevitable romantic conclusion, but not before a lot of sparks fly and some major disagreements take place. Deals with some serious issues, e.g. prejudice, women's rights.

Other books you might like:
Ann Gabriel, *South Texas*, 1990
    Mainstream elements
Julie Garwood, *The Bride*, 1989
    Different period/Forced marriage
Peggy Hanchar, *Tomorrow's Dream*, 1989
Betina Lindsey, *Waltz with the Lady*, 1990
    Wyoming and women's suffrage
Vivian Vaughn, *Texas Gamble*, 1990

864

SHIRL HENKE

Night Wind's Woman
(New York: Leisure, 1990)

Story type: Historical/American West
Major character(s): Orlena Valdez, Gentlewoman (governor's niece); Night Wind, Indian (half Apache), Warrior
Time period(s): 1770s (1774)
Locale(s): New Mexico

Summary: Seeking to avenge the cruel treatment of his people by the Spaniards, Night Wind, the legendary half-Apache warrior, plans to kidnap the Spanish governor's son—but ends up with his feisty niece instead. Proud and defiant, Orlena is different from any woman Night Wind has known; and he intends to have her. Their love faces severe tests but, of course, eventually triumphs. Interesting characters and good cultural detail in this passionate, rather serious story.

Other books you might like:
Beverly Bird, *Comes the Rain*, 1990
Genell Dellin, *Cherokee Dawn*, 1990
Genell Dellin, *Cherokee Nights*, 1991
Lindsay McKenna, *Sun Woman*, 1991
Deborah Smith, *Beloved Woman*, 1991

865

SHIRL HENKE

Paradise and More
(New York: Leisure, 1992)

Story type: Historical/Renaissance
Major character(s): Magdalena Valdes, Noblewoman; Aaron Torres, Military Personnel (commander for Columbus)
Time period(s): 15th century (1490s)
Locale(s): Spain; Caribbean

Summary: Although Magdalena's hopes to marry Aaron Torres are ruined when her father uses the Inquisition to destroy Aaron's family, she never forgets him, even though

he has gone to the New World; and when her life becomes unbearable in Spain, she flees and joins Aaron, claiming to be his betrothed. Aaron resists, but Magdalena is determined to both marry him and help stop an imminent war between the Spaniards and the Indians. She eventually does both, but not before the long arm of the Inquisition nearly ruins their lives. A highly passionate, sweeping historical romance filled with well-done historical detail.

Other books you might like:
Laura Gilmour Bennett, *By All That Is Sacred*, 1991
    time change elements
Bertrice Small, *Lost Love Found*, 1992
Julie Tetel, *Swept Away*, 1989
Kathleen E. Woodiwiss, *Shanna*, 1977

866

SHIRL HENKE

Return to Paradise
(New York: Leisure, 1992)

Story type: Historical/Renaissance; Historical/Exotic
Major character(s): Benjamin Torres, Doctor; Rodrigo "Rigo" De La Casas, Mercenary (long-lost brother of Benjamin); Miriam Toulon, Doctor
Time period(s): 16th century (1524)
Locale(s): Indres, Europe; Fictional Country (New World)

Summary: Dr. Benjamin Torres comes face to face with his long-lost half-brother, Rigo, and ends up saving his life—irrevocably changing his own in the process. A sweeping adventure of love, revenge, prejudice, and acceptance that takes its characters from the battlefields of Europe to the wild and exotic New World. A fast-paced, passionate double love story. Sequel to *Paradise and More*.

Other books you might like:
Beverly Byrne, *A Lasting Fire*, 1991
    first of a Trilogy
Virginia Henley, *The Pirate and the Pagan*, 1990
Iris Johansen, *The Wind Dancer*, 1991
    first of a Trilogy
Bertrice Small, *Lost Love Found*, 1992
Kathleen E. Woodiwiss, *So Worthy My Love*, 1989

867

SHIRL HENKE

Summer Has No Name
(New York: Severn House, 1990)

Story type: Contemporary/Mainstream
Major character(s): Marti Beaumont, Vintner (daughter of), Widow(er); Adam Moreland, Heir, Worker (in vineyards)
Time period(s): 20th century
Locale(s): Napa Valley, California

Summary: Young Marti Beaumont can hardly believe that the handsome new field worker in their family's vineyard is interested in her instead of her beautiful sister Reba. However, as their love grows, so does Reba's jealousy; and she sets a plan in motion that tears the lovers apart, sending a beaten and angry Adam to his wealthy father to reclaim his heritage and Marti to France to be married. When they meet again, Marti is widowed and Adam is bent on revenge.

Other books you might like:
Sally Beauman, *Destiny*, 1987
Georgia Bockoven, *A Marriage of Convenience*, 1991
Judy Gill, *Bad Billy Culver*, 1991
Danielle Steel, *Thurston House*, 1983
    three-generational saga
Patricia Strothers, *Silvermore*, 1989

868
SHIRL HENKE

Terms of Love
(New York: Leisure, 1992)

Story type: Historical/American West
Major character(s): Cassandra Clayton, Heiress; Steve Loring, Fugitive
Time period(s): 19th century
Locale(s): Colorado

Summary: Compelled by her father's will to marry and produce a son or forfeit her freighting business, tough and independent Cassie Clayton finds the ideal, low-profile man—Steve Loring, fugitive. Steve, however, wants more—and so, eventually, does Cassie, but it isn't until Steve solves the problems in his past that they are free to build a lasting life together. Hot love scenes, memorable characters, and a well-told story.

Other books you might like:
Rebecca Brandewyne, *Rainbow's End*, 1991
Theresa DiBenedetto, *Western Winds*, 1991
Johanna Lindsey, *Prisoner of My Desire*, 1991
    medieval setting
Susan Johnson, *Forbidden*, 1991

869
VIRGINIA HENLEY

The Dragon and the Jewel
(New York: Dell, 1991)

Story type: Historical/Medieval
Major character(s): Eleanor, Royalty (princess), Historical Figure; Simon de Montfort, Knight, Historical Figure
Time period(s): 13th century
Locale(s): England

Summary: This is another story of the Plantagenets. It centers around Princess Eleanor, sister to King Henry. She is married at nine and widowed at sixteen. She is so distraught over her husband's death that she takes a vow of chastity which she keeps until she meets the Norman Simon de Montfort. He vows to make her his, but it is Eleanor who makes him hers!

Other books you might like:
Shannon Drake, *Princess of Fire*, 1989
Brenda Joyce, *The Conqueror*, 1990
Mary Lide, *Ann of Cambray*, 1984
Jean Plaidy, *The Lion Justice*, 1975

870
VIRGINIA HENLEY

The Falcon and the Flower
(New York: Dell, 1989)

Story type: Historical/Medieval
Major character(s): Jasmine, Noblewoman, Bastard Daughter; Falcon de Burgh, Nobleman, Knight
Time period(s): 13th century
Locale(s): England

Summary: Raised in the arts of white witchery and taught to distrust men, Jasmine resists overtures from handsome, wealthy Falcon de Burgh; but he persists, and in spite of competition from King John himself, succeeds in winning his love.

Other books you might like:
Jude Deveraux, *The Taming*, 1989
Julie Garwood, *The Bride*, 1989
Johanna Lindsey, *When Love Awaits*, 1986
Marylyle Rogers, *Hidden Hearts*, 1989
Kathleen E. Woodiwiss, *The Wolf and the Dove*, 1974

871
VIRGINIA HENLEY
BRENDA JOYCE, Co-Author
FERN MICHAELS, Co-Author
JO GOODMAN, Co-Author

A Gift of Joy
(New York: Zebra, 1995)

Story type: Anthology; Holiday Themes
Time period(s): Indeterminate Past; 1990s
Locale(s): United States; Ireland; England

Summary: An eclectic collection of sensual Christmas novellas that include contemporary and historical, European and American settings. Included are "Christmas Eve" by Virginia Henley, "The Miracle" by Brenda Joyce, "The Bright Red Ribbon," by Fern Michaels, and "My True Love" by Jo Goodman.

Other books you might like:
Jane Bonander, *Avon Books Presents: A Christmas Together*, 1995
    historical Christmas anthology
Janet Dailey, *Santa's Little Helpers*, 1995
    contemporary Christmas anthology
Ann LaFarge, *The Joy of Christmas*, 1995
    contemporary Christmas anthology
Ellen Tanner Marsh, *A Christmas Embrace*, 1995
    snowstorms, Christmas, and a new beginning
Judith McNaught, *A Holiday of Love*, 1995
    historical Christmas anthology

872

VIRGINIA HENLEY

The Pirate and the Pagan
(New York: Dell, 1990)

Story type: Historical/Seventeenth Century
Major character(s): Summer St. Catherine, Noblewoman; Ruark Helford, Nobleman, Privateer
Time period(s): 17th century (Restoration England)
Locale(s): England

Summary: Realizing that smuggling is not the long term answer to her financial problems, Lady Summer St. Catherine takes herself to court in search of a wealthy husband—and she finds one in the form of devastatingly attractive Lord Ruark Helford. But Ruark is not quite what he seems and Summer is caught up in a struggle both political and personal as she seeks to come to terms with her feelings for her husband and his devil-may-care pirate brother Rory. A none-too-surprising twist at the end makes everything work out just fine in this lusty, highly descriptive novel of Restoration England.

Other books you might like:
Ashland Price, *Wild Irish Heather*, 1991
Rosemary Rogers, *Sweet Savage Love*, 1973
Bertrice Small, *Skye O'Malley*, 1980
Lynda Trent, *The Black Hawk*, 1991
Kathleen E. Woodiwiss, *Shanna*, 1977

873

VIRGINIA HENLEY

Seduced
(New York: Dell, 1994)

Story type: Historical/Edwardian
Major character(s): Antonia Lamb, Noblewoman, Twin; Anthony Lamb, Nobleman, Twin; Adam Savage, Guardian
Time period(s): 1900s
Locale(s): India; England; Venice, Italy

Summary: When Antonia's twin brother, Anthony, drowns at sea, she sees a way to both save her home and infuriate her new guardian, Adam Savage. She will masquerade as her brother, Tony. Adam takes ''Tony'' under his wing and educates him in all the ''ways of men.'' Antonia learns a lot, especially about men. She also realizes that she is coming to care for Adam. Eventually, the truth comes out—just in time to uncover a plot to steal all his holdings. A bawdy, sexy tale set during a particularly licentious period.

Other books you might like:
Catherine Coulter, *The Wyndham Legacy*, 1994
 dark
Brenda Joyce, *Dark Fires*, 1991
 similar style
Brenda Joyce, *Scandalous Love*, 1992
 similar style
Christina Skye, *The Black Rose*, 1991
Christina Skye, *Come the Night*, 1994
 Regency era

874

CANDICE HERN

A Change of Heart
(New York: Signet, 1995)

Story type: Regency
Major character(s): Lady Mary Haviland, Spinster, Noblewoman; Jack Raeburn, Rake, Nobleman (Marquess of Pemberton)
Time period(s): 1810s
Locale(s): England

Summary: Intrigued by both the unconventional lady and her equally unusual offer to help him find a wife, the Marquess of Pemberton joins forces with Lady Mary Haviland with wonderfully romantic, but totally unintended, results. This traditional Regency provides characters that are true to their time and excellent descriptions.

Other books you might like:
Mary Chase Comstock, *Fortune's Mistress*, 1996
 another unconventional heroine/darker than most
Georgette Heyer, *Bath Tangle*, 1955
Carla Kelly, *Mrs. Drew Plays Her Hand*, 1994
Betina M. Krahn, *The Last Bachelor*, 1994
 sensual
Evelyn Richardson, *Lady Alex's Gamble*, 1995

875

CANDICE HERN

A Proper Companion
(New York: Jove, 1995)

Story type: Regency
Major character(s): Emily Townsend, Companion, Noblewoman (impoverished); Robert, Nobleman
Time period(s): 1810s
Locale(s): Bath, England; London, England

Summary: In London for the Season, Emily Townsend attracts the attention of her employer's grandson, Robert, even though he is betrothed to another. The condition that she must marry in order to inherit from her grandfather brings numerous suitors to her door, but none measure up to Robert. Time limits and a conniving uncle cause a few problems, but true love finally triumphs in true Regency style. Sweet, traditional, and well-written.

Other books you might like:
Emily Hendrickson, *The Scoundrel's Bride*, 1994
Emma Lange, *A Heart in Peril*, 1994
Dawn Lindsey, *The American Cousin*, 1995
Phyllis Taylor Pianka, *The Thackery Jewels*, 1994
Nancy Richards-Akers, *Miss Wickham's Betrothal*, 1992

876

TERRI HERRINGTON

Her Father's Daughter

(New York: Harper Collins, 1991)

Story type: Contemporary/Mainstream
Major character(s): Corey Dobias, Heiress
Time period(s): 1990s
Locale(s): United States

Summary: When wealthy Nikos Dobias forces his three daughters to compete for his vast holdings, one daughter, Corey, refuses, setting the stage for a power struggle that has unforseen and irrevocable repercussions.

Other books you might like:
Sandra Bregman, *Reach for the Dream*, 1990
Janet Dailey, *Aspen Gold*, 1991
Barbara Delinsky, *Facets*, 1990
Susan Howatch, *The Rich Are Different*, 1977
Sara Orwig, *Favors of the Rich*, 1991

877

TERRI HERRINGTON

Silena

(New York: Harper, 1993)

Story type: Historical/American West
Major character(s): Silena Rivers, Young Woman; Sam Hawkins, Gunfighter
Time period(s): 1890s
Locale(s): Nebraska

Summary: Determined to discover the truth about her past, Silena goes to Omaha to find her only link, sharpshooter Willy Hawkins; instead, she finds his son, Sam, who has taken over for his father. When Silena returns home and finds her father shot, it is Sam who helps her solve all the mysteries. A novel of love, trust, and relationships.

Other books you might like:
Rosanne Bittner, *Outlaw Hearts*, 1993
Suzanne Ellison, *Sunburst*, 1993
Kit Gardner, *The Stolen Heart*, 1993
Joan Johnston, *Kid Calhoun*, 1993

878

LORI HERTER

Confession

(New York: Berkley, 1992)

Story type: Gothic; Contemporary/Fantasy
Series: Vampire
Major character(s): Darienne Victoire, Vampire; David de Morrissey, Vampire, Writer (playwright); Harriet Dvorak, Housewife
Time period(s): 1990s
Locale(s): Chicago, Illinois

Summary: When Harriet Dvorak becomes involved in helping her cousin Veronica locate a cure for David de Morrissey's vampire curse, she finds herself falling victim to David's considerable charm and ends up revitalizing her own marriage as a result. Third in Herter's Vampire series.

Other books you might like:
Anne Rice, *Interview with the Vampire*, 1976
Anne Rice, *Queen of the Damned*, 1988
Cheri Scotch, *The Werewolf's Kiss*, 1992
Anne Stuart, *Night of the Phantom*, 1991

879

LORI HERTER

Eternity

(New York: Berkley, 1993)

Story type: Contemporary/Fantasy; Gothic
Series: Vampire
Major character(s): Darienne Victoire, Vampire; Matthew McDowell, Actor, Singer; David de Morrissey, Writer (playwright), Vampire
Time period(s): 1990s
Locale(s): Chicago, Illinois; London, England; Switzerland

Summary: David de Morrissey's tenuous hold on his change from vampire to mortal gives him reasons to seek reassurance from other vampires. Meanwhile, his old vampire friend, Darienne, seeks to turn the love of her life, mortal actor Matthew McDowell, into a vampire. Dark and suspenseful. Fourth in Herter's Vampire series.

Other books you might like:
Susan Kay, *Phantom*, 1992
Linda Lael Miller, *Forever and the Night*, 1993
Anne Rice, *Interview with the Vampire*, 1976
Cheri Scotch, *The Werewolf's Kiss*, 1992
Anne Stuart, *Night of the Phantom*, 1991

880

LORI HERTER

Obsession

(New York: Berkley, 1991)

Story type: Contemporary/Fantasy; Gothic
Series: Vampire
Major character(s): Veronica Ames, Journalist (writer for magazine); David de Morrissey, Vampire, Writer (playwright); Darienne Victoire, Vampire
Time period(s): 1990s
Locale(s): Chicago, Illinois

Summary: When magazine writer Veronica Ames arranges for an interview with the reclusive and mysterious playwright David de Morrissey, she does not expect to come face to face with a vampire, much less fall in love with one. Darkly romantic and highly sensual, this poignant love story sets a definite gothic mood and contains some unexpectedly offbeat characters.

Other books you might like:

Shannon Drake, *Avon Books Presents: Haunting Love Stories*, 1991

    Contains stories by Drake, Betina Krahn, Linda Lael Miller, Christina Skye and Katherine Sutcliffe

Anne Rice, *Interview with the Vampire*, 1976

Anne Rice, *The Witching Hour*, 1990

Peter Straub, *Ghost Story*, 1979

Anne Stuart, *Night of the Phantom*, 1991

881

LORI HERTER

Possession

(New York: Berkley, 1992)

Story type: Contemporary/Fantasy; Gothic

Series: Vampire

Major character(s): David de Morrissey, Vampire, Writer (playwright); Alexandra Peters, Artisan (violin maker), Musician; Darienne Victoire, Vampire

Time period(s): 1990s

Locale(s): Chicago, Illinois

Summary: The sophisticated, lonely vampire David de Morrissey becomes involved with beautiful and potentially dangerous violin maker Alexandra Peters, while his fellow vampire, Darienne Victoire, meets her match in the mysterious actor Matthew McDowall. Second in Herter's vampire series.

Other books you might like:

Shannon Drake, *Avon Books Presents: Haunting Love Stories*, 1991

Anne Rice, *Interview with the Vampire*, 1976

Anne Rice, *Queen of the Damned*, 1988

Anne Rice, *The Vampire Lestat*, 1985

Anne Stuart, *Night of the Phantom*, 1991

882

LORI HERTER

The Willow File

(New York: Silhouette, 1994)

Story type: Contemporary/Fantasy

Major character(s): Arianne Lacey, Store Owner (perfume shop); Ross Briarcliff, Lawyer

Time period(s): 1990s

Locale(s): San Diego, California

Summary: Seeking to clear his family's name, Ross searches the old hotel where his grandfather supposedly killed his fiancee, Willow. However, what he finds is Arianne, Willow's great-niece, who is being haunted by her long-dead aunt. Together Ross and Arianne solve the old mystery and find passion and love in the process.

Other books you might like:

Kristin Hannah, *When Lightning Strikes*, 1994

    time travel

Sabine Kells, *Shadows on a Sunset Sea*, 1994

Patricia Simpson, *Whisper of Midnight*, 1991

Antoinette Stockenberg, *Embers*, 1994

Antoinette Stockenberg, *Emily's Ghost*, 1992

883

NORAH HESS

Devil in Spurs

(New York: Leisure, 1990)

Story type: Historical/American West

Major character(s): Jonty Rand, Imposter (dresses as a boy), Bastard Daughter; Cord McBain, Guardian (of Jonty)

Time period(s): 19th century

Locale(s): Wyoming

Summary: Dressed as a boy and raised in a brothel, Jonty is anything but ordinary; but when her grandmother dies and she becomes the responsibility of macho Cord McBain, it takes all of her strength and wit to see this through. Adventure and a little love in the Old West.

Other books you might like:

Georgina Gentry, *Nevada Nights*, 1989

Jill Marie Landis, *Wild Flower*, 1989

Elizabeth Lowell, *Reckless Love*, 1990

Deborah Simmons, *Heart's Masquerade*, 1989

    Girl as cabin boy on a privateer

Lisa Ann Verge, *The Heart's Disguise*, 1990

    Similar idea, pirate-fashion

884

NORAH HESS

Hawke's Pride

(New York: Leisure, 1991)

Story type: Historical/American West

Major character(s): Rue Delawney, Bride; Hawke Masters, Rancher

Time period(s): 19th century

Locale(s): Colorado

Summary: Hawke needs a housekeeper; Rue needs to escape her cruel stepfather's abuse. Under the circumstances, the "sale" of Rue to Hawke by her unprincipled stepfather seems logical, except to her grandfather who forces them to wed. The road to true love, however, is not smooth; and Rue and Hawke are forced to deal with an ex-mistress and a vindictive stepfather before they can be truly happy together. Realistic and passionate.

Other books you might like:

Deborah Camp, *Black-Eyed Susan*, 1990

Dorothy Garlock, *Homeplace*, 1991

Dorothy Garlock, *Midnight Blue*, 1989

Kristin James, *The Yankee*, 1990

Victoria Pade, *The Doubletree*, 1990

885

NORAH HESS

Kentucky Bride
(New York: Leisure, 1992)

Story type: Historical/American West
Major character(s): D'lise Alexander, Frontierswoman; Kane Devlin, Mountain Man
Time period(s): 1780s (1781)
Locale(s): Kentucky

Summary: Woman-wary Kane Devlin rescues D'lise Alexander from her lecherous uncle, only to discover he has a beautiful, independent, and incredibly tempting woman on his hands — permanently. Distrust, jealousy, and a meddling ex-mistress make life difficult for the pair, but love eventually triumphs in this descriptive and warm story of life on the Kentucky frontier.

Other books you might like:
Dorothy Garlock, *Homeplace*, 1991
Robin Lee Hatcher, *Promise Me Spring*, 1991
Jill Marie Landis, *Come Spring*, 1922
Elizabeth Ann Michaels, *A Jewel So Rare*, 1992
Dana Ransom, *Dakota Dawn*, 1991

886

NORAH HESS

Mountain Rose
(New York: Leisure, 1993)

Story type: Historical/American West Coast
Major character(s): Reagan O'Keefe, Orphan; Chase Donlin, Trapper
Time period(s): 1860s (1868)
Locale(s): Idaho; Oregon

Summary: Trapper Chase Donlin is shocked when the little girl he has promised to care for turns out to be an eighteen-year-old beauty — and to save her from harrassment by the other men, he tells everyone that she is his wife. Happy to have a home, Reagan agrees and quickly settles into her new role. However, when she gets involved with a kidnapped Indian woman and her baby, she ends up as a hostage until the villain who kidnapped the woman in the first place is turned in. Through all this, Reagan and Chase grow to realize that their relationship is more than just pretense, and that they really do want to build a future together. Heartwarming.

Other books you might like:
Barbara Cummings, *Frontier Fire*, 1992
Pamela K. Forrest, *Autumn Ecstasy*, 1990
Jill Marie Landis, *Come Spring*, 1992
Jill Marie Landis, *Wild Flower*, 1989
Cait Logan, *Wild Dawn*, 1992

887

NORAH HESS

Wildfire
(New York: Berkley, 1989)

Story type: Historical/American West
Major character(s): Serena Bain, Southern Belle; Josh Quade, Wagonmaster (Yankee)
Time period(s): 1860s
Locale(s): Oregon Trail

Summary: Having lost everything, including her fiance, in the Civil War, Serena Bain sets out to join her brother in Oregon. The journey there, however, is filled with struggles and challenges, not the least of which is the fiery love/hate relationship which develops between Serena and wagonmaster Josh Quade.

Other books you might like:
Cheryl Black, *Comanche Love Song*, 1989
Janet Dailey, *The Pride of Hannah Wade*, 1985
Jessie Ford, *A Different Breed*, 1988
  Clairvoyance and reincarnation are part of this unusual historical
Jill Marie Landis, *Sunflower*, 1988
Terri Valentine, *Golden Lies*, 1988

888

BRENDA HIATT

Lord Dearborn's Destiny
(Toronto: Harlequin, 1993)

Story type: Regency
Major character(s): Elinor O'Day, Debutante; Forrest Dearborn, Nobleman; Rosalind Winston, Debutante
Time period(s): 1810s
Locale(s): England

Summary: When Forrest Dearborn is told by a gypsy that his destiny is a tall, willowy blonde, he naturally zeroes in on the lovely Rosalind, the reigning belle of the season. The only thing is, his cousin Elinor keeps intruding—and she's neither tall nor blonde! Could his fortune be wrong? Dare he take matters into his own hands? And if he does, will he make the right choice? Lively, witty, and well-crafted.

Other books you might like:
Marion Chesney, *The First Rebellion*, 1989
  Maria Waverly's Family Accounts Series
Norma Lee Clark, *The Infamous Rake*, 1990
Carola Dunn, *Two Corinthians*, 1989
Georgette Heyer, *Black Sheep*, 1990
  classic Regency

889

JUDITH HILL

Hearts Enslaved
(New York: Zebra, 1994)

Story type: Historical/Pre-history

Major character(s): Rhyca, Young Woman, Abuse Victim (rape victim); Galen Mauricius, Military Personnel (Roman centurion), Slave
Time period(s): Indeterminate Past
Locale(s): England

Summary: Centurion Galen Mauricius agrees to be captured and become a slave in order to try to bring peace between the Romans and the Celts. But the job is difficult, and it is made even more so by Rhyca, a scorned pregnant rape victim, who hates him. Eventually her opinion changes when he shows kindness to a crippled child. Although they think they have no chance for a relationship, they still take care of each other and fight superstition and treachery in their search for peace. A story of pre-Arthurian Britain.

Other books you might like:
Marion Zimmer Bradley, *The Mists of Avalon*, 1988
  classic story of Arthurian Britain
Mary Ellen Gronau, *Passionate Warriors*, 1989
  later time period
Teresa Medeiros, *Lady of Conquest*, 1989
Joan Wolf, *Born of the Sun*, 1991
Joan Wolf, *The Road to Avalon*, 1988

890
JUDITH HILL
Knight's Desire
(New York: Zebra, 1992)

Story type: Historical/Medieval
Major character(s): Lady Taryn Maitland, Noblewoman; Garret d'Aubigny, Nobleman
Time period(s): 12th century
Locale(s): England

Summary: When Garret saves Lady Taryn from a disastrous marriage by implying that he is her lover, the King takes matters into his own hands and insists that they marry. Neither wants this, but once they are wed, events take a decidedly interesting turn. Good historical detail and memorable characters.

Other books you might like:
Rexanne Becnel, *The Rose of Blacksword*, 1992
Tanya Anne Crosby, *Angel of Fire*, 1992
Katherine Deauville, *Blood Red Roses*, 1991
Helen Mittermeyer, *Princess of the Veil*, 1992
Sheila O'Hallion, *Ravished Bride*, 1992

891
SANDRA HILL
The Reluctant Viking
(New York: Love Spell, 1994)

Story type: Time Travel
Major character(s): Ruby Jordan, Businesswoman, Time Traveller; Thork, Warrior (Viking)
Time period(s): 1990s; 10th century (925)
Locale(s): Jorvik, England (York)

Summary: While listening to a self-improvement tape, successful businesswoman Ruby Jordan is swept from her current life, and failing marriage, to 10th century Jorvik and into the arms of Viking knight Thork, a man who looks exactly like her husband, Jack. This sensual, action-filled tale features a very contemporary, very determined, heroine, good dialogue, humor, and a nice sense of time and place. Interesting clash of modern and medieval ideas.

Other books you might like:
Diana Gabaldon, *Outlander*, 1991
Kristin Hannah, *When Lightning Strikes*, 1994
Merline Lovelace, *Somewhere in Time*, 1994
Susan Sizemore, *In My Dreams*, 1994
Susan Sizemore, *Wings of the Storm*, 1992

892
SANDRA HILL
The Tarnished Lady
(New York: Leisure, 1995)

Story type: Historical/Medieval
Major character(s): Lady Eadyth of Hawk's Lair, Noblewoman, Beekeeper; Eirik of Ravenshire, Nobleman
Time period(s): 10th century (946)
Locale(s): England

Summary: Eirik, Lord of Ravenshire, is shocked when Lady Eadyth of Hawk's Lair marches into his castle and proposes to him; he is, nevertheless, intrigued by this independent, mysterious woman who nearly succeeds in "tarnishing" her true silvery beauty. The resulting match is anything but easy, but the truth—and love—eventually set things to rights. Lively, passionate, with lots of conflict.

Other books you might like:
Tanya Anne Crosby, *Once upon a Kiss*, 1995
Julie Garwood, *Saving Grace*, 1993
  gentler, with humor
Arnette Lamb, *Chieftain*, 1994
Patricia Potter, *The Abduction*, 1991
Amanda Quick, *Desire*, 1994

893
LINDA HILTON
Desire's Slave
(New York: Zebra, 1992)

Story type: Historical/American West Coast
Major character(s): Genevieve du Pres, Southern Belle; Rio Jackson, Scout (for wagon train)
Time period(s): 19th century
Locale(s): Sacramento, California; New Orleans, Louisiana

Summary: Sold to the highest bidder by her disreputable, brothel-owning fiance, Genevieve du Pres is much relieved to be rescued by rugged wagon train scout Rio Jackson and taken to safety in the mountains. However, winter strands them in a deserted cabin, and despite their different backgounds, by the time spring arrives they have fallen in love. A passionate, funny, and tender story of love, trust, and sharing.

Other books you might like:
Barbara Cummings, *Frontier Fire*, 1991
Pamela K. Forrest, *Autumn Ecstasy*, 1990
Jill Marie Landis, *Come Spring*, 1992
Elizabeth Lowell, *Only Mine*, 1992
Dana Ransom, *Dakota Dawn*, 1991

894
LINDA HILTON

Secret Fires
(New York: Zebra, 1991)

Story type: Historical/American West
Major character(s): Glorianna "Anna" Johnson, Rancher, Widow(er); Grant Brookington, Rancher
Time period(s): 19th century
Locale(s): Wyoming

Summary: Married and widowed within the month, Anna finds herself with a ranch, a stepson, and a fierce determination to succeed. The only problem is that she doesn't know a thing about either ranching or child raising! However, the neighboring rancher, Grant Brookington, is more than willing to teach her and together they take care of an avaricious brother-in-law and assorted other problems—including Anna's misguided notion that falling in love means giving up her independence. Heartwarming and tender.

Other books you might like:
Catherine Lanigan, *A Promise Made*, 1991
Pamela Litton, *Stardust and Whirlwinds*, 1991
Victoria Pade, *The Doubletree*, 1990
Jodi Thomas, *The Tender Texan*, 1991

895
MARTHA HIX

Caress of Fire
(New York: Zebra, 1992)

Story type: Historical/American West
Series: McLaughlin Clan
Major character(s): Lisette Keller, Cook, Runaway; Gil McLaughlin, Rancher
Time period(s): 1860s (1869)
Locale(s): Chisholm Trail, Southwest; Texas

Summary: Determined to run away to Chicago, independent young Lisette Keller sets out to convince cattleman Gil McLaughlin to take her as his cook on the drive to Abilene. Against his better judgment, he agrees on one condition—that she marry him! Lively and passionate.

Other books you might like:
Linda Ladd, *Midnight Fire*, 1991
Linda Lael Miller, *My Darling Melissa*, 1991
Eugenia Riley, *Taming Kate*, 1992
DeLoras Scott, *Devil's Delight*, 1992
DeLoras Scott, *The Miss and the Maverick*, 1990

896
MARTHA HIX

Lone Star Loving
(New York: Zebra, 1992)

Story type: Historical/American West
Series: McLaughlin Clan
Major character(s): Charity McLaughlin, Smuggler; David Fierce Hawk, Lawyer, Lawman (U.S. Marshal)
Time period(s): 19th century
Locale(s): Texas

Summary: Charity McLaughlin is on the run and can't return home; she is being chased by both the law and her rejected suitor. In this case, the "law" is Marshal David Fierce Hawk, who coincidentally had been promised to Charity in marriage. Eventually, he captures her and takes her home to Texas, just as he had promised her grandmother he would. During the the the harrowing journey, Charity begins to realize that David is her childhood "fantasy lover," and things finally begin to fall into place. Fast-paced and passionate.

Other books you might like:
Rosanne Bittner, *Outlaw Hearts*, 1993
Rosanne Bittner, *Shameless*, 1993
Carol Finch, *Promise Me Moonlight*, 1993
Phoebe Fitzjames, *Oklahoma Angel*, 1993
Kit Gardner, *The Stolen Heart*, 1993

897
MARTHA HIX

Wild Texas Rose
(New York: Zebra, 1990)

Story type: Historical/American West
Major character(s): Mariah Rose McGuire, Fiance(e) (of the hero's neighbor); Whit Reagor, Rancher
Time period(s): 1880s (1882)
Locale(s): Texas

Summary: Mariah comes to Texas to marry Joseph and ends up trying to fend off his handsome, womanizing neighbor, to whom she is involuntarily attracted. Drought, range wars, and plenty of passionate action.

Other books you might like:
Betina Lindsey, *Waltz with the Lady*, 1990
Evelyn Rogers, *Texas Kiss*, 1989
Victoria Thompson, *Bold Texas Embrace*, 1987
Victoria Thompson, *Fortune's Lady*, 1990
Vivian Vaughn, *Texas Gamble*, 1990

898
TAMI HOAG

Dark Paradise
(New York: Bantam, 1994)

Story type: Contemporary; Romantic Suspense
Major character(s): Marilee Jennings, Court Reporter (former); J.D. Rafferty, Rancher

Time period(s): 1990s
Locale(s): New Eden, Montana

Summary: Marilee Jennings heads for Montana to visit her old friend, Lucy, only to arrive and be told that Lucy has been killed in a hunting accident. The bearer of this news is rancher J.D. Rafferty—a man who hates all outsiders, especially those who own ranches. Marilee suspects murder, and the deeper she probes, the more murders take place. Obviously, she is doing something the murderer doesn't like. Determined and courageous, Marilee eventually must do battle with the whole town.

Other books you might like:
Christine Michels, *Danger's Kiss*, 1994
Karen Robards, *Maggy's Child*, 1994
    dark and rather dangerous
Nora Roberts, *Carnal Innocence*, 1992
Nora Roberts, *Divine Evil*, 1992

899

TAMI HOAG

Lucky's Lady

(New York: Doubleday, 1992)

Story type: Contemporary/Mainstream
Major character(s): Serena Sheridan, Psychologist; Lucky Doucet, Guide
Time period(s): 1990s
Locale(s): Louisiana

Summary: When Serena Sheridan returns home to the Louisiana bayous to see her grandfather, she hires the sensual and dangerously handsome Lucky Doucet to guide her to the fish camp where her grandfather has gone. Their travels through the steamy swamp result in equally steamy passion, and in different ways, they each learn they have met their match.

Other books you might like:
Kit Bakker, *Julianne's Song*, 1990
    Cajun Melodies Series
Jennifer Blake, *Joy and Anger*, 1991
Elinor Lynley, *Song of the Bayou*, 1990
    historical Louisiana
Virginia Nielsen, *Jessica's Song*, 1990
    Cajun Melodies Series
Nora Roberts, *Carnal Innocence*, 1992

900

TAMI HOAG

Still Waters

(New York: Bantam, 1992)

Story type: Contemporary/Mainstream; Romantic Suspense
Major character(s): Elizabeth Stuart, Journalist, Divorced Person; Dan Jantzen, Police Officer (sheriff)
Time period(s): 1990s
Locale(s): Stillwater, Minnesota

Summary: A brutal murder and Elizabeth Stuart's hard-hitting stories force the Amish town of Stillwater to take another look at itself — and it doesn't like what it sees. When another murder is discovered, this time implicating Elizabeth's son, Elizabeth and town Sheriff Dan Jantzen must begin to look for unpleasant answers in unlikely places. Suspenseful and romantic with a dash of fun.

Other books you might like:
Jill Barkin, *Hot Streak*, 1990
Jennifer Blake, *Joy and Anger*, 1991
Nora Roberts, *Carnal Innocence*, 1992
Nora Roberts, *Divine Evil*, 1992
Phyllis A. Whitney, *The Glass Flame*, 1978

901

KARLA HOCKER

A Deceitful Heart

(New York: Zebra, 1993)

Story type: Regency; Historical/Fantasy
Major character(s): Lady Caroline Dundas, Noblewoman, Debutante; Simon Renshaw, Lawyer (barrister)
Time period(s): 1810s
Locale(s): England

Summary: Lady Caroline Dundas hasn't found a husband in the Colonies, so her father takes her to London to be presented to the ton by her grandfather, the Duke. Unfortunately, the old Duke has died in the interim and Caroline and her father arrive in the middle of a search for the rightful heir. Simon Renshaw, the family solicitor, has taken it upon himself to protect the family from dishonest claimants and he challenges her relationship to the late Duke. He is not immune to her beauty, however, and things take an unusual turn when a ghost gets into the fray. Charming and suspenseful.

Other books you might like:
Michelle Brandon, *Touch of Heaven*, 1992
    American West setting
Jude Deveraux, *Wishes*, 1989
    American setting
Kasey Michaels, *The Haunted Miss Hampshire*, 1992
Kasey Michaels, *Out of the Blue*, 1992
Laura Parker, *For Love's Sake Only*, 1991

902

KARLA HOCKER

June Love

(New York: Zebra, 1995)

Story type: Regency
Major character(s): Theadora Stone, Historian; Stuart Archer, Nobleman (Viscount Stanmore)
Time period(s): 1810s
Locale(s): Ravensbrook, England; London, England

Summary: Miss Theadora Stone is an historian enchanted with the mystery surrounding the long dead Lady Arbella and her child. Stuart Archer, Viscount Stanmore hires Thea to discover Lady Arbella's connection to his family. Both are eager to uncover the secrets of the past and as they work together, they discover they have more in common than just the dry and dusty past.

Other books you might like:
Jean R. Ewing, *Rogue's Reward*, 1995
  mystery elements
Jean R. Ewing, *Virtue's Reward*, 1995
  mystery elements
Dawn Lindsey, *The American Cousin*, 1995
  mystery elements
Kasey Michaels, *The Haunted Miss Hampshire*, 1992
  ghostly elements

903
KARLA HOCKER

Lady Maryann's Dilemma
(New York: Zebra, 1990)

Story type: Regency
Major character(s): Maryann Rivington, Noblewoman, Debutante; Stephen Farrell, Gentleman
Time period(s): 1810s
Locale(s): London, England

Summary: Determined not to make the marital mistakes of her sisters, independent Lady Maryann Rivington agrees to a betrothal to a wealthy older man who shares her ideas of a perfect marriage—each to his/her own! But then she meets Stephen Farrell, who causes her heart to act strangely; and her views on love and marriage change radically.

Other books you might like:
Mary Balogh, *Promise of Spring*, 1990
Clare Darcy, *Letty*, 1980
Amanda Scott, *The Dauntless Miss Wingrave*, 1989
Joan Smith, *Cousin Cecelia*, 1990
Sheila Walsh, *A Highly Respectable Marriage*, 1983

904
KATHRYN HOCKETT

Gentle Warrior
(New York: Zebra, 1992)

Story type: Historical/Medieval
Major character(s): Rorick Wolframson, Explorer, Settler; Wenona, Indian (Algonquin)
Time period(s): 9th century (875)
Locale(s): North America

Summary: When Viking Rorick is shipwrecked and washed ashore on the North American coast, he is astonished by the land and its people. He's regarded as a god by Wenona and her shaman mother, and as he comes to appreciate the Algonquin ways and customs, he comes to love Wenona, too. However, when Vikings show up to take him home, they both have some difficult decisions to make. A sensual love story that addresses some serious aspects of intercultural similarities and differences.

Other books you might like:
Kathryn Lynn Davis, *Sing to Me of Dreams*, 1990
Kathleen Herbert, *Bride of the Spear*, 1990
Lynn Armistead McKee, *Woman of the Mists*, 1991
Marylyle Rogers, *Chanting the Dawn*, 1991

Joan Wolf, *Daughter of the Red Deer*, 1991

905
KATHRYN HOCKETT

Outlaw Seduction
(New York: Zebra, 1993)

Story type: Historical/American West
Major character(s): Bliss Harrison, Bounty Hunter; Travis La Mont, Journalist, Photographer
Time period(s): 19th century (late)
Locale(s): West

Summary: Bounty hunter Bliss Harrison is after alleged bank robber Travis La Mont, but when she catches him she can't resist his attraction. In spite of her feelings, however, she takes him in; and it is only when he is endangered by the real robbers, that she rescues him and is convinced of his innocence. Lots of humor and fast-paced action.

Other books you might like:
Teresa Hart, *Hearts Are Wild*, 1993
Alisa McBride, *Love's Bounty*, 1993
  audio tape
Rebecca Paisley, *Rainbows and Rapture*, 1992
Dana Ransom, *Dakota Destiny*, 1993

906
JOAN HOHL

Compromises
(New York: Zebra, 1995)

Story type: Contemporary
Major character(s): Frisco Styer, Accountant; Lucas MacCanna, Businessman
Time period(s): 1990s
Locale(s): Philadelphia, Pennsylvania

Summary: Lucas MacCanna is willing to help Frisco Styer's father out of deep financial difficulty under one condition— that she move in with him! In a situation just made for romance, the possibilities are endless as these two strong willed adversaries learn to become friends and finally lovers. A humorous, realistic, battle-of-wills romance.

Other books you might like:
Barbara Bretton, *Maybe This Time*, 1995
Jayne Ann Krentz, *Perfect Partners*, 1992
Jayne Ann Krentz, *Wildest Hearts*, 1993
Susan Elizabeth Phillips, *Fancy Pants*, 1989
Susan Elizabeth Phillips, *It Had to Be You*, 1994

907

JOAN HOHL
BOBBY HUTCHINSON, Co-Author
EVELYN ROGERS, Co-Author
BOBBI SMITH, Co-Author

Love Beyond Time

(New York: Avon, 1994)

Story type: Anthology; Time Travel

Summary: This diverse collection of four novellas, each making use of the time-travel convention, includes: "Turquoise Yesterdays" by Joan Hohl, "Forever" by Bobby Hutchinson, "Always Paradise" by Evelyn Rogers, and "Time-Stolen Love" by Bobbi Smith.

Other books you might like:
Madeline Baker, *Enchanted Crossings*, 1994
   anthology
Sandra Canfield, *The Loving*, 1992
Merline Lovelace, *Somewhere in Time*, 1994
Constance O'Day-Flannery, *A Time for Love*, 1991

908

JOAN HOHL

Shadow's Kiss

(New York: Dell, 1994)

Story type: Historical/American West; Historical/Fantasy
Major character(s): Darcy Flynn, Heiress, Madam (brothel owner); Jonathan Stuart, Spirit, Gentleman
Time period(s): 19th century
Locale(s): Denver, Colorado

Summary: When proper and gentle Darcy Flynn discovers she owns an infamous Denver brothel, she plans to leave immediately. However, Jonathan Stuart, a Southern gentleman from the spirit world convinces her to stay. As she gets to know her "girls," she comes to regard them as worthwhile and teaches them to make new lives for themselves. Several love stories intertwine in this nicely done story; there's even love for Darcy and Jonathan.

Other books you might like:
Barbara Faith, *Gamblin' Man*, 1993
   no paranormal elements
Roslynn Griffith, *The Wind Casts No Shadow*, 1994
LaVyrle Spencer, *Forgiving*, 1990
   no paranormal elements
Antoinette Stockenberg, *Emily's Ghost*, 1992
   contemporary
Isabel Whitfield, *Bodie Bride*, 1992
   no paranormal elements/proper heroine

909

JOAN HOHL

Silver Thunder

(New York: Dell, 1992)

Story type: Historical/American West

Major character(s): Jessica Randall, Young Woman; Duncan "Segundo" Frazer, Foreman (ranch foreman), Indian (Half-Shoshone)
Time period(s): 1890s (1892)
Locale(s): Wyoming

Summary: Duncan Frazer has been in Scotland for twenty years and wants to return unrecognized to his home in Wyoming. He hopes to catch the cattle rustlers who want to ruin him and buy his ranch, so he takes a job as foreman at a neighboring ranch. The ranch, however, has more to offer than just a job — young Jessica, tomboy and feminist, intrigues him more than he would like, and between getting rid of the rustlers and getting Jessica, Duncan (Segundo) has his hands full.

Other books you might like:
Catherine Anderson, *Indigo Blue*, 1992
Gwen Cleary, *Victoria's Ecstasy*, 1990
Johanna Lindsey, *Savage Thunder*, 1989
Victoria Thompson, *Wild Texas Promise*, 1990

910

ARLENE HOLLIDAY

Wild Texas Blossom

(New York: Zebra, 1994)

Story type: Historical/American West
Major character(s): Sassy Mahoney, Young Woman; Ty Beaumont, Lawman (former Texas Ranger)
Time period(s): 19th century (late)
Locale(s): Texas; New Mexico

Summary: Appropriately named, Sassy can hold her own with any man—until she meets ex-Texas Ranger Ty Beaumont. Together they travel though the Southwest as husband and wife in a search to clear his name of past misdeeds. A revenge-driven hero and a "sassy" heroine result in plenty of passion and action in this highly sensual historical.

Other books you might like:
Carol Finch, *Promise Me Moonlight*, 1993
   highly sensual
Phoebe Fitzjames, *Oklahoma Angel*, 1993
   highly sensual
Brenda Joyce, *The Fires of Paradise*, 1991
   highly sensual/darker than most/chase elements
Rebecca Paisley, *Rainbows and Rapture*, 1992
   chase elements/sensual/humorous

911

STEF ANN HOLM

Firefly

(New York: Leisure, 1990)

Story type: Historical/American West
Major character(s): Kristianna Bergendahl, Farmer; Stone Boucher, Trapper, Runaway (from his heritage and father)
Time period(s): 1830s (1835)
Locale(s): Minnesota; St. Louis, Missouri

Summary: The son of a successful fur trader, Stone Boucher, decides, against his father's wishes, to experience the frontier wilderness first hand. However, the wilderness also contains Kristianna Bergendahl, a farmer who's views on the use of land differ vastly from Stone's. They do, however, agree on their feelings for one another, but they can't be happy until they resolve a number of basic issues, including Stone's estrangement from his father. Gentle and realistic.

Other books you might like:
Rosanne Bittner, *Montana Woman*, 1990
Ann Gabriel, *South Texas*, 1990
Dorothy Garlock, *Nightrose*, 1990
Norah Hess, *Wildfire*, 1989
Jill Marie Landis, *Rose*, 1990

912

STEF ANN HOLM

King of the Pirates
(New York: Pocket, 1994)

Story type: Historical/Exotic
Major character(s): Catherine Le Clerc, Widow(er); Danton Luis Cristobal, Pirate, Nobleman (banished marquis)
Time period(s): 1710s (1719)
Locale(s): Madagascar; Zanzibar

Summary: Marquis-turned-buccaneer Danton Cristobal likes his life as it is—without any attachments; but when he rescues a disagreeable widow, Catherine, and her daughter and takes them to his island home, his life will never be the same again. Danger and adventure abound as Catherine and Danton gain strength to deal with their separate pasts and forge a new future together. Exotic setting.

Other books you might like:
Elizabeth DeLancey, *Sea of Dreams*, 1992
Diana Haviland, *Pirate's Kiss*, 1992
Laura Kinsale, *Seize the Fire*, 1989
Laurie McBain, *Moonstruck Madness*, 1977
Meagan McKinney, *Till Dawn Tames the Night*, 1991

913

STEF ANN HOLM

Liberty Rose
(New York: Pocket, 1993)

Story type: Historical
Major character(s): Liberty Rose Courtney, Servant (chambermaid); Anthony Fielding, Rake, Landowner
Locale(s): England

Summary: In order to get her aunt out of debtor's prison, chambermaid Liberty Rose accepts the job of "temporary fiance" to alcoholic Anthony Fielding during his grandfather's visit. However, the pretense eventually becomes real as Liberty Rose brings love and healing into Anthony's life, and to the joy of his entire household. Sweet, gentle, and warm.

Other books you might like:
Marion Chesney, *Lady Fortescue Steps Out*, 1993
Katherine Kingsley, *King of Hearts*, 1993

Kathryn Kramer, *Lady Rogue*, 1991
Joan Smith, *The Spanish Lady*, 1993
Marlene Suson, *The Errant Earl*, 1989

914

STEF ANN HOLM

Seasons of Gold
(New York: Pocket, 1992)

Story type: Historical/American West
Major character(s): Holly Dancer, Widow(er), Mine Owner; Jackson Ledgeway Steele, Detective, Cowboy
Time period(s): 1870s (1877)
Locale(s): Deadwood Gulch, South Dakota

Summary: Independent, strong-willed Holly Dancer throws a wrench into Jack Steele's murder investigation. Although her shameful marriage gives her reason to murder her husband, she is innocent—but she isn't vindicated until she is captured by the real murderer! A sensual, adventurous mystery laced with humor.

Other books you might like:
Rosanne Bittner, *Montana Woman*, 1990
Ann Gabriel, *South Texas*, 1990
Norah Hess, *Wildfire*, 1989
Jill Marie Landis, *Sunflower*, 1988

915

STEF ANN HOLM

Weeping Angel
(New York: Pocket, 1995)

Story type: Historical/American West
Major character(s): Amelia Marshall, Spinster; Frank Brody, Saloon Keeper/Owner
Time period(s): 1890s (1897)
Locale(s): Weeping Angel, Idaho

Summary: Amelia Marshall considers herself an old maid who has better things to do than ogle Weeping Angel's newest saloon owner at the end of the railroad platform or wonder why he, of all people, has ordered a parlor piano. Amelia has ordered a piano herself, but when only one arrives on the afternoon train, she is determined that it won't be going into Frank Brody's saloon. When the two agree to share the piano, neither suspects that the temporary arrangement will lead to a lifetime of love.

Other books you might like:
Candace Camp, *Rosewood*, 1991
Pamela Morsi, *Courting Miss Hattie*, 1991
Pamela Morsi, *Runabout*, 1994
LaVyrle Spencer, *The Gamble*, 199
Jodi Thomas, *Forever in Texas*, 1995

916

DEE HOLMES

The Farrell Marriage

(New York: Silhouette, 1992)

Story type: Contemporary
Major character(s): Christine Farrell, Spouse; Reid Farrell, Spy (undercover agent)
Time period(s): 1990s
Locale(s): United States

Summary: Undercover agent Reid Farrell returns from the "dead" to try to pick up the pieces of his life with his wife and teen-aged children. But it will take a lot of convincing, and a lot of love and understanding, before his family will believe that he truly has gotten his priorities straight. Fascinating character-study.

Other books you might like:
Janet Dailey, *Terms of Surrender*, 1982
Sandra Marton, *Night Fires*, 1991
Patricia Potter, *Island of Dreams*, 1991
LaVyrle Spencer, *Bittersweet*, 1990

917

MARY MAYER HOLMES

Savage Tides

(New York: Popular Library, 1989)

Story type: Historical/Victorian America
Major character(s): Augusta Mayhew, Mail Order Bride; Elijah, Lighthouse Keeper
Time period(s): 1830s (1831)
Locale(s): Maine (coastal island)

Summary: When plain, dependable Augusta Mayhew answers a newspaper ad to become the bride of a "wickie," she is surprised to find that her groom is a handsome, twice-married, lighthouse keeper. Mystery and romance are the order of the day.

Other books you might like:
Diane Day, *The Stone House*, 1989
    Contemporary setting
Jo Ann Ferguson, *At the Rainbow's End*, 1989
    Yukon setting
Barbara Hargis, *Heart Song*, 1990
Elisabeth Ogilvie, *Jennie About to Be*, 1984
    Early 19th Century Scotland and Maine
Penelope Williamson, *A Wild Yearning*, 1990

918

VICTORIA HOLT

The Captive

(New York: Doubleday, 1989)

Story type: Gothic
Major character(s): Rosetta Cranleigh, Gentlewoman; Simon Perrivale, Nobleman (bastard son), Fugitive (from a murder charge)

Time period(s): 1800s
Locale(s): Mediterranean; Africa (Coast)

Summary: After being shipwrecked and stranded on an island with Simon, captured by pirates, and sold to a Turkish pasha, plucky Rosetta Cranleigh heads alone to England to become a governess to one of Simon's young relatives. Simon had been wrongly accused of the murder of his step-brother and Rosetta hopes to prove his innocence so that he can return to England.

Other books you might like:
Dorothy Eden, *Winterwood*, 1967
Isabelle Holland, *Counterpoint*, 1980
Sara Hylton, *The Whispering Glade*, 1985
Carola Salisbury, *An Autumn in Araby*, 1983
Carola Salisbury, *The Winter Bride*, 1970

919

VICTORIA HOLT

Snare of Serpents

(New York: Doubleday, 1990)

Story type: Gothic
Major character(s): Davina Glentyre, Teacher
Locale(s): Edinburgh, Scotland; Kimberley, South Africa

Summary: Accused but not convicted of murdering her father, Davina Glentyre takes her tattered reputation and leaves Scotland to reestablish a school in Kimberley, South Africa. Along the way she befriends Roger and Myra Lestrange; but when Myra becomes mysteriously sick, Davina must once again fight for her reputation as well as her life. Another offering from a classic gothic writer.

Other books you might like:
Catherine Gaskin, *Fiona*, 1970
Sharon Gillenwater, *Highland Whispers*, 1989
Sara Hylton, *The Talisman of Set*, 1984
Elsie Lee, *Dark Moon, Lost Lady*, 1976
Phyllis A. Whitney, *Blue Fire*, 1961

920

KAY HOOPER

Amanda

(New York: Bantam, 1995)

Story type: Contemporary; Gothic
Major character(s): Amanda Daulton, Heiress, Amnesiac (repressed childhood memories); Walker McLelland, Lawyer
Time period(s): 1990s
Locale(s): Glory, South (a plantation/estate)

Summary: She might be just another fortune hunter—or she might really be Amanda, Jesse Daulton's long-missing granddaughter. But whoever she is, Jesse claims her as his own and sets forces in motion that make her the target not only of bitter family resentment, but of a determined killer, as well. A 20-year-old murder is at the heart of this mystery and the threatened heroine, long-kept family secrets, and brooding atmosphere add a decidedly gothic touch. Sensual.

Other books you might like:
Tami Hoag, *Dark Paradise*, 1994
Karen Robards, *Maggy's Child*, 1994
Nora Roberts, *Divine Evil*, 1992
Maggie Shayne, *Kiss of the Shadow Man*, 1994
Phyllis A. Whitney, *Woman Without a Past*, 1991

921
KAY HOOPER

Crime of Passion
(New York: Avon, 1991)

Story type: Romantic Suspense
Major character(s): Lane Montana, Businesswoman, Detective (finder of lost objects); Trey Fortier, Police Officer (lieutenant)
Time period(s): 1990s
Locale(s): Atlanta, Georgia

Summary: When Lane Montana, "finder of lost objects," goes to a prospective client's house and finds him dead, she determines to find the killer before she is arrested as a suspect herself. Things become nicely complicated when she and police lieutenant Trey Fortier begin to fall in love. First in a series of three.

Other books you might like:
Lisbeth Chance, *Cutting Edge*, 1985
Sandra Marton, *Night Fires*, 1991
Elizabeth Peters, *Naked Once More*, 1989
Chloe Summers, *No Easy Task*, 1991
Sherryl Woods, *Body and Soul*, 1989
   first of a trilogy

922
KAY HOOPER
KATHLEEN KANE, Co-Author
KAREN LOCKWOOD, Co-Author
BONNIE K. WINN, Co-Author

Hearts of Gold
(New York: Jove, 1994)

Story type: Anthology; Holiday Themes
Time period(s): 19th century

Summary: This collection of Valentine's Day stories set during the 19th century includes "Masquerade," "Betrayed Hearts," "Perfect Mates," and "Heart of Erin." Contributors are Kay Hooper, Kathleen Kane, Karen Lockwood, and Bonnie K. Winn and the settings for the stories range from Regency England to the American West.

Other books you might like:
Mary Balogh, *A Regency Valentine*, 1991
   anthology of 5 Valentine's Day Regencies
Julie Caille, *A Valentine's Day Fancy*, 1992
   Regency Valentines
Emily Hendrickson, *Elizabeth's Rake*, 1993
   Regency with a Valentine's Day tie-in.
Rebecca Paisley, *Love Potion*, 1994
   4 novellas linked by Cupid's "love potion."

923
KAY HOOPER

The Matchmaker
(New York: Dell, 1991)

Story type: Historical/Victorian America
Major character(s): Cyrus Fortune, Wealthy (millionaire); Julia Drummond, Socialite
Time period(s): 1870s (1870); 1900s (1902)
Locale(s): Richmond, Virginia

Summary: Julia, hopelessly and unhappily married to a controlling, abusive husband, is threatened by enigmatic, rich, worldly Cyrus who wants her for himself.

Other books you might like:
Leigh Riker, *Morning Rain*, 1991
   contemporary
Eugenia Riley, *Rogue's Mistress*, 1991
Danielle Steel, *Crossings*, 1982

924
KAY HOOPER

Star-Crossed Lovers
(New York: Doubleday, 1990)

Story type: Contemporary
Major character(s): Michele Logan, Insurance Investigator; Ian Stuart, Architect
Time period(s): 1990s
Locale(s): Martinique; Atlanta, Georgia

Summary: Taught to hate each other from birth, Ian Stuart and Michele Logan fall in love with each other and then are faced with the seemingly insurmountable problem of getting their warring families to end a 500 year old feud. A Romeo and Juliet story with a touch of magic thrown in for good measure.

Other books you might like:
Rebecca Brandewyne, *Forever My Love*, 1982
   family feuds medieval setting
Jayne Ann Krentz, *The Golden Chance*, 1990
Judith McNaught, *Double Standards*, 1984
Laura Taylor, *Jade's Passion*, 1990
Katherine Vickery, *Flame Across the Highlands*, 1990
   family feuds medieval setting

925
KAY HOOPER

The Wizard of Seattle
(New York: Bantam, 1993)

Story type: Time Travel
Major character(s): Serena Smyth, Wizard (apprentice); Richard Merlin, Wizard, Businessman
Time period(s): 1990s; Indeterminate Past
Locale(s): Seattle, Washington; Atlantis, Mythical Place

Summary: Richard, multimillionaire businessman and Master Wizard, defies ancient taboos by taking a young woman,

Serena Smyth, as an apprentice. So much anger forces him and Serena back in time to Atlantis, where they find sinister, hateful people determined to destroy each other. Their future depends upon whether or not they can change the past. Dark, convoluted, and unusual.

Other books you might like:
Jessica Bryan, *Across a Wine-Dark Sea*, 1991
Jessica Bryan, *Dawn on a Jade Sea*, 1992
Marilyn Campbell, *Stolen Dreams*, 1994
Saranne Dawson, *The Enchanted Land*, 1992
 fairy-tale quality

926
JENNIFER HORSMAN

Awaken My Fire
(New York: Avon, 1992)

Story type: Historical/Medieval
Major character(s): Lady Roshelle Marie of Reales, Noble-woman (countess); Vincent de la Eresman, Nobleman (Duke of Suffolk)
Time period(s): 15th century (1422)
Locale(s): France

Summary: Young Countess Roshelle really believes the curse placed on her will cause any man to die who tries to take her virginity; after all, two are already dead. Vincent de la Eresman, however, is drawn to her, and as they begin to love and trust each other, powerful forces begin to move against them to keep their love from becoming a reality. A lyrical, mystical, and exquisitely sensual portrayal of the High Middle Ages.

Other books you might like:
Kathryn Lynn Davis, *Child of Awe*, 1990
Virginia Henley, *The Falcon and the Flower*, 1991
Helen Mittermeyer, *Princess of the Veil*, 1992
Judith Merkle Riley, *In Pursuit of the Green Lion*, 1990
Marylyle Rogers, *Dark Whispers*, 1991

927
JENNIFER HORSMAN

A Kiss in the Night
(New York: Avon, 1995)

Story type: Historical/Renaissance
Major character(s): Linness of Sauvage, Psychic, Imposter; Lord Paxton Gaillard Chamberlain, Knight, Nobleman
Time period(s): 16th century (1513-1519)
Locale(s): France

Summary: When Paxton literally snatches the condemned witch Linness of Sauvage from the burning stake, they end up sharing a night of passion and the knowledge that whatever happens, they are forever linked. But fate immediately separates them; and when Paxton returns to his home, Chateau Gaillard, six years later, it is to find Linness married to his twin brother. Divided loyalties, a love that will not be denied, and dangerous intrigue highlight a story that is lyrical, intensely romantic, and highly sensual.

Other books you might like:
Alice Borchardt, *Devoted*, 1995
 well-written and involving
Laura Kinsale, *For My Lady's Heart*, 1993
 emotionally involving
Mary Lide, *Ann of Cambray*, 1984
Elizabeth Lowell, *Enchanted*, 1994
 highly sensual and emotionally involving
Judith Merkle Riley, *In Pursuit of the Green Lion*, 1990
 appealing characters/more humorous

928
JENNIFER HORSMAN

Virgin Star
(New York: Avon, 1993)

Story type: Historical
Major character(s): Shalyn, Amnesiac; Sean Seanessy, Sea Captain
Locale(s): England; At Sea

Summary: When infamous Captain Sean Seanessy finds a beautiful, unconscious woman at his mansion door, he instinctively knows his life is in for major change. However, he is ready to set sail on a mission to the Orient and wants to discover her identity quickly, but Shalyn can only remember that her life is in danger! Eventually, of course, they set sail together—and then the real action begins. Fast-paced and lusty.

Other books you might like:
Susan Johnson, *Sinful*, 1992
Catherine Lanigan, *Romancing the Stone*, 1984
Susannah Leigh, *Jade Dawn*, 1993
Christina Skye, *The Ruby*, 1992
Katherine Sutcliffe, *Shadow Play*, 1991

929
JENNIFER HORSMAN

With One Look
(New York: Avon, 1994)

Story type: Historical/Victorian; Historical/Fantasy
Major character(s): Jade Terese Devon, Handicapped (blind), Religious (novice); Victor Nolte, Gentleman
Time period(s): 1860s
Locale(s): New Orleans, Louisiana

Summary: Intrigued by novice Jade Devon's blindness and sordid past, Victor Nolte is determined to solve the mysteries surrounding her and help her to see once again. Her convent superiors are no help, but Jade's own remarkable memory and uncanny skills help with the solution. Although he makes love to her, Victor claims not to want her love; but a final confrontation makes them both see the light. A dark, hot romance filled with voodoo, murder, and kidnapping.

Other books you might like:
Catherine Coulter, *The Wyndham Legacy*, 1994
 dark/earlier British setting

Christina Dodd, *Candle in the Window*, 1991
   blind heroine/totally different treatment/gentle
Brenda Joyce, *Scandalous Love*, 1992
   hot and passionate/British setting
Sue Rich, *Mistress of Sin*, 1994
   mystical and exotic
Cheri Scotch, *The Werewolf's Kiss*, 1992
   voodoo, New Orleans, and werewolves

930

PHYLLIS HOUSEMAN

There Is a Season
(Bensalem, Pennsylvania: Meteor, 1992)

Story type: Contemporary
Major character(s): Beth Cristie, Scientist (biologist); Joshua Hunter, Scientist (geologist); Phil Price, Filmmaker
Time period(s): 1990s
Locale(s): Mt. St. Helens, Washington

Summary: Engaged in monitoring its ongoing seismic activity, Beth and Joshua meet on Mt. St. Helens' slopes and end up having to deal with some personal seismic activity of their own. Other members of the various scientific teams add to the problems, and jealousy, anger, and the volcano itself contribute to some near disasters. Interesting and somewhat technical.

Other books you might like:
Jennifer Greene, *Pink Topaz*, 1992
Jayne Ann Krentz, *Silver Linings*, 1991
Paula Detmer Riggs, *Rough Passage*, 1991
Frances Williams, *The Road to Forever*, 1991

931

LINDA HOWARD

After the Night
(New York: Pocket, 1995)

Story type: Contemporary; Romantic Suspense
Major character(s): Faith Devlin Hardy, Widow(er), Businesswoman (travel company owner); Gray Rouillard, Businessman
Time period(s): 1990s; 1970s
Locale(s): Prescott, Louisiana

Summary: Driven from town one night twelve years ago by an angry Gray Rouillard, Faith Devlin, now successful and self-assured, has returned to find some answers. Despite Gray's fury, Faith is determined to get what she came for, but when she digs too deeply, the atmosphere becomes threatening and people start to disappear—just as Gray's father and Faith's mother did years before. Passionate, dark, and hard-hitting.

Other books you might like:
Rebecca Brandewyne, *Dust Devil*, 1996
Tami Hoag, *Dark Paradise*, 1994
Kay Hooper, *Amanda*, 1995
Nora Roberts, *Carnal Innocence*, 1992

932

LINDA HOWARD (Pseudonym of Linda Howington)

Angel Creek
(New York: Pocket, 1991)

Story type: Historical/American West
Major character(s): Dee Swann, Landowner; Lucas Cochran, Rancher
Time period(s): 1860s
Locale(s): Prosper, Colorado

Summary: Dee Swann "owns" Angel Creek, and the surrounding ranchers, including wealthy and arrogant Lucas Cochran, all want the water and will do just about anything to get it. But when Dee is wounded in a raid, Lucas takes her home to heal—and as they fall in love, Dee must face difficult questions about the reasons for Lucas' love and the differences in their lifestyles. Passionate and realistic.

Other books you might like:
LaRee Bryant, *Sweet Texas Fury*, 1990
Gwen Cleary, *Victoria's Ecstasy*, 1990
Pamela Litton, *Stardust and Whirlwinds*, 1991
Patricia Rice, *Cheyenne's Lady*, 1989

933

LINDA HOWARD

Dream Man
(New York: Pocket, 1995)

Story type: Contemporary; Romantic Suspense
Major character(s): Marlie Keen, Psychic; Dane Hollister, Detective—Police
Time period(s): 1990s
Locale(s): Orlando, Florida

Summary: Free from her debilitating visions for six years, psychic Marlie Keen suddenly "sees" a murder through the eyes of the killer and knows that her peace is over and she must do something to help. At first, Detective Dane Hollister is skeptical; but as they work together, he learns that her abilities are real—as real as the love that is beginning to develop between them. Passionate, dark, and suspenseful.

Other books you might like:
Suzanne Forster, *Come Midnight*, 1995
Tami Hoag, *Dark Paradise*, 1994
Marilyn Pappano, *In Sinful Harmony*, 1995
Nora Roberts, *Hidden Riches*, 1994
Meryl Sawyer, *Kiss in the Dark*, 1995

934

LINDA HOWARD (Pseudonym of Linda Howington)

A Lady of the West
(New York: Pocket, 1990)

Story type: Historical/American West
Major character(s): Victoria Waverly, Bride, Southern Belle (former); Jake Roper, Cowboy
Time period(s): 1860s

Locale(s): New Mexico

Summary: Her way of life destroyed by the Civil War, Victoria agrees to marry rancher Frank McClain in return for her family's financial security. However, the bargain proves to be a poor one, at least from Victoria's point of view. Frank is less than the ideal husband and the atmosphere at the ranch is tense, violent, and frightening. In addition, Victoria must deal with her conflicting feelings for Jake Roper, a man consumed with seeking revenge for his parent's death years earlier at the hands of McClain. Action-filled and hard-hitting, but still romantic.

Other books you might like:
Ann Gabriel, *South Texas*, 1989
Norah Hess, *Wildfire*, 1989
Leta Tegler, *Gabrielle*, 1990
Victoria Thompson, *Fortune's Lady*, 1990
Jeanne Williams, *No Roof but Heaven*, 1990

935

LINDA HOWARD (Pseudonym of Linda Howington)

The Touch of Fire
(New York: Pocket, 1992)

Story type: Historical/American West
Major character(s): Annie Parker, Doctor; Rafe McCay, Outlaw, Fugitive
Time period(s): 19th century
Locale(s): Silver Mesa, Arizona

Summary: When fugitive Rafe McCay abducts frontier doctor Annie Parker and demands that she treat his wounds, he finds that her magical hands will heal not only his body, but eventually his heart as well. Memorable characters and passionate action.

Other books you might like:
Barbara Ankrum, *Chase the Fire*, 1991
Barbara Cummings, *Blazing Passion*, 1991
Linda Ladd, *Dragon Fire*, 1992
Scotney St. James, *Northern Fire, Northern Star*, 1990

936

HANNAH HOWELL

Beauty and the Beast
(New York: Leisure, 1992)

Story type: Historical/Medieval
Major character(s): Gytha Raouille, Young Woman; Thyer Saitum, Heir
Time period(s): 14th century (1356)
Locale(s): England

Summary: Insecure about his appearance and fearful of trusting women, Thyer Saitum is appalled to learn that he is to marry the lovely Gytha Raouille — and he determines not to fall in love with her so she cannot hurt him! Naturally, things don't work out that way. An unusual story of love and trust featuring a unique hero and a very special heroine.

Other books you might like:
Christina Dodd, *Candle in the Window*, 1991
Jennifer Horsman, *Awaken My Fire*, 1992
Laura Kinsale, *Flowers From the Storm*, 1992
Laura Kinsale, *The Prince of Midnight*, 1990
Helen Mittermeyer, *Princess of the Veil*, 1992

937

HANNAH HOWELL

Conqueror's Kiss
(New York: Avon, 1991)

Story type: Historical/Medieval
Major character(s): Jennet Armstrong Graeme, Captive; Hacon Gillard, Warrior, Knight
Time period(s): 14th century (1318)
Locale(s): Berwick, Scotland

Summary: Jennet, captured as plunder by Sir Hacon Gillard, hates the wars and the warriors as she accompanies the Scottish armies in their battles against England.

Other books you might like:
Katherine Deauville, *Blood Red Roses*, 1991
Jane Feather, *Brazen Whispers*, 1990
Brenda Joyce, *The Conqueror*, 1990
    violent and lusty
Johanna Lindsey, *Prisoner of My Desire*, 1991
Katherine Vickery, *Flame Across the Highlands*, 1990

938

HANNAH HOWELL

Kentucky Bride
(New York: Avon, 1994)

Story type: Historical/American Revolution
Major character(s): Clover Sherwood, Gentlewoman (impoverished); Ballard MacGregor, Backwoodsman
Time period(s): 1790s (1794)
Locale(s): Pennsylvania; Kentucky

Summary: Left penniless, Clover needs support; Ballard MacGregor needs a wife to teach him genteel ways. Their ultimate marriage is one of convenience and they both have a lot to learn, but as they gradually work out their problems, their relationship becomes one of passion and love.

Other books you might like:
Pamela K. Forrest, *Autumn Ecstasy*, 1990
Norah Hess, *Kentucky Bride*, 1992
    similar setting/ different treatment
Cait Logan, *Wild Dawn*, 1992
Debbie Macomber, *Morning Comes Softly*, 1993
    contemporary marriage of convenience
LaVyrle Spencer, *Morning Glory*, 1989

939

HANNAH HOWELL

Silver Flame

(New York: Avon, 1992)

Story type: Historical/Medieval
Major character(s): Sine Catriona Brodie, Young Woman, Thief (pickpocket); Sir Gamel Logan, Knight (landless)
Time period(s): 14th century
Locale(s): Scotland

Summary: When twelve-year-old Sine Catriona Brodie is forced by her cruel mother to flee with her young brother, she ends up learning the pickpocket trade (Oliver Twist style) in order to survive. However, she yearns for revenge, and when she ends up married to one of her "victims" Sir Gamel Logan, they begin this mission in earnest. Political intrigue, adventure, humor, and passion are part of this unusual portrait of Medieval life.

Other books you might like:
Rexanne Becnel, *The Rose of Blacksword*, 1992
Tanya Anne Crosby, *Angel of Fire*, 1992
Jude Deveraux, *The Taming*, 1989
Judith Merkle Riley, *In Pursuit of the Green Lion*, 1990
Anita Mills, *Winter Roses*, 1992

940

HANNAH HOWELL

Stolen Ecstasy

(New York: Leisure, 1991)

Story type: Historical/American West
Major character(s): Leanne Summers, Captive (hostage); Hunter Walsh, Outlaw, Spy
Time period(s): 1870s
Locale(s): Colorado

Summary: Kidnapped and taken hostage by a dashing outlaw, Leanne quickly realizes that Hunter Walsh is not quite what he seems. When she discovers his real mission, she decides to help him with disastrous and funny results. Likeable characters in a fast-paced romp through the Old West.

Other books you might like:
JoAnn De Lazzari, *Scoundrel's Captive*, 1991
Linda Madl, *Sunny*, 1990
Patricia Pellicane, *Desperado Passion*, 1991
Lynda Trent, *Heaven's Embrace*, 1990

941

HANNAH HOWELL

Wild Conquest

(New York: Avon, 1993)

Story type: Historical/Colonial America
Major character(s): Pleasance Dunstan, Servant (indentured); Tearlach O'Duine, Frontiersman, Trader (Fur)
Time period(s): 1760s
Locale(s): American Colonies

Summary: As a result of trying to save her spoiled sister and family from scandal, Pleasance Dunstan ends up indentured to fur trader Tearlach O'Duine for a year in payment for her "crimes." The life proves hard and isolated, but Pleasance is more than a match for both her new situation and her master and as love and respect begin to grow between the reluctant pair, the roles of master and slave reverse.

Other books you might like:
Patricia Rice, *Rebel Dreams*, 1991
Karen Robards, *This Side of Heaven*, 1991
Maura Seger, *Fortune's Tide*, 1990
Penelope Williamson, *A Wild Yearning*, 1990

942

CORAL HOYLE (Pseudonym of Coral Hoyle Titus)

A Merry Go-Round

(Toronto: Harlequin, 1990)

Story type: Regency
Major character(s): Kate McClintock, Imposter (Contessa d'Allessandria), Gentlewoman; Maxim Wolverton, Nobleman
Time period(s): 1810s
Locale(s): England

Summary: In order to help her father pay off a debt, Kate McClintock attends a lavish Regency house party disguised as the Contessa d'Allessandria, newly in mourning. She has no qualms about deceiving her lecherous host, but one of his guests, Sir Maxim Wolverton, is an entirely different matter. Witty, nicely plotted, and immensely funny.

Other books you might like:
Joan Aiken, *If I Were You*, 1987
Georgette Heyer, *Arabella*, 1949
Judith McNaught, *Whitney, My Love*, 1985
Daisy Vivian, *Fair Game*, 1986
Sheila Walsh, *A Highly Respectable Marriage*, 1983

943

CHARLOTTE HUBBARD

Colorado Moonfire

(New York: Zebra, 1992)

Story type: Historical/American West
Major character(s): Lyla O'Riley, Housekeeper (at a saloon); Barry Thompson, Lawman (Marshal)
Time period(s): 1890s
Locale(s): Cripple Creek, Colorado

Summary: A spunky saloon housekeeper and a dashing marshal lead each other a merry chase as they pursue thieves, solve mysteries, and find love in the Colorado Rockies. Lots of Action. Sequel to *Colorado Captive*.

Other books you might like:
Carol Finch, *Moonlight Enchantment*, 1992
Linda Lael Miller, *Caroline and the Raider*, 1992
Evelyn Rogers, *Sweet Texas Magic*, 1992
Judith Steel, *Wild Colorado Passion*, 1991

944

CHARLOTTE HUBBARD

Gambler's Tempting Kisses

(New York: Zebra, 1991)

Story type: Historical/American West
Major character(s): Charity Scott, Singer; Dillon Devereau, Gambler, Businessman (casino owner)
Time period(s): 19th century
Locale(s): Kansas

Summary: When dashing gambler Dillon Devereau offers naive preacher's daughter Charity Scott a singing job and an opportunity to discover her vanished mother's fate, she eagerly agrees, never dreaming that she will also discover love in the process. A passionate, funny romp that leads its characters on a merry chase all over Kansas.

Other books you might like:
Lisa Bingham, *Distant Thunder*, 1992
Lindsey Hanks, *Long Texas Nights*, 1991
Catherine Hart, *Sweet Fury*, 1990
Carla Simpson, *Desperado's Caress*, 1991

945

JAN HUDSON

Call Me Sin

(New York: Bantam, 1992)

Story type: Contemporary
Major character(s): Ross Berringer, Lawman (Texas Ranger); Susan Sinclair, Store Owner (bookstore)
Time period(s): 1990s
Locale(s): United States

Summary: Susan Sinclair is intrigued by Texas Ranger Ross, but she doesn't think she needs any help in capturing the con artist who fleeced her grandmother. However, her resources only come from reading mysteries, so eventually she has to turn to Ross for his macho help. Light and lively.

Other books you might like:
Sandra Brown, *Texas! Sage*, 1991
Linda Ladd, *Frostfire*, 1990
Christine Monson, *Golden Nights*, 1990
Tracy Sinclair, *If the Truth Be Told*, 1992

946

JANIS REAMS HUDSON

Apache Heartsong

(New York: Zebra, 1995)

Story type: Historical/American West
Major character(s): La Risa Chee, Indian (Chiricahua Apache); Spencer Colton, Doctor
Time period(s): 1890s (1894)
Locale(s): Mount Vernon, Alabama; Arizona; Pennsylvania

Summary: When Dr. Spencer Colton agrees to bring Chiricahua Apache LaRisa Chee from her school in Pennsyl-

vania to her father's deathbed in Alabama, he has no idea he is going to have to marry her to do it. But he does and what starts out as a temporary marriage of necessity ends up one of love as they both come to terms with their prejudices and pride. A warm, sensitive story of the healing power of love.

Other books you might like:
Beverly Bird, *Comes the Rain*, 1990
Kathleen Eagle, *Heaven and Earth*, 1990
Kathleen Eagle, *Sunrise Song*, 1996
20th century settings
Kathleen Harrington, *Cherish the Dream*, 1990
Deborah Smith, *Beloved Woman*, 1991

947

JANIS REAMS HUDSON

Apache Legacy

(New York: Zebra, 1994)

Story type: Historical/American West
Series: Colton Saga
Major character(s): Jessica Colton, Young Woman; Blake Renard, Military Personnel, Hunter (of Apaches)
Time period(s): 1880s (1886)
Locale(s): Arizona

Summary: When Captain Blake Renard arrests Jessica's half-brother, she decides to follow along and set him free. However, Blake decides differently and keeps his eye on her. Blake's long-standing hatred of Indians makes him determined to keep Jessica away from her half-Apache brother—a situation which results in serious conflict. Nevertheless, their attraction for each other is strong, and as their love for each other grows, Blake begins to deal with his anger and hatred.

Other books you might like:
Madeline Baker, *Forbidden Fires*, 1990
elements of hate and prejudice
Linda Madl, *Sunny*, 1990
bounty hunter/good historical details/serious issues
Connie Mason, *Beyond the Horizon*, 1990
deals with prejudice and bigotry
Elizabeth Turner, *Midnight Rain*, 1994
revenge-driven hero

948

JANIS REAMS HUDSON

Apache Magic

(New York: Zebra, 1991)

Story type: Historical/American West
Major character(s): Daniella "Dani" Blackwood, Psychic; Travis Colton, Parent
Time period(s): 1860s (1861)
Locale(s): Arizona

Summary: Adopted and highly respected and named "Woman of Magic" by the Apache because of her courage, psychic Daniella Blackwood is driven by dreams to find Travis Colton, a man whose son has been taken by the Apache, and help him redeem his son. But as Daniella works to free his son, Travis works to free Daniella from the fear of men; and as they come to trust each other, they also find love. Realistic, sensitive, and passionate.

Other books you might like:
Rosanne Bittner, *Arizona Ecstasy*, 1989
Georgina Gentry, *Cheyenne Princess*, 1987
Susan Johnson, *Forbidden*, 1991
Brenda Joyce, *Darkest Heart*, 1989
Dana Ransom, *Dakota Dawn*, 1991

949

JANIS REAMS HUDSON

For the Thrill
(Bensalem, Pennsylvania: Meteor, 1992)

Story type: Contemporary
Major character(s): Maggie Randolph, Widow(er), Waiter/ Waitress; Alex Dillon, Cowboy (rodeo rider)
Time period(s): 1990s
Locale(s): Deep Fork, Oklahoma

Summary: Made a widow once by the dangers of the rodeo, the last thing single mom Maggie Randolph needs is another bull rider; but when Alex Dillon comes to town, she is forced to reassess her feelings. Warm and passionate.

Other books you might like:
Kathleen Eagle, *This Time Forever*, 1992
Cindy Gerard, *Temptation From the Past*, 1991
Jan Hudson, *Call Me Sin*, 1992
Laura Phillips, *To Love a Cowboy*, 1992

950

JANIS REAMS HUDSON

Wild Texas Flame
(New York: Zebra, 1992)

Story type: Historical/American West
Major character(s): Sunny Thornton, Young Woman; Asher McCord, Convict (former), Handicapped (paralysed)
Time period(s): 1880s
Locale(s): Texas

Summary: Although the entire town considers Ash McCord the lowest of the low, Sunny Thornton sees something in the ex-convict that no one else sees. When he is shot in the back during a bank robbery while protecting Sunny, she takes it upon herself to nurse him back to health, in spite of his objections, foul moods, and other difficulties. Their feelings for each other are confused, to say the least, but by the end of the story everything is properly sorted out.

Other books you might like:
Jill Marie Landis, *Come Spring*, 1992
Laura Kinsale, *Flowers From the Storm*, 1992
Laura Kinsale, *The Prince of Midnight*, 1990
Pamela Morsi, *Heaven Sent*, 1990

951

FAYE HUGHES

Gotta Have It
(New York: Bantam, 1994)

Story type: Contemporary
Major character(s): Michael Ann O'Donnell, Thief (jewel), Businesswoman (security company owner); Remy Ballou, Thief (cat burglar)
Time period(s): 1990s
Locale(s): New Orleans, Louisiana

Summary: Lovers and partners in crime three years before, Michael Ann and Remy meet again under "legitimate" circumstances and discover their love has not died. Sexy and explicit.

Other books you might like:
B.J. James, *The Heart of the Hunter*, 1995
Kristin James, *Once in a Blue Moon*, 1995
Mallory Rush, *Love Game*, 1995
    explicit sex/some bondage
Candace Schuler, *Passion and Scandal*, 1995
Tiffany White, *Naughty by Night*, 1995

952

TRACY HUGHES

White Lies and Alibis
(Toronto: Harlequin, 1990)

Story type: Contemporary
Major character(s): Kristen Jordan, Lawyer, Single Parent (Divorced); Luke Wade, Defendant
Time period(s): 1980s

Summary: Luke Wade is a man with a past out of attorney Kristen Jordan's teenage past—and when she ends up defending him against theft charges, she considers it an opportunity to explore any possible relationship between them. A touching story of love and loyalty.

Other books you might like:
Mary Lynn Baxter, *Winter Heat*, 1990
Billie Green, *Bad for Each Other*, 1990
Virginia Nielsen, *Jessica's Song*, 1990
Elizabeth Quinn, *Any Day Now*, 1989
Kathleen Gilles Seidel, *Maybe This Time*, 1990

953

JILLIAN HUNTER

A Deeper Magic
(New York: Pinnacle, 1994)

Story type: Historical/Victorian; Historical/Fantasy
Major character(s): Margaret Rose, Healer; Ian MacNeill, Doctor
Time period(s): 19th century (late)
Locale(s): Outer Islands, Scotland; Aberdeen, Scotland

Summary: Banished for improper behavior to the outer islands off the Scottish coast, Margaret Rose adjusts to her situation and becomes a healer in the local tradition. Eventually she is summoned home, but when Dr. Ian MacNeill comes to get her, she refuses to go. Despite their deep-seated medical and scientific differences, they fall in love and marry. Their ultimate return to Aberdeen brings old enemies to the fore, but fortunately, their love is strong enough to endure—and win. An interesting clash between new science and ancient magic.

Other books you might like:
Kathryn Lynn Davis, *All We Hold Dear*, 1995
   similar setting/broader in scope
Ruth Langan, *Texas Healer*, 1992
   healer/doctor conflict in American West
Coral Smith Saxe, *Enchantment*, 1994
   reality/magic conflict in an American setting

954

JILLIAN HUNTER

Tiger Dance

(New York: Avon, 1991)

Story type: Historical/Exotic
Major character(s): Lorna Fairchild, Gentlewoman; Ross St. James, Government Official
Locale(s): Kali Simpang, Malaysia

Summary: Upon discovering her fiance's infidelity, Lorna Fairchild boldly sets sail for the Malaysian island of Kali Simpang to join her father. However, her father proves to be missing, and in the process of trying to find him—and a priceless statue he is said to have stolen—Lorna finds danger, excitement, and love in the arms of dashing Ross St. James.

Other books you might like:
Leslie O'Grady, *Seek the Wild Shore*, 1989
Barbara Dawson Smith, *Fire on the Wind*, 1992
Katherine Sutcliffe, *Shadow Play*, 1991
Terri Valentine, *Sweet Paradise*, 1992
Frances Williams, *The Road to Forever*, 1991

955

NANCY HUTCHINSON

Wild Card

(New York: Harper, 1994)

Story type: Contemporary
Major character(s): Sarah McDonald, Writer; Ian Wild, Actor, Dancer (ballet)
Time period(s): 1990s
Locale(s): New Jersey; Montana; New York, New York

Summary: When Ian Wild's car breaks down, Sarah McDonald's peaceful life is turned upside down in a way she never expected. Both have lost their first mates and are drawn to each other; but when Sarah agrees to visit Ian's Montana ranch, she walks into a tense, uncomfortable situation surrounding the death of Ian's first wife. Sarah's curiosity and love for Ian help her to uncover a murder, but in doing so, she ends up at the mercy of the murderer. Nevertheless, love (and justice) do prevail at the end.

Other books you might like:
Tami Hoag, *Dark Paradise*, 1994
   similar setting/different treatment
Rachel Lee, *Cowboy Cop*, 1994
Linda Lael Miller, *The Legacy*, 1994
Joan Elliott Pickart, *The Bonnie Blue*, 1990

956

SHARON IHLE

The Bride Wore Spurs

(New York: Harper, 1995)

Story type: Historical/American West
Major character(s): Kathleen Lacey O'Carroll, Mail Order Bride; John Winterhawke, Frontiersman
Time period(s): 1870s (1878)
Locale(s): Wyoming

Summary: Kathleen Lacey O'Carroll is determined to be a successful mail order bride; however, she arrives in Wyoming to discover that the man she is to marry hasn't actually ordered her. John Winterhawke leads a hard life and the last thing he needs is a soft woman. Neverthless, Kathleen refuses to give up on either this strange, harsh land or the man she longs to call husband.

Other books you might like:
Jude Deveraux, *Eternity*, 1995
   another mail order bride
Stef Ann Holm, *Firefly*, 1990
Jane Kidder, *Mail-Order Temptress*, 1992
Debbie Macomber, *Morning Comes Softly*, 1993
Theresa Michaels, *Gifts of Love*, 1992

957

SHARON IHLE

Wild Rose

(New York: Harper, 1993)

Story type: Historical/American West Coast
Major character(s): Maxine McKain, Con Artist; Francisco Dane del Cordobes, Rancher
Time period(s): 19th century
Locale(s): California

Summary: When her ne'er-do-well father loses her to the dashing Dane del Cordobes in a poker game, Maxine McKain doesn't take kindly to the situation. However, destiny has a way of rectifying things, and before long Maxine is able to claim Dane on her own terms. Funny, passionate, and fast-paced.

Other books you might like:
Lori Copeland, *Promise Me Forever*, 1994
Lori Copeland, *Promise Me Today*, 1992
Joan Johnston, *Outlaw's Bride*, 1993
Pamela Morsi, *Garters*, 1992
Rebecca Paisley, *Rainbows and Rapture*, 1992

958

JEAN INNES (Pseudonym of Jean Saunders)

Buccaneer's Bride

(New York: Zebra, 1989)

Story type: Historical/Georgian
Major character(s): Sarah Huxley, Runaway (from an unwanted marriage); David "Robbie" Roberts, Pirate (Scotsman)
Time period(s): 1760s (1763)
Locale(s): At Sea; England

Summary: In order to avoid being married to a cousin she despises, Sarah Huxley flees to Black Robbie's pirate ship. Adventure, danger, and love await her in this historical with a twist.

Other books you might like:
Kathryn Davenport, *Pirate's Mistress*, 1989
Heather Graham, *A Pirate's Ransom*, 1989
Laurie McBain, *Moonstruck Madness*, 1977
    First in a trilogy
Joan Van Nuys, *Beloved Avenger*, 1989
Kathleen E. Woodiwiss, *Shanna*, 1977

959

ALISON IRVING

No Greater Love

(New York: St. Martin, 1991)

Story type: Historical/American West; Saga
Major character(s): Montrose Daventry, Plantation Owner (daughter of); Mason Regrett, Rancher
Time period(s): 1840s (1845)
Locale(s): Texas

Summary: The Daventry family favors independence for Texas; the Regretts want Texas to become a state. With the battle lines thus drawn, it seems unlikely that beautiful, independent Montrose Daventry and equally opinionated Mason Regrett would even be civil to each other, let alone fall in love—but they do. More than a love story, this is a sweeping tale of saga-like proportions chronicling the creation of a state—as reflected in the lives of those who lived through it.

Other books you might like:
Rebecca Brandewyne, *Heartland*, 1990
    Kansas history
Lori Copeland, *Sweet Hannah Rose*, 1991
Ann Gabriel, *South Texas*, 1990
Ginna Gray, *Quiet Fires*, 1991
Patricia Potter, *The Silver Link*, 1991

960

CHERLYN JAC (Pseudonym of Cheryl Biggs)

Night's Immortal Touch

(New York: Pinnacle, 1995)

Story type: Contemporary/Fantasy

Major character(s): Suzanne Beaumondier, Vampire; Clay Garnier, Detective—Police
Time period(s): 1990s
Locale(s): New Orleans, Louisiana

Summary: When his vampire sister's arrival coincides with a series of vicious murders, Alexandre Beaumondier is concerned that she may be responsible; and the developing relationship between Suzanne and Clay Garnier, the police officer investigating the crimes, simply adds complications. Dark and passionate. Follows *Night's Immortal Kiss.*

Other books you might like:
Jasmine Cresswell, *Prince of the Night*, 1995
    historical vampires
Lori Herter, *Obsession*, 1991
    first of Herter's Vampire Series
Sabine Kells, *A Deeper Hunger*, 1994
Linda Lael Miller, *Forever and the Night*, 1993
Anne Rice, *Interview with the Vampire*, 1976
    classic vampire tale

961

ELIZABETH JACKSON

A Brilliant Alliance

(New York: Signet, 1993)

Story type: Regency
Major character(s): Caroline Wentworth, Gentlewoman; Charles Ridley, Nobleman
Time period(s): 1810s
Locale(s): England

Summary: Romance is on Caro's mind, but only for her sister, not for herself and she is determined that her sister's debut will be a success. Her efforts are rewarded when all goes beautifully, but she is taken by surprise when she finds that she has attracted several suitors in the process! Light Regency fun.

Other books you might like:
Georgette Heyer, *Bath Tangle*, 1955
Georgette Heyer, *Frederica*, 1965
Barbara Metzger, *An Affair of Interest*, 1992
Melinda Pryce, *The Last Lord*, 1993
Margaret Westhaven, *Four in Hand*, 1993

962

LISA JACKSON

Treasures

(New York: Zebra, 1994)

Story type: Contemporary/Mainstream
Major character(s): Adria Nash, Heiress (supposed); Zachary Danvers, Hotel Owner
Time period(s): 1990s
Locale(s): United States

Summary: Plagued by women claiming to be his dead half-sister, London, Zachary Danvers scorns Adria Nash when she walks into his life, claiming she only wants the truth about herself. The heiress had been kidnapped as a child and

Zachary was at one time suspected of the deed. The feuding Danvers and Polidari families could each benefit from London's return, and Adria's appearance on the scene opens old wounds, reveals family secrets, and throws things into general chaos. Of course, the fact that she is falling in love with Zachary simply adds to the confusion.

Other books you might like:
Catherine Coulter, *Beyond Eden*, 1991
  long-lost heiress theme
Barbara Delinsky, *The Passions of Chelsea Kane*, 1992
Sharon Sala, *Honor's Promise*, 1992
  long-lost heiress theme
Pamela Simpson, *Fortune's Child*, 1992
  another long-lost heiress
Phyllis A. Whitney, *Woman Without a Past*, 1991
  romantic suspense and another long-lost heiress

963

LISA JACKSON

Wishes

(New York: Zebra, 1995)

Story type: Contemporary
Major character(s): Kate Summers, Widow(er), Parent (adoptive); Deagan O'Rourke, Rancher; Jon Summers, Teenager, Psychic
Time period(s): 1990s
Locale(s): Hopewell, Oregon

Summary: Fifteen years earlier, grieving the loss of her husband and child, Kate Summers agreed to take the illegitimate son of a Boston debutante and move across the country and raise him as her own. But now Daegan O'Rourke has learned of his son's existence and when he moves in next door, he not only comes to care about Jon, but he learns to love Kate as well. But others are also searching for Jon, some of whom don't want him to be found. A suspenseful tale of greed, deception, and cruelty—laced with touches of the paranormal.

Other books you might like:
Mary Lynn Baxter, *Sweet Justice*, 1994
Rebecca Brandewyne, *Dust Devil*, 1995
Barbara Delinsky, *The Passions of Chelsea Kane*, 1992
Karen Robards, *Maggy's Child*, 1994
Erin Yorke, *What Child Is This?*, 1993

964

LORETTA JACKSON
VICKIE BRITTON, Co-Author

Nightmare in Morocco

(New York: Avalon Books, 1989)

Story type: Romantic Suspense
Major character(s): Noa Parker, Tour Guide; Taber Rand, Tour Guide
Time period(s): 1980s
Locale(s): Tangier, Morocco

Summary: Haunted by frightening childhood memories of Tangier, Noa refuses to lead a tour group to Morocco, until

she meets handsome tour manager Taber Rand. Suddenly Morocco seems much more interesting and not quite so dangerous. But her peace is shattered when trouble on the tour begins—and Noa realizes her life is in danger.

Other books you might like:
Joan Aiken, *A Cluster of Separate Sparks*, 1972
  Greek setting
Alma Blair, *The Unwitting Witness*, 1990
Betty Dahlin, *Roman Butterfly*, 1989
  Italian setting
Jane Edwards, *Dangerous Odyssey*, 1990
Mary Stewart, *The Gabriel Hounds*, 1967
  Classic Romantic Suspense/Lebanese setting

965

ARLENE JAMES

A Perfect Gentleman

(New York: Silhouette, 1990)

Story type: Contemporary/Innocent
Major character(s): Sabre Callot, Heiress (Would-be); Kenyon Ames, Detective (Finds lost heirs)
Time period(s): 1980s
Locale(s): New Orleans, Louisiana

Summary: Sabre is completely unsophisticated and out of her depth when she goes from her Bayou home to New Orleans to meet her wealthy grandfather so he can choose an heir. Kenyon Ames takes pity on her and the result is a modern version of Pygmalion.

Other books you might like:
Cordia Byers, *Lady Fortune*, 1989
  Historical and sensual/Lost Heiress theme
Jude Deveraux, *Wishes*, 1989
Leigh Michaels, *Let Me Count the Ways*, 1989
Rebecca Paisley, *Barefoot Bride*, 1990
  Historical and sensual

966

B.J. JAMES

A Step Away

(New York: Silhouette, 1992)

Story type: Contemporary
Major character(s): Raven McCandless, Young Woman; David, Police Officer
Time period(s): 1990s
Locale(s): North Carolina

Summary: David takes time in a quiet remote retreat to recover from his fellow agent's death. Raven is also there to heal from her past experiences. He is an idealist with a conscience; she provides him with strength and teaches him that love is forgiveness. Danger and betrayal are surprising touches in this rather graceful romance.

Other books you might like:
Sandra Field, *Goodbye Forever*, 1990
Judy Gill, *Golden Swan*, 1990
Joey Light, *Sterling's Reasons*, 1991

Diana Palmer, *The Case of the Mesmerizing Boss*, 1992

967
DEANA JAMES (Pseudonym of Mona D. Sizer)

Acts of Love
(New York: Zebra 1992)

Story type: Historical/American West; Historical/Victorian
Major character(s): Miranda Drummond, Actress; Shreve Catherwood, Actor, Director
Time period(s): 1880s
Locale(s): United States; Mexico; England

Summary: In a fast-paced and sensual story that begins where *Acts of Passion* leaves off, Miranda and Shreve continue their worldly travels and productions, performing and enchanting their audiences despite illness, injury, and incredible difficulties. They manage to foil their nemesis, Frank de la Barca, and eventually realize that their love for each other is more important than anything else. Theatrical and passionate.

Other books you might like:
Sandra Chastain, *Sweetwater*, 1990
Elizabeth Kary, *Midnight Lace*, 1990
Lindsay McKenna, *Lord of Shadowhawk*, 1992
    different setting
Martha Rofheart, *The Savage Brood*, 1978
    five centuries in the life of a theatrical family

968
DEANA JAMES (Pseudonym of Mona D. Sizer)

Acts of Passion
(New York.: Zebra, 1992)

Story type: Historical/American West; Historical/Victorian America
Major character(s): Miranda Drummond, Actress; Shreve Catherwood, Actor, Director
Time period(s): 1860s (1866); 1880s
Locale(s): West

Summary: When her mother is coerced into marrying the man who was responsible for her father's death, young Miranda Drummond escapes and joins a traveling acting troupe. The years bring her career success as an actress and love in the form of actor Shreve Catherwood. However, revenge will wait until events come full circle and Miranda and her stepfather are together once again at the place where her father died. An unusual, passionate, vengeance-driven romance. To be followed by *Acts of Love*.

Other books you might like:
Sandra Chastain, *Sweetwater*, 1990
Kathy Jones, *Sweet Obsession*, 1990
Elizabeth Kary, *Midnight Lace*, 1990
Robin Leigh, *Rugged Splendor*, 1991
LaVyrle Spencer, *Forgiving*, 1990

969
DEANA JAMES (Pseudonym of Mona D. Sizer)

Masque of Sapphire
(New York: Zebra, 1990)

Story type: Historical/War of 1812
Major character(s): Judith Talbot-Harrow, Businesswoman (Family-owned shipping concern); Tabor O'Halloran, Businessman
Time period(s): 1810s
Locale(s): England; United States

Summary: When English-born Judith Talbot-Harrow arrives from England to help run the family shipping business in America, she locks horns with Tabor O'Halloran. Love follows, but only after tragedy strikes. This is a sister novel to Emma Merritt's *Masque of Jade*.

Other books you might like:
Catherine Coulter, *Night Storm*, 1990
Betina M. Krahn, *Passion's Ransom*, 1989
Emma Merritt, *Masque of Jade*, 1990
    Companion novel
Karen Robards, *Morning Song*, 1989

970
DEANA JAMES (Pseudonym of Mona D. Sizer)

Speak Only Love
(New York: Zebra, 1991)

Story type: Historical/Regency; Gothic
Major character(s): Vivian Marleigh, Handicapped (mute), Heiress; Piers Polwyche, Nobleman, Bridegroom (reluctant)
Time period(s): 1810s
Locale(s): England

Summary: Forced by circumstances into a marriage neither really wants, mute, gentle Vivian determines to win her husband's love—even though he seems set on ruining his life in drink and smuggling. A darkly different historical with definite gothic leanings.

Other books you might like:
Shannon Drake, *Emerald Embrace*, 1991
Elizabeth Kary, *Midnight Lace*, 1990
Amanda Quick, *Scandal*, 1991
Amanda Quick, *Seduction*, 1990
Amanda Quick, *Surrender*, 1990

971
DEANA JAMES (Pseudonym of Mona D. Sizer)

Wild Texas Heart
(New York: Zebra, 1990)

Story type: Historical/American West
Series: Gilliard Family Saga
Major character(s): Fancy Breckenridge, Widow(er), Amnesiac; Irons, Oil Industry Worker (wildcat oil driller)
Time period(s): 1900s

Locale(s): Texas

Summary: Widow Fancy Gilliard Breckenridge and wildcatter Irons join forces to find oil on her property and regain her home. Good description of the rough, early years of the oil industry combined with a sensual love story. The latest in the Gilliard family saga.

Other books you might like:
Ann Gabriel, *South Texas*, 1990
DiAnna June, *Yesterday's Promise*, 1991
Evelyn Rogers, *Texas Kiss*, 1989
Janelle Taylor, *Follow the Wind*, 1990
Vivian Vaughn, *Texas Gamble*, 1990

972

KRISTIN JAMES

The Yankee

(Toronto: Harlequin, 1990)

Story type: Historical/American West
Major character(s): Margaret Carlisle, Orphan; Andrew "Drew" Stone, Rancher
Time period(s): 1870s
Locale(s): Huxley, Texas

Summary: Margaret Carlisle needs a home of her own and someone to help her raise her younger sister and brother; Yankee Andrew Stone needs a wife who will help his eleven-year-old daughter be accepted into the closed society of the small Texas town. Their marriage, which begins as one of convenience, gradually evolves into one of mutual trust, affection, and passion—strong enough to withstand the outside influences which threaten it.

Other books you might like:
Deborah Camp, *Black-Eyed Susan*, 1990
Dorothy Garlock, *Homeplace*, 1991
Ginna Gray, *Quiet Fires*, 1991
Norah Hess, *Hawke's Pride*, 1991
Victoria Pade, *The Doubletree*, 1990

973

SAMANTHA JAMES

My Cherished Enemy

(New York: Avon, 1992)

Story type: Historical/Medieval
Major character(s): Kathryn of Ashbury, Noblewoman; Guy de Marche, Knight (crusader), Nobleman (Earl of Sedgwick)
Time period(s): 12th century (1155)
Locale(s): England

Summary: Orphaned when her father is killed by their uncle and taken hostage when her home is captured by returning crusader Lord Guy de Marche, Kathryn fights for her honor and her love as she and Guy battle their way through pride to understanding. A medieval captive-in-love-with-captor tale of love, passion, and violence .

Other books you might like:
Catherine Archer, *Rose Among Thorns*, 1992
Rexanne Becnel, *My Gallant Enemy*, 1990
Virginia Henley, *The Dragon and the Jewel*, 1991
Brenda Joyce, *The Conqueror*, 1990
Libby Sydes, *The Lion's Angel*, 1992

974

SAMANTHA JAMES

Outlaw Heart

(New York: Avon, 1993)

Story type: Historical/American West
Major character(s): Abby McKenzie, Saloon Hostess; Kane, Gunfighter
Time period(s): 1870s (1878)
Locale(s): Wyoming

Summary: Looking for her father's killer, Abby McKenzie assumes a saloon-girl identity to kidnap some help in the form of gunfighter Kane. As they pursue their quarry, Kane and Abby discover their feelings for each other are more than platonic, but Kane feels he is not good enough for Abby, and, as a result, almost loses her. Eventually, the killer is caught and Abby and Kane straighten everything out to both their satisfactions.

Other books you might like:
Virginia Brown, *Wildfire*, 1990
Elaine Coffman, *Escape Not My Love*, 1990
Wendy Garrett, *Western Enchantress*, 1993
Patricia Potter, *Notorious*, 1993
Evelyn Rogers, *Sweet Texas Magic*, 1992

975

CLAUDIA JAMESON

That Certain Yearning

(Toronto: Harlequin, 1990)

Story type: Contemporary/Innocent
Major character(s): Diane West, Vacationer; Nick Channing, Vacationer
Time period(s): 1980s

Summary: Diane escapes to a rented vacation cottage to come to terms with her father's remarriage. Nick comes to the same vacation spot because his sister has recently died, leaving him responsible for her young daughter and they both need a break. Nick and Diane are attracted to each other, but Diane resists, not wanting just a holiday romance.

Other books you might like:
Loretta Jackson, *Nightmare in Morocco*, 1989
Jan McDaniel, *Angels in the Sand*, 1989
Alice Sharpe, *Just One More Secret*, 1990
Lee Stafford, *A Song in the Wilderness*, 1990
Diana Whitney, *A Liberated Man*, 1990

976

KRISTA JANSSEN

Ride the Wind

(New York: Pocket, 1993)

Story type: Historical/Seventeenth Century
Major character(s): Deborah McDonald, Horse Trainer; James Cortez Bedford, Rake, Gypsy
Time period(s): 17th century (1691)
Locale(s): England

Summary: Deborah McDonald knows she can handle any horse—and any man; but when she meets Cort and Pegasus, she is in for a shock. She manages to tame the stallion, but Cort doesn't succumb as easily. After all, she is only the horsemaster's daughter. Things change, however, when the truth of her parentage is revealed—and she has two men fighting for her. Believable characters, an unusual setting, and lots of fire and sparks.

Other books you might like:
Mary Daheim, *Gypsy Baron*, 1992
Sandra DuBay, *Nightrider*, 1991
Susan Johnson, *Sinful*, 1992
Kat Martin, *Gypsy Lord*, 1992
Lynda Trent, *The Black Hawk*, 1991

977

KRISTA JANSSEN

Wind Rose

(New York: Pockct, 1994)

Story type: Historical/Colonial America
Major character(s): Amanda Sheffield, Gentlewoman, Fiance(e) (reluctant); Braden Hamilton, Nobleman, Privateer
Time period(s): 17th century (1692)
Locale(s): Salem, Massachusetts, American Colonies; Chesapeake Bay, Virginia, American Colonies; Bermuda

Summary: Willing to marry for money, Amanda is taken by privateer Lord Braden (whom she has loved since childhood) to her new, rich fiance in the American Colonies. However, aboard ship they succumb to passion, but continue on to the arranged marriage. Smallpox, an evil stepfather, a difficult fiance, and a witch trial all complicate things for the pair. Eventually, they are saved (by Cotton Mather, no less) and they happily head for Bermuda.

Other books you might like:
Judith E. French, *Fortune's Mistress*, 1990
Andrea Parnell, *Wild Glory*, 1990
Maura Seger, *The Taming of Amelia*, 1993
Elizabeth Speare, *The Witch of Blackbird Pond*, 1958
  classic YA title
Becky Lee Weyrich, *Silver Tears*, 1990

978

MIRANDA JARRETT

Mariah's Prize

(Toronto: Harlequin, 1994)

Story type: Historical/Colonial America
Series: Sparhawk
Major character(s): Mariah West, Shipowner; Gabriel Sparhawk, Privateer, Sea Captain
Time period(s): 18th century
Locale(s): At Sea; New England

Summary: Restless and missing the sea, Gabriel Sparhawk jumps at the chance to captain Mariah West's ship, *Revenge*, against the French. And, of course, he does need the money. Mariah accompanies him, and together they face not only the dangers of the sea and of war, but of treachery and other villainies, as well. A fast-paced tale of love and adventure on the high seas.

Other books you might like:
Elizabeth DeLancey, *Sea of Dreams*, 1992
  two sea-lovers/later time period
Christine Dorsey, *Sea Fires*, 1992
Shannon Drake, *Bride of the Wind*, 1992
  fast-paced, action-oriented
Robin Lee Hatcher, *The Magic*, 1993
  more nautical adventures

979

PAMELA JECKEL

Deepwater

(New York: Kensington, 1994)

Story type: Saga; Historical/Mainstream
Major character(s): Leah Handcock, Pioneer
Time period(s): 18th century
Locale(s): Carolinas, American Colonies

Summary: Beginning in the "Lost Colony of Roanoke," this saga traces the lives of Leah Handcock and four generations of her daughters and their diverse men as they build Deepwater Plantation and a dynasty of strong people who affect the development of the nation. Good historical detail.

Other books you might like:
Gwen Bristow, *Deep Summer*, 1937
  first in the Plantation Trilogy
Virginia Coffman, *The Gaynor Women*, 1978
  three generations of Virginia women — post-Civil War
Lonnie Coleman, *Beulah Land*, 1973
  first in the Beulah Land Series
Colleen McCullough, *The Thorn Birds*, 1977
  strong heroine/Australian setting

219

980
BEVERLY JENKINS

Night Song
(New York: Avon, 1994)

Story type: Historical/American West; Ethnic
Major character(s): Cara Lee Henson, Teacher; Chase Jefferson, Military Personnel (10th Colored Cavalry)
Time period(s): 1880s (1882)
Locale(s): Henry Adams Township, Kansas

Summary: After her grandfather's hanging, Cara Lee Henson has no use for Union soldiers, an attitude that can be difficult to have in the black Kansas settlement where she teaches school—a town that reveres the famous Tenth Colored Cavalry. Nevertheless, when Captain Chase Jefferson comes to town, she ends up seduced and eventually married to a man who was originally not the marrying kind. Strong-willed characters, good historical detail, and long sex scenes.

Other books you might like:
Rita Mae Brown, *High Hearts*, 1986
  mainstream/ Civil War/African American characters
Roberta Gayle, *Sunshine and Shadows*, 1995
  historical American West/African American characters
Shirley Hailstock, *Clara's Promise*, 1995
  historical American West/African American characters

981
BEVERLY JENKINS

Vivid
(New York: Avon, 1995)

Story type: Historical/Victorian America; Ethnic
Major character(s): Viveca ''Vivid'' Lancaster, Doctor; Nate Grayson, Political Figure (mayor)
Time period(s): 1870s (1876)
Locale(s): Niles, Michigan

Summary: Thrilled at being offered a practice in a small Michigan town, Dr. Viveca Lancaster is determined to succeed, and she isn't about to let anyone get in her way, especially not Nate Grayson, the devastatingly handsome, but surprisingly chauvinistic, mayor. Excellent characterizations, intriguing historical details, and colorful descriptions add to this sensual romance that focuses on the lives of African Americans after the Civil War.

Other books you might like:
Rita Mae Brown, *High Hearts*, 1986
  mainstream/Civil War/African American characters
Tanya Anne Crosby, *Sagebrush Bride*, 1993
  another woman doctor/Native American elements
Roberta Gayle, *Sunshine and Shadows*, 1995
  historical/American West/African American characters
Shirley Hailstock, *Clara's Promise*, 1995
  historical/American West/African American characters
Linda Howard, *The Touch of Fire*, 1992
  another woman doctor/historical/American West

982
LINDA JENKINS

Maverick's Lady
(New York: Kismet, 1992)

Story type: Contemporary
Major character(s): Bentley North, Businesswoman; Reid Hunter, Businessman
Time period(s): 1990s
Locale(s): United States

Summary: Bentley and Reid become co-workers but resist becoming involved even though they are attracted to each other. But when Reid has to spend months in Russia and China, upon his return their passions flare and their good intentions evaporate. Steamy love scenes and lots of emotional conflict.

Other books you might like:
Pamela Bauer, *Swinging on a Star*, 1992
Theresa Gladden, *Just Desserts*, 1991
Kay Hooper, *Enemy Mine*, 1989
Jayne Ann Krentz, *The Golden Chance*, 1990
Noelle Berry McCue, *Look Beyond the Dream*, 1990

983
ANNA JENNET

Reckless
(New York: Diamond, 1993)

Story type: Historical/Medieval
Major character(s): Ailis MacFarlane, Captive; Alexander MacDubb, Laird
Time period(s): 14th century (1375)
Locale(s): Scotland

Summary: When clan chieftain Alexander MacDubb kidnaps Ailis MacFarlane and her sister's children, it is purely an impersonal act of revenge against the lecherous Donald MacCordy; but when Ailis becomes pregnant with Alexander's child, things take on a more personal flavor. An authentic, fast-paced tale of medieval Scotland.

Other books you might like:
Paige Brantley, *Captive to His Kiss*, 1992
Katherine Deauville, *Blood Red Roses*, 1991
Samantha James, *My Cherished Enemy*, 1992
Brenda Joyce, *The Conqueror*, 1990
Virginia Lynn, *The Lyon's Prize*, 1992

984
MURIEL JENSEN

Everything
(Toronto: Harlequin, 1990)

Story type: Contemporary
Major character(s): Shannon Carlisle, Businesswoman (assistant manager); Marty Hale, Businessman (department store manager)
Time period(s): 1980s

Summary: In order to save it, Shannon Carlisle sells her family's department store to Henry Hale, who makes his son Marty the manager. Shannon remains on as assistant manager and she soon is more involved in the lives of Marty and his four sons than she ever thought possible.

Other books you might like:
Kathryn Blair, *Dancing in the Aisles*, 1990
Judy Gill, *Golden Swan*, 1990
Kay Wilding, *Rainbow's End*, 1990
Sherryl Woods, *Tea and Destiny*, 1990

985
MURIEL JENSEN

Merry Christmas, Mommy
(Toronto: Harlequin, 1995)

Story type: Contemporary; Holiday Themes
Major character(s): Karma Endicott, Accountant, Parent; Nathan Foster, Doctor
Time period(s): 1990s
Locale(s): Heron Point, Oregon

Summary: Accountant Karma Edicott wants her well-ordered life to include a baby, but not a husband. Thanks to a sperm bank, she will soon get her wish. Then a car accident lands her in the hospital ER with the baby coming early and a handsome doctor coaching her through it all. Karma still doesn't want a husband and Nathan Foster doesn't want to care, but the baby wants two parents. And that is what he gets! A lively, charmingly told story, complete with wonderfully relevant comments from the baby.

Other books you might like:
Debra Dier, *Christmas Angels*, 1995
　anthology
Debbie Macomber, *Touched by Angels*, 1995
Heather Graham Pozzessere, *An Angel's Touch*, 1995
Cathy Gillen Thacker, *The Night Before Christmas*, 1995
Mary Anne Wilson, *The Christmas Husband*, 1995

986
MURIEL JENSEN

Valentine Hearts and Flowers
(Toronto: Harlequin, 1992)

Story type: Contemporary
Major character(s): Jocelyn Foley, Planner (community development); Rob Donnelly, Restauranteur
Time period(s): 1990s
Locale(s): United States

Summary: Frumpy, red-headed Jocelyn and the town's handsome new restaurant owner receive Cupid's help in their highly improbable romance. A funny, sentimental love story peopled with heartwarmingly realistic characters.

Other books you might like:
Annette Broadrick, *A Loving Spirit*, 1991
Carole Buck, *Love and Laughter*, 1989
Jude Deveraux, *Wishes*, 1989
Jan McDaniel, *Angels in the Sand*, 1989

987
CAROL JERINA

The Bridegroom
(New York: Harper, 1993)

Story type: Historical/American West
Major character(s): Chloe Bliss, Fiance(e); Payne Trefarron, Twin; Prescott Trefarron, Twin, Fiance(e)
Time period(s): 1890s
Locale(s): Texas

Summary: Payne and Prescott, estranged twins, have their enmity deepened by Chloe, who is engaged to one but wants the other. Payne kidnaps her, Prescott searches for her, and other adversaries cross both paths. A lot of past history needs to be reconciled, but eventually Chloe solves the problems and gets her man.

Other books you might like:
Rosanne Bittner, *Texas Bride*, 1988
Ginna Gray, *Quiet Fires*, 1991
Alison Irving, *No Greater Love*, 1991
　saga
Barbara Leigh, *Web of Loving Lies*, 1993

988
CAROL JERINA

Flirting with Danger
(New York: Pocket, 1990)

Story type: Romantic Suspense
Major character(s): Catherine Harrison, Journalist (Newspaper); Tom Devlin, Journalist (Newspaper)
Time period(s): 1980s
Locale(s): Washington, District of Columbia

Summary: Put off by journalist Tom Devlin's notorious reputation with women, reporter Catherine Harrison manages to avoid him until they are both caught up in a sensational murder and scandal.

Other books you might like:
Jill Barkin, *Hot Streak*, 1990
　Mainstream
Delayne Camp, *Newsworthy Affair*, 1990
Billie Green, *Bad for Each Other*, 1990
Sherryl Woods, *Stolen Moments*, 1990

989
IRIS JOHANSEN

The Beloved Scoundrel
(New York: Bantam, 1994)

Story type: Historical/Georgian
Major character(s): Marianna Sanders, Artist (stained glass); Jordan Draken, Nobleman (Duke of Cambaron)
Time period(s): 18th century (late)
Locale(s): Europe; England

Summary: Stained glass artist Marianna Sanders holds secrets that could damage the mighty Napoleon. Jordan Draken, Duke of Cambaron, kidnaps Marianna and her brother, trying to find the secret she holds. Vowing never to give up the secret plans, Marianna finds herself in love with Jordan—and only just in time uses her artistic talents to save her brother from death. Good historical detail.

Other books you might like:
Mary Balogh, *Beyond the Sunrise*, 1992
    similar period
Shirl Henke, *Paradise and More*, 1992
Rosalind Laker, *Tree of Gold*, 1986
    Napoleonic era/good historical detail
Mary Jo Putney, *Petals in the Storm*, 1993
Christina Skye, *The Black Rose*, 1991
    captor/captive — violent

990

IRIS JOHANSEN

The Golden Barbarian

(New York: Doubleday, 1991)

Story type: Historical/Exotic
Major character(s): Theresa "Tess" Rubinoff, Royalty (niece to King of Tamrovia); Galen Ben Raschid, Royalty (Sheikh of Sedikhan)
Time period(s): 18th century (late); 19th century (early)
Locale(s): Tamrovia, Fictional Country; Sedikhan, Fictional Country

Summary: In love with spirited Tess Rubinoff from the time she was 12, Sheikh Galen Ben Raschid determines to make her his bride. Six years later, he makes her an offer she can't refuse; but when Tess sets about liberating the women of male-dominated Sedikhan, he wonders if he didn't get a bit more than he bargained for. An exciting, passionate romance with an enchanting heroine. First in the Sedikhan series.

Other books you might like:
Jane Feather, *Bold Destiny*, 1990
Victoria Holt, *The Captive*, 1989
Mary Lide, *Isobelle*, 1988
JoAnne Lindsey, *Captive Bride*, 1977
JoAnn Redd, *Desert Bride*, 1989

991

IRIS JOHANSEN

Midnight Warrior

(New York: Bantam, 1994)

Story type: Historical/Medieval; Historical/Fantasy
Major character(s): Brynn of Falkhaar, Healer; Gage Dumont, Nobleman, Warrior
Time period(s): 11th century (1066)
Locale(s): England; Wales

Summary: Given by her cruel master to Norman Lord Gage Dumont in order to help his dying friend, healer Brynn of Falkhaar uses her innate mystical talents to heal the wounded warrior and ends up attracting the interest of Gage in the process. Lively dialogue, believable, thoughtfully constructed characters, and complex plotting are featured in this sensual, and somewhat magical, historical.

Other books you might like:
Rexanne Becnel, *Where Magic Dwells*, 1994
Roberta Gellis, *The Silver Mirror*, 1989
Laura Kinsale, *For My Lady's Heart*, 1993
    uses some Middle English/complex
Kathleen Morgan, *Fire Queen*, 1994
Penelope Williamson, *Keeper of the Dream*, 1992

992

IRIS JOHANSEN

Reap the Wind

(New York: Bantam, 1991)

Story type: Contemporary; Romantic Suspense
Series: Wind Dancer Trilogy
Major character(s): Caitlin Vasaro, Businesswoman (perfumer); Alex Karazoc, Businessman
Time period(s): 1990s
Locale(s): France; United States

Summary: When Caitlin Vasaro needs help, Alex Karazoc obliges and once again the famous Wind Dancer is at the center of the plot. A fast-moving story of greed, murder, and international intrigue. Follows *The Wind Dancer* and *Storm Winds*, concluding the trilogy.

Other books you might like:
Jill Barkin, *Hot Streak*, 1990
Judith Michael, *Deceptions*, 1982
Nora Roberts, *Public Secrets*, 1990
Sidney Sheldon, *If Tomorrow Comes*, 1985

993

IRIS JOHANSEN

Storm Winds

(New York: Bantam, 1991)

Story type: Historical/French Revolution
Series: Wind Dancer Trilogy
Major character(s): Juliette de Clement, Student, Gentlewoman; Jean Marc Andreas, Banker
Time period(s): 18th century
Locale(s): France

Summary: The second book in the Wind Dancer Trilogy follows the legendary statue to France where its recovery involves the efforts of both the powerful banker Jean Marc Andreas and young Juliette de Clement. As they work to retrieve the statue, their love grows amid the turmoil, danger, and intrigue of the French Revolution. Complex plot, rich detail, and memorable characters.

Other books you might like:
Brian Cleeve, *Hester*, 1979
Ellen Tanner Marsh, *If This Be Magic*, 1991
Baroness Orczy, *The Scarlet Pimpernel*, 1905
    classic tale of the French Revolution
Serena Richards, *Rendezvous*, 1991

Elizabeth Thornton, *Scarlet Angel*, 1990

994

IRIS JOHANSEN

Tiger Prince
(New York: Fanfare, 1993)

Story type: Historical/Exotic; Historical/Mainstream
Major character(s): Jane Barnaby, Railroad Worker, Business-woman; Ruel McLaren, Adventurer
Time period(s): 1870s (1876)
Locale(s): Kansapore, India; Scotland

Summary: Ruthless, and used to living on the edge, Ruel McLaren goes to India in search of gold and ends up plaguing Jane Barnaby by trying to destroy her railroad building career. He even kidnaps her and spirits her away to Scotland and a mystical island in search of adventure. Both fiercely independent, they clash constantly; but they do fall in love, albeit slowly. Thoughtful, deep, and highly complex story peopled with unusual characters.

Other books you might like:
Olga Bicos, *White Tiger*, 1991
Kristin Hannah, *The Enchantment*, 1992
Mary Jo Putney, *Veils of Silk*, 1992
Christina Skye, *The Ruby*, 1992
Shelly Thacker, *Silver and Sapphires*, 1993

995

IRIS JOHANSEN

The Wind Dancer
(New York: Bantam, 1991)

Story type: Historical/Renaissance
Series: Wind Dancer Trilogy
Major character(s): Sanchia, Thief, Slave; Lionello Andreas, Nobleman (ruler of Mandara)
Time period(s): 16th century (1503)
Locale(s): Italy

Summary: When wealthy Lionello Andreas needs a thief to regain his family's treasured heirloom, The Wind Dancer, he buys the best he can find—the street-wise pickpocket, Sanchia. But Sanchia proves to be more than Lion had bargained for, and their business relationship quickly turns personal and passionate. A sensual, sometimes violent, story set against the richness and intrigue of Renaissance Italy. First in a trilogy.

Other books you might like:
Linda Lang Bartell, *Caressa*, 1990
Pamela Belle, *The Lodestar*, 1989
Roberta Gellis, *The Silver Mirror*, 1989
Samuel Shellabarger, *Prince of Foxes*, 1947
    Classic Romantic Adventure of the Renaissance
Bertrice Small, *Love Wild and Fair*, 1978

996

IRIS JOHANSEN

Winter Bride
(New York: Bantam, 1992)

Story type: Contemporary
Major character(s): Jed Corbin, Television Personality (anchor); Ysabel Belfort Corbin, Widow(er), Step-Parent (step-mother)
Time period(s): 1990s
Locale(s): Pacific Northwest

Summary: TV anchor Jed Corbin meets his beautiful, widowed step-mother after his estranged father's death. Ysabel had been a literal captive of his father and now she needs help in returning to her home. Jed finds he can resist neither Ysabel nor her mission.

Other books you might like:
Joanne Z. Adams, *Intimate Connections*, 1991
Sara Chance, *Fire in the Night*, 1989
Molly Rice, *Chance Encounter*, 1992
Jeanne Stephens, *At Risk*, 1989

997

MARTHA JOHNSON

Deadly Secret
(New York: Zebra, 1994)

Story type: Romantic Suspense
Major character(s): Anne Barnhart, Parent, Divorced Person; Ross McLaren, Friend
Time period(s): 1990s
Locale(s): United States

Summary: Anne Barnhart lives in fear that her murderous husband will return on her daughter's ninth birthday to kill again; and although she changes her life, she still can't escape the fact that coincidental murders are coming closer and closer to her. However, friend Ross McLaren convinces her to face her own fears and together they track down a vicious killer.

Other books you might like:
Mary Higgins Clark, *A Cry in the Night*, 1983
Mary Higgins Clark, *Where Are the Children?*, 1975
Tami Hoag, *Night Sins*, 1995
Gloria Murphy, *Simon Says*, 1994
Constance Rauch, *A Deep Disturbance*, 1990

998

SUSAN JOHNSON

Brazen
(New York: Bantam, 1995)

Story type: Historical/Victorian
Major character(s): Angela "Angel" de Grae, Noblewoman; Kit Braddock, Adventurer (yacht racer), Rake
Time period(s): 1890s (1986)
Locale(s): England

Summary: In her trademark sizzling style, Susan Johnson continues the Braddock Family saga with the story of beautiful, unhappily married Countess Angel de Grae and playboy Kit Braddock. Well-developed, appealing protagonists draw the reader into a passionate story of star-crossed lovers set against the opulent backdrop of late Victorian society. Erotic.

Other books you might like:
Thea Devine, *Tempted by Fate*, 1992
    highly sensual/Regency period
Shirl Henke, *Terms of Love*, 1992
    highly sensual/different setting
Jennifer Horsman, *Awaken My Fire*, 1992
    highly sensual/medieval setting
Jennifer Horsman, *A Kiss in the Night*, 1995
    highly sensual/Renaissance setting
Brenda Joyce, *Scandalous Love*, 1992
    highly sensual/similar time period

999

SUSAN JOHNSON

Forbidden

(New York: Bantam, 1991)

Story type: Historical/American West; Historical/Victorian
Major character(s): Daisy Black, Lawyer, Indian (Absarokee); Etienne Martel, Nobleman (Duc de Vec)
Time period(s): 1890s (1892)
Locale(s): Paris, France; Helena, Montana

Summary: In Paris on business, Absarokee attorney Daisy Black meets the aristocratic Duc de Vec with passionate and life-changing results. A scandalous love affair, a vindictive wife, and a heroine who is more than a match for the worldly hero make this highly sensual (in fact, downright HOT) novel a well-written, riveting read. Not for the faint-hearted.

Other books you might like:
Karen Robards, *Morning Song*, 1989
Nan Ryan, *The Legend of Love*, 1991
Nan Ryan, *Sun God*, 1990
Deborah Smith, *Beloved Woman*, 1991

1000

SUSAN JOHNSON

Golden Paradise

(Toronto: Harlequin, 1990)

Story type: Historical/Victorian
Major character(s): Lisaveta Kuzan-Lazaroff, Royalty (princess), Scholar (of erotic Persian poetry); Stefan Bariatinsky, Royalty (prince), Military Personnel (general)
Time period(s): 1870s (1877)
Locale(s): Russia

Summary: Spoiled, highly educated, and stubborn, Lisaveta and Stefan are outrageously perfect for each other—but it takes a while before they are both convinced of it. A sensual (but not quite so sensual as some of her earlier works) romp through the glittering world of Tsarist Russia featuring engag-

ing and memorable characters. Follows *Seized by Love* and *Love Storm*.

Other books you might like:
Jennifer Blake, *Royal Passion*, 1985
Shannon Drake, *Princess of Fire*, 1989
    different period/strong characters
Constance Heaven, *The House of Kuragin*, 1972
    1st of three novels about Tsarist Russia—not sensual
Linda Madl, *Sweet Ransom*, 1989

1001

SUSAN JOHNSON

Outlaw

(New York: Bantam, 1993)

Story type: Historical
Major character(s): Elizabeth Graham, Noblewoman (English), Captive; Johnnie Carre, Laird (Scottish), Privateer
Time period(s): 1700s
Locale(s): Scotland

Summary: Searing passion between Elizabeth and Johnnie wasn't in the plans when he kidnapped her to ransom his brother; but when they are faced with the political realities of their situation, they know that they will fight friends and enemies alike to be together. Treachery, intrigue, and passion abound in this hot romance.

Other books you might like:
Elizabeth Bonner, *A Vow to Keep*, 1993
Rebecca Brandewyne, *Forever My Love*, 1982
Jude Deveraux, *Highland Velvet*, 1982
Mary Lide, *Ann of Cambray*, 1984

1002

SUSAN JOHNSON

Pure Sin

(New York: Bantam, 1994)

Story type: Historical/American West
Major character(s): Lady Flora Bonham, Noblewoman, Anthropologist; Adam Serre, Nobleman (Comte de Chastellux), Indian (Absarokee)
Time period(s): 1860s (1867)
Locale(s): Montana

Summary: In Montana to study the Absarokee culture, Lady Flora Bonham seduces Adam Serre on the very night that his wife has run off with another man—and they begin a relationship more passionate than either has ever known. Adam's daughter, marauding Lakotas, and hostile enemies cause problems, but Flora and Adam overcome them all in this incredibly hot and steamy historical.

Other books you might like:
Sandra Chastain, *Rebel in Silk*, 1994
Johanna Lindsey, *Savage Thunder*, 1989
Elizabeth Lowell, *Only His*, 1991
Elizabeth Lowell, *Only Mine*, 1992
Nan Ryan, *Written in the Stars*, 1993

1003

SUSAN JOHNSON

Sinful

(New York: Doubleday, 1992)

Story type: Historical/Exotic; Historical/Georgian
Major character(s): Sinjin St. John, Nobleman (Duke of Seth), Horse Trainer; Chelsea Fergusson, Noblewoman (daughter of an Earl), Horse Trainer
Locale(s): England; Scotland; Tunisia

Summary: Chelsea Fergusson devises a scheme to lose her virginity to avoid an undesirable marriage and ends up pregnant and married to the notorious and spoiled Sinjin St. John, Duke of Seth. Sinjin's anger causes his exile, but Chelsea comes to his rescue — and eventually into his arms — but not before they have a number of close calls along the way. (Chelsea even ends up in a harem!) Highly sensual. Hot.

Other books you might like:
Virginia Henley, *The Pirate and the Pagan*, 1990
Brenda Joyce, *The Conqueror*, 1990
Lucy Kidd, *A Rose Without Thorns*, 1991
Elizabeth Lowell, *Only Mine*, 1992
Bertrice Small, *Skye O'Malley*, 1980

1004

JOAN JOHNSTON

The Barefoot Bride

(New York: Dell, 1992)

Story type: Historical/American West
Major character(s): Molly Gallagher, Bride; Seth Kendrick, Doctor
Time period(s): 1860s
Locale(s): Montana

Summary: Molly Gallagher and Seth Kendrick have something in common—they both need to marry again—and they arrange it all by mail. When Molly arrives in Montana, what she finds is a kind and caring man with a ten-year-old daughter dead set against the marriage. What he finds is a strong, attractive woman with two children. What they find together is a way to create love and a family.

Other books you might like:
Lisa Bingham, *Eden Creek*, 1991
Jill Marie Landis, *Rose*, 1990
Victoria Pade, *The Doubletree*, 1990
LaVyrle Spencer, *Morning Glory*, 1989
Gary D. Svee, *Incident at Pishkin Creek*,
Jeanne Williams, *Home Mountain*, 1990

1005

JOAN JOHNSTON

The Inheritance

(New York: Dell, 1995)

Story type: Historical/Victorian

Major character(s): Margaret "Daisy" Windermere, Widow(er), Noblewoman (Duchess of Severn); Nicholas Calloway, Nobleman (Duke of Severn), Bounty Hunter (Texan)
Time period(s): 1850
Locale(s): Texas; London, England; England

Summary: Content on his Texas ranch, Nicholas Calloway plans to go to England to claim his newly inherited title, sell the estate, and return to Texas. However, his cousin's widow, Daisy, is determined to keep the lands and protect the estate and its people. Marriage is a logical option to her, and Nick wants to find out about his heritage—and the fact that Daisy is intriguing and sensual doesn't hurt. Strong minded people in a delightful romance.

Other books you might like:
Anne Barbour, *Lord Glenraven's Return*, 1994
    similar situation/Regency era
Betina M. Krahn, *The Last Bachelor*, 1994
    similar time period/humorous
Rebecca Paisley, *Diamonds and Dreams*, 1991
    American-in-England theme/humorous
Maura Seger, *The Lady and the Laird*, 1992
    light, humorous inheritance plot/different setting/paranormal element

1006

JOAN JOHNSTON

Kid Calhoun

(New York: Dell, 1993)

Story type: Historical/American West
Major character(s): Anabeth Calhoun, Outlaw, Imposter (disguised as a boy); Jake Kearney, Lawman (Texas Ranger)
Time period(s): 19th century (late)
Locale(s): Colorado; New Mexico

Summary: In order to find the killer of her infamous desperado uncle, Anabeth Calhoun disguises herself as a boy, takes her uncle's name, and sets out to hunt the murderer down. Texas Ranger Jake Kearney is also hunting for both a killer and a cache of gold. Naturally, their paths converge, but there is a lot of action and a lot of interesting characters and sub-plots to sort out before the pair realize that they are truly meant for each other.

Other books you might like:
Terri Herrington, *Silena*, 1993
Pamela Morsi, *Courting Miss Hattie*, 1991
Pamela Morsi, *Garters*, 1992
Rebecca Paisley, *Barefoot Bride*, 1990
Rebecca Paisley, *Moonlight and Magic*, 1990

1007

JOAN JOHNSTON

Maverick Heart

(New York: Dell, 1995)

Story type: Historical/American West

Major character(s): Lady Verity Talbot, Noblewoman (Countess of Rushland), Widow(er); Miles Broderick, Nobleman (Viscount Linden)
Time period(s): 1870s (1875)
Locale(s): Wyoming

Summary: When Verity marries the enemy of the man she loves in order to save his life, her only consolation is that she is secretly carrying his child. She never dreams that they will meet years later in the Wyoming wilderness—and will have one more chance at love. Strong, appealing characters, kidnappings, chases, and lots of fast-paced action highlight this story of rekindled love.

Other books you might like:
Julie Garwood, *Prince Charming*, 1994
Jill Marie Landis, *Come Spring*, 1992
Pamela Morsi, *Garters*, 1992
Pamela Morsi, *Wild Oats*, 1993
Rebecca Paisley, *Heartstrings*, 1994

1008

JOAN JOHNSTON

Outlaw's Bride
(New York: Dell, 1993)

Story type: Historical/American West
Major character(s): Patch Kendrick, Young Woman; Ethan Hawk, Rancher, Prisoner (former)
Time period(s): 1880s
Locale(s): Texas

Summary: Patch's one goal has been to find and marry Ethan, even if he doesn't have time for her. Everything has gone wrong for him—scandal, false accusations, a dependent family—and Patch's lifelong chase is just too much. They might, however, have a chance to find the real criminal and make things right, if they could work together. Shootouts and mystery keep them busy in this charming, intense Western romance.

Other books you might like:
Jessica Douglass, *Wish Me a Rainbow*, 1992
Jill Marie Landis, *Wild Flower*, 1989
Pamela Morsi, *Garters*, 1992
Rebecca Paisley, *Barefoot Bride*, 1990
Rebecca Paisley, *Moonlight and Magic*, 1990

1009

JOAN JOHNSTON

Sweetwater Seduction
(New York: Dell, 1991)

Story type: Historical/American West
Major character(s): Eden Devlin, Spinster, Teacher; Burke Kerrigan, Gunfighter
Time period(s): 19th century
Locale(s): Sweetwater, Wyoming

Summary: When spinster schoolmarm Miss Eden Devlin convinces the women of Sweetwater to deny their husbands their marital rights until they can stop feuding and come to terms on the rancher/farmer issue, the men react by secretly contracting with hired gun Burke Kerrigan to seduce Miss Devlin. Of course events conspire to ensure that this is just what happens—only they fall in love with each other, too. Good secondary characters and depiction of Western small town society.

Other books you might like:
LaRee Bryant, *Sweet Texas Fury*, 1990
Emily Carmichael, *Visions of the Heart*, 1990
Stef Ann Holm, *Firefly*, 1990
Jill Marie Landis, *Rose*, 1990
Victoria Thompson, *Playing with Fire*, 1990

1010

VELDA JOHNSTON

Flight to Yesterday
(New York: St. Martin's, 1990)

Story type: Romantic Suspense
Major character(s): Sara Hargreaves, Convict (escaped), Waiter/Waitress; Mike Rolfe, Lawyer (aspiring), Hotel Owner
Time period(s): 1980s
Locale(s): San Joaquin Valley, California

Summary: When Sara Hargreaves, wrongly convicted of killing her former lover, escapes from prison, she is befriended by would-be lawyer/motel owner, Mike Rolfe. Together they try to gather enough information to unmask the real killer and prove Sara's innocence.

Other books you might like:
Mary Higgins Clark, *Stillwatch*, 1984
Mignon Eberhart, *A Fighting Chance*, 1986
Jane Aiken Hodge, *One Way to Venice*, 1975
Mary Stewart, *The Moon-Spinners*, 1962
    Mystery in Crete
Mary Stewart, *My Brother Michael*, 1959
    Mystery in Delphi

1011

PAULA JONAS

To Spite the Devil
(New York: Zebra, 1994)

Story type: Historical/American Revolution
Major character(s): Patience Harding, Loyalist, Spouse (abandoned wife); Tom Morrison, Patriot, Servant (indentured)
Time period(s): 18th century (late)
Locale(s): New York

Summary: Patience Harding, deserted wife and Loyalist, is loved by indentured servant and Patriot, Tom Morrison. When Tom is cheated by Patience's father, he escapes; but Patience, now in love with him, seeks and finds him, even as her English husband returns. His cruel plans for the slaves and the Patriots force Patience to join Tom's cause. Eventually they win, but not without a long and tragic fight. Mainstream aspects.

Other books you might like:
Linda Covington, *Wild Tory Rose*, 1992
Charles Durham, *Walk in the Light*, 1992
    mainstream view of period
Jane Aiken Hodge, *Judas Flowering*, 1976
    American Revolutionary War classic
Jane Aiken Hodge, *Wide Is the Water*, 1981
    Sequel to *Judas Flowering*
Robin Maderich, *Faith and Honor*, 1989

1012
ELLEN JONES
Beloved Enemy
(New York: Simon & Schuster, 1994)

Story type: Historical/Medieval
Major character(s): Eleanor of Aquitaine, Royalty, Historical Figure; Henry of Anjou, Royalty, Historical Figure
Time period(s): 12th century
Locale(s): France

Summary: This highly detailed historical chronicles the lives of Eleanor of Aquitane and Henry of Anjou. Eleanor's divorce from King Louis VIII and subsequent marriage to Henry shocked their people, and their fiery and passionate relationship is still one of the most romantic love stories in history. Set against the backdrop of the pageantry and grandeur of medieval France, this story of treachery and love follows *The Fatal Crown*.

Other books you might like:
Roberta Gellis, *Roselynde*, 1978
    first in the Roselynde Chronicles
Roberta Gellis, *The Sword and the Swan*, 1977
Sharon Kay Penman, *Here Be Dragons*, 1985
Sharon Kay Penman, *The Sunne in Splendour*, 1982
    the story of Anne Neville and Richard III
Anya Seton, *Katherine*, 1954
    the story of Katherin Swynford and John of Gaunt

1013
ELLEN JONES
The Fatal Crown
(New York: Avon, 1991)

Story type: Historical/Medieval
Major character(s): Maud, Royalty (Princess of England), Historical Figure; Stephen, Nobleman (Count of Mortain), Historical Figure
Time period(s): 12th century (1111-1154)
Locale(s): England; France

Summary: Maud and Stephen, both descendants of William the Conqueror, are caught up in the politics of the time. Their love blossoms even as they both fight for the crown of England. A bittersweet, touching romance chronicling the lives of real people.

Other books you might like:
Robyn Carr, *The Blue Falcon*, 1981
Hilda Lewis, *Wife to the Bastard*, 1966

Mary Lide, *Ann of Cambray*, 1984
Mary Lide, *Gifts of the Queen*, 1985
Jean Plaidy, *The Passionate Enemies*, 1979

1014
KATHY JONES
Sweet Obsession
(New York: Zebra, 1990)

Story type: Historical/American West
Major character(s): Kayley Ryan, Rancher; Jack Corbett, Convict (former), Rancher
Time period(s): 19th century
Locale(s): New Mexico

Summary: Kayley Ryan is hunting down the person who injured her father. Jack Corbett is looking for his ex-partner who framed him and took everything he had. There are sparks and passion aplenty when these two revenge-oriented people meet; but real love and happiness elude them until they can come to terms with their single-minded obsessions for vengeance.

Other books you might like:
Virginia Brown, *Wildfire*, 1990
Elaine Coffman, *Escape Not My Love*, 1990
Robin Leigh, *Rugged Splendor*, 1991
Gina Robins, *Mississippi Mistress*, 1990
LaVyrle Spencer, *Forgiving*, 1990

1015
KATHY JONES
Wild Western Desire
(New York: Zebra, 1993)

Story type: Historical/American West
Major character(s): Katie Halliday, Writer (aspiring); Rait Caldwell, Gunfighter, Guardian
Time period(s): 19th century (late)
Locale(s): Durango, Colorado

Summary: Aspiring author Katie Halliday needs a keeper—and she gets one in the form of gunfighter Rait Caldwell. However, her hairbrained escapades, her insatiable curiosity, and a few legendary gunfighters keep Rait's life from being anything but dull, and it isn't long before they both realize that their relationship is becoming something other than they had expected. Funny and fast-paced.

Other books you might like:
Pamela Morsi, *Courting Miss Hattie*, 1991
Pamela Morsi, *Garters*, 1992
Rebecca Paisley, *Barefoot Bride*, 1990
Rebecca Paisley, *Rainbows and Rapture*, 1992
Linda Sandifer, *Mountain Ecstasy*, 1992

1016
MELISSA LYNN JONES

An Uncommon Miss
(New York: Zebra, 1993)

Story type: Regency
Major character(s): Rachel Dorne, Gentlewoman, Heiress; Marcus Kinsworth, Nobleman (Marquis of Tynsdale)
Time period(s): 1810s
Locale(s): London, England
Summary: Complacent, well-ordered Lord Marcus Tynsdale feels that this is the year to choose a wife; but his plans quickly go awry when his coach is abruptly comandeered by Scottish spitfire Rachel Dorne in an effort to stop an abduction in progress. A series of explosive adventures follow as Rachel shocks and dazzles the ton and eventually captures the heart of her most reluctant Lord. Fun and games.

Other books you might like:
Anne Caldwell, *Scandal's Darling*, 1991
Cathleen Clare, *Felicia*, 1993
Mary Kingsley, *A Maddening Minx*, 1992
Sheila O'Hallion, *The Captured Heart*, 1991
Joan Smith, *Madcap Miss*, 1989

1017
JOANNA JORDAN

Destiny's Dream
(New York: Avon, 1990)

Story type: Historical/American West
Major character(s): Sybella Hartford, Gentlewoman (English); Hawk Devlin, Guide (Part-Apache), Prospector
Time period(s): 1880s (1887)
Locale(s): Superstition Mountains, Arizona
Summary: Intent on finding the Montoya goldmine, a legacy from the Spanish side of the family, proper Englishwoman Sybella Hartford comes to Arizona and hires Hawk Devlin to guide her into the Superstition Mountains—but she finds more than treasure in the process. A passionate story filled with desperados, recalcitrant camels, and desert hardships.

Other books you might like:
Janet Dailey, *Night Way*, 1981
   Contemporary setting
Carol Finch, *Thunder's Tender Touch*, 1989
Johanna Lindsey, *Savage Thunder*, 1989
Joanne Redd, *Apache Bride*, 1990
Bobbi Smith, *Arizona Caress*, 1989

1018
NICOLE JORDAN

Moonwitch
(Toronto: Harlequin, 1991)

Story type: Historical/Antebellum American South
Major character(s): Selena Markham, Southern Belle; Kyle Ramsey, Sea Captain, Plantation Owner

Time period(s): 19th century
Locale(s): Natchez, Mississippi; Mississippi River
Summary: To thwart a plan by her stepmother and fiance to get her land and to avoid an unwanted marriage, Selena sets out to seduce Captain Kyle Ramsey, a man about to give up the sea and return home to take charge of his plantation. Compromised, married, and taken to Kyle's Mississippi Plantation, Selena sets about healing the wounds in his family, restoring the plantation, and winning her husband's trust and love. Gentle, sensuous, and poignant.

Other books you might like:
Gwen Bristow, *Deep Summer*, 1937
   first of Plantation Trilogy
Karen Robards, *Morning Song*, 1989
Evelyn Rogers, *A Heart So Wild*, 1991
Kathleen E. Woodiwiss, *Come Love a Stranger*, 1984
Kathleen E. Woodiwiss, *The Flame and the Flower*, 1972

1019
NICOLE JORDAN

The Savage
(New York: Avon, 1994)

Story type: Historical/Post-American Civil War; Historical/American West
Major character(s): Summer Weston, Rancher; Lance Calder, Foreman (former ranch foreman), Indian (half-Comanche)
Time period(s): 1860s (1865)
Locale(s): Round Rock, Texas; Otter Creek, Indian Territory
Summary: Former ranch foreman Lance Calder returns to Summer's ranch to rescue her sister who has been captured by Comanches. His condition? Marriage. Summer agrees, but things aren't easy as they face prejudice and learn to deal with their feelings for each other. Explicit sex and realistic Native American detail.

Other books you might like:
Rosanne Bittner, *Unforgettable*, 1994
Cassie Edwards, *Wild Splendor*, 1993
Georgina Gentry, *Sioux Slave*, 1992
   sweet/savage elements
Susan Johnson, *Pure Sin*, 1994
   explicit
Johanna Lindsey, *Savage Thunder*, 1989

1020
NICOLE JORDAN

Touch Me with Fire
(New York: Avon, 1993)

Story type: Historical/Regency
Major character(s): Blaise St. James, Noblewoman, Servant (in disguise); Julian Morrow, Nobleman, Widow(er)
Time period(s): 1810s (1813)
Locale(s): England
Summary: To avoid an unwanted marriage, Blaise runs away to be with the gypsies. She is distracted—and attracted—by the arrogant, tragic, and wounded Lord Julian, but she refuses

to be his mistress. Eventually, passion wins out, but the revelation that she is a "lady" puts quite a different spin on things. Lots of sparks.

Other books you might like:
Virginia Brown, *Hidden Touch*, 1992
Thea Devine, *Tempted by Fire*, 1992
Kathryn Kramer, *Lady Rogue*, 1991
Kat Martin, *Gypsy Lord*, 1992
Anne Stuart, *Shadow Dance*, 1993

1021

NICOLE JORDAN

Wild Star
(New York: Avon, 1992)

Story type: Historical/American West
Major character(s): Jessica Sommers, Businesswoman (boarding house owner); Garrett Devlin, Gambler, Gunfighter
Time period(s): 1840s (1849)
Locale(s): Silver Plume, Colorado

Summary: Jessica Sommers and her father, Riley, try to hold together a primitive silver mine, but they need a nightly guard. When Garrett Devlin rides into town, he seems the answer to a prayer and so is hired. The attraction between Jessica and Garrett is instantaneous, but they both have some problems to work out before they can find happiness together.

Other books you might like:
Rebecca Brandewyne, *Rainbow's End*, 1991
Betty Brooks, *Love's Endless Flame*, 1992
Linda Howard, *Angel Creek*, 1991
Colleen Quinn, *Colorado Flame*, 1989
Charlotte Simms, *Silver Caress*, 1990

1022

BRENDA JOYCE

Beyond Scandal
(New York: Avon, 1995)

Story type: Historical/Victorian
Major character(s): Anne St. Georges, Noblewoman; Dominick St. Georges, Nobleman
Time period(s): 1850s (1852 & 1856)
Locale(s): England

Summary: Compromised, wed, and cruelly abandoned, Anne St. Georges is beginning to put her life back together and then her husband, Dominick, returns and throws everything into chaos. A dark, gothic tale, filled with passionate, unrefined sex and fast-paced action.

Other books you might like:
Susan Johnson, *Sinful*, 1992
    explicitly sexy
Nan Ryan, *Because You're Mine*, 1995
    different setting, similar sensuality levels
Anne Stuart, *To Love a Dark Lord*, 1994
    darkly sensual
Katherine Sutcliffe, *A Fire in the Heart*, 1990
    Victorian passion

Katherine Sutcliffe, *My Only Love*, 1993
sequel to *A Fire in the Heart*

1023

BRENDA JOYCE (Pseudonym of Brenda Joyce Senior)

The Conqueror
(New York: Dell, 1990)

Story type: Historical/Medieval
Major character(s): Ceidre, Noblewoman (Saxon), Bastard Daughter; Rolfe "the Relentless" de Warenne, Knight (Norman)
Time period(s): 11th century (1096)
Locale(s): England

Summary: Although he wants Ceidre from the moment he sees her, Saxon knight Rolfe the Relentless must marry Ceidre's half-sister, the Lady Alice, instead. However, in keeping with the custom of the times, marriage doesn't keep Rolfe from pursuing Ceidre; nor does it keep them from falling in love. Plenty of action, violence, and passion in true sweet/savage tradition.

Other books you might like:
Linda Lang Bartell, *Brianna*, 1986
Shannon Drake, *Princess of Fire*, 1989
Mary Ellen Gronau, *Passionate Warriors*, 1989
Penelope Neri, *Bold Breathless Nights*, 1989
Rosemary Rogers, *Sweet Savage Love*, 1973
    the original sweet/savage—different period

1024

BRENDA JOYCE (Pseudonym of Brenda Joyce Senior)

Dark Fires
(New York: Dell, 1991)

Story type: Historical/Victorian
Series: Bragg Family Saga
Major character(s): Jane Barclay, Ward, Noblewoman (granddaughter of a duke); Nicolas Bragg, Nobleman (Earl of Dragmore), Guardian
Time period(s): 1870s (1874-1876)
Locale(s): England; United States

Summary: Angry, bitter, and reclusive, Nicolas Bragg is furious at finding himself suddenly saddled with a teenaged ward—especially one as beautiful and innocent as Jane Barclay. Although he initially plans to marry her off, passion intervenes; but it takes separation and tragedy to show them that their love can banish the dark secrets that haunt them.

Other books you might like:
Rebecca Brandewyne, *Upon a Moon-Dark Moor*, 1988
Virginia Henley, *The Falcon and the Flower*, 1989
Amanda Quick, *Seduction*, 1990
Christina Skye, *The Black Rose*, 1991
Katherine Sutcliffe, *Love's Illusion*, 1991

1025

BRENDA JOYCE (Pseudonym of Brenda Joyce Senior)

Darkest Heart
(New York: Dell, 1989)

Story type: Historical/American West
Major character(s): Candice Carter, Debutante (Spoiled); Jack, Indian (Half Chiricauhua Apache)
Time period(s): 1860s
Locale(s): New Mexico

Summary: After shooting a man she thought she loved, spoiled, headstrong Candice Carter is rescued from certain death in the desert by Jack, a Chiricauhua Apache half-breed. Passion, adventure, and good historical detail regarding the Apaches.

Other books you might like:
Rosanne Bittner, *Arizona Ecstasy*, 1989
Janet Dailey, *The Pride of Hannah Wade*, 1985
Carol Finch, *Thunder's Tender Touch*, 1989
Johanna Lindsey, *Savage Thunder*, 1989
Janelle Taylor, *Savage Conquest*, 1985

1026

BRENDA JOYCE (Pseudonym of Brenda Joyce Senior)

The Fires of Paradise
(New York: Avon, 1991)

Story type: Historical/American West
Series: Bragg Family Saga
Major character(s): Lucy Bragg, Debutante (easterner); Shoz Savage, Fugitive (escaped convict and gunrunner)
Time period(s): 1890s (1897)
Locale(s): Paradise, Texas

Summary: High-spirited, spoiled, and naive, Eastern-bred Lucy Bragg heads to her grandfather's Texas ranch for his 80th birthday and ends up rescued, and then kidnapped by the dangerous and irresistable escaped convict, Shoz Savage. Fleeing from the woman who framed him and sent him to jail in the first place, Shoz escapes with Lucy in tow — across the desert Southwest and ends up falling in love with her. The rest of the Braggs are soon in hot pursuit, with interesting results. A fast-paced, highly sensual romantic adventure with definite sweet/savage elements. Fourth in the Bragg Family Saga.

Other books you might like:
Susan Johnson, *Forbidden*, 1991
Penelope Neri, *Cherish the Night*, 1992
Rosemary Rogers, *Sweet Savage Love*, 1973
Nan Ryan, *The Legend of Love*, 1991
Janelle Taylor, *Promise Me Forever*, 1991

1027

BRENDA JOYCE

The Game
(New York: Avon, 1995)

Story type: Historical/Elizabethan
Major character(s): Katherine Fitzgerald, Noblewoman (daughter of an earl); Liam O'Neill, Nobleman, Pirate
Time period(s): 16th century (1562)
Locale(s): England

Summary: On her way home from a convent, innocent Katherine Fitzgerald is kidnapped by pirate Liam O'Neill—and thus begins their fiery love/hate relationship. But Liam is playing "The Game" with everyone, Katherine's father, the Queen, and Ireland. A complex plot, lots of court intrigue, a fair amount of suspense, and Joyce's trademark sensuality keep things lively.

Other books you might like:
Virginia Henley, *Seduced*, 1994
    different setting/similar sensuality levels
Nan Ryan, *Because You're Mine*, 1995
    different setting/similar sensuality levels
Bertrice Small, *Skye O'Malley*, 1980
    similar style and setting
Bertrice Small, *Wild Jasmine*, 1992
Kathleen E. Woodiwiss, *So Worthy My Love*, 1989

1028

BRENDA JOYCE (Pseudonym of Brenda Joyce Senior)

Promise of the Rose
(New York: Avon, 1993)

Story type: Historical/Medieval
Major character(s): Mary, Royalty (Princess of Scotland); Stephen de Warenne, Nobleman, Knight
Time period(s): 11th century
Locale(s): England

Summary: Kidnapped by Norman knight Stephen de Warenne, Princess Mary of Scotland refuses to reveal her identity, chosing to sacrifice her virginity for her countrymen instead. Once the truth is known, however, Mary and Stephen are forced into marriage and they are faced with the problems of dealing with their vast political differences and their growing love for each other. Dark, intense, and passionate. Sequel to *The Conqueror*.

Other books you might like:
Shannon Drake, *Knight of Fire*, 1993
Shannon Drake, *Princess of Fire*, 1989
Anita Gordon, *The Defiant Heart*, 1993
Marylyle Rogers, *Dark Whispers*, 1991
Bertrice Small, *To Love Again*, 1993

1029

BRENDA JOYCE (Pseudonym of Brenda Joyce Senior)

Scandalous Love
(New York: Avon, 1992)

Story type: Historical/Victorian
Series: Bragg Family Saga
Major character(s): Nicole Bragg Shelton, Heiress, Noblewoman; Hadrian Braxton-Lowell, Nobleman (Duke of Clayborough)
Time period(s): 1890s (1898)

Locale(s): England

Summary: Impulsive, independent, and highly controversial, Nicole Shelton attracts the attention of Hadrian Braxton-Lowell, the Duke of Clayborough, at a country ball — but he wants a mistress and, in spite of her scandalous reputation, she is a naive innocent. Misunderstandings, prior commitments, and pride keep the pair at odds, but tragedy allows them to draw close and eventually realize their love.

Other books you might like:
Thea Devine, *Tempted by Fire*, 1992
Amanda Quick, *Ravished*, 1992
Amanda Quick, *Scandal*, 1991
Katherine Sutcliffe, *A Fire in the Heart*, 1990

1030

BRENDA JOYCE (Pseudonym of Brenda Joyce Senior)

Secrets

(New York: Avon, 1993)

Story type: Historical
Series: Bragg Family Saga
Major character(s): Regina Shelton, Amnesiac, Noblewoman; Slade Delanza, Rancher
Time period(s): 19th century

Summary: When Regina Shelton loses her memory in a train robbery, she finds herself claimed by Slade Delanza as "Elizabeth," the wealthy fiancee of his deceased brother, James, and the woman he must now nominally marry in order to save the family ranch. Confused, Regina acquiesces; but as she gradually realizes she is not Elizabeth but a wealthy, titled woman in her own right—and that she doesn't merely want a marriage in name only, Slade's life takes a very interesting turn. Tie-in to *Scandalous Love* (1992). Hard-hitting and highly sensual.

Other books you might like:
Lori Copeland, *Fool Me Once*, 1990
    another amnesiac/light, funny treatment
Johanna Lindsey, *Savage Thunder*, 1989
Diana Palmer, *Trilby*, 1993
Nan Ryan, *The Legend of Love*, 1991

1031

DONNA JULIAN

Slow Dance

(New York: Signet, 1995)

Story type: Contemporary; Romantic Suspense
Major character(s): Lily Dawn Hutton, Indian (half-Osage), Landowner (Rosehill); Sash Rivers, Fisherman
Time period(s): 1990s
Locale(s): Rosehill, South Carolina

Summary: When Lily Hutton returns to Rosehill for her mother's funeral and to settle the estate, she also intends to find answers to some old questions: Did her mother kill her father as everyone thinks, or did someone else, and why? But the town is not quite what it seems, and as Lily searches for the truth, she uncovers some dark, ugly secrets—secrets that

many would rather she left undiscovered. In addition, her growing feelings for her old friend Sash Rivers add to the complications. Dark, suspenseful, and skillful handling of sensitive racial issues.

Other books you might like:
Jennifer Blake, *Shameless*, 1994
Tami Hoag, *Still Waters*, 1992
Kay Hooper, *Amanda*, 1995
Nora Roberts, *Carnal Innocence*, 1992
Nora Roberts, *Divine Evil*, 1992

1032

DIANNA JUNE

Yesterday's Promise

(New York: Leisure, 1991)

Story type: Historical/American West
Major character(s): Faith Jennings, Heiress, Amnesiac; Cord McCamy, Gunfighter
Time period(s): 19th century
Locale(s): Texas

Summary: Upon her grandfather's death, Faith Jennings returns to Texas to inherit the family ranch, only to find her claim contested by her greedy cousin, Diego Montez. Faith is determined to stay; and with the help of gunfighter Cord McCamy (who seems so familiar to her), they end up thwarting Diego's many and varied schemes. Faith's amnesia adds an interesting twist to this fast-paced, sensual story.

Other books you might like:
Georgina Gentry, *Quicksilver Passion*, 1990
Martha Hix, *Wild Texas Rose*, 1990
Deana James, *Wild Texas Heart*, 1990
Janelle Taylor, *Follow the Wind*, 1990
Victoria Thompson, *Bold Texas Embrace*, 1987

1033

ANN JUSTICE

Sara's Family

(Bensalem, Pennsylvania: Meteor, 1992)

Story type: Contemporary
Major character(s): Sara Peters, Mountain Woman; Harrison Hixon, Lawyer
Time period(s): 1990s
Locale(s): North Carolina

Summary: Rigid, buttoned-up New Yorker Harrison Hixon literally tumbles into the chaotic, disorganized lives of Sara Peters and her "children" and he stays around to learn a thing or two about love and reality. Charming.

Other books you might like:
Candace Camp, *Rosewood*, 1991
    historical
Lori Copeland, *Darling Deceiver*, 1990
Judy Gill, *Golden Swan*, 1990
Debbie Macomber, *Father's Day*, 1991
Rebecca Paisley, *Moonlight and Magic*, 1990
    historical

1034

KARIN KALLMAKER

Car Pool

(Tallahassee, Florida: Naiad, 1993)

Story type: Lesbian/Contemporary
Major character(s): Anthea Rossignole, Businesswoman, Lesbian; Shay Sumoto, Scientist (geologist), Lesbian
Time period(s): 1990s
Locale(s): Berkeley, California; Palo Alto, California

Summary: Successful, upwardly mobile—and closeted—Anthea Rossignole is merely the fellow carpooler of geologist Shay Sumoto, until their relationship takes a more romantic turn. A nicely-paced novel of love and choices, both personal and ethical.

Other books you might like:
Sarah Aldridge, *Keep to Me, Stranger*, 1989
Katherine V. Forrest, *The Romantic Naiad*, 1993
  anthology
Elisabeth Newbold, *The City Within*, 1973

1035

KARIN KALLMAKER

In Every Port

(Tallahassee: Naiad Press, 1989)

Major character(s): Jessica Brian, Businesswoman (Management Consultant); Catherine "Cat" Merrill, Businesswoman (Sales Manager)
Time period(s): 1970s (1978)
Locale(s): San Francisco, California; New York, New York

Summary: Jessica, who swears she will settle down some day, is an organized high-powered businesswoman who travels all over the country. She meets Cat, her neighbor across the hall, and they form an immediate friendship which over time deepens into a new kind of love for both of them.

Other books you might like:
Sarah Aldridge, *Keep to Me, Stranger*, 1989
Sarah Aldridge, *The Latecomer*, 1974
Evelyn Kennedy, *Of Love and Glory*, 1989
  World War II
Elisabeth Newbold, *The City Within*, 1973
Valerie Taylor, *Rice and Beans*, 1989

1036

KARIN KALLMAKER

Painted Moon

(Tallahassee, Florida: Naiad, 1994)

Story type: Lesbian/Contemporary
Major character(s): Jackie Frakes, Architect (aspiring), Lesbian; Leah Beck, Artist, Lesbian
Time period(s): 1990s
Locale(s): Bishop, California

Summary: Stranded together in a mountain cabin during a Sierra snowstorm, budding architect Jackie Frakes and renowned artist Leah Beck come to terms with their individual pasts and begin to sort out their future together. Likable, well-developed characters in a well-written, and at times humorous, romance.

Other books you might like:
Sarah Aldridge, *Keep to Me, Stranger*, 1989
Catherine Ennis, *Up, Up and Away*, 1994
Katherine V. Forrest, *The Romantic Naiad*, 1993
  anthology of lesbian short fiction
Katherine V. Forrest, *Curious Wine*, 1983
  classic popular lesbian romance
Melissa Hartman, *The Sure Thing*, 1994

1037

ANDREA KANE

Dream Castle

(New York: Pocket, 1992)

Story type: Historical/Regency; Gothic
Major character(s): Kassandra Grey, Young Woman; Braden Sheffield, Nobleman (Duke of Sherburgh)
Time period(s): 1810s
Locale(s): England

Summary: Braden Sheffield has been Kassandra's dream hero for years, so when he rescues her from a life with a drunken father and takes her home to protect her, she falls head-over-heels in love with him. However, Kassie is woefully unprepared for marriage and, in spite of the fact that he is attracted to Kassie, Braden doesn't believe in love. In the meantime, strange and sinister things begin to happen and Kassie's nightmares return. Eventually, Kassie teaches Braden about love and he teaches her all about marriage, but not before they confront some old enemies and put past hatreds behind them. A highly sensual gothic in a Regency setting.

Other books you might like:
Mary Balogh, *The Secret Pearl*, 1991
  Regency treatment
Catherine Coulter, *Night Shadow*, 1990
Georgette Heyer, *Cousin Kate*, 1968
  a classic gothic Regency
Mary Lide, *The Legacy of Tregaran*, 1991
Marylyle Rogers, *Dark Whispers*, 1991
  different time period

1038

ANDREA KANE

Masques of Betrayal

(New York: Pocket, 1993)

Story type: Historical/Post-American Revolution
Major character(s): Jacqueline Holt, Activist, Spy; Dane Westerbrooke, Political Figure
Time period(s): 18th century (late)
Locale(s): New England

Summary: Dane, friend and associate of American political leaders, works to form a government for a new country. Jacqueline, a strong anti-federalist, does clandestine work for her cause but, despite their ideological differences, is quite attracted to Dane. Even marriage doesn't reconcile their differences as suspicion, betrayal, and accusation continue to cause them problems.

Other books you might like:
Caryn Cameron, *Liberty's Lady*, 1990
Barbara Cummings, *Rebel Wildfire*, 1992
Judith E. French, *Scarlet Ribbons*, 1989
Robin Maderich, *Faith and Honor*, 1989

1039

KATHLEEN KANE

Keeping Faith
(New York: Diamond, 1994)

Story type: Historical/Victorian America; Historical/American West
Series: Town Called Harmony
Major character(s): Faith Lind, Teacher; Kincaid Hutton, Widow(er)
Time period(s): 1870s (1874)
Locale(s): Harmony, Kansas

Summary: Harmony, Kansas, is the ideal place for Faith Lind to begin her teaching career, for widower Kincaid Hutton to recover from a disastrous marriage, and for his troubled daughter to be helped by Faith. Although he is grateful and attracted to Faith, Kincaid is reluctant to consider any kind of serious involvement. Harmony, however, lives up to its name and the town's residents eventually succeed in bringing the pair together in a warm and loving romance.

Other books you might like:
Candace Camp, *Heirloom*, 1992
Candace Camp, *Rosewood*, 1991
Jill Marie Landis, *Rose*, 1990
Pamela Morsi, *Garters*, 1992
  small town humor
Linda Shertzer, *Pickett's Fence*, 1994
  small town environment

1040

KATHLEEN KANE

Mountain Dawn
(New York: Berkley, 1992)

Story type: Historical/American West
Major character(s): Bridget Dugan, Fugitive (escaped prisoner); Jacob Fallon, Military Personnel (major), Lawman (marshal)
Time period(s): 19th century
Locale(s): Montana

Summary: When Jacob Fallon and Bridget Dugan meet on a riverboat, she is trying to avoid both jail and the killers who are after her and he is trying to find help for his emotionally disturbed young daughter. Bridget is able to reach her, but when she discovers that Jacob is the town marshal, she faces a seemingly unsolvable dilemma. Love and trust, however, do help things work out in the end.

Other books you might like:
Caroline Bourne, *Riverboat Seduction*, 1992
Deborah Camp, *My Wild Rose*, 1992
Gwen Cleary, *Riverboat Temptation*, 1992
DeLoras Scott, *Rogue's Honor*, 1992

1041

KATHLEEN KANE

Small Treasures
(New York: Charter, 1993)

Story type: Historical/American West
Major character(s): Abby Sutton, Orphan; Samuel Hart, Recluse
Time period(s): 19th century (late)
Locale(s): Colorado

Summary: Tiny Abby Sutton arrives at "her" cabin, only to find it inhabited by giant loner, Sam Hart. He scares most people, but Abby needs a place to stay—so she moves in! Eventually, her cheerfulness, stubbornness, and caring concern melt Sam's hard exterior; and when she brings an orphan boy home to live with them, Sam's reclusive life-style is happily doomed. Charming, gentle, and warm.

Other books you might like:
Pamela K. Forrest, *Autumn Ecstasy*, 1990
Dorothy Garlock, *Homeplace*, 1991
  realistic and somewhat dark
Jill Marie Landis, *Come Spring*, 1992
Cait Logan, *Wild Dawn*, 1992
Pamela Morsi, *Heaven Sent*, 1990

1042

JILLIAN KARR (Pseudonym of Jill Gregory and Karen Katz)

Something Borrowed, Something Blue
(New York: Doubleday, 1993)

Story type: Contemporary/Mainstream
Major character(s): Monique D'Arcy, Editor (magazine), Fiance(e); Richard Ives, Publisher (magazine), Fiance(e)
Time period(s): 1990s

Summary: Countess Monique D'Arcy, editor of the floundering *Perfect Bride* magazine, decides to pursue the intimacies of four "perfect" weddings to boost circulation. But things don't turn out quite as "perfectly" as she might have wished as she uncovers deceit, villainy, political scandal, blackmail, and buried pasts. But worst of all, she begins to question whether or not she really wants to go through with her own wedding to Richard Ives, the owner and publisher of *Perfect Bride*. Complex and engrossing.

Other books you might like:
Gila Berkowitz, *The Brides*, 1992
Barbara Delinsky, *More than Friends*, 1993
Barbara Delinsky, *A Woman Betrayed*, 1991
LaVyrle Spencer, *Vows*, 1988

1043

LEE KARR

Dark Cries of Gray Oaks

(New York: Zebra, 1989)

Story type: Gothic
Major character(s): Brianna Anderson, Companion; Gavin Rodene, Doctor
Locale(s): St. Augustine, Florida

Summary: Companion to emotionally disturbed teenager Cassie Danzel, Brianna seeks to protect her charge from danger—because someone wants Cassie dead. Brianna knows why, but now she must find out who.

Other books you might like:
Isabelle Holland, *Counterpoint*, 1980
Victoria Holt, *Mistress of Mellyn*, 1960
　　Classic modern gothic
Elsie Lee, *Dark Moon, Lost Lady*, 1976
Elsie Lee, *Wingarden*, 1971
Katherine Sutcliffe, *A Heart Possessed*, 1988

1044

LEONA KARR

Nightfire

(New York: Zebra, 1990)

Story type: Historical/Antebellum American South
Major character(s): Kallie Wainwright, Imposter (former barmaid), Southern Belle; Miles D'Argent, Guardian
Time period(s): 1850s (1854)
Locale(s): Natchez, Tennessee

Summary: When runaway Kallie finds herself the only survivor of a stagecoach holdup, she assumes the identity of a fellow passenger and begins a new life as a Southern Belle. However, a blackmailer and her romantic feelings for her guardian present a few problems. Romance and adventure in the Old South.

Other books you might like:
Leigh Bristol, *Sunswept*, 1990
　　Autralian setting
Margaret Mitchell, *Gone with the Wind*, 1936
　　Classic Civil War story
Karen Robards, *Morning Song*, 1989
Janelle Taylor, *Kiss of the Night Wind*, 1989
　　Post-Civil War impersonation
Kathleen E. Woodiwiss, *Come Love a Stranger*, 1984

1045

ELIZABETH KARY

Midnight Lace

(New York: Jove, 1990)

Story type: Historical/Victorian; Gothic
Major character(s): Grayson Ware, Noblewoman, Actress (aspiring); Duncan Palmer, Sea Captain, Nobleman (Marquis of Antire)

Time period(s): 1840s (1844)
Locale(s): London, England

Summary: Betrothed by her uncle to a man who represents everything she hates, Lady Grayson Ware plans to avoid marriage and fulfill her dreams of being an actress at the same time. She enlists the aid of Duncan Palmer, the scandal-tainted Marquis of Antire, and together they end up fighting to save Duncan's family business, solving an old family mystery and a new series of murders as well, and falling in love in the process. An interesting combination of sensual romance, gothic plotting, and humor.

Other books you might like:
Rebecca Brandewyne, *Upon a Moon-Dark Moor*, 1988
　　first in a trilogy
Daphne Du Maurier, *Rebecca*, 1938
　　classic gothic—a must if you haven't read it already
Amanda Quick, *Scandal*, 1991
Katherine Sutcliffe, *Love's Illusion*, 1989
Phyllis A. Whitney, *A Window on the Square*, 1962

1046

MICHELLE KASEY

The Somerville Farce

(New York: New American Library/Signet, 1991)

Story type: Regency
Major character(s): Trixy Stourbridge, Governess; Harry, Nobleman (Duke of Glynde)
Time period(s): 1810s
Locale(s): England

Summary: When the Duke of Glynde's younger brother, Willie, decides to avenge the near loss of the family fortunes to the unscrupulous Sommerville by kidnapping several of his assorted female relatives, the Duke has all he can do to set matters straight—and then the spunky Miss Trixy Stourbridge decides to blackmail him! Classic Regency fare.

Other books you might like:
Marian Devon, *Miss Osborne Misbehaves*, 1990
Carola Dunn, *Two Corinthians*, 1989
Dawn Lindsey, *Dunraven's Folly*, 1989
Judith Nelson, *Patience Is a Virtue*, 1989
Sheila Walsh, *The Incomparable Miss Brady*, 1980

1047

BARBARA KELLER

The Heart's Legacy

(New York: Harper, 1993)

Story type: Historical/Victorian; Historical/Mainstream
Major character(s): Celine Morand, Widow(er); Gerard Morand, Hero
Time period(s): 1860s; 1870s (1869-1871)
Locale(s): France; The Bayous, Louisiana; Martinique

Summary: Sterile, but determined to have an heir, Henri Morand blackmails his young wife, Celine, and his cousin Gerard into producing one for him. When he dies suddenly, they are forced to continue with the charade. Celine and

Gerard do fall in love, but circumstances keep them apart, at least for a time in this bittersweet novel that sweeps its characters from France to the Louisiana bayous and tropical Martinique. Features a strong heroine and mainstream elements.

Other books you might like:
Rosanne Bittner, *In the Shadow of the Mountains*, 1991
Lindsay Chase, *The Vow*, 1992
Catherine Lanigan, *A Promise Made*, 1991
Deborah Martin, *Creole Nights*, 1992
LaVyrle Spencer, *The Fulfillment*, 1979

1048
BARBARA KELLER

Heartbreak Trail
(New York: Harper, 1992)

Story type: Historical/American West
Major character(s): Martha Turner, Young Woman; Cole Wingate, Prisoner (accused murderer)
Time period(s): 1870s (1877)
Locale(s): Fort Apache, Arizona

Summary: When accused murderer Cole Wingate and Martha Turner find themselves the survivors of an Indian attack, they realize they have a chance to begin again — and they do — as Elizabeth and Stephen Baldwin, of the U. S. Military. Trust and love, however, do not come easily to them and they must endure a number of dangers and hardships before they can find the happiness they seek. Memorable characters in a realistic and sensual story of the Old West.

Other books you might like:
Stephanie Bartlett, *Highland Flame*, 1992
Rosanne Bittner, *Oregon Bride*, 1990
Dorothy Garlock, *Homeplace*, 1991
Dorothy Garlock, *Nightrose*, 1990
Dorothy Garlock, *Ribbon in the Sky*, 1991

1049
SABINE KELLS

A Deeper Hunger
(New York: Leisure, 1994)

Story type: Contemporary/Fantasy; Historical/Fantasy
Major character(s): Cailie Wellington, Orphan; Tresand, Vampire, Imposter (Alexander Creighton)
Time period(s): 1780s (1780); 1990s
Locale(s): Maui, Hawaii

Summary: After losing her family, Cailie is haunted by strange dreams and to elude them, she goes on vacation to Maui. Strangely, her hired escort, the enigmatic Alex, bears an uncanny resemblance to the man in her dreams—something that is not so surprising when it turns out that Alex is a vampire and has loved Cailie over and over again throughout the years. Unfortunately, she always dies by his hand. This time, however, he is determined that things will be different. Dark fantasy.

Other books you might like:
Lori Herter, *Confession*, 1992
Lori Herter, *Obsession*, 1991
Susan Krinard, *Prince of Dreams*, 1995
Linda Lael Miller, *Forever and the Night*, 1993
Cheri Scotch, *The Werewolf's Kiss*, 1992

1050
SABINE KELLS

Shadows on a Sunset Sea
(New York: Love Spell, 1994)

Story type: Contemporary/Fantasy
Major character(s): Carolyn Masters, Vacationer, Reincarnated Person; Tiernan O'Rourke, Spirit, Nobleman (Earl of Thornwyck)
Time period(s): 1990
Locale(s): Ireland

Summary: When sensible Carolyn Masters comes to Ireland to visit her aunt at ancient—and supposedly haunted—Thornwyck Castle, her skepticism eventually turns to belief when a series of events, including encounters with the dynamic castle ghost, make her realize that she has a deeper link to the castle, and the ghost, than she had dreamed. An evil villain, a brooding atmosphere, and time-spanning love complement this tale of passion and revenge.

Other books you might like:
Jasmine Cresswell, *To Catch the Wind*, 1993
    reincarnation/17th century England
Barbara Erskine, *Kingdom of Shadows*, 1988
    Scottish setting/ time travel elements/gothic atmosphere
Anya Seton, *Dragonwyck*, 1944
    classic gothic atmosphere/no paranormal elements
Antoinette Stockenberg, *Embers*, 1994
    past deeds avenged/American setting
Becky Lee Weyrich, *Forever, for Love*, 1989
    reincarnation and Jean Lafitte

1051
CARLA KELLY

Libby's London Merchant
(New York: New American Library/Signet, 1991)

Story type: Regency
Major character(s): Libby Aames, Spinster; Benedict Nesbitt, Nobleman (Duke of Knaresborough), Imposter (Chocolatier); Anthony Cook, Doctor
Time period(s): 1810s
Locale(s): England

Summary: Having dispatched her cousin and uncle to Brighton, Libby Aames is looking forward to a summer of peace and quiet, but a curricle accident decrees otherwise. Libby finds herself with a drunken Duke disguised as a chocolatier to nurse—and a doctor to help. A delightful Regency confection that deals with some rather serious issues.

Other books you might like:
Carola Dunn, *Two Corinthians*, 1989

Dawn Lindsey, *Dunraven's Folly*, 1989
Mary Jo Putney, *The Rake and the Reformer*, 1989
Mary Linn Roby, *My Lady's Mask*, 1979
Sheila Simonson, *Lady Elizabeth's Comet*, 1985

1052

CARLA KELLY

Marian's Christmas Wish
(New York: New American Library, 1989)

Story type: Regency
Major character(s): Marian Wynswich, Debutante; Gilbert Graham, Nobleman (Earl), Diplomat
Time period(s): 1810s
Locale(s): England

Summary: Seventeen-year-old Marian falls in love with Lord Gilbert, an ''older man'' with a secret life in this Regency with a Christmas setting.

Other books you might like:
Mary Balogh, *Promise of Spring*, 1990
    Unusual older-woman/younger-man theme
Georgette Heyer, *These Old Shades*, 1926
    Classic May/December Regency
Leslie Lynn, *The Rake's Redemption*, 1989
Joan Smith, *Madcap Miss*, 1989
Marlene Suson, *The Errant Earl*, 1989

1053

CARLA KELLY

Miss Billings Treads the Boards
(New York: Signet, 1993)

Story type: Regency
Major character(s): Katherine Billings, Actress (temporary), Governess; Henry Tweksbury-Hampton, Nobleman (marquess), Military Personnel
Time period(s): 1810s
Locale(s): England

Summary: Suddenly aware that life is passing him by, Henry Tweksbury-Hampton, Marquess of Grayson, makes some radical changes—and ends up unconscious by the roadside. Fortunately, he is rescued by an itinerant company of actors—and even more fortunately, the charming and perceptive Katherine Billings, governess temporarily turned actress, is part of the group. A funny, witty, and charming tale of two slightly off-beat people who find each other and themselves, in the process.

Other books you might like:
Rita Boucher, *The Scandalous Schoolmistress*, 1992
Susan Carroll, *Mistress of Mischief*, 1992
Catherine Reynolds, *The Highwayman*, 1993
Meg-Lynn Roberts, *An Alluring Lady*, 1992
Patricia Veryan, *Logic of the Heart*, 1991

1054

CARLA KELLY

Miss Grimsley's Oxford Career
(New York: Signet, 1992)

Story type: Regency
Major character(s): Ellen Grimsley, Feminist, Student; James Gatewood, Scholar (Shakespearean scholar), Nobleman (Lord Chesney)
Time period(s): 1810s
Locale(s): Oxford, England

Summary: Ellen jumps at the chance to attend a seminary in Oxford, but finds the curriculum woefully limited to the traditional womanly arts. Her consolation is meeting the vibrant scholar James Gatewood, who understands her plight. She rashly agrees to write papers for her failing brother and is delighted to draw the attention of a renowned Shakespearean scholar-in-residence—who turns out to be none other than her friend, James. Ellen's feminist inclinations are hard to reconcile with a traditional role as wife and mother, but a little intelligence and a lot of love and understanding make things work out in the end.

Other books you might like:
Jane Ashford, *The Bluestocking*, 1980
Elizabeth Peters, *Crocodile on the Sandbank*, 1975
Sheila Simonson, *A Cousinly Connexion*, 1984
Sheila Simonson, *Lady Elizabeth's Comet*, 1985
Joan Smith, *Madcap Miss*, 1989

1055

CARLA KELLY

Miss Whittier Makes a List
(New York: Signet, 1994)

Story type: Regency
Major character(s): Hannah Whittier, Gentlewoman, Castaway; Daniel Spark, Sea Captain
Time period(s): 1810s
Locale(s): At Sea; Charleston, North Carolina

Summary: Rescued after her ship is destroyed, Hannah Whittier instantly sees that the English Captain Spark doesn't match her list of necessary male qualities. He is overbearing, arrogant, and demanding—putting her to work, even to climbing the rigging. However, as French ships attack them, most of the crew is lost and Hannah becomes indispensible to Daniel, in more ways than one. Nevertheless, neither is willing to give up their lives for the other and they go their separate ways. However, a surprise is in store.

Other books you might like:
Julie Garwood, *The Gift*, 1991
    sensual and funny shipboard historical
Margaret Evans Porter, *Road to Ruin*, 1992
    wonderful characters/strong heroine and hero
Meg-Lynn Roberts, *An Alluring Lady*, 1992
Patricia Veryan, *Logic of the Heart*, 1991

1056

CARLA KELLY

Mrs. Drew Plays Her Hand

(New York: Signet, 1994)

Story type: Regency; Holiday Themes
Major character(s): Roxanna Drew, Widow(er); Fletcher Rand, Nobleman (Marquess of Winn)
Time period(s): 1810s
Locale(s): England

Summary: Seeking both safety from her lecherous brother-in-law and the solitude to work through her grief and put her family's world back together, vicar's widow Roxanna Drew takes her two young daughters and moves into the delapidated dowerhouse of a nearby estate, determined to make it livable before winter. However, the winter winds bring more than snow to her door; and when Fletcher Rand, Marquess of Winn, the estate's absentee owner, appears in search of shelter, she welcomes him into her home—and into her life, as well. Features warm, realistic characters, an emotionally involving story, and a high degree of sexual tension.

Other books you might like:
Mary Balogh, *Christmas Belle*, 1994
Mary Balogh, *Christmas Beau*, 1992
Jo Beverley, *The Christmas Angel*, 1992
Susan Carroll, *Christmas Belles*, 1992
Jeanne Savery, *A Christmas Treasure*, 1994

1057

EVELYN KENNEDY

Of Love and Glory

(Tallahassee: Naiad Press, 1989)

Major character(s): Jennifer Kincade, Military Personnel (U.S. Army Lieutenant), Nurse; Maggie Conover, Journalist
Time period(s): 1940s (1943)
Locale(s): London, England; Italy

Summary: Jennifer comes to London as a nurse for the U.S. Army during WWII with her husband, David. She meets Maggie in a bomb shelter and together they assist in the emergency delivery of a baby. They form an immediate friendship which soon blossoms into love, precipitating an emotional upheaval in both of their lives.

Other books you might like:
Sarah Aldridge, *All True Lovers*, 1978
   Depression setting
Sarah Aldridge, *Tottie: A Tale of the Sixties*, 1975
   Sixties setting
Catherine Ennis, *South of the Line*, 1989
   Civil War setting
Penny Hayes, *The Long Trail*, 1986
   Set in the Old West
Karin Kallmaker, *In Every Port*, 1989
   Contemporary setting

1058

LYNETTE KENT

No Illusion

(Bensalem, Pennsylvania: Meteor, 1993)

Story type: Contemporary
Major character(s): Chloe Smith, Magician, Divorced Person; Peter Carroll, Professor; Eric Carroll, Young Man
Time period(s): 1990s
Locale(s): Washington, District of Columbia

Summary: Chloe Smith is a mesmerizing magician, hiding from everyone the dark secrets of her life. Peter Carroll and his son, Eric, are entranced, but Chloe will only get so close. Unaware of her amazing talents and her own worth, she is overwhelmed by her shortcomings. Peter and Eric pursue her, but it takes a near tragedy to make them realize how important they are to each other. Believable characters and excellent descriptions.

Other books you might like:
Joanne Z. Adams, *Intimate Connections*, 1991
Kathryn Attalla, *Homeward Bound*, 1993
Carole Buck, *Love and Laughter*, 1989
Sharon Sala, *Always a Lady*, 1993

1059

LYNN KERSTAN
ALICIA RASLEY, Co-Author

Gwen's Christmas Ghost

(New York: Zebra, 1995)

Story type: Regency; Holiday Themes
Major character(s): Gwendolyn Sevaric, Spinster, Noblewoman; Valerian Caine, Nobleman, Spirit
Time period(s): 1810s (1816)
Locale(s): England

Summary: Faced with an eternity of boredom, Valerian Caine is given one last chance by the Heavenly Powers to return to his former, dissolute 17th century life. He must go to the future world of 1816, see to the happiness of a number of people, and end the family feud that he began years earlier, all in the four weeks before Christmas. Appealing characters, lots of wit and whimsy, and good research add to this lively Regency. Kerstan and Rasley have each written Regencies separately; this is their first collaboration.

Other books you might like:
Mary Chase Comstock, *A Midsummer's Magic*, 1994
   fantasy and humorous elements
Karen Harbaugh, *The Vampire Viscount*, 1995
   paranormal theme
Sandra Heath, *The Halloween Husband*, 1994
   fantasy elements
Barbara Metzger, *Father Christmas*, 1995
   holiday theme
Kasey Michaels, *The Haunted Miss Hampshire*, 1992
   fantasy elements

1060
LYNN KERSTAN

A Spirited Affair
(New York: Zebra, 1993)

Story type: Regency
Major character(s): Jillian Lamb, Debutante (reluctant), Farmer (sheep farmer); Earl of Coltrane, Nobleman, Guardian
Time period(s): 1810s
Locale(s): England

Summary: Jillian Lamb flies into the life of her guardian, the Earl of Coltrane, seeking money to save her sheep farm. Instead, the Earl decides she needs to be properly "launched" and wed, so he places her in the care of his aunt who sets about doing just that—with superb results! However, when the Earl finds himself surprisingly jealous of Jillian's plethora of suitors, he begins to reassess the situation and take some action of his own. Witty and funny.

Other books you might like:
Clare Darcy, *Georgina*, 1971
Georgette Heyer, *Sylvester, or the Wicked Uncle*, 1957
Sheila O'Hallion, *The Captured Heart*, 1991
Carol Proctor, *Unlikely Guardian*, 1990
Joan Smith, *The Spanish Lady*, 1993

1061
LUCY KIDD

A Rose Without Thorns
(New York: Bantam, 1991)

Story type: Historical/French Revolution
Major character(s): Susannah Brig, Gentlewoman; Nicholas Carrick, Actor
Time period(s): 1780s (1787)
Locale(s): London, England; Virginia

Summary: Susannah, spurned by her aristocratic aunt, escapes servitude by joining the fashionable Bohemian London underworld. She loses her heart to dashing actor Nicholas Carrick and as the French Revolution gains momentum, Susannah fights for her life, her liberty, and most of all, her love.

Other books you might like:
Mollie Ashton, *Terms of Surrender*, 1990
Catherine Coulter, *Night Shadow*, 1989
Iris Johansen, *Storm Winds*, 1991
Catherine Lyndell, *Stolen Dreams*, 1989

1062
JANE KIDDER

Mail-Order Temptress
(New York: Zebra, 1992)

Story type: Historical/American West; Historical/Victorian America

Major character(s): Kirsten Lundgren, Mail Order Bride; Eric Wellesley, Farmer
Time period(s): 1880s
Locale(s): Minnesota

Summary: Kirsten Lundgren certainly doesn't fill Eric's order for a bride. He wants a brawny work-horse and she is a tiny, ravishing beauty. Kirsten can only hope *The Bride's Handbook* will help! In addition, it doesn't help that there is another woman on the scene — jealous and possessive Elise. Eventually Kirsten learns how to deal with both farmlife and Eric and he realizes she is just the bride he has always wanted.

Other books you might like:
Stef Ann Holm, *Firefly*, 1990
Jill Marie Landis, *Come Spring*, 1992
Linda Lael Miller, *Daniel's Bride*, 1992
LaVyrle Spencer, *The Endearment*, 1982

1063
JANE KIDDER

Passion's Bargain
(New York: Zebra, 1994)

Story type: Historical/American West
Series: Wellesley Brothers
Major character(s): Megan Taylor, Businesswoman (lumber mill owner); Geoffrey Wellesley, Businessman (timber)
Time period(s): 1880s
Locale(s): Oregon

Summary: To save her lumber mill and escape an unwanted marriage, Megan Taylor blackmails Geoffrey Wellesley, a wealthy timber baron, into marriage. Geoff furiously resists—until passion wins him over. The arrival of Megan's former fiance causes a few problems, but nothing insurmountable. Funny, fast-paced, and hot.

Other books you might like:
Sandra Chastain, *Rebel in Silk*, 1994
 another assertive heroine/ sexy
Jayne Ann Krentz, *Wildest Hearts*, 1993
 contemporary "partners" /fast-paced, funny, and sexy.
Linda Lael Miller, *My Darling Melissa*, 1990
 another fast-paced marriage of convenience/similar setting.
Rebecca Paisley, *Rainbows and Rapture*, 1992
 another blackmailing heroine/funny and sensual

1064
JANE KIDDER

Passion's Gift
(New York: Zebra, 1995)

Story type: Historical/American West
Series: Wellesley Brothers
Major character(s): Elyse Graham, Widow(er), Frontierswoman; Nathan Wellesley, Lawman (Texas Ranger)
Time period(s): 1870s (1879)
Locale(s): Texas

Summary: Elyse Graham's outlaw brother is using her barn for a hideout, so when Texas Ranger Nathan Wellesley asks for a place to stay, she is forced to let him stay in the house—with surprisingly passionate results. Nathan goes on his way, but he has left a son behind; and when he returns a year later in search of more outlaws, he and Elyse are forced to come to terms with their feelings in order to face their future. Warm and passionate.

Other books you might like:
Joan Johnston, *Maverick Heart*, 1995
　lighter and more humorous
Linda Lael Miller, *Daniel's Bride*, 1992
Libby Sydes, *Until Spring*, 1993
Victoria Thompson, *Winds of Destiny*, 1994

■1065

APRIL KIHLSTROM

Dangerous Masquerade
(New York: Signet, 1992)

Story type: Regency
Major character(s): Rebecca Stanwood, Heiress (American); Oliver Ransford, Gentleman
Time period(s): 1810s
Locale(s): England

Summary: Acquiescing to her father's last wish, Rebecca Stanwood travels from America to England to be reunited with her estranged English family, only to find herself betrayed by her jealous stepbrother, almost sold to a lecherous villain, and eventually, disguised as a servant, working in the home of charming Oliver Ransford. Suspenseful, well-plotted, and filled with some unusually wicked villains.

Other books you might like:
Georgette Heyer, *Cousin Kate*, 1968
Barbara Metzger, *An Affair of Interest*, 1992
Amanda Quick, *Scandal*, 1991
　sensual
Lois Stewart, *Romantic Masquerade*, 1990
Marlene Suson, *The Fair Imposter*, 1992

■1066

KATHERINE KINCAID

Beloved Bondage
(New York: Zebra, 1993)

Story type: Historical
Major character(s): Mira, Spouse (of a Roman Senator); Lucas, Slave, Royalty (captive prince)
Time period(s): 1st century (40 A.D.)
Locale(s): Rome, Roman Empire

Summary: When Mira buys Lucas out of gladiator school to protect her aging senator husband, Lucas has no intention of being her slave and he even plots to kill her. However, when they both become Christians, their relationship changes for the better. Eventually their beliefs land them in the arena where Lucas' strength saves their lives; but it isn't until Caligula's murder that they are actually free. Love, passion,

and action in Ancient Rome. Interesting in that this time period has not recently been used in the romance genre.

Other books you might like:
Jack Holland, *The Fire Queen*, 1992
　similar time period — fantasy/adventure
Teresa Medeiros, *Lady of Conquest*, 1989
　Irish setting
Susan Schwartz, *The Grail of Hearts*, 1992
Henryk Sienkiewicz, *Quo Vadis?*, 1896
　classic Christian tale of Ancient Rome

■1067

KATHERINE KINCAID

Midnight Treasure
(New York: Zebra, 1992)

Story type: Historical/Exotic; Historical/Post-American Revolution
Major character(s): Kathleen Montgomery, Loyalist, Plantation Owner; Jonas Irons, Sea Captain
Time period(s): 1790s (1792)
Locale(s): Bahamas

Summary: Loyalist Kathleen Montgomery hates Americans, so when Captain Jonas Irons is shipwrecked near her island plantation, the sparks fly. Eventually, things change a bit, but in the meantime, the pair have parents, a voodoo priestess, and a hurricane to make their lives a bit more interesting. Fast-paced and sensual.

Other books you might like:
Catherine Coulter, *The Heiress Bride*, 1992
Wendy Garrett, *Sweet Southern Caress*, 1991
Laura Simon, *A Taste of Heaven*, 1989
Jane Toombs, *Traitor's Kiss*, 1992
JoAnn Wendt, *Beyond the Savage Sea*, 1990

■1068

KATHERINE KINCAID

Stormswept
(New York: Zebra, 1991)

Story type: Historical/American Civil War
Major character(s): Freedom Walker, Activist (abolitionist); Ty Carrington, Blockade Runner, Plantation Owner
Time period(s): 1860s (1863)
Locale(s): North Carolina

Summary: When Southerner Ty Carrington finds Freedom Walker aboard his ship, he assumes she is a Union spy and takes her captive. One thing leads to another and before long they are in love despite their obvious political differences. Their lives are complicated by family problems, jealousy, and the escalating war; but their love does see them through to the end.

Other books you might like:
Heather Graham, *Love Not a Rebel*, 1989
　American Revolution
Elizabeth Kary, *Let No Man Divide*, 1987

Maura Seger, *Perchance to Dream*, 1989
  South wins the War
Terri Valentine, *Yankee's Caress*, 1989
Lois Wolfe, *The Schemers*, 1991

1069

KATHERINE KINGSLEY

King of Hearts
(New York: Signet, 1993)

Story type: Regency
Major character(s): Hannah Janes, Gentlewoman; Peter Frazier, Nobleman (Earl of Blakesford)
Time period(s): 1810s
Locale(s): England

Summary: Mistaken for the undertaker when he arrives to find his uncle dead, Peter Frazier, now the new Earl of Blakesford, is appalled to find the people celebrating the old Earl's death! Clearly he must set things to rights and repair the damage his uncle has done, including making provision for irrepressible Hannah Janes and her half-brother. However, in order to inherit, he must marry. Hannah, of course, is the perfect choice, but it takes them both a while to come to that conclusion.

Other books you might like:
Jo Beverley, *The Stanforth Secrets: A Regency Romantic Intrigue*, 1989
Marion Chesney, *Lady Fortescue Steps Out*, 1993
Mary Kingsley, *A Maddening Minx*, 1992
Melinda McRae, *A Highly Respected Widow*, 1992
Sheila Simonson, *A Cousinly Connexion*, 1984

1070

KATHERINE KINGSLEY

A Natural Attachment
(New York: Signet, 1990)

Story type: Regency
Major character(s): Eliza Austerleigh, Landowner, Spinster; Edward Seaton, Nobleman (Lord)
Time period(s): 1810s
Locale(s): England

Summary: When an inheritance saves Eliza from the dreaded fate of being a companion, she thinks her life is settled and her problems are solved. But Lord Edward needs a mother for his illegitimate heir and he sets his sights on Eliza. She marries him before she knows the entire story and then must find a way to turn a marriage of convenience into a marriage of love. Witty and lively.

Other books you might like:
Mary Balogh, *Promise of Spring*, 1990
Georgette Heyer, *The Convenient Marriage*, 1934
Leslie Lynn, *The Rake's Redemption*, 1989
Judith McNaught, *Whitney, My Love*, 1985
Marlene Suson, *The Errant Earl*, 1989

1071

KATHERINE KINGSLEY

No Greater Love
(New York: Onyx, 1992)

Story type: Historical/Regency
Major character(s): Georgia Wells, Widow(er), Seamstress; Nicholas Daventry, Heir, Nobleman
Time period(s): 1810s (1819)
Locale(s): England

Summary: Informed that he must marry within the month or forfeit the inheritance of his family estate, Raven's Close, blacksheep Nicholas Daventry surprises everyone, his scheming step-aunt in particular, by marrying the charming but destitute widow in his aunt's employ, Georgia Wells. But far from being the solution, their marriage plunges them into true danger as they discover they must fight not only for their inheritance, but their lives and their love as well. Passionate, believable characters in a perceptive and nicely crafted romance.

Other books you might like:
Laura Kinsale, *The Shadow and the Star*, 1991
Judith McNaught, *Whitney, My Love*, 1985
Mary Jo Putney, *Silk and Shadows*, 1991
Amanda Quick, *Seduction*, 1990
Amanda Quick, *Scandal*, 1991

1072

MARY KINGSLEY (Pseudonym of Mary Kruger)

A Gentleman's Desire
(New York: Zebra, 1991)

Story type: Regency
Major character(s): Melissa Selby, Runaway; Justin, Nobleman (Earl of Challeigh)
Time period(s): 1810s
Locale(s): England

Summary: When a slightly tipsy Earl of Challeigh mistakes young Melissa Selby for a lightskirt, quite compromising her reputation, they are forced into a marriage that brings a number of surprises to them both. While Justin plays in London, Melissa takes his rundown estate in hand; and when he is forced to return home, he begins to realize just how special his wife is. Well plotted and peopled with interesting characters.

Other books you might like:
Gayle Buck, *Mutual Consent*, 1991
Clare Darcy, *Victoire*, 1974
Charlotte Louise Dolan, *The Substitute Bridegroom*, 1991
Georgette Heyer, *A Civil Contract*, 1961
Amanda Quick, *Seduction*, 1990
  sensual

1073

MARY KINGSLEY (Pseudonym of Mary Kruger)

A Maddening Minx
(New York: Zebra, 1992)

Story type: Regency
Major character(s): Sarah Chadwick, Governess; Phillip Thornton, Nobleman (Marquess of Pembroke)
Time period(s): 1810s
Locale(s): England
Summary: When Sarah is wounded by robbers, Phillip Thornton, the brooding and mysterious Marquess of Pembroke, rescues her and takes her to his castle to recuperate. In his magical domain Sarah's fears begin to subside, and as she searchers for answers to her many questions about her enigmatic host, Sarah falls in love. *Beauty and the Beast*, Regency-style.

Other books you might like:
Anne Caldwell, *Scandal's Darling*, 1991
Catherine Coulter, *Night Shadow*, 1989
  sensual
Joan Smith, *Madcap Miss*, 1989
Anne Stuart, *Night of the Phantom*, 1991
  sensual contemporary setting

1074

MARY KINGSLEY (Pseudonym of Mary Kruger)

The Rake's Reward
(New York: Zebra, 1991)

Story type: Regency
Major character(s): Cecily Randall, Debutante, Noblewoman (Duke of Marlow's daughter); Alexander Darcy, Nobleman (Viscount St. Claire), Spy (former)
Time period(s): 1810s
Locale(s): London, England
Summary: Attracted to spirited Lady Cecily Randall, the notorious rake and ex-spy Viscount St. Clair is dismayed to learn that she may be the woman he is seeking in connection with a former comrade's murder and an assassination plot. Misunderstandings, suspicion, and inventive plot twists abound in this intriguing Regency.

Other books you might like:
Anne Caldwell, *Scandal's Darling*, 1991
Cleo Chadwick, *A Midsummer Night's Kiss*, 1991
Emily Hendrickson, *Miss Wyndham's Escapade*, 1990
Joan Overfield, *Bride's Leap*, 1991
Amanda Quick, *Seduction*, 1990
  sensual

1075

MARY KINGSLEY (Pseudonym of Mary Kruger)

Scandal's Lady
(New York: Zebra, 1994)

Story type: Regency

Major character(s): Cassandra Aldrich, Governess; Nicholas St. John, Nobleman (Earl of Lynton), Military Personnel (former)
Time period(s): 1810s
Locale(s): England

Summary: Governess Cassandra Aldrich's discovery that the new earl, Nicholas St. John, is her old childhood friend puts her in a difficult situation. She absolutely cannot compromise her position and so she becomes reserved and secretive; society's strict codes must be observed. But he isn't happy either. He doesn't want to be a landowner and wishes he could talk about his old navy days to the Cassandra he knew. Building this relationship won't be easy, but it does all work out.

Other books you might like:
Christina Cordaire, *Daring Illusion*, 1994
April Kihlstrom, *Dangerous Masquerade*, 1992
Emma Lange, *A Second Match*, 1993
Barbara Metzger, *Lady in Green*, 1993

1076

LAURA KINSALE (Pseudonym of Amanda Moor Jay)

The Dream Hunter
(New York: Berkley, 1994)

Story type: Historical/Exotic; Historical/Victorian
Major character(s): Zenobia "Zenia" Stanhope, Noblewoman, Imposter (disguised as a Bedouin boy); Arden Mansfield, Nobleman (Viscount Winter), Adventurer
Time period(s): 1830s (1838-1839)
Locale(s): Syria; England

Summary: Determined to locate the legendary mare, String of Pearls, Arden Mansfield returns to the Middle East just in time to see his long-time friend, the eccentric Lady Hester Stanhope, buried—and ends up the unwitting protector and companion of her illegitimate daughter, Zenia (aka Selim). Although they bravely face the desert heat and violent tribesmen, their true adversaries are themselves; and it is in England that they each must finally come to terms with what they really want. A multi-dimensional story featuring complex, well developed characters and good historical detail.

Other books you might like:
Debra Dier, *A Quest of Dreams*, 1994
  an exotic quest
Kristin Hannah, *The Enchantment*, 1992
  another exotic quest
Victoria Holt, *The Captive*, 1989
  similar setting
Iris Johansen, *Tiger Prince*, 1993
  complex story/interesting characters
Mary Lide, *Isobelle*, 1988
  similary setting/lyrical treatment

1077

LAURA KINSALE (Pseudonym of Amanda Moor Jay)

Flowers From the Storm
(New York: Avon, 1992)

Story type: Historical
Major character(s): Maddy Timms, Young Woman (Quaker), Care Giver; Christian Langland, Nobleman (Duke of Jervaulx), Handicapped (brain-damaged)
Time period(s): 1820s
Locale(s): England

Summary: When Christian Langland, the rakehell Duke of Jervaulx, is committed to an insane asylum, gentle Quaker Maddy Timms takes it upon herself to help him. She is convinced he is not deranged and can recover — and she fights family, friends, and conscience to make it so. A loving, sensitive, and gentle tale of two incredibly strong people who overcome tremendous obstacles to be together.

Other books you might like:
Christina Dodd, *Candle in the Window*, 1991
Hannah Howell, *Beauty and the Beast*, 1992
Jill Metcalf, *Spring Blossom*, 1992
Helen Mittermeyer, *Princess of the Veil*, 1992
Amanda Quick, *Ravished*, 1992
    another physically challenged hero/very different treatment

1078

LAURA KINSALE (Pseudonym of Amanda Moor Jay)

For My Lady's Heart
(New York: Berkley, 1993)

Story type: Historical/Medieval
Major character(s): Melanthe del Monteverde, Royalty (Princess); Ruadrik ''Ruck'' of Wolfscar, Nobleman, Knight
Time period(s): 14th century
Locale(s): England; France

Summary: Years after the Princess Melanthe saves Ruck from death and destitution, Ruck has the opportunity to repay her generosity by becoming her champion and protector. An adventurous tale of political intrigue, dark and complex, featuring strong, imperfect characters, excellent attention to historical detail, and Middle English dialogue. Challenging and thought-provoking. Based on *Sir Gawain and the Green Knight*.

Other books you might like:
Laura Gilmour Bennett, *By All That Is Sacred*, 1991
    time travel elements
Rebecca Brandewyne, *Forever My Love*, 1982
Ellen Jones, *The Fatal Crown*, 1991
Mary Lide, *Ann of Cambray*, 1984
Judith Merkle Riley, *In Pursuit of the Green Lion*, 1990

1079

LAURA KINSALE (Pseudonym of Amanda Moor Jay)

The Prince of Midnight
(New York: Avon, 1990)

Story type: Historical/Georgian
Major character(s): Leigh Strachan, Noblewoman, Orphan; S.T. Maitland, Highwayman (Prince of Midnight); James Chilton, Religious (minister), Villain
Time period(s): 1770s (1772)
Locale(s): England; France

Summary: Bent on avenging the deaths of her family, emotionally frozen Leigh Strachan seeks the aid of the legendary Prince of Midnight, only to find he is not at all what she expected. This once intrepid highwayman is now a hearing-impaired recluse with vertigo problems. Nevertheless, he agrees to help as he is able, and together they defeat an incredibly evil villain, managing the heal themselves and each other, and fall in love at the same time. Engaging and unique.

Other books you might like:
Linda Lang Bartell, *Caressa*, 1990
Sharon Gillenwater, *Highland Whispers*, 1990
Teresa Medeiros, *Lady of Conquest*, 1989
Marylyle Rogers, *Hidden Hearts*, 1989

1080

LAURA KINSALE (Pseudonym of Amanda Moor Jay)

Seize the Fire
(New York: Avon, 1989)

Story type: Historical
Major character(s): Olympia St. Leger, Royalty (Exiled princess); Sheridan Drake, Sea Captain (Former naval officer), Hero (Reluctant)
Locale(s): Europe; England

Summary: When an exiled princess enlists the aid of an accidental hero who has no desire to become a real one, some interesting, surprising, and funny things happen. Adventure, romance, and three months on an island are all part of this unusual story.

Other books you might like:
Sarah Edwards, *Fire and Sand*, 1989
Julie Tetel, *Swept Away*, 1989
    Different period
Penelope Williamson, *A Wild Yearning*, 1990

1081

LAURA KINSALE (Pseudonym of Jay Amanda Moor)

The Shadow and the Star
(New York: Avon, 1991)

Story type: Historical/Exotic; Historical/Victorian
Major character(s): Leda Etoile, Seamstress; Samuel Gerard, Martial Arts Expert, Thief
Time period(s): 1880s
Locale(s): Hawaii; London, England

Summary: Gentleman, thief, and martial arts expert, Samuel Gerard has his life all planned out in great detail—until he meets quite conventional London seamstress Leda Etoile. She saves him, goes to work for him, and eventually marries him—but the problems caused by his double life challenge their love as well as lead them both into dangerous intrigues. Intricately plotted and sensual.

Other books you might like:
Elizabeth Adler, *Fortune Is a Woman*, 1992
Patricia Gaffney, *Lily*, 1991
Linda Ladd, *Dragon Fire*, 1992
Mary Jo Putney, *Silk and Shadows*, 1991

1082

SUSAN E. KIRBY

Leah's Love Song

(New York: Avalon, 1990)

Story type: Contemporary/Innocent
Major character(s): Leah Winters, Musician (pianist), Teacher (music); Shay Jackson, Teacher (physical education)
Time period(s): 1990s
Locale(s): Pencrest, Oklahoma

Summary: Leah Winters is torn between her love for Shay Jackson and her desire to have a career as a concert pianist.

Other books you might like:
Arlene James, *Finally Home*, 1989
Anne Ladley, *The Runaway Heart*, 1990
Lynda Stowe Landers, *A Season to Remember*, 1989
Marcine Smith, *Waltz with the Flowers*, 1989

1083

RAINY KIRKLAND

Bewitching Kisses

(New York: Zebra, 1991)

Story type: Historical/Colonial America
Major character(s): Sarah Townsend, Housekeeper (Puritan); Nicholas Beaumont, Shipowner
Time period(s): 17th century
Locale(s): Virginia, American Colonies; Salem, Massachusetts, American Colonies

Summary: Sold by her greedy relatives and sent as a slave to the Virginia Colonies, Sarah Townsend is rescued by wealthy shipper Nicholas Beaumont and hired as his housekeeper. Love follows in due course, but a misunderstanding sends Sarah fleeing to Salem—right into the Witch Trials. Fast-paced, warm, and sensual, this historical deals with a number of cultural issues and provides interesting historical detail.

Other books you might like:
Nancy Moulton, *Defiant Heart*, 1989
Andrea Parnell, *Wild Glory*, 1990
Karen Robards, *This Side of Heaven*, 1991
Valerie Sherwood, *This Loving Torment*, 1977
Becky Lee Weyrich, *Silver Tears*, 1990

1084

JULIE KISTLER

Flannery's Rainbow

(Toronto: Harlequin, 1992)

Story type: Contemporary/Fantasy
Major character(s): Flannery O'Shea, Scientist (botanist); Jack McKeegan, Businessman
Time period(s): 1990s
Locale(s): Boston, Massachusetts; Irisheer, Illinois

Summary: Jack McKeegan takes refuge from the fog in a pub where an old man dressed as a leprechaun lets him join the party. Later he finds himself naked and in the bed of the leprechaun's granddaughter, Flannery—and all his possessions have disappeared! Apparently, he has also lost his senses, for the pub is now deserted and falling apart. Flannery helps him straighten out the clothes and business part, but the magic lingers on. Charmingly done.

Other books you might like:
Annette Broadrick, *A Loving Spirit*, 1990
Jude Deveraux, *Wishes*, 1989
    historical setting
Cheryl Reavis, *Promise Me a Rainbow*, 1990

1085

SANDRA KITT

The Color of Love

(New York: Signet, 1995)

Story type: Contemporary; Ethnic
Major character(s): Leah Downey, Artist (publishing house art director); Jason Horn, Police Officer
Time period(s): 1990s
Locale(s): New York, New York

Summary: When police officer Jason Horn reacts to the death of his young son by getting drunk and ending up on Leah Downey's steps, she assumes he's one of the homeless and, impulsively, leaves him a cup of coffee. Thus begins a relationship that develops into something neither had anticipated. A well-done, emotionally compelling story that focuses on interracial relationships and the special problems that can face the couples involved

Other books you might like:
Kathleen Eagle, *This Time Forever*, 1992
    Native American emphasis
Cassie Edwards, *Wild Splendor*, 1993
    Native American emphasis
Bette Ford, *For Always*, 1995
    African American emphasis
Felicia Mason, *Body and Soul*, 1995
    African American emphasis/reverse May-December couple
Marianne Willman, *Silver Shadows*, 1993
    Native American emphasis

1086

SANDRA KITT

Serenade

(New York: Pinnacle, 1994)

Story type: Contemporary; Ethnic
Major character(s): Alexandra Morrow, Singer, Teacher (music); Parker Harrison, Musician
Time period(s): 1990s
Locale(s): United States

Summary: Unexpectedly reunited at the wedding of a mutual friend, Alexandra Morrow and Parker Harrison find themselves falling in love with each other all over again; however, past misunderstandings and present difficulties must be resolved before they can be truly happy together. Interesting detail of the contemporary music world. One of the first titles in Pinnacle's new Arabesque ethnic romance line, *Serenade* features an African American hero and heroine.

Other books you might like:
Bette Ford, *For Always*, 1995
Shirley Hailstock, *Whispers of Love*, 1994
Donna Hill, *Spirit of the Season*, 1994
    holiday anthology/three novellas
Francis Ray, *Forever Yours*, 1994
Margie Walker, *Sweet Refrain*, 1992

1087

LISA KLEYPAS

Midnight Angel

(New York: Avon, 1995)

Story type: Historical/Victorian
Major character(s): Lady Anastasia "Tasia" Ivanovna Kapterena, Noblewoman (Russian refugee), Governess; Lord Luke Stokehurst, Nobleman
Time period(s): 1870s
Locale(s): London, England; St. Petersburg, Russia

Summary: Accused of murder, Lady Tasia flees Russia and takes a job as governess to English Lord Luke Stokehurst's teen-age daughter. She's inexperienced, but intuitively knows how to make things better between Luke and his daughter. Haunted by fears of capture, reluctant to share her true identity, and in love with her employer, Tasia lives in constant turmoil, afraid to be happy, dreading that one day she will be forced to return to Russia. Demanding, powerful, passionate, and compelling.

Other books you might like:
Elaine Coffman, *A Time for Roses*, 1995
    Russian setting/different time period
Constance Heaven, *The House of Kuragin*, 1972
    first of a classic series
Kasey Michaels, *Legacy of the Rose*, 1992
Anita Mills, *Falling Stars*, 1993
    Russian setting

1088

LISA KLEYPAS

Only in Your Arms

(New York: Avon, 1992)

Story type: Historical/Antebellum American South
Major character(s): Lysette Kersaint, Gentlewoman, Runaway (from an unwanted marriage); Max Vallerand, Rake, Gentleman
Time period(s): 1800s (1805)
Locale(s): New Orleans, Louisiana

Summary: Rather than marry the cruel man her stepfather has "sold" her to, independent Lysette Kersaint escapes — right into the arms of the equally dangerous, wealthy rake, Max Vallerand. Driven by vengeance, Max intends to use Lysette to destroy her fiance, but when he marries her instead, their lives take an unexpected and passionate turn — eventually for the best. Good depiction of Creole life and some political/historical detail.

Other books you might like:
Kat Martin, *Creole Fires*, 1992
Eugenia Riley, *Rogue's Mistress*, 1991
Alexandra Ripley, *New Orleans Legacy*, 1987
Diane Gates Robinson, *Delta Desire*, 1991
Bobbi Smith, *Bayou Bride*, 1991

1089

LISA KLEYPAS

Only with Your Love

(New York: Avon, 1992)

Story type: Historical/Exotic
Major character(s): Celia Vallerand, Captive; Justin "The Griffin" Vallerand, Sea Captain, Pirate; Philippe Vallerand, Doctor
Time period(s): 1810s (1817)
Locale(s): Gulf of Mexico, At Sea

Summary: Celia Vallerand's sea voyage to America with her new husband, Philippe, turns into a nightmare when they are kidnapped and she is rescued by the legendary "Griffin," a man who bears a striking resemblance to her husband. A story of passion, risk, and adventure set against an appropriately sultry and exotic backdrop. Follows *Only in Your Arms*.

Other books you might like:
Marsha Bauer, *Pirate's Angel*, 1991
Christine Dorsey, *Captain's Captive*, 1991
Connie Mason, *Tempt the Devil*, 1990
Meagan McKinney, *Till Dawn Tames the Night*, 1991
Lynette Vinet, *Pirate's Bride*, 1989

1090

LISA KLEYPAS

Then Came You

(New York: Avon, 1993)

Story type: Historical

Major character(s): Lily Lawson, Gentlewoman; Alex Ruiford, Nobleman (Lord Wolverton), Widow(er)
Time period(s): 1820s
Locale(s): London, England
Summary: Appalled that her meek sister might actually marry Lord Wolverton, reckless, independent Lily marries him herself—only to find herself madly in love with a man who had really wanted to marry her sister, Penny, instead. The pair have a lot to overcome before they can find happiness and make their lives run smoothly.

Other books you might like:
Susan Carroll, *Christmas Belles*, 1992
    Regency
Kathleen Harrington, *Sunshine and Shadow*, 1993
Georgette Heyer, *The Convenient Marriage*, 1934
    classic Regency
Katherine Kingsley, *No Greater Love*, 1992
Betina M. Krahn, *The Last Bachelor*, 1994

`1091`

KRISTIE KNIGHT (Pseudonym of Nancy Knight)

The Garden Path

(Toronto: Harlequin, 1992)

Story type: Historical/Antebellum American South
Major character(s): Thalia Fremont, Southern Belle, Businesswoman (plantation manager); Justin Lionheart, Military Personnel (Captain)
Locale(s): United States (the Carolinas)
Summary: Capable and independent Thalia Fremont finds herself suddenly "undone" when she meets devastatingly attractive Justin Lionheart, a Virginian with a mysterious purpose. A conniving wastrel brother, an attempted forced marriage, and several murders further complicate things, but Thalia and Justin succeed in unmasking the villain and setting things to rights in a somewhat complex story. Filled with mystery, suspense, and plenty of Antebellum atmosphere.

Other books you might like:
Brenna Braxton-Barshon, *Southern Oaks*, 1991
Thea Devine, *Southern Seduction*, 1991
Wendy Garrett, *Sweet Southern Caress*, 1991
Nicole Jordan, *Moonwitch*, 1991
Kathleen E. Woodiwiss, *Come Love a Stranger*, 1984

`1092`

KRISTIE KNIGHT (Pseudonym of Nancy Knight)

No Man's Fortune

(Toronto: Harlequin, 1993)

Story type: Historical/Exotic
Major character(s): Fortune Anthony, Adventurer, Traveller; Beaumont Gregory, Gambler
Time period(s): 1840s (1848)
Locale(s): Panama
Summary: On their way to California, Fortune Anthony and her family are forced to stay in Panama when the ship scheduled to take them on the rest of the journey doesn't arrive. As they adjust to their situation, the adventurous Fortune attracts the attention of gambler Beau Gregory, and although the resourceful Fortune solves most of her family's difficulties, Beau eventually lends a hand. Love in an interesting historical setting.

Other books you might like:
Tena Carlyle, *Captive Treasure*, 1992
    Mexican treasure hunt
Nicole Jordan, *Wild Star*, 1992
    American West setting
Laura Simon, *A Taste of Heaven*, 1989
    Caribbean setting

`1093`

VIVIAN KNIGHT-JENKINS

Love's Timeless Dance

(New York: Love Spell, 1993)

Story type: Time Travel
Major character(s): Leanne Sullivan, Dancer (choreographer), Time Traveller; Iain McBride, Widow(er)
Time period(s): 1990s; 17th century (1692)
Locale(s): Glencoe, Scotland
Summary: Choreographer Leanne Sullivan gets so intensely into her Scottish dance that she is transported back 300 years and ends up in Iain MacBride's arms. Suspicious of the attractive stranger, who just might make trouble for his newly-married sister, Iain takes her off to his cottage for the night and ends up being ordered to become handfasted to Leanne as a result. Love soon follows, as does Leanne's realization that the historical massacre that took place in Glencoe is about to become a reality!

Other books you might like:
Jude Deveraux, *A Knight in Shining Armor*, 1989
Diana Gabaldon, *Dragonfly in Amber*, 1992
    sequel to *Outlander*
Diana Gabaldon, *Outlander*, 1991
Diana Gabaldon, *Voyager*, 1994
    sequel to *Dragonfly in Amber*
Shelly Thacker, *Forever His*, 1993

`1094`

VIVIAN KNIGHT-JENKINS

Passion's Timeless Hour

(New York: Leisure, 1992)

Story type: Time Travel
Major character(s): Rebecca Ann Warren, Time Traveller, Nurse (military); William Alexander Ransom, Military Personnel (Confederate lieutenant colonel)
Time period(s): 1960s (1968); 1860s (1863)
Locale(s): Tennessee; Vietnam
Summary: Nurse Lt. Rebecca wakes up from her Vietnam War injury and finds herself in a Civil War confederate medical tent. An attractive lieutenant colonel, spies, and the usual time travel dilemmas are part of this historical.

Other books you might like:
Barbara Bretton, *Somewhere in Time*, 1992
Sandra Canfield, *The Loving*, 1992
Lori Copeland, *Forever Ashley*, 1992
Jude Deveraux, *A Knight in Shining Armor*, 1989
Eugenia Riley, *A Tryst in Time*, 1992

1095
ANNE KNOLL

The Stolen Bride of Glengarra Castle
(New York: Zebra, 1990)

Story type: Gothic
Major character(s): Elly Kincaid, Bride (reluctant); Gavin Mitchell, Nobleman (owner of Castle Bonnie Brae)
Locale(s): Ireland

Summary: To save the man she has loved since childhood from exposure as a member of the revolutionary Fenians, Elly allows herself to be married off to Sir Gavin Mitchell, the brooding and enigmatic owner of the mysterious Castle Bonnie Brae. Eventually, of course, Elly and Gavin fall in love, but legendary evil and political realities make the going anything but smooth. Politics, intrigue, and sensuality in a traditional gothic setting.

Other books you might like:
Victoria Holt, *Bride of Pendorric*, 1962
Victoria Holt, *Menfreya in the Morning*, 1966
Sara Hylton, *The Whispering Glade*, 1985
Katherine Sutcliffe, *A Heart Possessed*, 1988
Beverly C. Warren, *Lost Ladies of Windswept Moor*, 1990

1096
KATHLEEN KORBEL (Pseudonym of Eileen Dreyer)

A Soldier's Heart
(New York: Silhouette, 1994)

Story type: Contemporary
Major character(s): Claire Henderson, Nurse (former; Vietnam veteran), Innkeeper (bed and breakfast owner); Tony Riordan, Military Personnel (Vietnam veteran)
Time period(s): 1990s
Locale(s): Virginia

Summary: When ex-marine Tony Riordan goes in search of the army nurse who refused to let him die at Chu Lai, he finds a woman outwardly happy, well-adjusted, and successful, but inwardly tormented by nightmares from Nam. Just as she once saved his life, it now becomes his goal to help her save her own. A sensitive, poignant, and loving story that deals with the issues of war, guilt, and post traumatic stress disorder and the havoc they can wreak on the lives of all involved. Well-written, hard-hitting, and emotionally involving. A 1995 Rita Award Winner.

Other books you might like:
Catherine Anderson, *Cheyenne Amber*, 1994
  historical "issues" romance
Catherine Anderson, *Coming Up Roses*, 1993
  historical "issues" romance

Kathleen Eagle, *Heaven and Earth*, 1990
  a caring hero
Kathleen Eagle, *This Time Forever*, 1992

1097
BETINA M. KRAHN

Behind Closed Doors
(New York: Avon, 1991)

Story type: Historical/Elizabethan
Major character(s): Corinna "Corrie" Huntington, Noblewoman (lady in waiting to Elizabeth I); Rugar Kalisson, Ambassador (Swedish)
Time period(s): 16th century (1576)
Locale(s): London, England

Summary: Summoned to court by Queen Elizabeth, sweet and innocent Corrie Huntington finds court life fascinating and dangerous as she first enjoys Elizabeth's protection and then must deal with her jealousy when she falls in love with the handsome Swedish ambassador, Rugar Kalisson. A funny, passionate tale of court intrigue.

Other books you might like:
Jude Deveraux, *A Knight in Shining Armor*, 1989
Patricia Grasso, *Emerald Enchantment*, 1992
Bertrice Small, *Skye O'Malley*, 1980
Susan Tanner, *Captive to a Dream*, 1991

1098
BETINA M. KRAHN

Caught in the Act
(New York: Avon, 1990)

Story type: Historical/Renaissance
Major character(s): Meredith "Merrie" Straffen, Heiress, Noblewoman; John "Gentleman Jack" Huntington, Rake
Time period(s): 16th century (1550s)
Locale(s): England

Summary: In order to maintain their pleasant lifestyle when the Earl of Straffen dies, his servants arrange for his young, and supposedly biddable, granddaughter to marry handsome rake John Huntington. Although he was paid to love her and then leave, Jack is drawn to Merrie; and together they must outwit the villains and set things right. Believable characters, witty dialog, and plenty of passion.

Other books you might like:
Cordia Byers, *Desire and Deceive*, 1990
Cordia Byers, *Lady Fortune*, 1989
Amanda Quick, *Seduction*, 1990
Bertrice Small, *Skye O'Malley*, 1980
Kathleen E. Woodiwiss, *So Worthy My Love*, 1989

1099

BETINA M. KRAHN

The Last Bachelor
(New York: Bantam, 1994)

Story type: Historical/Victorian
Major character(s): Antonia Paxton, Widow(er), Noble-woman; Remington Carr, Nobleman
Time period(s): 1880s (1882)
Locale(s): London, England

Summary: Acutely aware of the complete vulnerability of unmarried women and their almost total lack of legal rights in late Victorian England, a highly respectable widow, Lady Antonia Paxton, decides to do something about it—and sets about obtaining husbands for a series of poor, but gently-bred young women. Her methods, as well as her political activities, bring her to the attention of society's most confirmed and eligible bachelor, Lord Remington Carr; and when Antonia daringly issues a challenge to determine who has the most difficult time of it, women or men, Remington accepts—and the fun begins. Fast-paced, funny, and relevant.

Other books you might like:
Mary Balogh, *The Secret Pearl*, 1991
Julie Garwood, *Prince Charming*, 1994
Mary Jo Putney, *Thunder and Roses*, 1991
Amanda Quick, *Mistress*, 1994
Amanda Quick, *Scandal*, 1991

1100

BETINA M. KRAHN

Love's Brazen Fire
(New York: Zebra, 1989)

Story type: Historical/Post-American Revolution
Major character(s): Whitney Daniels, Businesswoman (Distillery Owner); Garner Townsend, Military Personnel (Major)
Time period(s): 1790s (1794/Whiskey Rebellion)
Locale(s): Rapture, Pennsylvania

Summary: Set during the Whiskey Rebellion of 1794, this is the witty and humorous story of the daughter of a distiller and the man sent to close the still down. Interesting characters and plot turns.

Other books you might like:
Catherine Coulter, *Night Storm*, 1990
Judith E. French, *Bold Surrender*, 1988
   Colonial Setting
Karen Harper, *Eden's Gate*, 1989
Laura Simon, *A Taste of Heaven*, 1989
Judith Steel, *Seduction's Raging Flame*, 1989

1101

BETINA M. KRAHN

Midnight Magic
(New York: Zebra, 1990)

Story type: Historical/Regency
Major character(s): Charity Standing, Debutante; Rane "Bulldog" Austen, Nobleman
Time period(s): 1810s
Locale(s): Devonshire, England

Summary: Unknowingly, beautiful and charming Charity Standing is a jinx. Disastrous things just seem to happen to other people when she's around. No one is immune, even the man she loves. However once she realizes her effect on people, she decides to take action; and she stubbornly determines to marry not the man she loves, but someone who "deserves" all the bad luck marriage to her will bring! Sexy, witty, and just plain fun.

Other books you might like:
Catherine Coulter, *Night Trilogy*, 1989-1990
   includes *Night Fire, Night Shadow, and Night Storm*
Julie Garwood, *Guardian Angel*, 1990
Judith McNaught, *Almost Heaven*, 1990
Amanda Quick, *Seduction*, 1990

1102

BETINA M. KRAHN

My Warrior's Heart
(New York: Avon, 1992)

Story type: Historical/Pre-history
Major character(s): Aaren, Warrior, Maiden; Jorund, Pacifist
Time period(s): Indeterminate Past
Locale(s): Scandinavia

Summary: Six-foot tall Aaren is a warrior maiden who cannot marry until she is bested in one-on-one combat. Strangely, this assignment has fallen to the peace-loving Jorund, who is dedicated to a non-violent life. Kidnapping, seduction, and passion are part of this unusual and highly sensual romance.

Other books you might like:
Rebecca Brandewyne, *Beyond the Starlit Frost*, 1991
Jessica Bryan, *Across a Wine-Dark Sea*, 1991
Lindsay Randall, *Silversword*, 1990
Marylyle Rogers, *Chanting the Dawn*, 1991
Joan Wolf, *Born of the Sun*, 1991

1103

BETINA M. KRAHN

Passion's Ransom
(New York: Zebra, 1989)

Story type: Historical/Post-American Revolution
Major character(s): Blythe Woolrich, Businesswoman (owner of family business), Captive; Gideon Prescott, Pirate (raider)
Time period(s): 1770s (1778)

Summary: With the family business to run, her relatives to care for, and foreclosure on her home imminent, Blythe Woolrich needs a bit of luck. Instead she is captured by a pirate and held for ransom! Humor, adventure, and love abound as Blythe tames the captain and his crew.

Other books you might like:
Kathryn Davenport, *Pirate's Mistress*, 1989
Heather Graham, *A Pirate's Pleasure*, 1989
Jean Innes, *Buccaneer's Bride*, 1989
Johanna Lindsey, *A Pirate's Love*, 1978
Joan Van Nuys, *Beloved Avenger*, 1989

1104

BETINA M. KRAHN

The Perfect Mistress

(New York: Bantam, 1995)

Story type: Historical/Victorian
Major character(s): Gabrielle LeCoeur, Bastard Daughter; Pierce St. James, Nobleman (Earl of Sandbourne), Rake
Time period(s): 1880s (1883)
Locale(s): London, England

Summary: Although raised to become the "perfect mistress," independent Gabrielle LeCoeur dreams of marriage, instead—but to keep her mother and her "aunts" happy, she needs to find a nominal lover. She finds him in Pierce St. James, the bored, libertine Earl of Sandbourne, who needs just the kind of undercover political help Gabrielle can provide. Their bargain, however, becomes something more than either had expected and they are forced to come to terms with their feelings for each other and the reality of their situation. A witty, graceful, and well-plotted story that deals with the serious issue of the vulnerability of women in Victorian society.

Other books you might like:
Mary Balogh, *The Secret Pearl*, 1991
  courtesan heroine/Regency period
Mary Chase Comstock, *Fortune's Mistress*, 1996
  courtesan heroine/Regency treatment
Josephine Edgar, *Duchess*, 1976
  classic mainstream mistress/turn-of-the-century London
Anita Mills, *Secret Nights*, 1994
  another "vulnerable heroine"/Regency period
Amanda Quick, *Mistress*, 1995
  similar subject/more of a romp/Regency period

1105

KATHRYN KRAMER

Highland Bride

(New York: Jove, 1991)

Story type: Historical/Elizabethan
Major character(s): Moira MacKinnon, Noblewoman; Ryan Paxton, Businessman, Saloon Keeper/Owner
Time period(s): 16th century (1586)
Locale(s): London, England

Summary: Irish Moira MacKinnon is inadvertently involved in a complex plan to free captured Queen Mary and ends up falling in love with English Ryan Paxton. More history than romance, this story delivers a great deal of information about the Elizabethan period.

Other books you might like:
Philippa Carr, *The Witch From the Sea*, 1975
Jude Deveraux, *A Knight in Shining Armor*, 1989
  time change elements
Victoria Holt, *My Enemy the Queen*, 1978
Kathleen E. Woodiwiss, *So Worthy My Love*, 1989

1106

KATHRYN KRAMER

Lady Rogue

(New York: Dell, 1991)

Story type: Historical/Regency
Major character(s): Dawn Leighton, Orphan, Gentlewoman (impoverished); Garrick Seton, Nobleman, Architect
Time period(s): 1810s
Locale(s): London, England

Summary: When Lord Garrick Seton is introduced to lovely, young Dawn Leighton, he has no idea she is the same guttersnipe who had once saved him from thugs. Love blossoms, but the past has a way of haunting the present and before they can find happiness, Dawn and Garrick must confront some very real dangers and lay to rest some old ghosts. A delightful combination of *Oliver Twist* and *Pygmalion* with Cinderella's fairy godmother thrown in for good measure.

Other books you might like:
Mallory Burgess, *Ballenrose*, 1991
Georgette Heyer, *These Old Shades*, 1926
  classic Regency
Catherine Lyndell, *Stolen Dreams*, 1989
Louisa Rawlings, *Promise of Summer*, 1989
Stephanie Stevens, *Defiant Angel*, 1991

1107

JAYNE ANN KRENTZ

Family Man

(New York: Pocket, 1993)

Story type: Contemporary
Major character(s): Katy Wade, Businesswoman, Restauranteur; Luke Gilchrist, Businessman, Restauranteur
Time period(s): 1990s
Locale(s): United States

Summary: When irrepressible Katy Wade convinces the Gilchrist family's black sheep, Luke, to come and save his family's ailing restaurant empire, she ends up in a conflict between loyalty and love that could prove as disastrous to her career as her heart. Lively and passionate.

Other books you might like:
Sandra Brown, *Texas! Sage*, 1991
Lacey Dancer, *Baby Makes Five*, 1992

Judith McNaught, *Double Standards*, 1992
Nadine Miller, *Iron and Lace*, 1992

1108
JAYNE ANN KRENTZ
The Golden Chance
(New York: Pocket, 1990)

Story type: Contemporary
Major character(s): Philadelphia "Phila" Fox, Social Worker (Former), Heiress (Of stock shares); Nicodemus "Nick" Lightfoot, Businessman (Consultant; prodigal son)
Time period(s): 1980s
Locale(s): Holloway, Washington; Seattle, Washington; Port Claxton, Washington

Summary: After inheriting shares from her best friend in the company owned by the powerful Casleton and Lightfoot families, Phila accepts the invitation of Nick Lightfoot, the family's prodigal son, and goes to Port Claxton to meet the relatives. Love, intrigue, and danger follow.

Other books you might like:
Carol Budd, *White Lies*, 1988
    Romantic suspense
Janet Dailey, *Heiress*, 1987
Judith McNaught, *Double Standards*, 1984
Judith Michael, *Possessions*, 1984
    More glitzy and mainstream
Nora Roberts, *The Welcoming*, 1989
    Silhouette Special Edition/Puget Sound setting

1109
JAYNE ANN KRENTZ
Grand Passion
(New York: Pocket, 1994)

Story type: Contemporary
Major character(s): Cleopatra Robbins, Innkeeper; Max Fortune, Heir, Businessman (hotel executive)
Time period(s): 1990s
Locale(s): Washington

Summary: Cleo Robbins, with the help of her family and friends, runs a successful inn along the Washington coast, never dreaming that her late handyman was a multi-millionaire. However, his former protege, Max Fortune, knows and is convinced that Cleo is a gold-digger who is only after his money. Eventually, of course, he sees the light, but by then he has already become involved with the family, the Inn, and especially Cleo. Fast-paced, sexy, and typically Krentz.

Other books you might like:
Susan Elizabeth Phillips, *Heaven, Texas*, 1995
    funny/witty dialog/lively characters
Susan Elizabeth Phillips, *It Had to Be You*, 1994
    woman business owner/alpha hero/funny
Karren Radko, *Dreams and Wishes*, 1993
    similar plot ideas
Antoinette Stockenberg, *Embers*, 1993
    another B & B setting/vastly different treatment

1110
JAYNE ANN KRENTZ
Perfect Partners
(New York: Pocket, 1992)

Story type: Contemporary
Major character(s): Letitia "Letty" Thornquist, Librarian, Businesswoman (company owner); Joel Blackstone, Businessman (CEO)
Time period(s): 1990s
Locale(s): Seattle, Washington

Summary: Ready for a complete change of pace, naive and somewhat frumpy-looking Letitia Thornquist leaves her library position in the Midwest and heads for Seattle to oversee her newly-inherited sporting goods company — much to the dismay of the current CEO, Joel Blackstone. Sparks and tempers fly as these two clash, but the results are predictably funny and passionate as Joel, in the process of trying to "show Letty a thing or two," discovers there is a lot he can learn from her.

Other books you might like:
Elizabeth Bennett, *Changes of Heart*, 1992
Elizabeth Krueger, *For the Children*, 1992
Judith McNaught, *Double Standards*, 1989
Judith McNaught, *Paradise*, 1991
    mainstream

1111
JAYNE ANN KRENTZ
Silver Linings
(New York: Pocket, 1991)

Story type: Contemporary
Major character(s): Mattie Sharpe, Art Dealer; Hugh Abbott, Adventurer, Spy (former)
Time period(s): 1990s
Locale(s): Pacific Islands

Summary: When art dealer Mattie Sharpe arrives on an isolated Pacific Island to acquire an antique sword, she ends up with a dead body, an old lover, and a lot of trouble. Lively action, well-drawn, interesting characters, and sizzling sensuality.

Other books you might like:
Susan Anderson, *Shadow Dance*, 1989
Jill Barkin, *Hot Streak*, 1990
Janet Dailey, *Masquerade*, 1990
Sandra Marton, *Night Fires*, 1991
Chloe Summers, *No Easy Task*, 1991

1112
JAYNE ANN KRENTZ
Sweet Fortune
(New York: Pocket, 1991)

Story type: Contemporary

Major character(s): Jessie Benedict, Businesswoman; Sam "Hatch" Hatchard, Businessman (CEO)
Time period(s): 1990s
Locale(s): United States
Summary: When Jessie Benedict's father decides to insure the success (and the successor) of his company by convincing Jessie to marry the new CEO, Sam Hatchard, he reckons without his daughter's independent spirit—and Jessie doesn't count on Hatch's persistence—and persuasive powers. Passionate, funny, and fast-paced.

Other books you might like:
Elizabeth Bennett, *Changes of Heart*, 1992
Sandra Brown, *Texas! Sage*, 1991
Susan Kyle, *True Colors*, 1991
Judith McNaught, *Double Standards*, 1984

1113
JAYNE ANN KRENTZ
Trust Me
(New York: Pocket, 1995)

Story type: Contemporary
Major character(s): Desdemona Wainwright, Caterer; Sam Stark, Businessman, Computer Expert
Time period(s): 1990s
Locale(s): Seattle, Washington
Summary: Multi-millionaire businessman Sam Stark needs the perfect wife—someone who is unemotional and able to handle his growing social obligations. So why does he find himself attracted to spunky Desdemona Wainwright, beloved member of a very emotional, eccentric family of actors? Unfortunately, the attraction of opposites isn't quite enough to bring these two together. It isn't until they work together to uncover an industrial spy and murderer that they realize that their feelings for each other are real. Funny, fast-paced.

Other books you might like:
Barbara Bretton, *Maybe This Time*, 1995
Susan Elizabeth Phillips, *Heaven, Texas*, 1995
Susan Elizabeth Phillips, *Kiss an Angel*, 1996
Sharon Sala, *Diamond*, 1994
    funny and fast-paced
Mary Anne Wilson, *The Christmas Husband*, 1995
    heroine needs a husband for the weekend

1114
JAYNE ANN KRENTZ
Wildest Hearts
(New York: Pocket, 1993)

Story type: Contemporary/Mainstream
Major character(s): Annie Lyncroft, Businesswoman; Oliver Rain, Businessman
Time period(s): 1990s
Locale(s): Seattle, Washington
Summary: In order to save the family business after her brother mysteriously disappears, Annie Lyncroft decides that a marriage to the firm's largest investor is the only solution—

and she's right—but they both get a lot more than they bargained for. Alpha hero and spunky heroine in a passionate and intriguing, fast-paced story.

Other books you might like:
Kay Hooper, *Star-Crossed Lovers*, 1990
Susan Kyle, *After Midnight*, 1993
Susan Kyle, *True Colors*, 1991
Marcia Martin, *Southern Secrets*, 1991
Susan Elizabeth Phillips, *Hot Shot*, 1991

1115
SUSAN KRINARD
Prince of Dreams
(New York: Bantam, 1995)

Story type: Contemporary/Fantasy
Major character(s): Diana Ransom, Psychologist; Nicholas Gale, Vampire
Time period(s): 1990s
Locale(s): San Francisco, California
Summary: Practical psychologist Diana Ransom wants to rescue her cousin Keely from a mysterious stranger; the immortal Nicholas Gale has the same concern. Strange, erotic dreams, an evil villain, and psychic links are all part of this unusual and highly sensual vampire paranormal.

Other books you might like:
Wendy Haley, *This Dark Paradise*, 1994
Karen Harbaugh, *The Vampire Viscount*, 1995
    Regency period
Lori Herter, *Obsession*, 1991
    first in her Vampire Series
Sabine Kells, *A Deeper Hunger*, 1994
Anne Rice, *Interview with the Vampire*, 1976
    first in her vampire saga

1116
SUSAN KRINARD
Prince of Wolves
(New York: Bantam, 1994)

Story type: Contemporary/Fantasy
Major character(s): Joelle Randall, Architect, Orphan; Luke Gevaudan, Guide, Werewolf
Time period(s): 1990s
Locale(s): British Columbia, Canada
Summary: Joelle Randall goes to the Canadian Rockies in search of the site of her parents' twelve-year-old plane crash and ends up discovering an aspect of herself she didn't know existed as well as a totally unlooked-for love. A passionate and lyrical story that features an unusually gentle portrayal of the werewolf mythologies.

Other books you might like:
Lori Herter, *Obsession*, 1991
    vampire story
Rachel Lee, *Thunder Mountain*, 1994
Cheri Scotch, *The Werewolf's Kiss*, 1992
    1st in a trilogy

Cheri Scotch, *The Werewolf's Sin*, 1994
    3rd in a trilogy
Anne Stuart, *Night of the Phantom*, 1991

1117

SUSAN KRINARD

Star-Crossed
(New York: Bantam, 1995)

Story type: Futuristic
Major character(s): Ariane Burke-Marchand, Noblewoman (heiress of the ruling family); Rook Galloway, Fugitive (Kalian)
Time period(s): Indeterminate Future
Locale(s): Spaceship; Esperance, Planet—Imaginary

Summary: Drawn by a bond she feels rather than understands, Lady Ariane goes to the prison colony on Tantalus to see Rook Galloway, the man she has long considered responsible for her brother's murder, and ends up his hostage. Eventually she becomes his partner and mate as they fight treachery and hatred in an effort to expose old secrets, right past wrongs, and set their people free. A futuristic with paranormal elements.

Other books you might like:
Justine Davis, *Lord of the Storm*, 1994
Justine Davis, *The Sky Pirate*, 1995
Amanda Glass, *Shield's Lady*, 1989
Kathleen Morgan, *The Knowing Crystal*, 1991
    first of a trilogy
Kathleen Morgan, *Heart's Lair*, 1991
    second of a trilogy

1118

ELIZABETH KRUEGER

For the Children
(New York: Silhouette, 1992)

Story type: Contemporary
Major character(s): Diana Rowe, Heiress; Reid Hudson, Single Parent
Time period(s): 1990s

Summary: Diana turns her back on her inherited wealth to help Reid's son learn to speak and to try to convince her CEO that she's serious about her work and can be trusted. In the process, she finds that she's in need of some restructuring herself. A romantic, complex tale.

Other books you might like:
Barbara Caitlin, *Shotgun Wedding*, 1992
Gail Douglas, *After Hours*, 1991
Judith McNaught, *Double Standards*, 1984
Rebecca Winters, *The Marriage Bracelet*, 1992

1119

BARBARA KYLE

A Dangerous Devotion
(New York: Onyx, 1995)

Story type: Historical/Renaissance; Historical/Mainstream
Major character(s): Isabel Thornleigh, Gentlewoman, Revolutionary; Carlos Valverde, Mercenary
Time period(s): 16th century (1550s)
Locale(s): England

Summary: Henry VIII is dead, Edward VI is dead, and Mary is on the throne-fanatically determined to return England to "the bosom of the one true Church." Bloody turmoil reigns and no Protestant is safe. Isabel Thornleigh has seen her family torn apart and now she must rescue her father from prison and probable death—and the only person who can help her is the Spanish mercenary Carlos Valverde, a man who distrusts the English as much as Isabel docs the Spanish. A fast-paced romantic adventure with excellent historical detail.

Other books you might like:
Gayle Feyrer, *The Prince of Cups*, 1995
    Italian Renaissance intrigue
Diana Gabaldon, *Outlander*, 1991
    good historical detail/Scottish setting
Judith Merkle Riley, *In Pursuit of the Green Lion*, 1990
Anya Seton, *Katherine*, 1954
    earlier time period/excellent historical detail
Anya Seton, *Devil Water*, 1962
    Jacobite rebellions/excellent historical detail

1120

SUSAN KYLE

After Midnight
(New York: Warner, 1993)

Story type: Contemporary
Major character(s): Nikki Seymour, Young Woman; Kane Lombard, Businessman (oilman), Widow(er)
Time period(s): 1990s
Locale(s): Texas

Summary: Nikki, recovering from pneumonia, rescues injured Kane Lombard, wealthy oil tycoon, from the surf. Although he can't remember who he is at first, in reality, Kane is at odds with Nikki's senator brother, a conservationist. Eventually Kane's memory returns, but by then it is too late to undo the damage, because Nikki and Kane are fast falling in love. Blackmail and political vendettas are part of this fast-paced, realistic contemporary.

Other books you might like:
Jennifer Blake, *Love and Smoke*, 1989
Kay Hooper, *Star-Crossed Lovers*, 1990
Jayne Ann Krentz, *Family Man*, 1993
Jayne Ann Krentz, *Wildest Hearts*, 1993
Marcia Martin, *Southern Storms*, 1992

1121
SUSAN KYLE

Escapade
(New York: Warner, 1992)

Story type: Contemporary
Major character(s): Amanda Todd, Publisher (half owner of a newspaper); Josh Lawson, Publisher (half owner of a newspaper)
Time period(s): 1990s
Locale(s): Bahamas; San Antonio, Texas

Summary: Amanda has known for years that she is capable of running her half of the newspaper, but she can't convince her partner, Josh. An inept manager and Josh's gambling brother add to the problems, and so does the fact that Amanda has fallen in love with Josh. Nevertheless, Amanda persists — and ultimately wins it all.

Other books you might like:
Ellen Fletcher, *Pure Instinct*, 1992
Georgia Helm, *Mad Hatter*, 1992
Marcia Martin, *Southern Secrets*, 1991
Kathleen Gilles Seidel, *Maybe This Time*, 1990

1122
SUSAN KYLE

Night Fever
(New York: Warner, 1990)

Story type: Contemporary
Major character(s): Rebecca Cullen, Secretary—Legal; Rourke Kilpatrick, Lawyer (District Attorney)
Time period(s): 1980s
Locale(s): Curry Station, Georgia

Summary: When Rebecca Cullen, the sole support of her retired grandfather and her two younger brothers, goes to see the DA after one of her brothers is arrested on drug charges, she finds him cold, unsympathetic, and incredibly attractive—and he finds her intriguing, in spite of her family's bad reputation with the law.

Other books you might like:
Kathy Clark, *Sight Unseen*, 1990
Barbara Faith, *Danger in Paradise*, 1990
Jayne Ann Krentz, *The Golden Chance*, 1990
Kay Wilding, *Rainbow's End*, 1990

1123
SUSAN KYLE

True Colors
(New York: Warner, 1991)

Story type: Contemporary
Major character(s): Meredith Ashe "Kip" Tennison, Widow(er) (Wealthy), Businesswoman; Cy Hardin, Rancher, Businessman
Time period(s): 1990s
Locale(s): Billings, Montana

Summary: When sophisticated, super-businesswoman Meredith Tennison sets out to take over Cy Hardin's business, she wants more than his company—she wants revenge. Six years ago, as a result of Cy's mother's treachery, she was poor, pregnant, and alone. Now she's back in town, unrecognized, and bent on settling old scores. In the process, she learns something about revenge, a lot about the Hardins, and more about herself.

Other books you might like:
Sally Beauman, *Destiny*, 1987
Barbara Taylor Bradford, *A Woman of Substance*, 1979
Barbara Delinsky, *Facets*, 1990
Judy Gill, *Bad Billy Culver*, 1991
Sara Orwig, *Favors of the Rich*, 1991

1124
LINDA LADD

Dragon Fire
(New York: Avon, 1992)

Story type: Historical/American West
Series: Fire Trilogy
Major character(s): Windsor Richmond, Healer, Martial Arts Expert; Stone Kincaid, Avenger
Time period(s): 19th century
Locale(s): San Francisco, California; Mexico; Indian Territory

Summary: Set on avenging the deaths of his friends, Stone Kincaid is shocked to be accosted by a nun, apparently set on killing him! It turns out to be a case of mistaken identity, however, and recognizing a kindred spirit in Stone, healer and martial arts master Windsor Richmond decides to use her healing arts on him. They endure Indian attacks, kidnappings, and assorted dangers as they pursue their quest, eventually finding love, passion, and fulfillment. Fast-paced action, exceptionally well-drawn characters, and a fascinating bit of Oriental philosophy make this an unusual and imaginative romance. Third in the Fire Trilogy.

Other books you might like:
Madeline Baker, *Prairie Heat*, 1991
Catherine Hart, *Tempest*, 1991
Laura Kinsale, *The Shadow and the Star*, 1991
Lynda Trent, *Heaven's Embrace*, 1990

1125
LINDA LADD

Frostfire
(New York: Avon, 1990)

Series: Fire Trilogy
Major character(s): Tyler MacKenzie, Con Artist, Southern Belle; Gray Kincaid, Businessman (Wealthy Railroad Baron)
Time period(s): 1870s (1871/Chicago Fire)
Locale(s): Chicago, Illinois; New Orleans, Louisiana; Mississippi

Summary: Southern belle con-artist Tyler MacKenzie sets out to wreak vengeance on her father's murderer, the dashing and rich railroad tycoon Gray Kincaid. Their relationship takes a passionate turn, however, when they find they cannot resist one another, despite deep-seated distrust on both their parts.

Other books you might like:
Sally Beauman, *Destiny*, 1987
   Mainstream/Revenge elements
Julie Garwood, *Guardian Angel*, 1990
   Revenge elements
Penelope Neri, *Bold Breathless Nights*, 1989
   Medieval setting/Revenge complications
Rosemary Rogers, *Sweet Savage Love*, 1974
   Classic Sweet-Savage/Post-Civil War setting
Kathleen E. Woodiwiss, *Ashes in the Wind*, 1979
   Civil War setting

1126

LINDA LADD

Midnight Fire
(New York: Avon, 1991)

Story type: Historical/American West
Series: Fire Trilogy
Major character(s): Carlisle Kincaid, Young Woman; Chase Lancaster, Diplomat (advisor to Juarez)
Time period(s): 1870s (1871-1872)
Locale(s): United States; Mexico

Summary: When adventurous Carly Kincaid goes to Mexico, ostensibly to visit but secretly to help her school friend and her brother overthrow the Juarez government, she discovers, too late, that she is on the wrong side and has endangered not only her own life, but that of the man she has come, reluctantly, to love. Sequel to *Frostfire*.

Other books you might like:
Leigh Bristol, *Twice Blessed*, 1991
Elaine Coffman, *Escape Not My Love*, 1990
Heather Graham, *One Wore Blue*, 1991
Linda Lael Miller, *My Darling Melissa*, 1990
Patricia Potter, *The Silver Link*, 1991

1127

LINDA LADD

White Rose
(New York: Topaz, 1994)

Story type: Historical/Exotic
Series: White Flower Trilogy
Major character(s): Cassandra Delaney, Spy (Confederate), Captive; Derek Courtland, Privateer (Australian), Blockade Runner
Time period(s): 1860s
Locale(s): Nassau, Bahamas; Rio de Janiero, Brazil; Melbourne, Australia

Summary: Cassandra Delaney, superspy for the Confederacy, hires Derek Courtland, blockade runner, for a dangerous mission. He surprises her by taking her captive and heading for his native Australia. The journey includes both a romantic interlude in Brazil and near disaster, but that is just the begin-

ning. Once they arrive in Melbourne, Derek's former lover surfaces and schemes against Cass, but the local Aborigines save the day. Fast-paced adventure.

Other books you might like:
Debra Dier, *A Quest of Dreams*, 1994
Robin Lee Hatcher, *The Magic*, 1993
   action/adventure
Meagan McKinney, *Till Dawn Tames the Night*, 1991
   exotic setting/sea voyage
Katherine Sutcliffe, *Once a Hero*, 1994
   Australian setting
Barbara Wood, *The Dreaming*, 1992
   New Zealand setting/more mystical

1128

JANIS LADEN

Moonlight Veil
(New York: Zebra, 1991)

Story type: Regency
Major character(s): Allegra Caulfield, Debutante; Nigel Havyes, Nobleman (Earl of Debenham)
Time period(s): 1810s
Locale(s): England

Summary: Irrepressible Allegra sets out to free her elder sister from an unwanted engagement to the Earl of Debenham and ends up married to the Earl herself. Funny, lively, and filled with likeable characters.

Other books you might like:
Jo Beverley, *An Unwilling Bride*, 1992
Georgette Heyer, *The Convenient Marriage*, 1934
Barbara Metzger, *An Affair of Interest*, 1992
Patricia Rice, *Touched by Magic*, 1992

1129

ANNE LADLEY

Moriah's Magic
(New York: Avalon, 1992)

Story type: Contemporary/Innocent
Major character(s): Moriah Cavanaugh, Writer (of romance novels); Gabriel Santiago, Wanderer, Biker
Time period(s): 1990s
Locale(s): New England

Summary: Moriah's writing and her life take a turn for the better (or at least become more interesting) when biker Gabe Santiago rides into town and causes her to see everything in a different light. Light and sweet.

Other books you might like:
Rita Balkey, *Passion's Fury*, 1989
   historical setting/sensual
Jillian Dagg, *Sungold*, 1992
Amanda Scott, *Bath Charade*, 1991
   Regency

ANNE LADLEY

Prescription for Love
(New York: Avalon, 1990)

Story type: Contemporary/Innocent
Major character(s): Maria Thompson, Nurse; Jason McNamara, Doctor
Time period(s): 1990s
Locale(s): Rhome, Ohio

Summary: When nurse Maria Thompson agrees to help young Doctor Jason McNamara achieve enough social polish to land a prestigious residency, she doesn't plan to fall in love—especially not with a man whose ambitions might end up breaking her heart.

Other books you might like:
Annette Broadrick, *The Gemini Man*, 1991
Martha Hix, *Texas Tycoon*, 1991
Laura Parrish, *Love's Quiet Corner*, 1989
Nancy Sheehan, *Harvest of Love*, 1990

1131

ANNE LADLEY

The Runaway Heart
(New York: Avalon, 1990)

Story type: Contemporary/Innocent
Major character(s): Miko Wyler, Designer (sportswear); Max Thompson, Lawyer
Time period(s): 1990s
Locale(s): Port William, Massachusetts; New York, New York

Summary: Miko Wyler's highly successful sportswear designs are causing controversy of the legal kind; and when her attorney boyfriend takes the opposition's side, she decides they weren't meant for each other after all and heads for New York and the larger world of fashion. True love wins out but not before Miko discovers some truths about herself and life, in general.

Other books you might like:
Susan E. Kirby, *Leah's Love Song*, 1990
Lynda Stowe Landers, *A Season to Remember*, 1989
La Verne St. George, *A Private Proposal*, 1990
Marcine Smith, *Waltz with the Flowers*, 1989

1132

ANN LAFARGE, Editor

The Joy of Christmas
(New York: Zebra, 1994)

Story type: Anthology; Holiday Themes
Time period(s): 1990s

Summary: A collection of six short stories by Zebra's To Love Again authors focusing on the warmth, joy, and love of the Holiday season. Included are: ''Home for Christmas'' by Claire Bocardo, ''Silver Bells'' by Eileen Hehl, ''A

Stranger's Touch'' by Martha Schroeder, ''Dori's Miracle'' by Joan Shapiro, ''A Rose for Christmas'' by Charlotte Sherman, and ''A Surprise for Sadie'' by Clara Wimberly.

Other books you might like:
Elaine Barbieri, *Mistletoe Marriages*, 1994
Rexanne Becnel, *Christmas Journey*, 1992
Kathleen Creighton, *A Christmas Love*, 1992
Maggie Daniels, *Moonlight and Mistletoe*, 1993
Ellen Tanner Marsh, *A Christmas Embrace*, 1994

1133

ARNETTE LAMB

Betrayed
(New York: Pocket, 1995)

Story type: Historical/Georgian
Series: MacKenzie Trilogy
Major character(s): Sarah MacKenzie, Teacher; Michael Elliot, Military Personnel, Nobleman
Time period(s): 1780s (1785)
Locale(s): Scotland

Summary: Devastated to learn that she isn't the daughter of Lachlan MacKenzie, Duke of Ross, Sarah breaks her engagement to impoverished Henry Elliot and devotes herself to teaching. But Henry's family is in dire straits and when his mother schemes to have Henry's younger brother, Michael, recently returned from India woo Sarah (and her dowry) instead things become interesting indeed. Well-drawn, appealing characters and an interesting premise involve the readers emotionally in this fast-paced story that is evocative of the era.

Other books you might like:
Diana Gabaldon, *Outlander*, 1991
  first in a series/time travel elements
Julie Garwood, *The Bride*, 1989
  humorous, fast-paced, good characterizations
Julie Garwood, *Saving Grace*, 1993
  humorous, well-drawn characters
Ruth Langan, *The Highlander*, 1994
Elizabeth Thornton, *Highland Fire*, 1994

1134

ARNETTE LAMB

The Betrothal
(New York: Pocket, 1992)

Story type: Historical/Georgian
Major character(s): Lady Marjorie Entwhistle, Spinster, Postal Worker (postmistress); Lord Blake Chesterfield, Nobleman
Time period(s): 1730s (1739)
Locale(s): England

Summary: Lady Marjorie, Postmistress of Bath, is independent and single — and she likes it that way; that is, she likes it until the dashing Blake Chesterfield appears, determined to change her mind. A witty, highly sensual romance rife with mysteries, secrets, and danger.

Other books you might like:
Mary Kingsley, *The Rake's Reward*, 1991
Catherine Linden, *Highland Flame*, 1991
Maura Seger, *Beloved Enemy*, 1992

1135
ARNETTE LAMB

Border Bride
(New York: Pocket, 1993)

Story type: Historical
Major character(s): Alpin McKay, Gentlewoman; Malcolm Kerr, Nobleman
Locale(s): Scotland

Summary: Alpin McKay returns to Scotland determined to get her land back by any means possible from Lord Malcolm, her childhood enemy. Malcolm sees her return as a chance for revenge, but their battle of wills, devious and determined, is unexpectedly jolted by the fact that they are falling in love with each other. Passionate and funny.

Other books you might like:
Diana Gabaldon, *Outlander*, 1991
Patricia Grasso, *Highland Belle*, 1991
Johanna Lindsey, *A Gentle Feuding*, 1984
Maura Seger, *The Lady and the Laird*, 1992

1136
ARNETTE LAMB

The Border Lord
(New York: Pocket, 1993)

Story type: Historical/Georgian
Major character(s): Lady Miriam McDonald, Noblewoman, Diplomat; Duncan Kerr, Nobleman, Outlaw
Time period(s): 1710s (1713)
Locale(s): Scotland

Summary: Lady Miriam is asked by Queen Anne to mediate a border dispute between Lord Duncan and his neighbor. As she efficiently hunts for the truth, she is unprepared for her discovery of his double life as an outlaw and a kind, but bumbling land owner—and her own strong attraction to him. Lots of humor and warm, engaging characters.

Other books you might like:
Mary Burkhardt, *Highland Ecstasy*, 1993
Catherine Linden, *Highland Flame*, 1991
Scotney St. James, *Highland Hearts*, 1993
Casey Stuart, *Highland Rogue*, 1991

1137
ARNETTE LAMB

Chieftain
(New York: Pocket Books, 1994)

Story type: Historical/Medieval

Major character(s): Johanna "Clare" Benison, Imposter (posing as her late twin sister), Twin; Drummond McQueen, Laird
Time period(s): 14th century (1308)
Locale(s): England; Scotland

Summary: When her twin sister dies, leaving a son, Johanna assumes Clare's identity as the widow of a Scottish chieftain. The laird, however, is not "late" after all; and when he returns from captivity, he falls for his "new" wife all over again, who now seems strangely different. Deception, secrets, and clan loyalties and responsibilities all play a part in this witty, detailed, and touching story.

Other books you might like:
Rexanne Becnel, *A Dove at Midnight*, 1993
Julie Garwood, *Saving Grace*, 1993
Linda Madl, *A Tender Magic*, 1993
Miriam Minger, *Wild Angel*, 1994
Amanda Quick, *Desire*, 1994

1138
ARNETTE LAMB

Highland Rogue
(New York: Pocket, 1991)

Story type: Historical/Georgian
Major character(s): Juliet White, Governess; Lachlan MacKenzie, Nobleman (Duke of Ross)
Time period(s): 1770s (1777)
Locale(s): Highlands, Scotland

Summary: Juliet's search to find her dead sister's child leads her to the castle of the infamous Duke of Ross in the Scottish Highlands, where she take the job of governess to his four illegitimate six-year-old daughters, one of whom may be her niece. The girls are mischievous and delightful, the father is a paradox—a devastating rake and a wonderful father—and Juliet loses her heart to both. Funny, warm, and highly sensual.

Other books you might like:
Kimberly Cates, *To Catch the Flame*, 1991
Catherine Coulter, *Night Shadow*, 1989
Catherine Linden, *Highland Flame*, 1991
    Renaissance political intrigue
Sheila Simonson, *The Bar Sinister*, 1986
    Regency
Casey Stuart, *Highland Rogue*, 1991

1139
ARNETTE LAMB

Maiden of Inverness
(New York: Pocket, 1995)

Story type: Historical/Medieval
Major character(s): Meridene Macgillivray, Noblewoman (Maiden of Inverness); Revas MacDuff, Leader (clan leader)
Time period(s): 13th century (1296)
Locale(s): Highlands, Scotland; England

Summary: In order to foil the ancient Scottish tradition that says that the husband of the Maiden of Inverness will rule the Highlands, King Edward marries Meridene, the young Maiden of Inverness, to a commoner, butcher's son Revas MacDuff, a boy who can never rule. Taken to England, Meridene learns to hate Scotland; and when Revas, who has never forgotten her comes for her, he has more on his hands than he bargained for. A fast-paced, lyrical romance with exceptionally well-done characterizations. Excellent historical detail.

Other books you might like:
Rexanne Becnel, *A Dove at Midnight*, 1993
Rexanne Becnel, *The Rose of Blacksword*, 1992
Kathryn Lynn Davis, *Child of Awe*, 1990
Julie Garwood, *Saving Grace*, 1993
Julie Garwood, *The Secret*, 1992

1140
ELIZABETH LAMBERT
Wings of Desire
(New York: Avon, 1989)

Story type: Historical
Major character(s): Cassie Jones, Pilot (Barnstormer); Linc Cameron, Pilot (World War I Flying Ace)
Time period(s): 1910s (1919)
Locale(s): Virginia; in the Air

Summary: In order to be able to compete as a team for the $50,000 prize in a cross country air race, feisty Cassie and wary Linc bow to the judges' insistence on the proprieties and get married. But what begins as a marriage of convenience is something far different by the end of the race. Humorous, passionate, and adventurous.

Other books you might like:
Barbara Bretton, *Midnight Lover*, 1989
Julie Garwood, *The Bride*, 1989
Mayo Lucas, *Camelot Jones*, 1989

1141
LYNDA STOWE LANDERS
A Season to Remember
(New York: Avalon, 1989)

Story type: Contemporary/Innocent
Major character(s): Tori Ashford, Journalist (sportswriter); Currie Volner, Sports Figure (baseball player)
Time period(s): 1980s
Locale(s): Dallas, Texas

Summary: Successful sportswriter Tori Ashford and baseball star Currie Volner fall in love, but their pride, fears, and careers keep getting in the way—until they finally get their priorities straight.

Other books you might like:
Lynn Bulock, *Roses for Caroline*, 1989
Arlene James, *Finally Home*, 1989
Jan McDaniel, *This Fragile Heart*, 1989
Laura Parrish, *Love's Quiet Corner*, 1989

Marcine Smith, *Waltz with the Flowers*, 1989

1142
JILL MARIE LANDIS
After All
(New York: Jove, 1995)

Story type: Historical/American West
Major character(s): Ena Eberhart, Dancer (former, in a dance hall), Cook; Chase Cassidy, Rancher
Time period(s): 1880s (1884)
Locale(s): Wyoming; Montana

Summary: Running from her past as a dance hall entertainer, Evangeline Eberhart takes a job as a cook for rancher Chase Cassidy and his difficult teen-age nephew. The odds are that she won't succeed—she has no culinary skills, Chase has a shady past, and the nephew, Lane, has already driven off several cooks. Misunderstandings and misconceptions abound and take a while to clear up in this gentle, sensual western romance.

Other books you might like:
Jane Bonander, *Dancing on Snowflakes*, 1995
Robin Lee Hatcher, *Liberty Blue*, 1995
Debbie Macomber, *Morning Comes Softly*, 1993
Theresa Michaels, *Gifts of Love*, 1992
Jodi Thomas, *Prairie Song*, 1992

1143
JILL MARIE LANDIS
Come Spring
(New York: Jove, 1992)

Story type: Historical/American West
Major character(s): Annika Storm, Captive, Young Woman; Buck Scott, Mountain Man, Trapper
Time period(s): 1890s (1892)
Locale(s): Colorado

Summary: Mistaken for trapper Buck Scott's mail-order bride, Annika Storm finds herself kidnapped from the train, ensconced in a mountain cabin, and in charge of a three-year-old — all before she can prove she is not Buck's intended. By the time he learns the truth, the winter snows have blocked the way out, and Buck and Annika must face a passionate winter together. A tender, gentle romance that follows *Sunflower* and *Rose*.

Other books you might like:
Robin Lee Hatcher, *Promise Me Spring*, 1991
Jane Kidder, *Mail-Order Temptress*, 1992
Constance O'Day-Flannery, *A Time for Love*, 1991
   time travel elements
Victoria Pade, *The Doubletree*, 1990

1144

JILL MARIE LANDIS

Jade
(New York: Berkley, 1991)

Story type: Historical/American West Coast; Romantic Suspense

Major character(s): Jade Douglas, Orphan; Jason "J.T." Harrington, Wealthy (millionaire)

Time period(s): 19th century

Locale(s): San Francisco, California

Summary: Returning from Paris, Jade is determined to find her father's murderer and reclaim a treasure in Chinese artifacts. Her best friend, however, decides that what Jade really needs is a husband—one like millionaire Jason Harrington—and, unbeknownst to Jade, she arranges just that! All is well until a misunderstanding separates the pair and Jade begins her dangerous quest on her own. A fast-paced mystery filled with greed, treachery, passion, and an intriguing sprinkling of Chinese alchemy.

Other books you might like:

Marsha Bauer, *Sweet Conquest*, 1990
Gwen Bristow, *Calico Palace*, 1970
Donna Fletcher, *San Francisco Surrender*, 1990
Terri Valentine, *Master of Her Heart*, 1990

1145

JILL MARIE LANDIS

Last Chance
(New York: Jove, 1995)

Story type: Historical/American West

Major character(s): Rachel Albright McKenna, Widow(er), Teacher (former); Lane Cassidy, Detective—Private (Pinkerton agent), Gunfighter

Time period(s): 1890s (1894)

Locale(s): Last Chance, Montana

Summary: Still in widow's weeds a year after her husband's death, Rachel McKenna is stunned when Lane Cassidy, one of her former students and now a noted gunslinger (and undercover Pinkerton agent), strides across the dance floor at the town's Fourth of July celebration and claims a waltz. Her defiant acceptance sets the town on its ear and scandalizes her starchy in-laws, but it also renews a friendship that eventally blossoms into love. A warm, tender, sensual American Western romance. Tie-in to *After All*.

Other books you might like:

Rosanne Bittner, *Embers of the Heart*, 1990
Robin Lee Hatcher, *Liberty Blue*, 1995
Susan Macias, *Tender Victory*, 1993
LaVyrle Spencer, *The Gamble*, 1987
Jodi Thomas, *The Tender Texan*, 1991

1146

JILL MARIE LANDIS

Past Promises
(New York: Jove, 1993)

Story type: Historical/American West

Major character(s): Jessica Stanbridge, Scientist (paleontologist); Rory Burnett, Rancher, Writer (aspiring poet)

Time period(s): 1890s

Locale(s): Cortez, Colorado

Summary: In search of "the" find of dinosaur bones that will prove her competence as a paleontologist once and for all, intrepid Jessica Stanbridge braves heat, flash-floods, and Ute animosity—and eventually vindicates herself as a professional and finds love in the arms of rancher Rory Burnett at the same time. Warm, tender, and filled with bits of interesting historical detail.

Other books you might like:

Tena Carlyle, *Captive Treasure*, 1992
Elizabeth Peters, *Crocodile on the Sandbank*, 1975
Amanda Quick, *Ravished*, 1992
    Regency paleontologist
Colleen Shannon, *Golden Fires*, 1993

1147

JILL MARIE LANDIS

Rose
(New York: Jove, 1990)

Story type: Historical/American West

Major character(s): Rosa Audi, Restauranteur, Immigrant (widow); Kase Storm, Lawman (U.S. marshall), Indian (half-Sioux)

Time period(s): 1880s (1887)

Locale(s): Busted Heel, Wyoming

Summary: Against the advice of her family, Rosa leaves Italy and travels to America to join her husband in Busted Heel, Wyoming, only to be told upon her arrival that her husband is dead—the innocent victim of a stray bullet. Kase Storm, the local Marshall, thinks she should return home; but Rosa thinks otherwise and opens a restaurant to support herself. Love blossoms between Rosa and Kase; but before they can be together, Kase realizes he must come to terms with his past and discover the truth about his natural father—and himself. Gentle, lyrical, and delightful.

Other books you might like:

Janet Dailey, *The Pride of Hannah Wade*, 1985
Kathleen Eagle, *Heaven and Earth*, 1990
Jessie Ford, *A Different Breed*, 1988
Betina Lindsey, *Waltz with the Lady*, 1990
Johanna Lindsey, *Savage Thunder*, 1989

1148
JILL MARIE LANDIS

Until Tomorrow
(New York: Jove, 1994)

Story type: Historical/American West
Major character(s): Cara James, Frontierswoman, Artisan (doll maker); Dake Reed, Military Personnel (former Union officer)
Time period(s): 1860s
Locale(s): Kansas; West; Gadsden, Alabama

Summary: Returning home after the Civil War, Dake Reed finds a newborn baby and promises the dying mother that he will take the child to relatives in Alabama. Cara, orphaned and planning to leave her prairie sod home for California, agrees to accompany Dake and take care of the baby in return for the money to finance her trip west. Unfortunately, murder, the Klan, and madness await them in Alabama. Nevertheless, during the journey they forge a loving relationship that allows them to survive and plan a future. Warm and tender.

Other books you might like:
Deborah Camp, *Black-Eyed Susan*, 1990
Robin Lee Hatcher, *Promise Me Spring*, 1991
Robin Lee Hatcher, *Where the Heart Is*, 1993
Jill Metcalf, *Autumn Leaves*, 1993
Jodi Thomas, *The Tender Texan*, 1991

1149
JILL MARIE LANDIS

Wild Flower
(New York: Jove, 1989)

Story type: Historical/American West
Major character(s): Dani, Trapper, Mountain Woman; Troy, Explorer
Time period(s): 1830s
Locale(s): Colorado (Rocky Mountains); Caribbean

Summary: When the man who raised her dies, Dani continues the only life she has ever known, that of a trapper. Discovered by Troy, an explorer searching for the man who killed his parents, Dani eventually helps him in his search and evolves from a wild mountain girl into a lovely young woman—and finds love in the process.

Other books you might like:
Rosanne Bittner, *Tennessee Bride*, 1988
Kathleen Eagle, *Private Treaty*, 1988
Jo Ann Ferguson, *At the Rainbow's End*, 1989
Catherine Hart, *Fallen Angel*, 1989
Elizabeth Lane, *Wind River*, 1989

1150
RUTH LANGAN

All That Glitters
(New York: Harper, 1994)

Story type: Contemporary

Major character(s): Alexandra Corday, Singer (aspiring); Matt Montrose, Photojournalist
Time period(s): 1990s
Locale(s): Los Angeles, California; Carmel, California

Summary: Choosing Dirk Montrose over his brother Matt, Alex Corday soon realizes her mistake and turns to Matt as her savior as he helps her support herself and further her singing career. Consumed by her career and caring for her young brother, Alex has little time for anything else, but the attraction between her and Matt is still there—and his money is a stepping stone to stardom. Dirk causes problems, of course, but all works out in the end.

Other books you might like:
Rosalyn Alsobrook, *Elusive Caress*, 1990
   historical career-oriented heroine
Jackie Collins, *American Star*, 1993
   mainstream show business glitz
Edith Layton, *The Gilded Cage*, 1991
   historical singing career vs. love
Sharon Sala, *Diamond*, 1994
   another singing heroine/different approach
Katherine Sinclair, *Through the Years*, 1994
   historical saga/two career oriented women (one a singer) plus a child

1151
RUTH LANGAN

Captive of Desire
(New York: Pocket, 1990)

Story type: Historical/Seventeenth Century
Major character(s): Alana O'Donnell, Heiress (Daughter of clan chief); Sloan Townsend, Chieftain (Of the Killenen men)
Time period(s): 17th century (1648)
Locale(s): Ireland

Summary: Sloan fully intends to kill Alana, thus wiping out the O'Donnell clan, until he sees her; then he decides to kidnap her instead. A captive-in-love-with-captor story with an Irish twist.

Other books you might like:
Rebecca Brandewyne, *Forever My Love*, 1982
Mary Ellen Gronau, *Passionate Warriors*, 1989
Johanna Lindsey, *A Gentle Feuding*, 1984
Elona Malterre, *Mistress of the Eagles*, 1990
   15th Century Ireland
Katherine Vickery, *Flame Across the Highlands*, 1990

1152
RUTH LANGAN

Christmas Miracle
(Toronto: Harlequin, 1992)

Story type: Historical/American West; Holiday Themes
Major character(s): Lizzie Spooner, Young Woman, Traveller; Cody Martin, Recluse, Frontiersman
Time period(s): 1860s (1866)

Locale(s): New Mexico

Summary: Having lost everything in the Civil War, Southerner Lizzie Spooner takes her sister, brother, and grandfather and optimistically heads for California and a new start. However, when a Christmas blizzard strands them on the doorstep of embittered, reclusive Cody Martin, it soon becomes clear that she doesn't need to go all the way West for a new and fulfilling life. A story of miracles and redeeming love.

Other books you might like:
Rexanne Becnel, *Christmas Journey*, 1992
Jill Marie Landis, *Come Spring*, 1992
Francine Rivers, *Redeeming Love*, 1991
LaVyrle Spencer, *Forgiving*, 1990

1153

RUTH LANGAN

Deception
(Toronto: Harlequin, 1993)

Story type: Historical/Seventeenth Century
Major character(s): Claire Leyton, Thief (pickpocket); Shane Driscoll, Nobleman (cousin to King Charles I)
Time period(s): 17th century (1665)
Locale(s): England

Summary: When Shane Driscoll needs a lady to present at court, he chooses Claire by default, a woman who has a wild history of crime and dishonesty. As he turns her into a lady (and a mistress), he forgives her past and then discovers that she is the notorious outlaw, "Rogue." However, her bravery helps save the throne and she discovers she has a strange heritage—so all works out well in the end.

Other books you might like:
Mallory Burgess, *Ballenrose*, 1991
Jane Feather, *Reckless Angel*, 1991
Julie Tetel, *And Heaven Too*, 1990
    funny and light
JoAnn Wendt, *The Golden Dove*, 1989
Kathleen Winsor, *Forever Amber*, 1944

1154

RUTH LANGAN

Highland Fire
(Toronto: Harlequin, 1991)

Story type: Historical/Renaissance
Major character(s): Megan MacAlpin, Amnesiac, Laird; Kieran O'Mara, Warrior
Time period(s): 16th century (1556)
Locale(s): England; Ireland

Summary: Attacked and rendered memoryless, beautiful warrior Megan MacAlpin is rescued by Kieran and Colin O'Mara and, under their protection, goes with them to their native Ireland. Her unremembered past, of course, returns to haunt her; and when she suddenly regains her memory in the midst of battle, she must choose between her love and her duty to her clan.

Other books you might like:
Rebecca Brandewyne, *Forever My Love*, 1982
Shannon Drake, *Damsel in Distress*, 1992
Mary Jo Putney, *Uncommon Vows*, 1991
Maura Seger, *Beloved Enemy*, 1992
Katherine Vickery, *Flame Across the Highlands*, 1990

1155

RUTH LANGAN

Highland Heart
(Toronto: Harlequin, 1992)

Story type: Historical/Renaissance
Major character(s): Lindsey Gordon, Noblewoman (Laird's daughter), Warrior; Jamie McDonald, Nobleman, Knight
Time period(s): 16th century
Locale(s): Edinburgh, Scotland

Summary: Jamie McDonald is assigned to protect Mary, Queen of Scots, but balks when lovely Lindsey insists on coming along. He changes his mind, however, when she saves his life and proves she can hold her own in battle; but the pair must endure intrigues, dangers, and kidnappings before they can make their love a reality.

Other books you might like:
Stephanie Bartlett, *Highland Rebel*, 1992
Patricia Grasso, *Highland Belle*, 1991
Victoria Holt, *My Enemy the Queen*, 1978
Margaret Irwin, *The Gay Galliard: The Love Story of Mary, Queen of Scots*, 1979
Amanda Scott, *Border Bride*, 1990

1156

RUTH LANGAN

The Highlander
(Toronto: Harlequin, 1994)

Story type: Historical
Major character(s): Lady Leonora Waltham, Noblewoman (English), Captive; Dillon Campbell, Laird
Locale(s): Scotland; England

Summary: Clan Chieftan Dillon Campbell kidnaps the English Lady Leonora while rescuing his brother from prison and carries her off. At first she tries to escape, but as she comes to know him, she begins to like and respect him—and he and his people come to respect and love her. Politics and passion abound in this prequel to the Highland series.

Other books you might like:
Rebecca Brandewyne, *No Gentle Love*, 1980
Jude Deveraux, *Highland Velvet*, 1982
Diana Gabaldon, *Outlander*, 1991
    time travel elements
Patricia Potter, *The Abduction*, 1991

1157

RUTH LANGAN

Texas Healer

(Toronto: Harlequin, 1992)

Story type: Historical/American West
Major character(s): Dan Conway, Doctor; Morning Light, Healer, Indian (Comanche)
Time period(s): 19th century
Locale(s): Texas

Summary: In spite of a deep hatred for the white man, Comanche healer Morning Light nurses Dr. Dan Conway back to health, falling in love with him in the process. Together they try to help her tribe overcome a multitude of serious problems, including a devastating measles epidemic, and as they develop a mutual respect and trust for each other, they come to realize that their future is together and not in separate worlds.

Other books you might like:
Deborah Camp, *Lady Legend*, 1992
Kathleen Harrington, *Cherish the Dream*, 1991
Pamela Litton, *Dance with the Devil*, 1992
Fela Dawson Scott, *Ghost Dancer*, 1992

1158

EMMA LANGE

A Heart in Peril

(New York: Signet, 1994)

Story type: Regency
Major character(s): Christina Godfrey, Heiress; John Aldric, Nobleman (impoverished marquess)
Time period(s): 1810s
Locale(s): England

Summary: Wealthy and happily single, Christina Godfrey attracts numerous unwanted fortune hunters—most of whom only want her money. Her dilemma is that the handsome rake, the Marquess of Aldric, also needs her money—but she can't resist his appeal. Finally, in order to escape an impossible liaison, she agrees to marry Aldric—and she gradually learns that he didn't just want her fortune after all.

Other books you might like:
Mary Balogh, *Dancing with Clara*, 1994
    marriage of convenience
Georgette Heyer, *The Grand Sophy*, 1950
Patricia Oliver, *Miss Drayton's Downfall*, 1994
    forced marriage
Evelyn Richardson, *The Willful Widow*, 1994

1159

EMMA LANGE

A Second Match

(New York: Signet, 1993)

Story type: Regency

Major character(s): Gwendolyn Tarrant, Companion, Widow(er); Lucian Montfort, Rake, Nobleman (Marquess of Warrick)
Time period(s): 1810s
Locale(s): England

Summary: Gwen has no money, but her job as companion to Lady Chumleigh insuring her freedom from her father and distasteful husband is enough, until Lady Chumleigh's nephew, Lucian, shows up. He's not the marrying kind, but he expects all women to adore him. Not so Gwen, which both intrigues and attracts him. Exciting and nicely written.

Other books you might like:
Mary Balogh, *The Snow Angel*, 1991
Melinda McRae, *A Highly Respected Widow*, 1992
Barbara Metzger, *An Affair of Interest*, 1992
Barbara Metzger, *Lady in Green*, 1993
Jeanne Savery, *The Last of the Winter Roses*, 1991

1160

CATHERINE LANIGAN

At Long Last Love

(New York: Avon, 1994)

Story type: Contemporary/Exotic
Major character(s): Lilli Mitchell, Archaeologist (aspiring); Zane McAllister, Adventurer
Time period(s): 1990s
Locale(s): Texas; New York; Andes, South America

Summary: Lilli and Zane were fast friends as teenagers, despite the fact that Lilli's life was filled with exotic adventurers, courtesy of her archaeologist father, and Zane's was much more conventional. Eventually, their different goals and family pressures pulled them apart; but ten years later they are together once again exploring the Andes, searching for gold—and finding love.

Other books you might like:
Virginia Brown, *Emerald Nights*, 1991
    similar setting/different treatment
Laura Hastings, *The Turtledove's Secret*, 1992
    romantic suspense
Rob MacGregor, *Indiana Jones and the Seven Veils*, 1991
    more South American fantasy adventures
Ann Maxwell, *The Diamond Tiger*, 1990
    another exotic quest
Katherine Sutcliffe, *Shadow Play*, 1991
    historical exotic adventure

1161

CATHERINE LANIGAN

A Promise Made

(New York: Avon, 1991)

Story type: Historical/American West
Major character(s): Lisa Parish, Rancher; Kevin Dalt, Rancher; Barrett Russell, Villain
Time period(s): 1880s
Locale(s): Houston, Texas; Louisiana

Summary: Betrayed, pregnant, and abandoned, Lisa Parish is not about to give up her dreams of making a success of her Texas ranch. Aided by the "family fortune" (a gift from pirate Jean Laffite) and several loyal friends, Lisa forges ahead and in the process settles some old debts, finds love, and founds a dynasty.

Other books you might like:
Rebecca Brandewyne, *Heartland*, 1990
Elaine Coffman, *Angel in Marble*, 1991
Ann Gabriel, *South Texas*, 1990
Jill Gregory, *Lone Star Lady*, 1990
Pamela Litton, *Stardust and Whirlwinds*, 1991

1162

JUDITH A. LANSDOWNE

Amelia's Intrigue
(New York: Zebra, 1995)

Story type: Regency
Major character(s): Amelia Mapleton, Debutante, Gentlewoman; Anthony Talbot, Gentleman
Time period(s): 1810s
Locale(s): London, England

Summary: Anthony Talbot, younger brother of the Earl of Rutlidge, has no intention of getting married; he has other things that need his attention—things that are infinitely more important, and more mysterious. Nevertheless, the beautiful Amelia Mapleton does catch his eye; and in spite of himself, he is intrigued. A delightful heroine, an admirable hero, and a cast of appealing secondary characters (including an earl who is a bit more than he seems) add to this story that holds more than a few surprises. Witty, nicely paced. First novel.

Other books you might like:
Donna Davidson, *Elizabeth's Gift*, 1994
  a touch of mystery/paranormal
Charlotte Louise Dolan, *The Black Widow*, 1992
  mysteries
Gail Eastwood, *The Captain's Dilemma*, 1995
  secrets
Jean R. Ewing, *Rogue's Reward*, 1995
  a dash of mystery and suspense
Jean R. Ewing, *Virtue's Reward*, 1995
  more mystery and suspense

1163

LIANA LAVERENTZ

Ashton's Secret
(Bensalem, Pennsylvania: Meteor, 1993)

Story type: Contemporary
Major character(s): Meghan Edwards, Photographer; Nicholas Hawkinson, Crime Suspect
Time period(s): 1990s
Locale(s): Ashton

Summary: Meghan goes to Ashton to try to find her sister's murder and encounters the devastatingly attractive chief suspect, Nicholas Hawkinson. She also meets and is pursued by rich Cole Benson, who keeps dropping hints about Nicholas' guilt. Nonetheless, Meghan and Nicholas are drawn to one another, and as they defend their privacy, they begin to unravel the town's convoluted, hostile relationships — and solve the crime. Mysterious and intriguing.

Other books you might like:
Lacey Dancer, *Forever Joy*, 1993
Christina Hamlett, *Charade*, 1993
Merline Lovelace, *Bits and Pieces*, 1993
Sandra Steffen, *Hold Back the Night*, 1992

1164

SUSAN KAY LAW

Home Fires
(New York: Harper, 1995)

Story type: Historical/Victorian America
Major character(s): Amanda "Amy Smith" Sellington, Fugitive (from powerful, abusive husband); Jakob Hall, Businessman (brewer)
Time period(s): 1870s (1873)
Locale(s): New Ulm, Minnesota

Summary: When Amanda Sellington takes her stepson Daniel and flees from her abusive husband and her New York home, a chance acquaintance with a woman on the train takes her to a new life in New Ulm, Minnesota. Calling herself Amy Smith, Amanda adjusts to life in the peaceful, small town and attracts the interest of brewer Jakob Hall. But Amanda has a past, including a domineering, cruel, and very much alive, husband, to deal with before she and Jakob can find the happiness they want. Warm, satisfying, and poignant.

Other books you might like:
Gwen Cleary, *Tender Heart*, 1994
Robin Lee Hatcher, *Liberty Blue*, 1995
Stef Ann Holm, *Firefly*, 1990
Jill Marie Landis, *Rose*, 1990
LaVyrle Spencer, *The Endearment*, 1982

1165

SUSAN KAY LAW

Traitorous Hearts
(New York: Harper, 1994)

Story type: Historical/American Revolution
Major character(s): Elizabeth Jones, Patriot; Jonathan Leighton, Spy (British)
Time period(s): 1770s (1774)
Locale(s): American Colonies

Summary: Handsome Jon Leighton acts so dim-witted that no one could possibly guess he is a British spy. In spite of this, or perhaps because of it, the awkwardly-tall colonial Elizabeth is drawn to him. Traitors, divided loyalties, and the War itself threaten their growing, but dangerous love, and though they are constantly torn apart, fate has a way of bringing them together again.

Other books you might like:
Gwen Bristow, *Celia Garth*, 1959
   deception and spies
Caryn Cameron, *Freedom Flame*, 1990
Millie Criswell, *Phantom Lover*, 1993
   more disguises/funnier treatment
Colleen Faulkner, *Temptation's Tender Kiss*, 1990
   more deception and treachery
Baroness Orczy, *The Scarlet Pimpernel*, 1905
   classic spy disguise story/England and France

1166

KATHY LAWRENCE

Tin Angel

(New York: Avon, 1989)

Story type: Historical/American West
Major character(s): Jessica Taggart, Heiress, Businesswoman (Gambling house/brothel); Jake Weston, Businessman (Gambling house/brothel)
Time period(s): 1870s
Locale(s): San Francisco, California

Summary: Thinking she had inherited part-ownership in her father's San Francisco restaurant, Jessica is shocked to learn she now owns a gambling house and brothel—along with her father's partner, Jake Weston. Arguments and old antagonisms keep the two apart even as their feelings draw them together.

Other books you might like:
Barbara Bretton, *Midnight Lover*, 1989
Deborah Camp, *Fallen Angel*, 1989
Dorothy Garlock, *Midnight Blue*, 1989
Georgina Gentry, *Nevada Nights*, 1989
Victoria Thompson, *Fortune's Lady*, 1990

1167

EDITH LAYTON

The Crimson Crown

(New York; New American Library, 1990)

Story type: Historical/Medieval
Major character(s): Megan Basewell, Noblewoman (lady in waiting at court); Lucas Lovet, Nobleman, Spy
Time period(s): 15th century (1488)
Locale(s): England

Summary: Sent by King Henry VII to gather information from the court of Lady Katherine, Perkin Warbeck's wife, Lucas Lovet is attracted to one of her ladies in waiting, Megan Basewell. Their love blossoms amid the intrigue as they battle their feelings for each other. Laced with a number of historical figures, this intricate court drama is filled with well-done, accurate historical detail.

Other books you might like:
Pamela Belle, *The Lodestar*, 1989
Roberta Gellis, *The Dragon and the Rose*, 1977
Roberta Gellis, *Roselynde*, 1978
   1st of the Roselynde Chronicles

Rosemary Jarman, *The Court's Illusion*, 1983
Rosemary Jarman, *Crown in Candlelight*, 1978

1168

EDITH LAYTON

Fireflower

(New York: Signet, 1989)

Story type: Historical/Seventeenth Century
Major character(s): Mary Monk, Prostitute (Would-be); Gideon Hawkes, Gentleman, Landowner (Dispossessed)
Time period(s): 17th century (1666)
Locale(s): London, England

Summary: Left with no other choice, Mary Monk sets out to support herself by becoming a prostitute. However, she falls in love with her first customer, Gideon Hawkes, a dispossessed Royalist landowner newly returned to England, and it changes both their lives.

Other books you might like:
Pamela Belle, *Alethea*, 1985
   Restoration period
Deborah Camp, *Fallen Angel*, 1989
   Another would-be prostitute
Philippa Carr, *Lament for a Lost Lover*, 1977
   Restoration period/rather serious
Jane Feather, *Reckless Angel*, 1989
   Charles I/Cromwell period
JoAnn Wendt, *The Golden Dove*, 1989

1169

EDITH LAYTON

The Gilded Cage

(New York: New American Library, 1991)

Story type: Historical/Victorian America
Major character(s): Lucy Markham, Actress, Singer; Josh Dylan, Financier, Businessman
Time period(s): 1870s (1879)
Locale(s): New York, New York

Summary: Naive as she is lovely, young singer Lucy Markham sets out to achieve success in the glittering, but somewhat tawdry, world of New York theatre and ends up attracting the attention of dashing Josh Dylan and landing the lead in a London production of *HMS Pinafore* at the same time. Her dilemma: her love or her career.

Other books you might like:
Rosalyn Alsobrook, *Elusive Caress*, 1990
   similar setting/sensual
Sandra Chastain, *Sweetwater*, 1990
   sensual
Susan E. Kirby, *Leah's Love Song*, 1990
   contemporary musical dilemma
Anne Ladley, *The Runaway Heart*, 1990
   contemporary
Laura Parrish, *Love's Quiet Corner*, 1989
   contemporary

1170

EDITH LAYTON

A Love for All Seasons
(New York: Signet, 1992)

Story type: Regency
Time period(s): 1810s
Locale(s): England

Summary: A collection of five Regency romances by Edith Layton focusing on the various seasons of the year. Each has a distinct flavor, but they add up to a delightful whole. Included are: "Spring's Promise," "Summer's Fruit," "Autumn Leaves," "Snow Broth," and "A Love for All Seasons."

Other books you might like:
Mary Balogh, *Promise of Spring*, 1990
Mary Balogh, *A Regency Valentine*, 1991
    anthology
Cleo Chadwick, *A Midsummer Night's Kiss*, 1992
Teresa DesJardien, *A June Bride*, 1991
Carla Kelly, *Marian's Christmas Wish*, 1989

1171

MARY LEASK

Sing Carols with the Angels
(New York: Avalon, 1995)

Story type: Contemporary/Innocent; Holiday Themes
Major character(s): Lynn MacDougal, Amnesiac; Adam Stone, Economist
Time period(s): 1990s
Locale(s): Canada

Summary: Injured and suffering from amnesia, Lynn MacDougal is overjoyed to get a job as assistant to scholar and economist Adam Stone. Ever practical, Lynn knows that she must get on with her life, even though she doesn't know exactly what that life is. Frightening nightmares and a growing realization that she is falling in love with Adam add to her problems, but by the end of the book the mystery is solved, her identity is once again her own, and she and Adam are planning a future together. Sweet and mild. Holiday focus is on fall and the Canadian Thanksgiving. Christmas makes its appearance only at the end.

Other books you might like:
Jo Beverley, *The Christmas Angel*, 1992
    Regency
Bethany Campbell, *The Snow Garden*, 1989
Carla Kelly, *Marian's Christmas Wish*, 1989
    Regency
Debbie Macomber, *Touched by Angels*, 1995
    paranormal elements
Emma Richmond, *Christmas Journeys*, 1995
    anthology

1172

RACHEL LEE

Cowboy Cop
(Toronto: Harlequin, 1995)

Story type: Contemporary
Series: Montana Mavericks
Major character(s): Dakota Winston, Detective—Police; Clint Calloway, Detective—Police
Time period(s): 1990s
Locale(s): Whitehorn, Montana

Summary: Detective Clint Calloway is not going to make it easy for rookie Dakota Winston when she ends up under his supervision in Whitehorn. Nevertheless, she is determined to prove that even "spoiled rich women" can make good detectives—and she does. Well done characters, a nicely wounded hero, and lots of sexual tension are pluses. The concluding volume in the Montana Mavericks series, Cowboy Cop solves the ongoing mystery and ties up most of the loose ends.

Other books you might like:
Cathie Linz, *Baby Wanted*, 1995
    Montana Mavericks Series
Pat Montana, *Storybook Cowboy*, 1995
Paula Detmer Riggs, *The Bachelor Party*, 1995
Sharon Sala, *The Miracle Man*, 1995
Ingrid Weaver, *True Lies*, 1995

1173

RACHEL LEE

Thunder Mountain
(New York: Silhouette, 1994)

Story type: Contemporary/Fantasy
Major character(s): Mercy Kendrick, Scientist (biologist); Gray Cloud, Indian
Time period(s): 1990s
Locale(s): Thunder Mountain, Wyoming

Summary: When wildlife biologist Mercy Kendrick goes to the sacred Thunder Mountain in Wyoming to find and study the wolves living on its slopes, she is helped by Gray Cloud, the defender and protector of the mountain. However, danger stalks them both from the intruders and the overwhelming power of the mountain itself, as they join forces to protect the wolves from destruction. A magnetic and magical tale steeped in Native American mysticism and lore.

Other books you might like:
Madeline Baker, *The Spirit Path*, 1993
Kathleen Eagle, *Heaven and Earth*, 1990
Kathleen Eagle, *Medicine Woman*, 1989
Susan Krinard, *Prince of Wolves*, 1994
    werewolf romance
Peggy Webb, *Witch Dance*, 1994

1174

REBECCA HAGAN LEE

Golden Chances
(New York: Charter, 1992)

Story type: Historical/American West
Major character(s): Faith Collins, Southern Belle; Reese Jordan, Rancher
Time period(s): 1870s
Locale(s): Richmond, Virginia; Wyoming

Summary: What Reese Jordan wants is a widow to bear him a child and then conveniently divorce him; what he gets is a sweet, virginal bride who needs the job! Confusion reigns, but by the time they sort it all out, they are in love and nothing else matters. Gentle and sensual.

Other books you might like:
Robin Lee Hatcher, *Promise Me Spring*, 1991
Jill Marie Landis, *Come Spring*, 1992
Jodi Thomas, *The Tender Texan*, 1991
Lynda Trent, *Beloved Wife*, 1992

1175

ANA LEIGH

Angel Hunter
(New York: Leisure, 1992)

Story type: Historical/Post-American Civil War
Major character(s): Angeleen Hunter, Young Woman, Thief (horse thief); Ruarke Stewart, Gambler
Time period(s): 19th century
Locale(s): St. Louis, Missouri

Summary: When Angeleen's father loses their stallion, Bold King, to Ruarke Stewart in a riverboat card game, Angeleen steals him back and rides off for St. Louis — only to end up sick and rescued by Ruarke. Passion and pregnancy soon follow, but marriage must wait until all their misunderstandings are resolved.

Other books you might like:
Caroline Bourne, *Riverboat Seduction*, 1992
Catherine Hart, *Temptation*, 1992
Catherine Lanigan, *A Promise Made*, 1991
Kat Martin, *Creole Fires*, 1992
Gina Robins, *Mississippi Madness*, 1990

1176

ANA LEIGH

Tender Is the Touch
(New York: Avon, 1994)

Story type: Historical/American West Coast
Major character(s): Sydney Delaney, Secretary (office assistant); Mike McAllister, Businessman (freight line owner)
Time period(s): 1880s (1882)
Locale(s): Seattle, Washington; Alaska

Summary: Determined to hold a man's job in Alaska, Sydney irritates Mike not only simply by being a woman, but by the fact that she is stubborn, won't listen to his advice, and is constantly getting into trouble. Of course, the fact that he is falling in love with her has nothing to do with anything. Nearly raped, killed, mauled by a bear, and frozen to death, Sydney finally begins to believe him, but by then she has fallen in love and has no intention of leaving Alaska. A warm, detailed, emotional story.

Other books you might like:
Cassie Edwards, *Savage Promise*, 1991
   Native American focus
Wendy Garrett, *Western Enchantress*, 1993
Kristin Hannah, *A Handful of Heaven*, 1991
Shirley Parenteau, *Golden Prospect*, 1991
Annalise Sun, *The Golden Mountain*, 1990

1177

BARBARA LEIGH

Web of Loving Lies
(Toronto: Harlequin, 1993)

Story type: Historical/American West
Major character(s): Beth Ann Calwalder, Young Woman; James Montgomery, Scout; Melissa Cadwalder, Young Woman
Time period(s): 19th century
Locale(s): Nebraska

Summary: Melissa wants James, but James wants young Beth Ann. However, when the scheming Melissa tricks James into an engagement, he and Beth Ann reluctantly say goodbye. Years later, Beth Ann has a chance to marry James by proxy, pretending to be Melissa—and then the life of lies begins and trouble abounds. Things do work out in the end, however.

Other books you might like:
Gwen Cleary, *Ecstasy's Masquerade*, 1989
Ginna Gray, *Quiet Fires*, 1991
Carol Jerina, *The Bridegroom*, 1993
Heather Graham Pozzessere, *Forbidden Fire*, 1991

1178

JO LEIGH

Special Effects
(Bensalem, Pennsylvania: Meteor, 1992)

Story type: Contemporary
Major character(s): Catlin Clark, Filmmaker (associate producer); Luke McKeever, Filmmaker (special effects)
Time period(s): 1990s
Locale(s): California (Southern California)

Summary: Associate film producer Catlin Clark is on her way up and nothing is going to stop her — certainly not handsome Luke McKeever, who has definite ambitions of his own. Besides, she knows how fickle the film crowd can be and she doesn't want to take any chances. Nevertheless, they are both attracted to each other, but it takes a tragedy to make them deal with what is really important to them both.

Other books you might like:
Jennifer Blake, *Joy and Anger*, 1991
Gail Douglas, *After Hours*, 1991
Marie Ferrarella, *Sapphire and Shadow*, 1991
Theresa Gladden, *Just Desserts*, 1991

1179

ROBIN LEIGH (Pseudonym of Robin Lee Hatcher)

The Hawk and the Heather
(New York: Avon, 1992)

Story type: Historical/Regency
Major character(s): Heather Fitzhugh, Heiress—Dispossessed; Tanner Montgomery, Nobleman (Duke of Hawksbury)
Time period(s): 1810s
Locale(s): Glen Royal, England; London, England

Summary: Determined to regain her home, Glen Royal, from the family that had won it from her father years before, Heather Fitzhugh inadvertently falls in love with the very man she is supposed to hate, Tanner Montgomery, tenth Duke of Hawksbury. But when the pair finally reconcile their differences, meddling, jealous outsiders work to destroy their fragile happiness. Fast-paced, passionate, and witty.

Other books you might like:
Kathryn Kramer, *Lady Rogue*, 1991
Laura Parker, *For Love's Sake Only*, 1991
Amanda Quick, *Rendezvous*, 1992
Amanda Quick, *Scandal*, 1991
Susan Wiggs, *The Raven and the Rose*, 1992

1180

ROBIN LEIGH

Rugged Splendor
(New York: Avon, 1991)

Story type: Historical/American West
Major character(s): Silver Matlock, Fiance(e) (jilted); Jared Newman, Bounty Hunter
Time period(s): 1870s
Locale(s): Central City, Colorado; Denver, Colorado; Virginia City, Nevada

Summary: When her unscrupulous fiance jilts her and then robs her parents' mercantile, Silver Matlock decides to get even. She convinces bounty hunter Jared Newman to help her and together they begin a chase that takes them across the West, in and out of mining towns, and from one hair-raising adventure to another in their search for a thief—and, it seems, a killer.

Other books you might like:
Virginia Brown, *Wildfire*, 1990
Lindsey Hanks, *Outlaw Lover*, 1990
Gina Robins, *Mississippi Mistress*, 1990
Ashley Snow, *Dangerous Desire*, 1990
LaVyrle Spencer, *Forgiving*, 1990

1181

SUSANNAH LEIGH

Jade Dawn
(New York: Topaz, 1993)

Story type: Historical/Exotic
Major character(s): Rachel Todd, Gentlewoman (missionary's daughter); Matthew Barron, Shipowner, Sea Captain
Time period(s): 1840s
Locale(s): At Sea; China

Summary: Rachel abhors opium, but the man she loves and his brother trade in it for a profit. Eventually, Matthew gives it up for love, but his vengeful brother and the opium kings of China don't approve of his choice. A story of personal growth, filled with action and conflict.

Other books you might like:
Laurel Collins, *The Jade Garden*, 1992
Jennifer Horsman, *Virgin Star*, 1993
Maggie Osborne, *Emerald Rain*, 1991
Katherine Sutcliffe, *Shadow Play*, 1991

1182

SUSANNAH LEIGH

The Turquoise Trail
(New York: Onyx, 1991)

Story type: Historical/American West
Major character(s): Diana Howard, Heiress; Cord Montgomery, Wagonmaster
Time period(s): 1840s (1846)
Locale(s): Southwest

Summary: When Diana Howard, desperate to avoid marrying against her will, proposes a marriage of convenience to wagonmaster Cord Montgomery, she has no idea that he has a violent agenda of his own, or that she will actually fall in love with her dark and mysterious husband. A fast-paced, passionate tale of greed and revenge.

Other books you might like:
Lisa Bingham, *Eden Creek*, 1991
Elizabeth Lowell, *Only His*, 1991
Connie Mason, *Beyond the Horizon*, 1990
Jodi Thomas, *The Tender Texan*, 1991

1183

TAMARA LEIGH

Pagan Bride
(New York: Bantam, 1995)

Story type: Historical/Renaissance; Historical/Exotic
Major character(s): Alessandra Bayard, Noblewoman; Lucien De Gautier, Captive (slave), Nobleman
Time period(s): 15th century (1454)
Locale(s): Algiers, Ottoman Empire; England

Summary: Realizing she has only a short time to live and that her daughter will be in danger when she dies, Alessandra's mother, an English captive and favorite wife of the ruler of the Ottoman Empire, charges slave Lucien De Gautier to return her daughter to her natural father in England; in return he will have his freedom. Independent Alessandra resists; Lucien insists. The voyage to England brings love—and then Lucien learns that Alessandra's father is his mortal enemy. Fast-paced, adventurous, and highly sensual

Other books you might like:
Jane Feather, *Bold Destiny*, 1990
Patricia Grasso, *Desert Eden*, 1993
Johanna Lindsey, *Silver Angel*, 1988
Miriam Minger, *Captive Rose*, 1991

1184
TAMARA LEIGH
Warrior Bride
(New York: Bantam, 1994)

Story type: Historical/Medieval
Major character(s): Lizanne Balmaine, Healer, Warrior; Rannulf Wardieu, Warrior
Time period(s): 12th century (1156)
Locale(s): England

Summary: Thinking he is the man who nearly killed her brother years earlier, warrior/healer Lizanne chains prisoner Rannulf Wardieu—but doesn't tell him the reasons she is suspicious of him. As a result, when he gains his freedom, he abducts her. Eventually, she is forced to marry him, and as she comes to know and love him, she wonders if he really was the person responsible for injuring her brother after all. Passionate action.

Other books you might like:
Elizabeth Bonner, *A Vow to Keep*, 1993
Catherine Coulter, *Earth Song*, 1990
Shannon Drake, *Knight of Fire*, 1993
Shannon Drake, *Princess of Fire*, 1989
Lynette Vinet, *Knight's Caress*, 1990

1185
MARILYN LEVY
Sounds of Silence
(New York: Fawcett Juniper, 1989)

Story type: Young Adult
Major character(s): Nikki, Student—High School (popular), Musician (pianist, loves jazz); Blake, Student—High School (new), Handicapped (deaf)
Time period(s): 1980s
Locale(s): Chicago, Illinois (Wilmette High School)

Summary: The growing friendship/romance between popular Nikki and hearing-impaired Blake causes her parents concern and costs her her friends in the "in crowd." Personal security, independence, and acceptance are several major themes in this story of growing up.

Other books you might like:
Barbara Beasley Murphy, *One Another*, 1986

Madeleine L'Engle, *And Both Were Young*, 1949
  Republished in 1986
Susan Sallis, *Only Love*, 1980
  Poignant, bittersweet, and serious
Tod Strasser, *Workin' for Peanuts*, 1983
Jean Ure, *See You Thursday*, 1983

1186
MARY LIDE
The Legacy of Tregaran
(New York: St. Martins, 1991)

Story type: Gothic
Major character(s): Alice Tregarn, Young Woman (poor); John Tregaran, Young Man, Wealthy
Time period(s): 1910s
Locale(s): Cornwall, England

Summary: In this prequel to *Tregaran*, Alice Tregarn and John Tregaran are two star-crossed lovers from feuding families who, through the efforts of a retired solicitor, are eventually reunited—but not before a number of horrifying, brutal, and chilling events take place. Good characters and a marvelously gothic atmosphere.

Other books you might like:
Rebecca Brandewyne, *Across a Starlit Sea*, 1989
Rebecca Brandewyne, *Upon a Moon-Dark Moor*, 1988
Charlotte Bronte, *Jane Eyre*, 1847
  classic gothic novel
Daphne Du Maurier, *Rebecca*, 1938
  classic gothic novel
Victoria Holt, *Mistress of Mellyn*, 1970
  classic modern gothic novel

1187
JOEY LIGHT
High Riding Heroes
(Bensalem, Pennsylvania: Meteor, 1993)

Story type: Contemporary
Major character(s): Victoria Clay, Businesswoman (theme park owner), Socialite (Eastern); Wes Cooper, Actor (teacher of "cowboys"), Police Officer (former state trooper)
Time period(s): 1990s
Locale(s): Oklahoma

Summary: When eastern socialite Victoria Clay learns she is part owner of a restored Western village in Oklahoma, she heads West, and meets Buck who owns the other half of the village and Wes Cooper, who has been hired to make the whole thing more authentic. The more involved she becomes, the more determined she becomes to stay—and the tension, and the passion, mount between Victoria and Wes. Dangerous mistakes, thievery, and kidnapping all add to the action.

Other books you might like:
Anne Marie Duquette, *On the Line*, 1993
Lass Small, *A Nothing Town in Texas*, 1991
Lois Wolfe, *Mask of Night*, 1993

266

Thelma Zirkelbach, *A Man of Few Words*, 1993

1188

JOEY LIGHT

Sterling's Reasons

(New York: Kismet, 1991)

Story type: Contemporary
Major character(s): Sterling Powell, Detective—Private, Widow(er); Joe MacDaniels, Police Officer (lieutenant)
Time period(s): 1990s
Locale(s): North Ocean City

Summary: Sent by her philanthropic boss to a beach resort to determine how he can best help Joe MacDaniels, a police officer who accidentally killed his partner, Sterling Powell finds this assignment is more dangerous than she had imagined—to both her life and her heart. Lively romance with some interesting plot twists.

Other books you might like:
Lori Copeland, *Darling Deceiver*, 1990
Sandra Field, *Goodbye Forever*, 1990
Judy Gill, *Golden Swan*, 1990
Jayne Ann Krentz, *The Golden Chance*, 1991
Kay Wilding, *Rainbow's End*, 1990

1189

JUDI LIND

Heart Song

(Bensalem, Pennsylvania: Meteor, 1992)

Story type: Contemporary
Major character(s): Lainie Hamilton, Health Care Professional (speech pathologist); Matt Wilbourne, Hotel Owner (resort owner; outdoorsman)
Time period(s): 1990s
Locale(s): Oregon

Summary: Still grieving over her brother's sudden death, Lainie Hamilton sets out on a quest to locate an eight-year-old son her brother had never seen. Her search leads her to the Oregon mountains and into the life of outdoorsman Matthew Wilbourne, a sexy widower and the adoptive father of Lainie's nephew. Emotional, poignant, and heartwarming.

Other books you might like:
Carole Dean, *California Man*, 1992
Elizabeth Krueger, *For the Children*, 1992
Arnette Lamb, *Highland Rogue*, 1991
  similar quest/historical
Marilyn Pappano, *Operation Homefront*, 1992

1190

CATHERINE LINDEN

Highland Flame

(New York: Leisure, 1991)

Story type: Historical/Elizabethan

Major character(s): Marina Dudley, Noblewoman; Alexander "Alex" Sinclair, Nobleman
Time period(s): 16th century (1586)
Locale(s): Highlands, Scotland; England

Summary: Young, abused Marina Dudley and Scottish nobleman Alex Sinclair find love amid the turmoil of the struggle between Mary, Queen of Scots, and Elizabeth I. Passion, violence, and political intrigue abound in this highly detailed historical.

Other books you might like:
Kathryn Kramer, *Desire's Deception*, 1989
  Mary, Queen of Scots
Arnette Lamb, *Highland Rogue*, 1991
Patricia Potter, *The Abduction*, 1991
Bertrice Small, *Skye O'Malley*, 1980
  swashbuckling action
Kathleen E. Woodiwiss, *So Worthy My Love*, 1989

1191

BETINA LINDSEY

The Serpent Beguiled

(New York: Pocket, 1992)

Story type: Historical/Exotic; Historical/Fantasy
Major character(s): Lilith Cardew, Bride (deserted), Handicapped (scarred); Adam Dunraven, Explorer
Time period(s): 1880s (1887)
Locale(s): England; Pacific Islands

Summary: Explorer Adam Dunraven fulfills an obligation to his friend Cardew by marrying and giving security to his disfigured daughter, Lilith — and then takes off on a Pacific Island expedition. Lilith, however, isn't content to stay at home, so she follows him and ends up shipwrecked on a mystical isle. Because of her ability to communicate with dolphins, the natives treat her as a goddess, and she matures and gains independence (and also heals her scar in the process) — just in time for Adam's arrival on the island. A passionate, mystical fantasy.

Other books you might like:
Clare Coleman, *Daughter of the Reef*, 1992
Kathryn Lynn Davis, *Sing to Me of Dreams*, 1990
Laura Kinsale, *The Prince of Midnight*, 1990
Helen Mittermeyer, *Princess of the Veil*, 1992
Gina Robins, *Always and Forever*, 1992

1192

BETINA LINDSEY

Swan Bride

(New York: Pocket, 1990)

Story type: Historical/Medieval; Historical/Fantasy
Series: Swan Maidens of Myr
Major character(s): Moria, Mythical Creature (part swan, part woman); Wulfsun, Warrior (Viking)
Time period(s): Indeterminate Past
Locale(s): England; Myr, Mythical Place

Summary: When swan sister Moria comes of age, she must assume the form of a swan, leave the land of Myr (a land without men), find a mate, and return home to bear her young. However, her first foray into the land of men results in her being shot by a hunter and then captured by Vikings. True to her mission, Moria works her magic on her captor, Wulfsun, but in the process they fall in love—creating a potentially disastrous situation for them both. Unique.

Other books you might like:
Jude Deveraux, *A Knight in Shining Armor*, 1989
  time change
Jude Deveraux, *Wishes*, 1989
  fantasy elements
Julie Garwood, *The Bride*, 1989
  medieval Setting/no fantasy elements
Mary Ellen Gronau, *Gentle Conqueror*, 1989
  medieval setting/no fantasy elements

1193
BETINA LINDSEY

Swan Star
(New York: Pocket, 1994)

Story type: Historical/Fantasy
Series: Swan Maidens of Myr
Major character(s): Arrah of Myr, Mythical Creature (Swan Maiden); Traeth of Rhune, Warrior, Nobleman
Time period(s): Indeterminate Past

Summary: When warrior Traeth of Rhune comes across the beautiful Swan Maiden Arrah and her adolescent sister swimming in the moonlight, he steals Arrah's swan skin and imprisons her in his keep. Despite this dubious beginning, their relationship develops into one of passion, and eventually love and respect. Adventurous with touches of humor, whimsy, and lyricism. This story concludes the Swan Trilogy.

Other books you might like:
Rexanne Becnel, *Where Magic Dwells*, 1994
Jessica Bryan, *Across a Wine-Dark Sea*, 1991
Saranne Dawson, *Awakenings*, 1994
Saranne Dawson, *From the Mist*, 1991
Marylyle Rogers, *Chanting the Dawn*, 1991

1194
BETINA LINDSEY

Swan Witch
(New York: Pocket, 1993)

Story type: Historical/Fantasy
Series: Swan Maidens of Myr
Major character(s): Eithne, Witch, Handicapped (mute); Bron, Knight
Time period(s): Indeterminate Past
Locale(s): Raith Morna, Fictional Country

Summary: On a quest for healing for his sword hand, Bron, the sea king's son, ventures into enchanted Raith Morna, and discovers that he must solve the mystery of Eithne, the mute daughter of the evil Sheelin, before he is free to leave. All

sorts of mythical creatures are part of this lyrical, sensual story of love, healing, and enchantment. Ties to *Swan Bride*.

Other books you might like:
Rexanne Becnel, *Where Magic Dwells*, 1994
Marylyle Rogers, *Chanting the Dawn*, 1991
Marylyle Rogers, *Chanting the Morning Star*, 1993
Penelope Williamson, *Keeper of the Dawn*, 1992

1195
BETINA LINDSEY

Waltz with the Lady
(New York: Pocket, 1990)

Story type: Historical/American West
Major character(s): India Simms, Suffragette; Gat Ransom, Cowboy, Guide
Time period(s): 1860s
Locale(s): Wyoming

Summary: India Simms, a Bostonian suffragette, travels throughout the Wyoming Territory speaking on women's rights escorted only by Gat Ransom. In the process, they discover danger, freedom, and love. Chronicles some of the events that gave women the vote in Wyoming.

Other books you might like:
Carol Finch, *Thunder's Tender Touch*, 1989
Norah Hess, *Wildfire*, 1989
Johanna Lindsey, *Savage Thunder*, 1989
Sara Orwig, *Albuquerque*, 1989
  Sequel to *San Antonio*
Gina Robins, *Texas Temptation*, 1989

1196
DAWN LINDSEY

The American Cousin
(New York: Signet, 1995)

Story type: Regency
Major character(s): Sorrel Kent, Young Woman (American); Lord Guy Wycherly, Nobleman (marquis), Military Personnel (former)
Time period(s): 18th century (late)
Locale(s): Cotswolds, England

Summary: Visiting American Sorrel Kent is ignominiously rescued from a fall by the dashing Marquis of Wycherly and promptly intrigues him with her brash Americanisms. Both are guests in her aunt's home, where it is assumed that he will make an offer for her beautiful, but hateful, cousin. However, threats on Sorrel's life make the Marquis protective of her and he risks both propriety and his future by spending time with her. Blackmail, jealousy, and a bit of a mystery add interest to this witty, well-done Regency.

Other books you might like:
Anne Barbour, *A Talent for Trouble*, 1992
  mystery element
Charlotte Louise Dolan, *The Black Widow*, 1992
  mystery element
Candice Hern, *A Proper Companion*, 1995

Barbara Metzger, *A Suspicious Affair*, 1994
  mystery element
Deborah Simmons, *Fortune Hunter*, 1992
  mystery element

1197

DAWN LINDSEY

The Barbarous Scot

(New York: Signet, 1992)

Story type: Regency
Major character(s): Drewe Carlisle, Noblewoman, Debutante; GlenRoss, Nobleman (Earl of GlenRoss)
Time period(s): 1810s
Locale(s): England; Highlands, Scotland

Summary: Beautiful, sophisticated Lady Drewe Carlisle sets out to add the handsome Scottish Earl of GlenRoss to her bevy of admirers and ends up compromised and married to him! Their removal to the Earl's primitive family fortress in the Scottish Highlands tests Drewe's resourcefulness and resolve to the limits. Surprisingly, she not only endures, but blossoms, as she discovers what her heart has been trying to tell her all along. A charming story of love and fulfillment.

Other books you might like:
Mary Balogh, *Promise of Spring*, 1990
Mary Balogh, *The Snow Angel*, 1991
Georgette Heyer, *The Unknown Ajax*, 1959
Judith McNaught, *Almost Heaven*, 1990
Amanda Quick, *Surrender*, 1990
  sensual

1198

DAWN LINDSEY

Dunraven's Folly

(New York: New American Library, 1989)

Story type: Regency
Major character(s): Cat Dunraven, Horse Trainer; Simon Grey, Nobleman, Military Personnel (Major)
Time period(s): 1810s
Locale(s): England

Summary: Simon is tired of being fawned over because of his war injury, but he doesn't expect the spunky granddaughter of his horse trainer to be rude and to avoid him at every turn. Mystery, love, and horseracing are here in abundance.

Other books you might like:
Carola Dunn, *Lavender Lady*, 1983
Emily Hendrickson, *The Gallant Lord Ives*, 1989
Georgette Heyer, *The Toll-Gate*, 1954
Gladys McGorian, *The Prince Regent's Silver Bell*, 1987
Sheila Simonson, *A Cousinly Connexion*, 1984

1199

JOHANNA LINDSEY

Angel

(New York: Avon, 1992)

Story type: Historical/American West
Major character(s): Cassandra Stuart, Matchmaker, Frontierswoman; Angel, Gunfighter
Time period(s): 1880s (1881)
Locale(s): Texas

Summary: When Cassie Stuart's plan to end a long-standing feud between two local families backfires, she sends for an old family friend to act as a peacemaker — and ends up with the legendary ''Angel of Death'' on her doorstep, instead. Humorous, fast-paced, and filled with interesting characters, including a toe-chewing black panther. Sequel to *Savage Thunder*.

Other books you might like:
Joan Johnston, *Sweetwater Seduction*, 1991
Pamela Morsi, *Garters*, 1992
Pamela Morsi, *Heaven Sent*, 1990
Rebecca Paisley, *Midnight and Magnolias*, 1992
Gina Robins, *Whispers of Love*, 1991

1200

JOHANNA LINDSEY

Defy Not the Heart

(New York: Avon, 1989)

Story type: Historical/Medieval
Major character(s): Reina de Champeney, Noblewoman; Ranulf Fitz Hugh, Mercenary (Landless bastard son), Knight
Time period(s): 12th century (Medieval; during the Crusades)
Summary: When Ranulf sends the attackers of Reina's castle into retreat, she is grateful. When he abducts her the next day to take her to Lord Rothwell and a forced marriage, she is shocked. But ever resourceful, she decides Ranulf is preferable to old Lord Rothwell and thus begins the pursuit.

Other books you might like:
Jude Deveraux, *The Taming*, 1989
Julie Garwood, *The Bride*, 1989
Roberta Gellis, *Roselynde*, 1978
  First of six Roselynde Chronicles
Kathleen E. Woodiwiss, *The Wolf and the Dove*, 1974

1201

JOHANNA LINDSEY

Gentle Rogue

(New York: Avon, 1990)

Story type: Historical/Regency
Series: Malory Family
Major character(s): Georgina Anderson, Imposter (poses as cabin boy); James Malory, Sea Captain, Privateer
Time period(s): 1810s

Locale(s): England; At Sea; Connecticut

Summary: Arriving in England to discover that her fiance has married someone else, American Georgina Anderson heads for home disguised as a cabin boy aboard Capt. James Malory's ship. The savvy captain quickly discovers her ruse; but curious, he lets her continue her charade. Love, of course, wins out, but not before the intrepid pair are swept up in a number of escapades—and then they must face Georgie's highly protective family in Connecticut. Last in a trilogy that includes *Love Only Once* and *Tender Rebel*.

Other books you might like:
Julie Garwood, *Guardian Angel*, 1990
Meagan McKinney, *Till Dawn Tames the Night*, 1991
Elizabeth Ann Michaels, *Destiny's Will*, 1991
Claudette Williams, *Heart of Fancy*, 1990

1202

JOHANNA LINDSEY

Keeper of the Heart
(New York: Avon, 1993)

Story type: Futuristic
Major character(s): Shanelle Ly-San-Ter, Noblewoman; Falon Van'yer, Warrior
Time period(s): Indeterminate Future
Locale(s): Sha-Ka'an, Planet—Imaginary

Summary: Shanelle must find a mate before her father decides to choose one for her. Determined to find one to her liking, she goes to the Sha-Ka'ani competitions and encounters Falon Van'yer, a warrior who could win her heart, if she could only be sure she could entrust it to him. Contains bondage fantasy elements. Sequel to *Warrior's Woman*.

Other books you might like:
Marilyn Campbell, *Stardust Dreams*, 1993
Marilyn Campbell, *Stolen Dreams*, 1994
Amanda Glass, *Shield's Lady*, 1989
    pseudonym of Jayne Ann Krentz
Jayne Ann Krentz, *Sweet Starfire*, 1986

1203

JOHANNA LINDSEY

Love Me Forever
(New York: Morrow, 1995)

Story type: Historical
Major character(s): Kimberly Richards, Heiress; Lachlan MacGregor, Laird (of Clan MacGregor)
Time period(s): 19th century
Locale(s): England; Scotland

Summary: Still in mourning for her mother, Kimberly Richards is commanded by her self-centered father to find an appropriate husband and wed, so he can do the same. The "husband" is a reality before she expects it, and although their relationship has far to go, they get there in appropriately passionate style. Sensual, fast paced, and compelling. Typically "Lindsey."

Other books you might like:
Catherine Coulter, *Night Shadow*, 1989
Catherine Coulter, *The Sherbrooke Bride*, 1992
Linda Lael Miller, *Angelfire*, 1990
Katherine Sutcliffe, *My Only Love*, 1993

1204

JOHANNA LINDSEY

The Magic of You
(New York: Avon, 1993)

Story type: Historical/Regency
Series: Malory Family
Major character(s): Amy Malory, Noblewoman; Warren Anderson, Businessman
Time period(s): 1810s (1819)
Locale(s): London, England; At Sea

Summary: Amy Malory sets her sights on her older cousin Warren and will go to any lengths to get him; even compromise is not beneath her. Shamelessly, she allows them both to be kidnapped, and she wins out finally when they are thrown together aboard an America-bound ship. What Amy wants, Amy gets.

Other books you might like:
Catherine Coulter, *Night Fire*, 1989
Julie Garwood, *Guardian Angel*, 1990
Brenda Joyce, *Scandalous Love*, 1992
Katherine Sutcliffe, *My Only Love*, 1993

1205

JOHANNA LINDSEY

Man of My Dreams
(New York: Avon, 1992)

Story type: Historical/Victorian
Major character(s): Megan Pentworthy, Gentlewoman; Ambrose St. James, Nobleman
Time period(s): 1880s
Locale(s): England

Summary: When Megan Pentworthy is snubbed by the local nobility, she vows to make the Duke of Worthington fall in love with her. Nevermind that she has never met him; she will figure out a way. The Duke, however, sets out to thwart her plans while he is travelling in disguise as a horse breeder. The sparks that fly between them in their inevitable clash of wills manage to set them both on fire.

Other books you might like:
Julie Garwood, *Guardian Angel*, 1990
Linda Lael Miller, *Angelfire*, 1989
Colleen Quinn, *Defiant Rose*, 1992
Laura Simon, *A Taste of Heaven*, 1989
Stephanie Stevens, *Defiant Angel*, 1991

1206

JOHANNA LINDSEY

Once a Princess

(New York: Avon, 1991)

Story type: Historical/Victorian America
Major character(s): Titiana ''Tanya'' Janacek, Royalty (princess), Saloon Hostess; Stefan Barany, Royalty (prince)
Time period(s): 19th century
Locale(s): Natchez, Mississippi; Cardinia, Fictional Country

Summary: When Crown Prince Stefan Barany arrives in America to claim the exiled Princess Titiana as his bride, instead of the gently bred girl he expects to find, he is confronted with a fiery, independent hoyden who insists she is not a princess and has no intention of going with him to Cardinia. However, Stefan takes things into his own hands and before long the pair are on their way—right into a web of intrigue, jealousy, and murder. A charmingly funny Cinderella story filled with typical Lindsey wit and passion.

Other books you might like:
Deborah Camp, *Fire Lily*, 1991
Millie Criswell, *Brazen Virginia Bride*, 1990
Constance O'Banyon, *Pirate's Princess*, 1989
Sheila O'Hallion, *American Princess*, 1989
    Regency flavor
Rebecca Paisley, *Barefoot Bride*, 1990

1207

JOHANNA LINDSEY

Prisoner of My Desire

(New York: Avon, 1991)

Story type: Historical/Medieval
Major character(s): Rowena Belleme, Noblewoman (Lady of Kirkborough); Warrick de Chaville, Nobleman (Lord of Fulkhurst), Knight
Time period(s): 12th century (1152)
Locale(s): England

Summary: Rowena must produce an heir to escape her brother-in-law. Warrick is kidnapped and held prisoner for that purpose. He escapes and makes Rowena a helpless captive of his anger and vengeance. However, love does triumph in this captive/captor romance.

Other books you might like:
Jude Deveraux, *The Taming*, 1989
Julie Garwood, *The Prize*, 1991
Hannah Howell, *Conqueror's Kiss*, 1991
Brenda Joyce, *The Conqueror*, 1990
    more violent than some
Mary Jo Putney, *Uncommon Vows*, 1991

1208

JOHANNA LINDSEY

Savage Thunder

(New York: Avon, 1989)

Story type: Historical/American West
Major character(s): Jocelyn Fleming, Noblewoman (Duchess of Eaton), Widow(er); Colt Thunder, Guide, Indian (Part-Cheyenne)
Time period(s): 1870s (1878)
Locale(s): Wyoming

Summary: When newly-widowed Jocelyn Fleming leaves England for Wyoming, the last thing she expects is to fall in love with the bitter, angry man she hires as a guide. Sparks, passion, and adventure abound.

Other books you might like:
Cheryl Black, *Comanche Love Song*, 1989
Kathleen Eagle, *Private Treaty*, 1988
Jessie Ford, *A Different Breed*, 1988
Norah Hess, *Wildfire*, 1989
Janelle Taylor, *Savage Conquest*, 1985

1209

JOHANNA LINDSEY

Surrender My Love

(New York: Avon, 1994)

Story type: Historical/Medieval
Series: Viking Saga
Major character(s): Lady Erika of Gronwood, Noblewoman; Selig Haardrad, Warrior (Viking), Settler
Time period(s): 9th century (879)
Locale(s): Gronwood, England

Summary: Viking Lord Selig Haardrad tries to bring peace between the Danes and the Celts; however, when he is ambushed and left for dead, he is saved only to be arrested as a spy. Lady Erika, having been insulted by him, wants him treated harshly. In revenge, he later takes her prisoner and even marries her to avert a war. Lots of passion, action, and treachery in this fast-paced story of early England. Last of the Viking Saga.

Other books you might like:
Tanya Anne Crosby, *Viking's Prize*, 1994
Shannon Drake, *Knight of Fire*, 1993
Shannon Drake, *Princess of Fire*, 1989
Heather Graham, *The Viking's Woman*, 1990
Kathleen E. Woodiwiss, *The Wolf and the Dove*, 1984

1210

JOHANNA LINDSEY

Until Forever

(New York: Avon, 1995)

Story type: Time Travel

Major character(s): Roseleen White, Professor (of history), Time Traveller; Thorn Blooddrinker, Warrior (Viking), Time Traveller
Time period(s): 1990s; 11th century (1066)
Locale(s): United States; England

Summary: Accidentally conjuring up a Viking warrior by means of the enchanted sword, Blooddrinkers Curse, the quite conventional history professor Roseleen White is shocked to find herself the ''owner'' of a dynamic, devastatingly attractive man—one who will do anything she wishes. But Roseleen's ''wishes'' are somewhat unusual; and when they travel through time to 1066 to see history in action, they end up changing history and the future, as well. Naturally, they set things to rights, but not before they fall in love—something that creates an entirely different set of problems for them. Passionate, fast-paced.

Other books you might like:
Jude Deveraux, *A Knight in Shining Armor*, 1989
  another out-of-time hero
Heather Graham, *The Viking's Woman*, 1990
  Viking action/no time travel elements
Kristin Hannah, *When Lightning Strikes*, 1994
Sandra Hill, *The Reluctant Viking*, 1994
  another Viking hero/time travel elements
Bertrice Small, *A Moment in Time*, 1991
  passionate action

1211

JOHANNA LINDSEY

Warrior's Woman

(New York: Avon, 1990)

Story type: Futuristic
Major character(s): Tedra De Arr, Warrior (Virgin), Security Officer; Challen Ly-San-Ter, Warrior (Chief), Barbarian
Time period(s): Indeterminate Future (2139 A.C. (After Colonization))
Locale(s): Kystran, Planet—Imaginary; Sha-Ka'an, Planet—Imaginary (Mother planet of the Barbarians)

Summary: When virgin warrior Tedra De Arr escapes a political rebellion on Kystran, she ends up on a planet that appears to be the mother planet of the barbarian warriors who helped with the coup. Unfortunately for her, women have few rights on this planet and she is forced to deal with the barbarian chief on his terms. A captive-in-love-with-captor story in a futuristic setting.

Other books you might like:
Amanda Glass, *Shield's Lady*, 1989
E.M. Hull, *The Sheik*, 1919
  The Classic captive-in-love-with-captor story
Anne McCaffrey, *Crystal Singer*,
Anne McCaffrey, *Killashandra*,
Janelle Taylor, *Moondust and Madness*, 1986

1212

GAIL LINK

Wolf's Embrace

(New York: Leisure, 1989)

Story type: Historical/Medieval
Major character(s): Duvessa O'Dalaigh, Heroine; Hugh Fitzgerald, Hero
Time period(s): 15th century (1476)
Locale(s): England

Summary: Duvessa and Hugh's elopement causes repercussions felt in succeeding generations. An interesting treatment of the period and the place of women in the social structure.

Other books you might like:
Rebecca Brandewyne, *Forever My Love*, 1982
  Similar time period/Scotland
Rebecca Brandewyne, *No Gentle Love*, 1980
Jude Deveraux, *The Taming*, 1989
  Similar time period
Roberta Gellis, *Roselynde*, 1978
Kathleen E. Woodiwiss, *The Wolf and the Dove*, 1974

1213

CATHIE LINZ

Midnight Ice

(New York: Silhouette, 1994)

Story type: Contemporary
Major character(s): Faith Bishop, Journalist (magazine editor), Traveller; Cal Masters, Journalist (magazine reporter), Traveller
Time period(s): 1990s
Locale(s): At Sea (on a cruise ship); Alaska

Summary: When Faith Bishop's cabinmate ends up with a broken leg and sells her passage to Faith's old friend and secret love, Cal Masters, the stage is set for a fast-paced, funny, and passionate Alaskan cruise. A kooky pair of Russians looking for diamonds in cold cream jars just adds to the fun. Short, sexy, and warm.

Other books you might like:
Lori Copeland, *Darling Deceiver*, 1990
Judy Gill, *Golden Swan*, 1990
Georgia Helm, *Mad Hatter*, 1992
Valerie Parv, *Tasmanian Devil*, 1990
Kathleen Gilles Seidel, *Maybe This Time*, 1990

1214

CATHIE LINZ

A Wife in Time

(New York: Silhouette, 1995)

Story type: Contemporary; Time Travel
Major character(s): Susannah Hall, Editor, Time Traveller; Kane Wilder, Computer Expert, Time Traveller
Time period(s): 1990s; 1880s (1884)
Locale(s): Savannah, Georgia

Summary: Magically drawn back to sultry Victorian Savannah in search of the solution to a 111-year-old mystery, Susannah Hall and her accidental—and hostile—time-travel partner, Kane Wilder, must confront their increasingly passionate feelings for each other and solve the mystery at the same time. Interesting characters and some creative love scenes enhance this light and lively time travel that actually does change history.

Other books you might like:
Barbara Bretton, *The Invisible Groom*, 1994
  paranormal humor
Barbara Bretton, *Somewhere in Time*, 1992
  time-travel humor
Nelle McFather, *Tears of Fire*, 1994
  time travel
Kasey Michaels, *Timely Matrimoney*, 1994
  light, funny contemporary/time-traveller from the past
Sharon Sala, *Annie and the Outlaw*, 1994
  paranormal elements

1215

PAMELA LITTON

Dance with the Devil

(Toronto: Harlequin, 1992)

Story type: Historical/American West
Major character(s): Libby "Spirit Woman" Cummings, Captive; Mando Fierro, Warrior (Comanchero)
Time period(s): 1870s (1874)
Locale(s): Mexico

Summary: Intrigued by the story of the red-haired captive, Spirit Woman, and her daring escape from the Comanche, the vengeance-driven Comanchero leader, Mando Fierro, sets out to find her. The resulting captive-in-love-with-captor story is filled with non-stop action and plenty of passion. Spin-off of *Stardust and Whirlwinds*.

Other books you might like:
Madeline Baker, *Comanche Flame*, 1992
Deborah Camp, *Lady Legend*, 1992
Ruth Langan, *Texas Healer*, 1992
Fela Dawson Scott, *Ghost Dancer*, 1992

1216

PAMELA LITTON

Scoundrel

(New York: Jove, 1994)

Story type: Historical/American West
Series: Brides of the West
Major character(s): Lucy Drummond, Teacher; Sam McQuaid, Lawman (marshal)
Time period(s): 19th century
Locale(s): Starlight, New Mexico

Summary: Rejected as a mail-order bride, Lucy Drummond decides to stay in New Mexico despite the open disapproval of the marshal and the townspeople. After all, she has responsibilities. She's the temperance spokesperson, a murder wit-

ness, and the new school teacher. Obviously, she can't go home. Eventually, she wins the respect of the town and the love of the marshal in this rather classic western romance.

Other books you might like:
Deborah Camp, *My Wild Rose*, 1992
Katherine Compton, *Outlaw Bride*, 1991
Debra Dier, *Surrender the Dream*, 1993
Joan Johnston, *Kid Calhoun*, 1993
Victoria Thompson, *Playing with Fire*, 1990

1217

PAMELA LITTON

Stardust and Whirlwinds

(Toronto: Harlequin, 1991)

Story type: Historical/American West
Major character(s): Amelia Cummings, Widow(er), Store Owner; Ross Tanner, Gunfighter (former)
Time period(s): 1870s (1873)
Locale(s): Santa Angela, Texas

Summary: Determined to make a success of her late husband's store in isolated Santa Angela, Texas, Amelia Cummings quickly makes an enemy of a man who would buy her out and, just as quickly, acquires a protector in the form of renegade Ross Tanner. Love blossoms between the two, but Amelia must come to terms with her feelings for the realities of frontier life before they can be happy.

Other books you might like:
Elaine Coffman, *Angel in Marble*, 1991
Jill Marie Landis, *Rose*, 1990
Catherine Lanigan, *A Promise Made*, 1991
LaVyrle Spencer, *Forgiving*, 1990

1218

GEORGETTE LIVINGSTON

Ekahi

(New York: Avalon, 1994)

Story type: Contemporary/Innocent; Romantic Suspense
Series: Holly St. James
Major character(s): Holly St. James, Detective—Private; Logan West, FBI Agent (drug enforcement), Imposter ("Charlton Stroud")
Time period(s): 1990s
Locale(s): Kauai, Hawaii

Summary: Hired by his wife to follow Logan West, private investigator Holly St. James finds herself outsmarted at every turn. Logan finally confronts and befriends her and eventually reveals that he is not who she thinks he is and is actually part of a massive drug surveillance team. Both fall in love during the chase, and all ends well.

Other books you might like:
Alma Blair, *The Unwitting Witness*, 1990
Alma Blair, *The Dark Side of Paradise*, 1990
S.R. Hawley, *Deadly Secrets*, 1990
Karen G. McCullough, *The Night Prowlers*, 1990

1219

GEORGETTE LIVINGSTON

The House in the Trees

(New York: Avalon, 1993)

Story type: Contemporary/Innocent
Major character(s): Sabrina Chandler, Artist; Joshua Brand, Landowner (island owner)
Time period(s): 1990s
Locale(s): Emerald Island, Pacific Islands

Summary: When Sabrina Chandler goes to a remote and beautiful Pacific island to recover from a devastating love affair, the last thing she wants is another man in her life, but Joshua Brand, the magnetic and dangerous owner of the island, causes her to reevaluate her thoughts. Exotic and innocent.

Other books you might like:
Alma Blair, *The Dark Side of Paradise*, 1990
Anne Ladley, *Moriah's Magic*, 1992
Karen Morrell, *Wish upon a Star*, 1992
Valerie Parv, *Tasmanian Devil*, 1990
 sensual

1220

CAROLYN LLEWELLYN

The Lady of the Labyrinth

(New York: Scribner, 1990)

Story type: Romantic Suspense
Major character(s): Alison Jordan, Researcher
Time period(s): 1980s
Locale(s): Sicily, Italy

Summary: Alison Jordan and her half-brother, Jay, go to a mountain castle in Sicily in search of their missing archaeologist father. An interesting blend of ancient myths and modern greed provide the backdrop for this adventurous story of old secrets and love. Some surprises are in store.

Other books you might like:
Joan Aiken, *A Cluster of Separate Sparks*, 1972
Evelyn Anthony, *Mission to Malaspiga*, 1974
Anne Maybury, *The Terracotta Palace*, 1971
Mary Stewart, *The Gabriel Hounds*, 1967
Mary Stewart, *Thunder on the Right*, 1957

1221

DIANE E. LOCK

True Love

(New York: Zebra, 1994)

Story type: Contemporary
Major character(s): Andrea Walsh, Parent, Spouse; Stuart Walsh, Spouse, Parent; Richard Osborne, Boyfriend (former)
Time period(s): 1990s
Locale(s): United States

Summary: Married for twenty years to the rather dull, ordinary Stuart, Andrea Walsh has fantasies about the man denied to her in her youth. When she has the chance to fulfill those fantasies at a reunion, she agonizes over her right to happiness, her wasted years of marriage, and her new-found passion. Her self-analysis finally liberates her and helps her put things in perspective.

Other books you might like:
Georgia Bockoven, *Moments*, 1994
 lovers' triangle
Betty Cothran, *Over the Moon*, 1994
Kathleen Gilles Seidel, *Maybe This Time*, 1990
LaVyrle Spencer, *Bittersweet*, 1990
Penelope Williamson, *Once in a Blue Moon*, 1993
 historical setting

1222

KAREN LOCKWOOD

Harvest Song

(New York: Diamond, 1993)

Story type: Historical/American West
Major character(s): Elizabeth Sheldon, Spinster; Zachary Danners, Doctor
Time period(s): 1890s (1899)
Locale(s): Boston, Massachusetts; Eden Creek, Idaho

Summary: When Elizabeth travels to Idaho to claim her aunt's apple orchard, she is unimpressed by her fellow traveller, Dr. Zach Danners, who is trying to forget his past. However, the town welcomes him with open arms, and Elizabeth begins to reassess her opinion of him. The more she is around him, the more she comes to like him and that creates problems for her because she is engaged to someone else. Everything works out in the end in this sweet story set in rural, Victorian Idaho.

Other books you might like:
Marilyn Cunningham, *Seasons of the Heart*, 1992
Patricia Gaffney, *Sweet Everlasting*, 1993
Sharon Harlow, *Country Kiss*, 1993
Stef Ann Holm, *Firefly*, 1990

1223

CAIT LOGAN

Delilah

(New York: Jove, 1995)

Story type: Historical/American West
Major character(s): Delilah Smith Morton, Widow(er), Rancher; Simon Oakes, Lawman (Royal Canadian Mounted Police)
Time period(s): 1880s (1884)
Locale(s): Washington

Summary: Delilah and her brother Richard work hard, barely surviving on their Washington ranch. When the winter kills their cattle, Richard heads for the gold fields. Enter Mountie Simon Oakes, searching for his brother's killer, whom he thinks is Richard. Fate lends a hand when he is caught in a blizzard and Delilah rescues him. Love quickly follows and so do the obvious complications. A well-written novel with good characterizations.

Other books you might like:
Kristin Hannah, *A Handful of Heaven*, 1991
Robin Lee Hatcher, *Liberty Blue*, 1995
Theresa Michaels, *Gifts of Love*, 1992
Patricia Potter, *Defiant*, 1995
    another struggling widow/wounded hero

1224
CAIT LOGAN
Night Fire
(New York: Diamond, 1994)

Story type: Historical/American West
Major character(s): Arielle Browning, Widow(er) (assumed); Luc D'Arcy, Wagonmaster
Time period(s): 1840s (1846)
Locale(s): Oregon Trail; Willamette Valley, Oregon

Summary: Determined to find her lost love in Oregon, Arielle Browning can't join the wagon train unless she is married. Luc D'Arcy, wounded, angry, and vengeance-driven, is on the trail of the men who kidnapped his women. Out of mutual need, they join forces, marry (platonically, of course), and head west. Their marriage takes on a more passionate character on the journey, and despite their determination to pursue their individual goals, a surprise at the end of the journey provides a satisfactory ending for them both.

Other books you might like:
Susannah Leigh, *The Turquoise Trail*, 1991
    similar premise
Elizabeth Lowell, *Only His*, 1991
Elizabeth Lowell, *Only Mine*, 1992
Evelyn Rogers, *Flame*, 1994
    marriage of convenience/revenge-driven hero

1225
CAIT LOGAN
Wild Dawn
(New York: Diamond, 1992)

Story type: Historical/American West
Major character(s): Lady Regina Mortimer-Hawkes, Captive, Noblewoman; MacGregor, Trapper
Time period(s): 1860s (1867)
Locale(s): Colorado

Summary: Lady Regina, abused and abandoned by her fiance, has a choice of freezing in the mountains or becoming a wife to MacGregor and a mother to his son—Lady Regina sensibly chooses not to freeze. However, when MacGregor tries to "manage her by the book," she rebels—and life becomes even more interesting for them both. Vengeance, hardship, and passion are part of this intense, fast-paced romance.

Other books you might like:
Dorothy Garlock, *Homeplace*, 1991
Jill Marie Landis, *Come Spring*, 1992
Johanna Lindsey, *Angel*, 1992

Johanna Lindsey, *Savage Thunder*, 1989

1226
MARY-BEN LORRIS
Sing Me to Sleep
(New York: Zebra, 1994)

Story type: Contemporary; Romantic Suspense
Major character(s): Jodie Turner, Public Relations; Luke Prentiss, Musician, Recluse
Time period(s): 1990s
Locale(s): United States

Summary: Recuperating at the lake from the traumatic death of her sister, Jodie empathizes with her physically and emotionally damaged neighbor, Luke Prentiss. Nevertheless she fights her attraction to him as she pursues the dangerous clues that eventually lead to her sister's killer. A sinister, dark, and involving mystery.

Other books you might like:
Sandra Canfield, *Dark Journey*, 1994
Suzanne Forster, *Shameless*, 1994
Joey Light, *Sterling's Reasons*, 1991
Maggie Shayne, *Kiss of the Shadow Man*, 1994
Antoinette Stockenberg, *Embers*, 1994
    fantasy elements

1227
MERLINE LOVELACE
Bits and Pieces
(Bensalem, Pennsylvania: Meteor, 1993)

Story type: Contemporary
Major character(s): Maura Phillips, Engineer (aircraft); Jake McAllister, Pilot (test pilot); Lisa McAllister, Scientist (amateur paleontologist)
Time period(s): 1990s
Locale(s): Eglin Air Force Base, Florida

Summary: Maura Phillips has a flair for the funky and exotic, giving the impression of being anything but the genius aircraft engineer she really is. As a result, test pilot Jake McAllister doesn't take her seriously, until she proves her point. Fast-paced, funny story of intrigue involving sabotage and exciting chases laced with love.

Other books you might like:
Jennifer Blake, *Joy and Anger*, 1991
Blythe Bradley, *To Love a Stranger*, 1993
Lacey Dancer, *Forever Joy*, 1993
Liana Laverentz, *Ashton's Secret*,

1228
MERLINE LOVELACE
Somewhere in Time
(New York: Silhouette, 1994)

Story type: Time Travel

Major character(s): Aurora Durant, Military Personnel (Captain, U. S. Air Force), Time Traveller; Lucius Antonius, Military Personnel (Roman Centurion)
Time period(s): 1990s; 2nd century (180)
Locale(s): Middle East

Summary: Crashlanding during a routine mission over the Middle Eastern desert, Captain Aurora Durant slips through time and finds herself in the second century A.D. and the captive of Roman centurion Lucius Antonius. As expected, clashes between the macho Lucius and the thoroughly modern Aurora abound as she asserts her independence and he tries to keep her in what he considers to be her place. A lively story set during a period not often used in romance.

Other books you might like:
Diana Gabaldon, *Outlander*, 1991
  complex
Kristin Hannah, *When Lightning Strikes*, 1994
Sandra Hill, *The Reluctant Viking*, 1994
Joan Hohl, *Love Beyond Time*, 1994
  anthology
Susan Sizemore, *Wings of the Storm*, 1992

1229

ELIZABETH LOWELL (Pseudonym of Ann Maxwell)

Enchanted

(New York: Avon, 1994)

Story type: Historical/Medieval; Historical/Fantasy
Major character(s): Ariane the Betrayed, Noblewoman, Bride (reluctant); Simon the Loyal, Nobleman, Warrior
Time period(s): 12th century
Locale(s): Stone Ring Keep, England

Summary: Raped by a man she trusted and then cruelly betrayed by her father, Ariane must come to terms with her fears before she can truly be a wife to her husband. Politics, magic, and revenge are all part of this mystical and highly sensual story of Britain during the reign of Henry I. Sequel to *Untamed* and *Forbidden*.

Other books you might like:
Marion Zimmer Bradley, *The Mists of Avalon*, 1988
Marsha Canham, *In the Shadow of Midnight*, 1994
Maura Seger, *Tapestry*, 1993
Flora M. Speer, *Castle of Dreams*, 1990
Penelope Williamson, *Keeper of the Dream*, 1992

1230

ELIZABETH LOWELL (Pseudonym of Ann Maxwell)

Lover in the Rough

(New York: Avon, 1994)

Story type: Contemporary
Major character(s): Reba Farrall, Mine Owner; Chance Walker, Scientist (gemologist), Adventurer
Time period(s): 1990s
Locale(s): Death Valley, California

Summary: Reba owns half of an old and dangerous mine as well as a number of valuable art objects. Now that Jeremy, the

person who had always cared for her, is gone, various unsavory characters are after both Reba and the art. When Chance comes to her rescue, Reba is relieved. However, despite her growing feelings for him, she can never forget that he wants something of her, too—the mine. A near disaster saves the day—and their love, as well.

Other books you might like:
Rebecca Brandewyne, *Rainbow's End*, 1991
  historical
Millie Criswell, *Diamond in the Rough*, 1994
  historical
Elizabeth Duke, *Outback Legacy*, 1992
Johanna Lindsey, *Angel*, 1992
  historical
Jodi Thomas, *The Texan and the Lady*, 1994
  historical

1231

ELIZABETH LOWELL (Pseudonym of Ann Maxwell)

Only His

(New York: Avon, 1991)

Story type: Historical/American West
Series: Rockies Trilogy
Major character(s): Willow Moran, Southern Belle; Caleb Black, Guide, Gunfighter
Time period(s): 1860s
Locale(s): West; Colorado

Summary: Her way of life devastated by the Civil War, Southerner Willow Moran gathers up her string of prize horses and sets off to find her gold-mining brother in Colorado—completely unaware that the man she hires to guide her into the mountains is seeking revenge on her brother and is using Willow to find him. Plenty of passion and action in this hot, yet heartwarming, historical.

Other books you might like:
Rosanne Bittner, *Montana Woman*, 1990
Norah Hess, *Wildfire*, 1989
Joanna Jordan, *Destiny's Woman*, 1990
Johanna Lindsey, *Savage Thunder*, 1989

1232

ELIZABETH LOWELL

Only Love

(New York: Avon, 1995)

Story type: Historical/American West
Major character(s): Shannon Connor Smith, Frontierswoman; Whip Moran, Drifter
Time period(s): 19th century
Locale(s): Colorado

Summary: Despite the fact that Shannon Smith is supposedly married to the notorious and dangerous Silent John, Whip Moran knows she is the woman for him and he sets out to win her. Eventually, he succeeds, and then he must deal with the fact that he, foot-loose though he is, is falling in love with her and is finding it harder and harder to leave. Highly sensual and fast-paced.

Other books you might like:
Linda Hilton, *Desire's Slave*, 1992
Linda Howard, *Angel Creek*, 1991
Johanna Lindsey, *Angel*, 1992
Patricia Potter, *Defiant*, 1995

1233

ELIZABETH LOWELL (Pseudonym of Ann Maxwell)

Only Mine
(New York: Avon, 1992)

Story type: Historical/American West
Series: Rockies Trilogy
Major character(s): Jessica Charteris, Noblewoman; Wolf Lonetree, Indian, Nobleman (illegitimate son of a viscount)
Time period(s): 1860s (1867)
Locale(s): Rocky Mountains; England

Summary: To avoid a forced marriage to dreadful Lord Gore, independent Lady Jessica Charteris decides her childhood friend Wolf Lonetree would make an ideal mate—and she traps him into marriage. Their journey to his Rocky Mountain home is uncomfortable and arduous and Wolf thinks Jessica will eventually ask for an annulment. However, she surprises him with her strength, endurance, and determination—and her love. Witty dialogue, nicely-handled love scenes. Second in the Rockies trilogy.

Other books you might like:
Madeline Baker, *Comanche Flame*, 1992
Genell Dellin, *Cherokee Dawn*, 1989
Kathleen Harrington, *Cherish the Dream*, 1990
Norah Hess, *Devil in Spurs*, 1990
Jill Marie Landis, *Wild Flower*, 1989

1234

ELIZABETH LOWELL (Pseudonym of Ann Maxwell)

Reckless Love
(Toronto: Harlequin, 1990)

Story type: Historical/American West
Major character(s): Janna Wayland, Mountain Woman; Tyrell MacKenzie, Hero
Time period(s): 1860s
Locale(s): Utah

Summary: Living as a boy in the Utah wilderness and tending a herd of wild horses, Janna rescues Ty MacKenzie from a band of Ute Indians—only to find that he is after Lucifer, the stallion of her herd.

Other books you might like:
Genell Dellin, *Cherokee Dawn*, 1990
Georgina Gentry, *Nevada Nights*, 1989
Norah Hess, *Devil in Spurs*, 1990
Jill Marie Landis, *Wild Flower*, 1989
Lisa Ann Verge, *The Heart's Disguise*, 1990
    Girl-as-sailor on high seas

1235

ELIZABETH LOWELL (Pseudonym of Ann Maxwell)

Untamed
(New York: Avon, 1993)

Story type: Historical/Medieval
Major character(s): Lady Margaret of Blackthorne, Witch (Glendruid), Noblewoman (Saxon); Dominic le Sabra, Knight (Norman crusader)
Time period(s): 12th century
Locale(s): England

Summary: Henry I believes that a marriage between Lady Margaret, a Glendruid witch, and his loyal knight, Dominic, will bring peace to the land, and Margaret and Dominic are willing to oblige. However, Dominic mainly wants sons, while, according to legend, Margaret must receive passion and pleasure from her husband if there is to be peace and prosperity. Naturally, they work this all out, but not before they are forced to deal with some rather evil outside forces that threaten to tear their growing love apart. Romantic and appropriately passionate.

Other books you might like:
Linda Lang Bartell, *Tender Warrior*, 1992
Katherine Deauville, *Blood Red Roses*, 1991
    realistic
Linda Madl, *A Tender Magic*, 1993
Libby Sydes, *The Lion's Angel*, 1992
Penelope Williamson, *Keeper of the Dream*, 1992
    fantasy elements

1236

ELIZABETH LOWELL

A Woman Without Lies
(New York: Avon, 1995)

Story type: Contemporary
Major character(s): Angelina ''Angel'' Lange, Artist (stained glass); Miles ''Hawk'' Hawkins, Businessman
Time period(s): 1990s
Locale(s): Vancouver, British Columbia, Canada

Summary: When stained-glass artist Angel Lange and cynical businessman Hawk Hawkins meet, the attraction is instantaneous and undeniable. But Angel is still recovering from the tragic loss of her parents and fiance and Hawk's assumptions about love are anything but positive. A compelling, emotionally tense story that explores the relationship between a woman who is afraid to risk love again, and a man who must learn to trust before he can ever be capable of love. A revised reissue of one of Lowell's more popular romances.

Other books you might like:
Kathleen Eagle, *This Time Forever*, 1992
    non-trusting hero/Native American emphasis/good characterization
Linda Howard, *MacKenzie's Mountain*, 1989
    classic wounded hero/intense
Jeane Renick, *Trust Me*, 1992
    trust and love/different, exotic setting

Nora Roberts, *Born in Fire*, 1995
  artist heroine/good characterizations and relationships
Nora Roberts, *Born in Ice*, 1995
  another hero who needs to learn to trust and love

1237

MAYO LUCAS

Camelot Jones
(New York: Avon, 1989)

Story type: Historical/American West
Major character(s): Camelot Jones, Mountain Woman (Ozarks); Elliot Hamilton, Banker (Tenderfoot from New York)
Time period(s): 19th century
Locale(s): Ozark Mountains, Arkansas; Missouri

Summary: When Camelot Jones and Elliot Hamilton are forced, innocent though they are, into a shotgun marriage, he agrees to take her to St. Louis so she can find the man who had promised to come back for her. But the trip holds a number of surprises for them both, including the wonders of falling in love—with each other.

Other books you might like:
Gwen Cleary, *Ecstasy's Masquerade*, 1989
Georgina Gentry, *Nevada Nights*, 1989
Rebecca George, *A Wild Desire*, 1989
Norah Hess, *Wildfire*, 1989
Janelle Taylor, *Kiss of the Night Wind*, 1989

1238

CATHERINE LYNDELL (Pseudonym of Margaret Ball)

Stolen Dreams
(New York: Pocket, 1989)

Story type: Historical/Georgian
Major character(s): Gillie Duval, Guttersnipe; Edward Craigie, Nobleman (Baron Kinsale)
Time period(s): 1740s (1742-1747)
Locale(s): London, England

Summary: While searching for his servant in the London slums, Edward is rescued by Gillie, a child of the streets. After she helps him find his servant, Edward assumes responsibility for her and sends her off to school. Gillie dreams of love; Edward becomes engaged to another. But things right themselves in the end.

Other books you might like:
Georgette Heyer, *Friday's Child*, 1946
  Orphan-becomes-young-lady theme/Regency treatment
Laura Parker, *A Wilder Love*, 1990
Louisa Rawlings, *Promise of Summer*, 1989
Katherine Sutcliffe, *A Fire in the Heart*, 1990

1239

ELINOR LYNLEY

Song of the Bayou
(New York: Onyx, 1990)

Story type: Historical/Antebellum American South
Major character(s): Susanna Paxton, Southern Belle; Nicholas Jourdain, Widow(er), Plantation Owner
Time period(s): 1850s (1854)
Locale(s): Louisiana

Summary: When lovely and landed Susanna Paxton falls in love with Cajun Nicholas Jourdain, she finds herself caught up in a dangerous and violent situation—one that threatens not only the Cajun people, but her own life as well. Vigilantes, black magic, and Cajun culture are all part of this action-filled romance.

Other books you might like:
Kit Bakker, *Julianne's Song*, 1990
  Cajun Melodies Series. Bk. 1
Marie Beaumont, *Catherine's Song*, 1990
  Cajun Melodies Series. Bk. 2
Jennifer Blake, *Midnight Waltz*, 1985
Virginia Nielsen, *Jessica's Song*, 1990
  Cajun Melodies Series. Bk. 3
Wanda Owen, *Deceptive Desires*, 1990

1240

LESLIE LYNN (Pseudonym of Elaine Sima and Sherrill Bodine)

The Rake's Redemption
(New York: Fawcett, 1989)

Story type: Regency
Major character(s): Juliana Grenville, Widow(er); Dominic, Nobleman (Marquis of Aubrey), Rake
Time period(s): 1810s (Regency period)
Locale(s): England

Summary: Tragically widowed at 17, Juliana Grenville, now 23, decides for a number of particular reasons, that it is time to seek a husband. But instead of the elderly gentleman she had pictured, the dashing Marquis of Aubrey appears on the scene. A secret past complicates matters.

Other books you might like:
Kimberly Cates, *Restless Is the Wind*, 1989
  A more serious Regency
Brian Cleeve, *Sara*, 1976
  A more serious Regency
Georgette Heyer, *These Old Shades*, 1926
  A "classic"
Sheila Simonson, *The Bar Sinister*, 1986
Marlene Suson, *The Errant Earl*, 1989

1241

LESLIE LYNN and Sherrill Bodine)

Scandal's Child
(New York: Fawcett, 1990)

Story type: Regency
Major character(s): Kathryn Thistlewaite, Noblewoman; Jules Deveraux, Nobleman (Comte de Saville)
Time period(s): 1810s
Locale(s): England; France

Summary: When the Comte de Saville's chance meeting with three orphans results in the accidental compromising of Lady Kathryn Thistlewaite, he dutifully offers marriage—but Kat has other ideas, and marriage isn't one of them. Eventually, however, fate decrees otherwise and the pair are wed; but they must deal with their true feelings for each other—and sinister outside influences—before they can be happy. Exciting and peopled with interesting secondary characters.

Other books you might like:
Janice Bennett, *Forever in Time*, 1990
   time change elements
Clare Darcy, *Lady Pamela*, 1975
Clare Darcy, *Victoire*, 1974
Emily Hendrickson, *The Gallant Lord Ives*, 1989
Georgette Heyer, *The Unknown Ajax*, 1960

1242

VIRGINIA LYNN

Lyon's Prize
(New York: Bantam, 1992)

Story type: Historical/Medieval
Major character(s): Lady Brenna Dunston, Noblewoman (shrew); Rey de Lyon, Knight
Time period(s): 11th century (1076)
Locale(s): England

Summary: Lady Brenna is such a shrew that no one will marry her — no one, that is, except Sir Rey de Lyon, who has great faith in his abilities to deal with her appropriately. The sparks fly and they fight constantly; it is only when she realizes that he is truly on her side that she can admit to them both that she loves him. Realistic, memorable characters in a poignant love story.

Other books you might like:
Tanya Anne Crosby, *Angel of Fire*, 1992
Katherine Deauville, *Blood Red Roses*, 1991
Jude Deveraux, *The Taming*, 1989
Julie Garwood, *The Prize*, 1991
Kristin Hannah, *The Enchantment*, 1992

1243

VIRGINIA LYNN

River's Dream
(New York: Doubleday, 1991)

Story type: Historical/American West

Major character(s): Drucilla Duckworth, Teacher, Heiress— Lost; Gray Morgan, Hero
Time period(s): 19th century
Locale(s): Tennessee; Texas

Summary: Upon her grandmother's death, unattractive overweight Drucilla Duckworth learns she is not an orphan after all but the daughter of a wealthy Texas rancher—who has wanted her all these years. Drucilla heads for Texas and her new life; and on the way she is rescued by her "knight in shining armor," Gray Morgan, who hardly notices her. That is not the case when they meet again several months later and Drucilla has evolved into the beautiful River Templeton— and Gray doesn't recognize her as the same person. Westernized Ugly Duckling/Swan story.

Other books you might like:
Laura Black, *Albany*, 1989
Cordia Byers, *Lady Fortune*, 1989
Jude Deveraux, *Wishes*, 1989
Colleen McCullough, *The Ladies of Missalonghi*, 1987

1244

MALCOLM MACDONALD

Hell Hath No Fury
(New York: St. Martin, 1992)

Story type: Romantic Suspense; Historical/Victorian
Major character(s): Daisy O'Lindon, Model; Napier Lyndon-Fury, Gentleman
Time period(s): 1880s
Locale(s): Ireland

Summary: The longstanding feud between the Fury's and the O'Lindon's sets the backdrop for this sweeping tale of love and revenge that focuses on the relationship between aristocratic Napier Lyndon-Fury and artist's model, Daisy O'Lindon — and its impact on both their families and their lives.

Other books you might like:
Beverly Byrne, *The Flames of Vengeance*, 1991
   2nd in the Mendoza Family Trilogy
Marcia Davenport, *Valley of Decision*, 1942
Pamela Hill, *The House of Cray*, 1982
Susan Howatch, *Cashelmara*, 1974
Colleen McCullough, *The Thorn Birds*, 1977

1245

SUSAN MACIAS

Tender Victory
(New York: Diamond, 1993)

Story type: Historical/American West
Major character(s): Rachel Steele, Widow(er); Luke Hawkins, Rancher
Time period(s): 1880s (1883)
Locale(s): Wyoming

Summary: Rachel Steele and her son, Mark, finally escape from her evil father-in-law and head for Wyoming and Luke, the long-standing love of her life. Luke, however, doesn't know that she was literally forced into marriage with his best friend and he still feels betrayed and resentful. Rachel must deal with memories and feelings of unworthiness and Luke must learn to trust again, but eventually things come together for the pair and the past is laid, permanently, to rest. Warm and tender.

Other books you might like:
Kit Gardner, *The Stolen Heart*, 1993
Anne Harmon, *Wyoming Wildfire*, 1993
Alison Irving, *No Greater Love*, 1991
Brenda Joyce, *Secrets*, 1993
  hard-hitting and realistic

1246

SHARON MACIVER

River Song
(New York: Diamond, 1991)

Story type: Historical/American West
Major character(s): Sunny ''Sunflower'' Callahan, Indian (Quechan/Irish); Cole Fremont, Rancher
Time period(s): 1880s (1886)
Locale(s): Yuma, Arizona; Phoenix, Arizona

Summary: Sunny, determined to find her mother's killer, is led to Cole Fremont, who can't forget his parents' massacre by the Indians. Their forbidden love causes racial hatreds to flare in this passionate and realistic novel that makes a strong statement about prejudice and intolerance, in general, and the treatment of Native Americans, in particular.

Other books you might like:
Shirl Henke, *Night Wind's Woman*, 1991
Connie Mason, *Beyond the Horizon*, 1990
Jan McKee, *Sweet Justice*, 1991
Patricia Potter, *The Silver Link*, 1991

1247

DOROTHY MACK

The Mock Marriage
(New York: New American Library, 1991)

Story type: Regency
Major character(s): Clairisse Deschamps, Actress, Gentlewoman (impoverished); Egon Hollister, Nobleman
Time period(s): 1810s
Locale(s): England

Summary: When Sir Egon Hollister decides to outwit his autocratic grandmother by ''temporarily'' marrying to gain his inheritance, he has no idea that his actress-wife is actually an impoverished gentlewoman—nor does he plan to fall in love with her. Funny, witty, and filled with engaging characters.

Other books you might like:
Georgette Heyer, *A Civil Contract*, 1961
Karla Hocker, *Lady Maryann's Dilemma*, 1990
Judith Nelson, *Lady's Choice*, 1990
Rebecca Paisley, *Barefoot Bride*, 1990
  American setting

Amanda Quick, *Seduction*, 1990
  sensual

1248

DEBBIE MACOMBER

Father's Day
(Toronto: Harlequin, 1991)

Story type: Contemporary/Innocent
Major character(s): Robin Masterson, Widow(er); Cole Camden, Widow(er)
Time period(s): 1990s
Locale(s): San Francisco Bay, California

Summary: An adventuresome ten-year-old and a loveable black labrador bring an independent, understanding widow and an angry, bitter widower together in this delightful, heartwarming story of loss and love.

Other books you might like:
Lori Copeland, *Darling Deceiver*, 1990
  sensual
Judy Gill, *Golden Swan*, 1990
  sensual
Victoria Gordon, *Love Thy Neighbor*, 1991
Wendy Martin, *Love on Trial*, 1990
Miriam Pace, *Warm Creature Comforts*, 1991

1249

DEBBIE MACOMBER

First Comes Marriage
(Toronto: Harlequin, 1991)

Story type: Contemporary/Innocent
Major character(s): Janine, Young Woman; Zachary Taylor, Businessman (company owner)
Time period(s): 1990s

Summary: When Aton Hartman merges his company with Zack Taylor's, he just knows that he has found the perfect husband for his granddaughter Janine. Unfortunately, Zack and Janine don't agree, and they fight grandpa's matchmaking attempts—but then they fall in love. Warm and funny.

Other books you might like:
Martha Hix, *Texas Tycoon*, 1991
Wendy Martin, *Love on Trial*, 1990
Helen R. Myers, *A Fine Arrangement*, 1991
Nora Roberts, *Courting Catherine*, 1991

1250

DEBBIE MACOMBER

A Little Bit of Country
(Toronto: Harlequin, 1990)

Story type: Contemporary/Innocent
Major character(s): Rorie Campbell, Vacationer; Clay Franklin, Rancher (Owner of stud farm)
Time period(s): 1980s
Locale(s): Oregon

Summary: When Rorie's car breaks down on an Oregon backroad, she is forced to accept the hospitality of local rancher Clay Franklin until her car can be repaired. Rorie and Clay are intensely attracted to each other, but things are complicated by Clay's fiancee with whom Rorie becomes friends.

Other books you might like:
Vanessa Grant, *Awakening Dreams*, 1990
Kasey Michaels, *His Chariot Awaits*, 1990
Laura Parrish, *Love's Quiet Corner*, 1989
Valerie Parv, *Tasmanian Devil*, 1990
  Somewhat more sensual

`1251`

DEBBIE MACOMBER

Marriage of Inconvenience
(New York: Silhouette, 1992)

Story type: Contemporary
Series: Those Manning Men Trilogy
Major character(s): Jamie Warren, Parent (would be); Rich Manning, Engineer
Time period(s): 1990s
Locale(s): United States

Summary: When Jamie Warren decides she wants to have a baby, she asks her best friend from high school, Rich Manning, to be the father—but Rich insists on getting married! Their miserable marriage is complicated by a number of things, including their not wanting to mess up their friendship. Funny, warm, and provocative. First in Those Manning Men trilogy.

Other books you might like:
Georgia Bockoven, *A Marriage of Convenience*, 1985
Barbara Caitlin, *Shotgun Wedding*, 1992
Elizabeth Krueger, *For the Children*, 1992
LaVyrle Spencer, *Separate Beds*, 1985

`1252`

DEBBIE MACOMBER

Morning Comes Softly
(New York: Harper, 1993)

Story type: Contemporary/Mainstream
Major character(s): Mary Warner, Mail Order Bride, Librarian; Travis Thompson, Rancher, Guardian
Time period(s): 1990s
Locale(s): Montana

Summary: Being a father does not come easily to bachelor rancher Travis Thompson, but he's not about to let anyone take his brother's three orphaned children away from him—so he does the obvious and advertises for a wife! His answer arrives in the form of Mary Warner, the ultimate stereotypical spinster librarian. But Mary is more than she appears, and gradually they become a family, and Travis and Mary find a love they thought they would never have. Heartwarming.

Other books you might like:
Georgia Bockoven, *A Marriage of Convenience*, 1991

Robin Lee Hatcher, *Promise Me Spring*, 1991
  historical setting
Victoria Pade, *The Doubletree*, 1991
LaVyrle Spencer, *Morning Glory*, 1989
Ann Howard White, *All but Love*, 1993

`1253`

DEBBIE MACOMBER

Rainy Day Kisses
(Toronto: Harlequin, 1990)

Story type: Contemporary/Innocent
Major character(s): Susannah Simmons, Businesswoman; Nate Townsend, Neighbor
Time period(s): 1990s

Summary: Susannah Simmons is on the way up and nothing is going to stop her—not even her growing attraction to her laid-back next door neighbor. Warm, funny, and witty.

Other books you might like:
Arlene James, *Finally Home*, 1989
Lynda Stowe Landers, *A Season to Remember*, 1989
Helen R. Myers, *Invitation to a Wedding*, 1990
Constance Walker, *One Perfect Springtime*, 1989

`1254`

DEBBIE MACOMBER

A Season of Angels
(New York: Harper, 1993)

Story type: Contemporary/Fantasy
Major character(s): Shirley, Angel (guardian angel); Goodness, Angel (guardian angel); Mercy, Angel (guardian angel)
Time period(s): 1990s
Locale(s): Seattle, Washington

Summary: When three heart-felt Christmas prayers wing their way to heaven, the Archangel Gabriel dispatches three of his most creative prayer ambassadors to see that these prayers are "appropriately" answered. A funny, heart-warming trio of unrelated love stories tied together by the off-beat and not always angelic machinations of Shirley, Goodness, and Mercy, heavenly messengers par excellence.

Other books you might like:
Rexanne Becnel, *Christmas Journey*, 1992
Janice Bennett, *A Christmas Keepsake*, 1991
Annette Broadrick, *A Loving Spirit*, 1990
Jude Deveraux, *Wishes*, 1989

`1255`

DEBBIE MACOMBER

Someday Soon
(New York: Harper, 1995)

Story type: Contemporary

Major character(s): Linette Collins, Widow(er), Store Owner; Cain McClellan, Mercenary (leader, "Deliverance Company")
Time period(s): 1990s
Locale(s): San Francisco, California; Montana

Summary: When the still-grieving young widow Linette Collins meets mercenary Cain McClellan, the attraction is as compelling as it is unwelcome. She doesn't want to risk burying another man she loves and he can't afford the distraction of a wife. Nicely done main and secondary characters with a surprising amount of action and violence in this typical "hearth and home" romance.

Other books you might like:
Judith Janeway, *A Convenient Arrangement*, 1995
Lindsay Longford, *The Cowboy, the Baby, and the Runaway Bride*, 1995
Myrna Mackenzie, *The Daddy List*, 1995
Elizabeth Sites, *Stranger in Her Arms*, 1995
  another wounded hero
Karen van der Zee, *Making Magic*, 1995

1256

DEBBIE MACOMBER

Touched by Angels

(New York: Harper, 1995)

Story type: Contemporary/Fantasy; Holiday Themes
Major character(s): Shirley, Angel; Goodness, Angel; Mercy, Angel
Time period(s): 1990s
Locale(s): New York, New York

Summary: In the concluding volume of this popular trilogy, "prayer ambassadors" Shirley, Goodness, and Mercy, are up to their unconventional and often "unangelic" doings as they help a diverse group of people find love and happiness. The setting is Christmas in New York City; the mood is warm and loving. Follows *A Season of Angels* (Harper, 1993) and *The Trouble with Angels* (Harper, 1994)

Other books you might like:
Mary Balogh, *Angel Christmas*, 1994
  angelic Christmas anthology
Mary Chase Comstock, *A Christmas Wish*, 1995
Jude Deveraux, *Wishes*, 1989
  non-Christmas angel theme
Heather Graham Pozzessere, *An Angel's Touch*, 1995
Mary Anne Wilson, *The Christmas Husband*, 1995

1257

DEBBIE MACOMBER

The Trouble with Angels

(New York: Harper, 1994)

Story type: Contemporary/Fantasy
Major character(s): Shirley, Angel (guardian angel); Goodness, Angel (guardian angel); Mercy, Angel (guardian angel)
Time period(s): 1990s

Locale(s): Los Angeles, California

Summary: Once again the Archangel Gabriel reluctantly dispatches his three off-beat and somewhat unpredictable prayer ambassadors, Shirley, Goodness, and Mercy, to answer three very different Christmas prayers. The results are funny, occasionally poignant, and always heartwarming. Sequel to *A Season of Angels*.

Other books you might like:
Michelle Brandon, *Heaven on Earth*, 1993
  historical
Annette Broadrick, *A Loving Spirit*, 1990
Jude Deveraux, *Wishes*, 1989
  historical
Heather Graham, *Spirit of the Season*, 1993
Peg Sutherland, *Yes, Virginia*, 1993

1258

SELENA MACPHERSON

Rough and Tender

(New York: Avon, 1991)

Story type: Historical/American West
Major character(s): Raven Delacour, Young Woman; Eben St. Claire, Frontiersman
Time period(s): 1800s (1807-1808)
Locale(s): Midwest; Pittsburgh, Pennsylvania

Summary: When Eben St. Claire promises a dying trapper to take his daughter to Pennsylvania, he has no idea just how difficult that will be. It's bad enough that independent Raven Delacour fights him every step of the way, but when they fall in love, things really become complicated. Ex-lovers and old friends add to the fiery confusion.

Other books you might like:
Caroline Bourne, *Allegheny Captive*, 1990
Leigh Bristol, *Twice Blessed*, 1991
Elaine Coffman, *Escape Not My Love*, 1990
Betina Lindsey, *Waltz with the Lady*, 1990
DeLoras Scott, *The Miss and the Maverick*, 1990

1259

ROBIN MADERICH

Faith and Honor

(New York: Popular Library, 1989)

Story type: Historical/American Revolution
Major character(s): Faith Mary Asher, Widow(er), Spy (American); Fletcher Irons, Military Personnel (British), Nobleman
Time period(s): 1770s (1775-1781)
Locale(s): New England

Summary: Even though they are on opposite sides during the Revolutionary War, Faith and Fletcher fall in love. Circumstances keep them apart; but with the end of the war, they can finally be together. More realistic than some.

Other books you might like:
Gwen Bristow, *Celia Garth*, 1959
    American Revolution
Heather Graham, *Love Not a Rebel*, 1989
    Dell's American Woman Series 1
Karen Harper, *Eden's Gate*, 1989
    French and Indian War
Christina Savage, *Hearts of Fire*, 1984
Terri Valentine, *Yankee's Caress*, 1989
    American Civil War

1260
LINDA MADL
Sunny
(New York: Pocket, 1990)

Story type: Historical/American West
Major character(s): Sunny Lang, Heiress, Farmer; Cale McFarland, Bounty Hunter
Time period(s): 1870s (1875)
Locale(s): Arkansas

Summary: Bounty hunter Cale McFarland finds himself in a dilemma when he falls in love with Sunny, the sister of one of the men he was sent to track down. Things get even more complex when Sunny is kidnapped, her brother murdered, and she and Cale are forced to join forces to find a stash of gold before the "bad guys" do. Good period detail, lively action, and a serious look at the problem of good and evil are part of this romantic historical.

Other books you might like:
Rosanne Bittner, *Embers of the Heart*, 1990
Jessie Ford, *A Different Breed*, 1988
Nancy Moulton, *Defiant Heart*, 1989

1261
LINDA MADL
Sweet Ransom
(New York: Pocket, 1989)

Story type: Historical/Seventeenth Century
Major character(s): Elise Chatham Polonsky, Noblewoman (Countess); Nikholai "The Wolf" Fomin, Outlaw (Cossack leader)
Time period(s): 17th century (1669)
Locale(s): Russia

Summary: Held for ransom by the dashing leader of a Cossack band, fiery Countess Elise Polonsky learns to appreciate the ways of a different culture and comes to love the man who holds her captive.

Other books you might like:
Phoebe Conn, *By Love Enslaved*, 1989
    Different period/similar ambiance
Julie Garwood, *The Bride*, 1989
    Different period/similar characters
Betina M. Krahn, *Passion's Ransom*, 1989

1262
LINDA MADL
A Tender Magic
(New York: Pocket, 1993)

Story type: Historical/Medieval
Major character(s): Lady Leandra of Lyonesse, Noblewoman, Fiance(e) (reluctant); Garrett Bernay, Nobleman, Knight
Time period(s): 14th century (1346)
Locale(s): England

Summary: Lady Leandra would rather not be marrying Sir Reginald and Sir Garrett would rather not be escorting her to the wedding; nevertheless, that is exactly what they are both doing, until they are tricked into drinking a witch's love potion that Leandra was planning to use to make her "love" her intended bridegroom. Surprisingly, it works! And then Garrett and Leandra must deal with the results. A passionate love story with a fairy tale ending.

Other books you might like:
Julie Garwood, *The Bride*, 1989
Julie Garwood, *The Prize*, 1991
Elizabeth Lowell, *Untamed*, 1993
Judith Merkle Riley, *In Pursuit of the Green Lion*, 1990
Penelope Williamson, *Keeper of the Dream*, 1992

1263
LEE MAGNER
The Mistress of Foxgrove
(New York: Silhouette, 1989)

Story type: Contemporary
Major character(s): Elaine Faust, Landowner (Sister of the owner), Equestrian; Beau Lamond, Horse Trainer (Stable Manager)
Time period(s): 1980s
Locale(s): United States (Foxgrove)

Summary: Returning to the family estate, Foxgrove, to recover from a scandal, Elaine finds herself attracted to the stable manager, a man who for numerous reasons, has doubts about his self-worth. Related to *Master of the Hunt*.

Other books you might like:
Lori Copeland, *Tall Cotton*, 1990
Dee Holmes, *Black Horse Island*, 1990
Elizabeth Lowell, *Fire and Rain*, 1990
Julie Meyers, *In the Cards*, 1990

1264
ANTHEA MALCOLM (Pseudonym of Joan Grant and Tracy Grant)
Counterfeit Heart
(New York: Zebra, 1991)

Story type: Regency
Major character(s): Nicola, Gentlewoman; Charles, Gentleman
Time period(s): 1810s

Locale(s): England

Summary: A witty tale of two cousins who go in search of their respective "intendeds" and become embroiled in a host of other problems instead. Theft, kidnapping, and foreign intrigue are all part of this nicely-crafted Regency. Intricately plotted, well-researched, and peopled with delightfully different characters.

Other books you might like:
Carola Dunn, *Two Corinthians*, 1989
Barbara Metzger, *The Luck of the Devil*, 1991
Judith Nelson, *Lady's Choice*, 1990
Sheila Simonson, *Love and Folly*, 1988

1265

MARINA MALCOLM

Secret in the Shadows
(New York: Leisure, 1991)

Story type: Historical; Romantic Suspense
Major character(s): Amelia Donnelly, Gentlewoman, Orphan; Malcolm Laurence, Wealthy (millionaire); Philip Sheridan, Lawyer
Locale(s): Florida

Summary: Staying with her aunt in a Florida hotel, orphaned Amelia Donnelly finds herself caught in the middle of a dangerous intrigue—and faced with two highly eligible men to choose between. A light, fast-paced romantic mystery peopled with interesting characters.

Other books you might like:
Rita Balkey, *Passion's Fury*, 1989
Lisa Bingham, *Silken Dreams*, 1991
Victoria Holt, *The Secret Woman*, 1970
    Gothic elements
Elizabeth Peters, *Crocodile on the Sandbank*, 1975
    Victorian mystery Egyptian-style/First in the Amelia Peabody Series

---

1266

DOREEN OWENS MALEK

Torchlight
(Toronto: Harlequin, 1991)

Story type: Historical/Victorian America
Major character(s): Elizabeth Langdon, Gentlewoman, Mine Owner (daughter of); Sean Jameson, Miner
Time period(s): 1870s
Locale(s): Pottstown, Pennsylvania

Summary: When Elizabeth Langdon returns to her Pennsylvania home, she quickly becomes involved in a campaign to improve conditions in the local coal mines, much to the dismay of her mine-owner father and to the surprise of the miners, including their leader, Sean Jameson. A heartwarming, romantic story of a love that overcomes the barriers of class, wealth, and family expectations.

Other books you might like:
Elaine Barbieri, *Wishes on the Wind*, 1991

Sonya Birmingham, *Spitfire*, 1991
    miner's problems in the Old West
Lucy Elliot, *Private Paradise*, 1991
Constance O'Day-Flannery, *This Time Forever*, 1990
Joan Johnston, *Sweetwater Seduction*, 1991
    Old West setting

1267

ELONA MALTERRE

Mistress of the Eagles
(New York: Dell, 1990)

Story type: Historical/Medieval
Major character(s): Arrah O'Donnell, Noblewoman, Pirate; Seagan MacNamara, Nobleman
Time period(s): 15th century (1446)
Locale(s): Ireland; France

Summary: Arrah was just a young girl when Seagan first met her. When they meet again, she has become a strong woman and the captain of her own pirate ship. Love, passion, and tempers flare between these two independent spirits.

Other books you might like:
Morgan Llywelyn, *Grania: She-King of the Irish Seas*, 1985
    Historical characters
Laurie McBain, *Chance the Winds of Fortune*, 1980
Laurie McBain, *Moonstruck Madness*, 1977
Bertrice Small, *Skye O'Malley*, 1980
Lisa Ann Verge, *The Heart's Disguise*, 1990

1268

CAROL MARSH

The Silver Link
(New York: Dell, 1994)

Story type: Contemporary/Mainstream
Major character(s): Dana Armstrong, Heiress, Artist (painter); Marshall Fowler, Businessman; Peter Crane, Historian
Time period(s): 1990s
Locale(s): New York, New York; Grosse Pointe, Michigan; Malibu, California

Summary: Sheltered, naive heiress Dana Armstrong just knows she loves Marshall Fowler, the dashing auto heir who answers all her prayers. She ignores warnings by her father and best friend, Peter, and soon finds her life a living nightmare. Searching for the truth sends her to other men, compromises her career, and estranges her from Peter. It takes his departure to force her to mature and discover what she really wants in life.

Other books you might like:
Sally Beauman, *Destiny*, 1988
Catherine Coulter, *Beyond Eden*, 1991
Barbara Delinsky, *A Woman Betrayed*, 1991
Marie Ferrarella, *Sapphire and Shadow*, 1991
Johanna Kingsley, *Loving Touches*, 1995

1269

ELLEN TANNER MARSH

A Christmas Embrace
(New York: St. Martin's, 1994)

Story type: Contemporary; Holiday Themes
Major character(s): Rose Boyer, Veterinarian; Alex Boyer, Stock Broker
Time period(s): 1990s
Locale(s): Rancho San Dumas, California; Lancaster, Pennsylvania (in the country near Lancaster)

Summary: In an effort to revitalize their not-so-perfect marriage, veterinarian Rose Boyer gives her stock broker, workaholic husband a surprise Christmas gift—a romantic Christmas weekend in the picturesesque Pennsylvania Dutch country. Unfortunately, with snow, mixups, and Alex's ill-concealed resentment, the weekend promises to become a disaster—until the Christmas spirit lends a hand and helps them get their priorities in order.

Other books you might like:
Rexanne Becnel, *Christmas Journey*, 1992
Kathleen Creighton, *A Christmas Love*, 1992
Janet Dailey, *Mistletoe and Holly*, 1983
Heather Graham, *Spirit of the Season*, 1993
Monica Harris, *Spirit of the Season*, 1994
    African American holiday anthology

1270

ELLEN TANNER MARSH

If This Be Magic
(New York: Warner, 1990)

Story type: Historical/French Revolution
Major character(s): Townsend Grey, Gentlewoman; Ian Moncrieff, Nobleman (Duke of Boyne)
Time period(s): 1780s (1789-1790)
Locale(s): England; France

Summary: When Townsend meets Ian in a dismal fen in Norfolk, it is love at first sight. But when he takes her as his bride to the Court at Versailles, she begins to wonder why he married her. A story of mystery, danger, political intrigue, and love.

Other books you might like:
Brian Cleeve, *Hester*, 1979
Roberta Gellis, *The Silver Mirror*, 1989
    Different period/Court intrigue
Jill Gregory, *Moonlit Obsession*, 1986
Victoria Holt, *The Devil on Horseback*, 1977
Baroness Orczy, *The Scarlet Pimpernel*, 1905
    Classic tale of the French Revolution

1271

DEBORAH MARTIN

Creole Nights
(New York: Leisure, 1992)

Story type: Historical/Post-American Civil War
Major character(s): Elina Lannier, Young Woman Rene Bonnage, Gentleman (Creole)
Time period(s): 19th century
Locale(s): New Orleans, Louisiana

Summary: Elina and her brother go to New Orleans to find their father, but when Alex cheats infamous Rene Bonnage, they flee. Alex meets his end in a gaming hell, but Elina searches on — and finds that although her father is dead, he has a family in New Orleans — and Rene Bonnage is part of that family! Deceit, mystery, and passion follow in this intense and highly sensual romance.

Other books you might like:
Olga Bicos, *Santana Rose*, 1992
Kat Martin, *Creole Fires*, 1992
Linda Lael Miller, *Emma and the Outlaw*, 1991
Miriam Minger, *Defiant Imposter*, 1992
Karen Robards, *Morning Song*, 1991

1272

DEBORAH MARTIN

Silver Deceptions
(New York: Topaz, 1994)

Story type: Historical/Seventeenth Century
Major character(s): Arabella Taylor Maynard, Actress; Colin Jeffreys, Nobleman (Lord Hampton), Spy (former)
Time period(s): 17th century (1667)
Locale(s): London, England

Summary: Seeking revenge for her mother's death, Arabella acts the role of a wanton, hoping to trap the guilty party. However, complications result when both Lord Hampton and his friend Maynard are attracted to her. Treachery, intrigue, and danger enhance this complex story set in Restoration England.

Other books you might like:
Ruth Langan, *Deception*, 1993
Jean Plaidy, *The Pleasure of Love*, 1992
    good historical picture of Restoration England
Jeanette Baker Ramirez, *Lady of Lochabar*, 1993
Susan Wiggs, *The Lily and the Leopard*, 1991
Susan Wiggs, *The Mist and the Magic*, 1993

1273

KAT MARTIN

The Captain's Bride
(New York: Charter Diamond, 1990)

Story type: Historical/Antebellum American South
Major character(s): Gloria "Glory" Summerfield, Southern Belle; Nicholas Blackwell, Sea Captain

Time period(s): 1840s
Locale(s): South Carolina; At Sea; New York, New York

Summary: In an effort to get her mulatto half-brother out of the South, Glory applies to Captain Nicholas Blackwell for passage for herself and her "slave" aboard his New York-bound ship. Nicholas and Glory are at odds, even though they are attracted to each other, until a shipwreck forces them to realize their love for each other. Well-plotted and lively.

Other books you might like:
Jeanne E. Hansen, *Midnight Enchantment*, 1990
Wanda Owen, *Deceptive Desires*, 1990
Alexandra Ripley, *Charleston*, 1982
Linda Windsor, *Pirate's Wild Embrace*, 1990
Kathleen E. Woodiwiss, *Shanna*, 1977

1274

KAT MARTIN

Creole Fires

(New York: Dell, 1992)

Story type: Historical/Antebellum American South
Major character(s): Nicole St. Claire, Servant (indentured), Gentlewoman (impoverished); Alexandre du Villier, Plantation Owner
Time period(s): 19th century
Locale(s): New Orleans, Louisiana

Summary: Nicole St. Claire is bought as an indentured servant by planter Alex du Villier, and after a night of passion, he decides to make her his mistress. Nicole cannot reconcile herself to living in sin, but when she runs away, it results in even more trouble. Good period detail.

Other books you might like:
Brenna Braxton-Barshon, *Southern Oaks*, 1991
Thea Devine, *Southern Seduction*, 1991
Patricia Hagan, *Midnight Rose*, 1991
Jeanne E. Hansen, *Midnight Enchantment*, 1990
Sonya T. Pelton, *Love Hear My Heart*, 1990

1275

KAT MARTIN

Devil's Prize

(New York: St. Martin's, 1995)

Story type: Historical/Regency
Major character(s): Alexa Garrick, Debutante; Lord Damien Falon, Nobleman (Earl of Falon)
Time period(s): 1800s (1809)
Locale(s): London, England

Summary: Lord Damien Falon has plotted his revenge against Alexa Garrick in great detail, but his ruthless plans of seduction do not include marrying the woman who has destroyed his brother. Nevertheless, they wed; and Alexa, finding herself bound to a man who claims to hate her, wonders if the passion they share will be enough to sustain a marriage full of secrets and founded on deception. Passionate and realistic.

Other books you might like:
Patricia Camden, *Scarlet Kisses*, 1992
  a vengeful heroine
Iris Johansen, *The Beloved Scoundrel*, 1994
  forced relationship
Mary Jo Putney, *Thunder and Roses*, 1993
  forced relationship
Anne Stuart, *A Rose at Midnight*, 1993
  a vengeful heroine
Katherine Sutcliffe, *Miracle*, 1995

1276

KAT MARTIN

Gypsy Lord

(New York: St. Martin, 1992)

Story type: Historical/Georgian
Major character(s): Catherine Barrington, Noblewoman (Countess of Arondale), Captive; Dominic Edgemont, Nobleman (Lord Nightwyck), Gypsy (half)
Time period(s): 1800s (1805)
Locale(s): England

Summary: Although Dominic Edgemont prefers the gypsy life with his mother's family, he's not averse to using his aristocratic wealth to purchase an abused captive from a fellow gypsy. However, when the captive turns out to be of noble birth and fiesty to boot, he begins to wonder as to the wisdom of his decision. Fast-paced action, sparkling dialogue, and intense sexuality are part of this hard-hitting romance.

Other books you might like:
Iris Johansen, *The Golden Barbarian*, 1991
Mary Lide, *Isobelle*, 1988
Johanna Lindsey, *Captive Bride*, 1977
Lindsay McKenna, *King of Swords*, 1992
Patricia Pellicane, *Sweet Seduction*, 1992

1277

KAT MARTIN

Lover's Gold

(New York: Charter Diamond, 1991)

Story type: Historical/American West
Major character(s): Elaina McAllister, Gentlewoman (impoverished); Dan Morgan, Imposter, Gunfighter
Time period(s): 1870s (1878)
Locale(s): Pennsylvania; California

Summary: Although Dan Morgan cannot reveal his true identity to his childhood friend Elaina McAllister, he still has the power to save her from the murderous plans of her late father's former partners; but he doesn't count on falling in love with her. Exceedingly complex plot.

Other books you might like:
Constance Bennett, *Morning Sky*, 1991
Catherine Lanigan, *A Promise Made*, 1991
Joan Elliott Pickart, *The Bonnie Blue*, 1991
Terri Valentine, *Outlaw's Kiss*, 1991

1278

KAT MARTIN

Savannah Heat

(New York: Dell, 1993)

Story type: Historical/Exotic
Major character(s): Silver Jones, Runaway, Noblewoman (Lady Salena Hardwick Jones); Morgan Trask, Sea Captain
Time period(s): 1840s
Locale(s): Barbados; Texas; Yucatan Peninsula, Mexico

Summary: Silver Jones will do anything to keep from return to her abusive father—start fires, jump ship, what ever is needed to keep Morgan Trask from delivering her home. In spite of her annoying interferences in his secret mission to rescue his brother, he begins to admire Silver's spirit and courage. In addition, she is honest and caring, qualities he has not known in a woman. Passion between the two of them builds, despite a conflict of wills in this exciting and surprising, action-filled adventure.

Other books you might like:
Johanna Lindsey, *Gentle Rogue*, 1990
Linda Lael Miller, *Caroline and the Raider*, 1992
Deborah Simmons, *Heart's Masquerade*, 1989
Joan Van Nuys, *Beloved Avenger*, 1989

1279

MARCIA MARTIN

South of Paradise

(New York: Jove, 1993)

Story type: Contemporary
Major character(s): Victoria Blackwood, Con Artist; Richard Adams, Businessman
Time period(s): 1990s
Locale(s): North Carolina

Summary: Victoria, as four different people, beguiles and dupes older wealthy lawyers and takes their expensive cars. Richard, angry and determined to catch her, falls under her spell, too. Never one to let a man get to her emotionally, Victoria surprisingly finds herself attracted to Richard.

Other books you might like:
Lisbeth Chance, *Cutting Edge*, 1985
Mary Higgins Clark, *All around the Town*, 1992
Mary Higgins Clark, *Stillwatch*, 1984
Jeanne Stephens, *At Risk*, 1989
Corbett H. Thigpen, *The Three Faces of Eve*, 1957
   classic study of multiple personalities—not a romance

1280

MARCIA MARTIN

Southern Nights

(New York: Berkley, 1990)

Story type: Romantic Suspense

Major character(s): Maggie Hastings, Heiress (Yankee); Mark Fox, Heir—Dispossessed (Southerner)
Time period(s): 1980s
Locale(s): Charleston, South Carolina (Foxcroft Estate)

Summary: When William Fox wills his South Carolina estate, Foxcroft, to Yankee Maggie Hastings instead of his son Mark, he sets the stage for conflict and confrontation as well as the unraveling of some long-hidden family secrets. Strong and passionate.

Other books you might like:
Jill Barkin, *Hot Streak*, 1990
Sally Beauman, *Destiny*, 1990
Janet Dailey, *Masquerade*, 1990
Jayne Ann Krentz, *The Golden Chance*, 1990
Nora Roberts, *Public Secrets*, 1990

1281

MARCIA MARTIN

Southern Secrets

(New York: Jove, 1991)

Story type: Contemporary/Mainstream
Major character(s): Savannah King, Socialite; Danny Sawyer, Journalist (newspaper reporter)
Time period(s): 1990s
Locale(s): Kingsport, North Carolina

Summary: When they were children, Danny was the housekeeper's son and Savannah was beyond his reach. But when Danny comes back to Kingsport a self-made man, he finds Savannah struggling to take care of her mother and to keep their estate. Murder, romance, and passion are all part of this sensual love story.

Other books you might like:
Elaine Barbieri, *Wishes on the Wind*, 1991
   historical setting
Sandra Brown, *Breath of Scandal*, 1991
Rebecca George, *Call Home the Heart*, 1989
Lisa Gregory, *Seasons*, 1990
Judith McNaught, *Paradise*, 1991

1282

MARCIA MARTIN

Southern Storms

(New York: Jove, 1992)

Story type: Contemporary/Mainstream
Major character(s): Cara Chastain, Widow(er), Animal Lover; Lee Powers, Architect
Time period(s): 1990s
Locale(s): Walking Dune, North Carolina

Summary: Devoted to her son, her husband's memory, and saving a herd of wild Spanish mustangs, Cara Chastain has no intention of becoming emotionally involved again. But when attractive architect Lee Powers arrives in Walking Dune to plan a development that will threaten her beloved animals, her resolve flies out the window—and she finds herself falling in love with the very man she needs to fight. Sequel to *Southern Secrets*.

Other books you might like:
Jennifer Blake, *Love and Smoke*, 1989
Elizabeth Lowell, *Reckless Love*, 1990
    horses in the historical West
Laura Parrish, *Love's Quiet Corner*, 1989
    development vs. status quo theme
Peggy Roberts, *Mrs. Perfect*, 1992

1283

MICHELLE MARTIN

Queen of Hearts
(New York: Fawcett, 1994)

Story type: Regency
Major character(s): Samantha Adamson, Noblewoman; Lord Simon Cartwright, Nobleman
Time period(s): 1810s
Locale(s): London, England

Summary: Vibrant and self-assured, Samantha Adamson scandalizes the ton with her behavior and her mysterious past. She also attracts the attentions of the staid and proper Lord Cartwright, who in trying to save her from ruin, ends up falling in love with Samantha and becomes a little less starchy in the process.

Other books you might like:
Anne Barbour, *Lord Glenraven's Return*, 1994
Mary Chase Comstock, *An Impetuous Miss*, 1993
Charlotte Louise Dolan, *The Counterfeit Gentleman*, 1995
Georgette Heyer, *The Convenient Marriage*, 1934
Barbara Metzger, *Lady in Green*, 1993

1284

NANCY MARTIN

Monkey Wrench
(Toronto: Harlequin, 1992)

Story type: Contemporary
Series: Tyler
Major character(s): Susannah Atkins, Television Personality (Household Hints hostess); Joe Santori, Carpenter
Time period(s): 1990s
Locale(s): Milwaukee, Wisconsin; Tyler, Wisconsin

Summary: When Susannah Atkins returns to Tyler to visit her grandmother, Rose, she runs into Joe Santori, the man that Grandma has decided is The One for Susie. Lots of charm and small town ambience.

Other books you might like:
Dixie Dubois, *Home Fires*, 1992
Debbie Macomber, *First Comes Marriage*, 1991
Peggy Morse, *The Stillman Curse*, 1992
Alice Sharpe, *Wedding Bell Blues*, 1992
    innocent

1285

WENDY MARTIN

Love on Trial
(New York: Avalon, 1990)

Story type: Contemporary/Innocent
Major character(s): Kate Wynne, Lawyer; Brian Davis, Veterinarian
Time period(s): 1990s
Locale(s): Groveton, New Jersey

Summary: Successful, romantically wary attorney Kate Wynne finds herself the unwilling victim of her younger sister's matchmaking scheme involving an attractive veterinarian. Light and sweet.

Other books you might like:
Patricia Ellis, *Champagne and Wildflowers*, 1991
Debbie Macomber, *First Comes Marriage*, 1991
Helen R. Myers, *A Fine Arrangement*, 1991
La Verne St. George, *A Private Proposal*, 1990
Alice Sharpe, *A Storybook Love*, 1990

1286

SANDRA MARTON

Night Fires
(Toronto: Harlequin, 1991)

Story type: Contemporary; Romantic Suspense
Major character(s): Gabrielle Chiari, Businesswoman (flower-shop owner), Fugitive; James Forrester, Imposter
Time period(s): 1990s
Locale(s): New York, New York; New Orleans, Louisiana

Summary: Gabrielle Chiari thinks she has left her past behind when she leaves New York and goes into the flower business in New Orelans; but when mysterious James Forrester saves her life and then proceeds to pursue her, she wonders if she will ever be truly safe. Intriguingly different.

Other books you might like:
Susan Anderson, *Shadow Dance*, 1989
Janet Dailey, *Masquerade*, 1990
Jayne Ann Krentz, *Silver Linings*, 1991
Sidney Sheldon, *If Tomorrow Comes*, 1985
Chloe Summers, *No Easy Task*, 1991

1287

CONNIE MASON

Beyond the Horizon
(New York: Leisure, 1990)

Story type: Historical/American West
Major character(s): Shannon Brannigan, Southern Belle (former); Blade ''Swift Blade'' Stryker, Scout, Indian (half)
Time period(s): 1860s (1861)
Locale(s): Oregon Trail

Summary: Shannon Brannigan joins a wagon train hoping to catch up with her family who are heading west—and finds love, in the form of Blade Stryker, the enigmatic Indian scout. A romantic, fast-paced story that deals with, among other things, the issues of prejudice and bigotry.

Other books you might like:
Catherine Anderson, *Comanche Moon*, 1991
Rosanne Bittner, *Sioux Splendor*, 1990
Kathleen Harrington, *Cherish the Dream*, 1990
Norah Hess, *Wildfire*, 1989
Marianne Willman, *Yesterday's Shadows*, 1991

`1288`

CONNIE MASON

Brave Land, Brave Love
(New York: Leisure, 1992)

Story type: Historical/Exotic; Historical/Regency
Major character(s): Tia Fairfield, Runaway, Thief (pickpocket); Ben Penrod, Rancher
Time period(s): 1810s (1818)
Locale(s): England; Australia

Summary: A fast-paced, sexy story in which the heroine is forced to pretend to be the hero's wife and ends up falling in love with him — even though she is already married to someone else. Sweet/savage overtones.

Other books you might like:
Brenda Joyce, *Dark Fires*, 1991
Lindsay McKenna, *King of Swords*, 1992
Lindsay McKenna, *Lord of Shadowhawk*, 1992
Christina Skye, *The Black Rose*, 1991
Katherine Sutcliffe, *A Fire in the Heart*, 1990

`1289`

CONNIE MASON

Ice and Rapture
(New York: Leisure, 1993)

Story type: Historical/American West Coast
Major character(s): Margaret Afton, Journalist (reporter); Chase McGarrett, Rancher (cattleman)
Time period(s): 19th century (late)
Locale(s): Alaska

Summary: As an on-site reporter in Alaska, intrepid, highly independent, and hot-tempered Margaret Afton encounters outlaws, murderers, avalanches, wild rivers, and numerous other adventures in her journalistic pursuits and somehow, even finds time to fall in love with cattleman Chase McGarrett in the process. Fast-paced.

Other books you might like:
Colleen Faulkner, *Love's Sweet Bounty*, 1991
Jo Ann Ferguson, *At the Rainbow's End*, 1989
Peggy Hanchar, *Tomorrow's Dream*, 1989
Kristin Hannah, *A Handful of Heaven*, 1991
Shirley Parenteau, *Golden Prospect*, 1991

`1290`

CONNIE MASON

A Promise of Thunder
(New York: Leisure, 1993)

Story type: Historical/American West
Series: Women of the West
Major character(s): Storm Kennedy, Frontierswoman, Widow(er); Grady "Thunder" Stryker, Widow(er), Indian (half Lakota)
Time period(s): 1890s (1893)
Locale(s): Oklahoma

Summary: Grady's Indian family causes all kinds of trouble when he tries to make a life for himself away from them. Even when he marries Storm Kennedy, his sisters try to frighten her away with lies. Lots of action and adventure in this story set during the days of the Oklahoma land rush.

Other books you might like:
Michael Blake, *Dances with Wolves*, 1990
Constance O'Banyon, *Cheyenne Sunrise*, 1990
Dana Ransom, *Dakota Dawn*, 1991
Patricia Werner, *Cherokee Bride*, 1992

`1291`

CONNIE MASON

Tempt the Devil
(New York: Leisure, 1990)

Story type: Historical/Georgian
Major character(s): Devon Chatham, Noblewoman, Captive; Diablo, Pirate
Time period(s): 1710s (1715)
Locale(s): England; Barbados; At Sea

Summary: Taken captive during a daring gallow's rescue, Lady Devon Chatham falls in love with her pirate captor, Diablo. Passion and romance flourish until fate (and a jealous lover) interferes. Diablo and Devon, of course, are destined to be together, but not until he rights some old wrongs and clears his name. Action and adventure on the high seas.

Other books you might like:
Victoria Holt, *The Captive*, 1989
Jean Innes, *Buccaneer's Bride*, 1989
Johanna Lindsey, *A Pirate's Love*, 1978
Joan Van Nuys, *Beloved Avenger*, 1989
Kathleen E. Woodiwiss, *Shanna*, 1977

`1292`

CONNIE MASON

Wild Land, Wild Love
(New York: Leisure, 1992)

Story type: Historical/Exotic
Major character(s): Katherine Molly McKenzie, Rancher (sheep station owner); Robin Fletcher, Convict, Manager (of sheep station)
Locale(s): New South Wales, Australia

Summary: Kate travels to New South Wales to take over her father's sheep station, only to find it competently managed by convict Robin Fletcher. To make matters worse, she must marry Robin or lose the station. Misunderstandings, pride, jealousy, and treachery make it difficult for the pair to build any kind of relationship, but love does win out in the end. Vibrant picture of life in New South Wales.

Other books you might like:
Lois Battle, *The Past Is Another Country*, 1992
Dorothy Eden, *The Vines of Yarabee*, 1969
Colleen McCullough, *The Thorn Birds*, 1977
Linda Lael Miller, *Angelfire*, 1989
Lynette Vinet, *Wild, Wicked Eden*, 1990

1293

FELICIA MASON

Body and Soul

(New York: Pinnacle, 1995)

Story type: Contemporary; Ethnic
Major character(s): Toinette Blue, Administrator (welfare job program director), Spouse (abandoned); Robinson Mayview III, Lawyer
Time period(s): 1990s
Locale(s): United States

Summary: Beautiful, successful, and 47, Toinette Blue has a hard time believing that a younger man, particularly one as attractive and eligible as attorney Robinson Mayview, could be interested in her. But he is—and in spite of her objections, he refuses to give up. Humor, sensuality, and a few past secrets combine in this story that adds new dimension to the classic May-December theme. Warm and satisfying.

Other books you might like:
Bette Ford, *For Always*, 1995
     ethnic emphasis/sensitive
Sandra Kitt, *The Color of Love*, 1995
     ethnic emphasis
Pamela Morsi, *Courting Miss Hattie*, 1991
     historical/May-December relationship/not ethnic
Francis Ray, *Forever Yours*, 1994
     ethnic emphasis/humorous
Margie Walker, *Breathless*, 1995
     ethnic emphasis

1294

SONJA MASSIE

Far and Away

(New York: Berkley, 1992)

Story type: Historical/American West; Saga
Major character(s): Shannon Christie, Immigrant; Joseph Donelly, Immigrant
Time period(s): 19th century
Locale(s): Ireland; Boston, Massachusetts; Oklahoma

Summary: Privileged and independent, Shannon Christie escapes the turmoil in Ireland and ends up in America fighting for her life and fortune beside Joseph Donelly, a man with

reason to hate her family and everything it stands for. A sweeping picturesque movie tie-in.

Other books you might like:
Elaine Barbieri, *Tattered Silk*, 1991
Elaine Barbieri, *Wishes on the Wind*, 1991
Lucy Elliot, *Private Paradise*, 1991
Jill Marie Landis, *Rose*, 1990
Jill Marie Landis, *Sunflower*, 1988

1295

LAURA MATTHEWS

The Village Spinster

(New York: Signet, 1993)

Story type: Regency
Major character(s): Clarissa Driscoll, Teacher (of painting and deportment); Alexander Barrington, Nobleman (Earl of Kinsford)
Time period(s): 1810s
Locale(s): England

Summary: Clarissa Driscoll has enough on her mind trying to pay off her father's gambling debts with her small income as a teacher without having to worry about arrogant Lord Barrington complaining that her lessons are "too extreme" for his young siblings. She stands her ground and sparks fly, in more ways than one. Laced with wit and humor.

Other books you might like:
Rita Boucher, *The Scandalous Schoolmistress*, 1992
Cathleen Clare, *Felicia*, 1993
Georgette Heyer, *The Unknown Ajax*, 1959
Amanda Quick, *Scandal*, 1991
     sensual
Sheila Walsh, *The Arrogant Lord Alistair*, 1990

1296

ANN MAXWELL

The Diamond Tiger

(New York: Harper, 1992)

Story type: Contemporary/Mainstream; Romantic Suspense
Major character(s): Erin Shane Windsor, Mine Owner (Diamond) Cole Blackburn, Scientist (geologist)
Time period(s): 1990s
Locale(s): Australia

Summary: Erin's uncle leaves her a diamond mine and a poem full of clues—but no map! Geologist Cole Blackburn offers to help her find it, but the diamond cartel wants them both out of the way. The U.S. government and a Chinese tong are also involved, and the fact that Erin is suspicious that Cole is not what he seems just adds to the suspense. A well-crafted romantic mystery.

Other books you might like:
Barbara Delinsky, *Facets*, 1990
Jayne Ann Krentz, *Sweet Fortune*, 1991
Connie Mason, *Wild Land, Wild Love*, 1992
     historical Australia
Katherine Sinclair, *Far Horizons*, 1991

Barbara Wood, *The Dreaming*, 1992

1297
EVAN MAXWELL

All the Winters That Have Been
(New York: Harper Collins, 1995)

Story type: Contemporary
Major character(s): Helen Raven, Artist; Dane Corvin, Writer, Naturalist
Time period(s): 20th century (mid)
Locale(s): Puget Sound, Washington

Summary: Returning to the Pacific Northwest to be with his dying uncle, naturalist and writer Dane Corvin renews his relationship with the woman he has loved for two decades. Emotionally satisfying and sensitive, this novella focuses on universal themes and makes good use of imagry and metaphor. Nicely-crafted.

Other books you might like:
Lenore Caroll, *The Heart Remembers*, 1993
Marilyn Cunningham, *Seasons of the Heart*, 1992
Deborah Smith, *Miracle*, 1991
LaVyrle Spencer, *Bittersweet*, 1990
Robert James Waller, *The Bridges of Madison County*, 1992
    similar theme but ending will not satisfy many romance readers

1298
NORMA FOX MAZER
HARRY MAZER, Co-Author

Heartbeat
(New York: Bantam Starfire, 1989)

Story type: Young Adult
Series: Starfire
Major character(s): Hilary, Mechanic (auto, aspiring); Tod, Boyfriend
Time period(s): 1980s

Summary: Good friends Tod and Amos are both in love with Hilary, only Amos doesn't know how Tod feels—or that Hilary returns those feelings. When Amos develops a heart problem, things become even more complicated as the three learn something about love, friendship, and the realities of life.

Other books you might like:
Betty Bates, *Picking Up the Pieces*, 1981
Hila Coleman, *Don't Tell Me That You Love Me*, 1983
Madeleine L'Engle, *And Both Were Young*, 1949
    Republished in 1986
Marilyn Levy, *Sounds of Silence*, 1989
Richard Peck, *Close Enough to Touch*, 1981

1299
ALISA MCBRIDE

Love's Bounty
(Aurora, Colorado: Audio Entertainment, 1993)

Story type: Historical/American West
Major character(s): Kate Malone, Bounty Hunter; Dan Fields, Lawman (sheriff)
Time period(s): 1880s
Locale(s): Arizona

Summary: All independent, headstrong bounty hunter Kate Malone wants from the Sheriff Dan Fields is the whereabouts of a wanted murderer. What she gets is a partner—and a man who proves to be a greater threat to her future than the outlaw she is after! One of a new series of original romances on audio casette.

Other books you might like:
Kathryn Hockett, *Outlaw Seduction*, 1993
Linda Madl, *Sunny*, 1990
Rae Muir, *Gold Is the Game*, 1993
    audio tape
Andrea Parnell, *My Only Desire*, 1993

1300
MARY MCBRIDE

Riverbend
(Toronto: Harlequin, 1993)

Story type: Historical/American Civil War
Major character(s): Jessamine Dade, Southern Belle; Lee Kincannon, Hotel Owner, Military Personnel (Confederate soldier)
Time period(s): 1860s
Locale(s): New Orleans, Louisiana; St. Louis, Missouri

Summary: When Lee Kincannon agrees to help young Jessamine Dade return to her beloved plantation, Riverbend, he has no idea that four years later he will be seeking shelter in the same plantation as a wounded rebel. However, the road to love does not run smoothly for the pair, and they must deal not only with the war, but with grasping relatives, a love-struck suitor, and a jealous mistress before they can find the happiness they are seeking.

Other books you might like:
Jane Archer, *Bayou Passion*, 1991
Caroline Bourne, *Riverboat Seduction*, 1992
Christine Dorsey, *Kansas Kiss*, 1992
Diane Gates Robinson, *Delta Desire*, 1991

1301
HOLLY S. MCCLURE

Dreams of Joy
(New York: Avalon, 1990)

Story type: Contemporary/Innocent

Major character(s): Joy Carmichael, Entertainer (puppeteer), Television (creator of PBS children's show); Stephen Brooks, Businessman (real estate developer)
Time period(s): 1990s
Locale(s): Seattle, Washington

Summary: Classic story of love and conflict involving a woman determined to save the land and a man intent on developing it. Warm and funny.

Other books you might like:
Ruth Jean Dale, *Society Page*, 1991
Cindy T. Moss, *Love's Safe Harbor*, 1991
Laura Parrish, *Love's Quiet Corner*, 1989
Catherine Spencer, *Winter Roses*, 1991
Linda Varner, *A House Becomes a Home*, 1991

1302
AUDREY MCCONACHIE
No Blueprint for Love
(New York: Avalon, 1992)

Story type: Contemporary/Innocent
Major character(s): Paula Whittaker, Architect; Ross Anderson, Contractor, Widow(er)
Time period(s): 1990s
Locale(s): Seattle, Washington

Summary: Architect Paula Whittaker's career is on the fast track up. She has just been named head architect for the new hospital wing—and then things start to go wrong. She is attacked, missing drugs appear in her desk, and to top it off, she is disastrously attracted to contractor and widower Ross Anderson. Light romance with a dash of suspense.

Other books you might like:
Jillian Dagg, *Sungold*, 1992
Debbie Macomber, *Rainy Day Kisses*, 1990
La Verne St. George, *A Private Proposal*, 1990
Karen Rose Smith, *Garden of Fantasy*, 1992

1303
NOELLE BERRY MCCUE
Look Beyond the Dream
(New York: Silhouette, 1990)

Story type: Contemporary
Major character(s): Erin Daniels, Dietician (for health club chain); Logan Sinclair, Businessman (owner of health club chain)
Time period(s): 1990s

Summary: When Erin Daniels lands the job of dietitian for a string of health clubs, it means she will be traveling with the owner, handsome Logan Sinclair. Although powerfully attracted to each other, they try to resist involvement, knowing their romantic goals are not the same—he plays the field; she wants permanence. Romantic and sensual.

Other books you might like:
Patt Bucheister, *Once Burned, Twice as Hot*, 1990
Kay Hooper, *Enemy Mine*, 1989

Muriel Jensen, *Everything*, 1990
Valerie Parv, *Tasmanian Devil*, 1990

1304
KAREN G. MCCULLOUGH
The Night Prowlers
(New York: Avalon Books, 1990)

Story type: Romantic Suspense
Major character(s): Jan Lindell, Student (Graduate Assistant), Archaeologist; Gary Simpson, Architect, Landowner (son of)
Time period(s): 1980s
Locale(s): Virginia

Summary: When Jan Lindell takes a group of archeology students on a summer dig, they find more than the remains of an old inn. Threats and vandalism plague the project; ghost stories abound; and Jan's love life takes a turn for the better.

Other books you might like:
Jane Edwards, *Terror by Design*, 1990
Loretta Jackson, *Nightmare in Morocco*, 1989
    Moroccan setting
Elizabeth Peters, *Crocodile on the Sandbank*, 1975
    Historical/Archaeologist goes to Egypt
Elizabeth Peters, *Summer of the Dragon*, 1979
    Arizona setting
Mary Stewart, *This Rough Magic*, 1964
    Set on Corfu

1305
KAREN G. MCCULLOUGH
Programmed for Danger
(New York: Avalon, 1990)

Story type: Contemporary/Innocent; Romantic Suspense
Major character(s): Andrea Kingston, Computer Expert (programmer), Troubleshooter (systems analyst); David Purcell, Businessman (operations manager)
Time period(s): 1990s
Locale(s): Charlotte, North Carolina

Summary: Systems analyst Andrea Kingston comes to debug a seriously and maliciously infested computer system and finds that she has put both her life and her heart in danger.

Other books you might like:
Evelyn Anthony, *The Tamarind Seed*, 1971
Alma Blair, *The Unwitting Witness*, 1990
Mary Higgins Clark, *Stillwatch*, 1984
Jane Edwards, *Terror by Design*, 1990
Mary Stewart, *Airs Above the Ground*, 1965

1306
JAN MCDANIEL
Angels in the Sand
(New York: Avalon Books, 1989)

Story type: Contemporary/Innocent

Major character(s): Sarah Barnett, Restauranteur; Matt Gerrard, Journalist
Time period(s): 1980s
Locale(s): Winwood, Florida

Summary: From the time her father died when she was eighteen, Sarah had put her own life on hold and had devoted herself totally to providing for her family by keeping the family deli in operation. Now, six years later, she is suddenly faced with romance in the person of Matt Gerrard, and she is forced to deal with feelings she had only thought were for "other people."

Other books you might like:
Jane McBride Choate, *Badge of Love*, 1989
Rita Rainville, *Never on Sundae*, 1990
Joan Smith, *Sealed with a Kiss*, 1990
Alice Sharpe, *A Garland of Love*, 1990
Diana Whitney, *A Liberated Man*, 1990

1307

JAN MCDANIEL

This Fragile Heart
(New York: Avalon Books, 1989)

Story type: Contemporary/Innocent
Major character(s): Penny Arnette, Businesswoman (recently fired); Corey Zeller, Businessman (head, Mall Public Relations)
Time period(s): 1980s
Locale(s): Houston, Texas

Summary: When recently-fired Penny Arnette takes a temporary job as Santa Claus at a local shopping mall, she doesn't plan to become involved in business politics, achieve celebrity status, or fall in love—but, of course, she does all three.

Other books you might like:
Mary Blaynay, *Father Christmas*, 1989
Lynn Bulock, *Roses for Caroline*, 1989
Bethany Campbell, *The Snow Garden*, 1989
  Christmas theme
Lynda Stowe Landers, *A Season to Remember*, 1989
Laura Parrish, *Love's Quiet Corner*, 1989

1308

NELLE MCFATHER

Tears of Fire
(New York: Love Spell, 1994)

Story type: Time Travel; Contemporary/Fantasy
Major character(s): Fable Devereaux, Musician (country), Time Traveller
Time period(s): 1980s (1988-1989); 1860s
Locale(s): Nashville, Tennessee

Summary: Searching for answers to her sister's death, Fable is aided from the past by her grandmother, a distillery owner in 1859. As Fable drifts between the past and the present, she becomes involved in the Civil War and ends up in love with men in both time periods.

Other books you might like:
Lori Herter, *The Willow File*, 1994
Antoinette Stockenberg, *Embers*, 1994
Antoinette Stockenberg, *Emily's Ghost*, 1992
Marilyn Tracy, *Memory's Lamp*, 1994

1309

JOANNA MCGAURAN

A Love So Fierce
(New York: Dell, 1993)

Story type: Historical/Medieval
Major character(s): Brielle Le Fontin, Noblewoman; Adam Dunbarton, Nobleman, Knight
Time period(s): 14th century
Locale(s): England

Summary: Brielle adores her betrothed, Lord Adam Dunbarton, but her proud, stubborn manner doesn't appeal to him. Nevertheless, after they marry, he sees qualities, such as her honesty, that he likes. Their lives are anything but calm, however, as they struggle against many jealous enemies. Eventually, conflicts are settled and they are free to discover their love.

Other books you might like:
Suzanne Barclay, *Knight's Lady*, 1993
Katherine Deauville, *Blood Red Roses*, 1991
Julie Garwood, *The Secret*, 1992
Roberta Gellis, *The Silver Mirror*, 1989
Anita Gordon, *The Valiant Heart*, 1991

1310

JANET MCGIFFIN

Prescription for Death
(New York: Fawcett, 1994)

Story type: Romantic Suspense; Contemporary
Major character(s): Maxene St. Clair, Doctor; Joseph Grabowski, Police Officer
Time period(s): 1990s
Locale(s): United States

Summary: Fascinated by the autopsy of a victim of a "sculpture," Dr. Maxene St. Clair realizes there is more to this than she had first thought; and when she and the debonaire Joseph join forces, solving the mystery is only a matter of time. A witty and romantic mystery peppered with numerous escapades and close calls.

Other books you might like:
Evelyn Anthony, *The Doll's House*, 1992
Lacey Dancer, *Forever Joy*, 1993
Elizabeth Peters, *Borrower of the Night*, 1973
Sherryl Woods, *Hot Property*, 1992
Sherryl Woods, *Hot Secret*, 1992

1311

JACK MCGOWAN

Flame in the Night

(New York: Pocket, 1990)

Story type: Historical/Victorian
Major character(s): Cassie Harmon, Orphan (illegitimate), Debutante; Robert Harmon, Orphan, Businessman
Time period(s): 1840s (1842-1850)
Locale(s): Pennsylvania

Summary: In order to adopt her brother's newly orphaned illegitimate daughter, Marie Andelet agrees to take Cassie's step-brother, Robert, and her sister, Lucy, as well. But when Robert (not related to Cassie by blood) and Cassie fall in love, Marie has other plans.

Other books you might like:
Elaine Barbieri, *Wings of a Dove*, 1990
Rebecca George, *Call Home the Heart*, 1989
Barbara Hazard, *Call Back the Dream*, 1990
Jill Marie Landis, *Sunflower*, 1988
Rebecca Paisley, *Barefoot Bride*, 1990

1312

JAN MCKEE

Sweet Justice

(Toronto: Harlequin, 1991)

Story type: Historical/American West Coast
Major character(s): Jessica Cameron Miller, Widow(er); Morgan Rossiter, Lawman (temporary marshal)
Time period(s): 1880s (1882)
Locale(s): Moonshadow Valley, California; Kansas

Summary: When Morgan Rossiter comes to California looking for the woman who could testify against the man who killed his brother ten years earlier, he finds a respectable widow—not at all the kind of woman he had expected. Complex emotions and plotting, nicely done characters, and realistic depiction of the Old West.

Other books you might like:
Marsha Bauer, *Sweet Conquest*, 1990
Rosanne Bittner, *Oregon Bride*, 1990
Phoebe Conn, *Tempt Me with Kisses*, 1991
Barbara Hargis, *Heart Song*, 1990
Linda Madl, *Sunny*, 1990

1313

LYNN ARMISTEAD MCKEE

Touch the Stars

(New York: Diamond, 1992)

Story type: Historical/Pre-history
Major character(s): Mi-Sa, Shaman
Time period(s): Indeterminate Past
Locale(s): Everglades, Florida

Summary: Mi-Sa must endure prejudice and danger to take her rightful place as her tribe's spiritual leader in this exotic story set in the primitive, tropical Florida Everglades.

Other books you might like:
Jean M. Auel, *Clan of the Cave Bear*, 1980
Clare Coleman, *Daughter of the Reef*, 1992
Kathryn Lynn Davis, *Sing to Me of Dreams*, 1990
Linda Lay Shuler, *She Who Remembers*, 1988
Linda Lay Shuler, *Voice of the Eagle*, 1992

1314

LYNN ARMISTEAD MCKEE

Woman of the Mists

(New York: Diamond, 1991)

Story type: Historical/Pre-history
Major character(s): Teeka, Healer, Indian; Auro, Shaman, Indian; Kaho, Warrior, Indian
Time period(s): 7th century B.C.
Locale(s): Everglades, Florida

Summary: Forced to marry the fierce foreign warrior Kaho in order to avert a war, Teeka vows vengeance—and ends up finding love and fulfillment instead. Set in pre-Columbian Florida.

Other books you might like:
Kathryn Lynn Davis, *Sing to Me of Dreams*, 1990
Sue Harrison, *Mother Earth, Father Sky*, 1990
Linda Lay Shuler, *She Who Remembers*, 1990
Elizabeth Marshall Thomas, *Reindeer Moon*, 1987
Joan Wolf, *Daughter of the Red Deer*, 1991

1315

LINDSAY MCKENNA

Brave Heart

(Toronto: Harlequin, 1993)

Story type: Historical/American West
Major character(s): Serena "Brave Heart" Rogan, Abuse Victim, Activist; Black Wolf, Healer, Indian (Lakota)
Time period(s): 19th century
Locale(s): West

Summary: Wounded while defending a group of Lakota women from assault by rowdy miners, Serena Rogan, herself a victim of abuse, is nursed back to health by the tribal healer, Black Wolf. Their relationship gradually grows into one of trust and love as Black Wolf helps Serena heal in both body and spirit. But their happiness has attracted the envy and jealousy of others, and the pair must endure both loss and pain before they can truly be together. Sensitive and powerful portrayal of the Lakota culture.

Other books you might like:
Deborah Camp, *Lady Legend*, 1992
Kathleen Harrington, *Cherish the Dream*, 1990
Kathryn Hockett, *Gentle Warrior*, 1992
Ruth Langan, *Texas Healer*, 1992

1316

LINDSAY MCKENNA

King of Swords

(Toronto: Harlequin, 1992)

Story type: Historical/Georgian
Major character(s): Thorne Somerset, Healer, Noblewoman; Devlin Kyle, Military Personnel (Irish rebel captain)
Time period(s): 1800s (1803)
Locale(s): Spain

Summary: In Spain recovering from the death of her gypsy mother, Thorne Somerset is kidnapped and held hostage by Irish rebel Captain Devlin Kyle. Anger and enmity soon turn to love, but their happiness is shortened and Thorne is forced to marry Dev's sadistic rival. Everything works out in the end, but there is a lot of passionate, and sometimes brutal, action along the way. Sequel to *Lord of Shadowhawk.*

Other books you might like:
Rebecca Brandewyne, *Forever My Love,* 1982
   earlier time period
Connie Mason, *Brave Land, Brave Love,* 1992
Rosemary Rogers, *Surrender to Love,* 1982
Christina Skye, *The Black Rose,* 1991
Katherine Sutcliffe, *Shadow Play,* 1991

1317

LINDSAY MCKENNA

Lord of Shadowhawk

(Toronto: Harlequin, 1992)

Story type: Historical/Georgian
Major character(s): Alyssa Kyle, Handicapped (blind), Captive; Tristan "Tray" Trayhern, Handicapped (crippled), Nobleman (Lord of Shadowhawk)
Time period(s): 18th century (Irish Rebellion)
Locale(s): Wales; Ireland

Summary: When English nobleman Tray Trayherne discovers lovely, brutally beaten and blinded Alyssa among the prisoners his overly zealous brother has taken during a raid, he takes her to Shadowhawk to recover. His gentle care and concern gradually dispell Alyssa's hatred of all things English, but as they begin to fall in love, Tray fears that once Alyssa regains her sight she will be repelled by his crippled leg. His fears of rejection are groundless, but his concern over his brother's fanaticism are not; and before Tray and Alyssa can truly begin to build a life together, he must return to Ireland to rescue her once and for all from his brother's anti-Irish obsession.

Other books you might like:
Christina Dodd, *Candle in the Window,* 1991
   medieval setting
Laura Kinsale, *The Prince of Midnight,* 1990
Connie Mason, *Tempt the Devil,* 1990
Veronica Sattler, *A Dangerous Longing,* 1990

1318

LINDSAY MCKENNA

One Man's War

(New York: Silhouette, 1992)

Story type: Contemporary
Series: Moments of Glory Trilogy
Major character(s): Tess Ramsey, Volunteer (U.S. aid in Vietnam); Pete Mallory, Pilot
Time period(s): 1960s (1965)
Locale(s): Vietnam

Summary: Cocky "flyboy" Pete Mallory meets his commander's sister Tess, who is a US aid volunteer. As she concentrates on helping the Vietnamese people, he concentrates on her! Second in the Moments of Glory trilogy.

Other books you might like:
Lois Battle, *War Brides,* 1982
   WWII setting
Janet Dailey, *Silver Wings, Santiago Blue,* 1984
Jeane Eddy Westin, *Love and Glory,* 1985
   WWII setting

1319

LINDSAY MCKENNA

Point of Departure

(New York: Silhouette, 1993)

Story type: Contemporary
Series: That Special Woman
Major character(s): Callie Donovan, Military Personnel (naval intelligence lieutenant); Ty Ballard, Pilot
Time period(s): 1990s
Locale(s): United States

Summary: Brutally attacked by three men, Lt. Callie Donovan reports it and finds herself assigned to Ty Ballard for defense. He's a well-known "predator," and Callie's innocence attracts him. It takes a lot of courage to defy the "good old boy" network among his friends and to champion a female officer. But his gentle care for Callie gives both of them strength to love again.

Other books you might like:
Joanne Z. Adams, *Intimate Connections,* 1991
   mainstream
Sara Chance, *Fire in the Night,* 1989
Judith Duncan, *Beyond All Reason,* 1993
Jeanne Stephens, *At Risk,* 1989

1320

LINDSAY MCKENNA

Ride the Tiger

(New York: Silhouette, 1992)

Story type: Contemporary
Series: Moments of Glory Trilogy
Major character(s): Danielle "Dany" Villard, Plantation Owner; Gib Ramsey, Military Personnel (Marine Major)

Time period(s): 1960s (1965)
Locale(s): Vietnam

Summary: Dany, a plantation owner in Vietnam, tries to stay neutral between America and Vietnam as she and Marine Major Gib Ramsey become embroiled in the bloody, brutal war. His rescue when she needs it most leads to love. First in the Moments of Glory trilogy.

Other books you might like:
Thea Devine, *Southern Seduction*, 1991
Patricia Potter, *Dragonfire*, 1990
Jeane Eddy Westin, *Love and Glory*, 1985
Frances Williams, *The Road to Forever*, 1991

1321

LINDSAY MCKENNA

Sun Woman

(Toronto: Harlequin, 1991)

Story type: Historical/American West
Major character(s): Kutachna, Indian (Apache); Gibson McCoy, Military Personnel (sergeant)
Time period(s): 19th century
Locale(s): West

Summary: When Apache warrior Kutachna joins the army as a scout, she is subjected to prejudice, hatred, and even jealousy. One man, Gibson McCoy, believes in her and protects her; but when they fall in love, they both have decisions to make that will affect not only their own lives but those of people they love. Sensitive handling of Native American issues. Lots of Apache cultural detail.

Other books you might like:
Catherine Anderson, *Comanche Moon*, 1991
Beverly Bird, *Comes the Rain*, 1990
Rosanne Bittner, *Sioux Splendor*, 1990
Kathleen Harrington, *Cherish the Dream*, 1990
Shirl Henke, *Night Wind's Woman*, 1991

1322

MEAGAN MCKINNEY

Fair Is the Rose

(New York: Dell, 1993)

Story type: Historical/American West
Major character(s): Christal Van Allen, Captive, Fugitive; McCauley Cain, Lawman (U. S. Marshal), Outlaw (in disguise)
Time period(s): 1870s (1875)
Locale(s): New York; Wyoming

Summary: Falsely blamed for her parents' deaths, Christal Van Allen escapes from the asylum where she is being held and heads toward Wyoming. Her plans take an unexpected turn when her stagecoach is held up and she is taken hostage by the tough and gentle outlaw, McCauley Cain. Their feelings for each other grow, but when Cain is revealed as a U.S. Marshal, Christal flees. Nicely done characters. Sequel to *Lions and Lace*.

Other books you might like:
Caroline Bourne, *Love's Perfect Dream*, 1993
Genell Dellin, *Comanche Wind*, 1993
Robin Lee Hatcher, *Midnight Rose*, 1992
Linda Howard, *The Touch of Fire*, 1992

1323

MEAGAN MCKINNEY (Pseudonym of Ruth Goodman)

The Ground She Walks Upon

(New York: Delacorte, 1994)

Story type: Historical
Major character(s): Ravenna, Young Woman; Lord Niall Trevallyan, Nobleman
Time period(s): 1820s (1828); 1840s
Locale(s): Lir, Ireland

Summary: When an ancient Celtic cross "chooses" a baby to be Lord Niall Trevallyan's bride, he ignores the curse connected with the relic and refuses. Tragedy does, indeed, follow Trevallyan over the years, as the child, Ravenna, matures into a lovely young woman; nevertheless, even though famine and disaster loom, they both continue to defy the prediction. Eventually, love does win out, but they have to deal with pride, superstition, and prejudice before it does. Mystical, with a definite fairy tale quality.

Other books you might like:
Rexanne Becnel, *If This Be Magic*, 1994
   magical and mystical/medieval
Kathryn Lynn Davis, *All We Hold Dear*, 1995
   mystical/historical and contemporary
Coral Smith Saxe, *Enchantment*, 1994
   magic and spells
Penelope Williamson, *Keeper of the Dream*, 1992
   mystical/medieval
Erin Yorke, *Heaven's Gate*, 1992
   strong characters and conflicts/earlier time period

1324

MEAGAN MCKINNEY (Pseudonym of Ruth Goodman)

Lions and Lace

(New York: Dell, 1992)

Story type: Historical
Major character(s): Alana Van Allen, Socialite, Bride (reluctant); Trevor Sheridan, Financier
Time period(s): 20th century (early)
Locale(s): New York, New York

Summary: Out for revenge because the New York social set snubbed his young sister, wealthy, self-made Irish financier Trevor Sheridan methodically begins to ruin the rich offenders one by one. He blackmails the gentle Alana Van Allen into marriage for the purpose of gaining entry into the New York 400, but neither is prepared for the passion that develops between them. A somewhat dark and passionate tale of vengeance and love.

Other books you might like:
Elaine Barbieri, *Wishes on the Wind*, 1991

Sally Beauman, *Destiny*, 1987
Beverly Byrne, *The Flames of Vengeance*, 1991
Taylor Caldwell, *Ceremony of the Innocent*, 1991
Eugenia Riley, *Rogue's Mistress*, 1991

1325

MEAGAN MCKINNEY

Till Dawn Tames the Night
(New York: Dell, 1991)

Story type: Historical/Regency
Major character(s): Aurora Dayne, Orphan, Captive; Vashon, Pirate, Nobleman (dispossessed)
Time period(s): 1810s (1818)
Locale(s): England; At Sea; Tropical Island

Summary: When orphaned Aurora Dayne takes her sense of adventure and her lizard locket and boards a ship headed for the West Indies, she has no idea she holds the key to the location of a legendary emerald and is being pursued by a ruthless pirate, Vashon, and his cruel half-brother, Josiah Peterborough, to get it. Action, passion, and adventure abound in this dark tale of treachery and revenge.

Other books you might like:
Laura Kinsale, *Seize the Fire*, 1989
Johanna Lindsey, *Gentle Rogue*, 1990
Laurie McBain, *Moonstruck Madness*, 1977
Judith McNaught, *Almost Heaven*, 1990
Elizabeth Ann Michaels, *Destiny's Will*, 1991

1326

KAY MCMAHON

Betray the Night
(New York: Jove, 1991)

Story type: Historical/Victorian
Major character(s): Catherine Chase, Detective; T.J. Savage, Detective
Time period(s): 1840s (1845)
Locale(s): London, England

Summary: Catherine, unconventional and headstrong detective, believes that T.J. is a thief, but as it turns out, they are both trying to catch an art thief and solve the murder of Catherine's father. Their distrust of each other is at the center of their conflict, but the resulting sparks also inflame their passions.

Other books you might like:
Patricia Gaffney, *Thief of Hearts*, 1990
Elizabeth Kary, *Midnight Lace*, 1990
Patricia Pellicane, *Desperado Passion*, 1991
Michalann Perry, *Love's Windswept Embrace*, 1990

1327

KAY MCMAHON

Chase the Dawn
(New York: Jove, 1992)

Story type: Historical/American Civil War
Major character(s): Jonathan Stone, Gentleman; Adria Beaumont, Doctor
Time period(s): 1850s
Locale(s): Georgia

Summary: Yankee Doctor Adria Beaumont must deal with her political and personal feelings when she treats Southerner Jonathan Stone and ends up in love with him.

Other books you might like:
Barbara Cummings, *Blazing Passion*, 1991
Heather Graham, *One Wore Blue*, 1991
Cara Miles, *Surrender to the Fury*, 1992
Diane Gates Robinson, *The Falcon and the Swan*, 1992
Kathleen E. Woodiwiss, *Ashes in the Wind*, 1979

1328

KAY MCMAHON

Tender Lies
(New York: Zebra, 1990)

Story type: Historical/Georgian
Major character(s): Bevan O'Rourke, Fiance(e); Reid Hamilton, Amnesiac
Time period(s): 1790s (1798)
Locale(s): Ireland

Summary: To save her father's life, Bevan agrees to a marriage of convenience; but when she mistakes the shipwrecked victim of amnesia, Reid Hamilton, for her fiance, things begin to get complicated. Raids, murder, intrigue, and romance are part of this action-oriented historical.

Other books you might like:
Jude Deveraux, *The Taming*, 1989
    A forced marriage with interesting, if predictable, results
Julie Garwood, *The Bride*, 1989
Ruth Langan, *Captive of Desire*, 1990
Penelope Neri, *Bold Breathless Nights*, 1990
    Amnesia in an earlier time period
Katherine Vickery, *Flame Across the Highlands*, 1990

1329

JUDITH MCNAUGHT

Almost Heaven
(New York: Pocket, 1990)

Story type: Historical/Regency
Major character(s): Elizabeth Cameron, Noblewoman (Countess of Havenhurst), Heiress; Ian Thornton, Nobleman (Duke of Lundsford)
Time period(s): 1810s
Locale(s): England; Scotland

Summary: Intelligent, impulsive, and unconventional, Lady Elizabeth Cameron is ordered by her uncle to choose a husband from among several former suitors. Incensed, she determines to "persuade" them to withdraw their offers, and she succeeds admirably—except for Ian Thornton. Witty, warm, and fun.

Other books you might like:
Julie Garwood, *Guardian Angel*, 1990
Georgette Heyer, *Bath Tangle*, 1955
    Classic Regency
Georgette Heyer, *The Unknown Ajax*, 1959
    Classic Regency
Amanda Quick, *Seduction*, 1990
Claudette Williams, *Heart of Fancy*, 1990

1330

JUDITH MCNAUGHT
JUDE DEVERAUX, Co-Author
KIMBERLY CATES, Co-Author
ANDREA KANE, Co-Author
JUDITH O'BRIEN, Co-Author

A Gift of Love
(New York: Pocket, 1995)

Story type: Anthology; Holiday Themes
Locale(s): United States; England

Summary: This diverse anthology of Christmas novellas features stories by five of Pocket's premier authors. Included are: "Double Exposure" by Judith McNaught, "Just Curious" by Jude Deveraux, "Gabriel's Angel" by Kimberly Cates, "Yuletide Treasure" by Andrea Kane, and "Five Golden Rings" by Judith O'Brien.

Other books you might like:
Mary Balogh, *Angel Christmas*, 1994
    Christmas anthology
Elaine Barbieri, *Mistletoe Marriages*, 1994
    Christmas anthology
Jane Bonander, *Avon Books Presents: A Christmas Together*, 1994
    Christmas anthology
Virginia Henley, *A Gift of Love*, 1995
    Christmas anthology
Judith McNaught, *A Holiday of Love*, 1994
    Christmas anthology

1331

JUDITH MCNAUGHT
JUDE DEVERAUX, Co-Author
JILL BARNETT, Co-Author
ARNETTE LAMB, Co-Author

A Holiday of Love
(New York: Pocket, 1994)

Story type: Anthology; Holiday Themes

Summary: A quartet of diverse historical Christmas novellas. Included are: "Change of Heart" by Jude Deveraux, where a matchmaking twelve-year-old lends a hand; "Miracles" by

Judith McNaught, which features a rather retiring heroine, a disastrous proposal, and a miracle; "Daniel and the Angel" by Jill Barnett, which tells the tale of a banished angel and a lonely man; and "Hark! The Herald" by Arnette Lamb, where the Christmas season brings love to an unlikely pair in the Highlands.

Other books you might like:
Jo Beverley, *The Christmas Angel*, 1992
    a Regency-style Christmas
Jane Bonander, *Avon Books Presents: A Christmas Together*, 1994
    Tanya Ann Crosby, Jennifer Horsman, Joan Johnston, co-authors
Stella Cameron, *Avon Books Presents: A Christmas Collection*, 1992
    historical Christmas anthology
Carla Kelly, *Marian's Christmas Wish*, 1989
    Christmas romance Regency-style
Debbie Macomber, *The Trouble with Angels*, 1994
    a contemporary "angelic" Christmas romance

1332

JUDITH MCNAUGHT

Paradise
(New York: Pocket, 1991)

Story type: Contemporary/Mainstream
Major character(s): Meredith Bancroft, Businesswoman (family store president), Heiress; Matthew Farrell, Businessman (corporate tycoon), Worker (steel worker)
Time period(s): 1990s

Summary: Ruthlessly separated by the wiles of a deceptive and controlling father, Meredith and Matthew pursue their individual goals—only to find themselves pitted against one another eleven years later in a bitter corporate battle inspired by revenge. A fast-paced, passionate story rife with tragedy, greed and betrayal.

Other books you might like:
Sandra Brown, *Breath of Scandal*, 1991
Barbara Delinsky, *Facets*, 1990
Shirl Henke, *Summer Has No Name*, 1990
Kay Hooper, *Star-Crossed Lovers*, 1990
Deborah Smith, *Miracle*, 1991

1333

JUDITH MCNAUGHT

Perfect
(New York: Pocket, 1993)

Story type: Contemporary; Romantic Suspense
Major character(s): Julie Matheson, Teacher, Captive; Zach Benedict, Director (movie), Crime Suspect (murder)
Time period(s): 1990s
Locale(s): Colorado

Summary: Suspected of his straying wife's murder, movie mogul Zach Benedict ends up forcing lovely Julie Matheson to help him escape to a Colorado retreat, and in the process they both discover a love that they had never imagined. Warm, passionate, and elegant.

Other books you might like:
Jennifer Blake, *Joy and Anger*, 1991
Janet Dailey, *Aspen Gold*, 1991
Christiane Heggan, *Passions*, 1993
Karen Robards, *One Summer*, 1993

1334
MELINDA MCRAE
The Duke's Daughter
(New York: New American Library/Signet, 1991)

Story type: Regency
Major character(s): Miss Elizabeth, Noblewoman (Duke's daughter), Spinster; Somerset Graham, Nobleman (Earl of Wentworth)
Time period(s): 1810s
Locale(s): England

Summary: When the Earl of Wentworth is caught in a country snow storm, he seeks shelter in a nearby cottage owned by the mysterious and beautiful Miss Elizabeth. Intrigued, he begins to do some investigating and discovers she is not quite what she seems to be. Nicely plotted and peopled with enjoyable characters.

Other books you might like:
Elizabeth Brodnax, *The Marquis of Carabas*, 1991
Georgette Heyer, *Arabella*, 1949
Joan Smith, *Madcap Miss*, 1989
Lois Stewart, *Romantic Masquerade*, 1990
Daisy Vivian, *Counterfeit Lady*, 1987

1335
MELINDA MCRAE
A Highly Respected Widow
(New York: Signet, 1992)

Story type: Regency
Major character(s): Katherine Mayfield, Widow(er); Edward Beauchamp, Nobleman (Earl of Knowlton)
Time period(s): 1810s
Locale(s): England

Summary: Strangely dissatisfied with his profligate life, Edward Beauchamp, the Earl of Knowlton repairs to his country estate for solace. However, instead of quiet relaxation he finds a mischievous boy, a beautiful widow, and a love that he had been waiting for all his life. Delightfully complex characters.

Other books you might like:
Elizabeth Brodnax, *The Marquis of Carabas*, 1991
Georgette Heyer, *Arabella*, 1949
Georgette Heyer, *Black Sheep*, 1966
Mary Jo Putney, *The Rake and the Reformer*, 1989

1336
MELINDA MCRAE
Lady Leprechaun
(New York: Signet, 1993)

Story type: Regency
Major character(s): Emily Darrow, Noblewoman, Single Parent; Duke of Hartford, Nobleman, Single Parent
Time period(s): 1810s
Locale(s): England

Summary: Young Jeremy and Phillip set out on a "quest," and throw their respective mother and father into a tizzy trying to locate them. But when Lady Emily insists on accompanying the Duke of Hartford on his search, the chase becomes interesting indeed and eventually leads both to the children and to love. Fast-paced and charming.

Other books you might like:
Rita Boucher, *The Scandalous Schoolmistress*, 1992
Carola Dunn, *Two Corinthians*, 1989
Anthea Malcolm, *Counterfeit Heart*, 1991
Sheila Simonson, *The Bar Sinister*, 1986
Sheila Simonson, *Love and Folly*, 1988

1337
MELINDA MCRAE
Married by Mistake
(New York: Signet, 1992)

Story type: Regency
Major character(s): Florence Washburn, Bride, Gentlewoman; Thomas, Nobleman (Viscount Alford)
Time period(s): 1810s
Locale(s): England

Summary: When the profligate Lord Alford ends up accidentally married to his brother's fiancee — through his own mistake, incidentally — he repairs to an estate in Devon to await the expected annulment. However, matchmaking relatives send his wife to the same estate, with delightful and predictable results.

Other books you might like:
Jo Beverley, *An Arranged Marriage*, 1991
Gayle Buck, *Mutual Consent*, 1991
Amanda Quick, *Seduction*, 1990
Sheila Simonson, *A Cousinly Connexion*, 1984
Marlene Suson, *The Fair Imposter*, 1992

1338
MELINDA MCRAE
An Unlikely Attraction
(New York: Signet, 1991)

Story type: Regency
Major character(s): Sophrina Charlton, Noblewoman (Viscountess Teel); Penhurst, Nobleman (Earl of Penhurst)
Time period(s): 1810s

Locale(s): England

Summary: Struggling to forget her drowned husband's infidelity and begin a new life, Sophrina Charlton is drawn to the husband of the woman her husband ran off with. Love blooms—but when Rina's husband returns *alive* and wants her back, things become somewhat complicated. Nicely plotted.

Other books you might like:
Clare Darcy, *Lady Pamela*, 1975
Georgette Heyer, *Lady of Quality*, 1972
Amanda Quick, *Scandal*, 1991
   sensual
Sheila Simonson, *The Bar Sinister*, 1986

1339

JUDITH MCWILLIAMS

Suspicion

(Totonto: Harlequin, 1994)

Story type: Historical/Regency
Major character(s): Lucy Danvers, Noblewoman, Thief; Robert Standen, Nobleman
Time period(s): 1810s (1814)
Locale(s): France; London, England

Summary: In order to leave France and return to take her place in English society, impoverished Lucy Danvers steals passage money from Robert Standen. However, they meet once again in London, and he blackmails her into being his fiancee. Their relationship takes a bit of work; but together they straighten out family titles and eventually come to realize they have both made good choices.

Other books you might like:
Georgette Heyer, *Arabella*, 1949
   classic Regency
Georgette Heyer, *The Reluctant Widow*, 1946
   another classic Regency
Katherine Kingsley, *No Greater Love*, 1992
   another marriage of convenience
Laura Parker, *Caprice*, 1994
   deception and society
Amanda Quick, *Dangerous*, 1993
   another marriage of convenience/different treatment

1340

TERESA MEDEIROS

Lady of Conquest

(New York: Berkley, 1989)

Story type: Historical/Pre-history
Major character(s): Gelina O'Monoghan, Warrior (avenger of her family); Conn, Warrior, Ruler (High King of Erin)
Time period(s): 2nd century (123)
Locale(s): Ireland

Summary: Gelina sets out to avenge the downfall of her family and falls in love with Conn, the person she considers responsible, instead. Violent and bloody, this tale is more adventure than romance.

Other books you might like:
Blaine Anderson, *Love's Sweet Captive*, 1989
Shannon Drake, *Princess of Fire*, 1989
Mary Ellen Gronau, *Gentle Conqueror*, 1989
Mary Ellen Gronau, *Passionate Warriors*, 1989
Johanna Lindsey, *Fires of Winter*, 1980

1341

TERESA MEDEIROS

Once an Angel

(New York: Bantam, 1993)

Story type: Historical/Exotic
Major character(s): Emily Scarborough, Ward, Debutante; Justin Connors, Guardian
Time period(s): 19th century
Locale(s): New Zealand; England

Summary: Having spent most of her young life unhappily neglected in a boarding school, Emily Scarborough, in a bizarre twist of fate, ends up nude on a New Zealand beach in the arms of the very man who was supposed to be acting as her guardian. Passion, mystery, and humor in a poignant story, peopled with memorable characters.

Other books you might like:
Leigh Bristol, *Sunswept*, 1990
Betina Lindsey, *The Serpent Beguiled*, 1992
Julie Tetel, *Swept Away*, 1989
Marianne Willman, *Tilly and the Tiger*, 1990
Barbara Wood, *The Dreaming*, 1992

1342

TERESA MEDEIROS

Shadows and Lace

(New York: Berkley, 1990)

Story type: Historical/Medieval
Major character(s): Rowena, Noblewoman; Sir Gareth, Nobleman, Knight
Time period(s): 13th century (1279)
Locale(s): England

Summary: When Rowena's father gambles her into the service of Sir Gareth for a year, she complies—and then sets out to understand this complex man. Driven by revenge, Gareth seeks to solve the mystery of his stepmother's death, but he is drawn to Rowena and she becomes more important to him that he would have though possible. Passion, good characterizations, and excellent historical detail.

Other books you might like:
Rebecca Brandewyne, *No Gentle Love*, 1980
Jude Deveraux, *The Taming*, 1989
Johanna Lindsey, *Defy Not the Heart*, 1989
Johanna Lindsey, *When Love Awaits*, 1986
Kathleen E. Woodiwiss, *The Wolf and the Dove*, 1974

1343
ANNE MEREDITH

Love Across Time
(New York: St. Martin's, 1995)

Story type: Time Travel
Major character(s): Lindsey Callahan, Time Traveller; Devlin Windsor, Landowner
Time period(s): 1990s; 1850s
Locale(s): Natchez, Mississippi

Summary: Lindsey Callahan sees no reason for her having been sent back in time. Cryptic messages about a curse prove confusing, but her love for the cold, enigmatic Devlin and his son gives her a purpose. When a passionate embrace leads to scandal, Devlin insists that they marry, all the while accusing Lindsey of framing him. Her love for his young son finally turns Devlin around, but then Lindsey must worry about her imminent return to the present where she will lose them both.

Other books you might like:
Sandra Davidson, *The Heart Remembers*, 1995
    time travel elements
Kristin Hannah, *Once in Every Life*, 1993
    poignant time travel
Nelle McFather, *Tears of Fire*, 1994
    time travel elements
Judith O'Brien, *Ashton's Bride*, 1995
    time travel elements
Eugenia Riley, *Tempest in Time*, 1993
    time travel elements

1344
EMMA MERRITT

Beneath a Texas Star
(New York: Zebra, 1991)

Story type: Historical/American West
Major character(s): Clementina "Clem" Jones, Lawman (would-be sheriff); Wade Cameron, Journalist
Time period(s): 19th century
Locale(s): Lawful, Texas

Summary: When her sheriff father is killed, Clem Jones, the fastest gun around, decides to take over as sheriff herself. She runs into opposition, however, and the town decides to send for her uncle instead. Things begin to heat up when former-bounty-hunter-turned-New-York-journalist, Wade Cameron, comes to town and Clem suddenly finds her heart in danger. Lots of action and mystery, Texas-style.

Other books you might like:
Constance Bennett, *Morning Sky*, 1990
Catherine Hart, *Sweet Fury*, 1990
LaVyrle Spencer, *Forgiving*, 1990
Judith Steel, *Wild Colorado Passion*, 1991

1345
EMMA MERRITT

Lord of Fire
(New York: Avon, 1994)

Story type: Historical/Medieval
Major character(s): Lady Jarvia, Slave (former), Noblewoman; Malcolm MacDuncan, Laird
Time period(s): 7th century (625)
Locale(s): Scotland

Summary: Faced with the choice between a political marriage to Scottish chieftain Malcolm MacDuncan or banishment, Jarvia pragmatically agrees—and begins to plot her revenge. Power struggles, political intrigue, and deception abound in this sensual, rugged story. First of two books; to be followed by *Lord of Thunder*.

Other books you might like:
Katherine Deauville, *Daggers of Gold*, 1993
Julie Garwood, *The Bride*, 1989
    Witty and funny
Roberta Gellis, *The Silver Mirror*, 1989
Mary Ellen Gronau, *Passionate Warriors*, 1989
Teresa Medeiros, *Lady of Conquest*, 1993

1346
EMMA MERRITT

Masque of Jade
(New York: Zebra, 1990)

Story type: Historical/War of 1812
Major character(s): Laura Talbot-Harrow, Debutante, Gentlewoman; Clay Sutherland, Gambler
Time period(s): 1810s (1813)
Locale(s): Louisiana

Summary: Expected to marry "appropriately," Laura shocks society by falling in love with a gambler. Duels, murder, and treachery are all part of this romance set against the violence of the War of 1812. This is a sister novel to *Masque of Sapphire* by Deanna James.

Other books you might like:
Deana James, *Masque of Sapphire*, 1990
    Companion novel
Eugenia Price, *Savannah*, 1983
Alexandra Ripley, *Charleston*, 1982
Karen Robards, *Morning Song*, 1989
Kathleen E. Woodiwiss, *Come Love a Stranger*, 1984

1347
JILL METCALF

Autumn Leaves
(New York: Diamond, 1993)

Story type: Historical/Antebellum American South
Major character(s): Corinne Alexander, Child-Care Giver; Sean Garrick, Widow(er), Businessman
Time period(s): 1840s (1844)

Locale(s): Natchez, Mississippi

Summary: In a desperate effort to give her sister, Kenny, a better life, Corinne arranges for Kenny to inveigle her way into the home and heart of widower Sean Garrick and finds a new life—and love—for herself in the process.

Other books you might like:
Barbara Ankrum, *Renegade's Kiss*, 1993
Jill Marie Landis, *Come Spring*, 1992
Jill Marie Landis, *Until Tomorrow*, 1994
Victoria Pade, *The Doubletree*, 1990

1348
JILL METCALF

Family Reunion
(New York: Diamond, 1994)

Story type: Contemporary
Major character(s): Jennifer Downing, Young Woman; Chad Moran, Lawyer, Handicapped
Time period(s): 1990s

Summary: Although bitter at being confined to a wheel chair because of an accident, active, dynamic Chad Moran can't avoid Jennifer Downing's determination to see him happy and loved. Teenaged Silas, who caused his accident, adds to his anger and frustration, as does a local rapist. Through it all, Jennifer and Chad come to realize that their love for each other is what matters the most. A light, loving book on a serious subject.

Other books you might like:
Christina Dodd, *Lady in Black*, 1993
Judith Duncan, *Beyond All Reason*, 1993
Lindsay McKenna, *Lord of Shadowhawk*, 1992
    historical/disabilities and anger
Doreen Roberts, *Broken Wings*, 1992
Sharon Sala, *Always a Lady*, 1993

1349
JILL METCALF

Spring Blossom
(New York: Berkley, 1992)

Story type: Historical
Major character(s): Maggie Downing, Young Woman, Handicapped; Hunter Maguire, Farmer (horse farm owner)
Locale(s): United States; Canada

Summary: When Hunter Maguire sees Maggie Downing, he can hardly believe the cold, distant, scarred woman is the same vivacious, spirited girl he had known; so he decides to make things different. A unique story, a wonderful hero, and a lovely sweet and gentle romance.

Other books you might like:
Jude Deveraux, *Wishes*, 1989
Laura Kinsale, *Flowers From the Storm*, 1992
Jill Marie Landis, *Wild Flower*, 1989
Helen Mittermeyer, *Princess of the Veil*, 1992
    scarred Viking heroine

Pamela Morsi, *Courting Miss Hattie*, 1991

1350
BARBARA METZGER

An Affair of Interest
(New York: Fawcett, 1992)

Story type: Regency
Major character(s): Sydney Lattimore, Gentlewoman (impoverished); Forrest Mainwaring, Nobleman (Viscount)
Time period(s): 1810s
Locale(s): London, England

Summary: Deciding to remedy her family's financial situation by marrying her beautiful elder sister off to a wealthy gentleman, Sydney Lattimore sets out to acquire the needed money by disguising herself as a widow and applying to a somewhat disreputable "financial consultant." In the process she attracts the attention of Viscount Mainwaring, and the ensuing combination of mistaken identities and Sydney's outrageous schemes result in a fast-paced Regency romp that ends in love and a lot of laughter.

Other books you might like:
Gayle Buck, *The Waltzing Widow*, 1991
Julie Caille, *A Valentine's Day Fancy*, 1992
Georgette Heyer, *Frederica*, 1965
Janis Laden, *Moonlight Veil*, 1991

1351
BARBARA METZGER

An Angel for the Earl
(New York: Fawcett, 1994)

Story type: Regency; Historical/Fantasy
Major character(s): Lucinda Faire, Heiress; Kieren Sommerfield, Nobleman (Earl of Stanford), Rake (impoverished)
Time period(s): 1810s
Locale(s): London, England

Summary: After accidentally killing the man who was trying to seduce her, Lucinda Faire lapses into unconsciousness. When she learns that in order to get to heaven she must reform the notorious rake, Kieren Sommerfield, she wonders how on earth she will ever do it. Kieren's attractiveness makes it both difficult and easy as Lucinda suddenly realizes she has more than one reason to save both their souls. Funny, witty, and warm.

Other books you might like:
Mary Chase Comstock, *A Midsummer's Magic*, 1994
    paranormal elements
Donna Davidson, *Elizabeth's Gift*, 1994
    paranormal elements
Teresa DesJardien, *Haunted Hearts*, 1995
Teresa DesJardien, *Love's Magic*, 1995
    Druidic magic
Jude Deveraux, *Wishes*, 1989
    more "divine" intervention/non-Regency-style

1352

BARBARA METZGER

Father Christmas
(New York: Fawcett Crest, 1995)

Story type: Regency; Holiday Themes
Major character(s): Graceanne Warrington, Widow(er), Noblewoman; Leland Warrington, Nobleman (Duke of Ware)
Time period(s): 1810s
Locale(s): England

Summary: When the inebriated Duke of Ware decides to claim one of his late cousin's twin sons as heir, all in order to avoid marriage and its attendant inconveniences, the boy's mother takes exception and storms the Duke in his ''den'' to let him know exactly what she thinks of his plan. A well-matched hero and heroine, a pair of enterprising three-year-olds, and a host of marvelous secondary characters add to this lively, funny, well-done Regency.

Other books you might like:
Marian Devon, *Deck the Halls*, 1995
    holiday theme
Candice Hern, *A Change of Heart*, 1995
Carla Kelly, *Marian's Christmas Wish*, 1989
    holiday theme
Lynn Kerstan, *Gwen's Christmas Ghost*, 1995
    Alicia Rasley, co-author; paranormal elements
Joan Smith, *The Kissing Bough*, 1994

1353

BARBARA METZGER

Lady in Green
(New York: Fawcett Crest, 1993)

Story type: Regency
Major character(s): Annalise, Heiress, Housekeeper (in disguise); Ross Montclaire, Nobleman (Earl of Gardiner), Rake
Time period(s): 1810s
Locale(s): London, England

Summary: To escape an unwanted marriage, Annalise flees to a small house and disguises herself as an ugly housekeeper. However, when the renowned rake, the Earl of Gardiner, decides to rent the house as a trysting place, Annalise is equally determined that such things will not happen in her house! Fun and games ensue as Annalise in her double disguise as housekeeper and the mysterious Lady in Green turn the Earl's life upside down. Funny and lively.

Other books you might like:
Julie Caille, *An Impetuous Bride*, 1991
April Kihlstrom, *Dangerous Masquerade*, 1992
Emma Lange, *A Second Match*, 1993
Mary Jo Putney, *The Rake and the Reformer*, 1989
Jeanne Savery, *The Last of the Winter Roses*, 1991

1354

BARBARA METZGER

A Loyal Companion
(New York: Fawcett, 1993)

Story type: Regency
Major character(s): Fitz, Animal (dog); Sonya Randolph, Debutante, Animal Lover; Darius Conover, Military Personnel (soldier)
Time period(s): 1810s
Locale(s): England

Summary: When Sonya goes to London for the Season, her family sends faithful Fitz with her for protection. He also leads her on some merry ''people and hound'' escapades, and she even ends up rescuing dashing Darius Conover, currently out of favor with the ton. Darius, of course, is quite taken with Fitz, a feeling that is soon transferred to Fitz's enchanting mistress. A light, funny Regency that includes a delightful dog.

Other books you might like:
Julie Caille, *An Impetuous Bride*, 1991
Janis Laden, *Moonlight Veil*, 1991
Johanna Lindsey, *Angel*, 1992
    a pet panther in a sensual, American West setting
Judith Nelson, *Lady's Choice*, 1990
Veronica Sattler, *Sabelle*, 1992
    sensual

1355

BARBARA METZGER

The Luck of the Devil
(New York: Fawcett, 1991)

Story type: Regency
Major character(s): Rowanne Wimberly, Debutante; Carey Delverson, Nobleman (Duke of St. Dillon), Military Personnel (soldier)
Time period(s): 1810s
Locale(s): England

Summary: From their first highly memorable meeting at Almack's, Rowanne and Carey know that there is something special between them even though he goes off to war and she stays home to continue her obligatory social duties—and they don't meet again for years. However, when fate returns Carey to England and gifts him with unexpected family responsibilities, he and Rowanne renew their friendship with delightful and romantic results. A witty, intricately plotted Regency, peopled with well-developed characters.

Other books you might like:
Carla Kelly, *Libby's London Merchant*, 1991
Anthea Malcolm, *Counterfeit Heart*, 1991
Irene Saunders, *Lady Lucinde's Locket*, 1990
Sheila Simonson, *Lady Elizabeth's Comet*, 1985

1356

BARBARA METZGER

A Suspicious Affair

(New York: Fawcett, 1994)

Story type: Regency
Major character(s): Marisol Pendenning, Widow(er), Noble-woman; Carlinn Kimberly, Nobleman, Guardian; Jeremiah Dimm, Investigator
Time period(s): 1810s
Locale(s): London, England; Bath, England

Summary: While investigating the murder of pregnant Lady Marisol's husband, Jeremiah Dimm learns that he was not only a notorious bounder, but totally irresponsible when it came to choosing guardians for his forthcoming child. As a result, Jeremiah appoints the gruff Carlinn Kimberly, neighbor and magistrate, as guardian, even though he has no patience with Marisol. Nevertheless, the baby brings Carlinn and Marisol together, and Jeremiah solves the murder and other mysteries. Funny, witty, and clever with wonderful dialogue.

Other books you might like:
Anne Barbour, *Lord Glenraven's Return*, 1994
    humorous
Anne Barbour, *A Talent for Trouble*, 1992
    humorous
Sarah Eagle, *The Bedeviled Baron*, 1994
Evelyn Richardson, *The Willful Widow*, 1994

1357

JULIE MEYERS

In the Cards

(Toronto: Harlequin, 1990)

Story type: Contemporary
Major character(s): Rachel Locke, Librarian (research); Sandor Pulneshti, Boarder
Time period(s): 1980s
Locale(s): Cleveland, Ohio; Dalewood, Ohio

Summary: Rachel goes to take care of her aunt who has broken her hip and ends up being attracted to her aunt's dark, mysterious boarder. Danger, intrigue, and a secret past are part of this fast-paced romance.

Other books you might like:
Kathy Clark, *Sight Unseen*, 1990
Lee Magner, *The Mistress of Foxgrove*, 1989
Linda Turner, *An Unsuspecting Heart*, 1989
Kay Wilding, *Rainbow's End*, 1990

1358

BARBARA MICHAELS (Pseudonym of Barbara Mertz)

Into the Darkness

(New York: Simon and Schuster, 1990)

Story type: Gothic

Major character(s): Meg Venturi, Store Owner (jewelry business), Heiress; A.L. Riley, Store Owner (jewelry business)
Time period(s): 1980s
Locale(s): Seldon, Connecticut

Summary: When Meg returns to her New England home to take charge of the jewelry business she has inherited from her grandfather, she is surprised to find that not only does she share the business ownership with a mysterious man, but also that someone does not want her in town—and may be willing to go to any length to see that she leaves. New problems and old tragedies combine in this tense and suspenseful contemporary gothic.

Other books you might like:
Mary Higgins Clark, *Stillwatch*, 1984
Carola Salisbury, *Dark Inheritance*, 1975
    A chilling gothic set in an earlier time period
Mary Stewart, *Touch Not the Cat*, 1976
    Classic Modern Gothic/Romantic Suspense Author
Phyllis A. Whitney, *The Glass Flame*, 1978
Phyllis A. Whitney, *Spindrift*, 1975

1359

BARBARA MICHAELS (Pseudonym of Barbara Mertz)

Vanish with the Rose

(New York: Simon and Schuster, 1992)

Story type: Romantic Suspense; Gothic
Major character(s): Diana Randall, Lawyer, Imposter
Time period(s): 1990s

Summary: Attorney Diana Randall goes undercover as an expert on old roses to gain access to an historic estate in an effort to discover what really happened to her missing brother, Brad. Light romance, gripping suspense, and a dusting of the true supernatural served up in classic Michaels style.

Other books you might like:
Christina Hamlett, *Charade*, 1993

1360

ELIZABETH ANN MICHAELS

Destiny's Will

(New York: Pocket, 1991)

Story type: Historical/Regency
Major character(s): Cara Fairchild, Orphan, Gentlewoman; Justin Reynolds, Nobleman (Earl of Ellsworth), Sea Captain
Time period(s): 1810s (1811)
Locale(s): England; United States

Summary: Furious at being sent to live with the grandmother of the unknown Earl of Ellsworth who inherited her father's estate, Cara Fairchild decides America would be more interesting and sets sail on the first available ship. The voyage proves to be both dangerous and romantic as Cara and Captain Justin Reynolds fall victim to love and the politics of war.

Other books you might like:
Julie Garwood, *Guardian Angel*, 1990

Deana James, *Masque of Sapphire*, 1990
Johanna Lindsey, *Gentle Rogue*, 1990
Meagan McKinney, *Till Dawn Tames the Night*, 1991
Emma Merritt, *Masque of Jade*, 1990

1361

ELIZABETH ANN MICHAELS

A Jewel So Rare
(New York: Pocket, 1992)

Story type: Historical/Post-American Revolution
Major character(s): Annalese Renneau, Companion, Noblewoman; Cameron Slade, Gentleman
Time period(s): 1790s
Locale(s): United States

Summary: Sent to America to live with her aunt in order to avoid the Reign of Terror, French noblewoman Annalese Renneau arrives to find her aunt dead, her plans in shambles, and her need for a job imperative. With no other option, she accepts a position as companion to the charming, but confused, Flora Slade, and discovers both love and danger as she struggles to come to terms with her own past and help Cameron Slade deal with his own.

Other books you might like:
Karen Harper, *Eden's Gate*, 1989
Norah Hess, *Kentucky Bride*, 1992
Charlotte Simms, *Silver Caress*, 1990
Elizabeth Thornton, *Tender the Storm*, 1991

1362

KASEY MICHAELS (Pseudonym of Kathryn Seidick)

The Anonymous Miss Addams
(New York. Avon, 1989)

Story type: Regency
Major character(s): Miss Addams, Amnesiac, Gentlewoman; Pierre Claghorn Standish, Gentleman
Time period(s): 1810s
Locale(s): England

Summary: When Pierre takes a young amnesiac woman into his home as a "good deed," he doesn't expect to end up protecting her from an assassin. Neither does he expect to fall in love with her. Witty, suspenseful, and romantic.

Other books you might like:
Joan Aiken, *The Five-Minute Marriage*, 1977
Janice Bennett, *A Tempting Miss*, 1989
Emily Hendrickson, *Queen of the May*, 1989
Annabel Laine, *The Reluctant Heiress*, 1978
Jane Lovelace, *Rolissa*, 1985

1363

KASEY MICHAELS (Pseudonym of Kathryn Seidick)

Bride of the Unicorn
(New York: Pocket, 1993)

Story type: Historical/Regency

Major character(s): Caroline Monday, Heiress—Lost, Noblewoman; Morgan Blakely, Nobleman (Marquess of Clayton), Spy
Time period(s): 1810s
Locale(s): England; France

Summary: In a complicated quest for vengeance, Morgan Blakely, Marquess of Clayton, locates the long-lost heiress, Lady Caroline, and proceeds to turn her into the lady she is by birth, but not by upbringing. Morgan then Pygmalion-like, falls in love with his creation. Laced with passion and plenty of suspense.

Other books you might like:
Jo Beverley, *Deirdre and Don Juan*, 1993
Kathleen Harrington, *Sunshine and Shadow*, 1993
Judith McNaught, *Almost Heaven*, 1990
Amanda Quick, *Mistress*, 1994

1364

KASEY MICHAELS (Pseudonym of Kathryn Seidick)

The Haunted Miss Hampshire
(New York: Avon, 1992)

Story type: Regency
Major character(s): Cassandra Hampshire, Heiress; Earl of Haukedon, Nobleman
Time period(s): 1810s
Locale(s): England

Summary: Cassandra Hampshire is to be richer than her wildest dreams, provided she share her dead aunt's estate with the Earl of Haukedon. Not only is the Earl arrogant, but he doesn't believe Cassie when she swears she sees and hears her aunt's ghost. Typically fast-paced and witty Regency fare.

Other books you might like:
Michelle Brandon, *Touch of Heaven*, 1992
Anne Caldwell, *Scandal's Darling*, 1991
Jude Deveraux, *Wishes*, 1989
Amanda Quick, *Scandal*, 1991
Nancy Richards-Akers, *Miss Wickham's Betrothal*, 1992

1365

KASEY MICHAELS (Pseudonym of Kathryn Seidick)

His Chariot Awaits
(New York: Silhouette, 1990)

Story type: Contemporary/Innocent
Major character(s): Joey Abbot, Businesswoman (owner of Limousine Service), Writer; Daniel Quinn, Publisher, Widow(er)
Time period(s): 1980s
Locale(s): New York, New York

Summary: The first major contract for Abbot's Aristocratic Limousine Service turns out to be a chauvinistic widower, and in her brother's absence Joey Abbot has the job of being the chauffeur. Needless to say, in this case, the road to love is full of bumps, but there is a lot of humor and fun along the way.

Other books you might like:
Angela Carson, *Sweet Illusion*, 1990
Jane McBride Choate, *Badge of Love*, 1989
Debbie Macomber, *A Little Bit of Country*, 1990
Rita Rainville, *Never on Sundae*, 1990
Diana Whitney, *A Liberated Man*, 1990

1366

KASEY MICHAELS (Pseudonym of Kathryn Seidick)

The Illusion of Love
(New York: Pocket, 1994)

Story type: Historical/Regency
Major character(s): Sarah Towbridge, Heiress, Gentlewoman; Dante Muir, Nobleman, Amnesiac
Time period(s): 1810s (1814)
Locale(s): England

Summary: Needing money, Dante agrees to marry Sarah, a rather quiet, non-descript woman—and then he leaves for war, unaware that she is pregnant. When he returns, he is wounded and can't remember a thing. In the meantime, Sarah has taken over the estate, changing everything around and blossoming into a capable, lovely woman in the process. They put off making a decision about separating until Dante's memory returns, and as they wait, their relationship turns into love.

Other books you might like:
Jo Beverley, *An Unwilling Bride*, 1992
Regency marriage of convenience
Georgette Heyer, *A Civil Contract*, 1992
classic marriage of convenience
Mary Jo Putney, *Uncommon Vows*, 1991
amnesia, medieval-style
Amanda Quick, *Scandal*, 1991
highly capable heroine

1367

KASEY MICHAELS (Pseudonym of Kathryn Seidick)

Legacy of the Rose
(New York: Pocket, 1992)

Story type: Gothic; Historical/Mainstream
Major character(s): Kate Harvey, Nurse; Lucien Tremain, Military Personnel
Time period(s): 1810s (1812)
Locale(s): England

Summary: When Lucien returns home from the war with a shattered leg, he is devastated to find his mother dead and his father married to his fiancee, Melanie. When he collapses, he is cared for by Melanie's baby's wet-nurse, Kate — and as he comes to know her, he admires her more and more. A dark and very sensual tale, complete with torture scenes. Not a typical Michaels Regency — even though the time period is the same.

Other books you might like:
Judy Cuevas, *Black Silk*, 1991
Philippa Gregory, *Meridon*, 1992

Philippa Gregory, *Wideacre*, 1987
Pierre Choderlos de Laclos, *Les Liaisons Dangereuses*, 1782
classic/inspired the film *Dangerous Liaisons*.
Katherine Sutcliffe, *Shadow Play*, 1991

1368

KASEY MICHAELS (Pseudonym of Kathryn Seidick)

Masquerade in Moonlight
(New York: Pocket, 1994)

Story type: Historical/Regency
Major character(s): Marquerite Balfour, Noblewoman; Thomas Joseph Donovan, Diplomat (American)
Time period(s): 1810s (1810)
Locale(s): London, England

Summary: Lady Marquerite, intent on bringing her parents' murderers to justice, runs afoul of Thomas Donovan, who has his own reasons for hunting the same people. They can't trust each other, but they have a difficult time fighting their growing attraction for one another. Danger, intrigue, and passion abound in this somewhat dark and sensual romance.

Other books you might like:
Mary Balogh, *Deceived*, 1993
Alexandre Dumas, *The Count of Monte Cristo*, 1845
classic tale of revenge
Mary Jo Putney, *Petals in the Storm*, 1993
Mary Jo Putney, *Thunder and Roses*, 1993
Anne Stuart, *A Rose at Midnight*, 1993

1369

KASEY MICHAELS (Pseudonym of Kathryn Seidick)

Out of the Blue
(New York: Dell, 1992)

Story type: Time Travel; Regency
Major character(s): Cassandra Kelley, Editor (of Regency romances), Time Traveller; Marcus Pendelton, Nobleman (Marquess of Eastbourne)
Time period(s): 1990s; 1810s
Locale(s): London, England

Summary: While on a tourist visit to the Tower of London, Regency editor Cassandra Kelley wanders away from the tour and ends up in Regency England, face to face with dashing Marcus Pendelton, Marquess of Eastbourne. Gallantly, Marcus takes her in, and as their feelings for each other grow, they realize that love across time is a highly complicated undertaking. An intrigue that could have dire consequences for the Prince Regent and the future just adds to the fun. Witty, warm, and memorable.

Other books you might like:
Janice Bennett, *A Christmas Keepsake*, 1991
Janice Bennett, *A Touch of Forever*, 1992
Gayle Buck, *The Waltzing Widow*, 1991
Clare Darcy, *Letty*, 1980
Georgette Heyer, *A Civil Contract*, 1961

1370

KASEY MICHAELS

The Passion of an Angel
(New York: Pocket, 1995)

Story type: Historical/Regency
Major character(s): Prudence "Angel" MacAfee, Debutante, Ward; Banning Talbot, Nobleman (Marquess of Daventry), Guardian
Time period(s): 1810s
Locale(s): England

Summary: When Banning Talbot, Marquess of Daventry, returns to England to honor the request of his late friend and battle companion and act as guardian to his young sister, Banning finds not the lovely young "angel" he had expected, but a britches-clad hellion, determined to lead her own life. Sparks fly, but they cannot deny their mutual attraction. A lively, charming, and funny romance with a definite Regency flavor.

Other books you might like:
Anne Barbour, *My Cousin Jane*, 1995
　　Regency treatment/guardian-ward story
Jean R. Ewing, *Virtue's Reward*, 1995
　　another battlefield promise
Jane Feather, *Vixen*, 1994
　　guardian-ward story
Carla Kelly, *Marian's Christmas Wish*, 1989
Lynn Kerstan, *A Spirited Affair*, 1993

1371

KASEY MICHAELS (Pseudonym of Kathryn Seidick)

Timely Matrimony
(New York: Silhouette, 1994)

Story type: Time Travel
Major character(s): Suzi Harper, Critic (book reviewer), Vacationer; Harry Wilde, Time Traveller, Writer
Time period(s): 1990s
Locale(s): Ocean City, New Jersey

Summary: When he is swept overboard during a storm just off the American coast, Englishman Harry Wilde ends up not only in Suzi Harper's bed, but in her century, as well. Fast-paced, sensual, and funny.

Other books you might like:
Janice Bennett, *A Christmas Keepsake*, 1991
Constance O'Day-Flannery, *Timeless Passion*, 1986
Joan Overfield, *The Spirited Bluestocking*, 1992
　　Regency fantasy
Patricia Simpson, *The Legacy*, 1992
Susan Sizemore, *My Own True Love*, 1994

1372

LEIGH MICHAELS

Let Me Count the Ways
(Toronto: Harlequin, 1989)

Story type: Contemporary/Innocent
Major character(s): Sara Prentiss, Professor; Adam Merrill, Professor, Writer
Time period(s): 1980s
Locale(s): New England (Chandler College)

Summary: Usually it is the students who fall in love in college; this time it is their professors who have romance in mind. A story of two very different people that makes a good case for the theory that "opposites attract." Lots of college town atmosphere.

Other books you might like:
Lynn Bulock, *Roses for Caroline*, 1989
Karen Leabo, *Domestic Bliss*, 1990
Sandra K. Rhoades, *Foolish Deceiver*, 1990
Peggy Webb, *A Gift for Tenderness*, 1989

1373

THERESA MICHAELS (Pseudonym of Theresa DiBenedetto)

Gifts of Love
(Toronto: Harlequin, 1992)

Story type: Historical/American West
Major character(s): Erin Dunmore, Mail Order Bride; Mace Dalton, Widow(er), Rancher
Time period(s): 19th century
Locale(s): Washington

Summary: Pregnant and desperate, Erin Dunmore leaves her job in a San Francisco brothel and goes to Washington to become the mail-order bride of rancher Mace Dalton, a widower with two children. Although neither is looking for love, they are initially attracted to each other, but pride and mistrust keep them apart until disaster strikes and they are forced to come to terms with their feelings. Warm and sensual.

Other books you might like:
Madeline Baker, *Prairie Heat*, 1991
Lisa Bingham, *Eden Creek*, 1991
Constance O'Day-Flannery, *A Time for Love*, 1991
　　time travel
Victoria Pade, *The Doubletree*, 1990
Katherine Sutcliffe, *Dream Fever*, 1991
　　New Zealand setting

1374

CARA MILES (Pseudonym of Connie Mason)

Promise Me Forever
(New York: Avon, 1992)

Story type: Historical/War of 1812
Major character(s): Lily Montague, Debutante; Matthew Hawke, Privateer
Time period(s): 1810s

Locale(s): England

Summary: Captain Matthew Hawke marries Lily for her money and takes her *and* his mistress aboard ship. Eventually Matthew and Lily find love on a deserted island, but pirates do their best to interfere.

Other books you might like:
Christine Dorsey, *Captain's Captive*, 1991
Jean Innes, *Buccaneer's Bride*, 1989
Johanna Lindsey, *A Pirate's Love*, 1978
Joan Van Nuys, *Beloved Avenger*, 1989
Kathleen E. Woodiwiss, *Shanna*, 1977

1375

CARA MILES (Pseudonym of Connie Mason)

Surrender to the Fury

(New York: Avon, 1992)

Story type: Historical/American Civil War
Major character(s): Aimee Trevor, Southern Belle, Widow(er); Nick Drummond, Military Personnel (Union Army captain)
Time period(s): 1860s
Locale(s): Georgia

Summary: When Union Army Captain Nick Drummond brings his troops to occupy the Widow Trevor's Georgia plantation, he comes face to face with the woman who has haunted his dreams for five years, beautiful Aimee Trevor, widow, mother, and defiant southerner. Nick is determined to regain the trust he shattered years earlier, but circumstances, pride, and an old fiancee get in the way — at least temporarily. A sensual, fast-paced tale.

Other books you might like:
Micki Brown, *Once a Rebel*, 1992
Heather Graham, *One Wore Blue*, 1991
Heather Graham, *And One Wore Gray*, 1992
Kay McMahon, *Chase the Dawn*, 1992
Terri Valentine, *Yankee's Caress*, 1989

1376

LINDA LAEL MILLER

Angelfire

(New York: Pocket, 1989)

Story type: Historical/Victorian
Major character(s): Bliss Stafford, Runaway (from unwanted marriage); Jamie McKenna, Farmer
Time period(s): 19th century
Locale(s): New Zealand

Summary: In an effort to avoid one undesirable marriage, fiesty Bliss Stafford compromises her way into another and gets more than she bargained for—a passionate, determined husband who won't take ''no'' for an answer. Follows *Moonfire*, continuing the story of the McKennas.

Other books you might like:
Dorothy Eden, *An Important Family*, 1982
Meagan McKinney, *Till Dawn Tames the Night*, 1991

Laura Simon, *A Taste of Heaven*, 1989
Lynette Vinet, *Wild, Wicked Eden*, 1990

1377

LINDA LAEL MILLER

Caroline and the Raider

(New York: Pocket, 1992)

Story type: Historical/American West
Series: Orphan Train Trilogy
Major character(s): Caroline Chalmers, Teacher; Guthrie Hayes, Military Personnel (Civil War raider)
Time period(s): 1870s (1878)
Locale(s): Laramie, Wyoming

Summary: Caroline hires Civil War Raider Guthrie Hayes to help her fiance break out of jail, and ends up in love with Guthrie instead! Nevertheless, even though she no longer loves her betrothed, Caroline is determined to get him out of jail, and in doing so, she finds more trouble than she can handle. Guthrie to the rescue! Funny and passionate. Third in the Orphan Train trilogy.

Other books you might like:
Theresa DiBenedetto, *Western Winds*, 1991
Gina Robins, *Whispers of Love*, 1991
Victoria Thompson, *Wild Texas Promise*, 1990
Jeanne Williams, *No Roof but Heaven*, 1990

1378

LINDA LAEL MILLER

Daniel's Bride

(New York: Pocket, 1992)

Story type: Historical/American West
Major character(s): Jolie McKibben, Outlaw (alleged); Daniel Beckham, Widow(er), Farmer
Time period(s): 1870s (1877)
Locale(s): Washington (Washington Territory)

Summary: To save Jolie from being hanged as a bandit, Daniel Beckman marries her, even though he is still mourning the death of his wife and children. However, when two orphans show up needing parents, Jolie and Daniel oblige—and end up finding love and establishing a family. Sensual and realistic.

Other books you might like:
Emily Bradshaw, *Cactus Blossom*, 1991
Deborah Camp, *Black-Eyed Susan*, 1990
Katherine Compton, *Outlaw Bride*, 1991
Robin Lee Hatcher, *Promise Me Spring*, 1991
Victoria Pade, *The Doubletree*, 1990

1379

LINDA LAEL MILLER

Emma and the Outlaw

(New York: Pocket, 1991)

Story type: Historical/American West

Series: Orphan Train Trilogy
Major character(s): Emma Chalmers, Orphan; Steven Fairfax, Gunfighter
Time period(s): 1870s
Locale(s): Whitneyville, Idaho; Louisiana

Summary: Taken from her sisters on the Orphan Train and raised, quite properly incidentally, by the sympathetic town madam, Emma Chalmers has had anything but a conventional upbringing. But even that didn't prepare her for handsome outlaw Steven Fairfax and his devastating effect on her when he mistakes her for "one of the girls." Sizzling romance, a bit of mystery, and likeable characters enliven this, the second book in the Orphan Train Trilogy.

Other books you might like:
Elaine Barbieri, *Wings of a Dove*, 1990
Caroline Bourne, *Allegheny Captive*, 1990
Deborah Camp, *Fallen Angel*, 1989
Norah Hess, *Devil in Spurs*, 1990

1380

LINDA LAEL MILLER

Forever and the Night

(New York: Berkley, 1993)

Story type: Contemporary/Fantasy; Gothic
Major character(s): Neely Wallace, Assistant (political aide); Aidan Tremayne, Vampire, Artist
Time period(s): 1990s
Locale(s): Bright River, Connecticut

Summary: Longing to be human, reluctant vampire and artist Aidan Tremayne wants a future with political assistant Neely Wallace. She, however, is busy escaping mobs and gangsters and while she appreciates Aidan's help, he is, after all, a vampire. Nevertheless, she is attracted to him, and together they try to solve their almost overwhelming problems.

Other books you might like:
Lori Herter, *Confession*, 1992
Lori Herter, *Eternity*, 1993
Lori Herter, *Obsession*, 1991
Anne Rice, *Interview with the Vampire*, 1976
Cheri Scotch, *The Werewolf's Kiss*, 1992

1381

LINDA LAEL MILLER

The Legacy

(New York: Pocket, 1994)

Story type: Contemporary
Major character(s): Jacy Tiernan, Teacher; Ian Yarbro, Fiance(e) (former)
Time period(s): 1990s
Locale(s): Corroboree Springs, Australia

Summary: Ten years earlier, independent Jacy Tiernan left Australia when she learned her fiance, Ian Yarbro, had fathered a child. Now she has returned to help her father save his land, and she and Ian discover one another once again. The love is still there, but so is the pain. Nevertheless, to save her

land, Jacy agrees to marry Ian; and then the conflicts begin. Women's issues, passion, and a greedy neighbor with murder in his eye add to the action and intrigue.

Other books you might like:
Leigh Bristol, *Sunswept*, 1990
  historical setting
Elizabeth Duke, *Outback Legacy*, 1993
Nancy Hutchinson, *Wild Card*, 1994
Colleen McCullough, *The Thorn Birds*, 1977
  classic Australian saga
Donna Stephens, *Heart of the Wild*, 1993
  historical setting

1382

LINDA LAEL MILLER

Lily and the Major

(New York: Pocket, 1990)

Story type: Historical/Victorian America
Series: Orphan Train Trilogy
Major character(s): Lily Chalmers, Farmer, Orphan; Caleb Halliday, Military Personnel (major)
Time period(s): 1870s (1878)
Locale(s): Tylerville, Washington

Summary: Separated as a child from her two sisters via the Orphan Train, Lily wants two things: to find her sisters and to homestead her own land. She is already well on her way to achieving her goals when Major Caleb Halliday arrives on the scene determined to win Lily's affections. The encounters between these two fiercely independent people with diverse goals are fiery and passionate as they come to love and accept each other as they are.

Other books you might like:
Elaine Barbieri, *Wings of a Dove*, 1990
Rosanne Bittner, *Montana Woman*, 1990
Dorothy Garlock, *Homeplace*, 1991
Jill Gregory, *Lone Star Lady*, 1990
Stef Ann Holm, *Firefly*, 1990

1383

LINDA LAEL MILLER

My Darling Melissa

(New York: Pocket, 1990)

Story type: Historical/American West Coast
Major character(s): Melissa Corbin, Runaway (bride-to-be), Heiress; Quinn Rafferty, Businessman (lumber mill owner)
Time period(s): 1890s (1891)
Locale(s): Washington

Summary: Upon discovering that her intended husband plans to keep a mistress, Melissa leaves him standing at the altar and escapes in the private railroad car of Quinn Rafferty. Unwilling to return to face the wrath of her three brothers, Melissa strikes a bargain with Quinn. He will marry her in exchange for the benefits of being part of the Corbin family empire—and then the fireworks start.

Other books you might like:
Shirl Henke, *Moonflower*, 1989
Christine Monson, *Golden Nights*, 1990
Rebecca Paisley, *Barefoot Bride*, 1990
Victoria Thompson, *Bold Texas Embrace*, 1989
    Texas setting
Vivian Vaughn, *Texas Gamble*, 1990
    Texas setting

1384

LINDA LAEL MILLER

Pirates

(New York: Pocket, 1995)

Story type: Time Travel
Major character(s): Phoebe Turlow, Divorced Person, Time Traveller; Duncan Rourke, Pirate, Patriot
Time period(s): 1990s; 1780s (1780)

Summary: In an effort to get over her "divorce depression," Phoebe Turlow heads for the Caribbean and the island that was once home to the "patriot pirate" Duncan Rourke—and ends up in 1780 in his arms. Lots of lively action in this sensual, witty romance.

Other books you might like:
Sandra Davidson, *A Love for All Time*, 1993
    time travel elements
Christine Dorsey, *Sea of Dreams*, 1993
    more pirates
Meagan McKinney, *Till Dawn Tames the Night*, 1991
    pirates
Kasey Michaels, *Timely Matrimony*, 1994
    reverse time travel/funny, upbeat, lively
Becky Lee Weyrich, *Forever, for Love*, 1989
    pirates/time travel elements

1385

LINDA LAEL MILLER

Princess Annie

(New York: Pocket Star, 1994)

Story type: Historical/Victorian
Major character(s): Annie Trevarren, Debutante, Traveller; Prince Rafael St. James, Royalty (Crown Prince of Bavia)
Time period(s): 1890s (1895)
Locale(s): Bavia, Fictional Country

Summary: Annie's visit to the royal household in Bavia was supposed to be wonderful—but everything is going wrong. Annie can't stay out of trouble, her best friend, Princess Phaedra, refuses a prearranged marriage, the locals rebel, and the prince's former mistress is back. In addition, Annie is falling in love with the prince. Funny, fast-paced, and highly sensual. Follows *Taming Charlotte*.

Other books you might like:
Cordia Byers, *Lady Fortune*, 1989
    another American abroad
Johanna Lindsey, *Man of My Dreams*, 1992
Johanna Lindsey, *Once a Princess*, 1991

Sheila O'Hallion, *American Princess*, 1989
    another American abroad
Patricia Pellicane, *Sweet Seduction*, 1992

1386

LINDA LAEL MILLER

Taming Charlotte

(New York: Pocket, 1993)

Story type: Historical/Victorian
Major character(s): Charlotte Quade, Adventurer; Patrick Trevarren, Adventurer, Sea Captain
Time period(s): 1870s (1878)
Locale(s): Middle East; At Sea; United States

Other books you might like:
Susan Johnson, *Sinful*, 1992
Christina Skye, *The Ruby*, 1992
Bertrice Small, *Skye O'Malley*, 1980
Bertrice Small, *Wild Jasmine*, 1992

1387

LINDA LAEL MILLER

Yankee Wife

(New York: Pocket, 1993)

Story type: Historical/American West Coast
Major character(s): Lydia McQuire, Nurse, Mail Order Bride; Brigham Quade, Widow(er)
Time period(s): 1860s
Locale(s): California

Summary: Lydia answers Devon Quade's ad for a wife, but it's actually for his widowed brother, Brigham. However, neither Lydia nor Brigham want to marry, but he's a single parent and does need help. They grow close, but their strong wills and independent spirits create problems. Passion, surprising secrets, and interesting family relationships are part of this highly sensual historical.

Other books you might like:
Robin Lee Hatcher, *Midnight Rose*, 1992
Robin Lee Hatcher, *Promise Me Spring*, 1991
Victoria Pade, *The Doubletree*, 1990
Bronwyn Williams, *The Warfield Bride*, 1994
    different locale

1388

NADINE MILLER

Iron and Lace

(Bensalem, Pennsylvania: Meteor, 1992)

Story type: Contemporary
Major character(s): Shayna O'Malley, Widow(er), Teacher; Joshua Eddington, Businessman (foundry owner), Lobbyist
Time period(s): 1990s
Locale(s): Titusville, Indiana

Summary: When Washington lobbyist Joshua Eddington returns to Indiana to salvage the family foundry, he finds his hands full with more problems than he had anticipated — not the least of which is the independent and beautiful widow, Shayna O'Malley and her family.

Other books you might like:
Elaine Barbieri, *Wishes on the Wind*, 1991
   historical
Jayne Ann Krentz, *Family Man*, 1993
Jayne Ann Krentz, *The Golden Chance*, 1990
Marcia Martin, *Southern Secrets*, 1991

1389

ANITA MILLS

Autumn Rain
(New York: Onyx, 1993)

Story type: Historical/Regency
Major character(s): Elinor Ashton, Noblewoman (Lady Kingsley); Lucien de Clare, Nobleman (Earl of Longford), Rake
Time period(s): 1810s
Locale(s): London, England; Stoneleigh, England

Summary: Reluctantly married off to elderly Lord Kingsley in order to pay her father's gambling debts, young Elinor Ashton ends up becoming the toast of the ton, charming every man in sight, including Charlie, her husband's grandson and heir. Jealously, the old lord sends him off to war; and when tragedy results, he sets about plotting to assure himself of another heir by manipulating Elinor and social outcast Lucien de Clare into providing him with one. First in a proposed trilogy.

Other books you might like:
Lindsay Chase, *The Vow*, 1992
Barbara Keller, *The Heart's Legacy*, 1993
Judith McNaught, *Whitney, My Love*, 1985
Louisa Rawlings, *Promise of Summer*, 1989
Sheila Simonson, *A Cousinly Connexion*, 1989

1390

ANITA MILLS
ARNETTE LAMB, Co-Author
ROSANNE BITTNER, Co-Author

Cherished Moments
(New York: St. Martin s, 1994)

Story type: Anthology; Holiday Themes

Summary: This varied trio of historical novellas focuses on the joy of love and motherhood and includes the following: ''Memories'' by Anita Mills, a story of rekindled love set during the Regency period; ''Flowers From the Sea'' by Arnette Lamb, a tale of feuding clans, revenge, and love set in 17th century Scotland; and ''Indian Summer'' by Rosanne Bittner, a romance of forbidden love set in the American West.

Other books you might like:
Rosanne Bittner, *Wildest Dreams*, 1994

Julie Caille, *A Mother's Heart*, 1992
   anthology of six Regency short stories on the theme of motherhood.
Stella Cameron, *To Love and to Honor*, 1993
   anthology of four historical novellas focusing on marriage
Arnette Lamb, *Chieftain*, 1994
Anita Mills, *Secret Nights*, 1994

1391

ANITA MILLS

Comanche Moon
(New York: Topaz, 1995)

Story type: Historical/American West
Major character(s): Amanda Mary ''Maria'' Ross, Rancher, Orphan; Clay McAlester, Lawman (Texas Ranger)
Time period(s): 1870s (1873)
Locale(s): Texas

Summary: When Amanda learns that her mother and stepfather have been massacred in Texas, she leaves Boston to take over the enormous ranch she now owns. But danger lurks in unexpected places, and it takes the rough, Comanche-raised Texas Ranger Clay McAlester to save her life and show her a side to life she had never known existed. An adventurous novel of treachery, prejudice, and a love that surmounts the barriers of culture and pride.

Other books you might like:
Catherine Anderson, *Cheyenne Amber*, 1994
   hero raised by the Cheyenne/different issues
Catherine Anderson, *Comanche Magic*, 1990
Genell Dellin, *Comanche Wind*, 1992
Kathleen Eagle, *Heaven and Earth*, 1990
Kathleen Harrington, *Cherish the Dream*, 1990

1392

ANITA MILLS

Falling Stars
(New York: Topaz, 1993)

Story type: Historical
Major character(s): Kate Winstead, Noblewoman; Bell Townsend, Rake; Alexei Volsky, Nobleman (Russian)
Locale(s): Russia; England

Summary: Swept off her feet, Kate marries the dashing Count Alexei and leaves quiet England for a more tumultuous Russia. Soon she realizes life isn't all she had hoped and she enlists the aid of her countryman Bell Townsend to help her escape. Lots of action and conflict.

Other books you might like:
Constance Heaven, *The House of Kuragin*, 1972
   first of a trilogy set in Tsarist Russia
Linda Howard, *A Lady of the West*, 1990
   American West setting
Susan Johnson, *Golden Paradise*, 1990
Kathleen E. Woodiwiss, *Forever in Your Embrace*, 1992

1393

ANITA MILLS

The Fire and the Fury
(New York: Penguin, 1991)

Story type: Historical/Medieval
Series: Fire
Major character(s): Elizabeth of Riveaux, Noblewoman, Widow(er); Giles of Moray, Warrior, Nobleman
Time period(s): 12th century
Locale(s): England; Scotland

Summary: Determined to help defend her family's interests against their enemies, Elizabeth sets out for her grandmother's keep—and ends up being rescued from attackers by the fearless Butcher of Dunashee, Giles of Moray. Love quickly follows, but the political (and personal) problems for the pair are many, and they must deal with war, intrigue, and violence before they can settle down in relative peace. Another strong heroine. Fourth in the Fire Series.

Other books you might like:
Katherine Deauville, *Blood Red Roses*, 1991
Julie Garwood, *The Prize*, 1991
Roberta Gellis, *The Silver Mirror*, 1989
Anita Gordon, *The Valiant Heart*, 1991
Johanna Lindsey, *Defy Not the Heart*, 1989

1394

ANITA MILLS

Follow the Heart
(New York: Onyx, 1990)

Story type: Historical/Colonial America
Major character(s): Sarah Spender, Gentlewoman, Orphan; Adam Hastings, Military Personnel (army captain)
Time period(s): 1750s (1756-57)
Locale(s): England; American Colonies

Summary: Rescued from poverty and the unwanted dishonorable advances of her neighbor by an offer of marriage to handsome Captain Adam Hastings, Sarah Spender prepares to sail to the American Colonies with her new husband. However, circumstances keep her in England while he becomes involved with the French and Indian War. Missed communications and treachery result in misunderstandings that are corrected when they are reunited. Fiery and romantic.

Other books you might like:
Karen Harper, *Eden's Gate*, 1989
    similar time period
Nancy Moulton, *Defiant Heart*, 1989
    American Colonial Period
Veronica Sattler, *A Promise of Fire*, 1989
    American Revolution
Lynette Vinet, *Pirate's Bride*, 1989
Kathleen E. Woodiwiss, *Shanna*, 1977

1395

ANITA MILLS

Secret Nights
(New York: Topaz, 1994)

Story type: Historical/Regency
Major character(s): Elise Rand, Gentlewoman; Patrick Hamilton, Lawyer
Time period(s): 1810s
Locale(s): England

Summary: In an effort to save her father from the gallows, beautiful, wealthy Elise Rand offers herself to the ambitious barrister, Patrick Hamilton—on the condition that he take her father's case. She realizes, of course, that her reputation is doomed; what she doesn't know is that her heart will be in danger, as well. Good characterizations, nicely-handled language, and complex plotting are featured in this story that depicts a rather dark, but realistic, side of Regency life.

Other books you might like:
Mary Balogh, *Deceived*, 1993
Connie Brockway, *Promise Me Heaven*, 1994
Mary Jo Putney, *Petals in the Storm*, 1993
Mary Jo Putney, *Thunder and Roses*, 1993
Amanda Quick, *Mistress*, 1994

1396

ANITA MILLS

Winter Roses
(New York: Signet, 1992)

Story type: Historical/Medieval
Series: Fire
Major character(s): Arabella of Woolford, Widow(er), Noblewoman; William of Blacklieth, Nobleman
Time period(s): 13th century

Summary: Arabella's desire to protect her crippled son makes her vow never to wed again, so when her father betroths her to William of Blacklieth, a true giant of a man, her fears for her son are uppermost in her mind. However, in spite of rumor, a madman, and numerous misunderstandings, Arabella and William find happiness together at last. Well-drawn characters and nicely handled relationships. Fifth in the Fire Series.

Other books you might like:
Catherine Coulter, *Earth Song*, 1990
Edith Layton, *The Crimson Crown*, 1990
Marylyle Rogers, *Uncommon Vows*, 1990
Flora M. Speer, *Castle of the Heart*, 1990

1397

MIRIAM MINGER

Captive Rose
(New York: Avon, 1991)

Story type: Historical/Medieval
Major character(s): Leila Gervais, Doctor (trained in healing and sensual); Guy de Warenne, Knight (Crusader)

Time period(s): 13th century
Locale(s): Damascus, Syria; England

Summary: Raised from birth as the daughter of a respected Damascus physician, English Leila is trained in both the healing and sensual arts and is satisfied with her life, until it is invaded by crusader Guy de Warenne. Fascinated by Guy, Leila heals him and helps him escape—in return, he drugs her and takes her back to England with him. Lots of intrigue and danger. Interesting contrast in women's roles in two very different cultures.

Other books you might like:
Jane Feather, *Bold Destiny*, 1990
Virginia Henley, *The Falcon and the Flower*, 1989
Victoria Morrow, *Beneath a Pale Moon*, 1991
Bertrice Small, *Skye O'Malley*, 1980
Katherine Vickery, *Desire of the Heart*, 1990

1398

MIRIAM MINGER

Defiant Imposter

(New York: Avon, 1992)

Story type: Historical/Colonial America; Historical/Antebellum American South
Major character(s): Susanna Guthric, Imposter, Plantation Owner; Adam Thornton, Manager (of plantation), Servant (former indentured servant)
Time period(s): 18th century
Locale(s): Virginia, American Colonies

Summary: Assuming her dying friend's identity, Susanna goes to Virginia and takes control of the vast plantation, Briarwood—and, in spite of her intentions to marry a wealthy planter, finds herself attracted to the virile plantation manager Adam Thornton, a man who was once a servant. Blackmail, mistrust, and deception all play a part in this passionate story of two people who eventually learn to love and trust each other.

Other books you might like:
Rexanne Becnel, *Thief of My Heart*, 1991
Thea Devine, *Southern Seduction*, 1991
Patricia Hagan, *Midnight Rose*, 1991
Carla Simpson, *Always, My Love*, 1990

1399

MIRIAM MINGER

The Pagan's Prize

(New York: Jove, 1993)

Story type: Historical/Medieval
Major character(s): Zora, Royalty (Russian princess); Rurik, Nobleman (Viking lord), Warrior
Time period(s): 11th century (1024)
Locale(s): Chernigov, Russia; Novgorod, Russia; Norway

Summary: When Viking warrior Rurik rescues the Russian princess Zora from slavery, he has ulterior motives in mind — he plans to use her to thwart his uncle's warring ambitions. However, Zora wants none of it (or Rurik either) and spends

much of her time trying to escape. Bloody battles, daring rescues, hidden secrets, and passionate romance are here in abundance.

Other books you might like:
Phoebe Conn, *By Love Enslaved*, 1989
Anita Gordon, *The Valiant Heart*, 1991
Heather Graham, *The Viking's Woman*, 1990
Mary Ellen Gronau, *Passionate Warriors*, 1989
Helen Mittermeyer, *Princess of the Veil*, 1992

1400

MIRIAM MINGER

Wild Angel

(New York: Jove, 1994)

Story type: Historical/Medieval
Major character(s): Triona O'Toole, Orphan, Ward; Ronan O'Toole, Guardian, Chieftain (of the clan)
Locale(s): Ireland

Summary: Fiery and stubborn, Triona clashes violently with Ronan, her guardian and clan chieftain, as she seeks to avenge her father's death and avoid being controlled by Ronan in any way. Her willful ways, however, put others in danger—and the growing passion between Triona and Ronan simply adds to the complex plot. Fast-paced adventure.

Other books you might like:
Katherine Deauville, *Blood Red Roses*, 1991
Julie Garwood, *Saving Grace*, 1993
    laced with humor
Arnette Lamb, *Chieftain*, 1994
Anita Mills, *The Fire and the Fury*, 1991
Amanda Quick, *Desire*, 1994
    light and funny

1401

HELEN MITTERMEYER

Princess of the Veil

(New York: Doubleday, 1992)

Story type: Historical/Medieval
Major character(s): Iona, Royalty (Viking princess); Magnus Sinclair, Nobleman (clan leader), Warrior
Time period(s): 11th century
Locale(s): Scotland

Summary: Believing herself ugly and unmarriageable because of a violent childhood attack that left her disfigured in mind and body, Icelandic princess Iona sets sail intending to establish a retreat for women on a remote Scottish island. They are captured by a band of Scots led by Magnus Sinclair and as the two ancient enemy groups get to know each other, so do Magnus and Iona. When a compromising situation forces them to wed, things become both passionate and more sinister as an old enemy from the past tries once more to destroy Iona's happiness.

Other books you might like:
Christina Dodd, *Candle in the Window*, 1991
Heather Graham, *The Viking's Woman*, 1990

Laura Kinsale, *Flowers From the Storm*, 1992
Lindsay McKenna, *Lord of Shadowhawk*, 1992
Mary Jo Putney, *Uncommon Vows*, 1991

1402

KARYN MONK

Surrender to a Stranger
(New York: Bantam, 1995)

Story type: Historical/French Revolution
Major character(s): Jacqueline Doucette, Noblewoman; Armand St. James, Nobleman, Imposter ("Rescuer of French Nobility")
Time period(s): 1790s (1793)
Locale(s): France; England

Summary: Armand St. James, also known as The Black Prince and dedicated to saving French aristocrats from the guillotine, rescues Jacqueline Doucette on the eve of her execution and takes her to safety in England. She agrees to spend a night in his bed only if he will rescue her fiance, but when he is caught, Jacqueline heads for France to rescue him—and to seek vengeance on the man who had her father killed and tried to rape her. A suspenseful, realistic tale that will appeal to those who liked *A Tale of Two Cities* and *The Scarlet Pimpernel*. First novel.

Other books you might like:
Charles Dickens, *A Tale of Two Cities*, 1857
    story of the French Revolution
Jane Feather, *Velvet*, 1994
Iris Johansen, *Storm Winds*, 1991
Baroness Orczy, *The Scarlet Pimpernel*, 1905
    story of the French Revolution
Serena Richards, *Rendezvous*, 1991

1403

CAROLYN MONROE

Kiss of Bliss
(New York: Silhouette, 1992)

Story type: Contemporary/Innocent
Major character(s): Lanie Weatherford, Animal Lover (horse owner); Reece Masardi, Businessman (Feed Store Owner)
Time period(s): 1990s
Locale(s): United States

Summary: Lanie's pet miniature horse was her reason for moving to Bliss County and she badly needed the job at the local feed store. However, she didn't count on the owner being so stodgy and logical! Lanie's impulsiveness and Reece's seriousness threaten to keep them poles apart, but Winnie the horse, and fate, bring them together.

Other books you might like:
Debbie Macomber, *A Little Bit of Country*, 1990
Lee Magner, *The Mistress of Foxgrove*, 1989
Wendy Martin, *Love on Trial*, 1990
Shannon O'Connell, *That Darn Cat*, 1992
Laura Parrish, *Love's Quiet Corner*, 1989

1404

CHRISTINE MONSON

Golden Nights
(New York: Warner, 1990)

Story type: Historical/American West
Major character(s): Suzanne Maintree, Socialite (penniless), Bride (abandoned); Rafer Smith, Con Artist, Guide
Time period(s): 1860s (1869)
Locale(s): Colorado; Mississippi River

Summary: Abandoned on her wedding night and left with no money, Suzanne determines to track her husband down. In the company of her father-in-law and Rafer Smith, she journeys from Mexico to Colorado and finds adventure, danger and love.

Other books you might like:
Shirl Henke, *Moonflower*, 1990
Linda Lael Miller, *My Darling Melissa*, 1990
Kathleen E. Woodiwiss, *Ashes in the Wind*, 1979
    Similar writing style
Kathleen E. Woodiwiss, *Come Love a Stranger*, 1984

1405

CHRISTINE MONSON

This Fiery Splendor
(New York: Warner, 1991)

Story type: Historical/Victorian
Major character(s): Annalise Devon, Young Woman, Orphan; Derek Clavell, Nobleman, Military Personnel (colonel)
Time period(s): 1850s
Locale(s): England; India

Summary: Although missionary's daughter Annalise Devon and aristocratic Derek Clavell are drawn to each other, the differences in their social standings are insurmountable. Nevertheless, despite a fiance, the Sepoy uprising, and the rigid British social structure, love does win out—eventually—and Analise and Derek are free to be together.

Other books you might like:
E.M. Forster, *A Passage to India*, 1924
Victoria Holt, *The India Fan*, 1988
M.M. Kaye, *The Far Pavilions*, 1978

1406

KATE MOORE

An Improper Widow
(New York: Avon, 1995)

Story type: Regency
Major character(s): Susannah Bowen, Companion, Gentlewoman; Frances William Arden, Nobleman (Marques of Warne)
Time period(s): 1810s
Locale(s): England

Summary: Mysteriously stolen calling cards that end up in strange places, a highwayman who only demands a kiss, and some exceptionally well-done characters grace this traditional Regency that features intricate plotting and intriguing backstories—all based on *The Odyssey*. Witty, detailed, and accurate.

Other books you might like:
Jan Constant, *The Only Hope*, 1994
Gail Eastwood, *The Persistent Earl*, 1995
Jean R. Ewing, *Virtue's Reward*, 1995
Meg-Lynn Roberts, *Christmas Escapade*, 1994
Jeanne Savery, *A Reformed Rake*, 1994

1407

KATE MOORE

Sweet Bargain

(New York: Avon, 1993)

Story type: Regency
Major character(s): Isabel Shaw, Young Woman; Nick Seymour, Landowner
Time period(s): 1810s
Locale(s): England

Summary: When Isabel Shaw and her rather extensive family are refused permission to fish the lower Ashc river by the land's new owner, Nick Seymour, disappointment reigns; but when the fish are found poisoned, and Bel's younger brother is implicated, matters become serious. To top it all off, the son of the local squire spreads compromising rumors about Bel and Nick! It takes a lot to get everything appropriately settled, but love does win out in this elegant and charming Regency.

Other books you might like:
Carola Dunn, *Lavender Lady*, 1983
Georgette Heyer, *Frederica*, 1965
Sheila Simonson, *The Bar Sinister*, 1986
Sheila Simonson, *A Cousinly Connexion*, 1984

1408

MARGARET MOORE (Pseudonym of Margaret Wilkins)

China Blossom

(Toronto: Harlequin, 1992)

Story type: Historical/Victorian
Major character(s): Fragrant Blossom, Young Woman (concubine); Darcy Fitzroy, Gentleman, Businessman (shipping company owner)
Time period(s): 19th century
Locale(s): England

Summary: When Darcy Fitzroy is presented with a beautiful concubine as payment for a debt, his life is turned upside down as he tries to decide what to do with her. After all, respectable Victorian gentlemen don't own concubines! Desperate, he educates her and hopes to find her a husband; instead he ends up finding himself a wife. Funny, lively, and decidedly unusual.

Other books you might like:
Julie Garwood, *The Gift*, 1991
    different period
Pamela Morsi, *Garters*, 1992
Sheila O'Hallion, *The Captured Heart*, 1991
Amanda Quick, *Scandal*, 1991
    different period

1409

MARGARET MOORE (Pseudonym of Margaret Wilkins)

A Warrior's Quest

(Toronto: Harlequin, 1993)

Story type: Historical/Medieval
Major character(s): Fritha Kendrick, Orphan; Urien Fitzroy, Knight, Mercenary
Time period(s): 11th century
Locale(s): England

Summary: Urien Fitzroy, selling his knightly services to Lord Gervais, is surprised and angered by spitfire Fritha, who happens to be in the lord's charge. He is, however, intrigued in spite of himself. A jealous lady, knightly duties, and the antagonizing Fritha keep him busy, but love does win out in the end. Lots of action.

Other books you might like:
Linda Lang Bartell, *Brianna*, 1986
Catherine Coulter, *Earth Song*, 1990
Catherine Coulter, *Secret Song*, 1991
Jude Deveraux, *The Taming*, 1989
Julie Garwood, *The Prize*, 1991

1410

KATHLEEN MORGAN

A Certain Magic

(New York: St. Martin's, 1995)

Story type: Historical/Fantasy
Major character(s): Alena, Warrior; Galen Radbourne, Sorcerer (exiled)
Time period(s): Indeterminate Past
Locale(s): Cadwallan Isle, Mythical Place

Summary: Alena, a warrior determined to rescue her partner from an evil sorcerer, journeys to an isle of dragons and seeks help from the exiled sorcerer, Galen Radbourne. A young dragon is charmed by her, but even he cannot persuade Galen to go back to his brother's world of evil. Believing that his powers destroy those he loves, he struggles with his feelings for Alena until magic and dragon custom set things to rights.

Other books you might like:
Madeline Baker, *Warrior's Lady*, 1993
    more dragons
Saranne Dawson, *Awakenings*, 1994
    gentler, fairy-tale quality
Kay Hooper, *The Wizard of Seattle*, 1993
    darker
Tanya Huff, *The Fire's Stone*, 1990

Anne McCaffrey, *Dragonflight*, 1968
first in her classic dragon saga/some romance

1411

KATHLEEN MORGAN

Child of the Mist

(New York: Leisure, 1993)

Story type: Historical/Renaissance
Major character(s): Anne McGregor, Witch, Healer; Niall Campbell, Laird
Time period(s): 16th century
Locale(s): Scotland

Summary: Married to ensure clan peace, Niall Campbell and Anne McGregor discover that they must still deal with enemies who seek to kill them, and at the same time wrestle with their growing feelings of love.

Other books you might like:
Kathryn Lynn Davis, *Child of Awe*, 1990
Patricia Grasso, *Highland Belle*, 1991
Johanna Lindsey, *A Gentle Feuding*, 1984
Rebecca Sinclair, *Wild Scottish Embrace*, 1991
Katherine Vickery, *Flame Across the Highlands*, 1990

1412

KATHLEEN MORGAN

Crystal Fire

(New York: Leisure, 1992)

Story type: Futuristic
Series: Knowing Crystal Trilogy
Major character(s): Marissa Laomede, Warrior; Brace Ardane, Prisoner, Revolutionary
Time period(s): Indeterminate Future
Locale(s): Aranea, Planet—Imaginary

Summary: When Marissa rescues resistance fighter Brace Ardane from prison, she intends to turn him over to the evil Ferox in order to ransom her sister; however, love and growing respect interfere with her plans and the pair ends up being pursued by Ferox's soldiers from one exotic place to another. Third in the Knowing Crystal Trilogy.

Other books you might like:
Jackie Casto, *Dreams of Destiny*, 1990
Amanda Glass, *Shield's Lady*, 1989
Anne McCaffrey, *Crystal Singer*, 1982
Anne McCaffrey, *Killashandra*, 1985
Patricia Roenbuck, *Golden Temptress*, 1991

1413

KATHLEEN MORGAN

The Demon Prince

(New York: Love Spell, 1994)

Story type: Futuristic
Major character(s): Breanne, Maiden; Aidan, Royalty (prince)
Time period(s): Indeterminate

Locale(s): Anacreon, Planet—Imaginary

Summary: Powerful Prince Aidan returns to his kingdom from voluntary exile to find the evil sorceror Morloch bent on destruction. However, Breanne sees a softer side to the angry, vengeful prince and volunteers to marry him in order to fulfill the law demanding that he be married by the age of 30. Her love and wisdom help calm his nearly uncontrollable powers and with her help, he saves the kingdom. Fiery and witty.

Other books you might like:
Marion Zimmer Bradley, *Hawkmistress!*, 1982
Kay Hooper, *The Wizard of Seattle*, 1993
Tanya Huff, *The Fire's Stone*, 1990
Tanya Huff, *Gate of Darkness, Circle of Light*, 1989

1414

KATHLEEN MORGAN

Enchant the Heavens

(New York: Zebra, 1995)

Story type: Historical
Major character(s): Rhianna, Royalty (Celtic princess); Marcus, Military Personnel (Roman officer)
Time period(s): 1st century (55)
Locale(s): England; Rome, Italy

Summary: Celtic Princess Rhianna knows that her visions must be used to save her people and their traditions. Roman officer Marcus tries to govern fairly, but the brutality of prior invaders has caused deep prejudices to develop between Rhianna's family and the conquerors; and Rhianna finds it difficult to balance her need to help her people and her growing love for Marcus. Realistic descriptions of the Roman invasion and intriguing accounts of Celtic lore.

Other books you might like:
Marion Zimmer Bradley, *The Forest House*, 1994
similar time period/mystical
Judith Hill, *Hearts Enslaved*, 1994
similar time period
Joan Wolf, *Born of the Sun*, 1991
Celtic Britain/later time period
Joan Wolf, *The Road to Avalon*, 1991
Celtic Britain

1415

KATHLEEN MORGAN

Fire Queen

(New York: St. Martin's, 1994)

Story type: Historical/Fantasy
Major character(s): Lady Deidra, Noblewoman, Healer; Hawkwind, Nobleman, Mercenary
Time period(s): Indeterminate
Locale(s): Fictional Country

Summary: Determined to escape the nobility's confining lifestyle and become a warrior, Lady Deidra runs away and joins forces with the legendary Hawkwind and his band. Her true abilities, however, are not in combat, but in healing; and the knowledge that she possesses the ancient power of fire comes as both a surprising gift and a formidable challenge. Passion and fast-paced action.

Other books you might like:

Marion Zimmer Bradley, *Hawkmistress!*, 1982
  fantasy
Rebecca Brandewyne, *Swan Road*, 1994
Saranne Dawson, *Awakenings*, 1994
Coral Smith Saxe, *Enchantment*, 1994
  another heroine searching for her true talents

1416

KATHLEEN MORGAN

Heart's Lair

(New York: Leisure, 1991)

Story type: Futuristic
Series: Knowing Crystal Trilogy
Major character(s): Liane, Psychic, Healer; Karic, Royalty (Prince of the Cat People), Warrior
Time period(s): Indeterminate Future
Locale(s): Agrica, Planet—Imaginary

Summary: Second in the Knowing Crystal series, *Heart's Lair* follows the adventures of psychic healer Liane and Karic, Prince of the Cat People, as they struggle with cultural and biological differences to realize their love.

Other books you might like:

Jackie Casto, *Daughter of Destiny*, 1990
Jackie Casto, *Dreams of Destiny*, 1990
Saranne Dawson, *From the Mist*, 1991
Amanda Glass, *Shield's Lady*, 1989
Patricia Roenbuck, *Golden Temptress*, 1991

1417

KATHLEEN MORGAN

The Knowing Crystal

(New York: Leisure, 1991)

Story type: Futuristic
Series: Knowing Crystal Trilogy
Major character(s): Alia, Royalty; Teran, Criminal, Slave
Time period(s): Indeterminate Future
Locale(s): Carcer, Planet—Imaginary

Summary: Charged with finding the legendary knowing crystal and returning it to its rightful place among her people, Alia enlists the help of Teran, an exile who is destined not only to help her in her quest to bring enduring peace to the universe, but also to bring her love.

Other books you might like:

Jackie Casto, *Daughter of Destiny*, 1990
Jackie Casto, *Dreams of Destiny*, 1990
Amanda Glass, *Shield's Lady*, 1989
Johanna Lindsey, *Warrior's Woman*, 1990
Patricia Roenbuck, *Golden Temptress*, 1991

1418

KRISTIN MORGAN

First Comes Baby

(New York: Silhouette, 1992)

Story type: Contemporary/Innocent
Major character(s): Chelsey MacKenzie, Divorced Person, Parent (expectant mother); Jake, Hero (grandson)
Time period(s): 1990s
Locale(s): South

Summary: Jake tries to please his dying grandfather by inventing a marriage and an expectant wife—and then he has to produce one! Fortunately, Chelsey, a very pregnant divorcee fills the bill just fine—but then Grandfather recovers and insists they make things legitimate! Charming, romantic, and just plain fun.

Other books you might like:

Carla Cassidy, *Patchwork Family*, 1991
Debbie Macomber, *First Comes Marriage*, 1991
Debbie Macomber, *The Man You'll Marry*, 1992
Betty Neels, *The Final Touch*, 1992

1419

KAREN MORRELL

For the Love of Laura

(New York: Avalon, 1992)

Story type: Contemporary/Innocent
Major character(s): Laura Taylor, Teacher (of learning disabled children); Patrick Murphy, Widow(er), Businessman (nursery owner)
Time period(s): 1990s
Locale(s): Lakefield, Michigan

Summary: Handsome widower Patrick Murphy is determined to get to know his young son's teacher, Laura Taylor, better, but Laura won't date parents of her students. Interesting characters in a light romance where everyone wins.

Other books you might like:

Jo Beverley, *An Unwilling Bride*, 1992
  Regency setting
Lynn Bulock, *Roses for Caroline*, 1989
Victoria Thompson, *Playing with Fire*, 1990
  historical setting/sensual
Phyllis A. Whitney, *The Singing Stones*, 1990
  Gothic and suspense elements

1420

KAREN MORRELL

Wish upon a Star

(New York: Avalon, 1992)

Story type: Contemporary/Innocent
Major character(s): Annie Stewart, Waiter/Waitress, Vacationer; Phillipe Nadeau, Singer
Time period(s): 1990s
Locale(s): Iowa; Caribbean

Summary: When Annie wins a Caribbean cruise, she anticipates a wonderful holiday from her prosaic, small-town Iowa life but is very much on guard against men and "holiday romances." However, gorgeous Phillipe is persistent, and in spite of his reluctance to become seriously involved, he can't help himself. Zippy dialogue, exotic setting.

Other books you might like:
Bethany Campbell, *The Snow Garden*, 1989
   Christmas theme
Claudia Jameson, *That Certain Yearning*, 1990
Jan McDaniel, *Angels in the Sand*, 1989
Jeanne Savery, *The Last of the Winter Roses*, 1991
   Regency

1421
VICTORIA MORROW
An Angel in My Arms
(New York: Pocket, 1992)

Story type: Historical/American West
Major character(s): Lady Elizabeth Anne Ashton, Noblewoman; Beau Shannon, Rancher
Time period(s): 1860s (1864)
Locale(s): Montana

Summary: When Lady Elizabeth arrives at her grandparents' ranch in Montana, she finds that rugged Beau Shannon owns half the ranch. So she sets out to get it back and ends up in a game of strip poker with Beau! A passionate romance with lively characters.

Other books you might like:
Rosanne Bittner, *Montana Woman*, 1990
Theresa DiBenedetto, *Western Winds*, 1991
Georgina Gentry, *Apache Caress*, 1991
Susan Johnson, *Blaze*, 1986

1422
VICTORIA MORROW
Beneath a Pale Moon
(New York: Pocket, 1991)

Story type: Historical/Medieval
Major character(s): Charlotte "Cheryl" de Clare, Noblewoman; Garret Morgan, Knight
Time period(s): 12th century (1117)
Locale(s): Wales

Summary: Literally drugged into marriage to Norman Knight Garret Morgan by her determined grandmother, fiesty Welsh Lady Charlotte de Clare fights him every step of the way. It is only when her heritage is threatened that they join forces to fight the enemy—and find love in the bargain. Reminiscent of *Taming of the Shrew* with overtones of Chaucer.

Other books you might like:
Rexanne Becnel, *My Gallant Enemy*, 1990
Shannon Drake, *Princess of Fire*, 1989
Teresa Medeiros, *Shadows and Lace*, 1990
Miriam Minger, *Captive Rose*, 1991
Shelly Thacker, *Falcon on the Wind*, 1991

1423
VICTORIA MORROW
Jenny's Dream
(New York: Pocket, 1990)

Story type: Historical/American West
Major character(s): Jenny Bydalek, Immigrant, Orphan; Aaron Gannon, Hotel Owner (wealthy), Immigrant (Irish)
Time period(s): 1870s
Locale(s): Kansas City, Missouri; Alaska

Summary: Wealthy hotel owner Aaron Gannon takes pity on starving, orphaned Jenny, gives her a job, and ends up falling in love with her. This passionate story of two immigrants from different countries sweeps from Missouri to the rugged wilderness of Alaska as Jenny and Aaron come to terms with their feelings for each other.

Other books you might like:
Jo Ann Ferguson, *At the Rainbow's End*, 1989
Peggy Hanchar, *Tomorrow's Dream*, 1989
Elisabeth MacDonald, *Watch for the Morning*, 1978
Katherine Sutcliffe, *A Fire in the Heart*, 1990
   English setting

1424
PEGGY MORSE
The Stillman Curse
(Bensalem, Pennsylvania: Meteor, 1992)

Story type: Contemporary
Major character(s): Leandra Gallagher, Single Parent; Todd Stillman, Doctor
Time period(s): 1990s
Locale(s): Oklahoma City, Oklahoma

Summary: More than anything, Leandra doesn't want Todd Stillman to come back to town. Memories and rumors of the "Stillman Curse" are still too strong. However, Todd returns and he and Leandra's son, Trey, become friends, making life even more difficult for Leandra. But love has a way of appearing when least expected, and Laura and Todd must come to terms with not only their feelings, but the legendary "curse," as well.

Other books you might like:
Lynn Bulock, *In Your Dreams*, 1992
Lacey Dancer, *Baby Makes Five*, 1992
Lisa Gregory, *The Rainbow Promise*, 1989
Nancy Martin, *Monkey Wrench*, 1992

1425
PAMELA MORSI
Courting Miss Hattie
(New York: Bantam, 1991)

Story type: Historical/American West
Major character(s): Hattie Colfax, Farmer, Spinster; Reed Tyler, Farmer
Time period(s): 1890s

Locale(s): Arkansas

Summary: Independent, capable, and resigned to spinsterhood, Hattie Colfax has managed to run the best piece of land in the county single-handedly for years. She and her hired hand, young Reed Tyler, have also been just friends for years—and then widower Ancil Drayton starts calling on Miss Hattie. It doesn't take Reed long to discover that all Ancil wants is Miss Hattie's land and a mother for his children; it takes Reed only slightly longer to discover that he wants Miss Hattie for himself. A gentle, heartwarming story of a love that is all the more special because it is unexpected.

Other books you might like:
Jude Deveraux, *Wishes*, 1989
Lisa Gregory, *The Rainbow Season*, 1979
Joan Johnston, *Sweetwater Seduction*, 1991
Jill Marie Landis, *Rose*, 1990
LaVyrle Spencer, *Hummingbird*, 1990

1426
PAMELA MORSI
Garters
(New York: Jove, 1992)

Story type: Historical/Victorian America
Major character(s): Esme Crabb, Mountain Woman (hillbilly); Cleavis Rhy, Store Owner
Time period(s): 1880s
Locale(s): Vader, Tennessee

Summary: Esme Crabb is tired of having a cave for a house and living off of the town's charity because her father is the laziest man in Vader, Tennessee. So she sets out to marry the general store owner, Cleavis Rhy. Everything will be wonderful if she can just get Cleavis to agree! Soon the entire town is shaken by her outrageous behavior—and so is Cleavis. Funny and off beat.

Other books you might like:
Joan Johnston, *Sweetwater Seduction*, 1991
Jill Marie Landis, *Wild Flower*, 1989
Rebecca Paisley, *Barefoot Bride*, 1990
Rebecca Paisley, *Diamonds and Dreams*, 1991
Rebecca Paisley, *Midnight and Magnolias*, 1992

1427
PAMELA MORSI
Heaven Sent
(New York: Doubleday, 1990)

Story type: Historical/American West
Major character(s): Hannah Bunch, Spinster, Bride (reluctant); Henry Lee Watson, Bridegroom (reluctant), Businessman (illegal whiskey producer)
Time period(s): 19th century
Locale(s): Oklahoma

Summary: Determined to marry the man of her choice, innocent and naive pastor's daughter Hannah Bunch engineers a fool-proof plan—only to find herself compromised with the wrong man—lazy Henry Lee Watson. Marriage, however,

provides a number of surprises for them both, including love. Sweet, sensual and heartwarming.

Other books you might like:
Karen Bale, *Bold Montana Bride*, 1991
Diane Wicker Davis, *Heart of the Falcon*, 1990
Norah Hess, *Hawke's Pride*, 1991
Jill Marie Landis, *Sunflower*, 1989
Victoria Pade, *The Doubletree*, 1990

1428
PAMELA MORSI
Marrying Stone
(New York: Jove, 1994)

Story type: Historical/Victorian America
Major character(s): Meggie Best, Young Woman; J. Monroe Farley, Scholar (music)
Time period(s): 19th century
Locale(s): Ozarks

Summary: When straight-laced music scholar Monroe Farley comes to Meggie Best's Arkansas home to record native music, she just "knows" he is her fantasy prince, and so she pursues him ardently. When they are accidentally married by "jumping off the stone," they both agree that it will end when his work is done; but before that happens, Roe becomes the enchanted pursuer, and all ends well with the help of a delightful group of people.

Other books you might like:
Lori Copeland, *Sweet Hannah Rose*, 1991
Joan Johnston, *Sweetwater Seduction*, 1991
Rebecca Paisley, *Midnight and Magnolias*, 1992
LaVyrle Spencer, *The Endearment*, 1992
   warm

1429
PAMELA MORSI
Runabout
(New York: Jove, 1994)

Story type: Historical/American West
Major character(s): Tulsy Mae Bruder, Young Woman; Luther Briggs, Friend, Indian (half)
Time period(s): 1890s
Locale(s): Prattville, Oklahoma

Summary: Luther Briggs, a longtime friend of Tulsy Mae, isn't about to let her face people alone when she is jilted by the local doctor. Luther pretends to be her suitor and showers her with attention. However, their relationship soon becomes the focus of town gossip—and wouldn't you know? Their pretend romance soon becomes the real thing, much to the surprise of everyone concerned. Warm and humorous.

Other books you might like:
Lydia Browne, *Heart Strings*, 1993
   funny and lively
Lori Copeland, *Sweet Hannah Rose*, 1991
   humor and action

Jill Marie Landis, *Rose*, 1990
  warm and sensual
LaVyrle Spencer, *The Endearment*, 1992
  warm

1430

PAMELA MORSI

Wild Oats

(New York: Berkley, 1993)

Story type: Historical/American West
Major character(s): Cora Briggs, Divorced Person; Jedwin Sparrow, Undertaker
Time period(s): 1890s
Locale(s): Dead Dog, Oklahoma

Summary: Cora, shunned because she is divorced, decides she might as well play the game; but Jedwin's reputation—and the fact that he is really a good person—make the situation more serious. Love does follow, but it takes outside forces to set everything to rights.

Other books you might like:
Lydia Browne, *Heart Strings*, 1993
Lori Copeland, *Sweet Hannah Rose*, 1991
Jill Marie Landis, *Rose*, 1990
Rebecca Paisley, *Rainbows and Rapture*, 1992
Linda Sandifer, *Mountain Ecstasy*, 1992

1431

CINDY T. MOSS

Love's Safe Harbor

(New York: Avalon, 1991)

Story type: Contemporary/Innocent
Major character(s): Hilary Myles, Artisan (marine draftsman); Simon Daniels, Businessman (shipyard company owner)
Time period(s): 1990s
Locale(s): Maine; Halifax, Nova Scotia, Canada; At Sea

Summary: Marine draftsman Hilary Myles goes to Nova Scotia to try to save an old sailing ship, the *Northumberland*, from being destroyed and ends up at sea (and eventually in love) with the man who owns the company that is threatening to send the *Northumberland* to the scrapyard.

Other books you might like:
Ruth Jean Dale, *Society Page*, 1991
Holly S. McClure, *Dreams of Joy*, 1990
Catherine Spencer, *Winter Roses*, 1991
Linda Varner, *A House Becomes a Home*, 1991

1432

NANCY MOULTON

Defiant Heart

(New York: Avon Books, 1989)

Story type: Historical/Colonial America

Major character(s): Mariah Morgan, Heiress; James "Jamie" Lancaster, Heir (something of a vagabond), Shipowner (would-be)
Time period(s): 18th century (colonial period)
Locale(s): Massachusetts, American Colonies

Summary: When Mariah Morgan learns that her inheritance is a buried treasure, and that she and James Lancaster must work together to find it, she hopes to find it only so she can save the Boston charity hospital. She doesn't plan on the adventures that follow (bears, robbers, renegades, etc.).and she certainly doesn't plan to fall in love.

Other books you might like:
Cordia Byers, *Lady Fortune*, 1989
Judith E. French, *Scarlet Ribbons*, 1989
Jo Goodman, *Tempting Torment*, 1989
Jeanne E. Hansen, *Deception's Embrace*, 1989
Mayo Lucas, *Camelot Jones*, 1989

1433

RAE MUIR (Pseudonym of Marty Vogt)

Gold Is the Game

(Aurora, Colorado: Audio Entertainment, Inc., 1993)

Story type: Historical/American West Coast
Major character(s): Eliza Stafford, Widow(er), Journalist; Brand Hamilton, Printer, Businessman
Time period(s): 1850s
Locale(s): Grass Valley, California; Kelsey Bar, California

Summary: On a pilgrimage to discover her gold-seeking husband's grave, intrepid and liberated Eliza Stafford meets the enigmatic Brand Hamilton and learns that things are not always what they seem. Interesting post-gold rush historical detail. Audio format.

Other books you might like:
Jill Barnett, *Surrender a Dream*, 1991
Barbara Hargis, *Heart Song*, 1990
Jan McKee, *Sweet Justice*, 1991
Cynthia Wright, *Brighter than Gold*, 1990

1434

JUDITH NELSON

Lady's Choice

(New York: Berkley, 1990)

Story type: Regency
Major character(s): Frederica "Freddie" Farthingham, Noblewoman; Anthony "Tony" Chilesworth, Nobleman (Viscount)
Time period(s): 1810s
Locale(s): England

Summary: When childhood friends and adversaries Freddie and Tony are betrothed to each other in an effort by their parents to curb their exuberant ways, they reluctantly join forces and set out to thwart their families' matrimonial plans. A witty, charmingly told story of two people who fall in love with each other despite their intentions to the contrary.

Other books you might like:
Jo Beverley, *Lord Wraybourne's Betrothed*, 1988
Georgette Heyer, *Arabella*, 1949
　　classic regency author
Mary Jo Putney, *The Rogue and the Runaway*, 1990
Amanda Scott, *The Dauntless Miss Wingrave*, 1989
Sheila Walsh, *The Arrogant Lord Alistair*, 1990

1435
JUDITH NELSON

Patience Is a Virtue
(New York: Charter, 1989)

Story type: Regency
Major character(s): Patience Witherton, Gentlewoman, Debutante; Anthony Hampton, Nobleman (Marquess of Hamperston), Guardian
Time period(s): 1810s (Regency period)
Locale(s): England

Summary: Horrified at suddenly being made the guardian of two young ladies, Anthony determines to do his best; but the unconventional, outspoken hoyden, Patience, makes that difficult. Witty, lighthearted, and typically Regency.

Other books you might like:
Clare Darcy, *Victoire*, 1974
Glenna Finley, *The Marrying Kind*, 1989
Georgette Heyer, *Arabella*, 1949
　　Classic Regency author
Georgette Heyer, *These Old Shades*, 1926
　　Georgian setting/Regency flavor
Amanda Scott, *The Dauntless Miss Wingrave*, 1989

1436
PENELOPE NERI

Bold Breathless Nights
(New York: Zebra, 1989)

Story type: Historical/Medieval
Major character(s): Catriona McNair, Noblewoman, Amnesiac; Roarke Gilchrist, Nobleman, Bastard Son
Time period(s): 11th century (1067)
Locale(s): Scotland

Summary: Rescued by Roarke after her family has been brutally killed, Catriona finds herself in the arms of a passionate man with her memory gone. Puzzling questions, unexpected answers, revenge, and love.

Other books you might like:
Linda Lang Bartell, *Brianna*, 1986
Shannon Drake, *Princess of Fire*, 1989
Johanna Lindsey, *When Love Awaits*, 1986
Kathleen E. Woodiwiss, *The Wolf and the Dove*, 1974

1437
PENELOPE NERI

Cherish the Night
(New York: Zebra, 1992)

Story type: Historical/American West
Major character(s): Angelica "Angel" Brixton, Young Woman (nee Annie Higgins); Nick Durango, Cowboy (in Wild West Show), Bodyguard (Hired to protect Annie)
Time period(s): 1880s
Locale(s): England; Europe; United States

Summary: High-spirited Angel Brixton's escapades cause her father to hire American cowboy Nick Durango as her bodyguard as she tours Europe. Followed by kidnappers and other assorted villains as they make their tempestuous and passionate way through France, Italy, and Egypt, Nick and Angel manage to unmask a murderer and settle their personal affairs in the process. A non-stop, breathlessly-paced adventure.

Other books you might like:
Gwen Cleary, *Nevada Temptation*, 1990
Theresa DiBenedetto, *Western Winds*, 1991
Laura Parker, *A Wilder Love*, 1990
Rosemary Rogers, *Sweet Savage Love*, 1973

1438
PENELOPE NERI

Forever and Beyond
(New York: Zebra, 1990)

Story type: Time Travel; Historical/Fantasy
Major character(s): Kelly Michaels, Nurse, Reincarnated Person (of Blue Beads); White Wolf, Indian (half Comanche)
Time period(s): 1980s (1988); 19th century (late)
Locale(s): Arizona

Summary: When Kelly goes to Arizona to refocus her life after her divorce, instead of finding the peace she craves, she is swept up in a turbulent drama of love and revenge that began among the Comanche people 100 years earlier. The love of Blue Beads and White Wolf transcends time in a passionate and unusual love story that is a combination of Indian romance, reincarnation, and time travel.

Other books you might like:
Beverly Bird, *Comes the Rain*, 1990
Kathryn Lynn Davis, *Sing to Me of Dreams*, 1990
Heather Graham, *Every Time I Love You*, 1989
Kathleen Harrington, *Cherish the Dream*, 1990
Becky Lee Weyrich, *Forever, for Love*, 1989

1439
PENELOPE NERI

Forever in His Arms
(New York: Zebra, 1991)

Story type: Historical/Post-American Civil War

Major character(s): Jenny Lynn Delaney, Young Woman, Backwoodswoman; Tyler MacKenzie, Military Personnel (Union soldier), Backwoodsman
Time period(s): 1860s
Locale(s): Tennessee; Kentucky

Summary: Members of two feuding mountain families, Jennie Delaney and Tyler Mackenzie, fall in love; but when Jenny can't bring herself to leave her people for Tyler, he goes off to join the Union army. Devastated, Jenny follows him, and finds plenty of adventure along the way. A story filled with wonderful characters, strongly evoking the atmosphere of the 19th century mountain culture.

Other books you might like:
Rosanne Bittner, *Tennessee Bride*, 1988
Kay Hooper, *Star-Crossed Lovers*, 1991
   contemporary setting
Rebecca Paisley, *Barefoot Bride*, 1990
Michalann Perry, *Love's Windswept Embrace*, 1991
Kathleen E. Woodiwiss, *Ashes in the Wind*, 1979

1440
PENELOPE NERI
No Sweeter Paradise
(New York: Zebra, 1993)

Story type: Historical/Exotic
Major character(s): Lady Mariah Downing, Widow(er); Nathan Kincaid, Convict, Nobleman
Time period(s): 1790s (1790)
Locale(s): Pacific Islands

Summary: Shipwrecked on their way to Australia, convicted criminal Nathan (Jonathan) Kincaid and widow Lady Mariah Downing are cast ashore on a remote island and discover strength, endurance, and love as they deal with realities of life in a community of castaways. Passionate, strong characters.

Other books you might like:
Marsha Canham, *Under the Desert Moon*, 1992
   American West setting
Betina Lindsey, *The Serpent Beguiled*, 1992
Sue Rich, *Shadowed Vows*, 1992
Christina Skye, *The Ruby*, 1992
Julie Tetel, *Swept Away*, 1989

1441
DEBORAH NICHOLAS
Night Vision
(New York: Dell, 1993)

Story type: Romantic Suspense
Major character(s): Simone Gerard, Writer (mystery), Psychic; Mark Alvar, Publisher
Time period(s): 1990s
Locale(s): New Orleans, Louisiana

Summary: When mystery writer Simone Gerard's stories begin to parallel the lives of wealthy Mark Alvar's long-dead, detective parents, he becomes curious and buys the company that publishes Simone's books in hopes of learning more. But

Simone literally "dreams" her plots and when she realizes that there must be some kind of psychic connection between Mark's murdered parents and herself, she also realizes that somewhere there is a killer who must be feeling very threatened. Fast-paced, suspenseful action.

Other books you might like:
Elizabeth August, *The Virgin Wife*, 1993
Sandra Brown, *French Silk*, 1992
Nora Roberts, *Genuine Lies*, 1991
Pat Warren, *Nowhere to Run*, 1993

1442
VIRGINIA NIELSEN
Jessica's Song
(Toronto: Harlequin, 1990)

Story type: Contemporary
Series: Cajun Melodies
Major character(s): Jessica Owen, Scientist (marine biologist); Armand Le Blanc, Fisherman (Cajun)
Time period(s): 1980s
Locale(s): Houma, Louisiana

Summary: Jessica and Armand are attracted to each other in spite of the fact that she is a professor and he is an illiterate fisherman. Contains much descriptive material on the Cajun people and their livestyle.

Other books you might like:
Kit Bakker, *Julianne's Song*, 1990
   First in Cajun Melodies Series
Marie Beaumont, *Catherine's Song*, 1990
   Second in Cajun Melodies Series
Tracy Hughes, *White Lies and Alibis*, 1990
Elinor Lynley, *Song of the Bayou*, 1990
Vickie Lewis Thompson, *Connections*, 1990

1443
VIRGINIA NIELSEN
To Love a Pirate
(Toronto: Harlequin, 1993)

Story type: Historical/Antebellum American South
Major character(s): Maria-Theresa Dupre, Southern Belle, Plantation Owner; Jacques Bonnard, Pirate
Time period(s): 1810s (1814)
Locale(s): Louisiana

Summary: When Marie Dupre saves badly injured Jacques Bonnard, things seem to point to his being a traitor or a spy for the British. He is neither, but the family isn't sure, especially since the British will occupy their plantation. Vulnerable and suspicious, Marie flees into the bayou with Jacques for safety, and in the process learns to trust and finally love her pirate. Evocative of the era.

Other books you might like:
Brenna Braxton-Barshon, *Southern Oaks*, 1991
Wendy Garrett, *Sweet Southern Caress*, 1991
Lisa Kleypas, *Only in Your Arms*, 1992
Kristie Knight, *The Garden Path*, 1992

1444
MIRANDA NORTH
Forever Paradise
(New York: Zebra, 1990)

Story type: Historical/Exotic
Major character(s): Lydia Collins, Widow(er); Blake Spencer, Overseer
Time period(s): 17th century (1685)
Locale(s): Jamaica

Summary: When young widow Lydia Spencer discovers that her late husband has both willed the house to her and promised the same house to his bond servant, Blake Spencer, her life becomes a lot more complicated. Both want the house, of course, and therein lies the plot and conflict of this fast-paced, passionate adventure.

Other books you might like:
Barbara Bretton, *Midnight Lover*, 1989
Kathy Lawrence, *Tin Angel*, 1989
  Relutant partners
Laura Simon, *A Taste of Heaven*, 1989
  Reluctant partners in a tropical setting
Julie Tetel, *Swept Away*, 1989
  Tropical setting
Kathleen E. Woodiwiss, *Shanna*, 1977

1445
MARIAN OAKS
Love Lesson
(New York: Zebra, 1992)

Story type: Contemporary
Major character(s): Carolyn Whitaker, Divorced Person; John Adams, Divorced Person
Time period(s): 1990s
Locale(s): United States

Summary: Devastated by her husband's infidelity and their resulting failed marriage, Carolyn Whitaker struggles to put her life back together—and at the same time deal with her growing attraction to newly devorced John Adams. A sensual and moving story in the Zebra To Love Again line.

Other books you might like:
Kathleen Creighton, *A Christmas Love*, 1992
  holiday theme
Judy Gill, *Golden Swan*, 1990
Lisa Gregory, *The Rainbow Promise*, 1989
LaVyrle Spencer, *Bittersweet*, 1990
LaVyrle Spencer, *Morning Glory*, 1989

1446
CONSTANCE O'BANYON
Cheyenne Sunrise
(New York: Zebra, 1990)

Story type: Historical/American West

Major character(s): Alanna Caldwell, Indian (half Cheyenne); Nicholas "Nick" Ballanger, Military Personnel (captain)
Time period(s): 1870s (1876)
Locale(s): Indian Territory; Virginia

Summary: Raised by her maternal Cheyenne grandparents, Alanna Caldwell knows little of the white world and wishes she knew less; but when tragedy strikes and Captain Nick Ballanger is sent to escort her to her father's home in Virginia, she is forced to confront the other half of her ethnic heritage. She must also face her growing love for Nick, a man who has his own ghosts to lay before he can be free to fall in love.

Other books you might like:
Cheryl Black, *Comanche Love Song*, 1989
Cordia Byers, *Lady Fortune*, 1989
Cassie Edwards, *When Passion Calls*, 1990
Judith E. French, *Lovestorm*, 1990
Dana Ransom, *Wild Savage Love*, 1990

1447
CONSTANCE O'BANYON
Desert Song
(New York: Harper, 1995)

Story type: Historical/Exotic; Historical/Victorian
Major character(s): Lady Mallory Stanhope, Noblewoman, Captive; Michael DeWinter, Nobleman, Adventurer
Time period(s): 1840s (1845)
Locale(s): London, England; Sussex, England; Cairo, Egypt

Summary: Lady Mallory Stanhope nurses Michael DeWinter back to health and is dismayed when he leaves for the Egyptian desert to find his missing father. His capture by bandits and rescue by an Arab friend of his father's turns Michael into a renowned desert avenger. Following him, Mallory is kidnapped and gains her freedom by marrying Michael in an Arab ceremony. After more adventures, they make their way back to England, where Michael surprisingly refuses to release Mallory from their marriage vows. Fast-paced and adventurous.

Other books you might like:
Victoria Holt, *The Captive*, 1989
  similar premise and setting
E.M. Hull, *The Sheik*, 1919
  classic desert romance
Laura Kinsale, *The Dream Hunter*, 1994
  similar setting
Johanna Lindsey, *Captive Bride*, 1977
  similar setting
Bobbi Smith, *Capture My Heart*, 1992

1448
CONSTANCE O'BANYON
Forever My Love
(New York: Harper, 1991)

Story type: Historical/American Revolution
Major character(s): Royal Bradford, Gentlewoman; Damon Ruthland, Gentleman, Guardian

Time period(s): 1770s; 1780s (1774-1781)
Locale(s): England; Georgia

Summary: Packed off to school in England by her handsome guardian, Damon Ruthland, young Royal Bradford lives for the day when she can return home to Georgia—and to Damon. But war intervenes and it isn't until her best friend's brother is captured that she makes the journey home to enlist Damon's aid in freeing him. An unusual and tender love story.

Other books you might like:
Cordia Byers, *Lady Fortune*, 1989
Caryn Cameron, *Freedom Flame*, 1990
Millie Criswell, *Brazen Virginia Bride*, 1990
Veronica Sattler, *A Promise of Fire*, 1989
Maura Seger, *Fortune's Tide*, 1990
    fantasy premise/England won the War

1449

CONSTANCE O'BANYON

Pirate's Princess

(New York: Zebra, 1989)

Story type: Historical/Exotic
Major character(s): Jehane Beaudette, Royalty (exiled princess); Cord, Bodyguard
Time period(s): 1840s (1842)
Locale(s): Balmarhea Island, Fictional Country; United States

Summary: Raised together since childhood, Cord and Jehane have a relationship no one could break. Even when Cord learns that Jehane is an exiled princess and must return to her own country, he follows her and protects her against treachery and danger there. Love and devotion are primary themes.

Other books you might like:
Cordia Byers, *Lady Fortune*, 1989
Jude Deveraux, *A Knight in Shining Armor*, 1989
    Some fantasy elements
Sarah Edwards, *Crystal Rapture*, 1989
    Americans Abroad
Laura Kinsale, *Seize the Fire*, 1989

1450

JUDITH O'BRIEN

Ashton's Bride

(New York: Pocket, 1995)

Story type: Time Travel; Historical/American Civil War
Major character(s): Margaret Garnett, Professor (of history), Time Traveller; Ashton Johnson, Military Personnel (Confederate general)
Time period(s): 1990s; 1860s (1863-1864)
Locale(s): Magnolia, Tennessee; Richmond, Virginia

Summary: Margaret Garnett, the newest faculty member of Tennessee's Magnolia University, has the strangest feeling of being watched from the moment she sets foot on the old campus. Even stranger is discovering the man of her wildest dreams is the Confederate General Ashton Johnson, a man who died over a hundred years ago. But the strangest thing of all is waking up and finding herself transported back to 1863

and into the body of Ashton's fiancee. Exciting, engaging, tender, and humorous.

Other books you might like:
Sandra Canfield, *The Loving*, 1992
    time travel elements
Lori Copeland, *Forever Ashley*, 1992
    light and lively time travel
Kristin Hannah, *Once in Every Life*, 1993
    poignant time travel
Antoinette Stockenberg, *Emily's Ghost*, 1992
Becky Lee Weyrich, *Forever, for Love*, 1989
    time travel elements

1451

JUDITH O'BRIEN

Rhapsody in Time

(New York: Pocket, 1994)

Story type: Time Travel
Major character(s): Liz McShane, Editor; Alec Aaranson, Composer, Immigrant
Time period(s): 1990s; 1920s (1927)
Locale(s): New York, New York

Summary: Although Liz McShane always felt vaguely out of step in the 1990s, when she wakes up in 1927 after an accident, she isn't much happier. But things change when she meets Alec Aaranson and falls in love. However, Alec has a past which threatens to catch up with him and ruin his budding musical career—and Liz is the only one who can save him. The problem? She must return to the 1990s to do it. Good New York descriptions.

Other books you might like:
Diane Cory, *High Society*, 1990
    twenties setting/mainstream/no time travel elements
Rebecca Flanders, *The Sensation*, 1990
    light, 1920s setting/no time travel elements
Diana Gabaldon, *Outlander*, 1991
    classic time travel/different time and place
Becky Lee Weyrich, *Once upon Forever*, 1994
    time travel/different period/similar dilemma

1452

CONSTANCE O'DAY-FLANNERY

Once in a Lifetime

(New York: Zebra, 1992)

Story type: Contemporary/Fantasy
Major character(s): Maureen Malone, Writer; Bobby O'Connor, Spirit
Time period(s): 1990s; 1970s
Locale(s): United States

Summary: Maureen, the perfect wife and mother, has it all—until her husband leaves her because she isn't desirable. She is distraught until her friend Bobby, who has been dead for twenty years, suddenly appears. Their conversations and memories enable her to find the strength to continue and she changes from a meek and repressed girl into a strong, assertive, fulfilled woman.

Other books you might like:
Janice Bennett, *A Christmas Keepsake*, 1992
Annette Broadrick, *A Loving Spirit*, 1990
Julie Kistler, *Flannery's Rainbow*, 1992
Patricia Simpson, *Whisper of Midnight*, 1991

1453

CONSTANCE O'DAY-FLANNERY

Seasons

(New York: Warner, 1995)

Story type: Contemporary
Major character(s): Virginia "Ginny" Harrison, Businesswoman; Allyson (Allie) Barbera, Housewife; Nancy Lynch, Advertising
Time period(s): 1990s
Locale(s): Philadelphia, Pennsylvania

Summary: The three Sullivan sisters seem to have ideal lives. Allie has the perfect marriage, Ginny owns a successful business, and Nancy has an exciting advertising career. But beneath the facade all three have secrets—secrets that threaten to tear their worlds apart. Only when they confront their personal tragedies will they find the strength to move on with their lives and rediscover the special love that binds sisters together forever.

Other books you might like:
Gila Berkowitz, *The Brides*, 1992
Claire Bocardo, *Lovers and Friends*, 1995
Jillian Karr, *Something Borrowed, Something Blue*, 1993
Jean Stone, *Ivy Secrets*, 1996
Katherine Stone, *Pearl Moon*, 1995

1454

CONSTANCE O'DAY-FLANNERY

Second Chances

(New York: Zebra, 1992)

Story type: Contemporary/Fantasy
Major character(s): Jessica Meyers, Store Owner (dress shop), Care Giver; Lauren Heese, Spirit, Angel; Jack Lannigan, Spirit, Angel
Time period(s): 1990s
Locale(s): United States

Summary: When newly deceased advertising executive Lauren Reese and police officer Jack Lannigan end up as an unlikely pair of guardian angels, charged with the responsibility of helping Jessica Meyers get her life back together, they find that love and faith have a way of giving second chances to "everyone." A magical, poignant, and heartwarming story of love and death.

Other books you might like:
Jude Deveraux, *Wishes*, 1989
   historical setting
Pamela Simpson, *Partners in Time*, 1990
Patricia Simpson, *Whisper of Midnight*, 1991

1455

CONSTANCE O'DAY-FLANNERY

A Time for Love

(New York: Zebra, 1991)

Story type: Time Travel
Major character(s): Elizabeth MacKenzie, Businesswoman, Mail Order Bride; Jordan McCade, Rancher
Time period(s): 1990s; 1870s (1876)
Locale(s): Texas

Summary: Dragged from her dentist's chair through a time warp and deposited in the waiting arms of Jordan McCade, Elizabeth MacKenzie is mistaken for a mail-order bride and suddenly finds herself on her way to Texas—in the year 1876. Love and respect grow between the two as they establish their home; but Elizabeth must figure out how to solve the "time problem" before they can be truly happy.

Other books you might like:
Madeline Baker, *A Whisper on the Wind*, 1991
Jude Deveraux, *A Knight in Shining Armor*, 1989
Heather Graham, *Every Time I Love You*, 1988
Thomasina Ring, *Time-Spun Rapture*, 1990
Pamela Simpson, *Partners in Time*, 1990

1456

LESLIE O'GRADY

Seek the Wild Shore

(New York: Onyx, 1989)

Story type: Historical/Exotic
Major character(s): Maddie Dare, Journalist (Newspaper); Niles Marcus, Explorer (Botanical)
Time period(s): 1890s (1897)
Locale(s): South America (Amazon River)

Summary: Maddie, star reporter for the Morning Clarion, wants to do a feature on the Amazon; and she wants Niles, a botanical explorer, to guide her. Only Niles thinks women belong at home, not in the jungle. Nevertheless, when Maddie manufactures a non-existent fiance lost in the jungle, Niles agrees—and the adventures begin.

Other books you might like:
Rita Balkey, *Passion's Fury*, 1989
Betina Lindsey, *Waltz with the Lady*, 1990
Johanna Lindsey, *Savage Thunder*, 1989
Susan Sackett, *Passion's Golden Fire*, 1989
   Chitzen Itza setting
Laura Simon, *A Taste of Heaven*, 1989
   Caribbean setting

1457

SHEILA O'HALLION

American Princess

(New York: Pocket, 1989)

Story type: Historical/Victorian

Major character(s): Isabella Alexander, Heiress (''Terror of California''); David, Nobleman (duke)
Time period(s): 1880s (1881)
Locale(s): England

Summary: When spoiled Isabella bows to her father's dying wish that she travel to England to find a husband, she appalls London society and captures (and is literally captured by) the most eligible man around. Some Regency flavor.

Other books you might like:
Cordia Byers, *Lady Fortune*, 1989
Catherine Coulter, *Night Shadow*, 1989
Sarah Edwards, *Crystal Rapture*, 1989
   Americans Abroad series (St. Martin)

1458

SHEILA O'HALLION

The Captured Heart

(New York: Pocket, 1991)

Story type: Regency
Major character(s): Brianna Morris, Debutante, Ward; Andrew Ormsby, Nobleman (Duke of Ashford), Guardian (somewhat reluctant)
Time period(s): 1810s
Locale(s): England

Summary: From the moment irrepressible Brianna Morris becomes his ward, Andrew Ormsby, Duke of Ashford, knows his life will never be the same. Her outrageous behavior and artless charm both exasperate and attract the duke; and when Brianna decides he is the man for her, the duke's last hope for a peaceful and uneventful existence is dashed. A witty, sparkling Regency.

Other books you might like:
Clare Darcy, *Georgina*, 1971
Georgette Heyer, *The Corinthian*, 1941
Georgette Heyer, *Sylvester, or the Wicked Uncle*, 1957
Carol Proctor, *Unlikely Guardian*, 1990
Marlene Suson, *The Rake's Redemption*, 1989

1459

SHEILA O'HALLION

Ravished Bride

(New York: Pocket, 1992)

Story type: Historical/Medieval
Major character(s): Margaret Drummond, Royalty (Scottish princess); Jamie McDonel, Nobleman
Locale(s): England; Scotland

Summary: When pampered Princess Margaret is told she must marry the old king, by proxy, she rebels. Nevertheless, she is married anyway—but not to the king! She ends up married to his emissary, Jamie McDonel. Problems abound, but Jamie and Margaret eventually live happily ever after in the Highlands.

Other books you might like:
Rebecca Brandewyne, *Forever My Love*, 1982

Patricia Grasso, *Highland Belle*, 1991
Judith Hill, *Knight's Desire*, 1992
Karen Stratford, *Lavender Flame*, 1991
Casey Stuart, *Highland Rogue*, 1991

1460

PATRICIA OLIVER

Miss Drayton's Downfall

(New York: Signet, 1994)

Story type: Regency
Major character(s): Cassandra Drayton, Gentlewoman, Bride (reluctant); Phineas Ravenville, Nobleman (Earl of Mansfield), Rake
Time period(s): 1810s
Locale(s): England

Summary: Pregnant and devastated by her lover's death, Cassandra has no choice but to marry her lover's older brother, the Earl of Mansfield. Neither is happy with the arrangement, but she needs to be married and he gradually finds himself intrigued. Mutual respect soon follows—and so does love.

Other books you might like:
Susan Carroll, *Christmas Belles*, 1992
   holiday marriage of convenience
Marion Chesney, *The Desirable Duchess*, 1993
   another marriage of convenience
Georgette Heyer, *A Civil Contract*, 1961
Emma Lange, *A Heart in Peril*, 1994

1461

KATHERINE O'NEAL

Princess of Thieves

(New York: Bantam, 1993)

Story type: Historical/American West
Major character(s): Saranda Sherwin, Con Artist, Socialite; Mace Blackwood, Publisher (newspaper owner)
Time period(s): 19th century
Locale(s): Dodge City, Kansas; New York, New York

Summary: The Sherwin/Blackwood feud continues in spite of Mace's and Saranda's efforts to get things settled and back to normal. Both use disguises, are con-artists, and will go to any lengths to entrap and subdue the other. They even get Bat Masterson and Wyatt Earp involved! Adventurous, sizzling passion.

Other books you might like:
Suzannah Davis, *Angel Eyes*, 1993
Susan Johnson, *Blaze*, 1986
Susan Johnson, *Forbidden*, 1991
Brenda Joyce, *Darkest Heart*, 1989
Nan Ryan, *The Legend of Love*, 1991

1462

SARA ORWIG

Atlanta

(New York: Onyx, 1995)

Story type: Historical/Post-American Civil War
Major character(s): Claire Dryden, Fugitive, Parent (adopted); Fortune O'Brien, Parent
Time period(s): 1860s (1867)
Locale(s): Atlanta, Georgia

Summary: Fortune O'Brien is desperately searching for his son and the woman he believes has taken him. Claire Dryden would do anything to stay with the boy she promised to protect—including accepting Fortune's proposal of marriage. However, what begins as a marriage of convenience sparks passions they didn't know existed—and their pragmatic relationship soon becomes a romantic one as well.

Other books you might like:
Rosanne Bittner, *Wildest Dreams*, 1994
    Western saga/marriage of convenience
Nicole Jordan, *The Savage*, 1994
Victoria Pade, *The Doubletree*, 1990
Patricia Potter, *Defiant*, 1995
Libby Sydes, *Until Spring*, 1993

1463

SARA ORWIG

Denver

(New York: New American Libraries, 1990)

Story type: Historical/American West
Major character(s): Mary Katherine O'Malley, Fiance(e) (of Tigre's best friend); Tigre Dan "Dan Castle" Castillo, Miner (gold)
Time period(s): 19th century
Locale(s): Denver, Colorado

Summary: Silas and Dan not only save each other's lives but they become fast friends in the process. Looking for a new start, they head to the gold fields—and they strike it rich. The problem arises when Silas asks Dan to take some of his gold to his fiancee, Mary, while he stays to "make a million"—and Dan and Mary fall in love. Concludes the trilogy that began with *San Antonio* and *Albuquerque*.

Other books you might like:
Ann Gabriel, *South Texas*, 1990
Martha Hix, *Wild Texas Rose*, 1990
Colleen Quinn, *Colorado Flame*, 1989
Patricia Rice, *Cheyenne's Lady*, 1989
Charlotte Simms, *Silver Caress*, 1990

1464

SARA ORWIG

Favors of the Rich

(New York: Warner, 1991)

Story type: Contemporary/Mainstream

Major character(s): Cimarron Chisholm, Businesswoman (oil company owner); Fontaine Durand, Businessman (oil company owner); Nick Kaminski, Renegade
Time period(s): 20th century (1971-1980)
Locale(s): Southwest

Summary: Cimarron Chisholm works her way up in the oil industry, marries Fontaine Durand, the owner of White Star Oil, and eventually heads the company. Fast-paced, intriguing story of the oil industry, the people involved, and how one woman finds love and success in its midst.

Other books you might like:
Barbara Taylor Bradford, *A Woman of Substance*, 1979
Sandra Bregman, *Reach for the Dream*, 1990
Jacqueline Briskin, *Dreams Are Not Enough*, 1986
Terri Herrington, *Her Father's Daughter*, 1991
Judith Michael, *Possessions*, 1984

1465

SARA ORWIG

Sweeter than Sin

(New York: Warner, 1992)

Story type: Contemporary/Mainstream; Romantic Suspense
Major character(s): Alette Lachman, Artist, Landscaper; Jeff O'Neil, Businessman
Time period(s): 1990s
Locale(s): United States

Summary: When Alette Lachman finds herself charged with murder, simply because she resembles the murdered man's mistress, she finds an unexpected ally in Jeff O'Neil, the victim's best friend and her father's business competitor. As they work to solve the mystery, they also fall in love in this spicy novel of psychological suspense.

Other books you might like:
Jill Barkin, *Hot Streak*, 1990
Kay Hooper, *Crime of Passion*, 1991
Sandra Marton, *Night Fires*, 1991

1466

ELANE OSBORN

Skylark

(New York: Charter/Diamond, 1990)

Story type: Historical/Victorian
Major character(s): Hannah Bradley, Sports Figure (balloonist); Quinton Blackthorne, Nobleman (Earl of Chadwick)
Time period(s): 1890s (1895)
Locale(s): England; France

Summary: When Hannah goes to visit family in England, she doesn't plan on falling in love with her cousin's fiance. However, a daring balloon race to France and the discovery of the true object of her cousin's affections set everything to rights in this lively romp with a twist of mystery.

Other books you might like:
Joan Aiken, *The Smile of a Stranger*, 1978

Georgette Heyer, *Bath Tangle*, 1955
Elizabeth Lambert, *Wings of Desire*, 1989
  airplane race
Kasey Michaels, *The Anonymous Miss Addams*, 1989
Michalann Perry, *Love's Windswept Embrace*, 1990
  another balloonist heroine

1467

MAGGIE OSBORNE

Emerald Rain

(New York: St. Martins, 1991)

Story type: Historical/Exotic
Major character(s): Eulalie Pritchard, Spinster; March Addison, Guide, Shipowner (riverboat)
Time period(s): 1890s (1897)
Locale(s): Brazil

Summary: Intent on joining her fiance on his Brazilian rubber plantation, eminently proper Miss Eulalie Pritchard hires dashing and arrogant March Addison as her guide—and ends up falling in love with him. A sultry jungle romance with the added bonus of nicely done character development.

Other books you might like:
Virginia Brown, *Emerald Nights*, 1991
Leslie O'Grady, *Seek the Wild Shore*, 1989
Karen Robards, *Green Eyes*, 1991
Katherine Sutcliffe, *Shadow Play*, 1991
Janelle Taylor, *Whispered Kisses*, 1990

1468

MAGGIE OSBORNE

The Seduction of Samantha Kincade

(New York: Warner, 1995)

Story type: Historical/American West
Major character(s): Samantha Kincade, Bounty Hunter, Imposter (dresses as a boy); Trace Harden, Gambler
Time period(s): 19th century (late)
Locale(s): West

Summary: Sam Kincade's reputation as a bounty hunter is well-deserved. He's fast and he always gets his man. He's also a girl, although she manages to hide it from everyone—everyone except Trace Harden, the man who is after the same man Sam wants, Hannibal Cotwell, the man who destroyed her family. Humorous, sensual, and well-written. Abuse and abandonment issues are part of the backstories of several characters.

Other books you might like:
Robin Lee Hatcher, *Liberty Blue*, 1995
Linda Howard, *A Lady of the West*, 1991
  darker
Andrea Parnell, *My Only Desire*, 1993
  another female bounty hunter
Patricia Potter, *Defiant*, 1995
Patricia Potter, *Renegade*, 1994

1469

MAGGIE OSBORNE

The Wives of Bowie Stone

(New York: Warner, 1994)

Story type: Historical/American West
Major character(s): Rosie Mulvehey, Farmer, Spouse; Susan Stone, Teacher, Spouse; Bowie Stone, Military Personnel (former cavalry captain), Convict
Time period(s): 1880s (1880)
Locale(s): Gulliver County, Kansas; Washington, District of Columbia; Owls Butte, Wyoming

Summary: Hard drinking, unconventional Rosie Mulvehey needs help on her farm; convicted murderer Bowie Stone needs a reprieve from the gallows. The solution? Marriage. The Problem? Bowie already has a wife—but one who is miles away and already thinks he is dead. Funny, tender, and thought provoking, this story details the lives (and the growth) of two very different women linked by their marriage to the same man.

Other books you might like:
Rosanne Bittner, *Embers of the Heart*, 1990
Emily Bradshaw, *Cactus Blossom*, 1992
  another unconventional heroine
Katherine Compton, *Outlaw Bride*, 1991
  another hanging reprieve — this time for the heroine
Johanna Lindsey, *Angel*, 1992
  an unconventional heroine needing help/humorous
Pamela Morsi, *Courting Miss Hattie*, 1991

1470

JOAN OVERFIELD

Bride's Leap

(New York: Fawcett, 1991)

Story type: Regency
Major character(s): Margaret "Maggie" Chambers, Gentlewoman, Heiress; Ian Charles, Nobleman, Spy
Time period(s): 1810s
Locale(s): England

Summary: Sent to rusticate in the country and recover from his latest job-related injuries, British spy Sir Ian Charles runs straight into trouble—this time in the form of spirited heiress Maggie Chambers who has not only inherited a ghost-ridden estate, but who also seems to be a target for murder. Witty dialogue, engaging characters, and lively action in this Regency with a hint of the gothic. Sequel to *Journals of Lady X*.

Other books you might like:
Cleo Chadwick, *A Midsummer Night's Kiss*, 1991
Violet Hamilton, *A Traitorous Heart*, 1990
Emily Hendrickson, *Miss Wyndham's Escapade*, 1990
Mary Kingsley, *The Rake's Reward*, 1991
Annabel Laine, *The Reluctant Heiress*, 1978

1471

JOAN OVERFIELD

The Door Ajar

(New York: Zebra, 1995)

Story type: Regency; Time Travel
Major character(s): Miranda Winthrop, Heiress, Time Traveller; Alex Bramwell, Detective—Police (Scotland Yard)
Time period(s): 1810s (1811); 1990s
Locale(s): London, England

Summary: Stunned to learn on her wedding night that her husband has only married her for her money, Miranda flees before he can join her in bed and ends up miraculously in the 20th century, staring at a surprised and handsome stranger. Love soon follows, but Miranda learns that in order to save her 19th century husband from murder charges she must choose between love and duty. Well-written, lively action, and engaging characters.

Other books you might like:
Janice Bennett, *Forever in Time*, 1990
Janice Bennett, *A Touch of Forever*, 1992
Sandra Heath, *Magic at Midnight*, 1995
Kasey Michaels, *Out of the Blue*, 1992

1472

JOAN OVERFIELD

The Spirited Bluestocking

(New York: Zebra, 1992)

Story type: Regency
Major character(s): Elinore Denning, Scholar (bluestocking), Gentlewoman; Lucien Wendon, Nobleman (Marquess of Seabrook)
Time period(s): 1810s
Locale(s): England

Summary: Frustrated in his attempts to purchase an old, and reputedly haunted, estate near Brighton, the Marquess of Seabrook impersonates one of the ghosts in an effort to frighten the current owners into leaving. His plans are upset both by the intrepid Elinore Denning and a real ghost, both of who live in the house. Funny, witty, and typically Regency.

Other books you might like:
Jane Ashford, *The Bluestocking*, 1980
Rebecca Brandewyne, *Avon Books Presents: Bewitching Love Stories*, 1992
Carla Kelly, *Miss Grimsley's Oxford Career*, 1992
Kasey Michaels, *The Haunted Miss Hampshire*, 1992
Patricia Veryan, *Logic of the Heart*, 1991

1473

JOAN OVERFIELD

The Viscount's Vixen

(New York: Avon, 1992)

Story type: Regency

Major character(s): Phillipa Lambert, Scholar (bluestocking), Gentlewoman; Lord Alexander St. Ives, Nobleman (Viscount)
Time period(s): 1810s (1815)
Locale(s): London, England

Summary: Phillipa Lambert is a well-known bluestocking who vows she will never marry and she actually thinks women should be able to vote! When she finds out that the dashing Viscount Alexander St. Ives has wagered that he can get her to accompany him to the King's ball, she decides to give him what he deserves. However, they both gain more than they lose in this typically lighthearted Regency.

Other books you might like:
Jane Ashford, *The Bluestocking*, 1980
Georgette Heyer, *The Unknown Ajax*, 1960
Carla Kelly, *Miss Grimsley's Oxford Career*, 1990
Leslie Lynn, *Scandal's Child*, 1990
Amanda Quick, *Surrender*, 1990
   sensual

1474

WANDA OWEN

Deceptive Desires

(New York: Zebra, 1990)

Story type: Historical/Antebellum American South
Major character(s): Tiffany Renaud, Debutante (Spoiled); Chad Morrow, Hero
Time period(s): 19th century (mid-century)
Locale(s): Louisiana; At Sea

Summary: In this sequel to *Moonlit Splendor*, Tiffany and Chad meet aboard ship and are passionately drawn to each other. However, misunderstandings cause a rift between the two, threatening their love. Nevertheless, after various separations and unifications, they are finally together for good.

Other books you might like:
Jennifer Blake, *Midnight Waltz*, 1985
Sonya T. Pelton, *Love Hear My Heart*, 1990
Alexandra Ripley, *New Orleans Legacy*, 1987
Rosemary Rogers, *Sweet Savage Love*, 1974
   Classic sweet/savage
Kathleen E. Woodiwiss, *Come Love a Stranger*, 1984

1475

MIRIAM PACE

Warm Creature Comforts

(New York: Avalon, 1991)

Story type: Contemporary/Innocent
Major character(s): Sierra Sanchez, Veterinarian (zoo); Frank Woodard, Zoo Keeper
Time period(s): 1990s
Locale(s): Mariposa, California

Summary: Veterinarian Sierra Sanchez and zoo director Frank Woodard fight to keep the Mariposa Zoo from going under financially, and they find they share more than a love for animals.

Other books you might like:
Victoria Gordon, *Love Thy Neighbor*, 1991
Karen Leabo, *Runaway Bride*, 1991
La Verne St. George, *A Private Proposal*, 1990
Quinn Wilder, *High Heaven*, 1990

1476
VICTORIA PADE

The Doubletree
(Toronto: Harlequin, 1990)

Story type: Historical/American West
Major character(s): Glenna Ashe, Mail Order Bride; Jared Stratton, Rancher
Time period(s): 1880s (1886)
Locale(s): Kansas

Summary: When Glenna Ashe answers Jared Stratton's ad for a person to be his wife and a mother to his son, she hopes to find a new life on the Kansas ranch and some peace away from her brutal stepfather. Instead she discovers a son to love and a man to cherish, as her marriage of convenience gradually becomes the real thing!

Other books you might like:
Deborah Camp, *Black-Eyed Susan*, 1990
Pamela K. Forrest, *Autumn Ecstasy*, 1990
Barbara Hargis, *Heart Song*, 1990
Mary Mayer Holmes, *Savage Tides*, 1989
LaVyrle Spencer, *Morning Glory*, 1989

1477
LAURIE PAIGE

Sleeping with the Enemy
(Toronto: Harlequin, 1994)

Story type: Contemporary
Series: Montana Mavericks
Major character(s): Maggie Schaeffer, Investigator, Indian (Cheyenne); Jackson Hawk, Lawyer, Indian (Cheyenne)
Time period(s): 1990s
Locale(s): Laughing Horse Reservation, Montana; Washington, District of Columbia

Summary: Maggie Schaeffer, a congressman's investigator, is sent to report on the reservation and ends up clashing with Jackson Hawk, the Cheyenne attorney. His distrust of both Maggie and her agency makes things difficult, but when Maggie's boss's deals with a land baron come to light, the path suddenly becomes clear. Fast-paced and sensual.

Other books you might like:
Suzanne Ellison, *Arrowpoint*, 1992
Rachel Lee, *Cowboy Cop*, 1994
  final book in Montana Mavericks Series
Rachel Lee, *Thunder Mountain*, 1994
  paranormal elements
Lass Small, *A Nothing Town in Texas*, 1991

1478
REBECCA PAISLEY (Pseudonym of Rebecca Boado Rosas)

Barefoot Bride
(New York: Avon, 1990)

Story type: Historical/Victorian America
Major character(s): Keely "Chickadee" McBride, Mountain Woman; Saxon Blackwell, Heir, Gentleman
Time period(s): 19th century (late)
Locale(s): Boston, Massachusetts; North Carolina; Appalachians

Summary: Ordered by his autocratic grandmother to marry, Saxon tries to extend his bachelorhood by journeying to the mountains of North Carolina to buy property for the family business. An encounter with a grizzly bear puts him in the care of Chickadee McBride, a beautiful mountain girl—a girl he marries and takes home to the family, to the surprise of all concerned.

Other books you might like:
Rosanne Bittner, *Tennessee Bride*, 1988
Cheryl Black, *Comanche Love Song*, 1989
Cordia Byers, *Lady Fortune*, 1989
Jill Marie Landis, *Wild Flower*, 1989

1479
REBECCA PAISLEY

A Basket of Wishes
(New York: Dell, 1995)

Story type: Historical/Fantasy
Major character(s): Splendor, Mythical Creature (fairy), Royalty (fairy princess); Jourdian Amberville, Nobleman (Duke of Heathcourte)
Locale(s): England

Summary: As the result of a long-ago bargain, Splendor, Princess of the fairy kingdom of Pillywiggin, has three months to seduce and become pregnant by Jourdian Amberville, all in an effort to strengthen the weak bloodlines of her people. But Jourdian has to cooperate, and therein lies the problem. Funny, charming, and magical.

Other books you might like:
Linda Madl, *A Tender Magic*, 1993
  love potions/no fairies
Meagan McKinney, *The Ground She Walks Upon*, 1994
  fairytale-like quality/no fairies
Maggie Shayne, *Fairy Tale*, 1996
  fairies and mortals
Josepha Sherman, *Child of Faerie, Child of Earth*, 1992
  young adult/fairies and mortals

1480
REBECCA PAISLEY (Pseudonym of Rebecca Boado Rosas)

Diamonds and Dreams
(New York: Avon, 1991)

Story type: Historical

Major character(s): Goldie Mae, Young Woman; Saber Tremayne, Nobleman (Duke of Ravenhurst)
Time period(s): 19th century
Locale(s): United States; Hallensham, England

Summary: When spunky American Goldie Mae decides to help the small English village she has moved to by providing them with their own duke rather than the greedy estate manager they now have, her search for a man to pretend to be the absent duke nets her the real thing—and love in the process. Funny, gentle, and memorable.

Other books you might like:
Julie Garwood, *The Gift*, 1991
Mary Kingsley, *A Gentleman's Desire*, 1991
Mary Jo Putney, *Silk and Shadows*, 1991
Amanda Quick, *Rendezvous*, 1992

1481

REBECCA PAISLEY (Pseudonym of Rebecca Boado Rosas)

Heartstrings
(New York: Dell, 1994)

Story type: Historical/American West
Major character(s): Theodosia Worth, Scientist, Researcher; Roman Montana, Bodyguard
Time period(s): 19th century
Locale(s): West

Summary: Determined to conceive and bear a child for her sister, Theodosia Worth sets out, accompanied by her bodyguard, Roman Montana, to find the ideal father for the baby. Unfortunately, her first choice, the scholarly entomologist, Dr. Wallaby, doesn't work out, but Theodosia is determined—and her search yields some surprising results. A funny, fast-paced, witty romp through the Old West as Theodosia instructs Roman in the scientific facts of sex and he teaches her that everything isn't learned from a book.

Other books you might like:
Raine Cantrell, *Calico*, 1993
Lori Copeland, *Promise Me Today*, 1992
Kathy Jones, *Wild Western Desire*, 1993
Pamela Morsi, *Garters*, 1992
Pamela Morsi, *Wild Oats*, 1993

1482

REBECCA PAISLEY (Pseudonym of Rebecca Boado Rosas)

Midnight and Magnolias
(New York: Avon, 1992)

Story type: Historical/Exotic
Major character(s): Peachy McGee, Mountain Woman (hillbilly); Seneca, Royalty (Prince of Aventine)
Time period(s): 19th century
Locale(s): Aventine, Fictional Country; Possum Hollow, North Carolina

Summary: When Peachy McGee is told by a quack doctor that she is dying, she packs up her meager belongings, leaves Possum Hollow, North Carolina, and heads to the island of Aventine to catch herself a real live prince. And she does!

Prince Seneca marries her to spite his father. His father hates her, the peasants admire her, and Prince Seneca can't help but love her. Rife with Paisley's typical "down home" language.

Other books you might like:
Tena Carlyle, *Captive Treasure*, 1992
Laura Kinsale, *Seize the Fire*, 1989
Pamela Morsi, *Courting Miss Hattie*, 1992
Pamela Morsi, *Garters*, 1992
Elaine Rome, *Stark Lightning*, 1991

1483

REBECCA PAISLEY (Pseudonym of Rebecca Boado Rosas)

Moonlight and Magic
(New York: Avon, 1990)

Story type: Historical/American West
Major character(s): Chimera, Witch; Sterling Montoya, Cowboy
Time period(s): 19th century
Locale(s): Arizona

Summary: When Chimera, a self-styled witch, sees Sterling Montoya, she kn0ows her spell to conjure up a knight in shining armor has worked. However, Sterling isn't about to let some batty girl-witch and her band of orphans divert him from his purpose. Still, Chimera involves him in her battle against the evil Everett Sprague—a battle involving magic, Indians, orphans, and love.

Other books you might like:
Lisa Bingham, *Silken Dreams*, 1991
Lori Copeland, *Sweet Hannah Rose*, 1991
Jude Deveraux, *A Knight in Shining Armor*, 1989
Jill Marie Landis, *Wild Flower*, 1989

1484

REBECCA PAISLEY (Pseudonym of Rebecca Boado Rosas)

Rainbows and Rapture
(New York: Avon, 1992)

Story type: Historical/American West
Major character(s): Russia Valentine, Prostitute, Runaway; Santiago Zamora, Gunfighter
Time period(s): 19th century
Locale(s): New Mexico; Texas

Summary: To evade capture by her lecherous step-father, prostitute Russia Valentine blackmails the cynical gunslinger Santiago Zamora into helping her — and ends up finding love and true passion in the arms of her reluctant protector. Funny, action-filled, and sensual.

Other books you might like:
Gwen Cleary, *Ecstasy's Masquerade*, 1989
Elaine Coffman, *Escape Not My Love*, 1990
Pamela Morsi, *Courting Miss Hattie*, 1991
Pamela Morsi, *Garters*, 1992
Linda Sandifer, *Mountain Ecstasy*, 1992

1485

CATHERINE PALMER

Gunman's Lady

(New York: Diamond, 1993)

Story type: Historical/American West
Major character(s): Rosie Kingsley, Teacher; Bart Kingsley, Outlaw, Indian (half Apache)
Time period(s): 1880s (1883)
Locale(s): New Mexico

Summary: Briefly married as teenagers but separated for years, outlaw Bart Kingsley and society-miss-turned-teacher Rosie Kingsley meet again when she finds him under her bed, badly wounded, and running from the law. The spark is still there, but although he tries to reform, Bart's outlaw past continues to threaten their future. Fast-paced action.

Other books you might like:
Jenny Aiken, *Love Evergreen*, 1993
Elaine Barbieri, *Wishes on the Wind*, 1991
Rebecca George, *Call Home the Heart*, 1989
Nan Ryan, *Sun God*, 1990
  steamy and violent

1486

CATHERINE PALMER

Outlaw Heart

(New York: Diamond, 1992)

Story type: Historical/American West
Major character(s): Maria Isobel "Belle" Matar, Heiress; Noah Buchanan, Cowboy (trail boss), Writer (aspiring)
Time period(s): 19th century
Locale(s): Lincoln Town, New Mexico

Summary: Spanish heiress Isobel Matar comes to New Mexico from Spain to claim her land and find her father's murderer. The last thing she expects is to witness a murder and become a target herself. She is rescued by Noah Buchanan, who agrees to protect her by temporarily marrying her, but as they spend time together, their marriage becomes real. Civil unrest, gunfights, revenge, and murder are all part of this fast-paced, realistic story.

Other books you might like:
Ann Gabriel, *South Texas*, 1989
Lindsey Hanks, *Nevada Ecstasy*, 1992
Linda Howard, *A Lady of the West*, 1990
Pamela Litton, *Stardust and Whirlwinds*, 1991

1487

CATHERINE PALMER

The Wild Winds

(New York: Bantam, 1990)

Story type: Historical/Victorian America; Historical/Exotic
Major character(s): Teglan Lloyd, Heiress—Dispossessed, Imposter (disguised as a boy); Elijah Tate, Scientist (naturalist—marine biologist)

Time period(s): 1840s (1848)
Locale(s): Nantucket Island, Massachusetts; At Sea; Africa

Summary: Intent on exposing her unscrupulous uncle and regaining her whaling company, Teglan Lloyd disguises herself as a boy and becomes an assistant to marine biologist Elijah Tate aboard one of her own whalers. Elijah soon sees through her disguise and Teglan discovers that the whaler has other quarry in mind. Together they must fight for their lives and their love as they survive a forced marriage, a shipwreck, and captivity—all in a delightfully exotic setting.

Other books you might like:
Olga Bicos, *By My Heart Betrayed*, 1991
Catherine Coulter, *Night Storm*, 1990
Wendy Garrett, *Sweet Southern Caress*, 1991
Betina M. Krahn, *Passion's Ransom*, 1989
Lisa Ann Verge, *The Heart's Disguise*, 1990

1488

DIANA PALMER

The Case of the Mesmerizing Boss

(New York: Silhouette. 1992)

Story type: Contemporary
Major character(s): Tess Meriwether, Secretary; Dane, Detective
Time period(s): 1990s
Locale(s): Houston, Texas

Summary: When Tess inadvertently witnesses a drug deal, Dane takes her to safety at his ranch. Dane's tough exterior and Tess's shyness and insecurity are hard to reconcile, but they eventually manage to find love.

Other books you might like:
Carole Buck, *Knight and Day*, 1992
B.J. James, *A Step Away*, 1992
Sandra Marton, *Night Fires*, 1991
Molly Rice, *Chance Encounter*, 1992

1489

DIANA PALMER

King's Ransom

(New York: Silhouette, 1993)

Story type: Contemporary
Major character(s): Brianna Scott, Feminist, Roommate; Ahmed ben Rashid, Diplomat, Roommate
Time period(s): 1990s
Locale(s): United States

Summary: Brianna is persuaded to share her aparment with the chauvinistic Ahmed, a foreign diplomat from the Middle East, but she's not about to fulfill his ideal of a woman who serves him. However, they can't deny their mutual attraction and, despite culture clashes and differing values, they eventually manage to set their relationship to rights.

Other books you might like:
Emma Darcy, *The Falcon's Mistress*, 1990
Emma Darcy, *The Sheikh's Revenge*, 1993

Tracy Sinclair, *If the Truth Be Told*, 1992
Lass Small, *Dominic*, 1992
Joyce C. Ware, *And Be My Love*, 1993

1490

DIANA PALMER

Lacy

(New York: Ballantine, 1991)

Story type: Historical/Roaring Twenties
Major character(s): Lacy Jarrett, Heiress, Orphan; Coleman Whitehall, Rancher
Time period(s): 1910s; 1920s
Locale(s): Texas

Summary: A disastrous practical joke forces Cole and Lacy into marriage—a marriage that has to survive a war-changed Cole, a meddling brother, a pregnant sister's marriage to a gangster, a neighbor girl abandoned and pregnant by Cole's brother, and money problems. Lacy fights heroically to save this marriage and the farm, but Cole's pride and dark secrets threaten to drive them apart. Highly sensual.

Other books you might like:
Diane Cory, *High Society*, 1990
Diane Cory, *A Token of Jewels*, 1989
Rebecca Flanders, *The Sensation*, 1990
Katherine Sinclair, *A Distant Dawn*, 1991

1491

DIANA PALMER

Noelle

(New York: Ivy, 1995)

Story type: Historical/American West
Major character(s): Noelle Brown, Orphan, Companion; Jared Dunn, Lawyer, Gunfighter; Andrew Dunn, Businessman
Time period(s): 1900s
Locale(s): Fort Worth, Texas

Summary: When New York attorney and former gunslinger Jared Dunn heads for Texas to check up on a penniless orphan his grandmother has taken under her wing, he expects to find an unscrupulous, mercenary schemer. Instead, he finds a lively, quite unconventional innocent who ends up stealing his heart—and healing it, as well. Fast-paced, nicely plotted, with interesting characters.

Other books you might like:
Candace Camp, *Heirloom*, 1992
　　similar time period/heartwarming
Judy Cuevas, *Bliss*, 1995
　　similar time period/different treatment/wounded hero
Patricia Potter, *Lawless*, 1991
　　another wounded gunslinger hero
Katherine Sinclair, *Through the Years*, 1994
　　similar time period/mainstream saga with Southern flavor

1492

DIANA PALMER

Trilby

(New York: Ivy, 1993)

Story type: Historical/American West; Historical/Mainstream
Major character(s): Trilby Lang, Heiress; Thornton Vance, Rancher
Time period(s): 1910s
Locale(s): Arizona; New Mexico

Summary: Trilby, a Louisiana transplant, intrigues Arizona rancher Thorn Vance, but he thinks she is having an affair with his cousin. It isn't true, but when her fiance shows up, Thorn takes action. Their marriage leaves something to be desired and it takes a war with Mexico and Trilby's kidnapping for everyone to settle down and pay attention to the important things in life. A sweeping, multi-charactered story of love and distress in the early 20th Century west.

Other books you might like:
Ann Gabriel, *South Texas*, 1989
Linda Howard, *A Lady of the West*, 1990
Brenda Joyce, *Secrets*, 1993
Ann Wiley, *Angel in Disguise*, 1993

1493

MARILYN PAPPANO

In Sinful Harmony

(New York: Warner, 1995)

Story type: Contemporary; Romantic Suspense
Major character(s): Celine Hunter, Librarian; Will "Billy Ray" Beaumont, Drifter
Time period(s): 1990s
Locale(s): Harmony, Louisiana

Summary: Restless and bored, librarian Celine Hunter seriously considers leaving the small town of Harmony for more interesting territory—then Will Beaumont comes back to town, bringing all the excitement she could want with him. Love, mystery, and danger combine in this dark, well-plotted romance that verges on the mainstream.

Other books you might like:
Rebecca Brandewyne, *Dust Devil*, 1996
Tami Hoag, *Dark Paradise*, 1994
Tami Hoag, *Still Waters*, 1992
Karen Robards, *Walking After Midnight*, 1995
Nora Roberts, *Carnal Innocence*, 1992

1494

MARILYN PAPPANO

Operation Homefront

(New York: Silhouette, 1992)

Story type: Contemporary
Major character(s): Libby Harper, Divorced Person; Joe Mathieson, Military Personnel (Army Sergeant)
Time period(s): 1990s

Locale(s): United States

Summary: Young Justin's best friend turns out to be forty-year-old Sgt. Joe Mathieson, and his visit surprises Justin's mother, Libby. The lonely divorcee has only been concerned about a secure future for herself and her son, but mutual attraction eventually changes her priorities. Gently paced.

Other books you might like:
Susan Kyle, *Night Fever*, 1990
Lee Magner, *Song of the Mourning Dove*, 1992
Pat Warren, *The Long Road Home*, 1989
Kay Wilding, *Rainbow's End*, 1990

1495

SHIRLEY PARENTEAU

Golden Prospect

(Toronto: Harlequin, 1991)

Story type: Historical/American West
Major character(s): Julia Ames Everett, Singer, Gentlewoman; Duncan Adair, Guide, Fisherman
Time period(s): 1890s (1898)
Locale(s): Seattle, Washington; Dawson, Yukon Territory, Canada

Summary: Determined to find her father in the Yukon gold fields, sheltered and gently-raised Julia Everett joins a group of dancehall girls and heads north. Their somewhat reluctant guide, Duncan Adair, quickly realizes that Julia is not what she seems, and as he endeavors to protect her, much against her will, they fall in love. Fast-paced action during the turbulent days of the Klondike Gold Rush.

Other books you might like:
Colleen Faulkner, *Love's Sweet Bounty*, 1991
Jo Ann Ferguson, *At the Rainbow's End*, 1989
Peggy Hanchar, *Tomorrow's Dream*, 1989
Scotney St. James, *Northern Fire, Northern Star*, 1990
Annalise Sun, *The Golden Mountain*, 1990

1496

SHIRLEY PARENTEAU

The Naked Huntress

(Toronto: Harlequin, 1992)

Story type: Historical/American West Coast
Major character(s): Lyris Lowell, Journalist, Socialite; Nicholas Drake, Saloon Keeper/Owner
Time period(s): 1880s (1889)
Locale(s): Seattle, Washington

Summary: Nick will do anything to marry Lyris, even blackmail her by threatening to hang a nude painting of her in his bar if she doesn't! Her society family would be appalled if that picture ever saw the light of day, so Lyris agrees—and the battle is joined. Fast-paced, explosive, and highly sensual.

Other books you might like:
Susannah Leigh, *The Turquoise Trail*, 1991
Elizabeth Lowell, *Only His*, 1991
Linda Lael Miller, *Emma and the Outlaw*, 1991

Linda Lael Miller, *My Darling Melissa*, 1990

1497

GARDA PARKER

Arizona Temptation

(New York: Zebra, 1992)

Story type: Historical/American West
Major character(s): Laine Coleridge, Heiress, Hotel Owner; Travis Mitchum, Contractor
Time period(s): 1880s (1883)
Locale(s): Silver Grande, Arizona

Summary: When Boston-raised Laine Coleridge returns to Silver Grande, Arizona, to claim her inherited hotel, she runs into one man who would steal her hotel and another who would steal her heart. Funny, fast-paced, and filled with likeable characters.

Other books you might like:
Carol Finch, *Moonlight Enchantment*, 1992
Lindsey Hanks, *Long Texas Nights*, 1991
Kristin Hannah, *A Handful of Heaven*, 1991
Kathy Lawrence, *Tin Angel*, 1989
Pat Tracy, *The Flaming*, 1992

1498

GARDA PARKER

Blue Mountain Magic

(New York: Zebra, 1994)

Story type: Historical/Victorian America
Major character(s): Lila "Cat" Stockdale, Socialite; Seneca Pierce, Indian (Iroquois), Surveyor
Time period(s): 19th century
Locale(s): Adirondack Mountains, New York

Summary: Although Cat Stockdale initially agrees to an arranged marriage for the sake of her father's business ambitions, all plans are off when she meets the Iroquois surveyor, Seneca Pierce. Passion between Cat and Seneca lands them in a stormy marriage, but as both are unwilling to give up their way of life, a lot of compromise is needed. Good character and plot development.

Other books you might like:
Jenny Aiken, *Love Evergreen*, 1993
Pamela K. Forrest, *Wild Savage Love*, 1993
  earlier time period/gentler
Joan Van Nuys, *Beloved Intruder*, 1992
  earlier time period/Iroquois culture
Patricia Werner, *Cherokee Bride*, 1992

1499

GARDA PARKER

Out of the Blue

(New York: Zebra, 1992)

Story type: Contemporary/Mainstream

Major character(s): Majesty Wilde, Widow(er), Pilot (aspiring); Noah Decker, Businessman (lumber mill owner), Pilot

Time period(s): 1990s

Locale(s): Adirondack Mountains, New York

Summary: Maj Wilde goes to the mountains to recover from her husband's death and unhappy memories of betrayal, and forms a friendship with lumber mill owner Noah Decker. As they deal with a possible foreclosure, a troubled daughter, an empty marriage, and Maj's memories, their relationship deepens into love. A realistic and sensual romance between mature people.

Other books you might like:
Barbara Delinsky, *A Woman Betrayed*, 1991
Ray Sipherd, *The Courtship of Peggy McCoy*, 1990
LaVyrle Spencer, *Bittersweet*, 1990
Helen Van Slyke, *No Love Lost*, 1980

1500

GARDA PARKER

Temptation's Flame
(New York: Zebra, 1993)

Story type: Historical/Exotic; Historical/Mainstream

Major character(s): Nina Cole, Companion; Shane Merritt, Rancher (sheep)

Time period(s): 19th century

Locale(s): Australia

Summary: When Nina Cole arrives in Australia to find that her prospective employer has died, she answers Shane Merritt's ad for a companion to his mother. However, when they arrive at his sheep ranch, his mother doesn't want a companion at all—and she certainly doesn't want Nina! But the attraction between Shane and Nina has already begun, giving them the courage they need to defy his mother and build a new life of their own.

Other books you might like:
Connie Mason, *Wild Land, Wild Love*, 1992
Donna Stephens, *Heart of the Wild*, 1993
Katherine Sutcliffe, *Dream Fever*, 1991
Lynette Vinet, *Wild, Wicked Eden*, 1990
Barbara Wood, *The Dreaming*, 1992

1501

LAURA PARKER

Caprice
(New York: Dell, 1994)

Story type: Historical/Regency

Major character(s): Clarissa Willoughby, Widow(er), Imposter (Princess Soltana); Hadrian Blackburne, Nobleman (Lord Ramsbury), Rake

Time period(s): 1810s (1814)

Locale(s): London, England

Summary: Widowed Clarissa, coveting social acceptance, "becomes" the exotic Princess Soltana and enchants the town. Lord Ramsbury is captivated by her, but she soon tires

of the deception and wishes he could love her for herself—the plain Clarissa. Plenty of action combine with the hero and heroine's internal conflicts in this witty, funny, and intriguing historical. Fascinating secondary characters.

Other books you might like:
Loretta Chase, *The Lion's Daughter*, 1992
    interesting characters/nicely written
Charlene Cross, *Almost a Whisper*, 1994
Judith McWilliams, *Suspicion*, 1994
    more deception
Barbara Metzger, *An Affair of Interest*, 1992
    Regency disguises/funny and clever
Amanda Quick, *Mistress*, 1994
    another "imposter" heroine

1502

LAURA PARKER

For Love's Sake Only
(New York: Dell, 1991)

Story type: Historical/Regency

Major character(s): Regina Lindale, Noblewoman; Maxwell Kingsblood, Nobleman

Time period(s): 1800s

Locale(s): England

Summary: Married and widowed in less than a month, convent-raised Regina flees London and her mother-in-law to find solace in the countryside of her youth. But her plans are spoiled when her coach is commandeered by Maxwell Kingsblood. When he discovers her true identity, he insists that she be his guest at Kingsblood Hall. If that weren't bad enough, the two ghosts that haunt the hall decide that Regina is the woman for Maxwell and they will stop at nothing to bring the two together.

Other books you might like:
Annette Broadrick, *A Loving Spirit*, 1990
    contemporary ghosts
Betina M. Krahn, *Midnight Magic*, 1990
Judith McNaught, *Almost Heaven*, 1990
Patricia Simpson, *Whisper of Midnight*, 1991
    contemporary ghosts

1503

LAURA PARKER

Impetuous
(New York: Dell, 1995)

Story type: Historical/Regency

Major character(s): Lady Jane Blackburne, Teacher (tutor to Blake), Noblewoman; Gabriel Blake, Military Personnel (captain)

Time period(s): 1810s (1816)

Locale(s): London, England

Summary: When common soldier Gabriel Blake catches Lord Wellington's eye, Lady Jane agrees to help turn him into a "gentleman." He vaguely remembers her as his angel of mercy when he was wounded, but she has no memory of it.

She does, however, have strange, unexplained visions. As they come to know each other, they fall in love, but the past holds secrets for them both that must be dealt with before they can find happiness together. Fast-paced, sensual adventure.

Other books you might like:
Julie Caille, *The Rake and His Lady*, 1993
    different backgrounds
Christina Dodd, *Move Heaven and Earth*, 1995
    war recovery
Jill Gregory, *Forever After*, 1993
    mystery elements/Cinderella aspects
Kasey Michaels, *Bride of the Unicorn*, 1993
    Pygmalion theme

1504
LAURA PARKER

Moonshadow
(New York: Dell, 1992)

Story type: Historical/Fantasy; Historical/Victorian
Major character(s): Julianna Kingsblood, Noblewoman; Jos Trevelyn, Nobleman, Imposter
Time period(s): 19th century
Locale(s): England

Summary: When Julianna Kingsblood flees the London social scene and takes refuge at her grandparents' estate, instead of the peace and quiet she seeks, she ends up with a mysterious lover and the same two interfering ghosts that propelled her grandparents into matrimony. Funny, witty, and passionate.

Other books you might like:
Michelle Brandon, *Touch of Heaven*, 1992
Jude Deveraux, *Wishes*, 1989
Mary Kingsley, *A Maddening Minx*, 1992
    Regency
Colleen McCullough, *The Ladies of Missalonghi*, 1987
Patricia Simpson, *Whisper of Midnight*, 1991
    contemporary ghosts

1505
LAURA PARKER

A Wilder Love
(New York: Warner, 1990)

Story type: Historical/Victorian
Major character(s): Fanny Sweets, Thief (pickpocket), Orphan; Matthew Morningstar, Indian, Entertainer (in a Wild West show)
Time period(s): 1870s (1876)
Locale(s): New York, New York; West; England

Summary: Young pickpocket Fanny Sweets is attracted to Matthew Morningstar, one of the Indians in Buffalo Bill's Wild West Show, but he is wary of white women. Love wins out, but not before they lead each other a merry chase. The action moves from New York to the American West to England.

Other books you might like:
Betty Brooks, *Warrior's Embrace*, 1989

Janet Dailey, *The Pride of Hannah Wade*, 1985
Johanna Lindsey, *Savage Thunder*, 1989
Sheila O'Hallion, *American Princess*, 1989
Janelle Taylor, *Savage Conquest*, 1985

1506
DORIS PARMETT

Lies
(New York: Jove, 1993)

Story type: Contemporary/Mainstream
Major character(s): Samara Bonsseauc, Model, Designer (dress designer); Solange Gold, Socialite; David Orchin, Doctor (pediatrician)
Time period(s): 1970s (1979); 1980s (1986)
Locale(s): Paris, France; New York, New York; San Francisco, California

Summary: Separated as children, twins Solange and Samarra have no idea the other exists. However, when Samarra's mother dies in Paris, Samarra's father, a U.S. Senator, is thrilled to be reunited with her. Solange is less than pleased, and fearful of losing her inheritance, she sets about tricking David, Samarra's long-time friend and love, into marrying her. Eventually, of course, things work out, but not until a lot of time passes and old resentments and secrets are confronted.

Other books you might like:
Sally Beauman, *Destiny*, 1988
Shirley Conran, *Lace*, 1982
Barbara Delinsky, *The Passions of Chelsea Kane*, 1992
Elizabeth Gage, *Taboo*, 1993

1507
DORIS PARMETT

Risk
(New York: Jove, 1994)

Story type: Contemporary/Mainstream
Major character(s): Claire Jameson Brice, Socialite; Wendall Lawson, Doctor (Plastic surgeon)
Time period(s): 1990s
Locale(s): California; Connecticut; New York, New York

Summary: When her father is injured and reveals a secret past, socialite Claire Jameson's life (and love) explodes around her with devastating effects. Even Wendall Lawson, the sympathetic plastic surgeon called in to repair her father's damaged face, can't break through the resulting distrust. But Wendall is persistent, and as Claire gradually recovers and picks up the pieces, their relationship takes a turn for the better. Powerful.

Other books you might like:
Sandra Brown, *French Silk*, 1992
Janet Dailey, *The Glory Game*, 1989
Barbara Delinsky, *A Woman Betrayed*, 1991
Suzanne Forster, *Shameless*, 1994
Susan Elizabeth Phillips, *Fancy Pants*, 1989

1508

ANDREA PARNELL

My Only Desire
(New York: Zebra, 1993)

Story type: Historical/American West
Major character(s): Sunny Harlowe, Bounty Hunter, Detective; Price Ramsey, Actor, Crime Suspect
Time period(s): 1890s
Locale(s): California

Summary: Highly unconventional bounty hunter Sunny Harlowe is hired to track down Price Ramsey on suspicion of mine sabotage and worse. However, Sunny is smart enough to see that it is the mine-owner (who hired her) who has been doing all the things he is accusing Price of. Eventually, of course, Sunny finds Price and together they bring the real crook to justice.

Other books you might like:
Barbara Ankrum, *Renegade Bride*, 1992
Jill Gregory, *Cherished*, 1992
Elizabeth Lowell, *Reckless Love*, 1990
Linda Madl, *Sunny*, 1990
Alisa McBride, *Love's Bounty*, 1993
   audio tape

1509

ANDREA PARNELL

Wild Glory
(New York: Warner, 1990)

Story type: Historical/Colonial America
Major character(s): Glory Warren, Young Woman (Puritan), Witch (accused); Quade Wylde, Trapper
Time period(s): 17th century (1690s)
Locale(s): Massachusetts, American Colonies

Summary: When Glory Warren's carefree spirit gets her labeled as a witch, the only person she has to turn to is family friend, Quade Wylde. The trapper saves Glory's life and loses his heart. Romance and adventure in Puritan New England.

Other books you might like:
Nathaniel Hawthorne, *The Scarlet Letter*, 1850
   Classic Puritan tale
Hilda Lewis, *The Witch and the Priest*, 1970
   English setting/Historical characters
Nancy Moulton, *Defiant Heart*, 1989
Valerie Sherwood, *This Loving Torment*, 1977
Elizabeth Speare, *The Witch of Blackbird Pond*,
   Classic YA/More history than romance

1510

DELIA PARR

Evergreen
(New York: St. Martin's, 1995)

Story type: Historical/Victorian America

Major character(s): Moriah Lane, Convict, Abuse Victim; Royd Camden, Government Official (senator's aide), Investigator
Time period(s): 1820s (1828)
Locale(s): Pennsylvania

Summary: Unfairly sentenced to prison, Moriah Lane has two things to sustain her: Faith and the burning desire to expose a corrupt prison system. Her chance comes when Royd Camden comes to investigate the rumors of abuse, but she isn't sure she can trust him. She does, however, fall in love with him. He, in turn, is attracted to the beautiful, strong-willed Moriah, but is afraid to risk too much. Eventually, trust and truth are the only things that will bring these lovers together. A hard-hitting historical that deals with serious issues.

Other books you might like:
Catherine Anderson, *Cheyenne Amber*, 1994
   another abuse victim/good character development
Catherine Anderson, *Coming Up Roses*, 1993
   more abuse/good character development
Kathleen Eagle, *Sunrise Song*, 1996
   prison abuse/Native American elements
Laura Kinsale, *Flowers From the Storm*, 1992
   another improperly incarcerated main character/different treatment

1511

LAURA PARRISH

Love's Quiet Corner
(New York: Avalon, 1989)

Story type: Contemporary/Innocent
Major character(s): Kristen Edwards, Store Owner; Lucas Murray, Businessman (developer)
Time period(s): 1980s
Locale(s): Fairhill

Summary: Kristen and Lucas are definitely attracted to each other, but her attachment to the small town of Fairhill and his business interests almost keep them apart.

Other books you might like:
Lynn Bulock, *Roses for Caroline*, 1989
Arlene James, *Dream of a Lifetime*, 1989
Lynda Stowe Landers, *A Season to Remember*, 1989
Jan McDaniel, *This Fragile Heart*, 1989
Marcine Smith, *The Perfect Wife*, 1989

1512

VALERIE PARV

Tasmanian Devil
(Toronto: Harlequin, 1990)

Story type: Contemporary
Major character(s): Evelyn Consett, Businesswoman (Aspiring); Dane Balkan, Stock Broker
Time period(s): 1980s
Locale(s): Fiere Island, Australia

Summary: When Evelyn agrees to spend a month on an island in exchange for a job with her father's firm, she doesn't expect company—especially handsome, masculine company. But like it or not, Dane Balkan is there for the duration. Their relationship eventually becomes a romance, but it is one plagued with misunderstandings that threaten to destroy their love.

Other books you might like:
Patt Bucheister, *Once Burned, Twice as Hot*, 1990
Emma Darcy, *The Falcon's Mistress*, 1990
Vanessa Grant, *Awakening Dreams*, 1990
Debbie Macomber, *A Little Bit of Country*, 1990
    Innocent/Oregon setting
Anne McCaffrey, *Stitch-in-Snow*, 1984

1513

RACHEL COSGROVE PAYES

The Dark Towers of Trelochlen
(New York: Zebra, 1991)

Story type: Gothic
Major character(s): Tisha Hawkins, Governess; Andrew Redruth, Nobleman
Locale(s): Cornwall, England

Summary: A young, naive governess, an enigmatic, brooding Lord of the Manor, a castle on the windswept Cornish coast, and assorted murders and accidents combine in this chilling gothic written in classic first person style.

Other books you might like:
Victoria Holt, *The Shivering Sands*, 1969
Sara Hylton, *The Whispering Glade*, 1985
Lee Karr, *Dark Cries of Gray Oaks*, 1989
Mary Ellen Petty, *Lady of the Moors*, 1985
Carola Salisbury, *Dark Inheritance*, 1975

1514

PATRICIA PELLICANE

Desperado Passion
(New York: Zebra, 1991)

Story type: Historical/American West
Major character(s): Tanner Maddox, Lawman (U.S. Marshall); Elizabeth Garner, Thief (stagecoach robber), Businesswoman (boarding house owner)
Time period(s): 19th century
Locale(s): Willowbrook, Nevada

Summary: It's all very nice that Marshall Tanner Maddox is in town and is staying at the widow Garner's boarding house—except for one thing—Elizabeth Garner is the stagecoach bandit that the Marshall has come to catch! Lots of lively action in this Robin Hood tale of the Old West.

Other books you might like:
Virginia Brown, *Renegade Embrace*, 1990
Marylyle Rogers, *Hidden Hearts*, 1989
    medieval Robin Hood
Judith Steel, *Seduction's Raging Flame*, 1989
Cynthia Wright, *Brighter than Gold*, 1990

1515

PATRICIA PELLICANE

Sweet Seduction
(New York: Zebra, 1992)

Story type: Historical/Victorian
Major character(s): Meg Fairmont, Gypsy (half); Tristan Hall, Sea Captain
Time period(s): 1830s (1837)
Locale(s): England; United States; At Sea

Summary: In England for Victoria's coronation, wealthy American Meg Fairmont manages to visit her Gypsy grandmother's camp and ends up attracting, eluding, and finally being kidnapped by brash Captain Jack Howe. An adventure-filled sea voyage, a hurried marriage, a murderous stepmother, and abolitionist activities all keep this historical moving at a fast and passionate pace.

Other books you might like:
Cordia Byers, *Lady Fortune*, 1989
Johanna Lindsey, *Captive Bride*, 1977
Sheila O'Hallion, *American Princess*, 1989
Patricia Potter, *Rainbow*, 1991
Barbara Dawson Smith, *Fire on the Wind*, 1992

1516

SONYA T. PELTON

Love Hear My Heart
(New York: Zebra, 1990)

Story type: Historical/Antebellum American South
Major character(s): Cassandra St. James, Debutante, Runaway; Sylvester Diamond, Gentleman
Locale(s): Missouri

Summary: To avoid marrying one of her parents' matrimonial choices, Cassandra runs away, straight into the arms of a man she was trying to avoid. Passion, pregnancy, violence, and blackmail are part of this action-filled story set in the antebellum South.

Other books you might like:
Lonnie Coleman, *Beulah Land*, 1973
    Classic story of the Old South
Shirl Henke, *Moonflower*, 1989
Alexandra Ripley, *Charleston*, 1982
Karen Robards, *Morning Song*, 1989
Kathleen E. Woodiwiss, *Come Love a Stranger*, 1984
    Love and amnesia in the antebellum South

1517

MICHALANN PERRY

Love's Windswept Embrace
(New York: Zebra, 1990)

Story type: Historical/Victorian America
Major character(s): Aerial Windsor, Sports Figure (balloonist); Rye Berenger, Fugitive (from the law), Stowaway (in Aerial's balloon)

Time period(s): 1880s
Locale(s): Adirondack Mountains, New York
Summary: When intrepid balloonist Aerial Windsor sets out to break the existing long distance record, the last thing she expects is a stowaway on board—and the very man she had accused of murder some days earlier, at that! But Aerial will not turn back and Rye Berenger must go along for the ride. The close quarters and the long days and nights together bring about the expected results; and by the time the balloon crashes in a remote area of the Adirondacks, Rye and Aerial are in love. Adventure-filled, sensual, and great fun.

Other books you might like:
Caroline Bourne, *Allegheny Ecstasy*, 1990
Vanessa Grant, *Awakening Dreams*, 1990
    contemporary setting
Elizabeth Lambert, *Wings of Desire*, 1989
Elane Osborn, *Skylark*, 1990
Deborah Simmons, *Heart's Masquerade*, 1989

1518

CLARICE PETERS

The Absentee Earl
(Toronto: Harlequin, 1992)

Story type: Regency
Major character(s): Viola Challerton, Noblewoman; Richard, Nobleman (Earl of Avery)
Time period(s): 1810s
Locale(s): London, England

Summary: When the Earl of Avery returns to his bride after travelling for a year, he accuses her of only marrying him for his money. She counters with the rumor that he has a mistress — and the battle lines are drawn. The marriage seems doomed, but as Richard comes to know Viola better and he hears nothing but good things about her, he finds himself vying for her favor! Complex, witty, and unusual.

Other books you might like:
Anne Caldwell, *Scandal's Darling*, 1991
Leslie Lynn, *The Rake's Redemption*, 1989
Sue Rich, *Shadowed Vows*, 1992
Sheila Simonson, *A Cousinly Connexion*, 1984
Marlene Suson, *The Errant Earl*, 1989

1519

ELIZABETH PETERS (Pseudonym of Barbara Mertz)

The Snake, the Crocodile, and the Dog
(New York: Warner, 1992)

Story type: Romantic Suspense; Historical/Victorian
Series: Amelia Peabody
Major character(s): Amelia Peabody Emerson, Archaeologist; Radcliffe Emerson, Archaeologist
Time period(s): 1890s (1898)
Locale(s): Cairo, Egypt; England

Summary: When Amelia wishes dolefully that she and her husband could return to their more exciting courtship days, she has no idea that her dreams are about to come true — in nightmare form. Delightfully witty doings in Cairo revolving around an ancient Egyptian fairy tale, a strange disappearance, and amnesia. Latest in the Amelia Peabody Series.

Other books you might like:
Emily Hendrickson, *Miss Wyndham's Escapade*, 1990
    Regency
Jill Marie Landis, *Jade*, 1991
Amanda Quick, *Ravished*, 1992
Sheila Simonson, *Lady Elizabeth's Comet*, 1985
Mary Stewart, *The Gabriel Hounds*, 1967

1520

SUE PETERS

Unwilling Woman
(Toronto: Harlequin, 1989)

Story type: Contemporary/Innocent
Major character(s): Jess Donaldson, Designer (fashion); Max Beaumont, Nobleman (Earl of Blythe)
Time period(s): 1980s

Summary: When Luck leaves Max standing at the altar to elope with her true love, Jess, her best friend, is left to make things right. A contemporary version of the marriage-of-convenience plot.

Other books you might like:
Georgette Heyer, *A Civil Contract*, 1961
    Classic Regency Marriage-of-Convenience
Georgette Heyer, *The Convenient Marriage*, 1934
Lisa Jackson, *His Bride-to-Be*, 1990
Jane Shore, *The Cinderella Game*, 1990
Agnes Sligh Turnbull, *The Wedding Bargain*, 1966
    Sentimental

1521

MARY ELLEN PETTY

Lady of the Moors
(New York: Zebra, 1991)

Story type: Gothic
Major character(s): Melinda Westfall, Governess; Bart Cavendish, Gentleman
Locale(s): Cornwall, England

Summary: When Melinda Westfall goes to Trevlyn Hall to care for the young nephew of Bart Cavendish, she finds not only mystery, danger, and the answers to her own hidden past, but love and romance, as well. A lively, sensual gothic.

Other books you might like:
Dorothy Eden, *Winterwood*, 1967
Victoria Holt, *Menfreya in the Morning*, 1966
Anne Knoll, *The Stolen Bride of Glengarra Castle*, 1990
Rachel Cosgrove Payes, *The Dark Towers of Trelochlen*, 1991
Carola Salisbury, *The Winter Bride*, 1970

1522

LAURA PHILLIPS

Beginnings

(Bensalem, Pennsylvania: Meteor, 1992)

Story type: Contemporary
Major character(s): Abby Monroe, Animal Trainer (of dolphins); Matt Gardner, Troubleshooter
Time period(s): 1990s
Locale(s): United States

Summary: Matt Gardner is hired to investigate a troubled amusement park and ends up falling in love with Abby Monroe, the charming dolphin trainer.

Other books you might like:
Lori Copeland, *Darling Deceiver*, 1990
Wendy Martin, *Love on Trial*, 1990
    innocent
Carolyn Monroe, *Kiss of Bliss*, 1992
Miriam Pace, *Warm Creature Comforts*, 1991
    innocent

1523

LAURA PHILLIPS

Moon Showers

(Bensalem, Pennsylvania: Meteor, 1992)

Story type: Contemporary
Major character(s): Hillary Neill, Accountant, Heiress; Sam Langford, Professor
Time period(s): 1990s
Locale(s): Missouri

Summary: Hillary Neill and Sam Langford have a less than gentle meeting in her inherited historic mansion. A businesswoman from Chicago, she has come to Missouri to decide how to dispose of the house, but the more time she spends there, the more she comes to love the house—and neighbor Sam—in spite of the fact that she is haunted by his dead wife. Happy and witty.

Other books you might like:
Sandra Brown, *Texas! Sage*, 1991
Debbie Macomber, *First Comes Marriage*, 1991
Patricia Simpson, *Whisper of Midnight*, 1991
Sandra Steffen, *Hold Back the Night*, 1992
Judith Yoder, *A Matter of Compromise*, 1992

1524

LAURA PHILLIPS

To Love a Cowboy

(New York: Kismet, 1992)

Story type: Contemporary
Major character(s): Dee Williams, Photographer (children's book illustrator); Nick Ramsey, Cowboy (rodeo clown)
Time period(s): 1990s
Locale(s): United States

Summary: Dee Williams is shocked to find her childhood adversary and step-brother is one of the rodeo clowns she is photographing to illustrate a children's book. It has been years since she had admired and been rebuffed by Nick, and when their parents divorced, they hated each other. But the years have changed them both, and, surprisingly, their deep animosity gradually turns to love.

Other books you might like:
Judy Gill, *Golden Swan*, 1990
Tracy Hughes, *White Lies and Alibis*, 1990
Elizabeth Quinn, *Any Day Now*, 1989
Fayrene Preston, *Magnificent Affair*, 1992

1525

PATRICIA PHILLIPS

The Constant Flame

(New York: Leisure, 1993)

Story type: Historical/Medieval
Major character(s): Jessamyn Dacre, Noblewoman (Lady of the Castle); Rhys Trevaron, Nobleman
Time period(s): 15th century (1401)
Locale(s): Wales; England

Summary: Jessamyn, lady of the castle, manages the estate for her crippled brother. However, her life takes a romantic turn with the arrival of Lord Rhys, who seduces Jess and then leaves without explanation. Another woman, politics, and personal problems all must be dealt with before Jess and Rhys are free to find happiness with each other.

Other books you might like:
Rexanne Becnel, *Where Magic Dwells*, 1994
Roberta Gellis, *Roselynde*, 1984
    1st of the six Roselynde Chronicles
Jennifer Horsman, *Awaken My Fire*, 1992
Flora M. Speer, *Castle of the Heart*, 1990

1526

SUSAN ELIZABETH PHILLIPS

Fancy Pants

(New York: Pocket, 1989)

Story type: Contemporary/Mainstream
Major character(s): Francesca Day, Socialite (British); Dallie Beaudine, Sports Figure (Professional golfer)
Time period(s): 20th century (last half)
Locale(s): London, England; New York, New York; Texas

Summary: Used to wealth and privilege, Francesca Day has a hard time adjusting to being in America—and broke. Dallie Beaudine rescues her but has little patience for her spoiled-brat attitude. They both have a lot to learn (and do) before they finally can be happy together.

Other books you might like:
Janet Dailey, *The Glory Game*, 1989
Janet Dailey, *Heiress*, 1987
Judith Michael, *Possessions*, 1984
Danielle Steel, *Palomino*, 1981
Danielle Steel, *Passion's Promise*, 1976

1527

SUSAN ELIZABETH PHILLIPS

Heaven, Texas

(New York: Avon, 1995)

Story type: Contemporary
Major character(s): Gracie Snow, Filmmaker (film production assistant); Bobby Tom Denton, Sports Figure (ex-football player)
Time period(s): 1990s
Locale(s): Texas

Summary: When outwardly dowdy, but inwardly adventurous Gracie Snow is given the responsibility of seeing that ex-football star Bobby Tom Denton shows up at a film shoot on schedule, she takes her job seriously—and ends up on the road to Texas with the charming, obstinate, but incredibly appealing, Bobby Tom, himself. Funny, fast-paced, and filled with likable characters. Spin-off of *It Had to Be You.*

Other books you might like:
Barbara Bretton, *Maybe This Time*, 1994
Barbara Bretton, *One and Only*, 1994
Joan Hohl, *Compromises*, 1995
Jayne Ann Krentz, *Absolutely, Positively*, 1996
Jayne Ann Krentz, *Wildest Hearts*, 1993

1528

SUSAN ELIZABETH PHILLIPS

Hot Shot

(New York: Pocket, 1991)

Story type: Contemporary/Mainstream
Major character(s): Susannah Faulconer, Businesswoman (computer), Computer Expert; Sam Gamble, Computer Expert, Businessman (computer)
Time period(s): 1970s; 1980s
Locale(s): California

Summary: Susannah Faulconer, privileged daughter of a computer mogul, abandons her heritage (and fiance) and sets out with computer genius Sam Gamble to develop a practical home computer. Fast-paced, passionate account of the beginning of the personal computer industry in California.

Other books you might like:
Barbara Taylor Bradford, *A Woman of Substance*, 1979
Barbara Delinsky, *Facets*, 1990
Georgia Hampton, *Desire*, 1989
Terri Herrington, *Her Father's Daughter*, 1991
Sara Orwig, *Favors of the Rich*, 1991
    Texas oil industry

1529

SUSAN ELIZABETH PHILLIPS

It Had to Be You

(New York: Avon, 1994)

Story type: Contemporary

Major character(s): Phoebe Somerville, Sports Figure (football team owner), Heiress; Dan Calebrow, Coach (of a football team)
Time period(s): 1990s
Locale(s): Chicago, Illinois

Summary: When the rather notorious Phoebe Somerville inherits her father's professional football team, it is on the condition that the team win this year's conference championship; otherwise, ownership reverts to Phoebe's slimy cousin. The chances of winning are slim, and in the beginning Phoebe doesn't care; but when she realizes what winning and losing would mean for the people involved, she sets about proving that she is neither the failure nor the bimbo people had always thought her to be. A dynamic and sexy hero (Dan Calebrow) and some delightful secondary characters add to this funny, fast-paced story that considers some rather serious issues.

Other books you might like:
Barbara Bretton, *One and Only*, 1994
Sandra Brown, *Texas! Sage*, 1990
Janet Dailey, *Heiress*, 1987
Jayne Ann Krentz, *Perfect Partners*, 1993
Jayne Ann Krentz, *Wildest Hearts*, 1993

1530

PHYLLIS TAYLOR PIANKA

The Thackery Jewels

(Toronto: Harlequin, 1994)

Story type: Regency
Major character(s): Amethyst Thackery, Debutante; Emerald Thackery, Debutante; Topaz Thackery, Debutante
Time period(s): 1810s
Locale(s): London, England

Summary: Collectively known as "The Thackery Jewels," debutantes Amethyst, Emerald, and Topaz take the ton by storm and lead their guardian, Lady Udora, a merry chase as she sets about finding eligible husbands for them. But securing appropriate men for the hopelessly tenderhearted Amethyst, the intelligent and serious Emerald, and the daring and impulsive Topaz—all in a few short weeks—is not easy. Nevertheless, with a bit of luck—and the help of some delightful secondary characters, all three "jewels" are suitably "set" by the final page. Essentially a trilogy in a single volume. Light, traditional, and nicely descriptive of the period.

Other books you might like:
Clare Darcy, *Victoire*, 1974
Georgette Heyer, *Frederica*, 1965
Elizabeth Jackson, *A Brilliant Alliance*, 1993
Barbara Metzger, *An Affair of Interest*, 1992
Melinda Pryce, *The Last Lord*, 1993

1531

JOAN ELLIOTT PICKART

The Bonnie Blue

(New York: Doubleday, 1990)

Story type: Historical/American West
Major character(s): Becca Colton, Rancher; Mattie Muldoon, Businesswoman (bordello owner); Slade Ironbow, Gunfighter, Indian (half Apache)
Time period(s): 19th century
Locale(s): Dodge City, Kansas; Texas

Summary: When bordello owner Mattie Muldoon learns that her long lost daughter, Becca Colton, needs help to save her recently inherited Texas ranch, she turns to longtime friend, gunslinger Slade Ironbow for help. Slade rides to Becca's rescue and, in the process, loses his heart to the fiesty heiress. At the same time Mattie is developing "heart problems" of her own. An action-filled romance with the extra bonus of a nicely done secondary love story.

Other books you might like:
Constance Bennett, *Morning Sky*, 1991
Martha Hix, *Wild Texas Rose*, 1990
Kat Martin, *Lover's Gold*, 1991
Lass Small, *A Nothing Town in Texas*, 1991
Janelle Taylor, *Follow the Wind*, 1990

1532

JOAN ELLIOTT PICKART

Mixed Signals

(New York: Bantam, 1990)

Story type: Contemporary
Major character(s): Katha Logan, Businesswoman (computer typing service); Vince Santini, Police Officer (former)
Time period(s): 1980s
Locale(s): Los Angeles, California

Summary: Katha flamboyantly rescues Vince from a horde of reporters and then presents him with a problem she can't solve—someone is planning to steal this month's welfare checks by using a computer virus to alter the addresses and she wants to stop it. Katha and Vince solve the mystery and fall in love at the same time.

Other books you might like:
Linda Cajio, *Desperate Measures*, 1989
Deborah Smith, *Legends*, 1990
Linda Turner, *An Unsuspecting Heart*, 1989
Mary Anne Wilson, *Straight From the Heart*, 1989

1533

JEAN PLAIDY (Pseudonym of Eleanor Hibbert)

The Pleasure of Love

(New York: Putnam, 1992)

Story type: Historical/Mainstream; Historical/Seventeenth Century
Series: Queens of England

Major character(s): Catherine of Braganza, Royalty (queen), Historical Figure; Charles II, Royalty (king), Historical Figure; Barbara Palmer, Lover (of the king), Historical Figure
Time period(s): 17th century
Locale(s): England; Portugal

Summary: This is a fictionalized account of the relationship between Charles II of England and his wife, Catherine of Braganza. Interesting picture of Restoration England, the Court in particular.

Other books you might like:
Taylor Caldwell, *The Arm of Darkness*, 1943
Philippa Carr, *Lament for a Lost Lover*, same author/different pseudonym
Robyn Carr, *Chelynne*, 1980
Margaret Irwin, *The Stranger Prince*, 1937
JoAnn Wendt, *The Golden Dove*, 1989

1534

MARGARET EVANS PORTER

Dangerous Diversions

(New York: Signet, 1994)

Story type: Regency
Major character(s): Rosalie de Barante, Dancer (opera); Gervaise Marchant, Nobleman (Duke of Soliway)
Time period(s): 1810s
Locale(s): London, England

Summary: Opera dancer Rosalie de Barante isn't at all interested in becoming a mistress. Her career will always come first; something that is difficult for would-be suitors to understand. And then Gervaise Marchant saves her from being accosted by one of her "suitors," and he realises she is quite uncommon—and he is intrigued. Although an unlikely couple, they do seem to complement each other, and a happy romance develops.

Other books you might like:
Mary Balogh, *Christmas Belle*, 1994
theatrical heroine
Clare Darcy, *Caroline and Julia*, 1982
more theatrics
Marian Devon, *Lord Harlequin*, 1994
theatrical emphasis
Georgette Heyer, *Faro's Daughter*, 1941
Carla Kelly, *Miss Billings Treads the Boards*, 1993
heroine tries her hand at acting

1535

MARGARET EVANS PORTER

Road to Ruin

(New York: Signet, 1992)

Story type: Regency
Major character(s): Nerissa Newby, Spinster; Dominic Blythe, Nobleman
Time period(s): 1810s
Locale(s): England

Summary: Dominic is fleeing Bow Street Runners; Nerissa is escaping the ton gossips. When they find themselves in a coach together, their quick wits and a compromising situation provide a solution to both their problems—a marriage of convenience! An interesting story based on an old theme. The characterizations are superb.

Other books you might like:
Jo Beverley, *An Unwilling Bride*, 1992
Carla Kelly, *Libby's London Merchant*, 1991
Meg-Lynn Roberts, *An Alluring Lady*, 1992
Mary Linn Roby, *My Lady's Mask*, 1979
Patricia Veryan, *Logic of the Heart*, 1991

1536

PATRICIA POTTER

The Abduction
(Toronto: Harlequin, 1991)

Story type: Historical/Renaissance
Major character(s): Elsbeth Ker, Laird (Scottish chieftain); Alex Carey, Nobleman (English lord)
Time period(s): 16th century (1550s)
Locale(s): Borderlands, England; Borderlands, Scotland

Summary: When Scottish Laird Elsbeth Ker kidnaps English Lord Alex Carey in keeping with their long standing feud, they discover they would rather make love (and peace) than war—but traitors on both sides have other ideas. Fast-paced action and well-developed characters fill this gentle, passionate love story that is strongly evocative of the period.

Other books you might like:
Rebecca Brandewyne, *No Gentle Love*, 1989
Sandra DuBay, *Nightrider*, 1991
Catherine Linden, *Highland Flame*, 1991
Johanna Lindsey, *A Gentle Feuding*, 1984
Elizabeth Stuart, *Where Love Dwells*, 1990
    Medieval setting

1537

PATRICIA POTTER

Defiant
(New York: Bantam, 1995)

Story type: Historical/American West
Major character(s): Mary Jo Williams, Widow(er), Rancher; Wade Foster, Fugitive, Foreman (ranch)
Time period(s): 1870s (1876-1877)
Locale(s): El Paso, Texas; Cimarron Valley, Colorado

Summary: Having lost a husband and fiance, both Texas Rangers, to violence, Mary Jo Williams takes her young son and heads for the ranch she has inherited in Colorado to start a new life. But she needs help—and it comes in the form of a half-dead drifter, a man who, like Mary Jo, has past wounds that only time and love can heal. Warm, emotional, sensual, and gritty. A classic wounded hero story.

Other books you might like:
Rosanne Bittner, *Chase the Sun*, 1996
    emotionally wounded hero

Dorothy Garlock, *Sins of Summer*, 1994
Robin Lee Hatcher, *Liberty Blue*, 1995
    gentler
Maggie Osborne, *The Brides of Bowie Stone*, 1994
Maggie Osborne, *The Seduction of Samantha Kincade*, 1995

1538

PATRICIA POTTER

Dragonfire
(Toronto: Harlequin, 1990)

Story type: Historical/Victorian
Major character(s): Hope Townsend, Hotel Owner (British); Travis Farrell, Military Personnel (American marine major)
Time period(s): 1900s (1901 during Boxer Rebellion)
Locale(s): Peking, China

Summary: When Hope Townsend is rescued by American Major Travis Farrell during one of her attempts to save the missionaries during the Boxer Rebellion, the sparks fly from the start. He thinks she's a naive idealist; she thinks he just doesn't understand. Fate, however, lends a hand—and trapped together during the siege of the embassy, Hope and Travis resolve not only their political conflicts but their personal ones as well. Passion, action, and good historical detail.

Other books you might like:
Shirl Henke, *Night Flower*, 1990
Maura Seger, *Fortune's Tide*, 1990
Terri Valentine, *Master of Her Heart*, 1990

1539

PATRICIA POTTER

Island of Dreams
(New York: Harper Collins, 1991)

Story type: Romantic Suspense
Major character(s): Meara O'Hara, Journalist, Governess; David Michael Fielding, Spy
Time period(s): 20th century
Locale(s): Georgia

Summary: An ill-fated love affair has repercussions twenty years later in this story of passion, revenge, and enduring love.

Other books you might like:
Evelyn Anthony, *The Scarlet Thread*, 1990
Jennifer Blake, *Love and Smoke*, 1989
Janet Dailey, *Heiress*, 1987
Rebecca Forster, *A Delicate Matter*, 1989

1540

PATRICIA POTTER

Lawless
(New York: Doubleday, 1991)

Story type: Historical/American West

Major character(s): Willow Taylor, Teacher, Spinster; Lobo "Jess", Gunfighter
Time period(s): 19th century
Locale(s): West

Summary: When the infamous gunfighter, Lobo, hires on as "Jess" at Willow Taylor's ranch, he ends up not only saving her and her adopted children from danger, but he falls in love with her in the process. Tender and heartwarming.

Other books you might like:
Norah Hess, *Hawke's Pride*, 1991
Jill Marie Landis, *Rose*, 1990
Catherine Lanigan, *A Promise Made*, 1991
Pamela Litton, *Stardust and Whirlwinds*, 1991
Victoria Pade, *The Doubletree*, 1990

1541

PATRICIA POTTER

Lightning

(New York: Bantam, 1992)

Story type: Historical/American Civil War
Major character(s): Lauren Bradley, Twin, Spy (for Union Army); Adrian Talbot, Sea Captain, Smuggler (blockade runner for the South)
Time period(s): 1860s
Locale(s): Nassau, Bahamas; England; At Sea

Summary: Determined to avenge her twin brother's death, Lauren Bradley becomes a Union spy and goes to Nassau to sabotage the efforts of the man she considers responsible, blockade runner Captain Adrian Talbot. However, love complicates her efforts as she discovers the bitter side of revenge and learns that things are rarely so simple as they seem. Filled with action, adventure, and interesting characters.

Other books you might like:
Micki Brown, *Once a Rebel*, 1992
Heather Graham, *One Wore Blue*, 1991
Elizabeth Kary, *Let No Man Divide*, 1987
Katherine Kincaid, *Stormswept*, 1991
Lois Wolfe, *The Schemers*, 1991

1542

PATRICIA POTTER

Notorious

(New York: Bantam, 1993)

Story type: Historical/American West Coast
Major character(s): Catalina Hillard, Saloon Keeper/Owner; Marsh Canton, Saloon Keeper/Owner, Gunfighter (former)
Time period(s): 1850s
Locale(s): San Francisco, California

Summary: Rival saloon owner Catalina wants Marsh's saloon closed, but neither wit, manipulation, nor sex can persuade him. Her escapades bring them closer, however, and when they join together to fight outside forces, their own rivalry begins to take a backseat. Poignant and hard-hitting.

Other books you might like:
Jill Barnett, *Surrender a Dream*, 1991
   funny and fast-paced
Marsha Bauer, *Sweet Conquest*, 1990
Gwen Bristow, *Calico Palace*, 1970
Christina Dodd, *Treasure of the Sun*, 1991
   early California setting
Samantha James, *Outlaw Heart*, 1993

1543

PATRICIA POTTER

Rainbow

(New York: Bantam, 1991)

Story type: Historical/Antebellum American South
Major character(s): Meredith Seaton, Southern Belle, Heiress; Quinn Devereaux, Shipowner (riverboat owner), Gambler
Time period(s): 1850s
Locale(s): Mississippi River; Vicksburg, Mississippi; Louisiana

Summary: When her best friend and half-sister, Lissa, is sold away from her Mississippi plantation, young Meredith Seaton vows to find and set her free. Her quest becomes a passion—and as she secretly works to free the slaves, she attracts the attention of riverboat renegade Quinn Devereaux, who is also an undercover abolitionist. Especially well-done characterizations highlight this romantic adventure.

Other books you might like:
Wendy Garrett, *Sweet Southern Caress*, 1991
Patricia Hagan, *Midnight Rose*, 1991
Katherine Kincaid, *Stormswept*, 1991
Kat Martin, *The Captain's Bride*, 1990

1544

PATRICIA POTTER

Renegade

(New York: Doubleday, 1993)

Story type: Historical/American Civil War; Historical/American West
Major character(s): Susannah Fallon, Widow(er), Rancher; Rhys Redding, Prisoner, Blockade Runner
Time period(s): 1860s (1865)
Locale(s): Richmond, Virginia; Texas

Summary: Wounded and imprisoned in a Virginia jail, blockade runner Rhys Redding is intrigued by gentle, yet determined, Susannah Fallon, the sister of a fellow prisoner. Eventually, he helps her take her crippled brother, Carr, back to his Texas ranch. However, they arrive to find Carr's house destroyed and Susannah's ranch in danger from the notorious Martin brothers. Naturally, Rhys proves to be their salvation—and Susannah ends up being his. Passionate and heartwarming.

Other books you might like:
Heather Graham, *And One Rode West*, 1992
Martha Hix, *Wild Texas Rose*, 1990
Linda Howard, *A Lady of the West*, 1991

Patricia Rice, *Cheyenne's Lady*, 1989

1545

PATRICIA POTTER

The Silver Link

(Toronto: Harlequin, 1991)

Story type: Historical/American West
Series: Hampton Family
Major character(s): Antonia Ramirez, Rancher; Tristan Hampton, Military Personnel (army), Scout
Time period(s): 1840s (1846)
Locale(s): New Mexico

Summary: When army scout Tristan Hampton saves Antonia Ramirez from being raped by her own fiance, Ramon, Tris earns the gratitude (and love) of Antonia and the undying hatred of Ramon. Tristan and Antonia must fight for their love as they are driven apart by family, church, and treachery. Concludes the Hampton family series begun by *Swamp Fire* and *Samara*.

Other books you might like:
Elaine Barbieri, *Wings of a Dove*, 1990
Elaine Barbieri, *Wishes on the Wind*, 1991
Alison Irving, *No Greater Love*, 1991
Linda Ladd, *Midnight Fire*, 1991
Christine Monson, *This Fiery Splendor*, 1991

1546

CYNTHIA POWELL

The Bear Affair

(New York: Avalon, 1993)

Story type: Contemporary/Innocent
Major character(s): Taylor Berne, Manager (of hospital gift shop); Kayne Frost, Doctor
Time period(s): 1990s
Locale(s): United States

Summary: When hospital gift shop manager Taylor Berne and her teddy bears run afoul of the dashing, but icy, Dr. Kayne Frost, the scene is set for a clash of wills that will only be resolved by love. Light, innocent, and funny.

Other books you might like:
Jillian Dagg, *Sungold*, 1992
Debbie Macomber, *Rainy Day Kisses*, 1990
Karen Morrell, *For the Love of Laura*, 1992
Laura Parrish, *Love's Quiet Corner*, 1989

1547

JO-ANN POWER

Angel of Midnight

(New York: Pocket, 1995)

Story type: Historical/Medieval
Major character(s): Lady Angelica ''Angel'' Carlisle, Widow(er), Noblewoman; Nicholas St. Clair, Outlaw (Devil of Midnight)

Time period(s): 13th century (1215)
Locale(s): Yorkshire, England

Summary: Fearing for her fortune and her life, Lady Angelica decides to wed a man who can keep her safe and so she makes a bargain with the infamous outlaw, The Devil of Midnight—his freedom for marriage to her. A passionate, sensual story of Medieval England, complete with all the political intrigue and color of the times.

Other books you might like:
Katherine Deauville, *Blood Red Roses*, 1991
Shannon Drake, *Knight of Fire*, 1993
Shannon Drake, *Princess of Fire*, 1989
Caryl Wilson, *Firebrand's Bride*, 1992

1548

HEATHER GRAHAM POZZESSERE

An Angel's Touch

(New York: Kensington, 1995)

Story type: Contemporary/Fantasy; Holiday Themes
Major character(s): Cathy Angel, Angel (would-be); Don Angel, Angel (would-be)
Time period(s): 1990s
Locale(s): New York, New York

Summary: Killed in a train accident on Christmas Eve, Don and Cathy Angel end up in the presence of a yuppie Archangel Gabriel and are given the task of performing six miracles before Christmas Day to become angels themselves. All goes as predicted, but the ending is not quite the expected one.

Other books you might like:
Debra Dier, *Christmas Angels*, 1995
anthology
Virginia Henley, *A Gift of Joy*, 1995
anthology/no fantasy elements
Muriel Jensen, *Merry Christmas, Mommy*, 1995
no fantasy elements
Debbie Macomber, *Touched by Angels*, 1995
Emma Richmond, *Christmas Journeys*, 1995
anthology

1549

HEATHER GRAHAM POZZESSERE

Eyes of Fire

(Toronto: Mira, 1995)

Story type: Contemporary; Romantic Suspense
Major character(s): Samantha Carlyle, Businesswoman (island resort owner); Adam O'Connor, Investigator, Diver
Time period(s): 1990s
Locale(s): Seafire Isle, Caribbean

Summary: When a former lover suddenly registers as a guest at her Caribbean island resort, Samantha is shocked, furious, and curious. But when he saves her from being attacked in her bathtub by an intruder and he thinks her life is in danger, they reassess the situation and begin to work together to solve the mystery. Sunken treasure, greed, and murder are part of this fast-paced, suspenseful, and sexy story.

Other books you might like:
Jill Barkin, *Hot Streak*, 1990
Jennifer Blake, *Shameless*, 1994
Jayne Ann Krentz, *Sweet Fortune*, 1991
Ann Maxwell, *The Diamond Tiger*, 1992
Tracey Tillis, *Deadly Masquerade*, 1994

1550

HEATHER GRAHAM POZZESSERE

Forbidden Fire

(Toronto: Harlequin, 1991)

Story type: Historical/Victorian
Major character(s): Marissa Ayers, Imposter; Ian Tremayne, Hero
Time period(s): 1900s (1906); 1980s
Locale(s): Yorkshire, England; San Francisco, California

Summary: When Yorkshire-bred Marissa marries American Ian Tremayne so her friend and employer can receive her inheritance and marry the man of her choice, Marissa embarks on a journey that will take all the strength and determination she possesses to complete. Passion, long-kept secrets, and earthquakes combine in this sensual story of love and deception.

Other books you might like:
Leigh Bristol, *Sunswept*, 1990
Gwen Cleary, *Ecstasy's Masquerade*, 1989
Dorothy Eden, *The American Heiress*, 1980
Richard Peck, *Amanda/Miranda*, 1981

1551

HEATHER GRAHAM POZZESSERE

Slow Burn

(Don Mills, Ontario: Mira, 1994)

Story type: Contemporary; Romantic Suspense
Major character(s): Spencer Huntington, Businesswoman (restorer of historic buildings); David Delgado, Detective—Private
Time period(s): 1990s
Locale(s): Miami, Florida

Summary: When Spencer Huntington returns to Miami to discover the truth behind her husband's murder, she ends up joining forces with an old flame, police-officer-turned-private-detective David Delgado, and almost ends up getting them both killed in the process. A fast paced tale with surprising twists and some highly memorable scenes (e.g. the graveyard episode).

Other books you might like:
Jill Barkin, *Hot Streak*, 1990
Tami Hoag, *Still Waters*, 1992
Susan Kyle, *Night Fever*, 1990
Tracey Tillis, *Deadly Masquerade*, 1994
Sherryl Woods, *Hide and Seek*, 1994

1552

FAYRENE PRESTON

The Destiny

(New York: Doubleday, 1991)

Story type: Historical/Roaring Twenties
Major character(s): Arabella Linden, Socialite; Jake Deverell, Bastard Son, Businessman
Time period(s): 1920s (1928-1929)
Locale(s): Boston, Massachusetts

Summary: Reluctantly acknowledged and claimed as heir by Edward Deverell, his proud natural father, Jake Deverell enters a world of wealth and power he has previously only seen from afar. The tensions between father and son lead to some disastrous situations, but fate and love, in the form of beautiful Arabella Linden, intervene and things do work out in the end. Bootleggers, the mob, wild parties, and other accoutrements of the Twenties abound in this nicely detailed, fast-paced historical. Prequel to the SwanSea trilogy.

Other books you might like:
Leona Blair, *A World of Difference*, 1989
Sandra Bregman, *Reach for the Dream*, 1990
Diane Cory, *High Society*, 1990
Rebecca Flanders, *The Sensation*, 1990
Susan Howatch, *The Rich Are Different*, 1977

1553

FAYRENE PRESTON

Magnificent Affair

(New York: Bantam, 1992)

Story type: Contemporary
Major character(s): Ashley Whitfield, Fiance(e) (reluctant), Runaway; Max, Innkeeper
Time period(s): 1990s
Locale(s): California

Summary: Fleeing from an impending wedding, Ashley runs her Mercedes into the front porch of Max's peaceful inn. An unlikely romance develops between them in spite of her mother, her fiance's mother, and a mad assortment of wedding planners that descend upon them.

Other books you might like:
Mary Balogh, *The Snow Angel*, 1991
Sandra Chastain, *Penthouse Suite*, 1990
Judy Gill, *Golden Swan*, 1990
Amanda Quick, *Surrender*, 1990
historical

1554

ASHLAND PRICE

Viking Rose

(New York: Zebra, 1993)

Story type: Historical/Medieval
Major character(s): Alanna, Maiden (Irish); Storr, Scout (Viking)

Time period(s): 9th century (815)
Locale(s): Ireland (Erin)

Summary: Sent to survey the Irish countryside with the intent of capturing it, Viking scout Storr is surprised by the Irish Alanna as he bathes nude. Obligingly, he captures her and being uncommonly gentle, he treats her well. He does, however, still plunder the land. Eventually, they fall in love, but problems arise when Storr's relatives want him overthrown. Alanna to the rescue. Good cultural information in an unusually non-violent Viking tale.

Other books you might like:
Julie Garwood, *The Bride*, 1989
Heather Graham, *The Viking's Woman*, 1990
Mary Ellen Gronau, *Gentle Conqueror*, 1989
Marylyle Rogers, *Chanting the Dawn*, 1991
Marylyle Rogers, *The Eagle's Song*, 1992

1555

ASHLAND PRICE

Wild Irish Heather

(New York: Zebra, 1991)

Story type: Historical
Major character(s): Heather Monaghan, Fiance(e), Heiress; Sean Kerry, Kidnapper
Time period(s): 1700s (1707)
Locale(s): Ireland

Summary: Although engaged to another, beautiful heiress Heather Monaghan is attracted to dashing Sean Kerry, a rather interesting hero who abducts heiresses for prospective husbands. He fully intends to reform; but when circumstances keep interfering and he is forced to kidnap Heather, there seems to be little hope for their relationship. Funny, lively, and peopled with delightfully different characters.

Other books you might like:
Julie Garwood, *The Bride*, 1989
Virginia Henley, *The Pirate and the Pagan*, 1990
    Lustier and more violent than some
Laura Kinsale, *The Prince of Midnight*, 1990
Johanna Lindsey, *Defy Not the Heart*, 1989
Julie Tetel, *And Heaven Too*, 1990

1556

CAROL PROCTOR

Unlikely Guardian

(New York: Signet, 1990)

Story type: Regency
Major character(s): Philippa Raithby, Debutante, Equestrian; Evelyn Lovelace, Nobleman (Earl of Sinamor), Guardian (Rake)
Time period(s): 1810s
Locale(s): England

Summary: An altogether shocking choice as the guardian of a young girl, the Earl of Sinamor becomes intrigued with his young ward, Philippa, who prefers horses to men—including him! Pure Regency fun.

Other books you might like:
Clare Darcy, *Georgina*, 1971
Georgette Heyer, *Sylvester, or the Wicked Uncle*, 1957
Dawn Lindsey, *Dunraven's Folly*, 1989
Gladys McGorian, *The Prince Regent's Silver Bell*, 1987
Marlene Suson, *The Rake's Redemption*, 1989

1557

MELINDA PRYCE

The Last Lord

(New York: Diamond, 1993)

Story type: Regency
Major character(s): Susan Devane, Debutante; Patricia Devane, Debutante; Galen Sedgwick, Nobleman
Time period(s): 1810s
Locale(s): England

Summary: When Susan and Patricia Devane are informed that they must marry lords in order to inherit, Susan is appalled! She will marry only for love! On the other hand, Patricia loves the game. The problems arise when Lord Galen Sedgwick takes a serious liking to Susan, and then Patricia tells him that they are only out to marry well. Susan tries her best to convince him, but Patricia ends up sabatoging all her efforts. Unusual and interesting.

Other books you might like:
Mary Chase Comstock, *An Impetuous Miss*, 1993
Teresa DesJardien, *The Marriage Mart*, 1992
Carola Dunn, *Two Corinthians*, 1989
Elizabeth Jackson, *A Brilliant Alliance*, 1993
Joan Overfield, *The Viscount's Vixen*, 1992

1558

MARY JO PUTNEY

Dearly Beloved

(New York: Onyx Books, 1990)

Story type: Historical/Georgian
Major character(s): Diana Lindsay, Prostitute (courtesan); Gervase Brandelin, Nobleman
Time period(s): 18th century
Locale(s): London, England

Summary: Although Diana goes to London to become a courtesan, she wants more. She wants love, and she finds it in the arms of Gervase Brandelin. This historical deals realistically with a number of taboo topics often ignored in romance fiction.

Other books you might like:
Deborah Camp, *Fallen Angel*, 1989
    American West setting
Brian Cleeve, *Sara*, 1976
    Realistic Regency
Edith Layton, *Fireflower*, 1989
    Earlier period
Amanda Quick, *Seduction*, 1990
Patricia Rice, *Love Forever After*, 1990

1559

MARY JO PUTNEY

Petals in the Storm

(New York: Topaz, 1993)

Story type: Historical/Regency
Series: Fallen Angels
Major character(s): Magda Janos, Noblewoman (countess), Spy; Rafe Whitbourne, Rake, Spy
Time period(s): 1810s (1815)
Locale(s): Paris, France

Summary: Magda, spying to help Britain after the Napoleonic Wars, becomes partners with Rafe Whitbourne, the man she was once engaged to marry. Although they have a lot to straighten out, they cannot deny their feelings for each other, and as they get on with their spying, they renew their love, tackle new and old mysteries, and take Paris by storm. Evil, tension, and passion abound in this expansion of Putney's earlier Regency, *The Controversial Countess*.

Other books you might like:
Mary Balogh, *Beyond the Sunrise*, 1992
Shirl Henke, *Paradise and More*, 1992
Lindsay McKenna, *King of Swords*, 1992
Christina Skye, *The Black Rose*, 1991

1560

MARY JO PUTNEY

The Rake and the Reformer

(New York: Pocket, 1989)

Story type: Regency
Major character(s): Alys "A.E." Weston, Noblewoman, Steward; Richard "Reggie" Davenport, Landowner, Rake
Time period(s): 1810s (Regency period)
Locale(s): England (Strickland Estate)

Summary: Rake and reprobate, Reggie Davenport decides to reform when he learns he is now the owner of Strickland, his childhood home. Shocked to discover that his steward is a woman, once he meets the capable and lovely Lady Alys, he decides there might be more to her than meets the eye—and he is right. More sensual than most Regencies.

Other books you might like:
Brian Cleeve, *Sara*, 1976
    A more serious Regency
Clare Darcy, *Georgina*, 1971
Georgette Heyer, *Black Sheep*, 1966
Georgette Heyer, *Venetia*, 1958
Sheila Simonson, *The Bar Sinister*, 1986

1561

MARY JO PUTNEY

Silk and Secrets

(New York: Onyx, 1992)

Story type: Historical/Exotic; Historical/Victorian
Series: Silk Trilogy

Major character(s): Juliet Carlisle, Runaway, Warrior; Lord Ross Carlisle, Nobleman, Adventurer
Time period(s): 1840s (1841-1842)
Locale(s): Middle East; Asia

Summary: Lord Ross Carlisle has travelled far and wide searching for adventure since his young wife left him twelve years ago. Now his mother-in-law convinces him to go to Asia and the forbidden country of Bokhara to search for his wife's brother. Once there, he discovers that his long-lost wife has become a warrior and is leader of a group of friendly natives. They join forces to find her brother and, in the process, forge a new and lasting relationship for the future.

Other books you might like:
Olga Bicos, *White Tiger*, 1991
Jessica Bryan, *Across a Wine-Dark Sea*, 1991
    fantasy elements
Kristin Hannah, *The Enchantment*, 1992
Laura Kinsale, *Seize the Fire*, 1989
Bertrice Small, *Lost Love Found*, 1992

1562

MARY JO PUTNEY

Silk and Shadows

(New York: New American Library, 1991)

Story type: Historical/Victorian
Series: Silk Trilogy
Major character(s): Sara St. James, Noblewoman; Mikahl Khanauri, Royalty (Prince Peregrine of Kafirstan)
Time period(s): 1830s (1839)
Locale(s): London, England

Summary: When devastatingly attractive Mikahl Khanauri comes to England, it is for one purpose only—to avenge himself on the man who nearly destroyed him as a child. However, when he falls in love with Lady Sara St. James, one of the key weapons in his plan, things become truly complicated. Exotic, warm, and highly romantic.

Other books you might like:
Laura Kinsale, *The Shadow and the Star*, 1991
Rebecca Paisley, *Diamonds and Dreams*, 1991
Amanda Quick, *Rendezvous*, 1992
Amanda Quick, *Scandal*, 1991

1563

MARY JO PUTNEY

Thunder and Roses

(New York: Topaz, 1993)

Story type: Historical/Regency
Series: Fallen Angels
Major character(s): Clare Morgan, Teacher, Spinster; Nicholas Davies, Nobleman ("The Demon Earl"), Gypsy
Time period(s): 1810s
Locale(s): Wales

Summary: In order to save her beloved village from financial ruin, straight-laced Clare Morgan agrees to live (in name only) with the infamous "Demon Earl" for three months—

and finds herself falling in love with the very man she is determined to resist. A passionate, well-constructed story that explores the darker side of Regency life and the transcendent power of love.

Other books you might like:
Kathleen Harrington, *Sunshine and Shadow*, 1993
Laura Kinsale, *Flowers From the Storm*, 1992
Laura Kinsale, *The Prince of Midnight*, 1991
Amanda Quick, *Rendezvous*, 1992
Anne Stuart, *Shadow Dance*, 1993

1564
MARY JO PUTNEY

Uncommon Vows
(New York: New American Library/Signet, 1991)

Story type: Historical/Medieval
Major character(s): Meriel de Vere, Noblewoman, Amnesiac; Adrian de Lacey, Nobleman, Warrior
Time period(s): 12th century (1137-49)
Locale(s): England

Summary: When Adrian de Lacey discovers beautiful Meriel de Vere in a local forest, he assumes she is a commoner instead of the noblewoman she is and, suddenly besotted with her, takes her captive. Her true identity revealed, Adrian sets about wooing her but Meriel valiantly resists—until an accident results in her loss of memory. With her past a blank, Meriel and Adrian happily marry, and remain that way until another accident restores Meriel's first memory and erases the second, including her marriage to Adrian. Good depiction of medieval life and likeable characters.

Other books you might like:
Catherine Coulter, *Secret Song*, 1991
Christina Dodd, *Candle in the Window*, 1991
Teresa Medeiros, *Shadows and Lace*, 1990
Marylyle Rogers, *Hidden Hearts*, 1989
Susan Wiggs, *The Lily and the Leopard*, 1991

1565
MARY JO PUTNEY

Veils of Silk
(New York: Onyx, 1992)

Story type: Historical/Exotic; Historical/Victorian
Series: Silk Trilogy
Major character(s): Laura Stephanson, Orphan; Ian Cameron, Nobleman (Lord Falkirk)
Time period(s): 1840s (1847)
Locale(s): India; Scotland

Summary: Bitter and angry following his captivity in Central Asis, Ian Cameron has one last mission to fulfill—he needs to take a journal to the niece of a dying prisoner he had befriended. Their meeting, however, results in friendship which in time develops into love. An exotic, moving story set in Victorian Colonial India.

Other books you might like:
Justina Burgess, *Winds of Eden*, 1991

E.M. Forster, *A Passage to India*, 1924
Laura Kinsale, *The Shadow and the Star*, 1991
Christine Monson, *This Fiery Splendor*, 1991
Barbara Dawson Smith, *Fire on the Wind*, 1992

1566
AMANDA QUICK (Pseudonym of Jayne Ann Krentz)

Dangerous
(New York: Bantam, 1993)

Story type: Historical/Regency
Major character(s): Prudence Merryweather, Paranormal Investigator (of spectral phenomena); Sebastian Fleetwood, Nobleman (Earl of Angelstone), Detective—Private
Time period(s): 1810s
Locale(s): London, England

Summary: Prudence Merryweather has no time for marriage or men—investigating spectral phenomena is much more to her taste. However, when she and the notorious Earl of Angelstone find themselves in a compromising situation, there is nothing for it but to post the banns! Highlighted by fast-paced action, lively dialogue, and "ghostly" mysteries.

Other books you might like:
Jo Beverley, *Emily and the Dark Angel*, 1991
Jo Beverley, *My Lady Notorious*, 1993
Judith McNaught, *Almost Heaven*, 1990
Laura Parker, *Moonshadow*, 1992
Laura Parker, *Moonshadow*, 1992

1567
AMANDA QUICK (Pseudonym of Jayne Ann Krentz)

Deception
(New York: Bantam, 1993)

Story type: Historical/Regency
Major character(s): Olympia Wingfield, Spinster; Jared Ryder, Nobleman (Viscount Chillhurst), Imposter (posing as a tutor)
Time period(s): 1810s
Locale(s): Upper Tudway, England (in Dorset); London, England

Summary: On the shelf at 25, Olympia has her hands so full raising her three incorrigible nephews that she hardly has time for her first love, studying ancient legends and finding clues to hidden treasure. So naturally, when a nobleman posing as a tutor and "man of affairs" suddenly appears in her library to rescue her from her current chaotic state, she more than welcomes his help, little knowing that they are both seeking the same thing. Murder, blood feuds, and deceptions abound in this fast-paced, sensual love story of two originals who prove they are meant for each other, contrary to society's expectations.

Other books you might like:
Jane Feather, *Virtue*, 1993
Georgette Heyer, *Lady of Quality*, 1972
    classic Regency

Rebecca Paisley, *Moonlight and Magic*, 1990
    American West setting
Sheila Simonson, *The Bar Sinister*, 1986
Sheila Simonson, *Lady Elizabeth's Comet*, 1985

1568

AMANDA QUICK (Pseudonym of Jayne Ann Krentz)

Desire
(New York: Bantam, 1994)

Story type: Historical/Medieval
Major character(s): Lady Clare, Noblewoman, Spinster; Sir Gareth of Wyckmore, Knight
Time period(s): 12th century
Locale(s): Desire, England

Summary: Big, hard-headed Gareth needs a bride; delicate Lady Clare needs a man to save her island kingdom. However, getting these two opposites together presents a number of funny and passionate problems—all, of course, which are overcome in Quick's typically witty, fast-paced fashion. The time period is a bit of a departure from her usual Regency setting.

Other books you might like:
Julie Garwood, *The Bride*, 1989
Julie Garwood, *Saving Grace*, 1993
Arnette Lamb, *Chieftain*, 1994
Elizabeth Lowell, *Enchanted*, 1994
Elizabeth Lowell, *Untamed*, 1993

1569

AMANDA QUICK (Pseudonym of Jayne Ann Krentz)

Mistress
(New York: Bantam, 1994)

Story type: Historical/Regency
Major character(s): Iphiginia Bright, Teacher, Imposter (mistress); Marcus Valerius Cloud, Nobleman (Earl of Masters)
Time period(s): 1810s
Locale(s): London, England

Summary: Learning her aunt is being blackmailed, school mistress Iphiginia Bright boldly seeks the obvious solution. She will "become" the mistress of the recently-deceased Earl of Masters, who was a victim of the same blackmailer, insinuate herself into the *ton*, and discover the blackmailer's identity. She is succeeding admirably—until Marcus Valerius Cloud, the "dead" Earl, suddenly walks into the room and throws her plans, and her life, into passionate chaos. Funny, sensual, and fast-paced.

Other books you might like:
Connie Brockway, *Promise Me Heaven*, 1994
Judith McNaught, *Almost Heaven*, 1990
Anita Mills, *Secret Nights*, 1994
Anne Stuart, *To Love a Dark Lord*, 1994

1570

AMANDA QUICK (Pseudonym of Jayne Ann Krentz)

Mystique
(New York: Bantam, 1995)

Story type: Historical/Medieval
Major character(s): Alice, Noblewoman; Hugh the Relentless, Nobleman (Lord of Scarcliffe Keep)
Locale(s): England

Summary: All the Lady Alice wants is an education for her brother and a dowry so she can enter a convent and continue her research; all Sir Hugh wants is the legendary "green stone"—and Alice as a wife. The resulting bargain sends them on the trail of the stone, linked by a betrothal-of-convenience. Sparks, passion, and adventure are the order of the day as they complete their quest and are forced to deal with the terms of their agreement—and their feelings for each other. This fast-paced, funny story features lively, well-written dialogue, a spunky (and anachronistic) heroine, and a typically alpha hero.

Other books you might like:
Jude Deveraux, *The Taming*, 1989
Julie Garwood, *The Bride*, 1989
Julie Garwood, *Saving Grace*, 1993
Elizabeth Lowell, *Enchanted*, 1994
    more lyrical
Judith Merkle Riley, *In Pursuit of the Green Lion*, 1990
    paranormal elements/mainstream

1571

AMANDA QUICK (Pseudonym of Jayne Ann Krentz)

Ravished
(New York: Bantam, 1992)

Story type: Historical/Regency
Major character(s): Harriet Pomeroy, Archaeologist, Spinster; Gideon Westbrook, Nobleman (Viscount St. Justin), Handicapped (scarred)
Time period(s): 1810s
Locale(s): England

Summary: When archaeologist Harriet Pomeroy suspects smugglers are in her caves and might discover "her bones," she writes a letter to Gideon Westbrook, the absentee owner of the estate, requesting that he take action. He comes to her aid, though not so willingly as she would like, but together they deal with the problems of the smugglers and solve an old mystery in the process. Witty, sensual, and fast-paced.

Other books you might like:
Catherine Coulter, *Night Shadow*, 1989
Elizabeth Peters, *Crocodile on the Sandbank*, 1975
Elizabeth Peters, *The Snake, the Crocodile, and the Dog*, 1992
Sheila Simonson, *The Bar Sinister*, 1986
Sheila Simonson, *Lady Elizabeth's Comet*, 1985

1572

AMANDA QUICK (Pseudonym of Jayne Ann Krentz)

Reckless
(New York: Bantam, 1992)

Story type: Historical/Regency
Major character(s): Phoebe Layton, Noblewoman; Gabriel Banner, Gentleman, Pirate
Time period(s): 1810s
Locale(s): England

Summary: Although he fully intends to avenge himself on Phoebe's family for a series of past wrongs, when Gabriel Banner falls in love with Phoebe, his plans are changed. Deception, mystery, and passion in Regency England. Funny, witty, and typically "Quick."

Other books you might like:
Mary Balogh, *Beyond the Sunrise*, 1992
Loretta Chase, *The Lion's Daughter*, 1992
Laura Parker, *For Love's Sake Only*, 1991
Sue Rich, *Shadowed Vows*, 1992

1573

AMANDA QUICK (Pseudonym of Jayne Ann Krentz)

Rendezvous
(New York: Bantam, 1992)

Story type: Historical/Regency
Major character(s): Augusta Ballinger, Noblewoman; Harry Fleming, Writer, Spy ("Nemesis")
Time period(s): 1810s
Locale(s): England

Summary: Independent, free thinking Augusta puts herself in one dangerous situation after another, trying to clear her brother's name. She is alternately assisted and hampered by Harry, who writes history to hide his identity as the secret agent, Nemesis. Augusta, in keeping with her philosophy, does not intend to marry; but when a night of passion results in a quick marriage to Harry, she has reason to adjust her thoughts. Mystery, danger, and passion in a Regency setting.

Other books you might like:
Rebecca Paisley, *Diamonds and Dreams*, 1991
Mary Jo Putney, *Silk and Shadows*, 1991
Sheila Simonson, *Lady Elizabeth's Comet*, 1985
Susan Wiggs, *The Raven and the Rose*, 1992

1574

AMANDA QUICK (Pseudonym of Jayne Ann Krentz)

Scandal
(New York: Bantam, 1991)

Story type: Historical/Regency
Major character(s): Emily Faringdon, Spinster; Simon Traherne, Nobleman (Earl of Blade)
Time period(s): 1810s
Locale(s): England

Summary: Bent on avenging his father's ruin and death three years earlier, Simon Traherne sets about planning the downfall of his enemy through winning the heart of 24 year old Emily Faringdon. However, red-headed, bespectacled, intelligent, and financially astute, Emily is more than a match for his wiles—and with patience and determination, she proves to him that love is far preferable to revenge. Gothic overtones.

Other books you might like:
Charlene Cross, *A Heart So Innocent*, 1990
    Victorian
Julie Garwood, *The Gift*, 1991
Julie Garwood, *Guardian Angel*, 1990
Judith McNaught, *Almost Heaven*, 1990
Julie Tetel, *And Heaven Too*, 1990

1575

AMANDA QUICK (Pseudonym of Jayne Ann Krentz)

Seduction
(New York: Bantam, 1990)

Story type: Historical/Regency
Major character(s): Sophy Dorring, Spinster, Gentlewoman; Julian Sinclair, Nobleman (Earl of Ravenswood), Widow(er)
Time period(s): 1810s
Locale(s): England

Summary: Julian needs to marry again in order to produce an heir, but he wants a wife more biddable than his first, Elizabeth, proved to be. However, his choice, Sophy, turns out to be a willful, free-thinker intent on being dominated by no one. Mystery, intrigue and passion in a Regency setting.

Other books you might like:
Cordia Byers, *Lady Fortune*, 1989
    Earlier period/Strong heroine
Julie Garwood, *Guardian Angel*, 1990
Georgette Heyer, *The Unknown Ajax*, 1959
    Classic Regency author
Judith McNaught, *Almost Heaven*, 1990
Claudette Williams, *Heart of Fancy*, 1990

1576

AMANDA QUICK (Pseudonym of Jayne Ann Krentz)

Surrender
(New York: Bantam, 1990)

Story type: Historical/Regency; Gothic
Major character(s): Victoria Huntington, Spinster (by choice), Heiress; Lucas Colebrook, Nobleman (Earl of Stonevale)
Time period(s): 1810s
Locale(s): England

Summary: Lucas Colebrook needs an heiress and he thinks independent, adventuresome, "on the shelf" Victoria Huntington will do nicely. Victoria has other ideas, however, and marriage is not one of them—until they are forced into it as a result of one of their escapades. Lively, passionate, and funny with definite gothic elements.

Other books you might like:
Catherine Coulter, *Night Shadow*, 1989
Charlene Cross, *A Heart So Innocent*, 1990
Betina M. Krahn, *Midnight Magic*, 1990
Judith McNaught, *Almost Heaven*, 1990
Mary Jo Putney, *The Rake and the Reformer*, 1989

1577

COLLEEN QUINN

Colorado Flame
(New York: Zebra, 1989)

Story type: Historical/American West
Major character(s): Jessica Hayes, Journalist, Suffragette; Holden Keane, Detective—Private (Pinkerton's sharpshooter)
Time period(s): 19th century
Locale(s): Philadelphia, Pennsylvania; Sundance, Colorado

Summary: When her boss is killed in the process of investigating silver mine frauds, reporter Jessica Hayes knows her life is in danger. Accompanied by her ex-boyfriend, Holden Keane, a Pinkerton sharpshooter, Jessica arrives safely in Sundance to discover that she and Keane are now joint heirs to the Golden Nugget Saloon. Plenty of romance, action, and danger.

Other books you might like:
Rita Balkey, *Passion's Fury*, 1989
Linda Benjamin, *Midnight Chase*, 1989
   Unusual/hero is blind
Catherine Creel, *Nevada Captive*, 1989
Elizabeth Lane, *Wind River*, 1989
Rebecca Sinclair, *California Caress*, 1989

1578

COLLEEN QUINN

Defiant Rose
(New York: Pocket, 1992)

Story type: Historical/Victorian America
Major character(s): Rose Carney, Entertainer (clown), Businesswoman (circus owner); Michael Wharton, Banker
Time period(s): 1870s
Locale(s): Midwest; Philadelphia, Pennsylvania

Summary: Free-spirited, fun-loving Rose and sophisticated, and somewhat staid, banker Michael try to reconcile their different lifestyles in a romantic tale that centers around the joy and magic of the circus.

Other books you might like:
Brenna Braxton-Barshon, *Southern Oaks*, 1991
Patt Bucheister, *Once Burned, Twice as Hot*, 1990
Wendy Garrett, *Love's Magic Spell*, 1992
Laura Parker, *A Wilder Love*, 1990

1579

COLLEEN QUINN

Unveiled
(New York: Diamond, 1993)

Story type: Historical/Victorian America
Major character(s): Katie O'Connor, Companion, Imposter (employer's wealthy niece); Christopher Scott, Fortune Hunter
Time period(s): 19th century
Locale(s): Philadelphia, Pennsylvania; Cape May, New Jersey

Summary: Arriving in Cape May to become a companion to elderly Mrs. Pemberton, penniless Katie O'Connor is shocked to be claimed by her employer as her long-lost niece. But when Katie decides to go along with the deception, she finds herself involved with a dashing fortune hunter and caught up in a pretense that must eventually be exposed. Charming and sensual.

Other books you might like:
Dorothy Eden, *The American Heiress*, 1980
Virginia Lynn, *River's Dream*, 1991
Richard Peck, *Amanda/Miranda*, 1981
Heather Graham Pozzessere, *Forbidden Fire*, 1991

1580

COLLEEN QUINN

Wild Is the Night
(New York: Diamond, 1991)

Story type: Historical/American West
Major character(s): Amanda Emerson, Writer (penny novelist), Rancher; Luke Parker, Gunfighter
Time period(s): 19th century
Locale(s): Waco, Texas

Summary: When novelist Amanda Emerson inherits a ranch in Texas, she ends up pursued by a killer, guarded by a gunfighter, attacked by Indians, and forced into marriage—just like something out of one of her novels! Passion, action, and humor abound in this slightly off-beat love story.

Other books you might like:
Rita Balkey, *Passion's Fury*, 1989
Lori Copeland, *Sweet Hannah Rose*, 1991
Joan Johnston, *Texas Woman*, 1989
Victoria Thompson, *Sweet Texas Surrender*, 1991

1581

JULIA QUINN (Pseudonym of Julie Cotler)

Dancing at Midnight
(New York: Avon, 1995)

Story type: Historical/Regency
Major character(s): Lady Arabella "Belle" Blydon, Noblewoman; Lord John Blackwood, Nobleman, Handicapped (war-wounded)
Time period(s): 1810s (1816)
Locale(s): Oxfordshire, England

Summary: Intrigued by Lord John Blackwood, the wounded and enigmatic owner of the estate adjoining her uncle's, the unconventional Belle sets out to befriend him—in spite of the fact that he doesn't seem to like her. A charming, spirited—and myopic—heroine and a wounded hero of the first water join forces in a delightful, humorous romp with a fair amount of detail and just a dash of suspense.

Other books you might like:
Christina Dodd, *Move Heaven and Earth*, 1995
    another wounded hero/gothic atmosphere
Christina Dodd, *Priceless*, 1992
    another wounded hero/intrepid heroine/dashes of mystery
Amanda Quick, *Deception*, 1993
    dashes of mystery/fast-paced and witty
Amanda Quick, *Ravished*, 1992
    another wounded hero/fast-paced and witty
Anne Stuart, *To Love a Dark Lord*, 1994
    compelling/darker than some

`1582`
SHEILA RABE

Bringing Out Betsy
(New York: Zebra, 1994)

Story type: Regency
Major character(s): Betsy Brightham, Debutante; Lionel Hopewell, Nobleman (Duke of Littlefield)
Time period(s): 1810s
Locale(s): London, England

Summary: Thinking to ensure his inheritance, the elitist Duke of Littlefield reluctantly agrees to help with the London launching of the country daughter of his grandmother's schoolgirl friend—and ends up having his matrimonial future assured, as well. Features several interesting secondary characters and an accurate depiction of the tensions between the cits and the quality.

Other books you might like:
Marion Chesney, *Finessing Clarissa*, 1989
Jan Constant, *The Only Hope*, 1994
Clare Darcy, *Lydia: Or, Love in Town*, 1973
Georgette Heyer, *Arabella*, 1949
Barbara Metzger, *A Loyal Companion*, 1993

`1583`
KARREN RADKO

Dreams and Wishes
(Bensalem, Pennsylvania: Meteor, 1993)

Story type: Contemporary
Major character(s): Skye Carson, Innkeeper; Mac Morgan, Businessman (developer), Drifter (in disguise)
Time period(s): 1990s
Locale(s): Prospect, Oklahoma

Summary: Skye Carson can't turn away an obviously down-on-his-luck man when she has the only inn in town. However, Mac Morgan is anything but a drifter; on the contrary, he is a developer needing a break from business pressures, so he

stays. Romance blossoms and things seem rosy, until the truth of his identity surfaces. Eventually, all works out, with a little outside help.

Other books you might like:
Marissa Carroll, *Loveknot*, 1993
    final in the Tyler series
Jayne Ann Krentz, *Grand Passion*, 1993
Marcia Martin, *Southern Storms*, 1992
Laura Parrish, *Love's Quiet Corner*, 1989

`1584`
CATHERINE M. RAE

Julia's Story
(New York: St. Martin's 1989)

Story type: Historical
Major character(s): Julia Hastings, Socialite (impoverished); Seth Barnes, Bootlegger (former)
Time period(s): 1930s
Locale(s): New York, New York

Summary: As a result of the Depression, beautiful but impoverished socialite Julia Hastings is reduced to working as a sales clerk and living in a cold water flat. The chance discovery of some bonds seemingly changes her life for the better; but when the bonds' true owner, Seth Barnes, arrives on the scene and falls in love with Julia, things become complicated. Particularly good historical detail.

Other books you might like:
Leona Blair, *A World of Difference*, 1989
    Family Saga
Belva Plain, *Evergreen*, 1978
    Family Saga

`1585`
CARIN RAFFERTY

A Touch of Magic
(New York: Topaz, 1995)

Story type: Contemporary/Fantasy
Major character(s): Shana Morland, Witch; Ryan Alden, Doctor
Time period(s): 1990s
Locale(s): Sanctuary, Pennsylvania

Summary: Shana rescues mortal Ryan Alden from a motorcycle accident, using her witchcraft to heal and restrain him. She dares to meddle with an ancient deck of cards that tell of an ancient evil power over her which reaches out to touch Ryan, too. Shana must be truly in love to escape her evil pursuer, but Ryan's disbelief and reluctance challenge all her powers even though she knows that true love does exist for her and for him. Mystifying and supernatural.

Other books you might like:
Evelyn A. Crowe, *Reunited*, 1993
Sabine Kells, *Shadows on a Sunset Sea*, 1994
Susan Krinard, *Prince of Dreams*, 1995
Cheri Scotch, *The Werewolf's Sin*, 1994
    dark and violent/battle between good and evil

Maggie Shayne, *Out of This World Marriage*, 1995

1586

RITA RAINVILLE

Never on Sundae

(New York: Silhouette, 1990)

Story type: Contemporary/Innocent
Major character(s): Heather Brandon, Businesswoman ("Fat Farm" owner); Wade MacKenzie, Young Man
Time period(s): 1980s
Locale(s): Arizona (The Oasis)

Summary: Heather and Maude struggle to make a go of their desert "fat farm," but a neighboring bakery makes it very difficult. Maude's nephew, Wade, also makes life difficult for Heather, but in a very different way.

Other books you might like:
Jan McDaniel, *Angels in the Sand*, 1989
Kasey Michaels, *His Chariot Awaits*, 1990
Alice Sharpe, *Just One More Secret*, 1990
Jane Shore, *The Cinderella Game*, 1990

1587

JEANETTE BAKER RAMIREZ

Lady of Lochabar

(New York: Harper, 1993)

Story type: Historical/Seventeenth Century
Major character(s): Maggie MacDonald, Orphan; Simon Campbell, Laird (Laird of Diarmed)
Time period(s): 17th century (1667)
Locale(s): Scotland

Summary: When Simon of the Campbell clan is involved in the murder of Maggie MacDonald's parents, he rescues the 10 year old and takes her to his uncle's, promising to return some day. For ten years they dream of each other, but when he does return, the family will not allow the alliance and they are separated once more. Their love, however, does endure. Evokes the ruthlessness of the period, multi-dimensional, and provides good historical detail.

Other books you might like:
Chloe Gartner, *Mistress of the Highlands*, 1976
Jean Plaidy, *The Pleasure of Love*, 1992
Casey Stuart, *Highland Rogue*, 1991
Susan Wiggs, *The Mist and the Magic*, 1993

1588

LINDSAY RANDALL (Pseudonym of Susan Anderson)

Silversword

(New York: Leisure, 1990)

Story type: Historical
Major character(s): Mara, Adventurer; Aratar, Adventurer
Time period(s): Indeterminate Past
Locale(s): Earth (Northern Tundra)

Summary: Both mystic and mythic, this tale of Mara and Aratar's struggle to find their destinies is filled with legends, quests good and evil, and all the elements inherent in the fledgling mystic romance subgenre.

Other books you might like:
Nancy Harding, *Wind Child*, 1990
Anne McCaffrey, *Dragonriders of Pern Series*,
Rosemary Sutcliff, *A Light in the Forest*, 1980
    Part of an Arthurian trilogy/mystical and mythic
Jane Yolen, *Sister Light, Sister Dark*, 1989
    The myth/legend/history/story web articulated by a master

1589

DANA RANSOM

Dakota Dawn

(New York: Avon, 1991)

Story type: Historical/American West
Series: Dakota
Major character(s): Aurora Kincaid, Captive; Ethan Prescott, Mountain Man, Doctor
Time period(s): 19th century
Locale(s): Dakota Territory

Summary: Kidnapped by the Sioux, taken to wife by the chief's son, and sold into slavery by a jealous first wife, young, pregnant Aurora finally escapes—right into a blizzard! Her salvation comes in the form of trapper Ethan Prescott, who takes her in, helps with the birth of her child, and falls in love with her. Things become complicated, however, when Aurora is ostracized by her bigoted family and the Sioux want her son. Deftly handles a number of sensitive topics.

Other books you might like:
Rosanne Bittner, *Sioux Splendor*, 1990
Barbara Cummings, *Frontier Fire*, 1991
Kathleen Eagle, *Heaven and Earth*, 1990
Pamela K. Forrest, *Autumn Ecstasy*, 1990
Janis Reams Hudson, *Apache Magic*, 1991

1590

DANA RANSOM

Dakota Desire

(New York: Zebra, 1992)

Story type: Historical/American West
Major character(s): Genevieve Trowbridge, Fiance(e), Gentlewoman; Scott Prescott, Lawyer, Indian (half Sioux)
Time period(s): 19th century (late)
Locale(s): South Dakota

Summary: When attorney Scott Prescott takes his fiancee, Genevieve Trowbridge, to the Dakotas to meet the Sioux half of his family, he fully intends to return to his East Coast practice. However, an old promise to his Indian grandfather makes him reconsider and together Gena and Scott try to help his people. Complications ensue as Gena is not welcomed and it comes to light that Scott's other grandfather is a persecutor of the Sioux. Complex and powerful.

Other books you might like:
Beverly Bird, *Comes the Rain*, 1990
Jessie Ford, *A Different Breed*, 1988
Shirl Henke, *Night Wind's Woman*, 1990
Constance O'Banyon, *Cheyenne Sunrise*, 1990
Deborah Smith, *Beloved Woman*, 1991

`1591`

DANA RANSOM

Dakota Destiny
(New York: Zebra, 1993)

Story type: Historical/American West
Series: Dakota
Major character(s): Norah Denby, Con Artist; Rory Prescott, Gentleman
Time period(s): 19th century (late)
Locale(s): Deadwood, South Dakota

Summary: Greenhorn Rory Prescott is stunned by Norah Denby's beauty and her con game. Norah doesn't quite know what to make of Rory, either; but when they begin to fall in love, they realize the road won't be easy. Lots of family conflicts to resolve in this, the latest in the Dakota series.

Other books you might like:
Barbara Cummings, *Frontier Fire*, 1991
Pamela K. Forrest, *Autumn Ecstasy*, 1990
Teresa Hart, *Hearts Are Wild*, 1993
Kathryn Hockett, *Outlaw Seduction*, 1993

`1592`

DANA RANSOM

Temptation's Trail
(New York: Zebra, 1994)

Story type: Historical/American West
Major character(s): Amanda Duran, Orphan; Harmon Bass, Cowboy, Guide
Time period(s): 19th century (late)
Locale(s): Fort Davis, Texas

Summary: Wealthy Amanda hires half-Apache cowboy Harmon Bass to find her brother and some missing jewels. In spite of his looks, Harmon is an expert tracker, but Amanda isn't leaving anything to chance, so she goes along with him. However, Harmon is using this cover to avenge a past injustice, and this puts them both in constant danger. Eventually they unravel the mystery of the missing gems and come to terms with each other and their pasts.

Other books you might like:
Cait Logan, *Night Fire*, 1994
Susannah Leigh, *The Turquoise Trail*, 1991
Elizabeth Lowell, *Only His*, 1991
Elizabeth Lowell, *Only Mine*, 1992
Jodi Thomas, *The Texan and the Lady*, 1994
    gentler/another questing heroine

`1593`

DANA RANSOM

Texas Destiny
(New York: Zebra, 1994)

Story type: Historical/American West
Major character(s): Emily Marcus, Captive (of Apaches); Jack Bass, Lawman (Texas Ranger)
Time period(s): 19th century
Locale(s): Texas

Summary: When Texas Ranger Jack Bass is rescued from torture by a white woman dressed as an Apache, she turns out to be his commander's wife, Emily, who had been abducted years earlier. However, her return to ''civilization'' results in rejection and abuse from her husband—and she turns to Jack to help rescue her daughter, who is still with the Apaches. Tragedy and dark secrets cause problems, but love ultimately wins out. Sensual and intense.

Other books you might like:
Catherine Anderson, *Comanche Heart*, 1992
Cheryl Black, *Comanche Love Song*, 1989
    another returned captive
Janet Dailey, *The Pride of Hannah Wade*, 1985
    classic returned captive story
Linda Howard, *A Lady of the West*, 1990
    dark and violent/strong heroine/no Native American theme
Victoria Thompson, *Wild Texas Wind*, 1992
    another returned captive/realistic

`1594`

DANA RANSOM

Wild Savage Love
(New York: Zebra, 1990)

Story type: Historical/Colonial America
Major character(s): Evangeline Carey, Captive (of the Mohawk Indians); Royle Tanner, Businessman (fur trade)
Time period(s): 17th century (1684)
Locale(s): New York, American Colonies

Summary: When Evangeline Carey (Eyes-Like-Evening-Star) returns to white civilization eight years after she was captured by the Mohawks, she finds life restrictive and rigid; and when her uncle forces her into an arranged marriage, she finds it treacherous as well. However, in spite of the fact that he had expected a very different kind of bride, Royle Tanner sets out to understand and help her—and eventually he wins her love.

Other books you might like:
Madeline Baker, *Lacey's Way*, 1990
Cheryl Black, *Comanche Love Song*, 1989
Janet Dailey, *The Pride of Hannah Wade*, 1985
Cassie Edwards, *When Passion Calls*, 1990
Judith E. French, *Lovestorm*, 1990

1595

DANA RANSOM

Wild Wyoming Love

(New York: Zebra, 1991)

Story type: Historical/American West

Major character(s): Lucille "Lucy" Blessing, Banker, Widow(er); Sam Zachary, Imposter (ex-outlaw), Lawman (Marshal)

Time period(s): 1880s

Locale(s): Blessing, Wyoming

Summary: When former outlaw Sam Zachary arrives in Blessing, Wyoming, posing as the new marshal, he has larceny, not love, in mind. But a beautiful banker and his unexpected reaction to his new role work to change his mind. Lots of action and nicely handled character development.

Other books you might like:

Lisa Bingham, *Silken Dreams*, 1990
Catherine Hart, *Sweet Fury*, 1991
Emma Merritt, *Beneath a Texas Star*, 1991
Linda Shaw, *Odessa Gold*, 1991

1596

ALICIA RASLEY

Poetic Justice

(New York: Zebra, 1994)

Story type: Regency

Major character(s): Jessica Seton, Gentlewoman, Heiress; John Dryden, Businessman (rare book dealer), Privateer (former)

Time period(s): 1810s (1818)

Locale(s): England

Summary: Jessica Seton will do almost anything to keep her beloved literary collection out of the destructive hands of its present curator, even become involved with the infamous—and quite dashing—rare book dealer John Dryden. But true villainy is afoot, and an obsessed bibliophile must be dealt with before the manuscripts are safe and Jessica and John can begin to explore their growing feelings for each other. Well-researched and somewhat unusual.

Other books you might like:

Anne Barbour, *A Talent for Trouble*, 1992
Sarah Eagle, *The Marriage Gamble*, 1992
Amanda Quick, *Ravished*, 1992
  sensual
Evelyn Richardson, *Lady Alex's Gamble*, 1995
Sheila Simonson, *Lady Elizabeth's Comet*, 1985

1597

LOUISA RAWLINGS

Promise of Summer

(New York: Popular Library, 1989)

Story type: Historical/Georgian

Major character(s): Topaze Benoite, Thief, Imposter (posing as missing cousin); Lucien Renaudot, Bastard Son

Time period(s): 1730s (1739)

Summary: Driven by a desire for revenge against his cousin Veronique's family, Lucien convinces her pickpocket, look-alike, Topaze, to impersonate Veronique. Topaze makes the Pygmalion-like transition from guttersnipe to lady with ease, but long-forgotten secrets and unlooked-for dangers threaten both Topaze and Lucien as the plot takes a series of unusual turns.

Other books you might like:

Laura Black, *Albany*, 1984
Laura Black, *Glendraco*, 1977
Cordia Byers, *Lady Fortune*, 1989
Sarah Edwards, *Crystal Rapture*, 1989
Penelope Williamson, *Hearts Beguiled*, 1989

1598

LOUISA RAWLINGS

Stranger in My Arms

(Toronto: Harlequin, 1990)

Story type: Historical/Regency

Major character(s): Charmaine de Violette, Noblewoman (impoverished); Adam Bouchard, Military Personnel

Time period(s): 19th century (early)

Locale(s): France

Summary: Charmaine de Violette is caught in a conflict between her heart and her political convictions when she falls in love with Adam Bouchard, one of Napoleon's officers. Political intrigue, mistaken identity, and romance in a vividly detailed story set during a particulary flamboyant period in history.

Other books you might like:

Brian Cleeve, *Hester*, 1979
Iris Johansen, *Storm Winds*, 1991
Ellen Tanner Marsh, *If This Be Magic*, 1990
Baroness Orczy, *The Scarlet Pimpernel*, 1905
  classic tale of the French Revolution
Serena Richards, *Rendezvous*, 1991

1599

LOUISA RAWLINGS (Pseudonym of Sylvia Baumgartner)

Wicked Stranger

(Toronto: Harlequin, 1992)

Story type: Historical

Major character(s): Elizabeth Babcock, Spinster; Noel Bonchard, Military Personnel, Imposter (posing as his twin brother)

Time period(s): 19th century

Locale(s): Paris, France; New York, New York

Summary: Little does Noel Bouchard realize that when he impersonates his twin brother at a social gathering, he is setting the stage for his subsequent marriage to one of the most difficult, shrewish spinsters he has ever met! Elizabeth Babcock isn't about to let any man control her, but Noel sees through her facade and sets about winning her. A witty, "taming of the shrew" story.

Other books you might like:
Jane Feather, *Virtue*, 1993
Jill Gregory, *Forever After*, 1993
Amanda Quick, *Dangerous*, 1993
Amanda Quick, *Surrender*, 1990
Anne Stuart, *A Rose at Midnight*, 1993

1600
ANGIE RAY

Ghostly Enchantment
(New York: Harper, 1994)

Story type: Historical/Fantasy
Major character(s): Margaret Westbourne, Gentlewoman, Fiance(e); Bernard Denbeigh, Nobleman, Fiance(e); Philip Eglinton, Spirit
Time period(s): 19th century
Locale(s): England

Summary: When Margaret agrees to marry her childhood friend, Bernard Denbeigh, she doesn't expect to be acquiring a family ghost at the same time. Nevertheless, the dashing Philip comes with the castle, and when she finally meets him and learns of the curse on him, she determines to help—and arouses Bernard's jealousy in the process. Bernard's determination to win Margaret back reveals an entirely new side to his personality and suddenly Margaret begins to wonder who she really loves.

Other books you might like:
Sandra Heath, *The Halloween Husband*, 1994
Sabine Kells, *Shadows on a Sunset Sea*, 1994
Kasey Michaels, *The Haunted Miss Hampshire*, 1992
Laura Parker, *For Love's Sake Only*, 1991
Laura Parker, *Moonshadow*, 1992

1601
FRANCIS RAY

Forever Yours
(New York: Pinnacle, 1994)

Story type: Contemporary; Ethnic
Major character(s): Victoria Chandler, Businesswoman; Kane Taggart, Rancher
Time period(s): 1990s
Locale(s): United States

Summary: When her grandmother issues an ultimatum to either get married or lose her business, Victoria Chandler makes a deal with attractive rancher Kane Taggart—he gets the money he so desperately needs and she gets a husband—but only for a year. Problems arise, however, when they unexpectedly fall in love. Fast-paced, laced with humor, and peopled with likable characters. One of the first titles in Pinnacle's new Arabesque ethnic romance line, *Forever Yours* features an African American hero and heroine.

Other books you might like:
Bette Ford, *For Always*, 1995

Layle Guista, *Sweet Promise*, 1994
Donna Hill, *Spirit of the Season*, 1994
   holiday anthology/three novellas
Sandra Kitt, *Serenade*, 1994
Margie Walker, *Sweet Refrain*, 1994

1602
FRANCIS RAY

Undeniable
(New York: Pinnacle, 1995)

Story type: Contemporary; Ethnic
Major character(s): Rachel Malone, Heiress; Logan Prescott, Contractor
Time period(s): 1990s
Locale(s): Stanton, Texas

Summary: When Rachel Malone chooses her wealthy family over marriage to him, angry, bitter, and humiliated, Logan Prescott leaves Stanton, determined to succeed. But now he is back, successful beyond all expectations, and he intends to make Rachel and her family pay. A fast-paced, sensual story of pride, revenge, and love.

Other books you might like:
Angela Benson, *For All Time*, 1995
Bette Ford, *Forever After*, 1995
Carla Fredd, *Fire and Ice*, 1995
Sandra Kitt, *The Color of Love*, 1995

1603
PATRICK RAYMOND

Daniel and Esther
(New York: Margaret K. McElderry, 1990)

Story type: Young Adult
Major character(s): Esther, Student; Daniel, Student, Musician
Time period(s): 1930s
Locale(s): Europe

Summary: Set against the background of the Holocaust, this story depicts the growing relationship between Esther and Daniel as they learn about themselves and each other. A strong and tender story of first love.

Other books you might like:
Barbara Corcoran, *Axe-Time, Sword-Time*, 1976
   WWII/American setting
Anne Frank, *Anne Frank: A Diary of a Young Girl*, 1952
   Classic story of the Holocaust
Judith Kerr, *The Other Way Round*, 1975
   WWII setting
M.E. Kerr, *Gentlehands*, 1978
   Values and Nazi war criminals

1604

CHERYL REAVIS

The Prisoner

(Toronto: Harlequin, 1992)

Story type: Historical/American Civil War
Major character(s): Amanda Douglas, Captive, Southern Belle; John Howe, Military Personnel (Union officer)
Time period(s): 1860s (1865)
Locale(s): North Carolina

Summary: Punished from childhood by her fanatical preacher father for her mother's indiscretions, gentle Southerner Amanda Douglas is kidnapped by escaped POW Union Army Captain John Howe and taken to his Northern home — only to find she has left one prison for another. John's shallow and aristocratic mother makes Amanda's life miserable, but although she succeeds in separating the lovers, true love and old family secrets eventually bring about a satisfactorily happy ending. An insightful and warm sweet historical.

Other books you might like:
Micki Brown, *Once a Rebel*, 1992
Dorothy Garlock, *Ribbon in the Sky*, 1992
Heather Graham, *And One Wore Gray*, 1992
Terri Valentine, *Yankee's Caress*, 1989
Kathleen E. Woodiwiss, *Ashes in the Wind*, 1979

1605

CHERYL REAVIS

Promise Me a Rainbow

(New York: Berkley, 1990)

Story type: Contemporary
Major character(s): Catherine Holben, Nurse (teacher); Joe D'Amaro, Contractor (building)
Time period(s): 1980s

Summary: When Catherine innocently purchases a gnome sculpture, she has no idea that the former owner and his three children come along with the deal. More realistic than some.

Other books you might like:
Judy Gill, *Golden Swan*, 1990
Muriel Jensen, *Everything*, 1990
Muriel Jensen, *Side by Side*, 1989
Sherryl Woods, *Tea and Destiny*, 1990

1606

JOANNE REDD

Apache Bride

(New York: Dell, 1990)

Story type: Historical/American West
Major character(s): Alison Carr, Debutante (Bored); Ramon ''The Falcon'', Indian (half Apache), Chieftain
Time period(s): 1870s
Locale(s): Texas; Mexico

Summary: Bored with Baltimore society, Alison Carr goes to Mexico to join her father, but ends up being kidnapped by a devastatingly handsome Apache chief instead. Alison fights The Falcon at every turn, but eventually the mutual attraction proves to be too great and they fall in love.

Other books you might like:
Joanna Jordan, *Destiny's Dream*, 1990
Johanna Lindsey, *Captive Bride*, 1977
  In the tradition of *The Sheik*
Johanna Lindsey, *Savage Thunder*, 1989
Judith Steel, *Apache Heartbeat*, 1989
Janelle Taylor, *Savage Conquest*, 1985

1607

JOANNE REDD

Dance with Fire

(New York: Dell, 1992)

Story type: Historical/Colonial America
Major character(s): Fire Dancer, Indian (half-Chickasaw), Royalty (Indian princess); Evan Trevor, Military Personnel (British Army major), Nobleman
Time period(s): 18th century
Locale(s): Ohio Valley, Ohio (Chickasaw Territory)

Summary: Sent to solidify relations with the Chickasaw people and gain necessary intelligence into the activities of the French, British Major Evan Trevor ends up achieving his aims, reassessing his values, and falling in love with an independent and passionate Indian princess. Lots of historical and geographical detail.

Other books you might like:
Emily Carmichael, *Visions of the Heart*, 1990
Amy Christopher, *Captive Kiss*, 1992
Judith E. French, *Moonfeather*, 1990
Karen Harper, *Eden's Gate*, 1989
Janelle Taylor, *Forever Ecstasy*, 1991

1608

JOANNE REDD

Desert Bride

(New York: Dell, 1989)

Story type: Historical/Exotic
Major character(s): Lorna Winters, Young Woman; Nathan Sloan, Agent (American)
Time period(s): 1800s
Locale(s): Barbary Coast, Africa

Summary: Captured, rescued, sold, and married off, Lorna Winters decides she should have stayed in England—but that is before she falls in love with her rescuer and husband, Nathan Sloan. A distant relative of *The Sheik*.

Other books you might like:
Sarah Edwards, *Fire and Sand*, 1989
E.M. Hull, *The Sheik*, 1919
  The classic that started it all
Mary Lide, *Isobelle*, 1988
  Beautifully written

Johanna Lindsey, *Captive Bride*, 1977
  Desert setting
Johanna Lindsey, *A Pirate's Love*, 1978
  Captive-in-love-with-captor plot

1609
BARBARA REEVES

The Much Maligned Lord
(New York: Avon, 1993)

Story type: Regency
Major character(s): Emily Wilton, Gentlewoman; Holt Ingram, Nobleman (Lord Ravencroft), Rake
Time period(s): 1810s
Locale(s): London, England

Summary: Emily accidentally finds herself in Lord Ravencroft's life, but she's heard of his exploits and just can't risk her reputation, let alone her heart, on this well-known rake. However, all is not as it seems, and the pair do find a common meeting ground after all.

Other books you might like:
Mary Balogh, *The Notorious Rake*, 1992
Cathleen Clare, *Felicia*, 1993
Jan Constant, *The Only Hope*, 1994
Georgette Heyer, *Black Sheep*, 1966
Sheila Walsh, *The Arrogant Lord Alistair*, 1990

1610
JEANE RENICK

Trust Me
(New York: Harper Collins, 1992)

Story type: Contemporary/Exotic
Major character(s): Allison Shreve, Model, Vacationer (archaeological dig volunteer); Zachary Cross, Detective—Police, Vacationer (archaeological dig volunteer)
Time period(s): 1990s
Locale(s): Belize

Summary: Allison and Zachary badly need some R & R and plan to spend some time volunteering on an archaeological dig in Belize. Both need to recover from recent traumatic events and they have a hard enough time coming to terms with their personal problems without having to deal with drug smugglers, distraught women, stalking jaguars, damp caves, and scorpions. Nevertheless, they do, and in the process, they learn to love and trust each other. Suspense elements.

Other books you might like:
Carole Buck, *Knight and Day*, 1992
Joey Light, *Sterling's Reasons*, 1991
Leslie O'Grady, *Seek the Wild Shore*, 1989
Garda Parker, *Out of the Blue*, 1992

1611
CATHERINE REYNOLDS

The Highwayman
(Toronto: Harlequin, 1993)

Story type: Regency
Major character(s): Jane Lockwood, Spinster; Jon Edward Sebastian Manning, Nobleman (Viscount St. Clair), Rake
Time period(s): 1810s
Locale(s): England

Summary: Very proper Miss Jane is horrified that her drunken coachman has wounded "Highwayman" Jon Manning, so she takes him home to care for him. Nursing him, however, is such "improper" fun, and Jon is enjoying himself so much that he deliberately neglects to tell Jane of his true "rakish" identity. Eventually, of course, the truth surfaces and then they must determine whether their growing feelings for each other can overcome the obvious gulf between a highly virtuous woman and a renowned rake of the ton.

Other books you might like:
Jo Beverley, *My Lady Notorious*, 1993
  sensual
Suzannah Davis, *Angel Eyes*, 1993
  American West setting
Carla Kelly, *Miss Billings Treads the Boards*, 1992
Margaret Evans Porter, *Road to Ruin*, 1992
Patricia Rice, *Mad Maria's Daughter*, 1992

1612
MOLLY RICE

Chance Encounter
(Toronto: Harlequin, 1992)

Story type: Contemporary
Major character(s): Joanna Keller, Widow(er); Carl Donay, FBI Agent
Time period(s): 1990s

Summary: Carl Donay, an FBI agent investigating a terrorist group, becomes involved with Joanna, whose parents and husband have died and whose son is terminally ill. Her narrow, frightened world is wonderfully shaken up by this take-charge hero.

Other books you might like:
Iris Johansen, *Winter Bride*, 1992
Diana Palmer, *The Case of the Mesmerizing Boss*, 1992
Dallas Schulze, *Charity's Angel*, 1992
Chloe Summers, *No Easy Task*, 1991

1613
PATRICIA RICE

Cheyenne's Lady
(New York: New American Library, 1989)

Story type: Historical/American West
Major character(s): Maria Connelly, Rancher; Luke Walker, Gunfighter, Foreman

Time period(s): 1870s (1876)
Locale(s): West

Summary: When Irish Connelly sends for his old friend Luke Walker to help solve some local problems, he doesn't know he will be dead before Luke arrives—leaving his fiesty daughter, Maria, to deal with the gunslinger stranger. Adventure, treachery, and love are part of this action-filled story of the Old West.

Other books you might like:
Ann Gabriel, *South Texas*, 1990
Martha Hix, *Wild Texas Rose*, 1990
Betina Lindsey, *Waltz with the Lady*, 1990
Sara Orwig, *Albuquerque*, 1989
Vivian Vaughn, *Texas Gamble*, 1990

1614

PATRICIA RICE

Devil's Lady

(New York: NAL, 1992)

Story type: Historical/Victorian; Historical/Victorian America
Major character(s): Faith Montagne, Noblewoman; Morgan de Lacy, Nobleman (disenfranchised), Highwayman
Time period(s): 1850s (1851-1851)
Locale(s): Virginia; England

Summary: When Irish highwayman Morgan de Lacy rescues young Faith Montagne during a blizzard, he determines to make her aristocratic family pay for their treatment of her. He acquires her fortune, lands in jail, and eventually marries her — but when pride forces him to leave, she heads for the Colonies to do ''poor but honest'' work. Eventually, they are reunited and all is well. Fast-paced, funny, and sensual.

Other books you might like:
Mary Balogh, *The Snow Angel*, 1991
Catherine Coulter, *Secret Song*, 1991
Sandra DuBay, *Nightrider*, 1991
Janelle Taylor, *Promise Me Forever*, 1991
Shelly Thacker, *Midnight Raider*, 1992

1615

PATRICIA RICE

Love Forever After

(New York: New American Library, 1990)

Story type: Historical/Georgian
Major character(s): Penelope Carlisle, Noblewoman (Graham's wife); Graham Trevelyn, Nobleman (Viscount)
Time period(s): 18th century
Locale(s): England

Summary: Thrust abruptly into motherhood and the social scene by a marriage of convenience to reclusive Viscount Graham Trevelyn, Penelope accepts the challenge and gradually, in spite of her husband's reluctance to socialize, she draws him out and puts him back in touch with the world—and with love. An unsolved mystery adds intrigue.

Other books you might like:
Georgette Heyer, *The Convenient Marriage*, 1934
   Classic marriage-of-convenience plot
Judith McNaught, *Almost Heaven*, 1990
Mary Jo Putney, *Dearly Beloved*, 1990
Sheila Simonson, *The Bar Sinister*, 1986

1616

PATRICIA RICE

Mad Maria's Daughter

(New York: Signet, 1992)

Story type: Regency
Major character(s): Daphne Templeton, Gentlewoman; Gordon Griffin, Twin, Nobleman; Evan Griffin, Twin, Nobleman
Time period(s): 1810s
Locale(s): England

Summary: Tired of having to live down her mother's insane reputation, Daphne Templeton leaves the London social scene for a quiet, rural life and discovers that the country holds infinitely more adventure and excitement than the city. A dashing highwayman, a look-alike Lord, and political intrigue all combine in this fast-paced, entertaining Regency.

Other books you might like:
Cathleen Clare, *The Mistress of Mishap*, 1992
Violet Hamilton, *A Traitorous Heart*, 1990
Amanda Quick, *Scandal*, 1991
   sensual
Meg-Lynn Roberts, *An Alluring Lady*, 1992
Joan Smith, *Cousin Cecelia*, 1990

1617

PATRICIA RICE

Moon Dreams

(New York: Onyx, 1991)

Story type: Historical/Georgian
Major character(s): Alyson Hampton, Heiress, Psychic; Rory MacLean, Privateer, Laird
Time period(s): 1750s; 1760s (1759-1761)
Locale(s): England; American Colonies; Scotland

Summary: When young Alyson Hampton inherits her grandfather's large estate, she immediately becomes the object of her jealous, greedy cousin's marriage plans. Alyson flees to London, is rescued from her cousin's henchmen by privateer Rory MacLean, and eventually finds herself aboard his ship headed for America. Lots of action, intrigue, and romance with the added element of the unexplained—Alyson has ''The Sight.''

Other books you might like:
Kathryn Lynn Davis, *Child of Awe*, 1987
   Mystical elements
Catherine Gaskin, *Fiona*, 1970
Elizabeth Ann Michaels, *Destiny's Will*, 1991
Karen Stratford, *Lavender Flame*, 1991
Kathleen E. Woodiwiss, *Shanna*, 1977

1618
PATRICIA RICE

Paper Roses
(New York: Topaz, 1995)

Story type: Historical/American West
Major character(s): Evangeline Howell, Widow(er); Tyler Monteigne, Gambler

Summary: Heading for Texas to search for her parents, Evangeline hires gambler renegade Tyler Monteigne to escort her. Tyler is intrigued by her less-than-honest ways, and in spite of themselves they begin to care for each other. Robbers and assorted villains and scrapes all add to this lively adventure, liberally laced with wit and humor. First of a trilogy.

Other books you might like:
Kimberly Cates, *Only Forever*, 1992
　　another questing heroine
Lori Copeland, *Promise Me Forever*, 1994
　　lots of humor
Lori Copeland, *Promise Me Today*, 1992
　　lots of humor
Suzanne Ellison, *Sunburst*, 1993
　　another questing heroine

1619
PATRICIA RICE

Paper Tiger
(New York: Topaz, 1995)

Story type: Historical/Victorian America
Series: Paper Trilogy
Major character(s): Georgina Hanover, Gentlewoman, Fiance(e); Daniel Mulloney, Journalist, Imposter (calls himself Pecos Martin)
Time period(s): 19th century
Locale(s): Cutlerville, Ohio

Summary: Returning from a European tour, Georgina Hanover is expecting to settle down in her Ohio hometown and marry the man her father wants her to, ambitious Peter Mulloney. And then she meets a man on the train who turns her world upside down. The fact that he turns out to be Peter's long-lost brother simply adds to the problem, A highly entertaining heroine, an activist hero, and some interesting historical detail add to this lively, sensual read.

Other books you might like:
Elaine Barbieri, *Wishes on the Wind*, 1991
　　similar time period/labor unrest
Elaine Coffman, *Heaven Knows*, 1994
Joan Johnston, *Sweetwater Seduction*, 1991
　　fast-paced humor
Pamela Morsi, *Garters*, 1992
　　light, small-town atmosphere, funny

1620
PATRICIA RICE

Rebel Dreams
(New York: Onyx, 1991)

Story type: Historical/Colonial America; Historical/Georgian
Major character(s): Evelyn "E.A." Wellington, Businesswoman (storage company owner); Alex Hampton, Detective (investigator)
Time period(s): 1760s (1765)
Locale(s): Boston, Massachusetts, American Colonies; England

Summary: Sent to investigate the alleged smuggling activities of one E.A. Wellington, Alex Hampton is shocked to find his suspect is a woman—and a stubborn, independent, and incredibly lovable one, at that. Compromised, betrothed, and finally wed, the pair leave for England and Alex's newly inherited estate, but they both must come to terms with their feelings before they can make their marriage real.

Other books you might like:
Caryn Cameron, *Liberty's Lady*, 1990
Amy Christopher, *Rebel's Embrace*, 1991
Christine Dorsey, *Captain's Captive*, 1991
Christine Dorsey, *Traitor's Embrace*, 1990
Maura Seger, *Fortune's Tide*, 1990

1621
PATRICIA RICE

Shelter From the Storm
(New York: Onyx, 1993)

Story type: Historical/American Civil War
Major character(s): Laura Kincaid, Abuse Victim, Spinster; Cassius "Cash" Wickliffe, Landowner; Sallie, Cousin
Time period(s): 1860s
Locale(s): Kentucky

Summary: When Cash Wickliffe returns to his hometown, his childhood friend, Sallie, can't deny her feelings for him; Cash, however, determines to marry Sallie's beautiful cousin, Laura. A series of events results in Cash's marriage to Laura, Sallie's involvement in an abusive situation, and her eventual rescue by Cash. Poignant, emotional, and epic-like.

Other books you might like:
Margaret Mitchell, *Gone with the Wind*, 1936
Alexandra Ripley, *Scarlett*, 1991
Marianne Willman, *Yesterday's Shadows*, 1991
　　earlier Western setting
Kathleen E. Woodiwiss, *Ashes in the Wind*, 1979

1622
PATRICIA RICE

Texas Lily
(New York: Topaz, 1994)

Story type: Historical/American West

Major character(s): Lily Brown, Widow(er), Rancher; Cade de Suela, Indian (half Indian/half Mexican), Foreman
Time period(s): 1830s
Locale(s): Texas (near San Antonio)
Summary: Lily Brown has two goals: to care for her son, Roy, and to keep her ranch. It helps when Cade de Suela, despite prejudice and a strong woman boss, hires on as her foreman. The Texas war for independence, Cade's greedy half-brother, and other people and events interfere with their lives, but their love for each other and the land sustain them. Well-written, well-researched, well-reviewed.

Other books you might like:
Rebecca Brandewyne, *Heartland*, 1990
Ann Gabriel, *South Texas*, 1990
  good historical detail/mainstream elements
Jill Gregory, *Lone Star Lady*, 1990
  strong heroine
Linda Howard, *A Lady of the West*, 1990
  strong characters/darker and more violent than some
Catherine Lanigan, *A Promise Made*, 1991

1623
PATRICIA RICE
Touched by Magic
(New York: Onyx, 1992)

Story type: Historical/Georgian
Major character(s): Cassandra Howard, Noblewoman; Wyatt Mannering, Nobleman (Lord Merrick)
Time period(s): 18th century
Locale(s): England
Summary: Forced to marry the lecherous Sir Rupert, Cassie escapes on her wedding night and runs to Wyatt Mannering, Lord Merrick, a man who had once been willing to marry her. She and Wyatt flee to their country estates and their attraction to each other flares into passion. Guilt and dark secrets keep things in turmoil for a time, but eventually annulments and true love follow.

Other books you might like:
Judith McNaught, *Almost Heaven*, 1990
Mary Jo Putney, *Dearly Beloved*, 1990
Amanda Quick, *Seduction*, 1990
Sheila Simonson, *The Bar Sinister*, 1986

1624
SUE RICH
Mistress of Sin
(New York: Pocket, 1994)

Story type: Historical/Exotic; Historical/Fantasy
Major character(s): Moriah Morgan, Imposter (posing as a prostitute); Valsin Masters, Landowner (island owner), Recluse
Time period(s): 1850s (1851)
Locale(s): Bahamas
Summary: Posing as a prostitute, Moriah Morgan goes to Sin Master's remote island to search for her sister's murderer. Although several murders and a rather evil voodoo priestess conspire to stop her, Moriah is determined to learn who killed her sister and why Sin has retreated into exile. Dark forces and the wicked priestess nearly kill her, but eventually she and Sin find the real culprits—and discover love. Dark, mysterious, and sensual.

Other books you might like:
Jennifer Horsman, *With One Look*, 1994
  mystical and exotic/darker than some
Katherine Kincaid, *Midnight Treasure*, 1992
  a touch of voodoo with a very different emphasis
Cheri Scotch, *The Werewolf's Kiss*, 1992
  voodoo, New Orleans, and werewolves
Christina Skye, *The Ruby*, 1992
  island passion

1625
SUE RICH
The Scarlet Temptress
(New York: Pocket, 1991)

Story type: Historical/Colonial America
Major character(s): Samantha Fielding, Twin, Revolutionary; Jason Kincaid, Twin, Revolutionary; Nick Kincaid, Twin
Time period(s): 1770s (1774)
Locale(s): Virginia, American Colonies
Summary: Identical twins Samantha and Christine Fielding become politically and romantically involved with another pair of identical twins, Nick and Jason Kincaid, with somewhat confusing, but delightfully romantic, results.

Other books you might like:
Caryn Cameron, *Freedom Flame*, 1990
  sensual
Caryn Cameron, *Liberty's Lady*, 1990
  sensual
Carola Dunn, *Two Corinthians*, 1989
  Regency
Judith E. French, *Scarlet Ribbons*, 1989
  sensual
Anthea Malcolm, *Counterfeit Heart*, 1991
  Regency

1626
SUE RICH
Shadowed Vows
(New York: Pocket, 1992)

Story type: Historical/Georgian; Historical/Post-American Revolution
Major character(s): Lady Victoria Townsend, Noblewoman; Adam Remington, Nobleman, Indian (Shadow Hawk)
Time period(s): 1770s (1775); 1780s (1782)
Locale(s): American Colonies; England
Summary: When Adam Remington comes to England from the Colonies to claim his inheritance, he compromises young Victoria and is forced into marriage—and then he promptly disappears. Seven years later they both head to America—

Victoria to be reunited with her husband; Adam to seek revenge for being sold into salt mine slavery by Victoria's cousin. Together at last, they have a lot to work out, but in true romance fashion their problems are eventually solved to both of their satisfactions. Sensual.

Other books you might like:
Clarice Peters, *The Absentee Earl*, 1992
Amanda Quick, *Reckless*, 1992
Marlene Suson, *The Errant Earl*, 1989
Lynette Vinet, *Pirate's Bride*, 1989

1627
SUE RICH

The Silver Witch
(New York: Pocket, 1995)

Story type: Historical/Fantasy
Major character(s): Ashlee Walker, Recluse; Connor Westfield, Rake
Time period(s): 1820s (1821)
Locale(s): St. Augustine, Florida; Charleston, South Carolina

Summary: Badly scarred as the result of a laboratory accident, Ashlee Walker is resigned to life as a recluse, but strange dreams haunt her. Things become even more intriguing when Connor Westfield arrives, seeking her scientist father's help for his aunt's malaria, and they are both struck by the same sense of deja-vu—and the same attraction for each other. An old legend, a deserted swamp mansion haunted by a silver witch, and apparent reincarnation all add to this intriguing new-age romance.

Other books you might like:
Jude Deveraux, *Remembrance*, 1994
　reincarnation theme/different treatment
Kristin Hannah, *Once in Every Life*, 1993
　reincarnation/time travel elements/poignant
Sabine Kells, *A Deeper Hunger*, 1994
　vampire fantasy
Helen Mittermeyer, *Princess of the Veil*, 1992
　another scarred heroine
Maura Seger, *Forevermore*, 1994
　historical fantasy

1628
DENISE RICHARDS (Pseudonym of Kim Shreffler)

A Family Affair
(Bensalem, Pennsylvania: Meteor, 1992)

Story type: Contemporary
Major character(s): Marla Crandall, Stock Broker (assistant); Eric Westbrook, Innkeeper (ski lodge owner)
Time period(s): 1990s
Locale(s): United States

Summary: Shocked at her mother's announcement that she is not only getting married but also is pregnant, Marla Crandall joins forces with Eric Westbrook, the groom's brother, to stop the wedding from taking place — an alliance that eventually results in not one, but two, weddings.

Other books you might like:
Betty Barker, *Impossible Match*, 1992
Jayne Ann Krentz, *The Golden Chance*, 1990
Jayne Ann Krentz, *Sweet Fortune*, 1991
Nadine Miller, *Iron and Lace*, 1992

1629
SERENA RICHARDS

Rendezvous
(New York: Berkley, 1991)

Story type: Historical/Post-French Revolution
Major character(s): Isabelle Varens, Spy (French); Sinclair Carrington, Spy (English)
Time period(s): 18th century
Locale(s): France

Summary: Although imprisoned for her work rescuing French aristocrats from the guillotine, once she is released, Isabelle Varens cannot return to a quiet life, so she becomes a spy whose mission is to abduct Napoleon. Her teammate in this effort is master spy Sinclair Carrington, a secretive man she is loathe to trust but one with whom she falls dangerously in love. Passionate, suspenseful, and exceptionally well-plotted.

Other books you might like:
Mollie Ashton, *Terms of Surrender*, 1990
Brian Cleeve, *Hester*, 1979
Iris Johansen, *Storm Winds*, 1991
Baroness Orczy, *The Scarlet Pimpernel*, 1905
　classic tale of the French Revolution
Elizabeth Thornton, *Scarlet Angel*, 1990

1630
NANCY RICHARDS-AKERS

The Heart and the Heather
(New York: Avon, 1994)

Story type: Historical/Medieval
Major character(s): Isobel Kirkpatrick, Spouse (abandoned); Malcolm Kirkpatrick, Chieftain
Time period(s): 13th century
Locale(s): Western Highlands, Scotland

Summary: When Malcolm Kirkpatrick rescues Isobel Mac-William from warriors, they fall in love at first sight. Although both are wed, having been married as babies (to each other!) by their families, they can't resist each other and become "adulterers." Treachery, a vengeful grandfather, and their love eventually reveals the truth and they can be together at last.

Other books you might like:
Katherine Deauville, *The Amethyst Crown*, 1994
Denise Domning, *Summer Storm*, 1994
　unusual
Joanna McGauran, *By My Lady's Honor*, 1994
Emma Merritt, *Lord of Fire*, 1994
Emma Merritt, *Lord of Thunder*, 1994

1631

NANCY RICHARDS-AKERS

Lady Sarah's Charade

(New York: Avon, 1992)

Story type: Regency
Major character(s): Sarah Clement-Brooke, Noblewoman, Paranormal Investigator (ghost hunter); Beverley, Nobleman (Earl of Radnor)
Time period(s): 1790s
Locale(s): England

Summary: Sarah Clement-Brooke prefers ''ghost-hunting'' to any other activity, including romance. However, matchmaking Aunt Ophelia has ideas that include Sarah and the handsome, arrogant Earl of Radnor. To divert these plans, Sarah and the Earl decide to pretend courtship—leaving them both free to pursue their own interests; but as they go through the motions of romance, they find they are only fooling themselves! Happy romantic endings all around, even for Aunt Ophelia.

Other books you might like:
Marion Chesney, *The First Rebellion*, 1989
Carla Kelly, *Miss Grimsley's Oxford Career*, 1992
Elizabeth Peters, *The Curse of the Pharaohs*, 1981
Sheila Simonson, *Lady Elizabeth's Comet*, 1985

1632

NANCY RICHARDS-AKERS

Miss Wickham's Betrothal

(New York: Avon, 1992)

Story type: Regency
Major character(s): Lucy Wickham, Noblewoman, Debutante; Alex Paget, Nobleman (Earl)
Time period(s): 1810s
Locale(s): London, England

Summary: Lucy Wickham wants a hearth and home, but she really doesn't believe that she will find love. She does, however, find a fiance. Things take a turn for the unusual when she finds herself in love with his uncle, Alex Paget. Of course, everything turns out, but the journey to the satisfactory end is delightful.

Other books you might like:
Cathleen Clare, *The Mistress of Mishap*, 1992
Charlotte Louise Dolan, *The Black Widow*, 1992
Margaret Evans Porter, *Road to Ruin*, 1992
Amanda Quick, *Ravished*, 1992
Deborah Simmons, *Fortune Hunter*, 1992

1633

EVELYN RICHARDSON

Lady Alex's Gamble

(New York: Signet, 1995)

Story type: Regency

Major character(s): Lady Alexandra de Montmorency, Noblewoman (Earl of Harlewood's sister), Twin; Lord Christopher Wrotham, Nobleman, Military Personnel
Time period(s): 1810s
Locale(s): England

Summary: When her selfish twin brother's profligate ways leave Lady Alexandra de Montmorency no choice but to lose the family estate or marry a man she abhors, the intrepid Lady Alex assumes her brother's identity and heads for London, determined to gamble her way out of debt. Her adventures, however, net her more than money; and when the dashing and highly eligible Lord Wrotham appears on the scene, her life suddenly becomes complex in ways she had never imagined. Gentle, compelling, and involving.

Other books you might like:
Elisabeth Fairchild, *The Love Knot*, 1995
Candice Hern, *A Change of Heart*, 1995
Georgette Heyer, *Bath Tangle*, 1955
Georgette Heyer, *Faro's Daughter*, 1941
April Kihlstrom, *The Wicked Groom*, 1996

1634

EVELYN RICHARDSON

The Willful Widow

(New York: Signet, 1994)

Story type: Regency
Major character(s): Lady Diana Hatherill, Noblewoman; Lord Justin St. Claire, Nobleman
Time period(s): 1810s
Locale(s): England

Summary: All Lady Diana wants is to be left alone to lead her own life and protect her inheritance. The last thing she needs is interference from Lord Justin St. Clair. Nevertheless, that is just what she gets from this persistent hero who is determined to save his nephew from Diana but ends up falling in love with her himself.

Other books you might like:
Sarah Eagle, *The Reluctant Suitor*, 1991
Carla Kelly, *Miss Grimsley's Oxford Career*, 1992
Barbara Metzger, *An Affair of Interest*, 1992
Barbara Metzger, *Lady in Green*, 1993
Jeanne Savery, *The Last of the Winter Roses*, 1991

1635

PAULA DETMER RIGGS

Rough Passage

(New York: Silhouette, 1991)

Story type: Contemporary
Major character(s): Regan Delaney, Vacationer, Social Worker; Jake Cutter, Convict, Police Officer (former)
Time period(s): 1990s
Locale(s): California

Summary: While fighting a raging forest fire in southern California, convict Jake Cutter has a chance to escape to Mexico; but when he encounters lovely Regan Delaney, he knows he must sacrifice his chance to escape to take her to safety. A gritty, hard-hitting, passionate story about caring people in a rough, and at times unfair, world.

Other books you might like:
Janet Dailey, *Touch the Wind*, 1979
Vanessa Grant, *Awakening Dreams*, 1990
Anne McCaffrey, *Stitch in Snow*, 1984
Chloe Summers, *No Easy Task*, 1991
Kay Wilding, *Rainbow's End*, 1990

1636

LEIGH RIKER

Morning Rain

(New York: Harper, 1991)

Story type: Contemporary
Major character(s): Laurel Frasier Benedict, Socialite; Ryder McKendrick, Photojournalist
Time period(s): 1990s
Locale(s): Washington, District of Columbia

Summary: When Laurel Benedict, daughter of a prominent senator and wife to an ambitious politician, has an affair with photojournalist Ryder McKendrick, she finds herself caught between duty to her family and a love she cannot give up. Well-drawn characters set against the complex and somewhat sordid background of Washington politics.

Other books you might like:
Sandra Bregman, *Reach for the Dream*, 1990
Sandra Brown, *Mirror Image*, 1990
Belva Plain, *Evergreen*, 1978
Danielle Steel, *Crossings*, 1982
Helen Van Slyke, *A Necessary Woman*, 1979

1637

EUGENIA RILEY

Rogue's Mistress

(New York: Avon, 1991)

Story type: Historical/Victorian America
Major character(s): Mercy O'Shea, Ward, Spouse (reluctant); Julian Devereaux, Guardian
Time period(s): 1840s (1842)
Locale(s): New Orleans, Louisiana

Summary: To save her love from having to fight a duel with Julian Devereaux, her guardian, Mercy reluctantly agrees to marry Julian—and ends up loving a man she had hated for years. Lots of sparks and passion set against the glittering background of mid-nineteenth century New Orleans society.

Other books you might like:
Jennifer Blake, *Moonlight Waltz*, 1985
Brenda Joyce, *Dark Fires*, 1991
Alexandra Ripley, *New Orleans Legacy*, 1987
Karen Robards, *Forbidden Love*, 1990
Evelyn Rogers, *A Love So Wild*, 1991

1638

EUGENIA RILEY

Taming Kate

(New York: Avon, 1992)

Story type: Historical/American West
Major character(s): Kate Maloney, Young Woman (trouble-maker), Fiance(e); Charlie Durango, Bounty Hunter
Time period(s): 1850s (1859)
Locale(s): Texas

Summary: Ornery, belligerent, and fiery Kate Maloney is trouble to everyone. No one can handle her so the only solution is to marry her off! Only problem is that Kate doesn't want to get married—so she runs away and ends up captured by Comanches. Charlie Durango rescues her and wants to marry her, but it takes some doing to convince Kate that that is really what she wants, too. Sensual and fiery.

Other books you might like:
Robin Lee Hatcher, *Midnight Rose*, 1992
Linda Lael Miller, *Caroline and the Raider*, 1992
Penelope Neri, *Cherish the Night*, 1992
Rebecca Paisley, *Midnight and Magnolias*, 1992

1639

EUGENIA RILEY

Tempest in Time

(New York: Leisure, 1993)

Story type: Time Travel; Historical/Antebellum American South
Major character(s): Melissa "Missy" Monroe, Business-woman, Time Traveller; Jeff Dalton, Businessman, Fiance(e); Fabian Fontenot, Gentleman, Fiance(e)
Time period(s): 1850s; 1990s
Locale(s): Memphis, Tennessee

Summary: 1990s Missy isn't too anxious to marry shy, quiet Jeffrey but will do so to merge their companies; 1850s Melissa doesn't want to marry her arrogant, domineering fiance Fabian but has no choice. The solution miraculously comes on their wedding day when they exchange places through time and each finds the perfect mate. But can things stay as they are? Or will "time" once again take a hand? Intriguing and involved.

Other books you might like:
Sandra Canfield, *The Loving*, 1992
Sandra Davidson, *A Love for All Time*, 1993
Shannon Drake, *Avon Books Presents: Haunting Love Stories*, 1991
Kristin Hannah, *Once in Every Life*, 1993
Becky Lee Weyrich, *Forever, for Love*, 1989

1640

EUGENIA RILEY

A Tryst in Time

(New York: Leisure, 1992)

Story type: Time Travel; Historical/Post-American Civil War
Major character(s): Sarah Jennings, Artist; Damien Fontaine, Plantation Owner, Spirit
Time period(s): 1870s (1871); 20th century
Locale(s): Belle Fontaine, Louisiana

Summary: Hoping to find a new direction to life following her nervous breakdown, artist Sarah Jennings moves to an old Southern plantation and discovers ghosts, an inexplicable sense of "coming home," and a door into the past—and to love. A time travel novel with a touch of mystery and some unusual twists.

Other books you might like:
Peggy Darty, *The Crimson Roses of Fountain Court*, 1991
Diana Gabaldon, *Outlander*, 1991
Carla Simpson, *Always, My Love*, 1990
Kathleen E. Woodiwiss, *Come Love a Stranger*, 1984

1641

MILDRED RILEY

Journey's End

(New York: Zebra, 1995)

Story type: Historical/American West
Major character(s): Bethenia Cooper, Orphan; Haste Terrell, Cowboy, Detective—Private (Pinkerton agent)
Time period(s): 1870s (1875)
Locale(s): Boston, Massachusetts; Colorado

Summary: When Bethenia Cooper decides to find her uncle after her parents both die, she knows the only man who can get her to Colorado is the handsome cowboy, Haste Terrell. Haste, an undercover Pinkerton agent on assignment, doesn't relish the idea of escorting Bethenia; but when danger strikes on the trail, he discovers he cares for her more than he should. Both danger and love await them in Colorado.

Other books you might like:
Emily Bradshaw, *The Heart's Journey*, 1992
    another heroine heading west with a reluctant guide
Lori Copeland, *Promise Me Today*, 1992
    action and humor/a hero who is not what he seems
Joan Johnston, *Kid Calhoun*, 1993
    Colorado setting, fast-paced and funny
Elizabeth Lowell, *Only His*, 1991

1642

CONNIE RINEHOLD

More than Just a Night

(New York: Dell, 1991)

Story type: Historical/American West
Major character(s): Cameo Fielding, Frontierswoman; Zach McAllister, Spy

Time period(s): 1860s
Locale(s): United States

Summary: Cameo Fielding falls in love with Union spy Zach McAllister, who tragically disappears during battle. Later, when the new ranch manager, Sloane, mysteriously appears, Cameo is strangely attracted to him—for good reason as it turns out. Fast-paced and highly sensual.

Other books you might like:
Constance Bennett, *Morning Sky*, 1991
Linda Howard, *A Lady of the West*, 1990
Leta Tegler, *Gabrielle*, 1990
Victoria Thompson, *Fortune's Lady*, 1990

1643

CONNIE RINEHOLD

Unspoken Vows

(New York: Dell, 1995)

Story type: Historical/American West
Major character(s): Rachel Parrish, Rancher; Sir Henry Ashford, Nobleman (second son of an earl), Fugitive; Lucien Ashford, Nobleman (Earl of Fairleigh)
Time period(s): 1870s (1879); 1880s (1886)
Locale(s): Wyoming

Summary: Rachel Parrish, daughter of the Wyoming Territory's "best lady of ill repute," is not interested in following in her mother's footsteps and knows she has to get away. Determined to leave her past behind, she decides to reclaim her grandfather's homestead, but when she realizes she needs to be married to be considered respectable, she advertises for a husband. She gets one, but not the one she expects. Strong, appealing characters drive the action in this sensual, lively romance.

Other books you might like:
Rosanne Bittner, *Outlaw Hearts*, 1993
Peggy Hanchar, *Fancy Lady*, 1994
Teresa Hart, *Hearts Are Wild*, 1993
Theresa Michaels, *Gifts of Love*, 1992
    a heroine escaping her past
Patricia Potter, *Notorious*, 1993

1644

THOMASINA RING

Dream Catcher

(New York: Leisure, 1992)

Story type: Historical/American Revolution
Major character(s): Bethany Rose Stewart, Mountain Woman; Adam Barwick, Murderer (accused), Avenger
Time period(s): 18th century
Locale(s): Williamsburg, Virginia

Summary: Adam Barwick returns to his Virginia home bent on revenge for the treachery his step-brother had used to force him out of his home. When his horse is stolen, he takes out after the guilty parties and ends up finding Bethany Rose Stewart orphaned by a fire. He takes her to safety, and although her dreamy manner drives him crazy, she eventually proves to be a pragmatist, and love blossoms for them both.

Other books you might like:
Linda Covington, *Wild Tory Rose*, 1992
Constance O'Banyon, *Forever My Love*, 1991
Patricia Rice, *Moon Dreams*, 1991
Francine Rivers, *Redeeming Love*, 1991
   unusual
Becky Lee Weyrich, *Silver Tears*, 1990

1645

THOMASINA RING

Time-Spun Rapture

(New York: Leisure, 1990)

Story type: Time Travel
Major character(s): Astrid Van Fleet, Time Traveller; Thomas Arlington, Settler (Virginia colonist)
Time period(s): 1980s (1989); 17th century (1676)
Locale(s): Virginia

Summary: While camping in Virginia, Astrid Van Fleet falls asleep in 1989 and wakes up in 1676—in the middle of Bacon's Rebellion—about to be "rescued" from her sleeping bag by handsome colonist Thomas Arlington. Confused, she feigns amnesia until she can decide what to do. Inevitably, she becomes involved in the political events of the time; and while she and Tom fight for freedom, they also must fight their growing attraction to each other.

Other books you might like:
Jude Deveraux, *A Knight in Shining Armor*, 1989
   time change elements
Heather Graham, *Every Time I Love You*, 1988
   time change elements
Karen Harper, *Eden's Gate*, 1989
Andrea Parnell, *Wild Glory*, 1990
Becky Lee Weyrich, *Forever, for Love*, 1989
   time change elements

1646

THOMASINA RING

Time-Spun Treasure

(New York: Leisure, 1992)

Story type: Historical/American Revolution; Time Travel
Major character(s): Meredith Davis, Time Traveller, Health Care Professional (physical therapist); Benjamin Foxworth, Patriot
Time period(s): 1990s; 1770s (1774)
Locale(s): Virginia, American Colonies

Summary: Hurled from the present to pre-revolutionary Virginia, Meredith Davis suddenly has a baby and a new husband to contend with — and a family ghost as well. Family curses and treasure combine with a dash of political intrigue to produce a funny and engrossing time-travel romance.

Other books you might like:
Janice Bennett, *A Touch of Forever*, 1992
Barbara Bretton, *Somewhere in Time*, 1992

Lori Copeland, *Forever Ashley*, 1992
Jude Deveraux, *A Knight in Shining Armor*, 1989
Vivian Knight-Jenkins, *Passion's Timeless Hour*, 1992

1647

ALEXANDRA RIPLEY

Scarlett

(New York: Warner, 1991)

Story type: Historical/Post-American Civil War
Major character(s): Scarlett Butler, Plantation Owner; Rhett Butler, Businessman
Time period(s): 1870s
Locale(s): Georgia; Ireland

Summary: The story picks up where *Gone with the Wind* left off—Melly's funeral. Rhett has turned his back on Scarlett and already she is scheming to find a way to win him back. However, in order to find Rhett, Scarlett must find herself. She journeys home to Tara and then to Ireland and finally home to Rhett's arms. Long-awaited sequel to Margaret Mitchell's *Gone with the Wind*.

Other books you might like:
Jo Ann Algermissen, *Golden Bird*, 1990
Gwen Bristow, *Deep Summer*, 1937
   second in a trilogy
Lonnie Coleman, *Beulah Land*, 1973
   first of a trilogy
Margaret Mitchell, *Gone with the Wind*, 1936
   a "must" if you haven't read this classic
Kathleen E. Woodiwiss, *Ashes in the Wind*, 1979

1648

FRANCINE RIVERS

Redeeming Love

(New York: Bantam, 1991)

Story type: Historical/American West Coast
Major character(s): "Angel" Sarah Stafford, Prostitute (child); Michael Hosea, Farmer
Time period(s): 1830s (1837); 1850s
Locale(s): San Francisco, California; London, England

Summary: Sold into prostitution at the age of eight, Angel lives a tormented life of degradation, poverty, and loneliness until Michael takes her to his farm and into his life. Angel discovers a warmth and acceptance she has never known, and because of Michael's "redeeming love" she is able finally to come to terms with her past and put it behind her. Unique combination of sensual and inspirational elements. Loosely based on the Biblical story of the prophet Hosea.

Other books you might like:
Emilie Loring, *Swift Water*, 1929
   early 20th century setting
Bette M. Ross, *Gennie, the Huguenot Woman*, 1983
   inspirational
LaVyrle Spencer, *Forgiving*, 1990
LaVyrle Spencer, *Morning Glory*, 1989

1649

KAREN ROBARDS

Green Eyes

(New York: Avon, 1991)

Story type: Historical/Exotic
Major character(s): Anna Traherne, Plantation Owner (Ceylon), Widow(er); Julian Chase, Nobleman (Lord Ridley of Gordon Hall)
Time period(s): 19th century
Locale(s): England; Sri Lanka (Ceylon)

Summary: To escape her brother-in-law's lecherous attempts, young widow Anna Traherne takes the family emeralds and flees to her Ceylon plantation. Hot on her trail is the rightful owner of the jewels, Julian Chase; and he finds her with passionate results. A highly sensual, somewhat violent story in an exotic setting.

Other books you might like:
Virginia Henley, *The Pirate and the Pagan*, 1990
Meagan McKinney, *Till Dawn Tames the Night*, 1991
Katherine Sutcliffe, *Shadow Play*, 1991
Janelle Taylor, *Whispered Kisses*, 1990

1650

KAREN ROBARDS

Maggy's Child

(New York: Delacorte, 1994)

Story type: Contemporary/Mainstream; Romantic Suspense
Major character(s): Maggy Forrest, Socialite, Abuse Victim; Nick King, Businessman
Time period(s): 1990s
Locale(s): Louisville, Kentucky

Summary: Determined to win back Maggy, the love of his life, and settle an old score with her husband, Nick King returns to Louisville and becomes the catalyst that will turn Maggy's world upside down—and eventually set her free. A compelling story of love, spousal abuse, and revenge set against the silken facade of Kentucky blueblood society.

Other books you might like:
Jennifer Blake, *Love and Smoke*, 1989
Tami Hoag, *Dark Paradise*, 1994
Nora Roberts, *Divine Evil*, 1992
Katherine Stone, *Pearl Moon*, 1995
    different setting, spousal abuse, old secrets

1651

KAREN ROBARDS

Morning Song

(New York: Avon, 1989)

Story type: Historical/Antebellum American South
Major character(s): Jessica Lindsay, Southern Belle; Clive McIntock, Gambler (riverboat), Fortune Hunter (alias Stuart Edwards)
Time period(s): 1840s (1842)
Locale(s): Mississippi

Summary: Considering Clive a fortune hunter of the worst kind, Jessica makes life difficult for her cruel stepmother's new husband. But when Clive and Jessica fall in love with each other, life becomes difficult for them both.

Other books you might like:
Eugenia Price, *Savannah*, 1983
Alexandra Ripley, *Charleston*, 1982
Kathleen E. Woodiwiss, *Come Love a Stranger*, 1984
    Antebellum South
Kathleen E. Woodiwiss, *The Flame and the Flower*, 1972
    Antebellum South

1652

KAREN ROBARDS

Nobody's Angel

(New York: Delacorte, 1992)

Story type: Historical/Colonial America
Major character(s): Susannah Redman, Spinster; Ian Connelly, Nobleman (Marquis of Derne), Servant (indentured)
Time period(s): 18th century
Locale(s): American Colonies; England

Summary: Needing a new hired man, Susannah Redman buys the indenture of a bedraggled English convict only to find herself strangely attracted to this man who is not at all what he seems. A warm, passionate story that sweeps its characters from the simplicity of the American Colonies to the dazzling complexities of British high society and proves that true love does overcome all obstacles.

Other books you might like:
Cassie Edwards, *When Passion Calls*, 1990
Miriam Minger, *Defiant Imposter*, 1992
Dana Ransom, *Wild Savage Love*, 1990
Laura Simon, *A Taste of Heaven*, 1989
JoAnn Wendt, *The Golden Dove*, 1989

1653

KAREN ROBARDS

One Summer

(New York: Delacorte, 1993)

Story type: Contemporary; Romantic Suspense
Major character(s): Rachel Grant, Teacher (high school); Johnny Harris, Convict (ex-con)
Time period(s): 1990s
Locale(s): Tylerville, Kentucky

Summary: Teacher Rachel Grant firmly believes that one of her former students, Johnny Harris, is innocent of murder and rape. However, their small town thinks he is guilty and continues to ostracize him even after his release from prison after serving ten years. Things come to a head when another woman is killed, and Johnny is the prime suspect. A passionate story with an interesting, reverse-age difference twist.

Other books you might like:

Sandra Brown, *Breath of Scandal*, 1991
Carole Dean, *One Tough Cookie*, 1993
Jeane Gilbert-Lewis, *Common Ground*, 1993
Judith McNaught, *Perfect*, 1993

1654

KAREN ROBARDS

This Side of Heaven

(New York: Dell, 1991)

Story type: Historical/Colonial America
Major character(s): Caroline Wetherby, Refugee (from England); Matt Mathieson, Farmer (Pilgrim)
Time period(s): 17th century (1684)
Locale(s): Connecticut, American Colonies

Summary: Caroline, destitute and hating men, finds her Pilgrim family of men and boys a challenge instead of a refuge, especially her handsome, strong-willed brother-in-law.

Other books you might like:

Barbara Cummings, *Frontier Fire*, 1991
Rainy Kirkland, *Bewitching Kisses*, 1991
Anita Mills, *Follow the Heart*, 1990
Nancy Moulton, *Defiant Heart*, 1989
Becky Lee Weyrich, *Silver Tears*, 1990

1655

KAREN ROBARDS

Walking After Midnight

(New York: Doubleday, 1995)

Story type: Contemporary; Romantic Suspense
Major character(s): Summer McFee, Maintenance Worker (janitor); Steve Calhoun, Police Officer
Time period(s): 1990s
Locale(s): Murfreesboro, Tennessee

Summary: Summer McFee is well-acquainted with the hard knock realities of life, but nothing can prepare a woman to be kidnapped by a corpse! Steven Calhous isn't dead yet, but he soon will be if he can't figure out who is after him and why. Until he discovers Summer's role in his attempted murder, he's not letting her out of his sight. An unwilling participant in a deadly game, Summer soon realizes she's safer hiding out in the backwoods of Tennessee with Steve than turning to the police for help. A fast-paced thriller, laced with humor and a dash of the paranormal, that makes good use of the captive-in-love-with-captor plot pattern.

Other books you might like:

Jennifer Blake, *Shameless*, 1994
Rebecca Brandewyne, *Dust Devil*, 1996
Marilyn Pappano, *In Sinful Harmony*, 1995
Nora Roberts, *Carnal Innocence*, 1992
Tracey Tillis, *Deadly Masquerade*, 1994

1656

J.D. ROBB (Pseudonym of Nora Roberts)

Naked in Death

(New York: Berkley, 1995)

Story type: Romantic Suspense; Futuristic
Major character(s): Eve Dallas, Detective—Homicide; Roarke, Businessman (tycoon)
Time period(s): 21st century

Summary: When Lieutenant Eve Dallas is called in to investigate the unusual killing of a prostitute, all the evidence points to the enigmatic tycoon, Roarke—a man who Eve ends up being alternately attracted to and suspicious of as she works to solve the murder. A fast-paced and involving romantic suspense novel of the future. Unique.

Other books you might like:

Suzanne Forster, *Come Midnight*, 1991
    more murders/not futuristic
Wendy Haley, *Shadow Whispers*, 1992
    good characterizations/not futuristic
Tami Hoag, *Guilty as Sin*, 1996
    murder and suspense/not futuristic
Tami Hoag, *Night Sins*, 1995
    murder and suspense/not futuristic
Nora Roberts, *Carnal Innocence*, 1992
    same author/romantic suspense/not futuristic

1657

REBECCA ROBBINS

Lucky in Love

(New York: Avon, 1994)

Story type: Regency
Major character(s): Fanny McDonald, Noblewoman, Fiance(e) (reluctant); Malen Campbell, Nobleman (duke), Fiance(e)
Time period(s): 1810s
Locale(s): England

Summary: When Lady Fanny learns that her fiance is Malen Campbell of the hated Campbell clan, she refuses to marry him—even though she is attracted to him. His persistence wins in the end, but not before the couple engage in numerous, rather long and vitriolic exchanges. Not your typical Regency.

Other books you might like:

Jo Beverley, *An Arranged Marriage*, 1991
Jo Beverley, *An Unwilling Bride*, 1992
Mary Chase Comstock, *An Impetuous Miss*, 1993
Sarah Eagle, *The Reluctant Suitor*, 1991
Joan Overfield, *The Viscount's Vixen*, 1992

1658

ANN VICTORIA ROBERTS

Morning's Gate

(New York: Morrow, 1991)

Story type: Contemporary/Mainstream; Historical/World War I

Major character(s): Zoe Clifford, Artist; Steven Elliott, Sailor (merchant seaman); Liam Elliott, Military Personnel (Australian soldier)

Time period(s): 1990s (Gulf War); 1910s (1914-1917)

Locale(s): York, England; France (battlefields); Outback, Australia

Summary: Zoe Clifford, researching family history with her cousin Stephen, uncovers tragic love stories of her ancestors, in particular, Liam Elliott, a soldier in World War I. Her attraction to Liam's story uncovers remarkable parallels in her own life. Sequel to *Louisa Elliott*.

Other books you might like:

Colleen McCullough, *The Thorn Birds*, 1977
Anne Melville, *Blaine*, 1981
    part of the Lorimer Saga
Katherine Sinclair, *A Distant Dawn*, 1991
Marcella Thum, *The Thorn Trees*, 1991

1659

DOREEN ROBERTS

Broken Wings

(New York: Silhouette, 1992)

Story type: Contemporary

Major character(s): Lyn Barclay, Journalist; Ward Sullivan, Handicapped (blind), Pilot (Blue Angel Commander)

Time period(s): 1990s

Summary: Journalist Lyn Barclay tries to help Blue Angel Commander Ward Sullivan when he is blinded in a plane crash, but their past misunderstandings and his intense anger keep getting in the way.

Other books you might like:

Delayne Camp, *Newsworthy Affair*, 1990
Vanessa Grant, *Awakening Dreams*, 1990
Jennifer Greene, *Pink Topaz*, 1992
Elizabeth Lambert, *Wings of Desire*, 1990

1660

MEG-LYNN ROBERTS

An Alluring Lady

(New York: Zebra, 1992)

Story type: Regency

Major character(s): Jillian St. Erney, Widow(er), Governess; Jack Mackinnon, Rogue

Time period(s): 1810s

Locale(s): England

Summary: Literally thrown together along a country roadside as the result of an attack by a murderous gang of highwaymen, irrepressible Jillian St. Erney and charming adventurer Jack Mackinnon wend their way toward civilization and into each other's hearts as Jillian struggles with her feelings for this man who may not be what he seems. A witty, lively Regency romp.

Other books you might like:

Rita Boucher, *The Scandalous Schoolmistress*, 1992
Clare Darcy, *Letty*, 1980
Patricia Rice, *Mad Maria's Daughter*, 1992
Amanda Scott, *The Dauntless Miss Wingrave*, 1989
Patricia Veryan, *Logic of the Heart*, 1991

1661

MEG-LYNN ROBERTS

Christmas Escapade

(New York: Zebra, 1994)

Story type: Regency; Holiday Themes

Major character(s): Mary Marlowe, Companion, Gentlewoman; Peveril Standish, Nobleman (Viscount Lindford); Belinda Ramsbottom, Debutante

Time period(s): 1810s

Locale(s): England

Summary: When Peveril Standish, Viscount Lindford, bravely, if not a bit drunkenly, rescues two damsels in distress, he is instantly enamoured of the charms of the incredibly beautiful, but appallingly featherbrained Belinda Ramsbottom. However, it is eventually her companion, the lovely and logically sensible Mary Marlowe who wins his heart—even though she has to wait for him to grow up a bit to recognize what he really wants.

Other books you might like:

Susan Carroll, *Christmas Belles*, 1992
Sandra Heath, *A Christmas Courtship*, 1990
Carla Kelly, *Marian's Christmas Wish*, 1989
Carla Kelly, *Mrs. Drew Plays Her Hand*, 1994
Joan Smith, *The Kissing Bough*, 1994

1662

MEG-LYNN ROBERTS

Love's Gambit

(New York: Zebra, 1995)

Story type: Regency

Major character(s): Georgiana "Georgie" Carteret, Gentlewoman, Debutante; Augustus Sebastian Stanhope St. Regis, Nobleman (Viscount Sedgemoor), Rake

Time period(s): 1810s

Locale(s): England

Summary: Impish and fun-loving, the soon-to-be debutante Georgie Carteret decides the rigid, straight-laced Viscount Sedgemoor needs to be taken down a peg or two. When her efforts only succeed in making him angry, they end up in a situation that neither expected. A light, lively Regency with a marriage-of-convenience theme.

Other books you might like:
Julie Caille, *The Rake and His Lady*, 1993
Sarah Eagle, *The Marriage Gamble*, 1992
Kathleen Elliott, *A Special License*, 1995
Georgette Heyer, *The Convenient Marriage*, 1934
    classic Regency
Margaret Evans Porter, *Road to Ruin*, 1992

1663

NORA ROBERTS

Born in Fire

(New York: Jove, 1994)

Story type: Contemporary
Series: Born In Trilogy
Major character(s): Margaret Mary ''Maggie'' Concannon,
    Artist (glassmaker); Rogan Sweeney, Art Dealer (gallery
    owner)
Time period(s): 1990s
Locale(s): County Clare, Ireland; Dublin, Ireland

Summary: When gifted glassmaker Maggie Concannon agrees
to let art gallery owner and promoter Rogan Sweeney act as
her agent, she only thinks to earn enough money to take care
of some long-standing family obligations; she doesn't plan on
becoming a celebrity—or on falling in love with Rogan. Fiery
and fiercely independent, Maggie eventually learns that her
art can coexist with love and that all marriages don't have to
be as dismal as her parents'. Well-done characters and vivid
descriptions of both Ireland and glassmaking. First of a trilogy. To be followed by *Born in Ice*.

Other books you might like:
Sandra Brown, *Texas! Sage*, 1991
    passionate and fast-paced
Jayne Ann Krentz, *Perfect Partners*, 1992
    good conflicts/strong characters
Rosalind Laker, *The Silver Touch*, 1987
    historical/another determined artistic heroine
Katherine Stone, *Happy Endings*, 1994
    some similar conflicts/different styles
Katherine Stone, *Pearl Moon*, 1995
    sensitive characters/complex backstories

1664

NORA ROBERTS

Born in Ice

(New York: Jove, 1995)

Story type: Contemporary
Series: Born In Trilogy
Major character(s): Brianna Concannon, Innkeeper (bed and
    breakfast owner); Grayson Thorne, Writer (mystery)
Time period(s): 1990s
Locale(s): County Clare, Ireland

Summary: Calm, gentle Brianna Concannon is thoroughly
wedded to her home and family; restless writer Grayson
Thorne is proud to call no place ''home.'' When Grayson
comes to Brianna's B & B to write for several months, it is

obvious to them both that they have nothing in common.
Naturally they fall in love. Filled with well-drawn, believable
characters, this fast-paced novel provides an appealing love
story and an excellent sense of place. Follows *Born in Fire*;
followed by *Born in Shame*.

Other books you might like:
Maeve Binchy, *Circle of Friends*, 1990
    similar ambience
Maeve Binchy, *Firefly Summer*, 1987
    similar ambience
Maeve Binchy, *The Glass Lake*, 1994
Anne McCaffrey, *Stitch-in-Snow*, 1984
Rosamunde Pilcher, *Wild Mountain Thyme*, 1978

1665

NORA ROBERTS

Carnal Innocence

(New York: Bantam, 1992)

Story type: Romantic Suspense; Contemporary/Mainstream
Major character(s): Caroline Waverly, Musician (''retired''
    concert violinist); Tucker Longstreet, Plantation Owner
    (Sweetwater)
Time period(s): 1990s
Locale(s): Innocence, Mississippi

Summary: Concert violinist Caroline Waverly tries to ''retire'' quietly to her family's secluded bayou home but finds
that all is neither peaceful nor innocent in sleepy Innocence,
Mississippi. A serial killer is terrorizing the town and not only
is Caroline threatened, but the man she comes to love is a
suspect! Murder, deception, and passion are the order of the
day in this fast-paced, hard-hitting tale.

Other books you might like:
Jennifer Blake, *Joy and Anger*, 1991
Diane Chamberlain, *Secret Lives*, 1992
Catherine Coulter, *Beyond Eden*, 1991
Jessica Gregory, *Once Innocent*, 1991
Elise Title, *Stage Whispers*, 1992

1666

NORA ROBERTS

Divine Evil

(New York: Bantam, 1992)

Story type: Romantic Suspense
Major character(s): Clare Kimball, Artist (sculptor); Cameron
    Rafferty, Police Officer (sheriff)
Time period(s): 1990s
Locale(s): Emmetsboro, Maryland

Summary: Renowned sculptor Clare Kimball returns to her
hometown to lay some old ghosts to rest and finds herself
caught in a web of evil that stretches from the past into the
present and threatens her sanity, her life, and her love.
Chilling, explosive, and a bit terrifying.

Other books you might like:
Jill Barkin, *Hot Streak*, 1990
Jennifer Blake, *Joy and Anger*, 1991

Janet Dailey, *Masquerade*, 1990
Mollie Gregory, *Birthstone*, 1991
Tami Hoag, *Still Waters*, 1992

1667

NORA ROBERTS

Genuine Lies

(New York: Bantam, 1991)

Story type: Contemporary; Romantic Suspense
Major character(s): Julia Summers, Writer (biographer); Paul Winthrop, Writer (novelist); Eve Benedict, Actress
Time period(s): 1990s
Locale(s): Hollywood, California

Summary: In California to collaborate with legendary film star Eve Benedict on her memoirs, biographer Julia Summers is puzzled by the initial hostility of Eve's stepson, novelist Paul Winthrop, and puzzled by a series of incidents aimed at sabatoging the book. However, it is when Eve is murdered that Julia's problems really begin. Excellent characters, well-plotted, and fast-paced.

Other books you might like:
Jill Barkin, *Hot Streak*, 1991
Catherine Coulter, *Beyond Eden*, 1992
Mollie Gregory, *Birthstone*, 1991
Jayne Ann Krentz, *Silver Linings*, 1991
JoAnn Ross, *Secret Sins*, 1990

1668

NORA ROBERTS
PATRICIA POTTER, Co-Author
RUTH LANGAN, Co-Author

Harlequin Historical Christmas

(Toronto: Harlequin, 1990)

Story type: Holiday Themes; Historical
Time period(s): 18th century; 19th century
Locale(s): United States

Summary: A trilogy of Christmas historicals set in the United States including "In From the Cold" by Nora Roberts (American Revolution), "Miracle of the Heart" by Patricia Potter (Civil War), and "Christmas at Bitter Creek" by Ruth Langan (American West).

Other books you might like:
Jane Bonander, *Avon Books Presents: A Christmas Together*, 1994
Leigh Greenwood, *Their First Noel*, 1995
Anita Mills, *Cherished Moments*, 1994
Judith McNaught, *A Holiday of Love*, 1994

1669

NORA ROBERTS

Hidden Riches

(New York: Putnam, 1994)

Story type: Contemporary; Romantic Suspense

Major character(s): Dora Conroy, Antiques Dealer; Jed Skimmerhorn, Police Officer (former)
Time period(s): 1990s
Locale(s): Philadelphia, Pennsylvania

Summary: Dora Conroy, the hardworking owner of an antique shop, doesn't take kindly to having her life disturbed by her new tenant, Jed Skimmerhorn. His attitude and money irritate her no end; nevertheless, he does come in handy when a trail of murder, theft, and art smuggling leads to her door. Eventually, they set aside their differences long enough to deal with the mystery—and fall in love.

Other books you might like:
Sandra Brown, *French Silk*, 1992
Jude Deveraux, *Sweet Liar*, 1992
Linda Howard, *Dream Man*, 1995
Jayne Ann Krentz, *Silver Linings*, 1991
Heather Graham Pozzessere, *Slow Burn*, 1994

1670

PEGGY ROBERTS (Pseudonym of Peggy Henshar)

Mrs. Perfect

(New York: Zebra, 1992)

Story type: Contemporary
Major character(s): Ginny Logan, Widow(er), Advertising; Jason McCann, Widow(er), Writer; Alex Russel, Businessman, Advertising
Time period(s): 1990s
Locale(s): United States

Summary: Devastated by the back-to-back deaths of her husband and son, Ginny Logan suddenly finds herself raising her three grandchildren, balancing a demanding job, and dealing with a conniving co-worker. To gain a new perspective, she takes the children to her lake house where she finds peace and quite — and a neighbor and recent widower, Jason McCann. Ginny's prodigal daughter-in-law and her long-admiring boss add to the tension in this realistic and highly sensual contemporary romance. Part of Zebra's new "It's Never Too Late To Fall In Love" line.

Other books you might like:
Georgia Bockoven, *A Marriage of Convenience*, 1991
Judy Gill, *Golden Swan*, 1990
Marcia Martin, *Southern Storms*, 1992
Marilyn Pappano, *Operation Homefront*, 1992
LaVyrle Spencer, *Bittersweet*, 1990

1671

GINA ROBINS (Pseudonym of Connie Feddersen)

Always and Forever

(New York: Zebra, 1992)

Story type: Historical/Exotic; Historical/Antebellum American South
Major character(s): Candeliera Caron, Heiress; Nicolas Tiger, Privateer, Sea Captain
Time period(s): 1810s (1814-1815)
Locale(s): Sargasso Sea, At Sea; New Orleans, Louisiana

Summary: Lost at sea as a child, for the past eleven years Candel has been blissfully happy as priestess to a female-dominated remote island culture. The last thing she needs is to be "rescued" and returned to "civilization." However, when privateer Nicolas Tiger ends up on her island, that is exactly what happens. Her subsequent return results in culture shock in both directions as she and Nicolas battle for both dominance and love. Action-filled, passionate, and funny.

Other books you might like:
Cheryl Black, *Comanche Love Song*, 1989
Clare Coleman, *Daughter of the Reef*, 1992
Betina Lindsey, *The Serpent Beguiled*, 1992
Constance O'Banyon, *Cheyenne Sunrise*, 1990
Victoria Thompson, *Wild Texas Wind*, 1992

1672

GINA ROBINS (Pseudonym of Connie Feddersen)

Deception's Sweet Kiss
(New York: Zebra, 1990)

Story type: Historical/American West
Major character(s): Shiloh McBride, Heiress (railroad), Feminist; Holt Cantrell, Detective (Pinkerton agent), Imposter
Time period(s): 1860s (1867)
Locale(s): St. Louis, Missouri

Summary: Disguised as a shy, bumbling railroad millionaire, Pinkerton agent Holt Cantrell captures heiress and feminist Shiloh McBride instead of the crooks he was after. Filled with humor and charm.

Other books you might like:
Betty Brooks, *Wild Magnolia*, 1990
Lori Copeland, *Fool Me Once*, 1990
Betina M. Krahn, *Love's Brazen Fire*, 1989
     Earlier setting/witty, charming
Betina Lindsey, *Waltz with the Lady*, 1990
     Strong feminist heroine
Judith Steel, *Seduction's Raging Flame*, 1989
     Similar theme

1673

GINA ROBINS

Forbidden Kiss
(New York: Zebra, 1995)

Story type: Historical/American West
Major character(s): Casity Crockett, Fugitive, Mail Order Bride (substitute); Shayler McCain, Mountain Man, Miner (gold); Tweed Cramer, Miner (gold)
Time period(s): 1870s (1876)
Locale(s): Ogallala, Nebraska; Deadwood, South Dakota

Summary: Fleeing for her life after she witnesses the gunning down of her uncle, Casity Crockett literally grabs the last train out of town and ends up in the wilds of Dakota, mistaken for a mail order bride by Shayler McCain, the adopted son of the man who "ordered" her. Complications arise when Casity and Shay fall in love with each other—and the fact that the men who killed her uncle are hot on her trail add to the action. Fast-paced, passionate, and funny.

Other books you might like:
Lori Copeland, *Promise Me Forever*, 1994
     fast-paced/funny
Teresa Hart, *Hearts Are Wild*, 1993
Peggy Hanchar, *Fancy Lady*, 1994
Jill Marie Landis, *Come Spring*, 1992
     another mistaken mail-order bride/different treatment
Linda Lael Miller, *My Darling Melissa*, 1990

1674

GINA ROBINS (Pseudonym of Connie Feddersen)

Love's Sweetest Secret
(New York: Zebra, 1991)

Story type: Historical/Antebellum American South
Major character(s): Liberty Jordan, Fiance(e) (reluctant); Dylon Lockhart, Plantation Owner, Rake
Time period(s): 1760s (1764)
Locale(s): South Carolina

Summary: Liberty Jordan is a woman with a surfeit of fiances. Everyone, it seems, wants to marry her; and when one of her suitors kidnaps her, the other four are off in hot pursuit. Eventually, of course, she ends up with the right one. Funny, nicely plotted, and exceedingly lively.

Other books you might like:
Jeanne E. Hansen, *Midnight Enchantment*, 1990
Shirl Henke, *Moonflower*, 1989
Leona Karr, *Nightfire*, 1990
Margaret Mitchell, *Gone with the Wind*, 1938
     classic tale of the South
Sonya T. Pelton, *Love Hear My Heart*, 1990

1675

GINA ROBINS (Pseudonym of Connie Feddersen)

Mississippi Mistress
(New York: Zebra, 1990)

Story type: Historical/Victorian America
Major character(s): Cori Pierce, Entertainer (on a riverboat); Jacob Wolf, Shipowner (riverboat, partner), Sea Captain (riverboat)
Time period(s): 1850s (1856)
Locale(s): St. Louis, Missouri; Mississippi River

Summary: Determined to expose her father's killer, feisty Cori Pierce goes to work as an entertainer aboard a riverboat only to find herself falling in love with Jake Wolf, captain of the riverboat and partner of the man she holds responsible for her father's death. Jake and Cori eventually join forces in more ways than one and, after a number of funny and suspenseful adventures, solve the mystery and live happily ever after.

Other books you might like:
Caroline Bourne, *Allegheny Captive*, 1990
Leona Karr, *Nightfire*, 1990
Patricia Matthews, *Love's Raging Tide*, 1980
Karen Robards, *Morning Song*, 1989

Ashley Snow, *Dangerous Desire*, 1990
strong heroine with a mission/different setting

1676

GINA ROBINS (Pseudonym of Connie Feddersen)

Texas Temptation

(New York: Zebra, 1989)

Story type: Historical/American West
Major character(s): Catlin Quinn, Southern Belle; Lucas "Doc" Murdoch, Doctor (amateur; veterinarian also), Cowboy
Time period(s): 1860s (post-Civil War)
Locale(s): Texas

Summary: Having lost everything to the Civil War, Catlin is anti-men and determined to make it on her own. Then she meets Lucas and the battle begins.

Other books you might like:
Catherine Creel, *Nevada Captive*, 1989
Janet Dailey, *The Pride of Hannah Wade*, 1985
Norah Hess, *Wildfire*, 1989
Jill Marie Landis, *Sunflower*, 1988
Margaret Mitchell, *Gone with the Wind*, 1936
A classic "must", if you haven't already read it

1677

GINA ROBINS (Pseudonym of Connie Feddersen)

Whispers of Love

(New York: Pinnacle, 1991)

Story type: Historical/American West
Major character(s): Skylar MacRae, Debutante; Dakota Delany, Indian (adopted by the Comanche)
Time period(s): 19th century
Locale(s): Fort Phantom Hill, Texas

Summary: When Boston-bred Skylar MacRae leaves the army fort for a bit of privacy, she ends up with a wounded man at her feet and an unexpected mission. Action, passion, and humor abound as Skylar and Dakota fight to regain the sacred Indian lands—the lands now occupied by the fort! Especially well-done secondary characters.

Other books you might like:
Jessica Douglass, *All My Heart Can Hold*, 1991
Kathleen Harrington, *Cherish the Dream*, 1990
Johanna Lindsey, *Savage Thunder*, 1989
Linda Lael Miller, *Caroline and the Raider*, 1992

1678

DIANE GATES ROBINSON

Delta Desire

(New York: Zebra, 1991)

Story type: Historical/American West
Major character(s): Aimee Louvierre, Southern Belle; Sebastian "Shadow Panther" MacLeod, Indian (half-Chickasaw), Heir

Time period(s): 1790s (1794)
Locale(s): New Orleans, Louisiana; Tennessee

Summary: Although they have never met, when New Orleans beauty Aimee Louviere and arrogant Sebastian MacLeod (a.k.a. Shadow Panther, Chickasaw chief) see each other at Aimee's betrothal ball, they know they are destined to be together. Of course Aimee's fiance doesn't quite see it that way, but Shadow Panther takes care of that by simply kidnapping Aimee and carrying her off to his home. Lots of passion and Chickasaw lore.

Other books you might like:
Jane Archer, *Bayou Passion*, 1991
Catherine Hart, *Tempest*, 1991
Johanna Lindsey, *Savage Thunder*, 1989
Janelle Taylor, *Follow the Wind*, 1990

1679

DIANE GATES ROBINSON

The Eagle and the Rose

(New York: Zebra, 1993)

Story type: Historical/Colonial America
Major character(s): Lady Serena Marston, Noblewoman, Plantation Owner; Rafael Aquilera y Perez, Pirate
Locale(s): St. Augustine, Florida

Summary: Years after she first encountered the dashing pirate when he boarded her ship, Serena Marston meets Rafael Aguilera y Perez once again and they realize that the attraction they felt before is still there. However, obstacles in the form of old suspicions and vicious people keep the pair struggling to make their love a reality. Interesting early Spanish colonial setting.

Other books you might like:
Shannon Drake, *Bride of the Wind*, 1992
Heather Graham, *A Pirate's Promise*, 1989
Robin Lee Hatcher, *The Magic*, 1993
Kathleen E. Woodiwiss, *Shanna*, 1977

1680

DIANE GATES ROBINSON

The Falcon and the Swan

(New York: Zebra, 1992)

Story type: Historical/American Civil War
Major character(s): Ariane Valcour, Nurse (volunteer), Spy; Justin Pierce, Doctor, Military Personnel (Union Army Captain)
Time period(s): 1860s
Locale(s): Memphis, Tennessee

Summary: Although friends in childhood, Confederate spy Ariane Valcour and Union doctor Justin Pierce are now bitter enemies—she supporting the Southern cause by secretly writing newspaper articles as the notorious "Memphis Swan"; he trying to uncover the identity of the elusive journalist. Their feelings, however, get in the way, and eventually they are forced to make some very difficult decisions.

Other books you might like:
Micki Brown, *Once a Rebel*, 1992
Christine Dorsey, *Kansas Kiss*, 1992
Heather Graham, *And One Wore Gray*, 1992
Heather Graham, *One Wore Blue*, 1991

1681
SUZANNE ROBINSON

Lady Defiant
(New York: Doubleday, 1992)

Story type: Historical/Elizabethan
Major character(s): Oriel Richmond, Heiress; Blade Fitzstephen, Spy
Time period(s): 16th century (1560s)
Locale(s): England

Summary: Oriel's aunts and Blade's father want them to marry, but when Blade lashes out at his father and in his anger says inexcusable things about Oriel, she will have nothing to do with him. Eventually, Blade succeeds in wooing her and they do fall in love. Unfortunately, his job as agent for Queen Elizabeth keeps him out of the country a good part of the time and the dangers of his situation cause problems for them both. Passion, court intrigue, and adventure in Elizabethan England.

Other books you might like:
Mary Kingsley, *The Rake's Reward*, 1991
Ruth Langan, *Highland Fire*, 1991
Maura Seger, *Beloved Enemy*, 1992

1682
SUZANNE ROBINSON

Lady Gallant
(New York: Bantam, 1992)

Story type: Historical/Elizabethan
Major character(s): Eleanora "Nora" Becket, Noblewoman, Spy; Christian de Rivers, Nobleman, Spy
Time period(s): 16th century (1558)
Locale(s): England

Summary: Secretly working to secure Elizabeth's succession to the throne, dashing Christian de Rivers rescues Elizabeth's secret aide, Nora Becket. Although passionately attracted to each other, their separate secret lives cause problems for them both, but when the truth finally surfaces and they can begin to trust each other, they still must deal with danger and court intrigues before they can be happy together.

Other books you might like:
Jude Deveraux, *The Conquest*, 1991
Edith Layton, *The Crimson Crown*, 1990
Bertrice Small, *The Spitfire*, 1990
Sylvie Sommerfield, *Fires of Surrender*, 1990
Susan Wiggs, *The Lily and the Leopard*, 1991

1683
SUZANNE ROBINSON

Lord of Enchantment
(New York: Bantam, 1995)

Story type: Historical/Elizabethan
Major character(s): Lady Penelope Fairfax, Landowner, Psychic; Morgan "Tristan" St. John, Amnesiac, Spy (agent of the queen)
Time period(s): 16th century (1565)
Locale(s): Isle of Penance, England

Summary: Penelope Fairfax finds the shipwrecked Morgan St. John lying unconscious on her land, but when he wakes up, he can't remember anything. Naming him "Tristan," she and her household take care of the gentle man, who quickly becomes loved by all. Their attraction for each other grows; but when a stranger identifies Morgan as a different, strong, and dangerous man, their simple love is threatened. Humorous, enchanting, and filled with a cast of quirky characters.

Other books you might like:
Sandra Davidson, *Rosefire*, 1992
Karen Harper, *Passion's Rage*, 1992
Betina M. Krahn, *Behind Closed Doors*, 1991
Kasey Michaels, *The Illusion of Love*, 1994
    another hero who can't remember

1684
PATRICIA ROENBUCK

The Golden Conquest
(New York: Leisure, 1992)

Story type: Futuristic
Major character(s): Aylan, Psychic; Kolt, Psychic
Time period(s): Indeterminate Future
Locale(s): Rhiannon, Planet—Imaginary; Annan, Planet—Imaginary

Summary: Rescued from the attacks of an evil psychic, Aylan accompanies the gentle Kolt to his sylvan home on Annan, never dreaming that he is the same man who has haunted her dreams for years. Fast-paced and passionate. Follows *Golden Temptress*.

Other books you might like:
Marion Zimmer Bradley, *The Heritage of Hastur*, 1975
Jackie Casto, *Daughter of Destiny*, 1990
Anne McCaffrey, *Crystal Singer*, 1982
Kathleen Morgan, *Heart's Lair*, 1991
Kathleen Morgan, *The Knowing Crystal*, 1991

1685
PATRICIA ROENBUCK

Golden Temptress
(New York: Leisure, 1991)

Story type: Futuristic
Major character(s): Eirriel, Captive, Psychic; Captain Aubin, Spaceship Captain

Time period(s): Indeterminate Future
Locale(s): Dianthia, Planet—Imaginary; Spaceship

Summary: Rescued by Captain Aubin when she is captured by the invader Kedar, Eirriel enlists Aubin's help in freeing her people on the planet Dianthia. The pair must overcome numerous obstacles, including an evil telepath, a scheming woman, and enemy forces before they can achieve their goals and realize their love. Passionate and adventurous.

Other books you might like:
Jackie Casto, *Daughter of Destiny*, 1990
Jackie Casto, *Dreams of Destiny*, 1990
Amanda Glass, *Shield's Lady*, 1989
Johanna Lindsey, *Warrior's Woman*, 1990
Anne McCaffrey, *Killashandra*, 1985

1686

EVELYN ROGERS

Desert Fire

(New York: Zebra, 1992)

Story type: Historical/American West
Major character(s): Lady Charlotte Drake, Banker, Noblewoman; Maximilian Grant, Sports Figure (boxer), Gambler
Time period(s): 19th century
Locale(s): Las Vegas, Nevada

Summary: Charlotte and Maximilian meet on a train and spend days and nights having fun, never dreaming they will meet again Las Vegas. When they do, life becomes a bit more interesting as Charlotte and Max become partners in her bank and they join forces to search out treasure, enemies and old friends. Erotic, adventurous, and filled with memorable characters.

Other books you might like:
Marsha Canham, *Under the Desert Moon*, 1992
Susan Johnson, *Blaze*, 1986
Susannah Leigh, *The Turquoise Trail*, 1991
Nan Ryan, *The Legend of Love*, 1991

1687

EVELYN ROGERS

Flame

(New York: Zebra, 1994)

Story type: Historical/American West
Series: Chadwick Trilogy
Major character(s): Flame Chadwick, Young Woman (pregnant), Spouse (wife in name only); Matt Jackson, Scout, Military Personnel
Time period(s): 1870s (1876)
Locale(s): Fort Haraway, Texas

Summary: Pregnant and disgraced, Flame Chadwick flees west to marry Lieutenant Robert Anderson, whose dying wish is that his friend Matt Jackson marry her in his place. Unfortunately, Matt is a confirmed bachelor whose life is totally focused on tracking down a particular renegade Apache and he will allow nothing to interfere with his mission. He does,

however, agree to a marriage in name only, an arrangement that eventually becomes the real thing. Passion and action, Texas-style.

Other books you might like:
Arlene Holliday, *Wild Texas Blossom*, 1994
Janis Reams Hudson, *Apache Legacy*, 1994
   revenge-driven hero
Johanna Lindsey, *Angel*, 1992
   dangerous, "loner" hero
Cait Logan, *Night Fire*, 1994
   marriage of convenience/revenge-driven hero

1688

EVELYN ROGERS

A Love So Wild

(New York: Zebra, 1991)

Story type: Historical/Antebellum American South
Major character(s): Catherine Douchand, Saloon Hostess (casino); Adam Gase, Convict (framed ex-con)
Time period(s): 1830s
Locale(s): New Orleans, Louisiana

Summary: When Adam Gase decides to avenge himself on the man who had him falsely imprisoned for slave trafficking, he reckons without his victim's beautiful, independent mistress, Catherine Douchand. In spite of their antagonism, Adam and Catherine are drawn to each other; but old scores on both sides must be settled before they can be together.

Other books you might like:
Jennifer Blake, *Midnight Waltz*, 1985
Elinor Lynley, *Song of the Bayou*, 1990
Kat Martin, *The Captain's Bride*, 1990
Alexandra Ripley, *New Orleans Legacy*, 1987
Karen Robards, *Morning Song*, 1987

1689

EVELYN ROGERS

Sweet Texas Magic

(New York: Zebra, 1992)

Story type: Historical/American West
Major character(s): Lorelei Latham, Businesswoman (casino owner), Captive; Sam Delaney, Renegade
Time period(s): 19th century
Locale(s): New Orleans, Louisiana; Texas

Summary: Furious that Sam Delaney had the audacity to ruin her casino's opening night, Lorelei Latham takes matters into her own hands and ends up kidnapped and on her way to Texas in the company of the very man she had targeted for revenge. Lorelei's "allergy" to men adds an interesting twist to this fast-paced, passionate adventure.

Other books you might like:
Elaine Coffman, *Escape Not My Love*, 1990
Jill Gregory, *Cherished*, 1992
Hannah Howell, *Stolen Ecstasy*, 1991
Charlotte Hubbard, *Colorado Moonfire*, 1992
Rebecca Paisley, *Midnight and Magnolias*, 1992

1690

MARYLYLE ROGERS

Chanting the Dawn
(New York: Pocket, 1991)

Story type: Historical/Medieval; Historical/Fantasy
Major character(s): Brynna, Healer (Druid); Wulfayne, Warrior (Saxon)
Time period(s): 7th century (671)
Locale(s): England

Summary: When the young Druid healer Brynna rescues the unconscious Saxon warrior Wulfayne and takes him to her cave to recover, she recognizes him as the protector of her dreams but doesn't realize he will eventually become the love of her life. A mystical, lyrical tale filled with ancient magic and Druidic lore.

Other books you might like:
Betina Lindsey, *Swan Bride*, 1990
Lindsay Randall, *Silversword*, 1990
Flora M. Speer, *Castle of Dreams*, 1990
Joan Wolf, *Born of the Sun*, 1991

1691

MARYLYLE ROGERS

Chanting the Morning Star
(New York: Pocket, 1993)

Story type: Historical/Fantasy; Historical/Medieval
Major character(s): Llys, Religious (Druid), Orphan; Adam, Nobleman (Ealdorman of Oaklea), Warrior
Time period(s): 7th century (678)
Locale(s): Northumbria, England

Summary: When the warrior Adam is mysteriously wounded, he reluctantly finds himself in the care of the beautiful Druidic healer, Llys, a woman he distrusts because of her pagan beliefs and because he first sees her in a rather suspect situation with a corrupt bishop. Despite their differences, their feelings and respect for each other grow and they finally join forces to deal with enemies that would take over Northumbria. Magical and warm.

Other books you might like:
Rexanne Becnel, *Where Magic Dwells*, 1994
Betina Lindsey, *Swan Bride*, 1990
Betina Lindsey, *Swan Witch*, 1993
Judith Merkle Riley, *In Pursuit of the Green Lion*, 1990
Penelope Williamson, *Keeper of the Dream*, 1992

1692

MARYLYLE ROGERS

Dark Whispers
(New York: Pocket, 1991)

Story type: Historical/Medieval; Gothic
Major character(s): Alyce, Noblewoman; Rhodare "Demon Dare", Nobleman (Earl of Wythe)
Time period(s): 12th century

Locale(s): England
Summary: Twisted family hatreds and dark and demonic intrigues keep lovely Alyce and her childhood friend, Dare, from revealing their love. However, when Alyce's father is accused of treason, Dare rescues Alyce and takes her to his estate for protection. Treachery, political intrigue, and greed surround the pair as they struggle to make their love a reality.

Other books you might like:
Virginia Henley, *The Falcon and the Flower*, 1989
Gail Link, *Wolf's Embrace*, 1989
Flora M. Speer, *Castle of the Heart*, 1990
Katherine Vickery, *Desire of the Heart*, 1990

1693

MARYLYLE ROGERS

The Eagle's Song
(New York: Pocket, 1992)

Story type: Historical/Medieval
Major character(s): Lady Linnett, Noblewoman; Rhys ap Griffith, Royalty (dispossessed)
Time period(s): 11th century (1092)
Locale(s): Wales

Summary: Rhys ap Griffith, sometimes known as the legendary "Eagle," is determined to reclaim his family land and titles — and he has a plan. He will take the present occupants' children hostage and wait for results. However, he reckons without the gentle Lady Linnett and her sense of honor and fair play. Double dealing, treachery, and plenty of action are part of this passionate and heartwarming story.

Other books you might like:
Katherine Deauville, *Blood Red Roses*, 1991
Mary Lide, *Ann of Cambray*, 1984
Bertrice Small, *A Moment in Time*, 1991
	mystical elements
Caryl Wilson, *Firebrand's Lady*, 1992

1694

MARYLYLE ROGERS

Hidden Hearts
(New York: Pocket, 1989)

Story type: Historical/Medieval
Major character(s): Lady Amicia of Wryborn, Young Woman; Galen Fitz William, Young Man
Time period(s): 12th century
Locale(s): England

Summary: Rebellious, unloved, and unwanted, Amicia dreams of her hero, Robin Hood. When she meets Galen in the woods, she sees him in the same heroic light. Adventure, danger, and love follow in short order.

Other books you might like:
Jude Deveraux, *The Taming*, 1989
Roberta Gellis, *Roselynde*, 1978
	1st of the six Roselynde Chronicles
Virginia Henley, *The Falcon and the Flower*, 1989

Johanna Lindsey, *When Love Awaits*, 1986
Kathleen E. Woodiwiss, *The Wolf and the Dove*, 1974

1695

MARYLYLE ROGERS

The Keepsake
(New York: Pocket, 1993)

Story type: Historical/American West; Historical/Victorian
Major character(s): Elizabeth Hughes, Rancher, Bride; Grayson Brandt, Nobleman
Time period(s): 1880s (1882)
Locale(s): Wyoming; England

Summary: Tricked into marriage with English duke Grayson Brandt, Lizzie Hughes leaves her Wyoming ranch for Gray's English estate and finds love, mystery, danger, and a cause to fight for. A lyrical, enchanting story with well developed characters.

Other books you might like:
Cordia Byers, *Lady Fortune*, 1989
Patricia Pellicane, *Sweet Seduction*, 1992
Maura Seger, *Light on the Mountain*, 1992
Pat Tracy, *The Flaming*, 1992

1696

KRISTINE ROLOFSON

I'll Be Seeing You
(Toronto: Harlequin, 1993)

Story type: Contemporary
Major character(s): Janet Fridrick, Aged Person; Ray Sandetti, Aged Person
Time period(s): 1990s
Locale(s): Nebraska

Summary: Although very much in love following the War, Janet simply cannot leave her mother for Ray. Years (51, to be exact) later, they are reunited and with the help of their various 'children,' they are able to give love just one more chance.

Other books you might like:
Lenore Carroll, *The Heart Remembers*, 1993
Marilyn Cunningham, *Seasons of the Heart*, 1992
Kathleen Gilles Seidel, *Maybe This Time*, 1990
LaVyrle Spencer, *Bittersweet*, 1990

1697

ELAINE ROME (Pseudonym of Elaine Barbieri)

Stark Lightning
(New York: Harlequin, 1991)

Story type: Historical/American West
Major character(s): Valentine "Val" Stark, Rancher; Blake Walker, Rancher
Time period(s): 19th century
Locale(s): West

Summary: "Anything you can do, I can do better" is the operative phrase in this funny and romantic story as Val sets out to prove to Blake Walker, the new ranch manager her father hired, that she really doesn't need him. In the end, of course, they *both* win.

Other books you might like:
Martha Hix, *Wild Texas Rose*, 1990
Joan Johnston, *Sweetwater Seduction*, 1991
Victoria Thompson, *Sweet Texas Surrender*, 1991
Victoria Thompson, *Wild Texas Promise*, 1990

1698

JOANN ROSS

Secret Sins
(New York: St. Martin's, 1990)

Story type: Contemporary/Mainstream
Major character(s): Leigh Baron, Heiress (to Baron Studios); Matthew St. James, Actor, Writer (aspiring screenwriter)
Time period(s): 1970s
Locale(s): Hollywood, California

Summary: Her sister's jealousy and her father's domineering tendencies jeopardize Leigh Baron's relationship with Matthew St. James in this glitzy novel of the Hollywood film scene.

Other books you might like:
Kate Coscarelli, *Fame and Fortune*, 1984
   Glitz in Beverly Hills
Janet Dailey, *The Glory Game*, 1985
Catherine Mann, *Tinsel Town: A Novel*, 1985
Tracy Sinclair, *Miss Robinson Crusoe*, 1989
   Silhouette Special Edition
Danielle Steel, *Passion's Promise*, 1976

1699

MYRA ROWE

Cypress Moon
(New York: Warner, 1990)

Story type: Historical/Victorian America
Major character(s): Diana Hathaway, Thief (accidental); Lucas Greenwood, Plantation Owner
Time period(s): 1830s (1831)
Locale(s): Louisiana

Summary: To win a bet with his brother, Luke takes the beautiful young woman who stole his watch and proceeds to turn her, Pygmalion-style, into a cultured, elegant lady. His problem? He falls in love with her in the process. Also, Diana is not exactly what she seems.

Other books you might like:
Cordia Byers, *Lady Fortune*, 1989
Georgette Heyer, *Friday's Child*, 1946
   similar theme/Regency treatment
Catherine Lyndell, *Stolen Dreams*, 1989
Louisa Rawlings, *Promise of Summer*, 1989

1700

PATRICIA ROWE

Keepers of the Misty Time
(New York: Warner, 1994)

Story type: Historical/Pre-history
Major character(s): Ashan, Healer ("Moonkeeper"); Tor, Warrior
Time period(s): 91st century B.C. (9000 B.C.)
Locale(s): Pacific Northwest, North America

Summary: Ashan, the Chosen One, is Moonkeeper and care-taker of her tribe. She welcomes her celibate destiny, although she passionately loves the warrior Tor. When they finally give into their feelings, they both end up being exiled. Tor goes in search of a forbidden dream; Ashan learns to survive. They separately endure hardship and overcome obstacles, but they eventually find each other again—and a dream that will be the salvation of their people.

Other books you might like:
Jean M. Auel, *Clan of the Cave Bear*, 1980
Kathryn Lynn Davis, *Sing to Me of Dreams*, 1990
Linda Lay Shuler, *She Who Remembers*, 1988
Linda Lay Schuler, *The Voice of the Eagle*, 1992
Joan Wolf, *Daughter of the Red Deer*, 1991

1701

MALLORY RUSH

Love Game
(Toronto: Harlequin, 1995)

Story type: Contemporary
Major character(s): Chris Nicholson, Widow(er), Teacher; Greg Reynolds, Military Personnel (Marine captain)
Time period(s): 1990s
Locale(s): Texas

Summary: Divorced Marine Captain Greg Reynolds knows he isn't a good bet for marriage and just wants a fling; widowed teacher Chris Nicholson wants a father for her young daughter, but is tempted by an affair. Nevertheless, despite their different goals, their relationship becomes more than the finite affair they had expected and they are forced to come to terms with their feelings for each other. Highly erotic with elements of bondage and S & M.

Other books you might like:
Jill Barkin, *Hot Streak*, 1990
    sexy romantic suspense/Susan Johnson's pseudonym
Faye Hughes, *Gotta Have It*, 1995
    somewhat less erotic
Susan Johnson, *Forbidden*, 1991
    historical/erotic
Susan Johnson, *Golden Paradise*, 1990
    historical/erotic

1702

EVA RUTLAND

Gretna Bride
(Toronto: Harlequin, 1993)

Story type: Regency
Major character(s): Ventia Fielding, Noblewoman, Runaway; Victor Allen, Artist (painter); Duke of Hazelmere, Noble-man
Time period(s): 1810s
Locale(s): England

Summary: Ventia Fielding is ecstatic! She is going to marry the love of her life, the Duke of Hazelmere! Unfortunately, when she learns that, for the Duke, it is merely a marriage of convenience, she decides she can't marry him after all and runs away. Painter Victor Allen agrees to help her, but they end up compromised and are forced to marry. Love eventually follows, but not smoothly. Warm and funny with likeable characters.

Other books you might like:
Julie Caille, *The Rake and His Lady*, 1993
Marion Chesney, *The Desirable Duchess*, 1993
Clare Darcy, *Letty*, 1980
Sarah Eagle, *The Reluctant Suitor*, 1991
Linda Lael Miller, *My Darling Melissa*, 1990
    sensual/American setting

1703

NAN RYAN

Because You're Mine
(New York: Topaz, 1995)

Story type: Historical/American West
Major character(s): Sabella Rios, Heiress, Rancher; Burton Burnett, Rancher
Time period(s): 1880s
Locale(s): San Juan Capistrano, California; California

Summary: Deliberately and methodically, beautiful Sabella Rios sets out to seduce, marry, and destroy the current "owner" of the sprawling California rancho that she knows is hers. But Burt Burnett is a bit more than she bargained for; and when she ends up in love with him instead, things become a bit more complex. Strong characters, a pair of vile, unsavory villains, and graphic sex are all part of this fast-paced romance that features definite sweet/savage and rape elements.

Other books you might like:
Virginia Henley, *Desired*, 1995
    sweet/savage style
Brenda Joyce, *The Fires of Paradise*, 1991
    similar style
Brenda Joyce, *Secrets*, 1993
    similar style
Rosemary Rogers, *Sweet Savage Love*, 1973
    classic sweet/savage romance
Bertrice Small, *The Hellion*, 1996
    sweet/savage style

NAN RYAN

The Legend of Love
(New York: Dell, 1991)

Story type: Historical/American West
Major character(s): Elizabeth Montbleau Curtin, Southern Belle; West Quarternight, Spy, Guide
Time period(s): 1860s
Locale(s): Shreveport, Louisiana; New York, New York; New Mexico

Summary: After a night of unbridled passion in a Confederate prison cell just as the War is ending, Southerner Elizabeth Montbleau and Yankee West Quarternight go their separate ways, only to meet again on the New Mexican desert as Elizabeth goes in search of her missing husband. Realistic, passionate, and filled with non-stop action.

Other books you might like:
Susan Johnson, *Forbidden*, 1991
Brenda Joyce, *Darkest Heart*, 1989
Diane Gates Robinson, *Delta Desire*, 1991
Janelle Taylor, *Savage Conquest*, 1985

1705

NAN RYAN

A Lifetime of Heaven
(New York: Dell, 1994)

Story type: Historical/American West Coast
Major character(s): Kay Montgomery, Activist (Salvation Army captain); Nick McCabe, Saloon Keeper/Owner
Time period(s): 1880s (1883)
Locale(s): San Francisco, California

Summary: Kay Montgomery, a Salvation Army captain, clashes with saloon owner Nick McCabe as she converts his best employees and hurts his business. He has no luck in getting rid of her; she can't reform him either. Love and romance seem to be the only solution in this sexy romance.

Other books you might like:
Emily Bradshaw, *The Heart's Journey*, 1992
    an activist heroine/a disreputable hero/gentler treatment
Deborah Camp, *My Wild Rose*, 1992
    a temperance activist heroine/gentler treatment
Linda Howard, *Angel Creek*, 1991
    basic life-style conflicts/alpha hero
Susan Johnson, *Forbidden*, 1991
    highly sensual
Brenda Joyce, *Secrets*, 1993
    brutally sensual

1706

NAN RYAN

Love Me Tonight
(New York: Topaz, 1994)

Story type: Historical/American West

Major character(s): Helen Courtney, Widow(er) (impoverished), Farmer (farm owner); Kurt Northway, Military Personnel (Union Army captain), Single Parent
Time period(s): 1870s
Locale(s): Alabama

Summary: Poor, hardworking Southern widow Helen Courtney tries to keep her home intact, but she needs help. A former Yankee officer isn't exactly what she had in mind, but when ex-Union Captain Kurt Northway shows up with only his horse and young son to his name, she reluctantly accepts his offer to work. Trust and acceptance are slow in coming, and the fact that they are ostracized by the local townspeople doesn't help. Nevertheless, a bit of violence and a little help from a neighbor help them work things out. Brutal, violent, and steamy.

Other books you might like:
Sandra Chastain, *Rebel in Silk*, 1994
Susan Johnson, *Forbidden*, 1991
    highly and creatively sensual
Susan Johnson, *Pure Sin*, 1994
    highly sensual
Brenda Joyce, *The Fires of Paradise*, 1991
    similar style
Brenda Joyce, *Secrets*, 1991
    similar style

1707

NAN RYAN

Sun God
(New York: Dell, 1990)

Story type: Historical/American West
Major character(s): Amy Sullivan, Rancher; Luiz "Tonatiuh" Quintaro, Military Personnel (Captain)
Time period(s): 1850s (1856)
Locale(s): Texas; Mexico

Summary: Childhood sweethearts, Amy and Luiz are separated by her brothers, who tell her they've killed Luiz and then force her to marry another. When Amy and Luiz meet again ten years later, a widowed Amy is struggling to keep her ranch, and Luiz is determined to punish her for what he believes was her desertion of him. Aztec mysticism, gripping action, and steamy, and occasionally brutal, sex are all a part of this powerful love story.

Other books you might like:
Rebecca George, *Call Home the Heart*, 1989
    similar situation/different setting
Martha Hix, *Wild Texas Rose*, 1990
Brenda Joyce, *The Conqueror*, 1990
    different time period
Rosemary Rogers, *Sweet Savage Love*, 1973
Rosemary Rogers, *The Wildest Heart*, 1974

1708

NAN RYAN

Written in the Stars
(New York: Dell, 1993)

Story type: Historical/American West
Major character(s): Diane Buchanan, Entertainer (Wild West Show girl), Equestrian; Starkeeper, Captive
Time period(s): 19th century
Locale(s): West

Summary: When horsewoman Diane Buchanan joins her grandparents Wild West show, she is horrified to discover than an Indian captive is the star of the show. However, when she frees him, he captures her for revenge. Their captive/captor relationship results in growing feelings of love and eventually they go to his "people" where his true identitiy and secret mission are revealed. Passionate and realistic.

Other books you might like:
Rosanne Bittner, *Arizona Ecstasy*, 1989
Kathleen Eagle, *Heaven and Earth*, 1990
Georgina Gentry, *Sioux Slave*, 1992
Susan Johnson, *Forbidden*, 1991
Johanna Lindsey, *Savage Thunder*, 1989

1709

SUSAN SACKETT

Emerald Angel
(New York: Zebra, 1990)

Story type: Historical
Major character(s): Honor Wainwright, Young Woman; Rafe Farrell, Imposter (dockworker), Detective
Time period(s): 19th century
Locale(s): New York, New York

Summary: Rafe Farrell poses as a dockworker while investigating a shipping merchant suspected of gun running and ends up falling for the merchant's daughter, Honor. Mystery, deceit, and passion combine in this fast-paced romance.

Other books you might like:
Catherine Coulter, *Night Storm*, 1990
Betina M. Krahn, *Passion's Ransom*, 1989
Gina Robins, *Deception's Sweet Kiss*, 1990
Judith Steel, *Seduction's Raging Flame*, 1989

1710

SUSAN SACKETT

Passion's Golden Fire
(New York: Zebra, 1989)

Story type: Historical/Exotic
Major character(s): Sabine Payne, Archaeologist; Quinten Mannering, Archaeologist (member of the Royal Society)
Time period(s): 1880s (1885)
Locale(s): Chitzen Itza, Mexico (Yucatan Peninsula)

Summary: Sabine Payne accompanies her father to the dig at Chitzen Itza to take notes for him, expecting to find only heat, humidity, dirt, and hard work. In addition, she finds mystery, danger, and love in the person of archaeologist Quinten Mannering.

Other books you might like:
Rita Balkey, *Passion's Fury*, 1989
Kay Hooper, *Enemy Mine*, 1989
    Contemporary setting
Leslie O'Grady, *Seek the Wild Shore*, 1989

1711

KATHLEEN SAGE

Many Fires
(New York: Jove, 1995)

Story type: Historical/Post-American Civil War; Historical/American West
Major character(s): Elizabeth Wheaton, Healer, Captive (of the Cheyenne); Major James Ryerson, Military Personnel (major in Union Army)
Time period(s): 1860s (1867)
Locale(s): Vegetarian, Kansas

Summary: Captured and raised by the Cheyenne, Elizabeth Wheaton is known as the healer Many Fires. Captain James Ryerson knows her as the nurse who helped him on the battlefields of the Civil War; and it is to her that he brings his men when they need help. She agrees to help, but in in order to preserve Elizabeth's reputation, they pretend to be married-a pretense that eventually leads to the real thing. A unique, sensual story of two wounded protagonists and the healing power of love. Well-done characterizations. First novel.

Other books you might like:
Rosanne Bittner, *Chase the Sun*, 1996
    another emotionally wounded hero
Kathleen Eagle, *This Time Forever*, 1992
    wounded hero/contemporary setting/sensitive
Laura Kinsale, *Flowers From the Storm*, 1992
    classic wounded hero/different time period and setting
Patricia Potter, *Defiant*, 1996
    another wounded hero
Patricia Potter, *Renegade*, 1993
    another wounded hero

1712

SHARON SALA

Always a Lady
(Bensalem, Pennsylvania: Meteor, 1993)

Story type: Contemporary
Major character(s): Lily Brownfield, Secretary—Legal, Cook; Case Longren, Rancher; Todd Collins, Lawyer, Fiance(e) (former)
Time period(s): 1990s
Locale(s): Oklahoma

Summary: When Lily's fiance takes one look at her scarred face and breaks their engagement, she leaves her legal position and takes a job as a cook on an Oklahoma ranch. The hard work and the appreciative cowboys almost make her forget her face, but it takes the love and understanding of Case Longren to help her truly deal with her loss of self-worth and get her life back on track. Warm and realistic.

Other books you might like:
Judith Duncan, *Beyond All Reason*, 1993
Betina Lindsey, *The Serpent Beguiled*, 1992
    historical and exotic
Helen Mittermeyer, *Princess of the Veil*, 1992
    medieval setting
Ann Wiley, *Angel in Disguise*, 1993

1713
SHARON SALA

Annie and the Outlaw
(New York: Silhouette, 1994)

Story type: Contemporary/Fantasy
Major character(s): Annie Laurie O'Brien, Teacher; Gabriel Donner, Biker, Outlaw (former)
Time period(s): 1990s
Locale(s): United States

Summary: Given one last chance by God to make it into heaven, outlaw Gabriel Donner is to spend the next 150 years righting all the wrongs he encounters. His solitary task is almost completed when he rescues one last person, an inner city school teacher who is being plagued by her students—and Gabe suddenly isn't so sure he wants to go to heaven after all. Dark secrets, a high degree of sexual tension, likable characters, and dashes of humor contribute to this nicely plotted romantic fantasy.

Other books you might like:
Jude Deveraux, *Wishes*, 1989
Kristin Hannah, *When Lightning Strikes*, 1994
Constance O'Day-Flannery, *Second Chances*, 1992
Patricia Simpson, *Whisper of Midnight*, 1991
Antoinette Stockenberg, *Emily's Ghost*, 1992

1714
SHARON SALA

Diamond
(New York: Harper, 1994)

Story type: Contemporary
Major character(s): Diamond Houston, Singer (amateur); Jesse Eagle, Singer (country-western star)
Time period(s): 1990s
Locale(s): Nashville, Tennessee

Summary: When country superstar Jesse Eagle hears Diamond sing, he knows she can make it in Nashville. However, his agent—rejected by Diamond—sets out to destroy her fledgling career. Thinking Jesse is part of this, Diamond takes off on her own, determined to make it by herself. But Jesse tracks her down, with delightfully romantic results.

Other books you might like:
Jayne Ann Krentz, *The Golden Chance*, 1990
    fast-paced and funny
Ruth Langan, *All That Glitters*, 1994
    another singing heroine
Edith Layton, *The Gilded Cage*, 1991
    historical singer
Susan Elizabeth Phillips, *Heaven, Texas*, 1995
    fast-paced and funny

1715
SHARON SALA

Honor's Promise
(Bensalem, Pennsylvania: Meteor, 1992)

Story type: Contemporary
Major character(s): Honor O'Brien, Heiress—Lost; Trace Logan, Businessman
Time period(s): 1990s
Locale(s): Texas; Colorado

Summary: When Honor O'Brien is discovered to be the long-lost granddaughter of wealthy J.J. Malone, the man who found her, Trace Logan, realizes that everyone is not happy that she has been found. Jealousy, greed, and passion abound as Trace tries to protect the woman he has come to love.

Other books you might like:
Catherine Coulter, *Beyond Eden*, 1991
Terri Herrington, *Her Father's Daughter*, 1991
Jayne Ann Krentz, *The Golden Chance*, 1990
Phyllis A. Whitney, *Woman Without a Past*, 1991
    romantic suspense

1716
SHARON SALA

Lucky
(New York: Harper, 1995)

Story type: Contemporary
Series: Gambler's Daughters
Major character(s): Lucky Houston, Worker (card dealer); Nick Chenault, Businessman (casino owner)
Time period(s): 1990s
Locale(s): Las Vegas, Nevada

Summary: Lucky Houston knows how to deal cards, but she has a hard time dealing with her gambler father's death. Las Vegas seems to offer a solution from her life of poverty, so she heads for the casinos and a new start. But casino owner Nick Chennault causes problems in more ways than one. An involving story with well-drawn characters.

Other books you might like:
Anne Harmon, *Desert Flame*, 1993
    another heroine looking for a fresh start/warm and sensual
Ruth Langan, *Christmas Miracle*, 1992
    another heroine who finds a fresh start/holiday theme
DeLoras Scott, *Rogue's Honor*, 1992
    historical/another heroine wanting new beginnings

Erica Spindler, *Red*, 1995
   mainstream story/heroine leaves her past and heads for
   Hollywood

1717
MADELYN SANDERS

Darkness at Cottonwood Hall
(New York: Harlequin, 1993)

Story type: Gothic
Major character(s): Amanda Matthews, Nurse (psychiatric),
   Widow(er); Len Percy, Doctor (psychiatrist)
Time period(s): 1990s
Locale(s): Natchez, Mississippi

Summary: A much-needed job at Cottonwood Hall turns into
an all-consuming mystery for Amanda Matthews as she
watches her wealthy patients deal with strange ailments. Reluctant to investigate, she still is compelled to protect her
charges. Dr. Percy is sympathetic, and incredibly attractive,
but he also must be considered as one of the ghostly suspects.
Adventurous, dangerous, and suspenseful all the way.

Other books you might like:
Peggy Darty, *The Crimson Roses of Fountain Court*, 1991
Elsie Lee, *Wingarden*, 1971
Anne Stuart, *Night of the Phantom*, 1991
Ann Howard White, *All but Love*, 1993

1718
LINDA SANDIFER

Mountain Ecstasy
(New York: Zebra, 1992)

Story type: Historical/American West
Major character(s): Hattie Longmore, Divorced Person,
   Rancher; Jim Rider, Rancher, Drifter
Time period(s): 19th century
Locale(s): Eagle Rock, Idaho

Summary: Escaping from a disastrous divorce, Hattie
Longmore goes to join her brother and his young daughter on
his newly-purchased Idaho sheep ranch, only to find her
brother dead and herself part-owner of the ranch. She also
finds herself the reluctant partner of her brother's best friend,
the charming and footloose Jim Rider. In spite of themselves,
attraction sets in, and their efforts to keep from falling in love
and to make the ranch a success provide some hilarious
reading. Funny and fast-paced with some mystery thrown in
for good measure.

Other books you might like:
Jill Marie Landis, *Rose*, 1990
Pamela Morsi, *Courting Miss Hattie*, 1991
Pamela Morsi, *Garters*, 1992
Rebecca Paisley, *Barefoot Bride*, 1990
Rebecca Paisley, *Rainbows and Rapture*, 1992

1719
DEBORAH SATINWOOD

Angel Fire
(New York: Zebra, 1992)

Story type: Historical/Post-American Civil War
Major character(s): Angelina O'Brien, Southern Belle; Came-
   ron Forrester, Military Personnel
Time period(s): 1860s (1865)
Locale(s): Maryland

Summary: When Colonel O'Brien approaches Cameron Forrester with a scheme to save his young daughter from
marrying his mortal enemy, Cameron agrees—for a price. He
will marry Angelina, conveniently "die," and then retreat to
his Pennsylvania home and rebuild it with his earnings. Unfortunately, he falls in love with his gentle Angel. Powerful,
moving, and memorable.

Other books you might like:
Heather Graham, *And One Rode West*, 1992
Alexandra Ripley, *Scarlett*, 1991
LaVyrle Spencer, *The Endearment*, 1982
LaVyrle Spencer, *Years*, 1986
   World War I
Jodi Thomas, *The Tender Texan*, 1991

1720
VERONICA SATTLER

A Dangerous Longing
(New York: St. Martin's, 1990)

Story type: Historical/Georgian
Major character(s): Ariana Belmont, Young Woman; Sean
   O'Hara, Sea Captain
Time period(s): 18th century
Locale(s): Ireland; Caribbean; England

Summary: For 10 years Sean O'Hara has vowed vengeance on
Lord Harry Belmont for killing his brother in a stagecoach
robbery; but things become complicated when Sean falls in
love with Harry's daughter Ariana. Eventually, of course,
Sean discovers Lord Harry is not to blame (the villain in this
piece is Ariana's mother!), but a number of obstacles still
await the lovers before they can find happiness with each
other.

Other books you might like:
Meagan McKinney, *Till Dawn Tames the Night*, 1991
Judith McNaught, *Almost Heaven*, 1990
Mary Jo Putney, *Dearly Beloved*, 1990
Amanda Quick, *Scandal*, 1991

1721
VERONICA SATTLER

A Promise of Fire
(New York: St. Martin's, 1989)

Story type: Historical/American Revolution

Major character(s): Brittany Chambers, Spinster; Bryce Tremaine, Sea Captain
Time period(s): 1770s (1773)
Locale(s): Fredericksburg, Virginia

Summary: Because she refuses to marry against her will, fiery Brittany Chambers is sent to live with her aunt. Her escort is ship's captain Bryce Tremaine, a man with his own bitter agenda. Passion, adventure, and plenty of fire.

Other books you might like:
Judith E. French, *Lovestorm*, 1990
Betina Lindsey, *Waltz with the Lady*, 1990
Linda Lael Miller, *My Darling Melissa*, 1990
Valerie Sherwood, *This Loving Torment*, 1977

1722
VERONICA SATTLER

Sabelle
(New York: St. Martin, 1992)

Story type: Historical/Regency
Major character(s): Sabelle "Isabelle" Corstairs, Debutante, Animal Lover; Justin Hart, Nobleman (Duke of Haverleigh), Rake
Time period(s): 1810s
Locale(s): England

Summary: When intrepid animal rights activist Sabelle Corstairs accidentally ends up in the Duke of Haversleigh's bed (and seduced in the process!), she plans revenge — a revenge that works only too well. Fiery, sensual, and funny.

Other books you might like:
Mary Balogh, *The Snow Angel*, 1991
Mary Kingsley, *A Gentleman's Desire*, 1991
Judith McNaught, *Almost Heaven*, 1990
Amanda Quick, *Rendezvous*, 1992
Amanda Quick, *Surrender*, 1990

1723
IRENE SAUNDERS

Lady Lucinde's Locket
(New York: New American Library/Signet, 1990)

Story type: Regency
Major character(s): Lucinde Coldwell, Noblewoman, Widow(er); Anthony Mortimer, Nobleman (Earl of Grassington)
Time period(s): 1810s
Locale(s): Spain; London, England; Portugal

Summary: When Lucinde Coldwell's husband is killed in the peninsular campaign, she stays on to nurse the wounded. Her experience changes her into a thoughtful, mature woman. The only one who seems to understand her feelings about the soldiers and the war is her husband's best friend, Lord Anthony; but how will he feel when she begins to voice her opinions once they get back to London?

Other books you might like:
Kimberly Cates, *Restless Is the Wind*, 1989

Leslie Lynn, *The Rake's Redemption*, 1989
Mary Linn Roby, *My Lady's Mask*, 1979
Sheila Simonson, *A Cousinly Connexion*, 1984
Marlene Suson, *The Errant Earl*, 1989

1724
IRENE SAUNDERS

Talk of the Town
(New York: Signet 1991)

Story type: Regency
Major character(s): Catherine Howard, Gentlewoman; Edwin, Nobleman (Earl of Cloverdale)
Time period(s): 1810s
Locale(s): London, England

Summary: When country-bred Catherine Howard's reputation is nearly destroyed by her brother's ill-advised behavior, the Earl of Cloverdale gallantly marries her—with fascinating and unexpected results Intriguing.

Other books you might like:
Jo Beverley, *An Arranged Marriage*, 1991
Gayle Buck, *Mutual Consent*, 1991
Teresa DesJardien, *A June Bride*, 1991
Georgette Heyer, *The Convenient Marriage*, 1934
Leslie Lynn, *Scandal's Child*, 1990

1725
JEANNE SAVERY

A Christmas Treasure
(New York: Zebra, 1994)

Story type: Regency; Holiday Themes
Major character(s): Ernestine "Ernie" Matthewson, Gentlewoman; Ave Sommerton, Military Personnel (colonel), Nobleman
Time period(s): 1810s
Locale(s): England; Portugal

Summary: When her sister writes from Portugal that her husband is missing in action but she "knows" that he is not dead, Ernestine Matthewson is summarily dispatched by their overly-concerned father to go to the Peninsula and bring the obviously distraught Norry home. However, what Ernie finds is a perfectly sane, but very psychic, sister, a fascinatingly different lifestyle, and a dashing officer who threatens to turn her life upside down. Features good historical detail, interesting characters (some historical personalities), and a dash of the miraculous.

Other books you might like:
Gayle Buck, *The Waltzing Widow*, 1991
Georgette Heyer, *An Infamous Army*, 1937
   Classic Regency set during the Battle of Waterloo
Anthea Malcolm, *Counterfeit Heart*, 1991
Kate Moore, *The Mercenary Major*, 1993
Irene Saunders, *Lady Lucinde's Locket*, 1991

1726

JEANNE SAVERY

The Last of the Winter Roses

(New York: Walker, 1991)

Story type: Regency
Major character(s): Ardith Winter, Noblewoman, Spinster; St. John Worth, Nobleman (Marquis of Rohampton)
Time period(s): 1810s
Locale(s): England

Summary: Independent and happily single, Lady Ardith has no intention of marrying simply because her father wants an heir. But when a storm forces her to shelter at the home of her long-time friend, St. John Worth, she begins to see things a bit differently. Engaging characters and sparkling dialogue.

Other books you might like:
Mary Balogh, *The Snow Angel*, 1991
Julie Caille, *An Impetuous Bride*, 1991
Carola Dunn, *Two Corinthians*, 1989
Judith McNaught, *Whitney, My Love*, 1985

1727

JEANNE SAVERY

A Reformed Rake

(New York: Zebra, 1994)

Story type: Regency
Major character(s): Harriet Cole, Governess, Companion; Frederick Carrington, Rake, Nobleman
Time period(s): 1810s
Locale(s): Italy; England

Summary: While traveling in the Alps, Sir Frederick comes upon an attempted abduction. Although the intrepid Harriet, companion to the young lady being kidnapped, foils the act, Frederick decides to accompany the group back to England. Harriet, however, is not pleased. Frederick is a notorious rake, and she can hardly bring herself to be civil to him. Nevertheless, she does manage to see his true worth—eventually—in this story filled with interesting characters and sub-plots.

Other books you might like:
Brian Cleeve, *Sara*, 1976
  a more serious look at Regency England
Georgette Heyer, *Black Sheep*, 1966
Anthea Malcolm, *A Touch of Scandal*, 1991
  well-researched/more complex than many
Mary Jo Putney, *The Rake and the Reformer*, 1989
  reformed hero
Sheila Simonson, *The Bar Sinister*, 1986

1728

JENNIFER SAWYER, Editor

A Mother's Delight

(New York: Zebra, 1995)

Story type: Anthology; Regency
Time period(s): 1810s

Locale(s): England

Summary: This diverse anthology of six short stories focuses on the pains and pleasures of motherhood during the English Regency Period. Included are "Lady Charlotte Contrives" by Monique Ellis, "Gillian's Secret" by Violet Hamilton, "The Oriental Garden" by Isobel Linton, "Motherly Advice" by Sheila Rabe, "The Mother and the Marquess" by Jeanne Savery, and "Lost Love, New Love" by Lois Stewart. Stories vary as to style and quality.

Other books you might like:
Julie Caille, *A Mother's Heart*, 1992
  Regency anthology/motherhood theme
Carla Kelly, *Mrs. Drew Plays Her Hand*, 1994
  good mother/children depiction
Barbara Metzger, *A Suspicious Affair*, 1994
  a baby, a murder, and a mystery Regency-style
Anita Mills, *Cherished Moments*, 1994
  anthology on the theme of motherhood
Sheila Simonson, *The Bar Sinister*, 1986

1729

MERYL SAWYER

Blind Chance

(New York: Dell, 1989)

Story type: Contemporary
Major character(s): Alexa MacKenzie, Writer; Mark Kimbrough, Financier
Time period(s): 1980s
Locale(s): Mexico (Sea of Cortez); London, England

Summary: While consulting on a film version of her book, best-selling novelist Alexa MacKenzie ends up playing a small scene in the nude and having an affair with Mark Kimbrough. Both events have far-reaching effects on her life in this story of revenge, blackmail, and passion.

Other books you might like:
Sally Beauman, *Destiny*, 1987
Janet Dailey, *The Glory Game*, 1985
Rebecca Forster, *A Delicate Matter*, 1989
Catherine Mann, *Tinsel Town*, 1985
Danielle Steel, *Passion's Promise*, 1976

1730

MERYL SAWYER

Kiss in the Dark

(New York: Dell, 1995)

Story type: Contemporary; Romantic Suspense
Major character(s): Royce Winston, Journalist; Mitch Durant, Lawyer
Time period(s): 1990s
Locale(s): San Francisco, California

Summary: Royce Winston hates Mitch Durant, but there is no denying her attraction to him or the fact that she needs his help. Mitch, the best criminal attorney in San Francisco, is the only person who can clear her name and find out who is trying to frame her for theft and murder. Mitch can't change the events that he set in motion five years ago that destroyed Royce's family, but he is willing to risk his life to clear her name and find the killer who is after her.

Other books you might like:
Tami Hoag, *Night Sins*, 1995
Linda Howard, *Dream Man*, 1995
Meagan McKinney, *A Man to Slay Dragons*, 1996
Heather Graham Pozzessere, *Slow Burn*, 1994
Nora Roberts, *Genuine Lies*, 1992

1731

MERYL SAWYER

Midnight in Marrakesh

(New York: Dell, 1991)

Story type: Romantic Suspense; Contemporary/Mainstream
Major character(s): Lauren Winthrop, Art Dealer (manager of art gallery); Carlos Barzan, Financier (art); Ryan Westcott, Spy
Time period(s): 1990s
Locale(s): London, England; Marrakesh, Morocco

Summary: Laura Winthrop takes a job as manager of a prestigious London art gallery and ends up in a nightmare of intrigue and danger. Frauds, forgeries, drugs, and deceptions pepper the pages of this fast-paced, glitzy story of the art world and those who live in its thrall.

Other books you might like:
Janet Dailey, *The Glory Game*, 1985
Jayne Ann Krentz, *Silver Linings*, 1991
Judith Michael, *Deceptions*, 1982
Danielle Steel, *Passion's Promise*, 1976
Sherryl Woods, *Body and Soul*, 1989

1732

MERYL SAWYER

Promise Me Anything

(New York: Dell, 1994)

Story type: Contemporary; Romantic Suspense
Major character(s): Brett Lamont, Artisan (jewelry designer); Alex Savich, Businessman (diamond dealer)
Time period(s): 1990s

Summary: Brett and Alex need each other if they plan to make it in the diamond and jewelry design business. They join forces and together they plan to outwit the ruthless Diamond Club. Lots of fast-paced action and adventure.

Other books you might like:
Barbara Bretton, *One and Only*, 1994
Sandra Brown, *French Silk*, 1992
Deborah Gordon, *Beating the Odds*, 1992
Susan Kyle, *After Midnight*, 1993
Pat Warren, *Nowhere to Run*, 1993

1733

CORAL SMITH SAXE

Enchantment

(New York: Love Spell, 1994)

Story type: Historical/Fantasy
Major character(s): Bryony Talcott, Witch (Hag of Cold Springs Hollow); Adam Hawthorne, Investigator (of charlatans), Gentleman
Time period(s): 1780s (1787)
Locale(s): Cold Springs Hollow, Pennsylvania; Philadelphia, Pennsylvania

Summary: On a mission to prove the legendary Hag of Cold Springs Hollow is a fraud, Adam Hawthorne is surprised to discover his "witch" is not only a beauty, but that, much to her distress, she claims to have inherited no magical powers at all. Fascinated, he persists—and with the help of some delightful secondary characters, he finds himself in love with the woman he had set out to destroy. Passionate, gentle, and truly magical.

Other books you might like:
Rexanne Becnel, *Where Magic Dwells*, 1994
Wendy Garrett, *Carolina Dawn*, 1994
Kathleen Morgan, *Fire Queen*, 1994
    Faster paced/more action oriented
Becky Lee Weyrich, *Silver Tears*, 1990
    Salem Witch Trials setting
Penelope Williamson, *Keeper of the Dream*, 1992

1734

MARTHA SCHROEDER

The Law of Love

(New York: Zebra, 1994)

Story type: Contemporary
Major character(s): Caroline Faulkner, Student (law student), Divorced Person; Daniel Fratelli, Professor (law professor)
Time period(s): 1990s
Locale(s): United States

Summary: Tired of being a doormat to her ex-husband and her grown children, Caroline ignores their protests and belittling comments and enrolls in law school. Neither the difficult coursework nor Professor Daniel Fratelli's abominable attitude toward women can deter her. In fact, his attitude makes her so angry that she becomes a formidable opponent in the class and ends up intriguing and attracting him in the process.

Other books you might like:
Thelma Alexander, *True Texas Love*, 1994
Mary Lynn Baxter, *Winter Heat*, 1990
Kathleen Creighton, *Love and Other Surprises*, 1990
Muriel Jensen, *Everything*, 1990
Martha Schroeder, *Never Too Late*, 1994

1735

CANDACE SCHULER

The Right Direction

(Toronto: Harlequin, 1993)

Story type: Contemporary
Major character(s): Claire Kingston, Producer (movie); Rafe Santana, Director (movie)
Time period(s): 1990s
Locale(s): Hollywood, California

Summary: Claire's reputation as an icy, unapproachable professional intrigues movie director Rafe Santana, and when he takes time to discover the reasons for her aloofness, they both discover a passion hot enough to melt the ice. Fast-paced Hollywood tale.

Other books you might like:
Jackie Collins, *American Star*, 1993
    mainstream Hollywood glitz
Jo Leigh, *Special Effects*, 1992
Kathleen Gilles Seidel, *More than You Dreamed*, 1992
Tiffany White, *Naughty Talk*, 1993

1736

MARION SCHULTZ

Going Hollywood

(New York: Fawcett Juniper, 1989)

Story type: Young Adult
Major character(s): Christie Todd, Student—High School (on summer vacation); Danny Dodge, Actor (television)
Time period(s): 1980s
Locale(s): Hollywood, California

Summary: When Christie goes to Hollywood to spend the summer with her actor father, she meets Danny, a teenage television actor, who causes her to have second thoughts about the boyfriend she left at home.

Other books you might like:
Delores Beckman, *Who Loves Sam Grant?*, 1983
Barbara Girion, *In the Middle of a Rainbow*, 1983
Marjorie Holmes, *Sunday Morning*, 1982
Marilyn Levy, *Sounds of Silence*, 1989
Mary Towne, *Supercouple*, 1985

1737

DALLAS SCHULZE

Charity's Angel

(Toronto: Harlequin, 1992)

Story type: Contemporary
Major character(s): Charity Williams, Clerk (jewelry store); Gabe London, Police Officer (undercover)
Time period(s): 1990s

Summary: While working in a jewelry store, Charity is accidentally shot and paralyzed. Gabe, the policeman who shot her, feels responsible and tries to make amends. Love, of course, blossoms in the process, but it takes a bit of doing to overcome Charity's fears and Gabe's deep sense of guilt.

Other books you might like:
Charlotte Vale Allen, *Pieces of Dreams*, 1985
Emily Hendrickson, *The Gallant Lord Ives*, 1989
    Regency
Molly Rice, *Chance Encounter*, 1992

1738

DALLAS SCHULZE

Temptation's Price

(Toronto: Harlequin, 1992)

Story type: Historical/American West
Major character(s): Liberty Anne Ballard, Frontierswoman; Matt Prescott, Military Personnel, Scout (wagon scout)
Time period(s): 1860s (1860-1866)
Locale(s): Fort Bridge, Idaho

Summary: When Matt and Liberty Anne are attacked by Indians, Matt manages to keep them alive as they travel the 100 miles through the wilderness to her uncle's ranch. Once there, Matt is convinced that he should marry Liberty because she is now "compromised." However, both have serious doubts and Matt leaves to fight in the Civil War. When he returns six years later, they have both matured and are now ready to consider the future.

Other books you might like:
Jessica Douglass, *All My Heart Can Hold*, 1991
Robin Lee Hatcher, *Promise Me Spring*, 1991
Barbara Keller, *Heartbreak Trail*, 1992
Susannah Leigh, *The Turquoise Trail*, 1991
Diana Palmer, *Lacy*, 1991
    later period

1739

DALLAS SCHULZE

The Way Home

(New York: Dell, 1995)

Story type: Contemporary
Major character(s): Meg Harper, Abuse Victim, Teenager; Tyler McKendrick, Pilot, Accident Victim
Time period(s): 1930s
Locale(s): Regret, Iowa; Hollywood, California

Summary: When Tyler McKendrick, a successful Hollywood pilot, returns to his Iowa hometown to recuperate after an accident, he renews his friendship with Meg Harper, now almost grown up but still considered "trash" by Ty's upper-crust family, and ends up marrying her to save her from her abusive and lecherous stepfather. What begins as a marriage of convenience ends up as one in fact, but Ty and Meg have a lot of emotional growing to do before this happens. A sincere, solid story about real people you care about.

Other books you might like:
Debbie Macomber, *Morning Comes Softly*, 1993
    another marriage of convenience
Debbie Macomber, *Someday Soon*, 1995

Kathleen Gilles Seidel, *Maybe This Time*, 1990
  warm and sincere
LaVyrle Spencer, *Morning Glory*, 1989
  another marriage of convenience

1740
CHERI SCOTCH
The Werewolf's Kiss
(New York: Diamond, 1992)

Story type: Contemporary/Fantasy; Historical/Fantasy
Series: Werewolf Trilogy
Major character(s): Sylvie Marley, Teenager, Werewolf; Lucien Drago, Werewolf, Composer
Locale(s): Europe; New Orleans, Louisiana

Summary: Confused by her unexplained longings and feelings, 17-year-old Sylvie Marley, daughter of an esteemed Episcopal bishop, learns of her werewolf heritage and realizes that she must make an irrevocable choice. Chronicling the lengthy lives of several key characters, this unusual romance sweeps from ancient Rome to modern day New Orleans and combines classic werewolf lore with elements of voodoo and is punctuated by an occasional passage of pure, graphic horror.

Other books you might like:
Lori Herter, *Confession*, 1992
Lori Herter, *Obsession*, 1991
Susan Kay, *Phantom*, 1992
Anne Rice, *Interview with the Vampire*, 1976
Anne Rice, *The Vampire Lestat*, 1985

1741
CHERI SCOTCH
The Werewolf's Sin
(New York: Diamond, 1994)

Story type: Contemporary/Fantasy
Series: Werewolf Trilogy
Major character(s): Appollonius, Werewolf (good); Sylvie Drago, Werewolf; Lycaon, Werewolf (evil)
Time period(s): 1990s
Locale(s): New Orleans, Louisiana

Summary: In this concluding volume of The Werewolf Trilogy, ancient enemy werewolves Apollonius and Lycaon engage in their final battle—a battle that affects numerous characters in strange and unexpected ways. The "werewolf" aspects of this final volume often overshadow the romantic aspects of this story that is intense, violent, and dark.

Other books you might like:
Nancy Gideon, *Midnight Kiss*, 1994
  vampire story
Nancy Gideon, *Midnight Temptation*, 1994
  vampire Story
Susan Krinard, *Prince of Wolves*, 1994
  an unusual, gentler werewolf story
Anne Rice, *The Witching Hour*, 1991
Jane Toombs, *Under the Shadow*, 1992

1742
AMANDA SCOTT (Pseudonym of Lynn Scott Drennan)
Bath Charade
(New York: Signet, 1991)

Story type: Regency
Major character(s): Carolyn Hardy, Debutante; Sydney Saint Denis, Nobleman
Time period(s): 1810s
Locale(s): England

Summary: Young, spirited Carolyn Hardy just "knows" the great love of her life will be a dashing, brooding hero—just like the ones in the popular novels. Certainly, he will be nothing like her old friend, sophisticated, impeccably dressed, and remarkably calm and self-confident Sydney Saint Denis—or will he? A witty, heartwarming story in which Carolyn discovers that all heroes don't "go by the book."

Other books you might like:
Georgette Heyer, *Arabella*, 1949
Michelle Kasey, *The Somerville Farce*, 1991
Elisabeth Kidd, *A Hero for Antonia*, 1986
Kasey Michaels, *The Anonymous Miss Addams*, 1989
Judith Nelson, *Lady's Choice*, 1991

1743
AMANDA SCOTT
The Bawdy Bride
(New York: Pinnacle, 1995)

Story type: Historical/Georgian
Major character(s): Anne Davies, Noblewoman; Michael St. Ledgers, Nobleman
Time period(s): 1800s (1800)
Locale(s): England

Summary: Although she is determined to make a success of her arranged marriage, Anne Davies has more than enough to cope with as she struggles with an ancestral manor, two somewhat difficult children, and a complex husband. However, sinister and dangerous things are afoot, and it takes a bit of doing before the villain is caught and all is set to rights. A funny, somewhat dark, well-researched pre-Regency Georgian historical.

Other books you might like:
Jo Beverley, *Tempting Fortune*, 1995
Jane Feather, *Valentine*, 1995
Scotney St. James, *Highland Hearts*, 1993
  lighter
Arnette Lamb, *The Border Lord*, 1993
Amanda Quick, *Deception*, 1993
  lighter

1744

AMANDA SCOTT (Pseudonym of Lynn Scott Drennan)

Border Bride
(New York: Dell, 1990)

Story type: Historical/Renaissance
Major character(s): Mary Kate MacPherson, Noblewoman, Bride (reluctant); Adam Douglas, Nobleman, Laird
Time period(s): 16th century (1560s)
Locale(s): Scotland

Summary: When independent Mary Kate MacPherson realizes she can not escape marriage to the fierce border lord Adam Douglas, she relents—and then proceeds to make his life anything but peaceful. Jealously, treason, and high adventure are all part of this sensual, history-filled romance.

Other books you might like:
Jude Deveraux, *The Taming*, 1989
Julie Garwood, *The Bride*, 1989
Patricia Grasso, *Highland Belle*, 1991
Johanna Lindsey, *A Gentle Feuding*, 1984
Casey Stuart, *Highland Rogue*, 1991

1745

AMANDA SCOTT (Pseudonym of Lynn Scott Drennan)

Dangerous Illusions
(New York: Pinnacle, 1994)

Story type: Historical/Regency
Major character(s): Daintry Tarrant, Noblewoman; Gideon Deverill, Nobleman
Time period(s): 1810s (1815)
Locale(s): Cornwall, England; London, England

Summary: Lord Gideon must inform Lady Daintry of her fiance's death; unfortunately, both their families have feuded for years and he is less than welcome. Nevertheless, Daintry and Gideon become enamoured of each other and realize that if they are ever to be able to marry, they will need to discover the reasons for this ancient family feud. Their search results in a number of surprises and interesting twists—not all of them pleasant. Realistic pictures of Regency country life.

Other books you might like:
Catherine Anderson, *Coming Up Roses*, 1993
    abuse in a Western setting
Jean R. Ewing, *Virtue's Reward*, 1995
Carla Kelly, *Mrs. Drew Plays Her Hand*, 1994
    warm, rural Regency with a dash of serious realism
Johanna Lindsey, *A Gentle Feuding*, 1984
    16th century Scottish feud
Amanda Quick, *Deception*, 1993
    more feuds

1746

AMANDA SCOTT (Pseudonym of Lynn Scott Drennan)

The Dauntless Miss Wingrave
(New York: Signet, 1989)

Story type: Regency
Major character(s): Emily Wingrave, Gentlewoman (unmarried); Jack, Nobleman (Earl of Meriden), Guardian
Time period(s): 1810s (Regency period)
Locale(s): England

Summary: Emily finds it difficult to deal with the Earl of Meriden, her cousin, who stole a kiss from her years ago. Tempers flare on both sides—and suddenly they realize it is love, not hate, that is the cause.

Other books you might like:
Clare Darcy, *Letty*, 1980
Georgette Heyer, *The Grand Sophy*, 1950
Georgette Heyer, *Sprig Muslin*, 1956
Alice Chetwynd Ley, *The Intrepid Miss Haydon*, 1983
Judith Nelson, *Patience Is a Virtue*, 1989

1747

AMANDA SCOTT

Highland Fling
(New York: Pinnacle, 1995)

Story type: Historical/Georgian
Major character(s): Lady Maggie MacDrumin, Noblewoman, Spy; Lord Edward Carsley, Nobleman (Earl of Rothwell)
Time period(s): 1750s (1750)
Locale(s): London, England; Scotland

Summary: Maggie MacDrumin is a loyal Scot, determined to help her people in any way she can; Edward Carsley, Earl of Rothwell, is the current MacDrumin lord—but he is an absentee landlord. When an unexpected series of events lands Maggie in Edward's English home, she quickly determines that he needs to go to Scotland and help her clan. Although he resists, a government assignment soon has them headed north together and as they come to know each other, they fall in love. Passionate and occasionally dark.

Other books you might like:
Arnette Lamb, *Border Bride*, 1993
Arnette Lamb, *The Border Lord*, 1993
Maura Seger, *The Lady and the Laird*, 1992
Scotney St. James, *Highland Hearts*, 1993
Anne Stuart, *Highland Fling*, 1993
    anthology

1748

AMANDA SCOTT (Pseudonym of Lynn Scott Drennan)

The Rose at Twilight
(New York: Dell, 1993)

Story type: Historical/Medieval; Historical/Mainstream
Major character(s): Alys Wolveston, Noblewoman; Sir Nicholas Merion, Warrior

Time period(s): 14th century
Locale(s): England

Summary: When Lady Alys finds herself out of favor because there is now a new king, she flees for her own safety and ends up in the arms of Sir Nicholas, loyal Tudor knight. She still wants to go home but ends up immersed in a mystery and intrigue that could cost her life, and her heart, as well. A long, complex novel rife with politics, treachery, and court intrigue.

Other books you might like:
Jane Feather, *Brazen Whispers*, 1990
Roberta Gellis, *Roselynde*, 1978
 first of the Roselynde Chronicles
Roberta Gellis, *The Silver Mirror*, 1989
Laurie Grant, *Beloved Deceiver*, 1993
Sylvie Sommerfield, *Fires of Surrender*, 1990

1749
DELORAS SCOTT
Devil's Delight
(New York: Avon, 1992)

Story type: Historical/American West
Major character(s): Kate Whitfield, Young Woman, Rancher; Clint Morgan, Lawman (federal agent)
Time period(s): 1870s (1870)
Locale(s): Rawlins, Wyoming

Summary: Kate Whitfield has no intention of being taken care of, but it is decided that Clint Morgan should tame and marry her. Actually, he prefers to chase cattle thieves, but when Kate decides to come along, their close proximity leads to a romance that neither had foreseen. Rustlers, cattledrives, and a suspicious father keep things moving.

Other books you might like:
Carol Finch, *Moonlight Enchantment*, 1992
Martha Hix, *Caress of Fire*, 1992
Eugenia Riley, *Taming Kate*, 1992
Victoria Thompson, *Wild Texas Promise*, 1990

1750
DELORAS SCOTT
Fire and Ice
(Toronto: Harlequin, 1990)

Story type: Historical/American West
Major character(s): Jessy Turner, Widow(er); Cort Lancaster, Young Man
Time period(s): 1870s (1878)
Locale(s): Kansas

Summary: When Cort forces young widow Jessy to marry him, he gets more than he had bargained for. Someone is trying to kill him and Jessy is the prime suspect. Fast-paced Western action.

Other books you might like:
Barbara Bretton, *Midnight Lover*, 1989
Dorothy Garlock, *Midnight Blue*, 1989
Martha Hix, *Wild Texas Rose*, 1990

Colleen Quinn, *Colorado Flame*, 1989
Vivian Vaughn, *Texas Gamble*, 1990

1751
DELORAS SCOTT
The Miss and the Maverick
(Toronto: Harlequin, 1990)

Story type: Historical/American West
Major character(s): Carrie O'Brien, Fugitive; Luke Savage, Cowboy, Gunfighter (supposed)
Time period(s): 19th century
Locale(s): West; Colorado

Summary: When Carrie O'Brien steals her dishonest fiance's freight wagon and heads for Colorado, she has no idea what she is letting herself in for. Naive and totally unschooled in trail survival skills, Carrie must rely on Luke Savage, the man she has hired to drive her wagon—the same man who has been commissioned by Carrie's fiance to find her! Interesting times, as well as love, await these two as they wend their way West.

Other books you might like:
Deborah Camp, *Fallen Angel*, 1989
Elaine Coffman, *Escape Not My Love*, 1990
Kathleen Harrington, *Cherish the Dream*, 1990
Norah Hess, *Wildfire*, 1990
Christine Monson, *Golden Nights*, 1990

1752
DELORAS SCOTT
Rogue's Honor
(Toronto: Harlequin, 1992)

Story type: Historical/American West
Major character(s): Martha "Blossom" Jackson, Landowner, Saloon Keeper/Owner (former); Trace Lockhart, Businessman (lumber), Thief (former bank robber)
Time period(s): 1880s (1888)
Locale(s): Oklahoma; Bickerton, Missouri

Summary: Finally enjoying a respectable life in Oklahoma, former gambler and saloon owner Martha Jackson is not about to let anything or anyone destroy it—especially the fine, upstanding Trace Lockhart who wants her land! She turns fiesty and things get interesting as she must deal not only with Trace, but with a wily land speculator, as well. Funny and filled with surprises.

Other books you might like:
Deborah Camp, *My Wild Rose*, 1992
Thea Devine, *Tempted by Fire*, 1992
Kathleen Kane, *Mountain Dawn*, 1992
Rebecca Paisley, *Midnight and Magnolias*, 1992

1753

DELORAS SCOTT

Springtown

(Toronto: Harlequin, 1992)

Story type: Historical/Fantasy
Major character(s): Amanda Bradshaw, Runaway; Chance Boyer, Cowboy; Jack Quigley, Spirit
Time period(s): 1850s (1856)
Locale(s): California

Summary: To avoid an unwanted marriage, Amanda Bradshaw runs away and finds herself in a charming ghost town — but this one has an active ghost! Outlaws, lost gold, and a unique love triangle are all part of this fast-paced, and realistic (in spite of the ghost) story.

Other books you might like:
Jude Deveraux, *Wishes*, 1989
Dorothy Garlock, *Nightrose*, 1990
Linda Lael Miller, *Angelfire*, 1989
Thomasina Ring, *Time-Spun Treasure*, 1992
Patricia Simpson, *Whisper of Midnight*, 1991
   contemporary ghost

1754

FELA DAWSON SCOTT

Ghost Dancer

(New York: Leisure, 1992)

Story type: Historical/American West
Major character(s): Ghost Dancer "Angelique", Psychic, Religious (spiritual leader, Ghost Sioux); Cameron Wade, Military Personnel (army captain)
Time period(s): 1870s (1873)
Locale(s): South Dakota

Summary: Rescued from a Cheyenne ambush and nursed back to health by the legendary Ghost Dancer, mystical spiritual leader of the Ghost Sioux, Captain Cameron Wade is captivated by the beautiful, golden-haired woman. Realizing Ghost Dancer is white, he determines to "return her to her people" — but she refuses to go. It takes a greedy villain and a series of wagon attacks before Cameron and Ghost Dancer can come to terms with their love for each other and can learn to understand each other's worlds. Unique.

Other books you might like:
Deborah Camp, *Lady Legend*, 1992
Ruth Langan, *Texas Healer*, 1992
Pamela Litton, *Dance with the Devil*, 1992
Janelle Taylor, *Forever Ecstasy*, 1991

1755

THERESA SCOTT

Broken Promise

(New York: Lovespell, 1995)

Story type: Historical/Pre-history
Series: Hunters of the Ice Age

Major character(s): Star, Captive; Falcon, Kidnapper
Time period(s): 80th century B.C. (8000)
Locale(s): Palouse River Area, Washington; Palouse River Area, Idaho

Summary: The gentle, primitive Badgers lose their women routinely to the Jaguar tribe, and Star is captured even though she disguises herself. Falcon, a "lost" warrior strangely bereft of hopes and beliefs, claims her against her will; even though she continues to fight to return to her tribe, she comes to care for him. A poignant blend of fact and fiction. Latest in the Hunters of the Ice Age Series.

Other books you might like:
Jean M. Auel, *Clan of the Cave Bear*, 1980
   classic Ice Age story
Jean M. Auel, *The Mammoth Hunters*, 1985
J.H. Brennan, *Shiva Accused: An Adventure of the Ice Age*, 1991
   young adult adventure/some romance
Joan Wolf, *Daughter of the Red Deer*, 1991
   another captive/captor pre-history romance

1756

THERESA SCOTT

Dark Renegade

(New York: Dorchester, 1994)

Story type: Historical/Pre-history
Series: Hunters of the Ice Age
Major character(s): Summer, Young Woman; Talon, Warrior, Outcast
Time period(s): 91st century B.C. (9040 B. C.)
Locale(s): Snake River Plain, North America

Summary: Banished by his tribe, Talon steals Summer, the woman who has loved him for years, and sets out to make a new life for them both. His strange dissimilarity to his original family drives him to search for his true origins, and after overcoming a series of obstacles he finds a new tribe and achieves the status he has been seeking.

Other books you might like:
Jean M. Auel, *Clan of the Cave Bear*, 1980
Jean Auel, *The Mammoth Hunters*, 1985
Patricia Rowe, *Keepers of the Misty Time*, 1994
Linda Lay Shuler, *The Voice of the Eagle*, 1992
   early Native American culture
Joan Wolf, *Daughter of the Red Deer*, 1991
   early European (French) culture

1757

MAURA SEGER

Beloved Enemy

(New York: Harper, 1992)

Story type: Historical/Elizabethan
Major character(s): Dierdre O'Neill, Gentlewoman; John Delacroix, Spy, Warrior
Time period(s): 17th century (early)
Locale(s): Ireland

Summary: Determined to keep the Irish under control, Queen Elizabeth dispatches John Delacroix to infiltrate the O'Neill household and discover their plans. He is attracted to the lovely Dierdre, and when her father suspects his true mission and throws him in the dungeon, Dierdre releases him, only to become a hostage herself. Her ultimate rescue and his release leave their relationship in shreds, and it isn't until much later that they are given one more chance for happiness. A story of love and passion that overcomes ancient political and cultural differences.

Other books you might like:
Shannon Drake, *Damsel in Distress*, 1992
Iris Johansen, *The Wind Dancer*, 1991
Ruth Langan, *Highland Fire*, 1991
Miriam Minger, *Captive Rose*, 1991
Sylvie Sommerfield, *Fires of Surrender*, 1990

1758
MAURA SEGER

Forevermore
(New York: Harper, 1994)

Story type: Historical/Regency; Historical/Fantasy
Major character(s): Sarah Huxley, Spinster; William Devereaux Faulkner, Nobleman, Diplomat
Time period(s): 1800s
Locale(s): Aveburg, England; London, England

Summary: Intrigued by ancient Druid stones, Sarah finds herself having disturbing dreams about them—and when she discovers a dead gypsy, a friend sends for Sir William Faulkner, a diplomat renowned for settling disputes and solving mysteries. Unfortunately, more murders only add to the problem, as do hauntings, ghosts, and surrealistic visions. It takes a lot of work for Sarah and William to solve not only the mysteries of her dreams, but the secrets of their hearts as well.

Other books you might like:
Connie Brockway, *Promise Me Heaven*, 1994
charmingly gothic historical regency
Andrea Kane, *Dream Castle*, 1992
rather gothic historical Regency
Laura Parker, *For Love's Sake Only*, 1991
more Regency ghosts — with a light touch
Amanda Quick, *Dangerous*, 1993
a funny, lively approach to Regency "ghosts."
Barbara Wood, *The Dreaming*, 1992
exotic setting/mystical elements

1759
MAURA SEGER

Fortune's Tide
(New York: Avon, 1990)

Story type: Historical/Fantasy
Major character(s): Nora O'Connell Wentworth, Actress, Imposter (Boston socialite); Jason West, Privateer
Time period(s): 1770s (1778)

Locale(s): Alternate Earth

Summary: In an alternate reality in which America lost the Revolution, Dublin actress Nora Wentworth finds herself in England posing as a member of society and involved in a plan to help keep Washington, Jefferson, and Adams from being hanged as traitors. In the process she falls in love with privateer Jason West who is working to free the Americans. Interesting premise.

Other books you might like:
Christine Dorsey, *Traitor's Embrace*, 1990
Traditional Revolutionary War outcome
Robin Maderich, *Faith and Honor*, 1989
Traditional Revolutionary War outcome
Serena Richards, *Masquerade*, 1990
English setting
Lynette Vinet, *Pirate's Bride*, 1989
JoAnn Wendt, *The Golden Dove*, 1989
Earlier time period

1760
MAURA SEGER

Into the Storm
(New York: Warner, 1990)

Story type: Historical/War of 1812
Major character(s): Annabel Riordan, Saloon Keeper/Owner (Wild Geese Tavern); David de Montfort, Nobleman (Marquis), Diplomat (Napoleon's emissary)
Time period(s): 1810s (1813-1814)
Locale(s): Washington, District of Columbia

Summary: While in Washington on a political mission for Napoleon, Marquis David de Montfort is captivated by beautiful tavern owner Annabel Riordan. Although they become lovers, she refuses to be his mistress, so he returns to France alone. The birth of his son brings him back to Washington just in time to endure the British attacks on the city. This time David convinces Annabel to accompany him to France for the sake of their son. Likeable characters and fast action are highlights of this nicely-detailed historical.

Other books you might like:
Mollie Ashton, *Terms of Surrender*, 1990
Deana James, *Masque of Sapphire*, 1990
Emma Merritt, *Masque of Jade*, 1990
Elizabeth Ann Michaels, *Destiny's Will*, 1991
Serena Richards, *Rendezvous*, 1991

1761
MAURA SEGER

The Lady and the Laird
(Toronto: Harlequin, 1992)

Story type: Historical/Georgian; Historical/Fantasy
Major character(s): Katlin Sinclair, Noblewoman; Angus Wyndham, Laird
Time period(s): 1800s (1807)
Locale(s): Scotland

Summary: Katlin Sinclair inherits a castle from her uncle on one condition—that she live there for six months; otherwise it reverts to Angus Wyndham, since his ancestors were the original owners. Life is hard in the castle—no food, no servants, one resident ghost—but Kate endures with a lot of help, eventually, from Angus who has decided that he wants both Kate and the castle.

Other books you might like:
Diana Gabaldon, *Outlander*, 1991
   time change elements
Arnette Lamb, *Highland Rogue*, 1991
Ruth Langan, *Highland Heart*, 1992
Dawn Lindsey, *The Barbarous Scot*, 1992

1762

MAURA SEGER

Light on the Mountain

(Toronto: Harlequin, 1992)

Story type: Historical/Victorian
Major character(s): Morgana Penrhys, Teacher; David Harrell, Nobleman (Marquess of Montfort)
Time period(s): 1850s (1859)
Locale(s): London, England; Gynfelin, Wales

Summary: Instead of the peace and quiet he hopes to find when he returns to his estates, David, Marquess of Montfort, finds himself rescuing the beautiful, spirited schoolmarm from the advances of a student's father and becoming caught up in Morgana's concern for the plight of the local miners. A lyrical story of shared interests and blossoming love that overcomes gossip, greed, and the dictates of social class.

Other books you might like:
Stephanie Bartlett, *Highland Rebel*, 1992
Jessica Stirling, *Strathmore*, 1974
Victoria Thompson, *Playing with Fire*, 1990
Lynette Vinet, *Wild, Wicked Eden*, 1990

1763

MAURA SEGER

Perchance to Dream

(New York: Avon, 1989)

Story type: Historical/Fantasy
Major character(s): Susannah "Butterfly" Fitzgerald, Spy, Debutante; Rand Cabot, Spy (Yankee), Importer/Exporter
Time period(s): 1860s (Post-Civil War)
Locale(s): Alternate Earth

Summary: In a lively story based on the premise that the South won the War, Susannah and Rand work with Lincoln and Lee to reunite the states. Interesting idea and treatment.

Other books you might like:
Norah Hess, *Wildfire*, 1989
   Traditional Civil War outcome/post-war
Kathryn Kramer, *Destiny and Desire*, 1988
   Traditional Civil War outcome
Margaret Mitchell, *Gone with the Wind*, 1936
   A classic "must" if you haven't already read it

Janelle Taylor, *Destiny's Temptress*, 1986
   Traditional Civil War outcome
Kathleen E. Woodiwiss, *Ashes in the Wind*, 1979
   Traditional Civil War outcome

1764

MAURA SEGER

The Taming of Amelia

(Toronto: Harlequin, 1993)

Story type: Historical/Colonial America
Major character(s): Amelia Daniels, Heiress (Puritan); Garrick Marlowe, Sea Captain
Time period(s): 17th century
Locale(s): Belle Haven, Connecticut, American Colonies

Summary: Wealthy and orphaned, free-thinking Amelia Daniels convinces sea captain Garrick Marlowe (with a little help from Amelia's rejected suitor who sets fire to Garrick's ship) to go with her and establish a new colony in Connecticut. Despite the expected hardships, Belle Haven proves true to its name; and for a time, Amelia and Garrick are free to explore their new-found love for each other. Eventually, of course, the jealous and vindictive people they left behind complicate their lives, but their love does win out in the end. First in a projected series.

Other books you might like:
Emily Carmichael, *Visions of the Heart*, 1990
Barbara Cummings, *Wilderness Flame*, 1993
Pamela K. Forrest, *Wild Savage Heart*, 1993
Nancy Moulton, *Defiant Heart*, 1989
Penelope Williamson, *A Wild Yearning*, 1990

1765

MAURA SEGER

Tapestry

(New York: Harper, 1993)

Story type: Historical/Medieval
Major character(s): Lady Aveline, Noblewoman, Artist (tapestry designer); Renard d'Agounville, Lawman (High Sheriff of London), Warrior
Time period(s): 11th century (1070s)
Locale(s): England

Summary: To quell the growing possibility of unrest among the English populace, the Normans commission a tapestry to portray their own version of history, a tapestry that is to be designed and realized by Lady Aveline of the Thorney Cloister of English nuns and overseen by William's loyal warrior, Renard d'Agounville. Drawn to each other, Aveline and Renard must overcome old secrets and conflicting loyalties and deal with a series of murders before they can find happiness together. A lyrical, magical tale.

Other books you might like:
Rexanne Becnel, *Where Magic Dwells*, 1990
Kathryn Lynn Davis, *Child of Awe*, 1990
Mary Lide, *Ann of Cambray*, 1984
Marylyle Rogers, *The Eagle's Song*, 1992

Flora M. Speer, *Castle of the Heart*, 1990

1766

KATHLEEN GILLES SEIDEL

Maybe This Time

(New York: Pocket, 1990)

Story type: Contemporary
Major character(s): Emily Gordon, Agent (sports); Jeff Grant, Teacher (high school), Writer (novelist)
Time period(s): 1980s
Locale(s): Nancy Hanks, Illinois

Summary: Emily's senior year ended with a tragic car accident. Now, fifteen years later and a successful sports agent, she returns home to lay to rest some old ghosts, solve an old mystery, and, maybe, find an old love.

Other books you might like:
Sally Beauman, *Destiny*, 1987
Elizabeth Quinn, *Any Day Now*, 1989
LaVyrle Spencer, *Bittersweet*, 1990
Heidi Strasser, *Love's Memories*, 1988
Patricia Strothers, *Silvermore*, 1989

1767

KATHLEEN GILLES SEIDEL

More than You Dreamed

(New York: Pocket, 1992)

Story type: Contemporary
Major character(s): Jill Caslar, Young Woman; Doug Ringling, Filmmaker
Time period(s): 1990s
Locale(s): Hollywood, California

Summary: Proud of her father's legendary films, Jill Caslar is shocked to meet Doug Ringling who claims there is another version, one that was mysteriously supressed, of her father's most famous film. As she searches for the truth, Jill's feelings for Doug begin to grow; and when the evidence points to the validity of his theory, she realizes that the truth may be more than she can handle. Love and intrigue in a sparkling Hollywood setting.

Other books you might like:
Catherine Mann, *Tinsel Town: A Novel*, 1984
Nora Roberts, *Genuine Lies*, 1991
JoAnn Ross, *Secret Sins*, 1990
Tracy Sinclair, *Miss Robinson Crusoe*, 1989
Danielle Steel, *Passion's Promise*, 1976

1768

KATHLEEN GILLES SEIDEL

Till the Stars Fall

(New York: Onyx, 1994)

Story type: Contemporary/Mainstream

Major character(s): Krissa French, Manager (of a rock group), Housewife; Quinn Hunter, Musician (rock group), Doctor; Danny French, Musician (rock group), Activist (political)
Time period(s): 1970s; 1990s
Locale(s): Minnesota

Summary: Krissa, her brother Danny, and her lover Quinn thought they would be together forever—a marvelous rock band success. However, their mutual needs both inspired and destroyed their relationship, and eventually Krissa returned home to Minnesota, Quinn became a doctor, and Danny became a liberal activist. Their feelings, however, are still alive—sustaining them as well as tearing them apart. A well-written, powerful, realistic story.

Other books you might like:
Lenore Carroll, *The Heart Remembers*, 1993
Barbara Delinsky, *Commitments*, 1988
Shirl Henke, *Summer Has No Name*, 1990
LaVyrle Spencer, *Bittersweet*, 1990
Penelope Williamson, *Once in a Blue Moon*, 1993
  historical

1769

COLLEEN SHANNON

Golden Fires

(New York: Jove, 1993)

Story type: Historical/Victorian; Historical/Exotic
Major character(s): Lina Collier, Archaeologist; Jeremy Mayhew, Guide, Drifter
Time period(s): 1890s (1897)
Locale(s): France; Yucatan Peninsula, Mexico

Summary: Lina and her father, both archaeologists, need a guide to the Yucatan and Jeremy is the perfect choice. The expedition proves exciting and dangerous as they face numerous obstacles, both environmental and human, in their quest. Love and adventure in a steamy setting.

Other books you might like:
Jill Marie Landis, *Past Promises*, 1993
  Western archaeologist
Leslie O'Grady, *Seek the Wild Shore*, 1989
Jeane Renick, *Trust Me*, 1992
  contemporary setting
Susan Sackett, *Passion's Golden Fire*, 1989

1770

COLLEEN SHANNON

Surrender the Night

(New York: Jove, 1992)

Story type: Historical/Georgian
Major character(s): Katrina Lawson, Young Woman; Devon Cavanaugh, Hero; Will Farrow, Doctor
Time period(s): 1780s (1789)
Locale(s): London, England; Cornwall, England

Summary: Katrina Lawson seems to go from one predicament to another. First, she's rescued from becoming the sacrificial offering at a lewd ritual, then she escapes from a house where the hero wants her to be his mistress — only to end up in a brothel. Eventually, she is taken in by gentle Dr. Farrow and his family only to have the hero seek her out again. However, this time he wants to marry her, but she is having second thoughts for various reasons. All ends appropriately in this very sensual, fast-paced romance.

Other books you might like:
Johanna Lindsey, *Prisoner of My Desire*, 1991
    medieval setting
Mary Jo Putney, *Uncommon Vows*, 1991
Patricia Rice, *Touched by Magic*, 1992
Bertrice Small, *Lost Love Found*, 1992
Jennifer West, *Passion's Legacy*, 1991

1771
ALICE SHARPE

A Garland of Love
(New York: Avalon, 1990)

Story type: Contemporary/Innocent
Major character(s): Alison Simmons, Businesswoman (florist), Guardian (of a six-year-old child); Jack Foxx, Professor (literature), Child-Care Giver
Time period(s): 1980s
Locale(s): Eureka, California

Summary: When college professor Jack Foxx applies for the job as nanny for Alison's six-year-old nephew, it's all she can do to take him seriously. But when Jamie thinks he's great, she reconsiders.

Other books you might like:
Angela Carson, *Sweet Illusion*, 1990
Karen Leabo, *Domestic Bliss*, 1990
Jan McDaniel, *Angels in the Sand*, 1989
Lee Stafford, *A Song in the Wilderness*, 1990
Diana Whitney, *A Liberated Man*, 1990

1772
ALICE SHARPE

Just One More Secret
(New York: Avalon, 1990)

Story type: Contemporary/Innocent
Major character(s): Andrea Carber, Landscaper; Mark Tripper, Contractor (builds houses)
Time period(s): 1980s
Locale(s): Crescent Cove, California

Summary: Determined to start a new life after being falsely accused of embezzlement by her former employer, landscaper Andrea Carber has things well in hand in Crescent Cove—until she meets Mark Tripper. Their growing relationship, both personal and professional, demands that Andrea tell him of her past; but before she can, her past walks back into her life.

Other books you might like:
Angela Carson, *Sweet Illusion*, 1990
Jane McBride Choate, *Badge of Love*, 1989
Rita Rainville, *Never on Sundae*, 1990

Lee Stafford, *A Song in the Wilderness*, 1990
Diana Whitney, *A Liberated Man*, 1990

1773
ALICE SHARPE

The Vanishing Bridegroom
(New York: Avalon, 1990)

Story type: Contemporary/Innocent; Romantic Suspense
Major character(s): Kate Brewster, Bride (deserted), Businesswoman (welcome wagon-type service); Matt Vothers, Bridegroom (disappearing)
Time period(s): 1990s
Locale(s): San Francisco, California; Hawaii

Summary: When Matt leaves her standing at the altar, Kate Brewster knows something is very wrong; and when she tracks Matt to Hawaii and begins hearing some strange things about his behavior, she is sure of it. Mystery, intrigue, and romance.

Other books you might like:
Alma Blair, *The Dark Side of Paradise*, 1990
Marion Smith Collins, *Home to Stay*, 1991
Lucy Keane, *False Impressions*, 1990
Karen G. McCullough, *Programmed for Danger*, 1990
Mary Stewart, *My Brother Michael*, 1959

1774
ALICE SHARPE

Wedding Bell Blues
(New York: Avalon, 1992)

Story type: Contemporary/Innocent
Major character(s): Kylie Armstrong, Businesswoman (wedding consultant); Theo Brighton, Veterinarian
Time period(s): 1990s
Locale(s): United States

Summary: Although still wary of men as a result of being jilted, Kylie Armstrong does a good job of managing other people's weddings. However, when her great aunts decide she should get married and take it upon themselves to find her a husband, Kylie ends up with three men fighting for her attention.

Other books you might like:
Debbie Macomber, *First Comes Marriage*, 1991
Helen R. Myers, *Invitation to a Wedding*, 1990
Sue Peters, *Unwilling Woman*, 1989
Gina Robins, *Love's Sweetest Secret*, 1991
    another sought-after heroine/sensual/historical

1775
ALICE SHARPE

Yesterday's Dream
(New York: Avalon, 1991)

Story type: Contemporary/Innocent; Romantic Suspense

Major character(s): Zoe Drysdale, Businesswoman (boat maintenance business); John Nix, Businessman (investment counselor)
Time period(s): 1990s
Locale(s): Monterey, California; Mexico

Summary: Someone is trying to ruin Zoe Drysdale's boat maintenance business; and when Zoe investigates, one of her former customers ends up dead. With the help of John Nix, Zoe eventually solves the mystery, but not before she becomes involved in a web of intrigue and love that takes her all the way to Mexico.

Other books you might like:
Alma Blair, *The Unwitting Witness*, 1990
Judith Bowen, *Man of Steel*, 1991
Elizabeth Peters, *Summer of the Dragon*, 1979
Nora Roberts, *Courting Catherine*, 1991
Mary Stewart, *This Rough Magic*, 1964

1776

LINDA SHAW

Odessa Gold
(Toronto: Harlequin, 1991)

Story type: Historical/American West; Historical/Victorian America
Major character(s): Genevieve "Jenny" Carlyle, Young Woman; Odessa Gold, Convict (former)
Time period(s): 1890s
Locale(s): United States

Summary: When Jenny Carlyle impulsively comes to the aid of newly-released convict Odessa Gold by claiming to be his wife, she begins a fascinating and passionate relationship destined to last a lifetime. Adventure, danger, and love are part of this lively historical.

Other books you might like:
Robin Lee Hatcher, *Promised Sunrise*, 1990
Norah Hess, *Wildfire*, 1989
Dana Ransom, *Wild Wyoming Love*, 1991
Lynda Trent, *Heaven's Embrace*, 1990

1777

MAGGIE SHAYNE (Pseudonym of Margaret Benson)

Forgotten Vows
(New York: Silhouette, 1994)

Story type: Contemporary; Romantic Suspense
Major character(s): Joey Bradshaw, Psychic; Ash Coye, Journalist (newspaper reporter)
Time period(s): 1990s
Locale(s): United States

Summary: When newspaper reporter Ash Coye ends up in a hospital with amnesia, clairvoyant Joey Bradshaw sees a perfect opportunity to save her sister—and Ash, a man she has never met—from becoming a serial killer's next victims. She will present herself as Ash's new wife, keep him safe, and ensure the safety of her sister at the same time. What she doesn't count on, however, is falling in love with Ash, the

man who is determined to unmask the killer—and who considers Joey a prime suspect. Tense and passionate.

Other books you might like:
Sandra Canfield, *Dark Journey*, 1994
Janet Dailey, *Masquerade*, 1990
Wendy Haley, *Shadow Whispers*, 1992
Nora Roberts, *Divine Evil*, 1992
Tracey Tillis, *Deadly Masquerade*, 1994

1778

MAGGIE SHAYNE (Pseudonym of Margaret Benson)

Kiss of the Shadow Man
(New York: Silhouette, 1994)

Story type: Romantic Suspense; Gothic
Major character(s): Caitlin Rossi, Amnesiac; Dylan Rossi, Architect
Time period(s): 1990s
Locale(s): Eden, Connecticut

Summary: When she loses her memory in a car accident, Caitlin Rossi wakes up to a bizarre household, a hostile husband, and the knowledge that someone is trying to kill her—none of which, of course, she remembers. A gothicly mysterious, sensual, and sometimes violent romance with no overt paranormal aspects.

Other books you might like:
Sandra Brown, *Mirror Image*, 1990
Janet Dailey, *Masquerade*, 1990
Mary-Ben Lorris, *Sing Me to Sleep*, 1994
Judith Michael, *Deceptions*, 1982
Deborah Nicholas, *Night Vision*, 1993

1779

MAGGIE SHAYNE

Out of This World Marriage
(New York: Silhouette, 1995?)

Story type: Contemporary/Fantasy; Gothic
Major character(s): Janella, Alien; Thomas Duffy, Doctor
Time period(s): 1990s
Locale(s): Sumac, Iowa

Summary: Thomas' brief childhood encounter with a young alien girl has faded to little more than a dream; but when Janella returns as a beautiful, desirable woman, the dream suddenly becomes real—and more passionate and dangerous than he ever could have imagined. The fact that women are dominant in Janella's culture provides an interesting twist to this intriguing story.

Other books you might like:
Madeline Baker, *Enchanted Crossings*, 1994
  anthology
Lori Herter, *The Willow File*, 1994
  Gothic
Sabine Kells, *A Deeper Hunger*, 1994
  dark fantasy
Anne Stuart, *Night of the Phantom*, 1991
  paranormal elements/Gothic

Marilyn Tracy, *Memory's Lamp*, 1994
  futuristic elements

1780
NANCY SHEEHAN
Harvest of Love
(New York: Avalon, 1990)

Story type: Contemporary/Innocent
Major character(s): Darcy Lewis, Nurse (gerontologist), Social Worker; Luke Randall, Doctor
Time period(s): 1990s
Locale(s): Illinois

Summary: Young Doctor Luke Randall, fresh from high-powered University Hospital in Chicago, comes to work at several rural nursing homes and discovers he has a lot to learn about people and about love; and with the help of gerontologist Darcy Lewis, he succeeds.

Other books you might like:
Bethany Campbell, *Every Woman's Dream*, 1991
Anne Ladley, *Prescription for Love*, 1990
Wendy Martin, *Love on Trial*, 1990
Catherine Spencer, *Winter Roses*, 1991

1781
NANCY SHEEHAN
The Heart's Journey
(New York: Avalon, 1992)

Story type: Contemporary/Innocent
Major character(s): Kari McNeal, Young Woman, Businesswoman (financial adviser); Reed Drake, Sports Figure (skier), Businessman (developer)
Time period(s): 1990s
Locale(s): West Granville, Massachusetts

Summary: When Kari McNeal goes to see to her late grandmother's affairs in Massachusetts, she finds love in the form of a handsome ex-Olympic skier — and a family she didn't know she had.

Other books you might like:
Marjorie Everitt, *Somewhere Near Paradise*, 1992
Sandra Field, *Goodbye Forever*, 1990
Claudia Jameson, *That Certain Yearning*, 1990
Debbie Macomber, *A Little Bit of Country*, 1990

1782
JORY SHERMAN
Eagles of Destiny
(New York: Zebra, 1990)

Story type: Historical/American West
Major character(s): Estrellita De Rojas, Heiress, Noblewoman (Spanish); Jeremiah York, Trapper
Time period(s): 1830s
Locale(s): St. Louis, Missouri; Southwest

Summary: Attracted to each other in spite of their differences, aristocratic heiress Estrellita De Rojas and poor, westward-bound Jeremiah York must brave both parents and Comanches in their efforts to be together. This story doesn't end where one might expect; there is more to come.

Other books you might like:
Rosanne Bittner, *Sweet Mountain Magic*, 1990
Ann Gabriel, *South Texas*, 1990
Shirl Henke, *Night Flower*, 1990
Norah Hess, *Wildfire*, 1989
Dana Fuller Ross, *Wagons West series*, 1979
  More action than romance

1783
LINDA SHERTZER
Pickett's Fence
(New York: Diamond, 1994)

Story type: Historical/Victorian America; Historical/American West
Major character(s): Rachel Williams, Widow(er), Farmer; Tom Pickett, Farmer
Time period(s): 1870s (1872)
Locale(s): Kansas

Summary: A bull, a boy, and a killer combine to bring struggling farmers Rachel Williams and Tom Pickett together in a warm and loving story. Country charm with a bit of mystery thrown in.

Other books you might like:
Candace Camp, *Rosewood*, 1991
Anne Harmon, *Desert Flame*, 1992
  gently mysterious
Robin Lee Hatcher, *Where the Heart Is*, 1993
Kathleen Kane, *Keeping Faith*, 1994
Jill Marie Landis, *Rose*, 1990

1784
VALERIE SHERWOOD
Lisbon
(New York: New American Library, 1989)

Story type: Historical/Georgian
Major character(s): Charlotte Vayle, Gentlewoman; Tom Westing, Sailor (son of a pirate)
Time period(s): 1730s (1730-1735)
Locale(s): Europe; Lisbon, Portugal

Summary: Believing Tom, the man she loves, is dead, Charlotte agrees to marry Rowan to escape from her uncle. However, when she discovers that Tom is alive and that Rowan knew it all along, Charlotte learns just how cruel and deceitful her husband can be.

Other books you might like:
Barbara Hazard, *Call Back the Dream*, 1990
Marjorie Shoebridge, *To Love a Stranger*, 1990
Lisa Ann Verge, *Blaze of Passion*, 1989

1785

JUNE LUND SHIPLETT

Boston Renegade

(Toronto: Harlequin, 1992)

Story type: Historical/American West
Major character(s): Hannah Winters, Teacher, Rancher; Blake Morgan, Drifter, Guide
Time period(s): 1870s (1872)
Locale(s): Boston, Massachusetts; Hangtown, Texas

Summary: Hannah Winters and her friend leave staid Boston to run her inherited ranch in Texas. On the way, they are joined by Blake Morgan, a handsome drifter who decides to escort them to the ranch. He helps her in a variety of ways, even saving her life at one point, but Hannah is determined to run the ranch on her own, even though Blake seems more than willing to help. Sweet and lively.

Other books you might like:
DeLoras Scott, *Bittersweet*, 1988
DeLoras Scott, *Fire and Ice*, 1990
DeLoras Scott, *The Miss and the Maverick*, 1990
Victoria Thompson, *Sweet Texas Surrender*, 1991
Bonnie K. Winn, *Summer Rose*, 1992

1786

JANE SHORE

The Cinderella Game

(New York: Avalon, 1990)

Story type: Contemporary/Innocent
Major character(s): Sandy Childs, Clerk (in a fabric store), Designer (would-be fashion designer); Jason Grant, Director (theatre), Heir
Time period(s): 1980s
Locale(s): Brae-Mill

Summary: Sandy has always wanted to be a dress designer and now, thanks to theatre director Jason Grant, she is an apprentice in the local clothing factory. Their relationship takes a romantic turn and life seems very good to Sandy—until someone decides to sabotage the current play.

Other books you might like:
Sheila Fyfe, *Appointment with Love*, 1990
Rosalind Laker, *Banners of Silk*, 1981
    Historical setting
Kasey Michaels, *His Chariot Awaits*, 1990
Sue Peters, *Unwilling Woman*, 1989
Rita Rainville, *Never on Sundae*, 1990

1787

LINDA LAY SHULER

Voice of the Eagle

(New York: Morrow, 1992)

Story type: Historical/Pre-history
Major character(s): Kwani, Indian (Anasazi), Shaman
Time period(s): 13th century

Locale(s): West, North America

Summary: Spiritual leader of the Anasazi Kwani travels with her mate and young son across the plains and ends up saving the city of Cicuya and its people. Continues *She Who Remembers*.

Other books you might like:
Jean M. Auel, *Clan of the Cave Bear*, 1980
Beverly Bird, *Comes the Rain*, 1991
Kathryn Lynn Davis, *Sing to Me of Dreams*, 1990
Lynn Armistead McKee, *Touch the Stars*, 1992
Joan Wolf, *Daughter of the Red Deer*, 1991

1788

DEBORAH SIMMONS (Pseudonym of Deborah Siegenthal)

Fortune Hunter

(Toronto: Harlequin, 1992)

Story type: Regency
Major character(s): Melissa Hampton, Gentlewoman, Heiress; Leighton Somerset, Nobleman (impoverished viscount)
Time period(s): 1810s
Locale(s): England

Summary: Melissa has money, but no title; Leighton has a title, but no money. The match seems ideal, especially to infatuated Melissa. However, once they are married their problems start — Leighton's ex-lover tries to separate them and a murderer is making attempts on Melissa's life. All Melissa wants is to settle down with Leighton, money or no money. A sparkling, funny, and sometimes frightening, romp through Regency England.

Other books you might like:
Dorothy Eden, *Melbury Square*, 1970
Rosemary Edghill, *The Ill-Bred Bride*, 1990
Georgette Heyer, *A Civil Contract*, 1962
Dorothy Mack, *The Mock Marriage*, 1991
Amanda Quick, *Seduction*, 1990

1789

DEBORAH SIMMONS (Pseudonym of Deborah Siegenthal)

Heart's Masquerade

(New York: Avon, 1989)

Story type: Historical
Major character(s): Catherine "Cat" Amberly, Runaway; Ransom Du Prey, Privateer
Locale(s): At Sea; Barbados

Summary: Seeking escape from her cousin Edward who wants to kill her, Catherine poses as a boy and becomes "Cat," a cabin boy aboard the Barbados-bound privateer *Reckless*. Adventure, pirates, attempted murder, and romance are all in store for Cat and Captain Ransom Du Prey.

Other books you might like:
Kathryn Davenport, *Pirate's Mistress*, 1989
Georgina Gentry, *Nevada Nights*, 1989
    Old West; heroine poses as a boy

Jill Marie Landis, *Wild Flower*, 1989
  Western/Caribbean settings
Joan Van Nuys, *Beloved Avenger*, 1989

`1790`

SUZANNE SIMMONS

Diamond in the Rough
(New York: Topaz, 1994)

Story type: Historical/Regency
Major character(s): Juliet Jones, Spinster, Heiress; Lawrence Wicke, Nobleman
Time period(s): 19th century
Locale(s): New York; England

Summary: In need of a rich wife, the destitute duke, Lawrence, pursues the innocent, intelligent Juliet right to the altar—and then she discovers his scheme. Unwilling to settle for anything less than love, Juliet keeps her distance, but she also agrees to join forces with Lawrence and help him defeat his enemies. Naturally, their close proximity leads to love—and a satisfactory marriage relationship. Witty, fast-paced, and funny.

Other books you might like:
Jo Beverley, *Deirdre and Don Juan*, 1993
  Regency
Connie Brockway, *Promise Me Heaven*, 1994
Julie Garwood, *The Gift*, 1991
Amanda Quick, *Seduction*, 1990
Amanda Quick, *Surrender*, 1990

`1791`

TRANA MAE SIMMONS

Bittersweet Promises
(New York: Love Spell, 1994)

Story type: Historical/Victorian America; Historical/Post-American Civil War
Major character(s): Shanna Van Alstyne, Fugitive (from her vindictive father); Cody Garrett, Rescuer
Time period(s): 1860s (1866)
Locale(s): New York; Liberty, Missouri

Summary: Shanna promises her mother that she will find a man to marry who will save her and her young brother from her vengeful father. But when the bullets start to fly and her money is stolen, she has no choice but to stay for a while with the aunt of Cody Garrett, the man who rescued her from the gunfire. Love blooms, but it takes a bit of doing before everything works out. Funny and sensual.

Other books you might like:
Julie Garwood, *Prince Charming*, 1994
  funny and fast-paced/similar time period
Kathleen Kane, *Keeping Faith*, 1994
  small town ambience
Susan Kay Law, *Home Fires*, 1995
  another fugitive heroine
Bobbi Smith, *Beneath Passion's Skies*, 1993
  another fugitive heroine heading West

`1792`

CHARLOTTE SIMMS and Charla Chin)

Silver Caress
(New York: Avon, 1990)

Story type: Historical/American West
Major character(s): Felicity Howard, Housekeeper, Religious (former nun); Jake McCullough, Mine Owner (unwilling partner of Felicity)
Time period(s): 19th century
Locale(s): Silverton, Colorado

Summary: Falsely accused and expelled from a Philadelphia convent, Felicity (Sister Fidelis) heads to Colorado to keep house for her "pen pal," Joseph McCullough and start a new life. Unfortunately, when she arrives, Joseph is dead and Felicity is the owner of his house and half of his mine—much to the dismay of Joseph's son, Jake. Sparks fly between the two, but love wins out in the end.

Other books you might like:
Thea Devine, *Montana Mistress*, 1990
Patricia Gaffney, *Thief of Hearts*, 1990
Kathy Lawrence, *Tin Angel*, 1989
Sara Orwig, *Denver*, 1990
Colleen Quinn, *Colorado Flame*, 1989

`1793`

LAURA SIMON

Dreams of Paradise
(New York: Berkley, 1991)

Story type: Historical/Victorian America
Major character(s): Hazel Meriweather, Gentlewoman, Artist (fabric designer); Marco MacGregor, Hero
Time period(s): 19th century
Locale(s): Milan, Italy; Massachusetts

Summary: Hazel travels to Milan and spends a glorious summer in the arms of Marco MacGregor. In spite of their mutual love, Hazel returns to her impending marriage to a Boston businessman. Then tragedy strikes and Hazel is left on her own. Through her courage, talent, and determination, she takes control of her life and in the process, finds success and love.

Other books you might like:
Leona Blair, *A World of Difference*, 1989
  saga
Sandra Bregman, *Reach for the Dream*, 1990
Rebecca George, *Call Home the Heart*, 1989
Jill Marie Landis, *Rose*, 1990
LaVyrle Spencer, *Bittersweet*, 1990
  similar theme/contemporary setting

1794
LAURA SIMON

Garden of Dreams
(New York: Berkley, 1992)

Story type: Historical/Victorian America
Major character(s): Nina Colangelo, Immigrant, Business-woman (seed catalogues); Wim Pieter De Groot, Immigrant, Businessman (flower bulbs)
Time period(s): 1880s; 1890s
Locale(s): New York; Connecticut; Italy

Summary: Although they meet briefly, but memorably, as new immigrants, it is years before Nina Colangelo and Wim de Groot encounter each other again—this time as enterprising adults, determined to succeed in their new country—and this time they fall in love. Ethnic prejudice, class differences, and family pressures create problems for the pair, but love and commitment win out in the end.

Other books you might like:
Elaine Barbieri, *Tattered Silk*, 1991
Elaine Barbieri, *Wishes on the Wind*, 1991
Jill Marie Landis, *Rose*, 1990
Belva Plain, *Evergreen*, 1978
Lucy Elliot, *Private Paradise*, 1991

1795
LAURA SIMON

A Taste of Heaven
(New York: Berkley, 1989)

Story type: Historical/Exotic
Major character(s): Allegra Pembroke, Plantation Owner, Businesswoman (chocolate factory); Oliver MacKenzie, Plantation Owner, Businessman (shipping company owner)
Time period(s): 1890s
Locale(s): Grenada (L'Etoile—cocoa plantation); England

Summary: Impulsively abandoning her proper, boring life in New England, Allegra goes to Grenada in search of the adventuring father she has never known. But when he is accidentally killed before she can even meet him, Allegra inherits not only his business responsibilities but a charmingly unconventional partner as well. Love blossoms as Allegra battles her rigid upbringing and comes into her own as an independent, astute businesswoman.

Other books you might like:
Barbara Bretton, *Midnight Lover*, 1989
  Reluctant partners theme
Cordia Byers, *Lady Fortune*, 1989
Kathy Lawrence, *Tin Angel*, 1989
  Reluctant partners theme
Julie Tetel, *Swept Away*, 1989
  Tropical setting/Earlier time period

1796
SONIA SIMONE

Scandalous
(New York: Avon, 1994)

Story type: Historical/Antebellum American South
Major character(s): Liberty Brooks, Activist (abolitionist), Secretary; Zeke Malloy, Political Figure, Activist (abolitionist)
Time period(s): 1850s
Locale(s): New Orleans, Louisiana

Summary: When secretary Liberty Brooks becomes involved with the underground railway, she is captured to be sold as a slave—and suddenly it is her employer, avid abolitionist Zeke Malloy, who must set things to rights. Well-researched and filled with interesting historical detail.

Other books you might like:
Wendy Garrett, *Sweet Southern Caress*, 1991
Patricia Hagan, *Midnight Rose*, 1991
Shirl Henke, *Night Flower*, 1990
Patricia Potter, *Rainbow*, 1991

1797
CARLA SIMPSON

Always, My Love
(New York: Pinnacle, 1990)

Story type: Historical/Fantasy; Historical/Post-American Civil War
Major character(s): Amanda Spencer, Plantation Owner, Reincarnated Person; Coleton James, Overseer (plantation), Plantation Owner (former)
Time period(s): 1860s (1865)
Locale(s): Louisiana

Summary: When Coleton James returns home to Ombre Rose, his Louisiana plantation, after the Civil War, he is in for a number of surprises. Not only has his plantation been bought by a beautiful Northerner, but this woman is the embodiment of Cole's former fiancee—who died twenty years ago. A mystical story of love, revenge, and second chances.

Other books you might like:
Jo Ann Algermissen, *Golden Bird*, 1990
Lonnie Coleman, *Beulah Land*, 1973
  first in a trilogy
Karen Robards, *Morning Song*, 1989
Bobbi Smith, *Bayou Bride*, 1991
Kathleen E. Woodiwiss, *Come Love a Stranger*, 1984

1798
CARLA SIMPSON

Desperado's Caress
(New York: Zebra, 1991)

Story type: Historical/American West
Major character(s): Revel Tyson, Detective (Pinkerton agent); Jake Reno, Outlaw (former)

Time period(s): 1880s (1881)
Locale(s): Arizona

Summary: A Pinkerton agent with revenge on her mind, Revel Tyson saves Jake Reno from the gallows in return for his help in locating the man who killed her father; but when Jake leaves town without her, she sets off in pursuit! A funny, passionate, action-filled romp across the Southwest.

Other books you might like:
Charlotte Hubbard, *Gambler's Tempting Kisses*, 1991
Christine Monson, *Golden Nights*, 1990
Gina Robins, *Deception's Sweet Kiss*, 1990
Victoria Thompson, *Playing with Fire*, 1990

1799
CARLA SIMPSON

Seduced
(New York: Pinnacle, 1993)

Story type: Historical/American West Coast
Major character(s): Allison Caulfield, Socialite; Dalton Malone, Renegade
Time period(s): 19th century
Locale(s): San Francisco, California

Summary: Allison, new to "rough and ready" San Francisco, is unprepared for the difficulties she experiences as she attempts to find her father's killer. Dalton has absolutely no use for her, and she does get in his way! Nevertheless, passion takes over, and amid danger and adventure, they finally learn to love and care for each other.

Other books you might like:
Lori Copeland, *Promise Me Tomorrow*, 1994
Carol Finch, *Moonlight Enchantment*, 1992
Patricia Hagan, *Orchids in Moonlight*, 1993
Jill Marie Landis, *Jade*, 1991

1800
CARLA SIMPSON

Seductive Caress
(New York: Zebra, 1992)

Story type: Historical/Victorian; Romantic Suspense
Major character(s): Jessamyn Forsythe, Artist; Devlin Burke, Detective
Time period(s): 1880s (1888)
Locale(s): London, England

Summary: Jessamyn's sister is missing, and she is determined to find her, in spite of the fact that Jack the Ripper is running rampant in White Chapel. Her efforts lead her into dangerous territory, and when her landlady is murdered, Detective Devlin Burke takes her home with him and out of danger. A romantic love story centering on one of the most chilling and frightening crime sequences in modern history.

Other books you might like:
Thea Devine, *Tempted by Fire*, 1992
Elizabeth Kary, *Midnight Lace*, 1990
Kay McMahon, *Betray the Night*, 1991

Erin Yorke, *Dangerous Deceptions*, 1992

1801
PAMELA SIMPSON

Fortune's Child
(New York: Bantam, 1992)

Story type: Contemporary/Mainstream
Major character(s): Christina Grant-Fortune, Banker, Heiress; Ross McKenna, Businessman (CEO)
Time period(s): 1990s
Locale(s): San Francisco, California

Summary: When a woman professing to be Christina Fortune reappears after an absence of 20 years to claim her late father's controlling interest in Fortune Shipping, she finds a family in ferment and her own life in danger as she works to save her company and discover who originally forced the 15-year-old Christina to run away years before. Romance, intrigue, and fascinating characters are all part of this fast-paced, mainstream romance.

Other books you might like:
Sally Beauman, *Destiny*, 1987
Elizabeth Bennett, *Changes of Heart*, 1992
Catherine Coulter, *Beyond Eden*, 1991
Barbara Delinsky, *Facets*, 1990
Barbara Delinsky, *A Woman Betrayed*, 1991

1802
PAMELA SIMPSON

Partners in Time
(New York: Bantam, 1990)

Story type: Time Travel
Major character(s): C.J. Grant, Detective—Private, Actress (former); Sam Hackett, Lawman (U.S. Marshal)
Time period(s): 1980s (1989); 1880s (1882)
Locale(s): California

Summary: When an earthquake sends Marshal Sam Hackett from 1882 into 1989, he has some adjusting to do. Private-eye C.J. Grant helps him and things become more interesting when he discovers the man she is currently tracking is a descendant of the one that Sam was chasing in 1882. Humor, mystery, and romance grace this fast-paced story.

Other books you might like:
Janice Bennett, *A Timeless Affair*, 1990
  Time change/Regency period
Jude Deveraux, *A Knight in Shining Armor*, 1989
  Time change/Elizabethan period
Heather Graham, *Every Time I Love You*, 1989
  Time change/Pre-Revolutionary America
Colleen Quinn, *Colorado Flame*, 1989
  Mystery and adventure in a Western setting
Becky Lee Weyrich, *Forever, for Love*, 1989
  Time change/Early 19th century

1803
PATRICIA SIMPSON

The Legacy
(New York: Harper, 1992)

Story type: Contemporary/Fantasy
Major character(s): Jessica Ward, Neighbor, Scientist (astronomer); Cole Nichols, Heir—Dispossessed, Sports Figure (football player) Cosimo Cavanetti, Spirit
Time period(s): 1990s
Locale(s): Seattle, Washington

Summary: When Cole Nichols returns home to make peace with his dying father, he finds his family in chaos and the family winery on the edge of ruin—and it doesn't help matters that he has been having mysterious flashbacks to the 12th century! His old friend and neighbor Jessica Ward has also been seeing things—a monk who wanders about the winery. Together they work to find answers—and as they begin to solve the problems of the present, they find they are simultaneously setting to rights the wrongs of the past.

Other books you might like:
Laura Gilmour Bennett, *By All That Is Sacred*, 1991
Diana Gabaldon, *Dragonfly in Amber*, 1992
Diana Gabaldon, *The Outlander*, 1991
Constance O'Day-Flannery, *Once in a Lifetime*, 1992

1804
PATRICIA SIMPSON

The Night Orchid
(New York: Harper, 1994)

Story type: Time Travel
Major character(s): Marissa Quinn, Young Woman; Alek, Time Traveller, Warrior (Druid); Kyle Woodward, Scientist
Time period(s): 1990s; 5th century B.C.
Locale(s): Seattle, Washington

Summary: Suspicious of her sister Leslie's strange disappearance, Marissa Quinn gets no satisfactory answers from Leslie's boss, Dr. Woodward. However, things begin to fall into place when the Druid warrior Alek, suddenly appears and kidnaps Marissa to help him function in this alien world. As they piece things together, they realize that time-change scientist Dr. Woodward is responsible—and they are forced to confront and challenge him to bring Leslie back and restore Alek to his own time. Meantime, Marissa and Alek have fallen in love—a circumstance that adds challenges of its own.

Other books you might like:
Diana Gabaldon, *Outlander*, 1991
  first of a near-classic time travel series
Joan Hohl, *Love Beyond Time*, 1994
  time travel anthology
Kay Hooper, *The Wizard of Seattle*, 1993
  a rather dark time travel
Susan Sizemore, *Wings of the Storm*, 1992
  time travel/enterprising heroine

Flora M. Speer, *A Love Beyond Time*, 1994
  time travel/8th century France

1805
PATRICIA SIMPSON

Whisper of Midnight
(New York: Harper, 1991)

Story type: Romantic Suspense; Contemporary/Fantasy
Major character(s): Jamie Kent, Photographer
Time period(s): 1990s
Locale(s): Port Orchard, Washington

Summary: When Jamie Kent returns to her Washington home to help her brother, she literally encounters a ghost from her past—a sea captain who has haunted her dreams for years. However, as Jamie comes to know her ghostly visitor, her fear changes to something else—with far-reaching consequences. An unwanted fiance, would-be thieves, and old secrets add to the excitement of this romantic mystery. Reminiscent of both *Ghost* and *The Ghost and Mrs. Muir*.

Other books you might like:
Jude Deveraux, *A Knight in Shining Armor*, 1989
  time change elements
Barbara Michaels, *Ammie, Come Home*, 1969
Penelope Neri, *Forever and Beyond*, 1990
Becky Lee Weyrich, *Forever, For Love*, 1989

1806
KATHERINE SINCLAIR

A Distant Dawn
(New York: Berkley, 1991)

Story type: Historical/World War I; Saga
Major character(s): Jane Weatherly, Friend, Suffragette; Claudia Abelard, Heiress
Time period(s): 1910s
Locale(s): England

Summary: Close friends in spite of their class differences, aristocratic Claudia and stableman's daughter Jane survive the sinking of the *Lusitania* only to find themselves caught up in a war that threatens not only the lives of those they love but their entire social structure as well. Adventure, betrayal, and passion in a world turned upside down. Good historical detail.

Other books you might like:
Diane Cory, *A Token of Jewels*, 1989
Dorothy Eden, *The American Heiress*, 1980
Heather Hay, *Heritage*, 1988
Marcella Thum, *The Thorn Trees*, 1991

1807
KATHERINE SINCLAIR

Far Horizons
(New York: Berkley, 1991)

Story type: Historical

Major character(s): Bethany Newton, Fugitive, Convict; Mary Fielding, Noblewoman; Alison Banks, Child-Care Giver

Time period(s): 19th century

Locale(s): England; Australia; United States

Summary: Sweeping from the upper class British social scene to the Australian penal colony and the United States, this historical chronicles the lives and loves of three women who are bound together by a single child.

Other books you might like:

Sally Beauman, *Destiny*, 1987

Leigh Bristol, *Sunswept*, 1990

Dorothy Eden, *The Vines of Yarabee*, 1969

Valerie Sherwood, *Lisbon*, 1989

1808

KATHERINE SINCLAIR

Through the Years

(New York: Berkley, 1994)

Story type: Historical/Mainstream

Major character(s): Maggie Nesbitt, Seamstress, Designer (dress designer); Cordelia "Delia", Singer, Orphan

Time period(s): 1900s

Locale(s): Natchez, Mississippi; New Orleans, Louisiana; San Francisco, California

Summary: Delia is an orphan and, eventually, a famous singer; Maggie is a seamstress and, eventually, a successful dress designer. Their link? Delia's daughter, who is abandoned and then raised by Maggie. This sweeping story of two determined women who pursue separate, but eventually convergent, paths sweeps from the sultry and proper South to the "wilds" of California (just in time for the Great San Francisco earthquake) and features strong heroines and good characterizations in general.

Other books you might like:

Elaine Barbieri, *Tattered Silk*, 1991

   strong heroine/career goals

Gwen Bristow, *Calico Palace*, 1991

   San Francisco setting/another strong heroine

Heather Hay, *Heritage*, 1988

   two women/similar time period/different setting

Belva Plain, *Crescent City*, 1984

   saga of 19th century New Orleans

1809

KATHERINE SINCLAIR

Visions of Tomorrow

(New York: Charter, 1989)

Story type: Historical/Edwardian

Major character(s): Megan Thomas Robards, Doctor; Joanna Traherne, Gentlewoman

Time period(s): 1900s

Locale(s): Cornwall, England; New Mexico

Summary: When she is accused of killing her best friend, Megan escapes to New Mexico with the help of John McQuinn. Joanna, however, is not dead, but for a number of reasons cannot return home to clear Megan's name. A story of hardships, betrayal, and survival—with soap opera elements.

Other books you might like:

Heather Hay, *Heritage*, 1988

   Edwardian tale of two sisters

Cynthia Victor, *Consequences*, 1989

   A single event changes the lives of two sisters/Mainstream

Gay Courter, *The Midwife*, 1981

   Mainstream fiction

Nancy Zaroulis, *The Last Waltz*, 1984

1810

REBECCA SINCLAIR

California Caress

(New York: Zebra, 1989)

Story type: Historical/American West

Major character(s): Hope Bennett, Mine Owner, Southern Belle (Former); Drake Frazier, Gunfighter

Time period(s): 1850s (1851)

Locale(s): California; Boston, Massachusetts; Virginia

Summary: When Hope Bennett enlists the aid of notorious gunslinger Drake Frazier to save both her family's gold claim and her brother's life, she has no intention of paying his price—a night in bed with her. True love wins out eventually, but not before the pair have a number of adventures.

Other books you might like:

Barbara Bretton, *Midnight Lover*, 1989

Deborah Camp, *Fallen Angel*, 1989

Gwen Cleary, *Ecstasy's Masquerade*, 1989

Georgina Gentry, *Nevada Nights*, 1989

Norah Hess, *Wildfire*, 1989

1811

REBECCA SINCLAIR

Forbidden Desires

(New York: Zebra, 1992)

Story type: Historical/American West

Major character(s): Emilee Hogan, Teacher; Cade MacAllister, Bounty Hunter

Time period(s): 1870s

Locale(s): Halston, Nebraska

Summary: Cade MacAllister is after Emilee Hogan because she killed his brother; Emilee is running from him because she knows he won't listen to her explanations. She also has a deed to a mine that a number of other people want, so a lot of other people are chasing her, too. Cade and Emilee do get together and solve their problems, but not before a lot of high-powered action takes place. Sensual and fast-paced.

Other books you might like:

Barbara Ankrum, *Renegade Bride*, 1992

Jill Gregory, *Cherished*, 1992

Rebecca Paisley, *Midnight and Magnolias*, 1992

Rochelle Wayne, *Nevada Flame*, 1992

1812
REBECCA SINCLAIR

Wild Scottish Embrace
(New York: Zebra, 1991)

Story type: Historical/Renaissance
Major character(s): Marea MacKenzie, Noblewoman (Scottish), Healer; Chase Graham, Nobleman (English)
Time period(s): 16th century (1570s)
Locale(s): Scotland

Summary: Ten years after Chase Graham saved Marea MacKenzie's life and virtue during a raid on her keep, Marea, now a healer disguised as an old woman, has the opportunity to return the favor—with predictably passionate results. Their relationship is hampered somewhat by the fact that Chase is the son of the man who killed Marea's father and now holds her keep; but in spite of this and assorted other difficulties, love does prevail. Fast-paced and highly descriptive.

Other books you might like:
Kathryn Lynn Davis, *Child of Awe*, 1990
Jude Deveraux, *The Taming*, 1989
Patricia Grasso, *Highland Belle*, 1991
Johanna Lindsey, *A Gentle Feuding*, 1984
Katherine Vickery, *Flame Across the Highlands*, 1990

1813
TRACY SINCLAIR

If the Truth Be Told
(New York: Silhouette, 1992)

Story type: Contemporary
Major character(s): Chelsey Claiborne, Businesswoman (investment counselor); Roberto de Machado, Wealthy (millionaire)
Time period(s): 1990s
Locale(s): Spain

Summary: When Chelsey wonders what macho Spanish millionaire Roberto de Machado sees in her teen-age sister, she flies to Spain to find out—and realizes that *she* is what Roberto wants. A new twist on a classic formula.

Other books you might like:
Donna Carlisle, *Matchmaker, Matchmaker*, 1990
Jan Hudson, *Call Me Sin*, 1992
Jayne Ann Krentz, *Lady's Choice*, 1989
Lass Small, *Dominic*, 1992
Danielle Steel, *Passion's Promise*, 1976

1814
TRACY SINCLAIR

Miss Robinson Crusoe
(New York: Silhouette, 1989)

Story type: Contemporary
Major character(s): Bliss Goodwin, Castaway; Hunter Lord, Producer (Hollywood)
Time period(s): 1980s

Locale(s): Hollywood, California

Summary: When Bliss Goodwin is rescued after being shipwrecked, everyone wants to produce her story. With the help of Hunter Lord she avoids most of the pitfalls, except for one—falling in love with Hunter, who doesn't believe in marriage.

Other books you might like:
Christine Flynn, *Renegade*, 1989
Catherine Mann, *Tinsel Town*, 1985
Danielle Steel, *Passion's Promise*, 1976

1815
RAY SIPHERD

The Courtship of Peggy McCoy
(New York: St. Martin's, 1990)

Story type: Contemporary
Major character(s): Peggy McCoy, Military Personnel (WAVE Commander); Charles Deering, Military Personnel (Rear Admiral)
Time period(s): 1990s
Locale(s): United States

Summary: Age is no barrier to romance in this gentle, delightful tale of two independent "old salts" who find love at a time in their lives when other people are simply enjoying their grandchildren.

Other books you might like:
Betty Cothran, *Over the Moon*, 1994
Garda Parker, *Out of the Blue*, 1992

1816
SUSAN SIZEMORE

My Own True Love
(New York: Harper, 1994)

Story type: Time Travel
Major character(s): Sara Dayny, Accountant, Time Traveller; Lewis Morgan, Spy (British)
Time period(s): 1810s (1811)
Locale(s): Minnesota; London, England

Summary: Travelling through time to 1811, accountant Sara Dayny discovers Lewis Morgan, her own true love—but he turns out to be a British spy and he needs her for his schemes. All goes as Lewis has planned, gypsy marriage and all, until they fall in love; then things become even more complex. Realistic and fast-paced.

Other books you might like:
Barbara Bretton, *Somewhere in Time*, 1992
Diana Gabaldon, *Outlander*, 1991
Kristin Hannah, *When Lightning Strikes*, 1994
Kasey Michaels, *Timely Matrimony*, 1994
Becky Lee Weyrich, *Sweet Forever*, 1992

1817

SUSAN SIZEMORE

Wings of the Storm
(New York: Harper, 1992)

Story type: Time Travel
Major character(s): Jane Florian, Time Traveller, Scientist; Davvyd Ap Bleddyn, Knight
Time period(s): 1990s; 13th century
Locale(s): England

Summary: Forced back into the 13th century by a coworker, scientist and medievalist Jane Florian sets about using her knowledge and skills to survive—and ends up managing a castle, involved in treason, and in love with a heroic Welsh knight. Good historical detail.

Other books you might like:
Laura Gilmour Bennett, *By All That Is Sacred*, 1991
Jude Deveraux, *A Knight in Shining Armor*, 1989
Diana Gabaldon, *Dragonfly in Amber*, 1992
　　Sequel to *Outlander*
Diana Gabaldon, *Outlander*, 1991

1818

CHRISTINA SKYE (Pseudonym of Roberta Helmer)

The Black Rose
(New York: Dell, 1991)

Story type: Historical/Regency
Major character(s): Theresa ''Tess'' Leighton, Saloon Keeper/Owner, Smuggler; Dane St. Pierre, Nobleman (Viscount Ravenhurst)
Time period(s): 1810s
Locale(s): Camber Sands, England (south coast of England)

Summary: When Viscount Ravenhurst is assigned to find the infamous smuggler, ''The Romany Fox,'' he has no idea that his search will lead him to Tess Leighton, the woman who broke his heart. Determined to cause her the same kind of pain he experienced at her hands, he sets out to torture her—body and heart—but learns how closely intertwined are pain, pleasure, and love. Hot, explicit sex.

Other books you might like:
Rebecca Brandewyne, *Forever My Love*, 1982
Julie Garwood, *Guardian Angel*, 1990
Brenda Joyce, *Dark Fires*, 1991
Katherine Sutcliffe, *Love's Illusion*, 1989
Lynette Vinet, *Pirate's Bride*, 1989

1819

CHRISTINA SKYE

Come the Dawn
(New York: Dell, 1995)

Story type: Historical/Regency
Major character(s): India Delamere, Noblewoman; Devlyn Carlisle, Nobleman (Earl of Thornewood)
Time period(s): 1810s

Locale(s): England

Summary: Stunned and overjoyed when Devlyn Carlisle, the man to whom she had secretly been married, suddenly returns to London a year after he had been listed among the missing at Waterloo, India Delamere is faced with more than simply a returning husband. Amnesia, a dangerous mystery, and some wonderfully interesting characters are all elements in this intricately plotted, occasionally confusing story.

Other books you might like:
Stella Cameron, *Charmed*, 1995
Catherine Coulter, *The Valentine Legacy*, 1995
Jane Feather, *Valentine*, 1995
Jane Feather, *Velvet*, 1994
Katherine Sutcliffe, *Miracle*, 1995

1820

CHRISTINA SKYE (Pseudonym of Roberta Helmer)

Hour of the Rose
(New York: Avon, 1994)

Story type: Time Travel; Contemporary/Fantasy
Major character(s): Kelly Hamilton, Archaeologist, Psychic; Michael Burke, Nobleman (Viscount Dunwell), Military Personnel (former)
Time period(s): 1990s; 11th century
Locale(s): England

Summary: American archaeologist Kelly Hamilton and former English Commander Michael Burke are thrown together in a search for a buried urn containing microfiche. Kelly has used her second sight to help the U.S. government in the past, and now both governments want her help. Ghosts, reincarnation, and suspense add to the adventure as Kelly and Michael fight their basic distrust of each other and eventually solve the mystery and realize that they are truly meant for each other. Complex and intricate plot.

Other books you might like:
Laura Gilmour Bennett, *By All That Is Sacred*, 1991
　　another quest through time/ different treatment
Shannon Drake, *Avon Books Presents: Haunting Love Stories*, 1991
　　fantasy anthology
Kathleen Morgan, *The Demon Prince*, 1994
Shelly Thacker, *Forever His*, 1993
　　time travel

1821

CHRISTINA SKYE (Pseudonym of Roberta Helmer)

The Ruby
(New York: Dell, 1992)

Story type: Historical/Exotic; Historical/Victorian
Major character(s): Barrett Winslow, Adventurer, Amnesiac; Deveril Pagan St. Cyr, Plantation Owner
Time period(s): 1860s (1864)
Locale(s): London, England; Sri Lanka

Summary: Barrett and Deveril first meet in London, both are disguised and Barrett is running for her life. Their meeting is passionate and brief, but they are destined to meet again when Barrett is washed up on the shore of Deveril's island. Unfortunately, she has lost her memory, but he still remembers their first encounter. A 46 carat ruby, an exotic Ceylon setting, and a vile villain add to this highly sensual romance. Sweet/savage overtones.

Other books you might like:
Virginia Brown, *Emerald Nights*, 1991
Maggie Osborne, *Emerald Rain*, 1991
Karen Robards, *Green Eyes*, 1991
Bobbi Smith, *Capture My Heart*, 1992
Katherine Sutcliffe, *Shadow Play*, 1991

1822

BERTRICE SMALL

Lost Love Found

(New York: Ballantine, 1992)

Story type: Historical/Elizabethan
Major character(s): Valentina St. Michael, Widow(er), Noblewoman (lady-in-waiting to Elizabeth I); Tom Ashburne, Nobleman
Time period(s): 17th century (1650)
Locale(s): England; Constantinople, Turkey

Summary: Newly widowed Valentina joins the aging Queen Elizabeth's court to find continual intrigue—and a clue to her true parentage. Journeying to Turkey in search of her heritage, she is abducted, assaulted, and aided by the same woman who had helped her mother. Of course, she finds love along the way. Non-stop action, lots of passion and adventure, and a typically strong, intrepid heroine.

Other books you might like:
Jane Feather, *Bold Destiny*, 1990
Shirl Henke, *Paradise and More*, 1992
Virginia Henley, *The Pirate and the Pagan*, 1990
Mary Lide, *Isobelle*, 1988
Miriam Minger, *Captive Rose*, 1991

1823

BERTRICE SMALL

The Love Slave

(New York: Ballantine, 1995)

Story type: Historical/Medieval
Major character(s): Regan "Zaynah" MacDuff, Slave (love slave in training); Karim Al Malina, Teacher (of the love arts)
Time period(s): 10th century
Locale(s): Scotland; Spain

Summary: Sent by her treacherous family to a convent as a young girl, Scotswoman Regan MacDuff ends up in Moorish Spain as the possession of the Caliph and in the care of Karim to be trained as a love slave in all the erotic arts of the ancient world. Accepting her fate, she learns all Karim has to teach her, eventually becoming the Caliph's harem favorite. However, her heart belongs to Karim, and even though their chances of a life together are remote, they never stop loving

each other. An erotic, adventurous romance filled with explicit sex. Sweet/savage elements.

Other books you might like:
Jane Feather, *Bold Destiny*, 1990
Patricia Grasso, *Desert Eden*, 1993
exotic setting/sensual
Susan Johnson, *Forbidden*, 1991
similar sensuality levels
Susan Johnson, *Sinful*, 1993
similar sensuality levels
Mary Lide, *Isobelle*, 1988
exotic setting/more lyrical

1824

BERTRICE SMALL

A Moment in Time

(New York: Ballantine, 1991)

Story type: Historical/Fantasy; Historical/Medieval
Major character(s): Wynne of Gwernach, Noblewoman; Madoc of Powys, Royalty (prince)
Time period(s): 11th century (1060s)
Locale(s): Wales

Summary: In this story of reincarnation and a love that spans the ages, Wynne and Madoc fight the fates, vindictive and greedy relatives, and their own personalities to finally make their love a reality. Magical, mystical, and highly sensual.

Other books you might like:
Jude Deveraux, *A Knight in Shining Armor*, 1989
Shannon Drake, *Princess of Fire*, 1989
Barbara Erskine, *Kingdom of Shadows*, 1988
Penelope Neri, *Forever and Beyond*, 1990
American West setting
Carla Simpson, *Always, My Love*, 1990
American South setting

1825

BERTRICE SMALL

The Spitfire

(New York: Ballantine, 1990)

Story type: Historical/Medieval
Major character(s): Arabella Grey, Noblewoman (cousin to Richard III); Tavis Stewart, Nobleman (Earl of Dummor)
Time period(s): 15th century (1490s)
Locale(s): Scotland; England

Summary: To avenge the death of his betrothed, Tavis Stewart storms the wedding of the murderer, Sir Jasper Keane, kidnaps Arabella Grey, the bride-to-be, and marries her himself. In spite of these beginnings, Tavis and Arabella fall in love and begin a passionate marriage. However, Arabella still yearns for her estate, Greyfaire; and when Tavis refuses to help her, she plans to reclaim it herself. Betrayal, intrigue, and lively action follow Arabella in her struggle to regain her heritage and her love.

Other books you might like:
Rexanne Becnel, *My Gallant Enemy*, 1990

Rosemary Jarman, *Crown in Candlelight*, 1978
Brenda Joyce, *The Conqueror*, 1990
Anya Seton, *Katherine*, 1954

1826

BERTRICE SMALL

To Love Again

(New York: Ballantine, 1993)

Story type: Historical/Medieval
Major character(s): Cailin Drusus, Captive (Celtic), Fugitive; Wulf Ironfist, Warrior (Saxon); Flavius Aspar, Military Personnel
Time period(s): 5th century
Locale(s): England; Constantinople, Byzantium

Summary: In Britain, Cailin flees to a Celtic chieftain relative when her home is confiscated and her family murdered. She marries a Saxon warrior, Wulf, but is torn from him and sold to be a mistress of Aspar, a Byzantine general. Aspar is kind to her, but she still loves Wulf. She recognizes him as a gladiator and must deal with her conflicting emotions, eventually being forced to choose between love and a harsh life in Britain and loyalty and the luxuries of a life with Aspar. A highly sensual, sweet/savage romance.

Other books you might like:
Shannon Drake, *Knight of Fire*, 1993
Anita Gordon, *The Defiant Heart*, 1993
Brenda Joyce, *The Conqueror*, 1990
Brenda Joyce, *Promise of the Rose*, 1993

1827

BERTRICE SMALL

Wild Jasmine

(New York: Ballantine, 1992)

Story type: Historical/Seventeenth Century
Major character(s): Jasmine "Yasaman" de Marisco, Royalty (princess); Lord Rowan Lindley, Nobleman
Time period(s): 17th century
Locale(s): India; England; Ireland

Summary: Skye O'Malley's granddaughter, Jasmine, proves to be as adventurous as her famous grandmother. Raised as an Indian princess, Jasmine is sent to England to escape her half-brother's incestuous advances, where she finds herself pursued by lords, earls, and princes. She marries Rowan Lindley and they are happy until he is murdered. This story abounds in passion, action, and court intrigue and is a fitting conclusion to the lives of Skye, her daughter Velvet, and Jasmine.

Other books you might like:
Shirl Henke, *Paradise and More*, 1992
Betina M. Krahn, *Behind Closed Doors*, 1991
Miriam Minger, *Captive Rose*, 1991
Suzanne Robinson, *Lady Gallant*, 1992
Kathleen E. Woodiwiss, *So Worthy My Love*, 1989

1828

LASS SMALL

A Nothing Town in Texas

(New York: Harper, 1991)

Story type: Contemporary
Major character(s): Naomi Wentworth, Activist; Decker Jones, Spy (CIA), Cowboy
Time period(s): 1990s
Locale(s): Sawbuck, Texas

Summary: Summoned by his devious ranch-owning uncle to keep determined Naomi Wentworth from reviving the sorry town of Sawbuck, ex-CIA agent Decker Jones moves into town—and inadvertently sparks a revitalization effort that sweeps through the populace, carrying Decker along with it. The town blossoms and so does Decker and Naomi's love.

Other books you might like:
Constance Bennett, *Morning Sky*, 1991
Deana James, *Wild Texas Heart*, 1990
Kat Martin, *Lover's Gold*, 1991
Joan Elliott Pickart, *The Bonnie Blue*, 1990
Janelle Taylor, *Follow the Wind*, 1990

1829

BARBARA DAWSON SMITH

Fire at Midnight

(New York: Avon, 1992)

Story type: Historical/Victorian; Romantic Suspense
Major character(s): Norah Rutherford, Widow(er), Artist (jewelry designer); Lord Kit Coleridge, Nobleman, Rake
Time period(s): 1880s (1887)
Locale(s): London, England

Summary: Jewelry designer Norah Rutherford is a prime suspect in the murder of Maurice Rutherford. When Lord Kit Coleridge comes to her aid, her life undergoes some major changes. An exciting, exotic, passionate, and suspenseful tale.

Other books you might like:
Susan Johnson, *Forbidden*, 1991
Rosalind Laker, *The Jewelled Path*, 1983
Mary Jo Putney, *Silk and Shadows*, 1991
Katherine Sutcliffe, *A Fire in the Heart*, 1990
Catherine Wyatt, *A Rose in the Shadows*, 1992

1830

BARBARA DAWSON SMITH

Fire on the Wind

(New York: Avon, 1992)

Story type: Historical/Victorian; Historical/Exotic
Major character(s): Sarah Faulkner, Writer, Spinster; Damien Coleridge, Nobleman, Photographer
Time period(s): 1830s (1836); 1850s (1857)
Locale(s): London, England; Bombay, India; Himalayas, India

Summary: An armed Indian rebellion forces proper Englishwoman Sarah and renegade Damien to flee for safety with Damien's new-born, half-caste son. As they travel and struggle to survive, they collaborate on a book about India (she is an editorial writer and he is a photographer)—and they fall in love. Good historical detail about a fascinating, violent period in India's past.

Other books you might like:
E.M. Forster, *A Passage to India*, 1924
Victoria Holt, *The India Fan*, 1988
M.M. Kaye, *The Far Pavilions*, 1978
Christine Monson, *Rangoon*, 1985
Christine Monson, *This Fiery Splendor*, 1991

1831
BARBARA DAWSON SMITH
A Glimpse of Heaven
(New York: St. Martin's, 1995)

Story type: Historical/Regency; Gothic
Major character(s): Catherine Snow, Widow(er); Burke Grisham, Nobleman (Earl of Thornwald)
Time period(s): 1810s (1816)
Locale(s): England

Summary: When Burke Grisham goes to Yorkshire to fulfill his friend's dying request to look after his wife, he not only comes face to face with the woman who has inexplicably been haunting his dreams and whose past and future he intuitively knows, but one who is being treated like a servant by her in-laws in true Cinderella fashion (complete with wicked mother-in-law and two simpering sisters-in-law). He vows to help her, but Catherine despises him as the man who led her husband to ruin—and finally to his death at Waterloo—and she doesn't make it easy. Features excellent characterizations, gothic and paranormal elements, and an emotionally wounded hero.

Other books you might like:
Mary Balogh, *Deceived*, 1993
Christina Dodd, *Move Heaven and Earth*, 1995
  another wounded hero/gothic atmosphere
Georgette Heyer, *An Infamous Army*,
  classic Regency Waterloo tale
Christina Skye, *Come the Dawn*, 1995

1832
BOBBI SMITH
Arizona Caress
(New York: Zebra, 1989)

Story type: Historical/American West
Major character(s): Rori "Aurora" Prescott, Indian (half Pima Indian); Chance Broderick, Sea Captain
Time period(s): 1870s
Locale(s): Arizona; Boston, Massachusetts

Summary: When Chance Broderick leaves Boston to go to Arizona and help his brother save his gold mine, he doesn't plan to fall in love with Rori, the feisty daughter of his guide—but he does, and his life is never the same again.

Other books you might like:
Janet Dailey, *The Pride of Hannah Wade*, 1985
Judith Steel, *Apache Heartbeat*, 1989
Janelle Taylor, *Bittersweet Ecstasy*, 1987
Janelle Taylor, *Savage Conquest*, 1985
Janelle Taylor, *Sweet Savage Heart*, 1986

1833
BOBBI SMITH
Bayou Bride
(New York: Avon, 1991)

Story type: Historical/Antebellum American South
Major character(s): Jordan St. James, Servant (indentured), Bride (pretend); Dominic Kane, Plantation Owner, Heir
Time period(s): 19th century
Locale(s): Louisiana

Summary: To avoid being disinherited, Dominic Kane must find a bride before his father dies. Unfortunately Nick neither has a bride in mind nor wants one; so he convinces indentured servant, Jordan St. James, to play the part. It's when they fall in love with each other that the complications begin. Good characterizations and witty dialogue.

Other books you might like:
Lonnie Coleman, *Beulah Land*, 1973
  first of a trilogy
Thea Devine, *Southern Seduction*, 1991
Wendy Garrett, *Sweet Southern Caress*, 1991
Leona Karr, *Nightfire*, 1990
Kathleen E. Woodiwiss, *The Flame and the Flower*, 1972

1834
BOBBI SMITH
Beneath Passion's Skies
(New York: Zebra, 1993)

Story type: Historical/Victorian America; Historical/American West
Major character(s): Sarah Windsor, Fugitive; Angela Windsor, Fugitive
Time period(s): 1850s
Locale(s): Philadelphia, Pennsylvania; West; Midwest

Summary: To save their young nephew, Christopher, from his murderous father, Angela and Sarah Windsor escape with him and head toward California, hoping to confuse their pursuer by taking separate routes. Along the way, they endure hardships, meet a number of fascinating people, and both women find love. However, before they can settle down in happiness, they must meet Christopher's father in a final, devastating confrontation. Complex, and peopled with unusual characters.

Other books you might like:
Gwen Cleary, *Ecstasy's Masquerade*, 1989
Dorothy Garlock, *Homeplace*, 1991
Julie Garwood, *Prince Charming*, 1994

Kay Wilding, *Rainbow's End*, 1990
contemporary

1835

BOBBI SMITH

Capture My Heart
(New York: Zebra, 1992)

Story type: Historical/Exotic; Historical/Georgian
Major character(s): Victoria Lawrence, Captive; Alexander "Serad" Wakefield, Nobleman, Pirate
Time period(s): 18th century; 19th century (1789-1807)
Locale(s): England; Algeria

Summary: This complicated story of romance, villainy, and mistaken identities is rife with pirates, harems, prisons, and poison. Kidnapped and taken to Algeria as a child, Serad grows up to become a feared Barbary Pirate. Eventually, he learns of his true birth and angrily heads to England to sort things out. The lovely Victoria, an escapee from his harem, only adds to the passion and the adventure as Serad seeks to right old wrongs and see that the villains are all justly rewarded.

Other books you might like:
Susan Johnson, *Sinful*, 1992
Amanda Quick, *Scandal*, 1991
Christina Skye, *The Ruby*, 1992
Jennifer West, *Passion's Legacy*, 1991
Kathleen E. Woodiwiss, *Shanna*, 1977

1836

BOBBI SMITH

Dream Warrior
(New York: Zebra, 1993)

Story type: Historical/American West
Major character(s): Cari McCord, Young Woman; Bruce Marshal Silver Wolf, Indian (Cheyenne), Government Official (Bureau of Indian Affairs)
Time period(s): 19th century
Locale(s): Wyoming

Summary: Cari, ignoring her mother's prejudices, never forgets Silver Wolf, who saved her as a child. Both go east to school and then return to Wyoming, Silver Wolf as an educated BIA agent. Prejudice, greed, a murder, and treacherous enemies conspire to keep Cari and Wolf apart; but trust and love overcome everything and all is well.

Other books you might like:
Rosanne Bittner, *Sioux Splendor*, 1990
Genell Dellin, *Comanche Wind*, 1993
Kathleen Eagle, *Heaven and Earth*, 1990
Cassie Edwards, *Wild Splendor*, 1993
Kathleen Harrington, *Cherish the Dream*, 1990

1837

BOBBI SMITH

Kiss Me Forever
(New York: Zebra, 1991)

Story type: Historical/Exotic
Major character(s): Francesca Salazar, Gentlewoman; Slater MacKenzie, Spy
Time period(s): 1850s
Locale(s): Cuba; New Orleans, Louisiana

Summary: Brutally separated by her father after they have been married only a few months, Slater MacKenzie is kidnapped and told Francesca is dead, while Francesca believes Slater has abandoned her—leaving her to bear his child alone. When they eventually meet again, they each think the other betrayed them, but when Slater kidnaps Francesca and his son, things are put into the proper perspective. Lots of passionate action in this unique romance.

Other books you might like:
Dorothy Garlock, *Ribbon in the Sky*, 1991
Rebecca George, *Call Home the Heart*, 1989
Nan Ryan, *Sun God*, 1990
Janelle Taylor, *Promise Me Forever*, 1991

1838

DEBORAH SMITH

Beloved Woman
(New York: Bantam, 1991)

Story type: Historical/American West
Major character(s): Katherine Blue Song, Indian (Cherokee), Doctor; Justis Gallatin, Miner
Time period(s): 1830s
Locale(s): New York; Georgia; California

Summary: Katherine is determined to survive and help her people, the Cherokee, without any outside help—especially not from rough miner Justis Gallatin. Nevertheless, Justis persists, and Katherine comes to value and love him for the man he is. A powerful love story interwoven with the tragic events of the Trail of Tears, sweeping from New York to California in a flurry of fast-paced, dramatic adventure and highly charged romantic action.

Other books you might like:
Catherine Anderson, *Comanche Moon*, 1991
Rosanne Bittner, *Arizona Ecstasy*, 1989
Jessie Ford, *A Different Breed*, 1988
Shirl Henke, *Night Wind's Woman*, 1991
Constance O'Banyon, *Cheyenne Sunrise*, 1990

1839

DEBORAH SMITH

Legends
(New York: Bantam, 1990)

Story type: Contemporary

Major character(s): Elgiva MacRoth, Artisan (weaver), Kidnapper; Douglas Kincaid, Businessman (billionaire)
Time period(s): 1980s
Locale(s): New York, New York; Scotland

Summary: In order to save her clan's town, Elgiva kidnaps the billionaire who is planning to buy it. But love has a way of interfering with even the best laid plans. A passionate twist on the captive-in-love-with-captor theme.

Other books you might like:
Gail Douglas, *The Dreamweavers: Bewitching Lady*, 1990
Judith McNaught, *Almost Heaven*, 1990
   Historical, set in Scotland
Joan Elliott Pickart, *Mixed Signals*, 1990
Elise Title, *Out of the Blue*, 1989

1840
DEBORAH SMITH
Miracle
(New York: Bantam, 1991)

Story type: Contemporary/Mainstream
Major character(s): Amy Miracle, Writer, Entertainer (comedienne); Sebastien de Savin, Doctor
Time period(s): 1990s
Locale(s): Georgia; California

Summary: Shy, gentle Amy Miracle and the reserved, sophisticated doctor, Sebastien de Savin, meet and fall in love when she is just out of high school. However, fate separates them and it is ten years before they are reunited and are able to come to terms with their feelings and overcome the past. Well-developed characters.

Other books you might like:
Shirl Henke, *Summer Has No Name*, 1990
Judith McNaught, *Paradise*, 1991
Kathleen Gilles Seidel, *Maybe This Time*, 1990
LaVyrle Spencer, *Bittersweet*, 1990
Patricia Strothers, *Silvermore*, 1989

1841
DEBORAH SMITH
Sara's Surprise
(New York: Bantam, 1990)

Story type: Contemporary
Major character(s): Sara Scarborough, Scientist (botanist), Captive (former political prisoner); Kyle Surprise, Importer/Exporter, Detective—Private
Time period(s): 1980s
Locale(s): Kentucky

Summary: Hiding from the world in her secluded castle, Moonspell Keep, Sara is surprised and dismayed to find Kyle knocking at her door. Both want to put the memories of a terrible imprisonment and a tragic, daring rescue behind them, but they must slay their own dragons before they can be truly free to love again.

Other books you might like:
Janet Dailey, *Terms of Surrender*, 1982
Anne Lacey, *Rapture Deep*, 1988
Victoria Pade, *Twice Shy*, 1989
Danielle Steel, *Palomino*, 1981
Pat Warren, *The Long Road Home*, 1989

1842
DEBORAH SMITH
Silk and Stone
(New York: Bantam, 1994)

Story type: Contemporary; Contemporary/Fantasy
Major character(s): Samantha "Sam" Ryder, Young Woman, Artisan (weaver); Jake Raincrow, Indian, Psychic; Alexandra Vanderveer, Socialite (Samantha's aunt)

Summary: Greedy, possessive Alexandra Vanderveer wants it all, including the fabled Pandora Ruby and her niece Samantha. However, Jake's sister is the ruby's rightful owner, Jake is in love with Samantha, and Samantha doesn't want to be controlled—a series of events that produces an interesting story. A classic clash between good and evil with a touch of the mystical for good measure.

Other books you might like:
Barbara Delinsky, *Facets*, 1990
Kathleen Eagle, *Fire and Rain*, 1992
Kathleen Eagle, *This Time Forever*, 1994
Rachel Lee, *Thunder Mountain*, 1994
Peggy Webb, *Witch Dance*, 1994

1843
JOAN SMITH
Cousin Cecelia
(New York: Fawcett, 1990)

Story type: Regency
Major character(s): Cecelia Cummings, Matchmaker; Lord Wickham, Nobleman
Time period(s): 1810s
Locale(s): Laycombe, England

Summary: When matchmaker Cecelia Cummings is summoned to Laycombe to bring the young gentlemen of the area up to scratch, she finds a formidable opponent in Lord Wickham, who is newly rusticating in the country and is exerting a decidedly bad influence on the local bachelors. Cecelia, of course, proves equal to the challenge; but she also ends up losing her heart in the process. Charmingly regency.

Other books you might like:
Marion Chesney, *Refining Felicity*, 1988
   1st in School for Manners Series
Marion Chesney, *The Miser of Mayfair*, 1986
   1st in A House for the Season Series
Clare Darcy, *Georgina*, 1971
Georgette Heyer, *Lady of Quality*, 1972
Judith Nelson, *Patience Is a Virtue*, 1989

▮1844▮

JOAN SMITH

The Kissing Bough

(New York: Fawcett Crest, 1994)

Story type: Regency; Holiday Themes
Major character(s): Jane Ramsey, Gentlewoman, Spinster; Nicholas Morgan, Nobleman, Heir
Time period(s): 1810s
Locale(s): England

Summary: When Nicholas Morgan returns from the war in Spain and notifies his friends and family that he has a surprise for them and is "ready to settle down at last," everyone assumes that he has marriage to his childhood companion, Jane Ramsey, in mind. Then he shows up with an incredibly beautiful, but equally vain and vulgar, brewer's daughter as his fiancee—and the stage is set for an intriguing Holiday celebration. Light, fast-paced, and features some wonderfully obnoxious secondary characters.

Other books you might like:
Mary Balogh, *Christmas Belle*, 1994
Susan Carroll, *Christmas Belles*, 1992
Marion Chesney, *The Dreadful Debutante*, 1995
Mary Chase Comstock, *A Christmas Wish*, 1994
  anthology
Meg-Lynn Roberts, *Christmas Escapade*, 1994

▮1845▮

JOAN SMITH

Madcap Miss

(New York: Fawcett/Ballantine, 1989)

Story type: Regency
Major character(s): Grace Farnsworth, Governess (unemployed), Imposter; Lord Whewett, Nobleman
Time period(s): 1810s
Locale(s): England

Summary: When Grace Farnsworth agrees to pose as Lord Whewett's young daughter, it all seems harmless fun—until complications set in. Witty and just plain Regency fun.

Other books you might like:
Marion Chesney, *The Adventuress*, 1987
  A House for the Season Series 5
Georgette Heyer, *Arabella*, 1949
  Classic Regency author
Carla Kelly, *Marian's Christmas Wish*, 1989
Elizabeth Law, *Double Deception*, 1987
Daisy Vivian, *Counterfeit Lady*, 1987

▮1846▮

JOAN SMITH

The Spanish Lady

(New York: Fawcett, 1993)

Story type: Regency

Major character(s): Lady Helena, Noblewoman, Debutante; Edward Hadley, Gentleman
Time period(s): 1810s
Locale(s): England

Summary: The last thing Edward wants to do is serve as escort for his beautiful cousin, Lady Helena, for the coming Season, or so he tells himself. Why, then, does he feel so jealous of the myriad suitors she eventually attracts? Their families, of course, think they would make a marvelous match; and, just as naturally, they fight it all the way, leading each other in and out of numerous escapades before they realize that their families were right all along.

Other books you might like:
Stef Ann Holm, *Liberty Rose*, 1993
Lynn Kerstan, *A Spirited Affair*, 1993
Louisa Rawlings, *Wicked Stranger*, 1993
  sensual
Nancy Richards-Akers, *Lady Sarah's Charade*, 1992
Jeanne Savery, *The Last of the Winter Roses*, 1991

▮1847▮

KAREN ROSE SMITH

Garden of Fantasy

(Bensalem, Pennsylvania: Meteor, 1992)

Story type: Contemporary
Major character(s): Beth Terrell, Architect (landscape); Nash Winchester, Architect
Time period(s): 1990s
Locale(s): Lancaster, Pennsylvania

Summary: Beth Terrell and Nash Winchester both want the landscaping contract for a new resort—and they will stop at almost nothing to get it. However, in spite of their rivalry, they are attracted to each other, which makes the situation even more difficult.

Other books you might like:
Delayne Camp, *Newsworthy Affair*, 1990
Kathryn Kramer, *Lady Rogue*, 1991
Audrey McConachie, *No Blueprint for Love*, 1992
  innocent
Karen G. McCullough, *The Night Prowlers*, 1990
  innocent

▮1848▮

EBONI SNOE (Pseudonym of Gwyn McGee)

The Passion Ruby

(New York: Pinnacle, 1995)

Story type: Contemporary; Ethnic
Major character(s): Sienna Russell, Fugitive; Hennessy "Hawk" Jackson, Adventurer
Time period(s): 1990s
Locale(s): South; Martinique

Summary: A precious stone, a bracelet, a journal, and a strange legend send Sienna Russell and the enigmatic Hawk on a journey into danger and love as they try to solve the mystery of the Stonekeeper. Passionate, adventurous, and exotic.

Other books you might like:
La Florya Gauthier, *Whispers in the Sand*, 1995
    African American characters/exotic setting
Donna Julian, *Slow Dance*, 1995
    mystery Southern-style
Deborah Smith, *Silk and Stone*, 1994
    rubies and quests/no ethnic emphasis
Amberlina Wicker, *Private Matters*, 1995
    suspenseful/African American characters

1849

ASHLEY SNOW

Dangerous Desire
(New York: Zebra, 1990)

Story type: Historical/American Revolution
Major character(s): Justine "Jess" Maury, Spy (British agent); Rhys Llewellen, Sea Captain, Privateer
Time period(s): 1770s
Locale(s): Baghdad, Middle East; United States

Summary: When intrepid Jess Maury decides to complete her late father's undercover mission for the British crown, she only plans to deliver a message to Baghdad, not fall in love with the captain of the ship that will take her there. But love and circumstances decree otherwise and Jess suddenly finds herself in love with "the enemy" and in the middle of a dangerous game.

Other books you might like:
Gwen Bristow, *Celia Garth*, 1959
Judith E. French, *Scarlet Ribbons*, 1989
Heather Graham, *Love Not a Rebel*, 1989
Robin Maderich, *Faith and Honor*, 1989
Christina Savage, *Hearts of Fire*, 1984

1850

LINDA SOLE

The Last Summer of Innocence
(New York: St. Martin's, 1992)

Story type: Historical/World War I
Major character(s): Kate Linton, Young Woman; Harry Redfern, Nobleman
Time period(s): 1910s
Locale(s): Cambridge, England

Summary: When Kate Linton's mother sends her to live with her distant cousin on his country estate, Kate finds herself in a luxurious environment, rife with secrets and deceptions that will eventually threaten her happiness. A novel of love and treachery set during the tumultuous years of World War I.

Other books you might like:
Diane Cory, *High Society*, 1990
Diane Cory, *A Token of Jewels*, 1989
Diana Palmer, *Lacy*, 1992
Katherine Sinclair, *A Distant Dawn*, 1991

1851

SYLVIE SOMMERFIELD

Fires of Surrender
(New York: Zebra, 1990)

Story type: Historical/Medieval
Major character(s): Kathryn McLeod, Noblewoman; Anne McLeod, Noblewoman
Time period(s): 15th century (1488)
Locale(s): England; Scotland

Summary: Sent to Scotland on a political mission by Henry VII, Englishman Sir Andrew Craighton poses as a servant in the house of the powerful McLeod family—and proceeds to fall in love with one of the daughters, the beautiful Lady Anne. On the other hand, her sister, fiery, tempestuous Lady Kathryn, attracts the attention of Donovan Macadam who has been sent by Scotland's new King James IV to take control of the McLeods. Danger, adventure, and political intrigue abound in this passionate double-love story as the characters try to avert an assassination attempt and arrange for peace.

Other books you might like:
Pamela Belle, *The Lodestar*, 1989
Rebecca Brandewyne, *Forever My Love*, 1982
Jude Deveraux, *Highland Velvet*, 1982
Roberta Gellis, *The Roselynde Chronicles Series*, 1978-1983
Roberta Gellis, *The Silver Mirror*, 1989

1852

SYLVIE SOMMERFIELD

Love's Stolen Promise
(New York: Pinnacle, 1992)

Story type: Historical/Post-American Civil War
Major character(s): Whitney Clayborn, Southern Belle; Mitch Flannery, Farmer, Military Personnel
Time period(s): 1850s; 1860s
Locale(s): United States

Summary: Southern belle Whitney Clayborn and poor Mitch Flannery are in love but are separated by an angry father — and the war. When the dust settles, Whitney's family is living in a rude cabin and Mitch returns to try to win Whitney's love all over again. A complex story, good characterizations, and a vivid portrayal of the South.

Other books you might like:
Caroline Bourne, *Riverboat Seduction*, 1992
Micki Brown, *Once a Rebel*, 1992
Heather Graham, *And One Rode West*, 1992
Heather Graham, *One Wore Blue*, 1991
Margaret Mitchell, *Gone with the Wind*, 1993

1853

FLORA M. SPEER

Castle of Dreams
(New York: Pinnacle, 1990)

Story type: Historical/Medieval

Major character(s): Meredith, Healer; Guy, Warrior (Crusader), Landowner (castle)
Time period(s): 12th century
Locale(s): Wales

Summary: Set against the background of the conquest of Wales, this is a complex story of the contrasts and conflicts inherent in any invasion, brought to life through the characters of healer Meredith and warrior and crusader Guy. Rich in historical detail; more history than romance.

Other books you might like:
Mary Ellen Gronau, *Gentle Conqueror*, 1989
Virginia Henley, *The Falcon and the Flower*, 1989
Mary Lide, *Ann of Cambray*, 1984
Gail Link, *Wolf's Embrace*, 1989
Norah Lofts, *Madselin*, 1969

1854

FLORA M. SPEER

Castle of the Heart

(New York: Pinnacle, 1990)

Story type: Historical/Medieval
Major character(s): Arianna, Noblewoman; Thomas, Nobleman, Knight
Time period(s): 12th century
Locale(s): Wales; England

Summary: Although married to Selene, a woman who is slowly descending into madness because of her inability to reconcile her strong sensuality with her skewed idea of "goodness," Thomas is in love with Selene's cousin and companion, Ariana. However, neither will betray Selene; and it isn't until Thomas discovers just how cruelly he has been manipulated that he can rectify the situation. Strongly evocative of the era. Sequel to *Castle of Dreams*.

Other books you might like:
Robyn Carr, *The Blue Falcon*, 1981
Edith Layton, *The Crimson Crown*, 1990
Mary Lide, *Ann of Cambray*, 1984
Mary Lide, *Gifts of the Queen*, 1985
Katherine Vickery, *Desire of the Heart*, 1990

1855

FLORA M. SPEER

A Love Beyond Time

(New York: Love Spell, 1994)

Story type: Time Travel
Major character(s): Danise, Noblewoman; Mike Bailey, Time Traveller, Archaeologist
Time period(s): 8th century
Locale(s): France

Summary: Swept back in time to Charlemagne's 8th century Francia, archaeologist Mike Bailey awakes to find himself in the company of the beautiful Danise—with no memory of who he is or where he has come from. Gradually, his memory returns and with it the realization that he may never return to the present. However, just as he is accepting his situation—

and his growing love for Danise, the present interferes, with nearly disastrous results. Battles, politics, and lots of historical detail are part of this unusually set romance.

Other books you might like:
Laura Gilmour Bennett, *By All That Is Sacred*, 1991
Rebecca Brandewyne, *Swan Road*, 1994
Susan Sizemore, *In My Dreams*, 1994
Susan Sizemore, *Wings of the Storm*, 1992
Judith Tarr, *His Majesty's Elephant*, 1993
    Young Adult fantasy set during Charlemagne's rule

1856

FLORA M. SPEER

No Other Love

(New York: Lovespell, 1993)

Story type: Time Travel
Major character(s): Merin, Historian; Herne, Doctor
Time period(s): Indeterminate Future
Locale(s): Planet—Imaginary

Summary: On a mission to a planet ruled by telepaths, Physician Herne and the historian Merin work together to uncover archaeological remains and study the planet's atmosphere. But when they are suddenly thrust back in time to the days of the original inhabitants, they are faced with conflicts and decisions that will have far-reaching ramifications, and they discover a love that will last through time.

Other books you might like:
Marion Zimmer Bradley, *The Heritage of Hastur*, 1975
Marilyn Campbell, *Stolen Dreams*, 1994
    a futuristic time-travel
Kathleen Morgan, *The Knowing Crystal*, 1991
Patricia Roenbuck, *The Golden Conquest*, 1992
Patricia Roenbuck, *Golden Temptress*, 1991

1857

LAVYRLE SPENCER

Bittersweet

(New York: Putnam, 1990)

Story type: Contemporary
Major character(s): Maggie Stearn, Widow(er) (wealthy), Innkeeper (bed and breakfast owner); Eric Severson, Businessman (charter fishing boats), Sailor
Time period(s): 1980s
Locale(s): Fish Creek, Wisconsin

Summary: Returning to her hometown after the death of her husband, wealthy Maggie Stearn encounters her now-married first love and is forced to deal with old emotions—and new realities.

Other books you might like:
Sally Beauman, *Destiny*, 1987
    Mainstream
Rebecca George, *Call Home the Heart*, 1989
    19th Century
Lisa Gregory, *The Rainbow Promise*, 1989
Elizabeth Quinn, *Any Day Now*, 1990

Patricia Strothers, *Silvermore*, 1989
Mainstream

1858
LAVYRLE SPENCER

Bygones
(New York: Putnam, 1992)

Story type: Contemporary
Major character(s): Bess Curran, Divorced Person; Michael Curran, Divorced Person
Time period(s): 1990s
Locale(s): United States

Summary: Bess and Michael Curran, bitterly divorced, are forced to confront each other, their children, and surroundings that are saturated with memories. As they learn to cooperate in their daughter's wedding plans, they begin to look at each other with renewed sensitivity, making the inevitable comparisons with their current loves. A believable and emotional look at a loving couple.

Other books you might like:
Georgia Bockoven, *A Marriage of Convenience*, 1991
Janet Dailey, *Terms of Surrender*, 1982
Lisa Gregory, *The Rainbow Promise*, 1989
Judith Yoder, *A Matter of Compromise*, 1992

1859
LAVYRLE SPENCER

Forgiving
(New York: Putnam, 1990)

Story type: Historical/American West
Major character(s): Sarah Merritt, Journalist (newspaper owner); Noah Campbell, Lawman (sheriff)
Time period(s): 19th century
Locale(s): Dakota Territory

Summary: Sarah Merritt heads for the Dakota Territory intent on doing two things—finding her runaway sister, Addie, and establishing her own newspaper. She does both in spite of the numerous clashes with the local sheriff with whom she eventually falls in love. Addie and Sarah, however, have a number of issues to resolve between them before all can be forgiven.

Other books you might like:
Madeline Baker, *Forbidden Fires*, 1990
Jude Deveraux, *Mountain Laurel*, 1990
Stef Ann Holm, *Firefly*, 1990
Jill Marie Landis, *Rose*, 1990
Scotney St. James, *Northern Fire, Northern Star*, 1990

1860
LAVYRLE SPENCER

November of the Heart
(New York: Putnam, 1993)

Story type: Historical/Victorian America

Major character(s): Lorna Barnett, Gentlewoman, Single Parent (unwed mother); Jens Harken, Artisan (boat builder), Servant
Time period(s): 1890s (1895)
Locale(s): White Bear Lake, Minnesota; St. Paul, Minnesota

Summary: When wealthy debutante Lorna Barnett falls in love with her family's employee, Norwegian immigrant Jens Harken, the world seems aligned against them; and it isn't until Lorna realizes what is really important in her life that the couple (and everyone else, incidentally) can find happiness. Lots of boat building and sailing detail in a sensual, heart-warming story.

Other books you might like:
Elaine Barbieri, *Wishes on the Wind*, 1991
Lucy Elliot, *Private Paradise*, 1991
Lisa Gregory, *The Rainbow Promise*, 1989
Jill Marie Landis, *Sunflower*, 1988
Laura Simon, *Garden of Dreams*, 1992

1861
MARY SPENCER

The Vow
(New York: Harper, 1994)

Story type: Historical/Medieval
Major character(s): Lady Margaret, Noblewoman; Sir Eric, Knight, Adoptee
Time period(s): 15th century (1403)
Locale(s): Shrewsbury, England

Summary: Sir Eric, the gallant, responsible, awe-inspiring "perfect" knight, is really a bit insecure. And it doesn't help his self-image when he is sent on the less-than-glorious mission to retrieve his friend's daughter, the independent Lady Margot. The fact that Margot has intended to marry him since childhood just adds to the complictions, and it takes all of Eric's ingenuity to both evade and rescue her at the same time. Eventually, things work out—he sees his true worth and love enters the picture.

Other books you might like:
Julie Garwood, *Lyon's Lady*, 1988
Julie Garwood, *The Prize*, 1991
Betina M. Krahn, *My Warrior's Heart*, 1992
    gentle hero/assertive heroine
Susan Tanner, *Captive to a Dream*, 1991
    childhood friends/different treatment

1862
ERICA SPINDLER

Red
(Toronto: Mira, 1995)

Story type: Contemporary/Mainstream
Major character(s): Becky Lynn Lee, Model; Jack Gallagher, Photographer
Time period(s): 1990s
Locale(s): Hollywood, California

Summary: A victim of abuse and rape, Becky Lynn Lee leaves the Mississippi Delta and heads for California to make her fortune. Surprisingly, she does, as a high fashion photography model. But success has its price, and Becky must face pain and betrayal—and her past—before she finds true happiness. A fast-paced, mainstream novel filled with tarnished Hollywood glitz and some fascinating characters.

Other books you might like:
Sally Beauman, *Destiny*, 1987
Jackie Collins, *Hollywood Star*, 1993
   more Hollywood glitz
Catherine Mann, *Tinsel Town*, 1985
Carol Marsh, *The Silver Link*, 1994
JoAnn Ross, *Secret Sins*, 1990

1863

LA VERNE ST. GEORGE

A Private Proposal

(New York: Avalon, 1990)

Story type: Contemporary/Innocent
Major character(s): Hayley Lancaster, Businesswoman (information specialist); David Mansfield, Businessman (company owner)
Time period(s): 1990s
Locale(s): Pittsburgh, Pennsylvania

Summary: Information specialist Hayley Lancaster is thrilled when her ideas meet with the approval of David Mansfield, the company president, and he makes her part of the proposal team for a prestigious project. However, when Hayley begins to fall for him, things get complicated; and when David discovers she is good friends with one of his prime competitors, his admiration turns to jealousy and suspicion.

Other books you might like:
Annette Broadrick, *The Gemini Man*, 1991
Patricia Ellis, *Champagne and Wildflowers*, 1991
Lynda Stowe Landers, *A Season to Remember*, 1989
Wendy Martin, *Love on Trial*, 1990
Diana Palmer, *Harden*, 1991

1864

SCOTNEY ST. JAMES (Pseudonym of Linda Varner)

Highland Hearts

(New York: Zebra, 1993)

Story type: Historical/Georgian
Major character(s): Meg MacLinn, Heiress—Dispossessed, Noblewoman; Lord Ransom St. Clair, Privateer (smuggler), Nobleman
Time period(s): 1760s
Locale(s): Scotland

Summary: Ransom St. Clair returns to Scotland to accomplish the impossible task of renovating the crumbling stronghold Wolfcraig and encounters the lovely Meg MacLinn who has come to claim Wolfcraig as her own. Although he originally has other ideas, they strike a bargain: they will marry, he will get the castle, renovate it, and be freed of his debt to the

King—and then he will turn the castle over to Meg. All goes as planned, and then they fall in love. Funny, complex, and filled with adventure.

Other books you might like:
Mary Burkhardt, *Highland Ecstasy*, 1993
Patricia Grasso, *Highland Belle*, 1991
Arnette Lamb, *The Border Lord*, 1993
Kathleen Morgan, *Child of the Mist*, 1993
Katherine Vickery, *Flame Across the Highlands*, 1990

1865

SCOTNEY ST. JAMES (Pseudonym of Lynda Varner)

Northern Fire, Northern Star

(New York: Zebra, 1990)

Story type: Historical/Canadian West
Major character(s): Alexandra MacKenzie, Doctor; Rhys Morgan, Settler
Time period(s): 1800s (1804)
Locale(s): Lake of the Woods, Canada

Summary: Determined to escape the prejudice against women doctors and practice her profession in a freer environment, Alexandra MacKenzie takes her grandfather's place and accompanies a group of mail-order brides heading for the Canadian frontier. Her hopes, however, meet furious resistance from Rhys Morgan who doesn't want a beautiful, unmarried woman on his hands. The sparks fly constantly as these two strong-willed characters inevitably battle their way into love.

Other books you might like:
Judy Alter, *Mattie*, 1988
Jo Ann Ferguson, *At the Rainbow's End*, 1989
Peggy Hanchar, *Tomorrow's Dream*, 1989
Kathleen Harrington, *Cherish the Dream*, 1990
LaVyrle Spencer, *Forgiving*, 1990

1866

CHERYL ST. JOHN

Rain Shadow

(Toronto: Harlequin, 1994)

Story type: Historical/American West
Major character(s): Rain Shadow, Adoptee (by Lakota Sioux), Entertainer; Anton Neubauer, Farmer, Immigrant
Time period(s): 19th century
Locale(s): Midwest

Summary: Rain Shadow, raised by the Sioux and now part of Buffalo Bill's Wild West Show, has her injured child treated by Anton Neubauer, a German farmer. She moves her teepee into his front yard, unwilling to live in his house. Despite his anger that she won't see things his way and stubbornness on both their parts, their relationship grows and Rain Shadow finds she cares more and more for this gentle man.

Other books you might like:
Catherine Anderson, *Cheyenne Amber*, 1994
   Cheyenne-raised hero
Candace Camp, *Heirloom*, 1992
   gentle, warm, and rural

Kathleen Eagle, *Heaven and Earth*, 1990
Native American elements
Jill Marie Landis, *Sunflower*, 1988
heartwarming
Kathleen Sage, *Many Fires*, 1995
Cheyenne-raised heroine

1867

ROBIN ST. THOMAS

Lie and Say You Love Me
(New York: Zebra, 1992)

Story type: Contemporary/Mainstream
Major character(s): Layne Fielding Blair, Socialite; Jack Goddard, Producer (theatre)
Time period(s): 1990s
Locale(s): New York, New York

Summary: Layne Fielding Blair, rich, powerful, and vengeful, will do anything to keep her philandering lover, producer Jack Goddard—even ruin the budding career of young actress Angela Holden. In spite of her machinations, Angela is a hit and on her way to stardom, Jack is off after Angela, and Layne plots her revenge from a jail cell. A classic tale of a woman scorned and the depths to which her need for revenge will take her.

Other books you might like:
Lois Battle, *The Past Is Another Country*, 1992
Sally Beauman, *Destiny*, 1987
Shirley Conran, *Lace*, 1982
Helen Van Slyke, *Public Tears, Private Smiles*, 1982

1868

LEE STAFFORD

A Song in the Wilderness
(Toronto: Harlequin, 1990)

Story type: Contemporary/Innocent
Major character(s): Amber Kingsland, Secretary, Single Parent (widow); Luke Tremayne, Journalist (guest lecturer)
Time period(s): 1980s
Locale(s): England; France

Summary: When journalist Luke Tremayne comes as a guest lecturer to the university where Amber Kingsland works, she must deal with her old feelings for him as she endeavors to keep him from learning that he is the father of her daughter.

Other books you might like:
Angela Carson, *Sweet Illusion*, 1990
Karen Leabo, *Domestic Bliss*, 1990
Leigh Michaels, *Let Me Count the Ways*, 1989
Alice Sharpe, *A Garland of Love*, 1990
Alice Sharpe, *Just One More Secret*, 1990

1869

DANIELLE STEEL

Daddy
(New York: Delacorte, 1989)

Story type: Contemporary/Mainstream
Major character(s): Oliver Watson, Advertising (executive)
Time period(s): 1980s
Locale(s): New York, New York

Summary: Oliver has the ideal life—until his wife escapes to pursue her education at Harvard, his mother dies of Alzheimers, and his son becomes a father and a school dropout. With the help of his father, Oliver eventually picks up the pieces of his life and makes a fresh start. More mainstream than romance, somewhat soapy, but classic Steel.

Other books you might like:
Janet Dailey, *Heiress*, 1987
Judith Michael, *Possessions*, 1984
A woman, forced by circumstances, changes dynamically
Judith Michael, *Private Affairs*, 1986
A couple tries to rebuild their relationship
Helen Van Slyke, *A Necessary Woman*, 1980
A woman struggles with dependents and her own desires

1870

DANIELLE STEEL

No Greater Love
(New York: Delacorte, 1992)

Story type: Saga
Major character(s): Edwina Winfield, Child-Care Giver (for siblings), Spinster
Time period(s): 20th century (1910-1930)
Locale(s): Europe; San Francisco, California; Hollywood, California

Summary: Edwina Winfield's mother, father, and fiance all go down with the *Titanic*, leaving her to care for her five young brothers and sisters. When they eventually all leave home, Edwina finally frees herself from her haunting memories and discovers a different and exciting life. Her struggles span a number of years and include the major events of the era—WW I, the Roaring Twenties, and the rise of Hollywood.

Other books you might like:
Elizabeth Adler, *Fortune Is a Woman*, 1992
Rebecca Forster, *A Delicate Matter*, 1989
LaVyrle Spencer, *The Gamble*, 1989
Helen Van Slyke, *A Necessary Woman*, 1980

1871

JUDITH STEEL

Seduction's Raging Flame
(New York: Zebra, 1989)

Story type: Historical/American West

Major character(s): Patricia Jean "Trishia" Bonner, Thief (train robber); Lane Hollister, Detective (searching for the train robber)
Time period(s): 19th century
Locale(s): Colorado

Summary: Lane Hollister has no idea that the train robber he is searching for is none other than the woman he loves, Patricia Jean Bonner, who is seeking to avenge her father. Love wins out in the end, of course, and all wrongs are appropriately righted.

Other books you might like:
LaRee Bryant, *Arizona Captive*, 1989
Deborah Camp, *Fallen Angel*, 1989
Colleen Faulkner, *Passion's Savage Moon*, 1989
Georgina Gentry, *Nevada Nights*, 1989
Jeanne E. Hansen, *Deception's Embrace*, 1989

1872

JUDITH STEEL

Wild Colorado Passion

(New York: Zebra, 1991)

Story type: Historical/American West
Major character(s): Lorelei Abbott, Store Owner; Holt Dolan, Rancher, Lawman (sheriff)
Time period(s): 1880s (1881)
Locale(s): Daring, Colorado

Summary: When beautiful, headstrong, gun-hating store owner Lorelei Abbott and tough, gunslinging rancher Holt Dolan meet, their mutual antagonism and involuntary attraction to each other set sparks flying—and when Holt takes on the job of town sheriff, things go from bad to worse. Gunfights, kidnappings, and other accoutrements of life in the Old West keep this rollicking adventure moving at a fast clip.

Other books you might like:
Emily Carmichael, *Visions of the Heart*, 1990
Elaine Coffman, *Escape Not My Love*, 1990
Catherine Hart, *Sweet Fury*, 1990
Emma Merritt, *Beneath a Texas Star*, 1991
Victoria Thompson, *Playing with Fire*, 1990

1873

SANDRA STEFFEN

Hold Back the Night

(Bensalem, Pennsylvania: Meteor, 1992)

Story type: Contemporary
Major character(s): Starr Davidson, Young Woman, Orphan; Shane Wells, Police Officer (Undercover)
Time period(s): 1990s
Locale(s): Pinesburg, Michigan

Summary: When orphaned Starr Davidson returns to her hometown to care for her adopted Uncle Mick, she finds that ex-cop Shane Wells has not only invaded her cherished lighthouse, but is claiming to be Uncle Mick's long-lost grandson, as well. Both threatened and attracted by this disturbing man, Starr tries to come to terms with her conflicting feelings —

and at the same time help Shane deal with a tragedy from his past. A mystery surrounding the lighthouse and an old diary add interest to this gentle contemporary.

Other books you might like:
B.J. James, *A Step Away*, 1992
Joey Light, *Sterling's Reasons*, 1991
Laura Phillips, *Moon Showers*, 1992
Pat Warren, *Bright Hopes*, 1992

1874

DONNA STEPHENS

Heart of the Wild

(New York: Avon, 1993)

Story type: Historical/Exotic
Major character(s): Darcy McCall, Doctor; Jim Burleson, Rancher
Time period(s): 1890s
Locale(s): Australia

Summary: Jim Burleson needs a doctor around his outback ranch, but no way will he accept a woman and a Yank! Dr. Darcy McCall is just as determined to say on the job and she proceeds to befriend the help and the natives. The pair soon begin to see the good points in each other, but their cultural differences are almost too great for romance. It is only when they are threatened by outside forces that they join together for survival and find love in the process. Strong characters.

Other books you might like:
Leigh Bristol, *Sunswept*, 1990
Connie Mason, *Brave Land, Brave Love*, 1992
Connie Mason, *Wild Land, Wild Love*, 1992
Garda Parker, *Temptation's Flame*, 1992
Lynette Vinet, *Wild, Wicked Eden*, 1990

1875

JEANNE STEPHENS

At Risk

(New York: Silhouette, 1989)

Story type: Contemporary
Major character(s): Darcy Gilbert, Journalist (T.V. newscaster), Abuse Victim (battered wife); Zach Shaffer, Doctor
Time period(s): 1980s

Summary: An abuse victim in a former marriage, T.V. anchorwoman Darcy Gilbert sets out to help others in similar circumstances. Threats, personal danger, and love all follow in due course.

Other books you might like:
Susan Anderson, *Shadow Dance*, 1989
Sara Chance, *Fire in the Night*, 1989
    Silhouette Intimate Moments
Mary Anne Wilson, *Straight From the Heart*, 1989
    Silhouette Intimate Moments
Sherryl Woods, *Body and Soul*, 1989

STEPHANIE STEVENS

Defiant Angel

(New York: Avon, 1991)

Story type: Historical/Regency
Major character(s): Tiffany Courtland, Noblewoman (hoyden); Clinton Barencourte, Nobleman (Duke of Wentworth)
Time period(s): 1810s
Locale(s): England
Summary: Sent to Paris by her insensitive father to "grow up" and to forget about her childhood friend and love, Lady Tiffany Courtland does indeed grow up—and when she does, she takes Paris by storm. She even catches the attention of the arrogant and powerful Clinton Barencourte, Duke of Wentworth, a man who represents everything Tiffany despises. Sparks fly constantly between these two as Clinton relentlessly pursues her and Tiffany defiantly resists. A witty, highly sensual tale.

Other books you might like:
Shirlee Busbee, *Whisper to Me of Love*, 1991
Catherine Coulter, *Night Fire*, 1989
Catherine Coulter, *Night Shadow*, 1989
Kathryn Kramer, *Lady Rogue*, 1991
Amanda Quick, *Surrender*, 1990

1877

LOIS STEWART

The Duke's Mistress

(New York: Zebra, 1993)

Story type: Regency
Major character(s): Hilary Vane, Gentlewoman, Teacher; Jonathan Rayner, Nobleman, Landlord
Time period(s): 1810s
Locale(s): England
Summary: Hilary plans to open a girls' school for the Duke's tenant farmers' daughters; the Duke, however, strongly opposes it—and there-in hangs the conflict. Jonathan's sister and Hilary's brother add an interesting subplot and create numerous problems for our heroine and hero, but love will out in this fast-paced, witty story of Regency England.

Other books you might like:
Rita Boucher, *The Scandalous Schoolmistress*, 1992
Mary Chase Comstock, *A Midsummer's Magic*, 1994
Carola Dunn, *Two Corinthians*, 1989
Georgette Heyer, *Lady of Quality*, 1972
Joan Smith, *Cousin Cecelia*, 1990

LOIS STEWART

Romantic Masquerade

(New York: Zebra, 1990)

Story type: Regency

Major character(s): Sabrina Neville, Widow(er), Imposter (Hungarian countess); Jareth Tremayne, Gambler, Nobleman
Time period(s): 1810s
Locale(s): London, England
Summary: When intrepid Sabrina Neville sets out to pay her brother's debt of honor by tricking gambler Lord Jareth Tremayne out of the necessary funds, she begins a deception that could save the family fortune but break her heart in the process. Funny and witty.

Other books you might like:
Janice Bennett, *A Tempting Miss*, 1989
Elizabeth Brodnax, *The Marquis of Carabas*, 1991
Georgette Heyer, *Faro's Daughter*, 1942
Melinda McRae, *The Duke's Daughter*, 1991

1879

MARIAH STEWART

Moments in Time

(New York: Pocket, 1995)

Story type: Contemporary
Major character(s): Maggie Borders, Spouse; J.D. "Jamey" Borders, Musician (rock star)
Time period(s): 1990s
Locale(s): London, England
Summary: Maggie, insisting on a divorce, must sit with her husband J.D., a famous musician, for a live, in-depth TV interview. His former lover, Glory, has been caught in J.D.'s hotel room and even though he is the victim of a set up, Maggie isn't listening. It's up to him to convince her—on television. As the interview proceeds the couple relive their colorful past and see new facets in each other, forcing them to re-examine their life together. Clever and nostalgic.

Other books you might like:
Rexanne Becnel, *Christmas Journey*, 1992
  marriage renewal theme
Diane E. Lock, *True Love*, 1994
  similar theme
Kathleen Gilles Seidel, *Maybe This Time*, 1990
LaVyrle Spencer, *Bygones*, 1993
  marriage renewal theme

1880

MARY STEWART

The Stormy Petrel

(New York: Morrow, 1991)

Story type: Romantic Suspense
Major character(s): Rose Fenemore, Writer (Poet), Scholar (Cambridge Don); Ewen MacKay, Vacationer; John Parsons, Scientist (geologist)
Time period(s): 1990s
Locale(s): The Hebrides, Scotland
Summary: Seeking solitude, Cambridge don Rose Fenemore impulsively rents a small Scottish island for the summer and settles down to peacefully write poetry. However, her quiet

idyll is short-lived as several somewhat mysterious men intrude, bringing with them danger and love. A beautifully written story from a writer who set the original standards for the Romantic Suspense genre.

Other books you might like:
Joan Aiken, *A Cluster of Separate Sparks*, 1972
Alma Blair, *The Dark Side of Paradise*, 1990
Jane Aiken Hodge, *Secret Island*, 1985
Elizabeth Peters, *The Camelot Caper*, 1969
Phyllis A. Whitney, *Rainsong*, 1984
    contemporary Gothic

`1881`
ANTOINETTE STOCKENBERG

Embers
(New York: Dell, 1994)

Story type: Contemporary/Fantasy
Major character(s): Meg Hazard, Innkeeper (Bed & Breakfast owner); Tom Wyler, Detective—Police, Vacationer
Time period(s): 1990s
Locale(s): Bar Harbor, Maine

Summary: When Meg Hazard rents a room to vacationing— and somewhat notorious—police detective Tom Wyler, she has no idea of the strange turn her life is about to take—or the part he will play in it. A Victorian dollhouse, a very real ghost, and an old mysterious tragedy lead the normally pragmatic Meg into a dangerous search to uncover long-kept secrets and to eventually unmask a murderer. Engaging and well-written.

Other books you might like:
Kristin Hannah, *Once in Every Life*, 1993
    time travel
Lori Herter, *The Willow File*, 1994
Sabine Kells, *Shadows on a Sunset Sea*, 1994
Patricia Simpson, *Whisper of Midnight*, 1991
LaVyrle Spencer, *Morning Glory*, 1989
    no fantasy elements

`1882`
ANTOINETTE STOCKENBERG

Emily's Ghost
(New York: Dell, 1992)

Story type: Romantic Suspense; Contemporary/Fantasy
Major character(s): Emily Bowditch, Journalist (newspaper reporter); Arthur Lee Alden, Political Figure (senator); Fergus O'Malley, Spirit
Time period(s): 1990s
Locale(s): Boston, Massachusetts

Summary: Newspaper reporter Emily Bowditch contacts Senator Arthur Lee Alden regarding his proposed funding for psychic research. To illustrate his point he takes her to a seance—but she is the one who ends up with the ghost—one Fergus O'Malley, wrongly hanged for murder a century earlier! Emily takes his case, and as she begins her investigation she is confused by her attraction to him, especially since she also cares for the senator. Romantic, intriguing, and poignant.

Other books you might like:
Janice Bennett, *A Christmas Keepsake*, 1991
Annette Broadrick, *A Loving Spirit*, 1990
Constance O'Day-Flannery, *A Time for Love*, 1991
Patricia Simpson, *Whisper of Midnight*, 1991
Becky Lee Weyrich, *Sweet Forever*, 1992

`1883`
ANTOINETTE STOCKENBERG

Time After Time
(New York: Dell, 1995)

Story type: Contemporary/Fantasy
Major character(s): Liz Coppersmith, Businesswoman (events planner); Jack Eastman, Businessman (shipyard owner)
Time period(s): 1990s
Locale(s): Newport, Rhode Island

Summary: Determined to make a success of her new venture, Parties Plus, Liz Coppersmith is elated when Jack Eastman, a member of one of Newport's elite families, asks her plan a birthday party for his five-year-old half sister. But things don't go as planned and their relationship is anything but smooth. An old trunk, some love letters from the past, and a handsome ghost shed some light on long forgotten Eastman family secrets, secrets that can profoundly affect Jack and Liz in the present. Eerie, romantic, and passionate.

Other books you might like:
Evelyn A. Crowe, *Reunited*, 1993
Lori Herter, *The Willow File*, 1994
Sabine Kells, *Shadows on a Sunset Sea*, 1994
Patricia Simpson, *Whisper of Midnight*, 1991
Becky Lee Weyrich, *Forever, for Love*, 1989

`1884`
JEAN STONE

First Loves
(New York: Bantam, 1995)

Story type: Contemporary/Mainstream
Major character(s): Meg Cooper, Lawyer (criminal defense); Alissa Page, Socialite; Zoe Hartman, Actress (former film star)
Time period(s): 1990s
Locale(s): New York, New York; Los Angeles, California

Summary: While at the same spa for vastly different reasons, Alissa, Meg, and Zoe meet and become unlikely friends. Reminiscing about first loves, they challenge themselves to find these men to see if they should have stayed with them. But their searches net them more than they expect—and new goals, new directions, new concepts, and new lives are the result.

Other books you might like:
Lois Battle, *War Brides*, 1982
    earlier time period/mainstream
Gila Berkowitz, *The Brides*, 1992
Claire Bocardo, *Lovers and Friends*, 1995
    part of To Love Again Series

Constance O'Day-Flannery, *Seasons*, 1995
Kathleen Gilles Seidel, *Maybe This Time*, 1990

1885

KATHERINE STONE

Pearl Moon
(New York: Fawcett Columbine, 1995)

Story type: Contemporary/Mainstream
Major character(s): Maylene Kwan, Architect; Sam Coulter, Businessman (developer); Allison Parish Whitaker, Photographer
Time period(s): 1990s
Locale(s): Texas; Hong Kong

Summary: At war with both her dual heritage and the parents who betrayed her, beautiful Amerasian Maylene Kwan flees her beloved Hong Kong to start a new life. But fate forces her to return, and suddenly, she is on a collision course, not only with her past, but with the half-sister she has never met and a man who threatens her with love. With deft and vivid imagry that captures the exotic beauty and mystical feel of Hong Kong, Stone takes the lives of two sisters raised worlds apart and weaves them into a lyrical, emotionally involving whole that succeeds in blending mainstream themes with powerful love stories.

Other books you might like:
Barbara Delinsky, *The Passions of Chelsea Kane*, 1992
    emotionally involving/self-discovery aspects
Barbara Delinsky, *Suddenly*, 1994
    emotionally involving/self-discovery aspects
Doris Parmett, *Lies*, 1993
    separated sisters/different treatment
LaVyrle Spencer, *Sweet Memories*, 1989
    self-acceptance aspects/emotionally involving
Penelope Williamson, *Once in a Blue Moon*, 1993
    emotionally involving/lyrical writing-style

1886

KAREN STRATFORD

Lavender Flame
(New York: Avon, 1991)

Story type: Historical/Georgian
Major character(s): Catriona Ferguson, Bride (reluctant); Robert MacLean, Warrior (Highlander)
Time period(s): 1730s (1736)
Locale(s): Scotland

Summary: In the process of escorting Catriona Ferguson home to wed his cruel cousin and thus end an ancient feud, Robbie MacLean falls in love with his beautiful charge. Although she returns his regard, Catriona is willing to abide by her grandfather's wishes—until Robbie's fiancee dies and Catriona is accused of witchcraft. Then she and Robbie escape and the chase is on. Violence, treachery, and passion are the order of the day in this poetically written novel of the Highlands.

Other books you might like:
Rebecca Brandewyne, *Forever My Love*, 1982

Kathryn Lynn Davis, *Child of Awe*, 1987
Johanna Lindsey, *A Gentle Feuding*, 1984
Patricia Rice, *Moon Dreams*, 1991
Katherine Vickery, *Flame Across the Highlands*, 1990

1887

ANNE STUART
CAITLIN MCBRIDE, Co-Author
JILL BARNETT, Co-Author
LINDA SHERTZER, Co-Author

Highland Fling
(New York: Jove, 1993)

Story type: Anthology; Historical
Locale(s): Scotland

Summary: A collection of four novellas steeped in the atmosphere and tradition of Scotland. Included are stories by Anne Stuart, Caitlin McBride, Jill Barnett, and Linda Shertzer.

Other books you might like:
Diana Gabaldon, *Outlander*, 1991
    first of a series set in Scotland; time travel elements
Julie Garwood, *The Bride*, 1989
Julie Garwood, *The Secret*, 1992
Amanda Scott, *Border Bride*, 1990
Maura Seger, *The Lady and the Laird*, 1992

1888

ANNE STUART (Pseudonym of Anne Stuart Ohlrogge)

Night of the Phantom
(Toronto: Harlequin, 1991)

Story type: Gothic
Major character(s): Megan Carey, Businesswoman; Ethan Winslowe, Recluse, Wealthy (millionaire)
Time period(s): 1990s
Locale(s): Illinois

Summary: Sent by her less than scrupulous father to confront an eccentric millionaire who is threatening to expose him, Megan Carey anticipates nothing more difficult, or unusual, than some hard-headed business negotiations. Instead, she finds an isolated mansion, a belligerant butler, and a hero who only appears after dark. Sensual, romantic, and highly reminiscent of *Beauty and the Beast*.

Other books you might like:
Shannon Drake, *Avon Books Presents: Haunting Love Stories*, 1991
Lori Herter, *Obsession*, 1991
Lori Herter, *Possession*, 1992
Anne Rice, *Interview with the Vampire*, 1976
Anne Rice, *The Witching Hour*, 1990

1889

ANNE STUART (Pseudonym of Anne Stuart Ohlrogge)

A Rose at Midnight
(New York: Avon, 1993)

Story type: Historical/Post-French Revolution
Major character(s): Ghislaine "Gilly" de Lorgny, Orphan, Cook; Nicholas Blackthorne, Gentleman
Time period(s): 1800s (1803)
Locale(s): England; France

Summary: Orphaned and left destitute by the Reign of Terror, Gilly de Lorgny lives for the day when she can wreak vengeance on the one man who could have saved her, Englishman Nicholas Blackthorne. Now working as a cook, she gets her chance and poisons his food. However, he doesn't die, he just becomes furious, kidnaps her and spirits her away to his hunting lodge. Old passions resurface and Gilly begins to view Nicholas a bit differently; and Nicholas, remorseful at not having been able to help her years ago, takes her to Europe where they can settle the past once and for all.

Other books you might like:
Brenna Braxton-Barshon, *Through All Eternity*, 1992
Brenda Joyce, *Dark Fires*, 1991
Andrea Kane, *Dream Castle*, 1992
Louisa Rawlings, *Wicked Stranger*, 1993
Elizabeth Thornton, *Scarlet Angel*, 1990

1890

ANNE STUART (Pseudonym of Anne Stuart Ohlrogge)

Shadow Dance
(New York: Avon, 1993)

Story type: Historical/Regency
Major character(s): Sophie de Quincey, Noblewoman; Valerian Romney, Crime Suspect (accused murderer); Juliette MacGowan, Runaway, Abuse Victim
Time period(s): 1810s (1815)
Locale(s): England

Summary: Disguised as a boy to escape an abusive husband, Juliette is taken in by the Romneys; however, Phelan Romney sees through her disguise and falls in love with her. On the other hand, Phelan's brother Valerian, who is accused of murder disguises himself as a woman and proceeds to fall in love with a local member of the nobility, Sophie de Quincy. Sophie, however, doesn't see through the disguise and comes to admire and love the woman! Straightening this all out takes some time.

Other books you might like:
Georgette Heyer, *Cousin Kate*, 1968
  classic Regency with gothic elements
Georgette Heyer, *These Old Shades*, 1926
  classic Regency
Nicole Jordan, *Touch Me with Fire*, 1993
Andrea Kane, *Dream Castle*, 1992
Mary Jo Putney, *Thunder and Roses*, 1993

1891

ANNE STUART (Pseudonym of Anne Stuart Ohlrogge)

To Love a Dark Lord
(New York: Avon, 1994)

Story type: Historical/Georgian
Major character(s): Emma Langolet, Heiress, Orphan; James Patrick, Nobleman (Earl of Killoran)
Time period(s): 1770s (1775)
Locale(s): London, England

Summary: When the bored Earl of Killoran comes across Emma Langolet calmly standing in a pool of blood with a corpse at her feet, he takes pity on her and rescues her—little realizing that she will end up "saving" him, as well. A dark, passionate, highly involving story that features strong, well-developed characters.

Other books you might like:
Mary Balogh, *The Notorious Rake*, 1992
Jo Beverley, *Tempting Fortune*, 1995
Georgette Heyer, *These Old Shades*, 1926
Mary Jo Putney, *Thunder and Roses*, 1993
Amanda Quick, *Mistress*, 1994

1892

CASEY STUART

Highland Rogue
(New York: Zebra, 1991)

Story type: Historical/Seventeenth Century
Major character(s): Maura Campbell, Ward (of Oliver Cromwell); "Black Alexander" MacLaren, Laird
Time period(s): 17th century (1650s)
Locale(s): England; Scotland

Summary: Scheduled to be married momentarily to the cruel man of her guardian Oliver Cromwell's choosing, Maura Campbell is quite pleased to be kidnapped and carried off to the Highlands—even if her abductor is the fabled "Black Alexander" MacLaren, himself! In the wild, romantic setting, their love blossoms; but realities intrude, bringing treachery, violence, and separation. Gentle, sensual, and mature characters.

Other books you might like:
Kimberly Cates, *Crown of Mist*, 1988
Jane Feather, *Reckless Angel*, 1989
Chloe Gartner, *Mistress of the Highlands*, 1976
Patricia Grasso, *Highland Belle*, 1991
Amanda Scott, *Border Bride*, 1990

1893

DIANA STUART

The Moon Pool
(New York: Silhouette, 1991)

Story type: Contemporary
Major character(s): Robert Pierson, Doctor; Maya Najero, Nurse (Yaqui)

Time period(s): 1990s
Locale(s): San Joaquin Valley, California

Summary: Unexpectedly finding themselves working together in a small clinic in an impoverished area of the San Joaquin Valley, former sweethearts Robert and Maya are once again attracted to each other; and once again they must confront the problems of family opinion, prejudice, and commitment. Mystical and heartwarming.

Other books you might like:
Delayne Camp, *Newsworthy Affair*, 1990
Janet Dailey, *Terms of Surrender*, 1982
Tracy Hughes, *White Lies and Alibis*, 1990
Miriam Pace, *Warm Creature Comforts*, 1991
    innocent sweet
Laura Taylor, *Jade's Passion*, 1990

1894

ELIZABETH STUART

Bride of the Lion

(New York: St. Martin's, 1995)

Story type: Historical/Medieval
Major character(s): Jocelyn Montagne, Noblewoman; Robert De Langley, Nobleman ("Lion of Normandy")
Time period(s): 12th century (1152)
Locale(s): England

Summary: Intent on reclaiming the lands which had been taken from him, Robert de Langley, the Lion of Normandy, descends upon the castle of his old enemy, Lord William Montagne, and finds himself facing a small, raven-haired beauty, armed with nothing but a knife and the will to defend herself. Intrigued, yet determined, Robert holds Jocelyn and her sister hostage for his lands, but in the process, he realizes he is coming to care for the daughter of his hated enemy. Well-written, compelling, good historical details.

Other books you might like:
Rexanne Becnel, *A Dove at Midnight*, 1993
Alice Borchardt, *Devoted*, 1995
Roberta Gellis, *Roselynde*, 1978
    1st of the Roselynde Chronicles
Iris Johansen, *Lion's Bride*, 1996

1895

ELIZABETH STUART

Where Love Dwells

(New York: St. Martin's, 1990)

Story type: Historical/Medieval
Major character(s): Elen of Teifi, Noblewoman (Welsh); Richard of Kent, Nobleman (English)
Time period(s): 13th century (1283)
Locale(s): Wales

Summary: When the Welsh rebel Lady Elen is captured in a raid by Englishman Richard of Kent, she defies Richard at every turn and continues to work for the Welsh cause. Their growing attraction to each other, however, results in love—and with love comes understanding and healing—until out-

side forces threaten to destroy what they have begun to build together. Passion and politics in 13th century Wales.

Other books you might like:
Rebecca Brandewyne, *No Gentle Love*, 1989
Shannon Drake, *Princess of Fire*, 1989
Roberta Gellis, *The Silver Mirror*, 1989
Johanna Lindsey, *A Gentle Feuding*, 1984
Johanna Lindsey, *When Love Awaits*, 1986

1896

CHLOE SUMMERS

No Easy Task

(New York: Kismet, 1991)

Story type: Contemporary
Major character(s): Doone Daniels, Courier; Hunter MacKenzie, Detective—Private
Time period(s): 1990s
Locale(s): Eagle Island

Summary: When Doone Daniels delivers a package to Hunter MacKenzie, she unwittingly sets in motion a plan that will endanger his life—at the hands of Doone's boss.

Other books you might like:
Carol Jerina, *Flirting with Danger*, 1990
Velda Johnston, *Flight to Yesterday*, 1990
Jayne Ann Krentz, *Silver Linings*, 1991
Sandra Marton, *Night Fires*, 1991
Paula Detmer Riggs, *Rough Passage*, 1991

1897

ANNALISE SUN

The Golden Mountain

(New York: Pocket, 1990)

Story type: Historical/American West Coast; Historical/Canadian West
Major character(s): Cassandra Thornton, Photographer; Jared Duran, Young Man; King Duran, Young Man
Time period(s): 1890s
Locale(s): Seattle, Washington; Klondike, Yukon Territory, Canada

Summary: Cass Thornton's search for her 14-year-old half-sister, Tea Rose, takes her from the sinister warrens of Seattle's Chinatown to the wild and dangerous gold fields of the Klondike. She is aided by two attractive, yet very different, brothers—each with his own agenda. Along the way she must sort out her feelings for them both. Realistic setting and good characterizations.

Other books you might like:
Jude Deveraux, *Mountain Laurel*, 1990
Rene J. Garrod, *Temptation's Wild Embrace*, 1990
Peggy Hanchar, *Tomorrow's Dream*, 1989
Terri Valentine, *Master of Her Heart*, 1990

1898

MARLENE SUSON

Devil's Bargain

(New York: Avon, 1992)

Story type: Regency
Major character(s): Portia "Tia" Easton, Noblewoman; Marc Hamilton, Nobleman (Duke of Castleton)
Time period(s): 1810s
Locale(s): London, England

Summary: High-spirited Portia dreams of being rescued by a gallant gentleman who will take care of her and her younger brother. To her delight, the Duke of Castleton decides he needs to marry—and he chooses her! Her delight changes to disgust, however, when she finally meets the aloof and icy aristocrat, but her situation is dire and she is forced to accept his offer. In London their world becomes truly dangerous; and as Marc withdraws even more, Tia wonders if she can tell her husband of her fears.

Other books you might like:
Anne Caldwell, *Scandal's Darling*, 1991
Georgette Heyer, *These Old Shades*, 1926
Annabel Laine, *The Reluctant Heiress*, 1978
Leslie Lynn, *The Rake's Redemption*, 1989

1899

MARLENE SUSON

The Errant Earl

(New York: Fawcett, 1989)

Story type: Regency
Major character(s): Kit Kendall, Noblewoman, Spouse (neglected wife); Scott Kendall, Military Personnel (lieutenant colonel), Nobleman (Lord Kingsley)
Time period(s): 1810s (Regency period)
Locale(s): England (Scarlet Oaks Estate)

Summary: When Scott Kendall returns from six years of war to take over the responsibilities of his estate, Scarlet Oaks, he must deal with an angry, estranged wife, a son who doesn't know him, and a deteriorating estate.

Other books you might like:
Kimberly Cates, *Restless Is the Wind*, 1989
　A more serious Regency
Brian Cleeve, *Sara*, 1976
　A more serious Regency
Elisabeth Kidd, *Lady Lu*, 1989
Leslie Lynn, *The Rake's Redemption*, 1989
Sheila Simonson, *A Cousinly Connexion*, 1984

1900

MARLENE SUSON

The Lily and the Hawk

(New York: Avon, 1993)

Story type: Historical/Regency

Major character(s): Lily Culhane, Actress; Damon St. Clair, Nobleman (Earl of Hawkhurst)
Time period(s): 19th century
Locale(s): England

Summary: Damon St. Clair seeks out and confronts the mysterious Lily Culhane when his married nephew appears to be smitten by the lady. However, she isn't at all what the ton thinks; in reality, she is a recluse and highly unavailable. However, by the time Damon realizes his mistake, Lily is in no mood to deal with him. In a twist of fate, circumstances force Lily and her sister to take refuge with Damon—and then the romance begins. Witty and unusual.

Other books you might like:
Brenda Joyce, *Scandalous Love*, 1992
　somewhat "ungentle"
Betina M. Krahn, *The Last Bachelor*, 1994
Arnette Lamb, *The Betrothal*, 1992
Amanda Quick, *Scandal*, 1991

1901

KATHERINE SUTCLIFFE

Dream Fever

(New York: Avon, 1991)

Story type: Historical/Exotic
Major character(s): Summer O'Neile, Mail Order Bride; Nicholas Sabre, Rancher (Sheep)
Time period(s): 1860s (1860)
Locale(s): London, England; Lyttleton, New Zealand

Summary: Nicholas, bitter and exiled, and Summer, fleeing from a crime, battle each other and the New Zealand locals who try to keep them from making a new life for themselves.

Other books you might like:
Leigh Bristol, *Sunswept*, 1990
Linda Lael Miller, *Angelfire*, 1989
Linda Lael Miller, *Moonfire*, 1988
Leslie O'Grady, *Seek the Wild Shore*, 1989
Lynette Vinet, *Wild, Wicked Eden*, 1990

1902

KATHERINE SUTCLIFFE

A Fire in the Heart

(New York: Avon, 1990)

Story type: Historical/Victorian
Major character(s): Bonnie Eden, Runaway, Servant (maid); Damien Warwick, Nobleman
Time period(s): 1860s
Locale(s): England

Summary: When Lord Damien Warwick reluctantly takes young runaway Bonnie Eden into his home and gives her a job as a maid, he doesn't plan to fall in love with her. Nevertheless, he does—and when he belatedly realizes it, Bonnie has run away again; and in order to win her, Lord Damien must first find her.

Other books you might like:
Charlene Cross, *Masque of Enchantment*, 1990
Catherine Lyndell, *Stolen Dreams*, 1989
Linda Lael Miller, *My Darling Melissa*, 1990
Barbara Dawson Smith, *Silver Splendor*, 1989

1903
KATHERINE SUTCLIFFE

Miracle
(New York: Jove, 1995)

Story type: Historical/Georgian
Major character(s): Miracle Cavendish, Noblewoman; Clayton Hawthorne, Nobleman, Twin
Time period(s): 1800s
Locale(s): Salisbury, England; Isle of Wight, England

Summary: Clayton Hawthorne, an unwilling participant in a scheme to find his twin brother a wife, travels to the Isle of Wight to convince the free-spirited Miracle Cavendish to marry him, or rather, his brother Trey. Miracle couldn't stand Trey when she had met him earlier, but this time he seems "different," and she certainly can't explain why she suddenly finds herself falling in love with him. It isn't until they return to England that the play goes awry and Clayton realizes that he is in love with the woman he has arranged for his brother to marry!

Other books you might like:
Stella Cameron, *Fascination*, 1993
    darker
Jane Feather, *Valentine*, 1995
Jane Feather, *Virtue*, 1993
Mary Jo Putney, *Thunder and Roses*, 1993
Christina Skye, *Come the Dawn*, 1995

1904
KATHERINE SUTCLIFFE

My Only Love
(New York: Berkley, 1993)

Story type: Historical/Victorian
Major character(s): Olivia Devonshire, Gentlewoman; Miles Kemball Warwick, Mine Owner
Time period(s): 19th century
Locale(s): England

Summary: Olivia Devonshire is a woman with a reputation. Miles Warwick is a man in need of money. So when Olivia's father offers to "sell" Olivia to Miles for a price, they both agree and end up turning their marriage of convenience into a most passionate and satisfactory relationship. Sequel to *A Fire in the Heart*.

Other books you might like:
Elizabeth August, *Pirate's Bride*, 1992
Phoebe Conn, *Desire*, 1993
Johanna Lindsey, *The Magic of You*, 1993
Linda Lael Miller, *My Darling Melissa*, 1990
    American setting

1905
KATHERINE SUTCLIFFE

Once a Hero
(New York: Jove, 1994)

Story type: Historical/Exotic
Major character(s): Bronte Haviland, Administrator (of an orphanage and school); Brandon Tremain, Prisoner, Imposter (posing as traitor)
Time period(s): 19th century
Locale(s): New South Wales, Australia

Summary: Bronte, the warden's daughter, finds her dream hero, Brandon Tremain, in a most unlikely place—prison. She tries to stay aloof, but she can't deny she has fallen in love with him. Passion, adventure, and suspense quickly follow.

Other books you might like:
Brenda Joyce, *Secrets*, 1993
    Western-style passion
Linda Ladd, *White Rose*, 1994
    Australian setting
Connie Mason, *Brave Land, Brave Love*, 1992
    Australian setting
Nan Ryan, *The Legend of Love*, 1991
    Western-style passion
Lynette Vinet, *Wild, Wicked Eden*, 1990
    New Zealand setting

1906
KATHERINE SUTCLIFFE

Shadow Play
(New York: Avon, 1991)

Story type: Historical/Exotic; Historical/Victorian
Major character(s): Sarah St. James, Gentlewoman; Morgan Kane, Adventurer
Time period(s): 1870s
Locale(s): Guyana (British Guiana); Brazil; England

Summary: Desperate to save her late father's fortune and reputation, Sarah St. James hires legendary adventurer Morgan Kane to take her to the Amazon jungle stronghold of cruel and sadistic rubber baron Rudolopho King to steal rubber plant seeds and to avenge her father's death. Morgan has his own dark reasons for hating King; and together Sarah and Morgan battle the jungle, each other, and eventually King himself in this realistic, violent, and brutal adventure/romance with a strong allegorical quality.

Other books you might like:
Virginia Henley, *The Pirate and the Pagan*, 1990
Karen Robards, *Green Eyes*, 1991
Karen Robards, *Wild Orchids*, 1986
Janelle Taylor, *Whispered Kisses*, 1990

1907

PEG SUTHERLAND

Yes, Virginia

(Toronto: Harlequin, 1993)

Story type: Contemporary/Fantasy; Holiday Themes
Major character(s): Virginia Holly, Journalist (reporter); Nick Costhaler, Artisan (toy maker), Guide
Time period(s): 1990s
Locale(s): North Pole, Mythical Place

Summary: Journalist Virginia Holly is assigned to check into a fax requesting a replacement for Santa and Mrs. Claus, who want to retire in Miami. Virginia and Nick, a toy maker, make the trip north and find more than magic; they find each other, a whole new way of life, and a whole new world of love. Myth and technology combine in a lovely Christmas story.

Other books you might like:
Rexanne Becnel, *Christmas Journey*, 1992
Janice Bennett, *A Christmas Keepsake*, 1992
Heather Graham, *Spirit of the Season*, 1993
Ruth Langan, *Christmas Miracle*, 1992
　　historical American West
Debbie Macomber, *A Season of Angels*, 1993

1908

LIBBY SYDES

Bayou Dreams

(New York: Dell, 1991)

Story type: Historical/War of 1812
Major character(s): Acadiana "Cade" Hamilton, Plantation Owner, Southern Belle (atypical); Jonas Courtland, Plantation Owner
Time period(s): 1810s (1814)
Locale(s): New Orleans, Louisiana

Summary: Jonas Courtland will do anything to regain his family's land, even marry the fiesty spitfire who now owns it. But independent Acadiana Hamilton has other ideas, and they don't include a husband. Funny, passionate, and interestingly plotted, this lively romance is set in the Louisiana of Jean Lafitte and it is nicely evocative of the era.

Other books you might like:
Elinor Lynley, *Song of the Bayou*, 1990
Emma Merritt, *Masque of Jade*, 1990
Alexandra Ripley, *Charleston*, 1982
Laura Simon, *A Taste of Heaven*, 1989
　　Caribbean setting
Becky Lee Weyrich, *Forever, My Love*, 1989
　　fantasy elements

1909

LIBBY SYDES

The Lion's Angel

(New York: Dell, 1992)

Story type: Historical/Medieval

Major character(s): Lady LeClair of Ravenwood, Noblewoman; Lord Borgia de St. Brieuc, Knight
Time period(s): 11th century (1067)
Locale(s): England

Summary: Good and kind Lady LeClaire struggles to keep her sisters and serfs in their homes, even though William the Conqueror sends Borgia de St. Brieuc to claim their home. The sparks between the two are immediate, and William's suggestion of "joint ownership" only intensifies the conflict. Lots of fire and passion in this story of goodness put to the test.

Other books you might like:
Catherine Archer, *Rose Among Thorns*, 1992
Samantha James, *My Cherished Enemy*, 1992
Flora M. Speer, *Castle of Dreams*, 1992
Elizabeth Stuart, *Where Love Dwells*, 1990
Kathleen E. Woodiwiss, *The Wolf and the Dove*, 1974

1910

LIBBY SYDES

Until Spring

(New York: Dell, 1993)

Story type: Historical/American West; Historical/Post-American Civil War
Major character(s): Addy Smith, Widow(er); Zeke Claiborne, Widow(er)
Time period(s): 19th century
Locale(s): Laramie, Wyoming

Summary: Addy, alone and eluding her scheming brother-in-law, accepts Zeke as a husband and his three children as her own. Zeke is wounded and Addy is challenged by the ranch and a family; as she deals with it all, she wins Zeke's respect. As their relationship develops, true love and caring take root; but old secrets threaten their happiness until they can be resolved.

Other books you might like:
Robin Lee Hatcher, *Promise Me Spring*, 1991
Jill Marie Landis, *Come Spring*, 1992
Jill Marie Landis, *Rose*, 1990
Victoria Pade, *The Doubletree*, 1990
LaVyrle Spencer, *Morning Glory*, 1989

1911

SUSAN TANNER

Captive to a Dream

(New York: Leisure, 1991)

Story type: Historical/Renaissance
Major character(s): Rhea, Noblewoman; Gavin "Berenhard" MacAmlaid, Knight, Bastard Son
Time period(s): 16th century (1517)
Locale(s): Highlands, Scotland

Summary: Friends as children but separated by their parents, Rhea and Gavin meet again as adults with passionate and violent results. Revenge, madness, and court intrigue are all part of this fast-paced sequel to *Highland Captive*.

Other books you might like:
Jude Deveraux, *A Knight in Shining Armor*, 1989
Roberta Gellis, *The Silver Mirror*, 1989
Betina M. Krahn, *Behind Closed Doors*, 1991
Kathleen E. Woodiwiss, *So Worthy My Love*, 1989

1912
JANELLE TAYLOR

Chase the Wind
(New York: Kensington, 1994)

Story type: Historical/American West
Major character(s): Bethany Wind, Government Official; Navarro Breed, Government Official
Time period(s): 19th century
Locale(s): Arizona

Summary: Assigned to stop a shipment of arms and avert a bloody confrontation with Geronimo, undercover agents Navarro Breed and Bethany Wind agree to a temporary marriage and head for Arizona. Both are disillusioned with both love and marriage and are only concerned with stopping the gunrunners—but by the time they have accomplished their goals, trust and love have replaced suspicion and fear, and their marriage is no longer merely a sham. Fast-paced and action filled.

Other books you might like:
Genell Dellin, *Comanche Wind*, 1993
Kathleen Eagle, *Heaven and Earth*, 1990
Cassie Edwards, *Wild Splendor*, 1993
Diane Gates Robinson, *Delta Desire*, 1991
Bobbi Smith, *Dream Warrior*, 1993

1913
JANELLE TAYLOR

Destiny Mine
(New York: Kensington, 1995)

Story type: Historical/Post-American Revolution
Major character(s): Kionee, Indian (Hanueva), Warrior; Stalking Wolf, Indian (Cheyenne), Warrior
Time period(s): 1790s (1797)
Locale(s): Bighorn Mountains, Wyoming

Summary: Since the age of five, Kionee, hunter-guardian for her family and member of the Hanueva tribe, has taken on the duties of a warrior and, with other tiva of her tribe, has ceased to live as a woman. Kionee is resigned to her sacred honor as a chosen one—until she meets Stalking Wolf of the Cheyenne. In spite of the fact that their love is forbidden, they fall in love and wonder if it is, perhaps, the will of the earth god.

Other books you might like:
Catherine Anderson, *Comanche Moon*, 1991
    Native American themes
Beverly Bird, *Comes the Rain*, 1990
    Native American themes
Genell Dellin, *Cherokee Sundown*, 1992
    Native American themes

Kelly Ferjutz, *Windsong*, 1994
    Native American themes

1914
JANELLE TAYLOR

Follow the Wind
(New York: Zebra, 1990)

Story type: Historical/American West
Major character(s): Jessica Lane, Rancher; Navarro Breed, Gunfighter; Nathan Cordell, Foreman
Time period(s): 1870s (1876)
Locale(s): Texas

Summary: Jessica will do anything to keep her family's land from being taken over by a greedy neighbor, including enlisting the aid of gunfighter Navarro Breed. But their problems are compounded by love, jealousy, and a traitor bent on destroying Jessica's happiness. Lots of action and passion, Texas-style.

Other books you might like:
Constance Bennett, *Morning Sky*, 1991
Deana James, *Wild Texas Heart*, 1990
DiAnna June, *Yesterday's Promise*, 1991
Catherine Lanigan, *A Promise Made*, 1991
Joan Elliott Pickart, *The Bonnie Blue*, 1990

1915
JANELLE TAYLOR

Forever Ecstasy
(New York: Zebra, 1991)

Story type: Historical/American West
Major character(s): Morning Star, Indian (Lakota/Sioux); Joe "Sky Warrior" Lawrence, Imposter, Diplomat (of a sort)
Time period(s): 1850s (1851)
Locale(s): United States

Summary: In order to find the people who killed his friend, Tanner, and also expose a slippery traitor, Snakeman, Joe Lawrence assumes his friend's identity and travels West. But when he meets and begins to fall in love with Tanner's cousin, Morning Star, his role of avenger and peacemaker becomes much more complicated. Last, and eighth, in the Gray Eagle/Alissa Ecstasy Series.

Other books you might like:
Kathleen Harrington, *Cherish the Dream*, 1990
Penelope Neri, *Forever and Beyond*, 1990
    time change elements
Constance O'Banyon, *Cheyenne Sunrise*, 1990
Deborah Smith, *Beloved Woman*, 1991

1916
JANELLE TAYLOR

Kiss of the Night Wind
(New York: Zebra, 1989)

Story type: Historical/American West

Major character(s): Carrie Sue Stover, Runaway, Teacher; T.J. Rogue, Gunfighter
Time period(s): 1880s
Locale(s): Tucson, Arizona

Summary: Fleeing from an unhappy past, Carrie Sue Stover starts life over as a schoolmarm. In the process she meets T.J. Rogue, a man in a similar situation, and then the complications begin. True love, of course, wins out in the end, in spite of misunderstandings that severely test their feelings for each other.

Other books you might like:
Linda Benjamin, *Midnight Chase*, 1989
LaRee Bryant, *Arizona Captive*, 1989
Elizabeth Lane, *Wind River*, 1989
Colleen Quinn, *Colorado Flame*, 1989
Rebecca Sinclair, *California Caress*, 1989

1917

JANELLE TAYLOR

The Last Viking Queen
(New York: Zebra, 1994)

Story type: Historical/Fantasy; Historical/Medieval
Major character(s): Alysa Malvern Crisdean, Royalty (princess), Witch; Gavin, Spouse; Erik, Warrior (Viking)
Time period(s): 5th century
Locale(s): England

Summary: Princess Alysa and her husband, Gavin, fight evil forces that threaten her people; and when Gavin disappears, Alysa goes right to the enemy camp to find him. Once there, she is fascinated by the Viking, Erik, but she still yearns for Gavin. Using her wits and magical powers, she plans a strategy that eventually defeats the invaders and returns Gavin to her.

Other books you might like:
Rebecca Brandewyne, *Beyond the Starlit Frost*, 1991
   Sequel to *Passion Moon Rising*
Rebecca Brandewyne, *Passion Moon Rising*, 1988
   fantasy elements
Heather Graham, *The Viking's Woman*, 1990
   Viking tale
Johanna Lindsey, *Fires of Winter*, 1980
   more Vikings, but with a captor/captive emphasis
Lindsay Randall, *Silversword*, 1990
   fantasy elements

1918

JANELLE TAYLOR

Promise Me Forever
(New York: Zebra, 1991)

Story type: Historical/Victorian America
Major character(s): Rachel McCandeless, Widow(er) ("Black Widow"); Daniel Slade "Mac" McCandeless, Rogue
Time period(s): 1880s (1885)
Locale(s): Georgia; Cuba

Summary: When young Rachel McCandeless becomes a widow for the third time, she sets out to clear her "black widow" reputation and find the answers to her husband's mysterious deathbed comments. Aided by her husband's brother (who keeps his identity hidden because he is suspicious of Rachel), Rachel's quest leads her across the South and inevitably to Cuba, where the dangers and the stakes increase dramatically. Fascinating portrayal of the woman's role in the Southern society of the late Victorian Era.

Other books you might like:
Jane Archer, *Rebel Seduction*, 1990
Evelyn Rogers, *A Love So Wild*, 1991
Myra Rowe, *Cypress Moon*, 1990
Bobbi Smith, *Kiss Me Forever*, 1991

1919

JANELLE TAYLOR

Whispered Kisses
(New York: Zebra, 1990)

Story type: Historical/Exotic
Major character(s): Laura Leigh Webster, Heiress; Jace Elliott, Guide
Time period(s): 1890s (1896)
Locale(s): London, England; Africa

Summary: An African safari brings heiress Laura Leigh Webster both love and danger as she and Jace Elliott try to solve the mysteries of his past.

Other books you might like:
Isak Dinesen, *Out of Africa*, 1989
   Mainstream
C.S. Forester, *The African Queen*, 1940
Leslie O'Grady, *Seek the Wild Shore*, 1989
Susan Sackett, *Passion's Golden Fire*, 1989
   Chitzen Itza setting
Laura Simon, *A Taste of Heaven*, 1989
   Caribbean setting

1920

LAURA TAYLOR

Jade's Passion
(Toronto: Harlequin, 1990)

Story type: Contemporary
Major character(s): Jade Howell, Teacher, Child-Care Giver (for homeless children); Reed Townsend, Contractor, Philanthropist
Time period(s): 1990s
Locale(s): United States

Summary: Jade Howell and Reed Townsend fight and finally give in to their feelings for each other, in spite of the fact that they think their relationship has no future. However, once they learn to trust their feelings and each other, they realize that love can blossom and thrive in spite of a number of obstacles. Passionate and sensitive.

Other books you might like:
Elizabeth Barnes, *In Spite of Themselves*, 1991

Rita Clay Estrada, *The Lady Says No*, 1991
Kay Hooper, *Star-Crossed Lovers*, 1990
Linda Lael Miller, *Glory, Glory*, 1990
Diana Stuart, *The Moon Pool*, 1991

1921
LUCY TAYLOR

Avenue of Dreams
(New York: New American Libraries, 1990)

Story type: Saga
Major character(s): Chiara Sardanno, Immigrant (Italian), Seamstress; Mike Marcassa, Immigrant (Italian); Stewart Austin, Businessman, Wealthy
Time period(s): 20th century (1st half)
Locale(s): Italy; Detroit, Michigan

Summary: Italian immigrant Chiara struggles to realize her dreams for love and success in the face of heartbreaking tragedy, illicit love, and world turmoil. A triumphant story of love and hope spanning three generations set against the turbulance of early to mid 20th century America.

Other books you might like:
Helen Barolini, *Umbertina*, 1979
Barbara Taylor Bradford, *A Woman of Substance*, 1979
Sandra Bregman, *Reach for the Dream*, 1990
Catherine Cookson, *The Whip*, 1983
Belva Plain, *Evergreen*, 1979

1922
LETA TEGLER

Gabrielle
(New York: Avon, 1990)

Story type: Historical/American Civil War
Major character(s): Gabrielle St. Claire, Southern Belle, Spy (suspected); Cade Montana, Rancher
Time period(s): 1860s (1861)
Locale(s): New Orleans, Louisiana; Texas

Summary: When Gabrielle is discovered passing secret messages between her sister and her lover, she is suspected of being a spy and is summarily sent to stay on Cade Montana's ranch in Texas. But Texas is not New Orleans, and Gabrielle must deal not only with unaccustomed ''hardships,'' but her growing attraction to Cade as well. Lots of humor and adventure.

Other books you might like:
Deborah Camp, *Black-Eyed Susan*, 1990
Jessie Ford, *A Different Breed*, 1988
Norah Hess, *Wildfire*, 1989
Linda Howard, *A Lady of the West*, 1990
Terri Valentine, *Yankee's Caress*, 1989

1923
JULIE TETEL

And Heaven Too
(New York: Warner, 1990)

Story type: Historical/Seventeenth Century
Major character(s): Judith Beaufort, Noblewoman; Charles Lambert, Nobleman, Art Dealer
Time period(s): 17th century (1639)
Locale(s): London, England

Summary: When Lord Charles Lambert's priceless painting is stolen, he instigates a kidnapping—and ends up with a drenched and angry Lady Judith instead of the appropriate thief. The quest for the missing painting leads to some intriguing secrets; and in a manner worthy of Shakespeare's comedies the painting is found, a plot is foiled, and the hero and heroine fall in love.

Other books you might like:
Mallory Burgess, *Ballenrose*, 1991
Shirl Henke, *Moonflower*, 1989
Ashland Price, *Wild Irish Heather*, 1991
Lynda Trent, *The Tryst*, 1986

1924
JULIE TETEL

Sweet Suspicions
(Toronto: Harlequin, 1992)

Story type: Historical/Georgian
Major character(s): Caroline Hutton, Gentlewoman (impoverished); Richard Worth, Military Personnel
Time period(s): 1710s (1714)
Locale(s): England

Summary: Poor, but well-born Caroline Hutton fufills the requirements that Richard Worth has for a bride; however, Caroline is only interested in settling her father's estate. But when they meet at a ball, they are both fascinated with each other. The problems begin when a suitor of Caroline's is killed and Richard is accused. A suspenseful and sensual romance.

Other books you might like:
Mary Jo Putney, *Silk and Shadows*, 1991
Amanda Quick, *Rendezvous*, 1992
Amanda Quick, *Ravished*, 1992
Barbara Dawson Smith, *Fire at Midnight*, 1992
Catherine Wyatt, *A Rose in the Shadows*, 1992

1925
JULIE TETEL

Swept Away
(New York: Popular Library, 1989)

Story type: Historical/Exotic
Major character(s): Eve Marie Sedgwick, Widow(er), Castaway; Adam Winthrop, Shipowner, Castaway
Time period(s): 17th century (1688)

Locale(s): At Sea; Caribbean

Summary: En route from England to Philadelphia, their ship sinks and Eve Marie Sedgwick and Adam Winthrop, the ship's owner, are castaway on a Caribbean island. The local Arawek Indians assume they are married; and the situation proves awkward, funny, and passionate.

Other books you might like:
Julie Garwood, *The Bride*, 1989
    Different period but witty and humorous
Shirl Henke, *Moonflower*, 1989
Laura Kinsale, *Seize the Fire*, 1989
Tracy Sinclair, *Miss Robinson Crusoe*, 1989

1926

SHELLY THACKER (Pseudonym of Shelly Thacker Meinhardt)

Falcon on the Wind
(New York: Avon, 1991)

Story type: Historical/Medieval
Major character(s): Laurien D'Amboise, Noblewoman; Connor of Glenshiel, Nobleman, Warrior
Time period(s): 13th century (1251)
Locale(s): Scotland

Summary: When Laurien is abruptly kidnapped by Connor on her wedding day, she is much relieved; but when she learns that she is only being held for political ransom and will be returned to her villainous fiance once certain conditions are met, she plans to escape. Laurien and Connor do eventually fall in love, despite their violent and fiery clashes in this nicely done captor/captive medieval tale.

Other books you might like:
Rexanne Becnel, *My Gallant Enemy*, 1990
Catherine Coulter, *Secret Song*, 1991
    third in trilogy
Johanna Lindsey, *Defy Not the Heart*, 1989
Victoria Morrow, *Beneath a Pale Moon*, 1991
Marylyle Rogers, *Proud Hearts*, 1990

1927

SHELLY THACKER (Pseudonym of Shelly Thacker Meinhardt)

Forever His
(New York: Avon, 1993)

Story type: Time Travel
Major character(s): Celine Fontaine, Socialite; Gaston De Varennes, Knight, Mercenary
Time period(s): 14th century; 1990s
Locale(s): France

Summary: Sir Gaston is stunned to find his fiancee in his bed and, suddenly, he knows he is being tricked by her father. Celine, fresh from a jaunt in time from the 1990s to the 1300s, is confused but doesn't understand. She adapts, but needs to return to her time or face death. She falls in love with Gaston, and they marry, but she knows he doesn't believe her story of coming from the future. Politics and passion in an adventurous romance.

Other books you might like:
Laura Gilmour Bennett, *By All That Is Sacred*, 1991
Diana Gabaldon, *Outlander*, 1991
Vivian Knight-Jenkins, *Love's Timeless Dance*, 1993
Susan Sizemore, *Wings of the Storm*, 1992
Terri Valentine, *Sands of Time*, 1993
    Middle Eastern time travel

1928

SHELLY THACKER (Pseudonym of Shelly Thacker Meinhardt)

Midnight Raider
(New York: Avon, 1922)

Story type: Historical/Medieval
Major character(s): Elizabeth Thornton, Highwayman, Prisoner (former); Pierce Wolverton, Nobleman (Earl of Darkridge), Highwayman
Time period(s): 13th century
Locale(s): England

Summary: Elizabeth sets out to rob the carriages of the man who sent her to prison, and she finds that Pierce Wolverton seeks revenge against the same man. They join forces and discover a passion that could either kill or save them. Lots of swashbuckling adventure.

Other books you might like:
Rexanne Becnel, *My Gallant Enemy*, 1990
Kimberly Cates, *To Catch the Flame*, 1991
Catherine Coulter, *Secret Song*, 1991
Shannon Drake, *Princess of Fire*, 1989

1929

SHELLY THACKER (Pseudonym of Shelly Thacker Meinhardt)

Silver and Sapphires
(New York: Avon, 1993)

Story type: Historical/Exotic
Major character(s): Ashiana de Canti e Calda, Royalty (princess), Imposter (slave-girl); Saxon D'Avenant, Smuggler
Time period(s): 1750s
Locale(s): India; England

Summary: To prove her love for her clan, Princess Ashiana embarks on a quest to find a stolen stone and return it to her people. Disguised as a slave, she is given to smuggler Saxon D'Avenant, who is also on a stone-finding mission. Their goal is to find all the stones (nine in all) and return them to their rightful place, because only then will harmony and light be restored. Passionate, brutal, and fast-paced action. Sweet/savage elements.

Other books you might like:
Virginia Henley, *The Pirate and the Pagan*, 1990
Iris Johansen, *Tiger Prince*, 1993
Susan Johnson, *Sinful*, 1993
Christina Skye, *The Ruby*, 1992
Katherine Sutcliffe, *Shadow Play*, 1991

1930

JODI THOMAS

Forever in Texas

(New York: Jove, 1995)

Story type: Historical/American West
Major character(s): Hannah Randell, Fugitive, Imposter (posing as a teacher); Sanford Colston, Political Figure (school board member)
Time period(s): 19th century
Locale(s): Saints Roost, Texas

Summary: Failing in his attempt to hire a school teacher for the small Texas town of Saints Roost, Ford Colston is even more chagrined when a beautiful thief steals his clothes—and then kisses him! However, when she shows up in Saints Roost claiming to be the teacher he hired and an embrace results in a forced marriage, both of their lives change dramatically. The past intrudes to add a bit of danger, but things work out in the end. Lively action, tender sensuality, and humor add to this story that does allude to a few serious social issues.

Other books you might like:
Gwen Cleary, *Tender Heart*, 1994
Pamela K. Forrest, *Desert Angel*, 1994
Robin Lee Hatcher, *Where the Heart Is*, 1993
Jill Marie Landis, *Come Spring*, 1992
Pamela Morsi, *Runabout*, 1994

1931

JODI THOMAS

The Tender Texan

(New York: Diamond, 1991)

Story type: Historical/American West
Major character(s): Anne Marie Meyer, Immigrant (German), Settler; Chance Wyatt, Cowboy
Time period(s): 1830s (1836)
Locale(s): Texas

Summary: When widowed immigrant Anna Marie Meyer pays Chance Wyatt $100 to marry her platonically for a year so she can claim her land, she ends up with a husband who needs her as much as she needs him—but Chance must deal with his past tragedies and Anna must come to terms with her feelings before they can find happiness together. A gentle, sensual love story.

Other books you might like:
Lisa Gregory, *The Rainbow Promise*, 1989
Lisa Gregory, *The Rainbow Season*, 1979
Jill Marie Landis, *Rose*, 1990
Victoria Pade, *The Doubletree*, 1990
LaVyrle Spencer, *The Endearment*, 1982

1932

JODI THOMAS

The Texan and the Lady

(New York: Diamond, 1994)

Story type: Historical/American West
Major character(s): Jennie Munday, Runaway (pastor's daughter); Austin McCormick, Lawman (U. S. Marshal)
Time period(s): 1880s
Locale(s): Kansas; Iowa

Summary: Escaping her boring life, Jennie heads West and discovers that her "hero" is actually a cold U.S. Marshal who is on the trail of former enemies. He isn't happy when Jennie insists on joining the search, but he eventually relents. Treachery, murder, and a host of other dangers plague them, but justice (and love) do prevail in the end. Tender.

Other books you might like:
Rosanne Bittner, *Embers of the Heart*, 1990
Jill Marie Landis, *Rose*, 1990
Elizabeth Lowell, *Lover in the Rough*, 1994
LaVyrle Spencer, *The Endearment*, 1992
LaVyrle Spencer, *The Gamble*, 1987

1933

VICTORIA THOMPSON

Fortune's Lady

(New York: Avon, 1990)

Story type: Historical/American West
Major character(s): Suzanne Prentice, Widow(er), Saloon Hostess; Jared Caine, Gambler
Time period(s): 19th century (late)
Locale(s): Dodge City, Kansas

Summary: Forced by financial circumstances to work in a saloon to provide for her young son, Suzanne endures the censure of the townswomen and unwelcome advances by men. But when Jared, the Faro dealer at the saloon, is wounded by a card cheat, she takes him home to nurse him— and ends up falling in love.

Other books you might like:
Barbara Bretton, *Midnight Lover*, 1989
Deborah Camp, *Fallen Angel*, 1989
Dorothy Garlock, *Midnight Blue*, 1989
Georgina Gentry, *Nevada Nights*, 1989
Kathy Lawrence, *Tin Angel*, 1990

1934

VICTORIA THOMPSON

Playing with Fire

(New York: Avon, 1990)

Story type: Historical/American West
Major character(s): Isabel Forester, Teacher; Eben Walker, Blacksmith
Time period(s): 19th century
Locale(s): Bittercreek, Texas

Summary: When sheltered Isabel Forester leaves New York for Bittercreek, Texas, she simply intends to become the new schoolmarm. However, in a town with a scarcity of single women, she quickly becomes a highly desirable commodity—and when she becomes the prize in the local lottery, things really become interesting. A funny, gentle romance peopled with memorable, enjoyable characters set against a believable Western background.

Other books you might like:
Rosanne Bittner, *Embers of the Heart*, 1990
Emily Carmichael, *Visions of the Heart*, 1990
Jude Deveraux, *Mountain Laurel*, 1990
Jane Kidder, *Silver Caress*, 1990
Jill Marie Landis, *Rose*, 1990

1935

VICTORIA THOMPSON

Sweet Texas Surrender

(New York: Zebra, 1991)

Story type: Historical/American West
Major character(s): Sarah Hadley, Widow(er), Rancher; Travis Taylor, Gunfighter
Time period(s): 19th century
Locale(s): Texas

Summary: Widowed rancher Sarah Hadley needs help protecting her sheep from her treacherous cattlemean neighbors. But when she hires the mysterious gunslinger Travis Taylor, she gets far more than just another employee as Travis proves to be her champion, rescuer, friend, and eventually, lover. She's tall and independent; he's short and has a past—but love has a way of putting everything into proper perspective.

Other books you might like:
Ann Gabriel, *South Texas*, 1989
Dorothy Garlock, *Midnight Blue*, 1989
Jill Marie Landis, *Sunflower*, 1989
Pamela Litton, *Stardust and Whirlwinds*, 1991
Colleen Quinn, *Wild Is the Night*, 1991

1936

VICTORIA THOMPSON

Wild Texas Promise

(New York: Zebra, 1990)

Story type: Historical/American West
Major character(s): Eden Campbell, Rancher; Lincoln "Linc" Scott, Gunfighter
Time period(s): 19th century
Locale(s): Texas

Summary: Eden Campbell is strong, determined, and can fight her own battles. She certainly doesn't need a husband. Linc Scott is a footloose gunfighter who won't be tied down. He certainly doesn't need a wife. However, circumstances prove them both wrong as they join forces to battle cattle rustlers and fall in love in spite of themselves. Strong characters and plenty of action.

Other books you might like:
Dorothy Garlock, *Midnight Blue*, 1989
Martha Hix, *Wild Texas Rose*, 1990
Jill Marie Landis, *Sunflower*, 1988
Vivian Vaughn, *Texas Gamble*, 1990
Jeanne Williams, *No Roof but Heaven*, 1990

1937

VICTORIA THOMPSON

Wild Texas Wind

(New York: Zebra, 1992)

Story type: Historical/American West
Major character(s): Rebekah Tate, Captive (of the Comanche); Sean MacDougal, Trader
Time period(s): 1830s (1836)
Locale(s): Texas

Summary: Held in brutal captivity by the Comanche for seven years, Rebekah Tate is released as a result of a bargaining scheme by would-be hero Sean MacDougal — but she is heartbroken to learn that she must leave her young biracial son behind. Eventually, of course, Sean sees to it that the boy is released, but then the bigotry that has been simmering beneath the surface of the town boils over and Rebekah must face the prejudice of the white world. Passionate, realistic, and compelling.

Other books you might like:
Catherine Anderson, *Comanche Heart*, 1992
Madeline Baker, *Forbidden Fires*, 1990
Janet Dailey, *The Pride of Hannah Wade*, 1985
Gina Robins, *Always and Forever*, 1992

1938

VICTORIA THOMPSON

Winds of Destiny

(New York: Zebra, 1994)

Story type: Historical/American West
Series: Tates of Texas
Major character(s): Becky Tate, Indian (half Comanche), Activist (educates black children); Clint Masterson, Lawman (Texas Ranger)
Time period(s): 1880s
Locale(s): Texas; New Orleans, Louisiana

Summary: Becky Tate has given up on finding a respectable man to love—and then Texas Ranger Clint Masterson enters the scene. He restores order to a difficult situation (her father illegally fenced off some land) and then rescues Becky when her school for black children stirs up more trouble in the community. Although Clint is drawn to Becky and wants to protect her, he won't marry her because of his past. Becky, however, has other ideas.

Other books you might like:
Betina M. Krahn, *The Last Bachelor*, 1994
    another activist — Regency style/lots of humor
Pamela Morsi, *Courting Miss Hattie*, 1991

Pamela Morsi, *Garters*, 1992
a rather outrageous, determined heroine
Rebecca Paisley, *Moonlight and Magic*, 1990
children, humor, and another heroine who knows what she wants.

1939

ALEXANDRA THORNE

Boundless
(New York: Pinnacle, 1994)

Story type: Historical/American West
Major character(s): Elke Von Braun Sonnschein, Immigrant, Businesswoman (bakery owner); Patrick Pride, Rancher
Time period(s): 1860s
Locale(s): Fredericksburg, Texas

Summary: Orphaned and newly arrived in America, fourteen-year-old Elke Von Braun is determined to make a place for herself in her rough, new country. Marriage to the kindly Otto Sonnschein brings security; but when the magnetic Patrick Pride comes into her life, Elke realizes that nothing will ever be the same again. Good historical detail of the German immigrants in Texas. Prequel to Thorne's contemporary romance, *Lawless*.

Other books you might like:
Elaine Barbieri, *More Precious than Gold*, 1992
saga elements
Ann Gabriel, *South Texas*, 1990
good historical detail/mainstream
Ginna Gray, *Quiet Fires*, 1991
earlier time period/marriage of convenience/good historical detail
Jill Marie Landis, *Rose*, 1990
immigrant theme (Italian heroine)
Jill Marie Landis, *Sunflower*, 1988
immigrant theme (Dutch heroine)

1940

ALEXANDRA THORNE

Lawless
(New York: Pinnacle, 1994)

Story type: Contemporary/Mainstream
Major character(s): Caitlin Pride, Model, Rancher; James Comanche Killian, Foreman
Time period(s): 1990s
Locale(s): Texas

Summary: When high-fashion model Caitlin Pride goes home to Texas to be with her dying father, she has no idea that she will end up running the family ranch—and being forced to deal with her childhood sweetheart, ranch manager James Comanche Killian. Greed, treachery, and passion abound in this fast-paced story of contemporary Texas.

Other books you might like:
Jennifer Blake, *Shameless*, 1994
Southern setting
Sandra Brown, *Breath of Scandal*, 1991

Marcia Martin, *Southern Storms*, 1992
Karen Robards, *One Summer*, 1993
Nora Roberts, *Divine Evil*, 1992

1941

ELIZABETH THORNTON (Pseudonym of Mary George)

Dangerous to Love
(New York: Bantam, 1994)

Story type: Historical/Georgian
Major character(s): Serena Ward, Gentlewoman, Rebel (Jacobite); Julian Raynor, Gentleman, Rake
Time period(s): 1740s
Locale(s): London, England

Summary: When Jacobite sympathizer Serena Ward is mistaken for a common prostitute by the notorious rake Julian Raynor, a surprise raid of the Thatched Tavern by the militia sends her straight to his bed—and into his life, as well. A novel of deception, intrigue, and revenge set during the turbulent period following the Battle of Culloden.

Other books you might like:
Jo Beverley, *My Lady Notorious*, 1993
Kimberly Cates, *Crown of Dreams*, 1993
Susan Sizemore, *My First Duchess*, 1993
Casey Stuart, *Highland Rogue*, 1991
Patricia Veryan, *Had We Never Loved*, 1992

1942

ELIZABETH THORNTON (Pseudonym of Mary George)

Highland Fire
(New York: Pinnacle, 1994)

Story type: Historical/Regency
Major character(s): Caitlin Randal, Revolutionary; Iaian Randal, Nobleman, Revolutionary (rebel leader)
Time period(s): 1810s (1815)
Locale(s): Scotland

Summary: Thinking she is illegitimate, Caitlin defies her grandfather and joins the rebels. However, she is mistaken for a prostitute and catches the eye of the rebel leader, Iaian Randal, who pursues her relentlessly. The story features a strong-willed heroine, a stubborn hero, and a determined grandfather in a fast-paced, adventurous tale.

Other books you might like:
Mary Balogh, *Beyond the Sunrise*, 1992
Connie Brockway, *Promise Me Heaven*, 1994
Patricia Potter, *The Abduction*, 1991
Mary Jo Putney, *Dearly Beloved*, 1990
Rebecca Sinclair, *Wild Scottish Embrace*, 1991

1943

ELIZABETH THORNTON (Pseudonym of Mary George)

Scarlet Angel
(New York: Pinnacle, 1990)

Story type: Historical/Georgian; Historical/French Revolution

Major character(s): Gabrielle de Brienne, Captive; Cam Colburne, Nobleman (Duke of Dyson)
Time period(s): 1800s (1803)
Locale(s): England; France

Summary: Eleven years before Gabrielle and Cam separately endured the horrors of the French Revolution, but from different vantage points—his British, hers French. Now, bent on avenging the deaths of his stepmother and sister, Cam kidnaps Gabrielle, the granddaughter of the man he holds responsible, and takes her to England as his hostage. Blackmail, a forced marriage, and political intrigue are all part of this lively romance set during a particularly bloody historical period.

Other books you might like:
Mollie Ashton, *Terms of Surrender*, 1990
Brian Cleeve, *Hester*, 1979
Jane Feather, *Reckless Angel*, 1989
Ellen Tanner Marsh, *If This Be Magic*, 1990

1944

ELIZABETH THORNTON (Pseudonym of Mary George)

Tender the Storm

(New York: Pinnacle, 1991)

Story type: Historical/Post-French Revolution
Major character(s): Zoe Devereaux, Gentlewoman, Refugee (French Revolution); Rolfe, Nobleman (Marquess of Rivard), Government Official
Time period(s): 1810s (1814)
Locale(s): France; England

Summary: Rescued from the guillotine and swept to safety in England, young Zoe Devereaux is shocked to discover her hero is, in reality, a notorious rake. Nevertheless, when circumstances demand marriage, the pair oblige with interesting results. A difficult mother-in-law and a romantic misunderstanding send Zoe to France in search of her inheritance and a divorce—but she reckons without her husband's creative persistence in tracking down the woman he loves.

Other books you might like:
Jill Gregory, *Moonlit Obsession*, 1986
Victoria Holt, *The Devil on Horseback*, 1977
Ellen Tanner Marsh, *If This Be Magic*, 1991
Louisa Rawlings, *Stranger in My Arms*, 1990
Serena Richards, *Rendezvous*, 1991

1945

ELIZABETH THORNTON (Pseudonym of Mary George)

Velvet Is the Night

(New York: Pinnacle, 1992)

Story type: Historical/Post-French Revolution
Major character(s): Claire Devereux, Gentlewoman; Adam Dillon, Rake, Imposter
Time period(s): 18th century
Locale(s): France; United States

Summary: When young, beautiful Claire agrees to become the mistress of the infamous Commissioner of Rouen, Philippe Dubet, in order to win safety for herself and her siblings

during the Reign of Terror, she ends up in bed and in love with Adam Dillon, the Americanized half-brother of Philippe—a man who is bent on revenge. Passionate, realistic, and filled with excellent historical detail. Follows *Tender the Storm*.

Other books you might like:
Mollie Ashton, *Terms of Surrender*, 1990
Jill Gregory, *Moonlit Obsession*, 1986
Victoria Holt, *The Devil on Horseback*, 1977
Baroness Orczy, *The Scarlet Pimpernel*, 1905
    classic adventure tale of the French Revolution
Serena Richards, *Rendezvous*, 1991

1946

MARCELLA THUM

The Thorn Trees

(New York: Ballantine, 1991)

Story type: Historical/World War I
Major character(s): Kate Cantrell, Actress; Cody Prentice, Plantation Owner (coffee); Roger Westmacott, Plantation Owner (coffee)
Time period(s): 1910s (1914-1918)
Locale(s): England; Kenya

Summary: Married to one man but attracted to another, Kate is a prime suspect when her husband is fatally poisoned—even the man she loves has doubts. But World War I intervenes and the pair are separated, and it isn't until a tragedy brings Cody back to England that all mysteries are solved, all wrongs righted, and the lovers are finally united. Nicely-drawn characters in an interesting and somewhat exotic setting.

Other books you might like:
Diane Cory, *A Token of Jewels*, 1989
Victoria Holt, *Snare of Serpents*, 1990
Katherine Sinclair, *A Distant Dawn*, 1991
Katherine Sinclair, *Far Horizons*, 1991

1947

TRACEY TILLIS

Deadly Masquerade

(New York: Dell, 1994)

Story type: Contemporary; Romantic Suspense
Major character(s): Kelly Wylie, Police Officer (Internal Affairs); Nicholas Abella, Police Officer (Detective Sergeant)
Time period(s): 1990s
Locale(s): Sedgwick City, Indiana; The Bayous, Louisiana

Summary: When prosecutor Peter Cain is gunned down and his bodyguard, a police officer with a pristine record, disappears, it becomes a case for Internal Affairs. IA Sergeant Kelly Wylie is reluctantly forced to appeal to Sergeant Nick Abella, the brother of the missing cop, to help her find some answers. Their search sweeps them from the Indiana slums to the bayous of Cajun Louisiana, all the while bringing them closer not only to the solution to the crime (and the assassin who stalks them), but to a passionate romantic relationship that neither had wanted. A fast-paced, intense, and intricately plotted story, featuring thoughtfully developed characters.

Other books you might like:
Jill Barkin, *Hot Streak*, 1990
Jude Deveraux, *Sweet Liar*, 1992
Heather Graham Pozzessere, *Slow Burn*, 1994
Nora Roberts, *Genuine Lies*, 1991
Sherryl Woods, *Hide and Seek*, 1994

1948

TRACEY TILLIS

Night Watcher

(New York: Bantam, 1995)

Story type: Contemporary; Romantic Suspense
Major character(s): Julie Connor, Journalist; Michael Quinn, Police Officer (undercover)
Time period(s): 1990s
Locale(s): Michigan City, Illinois

Summary: Julie Connor is a top-notch investigative reporter, well acquainted with the seedier side of society. But when one of her sources turns up dead, she finds herself caught up in a dangerous investigation that is way over her head. She is rescued by the mysterious Michael Quinn, who appears out of nowhere to save her life. She doesn't know who he is or how he fits into the twisted plot, but he may be the only one who can keep her alive.

Other books you might like:
Tami Hoag, *Guilty as Sin*, 1996
Tami Hoag, *Still Waters*, 1992
Heather Graham Pozzessere, *Slow Burn*, 1994
Nora Roberts, *Carnal Innocence*, 1992
Meryl Sawyer, *Kiss in the Dark*, 1995

1949

ELISE TITLE

Hot Property

(Toronto: Mira, 1995)

Story type: Contemporary/Mainstream; Romantic Suspense
Major character(s): Kate Paley, Businesswoman (studio executive); Adrian Needham, Director (film); Doug Garrison, Businessman (studio executive)
Time period(s): 1990s
Locale(s): Hollywood, California

Summary: Ambitious, driven studio executive Kate Paley has no time for anything but success; when she is finally given a chance to prove herself as president of Paradine's motion picture division by the CEO, she is thrilled. However, a jealous, vengeful boss, a former protege who is being stalked, and a British film director (who is also the only man she has ever loved) all impact her life in different ways—and as she is forced to deal with these situations, she also learns what is truly important. A fast-paced, engrossing, suspenseful look at the seamier side of the Hollywood scene.

Other books you might like:
Jackie Collins, *American Star*, 1993
    mainstream Hollywood glitz
JoAnn Ross, *Secret Sins*, 1990
Meryl Sawyer, *Blind Chance*, 1989
Erica Spindler, *Red*, 1995
    Hollywood setting

1950

JANE TOOMBS

Midnight Whispers

(New York: Zebra, 1989)

Story type: Historical/American West
Major character(s): Nona Willard, Teacher; Spencer Quinlan, Journalist (newspaper)
Time period(s): 1870s
Locale(s): West

Summary: When the man she loves marries her sister, Nona resigns herself to a life without love—and then she meets Spencer. Includes a number of historical characters (e.g. General Custer) and good historical detail.

Other books you might like:
LaRee Bryant, *Arizona Captive*, 1989
Georgina Gentry, *Nevada Nights*, 1989
Norah Hess, *Wildfire*, 1989
Jill Marie Landis, *Wild Flower*, 1989
Janelle Taylor, *Kiss of the Night Wind*, 1989

1951

JANE TOOMBS

Passion's Melody

(New York: Zebra, 1994)

Story type: Historical
Major character(s): Snow Flower, Healer, Shaman; Kegan Kendall, Spy (British)
Time period(s): 1810s (1812)
Locale(s): Lake Michigan, Michigan; New York; England

Summary: Rescued from murderous Sioux by British spy Kegan Kendall, gentle healer Snow Flower learns to love him and they marry. However, when his brother dies, Kegan leaves for England. Certain she has been betrayed, Snow Flower goes to New York and earns money for her passage to England. She arrives to find Kegan engaged, and it takes all of her mystical powers and talents to win him back.

Other books you might like:
Rosanne Bittner, *Sioux Splendor*, 1990
    later time period/American setting/separation plot device
Elaine Coffman, *Somewhere Along the Way*, 1992
    determined hero/European-American settings
April Kihlstrom, *Dangerous Masquerade*, 1992
Johanna Lindsey, *The Magic of You*, 1993
    determined heroine/different approach

1952

JANE TOOMBS

Riverboat Rogue
(New York: Zebra, 1990)

Story type: Historical/American West
Major character(s): Merribeth, Musician (piano player); Brent O'Neal, Gambler (riverboat)
Time period(s): 1860s
Locale(s): New Orleans, Louisiana; San Francisco, California; Virginia City, Nevada

Summary: Merribeth's search for her sister takes her from New Orleans through San Francisco to Virginia City. Along the way she is aided by dashing gambler Brent O'Neal with whom she eventually falls in love.

Other books you might like:
Carol Finch, *Thunder's Tender Touch*, 1989
Georgina Gentry, *Nevada Nights*, 1989
Norah Hess, *Wildfire*, 1989
Mayo Lucas, *Camelot Jones*, 1989
Janelle Taylor, *Kiss of the Night Wind*, 1989

1953

JANE TOOMBS

Traitor's Kiss
(New York: Zebra, 1992)

Story type: Historical/Exotic; Gothic
Major character(s): Nara Winfield, Heiress; Rolfe Daniels, Heir, Sailor
Time period(s): 19th century
Locale(s): England; Singapore; India

Summary: While in England to claim her inheritance, American Nara Winfield is saved from drowning by Rolfe Daniels, the man who also claims to be the rightful heir! Her family likes him; she thinks he's a usurper. Nevertheless, he goes with them when they head for Singapore to search for a long-lost brother. Imposters, poisonous snakes, death, and even abduction into a harem are all they find—the real surprise comes once they have returned to England. An exotic, sensual romance with gothic leanings.

Other books you might like:
Olga Bicos, *White Tiger*, 1991
Jillian Hunter, *Tiger Dance*, 1991
Katherine Kincaid, *Midnight Treasure*, 1992
Katherine Sutcliffe, *Shadow Play*, 1991
Jennifer West, *Passion's Legacy*, 1991

1954

MARILYN TRACY

Memory's Lamp
(New York: Silhouette, 1994)

Story type: Contemporary/Fantasy
Major character(s): Sandy Rush, Saleswoman; Cliff Broderick, Archaeologist

Time period(s): 1990s
Locale(s): Washington, District of Columbia

Summary: Dying archaeologist Rachel Dorfman transfers her memories into the mind of naive and innocent Sandy Rush. Sandy is catapulted into a world of magic, murder, and the unexplained as she races against time to locate the Provenance Stone, close a time portal, and save herself from destruction. Highly sensual, fast-paced, and involving.

Other books you might like:
Madeline Baker, *Enchanted Crossings*, 1994
    anthology
Olga Bicos, *More than Magic*, 1994
Cheri Scotch, *The Werewolf's Sin*, 1994
    another good and evil struggle, werewolf-style/ 3rd in series
Anne Stuart, *Night of the Phantom*, 1991

1955

PAT TRACY

The Flaming
(Toronto: Harlequin, 1992)

Story type: Historical/Victorian; Historical/American West
Major character(s): Anya Delangue, Spinster, Heiress; Morgan Grayson, Rancher, Heir
Time period(s): 1860s (1865)
Locale(s): England

Summary: Resigned to a life of genteel spinsterhood, innocent Anya Delangue is stunned to discover that, much to her selfish sister's dismay, her late brother-in-law has willed her his holdings if she marries his nephew, Texas rancher Morgan Grayson. The obvious conflicts between the naive Anya and the bold American propel the story to its expected, passionate conclusion but not before they deal with attempted murder and jealous relatives who try to keep them apart. Nicely crafted.

Other books you might like:
Jude Deveraux, *Wishes*, 1989
Catherine Hart, *Temptation*, 1992
Garda Parker, *Arizona Temptation*, 1992
Victoria Thompson, *Playing with Fire*, 1990
Lynette Vinet, *Wild, Wicked Eden*, 1990

1956

LYNDA TRENT

Beloved Wife
(Toronto: Harlequin, 1992)

Story type: Historical/American West
Major character(s): Ammity Becker, Mail Order Bride, Orphan; Clay Morgan, Rancher
Time period(s): 1880s (1887)
Locale(s): Texas

Summary: Believing she is pregnant and in need of a change, Ammity heads West as a mail-order bride. When she arrives, she discovers a "family" ready to marry her — a family of seven. They certainly do need someone to take care of them, but Clay, the man Ammity is to marry, is still grieving and is unwilling to get close to anyone. This changes, of course, and in time this story warms to a wonderful, sensual romance.

Other books you might like:
Candace Camp, *Rosewood*, 1991
Rebecca Hagan Lee, *Golden Chances*, 1992
Linda Lael Miller, *Daniel's Bride*, 1992
Victoria Pade, *The Doubletree*, 1990

1957

LYNDA TRENT

The Black Hawk
(Toronto: Harlequin, 1991)

Story type: Historical/Renaissance
Major character(s): Bianca Stanford, Noblewoman; Robert Chandler, Privateer (former)
Time period(s): 16th century
Locale(s): England

Summary: To save her father from prison and rescue the family home, Lady Bianca Stanford marries ex-privateer Robert Chandler; and then they both set about rebuilding the crumbling estate. In the process, of course, mutual respect turns into love; but before they can really settle down to wedded bliss, they must deal with a series of villains and assorted troublemakers, largely from within their own families. Fast-paced, good historical detail, and intricately plotted.

Other books you might like:
Diane Wicker Davis, *Heart of the Falcon*, 1990
Jude Deveraux, *The Taming*, 1989
Roberta Gellis, *Roselynde*, 1978
    1st of the Roselynde Chronicles
Virginia Henley, *The Pirate and the Pagan*, 1990
Laurie McBain, *Chance the Winds of Fortune*, 1982

1958

LYNDA TRENT

Everlasting
(New York: Harper, 1991)

Story type: Saga
Major character(s): Amelia Radcliffe, Spinster; Electra Radcliffe, Designer (fashion)
Time period(s): 20th century (1920-1980s)
Locale(s): Willowbrook, Virginia; New York, New York

Summary: When the death of their father leaves them penniless, Amelia and Electra Radcliffe are forced to take radical measures to save their home, including Electra's literally selling herself to meet household expenses. Electra's flashy, materially successful, scandalous existence contrasts with Amelia's more mundane lifestyle; but eventually they both find love.

Other books you might like:
Leona Blair, *A World of Difference*, 1989
Sandra Bregman, *Reach for the Dream*, 1990
Virginia Coffman, *The Gaynor Women*, 1978
Belva Plain, *Evergreen*, 1978

1959

LYNDA TRENT

Follow Your Heart
(Toronto: Harlequin, 1992)

Story type: Contemporary
Major character(s): Amaris Channing, Psychic, Waiter/Waitress; Blake Mayfield, Political Figure (candidate), Businessman
Time period(s): 1990s
Locale(s): United States

Summary: Waitress Amaris Channing has psychic powers and her abilities intrigue Blake Mayfield, a wealthy politician. When she slips past his security to return his money clip and then abruptly disappears, he sets out to find her—only to discover that their deep-seated social class judgments keep them apart.

Other books you might like:
Caroline Bourne, *Allegheny Ecstasy*, 1990
Sandra Chastain, *Penthouse Suite*, 1990
Kathy Clark, *Sight Unseen*, 1990
Phyllis A. Whitney, *Rainbow in the Mist*, 1989

1960

LYNDA TRENT

Heaven's Embrace
(Toronto: Harlequin, 1990)

Story type: Historical/American West
Major character(s): Kate O'Connell, Religious (novice); Jess Darnell, Gunfighter, Lawman (ex-sheriff)
Time period(s): 1830s (1835)
Locale(s): Texas

Summary: When a holy relic is stolen by Salazar's murderous band of outlaws, the only survivor of the attack is novice Sister Mary Catherine (Kate). Aided by gunfighter Jess Darnell, who has his own score to settle with Salazar, Kate sets out to retrieve the relic and ends up putting her heart, as well as her life, in danger. Passion and adventure in the Old West.

Other books you might like:
Carol Finch, *Thunder's Tender Touch*, 1989
Catherine Hart, *Tempest*, 1991
Kathy Jones, *Sweet Obsession*, 1990
Catherine Lanigan, *A Promise Made*, 1991
Christine Monson, *Golden Nights*, 1990

1961

LYNDA TRENT

Rachel
(Toronto: Harlequin, 1992)

Story type: Historical/Victorian
Major character(s): Rachel Pennington, Spinster; Jared Prescott, Landowner
Time period(s): 1850s

Locale(s): England

Summary: Approaching spinsterhood, but determined to marry only for love, independent Rachel Pennington finds few eligible men to choose from until the mysterious, and somewhat reclusive, Jared Prescott moves into a nearby estate. He, Rachel decides, is The One—and nothing, not even a dictatorial father, a dark secret, or murder can keep her from achieving her goal. (Not that Jared minds, of course.) Well plotted with interesting characters.

Other books you might like:
Judith McNaught, *Almost Heaven*, 1990
Amanda Quick, *Rendezvous*, 1992
Amanda Quick, *Seduction*, 1990
Jeanne Savery, *The Last of the Winter Roses*, 1991
  Regency treatment
Marianne Willman, *Tilly and the Tiger*, 1990

1962

THOMAS TRYON

The Wings of the Morning
(New York: Fawcett, 1992)

Story type: Gothic
Major character(s): Georgiana Ross, Handicapped (mute)
Locale(s): Pequod Landing

Summary: Young, mute Georgiana Ross is a chief victim of the long-standing family feud between the farming Talcotts and the sea-faring Grimes. A gothic tale filled with dark family secrets, betrayals, and illicit passions. First of a series.

Other books you might like:
Rebecca Brandewyne, *Upon a Moon-Dark Moor*, 1988
Daphne Du Maurier, *Rebecca*, 1938
Philippa Gregory, *Wideacre*, 1987
  first of a trilogy
Susan Howatch, *Penmarric*, 1971
Elizabeth Kary, *Midnight Lace*, 1990

1963

JOY TUCKER

Traitor's Kiss
(New York: Avon, 1993)

Story type: Historical/Elizabethan
Major character(s): Lady Kat Preston, Noblewoman, Courtier (lady-in-waiting); Lord Robin Hawking, Nobleman, Agent (of Queen Elizabeth I)
Time period(s): 16th century
Locale(s): England

Summary: When Kat Preston, lady-in waiting to Queen Elizabeth, learns that a plot to free Mary Stuart may involve her home, she seeks out the Queen's agent, notorious rake Robin Hawking. Unfortunately, he misunderstands her presence in his rooms and he becomes infatuated with Kat, arousing the jealousy of the Queen and causing all kinds of potentially deadly problems for Kat. Lots of action and intrigue.

Other books you might like:
Sandra Davidson, *Rosefire*, 1992
Karen Harper, *Passion's Reign*, 1992
Betina M. Krahn, *Behind Closed Doors*, 1991
Suzanne Robinson, *Lady Defiant*, 1992
Erin Yorke, *Heaven's Gate*, 1992

1964

ELIZABETH TURNER

Midnight Rain
(New York: Avon, 1994)

Story type: Historical/American West
Major character(s): Alana Fairchild, Singer (saloon); Trey Matthews, Railroad Worker
Time period(s): 1880s (1886)
Locale(s): San Diego, California

Summary: Alana and Trey's relationship is anything but peaceful as they fight, separate, reconcile, and love. Trey is seeking vengeance for his brother's death and he suspects Alana. This does, of course, put a strain on them both, but they eventually discover the truth and all works out in the end. Love and hate in early California.

Other books you might like:
JoAnn De Lazzari, *Scoundrel's Desire*, 1993
  early California
Christina Dodd, *Treasure of the Sun*, 1991
  early California/good historical detail
Robin Lee Hatcher, *Midnight Rose*, 1991
Janis Reams Hudson, *Apache Legend*, 1994
  revenge-driven hero
Linda Madl, *Sunny*, 1990
  revenge elements

1965

TERRI VALENTINE

Master of Her Heart
(New York: Zebra, 1990)

Story type: Historical/American West Coast
Major character(s): Garnet Sinclair, Teacher (in China), Captive (of white slave traders); Bain Carson, Twin (of dead slave-trading brother)
Time period(s): 1870s
Locale(s): San Francisco, California; China; England

Summary: When Garnet Sinclair tries to save her students from the white slave traders, she is kidnapped in their stead and suddenly finds herself aboard ship, headed for the auction blocks of San Francisco. She is rescued by Bain Carson (posing as his dead, slave-trading brother, Drew) who buys her to help him communicate with his half-Asian niece; but the deception Bain has begun creates all sorts of problems when he and Garnet fall in love with each other.

Other books you might like:
Rene J. Garrod, *Temptation's Wild Embrace*, 1990
  same locale and time period
Patricia Potter, *Dragonfire*, 1990

Janelle Taylor, *Kiss of the Night Wind*, 1989
JoAnn Wendt, *The Golden Dove*, 1989

1966

TERRI VALENTINE

Outlaw's Kiss

(New York: Zebra, 1991)

Story type: Historical/American West
Major character(s): Serra Paletot, Orphan, Imposter ("Serenity Langston"); Tyler Ramsey, Orphan
Time period(s): 1880s
Locale(s): Joplin, Missouri; New York, New York

Summary: Convinced by means of hypnotic suggestion that she is actually the long lost daughter of John Langston, orphaned Serra is on her way to meet her father when she is rudely abducted by Tyler Ramsey, an old childhood friend, who is out to prove that "Serenity" is an imposter. Love comes to Ty and Serra, but not before Serra confronts her past and a villain's schemes are foiled. Gentle and moving.

Other books you might like:
Elaine Barbieri, *Wings of a Dove*, 1990
Rexanne Becnel, *Thief of My Heart*, 1991
Kat Martin, *Lover's Gold*, 1991
Linda Lael Miller, *Lily and the Major*, 1990
Robin LeAnne Wiete, *Fortune's Lady*, 1990

1967

TERRI VALENTINE

Sands of Time

(New York: Zebra, 1992)

Story type: Time Travel
Major character(s): Chelsea Browne, Doctor; Khalil, Ruler (sheikh)
Time period(s): 1990s; 15th century (1490s)
Locale(s): Saudi Arabia

Summary: Dr. Chelsea Browne, clinic-worker in Saudi Arabia, must go to save a Sheikh's life. A sandstorm takes them back 500 years and although 1990 presents cultural differences, 1490 is impossible! Independent Chelsea and arrogant Khalil struggle with their roles, time change, and their growing love. Enemies don't help. A realistic look at cultural differences.

Other books you might like:
Iris Johansen, *The Golden Barbarian*, 1991
Vivian Knight-Jenkins, *Love's Timeless Dance*, 1993
　Scottish setting
JoAnne Redd, *Desert Bride*, 1989
　no time travel elements
Susan Sizemore, *Wings of the Storm*, 1992
Shelly Thacker, *Forever His*, 1993
　French medieval setting

1968

TERRI VALENTINE

Sweet Paradise

(Toronto: Harlequin, 1992)

Story type: Historical/Exotic
Major character(s): Cray Branson, Photographer; Reba Van Hausen, Activist (conservationist)
Locale(s): Africa

Summary: Reba abhors the hunters who invade her African paradise and is suspicious of Cray's government photography mission. Their safari proves to be a dangerous journey as someone tries to destroy Cray's work and spread seeds of mistrust among the company. As Reba and Cray learn to respect each other, their love grows, but it is ultimately threatened by a devastating revelation that may separate them forever. Passion and intrigue in an exotic setting.

Other books you might like:
Jillian Hunter, *Tiger Dance*, 1991
Catherine Palmer, *The Burning Plains*, 1988
Catherine Palmer, *Land of Enchantment*, 1991
Mike Resnick, *Ivory: A Legend of Past and Future*, 1988
Frances Williams, *The Road to Forever*, 1991

1969

TERRI VALENTINE

Yankee's Caress

(New York: Zebra, 1989)

Story type: Historical/American Civil War
Major character(s): Danica "Danni" Navarro, Widow(er) (Southerner), Store Owner; Fox McClure, Spy, Yankee
Time period(s): 1860s (1862)
Locale(s): Vicksburg, Mississippi

Summary: Rescued from a runaway wagon by a daring stranger, Danica is surprised to learn he is a Yankee spy. He is tried for murder and she is subjected to town censure; but love has a way of making things turn out right in the end.

Other books you might like:
Kathryn Kramer, *Destiny and Desire*, 1988
Robin Maderich, *Faith and Honor*, 1989
　American Revolution
Maura Seger, *Perchance to Dream*, 1989
　The South wins the war
Janelle Taylor, *Destiny's Temptation*, 1986
Kathleen E. Woodiwiss, *Ashes in the Wind*, 1979

1970

JOAN VAN NUYS

Beloved Avenger

(New York: Avon, 1989)

Story type: Historical/Post-American Revolution
Major character(s): Fairburn, Heiress, Fiance(e) (of hero's enemy); Lucien Thorne, Pirate (former ship's captain)
Time period(s): 1780s

Locale(s): At Sea; England; United States

Summary: When Lucien inadvertently captures Sarina Fairburn, the intended bride of the man who killed his brother and ruined his name, he vows vengeance—but finds love instead.

Other books you might like:
Kathryn Davenport, *Pirate's Mistress*, 1989
Heather Graham, *A Pirate's Pleasure*, 1989
Jean Innes, *Buccaneer's Bride*, 1989
Laurie McBain, *Moonstruck Madness*, 1977
   1st of a trilogy
Kathleen E. Woodiwiss, *Shanna*, 1977

1971
JOAN VAN NUYS
Beloved Intruder
(New York: Avon, 1992)

Story type: Historical/Post-American Revolution
Major character(s): Hope Caldwell, Doctor, Teacher; Firewalker, Indian (Delaware chief)
Time period(s): 18th century (1774-1788)
Locale(s): Pennsylvania

Summary: To escape vicious gossip, Hope and her doctor father move to the Pennsylvania frontier and practice their medical skills among the Indians and settlers. As she works more and more closely with the Delawares, they come to trust and respect her and when a treacherous fur trader tries to stir things up and sell her to the Iroquois, Firewalker, the next chief, comes to her rescue. Complex picture of life along the Colonial frontier.

Other books you might like:
Kate Cameron, *Orenda*, 1992
Charles Durham, *Walk in the Light*, 1992
   mainstream
Judith E. French, *Moon Dancer*, 1991
Judith E. French, *Moonfeather*, 1990

1972
JOAN VAN NUYS
Unwilling Betrayer
(New York: Leisure, 1992)

Story type: Historical/Medieval
Major character(s): Brianna Kinrade, Noblewoman (Irish), Spy; Wulf Thorsson, Nobleman (Norwegian), Military Personnel
Time period(s): 11th century (1013)
Locale(s): Ireland

Summary: On a secret mission from her foster father, High King Brian Boru, to the Viking stronghold, Irish noblewoman Brianna Kinrade is first mistaken for a slave and then rescued by Norwegian Wulf Thorsson, the leader of the Viking army. Realizing she is suddenly in a perfect position to spy for Ireland, Brianna remains with Wulf, enmeshing herself in not only a tangled political intrigue but a passionate relationship with Wulf, as well. Fast-paced and filled with historical detail.

Other books you might like:
Linda Lang Bartell, *Brianna*, 1986
Heather Graham, *The Viking's Woman*, 1990
Mary Ellen Gronau, *Gentle Conqueror*, 1989
Johanna Lindsey, *Fires of Winter*, 1980
Katherine Vickery, *Flame Across the Highlands*, 1990

1973
LINDA VARNER
As Sweet as Candy
(New York: Silhouette, 1992)

Story type: Contemporary/Innocent
Major character(s): Jenny Robbins, Child-Care Giver (manager); Ben Ryder, Veterinarian
Time period(s): 1990s
Locale(s): United States

Summary: Jenny and Ben team up to baby-sit his niece, and *she* sets out to bring the two together. Not an easy task since Ben is rather set in his ways and has his life all planned out, and Jenny is a take-charge kind of manager. But with the help of his "angelic" niece, the pair find they have a lot in common, including love.

Other books you might like:
Marie Ferrarella, *Man Trouble*, 1991
Debbie Macomber, *First Comes Marriage*, 1991
Debbie Macomber, *Rainy Day Kisses*, 1990
Helen R. Myers, *Three Little Chaperones*, 1992
Nora Roberts, *Courting Catherine*, 1991

1974
VIVIAN VAUGHN
Silver Surrender
(New York: Zebra, 1992)

Story type: Historical/American West
Series: Jarret Family
Major character(s): Aurelia Mazon, Young Woman, Thief (train robber); Carson Jarret, Lawman (Texas Ranger)
Time period(s): 19th century
Locale(s): Mexico

Summary: Lovely, wealthy Aurelia wants to escape to the city, but when her train-robbing antics land a handsome American in jail, she helps him escape — and then falls in love with him. Unfortunately, her family has chosen someone else for her — a cold, hard mine-owner who causes no end of problems for them both. Nevertheless, they persevere and all is well by the end of the story. A sensual, fast-paced romance.

Other books you might like:
Linda Ladd, *Midnight Fire*, 1991
Gina Robins, *Deception's Sweet Kiss*, 1990
Judith Steel, *Seduction's Raging Flame*, 1989
Rochelle Wayne, *Nevada Flame*, 1992

1975
VIVIAN VAUGHN

Texas Gamble
(New York: Zebra, 1990)

Story type: Historical/American West
Major character(s): Serita Cortivas, Landowner; Giddeon Duval, Sea Captain
Time period(s): 1830s (1839)
Locale(s): Texas

Summary: When Serita's father "loses" her in a card game to Giddeon Duval, they marry each other reluctantly—each wanting something the other has. But they don't count on falling in love. Lots of Texas history.

Other books you might like:
Barbara Bretton, *Midnight Lover*, 1989
Ann Gabriel, *South Texas*, 1990
    Somewhat mainstream
Martha Hix, *Wild Texas Rose*, 1990
Kay McMahon, *Bandit's Brazen Kiss*, 1990
Victoria Thompson, *Bold Texas Embrace*, 1989

1976
LISA ANN VERGE

The Heart's Disguise
(New York: Popular Library, 1990)

Story type: Historical/Seventeenth Century
Major character(s): Adriana Joubet, Imposter (Poses as a cabin boy), Sailor; Roarke Cameron, Pirate ("Sea Wolf")
Time period(s): 17th century (1690s)
Locale(s): At Sea; Carolinas, American Colonies

Summary: Dressed as a boy from birth, Adriana does what all men of St. Malo do, she becomes a sailor. Her secret is safe until she sails with Roarke Cameron, the infamous Sea Wolf. Betrayal, love, and revenge are part of this fast-paced adventure.

Other books you might like:
Catherine Coulter, *Night Storm*, 1990
    Third in "Night" trilogy
Heather Graham, *A Pirate's Pleasure*, 1989
Jean Innes, *Buccaneer's Bride*, 1989
Joan Van Nuys, *Beloved Avenger*, 1989
Kathleen E. Woodiwiss, *Shanna*, 1977

1977
LISA ANN VERGE

Sweet Harvest
(Bensalem, Pennsylvania: Meteor, 1992)

Story type: Contemporary
Major character(s): Amanda Karlson, Vintner; Garrick Kane, Businessman (winery owner)
Time period(s): 1990s
Locale(s): Napa Valley, California

Summary: When Amanda Karlson accepts the job as head winemaker at a Napa Valley winery, she is determined to keep things strictly on a business basis with her handsome boss, Garrick Kane. Garrick, however, has other ideas and bit by bit he convinces Amanda that sometimes business and pleasure do mix. Good characterizations and interesting winemaking details.

Other books you might like:
Sally Falcon, *Stolen Kisses*, 1992
Theresa Gladden, *Just Desserts*, 1991
Shirl Henke, *Summer Has No Name*, 1990
Judith McNaught, *Double Standards*, 1984
Danielle Steel, *Thurston House*, 1983
    historical Napa Valley

1978
PATRICIA VERYAN

Ask Me No Questions
(New York: St. Martin's, 1993)

Story type: Historical/Georgian
Series: Tales of the Jewelled Men
Major character(s): Ruth Allington, Widow(er), Artist; Gordon Chandler, Heir
Time period(s): 1740s
Locale(s): England

Summary: Another in Veryan's romantic adventure series Tales of the Jewelled Men. This time Gideon Rossiter and company save Gordon Chandler's lovely estate, Lac Brilliant, from falling into the hands of the infamous Jewelled Men despite a series of deceptions, treacheries, and assorted plots. Complex and romantic.

Other books you might like:
Mary Kingsley, *The Rake's Reward*, 1991
Joan Overfield, *Bride's Leap*, 1991
Marlene Suson, *Devil's Bargain*, 1992
Winifred Witton, *The Denville Diamond*, 1991

1979
PATRICIA VERYAN

Had We Never Loved
(New York: St. Martin's, 1992)

Story type: Historical/Georgian
Series: Tales of the Jewelled Men
Major character(s): Horatio Clement Laindon, Nobleman (Viscount Glendenning); Amy Consett, Gypsy
Time period(s): 18th century
Locale(s): England; Scotland

Summary: When his family is accused of supporting the Stuart cause, Horatio Laindon begins a search for the one thing that will save them, a missing heirloom pin. Fast-paced action, a charming Gypsy heroine, and a memorable love story combine in this romantic adventure laced with political intrigue and conspiracy.

Other books you might like:
Georgette Heyer, *The Masqueraders*, 1928

Pamela Hill, *The Malvie Inheritance*, 1973
Catherine Linden, *Highland Flame*, 1991
    Renaissance political intrigue
Jean Saunders, *Scarlet Rebel*, 1984
Daisy Vivian, *Rose White, Rose Red*, 1986

1980

PATRICIA VERYAN

Logic of the Heart
(New York: Fawcett, 1991)

Story type: Regency
Major character(s): Susan Henley, Widow(er); Valentine
    Montclair, Gentleman
Time period(s): 1810s
Locale(s): England

Summary: Inheritances, unscrupulous relatives, thieves, and
all sorts of skulduggery are part of this delightful Regency in
which two people lay claim to the same cottage and find that
they have more in common than just a piece of real estate.
Interesting characters, lively action, and charming dialogue.

Other books you might like:
Marian Devon, *Miss Osborne Misbehaves*, 1990
June Drummond, *The Bluestocking*, 1986
Rosemary Edghill, *The Ill-Bred Bride*, 1990
Annabel Laine, *The Reluctant Heiress*, 1978
Sheila Simonson, *A Cousinly Connexion*, 1984

1981

KATHERINE VICKERY

Desire of the Heart
(New York: Pocket, 1990)

Story type: Historical/Medieval
Major character(s): Kendra, Noblewoman (impoverished);
    Geoffrey de Bron, Nobleman, Religious
Time period(s): 12th century (1162)
Locale(s): England

Summary: Grieving over the death of her sister, Saxon noblewoman Kendra attacks the man responsible, cruel Norman
Reynard de Bron. However, her spirit and beauty attracts his
brother, Geoffrey, who saves her from death by asking that
she be given to him. Their attraction for each other flares into
love—a love complicated by the fact that he is a cleric and,
therefore, is not free to marry. However, love eventually finds
a way in this vivid depiction of the brutality, intrigue, and
romance that were a part of Henry II's England.

Other books you might like:
Cecelia Holland, *The Earl*, 1971
Brenda Joyce, *The Conqueror*, 1991
    sweet savage elements
Miriam Minger, *Captive Rose*, 1991
Flora M. Speer, *Castle of Dreams*, 1990
Flora M. Speer, *Castle of the Heart*, 1990

1982

KATHERINE VICKERY

Flame Across the Highlands
(New York: Pocket, 1990)

Story type: Historical/Medieval
Major character(s): Brianna Nic Lachlan, Noblewoman (of the
    Clan MacQuarie); Ian Mac Niall, Warrior (of the Clan
    Campbell)
Time period(s): 14th century
Locale(s): Scotland

Summary: The ancient rivalry between the clans MacQuarie
and Campbell result in a twisted plan of revenge that
inadvertently brings Brianna and Ian together and forces them
to fight for their lives and their love.

Other books you might like:
Linda Lang Bartell, *Brianna*, 1986
Rebecca Brandewyne, *Forever My Love*, 1982
Jude Deveraux, *Highland Velvet*, 1982
Julie Garwood, *The Bride*, 1989
Johanna Lindsey, *A Gentle Feuding*, 1984

1983

LYNETTE VINET

Knight's Caress
(New York: Zebra, 1993)

Story type: Historical/Medieval
Major character(s): Amberlie de Fontaine, Widow(er), Noble-
    woman; Tedric of Woodrose, Nobleman
Time period(s): 11th century (1067)
Locale(s): England

Summary: Bent on revenge for his father's death, Tedrick
kidnaps the Lady Amberlie intending to hold her for ransom
but instead he ends up simply holding her! She knows she
shouldn't respond to him because he is the enemy, after all;
but politics proves less strong than love and when King William decrees their marriage, it just might be the solution to
their problems.

Other books you might like:
Rexanne Becnel, *A Dove at Midnight*, 1993
Catherine Coulter, *Earth Song*, 1990
Tanya Anne Crosby, *Angel of Fire*, 1992
Jude Deveraux, *The Taming*, 1989
Julie Garwood, *The Prize*, 1991

1984

LYNETTE VINET

Pirate's Bride
(New York: Zebra, 1989)

Story type: Historical/American Revolution
Major character(s): Bethlyn Talbot, Spouse (Abandoned); Ian
    ''Hawk'' Bristol, Pirate
Time period(s): 1770s (1777)
Locale(s): At Sea (High seas, sailing for America)

Summary: Bound by the terms of his mother's will, Ian Bristol marries his stepsister, Bethlyn; then he deserts his bride and sails for America. On her way to find him, Bethlyn's ship is attacked by the pirate Hawk; and she discovers love, adventure, a cause to fight for, and a new side to her husband.

Other books you might like:
Kathryn Davenport, *Pirate's Mistress*, 1989
Heather Graham, *A Pirate's Pleasure*, 1989
   North American Woman 2
Betina M. Krahn, *Passion's Ransom*, 1989
Valerie Sherwood, *This Loving Torment*, 1977
Kathleen E. Woodiwiss, *Shanna*, 1989

1985

LYNETTE VINET

Wild, Wicked Eden

(New York: Zebra, 1990)

Story type: Historical/Exotic; Historical/Victorian
Major character(s): Eden Flynn, Widow(er), Mine Owner; Damon Alexander, Mine Owner
Time period(s): 1870s
Locale(s): Queenstown, New Zealand

Summary: Eden Flynn honors her husband's dying wish and heads to New Zealand to take over his share of a gold mine and runs right into trouble in the form of Damon Alexander, her husband's nephew and partner. Naturally, they fall in love; but Damon's distrust of women (aided by strategic comments from his rival) and the reappearance of a vindictive wife, make Eden's and Damon's path to happiness anything but easy.

Other books you might like:
Barbara Bretton, *Midnight Lover*, 1989
Georgina Gentry, *Nevada Nights*, 1989
Meagan McKinney, *Till Dawn Tames the Night*, 1991
Leslie O'Grady, *Seek the Wild Shore*, 1989
Laura Simon, *A Taste of Heaven*, 1989

1986

TINA WAINSCOTT

On the Way to Heaven

(New York: St. Martin's, 1995)

Story type: Contemporary; Reincarnation
Major character(s): Chris Copestakes, Student, Reincarnated Person; Jamie DiBarto, Businessman (resort owner)
Time period(s): 1990s
Locale(s): California; Constantine, Jamaica

Summary: Chris Copestakes thinks she has died only to discover she has been given a second chance at life—in someone else's body! She awakes to find she is inhabiting the body of the selfish and beautiful socialite wife of Jamie DiBarto. Chris has to do some quick thinking in an unfamiliar world in order to keep her "new" husband and find the person who had originally killed her. Tender, emotional, and with a dash of humor. Golden Heart winner. First novel.

Other books you might like:
Margot Dalton, *Angels in the Light*, 1993
Margot Dalton, *Tangled Lives*, 1996
   similar theme/no paranormal elements
Linda Renee De Jong, *Shattered Illusions*, 1992
   similar theme/no paranormal elements
Kristin Hannah, *Once in Every Life*, 1993
   emotional/reincarnation theme
Maggie Shayne, *Kiss of the Shadow Man*, 1994
   similar theme/no paranormal elements

1987

CONSTANCE WALKER

One Perfect Springtime

(New York: Avalon, 1989)

Story type: Contemporary/Innocent
Major character(s): Jennifer Lowell, Photojournalist; Jason King, Principal (assistant)
Time period(s): 1980s
Locale(s): Midwest (near Chicago)

Summary: Photojournalist Jennie Lowell and high school assistant principal Jason King are attracted to each other from their first meeting. But when Jennie wants to do a controversial story on several of Jason's students, it threatens their relationship.

Other books you might like:
Lynn Bulock, *Roses for Caroline*, 1987
Jane McBride Choate, *Badge of Love*, 1989
Lynda Stowe Landers, *A Season to Remember*, 1989
Kathleen Gilles Seidel, *Maybe This Time*, 1990
Peggy Webb, *Harvey's Missing*, 1990

1988

MARGIE WALKER

Breathless

(New York: Pinnacle, 1995)

Story type: Contemporary; Ethnic
Major character(s): Monique Robbins, Businesswoman (nightclub owner); Solomon Thomas, Businessman (nightclub manager)
Time period(s): 1990s
Locale(s): United States

Summary: In spite of the fact that Monique Robbins doesn't want a man running her club, that's exactly what she gets. And not only does Solomon Thomas agree to manage T's Place, but he demands total control. The fireworks are set to go off when these two are forced to deal not only with their business relationship, but their growing personal feelings for each other, as well. A threat from Monique's past provides a bit of suspense in this fast-paced romance.

Other books you might like:
Bette Ford, *Forever After*, 1995
Gwynne Forster, *Sealed with a Kiss*, 1995
Sandra Kitt, *Serenade*, 1994
   gentler pacing

Francis Ray, *Forever Yours*, 1994

1989

SHEILA WALSH

The Arrogant Lord Alistair
(New York: Signet 1990)

Story type: Regency
Major character(s): Charity Wyngate, Gentlewoman (impoverished), Guardian; Lord Alistair, Nobleman
Time period(s): 1810s
Locale(s): England

Summary: When Charity Wyngate asks the Duke of Orme to help his newly orphaned grandchildren (Charity's niece and nephew), both the Duke and his son, Lord Alistair, assume she is a fortune hunter. Nevertheless, the Duke agrees to help, but only if Charity reliquishes custody and agrees never to see the children again. Reluctantly, Charity agrees; but as her love and concern for the children become obvious, the attitudes of the men change and Lord Alistair begins to see her in a totally different light.

Other books you might like:
Carola Dunn, *Lavender Lady*, 1985
Georgette Heyer, *Frederica*, 1965
Judith Nelson, *Patience Is a Virtue*, 1989
Amanda Scott, *The Dauntless Miss Wingrave*, 1989
Sheila Simonson, *The Bar Sinister*, 1986

1990

REBECCA WARD (Pseudonym of Maureen Wartski)

Wild Rose
(New York: Fawcett, 1993)

Story type: Regency
Major character(s): Rosamund St. Helm, Debutante (Canadian); Julian Dane, Nobleman (Earl of Hawkley)
Time period(s): 1810s
Locale(s): England

Summary: Canadian-raised Rosa St. Helm returns to London society after her parents' deaths, but her western upbringing is too bold and democratic for the ton, so her brother asks Julian to keep an eye on Rosa and her Canadian friend, Lucy. Julian obliges, but he has a hard time understanding her unconventional ideas, particularly her need to protect three Mohawk Indians, whom she ends up making the hit of the Season! Eventually, of course, Rosa and Julian discover each other, and, despite vast differences love does triumph over all.

Other books you might like:
Roberta Eckert, *Heir to Vengeance*, 1990
Sheila O'Hallion, *American Princess*, 1989
　　later time period
Carol Proctor, *Unlikely Guardian*, 1990
Mary Linn Roby, *My Lady's Mask*, 1979

1991

CIJI WARE

Wicked Company
(New York: Bantam, 1992)

Story type: Historical/Mainstream; Saga
Major character(s): Sophie McGann, Writer, Printer (Of playbills)
Time period(s): 18th century
Locale(s): England; Scotland

Summary: This lavish tale of the 18th century English theatre world focuses on the volatile life of writer Sophie McGann and the men who seek to help her, use her, and love her as she struggles for happiness and recognition in a time when the talents of women were often overlooked. Sweeping, realistic, and dramatic.

Other books you might like:
Elizabeth Buchan, *Daughters of the Storm*, 1988
Colleen Faulkner, *Sweet Deception*, 1992
Rosalind Laker, *Tree of Gold*, 1986
Rosalind Laker, *The Silver Touch*, 1987
Martha Rofheart, *The Savage Brood*, 1978
　　Five century Theatre Saga

1992

TERESA WARFIELD

Cherokee Bride
(New York: Diamond, 1994)

Story type: Historical/American West
Major character(s): Danagasta, Indian (Cherokee), Royalty (chief's daughter); Grant Claiborne, Government Official (Indian Affairs agent)
Time period(s): 1800s (1807-1809)
Locale(s): Big Water, Tennessee; Baltimore, Maryland

Summary: Danagasta suspects Indian agent Grant Claiborne of being a supplier of whiskey to her tribe and takes him prisoner after she rescues him from drowning. Actually, he's there to help the tribe adapt to moving, and when Danagasta is ordered to care for him, she bitterly takes her revenge and tricks him into marriage. Passion lends a hand and everything does work out eventually. Highly sensual.

Other books you might like:
Genell Dellin, *Cherokee Dawn*, 1990
　　Cherokee Nation Series — 1
Genell Dellin, *Cherokee Nights*, 1991
　　Cherokee Nation Series — 2
Genell Dellin, *Cherokee Sundown*, 1992
　　Cherokee Nation Series — 3
Deborah Smith, *Beloved Woman*, 1991
　　well-done story of Cherokee Removal/ totally different feel

1993

PAT WARREN

Bright Hopes

(Toronto: Harlequin, 1992)

Story type: Contemporary
Series: Tyler
Major character(s): Pam Casals, Coach (high school football), Handicapped (multiple sclerosis); Patrick Kelsey, Coach (high school basketball)
Time period(s): 1990s
Locale(s): Tyler, Wisconsin

Summary: With her MS in temporary remission, former Olympic medalist Pam Casals comes to Tyler to coach the high school football team and runs headlong into opposition from the basketball coach, attractive Patrick Kelsey. Of course, she also runs into love at the same time — and then must confront the complications that her new-found relationship brings to her life. Second in the projected 12 book series set in the small Midwestern town of Tyler.

Other books you might like:
Molly Rice, *Chance Encounter*, 1992
Doreen Roberts, *Broken Wings*, 1992
Sandra Steffen, *Hold Back the Night*, 1992
Rebecca Winters, *The Marriage Bracelet*, 1992

1994

PAT WARREN

The Long Road Home

(New York: Silhouette, 1989)

Story type: Contemporary
Major character(s): Carrie McKamey Weston, Artist (landscape); Brock Logan, Businessman
Time period(s): 1980s
Locale(s): Carmel, California

Summary: Brock comes to Carmel to find his boss's daughter and reunite her with her father. But Carrie wants only to be left alone to paint and to raise her seven-year-old son. Love, however, has a way of changing things.

Other books you might like:
Janet Dailey, *Terms of Surrender*, 1982
Anne Lacey, *Rapture Deep*, 1988
    Silhouette Special Editions
Anne McCaffrey, *Stitch-in-Snow*, 1984
Victoria Pade, *Twice Shy*, 1989
    Silhouette Special Editions
Danielle Steel, *Palomino*, 1981

1995

PAT WARREN

Nowhere to Run

(New York: Zebra, 1993)

Story type: Romantic Suspense

Major character(s): Carly Weston, Socialite; Sam English, Detective, Police Officer
Time period(s): 1990s
Locale(s): Detroit, Michigan

Summary: After Carly Weston's wealthy father is murdered by a serial killer, detective Sam English must outthink the deranged man who has targeted Carly as his next victim.

Other books you might like:
Deborah Nicholas, *Night Vision*, 1993
Nora Roberts, *Divine Evil*, 1992
Tracey Tillis, *Deadly Masquerade*, 1994
Rebecca York, *What Child Is This?*, 1993

1996

PATRICIA WATTERS

Come Be My Love

(New York: Avon, 1993)

Story type: Historical/Canadian West
Major character(s): Sarah Ashley, Suffragette, Businesswoman; Jon Cromwell, Widow(er), Political Figure (governor)
Time period(s): 1860s (1863)
Locale(s): Vancouver, British Columbia, Canada

Summary: Businesswoman Sarah Ashley begins to think Vancouver isn't the best place to sell her new line of progressive women's wear. Everyone is conspiring against her and the arrogant governor, Jon Cromwell is leading the attack. Nevertheless, she endures and even converts the governor's daughter; but the violence and hatred are almost her undoing. Even her stepbrothers are involved. Eventually, of course, Jon "sees the light," risking his office and reputation, as well as his heart, in a lively, accurate story of the Northwestern frontier.

Other books you might like:
Sonya Birmingham, *Spitfire*, 1991
Deborah Camp, *My Wild Rose*, 1992
Debra Dier, *Surrender the Dream*, 1993
Linda Howard, *Angel Creek*, 1991

1997

ROCHELLE WAYNE

Nevada Flame

(New York: Zebra, 1992)

Story type: Historical/American West
Major character(s): Laura Mills, Fugitive; Craig Branston, Bounty Hunter (former)
Time period(s): 1880s
Locale(s): Death Valley, California; West

Summary: Laura Mills has problems — her father died, her brother took off, her mother is losing the ranch, and she is wanted for murder! Naturally, she isn't guilty, but that doesn't stop bounty hunters from coming after her. Craig Branston, who has been hired to find her, saves her and together they head for Death Valley to look for her brother. Several other love stories add to this action-filled romance.

Other books you might like:
Barbara Ankrum, *Renegade Bride*, 1992
Madeline Baker, *Prairie Heat*, 1991
Rebecca Sinclair, *Forbidden Desires*, 1992
Vivian Vaughn, *Silver Surrender*, 1992

1998
PEGGY WEBB

Witch Dance
(New York: Bantam, 1994)

Story type: Contemporary; Romantic Suspense
Major character(s): Kate Malone, Doctor; Eagle Mingo, Indian (Chickasaw), Chieftain (of the tribe)
Time period(s): 1990s
Locale(s): Chickasaw Tribal Lands, Oklahoma

Summary: Talented Dr. Kate Malone goes to the Chickasaw Tribal Lands in Oklahoma to practice medicine, determined to make a difference. What she finds, however, is hostility, wariness, and true danger as she fights to bring healing to the people and keep from getting killed in the process. A passionate story filled with Chickasaw lore and magnetic characters.

Other books you might like:
Janet Dailey, *Night Way*, 1981
Kathleen Eagle, *Heaven and Earth*, 1990
   historical
Kathleen Eagle, *This Time Forever*, 1992
Rachel Lee, *Thunder Mountain*, 1994
Deborah Smith, *Beloved Woman*, 1991

1999
THERESA WEIR

Iguana Bay
(New York: Silhouette, 1990)

Story type: Contemporary
Major character(s): Elisa Ramsey, Teacher; Dylan Davis, Police Officer (former)
Time period(s): 1990s
Locale(s): Iguana Bay, Florida

Summary: Driven by vengeance, ex-cop Dylan Davis kidnaps the one person who can provide the man who killed his girlfriend with an alibi, Elisa Ramsey, a young, naive school teacher. Fast-paced action and good characterization in this captive-in-love-with-captor tale.

Other books you might like:
Jill Barkin, *Hot Streak*, 1990
Janet Dailey, *Masquerade*, 1990
Carol Jerina, *Flirting with Danger*, 1990
Marcia Martin, *Southern Nights*, 1990
Sherryl Woods, *Body and Soul*, 1989

2000
JOANN WENDT

Beyond the Savage Sea
(New York: Warner, 1990)

Story type: Historical/Seventeenth Century
Series: Lovestruck
Major character(s): Edwinna Crawford, Plantation Owner; Drake Steel, Businessman (wine merchant)
Time period(s): 17th century (1659)
Locale(s): Barbados; England

Summary: In order to save her sugar plantation from her scheming uncle, Edwinna must marry within 24 hours. Her unlikely choice is an English wine merchant about to be executed for piracy. The resulting marriage of convenience is anything but convenient; but as their friendship grows, so does their love—despite tragic violence, changing political conditions, and a reappearing first wife.

Other books you might like:
Pamela Belle, *Alethea*, 1985
Barbara Bretton, *Midnight Lover*, 1989
   reluctant partners theme
Edith Layton, *Fireflower*, 1989
Laura Simon, *A Taste of Heaven*, 1989
   reluctant partners theme/Caribbean setting
Kathleen E. Woodiwiss, *Shanna*, 1977

2001
JOANN WENDT

The Golden Dove
(New York: Warner, 1989)

Story type: Historical/Seventeenth Century
Major character(s): Jericho Jones, Slave, Teacher; Lord Dove DuMont, Nobleman (younger son; royalist)
Time period(s): 17th century (1660s)
Locale(s): England; American Colonies

Summary: Taken from her mother as a baby and sold as a bondslave, Jericho is eventually won in a dice game at the awkward age of eleven by British Lord Dove DuMont—an event that changes both their lives. Adventure, passion, and political intrigue all set against the background of Colonial America and Restoration England.

Other books you might like:
Pamela Belle, *Alethea*, 1985
Philippa Carr, *Lament for a Lost Lover*, 1977
   More serious Restoration romance
Kimberly Cates, *Crown of Mist*, 1988
Jane Feather, *Reckless Angel*, 1989
   Similar time period
Edith Layton, *Fireflower*, 1989

2002
SALLY WENTWORTH
Strange Encounter
(Toronto: Harlequin, 1990)

Story type: Contemporary
Major character(s): Kelly Baxter, Orphan; Byron Thorne, Steward
Time period(s): 1980s
Locale(s): England

Summary: Recovering from the death of her parents, Kelly Baxter goes to Ashdon Hall, her cousin's English estate, and finds mystery, romance, and love.

Other books you might like:
Barbara Michaels, *Be Buried in the Rain*, 1985
Elisabeth Ogilvie, *Bellwood*, 1967
Mary Stewart, *The Ivy Tree*, 1961
Phyllis A. Whitney, *Silverhill*, 1967
Phyllis A. Whitney, *Silversword*, 1987

2003
PATRICIA WERNER
Cherokee Bride
(New York: Zebra, 1992)

Story type: Historical/American West
Major character(s): Kit Newcomb, Young Woman; Red Hawk, Indian (Cherokee)
Time period(s): 1820s (1829)
Locale(s): Washington, District of Columbia; Georgia

Summary: Kit Newcomb's trip to Washington gives her a chance to work with some important and influential people; she also gets to know Red Hawk, a Cherokee who is pleading for government help in keeping his tribe's lands in Georgia. Despite her father's wishes and deep hatred of Indians in general, Kit continues to see Red Hawk and their love blossoms. The Cherokee Tragedy, of course, overshadows their relationship, but they continue to fight and their strength and courage make their relationship last.

Other books you might like:
Rosanne Bittner, *Sioux Splendor*, 1990
Genell Dellin, *Cherokee Sundown*, 1992
Constance O'Banyon, *Cheyenne Sunrise*, 1990
Deborah Smith, *Beloved Woman*, 1991

2004
JENNIFER WEST
Passion's Legacy
(Toronto: Harlequin, 1991)

Story type: Historical/Georgian; Historical/Exotic
Major character(s): Melissa Danfort, Noblewoman (granddaughter of a Duke); Brandon De Forrest, Nobleman (disenfranchised), Shipowner (shipping company owner)
Time period(s): 1730s (1735)
Locale(s): England; India

Summary: In a fast-paced adventure that sweeps from England to India and back again, Melissa and Brandon must deal with treachery, greed, and violence before they can realize their love.

Other books you might like:
Sandra DuBay, *Nightrider*, 1991
Christine Monson, *This Fiery Splendor*, 1991
  earlier time period
Patricia Rice, *Moon Dreams*, 1991
Karen Stratford, *Lavender Flame*, 1991

2005
MARGARET WESTHAVEN (Pseudonym of Peggy M. Hansen)
Country Dance
(New York: Signet, 1991)

Story type: Regency
Major character(s): Marianna Chapin, Dancer, Gentlewoman; Henry Duke, Gentleman
Time period(s): 1810s
Locale(s): Dorset, England

Summary: Considered ineligible for the *ton* marriage mart because of her past, Marianna Chapin surprises everyone, including herself and her less-than-kind stepmother, by charming the dashing and sophisticated Henry Duke. Several secondary love stories add to the lively action.

Other books you might like:
Georgette Heyer, *Venetia*, 1959
Leslie Lynn, *Scandal's Child*, 1990
Melinda McRae, *The Duke's Daughter*, 1991
Amanda Quick, *Scandal*, 1991
  sensual
Winifred Witton, *The Denville Diamond*, 1991

2006
MARGARET WESTHAVEN (Pseudonym of Peggy M. Hansen)
Four in Hand
(New York: Signet, 1993)

Story type: Regency
Major character(s): Lady Jane Averham, Noblewoman, Widow(er); Archibald McGowan, Nobleman
Time period(s): 1810s
Locale(s): Vienna, Austria

Summary: Lady Jane Averham's main concern is to find husbands for her teenage daughters; but to her surprise, Archie McGowan, quite the eligible bachelor, takes a liking to her, in spite of the fact that she is much older than he! They have great chemistry, but marriage is another thing—after all, people will talk. Funny, witty, and rife with fascinating subplots.

Other books you might like:
Gayle Buck, *The Waltzing Widow*, 1991
Elizabeth Jackson, *A Brilliant Alliance*, 1993
Barbara Metzger, *An Affair of Interest*, 1992

Pamela Morsi, *Courting Miss Hattie*, 1991
Gail Whitaker, *The Blade and the Bath Miss*, 1993

2007
BECKY LEE WEYRICH

Forever, for Love
(New York: Pocket, 1989)

Story type: Historical/Fantasy
Major character(s): Pandora Sherwood, Psychic, Reincarnated Person (Lafitte's wife); Jean Lafitte, Pirate, Historical Figure
Time period(s): 20th century; 1810s
Locale(s): Galveston Island, Texas

Summary: In this historical that involves reincarnation and time travel (of a sort), Pandora returns to a past in which she is pirate Jean Lafitte's wife in order to find love and happiness in her present life. A story of love enduring throughout time.

Other books you might like:
Kathryn Davenport, *Pirate's Mistress*, 1989
    Swashbuckling romance
Jude Deveraux, *A Knight in Shining Armor*, 1989
    Elizabethan/present time change
Barbara Erskine, *Kingdom of Shadows*, 1989
    Scottish time change/Strong historical elements
Heather Graham, *Every Time I Love You*, 1989
    Pre-Revolutionary America/present time change

2008
BECKY LEE WEYRICH

Once upon Forever
(New York: Pinnacle, 1994)

Story type: Time Travel
Major character(s): Larissa Courtney, Time Traveller (aka Cluney Summerland); Hunter Breckinridge, Military Personnel (Union soldier); Jeff Layton, Fiance(e)
Time period(s): 1860s; 1990s
Locale(s): Kentucky

Summary: As soon as they are married, Larissa Courtney and Hunter Breckinridge are separated—he leaves to fight for the Union and she disappears over the ''moonbow'' and wakes up in the 20th century. A modern-day fiance(e), Hunter's old diary, modern medicine, and a lot of time travel for everyone concerned eventually help Larissa resolve her dilemma.

Other books you might like:
Diana Gabaldon, *Outlander*, 1991
    classic time travel/different period and place
Judith O'Brien, *Rhapsody in Time*, 1994
    time travel
Eugenia Riley, *Tempest in Time*, 1993
    time travel
Eugenia Riley, *A Tryst in Time*, 1992
    time travel
Maura Seger, *Perchance to Dream*, 1989
    post-Civil War fantasy/ not time travel

2009
BECKY LEE WEYRICH

Silver Tears
(New York: Pocket, 1990)

Story type: Historical/Colonial America
Major character(s): Alice Balfour, Witch (accused), Widow(er); Christopher Gunn, Diplomat, Backwoodsman
Time period(s): 17th century (1690s)
Locale(s): American Colonies

Summary: Accused of witchcraft, Alice escapes death when elderly Lord Balfour comes to her aid, marries her, and arranges for her future. This includes naming the man she is to marry when he dies—Christopher Gunn of the American Colonies. Christopher, however, is not at all what Alice expects, but his rough exterior hides a sensitive person whom Alice comes to love. Fast-paced action and passion with the drama of the Salem Witch Trials thrown in for good measure.

Other books you might like:
Andrea Parnell, *Wild Glory*, 1990
Valerie Sherwood, *This Loving Torment*, 1990
Elizabeth Speare, *The Witch of Blackbird Pond*, 1958
    YA classic
Karen Stratford, *Lavender Flame*, 1991

2010
BECKY LEE WEYRICH

Sweet Forever
(New York: Pinnacle, 1992)

Story type: Time Travel; Historical/Fantasy
Major character(s): Julianna Doran, Time Traveller; Brom Vanderzee, Pirate, Sea Captain; Elliot Creighton, Fiance(e), Actor
Time period(s): 1890s (1899); 17th century (1690's)
Locale(s): United States; American Colonies

Summary: When a Ouija board gives Julianna Doran a tantalizing glimpse of dashing 17th century Brom Vanderzee, she begins a quest that alternately sweeps her into the past and Brom into her world with passionate results. Mystical and sensuous. Interesting in that the story takes place in two historical time perionds rather than one plus the present.

Other books you might like:
Laura Gilmour Bennett, *By All That Is Sacred*, 1991
Jude Deveraux, *A Knight in Shining Armor*, 1989
Diana Gabaldon, *Outlander*, 1991
Thomasina Ring, *Time-Spun Rapture*, 1990
Antoinette Stockenberg, *Emily's Ghost*, 1992

2011
BECKY LEE WEYRICH

Whispers in Time
(New York: Pinnacle, 1993)

Story type: Time Travel

Major character(s): Carol Marlowe, Psychic, Detective ("Camille Mazeret"); Frank Longpre, Police Officer ("Victor Navar")
Time period(s): 1990s; 1840s
Locale(s): New Orleans, Louisiana

Summary: When Carol Marlowe, psychic detective, is asked by Frank Longpre to investigate a 100 year old body, it seems to fit in with visions and dreams she has been having. The body seems to "speak" to her and when she somehow ends up in the 1840s, she finds that Frank has great similarity to Vic Navar, and she has become Camille. Interesting and appealing.

Other books you might like:
Sandra Canfield, *The Loving*, 1992
Constance O'Day-Flannery, *Second Chances*, 1992
    fantasy
Pamela Simpson, *Partners in Time*, 1990
Antoinette Stockenberg, *Emily's Ghost*, 1992

2012

GAIL WHITAKER

The Blade and the Bath Miss

(Toronto: Harlequin, 1992)

Story type: Regency
Major character(s): Lady Emma Harding, Noblewoman; Tristan, Nobleman (Marquis of Chadwick)
Time period(s): 1810s
Locale(s): England

Summary: When Tristan, Marquis of Chadwick, rescues Lady Emma Harding from the unwanted attentions of a travelling companion, he is enchanted by the young debutante, and nobly decides to find her a suitable husband and watch over her. After all, she is only 19 and he is an ancient 39! Eventually, he realizes that this kind of platonic relationship isn't at all what he wants—and then his pursuit begins in earnest. Emma, of course, has realized all along that Tristan is hers. Very Regency.

Other books you might like:
Georgette Heyer, *These Old Shades*, 1926
    classic Regency
Kathryn Kramer, *Lady Rogue*, 1991
    sensual
Amanda Quick, *Ravished*, 1992
    sensual
Joan Smith, *Cousin Cecelia*, 1990
Margaret Westhaven, *Four in Hand*, 1993

2013

ANN HOWARD WHITE

All but Love

(Bensalem, Pennsylvania: Meteor, 1993)

Story type: Contemporary
Major character(s): Catherine Chambers, Doctor (pediatric surgeon); Mark Garrett, Contractor, Single Parent
Time period(s): 1990s

Locale(s): St. Croix, Virgin Islands of the United States
Summary: When childless widow Dr. Catherine Chambers treats Beth Garrett after an accident, she discovers that the little girl is a pawn in a bitter custody fight and that her father, Mark, needs to establish a "proper" home for her. Catherine and Mark agree to marry, platonically, of course, to accomplish this. Naturally, things don't stay that way.

Other books you might like:
Elizabeth Krueger, *For the Children*, 1992
Judi Lind, *Heart Song*, 1992
Debbie Macomber, *Morning Comes Softly*, 1993
Victoria Pade, *The Doubletree*, 1990
    historical setting

2014

TIFFANY WHITE

Naughty Talk

(Toronto: Harlequin, 1993)

Story type: Contemporary
Major character(s): Nicole Hart, Writer (aspiring), Waiter/Waitress; Anthony Gawain, Television Personality (talk show host)
Time period(s): 1990s
Locale(s): United States

Summary: Nicole, aspiring writer, poses as a sex therapist to get on Anthony's talk show. It seems to be a great idea at the beginning, but when he tries to date her, she has to maintain the deception and that isn't easy. It all works out eventually, but the lies don't help.

Other books you might like:
Joanne Z. Adams, *Intimate Connections*, 1991
Gloria Alvarez, *Heart Waves*, 1992
Sally Falcon, *Stolen Kisses*, 1992
Candace Schuler, *The Right Direction*, 1993

2015

ISABEL WHITFIELD (Pseudonym of Tamara B. Ganahl)

Bodie Bride

(Toronto: Harlequin, 1992)

Story type: Historical/American West
Major character(s): Margaret Warren, Spinster; John Banning, Young Man
Time period(s): 1870s (1879)
Locale(s): Bodie, California

Summary: Prudish and proper Margaret Warren is shocked and dismayed by brawling, rugged Bodie, California. In addition she is terrified of men, of having children, and marriage in general. This proves to to be something of a problem when her father brings home John Banning and invites him to stay and marry his daughter! Gentle John doesn't push, and gradually Margaret allows her feelings for him to overcome her fears. A sweet romance with a caring hero.

Other books you might like:
Candace Camp, *Rosewood*, 1991

Theresa DiBenedetto, *Silver Mist*, 1991
Anne Harmon, *Desert Flame*, 1992
Jodi Thomas, *The Tender Texan*, 1991
Victoria Thompson, *Playing with Fire*, 1990

2016
DIANA WHITNEY

A Liberated Man
(New York: Silhouette, 1990)

Story type: Contemporary/Innocent
Major character(s): Shannon Doherty, Maintenance Worker (plumber); Mitch Wheeler, Artist (cartoonist)
Time period(s): 1980s
Locale(s): Los Angeles, California

Summary: Cartoonist Mitch Wheeler is fighting for custody of his dead brother's three children, but his bachelorhood is a definite minus. Shannon loves kids, and Mitch as well, but has a secret in her past that might ruin everything.

Other books you might like:
Angela Carson, *Sweet Illusion*, 1990
Dorsey Kelley, *Montana Heat*, 1990
Kasey Michaels, *His Chariot Awaits*, 1990
Alice Sharpe, *Just One More Secret*, 1990
Lee Stafford, *A Song in the Wilderness*, 1990

2017
PHYLLIS A. WHITNEY

Rainbow in the Mist
(New York: Doubleday, 1989)

Story type: Gothic
Major character(s): Christy Loren, Psychic (reluctant clairvoyant); Hayden Mitchell, Businessman (nursery owner)
Time period(s): 1980s
Locale(s): Blue Ridge Mountains, Virginia

Summary: Fleeing to Virginia's Blue Ridge Mountains to escape the notoriety and consequences of being able to clairvoyantly locate missing people, Christy is unwittingly drawn into the mystery of the missing, fey-like Dierdre. As she struggles to solve the mystery, Christy also comes to terms with her true psychic powers, as well as her growing feelings for the husband of the missing woman.

Other books you might like:
Susan Howatch, *April's Grave*, 1969
Barbara Michaels, *Ammie, Come Home*, 1969
Barbara Michaels, *Here I Stay*, 1983
Barbara Michaels, *Someone in the House*, 1981
Mary Stewart, *Nine Coaches Waiting*, 1958

2018
PHYLLIS A. WHITNEY

The Singing Stones
(New York: Doubleday, 1990)

Story type: Gothic
Major character(s): Lynn McLeod, Psychologist (Child psychologist); Stephen Asche, Architect
Time period(s): 1980s
Locale(s): Blue Ridge Mountains, Virginia

Summary: When child psychologist Lynn McLeod goes to the Blue Ridge Mountains in Virginia to help Jilly, her ex-husband's 10 year old daughter by another marriage, recover from several traumatic experiences, she becomes enmeshed in murder with a good dash of the occult thrown in. All this, of course, is tied together with a slender thread of romance.

Other books you might like:
Lee Karr, *Dark Cries of Gray Oaks*, 1989
Elsie Lee, *Wingarden*, 1971
Barbara Michaels, *The Crying Child*, 1971
Barbara Michaels, *Here I Stay*, 1983
    Ghostly happenings in a Victorian mansion
Elisabeth Ogilvie, *Bellwood*, 1968

2019
PHYLLIS A. WHITNEY

Woman Without a Past
(New York: Doubleday, 1991)

Story type: Romantic Suspense; Gothic
Major character(s): Molly Hunt, Writer (mystery novelist), Heiress—Lost; Charles Landry, Gentleman
Time period(s): 1990s
Locale(s): Charleston, South Carolina

Summary: When Charles Landry recognizes writer Molly Hunt as his fiancée's long-lost twin sister, he brings her to Charleston to be reunited with her family—and sets in motion forces that eventually threaten Molly's life. Murder and suspense in traditional Whitney fashion.

Other books you might like:
Kay Hooper, *Crime of Passion*, 1991
Susan Howatch, *April's Grave*, 1969
Barbara Michaels, *Be Buried in the Rain*, 1983
Mary Stewart, *The Stormy Petrel*, 1991

2020
ROBIN LEANNE WIETE

Fortune's Lady
(New York: Onyx, 1990)

Story type: Historical/American West
Major character(s): Marianne Blakemore, Runaway, Imposter (mail order bride); Nick Fortune, Hero
Time period(s): 1880s (1888)
Locale(s): Washington

Summary: Running away until she can prove she is innocent of her uncle's murder, Marianne is injured in a train wreck. Nick rescues her thinking she is his mail order bride; and to avoid capture, Marianne goes along with the deception. But then she falls in love with Nick and is forced to make some difficult choices.

Other books you might like:
Gwen Cleary, *Ecstasy's Masquerade*, 1989
   Another deceptive runaway
Lori Copeland, *Fool Me Once*, 1990
Rebecca George, *A Wild Desire*, 1989
Mary Mayer Holmes, *Savage Tides*, 1989
Janelle Taylor, *Kiss of the Night Wind*, 1989

2021

ROBIN LEANNE WIETE

Freedom Angel
(New York: New American Libraries, 1990)

Story type: Historical
Major character(s): Kelsey Tremayne, Plantation Owner (joint owner with Garrett); Garrett O'Neill, Plantation Owner (joint owner with Kelsey)
Time period(s): 19th century
Locale(s): Great Lakes (on Lake Ontario)

Summary: Kelsey Tremayne returns from England to her family estate along Lake Ontario and renews a childhood relationship with Garrett O'Neill, now the joint owner of Riverview Plantation with Kelsey. Although they loved each other years before—and still do—trust does not come so easily; and it takes a great deal of understanding on both their parts before they can be happy together. A passionate, sensitive love story intertwined with the danger and excitement of the Underground Railroad movement.

Other books you might like:
Emily Carmichael, *Visions of the Heart*, 1990
Stef Ann Holm, *Firefly*, 1990
Kathy Lawrence, *Tin Angel*, 1989
Laura Simon, *A Taste of Heaven*, 1989

2022

ROBIN LEANNE WIETE

When Morning Comes
(New York: Onyx, 1993)

Story type: Historical/Post-American Revolution
Major character(s): Rebecca Osborne, Widow(er); Aaron "Cain" Cambridge, Healer (for the Shawnee), Amnesiac
Time period(s): 18th century (1782-1792)
Locale(s): Ohio

Summary: When, in order to save her son's leg, Rebecca goes in search of the legendary Cain, healer of the Shawnee, she is shocked to find that he is the missing surgeon Aaron Cambridge, her son's father! Even though he has had amnesia, guilt, and army desertion to deal with, Rebecca isn't quite ready to forgive him for deserting her and their son; and when he finally turns himself in and resumes his career, the sparks

are still flying. Eventually, they reconcile their differences and join forces to clear his name, help him regain his memory, and in the process, they bring peace to the frontier. Realistic.

Other books you might like:
Rosanne Bittner, *Embers of the Heart*, 1990
Pamela K. Forrest, *Wild Savage Heart*, 1993
Dorothy Garlock, *Homeplace*, 1991
Norah Hess, *Kentucky Bride*, 1992
Joan Van Nuys, *Beloved Intruder*, 1992

2023

SUSAN WIGGS

Circle in the Water
(New York: Harper, 1994)

Story type: Historical/Renaissance
Major character(s): Juliana Romanov, Royalty (princess), Gypsy; Stephen de Lacey, Nobleman (Baron of Wimberleigh)
Time period(s): 16th century (1530s)
Locale(s): England

Summary: When Henry VIII takes revenge against Stephen de Lacey, the arrogant Baron of Wimberleigh, by forcing him to marry a gypsy hoyden who was trying to steal his horse, he has no idea that the girl is actually an incognito Russian princess—and that by ordering the marriage, he is actually insuring Stephen and Juliana's ultimate happiness. Excitement, deception, and danger combine in this story set during one of the most colorful periods in English history.

Other books you might like:
Sandra Davidson, *Rosefire*, 1992
   another "hidden" princess
Christina Dodd, *The Greatest Lover in All England*, 1993
   a missing heiress/humorous treatment
Betina M. Krahn, *Behind Closed Doors*, 1992
Erin Yorke, *Heaven's Gate*, 1992

2024

SUSAN WIGGS

Jewel of the Sea
(New York: Tor, 1993)

Story type: Historical/Mainstream
Major character(s): Paloma, Slave; Armando, Adventurer; Will, Musician
Time period(s): 16th century
Locale(s): South America; England; At Sea

Summary: Fate unites Paloma, Armando, Will, and Gabriella, four renegades, and together they search for and find new lives in the Spanish colonies. An intricate, sweeping novel set during one of the most colorful and intriguing periods of history.

Other books you might like:
Beverly Byrne, *A Lasting Fire*, 1991
   first of a trilogy
Suzanne Ellison, *Eagle Knight*, 1991
Shirl Henke, *Paradise and More*, 1992

Shirl Henke, *Return to Paradise*, 1992
Iris Johansen, *The Wind Dancer*, 1991
  first of a trilogy

2025

SUSAN WIGGS

The Lily and the Leopard
(New York: Harper, 1991)

Story type: Historical/Medieval
Major character(s): Lianna, Noblewoman, Heiress; Enguarrand ''Rand'' Fitzmarc, Nobleman, Knight
Time period(s): 15th century (1414-1415)
Locale(s): England; France

Summary: Seeking emotional solace from a treacherous, but self-imposed, marriage, Lianna flees to the woods and into the arms of the very man she was supposed to have married, English knight Sir Rand Fitzmarc. Drama, violence, intrigue, and passion abound in this colorful and nicely detailed medieval historical.

Other books you might like:
Rexanne Becnel, *My Gallant Enemy*, 1990
Jude Deveraux, *The Conquest*, 1991
Julie Garwood, *The Bride*, 1989
Johanna Lindsey, *Defy Not the Heart*, 1989
Kathleen E. Woodiwiss, *The Wolf and the Dove*, 1971

2026

SUSAN WIGGS

The Mist and the Magic
(New York: Harper, 1993)

Story type: Historical/Seventeenth Century
Major character(s): Caitlin McBride, Rebel (leader); John Wesley Hawkins, Spy
Time period(s): 17th century (1658)
Locale(s): England; Ireland

Summary: John Wesley Hawkins, Royalist spy, is sent by Cromwell to capture the leader of a band of rebels who keep harrassing the British forces—and he keeps John's three-year-old daughter as hostage. When John meets Caitlin, the rebel leader, he is enchanted, and torn between his love for her and his fear for his daughter's safety. A believable love story combined with an intricate tale of political intrigue. Interesting historical detail.

Other books you might like:
Jane Feather, *Reckless Angel*, 1989
Chloe Gartner, *Mistress of the Highlands*, 1976
Jean Plaidy, *The Pleasure of Love*, 1992
  Mainstream Restoration Historical
Jeanette Baker Ramirez, *Lady of Lochabar*, 1993

2027

SUSAN WIGGS

The Raven and the Rose
(New York: Harper, 1992)

Story type: Historical/Regency
Major character(s): Lorilie le Clerc, Healer; Daniel Severin, Mercenary
Time period(s): 1810s
Locale(s): Paris, France; Switzerland

Summary: Tough, cynical Daniel is sent by Empress Josephine to locate a missing relative and in the process he is caught in an avalanche in the Alps. Rescued by Lorilie, he is taken to the hospice where she was raised and as he recovers, Lorilie falls in love with him. In a series of unusual events, they try to escape Napoleon's army, are forced to wed, and are then sent to Paris on a mission. But danger and intrigue await them not only in Paris, but in the Alps as well. Detailed descriptions of Napoleon and Josephine in this sensual romance.

Other books you might like:
Iris Johansen, *Storm Winds*, 1991
Amanda Quick, *Rendezvous*, 1992
Louisa Rawlings, *Stranger in My Arms*, 1990
Serena Richards, *Rendezvous*, 1991

2028

SUSAN WIGGS

Vows Made in Wine
(New York: Harper, 1995)

Story type: Historical/Renaissance
Major character(s): Lark Merrifield, Activist (rescues people from execution); Oliver de Lacey, Nobleman (Baron Wimberleigh)
Time period(s): 16th century
Locale(s): England

Summary: Lark Merrifield's mission in life is to save people from death at the hands of Bloody Mary; and when she ends up nursing the debauched Lord Oliver de Lacey (a hanging victim who didn't quite die) back to relative good health, she has no idea of the future role he will play in her life—or he in hers. A passionate, fast-paced romance that provides a good feel for the period.

Other books you might like:
Sandra Davidson, *Rosefire*, 1992
Christina Dodd, *Outrageous*, 1994
Betina M. Krahn, *Behind Closed Doors*, 1992
Barbara Kyle, *A Dangerous Devotion*, 1994
  similar time period/mainstream elements
Barbara Kyle, *A Dangerous Temptation*, 1994

2029

JENNIFER WILDE (Pseudonym of Tom Huff)

They Call Her Dana

(New York: Ballantine, 1989)

Story type: Historical/Mainstream
Major character(s): Dana O'Malley, Bastard Daughter
Time period(s): 1830s
Locale(s): New Orleans, Louisiana

Summary: Escaping from the poverty of the bayous, illegitimate Dana heads for New Orleans in search of her destiny. She achieves fame, fortune, and love; and she eventually discovers the long-hidden secrets of her past.

Other books you might like:
Sally Beauman, *Destiny*, 1987
Philippa Gregory, *Wideacre*, 1987
Rosalind Laker, *Banners of Silk*, 1981
    Strong woman/European setting
Elinor Lynley, *Song of the Bayou*, 1990
    Louisiana setting/different emphasis
Alexandra Ripley, *New Orleans Legacy*, 1987

2030

LAUREN WILDE (Pseudonym of Anne Redd)

Sweet Savage Splendor

(New York: Zebra 1993)

Story type: Historical/American Revolution
Major character(s): Felicia Edwards, Frontierswoman; Hawk, Frontiersman, Indian (Cherokee)
Time period(s): 18th century (late)
Locale(s): Carolinas, American Colonies

Summary: Believing that Felicia Edwards is the mistress of the man who killed his father, Cherokee rebel Hawk kidnaps her with the intention of using her to bait a trap for the villain. Felicia, however, is not Colonel Tarelton's lover after all; she is, however, a loyal Tory and knows that Hawk is her "enemy." Nevertheless, as they spend time together, their mutual love and respect grows. Interesting historical and Cherokee cultural detail.

Other books you might like:
Amy Christopher, *Captive Kiss*, 1992
    later time period
Pamela K. Forrest, *Wild Savage Heart*, 1993
JoAnne Redd, *Dance with Fire*, 1992
    same author/different pseudonym
Joan Van Nuys, *Beloved Intruder*, 1992
Robin LeAnne Wiete, *When Morning Comes*, 1993

2031

KAY WILDING

Rainbow's End

(Toronto: Harlequin, 1990)

Story type: Contemporary

Major character(s): Thea Cameron, Single Parent, Runaway (from dangerous ex-husband); Quint Richards, Lawyer (district attorney)
Time period(s): 1980s
Locale(s): Planter's Junction, Georgia

Summary: Fleeing with her children from her knife-wielding ex-husband, Thea seeks refuge with her aunt—only to find Aunt Maudie laid up with a broken hip and an old flame, turned DA, ensconced with his two children in her aunt's house. Naturally, Thea stays—and then the complications start.

Other books you might like:
Judy Gill, *Golden Swan*, 1990
Muriel Jensen, *Everything*, 1990
Susan Kyle, *Night Fever*, 1990
Julie Meyers, *In the Cards*, 1990

2032

TERRI LYNN WILHELM

Fool of Hearts

(New York: Harper, 1995)

Story type: Historical/Georgian
Major character(s): Lady Gillian Ellicott, Noblewoman; Calum MacFuaran, Nobleman (Marquess of Iolar), Heir
Time period(s): 18th century (1783)
Locale(s): Yorkshire, England

Summary: The Lady Gillian Ellicott can't keep an unsavory relative from inheriting her father's estate, but she can keep the world from discovering her father's death. Gillian concocts a desperate plan to find a husband and have a baby before any of her ruthless relatives can claim the estate. But when Calum MacFuaran, the Marquess of Iolar and heir to the estate, arrives, Gillian's plans begin to crumble. Sensual, realistic, and intriguing.

Other books you might like:
Jo Beverley, *My Lady Notorious*, 1993
    similar time period
Stella Cameron, *Fascination*, 1993
Iris Johansen, *The Beloved Scoundrel*, 1994
    similar time period
Kat Martin, *Devil's Prize*, 1995

2033

BRONWYN WILLIAMS

Gideon's Fall

(Toronto: Harlequin, 1991)

Story type: Historical/Colonial America
Major character(s): Prudence "Haskell" Andros, Thief; Gideon McNair, Sea Captain; Pride Andros, Thief
Time period(s): 1720s (1728)
Locale(s): Georgia, American Colonies; At Sea

Summary: When whaler captain Gideon McNair catches two young thieves stealing from him, he puts them to work in his whaling camp as recompense. However, "Haskell" (one of the thieves) is really Prudence, and when Gideon discovers her true identity—and comes to grips with his feelings for her—he has some decisions to make. Action and adventure in Colonial America.

Other books you might like:
Catherine Coulter, *Night Storm*, 1990
Heather Graham, *A Pirate's Pleasure*, 1989
Karen Harper, *Eden's Gate*, 1989
Lisa Ann Verge, *The Heart's Disguise*, 1990

`2034`
BRONWYN WILLIAMS

The Warfield Bride
(New York: Topaz, 1994)

Story type: Historical/Victorian America
Major character(s): Hannah Ballinger, Mail Order Bride, Widow(er); Penn Warfield, Sea Captain (keeper of a Life-saving Station)
Time period(s): 1890s (1899)
Locale(s): Hatteras Island, North Carolina

Summary: Determined to see his four brothers safely wed, Penn Warfield sends for a mail-order bride for his brother Adam and ends up falling in love with the lovely, enchanting—and pregnant—widow, Hannah Ballinger, himself. The lonely, windswept island on the Outer Banks of North Carolina makes an interesting setting.

Other books you might like:
Sharon Harlow, *Country Kiss*, 1993
Jill Marie Landis, *Come Spring*, 1992
Debbie Macomber, *Morning Comes Softly*, 1994
   contemporary
Victoria Pade, *The Doubletree*, 1990
LaVyrle Spencer, *Morning Glory*, 1989

`2035`
CLAUDETTE WILLIAMS

Heart of Fancy
(New York: Ballantine, 1990)

Story type: Historical/Regency
Major character(s): Fancy Kingston, Gentlewoman (impoverished); Robert Torington, Nobleman (lord), Rake
Time period(s): 1810s
Locale(s): England

Summary: On her way to stay with her aunt, penniless Fancy Kingston is kidnapped from the stagecoach by a group of thrill-seeking young men. However, her attraction to the leader, Robert Torington, and his to her, has some consequences they never intended.

Other books you might like:
Janice Bennett, *A Timeless Affair*, 1990
   Time change/Regency London
Julie Garwood, *Guardian Angel*, 1990
Sharon Gillenwater, *Highland Whispers*, 1989
   Gothic touch
Amanda Quick, *Seduction*, 1990

Joan Van Nuys, *Beloved Avenger*, 1989
   Kidnapping pirate-style

`2036`
FRANCES WILLIAMS

The Road to Forever
(New York: Silhouette, 1991)

Story type: Contemporary/Exotic
Major character(s): Tara Morgan, Travel Agent, Courier (for U.S. government); Kent Masterson, Photographer (for U.S. government)
Time period(s): 1990s
Locale(s): Himalayas, China

Summary: On secret government business in the Himalayas, photographer Kent Masterson and travel agent Tara Morgan become involved in both religion and politics as they rescue a child and flee from the Chinese army through the high mountain passes. Exotic locale, interesting characters, and suspenseful action.

Other books you might like:
Evelyn Anthony, *A Place to Hide*, 1987
Lisbeth Chance, *Baja Run*, 1986
Jayne Ann Krentz, *Silver Linings*, 1991
Sandra Marton, *Night Fires*, 1991
Mary Stewart, *Madam, Will You Talk?*, 1955

`2037`
PENELOPE WILLIAMSON

Keeper of the Dream
(New York: Dell, 1992)

Story type: Historical/Medieval; Historical/Fantasy
Major character(s): Arianna, Noblewoman, Psychic; Raine, Knight, Bastard Son; Taliesin, Servant (squire), Minstrel (bard)
Time period(s): 12th century (1157)
Locale(s): Wales

Summary: Forced to wed for political reasons, Lady Arianna and Sir Raine the Bastard battle their way to understanding, and with the help of the bard Taliesin, create a love that transcends time and political adversaries. Arianna's gift of "sight" and the magic of Taliesin add a mystical quality to this enchanted and sensual tale.

Other books you might like:
Marion Zimmer Bradley, *The Mists of Avalon*, 1988
Marsha Canham, *Through a Dark Mist*, 1992
Marylyle Rogers, *Chanting the Dawn*, 1991
Flora M. Speer, *Castle of Dreams*, 1990
Joan Wolf, *Born of the Sun*, 1991

2038

PENELOPE WILLIAMSON

Once in a Blue Moon

(New York: Dell, 1993)

Story type: Historical
Major character(s): Jessalyn Letty, Horse Trainer (stable owner); McCady Trelawny, Nobleman, Rake
Locale(s): Cornwall, England

Summary: Tormented McCady Trelawny and spirited Jessalyn Letty are drawn to each other, but she is poor and he needs money, so they each go their separate ways. Years later, they meet again and realize they are still in love. But happiness does not come easily, and the pair must surmount a great many obstacles before they can make their love a safe and secure reality. Lyrical, complex, and emotional.

Other books you might like:
Mary Balogh, *Beyond the Sunrise*, 1992
Shirl Henke, *Paradise and More*, 1992
Shirl Henke, *Summer Has No Name*, 1990
  contemporary setting
LaVyrle Spencer, *Bittersweet*, 1990
  contemporary setting

2039

PENELOPE WILLIAMSON

A Wild Yearning

(New York: Avon, 1990)

Story type: Historical/Colonial America
Major character(s): Delia McQuaid, Mail Order Bride; Ty Savitch, Doctor, Guide
Time period(s): 1720s
Locale(s): Boston, Massachusetts; Maine

Summary: On her way to join her soon-to-be-husband in Maine, mail order bride Delia McQuaid falls in love with her guide, Ty Savitch. True love eventually wins out, but not before the two confront and solve a number of difficult problems.

Other books you might like:
Jo Ann Ferguson, *At the Rainbow's End*, 1989
  Another mail order bride
Mary Mayer Holmes, *Savage Tides*, 1989
  Mail order bride plot device
Nancy Moulton, *Defiant Heart*, 1989
Robin LeAnne Wiete, *Fortune's Lady*, 1990
  Heroine is mistaken for a mail order bride/West Coast setting

2040

MARIANNE WILLMAN

Silver Shadows

(New York: Harper, 1993)

Story type: Historical/American West; Historical/Mainstream

Major character(s): Cassandra Lucton, Frontierswoman; Grayson "Gray Wolf" Howard, Indian (half-Cheyenne)
Time period(s): 19th century (late)
Locale(s): Colorado

Summary: Thinking that Tyler Lucton is responsible for the death of his Cheyenne wife, Grayson Howard seeks revenge; but Tyler's wife, Cassandra, deters him. As a result, when Cassandra Lucton is widowed by the sudden death of her husband, Gray wants to protect and care for her—even marry her. They are drawn to each other, but must fight the treachery, jealousy, and prejudice that surround them as they strive toward happiness. An in-depth historical novel with saga elements.

Other books you might like:
Elaine Barbieri, *More Precious than Gold*, 1992
Kathleen Eagle, *This Time Forever*, 1992
  contemporary setting
Linda Howard, *A Lady of the West*, 1990

2041

MARIANNE WILLMAN

Tilly and the Tiger

(Toronto: Harlequin, 1990)

Story type: Historical/Exotic
Major character(s): Matilda "Tilly" Templeton, Spinster; Lucas "Tiger" Flynn, Adventurer
Time period(s): 1850s (1858)
Locale(s): Jamaica; Central America

Summary: English Miss Tilly Templeton accepts her old school friend's invitation to visit her in Jamaica and ends up shipwrecked, attacked, captured, and in love with a disreputable rogue. Not bad, she decides, for a proper spinster who up until now has only *dreamed* of adventure.

Other books you might like:
Laura Kinsale, *Seize the Fire*, 1989
Meagan McKinney, *Till Dawn Tames the Night*, 1991
Leslie O'Grady, *Seek the Wild Shore*, 1989
Susan Sackett, *Passion's Golden Fire*, 1989
Julie Tetel, *Swept Away*, 1989

2042

MARIANNE WILLMAN

Yesterday's Shadows

(New York: Harper, 1991)

Story type: Historical/American West; Saga
Major character(s): Bettany Ann Howard, Widow(er); Wolf Star Logan, Warrior, Adoptee (by the Cheyenne)
Time period(s): 1840s (1840-1841)
Locale(s): West

Summary: Saved by one man but taken to wife by another, Bettany Howard is irresistably drawn to her rescuer, Wolf Star Logan. Eventually, circumstances bring them together, but old secrets and past sins must be dealt with before Bettany and Logan can find happiness. Complex, mystical, and passionate.

Other books you might like:
Catherine Anderson, *Comanche Moon*, 1991
Madeline Baker, *A Whisper on the Wind*, 1991
    time change elements
Shirl Henke, *Golden Lady*, 1986
Penelope Neri, *Forever and Beyond*, 1990
    time change elements
Nan Ryan, *Desert Storm*, 1987

2043

CARYL WILSON

Firebrand's Lady
(New York: Pocket, 1992)

Story type: Historical/Medieval
Major character(s): Morgana, Noblewoman; Blaise de Rouen, Knight
Time period(s): 11th century
Locale(s): England; Ireland

Summary: In order to help her people, Saxon maid Morgana becomes a spy in the Norman Court. Even her love for Norman knight Blaise de Rouen can't change her loyalty — but when he callously betrays her and she is forced to wed another, matters take a darker turn. A sensual, realistic, and graphic story that accurately details the harshness as well as the glories of Medieval life.

Other books you might like:
Marsha Canham, *Through a Dark Mist*, 1992
Katherine Deauville, *Blood Red Roses*, 1991
Marylyle Rogers, *The Eagle's Song*, 1992
Bertrice Small, *A Moment in Time*, 1991
    mystical elements

2044

CARYL WILSON

Tonight and Forever
(New York: Pocket, 1993)

Story type: Historical/American Civil War
Major character(s): Courtney Asquith, Dancer (ballerina), Servant (in disguise); Sean Caddell, Shipowner, Smuggler
Time period(s): 19th century (1859-1862)
Locale(s): England; Charleston, South Carolina; New Orleans, Louisiana

Summary: Seeking revenge for her dead sister, Courtney falls for the very man she wants to destroy. He saves her from attack and then takes her, disguised as a servant, to America. Facing family secrets, deep mistrust of each other, betrayal, and the Civil War, they eventually turn to each other and discover love and, finally, trust.

Other books you might like:
Thea Devine, *Southern Seduction*, 1991
Katherine Kincaid, *Stormswept*, 1991
Patricia Potter, *Lightning*, 1992
Gina Robbins, *Always and Forever*, 1992

2045

GAYLE WILSON

The Heart's Desire
(Toronto: Harlequin, 1994)

Story type: Historical/Regency
Major character(s): Lady Emily Harland, Noblewoman; Dominic Maitland, Spy, Handicapped (crippled)
Time period(s): 1810s (1813-1814)
Locale(s): London, England

Summary: After the war, the widowed Lady Emily returns to England, only to have her father and Dominic Maitland try to draw her into their spying activities. Intrigued by the duke, Emily pursues him; feeling inadequate, the crippled Dominic resists and resigns himself to a lonely life. Political intrigue adds spice to this romance where forgiveness and love are a long time coming.

Other books you might like:
Danelle Harmon, *Captain of My Heart*, 1992
    another aggressive heroine — Georgian-style
Laura Kinsale, *The Prince of Midnight*, 1990
    another handicapped hero
Mary Jo Putney, *Petals in the Storm*, 1993
Mary Jo Putney, *Thunder and Roses*, 1992

2046

MARY ANNE WILSON

The Christmas Husband
(Toronto: Harlequin, 1995)

Story type: Contemporary; Holiday Themes
Major character(s): Dr. Love, Radio Personality (talk show host); Steven York, Businessman
Time period(s): 1990s
Locale(s): San Francisco, California; Lake Tahoe, California

Summary: When talk show host "Dr. Love" suddenly needs a husband for the weekend, she accidentally ends up paired with Steven York, one of the more eligible single fathers in town. An engaging child and and a wonderfully efficient male housekeeper almost steal the show in this light holiday romance.

Other books you might like:
Elaine Barbieri, *Mistletoe Marriages*, 1994
    anthology
Bethany Campbell, *The Man Who Came for Christmas*, 1993
Kathleen Creighton, *A Christmas Love*, 1992
Janet Dailey, *Santa's Little Helpers*, 1995
    anthology
Debbie Macomber, *Touched by Angels*, 1995
    last of a trilogy

2047

PATRICIA WILSON

Guardian Angel

(Toronto: Harlequin, 1990)

Story type: Contemporary
Major character(s): Tara Frost, Public Relations; Ben Shapiro, Public Relations
Time period(s): 1980s

Summary: Tara's boss, Ben, is domineering and somewhat autocratic; but he is kind and generous when it comes to helping Tara care for her paralyzed mother. As she accepts more help from him, Tara begins to feel more and more in his control; but she also starts to fall in love with him—adding to the confusion.

Other books you might like:
Angela Carson, *Sweet Illusion*, 1990
    Similar theme, innocent rendering
Maggie Charles, *The Snow Image*, 1989
Kathleen Creighton, *Love and Other Surprises*, 1990
Connie Rinehold, *Silken Threads*, 1989

2048

CLARA WIMBERLY

The Emerald Tears of Foxfire Manor

(New York: Zebra, 1990)

Story type: Gothic
Major character(s): Kathryn McClary, Orphan; Matthew Kincaid, Young Man
Time period(s): 1860s (1864)
Locale(s): South Carolina (Foxfire Manor)

Summary: Left destitute and unprotected by the Civil War, Kathryn turns to Robert Kincaid of Foxfire Manor. However, his premature death and the unusual and menacing things that have begun to happen leave her vulnerable once more, and she turns to another Kincaid, Robert's brother, Matthew.

Other books you might like:
Dorothy Eden, *Darkwater*, 1964
Dorothy Eden, *The Shadow Wife*, 1968
Victoria Holt, *Mistress of Mellyn*, 1960
    Classic gothic
Lee Karr, *Dark Cries of Gray Oaks*, 1989
Beverly C. Warren, *Lost Ladies of Windswept Moor*, 1990

2049

LINDA WINDSOR

Pirate's Wild Embrace

(New York: Zebra, 1990)

Story type: Historical
Major character(s): Shannon Brennan, Young Woman (pirate's daughter); Morgan Hawke, Hero
Time period(s): 19th century
Locale(s): England

Summary: Seeking to avenge the death of his father, Morgan Hawke agrees to help Shannon, the daughter of the pirate who murdered his father, escape from the buccaneers' stronghold. When he returns her to her family in England, her welcome is not all she had hoped as deceit and treachery become the order of the day.

Other books you might like:
Laura Black, *Albany*, 1984
Cordia Byers, *Lady Fortune*, 1989
    Another "unwelcome" heroine
Sarah Edwards, *Crystal Rapture*, 1989
Jean Innes, *Buccaneer's Bride*, 1989
Laura Simon, *A Taste of Heaven*, 1989

2050

JULIA WINFIELD

Tug of Hearts

(New York: Bantam, 1989)

Story type: Young Adult
Series: Private Eyes
Major character(s): Christine Harter, Student, Detective—Amateur; Andy Mellon, Student—College (in the fall)
Time period(s): 1980s

Summary: Problems with a current boyfriend and a long-time former boyfriend keep Christine busy as she tries to solve the mystery of a missing will.

Other books you might like:
Mary Higgins Clark, *Stillwatch*, 1984
    For more mature YAs
Norma Johnston, *The Watcher in the Mist*, 1986
Joyce Anne Schneider, *Darkness Falls*, 1989
Mary Stewart, *The Moon-Spinners*, 1962

2051

BONNIE K. WINN

Summer Rose

(New York: Diamond, 1992)

Story type: Historical/American West
Major character(s): Cassandra Dalton, Heiress, Rancher (sheep); Shane Lancer, Rancher (cattle)
Time period(s): 19th century
Locale(s): Keenonburg, Texas

Summary: Cassie, her friend, and her young brother leave the Boston tenements to claim the Texas sheep ranch her uncle has left her. Surprised by the cattle town's hostility (they won't even sell her supplies), she is determined to succeed, even if she has to learn sheep ranching from a book! When cattle rancher Shane Lancer befriends her, the townsfolk gradually warm up, but after a dispute over water when Cassie dams up the town's supply, real problems begin. Funny, sensuous, and action-filled.

Other books you might like:
Theresa DiBenedetto, *Western Winds*, 1991
Linda Howard, *Angel Creek*, 1991
DiAnna June, *Yesterday's Promise*, 1991

June Lund Shiplett, *Boston Renegade*, 1992

2052

ANNE MARIE WINSTON

Unlikely Eden

(New York: Silhouette, 1993)

Story type: Contemporary/Exotic
Major character(s): Meredith Bayliss, Scientist (botanist); Jared Adamson, Scientist (ecologist)
Time period(s): 1990s
Locale(s): Venezuela

Summary: Part of the same scientific expedition to the Venezuelan jungle, Merry and Jared are highly unlikely lovers. Nevertheless, their proximity to each other, their similar interests, and their lush, tropical surroundings spark a passion that, eventually, neither can resist.

Other books you might like:
Lacey Dancer, *Lightning Strikes Twice*, 1993
Leslie O'Grady, *Seek the Wild Shore*, 1989
   historical
Jeane Renick, *Trust Me*, 1992
Susan Sackett, *Passion's Golden Fire*, 1989
   historical

2053

REBECCA WINTERS

The Marriage Bracelet

(New York: Harlequin, 1992)

Story type: Contemporary
Major character(s): Heather Martin, Teacher; Nick Antonovic, Businessman (timber); Branko Antonovic, Teenager, Gypsy
Time period(s): 1990s
Locale(s): Pacific Northwest

Summary: Eighteen-year-old Branko Antonovic develops a serious infatuation for Heather Martin, his ESL teacher, when she shows concern for his culture shock and grief over his mother's death. Heather expects Branko's father, Nick, to also be an immigrant Gypsy, and is surprised to find him an educated, successful businessman. When Nick and Heather become attracted to each other, Branko is devastated and flees to the woods, with near disastrous consequences.

Other books you might like:
Kathleen Creighton, *Love and Other Surprises*, 1990
Elizabeth Krueger, *For the Children*, 1992
Marilyn Pappano, *Operation Homefront*, 1992
Sophie Weston, *Gypsy in the Night*, 1992

2054

EILEEN WINWOOD

A Worthy Engagement

(New York: Berkley, 1993)

Story type: Regency

Major character(s): Lady Alessandra Ridgely, Noblewoman; Lucien Tremaine, Nobleman (Marquess of Canfield)
Time period(s): 1810s
Locale(s): England

Summary: When Lucien, Marquess of Canfield, provokes the usually proper Alessandra Ridgely into highly unladylike behavior, the end result is betrothal! Surprisingly, their relationship flares into a passion that neither they nor society at large had expected.

Other books you might like:
Jo Beverley, *An Arranged Marriage*, 1991
Sarah Eagle, *The Marriage Gamble*, 1992
Margaret Evan Porter, *Road to Ruin*, 1992
Susan Sizemore, *My First Duchess*, 1993
   sensual
Patricia Veryan, *Logic of the Heart*, 1992

2055

WINIFRED WITTON (Pseudonym of Winifred Witton Smith)

The Denville Diamond

(Toronto: Harlequin, 1991)

Story type: Regency
Major character(s): Violet Langford, Gentlewoman (impoverished), Imposter; Bentley Frome, Nobleman, Imposter
Time period(s): 1810s
Locale(s): England

Summary: Take one heirloom diamond, one unwanted fiance, and two missing pairs of spectacles. Add two unusual protagonists and mix well with assorted members of the Regency *ton*. Season with humor, wit, and deception. Place all in a country houseparty and let bubble until done. Result: One hilarious, sparkling, and delectable Regency.

Other books you might like:
Clare Darcy, *Lady Pamela*, 1975
June Drummond, *The Bluestocking*, 1986
Coral Hoyle, *A Merry Go-Round*, 1990
Daisy Vivian, *Fair Game*, 1986
Margaret Westhaven, *Country Dance*, 1991

2056

JOAN WOLF

Born of the Sun

(New York: Onyx, 1991)

Story type: Historical/Medieval
Series: Chronicles of the Dark Ages
Major character(s): Princess Niniane, Royalty (Celtic); Ceawlin, Royalty, Bastard Son (of the Saxon king)
Time period(s): 6th century (555-575)
Locale(s): England

Summary: In this classic story of early Britain the Celtic Britons battle the Saxons for control. Celtic Niniane and Saxon Ceawlin marry and struggle to bring peace to their peoples. Vivid historical detail, well-drawn characters, and fast-paced action are all part of this well-told story from a magical period of history. Follows *The Road to Avalon*, first in the Chronicles of the Dark Ages.

Other books you might like:
Marion Zimmer Bradley, *The Mists of Avalon*, 1988
Roberta Gellis, *Roselynde*, 1978
   1st of the Roselynde Chronicles
Teresa Medeiros, *Lady of Conquest*, 1989
Rosemary Sutcliff, *A Light in the Forest*,
   1st of Arthurian Trilogy

2057

JOAN WOLF

Daughter of the Red Deer

(New York: Dutton, 1991)

Story type: Historical/Pre-history
Major character(s): Alin, Prehistoric Human (healer), Leader; Mar, Prehistoric Human, Warrior; Atlan, Prehistoric Human, Chieftain
Time period(s): 120th century B.C.
Locale(s): Vezere Valley, France

Summary: Trained from birth to take her mother's place as high priestess and leader of her clan, Alin's world changes abruptly when she and the other young women of the tribe are kidnapped by a patriarchal clan whose women have tragically died. A gentle and passionate story of love and divided loyalties set against the misty backdrop of pre-history in the country that will become France. Lots of interesting cultural detail.

Other books you might like:
Jean M. Auel, *Clan of the Cave Bear*, 1980
Kathryn Lynn Davis, *Sing to Me of Dreams*, 1990
Sue Harrison, *Mother Earth, Father Sky*, 1990
Kathleen Herbert, *Bride of the Spear*, 1990
Linda Lay Shuler, *She Who Remembers*, 1988

2058

LOIS WOLFE

Mask of Night

(New York: Doubleday, 1993)

Story type: Historical/American Civil War
Major character(s): Katie Henslowe, Manager (of a theatre troupe); Matt Dennigan, Detective—Private
Time period(s): 1860s
Locale(s): St. Louis, Missouri

Summary: When wealthy Julian Gates offers to open a theatre, Katie's Shakespearean troupe is overjoyed, little realizing that Julian is not the benevolent person he appears to be. It takes all of Katie's and investigator Matt Dennigan's ingenuity to finally unravel Julian s sinister scheme.

Other books you might like:
Lois Greiman, *Surrender My Heart*, 1993
Deana James, *Acts of Love*, 1992
Deana James, *Acts of Passion*, 1992
Martha Rofheart, *The Savage Brood*, 1978
   theatre saga

Patricia Watters, *Come Be My Love*,

2059

LOIS WOLFE

The Schemers

(New York: Bantam, 1991)

Story type: Historical/American Civil War
Major character(s): Devon Picard, Activist (abolitionist); Gentry Morgan, Indian (half Cherokee), Spy
Time period(s): 1860s
Locale(s): South; Indian Territory; Nassau, Bahamas

Summary: A reluctant southern spy and a double agent with a hidden agenda meet amid the turmoil of the Civil War and join forces in routing a traitor and a murderer. Fast action, intrigue, and treachery abound in this passionate story of love, hate, and revenge.

Other books you might like:
Elizabeth Kary, *Love, Honor and Betray*, 1986
Katherine Kincaid, *Stormswept*, 1991
Robin Maderich, *Faith and Honor*, 1989
   American Revolution
Maura Seger, *Perchance to Dream*, 1989
   The South Wins the War
Terri Valentine, *Yankee's Caress*, 1989

2060

BARBARA WOOD

The Dreaming

(New York: Avon, 1992)

Story type: Historical/Exotic; Saga
Major character(s): Joanna Drury, Orphan, Immigrant; Hugh Westbrook, Rancher (sheep)
Time period(s): 1870s; 1880s (1871-1886)
Locale(s): Melbourne, Australia

Summary: Joanna Drury goes to Australia to find answers to her grandparents' disappearance and her mother's mysterious death. Even her marriage to rancher Hugh Westbrook can't dispel the superstitions and strange dreams that plague her. However, her contacts with the aborigines and their "dreaming" lead her along new paths and the suspense increases throughout the book right up to the chilling finale.

Other books you might like:
Lois Battle, *The Past Is Another Country*, 1992
Leigh Bristol, *Sunswept*, 1990
Ann Maxwell, *The Diamond Tiger*, 1992
Colleen McCullough, *The Thorn Birds*, 1977
Katherine Sinclair, *Far Horizons*, 1991

2061

KATHLEEN E. WOODIWISS

Forever in Your Embrace

(New York: Avon, 1992)

Story type: Historical/Seventeenth Century

Major character(s): Synnovea Zenkavna, Noblewoman (countess); Tyrone Rycroft, Military Personnel (British colonel)
Time period(s): 17th century (1620)
Locale(s): Russia

Summary: In order to escape an unwanted marriage, lovely Countess Synnovea sets up the man who had rescued her when she was kidnapped, English Colonel Tyrone Rycroft, as her "spoiler"—hoping that as a "non-virgin" she will no longer be desirable. However, the Tsar insists that they marry and Rycroft is furious—and their marriage is off to a disastrous start. Action, violence, and threats of sexual abuse abound in this latest offering from one of the romance genre's original Hot Historical writers.

Other books you might like:
Judith Hill, *Knight's Desire*, 1992
Susan Johnson, *Golden Paradise*, 1990
Susan Johnson, *Love Storm*, 1981
Susan Johnson, *Seized by Love*, 1978
Linda Madl, *Sweet Ransom*, 1989

`2062`

KATHLEEN E. WOODIWISS

So Worthy My Love

(New York: Avon, 1989)

Story type: Historical/Renaissance; Historical/Elizabethan
Major character(s): Elise Radbourne, Noblewoman; Maxim Seymour, Nobleman (Marquess of Bradbury), Fugitive (Political)
Time period(s): 16th century (1585)
Locale(s): London, England; Germany

Summary: Attempting a revenge kidnapping, political fugitive Maxim Seymour inadvertently ends up with the wrong woman—a mistake that changes his life and that of Elise Radbourne, the kidnap victim.

Other books you might like:
Jude Deveraux, *A Knight in Shining Armor*, 1989
    Fantasy time change elements/present to 16th century
Kathryn Kramer, *Desire's Deception*, 1989
    Mary, Queen of Scots/Much historical detail
Miriam Minger, *Stolen Splendor*, 1989
Bertrice Small, *Skye O'Malley*, 1980
    Adventure, politics, and love in the 16th century
Lynda Trent, *The Tryst*, 1986
    Impersonation in an Elizabethan setting

`2063`

KATHLEEN E. WOODIWISS
CATHERINE ANDERSON, Co-Author
LORETTA CHASE, Co-Author
LISA KLEYPAS, Co-Author

Three Weddings and a Kiss

(New York: Avon, 1995)

Story type: Anthology; Historical
Time period(s): 19th century

Locale(s): United States; England; Canada

Summary: Focusing on the insitution of marriage, this diverse collection of historical romances sweeps from the wilds of the Canadian Rockies through the sultry Antebellum South to the glitter of Regency England and the gloom of darkly mysterious Dartmoor. Includes three novellas: "Fancy Free" by Catherine Anderson, "The Mad Earl's Bride" by Loretta Chase, and "Promises" by Lisa Kleypas. Also included is "The Kiss" by Kathleen E. Woodiwiss, a very short story that is a sequel to her ground-breaking novel *The Flame and the Flower*.

Other books you might like:
Catherine Anderson, *Tall, Dark, and Dangerous*, 1994
    historical anthology
Kimberly Cates, *One Night with a Rogue*, 1995
    anthology
Kay Hooper, *Hearts of Gold*, 1994
    Valentine's Day anthology
Amanda Quick, *Desire*, 1994
    funny and passionate/medieval bride and groom
Kathleen E. Woodiwiss, *The Flame and the Flower*, 1972
    prequel to "The Kiss"

`2064`

ELEANOR WOODS

Above Suspicion

(Toronto: Harlequin, 1990)

Story type: Contemporary
Major character(s): Jenny Castle, Businesswoman (kennel owner); Jonah McCal, Detective—Private
Time period(s): 1980s
Locale(s): New Orleans, Louisiana; Jefferson City, Louisiana

Summary: When Jonah McCal is hired to investigate the disappearance of a number of dogs, he enlists the aid of kennel owner Jenny Castle. Matters take an interesting turn when Jonah begins to fall in love with Jenny, in spite of the fact that he suspects her of being involved with the "dognappings."

Other books you might like:
Lori Copeland, *Tall Cotton*, 1990
Barbara Faith, *Danger in Paradise*, 1990
Linda Turner, *An Unsuspecting Heart*, 1989
Linda Randall Wisdom, *Sins of the Past*, 1990

`2065`

SHERRYL WOODS

Body and Soul

(New York: Popular Library, 1989)

Story type: Romantic Suspense
Series: Amanda Roberts
Major character(s): Amanda Roberts, Journalist (newspaper reporter); Joe Donelli, Police Officer (former), Farmer
Time period(s): 1980s
Locale(s): Atlanta, Georgia

Summary: When reporter Amanda Roberts' aerobics instructor ends up dead, Amanda senses a story—and becomes the next target of the killer. Her ex-cop boyfriend, Joe Donelli, wants her out of it, but Amanda can't let go and they both end up becoming involved, and, of course, solving the crime.

Other books you might like:
Susan Anderson, *Shadow Dance*, 1989
D.B. Baylor, *Fatal Obsession*, 1989
Mary Higgins Clark, *Stillwatch*, 1984
Elizabeth Peters, *Naked Once More*, 1989

2066

SHERRYL WOODS

Hide and Seek

(New York: Warner, 1994)

Story type: Contemporary; Romantic Suspense
Series: Amanda Roberts
Major character(s): Amanda Roberts, Journalist; Joe Donelli, Police Officer (former), Farmer
Time period(s): 1990s

Summary: Amanda and Joe's evolving love story is interrupted by her frantic quest for a killer who has come too close to her. The closer Amanda gets, the greater the danger; and the ultimate chase almost spells disaster for Joe and Amanda. Latest in the Amanda Roberts series.

Other books you might like:
Lacey Dancer, *Forever Joy*, 1993
Tami Hoag, *Still Waters*, 1992
Susan Kyle, *Night Fever*, 1993
Heather Graham Pozzessere, *Slow Burn*, 1994
Tracey Tillis, *Deadly Masquerade*, 1994

2067

SHERRYL WOODS

Hot Property

(New York: Dell, 1992)

Story type: Contemporary; Romantic Suspense
Major character(s): Molly DeWitt, Detective—Amateur; Michael O'Hara, Detective—Police
Time period(s): 1990s
Locale(s): United States

Summary: When Molly DeWitt finds the president of her condominium association dead on the lounge floor — stabbed with her own knife — she decides to investigate, much to the irritation of handsome, but macho, police detective Michael O'Hara. The attraction between the two is obvious, but the romance remains unresolved, leaving the door open for the future adventures of these appealing characters. Funny and nicely plotted.

Other books you might like:
Jill Barkin, *Hot Streak*, 1991
Wendy Haley, *Shadow Whispers*, 1992
Kay Hooper, *Crime of Passion*, 1991
Carol Jerina, *Flirting with Danger*, 1990
Theresa Weir, *Iguana Bay*, 1990

2068

SHERRYL WOODS

Hot Secret

(New York: Dell, 1992)

Story type: Romantic Suspense
Major character(s): Molly DeWitt, Detective—Amateur; Michael O'Hara, Detective—Police, Police Officer
Time period(s): 1990s
Locale(s): Florida

Summary: When a brilliant, but controversial, film director is murdered in the leading lady's dressing room, police detective Michael O'Hara has his hands full, not only with solving the crime, but with dealing with the charming and inquisitive amateur sleuth, Molly DeWittt. Follows "Hot Property.".

Other books you might like:
Deborah Gordon, *Beating the Odds*, 1992
Wendy Haley, *Shadow Whispers*, 1992
Carol Jerina, *Flirting with Danger*, 1990
Antoinette Stockenberg, *Emily's Ghost*, 1992
fantasy time-change elements

2069

SHERRYL WOODS

Stolen Moments

(New York: Popular Library, 1990)

Story type: Romantic Suspense
Series: Amanda Roberts
Major character(s): Amanda Roberts, Journalist (newspaper reporter); Joe Donelli, Police Officer (former), Detective
Time period(s): 1980s
Locale(s): Georgia

Summary: Amanda and Joe are back together again, this time involved in the disappearance of Southern artifacts. Eventually, the mystery is solved and their somewhat rocky relationship comes to a satisfying resolution.

Other books you might like:
Susan Anderson, *Shadow Dance*, 1989
Jill Barkin, *Hot Streak*, 1990
D.B. Baylor, *Fatal Obsession*, 1989
Mary Higgins Clark, *Stillwatch*, 1984
Carol Jerina, *Flirting with Danger*, 1990

2070

CYNTHIA WRIGHT

Barbados

(New York: Ballantine, 1995)

Story type: Historical/Regency; Historical/Exotic
Major character(s): Adrienne Beauvisage, Governess, Companion; Nathan Raveneau, Guardian, Pirate
Time period(s): 1810s (1818)
Locale(s): England; Barbados

Summary: Knowing his daughter's penchant for adventure (and trouble), Nicholai Beauvisage hires Nathan Raveneau, the son of an old friend, to act as Adrienne's protector. When Nathan realizes she is in danger, he takes her aboard his ship and they set sail for Barbados. It is only then that Adrienne discovers that he is in reality the notorious pirate, "The Scapegrace." Proximity encourages passion and when they reach his plantation, marriage follows. But vengeance, danger, and more adventure await and must be taken care of before they can both be truly happy. Exotic and romantic.

Other books you might like:
Judith E. French, *Fortune's Mistress*, 1993
Kit Gardner, *Island Star*, 1994
Lisa Kleypas, *Only with Your Love*, 1992
Kathleen E. Woodiwiss, *Shanna*, 1977
    classic pirate tale

2071

CYNTHIA WRIGHT

Brighter than Gold
(New York: Ballantine, 1990)

Story type: Historical/American West
Major character(s): Kate McKenzie, Journalist (newspaper), Businesswoman (saloon-keeper's daughter); Jack Adams, Prospector
Time period(s): 1860s (1864)
Locale(s): California

Summary: Journalist Kate McKenzie applauds the actions of the Robin Hood-like Griffin as he steals from a pair of greedy mine owners—until her father is killed and all the evidence points to the elusive Griffin. But just who he is and how he relates to the man Kate loves, Jack Adams, are questions that form the key motivations in this fast-paced historical.

Other books you might like:
Rene J. Garrod, *Temptation's Wild Embrace*, 1990
Marylyle Rogers, *Hidden Hearts*, 1989
    Medieval Robin Hood
Dana Fuller Ross, *California!*, 1981
    Wagons West series/Action, some romance
Rebecca Sinclair, *California Caress*, 1989
Lynette Vinet, *Pirate's Bride*, 1989
    Another incognito hero/High seas setting

2072

CYNTHIA WRIGHT

Wildblossom
(New York: Ballantine, 1994)

Story type: Historical/American West
Major character(s): Shelby Matthews, Rancher; Geoffrey Weston, Nobleman (English)
Time period(s): 19th century
Locale(s): Cody, Wyoming; England

Summary: New ranch owner Shelby Matthews needs money and gambles away half her ranch to Lord Geoffrey Weston who is in Wyoming on vacation. They work together and

enjoy each other until he's called home. Torn between duty and Shelby, Geoffrey returns to England; all seems lost until Shelby shows up as a Buffalo Bill Wild West performer. They rekindle their love affair, but they both have a lot of compromising to do.

Other books you might like:
Gwen Cleary, *Victoria's Ecstasy*, 1990
Joan Hohl, *Silver Thunder*, 1992
Joan Johnston, *The Inheritance*, 1995

2073

JESSICA WULF

The Irish Rose
(New York: Zebra, 1994)

Story type: Historical/American West
Major character(s): Alina Gallagher, Orphan, Accountant (bookkeeper); Beauregard Parker, Rancher
Time period(s): 1890s
Locale(s): Laramie, Wyoming

Summary: After her father's death, Alina flees home to avoid both greedy relatives and an arranged marriage. Although she escapes detection for a while, eventually "the marriage" looms on the horizon and rancher Beau Parker comes to her rescue—by marrying her himself. This action sparks anger and greed from a variety of sources, and Alina and Beau find themselves dealing with kidnapping, stealing, and trickery—and a newly-found love.

Other books you might like:
Jenny Aiken, *Love Evergreen*, 1993
Samantha James, *Outlaw Heart*, 1993
Diana Palmer, *Lacy*, 1991
Diana Palmer, *Trilby*, 1993
Katherine Sutcliffe, *Dream Fever*, 1991

2074

CATHERINE WYATT

Beneath a Harvest Moon
(New York: Zebra, 1993)

Story type: Historical/Canadian West
Major character(s): Alexandra Merrit, Young Woman; Morgan Glendower, Doctor, Recluse
Time period(s): 1860s
Locale(s): Canada

Summary: In order to check out the past of her father's prospective wife, Alexandra goes to stay with her grandmother in Canada and meets Morgan Glendower, a reclusive, resentful doctor who is hiding from the world. In spite of their initial, mutual distrust, they gradually begin a relationship which leads to love.

Other books you might like:
Kristin Hannah, *A Handful of Heaven*, 1991
Linda Howard, *The Touch of Fire*, 1992
Shirley Parenteau, *Golden Prospect*, 1991
Scotney St. James, *Northern Fire, Northern Star*, 1990

2075
CATHERINE WYATT

A Rose in the Shadows
(New York: Zebra, 1992)

Story type: Historical/Victorian America
Major character(s): Kate Warne, Detective; Alec Dalton, Detective
Time period(s): 1850s (1855)
Locale(s): New York, New York; Chicago, Illinois

Summary: Totally convinced of her ability, young widow Kate Warne insists that she be hired as a Pinkerton detective. Amazingly, she succeeds, but when she must pair up with handsome Alec Dalton, they argue over everything. In spite of this, they are a great team, and as they work together, they slowly begin to appreciate one another. Attraction and love soon follow, but then the blossoming of Kate's promising career begins to create conflict. Interesting characters in a lively story.

Other books you might like:
Kay Hooper, *Crime of Passion*, 1991
Kay McMahon, *Betray the Night*, 1991
   British setting
Gina Robins, *Deception's Sweet Kiss*, 1990
Barbara Dawson Smith, *Fire at Midnight*, 1992
Erin Yorke, *Dangerous Deceptions*, 1992

2076
PATRICIA WYNN

The Bumblebroth
(New York: Fawcett Crest, 1995)

Story type: Regency
Major character(s): Mathilda, Noblewoman (Duchess of Upavon); William Westbury, Nobleman
Time period(s): 1810s
Locale(s): England

Summary: Lord Westbury's mother is determined that he will marry the Duchess of Upavon's fifteen-year-old daughter in order to reclaim some ancestral lands. But once Westbury meets Mathilda, the duchess, herself, there is do doubt which lady he will pursue. Light and diverting.

Other books you might like:
Georgette Heyer, *Bath Tangle*, 1955
   classic Regency
Georgette Heyer, *Frederica*, 1965
   classic Regency
Elizabeth Jackson, *A Brilliant Alliance*, 1993
   similar idea
Phyllis Taylor Pianka, *The Thackery Jewels*, 1994

2077
JUDITH YODER

A Matter of Compromise
(Toronto: Harlequin, 1992)

Story type: Contemporary
Major character(s): Susan O'Toole, Paralegal; Tony Brandon, Lawyer
Time period(s): 1990s
Locale(s): Washington, District of Columbia

Summary: There are bitter feelings between Tony and Susan because four years ago he inadvertently closed Susan's legal aid business. Now they still have problems trusting each other, but their common interest in keeping a group of senior citizens from being evicted makes for close contact. Gradually they build a relationship and begin to put the past behind them.

Other books you might like:
Delayne Camp, *Newsworthy Affair*, 1990
Kay Hooper, *Star-Crossed Lovers*, 1990
Carol Jerina, *Flirting with Danger*, 1990
Kathleen Gilles Seidel, *Maybe This Time*, 1990
LaVyrle Spencer, *Bygones*, 1992

2078
REBECCA YORK

What Child Is This?
(Toronto: Harlequin, 1993)

Story type: Contemporary; Romantic Suspense
Major character(s): Erin Morgan, Researcher; Travis Stone, Adoptee
Time period(s): 1990s
Locale(s): United States

Summary: When Erin, a specialist in locating birth parents, agrees to help her former boyfriend Travis find his own birth parents, they end up involved not only in solving a mystery but trying to outwit a murderer as well. Suspenseful and fast-paced.

Other books you might like:
Elizabeth August, *The Virgin Wife*, 1993
Christiane Heggan, *Passions*, 1993
Tracey Tillis, *Deadly Masquerade*, 1994
Pat Warren, *Nowhere to Run*, 1993

2079
ERIN YORKE (Pseudonym of Susan Yasnick and Chris Healy)

Dangerous Deceptions
(Toronto: Harlequin, 1992)

Story type: Historical/Victorian
Major character(s): Anne Hargraves, Singer, Spy (British Intelligence); Ian Kendrick, Spy (British Intelligence)
Time period(s): 1880s (1887)
Locale(s): London, England

Summary: Queen Victoria is in danger of being assassinated, and Anne Hargraves and Ian Kendrick are using their spying skills to prevent it from happening. Both work for British Intelligence, but neither knows about the other, and as the story progresses, they become more and more attracted to each other and, at the same time, more and more suspicious of each other. Eventually, all secrets are revealed and the Queen is saved.

Other books you might like:
Patricia Gaffney, *Thief of Hearts*, 1990
Elizabeth Kary, *Midnight Lace*, 1991
Jayne Ann Krentz, *Rendezvous*, 1992
Kay McMahon, *Betray the Night*, 1991
Carla Simpson, *Seductive Caress*, 1992

2080

ERIN YORKE (Pseudonym of Susan Yasnick and Chris Healy)

Heaven's Gate
(Toronto: Harlequin, 1992)

Story type: Historical/Renaissance
Major character(s): Regan Davies, Noblewoman; Connor O'Carroll, Nobleman (Earl of Kincaid)
Time period(s): 16th century (1567)
Locale(s): Ireland

Summary: Banished from Elizabeth's court and sent to reclaim her late father's Irish estate, Lady Regan Davies finds herself in conflict with the original owner of her estate, the dispossessed Irish Earl of Kincaid, Connor O'Carroll. Connor, however, is in disguise; and as he covertly orchestrates a series of events to frighten Regan into leaving, he is also falling under her spell. An action-filled story of two determined and independent people who fall in love in spite of themselves.

Other books you might like:
Kimberleigh Caitlin, *Wildwitch*, 1991
Betina M. Krahn, *Behind Closed Doors*, 1991
Betina M. Krahn, *Caught in the Act*, 1990
Catherine Linden, *Highland Flame*, 1991
Bertrice Small, *Skye O'Malley*, 1980

2081

MOLLEEN ZANGER

Gardenias Where There Are None
(Tallahassee, Florida: Naiad, 1994)

Story type: Contemporary/Fantasy; Lesbian/Contemporary

Major character(s): Melanie Myer, Student, Lesbian; Camille, Spirit
Time period(s): 1990s
Locale(s): Michigan

Summary: Graduate student Melanie Myer rents a long-vacant house in rural Michigan and ends up being courted by the ghost of a woman who died almost 80 years ago. Filled with all the standard accoutrements of the paranormal (cold spots, strange fragrances, moving objects, intuitive knowledge) and a few that are more unusual (communicating with the ghost via computer), this story features well-defined characters and a nicely-handled (and quite romantic) relationship between Camille and Mel. Fast-paced, well-written, and sexually explicit.

Other books you might like:
Nancy Tyler Glenn, *Clicking Stones*, 1989
Lori Herter, *The Willow File*, 1994
   non-lesbian romance
Karen M.C. Minns, *Virago*, 1990
   vampire story
Ouida Rozier, *Shadows After Dark*, 1993
   fantasy
Antoinette Stockenberg, *Embers*, 1994
   non-lesbian ghost story

2082

THELMA ZIRKELBACH

A Man of Few Words
(Bensalem, Pennsylvania: Meteor, 1993)

Story type: Contemporary
Major character(s): Kelly Connery, Health Care Professional (speech pathologist); Grant Stuart, Rancher
Time period(s): 1990s
Locale(s): Texas

Summary: Grant Stuart wants the best speech teacher for his son and Kelly truly wants to help, so in spite of some misgivings, she agrees to teach young Sean Stuart at his father's ranch. Busy, taciturn, and emotionally distant, Grant has no plans for any romantic involvements, but Kelly changes his mind.

Other books you might like:
Kathy Clark, *Stand by Your Man*, 1993
Anne Marie Duquette, *On the Line*, 1993
Joey Light, *High Riding Heroes*, 1993
Joey Light, *Sterling's Reasons*, 1991

Series Index

This index alphabetically lists series to which books featured in the entries belong. Beneath each series name, book titles are listed alphabetically with author names. Numbers refer to the entries that feature each title.

Time Period Index

This index chronologically lists the time settings in which the featured books take place. Main headings refer to a century; where no specific time is given, the headings INDETERMINATE PAST, INDETERMINATE FUTURE, and INDETERMINATE are used. The 18th through 21st centuries are broken down into decades when possible. (Note: 1800s, for example, refers to the first decade of the 19th century.) Featured titles are listed alphabetically beneath time headings, with author names and entry numbers also provided.

INDETERMINATE PAST

Angel Christmas - Mary Balogh 53
A Certain Magic - Kathleen Morgan 1410
Daughter of the Reef - Clare Coleman 375
Fire Queen - Deborah Grambien 743
A Gift of Joy - Virginia Henley 871
Hearts Enslaved - Judith Hill 889
Irish Magic - Roberta Gellis 709
My Warrior's Heart - Betina M. Krahn 1102
Silversword - Lindsay Randall 1588
Sister of the Sun - Clare Coleman 376
Swan Bride - Betina Lindsey 1192
Swan Star - Betina Lindsey 1193
Swan Witch - Betina Lindsey 1194
Touch the Stars - Lynn Armistead McKee 1313
Warrior's Lady - Madeline Baker 48
The Wizard of Seattle - Kay Hooper 925

120th CENTURY B.C.

Daughter of the Red Deer - Joan Wolf 2057

91st CENTURY B.C.

Dark Renegade - Theresa Scott 1756
Keepers of the Misty Time - Patricia Rowe 1700

80th CENTURY B.C.

Broken Promise - Theresa Scott 1755

13th CENTURY B.C.

Across a Wine-Dark Sea - Jessica Bryan 239

7th CENTURY B.C.

Woman of the Mists - Lynn Armistead McKee 1314

5th CENTURY B.C.

The Night Orchid - Patricia Simpson 1804

1st CENTURY

Beloved Bondage - Katherine Kincaid 1066
Enchant the Heavens - Kathleen Morgan 1414

2nd CENTURY

Lady of Conquest - Teresa Medeiros 1340
Somewhere in Time - Merline Lovelace 1228

5th CENTURY

The Last Viking Queen - Janelle Taylor 1917
To Love Again - Bertrice Small 1826

6th CENTURY

Born of the Sun - Joan Wolf 2056

7th CENTURY

Chanting the Dawn - Marylyle Rogers 1690
Chanting the Morning Star - Marylyle Rogers 1691
Heartspell - Blaine Anderson 15
Lord of Fire - Emma Merritt 1345

8th CENTURY

A Love Beyond Time - Flora M. Speer 1855

9th CENTURY

By Love Enslaved - Phoebe Conn 385
Dawn on a Jade Sea - Jessica Bryan 240
Gentle Warrior - Kathryn Hockett 904
Surrender My Love - Johanna Lindsey 1209
Swan Road - Rebecca Brandewyne 204
Viking Rose - Ashland Price 1554
The Viking's Woman - Heather Graham 742

10th CENTURY

The Defiant Heart - Anita Gordon 732
Devoted - Alice Borchardt 184
Gentle Conqueror - Mary Ellen Gronau 772
Lord of Hawkfell Island - Catherine Coulter 405
The Love Slave - Bertrice Small 1823
Passionate Warriors - Mary Ellen Gronau 773
The Reluctant Viking - Sandra Hill 891
The Tarnished Lady - Sandra Hill 892
The Valiant Heart - Anita Gordon 733

11th CENTURY

Blood Red Roses - Katherine Deauville 493
Bold Breathless Nights - Penelope Neri 1436
The Conqueror - Brenda Joyce 1023

Daggers of Gold - Katherine Deauville 494
The Eagle's Song - Marylyle Rogers 1693
Firebrand's Lady - Caryl Wilson 2043
Hour of the Rose - Christina Skye 1820
Knight of Fire - Shannon Drake 566
Knight's Caress - Lynette Vinet 1983
The Lion's Angel - Libby Sydes 1909
Lyon's Prize - Virginia Lynn 1242
Midnight Warrior - Iris Johansen 991
A Moment in Time - Bertrice Small 1824
The Pagan's Prize - Miriam Minger 1399
Princess of Fire - Shannon Drake 567
Princess of the Veil - Helen Mittermeyer 1401
The Prize - Julie Garwood 705
Promise of the Rose - Brenda Joyce 1028
Rose Among Thorns - Catherine Archer 27
Tapestry - Maura Seger 1765
Tender Warrior - Linda Lang Bartell 93
Until Forever - Johanna Lindsey 1210
Unwilling Betrayer - Joan Van Nuys 1972
A Warrior's Quest - Margaret Moore 1409

12th CENTURY

The Amethyst Crown - Katherine Deauville 492
Angel of Fire - Tanya Anne Crosby 431
Autumn's Flame - Denise Domning 546
Beloved Enemy - Ellen Jones 1012
Beneath a Pale Moon - Victoria Morrow 1422
The Bride - Julie Garwood 699
Bride of the Lion - Elizabeth Stuart 1894
Candle in the Window - Christina Dodd 534
Castle of Dreams - Flora M. Speer 1853
Castle of the Heart - Flora M. Speer 1854
Castles in the Air - Christina Dodd 535
Damsel in Distress - Shannon Drake 564
Dark Whispers - Marylyle Rogers 1692
Defy Not the Heart - Johanna Lindsey 1200
Desire - Amanda Quick 1568
Desire of the Heart - Katherine Vickery 1981
Emerald Fire - Laurie Grant 745
Enchanted - Elizabeth Lowell 1229
The Fatal Crown - Ellen Jones 1013
The Fire and the Fury - Anita Mills 1393
Hidden Hearts - Marylyle Rogers 1694
Keeper of the Dream - Penelope Williamson 2037
Knight's Desire - Judith Hill 890
My Cherished Enemy - Samantha James 973
Once upon a Kiss - Tanya Anne Crosby 433
Prisoner of My Desire - Johanna Lindsey 1207
The Rose of Blacksword - Rexanne Becnel 113
Splendor - Charlene Cross 440
Summer Storm - Denise Domning 547

1840s

Almost a Whisper - Charlene Cross 436
Angel in Marble - Elaine Coffman 368
Autumn Leaves - Jill Metcalf 1347
Betray the Night - Kay McMahon 1326
Blossom - Constance Bennett 120
Bold Destiny - Jane Feather 628
The Captain's Bride - Kat Martin 1273
Cheyenne Dreams - Peggy Hanchar 790
Desert Song - Constance O'Banyon 1447
Ecstasy's Masquerade - Gwen Cleary 363
Flame in the Night - Jack McGowan 1311
For All the Right Reasons - Elaine Coffman 370
The Ground She Walks Upon - Meagan
  McKinney 1323
A Heart So Innocent - Charlene Cross 438
Heaven and Earth - Kathleen Eagle 581
The Jacaranda Tree - Rebecca Brandewyne 202
Jade Dawn - Susannah Leigh 1181
Masque of Enchantment - Charlene Cross 439
Midnight Lace - Elizabeth Kary 1045
Morning Song - Karen Robards 1651
Night Fire - Cait Logan 1224
Night Flower - Shirl Henke 863
No Greater Love - Alison Irving 959
No Man's Fortune - Kristie Knight 1092
Only Forever - Kimberly Cates 330
Orchids in Moonlight - Patricia Hagan 781
Pirate's Princess - Constance O'Banyon 1449
Promises to Keep - Nina Beaumont 107
Renegade Embrace - Virginia Brown 235
Rogue's Mistress - Eugenia Riley 1637
Savannah Heat - Kat Martin 1278
Scoundrel's Desire - JoAnn De Lazzari 489
Silk and Secrets - Mary Jo Putney 1561
The Silver Link - Patricia Potter 1545
Somewhere Along the Way - Elaine Coffman 372
Sultry Nights - Charla Cameron 281
Sweet Mountain Magic - Rosanne Bittner 162
Treasure of the Sun - Christina Dodd 541
The Turquoise Trail - Susannah Leigh 1182
Veils of Silk - Mary Jo Putney 1565
The Vow - Lindsay Chase 337
Whispers in Time - Becky Lee Weyrich 2011
Wild Star - Nicole Jordan 1021
The Wild Winds - Catherine Palmer 1487
Yesterday's Shadows - Marianne Willman 2042

1850s

Beneath Passion's Skies - Bobbi Smith 1834
Beyond Scandal - Brenda Joyce 1022
Black Silk - Judy Cuevas 443
California Caress - Rebecca Sinclair 1810
Capture the Night - Geralyn Dawson 482
Caress - Rosanne Bittner 153
Chase the Dawn - Kay McMahon 1327
Comanche Flame - Genell Dellin 507
Devil's Lady - Patricia Rice 1614
Fire on the Wind - Barbara Dawson Smith 1830
Forever Ecstasy - Janelle Taylor 1915
A Forever Kind of Love - Patricia Hagan 778
The Forever Tree - Rosanne Bittner 155
Gold Is the Game - Rae Muir 1433
Heaven Knows - Elaine Coffman 371
The Inheritance - Joan Johnston 1005
The Jacaranda Tree - Rebecca Brandewyne 202
Kiley's Storm - Suzanne Elizabeth 599
Kiss Me Forever - Bobbi Smith 1837
Light on the Mountain - Maura Seger 1762
Love Across Time - Anne Meredith 1343
Love's Stolen Promise - Sylvie Sommerfield 1852
The Master's Bride - Suzannah Davis 481
Midnight Rose - Robin Lee Hatcher 830
Mississippi Mistress - Gina Robins 1675
Mistress of Sin - Sue Rich 1624
Mountain Laurel - Jude Deveraux 516
Nightfire - Leona Karr 1044
Notorious - Patricia Potter 1542
Once a Rebel - Micki Brown 226

Oregon Bride - Rosanne Bittner 158
Prince of the Night - Jasmine Cresswell 420
Rachel - Lynda Trent 1961
Rainbow - Patricia Potter 1543
Redeeming Love - Francine Rivers 1648
Riverboat Temptation - Gwen Cleary 365
A Rose in the Shadows - Catherine Wyatt 2075
Scandalous - Sonia Simone 1796
Secrets of a Midnight Moon - Jane Bonander 181
Shameless - Rosanne Bittner 160
Song of the Bayou - Elinor Lynley 1239
Southern Seduction - Thea Devine 522
Springtown - DeLoras Scott 1753
Stolen Fire - Danette Chartier 335
Sun God - Nan Ryan 1707
Surrender My Heart - Lois Greiman 770
Surrender the Dream - Debra Dier 531
Taming Kate - Eugenia Riley 1638
Tangled - Mary Balogh 69
Tarnished Hearts - Raine Cantrell 311
Tempest in Time - Eugenia Riley 1639
Tempt Me with Kisses - Phoebe Conn 387
This Fiery Splendor - Christine Monson 1405
Thunder's Tender Touch - Carol Finch 647
Tilly and the Tiger - Marianne Willman 2041
When Lightning Strikes - Rexanne Becnel 115
When Passion Calls - Cassie Edwards 594
Wings of a Dove - Elaine Barbieri 76
The Wings of Morning - Karen Harper 812

1860s

Acts of Passion - Deana James 968
All My Heart Can Hold - Jessica Douglass 559
Always, My Love - Carla Simpson 1797
And One Rode West - Heather Graham 736
And One Wore Gray - Heather Graham 737
Angel Creek - Linda Howard 932
Angel Fire - Deborah Satinwood 1719
An Angel in My Arms - Victoria Morrow 1421
Apache Magic - Janis Reams Hudson 948
Ashton's Bride - Judith O'Brien 1450
Atlanta - Sara Orwig 1462
The Barefoot Bride - Joan Johnston 1004
Because of You - Micki Brown 225
Beneath a Harvest Moon - Catherine Wyatt 2074
Beyond the Horizon - Connie Mason 1287
Bittersweet Promises - Trana Mae Simmons 1791
Blossom - Constance Bennett 120
Boundless - Alexandra Thorne 1939
Brighter than Gold - Cynthia Wright 2071
Cactus Blossom - Emily Bradshaw 195
Captive Treasure - Tena Carlyle 314
Caress of Fire - Martha Hix 895
Chase the Fire - Barbara Ankrum 22
Cherokee Dawn - Genell Dellin 504
Cheyenne Amber - Catherine Anderson 16
Christmas Miracle - Ruth Langan 1152
Comanche Moon - Catherine Anderson 18
Come Be My Love - Patricia Watters 1996
Dancing on Snowflakes - Jane Bonander 180
The Daring - Patricia Hagan 777
Darkest Heart - Brenda Joyce 1025
Dearest Enemy - Stephanie Bartlett 94
Deception's Sweet Kiss - Gina Robins 1672
Distant Thunder - Lisa Bingham 145
Dream Fever - Katherine Sutcliffe 1901
Embers of the Heart - Rosanne Bittner 154
Emerald Embrace - Shannon Drake 565
The Emerald Tears of Foxfire Manor - Clara
  Wimberly 2048
The Falcon and the Swan - Diane Gates
  Robinson 1680
A Fire in the Heart - Katherine Sutcliffe 1902
Flame Lily - Candace Camp 289
The Flames of Vengeance - Beverly Byrne 265
The Flaming - Pat Tracy 1955
Forever in His Arms - Penelope Neri 1439
A Forever Kind of Love - Patricia Hagan 778
Gabrielle - Leta Tegler 1922

Golden Bird - Jo Ann Algermissen 9
Golden Nights - Christine Monson 1404
The Heart's Legacy - Barbara Keller 1047
Irresistible - Catherine Hart 820
The Jade Garden - Laurel Collins 378
Kansas Kiss - Christine Dorsey 550
Lady Legend - Deborah Camp 296
A Lady of the West - Linda Howard 934
Legacy - Leigh Bristol 217
The Legend of Love - Nan Ryan 1704
Lightning - Patricia Potter 1541
Lone Star Lady - Jill Gregory 764
Love a Dark Rider - Shirlee Busbee 258
Love's Stolen Promise - Sylvie Sommerfield 1852
Many Fires - Kathleen Sage 1711
Mask of Night - Lois Wolfe 2058
Midnight Blue - Dorothy Garlock 687
Montana Mistress - Carol Finch 644
Montana Woman - Rosanne Bittner 157
Moonlight Enchantment - Carol Finch 645
More than Just a Night - Connie Rinehold 1642
Mountain Rose - Norah Hess 886
Nevada Nights - Georgina Gentry 713
Once a Rebel - Micki Brown 226
Once upon Forever - Becky Lee Weyrich 2008
One Wore Blue - Heather Graham 739
Only His - Elizabeth Lowell 1231
Only Mine - Elizabeth Lowell 1233
Passion's Timeless Hour - Vivian Knight-
  Jenkins 1094
Perchance to Dream - Maura Seger 1763
Prince Charming - Julie Garwood 704
The Prisoner - Cheryl Reavis 1604
Promised Sunrise - Robin Lee Hatcher 832
Pure Sin - Susan Johnson 1002
Quicksilver Passion - Georgina Gentry 714
Rebel Seduction - Jane Archer 30
Reckless Love - Elizabeth Lowell 1234
The Redhead and the Preacher - Sandra
  Chastain 344
Renegade - Patricia Potter 1544
Renegade Bride - Barbara Ankrum 23
Renegade's Kiss - Barbara Ankrum 24
The Return - Diane Haeger 776
Riverbend - Mary McBride 1300
Riverboat Rogue - Jane Toombs 1952
Riverboat Seduction - Caroline Bourne 192
The Ruby - Christina Skye 1821
Sagebrush Bride - Tanya Anne Crosby 434
Sapphire - Venita Helton 849
The Savage - Nicole Jordan 1019
The Schemers - Lois Wolfe 2059
Shelter From the Storm - Patricia Rice 1621
Sioux Splendor - Rosanne Bittner 161
South of the Line - Catherine Ennis 611
Storm Dancers - Allison Hayes 838
Stormswept - Katherine Kincaid 1068
Surrender to the Fury - Cara Miles 1375
Sweet Texas Fury - LaRee Bryant 242
Tears of Fire - Nelle McFather 1308
Temptation's Price - Dallas Schulze 1738
Texas Temptation - Gina Robins 1676
Thief of Hearts - Patricia Gaffney 679
Until Tomorrow - Jill Marie Landis 1148
Waltz with the Lady - Betina Lindsey 1195
White Rose - Linda Ladd 1127
White Tiger - Olga Bicos 142
Wild Dawn - Cait Logan 1225
Wild Mountain Honey - Carol Finch 648
Wildest Dreams - Rosanne Bittner 164
Wildfire - Norah Hess 887
The Wings of Morning - Karen Harper 812
With One Look - Jennifer Horsman 929
Yankee Wife - Linda Lael Miller 1387
Yankee's Caress - Terri Valentine 1969

1870s

Almost Home - Debra Cowan 414
Angel Eyes - Suzannah Davis 478

Geographic Index

This index provides access to all featured books by geographic settings, such as countries, continents, oceans, and planets. States and provinces are indicated for the United States and Canada. Also interfiled are headings for fictional place names, such as Spaceships, Imaginary Planets, etc. Sections are further broken down by city or the specific name of the inaginary locale. Book titles are listed alphabetically under headings, and author names and entry numbers are also provided.

AFGHANISTAN

Bold Destiny - Jane Feather 628

AFRICA

The Captive - Victoria Holt 918
Sweet Paradise - Terri Valentine 1968
Whispered Kisses - Janelle Taylor 1919
The Wild Winds - Catherine Palmer 1487

Barbary Coast
Desert Bride - JoAnne Redd 1608
Sea Fires - Christine Dorsey 551

ALBANIA

The Lion's Daughter - Loretta Chase 339

ALGERIA

Capture My Heart - Bobbi Smith 1835

Sahara Desert
Crossing Eden - Emma Gordon 735

ALTERNATE EARTH

Fortune's Tide - Maura Seger 1759
Perchance to Dream - Maura Seger 1763

AMERICAN COLONIES

The Conquest - Lucy Elliot 602
Follow the Heart - Anita Mills 1394
Freedom Flame - Caryn Cameron 279
The Golden Dove - JoAnn Wendt 2001
Master of My Dreams - Danelle Harmon 809
Moon Dreams - Patricia Rice 1617
Moonfeather - Judith E. French 670
Nobody's Angel - Karen Robards 1652
Pirate's Angel - Marsha Bauer 99
Pirate's Bride - Elizabeth August 35
A Pirate's Pleasure - Heather Graham 740
Shadowed Vows - Sue Rich 1626
Silver Tears - Becky Lee Weyrich 2009
Somewhere in Time - Barbara Bretton 216
Sweet Forever - Becky Lee Weyrich 2010
Temptation's Tender Kiss - Colleen Faulkner 627
Traitorous Hearts - Susan Kay Law 1165
Wild Conquest - Hannah Howell 941

Winds of Glory - Gretchen Genet 711
Block Island
Blazing Passion - Barbara Cummings 445

Carolinas
Deepwater - Pamela Jeckel 979
The Heart's Disguise - Lisa Ann Verge 1976
Sea Fires - Christine Dorsey 551
Sweet Savage Splendor - Lauren Wilde 2030

Charlestown
Kissed - Tanya Anne Crosby 432

CONNECTICUT

This Side of Heaven - Karen Robards 1654

Belle Haven
The Taming of Amelia - Maura Seger 1764

GEORGIA

Gideon's Fall - Bronwyn Williams 2033
Rebel Wildfire - Barbara Cummings 447

MARYLAND

Flames of Love - Colleen Faulkner 624
Moon Dancer - Judith E. French 669
Sweet Deception - Colleen Faulkner 626

MASSACHUSETTS

Defiant Heart - Nancy Moulton 1432
A Love for All Time - Sandra Davidson 470
Wild Glory - Andrea Parnell 1509

Boston
Rebel Dreams - Patricia Rice 1620
Rebel's Captive - Amy Christopher 356

Salem
Bewitching Kisses - Rainy Kirkland 1083
Wind Rose - Krista Janssen 977

NEW ENGLAND

Fortune's Mistress - Judith E. French 667

NEW HAMPSHIRE

Frontier Fire - Barbara Cummings 446

NEW YORK

The Claim - Lucy Elliot 601
Wild Savage Love - Dana Ransom 1594

Mohawk Valley
Eden's Gate - Karen Harper 810

PENNSYLVANIA

Wilderness Flame - Barbara Cummings 448

SOUTH CAROLINA

Wild Savage Heart - Pamela K. Forrest 661

VIRGINIA

Bewitching Kisses - Rainy Kirkland 1083
Brazen Virginia Bride - Millie Criswell 423
Bride of the Wind - Shannon Drake 563
Defiant Imposter - Miriam Minger 1398
Lovestorm - Judith E. French 668
The Raider's Bride - Kimberly Cates 331
The Scarlet Temptress - Sue Rich 1625
Time-Spun Treasure - Thomasina Ring 1646

Chesapeake Bay
Wind Rose - Krista Janssen 977

Fredericksburg
Phantom Lover - Millie Criswell 428

Williamsburg
Rebel Wildfire - Barbara Cummings 447

ASIA

Silk and Secrets - Mary Jo Putney 1561

AT SEA

Beloved Avenger - Joan Van Nuys 1970
Blazing Passion - Barbara Cummings 445
Buccaneer's Bride - Jean Innes 958
The Captain's Bride - Kat Martin 1273
Captain's Captive - Christine Dorsey 549
Deceptive Desires - Wanda Owen 1474
Desert Eden - Patricia Grasso 747
Desire - Phoebe Conn 386
Devil's Deception - Suzannah Davis 480
A Durable Fire - Virginia Bernhard 129
Forever After - Bette Ford 657

Gentle Rogue - Johanna Lindsey 1201
Gideon's Fall - Bronwyn Williams 2033
The Heart's Disguise - Lisa Ann Verge 1976
Heart's Masquerade - Deborah Simmons 1789
Jade Dawn - Susannah Leigh 1181
Jewel of the Sea - Susan Wiggs 2024
Lightning - Patricia Potter 1541
Love's Safe Harbor - Cindy T. Moss 1431
The Magic - Robin Lee Hatcher 829
The Magic of You - Johanna Lindsey 1204
Mariah's Prize - Miranda Jarrett 978
Midnight Ice - Cathie Linz 1213
Miss Whittier Makes a List - Carla Kelly 1055
Only for Love - Elaine Barbieri 73
Pirate's Angel - Marsha Bauer 99
Pirate's Bride - Elizabeth August 35
Pirate's Bride - Lynette Vinet 1984
Sea of Dreams - Elizabeth DeLancey 497
Sea of Dreams - Christine Dorsey 552
Sweet Abandon - Sara Blayne 175
Sweet Seduction - Patricia Pellicane 1515
Sweet Southern Caress - Wendy Garrett 696
Swept Away - Julie Tetel 1925
Taming Charlotte - Linda Lael Miller 1386
Tempt the Devil - Connie Mason 1291
Till Dawn Tames the Night - Meagan
  McKinney 1325
Virgin Star - Jennifer Horsman 928
When Midnight Comes - Robin Burcell 253
The Wild Winds - Catherine Palmer 1487

Gulf of Mexico
Only with Your Love - Lisa Kleypas 1089

Sargasso Sea
Always and Forever - Gina Robins 1671

ATLANTIC OCEAN

Heaven on Earth - Michelle Brandon 205

AUSTRALIA

Brave Land, Brave Love - Connie Mason 1288
The Diamond Tiger - Ann Maxwell 1296
Dream Time - Paris Afton Bonds 182
Far Horizons - Katherine Sinclair 1807
Heart of the Wild - Donna Stephens 1874
Outback Legacy - Elizabeth Duke 570
The Past Is Another Country - Lois Battle 97
Temptation's Flame - Garda Parker 1500

Corroboree Springs
The Legacy - Linda Lael Miller 1381

Fiere Island
Tasmanian Devil - Valerie Parv 1512

Melbourne
The Dreaming - Barbara Wood 2060
White Rose - Linda Ladd 1127

New South Wales
The Jacaranda Tree - Rebecca Brandewyne 202
Once a Hero - Katherine Sutcliffe 1905
Wild Land, Wild Love - Connie Mason 1292

Outback
Morning's Gate - Ann Victoria Roberts 1658

AUSTRIA

The Princess Royal - Virginia Coffman 374

Vienna
Four in Hand - Margaret Westhaven 2006
Promises to Keep - Nina Beaumont 107
Sapphire Magic - Nina Beaumont 108

BAHAMAS

Escapade - Susan Kyle 1121
Midnight Treasure - Katherine Kincaid 1067
Mistress of Sin - Sue Rich 1624
Wild Wind - Jane Archer 31

Grand Abaco Island
Tradewinds - Annee Cartier 326

Nassau
Lightning - Patricia Potter 1541
Rebel's Captive - Amy Christopher 356
The Schemers - Lois Wolfe 2059
White Rose - Linda Ladd 1127

BARBADOS

Barbados - Cynthia Wright 2070
Beyond the Savage Sea - JoAnn Wendt 2000
Heart's Masquerade - Deborah Simmons 1789
Island Star - Kit Gardner 684
Savannah Heat - Kat Martin 1278
Tempt the Devil - Connie Mason 1291

BELGIUM

Virtue - Jane Feather 635

Brussels
The Waltzing Widow - Gayle Buck 248

BELIZE

Trust Me - Jeane Renick 1610

BERMUDA

The Heart Remembers - Barbara Hazard 842
Wind Rose - Krista Janssen 977

BRAZIL

Emerald Rain - Maggie Osborne 1467
Shadow Play - Katherine Sutcliffe 1906

Rio de Janiero
A Quest of Dreams - Debra Dier 530
White Rose - Linda Ladd 1127

BYZANTIUM

The Defiant Heart - Anita Gordon 732

Constantinople
To Love Again - Bertrice Small 1826

CANADA

Beneath a Harvest Moon - Catherine Wyatt 2074
Better than Before - Judith Duncan 572
Sing Carols with the Angels - Mary Leask 1171
The Spirit Path - Madeline Baker 47
Spring Blossom - Jill Metcalf 1349
Three Weddings and a Kiss - Kathleen E.
  Woodiwiss 2063
Tomorrow's Dream - Peggy Hanchar 792

Kinikinik Lake
Golden Swan - Judy Gill 725

Lake of the Woods
Northern Fire, Northern Star - Scotney St.
  James 1865

ALBERTA
Beyond All Reason - Judith Duncan 573

BRITISH COLUMBIA
Awakening Dreams - Vanessa Grant 746
Prince of Wolves - Susan Krinard 1116

Salt Spring Island
California Man - Carole Dean 490

Vancouver
After Hours - Gail Douglas 556
Come Be My Love - Patricia Watters 1996
A Woman Without Lies - Elizabeth Lowell 1236

Vancouver Island
Sing to Me of Dreams - Kathryn Lynn Davis 477

NOVA SCOTIA

Halifax
Love's Safe Harbor - Cindy T. Moss 1431

ONTARIO
Visions of the Heart - Emily Carmichael 317

QUEBEC
Captive Kiss - Amy Christopher 355
Capture - Emily French 665
The Conquest - Lucy Elliot 602

Montreal
Captain's Captive - Christine Dorsey 549

YUKON TERRITORY
Western Enchantress - Wendy Garrett 697

Dawson
Golden Prospect - Shirley Parenteau 1495
A Handful of Heaven - Kristin Hannah 797

Klondike
The Golden Mountain - Annalise Sun 1897

CARIBBEAN

A Dangerous Longing - Veronica Sattler 1720
Fortune's Mistress - Judith E. French 667
Only for Love - Elaine Barbieri 73
Paradise and More - Shirl Henke 865
Pirate's Kiss - Diana Haviland 834
Swept Away - Julie Tetel 1925
Wild Flower - Jill Marie Landis 1149
Wish upon a Star - Karen Morrell 1420

Arawak Island
Fortune's Bride - Judith E. French 666

Bellington Cay
To Love a Stranger - Blythe Bradley 194

St. Dominique
Sweet Abandon - Sara Blayne 175

Seafire Isle
Eyes of Fire - Heather Graham Pozzessere 1549

CENTRAL AMERICA

Lightning Strikes Twice - Lacey Dancer 459
Tilly and the Tiger - Marianne Willman 2041

CHINA

Dawn on a Jade Sea - Jessica Bryan 240

481

A Knight in Shining Armor - Jude Deveraux   515
Knight of Fire - Shannon Drake   566
Knight's Caress - Lynette Vinet   1983
Knight's Desire - Judith Hill   890
Knight's Lady - Suzanne Barclay   83
Lady Alex's Gamble - Evelyn Richardson   1633
The Lady and the Wolf - Julie Beard   105
Lady Defiant - Suzanne Robinson   1681
Lady Gallant - Suzanne Robinson   1682
Lady Leprechaun - Melinda McRae   1336
Lady Sarah's Charade - Nancy Richards-Akers   1631
Lady Vengeance - Sarah Eagle   585
Lady's Choice - Judith Nelson   1434
The Last Lord - Melinda Pryce   1557
The Last of the Winter Roses - Jeanne Savery   1726
The Last Viking Queen - Janelle Taylor   1917
Legacy of the Rose - Kasey Michaels   1367
Libby's London Merchant - Carla Kelly   1051
Liberty Rose - Stef Ann Holm   913
Lightning - Patricia Potter   1541
The Lily and the Hawk - Marlene Suson   1900
The Lily and the Leopard - Susan Wiggs   2025
The Lion's Angel - Libby Sydes   1909
Logic of the Heart - Patricia Veryan   1980
Lord Dearborn's Destiny - Brenda Hiatt   888
Lord Harlequin - Marian Devon   525
Lost Love Found - Bertrice Small   1822
A Love for All Seasons - Edith Layton   1170
Love Forever After - Patricia Rice   1615
The Love Knot - Elisabeth Fairchild   619
Love Me Forever - Johanna Lindsey   1203
A Love So Fierce - Joanna McGauran   1309
Love's Gambit - Meg-Lynn Roberts   1662
A Loyal Companion - Barbara Metzger   1354
The Luck of the Devil - Barbara Metzger   1355
Lucky in Love - Rebecca Robbins   1657
Lucy's Christmas Angel - Sandra Heath   845
Lyon's Prize - Virginia Lynn   1242
Mad Maria's Daughter - Patricia Rice   1616
Madcap Johnny - Jeanne Carmichael   318
Madcap Miss - Joan Smith   1845
A Maddening Minx - Mary Kingsley   1073
Maiden of Inverness - Arnette Lamb   1139
Man of My Dreams - Johanna Lindsey   1205
Marian's Christmas Wish - Carla Kelly   1052
The Marriage Gamble - Sarah Eagle   586
The Marriage Mart - Teresa DesJardien   510
Married by Mistake - Melinda McRae   1337
Masque of Enchantment - Charlene Cross   439
Masque of Sapphire - Deana James   969
Master of Her Heart - Terri Valentine   1965
Master of My Dreams - Danelle Harmon   809
Meridon - Philippa Gregory   768
A Merry Go-Round - Coral Hoyle   942
Midnight Raider - Shelly Thacker   1928
Midnight Warrior - Iris Johansen   991
Midsummer Night's Madness - Jill Barnett   90
A Misbegotten Match - Rita Boucher   186
Miss Billings Treads the Boards - Carla Kelly   1053
Miss Drayton's Downfall - Patricia Oliver   1460
Miss Gabriel's Gambit - Rita Boucher   187
Miss Wyndham's Escapade - Emily Hendrickson   854
The Mist and the Magic - Susan Wiggs   2026
The Mistress of Mishap - Cathleen Clare   358
The Mock Marriage - Dorothy Mack   1247
Moon Dreams - Patricia Rice   1617
Moonfeather - Judith E. French   670
Moonlight Charade - Judy Christenberry   353
Moonlight Veil - Janis Laden   1128
Moonshadow - Laura Parker   1504
A Mother's Delight - Jennifer Sawyer   1728
Move Heaven and Earth - Christina Dodd   538
Mrs. Drew Plays Her Hand - Carla Kelly   1056
Mutual Consent - Gayle Buck   247
My Cherished Enemy - Samantha James   973
My Gallant Enemy - Rexanne Becnel   112
My Lady Notorious - Jo Beverley   136
My Only Love - Katherine Sutcliffe   1904
Mystique - Amanda Quick   1570

A Natural Attachment - Katherine Kingsley   1070
Night Storm - Catherine Coulter   407
Nightrider - Sandra DuBay   568
No Greater Love - Katherine Kingsley   1071
A Noble Deception - Sara Blayne   174
Nobody's Angel - Karen Robards   1652
Once an Angel - Teresa Medeiros   1341
Once upon a Kiss - Tanya Anne Crosby   433
One Night with a Rogue - Kimberly Cates   329
The Only Hope - Jan Constant   389
Only Mine - Elizabeth Lowell   1233
Outrageous - Christina Dodd   539
Pagan Bride - Tamara Leigh   1183
The Panther and the Rose - Mary Burkhardt   257
The Passion of an Angel - Kasey Michaels   1370
Passion's Legacy - Jennifer West   2004
Passion's Melody - Jane Toombs   1951
Patience Is a Virtue - Judith Nelson   1435
The Persistent Earl - Gail Eastwood   589
The Pirate and the Pagan - Virginia Henley   872
Pirates and Promises - Anne Caldwell   274
Pirate's Angel - Marsha Bauer   99
Pirate's Wild Embrace - Linda Windsor   2049
Pirouette - Madeline Hale   782
The Pleasure of Love - Jean Plaidy   1533
Poetic Justice - Alicia Rasley   1596
Priceless - Christina Dodd   540
The Prince of Midnight - Laura Kinsale   1079
Princess of Fire - Shannon Drake   567
Prisoner of My Desire - Johanna Lindsey   1207
The Prize - Julie Garwood   705
Promise Me Forever - Cara Miles   1374
Promise of the Rose - Brenda Joyce   1028
Queen of the May - Emily Hendrickson   855
The Quest - Juliana Garnett   692
Rachel - Lynda Trent   1961
The Rake and His Lady - Julie Caille   269
The Rake and the Redhead - Emily Hendrickson   856
The Rake and the Reformer - Mary Jo Putney   1560
The Rake's Redemption - Leslie Lynn   1240
Ravished - Amanda Quick   1571
Ravished Bride - Sheila O'Hallion   1459
Rebel Dreams - Patricia Rice   1620
Rebel Wildfire - Barbara Cummings   447
Reckless - Amanda Quick   1572
Reckless Angel - Jane Feather   631
A Reformed Rake - Jeanne Savery   1727
A Regency Christmas II - Mary Balogh   63
A Regency Christmas VI - Mary Balogh   64
A Regency Christmas VII - Mary Balogh   65
A Regency Valentine - Mary Balogh   66
The Reluctant Suitor - Sarah Eagle   587
Remembrance - Jude Deveraux   517
Rendezvous - Amanda Quick   1573
The Return - Diane Haeger   776
Ride the Wind - Krista Janssen   976
Road to Ruin - Margaret Evans Porter   1535
Rogue's Reward - Jean R. Ewing   617
Rose Among Thorns - Catherine Archer   27
A Rose at Midnight - Anne Stuart   1889
The Rose at Twilight - Amanda Scott   1748
The Rose of Blacksword - Rexanne Becnel   113
Rosefire - Sandra Davidson   471
Sabelle - Veronica Sattler   1722
Sapphire and Shadow - Marie Ferrarella   639
Saving Grace - Julie Garwood   706
Scandal - Amanda Quick   1574
Scandalous - Pamela Caldwell   276
Scandalous Love - Brenda Joyce   1029
Scandal's Child - Leslie Lynn   1241
Scandal's Darling - Anne Caldwell   275
Scandal's Lady - Mary Kingsley   1075
Scarlet Angel - Elizabeth Thornton   1943
The Scarlet Thread - Evelyn Anthony   26
Sea of Dreams - Elizabeth DeLancey   497
Sea of Dreams - Christine Dorsey   552
A Second Match - Emma Lange   1159
The Secret - Julie Garwood   707
Secret Nights - Anita Mills   1395

Secret Song - Catherine Coulter   408
Seduced - Virginia Henley   873
Seduction - Amanda Quick   1575
Seize the Fire - Laura Kinsale   1080
The Serpent Beguiled - Betina Lindsey   1191
Shadow Dance - Anne Stuart   1890
Shadow Play - Katherine Sutcliffe   1906
Shadowed Vows - Sue Rich   1626
Shadows and Lace - Teresa Medeiros   1342
The Sherbrooke Bride - Catherine Coulter   409
Silver and Sapphires - Shelly Thacker   1929
The Silver Mirror - Roberta Gellis   710
Sinful - Susan Johnson   1003
Skylark - Elane Osborn   1466
The Snake, the Crocodile, and the Dog - Elizabeth Peters   1519
The Snow Angel - Mary Balogh   68
The Somerville Farce - Michelle Kasey   1046
A Song in the Wilderness - Lee Stafford   1868
The Spanish Lady - Joan Smith   1846
Speak Only Love - Deana James   970
A Spirited Affair - Lynn Kerstan   1060
The Spirited Bluestocking - Joan Overfield   1472
The Spitfire - Bertrice Small   1825
Splendor - Charlene Cross   440
Stolen Fire - Danette Chartier   335
Strange Encounter - Sally Wentworth   2002
The Substitute Bridegroom - Charlotte Louise Dolan   545
Summer Storm - Denise Domning   547
Summer Storm - Denise Domning   547
Sunshine and Shadow - Kathleen Harrington   816
Surrender - Amanda Quick   1576
Surrender to a Stranger - Karyn Monk   1402
Susannah's Secret - Judy Christenberry   354
Swan Bride - Betina Lindsey   1192
Swan Road - Rebecca Brandewyne   204
Sweet Bargain - Kate Moore   1407
Sweet Illusion - Angela Carson   325
Sweet Seduction - Patricia Pellicane   1515
Sweet Suspicions - Julie Tetel   1924
The Taming - Jude Deveraux   519
Tangled - Mary Balogh   69
Tapestry - Maura Seger   1765
The Tarnished Lady - Sandra Hill   892
A Taste of Heaven - Laura Simon   1795
Tempt the Devil - Connie Mason   1291
Tempted by Fire - Thea Devine   523
Tempting Fortune - Jo Beverley   138
A Tender Magic - Linda Madl   1262
Tender the Storm - Elizabeth Thornton   1944
Thief of Hearts - Patricia Gaffney   679
This Fiery Splendor - Christine Monson   1405
The Thorn Trees - Marcella Thum   1946
Three Weddings and a Kiss - Kathleen E. Woodiwiss   2063
Through a Dark Mist - Marsha Canham   307
Through All Eternity - Brenna Braxton-Barshon   210
Till Dawn Tames the Night - Meagan McKinney   1325
A Time for Roses - Elaine Coffman   373
Timeless - Jasmine Cresswell   421
To Catch the Flame - Kimberly Cates   332
To Catch the Wind - Jasmine Cresswell   422
To Love Again - Bertrice Small   1826
To Love and to Honor - Phoebe Conn   388
A Token of Jewels - Diane Cory   400
Tonight and Forever - Caryl Wilson   2044
Touch Me with Fire - Nicole Jordan   1020
A Touch of Forever - Janice Bennett   126
Touched by Magic - Patricia Rice   1623
A Traitorous Heart - Violet Hamilton   787
Traitor's Kiss - Jane Toombs   1953
Traitor's Kiss - Joy Tucker   1963
Uncommon Vows - Mary Jo Putney   1564
An Unlikely Attraction - Melinda McRae   1338
Unlikely Guardian - Carol Proctor   1556
Untamed - Elizabeth Lowell   1235
Until Forever - Johanna Lindsey   1210

Northumbria
Chanting the Morning Star - Marylyle Rogers   1691

Oxford
Miss Grimsley's Oxford Career - Carla Kelly   1054

Oxfordshire
Dancing at Midnight - Julia Quinn   1581

Ravencroft
Lord Glenraven's Return - Anne Barbour   80

Ravensbrook
June Love - Karla Hocker   902

Renford
Tender Warrior - Linda Lang Bartell   93

Rookeshaven
A Midsummer's Magic - Mary Chase Comstock   384

Salisbury
Miracle - Katherine Sutcliffe   1903

Shipton
A Lady in Disguise - Mellyora Ashley   32

Shrewsbury
The Vow - Mary Spencer   1861

Somerset
Move Heaven and Earth - Christina Dodd   538

Stone Ring Keep
Enchanted - Elizabeth Lowell   1229

Stoneleigh
Autumn Rain - Anita Mills   1389

Stratford
Call Home the Heart - Rebecca George   718

Sussex
Desert Song - Constance O'Banyon   1447

Upper Tudway
Deception - Amanda Quick   1567

Wycherley
To Love and to Cherish - Patricia Gaffney   680

York
Morning's Gate - Ann Victoria Roberts   1658

Yorkshire
Angel of Midnight - Jo-Ann Power   1547
Fool of Hearts - Terri Lynn Wilhelm   2032
Forbidden Fire - Heather Graham Pozzessere   1550
Fortune Is a Woman - Elizabeth Adler   4
The Jacaranda Tree - Rebecca Brandewyne   202
Lord Carew's Bride - Mary Balogh   60

EUROPE

The Beloved Scoundrel - Iris Johansen   989
Cherish the Night - Penelope Neri   1437
Daniel and Esther - Patrick Raymond   1603
Lisbon - Valerie Sherwood   1784
No Greater Love - Danielle Steel   1870
Remember - Barbara Taylor Bradford   193
The Scarlet Thread - Evelyn Anthony   26
Seize the Fire - Laura Kinsale   1080
Surrender in Scarlet - Patricia Camden   278
The Werewolf's Kiss - Cheri Scotch   1740

Indres
Return to Paradise - Shirl Henke   866

FICTIONAL COUNTRY

Fire Queen - Kathleen Morgan   1415
Return to Paradise - Shirl Henke   866
Warrior's Lady - Madeline Baker   48

Aventine
Midnight and Magnolias - Rebecca Paisley   1482

Balmarhea Island
Pirate's Princess - Constance O'Banyon   1449

Bavia
Princess Annie - Linda Lael Miller   1385

Cardinia
Once a Princess - Johanna Lindsey   1206

Innerworld
Stolen Dreams - Marilyn Campbell   303

Katandi
Awakenings - Saranne Dawson   483

Lichtenbourg
The Princess Royal - Virginia Coffman   374

Llantis
Awakenings - Saranne Dawson   483

Mendorra
Dangerous Charade - Madeline Harper   813

Perreault
One and Only - Barbara Bretton   215

Raith Morna
Swan Witch - Betina Lindsey   1194

Rhafhar
The Falcon's Mistress - Emma Darcy   463

Sedikhan
The Golden Barbarian - Iris Johansen   990

Tamrovia
The Golden Barbarian - Iris Johansen   990

Volas
From the Mist - Saranne Dawson   485

FRANCE

Across Time - Nina Beaumont   106
Angel of Fire - Tanya Anne Crosby   431
Awaken My Fire - Jennifer Horsman   926
Beloved Deceiver - Laurie Grant   744
Beloved Enemy - Ellen Jones   1012
Bliss - Judy Cuevas   444
Brazen Whispers - Jane Feather   629
Bride of the Unicorn - Kasey Michaels   1363
Captive to His Kiss - Paige Brantley   207
Captives of the Night - Loretta Chase   338
Capture the Night - Geralyn Dawson   482
Changes of Heart - Elizabeth Bennett   122
Courtesan - Diane Haeger   775
Devoted - Alice Borchardt   184
Dragonfly in Amber - Diana Gabaldon   673
The Fatal Crown - Ellen Jones   1013
For My Lady's Heart - Laura Kinsale   1078
Forever His - Shelly Thacker   1927
Golden Fires - Colleen Shannon   1769
The Heart's Legacy - Barbara Keller   1047
Highland Whispers - Sharon Gillenwater   726
If This Be Magic - Ellen Tanner Marsh   1270
A Kiss in the Night - Jennifer Horsman   927
The Lily and the Leopard - Susan Wiggs   2025
A Love Beyond Time - Flora M. Speer   1855
Madcap Johnny - Jeanne Carmichael   318
Masquerade - Janet Dailey   454
Mistress of the Eagles - Elona Malterre   1267
Morning's Gate - Ann Victoria Roberts   1658
The Prince of Midnight - Laura Kinsale   1079
Reap the Wind - Iris Johansen   992
Rendezvous - Serena Richards   1629
A Rose at Midnight - Anne Stuart   1889
Scandal's Child - Leslie Lynn   1241
Scarlet Angel - Elizabeth Thornton   1943
Scarlet Kisses - Patricia Camden   277

Sea of Dreams - Christine Dorsey   552
The Silver Mirror - Roberta Gellis   710
Skylark - Elane Osborn   1466
A Song in the Wilderness - Lee Stafford   1868
Storm Winds - Iris Johansen   993
Stranger in My Arms - Louisa Rawlings   1598
Sunshine and Shadow - Kathleen Harrington   816
Surrender to a Stranger - Karyn Monk   1402
Suspicion - Judith McWilliams   1339
Tender the Storm - Elizabeth Thornton   1944
Terms of Surrender - Mollie Ashton   33
Through All Eternity - Brenna Braxton-Barshon   210
Velvet - Jane Feather   633
Velvet Is the Night - Elizabeth Thornton   1945
Viking's Prize - Tanya Anne Crosby   435

Bordeaux
The Sorceress - Claire Delacroix   495

Brittany
Gentle Conqueror - Mary Ellen Gronau   772

Nice
The Dreamweavers: Sophisticated Lady - Gail Douglas   558

Normandy
In the Shadow of Midnight - Marsha Canham   306
Splendor - Charlene Cross   440

Paris
Beyond Eden - Catherine Coulter   402
Dance of Deception - Suzannah Davis   479
Forbidden - Susan Johnson   999
Gilded Dreams - Kristy Daniels   461
Lies - Doris Parmett   1506
Lord of Scoundrels - Loretta Chase   340
Michaela - Sarah Aldridge   7
Petals in the Storm - Mary Jo Putney   1559
Promise Me Heaven - Connie Brockway   221
The Raven and the Rose - Susan Wiggs   2027
Wicked Stranger - Louisa Rawlings   1599

Puivaillon
By All That Is Sacred - Laura Gilmour Bennett   127

Vezere Valley
Daughter of the Red Deer - Joan Wolf   2057

FRENCH POLYNESIA

Tahiti
Daughter of the Reef - Clare Coleman   375

GERMANY

So Worthy My Love - Kathleen E. Woodiwiss   2062

GREECE

Dangerous Odyssey - Jane Edwards   597

GRENADA

A Taste of Heaven - Laura Simon   1795

GUYANA

Shadow Play - Katherine Sutcliffe   1906

HONG KONG

Fortune Is a Woman - Elizabeth Adler   4
Pearl Moon - Katherine Stone   1885

IN THE AIR

Wings of Desire - Elizabeth Lambert   1140

Eader Island
All We Hold Dear - Kathryn Lynn Davis   476

Edinburgh
Highland Heart - Ruth Langan   1155
Snare of Serpents - Victoria Holt   919

Glasgow
All We Hold Dear - Kathryn Lynn Davis   476

Glen Affric
All We Hold Dear - Kathryn Lynn Davis   476

Glencoe
Love's Timeless Dance - Vivian Knight-Jenkins   1093

Hawkstone
Masque of Enchantment - Charlene Cross   439

The Hebrides
The Stormy Petrel - Mary Stewart   1880

Highlands
The Barbarous Scot - Dawn Lindsey   1197
Captive to a Dream - Susan Tanner   1911
Highland Flame - Catherine Linden   1190
Highland Rogue - Arnette Lamb   1138
Maiden of Inverness - Arnette Lamb   1139
Saving Grace - Julie Garwood   706

Isle of Skye
Highland Rebel - Stephanie Bartlett   96

Loch Earn
Highland Whispers - Sharon Gillenwater   726

Outer Islands
A Deeper Magic - Jillian Hunter   953

Western Highlands
The Heart and the Heather - Nancy Richards-Akers   1630

SINGAPORE

Traitor's Kiss - Jane Toombs   1953

SOUTH AFRICA

Kimberley
Snare of Serpents - Victoria Holt   919

SOUTH AMERICA

Jewel of the Sea - Susan Wiggs   2024
Seek the Wild Shore - Leslie O'Grady   1456

Amazon Jungle
Eden's Angel - Katherine Compton   379

Andes
At Long Last Love - Catherine Lanigan   1160

SPACESHIP

Golden Temptress - Patricia Roenbuck   1685
The Sky Pirate - Justine Davis   474
Star-Crossed - Susan Krinard   1117
Stardust Dreams - Marilyn Campbell   302

Sunbird
Lord of the Storm - Justine Davis   473

SPAIN

Beyond the Sunrise - Mary Balogh   54
The Eagle and the Dove - Jane Feather   630
The Firebirds - Beverly Byrne   264
If the Truth Be Told - Tracy Sinclair   1813
King of Swords - Lindsay McKenna   1316

Lady Lucinde's Locket - Irene Saunders   1723
A Lasting Fire - Beverly Byrne   266
Love and Triumph - Patricia Hagan   779
The Love Slave - Bertrice Small   1823
Paradise and More - Shirl Henke   865

Cordoba
The Flames of Vengeance - Beverly Byrne   265

Costa del Sol
One Tough Cookie - Carole Dean   491

Madrid
Desire - Phoebe Conn   386

SRI LANKA

Green Eyes - Karen Robards   1649
The Jade Garden - Laurel Collins   378
The Ruby - Christina Skye   1821

SWITZERLAND

Eternity - Lori Herter   879
Lucy's Christmas Angel - Sandra Heath   845
The Raven and the Rose - Susan Wiggs   2027

SYRIA

The Dream Hunter - Laura Kinsale   1076

Damascus
Captive Rose - Miriam Minger   1397

TROPICAL ISLAND

Till Dawn Tames the Night - Meagan McKinney   1325

TUNISIA

Sinful - Susan Johnson   1003

TURKEY

Desert Eden - Patricia Grasso   747

Constantinople
Lost Love Found - Bertrice Small   1822

UNITED STATES

Acts of Love - Deana James   967
Angel Christmas - Mary Balogh   53
Angels in the Light - Margot Dalton   456
Annie and the Outlaw - Sharon Sala   1713
As Sweet as Candy - Linda Varner   1973
The Bear Affair - Cynthia Powell   1546
Beating the Odds - Deborah Gordon   734
Beginnings - Laura Phillips   1522
Beloved Avenger - Joan Van Nuys   1970
Bleeding Hearts - Jane Haddam   774
Blue Orchids - Julia Fenton   637
Body and Soul - Felicia Mason   1293
Breathless - Margie Walker   1988
Bygones - LaVyrle Spencer   1858
Call Home the Heart - Rebecca George   718
Call Me Sin - Jan Hudson   945
Captain's Captive - Christine Dorsey   549
Cherish the Night - Penelope Neri   1437
Christmas Angels - Debra Dier   529
A Christmas Love - Kathleen Creighton   416
The Courtship of Peggy McCoy - Ray Sipherd   1815
Dangerous Desire - Ashley Snow   1849
Dark Fires - Brenda Joyce   1024
Deadly Secret - Martha Johnson   997
Destiny's Will - Elizabeth Ann Michaels   1360

Devil's Deception - Suzannah Davis   480
Diamonds and Dreams - Rebecca Paisley   1480
A Durable Fire - Virginia Bernhard   129
A Family Affair - Denise Richards   1628
Family Man - Jayne Ann Krentz   1107
Far Horizons - Katherine Sinclair   1807
The Farrell Marriage - Dee Holmes   916
Flame Lily - Candace Camp   289
Follow Your Heart - Lynda Trent   1959
Forever Ecstasy - Janelle Taylor   1915
Forever Yours - Francis Ray   1601
Forgotten Vows - Maggie Shayne   1777
The Garden Path - Kristie Knight   1091
A Gift of Joy - Virginia Henley   871
A Gift of Love - Judith McNaught   1330
Harlequin Historical Christmas - Nora Roberts   1668
Her Father's Daughter - Terri Herrington   876
Holiday Cheer - Rochelle Alers   8
Hot Property - Sherryl Woods   2067
Jade's Passion - Laura Taylor   1920
A Jewel So Rare - Elizabeth Ann Michaels   1361
King's Ransom - Diana Palmer   1489
Kiss of Bliss - Carolyn Monroe   1403
Knight and Day - Carole Buck   244
The Law of Love - Martha Schroeder   1734
Love and Other Surprises - Kathleen Creighton   417
Love Lesson - Marian Oaks   1445
Love Not a Rebel - Heather Graham   738
Love's Stolen Promise - Sylvie Sommerfield   1852
A Marriage of Convenience - Georgia Bockoven   177
Marriage of Inconvenience - Debbie Macomber   1251
Masque of Sapphire - Deana James   969
Maverick's Lady - Linda Jenkins   982
Midnight Fire - Linda Ladd   1126
Midsummer Night's Madness - Jill Barnett   90
Mirror Image - Sandra Brown   229
The Mistress of Foxgrove - Lee Magner   1263
More than Friends - Barbara Delinsky   500
More than Just a Night - Connie Rinehold   1642
Mrs. Perfect - Peggy Roberts   1670
Naughty Talk - Tiffany White   2014
Odessa Gold - Linda Shaw   1776
On the Line - Anne Marie Duquette   576
Once in a Lifetime - Constance O'Day-Flannery   1452
One Night with a Rogue - Kimberly Cates   329
Operation Homefront - Marilyn Pappano   1494
Pirate's Princess - Constance O'Banyon   1449
Pirouette - Madeline Hale   782
Point of Departure - Lindsay McKenna   1319
Prescription for Death - Janet McGiffin   1310
Pretty Maids in a Row - Marilyn Campbell   301
Reap the Wind - Iris Johansen   992
Renegade's Kiss - Barbara Ankrum   24
The Romantic Naiad - Katherine V. Forrest   658
Santa's Little Helpers - Janet Dailey   455
Sapphire and Shadow - Marie Ferrarella   639
The Scarlet Thread - Evelyn Anthony   26
Sea of Dreams - Elizabeth DeLancey   497
Seasons of Love - Elaine Barbieri   74
Second Chances - Constance O'Day-Flannery   1454
Serenade - Sandra Kitt   1086
Shadow Whispers - Wendy Haley   785
Shadows and Secrets - Carol Blake Gerrond   721
Shattered Illusions - Linda Renee De Jong   487
Sight Unseen - Kathy Clark   359
Silhouette Christmas Stories 1990 - Kathleen Creighton   418
Sing Me to Sleep - Mary-Ben Lorris   1226
Somewhere in Time - Barbara Bretton   216
Spirit of the Season - Heather Graham   741
Spirit of the Season - Monica Harris   817
Spring Blossom - Jill Metcalf   1349
Suspicion's Gate - Justine Davis   475
Sweet Forever - Becky Lee Weyrich   2010
Sweet Fortune - Jayne Ann Krentz   1112
Sweet Justice - Mary Lynn Baxter   103
Sweet Seduction - Patricia Pellicane   1515
Sweeter than Sin - Sara Orwig   1465

Taming Charlotte - Linda Lael Miller   1386
Their First Noel - Leigh Greenwood   760
This Time Forever - Kathleen Eagle   583
Three Weddings and a Kiss - Kathleen E.
   Woodiwiss   2063
To Love a Cowboy - Laura Phillips   1524
To Love and to Honor - Phoebe Conn   388
Treasures - Lisa Jackson   962
True Love - Diane E. Lock   1221
Under His Spell - Ellen Archer   28
Until Forever - Johanna Lindsey   1210
Valentine Hearts and Flowers - Muriel Jensen   986
Velvet Is the Night - Elizabeth Thornton   1945
Wedding Bell Blues - Alice Sharpe   1774
What Child Is This? - Rebecca York   2078
Wild Tory Rose - Linda Covington   413
The Wings of Morning - Karen Harper   812
A Woman Betrayed - Barbara Delinsky   503

Ashton
Ashton's Secret - Liana Laverentz   1163

Brae-Mill
The Cinderella Game - Jane Shore   1786

Cameron
Dangerous Bequest - Lee Anderson   21

Cherokee Nation
Cherokee Nights - Genell Dellin   505

Cloverdale
Darling Deceiver - Lori Copeland   390

Dakota Territory
Cheyenne Dreams - Peggy Hanchar   790
Dakota Dawn - Dana Ransom   1589
Forgiving - LaVyrle Spencer   1859
Sagebrush Bride - Tanya Anne Crosby   434
Sioux Slave - Georgina Gentry   716

Eagle Island
No Easy Task - Chloe Summers   1896

Fairhill
Love's Quiet Corner - Laura Parrish   1511

Iroquois Nation
Orenda - Kate Cameron   282

North Ocean City
Sterling's Reasons - Joey Light   1188

Oregon Trail
Beyond the Horizon - Connie Mason   1287
Irresistible - Catherine Hart   820
Night Fire - Cait Logan   1224
Promised Sunrise - Robin Lee Hatcher   832
When Lightning Strikes - Rexanne Becnel   115
Wildfire - Norah Hess   887

Pequod Landing
The Wings of the Morning - Thomas Tryon   1962

Smoky Mountains
Baby Makes Five - Lacey Dancer   457

Willow Ridge
Over the Moon - Betty Cothran   401

ALABAMA

Love Me Tonight - Nan Ryan   1706

Gadsden
Until Tomorrow - Jill Marie Landis   1148

Mount Vernon
Apache Heartsong - Janis Reams Hudson   946

ALASKA

Ice and Rapture - Connie Mason   1289
Jenny's Dream - Victoria Morrow   1423

Love's Sweet Bounty - Colleen Faulkner   625
Midnight Ice - Cathie Linz   1213
Savage Promise - Cassie Edwards   593
Tender Is the Touch - Ana Leigh   1176
Tomorrow's Dream - Peggy Hanchar   792

Juneau
The Wailing Winds of Juneau Abbey - Peggy
   Darty   466

APPALACHIANS

Barefoot Bride - Rebecca Paisley   1478

ARIZONA

Angel Eyes - Suzannah Davis   478
Apache Heartsong - Janis Reams Hudson   946
Apache Legacy - Janis Reams Hudson   947
Apache Magic - Janis Reams Hudson   948
Arizona Caress - Bobbi Smith   1832
Arizona Lovestorm - Wendy Garrett   693
Blossom - Constance Bennett   120
Chase the Wind - Janelle Taylor   1912
Desert Angel - Pamela K. Forrest   660
Desert Flame - Anne Harmon   806
Desperado's Caress - Carla Simpson   1798
Forever and Beyond - Penelope Neri   1438
Formula for Murder - S.R. Hawley   836
A Gentle Taming - Adrienne Day   486
Love's Bounty - Alisa McBride   1299
Mad Hatter - Georgia Helm   848
Moonlight and Magic - Rebecca Paisley   1483
Never on Sundae - Rita Rainville   1586
Pink Topaz - Jennifer Greene   755
Scarlet Sunset, Silver Nights - Leigh Greenwood   759
Trilby - Diana Palmer   1492
Wild Splendor - Cassie Edwards   595
Wild Wind - Jane Archer   31

Dragoon Mountains
Desert Sunrise - Raine Cantrell   310

Fort Apache
Heartbreak Trail - Barbara Keller   1048

Phoenix
Deadly Secrets - S.R. Hawley   835
River Song - Sharon MacIver   1246

Prescott
Desert Sunrise - Raine Cantrell   310

Purgatory
Temptation's Fire - Millie Criswell   429

Rainbow Rock
Ride the Rainbow Home - Susan Aylworth   39

Silver Grande
Arizona Temptation - Garda Parker   1497

Silver Mesa
The Touch of Fire - Linda Howard   935

Superstition Mountains
Destiny's Dream - Joanna Jordan   1017

Sycamore Flats
Laurel - Leigh Greenwood   758

Tombstone
Fallen Angel - Deborah Camp   294

Tucson
Kiss of the Night Wind - Janelle Taylor   1916

Yuma
River Song - Sharon MacIver   1246

ARKANSAS

Courting Miss Hattie - Pamela Morsi   1425

Promise Me Moonlight - Carol Finch   646
Sunny - Linda Madl   1260
Tall Cotton - Lori Copeland   396
Thunder's Tender Touch - Carol Finch   647

Eureka Springs
My Wild Rose - Deborah Camp   297
Runaway Heart - Tena Carlyle   315

Little Rock
Stolen Kisses - Sally Falcon   622

Ozark Mountains
Camelot Jones - Mayo Lucas   1237

CALIFORNIA

Because You're Mine - Nan Ryan   1703
Beloved Woman - Deborah Smith   1838
Brighter than Gold - Cynthia Wright   2071
California Caress - Rebecca Sinclair   1810
Cherokee Nights - Genell Dellin   505
A Delicate Matter - Rebecca Forster   662
For All the Right Reasons - Elaine Coffman   370
Hot Shot - Susan Elizabeth Phillips   1528
Lover's Gold - Kat Martin   1277
Magnificent Affair - Fayrene Preston   1553
Midnight Rose - Robin Lee Hatcher   830
Miracle - Deborah Smith   1840
Moments - Georgia Bockoven   178
My Only Desire - Andrea Parnell   1508
On the Way to Heaven - Tina Wainscott   1986
Orchids in Moonlight - Patricia Hagan   781
Partners in Time - Pamela Simpson   1802
Renegade Embrace - Virginia Brown   235
Risk - Doris Parmett   1507
Rough Passage - Paula Detmer Riggs   1635
Secrets of a Midnight Moon - Jane Bonander   181
Shameless - Suzanne Forster   664
Special Effects - Jo Leigh   1178
Springtown - DeLoras Scott   1753
Surrender a Dream - Jill Barnett   91
Sweet Conquest - Marsha Bauer   100
Tempt Me with Kisses - Phoebe Conn   387
Treasure of the Sun - Christina Dodd   541
Wild Rose - Sharon Ihle   957
Yankee Wife - Linda Lael Miller   1387

Balboa Island
Does Cupid Do Take-Out? - Kathryn E. Coulter   412

Berkeley
Car Pool - Karin Kallmaker   1034

Beverly Hills
Birthstone - Mollie Gregory   767

Bishop
Painted Moon - Karin Kallmaker   1036

Bodie
Bodie Bride - Isabel Whitfield   2015

Carmel
All That Glitters - Ruth Langan   1150
The Long Road Home - Pat Warren   1994

Crescent Cove
Just One More Secret - Alice Sharpe   1772

Deadman's Gulch
Rawhide and Lace - Margaret Brownley   238

Death Valley
Lover in the Rough - Elizabeth Lowell   1230
Nevada Flame - Rochelle Wayne   1997

Eureka
A Garland of Love - Alice Sharpe   1771

Fort Tejon
Sunburst - Suzanne Ellison   610

Seasons - Lisa Gregory 766
Sioux Splendor - Rosanne Bittner 161
Sleeping with the Enemy - Laurie Paige 1477
The Wives of Bowie Stone - Maggie Osborne 1469

FLORIDA

Forever Joy - Lacey Dancer 458
Hot Secret - Sherryl Woods 2068
Penthouse Suite - Sandra Chastain 342
Sapphire - Venita Helton 849
Secret in the Shadows - Marina Malcolm 1265
Sultry Nights - Charla Cameron 281
Swept Away - Cay David 467

Eglin Air Force Base
Bits and Pieces - Merline Lovelace 1227

Everglades
Touch the Stars - Lynn Armistead McKee 1313
Woman of the Mists - Lynn Armistead McKee 1314

Florida Keys
Heaven on Earth - Michelle Brandon 205

Iguana Bay
Iguana Bay - Theresa Weir 1999

Miami
Bliss - Judy Cuevas 444
Slow Burn - Heather Graham Pozzessere 1551

Orlando
Dream Man - Linda Howard 933

Rainy
Silver Mist - Theresa DiBenedetto 527

St. Augustine
Dark Cries of Gray Oaks - Lee Karr 1043
The Eagle and the Rose - Diane Gates
   Robinson 1679
The Heart Remembers - Sandra Davidson 469
The Silver Witch - Sue Rich 1627

Shell Bay
Terror by Design - Jane Edwards 598

Winwood
Angels in the Sand - Jan McDaniel 1306

GEORGIA

Beloved Woman - Deborah Smith 1838
Chase the Dawn - Kay McMahon 1327
Cherokee Bride - Patricia Werner 2003
Forever My Love - Constance O'Banyon 1448
Island of Dreams - Patricia Potter 1539
Jasmine and Silk - Sandra Chastain 341
Miracle - Deborah Smith 1840
Promise Me Forever - Janelle Taylor 1918
Rebel Seduction - Jane Archer 30
Scarlett - Alexandra Ripley 1647
Southern Seduction - Thea Devine 522
Stolen Moments - Sherryl Woods 2069
Surrender to the Fury - Cara Miles 1375
Tarnished Hearts - Raine Cantrell 311

Atlanta
Atlanta - Sara Orwig 1462
Body and Soul - Sherryl Woods 2065
Crime of Passion - Kay Hooper 921
Star-Crossed Lovers - Kay Hooper 924

Blue Ridge Mountains
Moonlight and Mistletoe - Maggie Daniels 462

Cherokee Nation
Cherokee Sundown - Genell Dellin 506

Curry Station
Night Fever - Susan Kyle 1122

Galilee
Summer of the Soldiers - Sandra Chastain 345

Planter's Junction
Rainbow's End - Kay Wilding 2031

Savannah
A Wife in Time - Cathie Linz 1214

Smith Springs
When Someday Comes - Faith E.W. Garner 691

Sweetwater
Sweetwater - Sandra Chastain 346

Windlea
Sweet Southern Caress - Wendy Garrett 696

Winslow
Summer of the Soldiers - Sandra Chastain 345

GREAT LAKES

Freedom Angel - Robin LeAnne Wiete 2021

HAWAII

The Dark Side of Paradise - Alma Blair 166
The Master's Bride - Suzannah Davis 481
The Shadow and the Star - Laura Kinsale 1081
The Vanishing Bridegroom - Alice Sharpe 1773

Kauai
Ekahi - Georgette Livingston 1218

Maui
A Deeper Hunger - Sabine Kells 1049

IDAHO

Mountain Rose - Norah Hess 886
Promise Me Spring - Robin Lee Hatcher 831
Sins of Summer - Dorothy Garlock 690

Blue Springs Ranch
Liberty Blue - Robin Lee Hatcher 828

Boise
Promised Sunrise - Robin Lee Hatcher 832

Eagle Rock
Mountain Ecstasy - Linda Sandifer 1718

Eden Creek
Harvest Song - Karen Lockwood 1222

Florence
Whisper My Name - Raine Cantrell 312

Fort Bridge
Temptation's Price - Dallas Schulze 1738

Homestead
Where the Heart Is - Robin Lee Hatcher 833

Hope
Seasons of the Heart - Marilyn Cunningham 449

Palouse River Area
Broken Promise - Theresa Scott 1755

Weeping Angel
Weeping Angel - Stef Ann Holm 915

Whitneyville
Emma and the Outlaw - Linda Lael Miller 1379

ILLINOIS

Harvest of Love - Nancy Sheehan 1780
Night of the Phantom - Anne Stuart 1888
Silken Dreams - Lisa Bingham 147

Chennowah Grove
Somewhere Near Paradise - Marjorie Everitt 616

Chicago
Confession - Lori Herter 878
Eternity - Lori Herter 879
Frostfire - Linda Ladd 1125
Intimate Connections - Joanne Z. Adams 2
Island Star - Kit Gardner 684
It Had to Be You - Susan Elizabeth Phillips 1529
Obsession - Lori Herter 880
Possession - Lori Herter 881
A Rose in the Shadows - Catherine Wyatt 2075
Silken Promises - Lisa Bingham 148
The Snow Garden - Bethany Campbell 300
Sounds of Silence - Marilyn Levy 1185
When Lightning Strikes - Rexanne Becnel 115

Irisheer
Flannery's Rainbow - Julie Kistler 1084

Michigan City
Night Watcher - Tracey Tillis 1948

Nancy Hanks
Maybe This Time - Kathleen Gilles Seidel 1766

St. Louis
High Society - Diane Cory 399

INDIAN TERRITORY

Cheyenne Sunrise - Constance O'Banyon 1446
Dragon Fire - Linda Ladd 1124
The Schemers - Lois Wolfe 2059

Otter Creek
The Savage - Nicole Jordan 1019

INDIANA

Sedgwick City
Deadly Masquerade - Tracey Tillis 1947

Titusville
Iron and Lace - Nadine Miller 1388

IOWA

Homeplace - Dorothy Garlock 686
The Texan and the Lady - Jodi Thomas 1932
Travelin' Man - Lois Faye Dyer 579
Wish upon a Star - Karen Morrell 1420

Regret
The Way Home - Dallas Schulze 1739

Sumac
Out of This World Marriage - Maggie Shayne 1779

KANSAS

American Star - Jackie Collins 377
Angel of Fire - Jessica Douglass 560
The Doubletree - Victoria Pade 1476
Fire and Ice - DeLoras Scott 1750
Gambler's Tempting Kisses - Charlotte Hubbard 944
Kansas Kiss - Christine Dorsey 550
Outlaw Hearts - Rosanne Bittner 159
Pickett's Fence - Linda Shertzer 1783
Renegade Angel - Phoebe Fitzjames 650
Sweet Justice - Jan McKee 1312
Tempest - Catherine Hart 822
The Texan and the Lady - Jodi Thomas 1932
Until Tomorrow - Jill Marie Landis 1148
Wildfire - Virginia Brown 236

Abilene
Embers of the Heart - Rosanne Bittner 154
Fern - Leigh Greenwood 757

Dodge City
The Bonnie Blue - Joan Elliott Pickart 1531
Fortune's Lady - Victoria Thompson 1933

Niles
Vivid - Beverly Jenkins   981

Pinesburg
Hold Back the Night - Sandra Steffen   1873

MIDWEST

Beneath Passion's Skies - Bobbi Smith   1834
Bride of the Wilderness - Elizabeth Grayson   753
Country Kiss - Sharon Harlow   805
Defiant Rose - Colleen Quinn   1578
One Perfect Springtime - Constance Walker   1987
Rain Shadow - Cheryl St. John   1866
Rough and Tender - Selena MacPherson   1258

Riverbend
What the Lady Wants - Jennifer Crusie   442

MINNESOTA

Firefly - Stef Ann Holm   911
Mail-Order Temptress - Jane Kidder   1062
My Own True Love - Susan Sizemore   1816
Till the Stars Fall - Kathleen Gilles Seidel   1768

New Ulm
Home Fires - Susan Kay Law   1164

Pinedale
Sungold - Jillian Dagg   450

St. Paul
November of the Heart - LaVyrle Spencer   1860

Stillwater
Still Waters - Tami Hoag   900

White Bear Lake
November of the Heart - LaVyrle Spencer   1860

MISSISSIPPI

Captain of My Heart - Danelle Harmon   808
Frostfire - Linda Ladd   1125
Morning Song - Karen Robards   1651

Biloxi
Priceless - Mary Lynn Baxter   102

Innocence
Carnal Innocence - Nora Roberts   1665

Natchez
Autumn Leaves - Jill Metcalf   1347
Darkness at Cottonwood Hall - Madelyn
   Sanders   1717
Love Across Time - Anne Meredith   1343
Moonwitch - Nicole Jordan   1018
Once a Princess - Johanna Lindsey   1206
Through the Years - Katherine Sinclair   1808

Vicksburg
Rainbow - Patricia Potter   1543
Yankee's Caress - Terri Valentine   1969

MISSISSIPPI RIVER

Allegheny Captive - Caroline Bourne   189
Golden Nights - Christine Monson   1404
Mississippi Flame - Cheryl Biggs   143
Mississippi Mistress - Gina Robins   1675
Moonwitch - Nicole Jordan   1018
Promise Me Forever - Lori Copeland   393
Rainbow - Patricia Potter   1543
South of the Line - Catherine Ennis   611

MISSOURI

Almost Home - Debra Cowan   414
Camelot Jones - Mayo Lucas   1237

Caress - Rosanne Bittner   153
Love Hear My Heart - Sonya T. Pelton   1516
Moon Showers - Laura Phillips   1523
Renegade Angel - Phoebe Fitzjames   650

Bickerton
Rogue's Honor - DeLoras Scott   1752

Culverton
Heart Strings - Lydia Browne   237

Joplin
Outlaw's Kiss - Terri Valentine   1966

Kansas City
Jenny's Dream - Victoria Morrow   1423
Newsworthy Affair - Delayne Camp   298

Liberty
Bittersweet Promises - Trana Mae Simmons   1791

St. Joseph
Nevada Nights - Georgina Gentry   713
When Lightning Strikes - Rexanne Becnel   115

St. Louis
Angel Hunter - Ana Leigh   1175
Black-Eyed Susan - Deborah Camp   292
Deception's Sweet Kiss - Gina Robins   1672
Eagles of Destiny - Jory Sherman   1782
Ecstasy's Masquerade - Gwen Cleary   363
Firefly - Stef Ann Holm   911
In Your Dreams - Lynn Bulock   250
Mask of Night - Lois Wolfe   2058
Mississippi Mistress - Gina Robins   1675
Riverbend - Mary McBride   1300

MONTANA

After All - Jill Marie Landis   1142
An Angel in My Arms - Victoria Morrow   1421
The Barefoot Bride - Joan Johnston   1004
Bold Montana Bride - Karen Bale   50
Ecstasy's Masquerade - Gwen Cleary   363
Montana Mistress - Thea Devine   521
Montana Mistress - Carol Finch   644
Morning Comes Softly - Debbie Macomber   1252
Mountain Dawn - Kathleen Kane   1040
Nightrose - Dorothy Garlock   688
Prince Charming - Julie Garwood   704
Pure Sin - Susan Johnson   1002
Renegade Bride - Barbara Ankrum   23
Someday Soon - Debbie Macomber   1255
Wild Card - Nancy Hutchinson   955
Wildest Dreams - Rosanne Bittner   164

Billings
True Colors - Susan Kyle   1123

Butte
Meant to Be - Elizabeth DeLancey   496

Elkhorn
Outcast - Emily Carmichael   316

Helena
Forbidden - Susan Johnson   999

Last Chance
Last Chance - Jill Marie Landis   1145

Laughing Horse Reservation
Sleeping with the Enemy - Laurie Paige   1477

Mountain Valley
For the Roses - Julie Garwood   701

New Eden
Dark Paradise - Tami Hoag   898

Stiles
Meant to Be - Elizabeth DeLancey   496

Whitehorn
Cowboy Cop - Rachel Lee   1172

NEBRASKA

Heirloom - Candace Camp   290
I'll Be Seeing You - Kristine Rolofson   1696
The Man Who Came for Christmas - Bethany
   Campbell   299
Midnight Fire - Madeline Baker   45
Ribbon in the Sky - Dorothy Garlock   689
Silena - Terri Herrington   877
Storm Dancers - Allison Hayes   838
Web of Loving Lies - Barbara Leigh   1177

Halston
Forbidden Desires - Rebecca Sinclair   1811

Ogallala
Forbidden Kiss - Gina Robins   1673

NEVADA

Dancing on Snowflakes - Jane Bonander   180
Maybe This Time - Barbara Bretton   213
When Destiny Calls - Suzanne Elizabeth   600

Carson City
Nevada Temptation - Gwen Cleary   364

Castletown
Nevada Ecstasy - Lindsey Hanks   794

Las Vegas
Crystal Days - Carole Nelson Douglas   554
Crystal Nights - Carole Nelson Douglas   555
Desert Fire - Evelyn Rogers   1686
The Invisible Groom - Barbara Bretton   212
Lucky - Sharon Sala   1716

Virginia City
Renegade Bride - Barbara Ankrum   23
Riverboat Rogue - Jane Toombs   1952
Rugged Splendor - Robin Leigh   1180

Willowbrook
Desperado Passion - Patricia Pellicane   1514

NEW ENGLAND

Captive Kiss - Amy Christopher   355
Faith and Honor - Robin Maderich   1259
Fire Lily - Deborah Camp   295
Let Me Count the Ways - Leigh Michaels   1372
Mariah's Prize - Miranda Jarrett   978
Masques of Betrayal - Andrea Kane   1038
Moriah's Magic - Anne Ladley   1129

Norwich Notch
The Passions of Chelsea Kane - Barbara
   Delinsky   501

NEW JERSEY

Maybe This Time - Barbara Bretton   213
Wild Card - Nancy Hutchinson   955

Cape May
Unveiled - Colleen Quinn   1579

Groveton
Love on Trial - Wendy Martin   1285

Ocean City
Timely Matrimony - Kasey Michaels   1371

Patterson
Tattered Silk - Elaine Barbieri   75

NEW MEXICO

All My Heart Can Hold - Jessica Douglass   559

Astoria
A Light for My Love - Alexis Harrington   814

Heron Point
Merry Christmas, Mommy - Muriel Jensen   985

Hopewell
Wishes - Lisa Jackson   963

Jacksonville
Dearest Enemy - Stephanie Bartlett   94

Portland
Jesse's Renegade - Nancy Bush   260

Willamette River
Riverboat Temptation - Gwen Cleary   365

Willamette Valley
Night Fire - Cait Logan   1224

Wolf's Landing
Indigo Blue - Catherine Anderson   19

OZARKS

Marrying Stone - Pamela Morsi   1428

PACIFIC NORTHWEST

The Marriage Bracelet - Rebecca Winters   2053
Song of the Warrior - Georgina Gentry   717
Winter Bride - Iris Johansen   996

PENNSYLVANIA

Apache Heartsong - Janis Reams Hudson   946
Beloved Intruder - Joan Van Nuys   1971
Evergreen - Delia Parr   1510
Flame in the Night - Jack McGowan   1311
Kentucky Bride - Hannah Howell   938
Lover's Gold - Kat Martin   1277
Wishes on the Wind - Elaine Barbieri   77

Allegheny Mountains
Allegheny Captive - Caroline Bourne   189

Black Wall
Passion's Bold Fire - Rosalyn Alsobrook   12

Chadds Ford
Storm Dancers - Allison Hayes   838

Cold Springs Hollow
Enchantment - Coral Smith Saxe   1733

Lancaster
A Christmas Embrace - Ellen Tanner Marsh   1269
Garden of Fantasy - Karen Rose Smith   1847

Philadelphia
Beneath Passion's Skies - Bobbi Smith   1834
Colorado Flame - Colleen Quinn   1577
Compromises - Joan Hohl   906
Defiant Rose - Colleen Quinn   1578
Enchantment - Coral Smith Saxe   1733
Hidden Riches - Nora Roberts   1669
Seasons - Constance O'Day-Flannery   1453
Traitor's Embrace - Christine Dorsey   553
Unveiled - Colleen Quinn   1579
Walk in the Light - Charles Durham   577

Pittsburgh
A Private Proposal - La Verne St. George   1863
Rough and Tender - Selena MacPherson   1258

Pottstown
Torchlight - Doreen Owens Malek   1266

Rapture
Love's Brazen Fire - Betina M. Krahn   1100

Sanctuary
A Touch of Magic - Carin Rafferty   1585

Wayne's Crossing
Sweet Everlasting - Patricia Gaffney   678

RHODE ISLAND

Newport
Time After Time - Antoinette Stockenberg   1883

Waverly
The Christmas Wish - Rexanne Becnel   110

ROCKY MOUNTAINS

Mountain Laurel - Jude Deveraux   516
Only Mine - Elizabeth Lowell   1233

SOUTH

First Comes Baby - Kristin Morgan   1418
The Passion Ruby - Eboni Snoe   1848
The Schemers - Lois Wolfe   2059
Shameless - Jennifer Blake   173
Southern Oaks - Brenna Braxton-Barshon   209

Glory
Amanda - Kay Hooper   920

Palmetto
Breath of Scandal - Sandra Brown   227

SOUTH CAROLINA

The Captain's Bride - Kat Martin   1273
The Emerald Tears of Foxfire Manor - Clara Wimberly   2048
Fortune's Bride - Judith E. French   666
Love's Sweetest Secret - Gina Robins   1674

Charleston
Legacy - Leigh Bristol   217
The Silver Witch - Sue Rich   1627
Southern Nights - Marcia Martin   1280
Surrender My Heart - Lois Greiman   770
Tonight and Forever - Caryl Wilson   2044
Woman Without a Past - Phyllis A. Whitney   2019

Rosehill
Slow Dance - Donna Julian   1031

SOUTH DAKOTA

Dakota Desire - Dana Ransom   1590
Ghost Dancer - Fela Dawson Scott   1754
Reason to Believe - Kathleen Eagle   582
Sioux Splendor - Rosanne Bittner   161
A Whisper on the Wind - Madeline Baker   49

Black Hills
The Spirit Path - Madeline Baker   47

Deadwood
Dakota Destiny - Dana Ransom   1591
Forbidden Kiss - Gina Robins   1673
More Precious than Gold - Elaine Barbieri   72

Deadwood Gulch
Seasons of Gold - Stef Ann Holm   914

Lakota Reservation
Fire and Rain - Kathleen Eagle   580

SOUTHWEST

Eagles of Destiny - Jory Sherman   1782
Favors of the Rich - Sara Orwig   1464
Prairie Heat - Madeline Baker   46
The Turquoise Trail - Susannah Leigh   1182
Wild Mountain Honey - Carol Finch   648

Chisholm Trail
Caress of Fire - Martha Hix   895

TENNESSEE

Delta Desire - Diane Gates Robinson   1678
Forever in His Arms - Penelope Neri   1439
A Forever Kind of Love - Patricia Hagan   778
Once a Rebel - Micki Brown   226
Passion's Timeless Hour - Vivian Knight-Jenkins   1094
River's Dream - Virginia Lynn   1243
South of the Line - Catherine Ennis   611

Appalachian Mountains
Mountain Mystic - Debra Dixon   533

Big Water
Cherokee Bride - Teresa Warfield   1992

Blue Ridge Mountains
The Daring - Patricia Hagan   777

Magnolia
Ashton's Bride - Judith O'Brien   1450

Memphis
Because of You - Micki Brown   225
The Falcon and the Swan - Diane Gates Robinson   1680
Tempest in Time - Eugenia Riley   1639

Murfreesboro
Walking After Midnight - Karen Robards   1655

Nashville
Diamond - Sharon Sala   1714
Tears of Fire - Nelle McFather   1308

Natchez
Nightfire - Leona Karr   1044

Vader
Garters - Pamela Morsi   1426

TEXAS

After Midnight - Susan Kyle   1120
Angel - Johanna Lindsey   1199
Apache Bride - JoAnne Redd   1606
At Long Last Love - Catherine Lanigan   1160
Bayou Passion - Jane Archer   1245
Beloved Wife - Lynda Trent   1956
The Bonnie Blue - Joan Elliott Pickart   1531
The Bridegroom - Carol Jerina   987
Cactus Blossom - Emily Bradshaw   195
Capture the Night - Geralyn Dawson   482
Caress of Fire - Martha Hix   895
Comanche Moon - Catherine Anderson   18
Comanche Moon - Anita Mills   1391
Comanche Wind - Genell Dellin   508
Desperado - Rebecca Brandewyne   200
Escape Not My Love - Elaine Coffman   369
Fancy Pants - Susan Elizabeth Phillips   1526
A Fire in the Blood - Shirl Henke   861
Follow the Wind - Janelle Taylor   1914
Gabrielle - Leta Tegler   1922
Golden Bird - Jo Ann Algermissen   9
Heaven, Texas - Susan Elizabeth Phillips   1527
Heaven's Embrace - Lynda Trent   1960
Honor's Promise - Sharon Sala   1715
The Inheritance - Joan Johnston   1005
Lacy - Diana Palmer   1490
Lawless - Alexandra Thorne   1940
Lone Star Lady - Jill Gregory   764
Lone Star Loving - Martha Hix   896
Love a Dark Rider - Shirlee Busbee   258
Love Game - Mallory Rush   1701
Love So Wild - Elaine Crawford   415
Love's Endless Flame - Betty Brooks   223
A Man of Few Words - Thelma Zirkelbach   2082
Midnight Fire - Madeline Baker   45
Moonflower - Shirl Henke   862
Night Flower - Shirl Henke   863
No Greater Love - Alison Irving   959

Puget Sound
All the Winters That Have Been - Evan
　Maxwell　1297
Bad Billy Culver - Judy Gill　724

Rock Falls
Hot as Sin - Debra Dixon　532

San Juan Island
Once in Every Life - Kristin Hannah　799

Seattle
Charade - Christina Hamlett　788
Dangerous Odyssey - Jane Edwards　597
Dreams of Joy - Holly S. McClure　1301
The Golden Chance - Jayne Ann Krentz　1108
The Golden Mountain - Annalise Sun　1897
Golden Prospect - Shirley Parenteau　1495
The Legacy - Patricia Simpson　1803
The Naked Huntress - Shirley Parenteau　1496
The Night Orchid - Patricia Simpson　1804
No Blueprint for Love - Audrey McConachie　1302
Once in Every Life - Kristin Hannah　799
Perfect Partners - Jayne Ann Krentz　1110
A Season of Angels - Debbie Macomber　1254
Tender Is the Touch - Ana Leigh　1176
Trust Me - Jayne Ann Krentz　1113
Wildest Hearts - Jayne Ann Krentz　1114
The Wizard of Seattle - Kay Hooper　925

Tylerville
Lily and the Major - Linda Lael Miller　1382

WEST
Acts of Passion - Deana James　968
And One Rode West - Heather Graham　736
Apache Caress - Georgina Gentry　712
Beneath Passion's Skies - Bobbi Smith　1834
Brave Heart - Lindsay McKenna　1315
Calico - Raine Cantrell　309
Cherish the Dream - Kathleen Harrington　815
Cheyenne's Lady - Patricia Rice　1613
Cheyenne's Shadow - Deborah Camp　293
Comanche Flame - Madeline Baker　41
Diamond in the Rough - Millie Criswell　426
Distant Thunder - Lisa Bingham　145
Endless Seduction - Rosalyn Alsobrook　11
Forbidden Fires - Madeline Baker　43
Forever Gold - Catherine Hart　819
Hearts Are Wild - Teresa Hart　824
The Heart's Journey - Emily Bradshaw　197
Heartstrings - Rebecca Paisley　1481
Heaven on Earth - Michelle Brandon　205
Hostage Heart - Lisa Hendrix　859
Lawless - Patricia Potter　1540
Love's Sweet Bounty - Colleen Faulkner　625
Midnight Whispers - Jane Toombs　1950
The Miss and the Maverick - DeLoras Scott　1751
Mississippi Flame - Cheryl Biggs　143
Nevada Flame - Rochelle Wayne　1997
Nevada Nights - Georgina Gentry　713
Only His - Elizabeth Lowell　1231
Orchids in Moonlight - Patricia Hagan　781
Outlaw Hearts - Rosanne Bittner　159
Outlaw Seduction - Kathryn Hockett　905
Quiet Fires - Ginna Gray　751
The Redhead and the Preacher - Sandra
　Chastain　344
The Seduction of Samantha Kincade - Maggie
　Osborne　1468
Stark Lightning - Elaine Rome　1697
Sun Woman - Lindsay McKenna　1321
Tall, Dark, and Dangerous - Catherine Anderson　20
Tender Heart - Gwen Cleary　366
Until Tomorrow - Jill Marie Landis　1148

When Passion Calls - Cassie Edwards　594
Wild Sweet Ecstasy - Jo Goodman　731
A Wilder Love - Laura Parker　1505
Written in the Stars - Nan Ryan　1708
Yesterday's Shadows - Marianne Willman　2042

Fortune Flats
When Lightning Strikes - Kristin Hannah　801

WISCONSIN

Echo Moon Island
Secrets of Echo Moon - Jill Giencke　722

Fish Creek
Bittersweet - LaVyrle Spencer　1857

Milwaukee
Arrowpoint - Suzanne Ellison　607
Monkey Wrench - Nancy Martin　1284
A Token of Jewels - Diane Cory　400

Tyler
Arrowpoint - Suzanne Ellison　607
Bright Hopes - Pat Warren　1993
Loveknot - Marissa Carroll　320
Monkey Wrench - Nancy Martin　1284

WYOMING
After All - Jill Marie Landis　1142
The Bride Wore Spurs - Sharon Ihle　956
Cheyenne Surrender - Madeline Baker　40
Dangerous Charade - Madeline Harper　813
Devil in Spurs - Norah Hess　883
Dream Warrior - Bobbi Smith　1836
Fair Is the Rose - Meagan McKinney　1322
Golden Chances - Rebecca Hagan Lee　1174
The Heart Remembers - Lenore Carroll　319
The Keepsake - Marylyle Rogers　1695
Maverick Heart - Joan Johnston　1007
Midnight Blue - Dorothy Garlock　687
Outlaw Heart - Samantha James　974
Savage Thunder - Johanna Lindsey　1208
Scoundrel's Captive - JoAnn De Lazzari　488
Secret Fires - Linda Hilton　894
Silver Thunder - Joan Hohl　909
Snow Angel - Susan Amarillas　14
Tarnished Hearts - Raine Cantrell　311
Tender Victory - Susan Macias　1245
Unspoken Vows - Connie Rinehold　1643
Victoria's Ecstasy - Gwen Cleary　367
Waltz with the Lady - Betina Lindsey　1195

Bighorn Mountains
Destiny Mine - Janelle Taylor　1913

Blessing
Wild Wyoming Love - Dana Ransom　1595

Busted Heel
Rose - Jill Marie Landis　1147

Cheyenne
A Fire in the Blood - Shirl Henke　861
Wyoming Wildfire - Anne Harmon　807

Cody
Wildblossom - Cynthia Wright　2072

Collins
Outlaw Lover - Lindsey Hanks　795

Crow Territory
Lady Legend - Deborah Camp　296

Laramie
Caroline and the Raider - Linda Lael Miller　1377
The Irish Rose - Jessica Wulf　2073

The Stolen Heart - Kit Gardner　685
Until Spring - Libby Sydes　1910

Owls Butte
The Wives of Bowie Stone - Maggie Osborne　1469

Rawlins
Devil's Delight - DeLoras Scott　1749

Star Valley
A Child's Promise - Deborah Bedford　117

Sweetwater
Sweetwater Seduction - Joan Johnston　1009

Thunder Mountain
Thunder Mountain - Rachel Lee　1173

Willow Creek
Rebel in Silk - Sandra Chastain　343

Willow Springs
Morning Sky - Constance Bennett　121

VATICAN CITY

The Turtledove's Secret - Laura Hastings　827

VENEZUELA

Unlikely Eden - Anne Marie Winston　2052

VIETNAM

One Man's War - Lindsay McKenna　1318
Passion's Timeless Hour - Vivian Knight-
　Jenkins　1094
Ride the Tiger - Lindsay McKenna　1320

VIRGIN ISLANDS OF THE UNITED STATES

St. Croix
All but Love - Ann Howard White　2013

WALES

Beneath a Pale Moon - Victoria Morrow　1422
Blood Red Roses - Katherine Deauville　493
Castle of Dreams - Flora M. Speer　1853
Castle of the Heart - Flora M. Speer　1854
The Constant Flame - Patricia Phillips　1525
The Eagle's Song - Marylyle Rogers　1693
In the Shadow of Midnight - Marsha Canham　306
Keeper of the Dream - Penelope Williamson　2037
Lord of Shadowhawk - Lindsay McKenna　1317
Midnight Warrior - Iris Johansen　991
A Moment in Time - Bertrice Small　1824
Thunder and Roses - Mary Jo Putney　1563
Where Love Dwells - Elizabeth Stuart　1895

Gynfelin
Light on the Mountain - Maura Seger　1762

Radnor Forest
Where Magic Dwells - Rexanne Becnel　116

WEST INDIES

The Black Angel - Cordia Byers　261

ZANZIBAR

King of the Pirates - Stef Ann Holm　912

Story Type Index

This index is a listing of all the story types arranged in alphabetical order. An alphabetical listing of the featured book titles that fall under each story type is provided, along with author names and entry numbers. For definitions of the story types, see the "Key to Story Types" following the Introduction.

ROMANCE

Under the Desert Moon - Marsha Canham   308
Unforgettable - Rosanne Bittner   163
Unspoken Vows - Connie Rinehold   1643
Until Spring - Libby Sydes   1910
Until Tomorrow - Jill Marie Landis   1148
Victoria's Ecstasy - Gwen Cleary   367
Virgin Fire - Elizabeth Chadwick   334
Waltz with the Lady - Betina Lindsey   1195
Web of Loving Lies - Barbara Leigh   1177
Weeping Angel - Stef Ann Holm   915
Western Winds - Theresa DiBenedetto   528
When Lightning Strikes - Rexanne Becnel   115
When Passion Calls - Cassie Edwards   594
Where the Heart Is - Robin Lee Hatcher   833
Whisper My Name - Raine Cantrell   312
Whispers of Love - Gina Robins   1677
Wild Colorado Passion - Judith Steel   1872
Wild Dawn - Cait Logan   1225
A Wild Desire - Rebecca George   719
Wild Flower - Jill Marie Landis   1149
Wild Is the Night - Colleen Quinn   1580
Wild Magnolia - Betty Brooks   224
Wild Mountain Honey - Carol Finch   648
Wild Oats - Pamela Morsi   1430
Wild Splendor - Cassie Edwards   595
Wild Star - Nicole Jordan   1021
Wild Sweet Ecstasy - Jo Goodman   731
Wild Texas Blossom - Arlene Holliday   910
Wild Texas Flame - Janis Reams Hudson   950
Wild Texas Heart - Deana James   971
Wild Texas Promise - Victoria Thompson   1936
Wild Texas Rose - Martha Hix   897
Wild Texas Wind - Victoria Thompson   1937
Wild Western Desire - Kathy Jones   1015
Wild Wind - Jane Archer   31
Wild Wyoming Love - Dana Ransom   1595
Wildblossom - Cynthia Wright   2072
Wildest Dreams - Rosanne Bittner   164
Wildfire - Virginia Brown   236
Wildfire - Norah Hess   887
The Wind Casts No Shadow - Roslynn Griffith   771
Winds of Destiny - Victoria Thompson   1938
Windsong - Kelly Ferjutz   638
Wish Me a Rainbow - Jessica Douglass   561
The Wives of Bowie Stone - Maggie Osborne   1469
Written in the Stars - Nan Ryan   1708
Wyoming Wildfire - Anne Harmon   807
The Yankee - Kristin James   972
Yesterday's Promise - DiAnna June   1032
Yesterday's Shadows - Marianne Willman   2042

Historical/American West Coast
California Temptress - Millie Criswell   424
Crooked Hearts - Patricia Gaffney   676
Desire's Slave - Linda Hilton   893
The Forever Tree - Rosanne Bittner   155
Gold Is the Game - Rae Muir   1433
The Golden Mountain - Annalise Sun   1897
Ice and Rapture - Connie Mason   1289
If You Believe - Kristin Hannah   798
Jade - Jill Marie Landis   1144
A Lifetime of Heaven - Nan Ryan   1705
A Light for My Love - Alexis Harrington   814
Master of Her Heart - Terri Valentine   1965
Midnight Rose - Robin Lee Hatcher   830
Mountain Rose - Norah Hess   886
My Darling Melissa - Linda Lael Miller   1383
The Naked Huntress - Shirley Parenteau   1496
Notorious - Patricia Potter   1542
Once in Every Life - Kristin Hannah   799
Paradise in His Arms - Elizabeth Daniels   460
Rawhide and Lace - Margaret Brownley   238
Redeeming Love - Francine Rivers   1648
Renegade Embrace - Virginia Brown   235
Riverboat Temptation - Gwen Cleary   365
San Francisco Surrender - Donna Fletcher   652
Scoundrel's Desire - JoAnn De Lazzari   489
Seduced - Carla Simpson   1799
Surrender a Dream - Jill Barnett   91

Surrender the Dream - Debra Dier   531
Sweet Conquest - Marsha Bauer   100
Sweet Justice - Jan McKee   1312
Tempt Me with Kisses - Phoebe Conn   387
Temptation's Wild Embrace - Rene J. Garrod   698
Tender Is the Touch - Ana Leigh   1176
Wild Heather - Millie Criswell   430
Wild Rose - Sharon Ihle   957
Yankee Wife - Linda Lael Miller   1387

Historical/Antebellum American South
Always and Forever - Gina Robins   1671
Arrow to the Heart - Jennifer Blake   169
Autumn Leaves - Jill Metcalf   1347
Bayou Bride - Bobbi Smith   1833
The Captain's Bride - Kat Martin   1273
Caress - Rosanne Bittner   153
Carolina Dawn - Wendy Garrett   694
Creole Fires - Kat Martin   1274
Deceptive Desires - Wanda Owen   1474
Defiant Imposter - Miriam Minger   1398
The Garden Path - Kristie Knight   1091
Jasmine and Silk - Sandra Chastain   341
Love Hear My Heart - Sonya T. Pelton   1516
A Love So Wild - Evelyn Rogers   1688
Love's Sweetest Secret - Gina Robins   1674
Midnight Enchantment - Jeanne E. Hansen   802
Midnight Rogue - Elaine Barbieri   70
Midnight Rose - Patricia Hagan   780
Moonflower - Shirl Henke   862
Moonwitch - Nicole Jordan   1018
Morning Song - Karen Robards   1651
Nightfire - Leona Karr   1044
Only in Your Arms - Lisa Kleypas   1088
Rainbow - Patricia Potter   1543
Scandalous - Sonia Simone   1796
Song of the Bayou - Elinor Lynley   1239
Southern Oaks - Brenna Braxton-Barshon   209
Southern Seduction - Thea Devine   522
Sultry Nights - Charla Cameron   281
Surrender My Heart - Lois Greiman   770
Sweet Southern Caress - Wendy Garrett   696
Tarnished Hearts - Raine Cantrell   311
Tempest in Time - Eugenia Riley   1639
To Love a Pirate - Virginia Nielsen   1443

Historical/Canadian West
Beneath a Harvest Moon - Catherine Wyatt   2074
Come Be My Love - Patricia Watters   1996
The Golden Mountain - Annalise Sun   1897
A Handful of Heaven - Kristin Hannah   797
Northern Fire, Northern Star - Scotney St. James   1865
Western Enchantress - Wendy Garrett   697

Historical/Colonial America
Bewitching Kisses - Rainy Kirkland   1083
Blazing Passion - Barbara Cummings   445
Brazen Virginia Bride - Millie Criswell   423
Bride of the Wind - Shannon Drake   563
Captive Kiss - Amy Christopher   355
Dance with Fire - JoAnne Redd   1607
Defiant Heart - Nancy Moulton   1432
Defiant Imposter - Miriam Minger   1398
A Durable Fire - Virginia Bernhard   129
The Eagle and the Rose - Diane Gates Robinson   1679
Eden's Gate - Karen Harper   810
Flames of Love - Colleen Faulkner   624
Follow the Heart - Anita Mills   1394
Frontier Fire - Barbara Cummings   446
Gideon's Fall - Bronwyn Williams   2033
Kissed - Tanya Anne Crosby   432
A Love for All Time - Sandra Davidson   470
Lovestorm - Judith E. French   668
The Magic - Robin Lee Hatcher   829
Mariah's Prize - Miranda Jarrett   978
Master of My Dreams - Danelle Harmon   809
Moon Dancer - Judith E. French   669
Moonfeather - Judith E. French   670

Nobody's Angel - Karen Robards   1652
Pirate's Angel - Marsha Bauer   99
Pirate's Bride - Elizabeth August   35
A Pirate's Pleasure - Heather Graham   740
The Raider's Bride - Kimberly Cates   331
Rebel Dreams - Patricia Rice   1620
The Scarlet Temptress - Sue Rich   1625
Sea Fires - Christine Dorsey   551
Silver Tears - Becky Lee Weyrich   2009
The Taming of Amelia - Maura Seger   1764
This Side of Heaven - Karen Robards   1654
Wild Conquest - Hannah Howell   941
Wild Glory - Andrea Parnell   1509
Wild Savage Heart - Pamela K. Forrest   661
Wild Savage Love - Dana Ransom   1594
A Wild Yearning - Penelope Williamson   2039
Wilderness Flame - Barbara Cummings   448
Wind Rose - Krista Janssen   977

Historical/Edwardian
Bliss - Judy Cuevas   444
Seduced - Virginia Henley   873
Visions of Tomorrow - Katherine Sinclair   1809

Historical/Elizabethan
Behind Closed Doors - Betina M. Krahn   1097
Beloved Enemy - Maura Seger   1757
Emerald Enchantment - Patricia Grasso   748
The Game - Brenda Joyce   1027
The Greatest Lover in All England - Christina Dodd   536
The Heiress - Jude Deveraux   513
Highland Bride - Kathryn Kramer   1105
Highland Flame - Catherine Linden   1190
Lady Defiant - Suzanne Robinson   1681
Lady Gallant - Suzanne Robinson   1682
Lord of Enchantment - Suzanne Robinson   1683
Lost Love Found - Bertrice Small   1822
Rosefire - Sandra Davidson   471
So Worthy My Love - Kathleen E. Woodiwiss   2062
Traitor's Kiss - Joy Tucker   1963
Wildwitch - Kimberleigh Caitlin   272

Historical/Exotic
Always and Forever - Gina Robins   1671
Barbados - Cynthia Wright   2070
The Black Angel - Cordia Byers   261
Bold Destiny - Jane Feather   628
Brave Land, Brave Love - Connie Mason   1288
Captive Treasure - Tena Carlyle   314
Capture My Heart - Bobbi Smith   1835
Capture the Night - Geralyn Dawson   482
Daughter of the Reef - Clare Coleman   375
The Defiant Heart - Anita Gordon   732
Desert Bride - JoAnne Redd   1608
Desert Eden - Patricia Grasso   747
Desert Song - Constance O'Banyon   1447
Desire - Phoebe Conn   386
Dream Fever - Katherine Sutcliffe   1901
The Dream Hunter - Laura Kinsale   1076
The Dreaming - Barbara Wood   2060
The Eagle and the Dove - Jane Feather   630
Eagle Knight - Suzanne Ellison   608
Eden's Angel - Katherine Compton   379
Emerald Nights - Virginia Brown   233
Emerald Rain - Maggie Osborne   1467
The Enchantment - Kristin Hannah   796
Fire on the Wind - Barbara Dawson Smith   1830
Forever Paradise - Miranda North   1444
Fortune's Mistress - Judith E. French   667
The Golden Barbarian - Iris Johansen   990
Golden Fires - Colleen Shannon   1769
Green Eyes - Karen Robards   1649
Heart of the Wild - Donna Stephens   1874
Imagine - Jill Barnett   88
Island Star - Kit Gardner   684
Jade Dawn - Susannah Leigh   1181
The Jade Garden - Laurel Collins   378
King of the Pirates - Stef Ann Holm   912
Kiss Me Forever - Bobbi Smith   1837

Castles in the Air - Christina Dodd   535
Chanting the Dawn - Marylyle Rogers   1690
Chanting the Morning Star - Marylyle Rogers   1691
Chieftain - Arnette Lamb   1137
The Conqueror - Brenda Joyce   1023
Conqueror's Kiss - Hannah Howell   937
The Conquest - Jude Deveraux   511
The Constant Flame - Patricia Phillips   1525
The Crimson Crown - Edith Layton   1167
Daggers of Gold - Katherine Deauville   494
Damsel in Distress - Shannon Drake   564
Dark Whispers - Marylyle Rogers   1692
The Defiant Heart - Anita Gordon   732
Defy Not the Heart - Johanna Lindsey   1200
Desire - Amanda Quick   1568
Desire and Deceive - Cordia Byers   262
Desire of the Heart - Katherine Vickery   1981
Devoted - Alice Borchardt   184
A Dove at Midnight - Rexanne Becnel   111
The Dragon and the Jewel - Virginia Henley   869
The Eagle's Song - Marylyle Rogers   1693
Earth Song - Catherine Coulter   403
Emerald Fire - Laurie Grant   745
Enchanted - Elizabeth Lowell   1229
The Falcon and the Flower - Virginia Henley   870
Falcon on the Wind - Shelly Thacker   1926
The Fatal Crown - Ellen Jones   1013
The Fire and the Fury - Anita Mills   1393
Firebrand's Lady - Caryl Wilson   2043
Fires of Surrender - Sylvie Sommerfield   1851
Flame Across the Highlands - Katherine
   Vickery   1982
For My Lady's Heart - Laura Kinsale   1078
Gentle Conqueror - Mary Ellen Gronau   772
Gentle Warrior - Kathryn Hockett   904
The Heart and the Heather - Nancy Richards-
   Akers   1630
Heart's Awakening - Paige Brantley   208
Heartspell - Blaine Anderson   15
Hidden Hearts - Marylyle Rogers   1694
In the Shadow of Midnight - Marsha Canham   306
Keeper of the Dream - Penelope Williamson   2037
Knight of Fire - Shannon Drake   566
Knight's Caress - Lynette Vinet   1983
Knight's Desire - Judith Hill   890
Knight's Lady - Suzanne Barclay   83
The Lady and the Wolf - Julie Beard   105
The Last Viking Queen - Janelle Taylor   1917
The Lily and the Leopard - Susan Wiggs   2025
The Lion's Angel - Libby Sydes   1909
The Lodestar - Pamela Belle   118
Lord of Fire - Emma Merritt   1345
Lord of Hawkfell Island - Catherine Coulter   405
The Love Slave - Bertrice Small   1823
A Love So Fierce - Joanna McGauran   1309
Lyon's Prize - Virginia Lynn   1242
Maiden of Inverness - Arnette Lamb   1139
Midnight Raider - Shelly Thacker   1928
Midnight Warrior - Iris Johansen   991
Mistress of the Eagles - Elona Malterre   1267
A Moment in Time - Bertrice Small   1824
My Cherished Enemy - Samantha James   973
My Gallant Enemy - Rexanne Becnel   112
Mystique - Amanda Quick   1570
Once upon a Kiss - Tanya Anne Crosby   433
The Pagan's Prize - Miriam Minger   1399
Passionate Warriors - Mary Ellen Gronau   773
Princess of Fire - Shannon Drake   567
Princess of the Veil - Helen Mittermeyer   1401
Prisoner of My Desire - Johanna Lindsey   1207
The Prize - Julie Garwood   705
Promise of the Rose - Brenda Joyce   1028
The Quest - Juliana Garnett   692
Ravished Bride - Sheila O'Hallion   1459
Reckless - Anna Jennet   983
Rose Among Thorns - Catherine Archer   27
The Rose at Twilight - Amanda Scott   1748
The Rose of Blacksword - Rexanne Becnel   113
Saving Grace - Julie Garwood   706

Secret Song - Catherine Coulter   408
Shadows and Lace - Teresa Medeiros   1342
Silver Flame - Hannah Howell   939
The Silver Mirror - Roberta Gellis   710
The Sorceress - Claire Delacroix   495
The Spitfire - Bertrice Small   1825
Splendor - Charlene Cross   440
Summer Storm - Denise Domning   547
Surrender My Love - Johanna Lindsey   1209
Swan Bride - Betina Lindsey   1192
The Taming - Jude Deveraux   519
Tapestry - Maura Seger   1765
The Tarnished Lady - Sandra Hill   892
A Tender Magic - Linda Madl   1262
Tender Warrior - Linda Lang Bartell   93
Through a Dark Mist - Marsha Canham   307
To Love Again - Bertrice Small   1826
Uncommon Vows - Mary Jo Putney   1564
Untamed - Elizabeth Lowell   1235
Unwilling Betrayer - Joan Van Nuys   1972
The Valiant Heart - Anita Gordon   733
Viking Rose - Ashland Price   1554
Viking's Prize - Tanya Anne Crosby   435
The Viking's Woman - Heather Graham   742
The Vow - Mary Spencer   1861
A Vow to Keep - Elizabeth Bonner   183
Warrior Bride - Tamara Leigh   1184
A Warrior's Quest - Margaret Moore   1409
Where Love Dwells - Elizabeth Stuart   1895
Where Magic Dwells - Rexanne Becnel   116
Wild Angel - Miriam Minger   1400
Winter Roses - Anita Mills   1396
Winter's Heat - Denise Domning   548
Wolf's Embrace - Gail Link   1212

Historical/Post-American Civil War
Always, My Love - Carla Simpson   1797
And One Rode West - Heather Graham   736
Angel Fire - Deborah Satinwood   1719
Angel Hunter - Ana Leigh   1175
Atlanta - Sara Orwig   1462
Bittersweet Promises - Trana Mae Simmons   1791
Creole Nights - Deborah Martin   1271
Flame Lily - Candace Camp   289
Forever in His Arms - Penelope Neri   1439
A Forever Kind of Love - Patricia Hagan   778
Golden Bird - Jo Ann Algermissen   9
Kansas Kiss - Christine Dorsey   550
Love's Stolen Promise - Sylvie Sommerfield   1852
Many Fires - Kathleen Sage   1711
Rebel Seduction - Jane Archer   30
Renegade's Kiss - Barbara Ankrum   24
Santana Rose - Olga Bicos   141
The Savage - Nicole Jordan   1019
Scarlett - Alexandra Ripley   1647
Thief of My Heart - Rexanne Becnel   114
A Tryst in Time - Eugenia Riley   1640
Until Spring - Libby Sydes   1910

Historical/Post-American Revolution
Allegheny Ecstasy - Caroline Bourne   190
Autumn Ecstasy - Pamela K. Forrest   659
Beloved Avenger - Joan Van Nuys   1970
Beloved Intruder - Joan Van Nuys   1971
Destiny Mine - Janelle Taylor   1913
A Jewel So Rare - Elizabeth Ann Michaels   1361
Love's Brazen Fire - Betina M. Krahn   1100
Masques of Betrayal - Andrea Kane   1038
Midnight Treasure - Katherine Kincaid   1067
Passion's Ransom - Betina M. Krahn   1103
Shadowed Vows - Sue Rich   1626
When Morning Comes - Robin LeAnne Wiete   2022

Historical/Post-French Revolution
Rendezvous - Serena Richards   1629
A Rose at Midnight - Anne Stuart   1889
Tender the Storm - Elizabeth Thornton   1944
Velvet Is the Night - Elizabeth Thornton   1945

Historical/Pre-history
Across a Wine-Dark Sea - Jessica Bryan   239
Broken Promise - Theresa Scott   1755
Dark Renegade - Theresa Scott   1756
Daughter of the Red Deer - Joan Wolf   2057
Fire Queen - Deborah Grambien   743
Hearts Enslaved - Judith Hill   889
Keepers of the Misty Time - Patricia Rowe   1700
Lady of Conquest - Teresa Medeiros   1340
My Warrior's Heart - Betina Krahn   1102
Touch the Stars - Lynn Armistead McKee   1313
Voice of the Eagle - Linda Lay Shuler   1787
Woman of the Mists - Lynn Armistead McKee   1314

Historical/Regency
Almost Heaven - Judith McNaught   1329
Autumn Rain - Anita Mills   1389
Barbados - Cynthia Wright   2070
Beyond the Sunrise - Mary Balogh   54
The Black Rose - Christina Skye   1818
Brave Land, Brave Love - Connie Mason   1288
Bride of the Unicorn - Kasey Michaels   1363
Caprice - Laura Parker   1501
Castles - Julie Garwood   700
Charmed - Stella Cameron   285
Come the Dawn - Christina Skye   1819
Dance of Deception - Suzannah Davis   479
Dancing at Midnight - Julia Quinn   1581
Dangerous - Amanda Quick   1566
Dangerous Illusions - Amanda Scott   1745
Dangerous Joy - Jo Beverley   133
Deceived - Mary Balogh   58
Deception - Amanda Quick   1567
Defiant Angel - Stephanie Stevens   1876
Destiny's Will - Elizabeth Ann Michaels   1360
Devil's Prize - Kat Martin   1275
Diamond in the Rough - Suzanne Simmons   1790
Dream Castle - Andrea Kane   1037
Dreaming - Jill Barnett   87
For Love's Sake Only - Laura Parker   1502
Forever After - Jill Gregory   763
Forevermore - Maura Seger   1758
Gentle Rogue - Johanna Lindsey   1201
The Gift - Julie Garwood   702
A Glimpse of Heaven - Barbara Dawson Smith   1831
Guardian Angel - Julie Garwood   703
The Hawk and the Heather - Robin Leigh   1179
Heart of Fancy - Claudette Williams   2035
Heart of the Falcon - Diane Wicker Davis   472
The Heart's Desire - Gayle Wilson   2045
The Heiress Bride - Catherine Coulter   404
Hidden Touch - Virginia Brown   234
Highland Fire - Elizabeth Thornton   1942
The Illusion of Love - Kasey Michaels   1366
Impetuous - Laura Parker   1503
Lady Rogue - Kathryn Kramer   1106
Lady Vengeance - Sarah Eagle   585
The Lily and the Hawk - Marlene Suson   1900
The Lion's Daughter - Loretta Chase   339
The Magic of You - Johanna Lindsey   1204
Masquerade in Moonlight - Kasey Michaels   1368
Midnight Magic - Betina M. Krahn   1101
Mistress - Amanda Quick   1569
Move Heaven and Earth - Christina Dodd   538
Night Shadow - Catherine Coulter   406
Night Storm - Catherine Coulter   407
No Greater Love - Katherine Kingsley   1071
The Painted Veil - Susan Carroll   324
The Passion of an Angel - Kasey Michaels   1370
Petals in the Storm - Mary Jo Putney   1559
Promise Me Heaven - Connie Brockway   221
The Rake and His Lady - Julie Caille   269
The Raven and the Rose - Susan Wiggs   2027
Ravished - Amanda Quick   1571
Reckless - Amanda Quick   1572
Rendezvous - Amanda Quick   1573
Sabelle - Veronica Sattler   1722
Scandal - Amanda Quick   1574
Scandalous - Pamela Caldwell   276

Character Name Index

This index alphabetically lists the major characters in each featured title. Each character name is followed by a description of the character. Citations also provide titles of the books featuring the character, listed alphabetically if there is more than one title; author names; and entry numbers.

A

Aames, Libby (Spinster)
Libby's London Merchant - Carla Kelly   1051

Aaranson, Alec (Composer; Immigrant)
Rhapsody in Time - Judith O'Brien   1451

Aaren (Warrior; Maiden)
My Warrior's Heart - Betina M. Krahn   1102

ab Gruffydd, Wynne (Witch; Guardian)
Where Magic Dwells - Rexanne Becnel   116

Abbot, Joey (Businesswoman; Writer)
His Chariot Awaits - Kasey Michaels   1365

Abbott, Hugh (Adventurer; Spy)
Silver Linings - Jayne Ann Krentz   1111

Abbott, Lorelei (Store Owner)
Wild Colorado Passion - Judith Steel   1872

Abelard, Claudia (Heiress)
A Distant Dawn - Katherine Sinclair   1806

Abella, Nicholas (Police Officer)
Deadly Masquerade - Tracey Tillis   1947

Acton, Eleanor (Debutante; Noblewoman)
Rogue's Reward - Jean R. Ewing   617

Acton, Richard (Nobleman; Military Personnel)
Virtue's Reward - Jean R. Ewing   618

Adair, Abby (Widow(er))
The Wings of Morning - Karen Harper   812

Adair, Duncan (Guide; Fisherman)
Golden Prospect - Shirley Parenteau   1495

Adair, Peyton (Radio)
Heart Waves - Gloria Alvarez   13

Adam (Nobleman; Warrior)
Chanting the Morning Star - Marylyle Rogers   1691

Adams, Jack (Prospector)
Brighter than Gold - Cynthia Wright   2071

Adams, John (Divorced Person)
Love Lesson - Marian Oaks   1445

Adams, Richard (Businessman)
South of Paradise - Marcia Martin   1279

Adamson, Jared (Scientist)
Unlikely Eden - Anne Marie Winston   2052

Adamson, Samantha (Noblewoman)
Queen of Hearts - Michelle Martin   1283

Addams (Amnesiac; Gentlewoman)
The Anonymous Miss Addams - Kasey
   Michaels   1362

Addison, March (Guide; Shipowner)
Emerald Rain - Maggie Osborne   1467

Adrienne (Captive; Royalty)
A Vow to Keep - Elizabeth Bonner   183

Afton, Margaret (Journalist)
Ice and Rapture - Connie Mason   1289

Aidan (Royalty)
The Demon Prince - Kathleen Morgan   1413

Ailinn of Briann (Captive)
The Defiant Heart - Anita Gordon   732

Al Kader, Sharif (Royalty)
The Sheikh's Revenge - Emma Darcy   464

Al Malina, Karim (Teacher)
The Love Slave - Bertrice Small   1823

Alanna (Maiden)
Viking Rose - Ashland Price   1554

Alaric of Anion (Nobleman)
Princess of Fire - Shannon Drake   567

Alden, Arthur Lee (Political Figure)
Emily's Ghost - Antoinette Stockenberg   1882

Alden, Ryan (Doctor)
A Touch of Magic - Carin Rafferty   1585

Alderney, Justin (Nobleman; Rake)
The Halloween Husband - Sandra Heath   844

Aldric, John (Nobleman)
A Heart in Peril - Emma Lange   1158

Aldrich, Cassandra (Governess)
Scandal's Lady - Mary Kingsley   1075

Alek (Time Traveller; Warrior)
The Night Orchid - Patricia Simpson   1804

Alena (Warrior)
A Certain Magic - Kathleen Morgan   1410

Alesandra (Royalty; Orphan)
Castles - Julie Garwood   700

Alessandra (Noblewoman)
A June Bride - Teresa DesJardien   509

Alexander, Corinne (Child-Care Giver)
Autumn Leaves - Jill Metcalf   1347

Alexander, Damon (Mine Owner)
Wild, Wicked Eden - Lynette Vinet   1985

Alexander, D'lise (Frontierswoman)
Kentucky Bride - Norah Hess   885

Alexander, Isabella (Heiress)
American Princess - Sheila O'Hallion   1457

Alexander, Jane (Widow(er))
Halfway to Paradise - Emily Bradshaw   196

Alia (Royalty)
The Knowing Crystal - Kathleen Morgan   1417

Alice (Noblewoman)
Mystique - Amanda Quick   1570

Alin (Prehistoric Human; Leader)
Daughter of the Red Deer - Joan Wolf   2057

Alistair, Lord (Nobleman)
The Arrogant Lord Alistair - Sheila Walsh   1989

Allen, Felicity (Singer)
Promises to Keep - Nina Beaumont   107

Allen, Laurette (Imposter; Gentlewoman)
Renegade Embrace - Virginia Brown   235

Allen, Victor (Artist)
Gretna Bride - Eva Rutland   1702

Allington, Ruth (Widow(er); Artist)
Ask Me No Questions - Patricia Veryan   1978

Allison, Jennifer "Jenny" (Heroine)
Wildfire - Virginia Brown   236

Althson, Lyting (Nobleman)
The Defiant Heart - Anita Gordon   732

Alton, Simon Hilliard (Nobleman; Fiance(e))
The Marriage Gamble - Sarah Eagle   586

Alvar, Mark (Publisher)
Night Vision - Deborah Nicholas   1441

Alyce (Noblewoman)
Dark Whispers - Marylyle Rogers   1692

Alyeka (Sorcerer)
The Enchanted Land - Saranne Dawson   484

Amberly, Catherine "Cat" (Runaway)
Heart's Masquerade - Deborah Simmons   1789

Amberville, Jourdian (Nobleman)
A Basket of Wishes - Rebecca Paisley   1479

Ames, Asher (Journalist)
Newsworthy Affair - Delayne Camp   298

Ames, Kenyon (Detective)
A Perfect Gentleman - Arlene James   965

Ames, Veronica (Journalist)
Obsession - Lori Herter   880

Amicia of Wryborn, Lady (Young Woman)
Hidden Hearts - Marylyle Rogers   1694

Anderson, Alexandra (Student; Time Traveller)
A Touch of Forever - Janice Bennett   126

Anderson, Brianna (Companion)
Dark Cries of Gray Oaks - Lee Karr   1043

Anderson, Ellen (Surveyor; Divorced Person)
Shifting Sands - Suzanne Ellison   609

Anderson, Georgina (Imposter)
Gentle Rogue - Johanna Lindsey   1201

Anderson, Kelsey (Teacher)
Dangerous Odyssey - Jane Edwards   597

Anderson, Rebecca (Young Woman)
Sweet Lullaby - Lorraine Heath   843

Anderson, Ross (Contractor; Widow(er))
No Blueprint for Love - Audrey McConachie   1302

Anderson, Warren (Businessman)
The Magic of You - Johanna Lindsey   1204

Andreas, Jean Marc (Banker)
Storm Winds - Iris Johansen   993

Andreas, Lionello (Nobleman)
The Wind Dancer - Iris Johansen   995

Andrews, Derek (Sea Captain)
Only for Love - Elaine Barbieri   73

Andros, Pride (Thief)
Gideon's Fall - Bronwyn Williams   2033

Andros, Prudence "Haskell" (Thief)
Gideon's Fall - Bronwyn Williams   2033

Angel (Gunfighter)
Angel - Johanna Lindsey   1199

Angel, Cathy (Angel)
An Angel's Touch - Heather Graham
   Pozzessere   1548

Angel, Don (Angel)
An Angel's Touch - Heather Graham
   Pozzessere   1548

Angelique (Runaway)
Sweet Abandon - Sara Blayne   175

Angelo, Nick (Actor)
American Star - Jackie Collins   377

Annalise (Heiress; Housekeeper)
Lady in Green - Barbara Metzger   1353

Anthony, Fortune (Adventurer; Traveller)
No Man's Fortune - Kristie Knight   1092

Antonius, Lucius (Military Personnel)
Somewhere in Time - Merline Lovelace   1228

Antonovic, Branko (Teenager; Gypsy)
The Marriage Bracelet - Rebecca Winters   2053

Antonovic, Nick (Businessman)
The Marriage Bracelet - Rebecca Winters   2053

Ap Bleddyn, Davvyd (Knight)
Wings of the Storm - Susan Sizemore   1817

ap Powel, Griffith (Mercenary)
Outrageous - Christina Dodd   539

Appollonius (Werewolf)
The Werewolf's Sin - Cheri Scotch   1741

Aquilera y Perez, Rafael (Pirate)
The Eagle and the Rose - Diane Gates
   Robinson   1679

Arabella of Woolford (Widow(er); Noblewoman)
Winter Roses - Anita Mills   1396

Aragon, Daniel (Doctor)
Tempt Me with Kisses - Phoebe Conn   387

Aragon, Rick (Lawyer; Government Official)
Appointment with Love - Sheila Fyfe   672

Aragon y Bourbon, Luis Augustin (Heir; Gypsy)
Desire - Phoebe Conn   386

Aratar (Adventurer)
Silversword - Lindsay Randall   1588

Archer, Stuart (Nobleman)
June Love - Karla Hocker   902

Ardane, Brace (Prisoner; Revolutionary)
Crystal Fire - Kathleen Morgan   1412

Arden, Frances William (Nobleman)
An Improper Widow - Kate Moore   1406

Ariane the Betrayed (Noblewoman; Bride)
Enchanted - Elizabeth Lowell   1229

Arianna (Noblewoman)
Castle of the Heart - Flora M. Speer   1854

Arianna (Noblewoman; Psychic)
Keeper of the Dream - Penelope Williamson   2037

Arianne (Noblewoman)
Rosefire - Sandra Davidson   471

Aric of Wycliffe (Knight; Outlaw)
The Rose of Blacksword - Rexanne Becnel   113

Arlington, Thomas (Settler)
Time-Spun Rapture - Thomasina Ring   1645

Armando (Adventurer)
Jewel of the Sea - Susan Wiggs   2024

Armitage, Elizabeth (Teacher; Spinster)
An Unwilling Bride - Jo Beverley   139

Armitage, Sebastian (Orphan; Plantation Owner)
A Misbegotten Match - Rita Boucher   186

Armitage, Susan (Child-Care Giver)
Black-Eyed Susan - Deborah Camp   292

Armstrong, Dana (Heiress; Artist)
The Silver Link - Carol Marsh   1268

Armstrong, Kylie (Businesswoman)
Wedding Bell Blues - Alice Sharpe   1774

Armstrong Graeme, Jennet (Captive)
Conqueror's Kiss - Hannah Howell   937

Arnette, Penny (Businesswoman)
This Fragile Heart - Jan McDaniel   1307

Arnold, Althea (Young Woman; Apothecary)
The Firelands - Karen Harper   811

Arrah of Myr (Mythical Creature)
Swan Star - Betina Lindsey   1193

Arundel, Harcourt "Harry" (Nobleman; Military
   Personnel)
The Bishop's Daughter - Susan Carroll   321

Asche, Stephen (Architect)
The Singing Stones - Phyllis A. Whitney   2018

Ashan (Healer)
Keepers of the Misty Time - Patricia Rowe   1700

Ashburne, Tom (Nobleman)
Lost Love Found - Bertrice Small   1822

Ashby, Henrietta "Harry" (Runaway)
Reckless Angel - Jane Feather   631

Ashcroft, Stacia (Heiress)
An Impetuous Bride - Julie Caille   267

Ashe, Glenna (Mail Order Bride)
The Doubletree - Victoria Pade   1476

Asher, Faith Mary (Widow(er); Spy)
Faith and Honor - Robin Maderich   1259

Ashford, Alissa (Imposter; Governess)
Masque of Enchantment - Charlene Cross   439

Ashford, Henry (Nobleman; Fugitive)
Unspoken Vows - Connie Rinehold   1643

Ashford, Jonathan (Plantation Owner)
Pirate's Bride - Elizabeth August   35

Ashford, Libby (Gentlewoman)
Blossom - Constance Bennett   120

Ashford, Lucien (Nobleman)
Unspoken Vows - Connie Rinehold   1643

Ashford, Sara (Young Woman)
Crossing Eden - Emma Gordon   735

Ashford, Tori (Journalist)
A Season to Remember - Lynda Stowe Landers   1141

Ashley, Linnea (Young Woman; Bride)
A Special License - Kathleen Elliott   604

Ashley, Sarah (Suffragette; Businesswoman)
Come Be My Love - Patricia Watters   1996

Ashton, Elinor (Noblewoman)
Autumn Rain - Anita Mills   1389

Ashton, Elizabeth Anne (Noblewoman)
An Angel in My Arms - Victoria Morrow   1421

Ashton, Mira (Imposter; Stowaway)
Captain of My Heart - Danelle Harmon   808

Aspar, Flavius (Military Personnel)
To Love Again - Bertrice Small   1826

Asquith, Courtney (Dancer; Servant)
Tonight and Forever - Caryl Wilson   2044

Atkins, Susannah (Television Personality)
Monkey Wrench - Nancy Martin   1284

Atlan (Prehistoric Human; Chieftain)
Daughter of the Red Deer - Joan Wolf   2057

Atley, Holt (Scientist)
White Tiger - Olga Bicos   142

Aubin (Spaceship Captain)
Golden Temptress - Patricia Roenbuck   1685

Audi, Rosa (Restauranteur; Immigrant)
Rose - Jill Marie Landis   1147

Audley, Phillip (Nobleman)
Forever After - Jill Gregory   763

Auro (Shaman; Indian)
Woman of the Mists - Lynn Armistead McKee   1314

Austen, Rane "Bulldog" (Nobleman)
Midnight Magic - Betina M. Krahn   1101

Austerleigh, Eliza (Landowner; Spinster)
A Natural Attachment - Katherine Kingsley   1070

Austin, Cord (Wagonmaster)
Orchids in Moonlight - Patricia Hagan   781

Austin, Stewart (Businessman; Wealthy)
Avenue of Dreams - Lucy Taylor   1921

Aveline (Noblewoman; Artist)
Tapestry - Maura Seger   1765

Avenil, Lily (Equestrian; Entertainer)
Wyoming Wildfire - Anne Harmon   807

Averham, Jane (Noblewoman; Widow(er))
Four in Hand - Margaret Westhaven   2006

Averil, Cassie (Businesswoman)
Matchmaker, Matchmaker - Donna Carlisle   313

Ayers, Marissa (Imposter)
Forbidden Fire - Heather Graham Pozzessere   1550

Aylan (Psychic)
The Golden Conquest - Patricia Roenbuck   1684

B

Babcock, Elizabeth (Spinster)
Wicked Stranger - Louisa Rawlings   1599

Baby (Computer)
Baby Makes Five - Lacey Dancer   457

Bailey, Mike (Time Traveller; Archaeologist)
A Love Beyond Time - Flora M. Speer   1855

Bain, Serena (Southern Belle)
Wildfire - Norah Hess   887

Baker, Taylor (Noblewoman; Fugitive)
Prince Charming - Julie Garwood   704

Balfour, Alice (Witch; Widow(er))
Silver Tears - Becky Lee Weyrich   2009

Balfour, Marquerite (Noblewoman)
Masquerade in Moonlight - Kasey Michaels   1368

Balkan, Dane (Stock Broker)
Tasmanian Devil - Valerie Parv   1512

Ballanger, Nicholas "Nick" (Military Personnel)
Cheyenne Sunrise - Constance O'Banyon   1446

Ballard, Liberty Anne (Frontierswoman)
Temptation's Price - Dallas Schulze   1738

Ballard, Ty (Pilot)
Point of Departure - Lindsay McKenna   1319

Ballenrose (Gentleman)
Ballenrose - Mallory Burgess   255

Ballinger, Augusta (Noblewoman)
Rendezvous - Amanda Quick   1573

Ballinger, Hannah (Mail Order Bride; Widow(er))
The Warfield Bride - Bronwyn Williams   2034

Ballou, Remy (Thief)
Gotta Have It - Faye Hughes   951

Balmaine, Lizanne (Healer; Warrior)
Warrior Bride - Tamara Leigh   1184

Balo (Nobleman)
Deeper than Roses - Charlene Cross   437

Bancroft, Meredith (Businesswoman; Heiress)
Paradise - Judith McNaught   1332

Banks, Alison (Child-Care Giver)
Far Horizons - Katherine Sinclair   1807

Banks, James (Doctor)
The Rainbow Promise - Lisa Gregory   765

Banner, Gabriel (Gentleman; Pirate)
Reckless - Amanda Quick   1572

Banning, Dallas (Editor; Detective)
Rebel in Silk - Sandra Chastain   343

Banning, John (Young Man)
Bodie Bride - Isabel Whitfield   2015

Bannon, Tom (Rancher; Lawyer)
Aspen Gold - Janet Dailey   453

Barany, Stefan (Royalty)
Once a Princess - Johanna Lindsey   1206

Barbera, Allyson (Allie) (Housewife)
Seasons - Constance O'Day-Flannery   1453

Barclay, Jane (Ward; Noblewoman)
Dark Fires - Brenda Joyce   1024

Barclay, Lyn (Journalist)
Broken Wings - Doreen Roberts   1659

Barencourte, Clinton (Nobleman)
Defiant Angel - Stephanie Stevens   1876

Bariatinsky, Stefan (Royalty; Military Personnel)
Golden Paradise - Susan Johnson   1000

Barnaby, Jane (Railroad Worker; Businesswoman)
Tiger Prince - Iris Johansen   994

Barnes, Seth (Bootlegger)
Julia's Story - Catherine M. Rae   1584

Barnett, Brandelene (Southern Belle; Plantation Owner)
Southern Oaks - Brenna Braxton-Barshon   209

Barnett, Lorna (Gentlewoman; Single Parent)
November of the Heart - LaVyrle Spencer   1860

Barnett, Sarah (Restauranteur)
Angels in the Sand - Jan McDaniel   1306

Barnhart, Anne (Parent; Divorced Person)
Deadly Secret - Martha Johnson   997

Baron, Kohl (Businessman; Gunfighter)
Nevada Temptation - Gwen Cleary   364

Baron, Leigh (Heiress)
Secret Sins - JoAnn Ross   1698

Baron, Olivia (Doctor)
Outcast - Emily Carmichael   316

Baron, Tamsyn "La Violette" (Mercenary; Noblewoman)
Violet - Jane Feather   634

Barrett, Hugh (Sea Captain; Shipowner)
Sweet Southern Caress - Wendy Garrett   696

Barrington, Alexander (Nobleman)
The Village Spinster - Laura Matthews   1295

Barrington, Catherine (Noblewoman; Captive)
Gypsy Lord - Kat Martin   1276

Barron, Alyssa (Widow(er))
Loveknot - Marissa Carroll   320

Barron, Matthew (Shipowner; Sea Captain)
Jade Dawn - Susannah Leigh   1181

Bartingham, Stephen (Knight)
The Lady and the Wolf - Julie Beard   105

Bartlett, Shane (Businessman)
Matchmaker, Matchmaker - Donna Carlisle   313

Barwick, Adam (Murderer; Avenger)
Dream Catcher - Thomasina Ring   1644

Barzan, Carlos (Financier)
Midnight in Marrakesh - Meryl Sawyer   1731

Bascom, Will (Doctor)
Highland Flame - Stephanie Bartlett   95

Basewell, Megan (Noblewoman)
The Crimson Crown - Edith Layton   1167

Bass, Harmon (Cowboy; Guide)
Temptation's Trail - Dana Ransom   1592

Bass, Jack (Lawman)
Texas Destiny - Dana Ransom   1593

Batthyny, Eleanora (Noblewoman)
Scarlet Kisses - Patricia Camden   277

Baxter, Jennifer (Teacher)
Escape Not My Love - Elaine Coffman   369

Baxter, Kelly (Orphan)
Strange Encounter - Sally Wentworth   2002

Baxter, Merideth (Noblewoman)
Sea of Dreams - Christine Dorsey   552

Bayard, Alessandra (Noblewoman)
Pagan Bride - Tamara Leigh   1183

Bayliss, Meredith (Scientist)
Unlikely Eden - Anne Marie Winston   2052

Bear (Warrior; Indian)
Song of the Warrior - Georgina Gentry   717

Beauchamp, Dominique (Noblewoman)
Once upon a Kiss - Tanya Anne Crosby   433

Beauchamp, Edward (Nobleman)
A Highly Respected Widow - Melinda McRae   1335

Beaudette, Jehane (Royalty)
Pirate's Princess - Constance O'Banyon   1449

Beaudine, Dallie (Sports Figure)
Fancy Pants - Susan Elizabeth Phillips   1526

Beaufort, Judith (Noblewoman)
And Heaven Too - Julie Tetel   1923

Beaumondier, Suzanne (Vampire)
Night's Immortal Touch - Cherlyn Jac   960

Beaumont, Adria (Doctor)
Chase the Dawn - Kay McMahon   1327

Beaumont, Francis (Crime Victim)
Captives of the Night - Loretta Chase   338

Beaumont, Jaine (Gambler)
Tempted by Fire - Thea Devine   523

Beaumont, Leila (Artist)
Captives of the Night - Loretta Chase   338

Beaumont, Marti (Vintner)
Bouquet - Shirl Henke   860

Beaumont, Marti (Vintner; Widow(er))
Summer Has No Name - Shirl Henke   867

Beaumont, Max (Nobleman)
Unwilling Woman - Sue Peters   1520

Beaumont, Nicholas (Shipowner)
Bewitching Kisses - Rainy Kirkland   1083

Beaumont, Rafe (Convict; Artisan)
Winter Heat - Mary Lynn Baxter   104

Beaumont, Stephen (Veteran; Farmer)
Dearest Enemy - Stephanie Bartlett   94

Beaumont, Ty (Lawman)
Wild Texas Blossom - Arlene Holliday   910

Beaumont, Will "Billy Ray" (Drifter)
In Sinful Harmony - Marilyn Pappano   1493

Beauvisage, Adrienne (Governess; Companion)
Barbados - Cynthia Wright   2070

Beck, Leah (Artist; Lesbian)
Painted Moon - Karin Kallmaker   1036

Becker, Ammity (Mail Order Bride; Orphan)
Beloved Wife - Lynda Trent 1956

Becker, Leah (Widow(er); Businesswoman)
Almost Home - Debra Cowan 414

Becket, Eleanora "Nora" (Noblewoman; Spy)
Lady Gallant - Suzanne Robinson 1682

Becket, Faith Ann (Frontierswoman)
Desert Sunrise - Raine Cantrell 310

Beckham, Daniel (Widow(er); Farmer)
Daniel's Bride - Linda Lael Miller 1378

Bedford, James Cortez (Rake; Gypsy)
Ride the Wind - Krista Janssen 976

Beg, Khalid (Royalty)
Desert Eden - Patricia Grasso 747

Belleme, Rowena (Noblewoman)
Prisoner of My Desire - Johanna Lindsey 1207

Belmont, Ariana (Young Woman)
A Dangerous Longing - Veronica Sattler 1720

Belmont, Theodora (Noblewoman)
Valentine - Jane Feather 632

Ben Raschid, Galen (Royalty)
The Golden Barbarian - Iris Johansen 990

ben Rashid, Ahmed (Diplomat; Roommate)
King's Ransom - Diana Palmer 1489

Benedict, Eve (Actress)
Genuine Lies - Nora Roberts 1667

Benedict, Grayson (Rancher)
Wyoming Wildfire - Anne Harmon 807

Benedict, Jessie (Businesswoman)
Sweet Fortune - Jayne Ann Krentz 1112

Benedict, Laurel Frasier (Socialite)
Morning Rain - Leigh Riker 1636

Benedict, Zach (Director; Crime Suspect)
Perfect - Judith McNaught 1333

Benison, Johanna "Clare" (Imposter; Twin)
Chieftain - Arnette Lamb 1137

Bennett, Caroline (Heiress; Businesswoman)
Midnight Lover - Barbara Bretton 214

Bennett, Ellie (Businesswoman)
Renegade - Christine Flynn 654

Bennett, Hope (Mine Owner; Southern Belle)
California Caress - Rebecca Sinclair 1810

Bennett, Rosa (Diplomat; Spy)
The Doll's House - Evelyn Anthony 25

Bennett, Tyler (Lawyer)
Temptation's Wild Embrace - Rene J. Garrod 698

Bennett, Victoria (Midwife)
Mountain Mystic - Debra Dixon 533

Bennington, Katherine (Heiress)
Travelin' Man - Lois Faye Dyer 579

Benoite, Topaze (Thief; Imposter)
Promise of Summer - Louisa Rawlings 1597

Berenger, Rye (Fugitive; Stowaway)
Love's Windswept Embrace - Michalann Perry 1517

Berg, Fernando "Nando" (Military Personnel; Nobleman)
Sapphire Magic - Nina Beaumont 108

Bergendahl, Kristianna (Farmer)
Firefly - Stef Ann Holm 911

Bernard, Celene Peugeot (Widow(er))
Bride of the Wilderness - Elizabeth Grayson 753

Bernay, Garrett (Nobleman; Knight)
A Tender Magic - Linda Madl 1262

Berne, Taylor (Manager)
The Bear Affair - Cynthia Powell 1546

Bernstein, Betsy (Interior Decorator)
Trespassing Hearts - Julie Ellis 605

Berringer, Christina (Noblewoman)
Sunshine and Shadow - Kathleen Harrington 816

Berringer, Ross (Lawman)
Call Me Sin - Jan Hudson 945

Best, Meggie (Young Woman)
Marrying Stone - Pamela Morsi 1428

Beverley (Nobleman)
Lady Sarah's Charade - Nancy Richards-Akers 1631

Bigod, Barbara (Noblewoman; Bastard Daughter)
The Silver Mirror - Roberta Gellis 710

Billings, Katherine (Actress; Governess)
Miss Billings Treads the Boards - Carla Kelly 1053

Bishop, Faith (Journalist; Traveller)
Midnight Ice - Cathie Linz 1213

Black, Caleb (Guide; Gunfighter)
Only His - Elizabeth Lowell 1231

Black, Daisy (Lawyer; Indian)
Forbidden - Susan Johnson 999

Black, James (Pirate; Bastard Son)
Fortune's Mistress - Judith E. French 667

Black Eagle (Indian; Warrior)
Capture - Emily French 665

Black Horse, Cleve (Indian; Prisoner)
This Time Forever - Kathleen Eagle 583

Black Wolf (Healer; Indian)
Brave Heart - Lindsay McKenna 1315

Black Wolf (Nobleman; Outlaw)
Through a Dark Mist - Marsha Canham 307

Blackburne, Hadrian (Nobleman; Rake)
Caprice - Laura Parker 1501

Blackburne, Jane (Teacher; Noblewoman)
Impetuous - Laura Parker 1503

Blackheath, Ian (Spy; Rake)
The Raider's Bride - Kimberly Cates 331

Blackstone, Emma (Socialite)
Desire - Georgia Hampton 789

Blackstone, Jack (Pirate; Sea Captain)
Sea Fires - Christine Dorsey 551

Blackstone, Jared (Privateer; Sea Captain)
Sea of Dreams - Christine Dorsey 552

Blackstone, Joel (Businessman)
Perfect Partners - Jayne Ann Krentz 1110

Blackthorne, Laurel (Widow(er); Outcast)
Laurel - Leigh Greenwood 758

Blackthorne, Nicholas (Gentleman)
A Rose at Midnight - Anne Stuart 1889

Blackthorne, Quinton (Nobleman)
Skylark - Elane Osborn 1466

Blackwell, Nicholas (Sea Captain)
The Captain's Bride - Kat Martin 1273

Blackwell, Saxon (Heir; Gentleman)
Barefoot Bride - Rebecca Paisley 1478

Blackwood, Daniella "Dani" (Psychic)
Apache Magic - Janis Reams Hudson 948

Blackwood, John (Nobleman; Handicapped)
Dancing at Midnight - Julia Quinn 1581

Blackwood, Mace (Publisher)
Princess of Thieves - Katherine O'Neal 1461

Blackwood, Victoria (Con Artist)
South of Paradise - Marcia Martin 1279

Blade, Coleman "Cole" (Lawman)
Long Texas Nights - Lindsey Hanks 793

Blair, Layne Fielding (Socialite)
Lie and Say You Love Me - Robin St. Thomas 1867

Blair-Coupland, Alison (Noblewoman; Actress)
The Brides of Eden - Clare Benedict 119

Blaise de Rouen (Knight)
Firebrand's Lady - Caryl Wilson 2043

Blake (Student—High School; Handicapped)
Sounds of Silence - Marilyn Levy 1185

Blake, Caroline (Teacher)
Roses for Caroline - Lynn Bulock 252

Blake, Gabriel (Military Personnel)
Impetuous - Laura Parker 1503

Blake, Gavin (Rancher)
Promise Me Spring - Robin Lee Hatcher 831

Blake, Robert (Spy)
Beyond the Sunrise - Mary Balogh 54

Blakely, Morgan (Nobleman; Spy)
Bride of the Unicorn - Kasey Michaels 1363

Blakemore, Marianne (Runaway; Imposter)
Fortune's Lady - Robin LeAnne Wiete 2020

Blakewell, Seth (Indian)
Heir to Vengeance - Roberta Eckert 590

Blessing, Lucille "Lucy" (Banker; Widow(er))
Wild Wyoming Love - Dana Ransom 1595

Bliss, Abigail (Frontierswoman; Writer)
When Lightning Strikes - Rexanne Becnel 115

Bliss, Chloe (Fiance(e))
The Bridegroom - Carol Jerina 987

Blood, Sebastian (Detective)
San Francisco Surrender - Donna Fletcher 652

Bloodaxe, Wulfgar (Warrior)
Swan Road - Rebecca Brandewyne 204

Blooddrinker, Thorn (Warrior; Time Traveller)
Until Forever - Johanna Lindsey 1210

Blue, Aubrey (Young Woman; Teacher)
Under the Desert Moon - Marsha Canham 308

Blue, Liberty "Libby" (Rancher; Fugitive)
Liberty Blue - Robin Lee Hatcher 828

Blue, Toinette (Administrator; Spouse)
Body and Soul - Felicia Mason 1293

Blue Song, Katherine (Indian; Doctor)
Beloved Woman - Deborah Smith 1838

Blydon, Arabella "Belle" (Noblewoman)
Dancing at Midnight - Julia Quinn 1581

Blythe, Dominic (Nobleman)
Road to Ruin - Margaret Evans Porter 1535

Bodman, Sarah (Businesswoman; Lesbian)
Up, Up and Away - Catherine Ennis 612

Bonchard, Noel (Military Personnel; Imposter)
Wicked Stranger - Louisa Rawlings 1599

Broderick, Miles (Nobleman)
Maverick Heart - Joan Johnston 1007

Brodfield, Phoebe (Widow(er); Noblewoman)
The Persistent Earl - Gail Eastwood 589

Brodie, Sine Catriona (Young Woman; Thief)
Silver Flame - Hannah Howell 939

Brody, Frank (Saloon Keeper/Owner)
Weeping Angel - Stef Ann Holm 915

Brody, John (Sailor; Imposter)
Thief of Hearts - Patricia Gaffney 679

Bron (Knight)
Swan Witch - Betina Lindsey 1194

Bronson, Daniel (Businessman)
One and Only - Barbara Bretton 215

Brookington, Grant (Rancher)
Secret Fires - Linda Hilton 894

Brooks, Belinda (Artist; Student)
Sweet Deception - Vanessa Hale 783

Brooks, Liberty (Activist; Secretary)
Scandalous - Sonia Simone 1796

Brooks, Stephen (Businessman)
Dreams of Joy - Holly S. McClure 1301

Brougham, Jervis (Nobleman)
Deck the Halls - Marian Devon 524

Brown, Cat (Imposter)
The Marquis of Carabas - Elizabeth Brodnax 222

Brown, Lily (Widow(er); Rancher)
Texas Lily - Patricia Rice 1622

Brown, Noelle (Orphan; Companion)
Noelle - Diana Palmer 1491

Brown, Susannah (Governess; Widow(er))
Susannah's Secret - Judy Christenberry 354

Browne, Chelsea (Doctor)
Sands of Time - Terri Valentine 1967

Brownell, Eli (Military Personnel)
The Conquest - Lucy Elliot 602

Brownell, Zeke (Vigilante)
The Claim - Lucy Elliot 601

Brownfield, Lily (Secretary—Legal; Cook)
Always a Lady - Sharon Sala 1712

Browning, Arielle (Widow(er))
Night Fire - Cait Logan 1224

Browning, Kendra (Detective—Homicide; Time Traveller)
When Midnight Comes - Robin Burcell 253

Bruder, Tulsy Mae (Young Woman)
Runabout - Pamela Morsi 1429

Bruycker, John (Psychic)
White Light - Wendy Haley 786

Bryn, Dilys (Debutante)
The Infamous Rake - Norma Lee Clark 361

Brynn of Falkhaar (Healer)
Midnight Warrior - Iris Johansen 991

Brynna (Healer)
Chanting the Dawn - Marylyle Rogers 1690

Buchanan, Cole (Businessman)
Masquerade - Janet Dailey 454

Buchanan, Diane (Entertainer; Equestrian)
Written in the Stars - Nan Ryan 1708

Buchanan, Noah (Cowboy; Writer)
Outlaw Heart - Catherine Palmer 1486

Buchanan, Tibbie (Health Care Professional; Single Parent)
Angel in Marble - Elaine Coffman 368

Bullard, Julie (Director)
Joy and Anger - Jennifer Blake 171

Bunch, Hannah (Spinster; Bride)
Heaven Sent - Pamela Morsi 1427

Burbridge, Elizabeth (Spinster; Teacher)
The Dream - Kit Gardner 683

Burch, Jane (Companion; Imposter)
My Cousin Jane - Anne Barbour 81

Burke, Devlin (Detective)
Seductive Caress - Carla Simpson 1800

Burke, Dillon (Engineer)
Breath of Scandal - Sandra Brown 227

Burke, Michael (Nobleman; Military Personnel)
Hour of the Rose - Christina Skye 1820

Burke-Marchand, Ariane (Noblewoman)
Star-Crossed - Susan Krinard 1117

Burleson, Jim (Rancher)
Heart of the Wild - Donna Stephens 1874

Burnett, Burton (Rancher)
Because You're Mine - Nan Ryan 1703

Burnett, Jake (Heir; Cowboy)
Sweet Lullaby - Lorraine Heath 843

Burnett, Lacy (Witch; Psychic)
Fortune's Mistress - Judith E. French 667

Burnett, Rory (Rancher; Writer)
Past Promises - Jill Marie Landis 1146

Burns, Katy (Spinster)
Nightrose - Dorothy Garlock 688

Burns, Maddie (Imposter; Businesswoman)
Sunswept - Leigh Bristol 218

Burnside, Talitha (Noblewoman; Artist)
A Talent for Trouble - Anne Barbour 82

Butler, Rhett (Businessman)
Scarlett - Alexandra Ripley 1647

Butler, Scarlett (Plantation Owner)
Scarlett - Alexandra Ripley 1647

Bydalek, Jenny (Immigrant; Orphan)
Jenny's Dream - Victoria Morrow 1423

C

Cabot, Rand (Spy; Importer/Exporter)
Perchance to Dream - Maura Seger 1763

Caddell, Sean (Shipowner; Smuggler)
Tonight and Forever - Caryl Wilson 2044

Caddo (Indian; Outlaw)
The Lady and the Outlaw - Katherine Compton 380

Cade, Nicolas (Criminal)
Renegade Embrace - Virginia Brown 235

Caden, Amanda (Plantation Owner)
Jasmine and Silk - Sandra Chastain 341

Cadwalder, Melissa (Young Woman)
Web of Loving Lies - Barbara Leigh 1177

Cain, McCauley (Lawman; Outlaw)
Fair Is the Rose - Meagan McKinney 1322

Cain, Walker (Bodyguard)
Always in My Dreams - Jo Goodman 730

Caine (Nobleman; Spy)
Guardian Angel - Julie Garwood 703

Caine, Charity (Young Woman)
Oklahoma Angel - Phoebe Fitzjames 649

Caine, Jared (Gambler)
Fortune's Lady - Victoria Thompson 1933

Caine, Karissa (Mine Owner; Saloon Hostess)
Passion's Bold Fire - Rosalyn Alsobrook 12

Caine, Valerian (Nobleman; Spirit)
Gwen's Christmas Ghost - Lynn Kerstan 1059

Calder, Lance (Foreman; Indian)
The Savage - Nicole Jordan 1019

Caldwell, Alanna (Indian)
Cheyenne Sunrise - Constance O'Banyon 1446

Caldwell, Hope (Doctor; Teacher)
Beloved Intruder - Joan Van Nuys 1971

Caldwell, Lathe (Doctor)
Endless Seduction - Rosalyn Alsobrook 11

Caldwell, Rait (Gunfighter; Guardian)
Wild Western Desire - Kathy Jones 1015

Calebrow, Dan (Coach)
It Had to Be You - Susan Elizabeth Phillips 1529

Calhoun, Anabeth (Outlaw; Imposter)
Kid Calhoun - Joan Johnston 1006

Calhoun, Annie (Outlaw)
Outlaw Bride - Katherine Compton 381

Calhoun, Cairo (Outlaw)
Promise Me Moonlight - Carol Finch 646

Calhoun, McKenzie Kathryn "Macky" (Fugitive; Imposter)
The Redhead and the Preacher - Sandra Chastain 344

Calhoun, Rachel (Doctor)
Walk in the Light - Charles Durham 577

Calhoun, Steve (Police Officer)
Walking After Midnight - Karen Robards 1655

Callahan, Dory (Single Parent)
Sins of Summer - Dorothy Garlock 690

Callahan, Jake (Rancher; Twin)
Homeward Bound - Kathryn Attalla 34

Callahan, Kane (Detective—Private)
Moonlight Enchantment - Carol Finch 645

Callahan, Lindsey (Time Traveller)
Love Across Time - Anne Meredith 1343

Callahan, Sunny "Sunflower" (Indian)
River Song - Sharon MacIver 1246

Callahan, Trevor (Rancher; Twin)
Homeward Bound - Kathryn Attalla 34

Callan, J. Barrett V (Businessman; Lawman)
A Margin in Time - Laura Hayden 837

Callot, Sabre (Heiress)
A Perfect Gentleman - Arlene James 965

Calloway, Clint (Detective—Police)
Cowboy Cop - Rachel Lee 1172

Calloway, Nicholas (Nobleman; Bounty Hunter)
The Inheritance - Joan Johnston 1005

Carroll, Eric (Young Man)
No Illusion - Lynette Kent   1058

Carroll, Peter (Professor)
No Illusion - Lynette Kent   1058

Carsley, Edward (Nobleman)
Highland Fling - Amanda Scott   1747

Carson, Bain (Twin)
Master of Her Heart - Terri Valentine   1965

Carson, Hunter (Banker)
Touch of Heaven - Michelle Brandon   206

Carson, Skye (Innkeeper)
Dreams and Wishes - Karren Radko   1583

Carstairs, Augusta (Gentlewoman; Actress)
A Tempting Miss - Janice Bennett   125

Carstairs, Claudia (Widow(er))
Lord Glenraven's Return - Anne Barbour   80

Carter, Candice (Debutante)
Darkest Heart - Brenda Joyce   1025

Carter, Clinton (Rancher)
Seasons of the Heart - Marilyn Cunningham   449

Carteret, Georgiana "Georgie" (Gentlewoman;
   Debutante)
Love's Gambit - Meg-Lynn Roberts   1662

Cartwright, Simon (Nobleman)
Queen of Hearts - Michelle Martin   1283

Casals, Pam (Coach; Handicapped)
Bright Hopes - Pat Warren   1993

Caslar, Jill (Young Woman)
More than You Dreamed - Kathleen Gilles
   Seidel   1767

Cassidy, Chase (Rancher)
After All - Jill Marie Landis   1142

Cassidy, Lane (Detective—Private; Gunfighter)
Last Chance - Jill Marie Landis   1145

Cassidy, Robert (Lawyer)
French Silk - Sandra Brown   228

Cassidy, Victoria Flemming (Captive)
Montana Mistress - Carol Finch   644

Castillo, Tigre Dan "Dan Castle" (Miner)
Denver - Sara Orwig   1463

Castle, Antonia (Feminist)
Heart Strings - Lydia Browne   237

Castle, Jenny (Businesswoman)
Above Suspicion - Eleanor Woods   2064

Castlereagh, Katrine (Gentlewoman)
Arrow to the Heart - Jennifer Blake   169

Catherine of Braganza (Royalty; Historical Figure)
The Pleasure of Love - Jean Plaidy   1533

Catherwood, Shreve (Actor; Director)
Acts of Love - Deana James   967
Acts of Passion - Deana James   968

Caulfield, Allegra (Debutante)
Moonlight Veil - Janis Laden   1128

Caulfield, Allison (Socialite)
Seduced - Carla Simpson   1799

Cavanagh, Miles (Guardian; Nobleman)
Dangerous Joy - Jo Beverley   133

Cavanaugh, Conn (Trapper; Settler)
Quiet Fires - Ginna Gray   751

Cavanaugh, Devon (Hero)
Surrender the Night - Colleen Shannon   1770

Cavanaugh, Jenny (Advertising; Imposter)
Moments - Georgia Bockoven   178

Cavanaugh, Kate (Feminist; Prostitute)
Storyville - Lois Battle   98

Cavanaugh, Matt (Gambler)
A Wild Desire - Rebecca George   719

Cavanaugh, Moriah (Writer)
Moriah's Magic - Anne Ladley   1129

Cavendish, Bart (Gentleman)
Lady of the Moors - Mary Ellen Petty   1521

Cavendish, Miracle (Noblewoman)
Miracle - Katherine Sutcliffe   1903

Ceawlin (Royalty; Bastard Son)
Born of the Sun - Joan Wolf   2056

Ceidre (Noblewoman; Bastard Daughter)
The Conqueror - Brenda Joyce   1023

Cenred (Entertainer)
The Amethyst Crown - Katherine Deauville   492

Chaco (Indian)
Arizona Ecstasy - Rosanne Bittner   152

Chadwick, Flame (Young Woman; Spouse)
Flame - Evelyn Rogers   1687

Chadwick, Miranda (Scientist)
Sea Fires - Christine Dorsey   551

Chadwick, Sarah (Governess)
A Maddening Minx - Mary Kingsley   1073

Challerton, Viola (Noblewoman)
The Absentee Earl - Clarice Peters   1518

Challoner, Luke (Doctor)
Sweet Illusion - Angela Carson   325

Chalmers, Caroline (Teacher)
Caroline and the Raider - Linda Lael Miller   1377

Chalmers, Emma (Orphan)
Emma and the Outlaw - Linda Lael Miller   1379

Chalmers, Lily (Farmer; Orphan)
Lily and the Major - Linda Lael Miller   1382

Chamberlain, Paxton Gaillard (Knight; Nobleman)
A Kiss in the Night - Jennifer Horsman   927

Chambers, Alexandra (Noblewoman; Bride)
The Sherbrooke Bride - Catherine Coulter   409

Chambers, Brittany (Spinster)
A Promise of Fire - Veronica Sattler   1721

Chambers, Catherine (Doctor)
All but Love - Ann Howard White   2013

Chambers, Jessica (Researcher; Scientist)
Formula for Murder - S.R. Hawley   836

Chambers, Margaret "Maggie" (Gentlewoman;
   Heiress)
Bride's Leap - Joan Overfield   1470

Chambers, Victoria (Thief)
San Francisco Surrender - Donna Fletcher   652

Champion, Jill (Heiress)
Dangerous Bequest - Lee Anderson   21

Chandler, Carolyn (Runaway)
Midnight Fire - Madeline Baker   45

Chandler, Cordell (Rancher)
Ecstasy's Masquerade - Gwen Cleary   363

Chandler, Gordon (Heir)
Ask Me No Questions - Patricia Veryan   1978

Chandler, Jamie (Traveller)
Orchids in Moonlight - Patricia Hagan   781

Chandler, Jarrett (Landowner)
Across a Starlit Sea - Rebecca Brandewyne   198

Chandler, Nicki (Businesswoman; Psychic)
Sight Unseen - Kathy Clark   359

Chandler, Robert (Privateer)
The Black Hawk - Lynda Trent   1957

Chandler, Sabrina (Artist)
The House in the Trees - Georgette Livingston   1219

Chandler, Sam (Gambler)
Nevada Ecstasy - Lindsey Hanks   794

Chandler, Victoria (Businesswoman)
Forever Yours - Francis Ray   1601

Chandon, Claire (Gentlewoman; Servant)
Eden's Gate - Karen Harper   810

Channing, Amaris (Psychic; Waiter/Waitress)
Follow Your Heart - Lynda Trent   1959

Channing, Derek (Businessman)
Charade - Christina Hamlett   788

Channing, Nick (Vacationer)
That Certain Yearning - Claudia Jameson   975

Channing-Downes, Submit (Widow(er);
   Noblewoman)
Black Silk - Judy Cuevas   443

Chanson, Alain (Businessman)
Changes of Heart - Elizabeth Bennett   122

Chapin, Marianna (Dancer; Gentlewoman)
Country Dance - Margaret Westhaven   2005

Chaplin, Anne (Art Dealer; Imposter)
In Spite of Themselves - Elizabeth Barnes   86

Charles (Gentleman)
Counterfeit Heart - Anthea Malcolm   1264

Charles, Ian (Nobleman; Spy)
Bride's Leap - Joan Overfield   1470

Charles II (Royalty; Historical Figure)
The Pleasure of Love - Jean Plaidy   1533

Charlton, Sophrina (Noblewoman)
An Unlikely Attraction - Melinda McRae   1338

Charteris, Jessica (Noblewoman)
Only Mine - Elizabeth Lowell   1233

Chase, Catherine (Detective)
Betray the Night - Kay McMahon   1326

Chase, Julian (Nobleman)
Green Eyes - Karen Robards   1649

Chassyn, Gryph (Psychic)
Shield's Lady - Amanda Glass   729

Chastain, Cara (Widow(er); Animal Lover)
Southern Storms - Marcia Martin   1282

Chastain, Devlin (Noblewoman)
Crown of Dreams - Kimberly Cates   328

Chastaine, Jake (Sea Captain)
A Light for My Love - Alexis Harrington   814

Chatham, Devon (Noblewoman; Captive)
Tempt the Devil - Connie Mason   1291

Chauncey, Philipa (Noblewoman; Fiance(e))
Charmed - Stella Cameron   285

Chavez Lopez, Santana Maria (Noblewoman)
The Forever Tree - Rosanne Bittner   155

Cook, Anthony (Doctor)
Libby's London Merchant - Carla Kelly   1051

Cooper, Bethenia (Orphan)
Journey's End - Mildred Riley   1641

Cooper, Gil (Principal)
The Christmas Wish - Rexanne Becnel   110

Cooper, Lauren (Rancher)
A Gentle Taming - Adrienne Day   486

Cooper, Meg (Lawyer)
First Loves - Jean Stone   1884

Cooper, Wes (Actor; Police Officer)
High Riding Heroes - Joey Light   1187

Copestakes, Chris (Student; Reincarnated Person)
On the Way to Heaven - Tina Wainscott   1986

Copper-Headed Woman (Healer; Adoptee)
Lady Legend - Deborah Camp   296

Coppersmith, Liz (Businesswoman)
Time After Time - Antoinette Stockenberg   1883

Corbett, Jack (Convict; Rancher)
Sweet Obsession - Kathy Jones   1014

Corbett of Colchester (Nobleman)
My Gallant Enemy - Rexanne Becnel   112

Corbin, Jed (Television Personality)
Winter Bride - Iris Johansen   996

Corbin, Melissa (Runaway; Heiress)
My Darling Melissa - Linda Lael Miller   1383

Corbin, Ysabel Belfort (Widow(er); Step-Parent)
Winter Bride - Iris Johansen   996

Cord (Bodyguard)
Pirate's Princess - Constance O'Banyon   1449

Corday, Alexandra (Singer)
All That Glitters - Ruth Langan   1150

Cordelia "Delia" (Singer; Orphan)
Through the Years - Katherine Sinclair   1808

Cordell, Nathan (Foreman)
Follow the Wind - Janelle Taylor   1914

Cormick, Bryce Darcy (Spy; Actor)
Dance of Deception - Suzannah Davis   479

Corstairs, Sabelle "Isabelle" (Debutante; Animal Lover)
Sabelle - Veronica Sattler   1722

Cortivas, Serita (Landowner)
Texas Gamble - Vivian Vaughn   1975

Corvin, Dane (Writer; Naturalist)
All the Winters That Have Been - Evan Maxwell   1297

Corvin, Daniel (Nobleman)
The Scandalous Schoolmistress - Rita Boucher   188

Costanza, Alaina "Lainie" (Writer; Time Traveller)
When Lightning Strikes - Kristin Hannah   801

Costello, Kate "Leather" (Musician; Entertainer)
Homeward Bound - Kathryn Attalla   34

Costhaler, Nick (Artisan; Guide)
Yes, Virginia - Peg Sutherland   1907

Cotter, Tracey (Businesswoman)
Stand by Your Man - Kathy Clark   360

Coulson, Megan (Captive)
Forever Gold - Catherine Hart   819

Coulter, Adam (Avenger)
Runaway Heart - Tena Carlyle   315

Coulter, Belinda (Singer)
The Daring - Patricia Hagan   777

Coulter, Jessica (Teacher)
The Daring - Patricia Hagan   777

Coulter, Sam (Businessman)
Pearl Moon - Katherine Stone   1885

Courtenay, Miles (Rake; Gambler)
The Lady and the Rake - Carola Dunn   574

Courtland, Alexandra (Revolutionary)
Brazen Virginia Bride - Millie Criswell   423

Courtland, Derek (Privateer; Blockade Runner)
White Rose - Linda Ladd   1127

Courtland, Jonas (Plantation Owner)
Bayou Dreams - Libby Sydes   1908

Courtland, Tiffany (Noblewoman)
Defiant Angel - Stephanie Stevens   1876

Courtney, Guinivere (Teacher)
The Scandalous Schoolmistress - Rita Boucher   188

Courtney, Helen (Widow(er); Farmer)
Love Me Tonight - Nan Ryan   1706

Courtney, Larissa (Time Traveller)
Once upon Forever - Becky Lee Weyrich   2008

Courtney, Liberty Rose (Servant)
Liberty Rose - Stef Ann Holm   913

Cox, Hillary (Writer)
Facets - Barbara Delinsky   499

Coye, Ash (Journalist)
Forgotten Vows - Maggie Shayne   1777

Crabb, Esme (Mountain Woman)
Garters - Pamela Morsi   1426

Crabtree, Emily (Widow(er); Rancher)
Desert Flame - Anne Harmon   806

Craddock, Matthew (Saloon Keeper/Owner)
Gamblin' Man - Barbara Faith   621

Craigie, Edward (Nobleman)
Stolen Dreams - Catherine Lyndell   1238

Cramer, Julie (Student; Tour Guide)
Roman Butterfly - Betty Dahlin   452

Cramer, Lillian "Lili" (Businesswoman; Researcher)
The Firebirds - Beverly Byrne   264

Cramer, Tweed (Miner)
Forbidden Kiss - Gina Robins   1673

Crandall, Marla (Stock Broker)
A Family Affair - Denise Richards   1628

Crandell, Blake (Nobleman)
Hidden Touch - Virginia Brown   234

Crane, Peter (Historian)
The Silver Link - Carol Marsh   1268

Cranleigh, Rosetta (Gentlewoman)
The Captive - Victoria Holt   918

Crawford, Edwinna (Plantation Owner)
Beyond the Savage Sea - JoAnn Wendt   2000

Crawford, Eva (Adoptee)
All We Hold Dear - Kathryn Lynn Davis   476

Crawford, Nick (Bachelor)
The Sensation - Rebecca Flanders   651

Creed, Montana (Heir; Farmer)
Surrender a Dream - Jill Barnett   91

Creeghan, Bruce (Nobleman)
Emerald Embrace - Shannon Drake   565

Creighton, Elliot (Fiance(e); Actor)
Sweet Forever - Becky Lee Weyrich   2010

Cribbage, Barbara (Young Woman)
Mutual Consent - Gayle Buck   247

Crisdean, Alysa Malvern (Royalty; Witch)
The Last Viking Queen - Janelle Taylor   1917

Cristie, Beth (Scientist)
There Is a Season - Phyllis Houseman   930

Cristobal, Danton Luis (Pirate; Nobleman)
King of the Pirates - Stef Ann Holm   912

Crocker, Daniel (Detective; Orphan)
Distant Thunder - Lisa Bingham   145

Crockett, Casity (Fugitive; Mail Order Bride)
Forbidden Kiss - Gina Robins   1673

Cromwell, Jon (Widow(er); Political Figure)
Come Be My Love - Patricia Watters   1996

Cross, Zachary (Detective—Police; Vacationer)
Trust Me - Jeane Renick   1610

Crosse, Emilie (Appraiser; Time Traveller)
Somewhere in Time - Barbara Bretton   216

Culhane, Jay (Lawman)
Escape Not My Love - Elaine Coffman   369

Culhane, Lily (Actress)
The Lily and the Hawk - Marlene Suson   1900

Cullen, Rebecca (Secretary—Legal)
Night Fever - Susan Kyle   1122

Culver, Billy (Businessman)
Bad Billy Culver - Judy Gill   724

Cummings, Amelia (Widow(er); Store Owner)
Stardust and Whirlwinds - Pamela Litton   1217

Cummings, Cecelia (Matchmaker)
Cousin Cecelia - Joan Smith   1843

Cummings, Libby "Spirit Woman" (Captive)
Dance with the Devil - Pamela Litton   1215

Curran, Bess (Divorced Person)
Bygones - LaVyrle Spencer   1858

Curran, Lila (Gentlewoman)
The Flames of Vengeance - Beverly Byrne   265

Curran, Michael (Divorced Person)
Bygones - LaVyrle Spencer   1858

Curtin, Elizabeth Montbleau (Southern Belle)
The Legend of Love - Nan Ryan   1704

Cutter, Jake (Military Personnel)
Does Cupid Do Take-Out? - Kathryn E. Coulter   412

Cutter, Jake (Convict; Police Officer)
Rough Passage - Paula Detmer Riggs   1635

D

Dacre, Jessamyn (Noblewoman)
The Constant Flame - Patricia Phillips   1525

Dade, Jessamine (Southern Belle)
Riverbend - Mary McBride   1300

d'Agenais, Achille (Nobleman)
Scarlet Kisses - Patricia Camden   277

d'Agounville, Renard (Lawman; Warrior)
Tapestry - Maura Seger   1765

D'Aix, Sir Alphonse (Nobleman; Bastard Son)
The Silver Mirror - Roberta Gellis   710

de Allesandro, Dante (Nobleman)
Caressa - Linda Lang Bartell 92

De Arr, Tedra (Warrior; Security Officer)
Warrior's Woman - Johanna Lindsey 1211

de Ath Ballister, Sebastian (Nobleman; Rake)
Lord of Scoundrels - Loretta Chase 340

de Barante, Rosalie (Dancer)
Dangerous Diversions - Margaret Evans Porter 1534

de Beaucaire, Gabrielle (Spy)
Velvet - Jane Feather 633

de Beauchamp, Philippa (Noblewoman)
Earth Song - Catherine Coulter 403

de Beaufort, Adrienne (Time Traveller; Reincarnated Person)
Across Time - Nina Beaumont 106

de Blanc, Rowan (Gentleman)
Arrow to the Heart - Jennifer Blake 169

de Borge, Simon (Knight)
Daggers of Gold - Katherine Deauville 494

de Brese, Magdalen (Noblewoman)
Brazen Whispers - Jane Feather 629

de Brienne, Gabrielle (Captive)
Scarlet Angel - Elizabeth Thornton 1943

de Briscourt, Servanne (Noblewoman)
Through a Dark Mist - Marsha Canham 307

de Bron, Geoffrey (Nobleman; Religious)
Desire of the Heart - Katherine Vickery 1981

de Burgh, Falcon (Nobleman; Knight)
The Falcon and the Flower - Virginia Henley 870

De Burgh, Isabeau "Beau" (Highwayman; Noblewoman)
To Catch the Flame - Kimberly Cates 332

de Canti e Calda, Ashiana (Royalty; Imposter)
Silver and Sapphires - Shelly Thacker 1929

de Castillo, Rigo (Military Personnel; Revolutionary)
Desperado - Rebecca Brandewyne 200

de Champeney, Reina (Noblewoman)
Defy Not the Heart - Johanna Lindsey 1200

de Chaville, Warrick (Nobleman; Knight)
Prisoner of My Desire - Johanna Lindsey 1207

de Claire, Ariel (Noblewoman)
In the Shadow of Midnight - Marsha Canham 306

de Clairmont, Hugh (Nobleman)
A Vow to Keep - Elizabeth Bonner 183

de Clare, Charlotte "Cheryl" (Noblewoman)
Beneath a Pale Moon - Victoria Morrow 1422

de Clare, Lucien (Nobleman; Rake)
Autumn Rain - Anita Mills 1389

de Clement, Juliette (Student; Gentlewoman)
Storm Winds - Iris Johansen 993

de Clerc, Ariana (Artisan)
Knight's Lady - Suzanne Barclay 83

De Dreux, Mercedes (Imposter; Thief)
Santana Rose - Olga Bicos 141

de Fontaine, Amberlie (Widow(er); Noblewoman)
Knight's Caress - Lynette Vinet 1983

De Forrest, Brandon (Nobleman; Shipowner)
Passion's Legacy - Jennifer West 2004

de Forte, Pierce (Pirate; Nobleman)
Bride of the Wind - Shannon Drake 563

de Fortenberry, Dienwald (Nobleman)
Earth Song - Catherine Coulter 403

de Fortesque, Daria (Noblewoman; Heiress)
Secret Song - Catherine Coulter 408

De Gautier, Lucien (Captive; Nobleman)
Pagan Bride - Tamara Leigh 1183

de Gervais, Guy (Nobleman)
Brazen Whispers - Jane Feather 629

de Gourney, Lucien "The Dragon" (Nobleman)
Through a Dark Mist - Marsha Canham 307

de Grae, Angela "Angel" (Noblewoman)
Brazen - Susan Johnson 998

De Groot, Wim Pieter (Immigrant; Businessman)
Garden of Dreams - Laura Simon 1794

de Jobourg, Constance (Noblewoman)
The Amethyst Crown - Katherine Deauville 492

De Jobourg, Fulk (Nobleman)
Blood Red Roses - Katherine Deauville 493

De La Casas, Rodrigo "Rigo" (Mercenary)
Return to Paradise - Shirl Henke 866

de la Eresman, Vincent (Nobleman)
Awaken My Fire - Jennifer Horsman 926

De La Rocques, Jeanne Marie (Captive; Orphan)
Capture - Emily French 665

de la Rosa, Elena (Gentlewoman)
Eagle Knight - Suzanne Ellison 608

de la Sol, Damian (Landowner)
Treasure of the Sun - Christina Dodd 541

de Lacey, Adrian (Nobleman; Warrior)
Uncommon Vows - Mary Jo Putney 1564

de Lacey, Oliver (Nobleman)
Vows Made in Wine - Susan Wiggs 2028

de Lacey, Stephen (Nobleman)
Circle in the Water - Susan Wiggs 2023

de Lacy, Morgan (Nobleman; Highwayman)
Devil's Lady - Patricia Rice 1614

De Langley, Robert (Nobleman)
Bride of the Lion - Elizabeth Stuart 1894

De Leroy, Michelle (Twin; Fiance(e))
Wild Magnolia - Betty Brooks 224

de Lontaine, Adelaine (Twin; Noblewoman)
Angel of Fire - Tanya Anne Crosby 431

de Lontaine, Chrestien (Twin; Noblewoman)
Angel of Fire - Tanya Anne Crosby 431

de Lorgny, Ghislaine "Gilly" (Orphan; Cook)
A Rose at Midnight - Anne Stuart 1889

de Lyon, Rey (Knight)
Lyon's Prize - Virginia Lynn 1242

de Machado, Roberto (Wealthy)
If the Truth Be Told - Tracy Sinclair 1813

de Marche, Guy (Knight; Nobleman)
My Cherished Enemy - Samantha James 973

de Marisco, Jasmine "Yasaman" (Royalty)
Wild Jasmine - Bertrice Small 1827

de Medici, Catherine (Royalty; Historical Figure)
Courtesan - Diane Haeger 775

de Moncelet, Madeleine (Noblewoman; Orphan)
Captive to His Kiss - Paige Brantley 207

de Mont St. Michel, Rolphe (Knight; Kidnapper)
Splendor - Charlene Cross 440

de Montefiori, Alexandro (Nobleman)
Across Time - Nina Beaumont 106

de Montfort, David (Nobleman; Diplomat)
Into the Storm - Maura Seger 1760

de Montfort, Simon (Knight; Historical Figure)
The Dragon and the Jewel - Virginia Henley 869

de Montmorency, Alexandra (Noblewoman; Twin)
Lady Alex's Gamble - Evelyn Richardson 1633

de Montrain, Katherine (Noblewoman; Outlaw)
Damsel in Distress - Shannon Drake 564

de Morrissey, David (Vampire; Writer)
Confession - Lori Herter 878

de Morrissey, David (Writer; Vampire)
Eternity - Lori Herter 879

de Morrissey, David (Vampire; Writer)
Obsession - Lori Herter 880
Possession - Lori Herter 881

de Mortain, Catherine (Noblewoman; Captive)
Splendor - Charlene Cross 440

de Navarro, Durango (Mine Owner; Gambler)
Rainbow's End - Rebecca Brandewyne 203

De Poitiers, Diane (Historical Figure; Noblewoman)
Courtesan - Diane Haeger 775

de Pontesse, Hugues (Knight; Diplomat)
The Sorceress - Claire Delacroix 495

de Quincey, Sophie (Noblewoman)
Shadow Dance - Anne Stuart 1890

de Rivers, Christian (Nobleman; Spy)
Lady Gallant - Suzanne Robinson 1682

De Rojas, Estrellita (Heiress; Noblewoman)
Eagles of Destiny - Jory Sherman 1782

de St. Benoit, Kaatje (Widow(er))
Surrender in Scarlet - Patricia Camden 278

de St. Brieuc, Borgia (Knight)
The Lion's Angel - Libby Sydes 1909

de Saint Vallier, Nardi (Artist; Nobleman)
Bliss - Judy Cuevas 444

de Savin, Sebastien (Doctor)
Miracle - Deborah Smith 1840

de Severies, Dominique "Sancha" (Noblewoman)
Heart's Awakening - Paige Brantley 208

de Suela, Cade (Indian; Foreman)
Texas Lily - Patricia Rice 1622

de Tourneay, Roland (Adventurer; Knight)
Secret Song - Catherine Coulter 408

De Varennes, Gaston (Knight; Mercenary)
Forever His - Shelly Thacker 1927

de Vere, Katherine (Noblewoman; Courtier)
Gypsy Baron - Mary Daheim 451

de Vere, Meriel (Noblewoman; Amnesiac)
Uncommon Vows - Mary Jo Putney 1564

de Violette, Charmaine (Noblewoman)
Stranger in My Arms - Louisa Rawlings 1598

de Vire, Elise (Widow(er); Spy)
Beloved Deceiver - Laurie Grant 744

de Warenne, Guy (Knight)
Captive Rose - Miriam Minger 1397

de Warenne, Rolfe "the Relentless" (Knight)
The Conqueror - Brenda Joyce 1023

Dillon, Adam (Rake; Imposter)
Velvet Is the Night - Elizabeth Thornton 1945

Dillon, Alex (Cowboy)
For the Thrill - Janis Reams Hudson 949

Dimm, Jeremiah (Investigator)
A Suspicious Affair - Barbara Metzger 1356

Dixon, Jo Ellen (Young Woman)
Summer of the Soldiers - Sandra Chastain 345

Dixon, Owen (Businessman)
Mad Hatter - Georgia Helm 848

d'Lucy, Blaec (Nobleman; Knight)
Once upon a Kiss - Tanya Anne Crosby 433

Dobias, Corey (Heiress)
Her Father's Daughter - Terri Herrington 876

Dobson, Julia Turner (Widow(er))
The Rainbow Promise - Lisa Gregory 765

Dodge, Danny (Actor)
Going Hollywood - Marion Schultz 1736

Doherty, Shannon (Maintenance Worker)
A Liberated Man - Diana Whitney 2016

Dolan, Holt (Rancher; Lawman)
Wild Colorado Passion - Judith Steel 1872

Dolan, Mike (Military Personnel)
Ribbon in the Sky - Dorothy Garlock 689

Domenici, Carlo (Dancer)
Pirouette - Madeline Hale 782

Dominic (Nobleman; Rake)
The Rake's Redemption - Leslie Lynn 1240

Dominic le Sabra (Knight)
Untamed - Elizabeth Lowell 1235

Donaldson, Jess (Designer)
Unwilling Woman - Sue Peters 1520

Donay, Carl (FBI Agent)
Chance Encounter - Molly Rice 1612

Donelli, Joe (Police Officer; Farmer)
Body and Soul - Sherryl Woods 2065
Hide and Seek - Sherryl Woods 2066

Donelli, Joe (Police Officer; Detective)
Stolen Moments - Sherryl Woods 2069

Donelly, Joseph (Immigrant)
Far and Away - Sonja Massie 1294

Donlin, Chase (Trapper)
Mountain Rose - Norah Hess 886

Donnelly, Amelia (Gentlewoman; Orphan)
Secret in the Shadows - Marina Malcolm 1265

Donnelly, Rob (Restauranteur)
Valentine Hearts and Flowers - Muriel Jensen 986

Donner, Gabriel (Biker; Outlaw)
Annie and the Outlaw - Sharon Sala 1713

Donovan, Andrew (Sea Captain)
Allegheny Captive - Caroline Bourne 189

Donovan, Callie (Military Personnel)
Point of Departure - Lindsay McKenna 1319

Donovan, Clee (Photojournalist)
Remember - Barbara Taylor Bradford 193

Donovan, Cole (Murderer)
Allegheny Ecstasy - Caroline Bourne 190

Donovan, Conner (Plantation Owner; Smuggler)
Wild Tory Rose - Linda Covington 413

Donovan, Jade (Singer)
Irresistible - Catherine Hart 820

Donovan, Michael (Police Officer)
A Loving Spirit - Annette Broadrick 220

Donovan, Reid (Businessman; Handicapped)
Lady in Black - Christina Dodd 537

Donovan, Thomas Joseph (Diplomat)
Masquerade in Moonlight - Kasey Michaels 1368

Doran, Julianna (Time Traveller)
Sweet Forever - Becky Lee Weyrich 2010

Dorian (Royalty)
Across a Wine-Dark Sea - Jessica Bryan 239

Dorn, Zachary (Advertising)
Changes of Heart - Elizabeth Bennett 122

Dorne, Rachel (Gentlewoman; Heiress)
An Uncommon Miss - Melissa Lynn Jones 1016

Dorring, Sophy (Spinster; Gentlewoman)
Seduction - Amanda Quick 1575

Doucet, Anne-Marie (Spy)
The Conquest - Lucy Elliot 602

Doucet, Lucky (Guide)
Lucky's Lady - Tami Hoag 899

Doucette, Jacqueline (Noblewoman)
Surrender to a Stranger - Karyn Monk 1402

Douchand, Catherine (Saloon Hostess)
A Love So Wild - Evelyn Rogers 1688

Douglas, Adam (Nobleman; Laird)
Border Bride - Amanda Scott 1744

Douglas, Amanda (Captive; Southern Belle)
The Prisoner - Cheryl Reavis 1604

Douglas, Arabella (Gentlewoman)
Sapphire Magic - Nina Beaumont 108

Douglas, Jade (Orphan)
Jade - Jill Marie Landis 1144

Downey, Leah (Artist)
The Color of Love - Sandra Kitt 1085

Downing, Jennifer (Young Woman)
Family Reunion - Jill Metcalf 1348

Downing, Maggie (Young Woman; Handicapped)
Spring Blossom - Jill Metcalf 1349

Downing, Mariah (Widow(er))
No Sweeter Paradise - Penelope Neri 1440

Downing, Sam (Outlaw)
Sweet Fury - Catherine Hart 821

Drago, Lucien (Werewolf; Composer)
The Werewolf's Kiss - Cheri Scotch 1740

Drago, Matt (Indian)
Lacey's Way - Madeline Baker 44

Drago, Sylvie (Werewolf)
The Werewolf's Sin - Cheri Scotch 1741

Drake, Andrew (Farmer)
Sungold - Jillian Dagg 450

Drake, Barrett (Imposter; Spy)
Promise Me Today - Lori Copeland 394

Drake, Charlotte (Banker; Noblewoman)
Desert Fire - Evelyn Rogers 1686

Drake, Jonathan (Doctor)
A Delicate Matter - Rebecca Forster 662

Drake, Juliet (Actress; Singer)
Heirloom - Candace Camp 290

Drake, Nicholas (Saloon Keeper/Owner)
The Naked Huntress - Shirley Parenteau 1496

Drake, Reed (Sports Figure; Businessman)
The Heart's Journey - Nancy Sheehan 1781

Drake, Sheridan (Sea Captain; Hero)
Seize the Fire-- Laura Kinsale 1080

Draken, Jordan (Nobleman)
The Beloved Scoundrel - Iris Johansen 989

Drayton, Cassandra (Gentlewoman; Bride)
Miss Drayton's Downfall - Patricia Oliver 1460

Drayton, John (Spy; Imposter)
Madcap Johnny - Jeanne Carmichael 318

Drew, Roxanna (Widow(er))
Mrs. Drew Plays Her Hand - Carla Kelly 1056

Driscoll, Clarissa (Teacher)
The Village Spinster - Laura Matthews 1295

Driscoll, Elizabeth (Young Woman)
Delacey's Angel - Monique Ellis 606

Driscoll, Shane (Nobleman)
Deception - Ruth Langan 1153

d'Rouchert, Cianda (Thief)
Stolen Fire - Danette Chartier 335

Drumayne, Gabriel (Teacher; Time Traveller)
Stolen Dreams - Marilyn Campbell 303

Drummond, Angela (Nurse)
The Scarlet Thread - Evelyn Anthony 26

Drummond, Daniel (Gentleman; Widow(er))
Reckless Angel - Jane Feather 631

Drummond, Julia (Socialite)
The Matchmaker - Kay Hooper 923

Drummond, Lucy (Teacher)
Scoundrel - Pamela Litton 1216

Drummond, Margaret (Royalty)
Ravished Bride - Sheila O'Hallion 1459

Drummond, Miranda (Actress)
Acts of Love - Deana James 967
Acts of Passion - Deana James 968

Drummond, Nick (Military Personnel)
Surrender to the Fury - Cara Miles 1375

Drury, Joanna (Orphan; Immigrant)
The Dreaming - Barbara Wood 2060

Drussard, Justine (Actress; Prostitute)
Fallen Angel - Deborah Camp 294

Drusus, Cailin (Captive; Fugitive)
To Love Again - Bertrice Small 1826

Dryden, Claire (Fugitive; Parent)
Atlanta - Sara Orwig 1462

Dryden, John (Businessman; Privateer)
Poetic Justice - Alicia Rasley 1596

Drysdale, Zoe (Businesswoman)
Yesterday's Dream - Alice Sharpe 1775

du Pres, Genevieve (Southern Belle)
Desire's Slave - Linda Hilton 893

Du Prey, Ransom (Privateer)
Heart's Masquerade - Deborah Simmons 1789

du Villier, Alexandre (Plantation Owner)
Creole Fires - Kat Martin 1274

Dubay, Gabrielle (Debutante; Captive)
Midnight Rogue - Elaine Barbieri 70

Duckworth, Drucilla (Teacher; Heiress—Lost)
River's Dream - Virginia Lynn 1243

Dudley, Marina (Noblewoman)
Highland Flame - Catherine Linden 1190

Duffy, Thomas (Doctor)
Out of This World Marriage - Maggie Shayne 1779

Dugan, Bridget (Fugitive)
Mountain Dawn - Kathleen Kane 1040

Dugan, Sara (Secretary; Apprentice)
Mad Hatter - Georgia Helm 848

Duke, Henry (Gentleman)
Country Dance - Margaret Westhaven 2005

Duke of Farrant (Nobleman)
The Desirable Duchess - Marion Chesney 347

Duke of Hartford (Nobleman; Single Parent)
Lady Leprechaun - Melinda McRae 1336

Duke of Hazelmere (Nobleman)
Gretna Bride - Eva Rutland 1702

DuMont, Dove (Nobleman)
The Golden Dove - JoAnn Wendt 2001

Dumont, Gage (Nobleman; Warrior)
Midnight Warrior - Iris Johansen 991

Dunay, Anna (Immigrant)
Reach for the Dream - Sandra Bregman 211

Dunbar, Celeste (Dentist)
Hearts Afire - Monique Gilmore 727

Dunbarton, Adam (Nobleman; Knight)
A Love So Fierce - Joanna McGauran 1309

Duncan, Terry (Doctor)
Wolf and the Angel - Kathleen Creighton 419

Dundas, Caroline (Noblewoman; Debutante)
A Deceitful Heart - Karla Hocker 901

Dunmore, Erin (Mail Order Bride)
Gifts of Love - Theresa Michaels 1373

Dunn, Andrew (Businessman)
Noelle - Diana Palmer 1491

Dunn, Jared (Lawyer; Gunfighter)
Noelle - Diana Palmer 1491

Dunraven, Adam (Explorer)
The Serpent Beguiled - Betina Lindsey 1191

Dunraven, Cat (Horse Trainer)
Dunraven's Folly - Dawn Lindsey 1198

Dunstan, Pleasance (Servant)
Wild Conquest - Hannah Howell 941

Dunston, Brenna (Noblewoman)
Lyon's Prize - Virginia Lynn 1242

Dupre, Maria-Theresa (Southern Belle; Plantation Owner)
To Love a Pirate - Virginia Nielsen 1443

Duran, Amanda (Orphan)
Temptation's Trail - Dana Ransom 1592

Duran, Jared (Young Man)
The Golden Mountain - Annalise Sun 1897

Duran, King (Young Man)
The Golden Mountain - Annalise Sun 1897

Durand, Fontaine (Businessman)
Favors of the Rich - Sara Orwig 1464

Durango, Charlie (Bounty Hunter)
Taming Kate - Eugenia Riley 1638

Durango, Dallas (Runaway; Imposter)
Nevada Nights - Georgina Gentry 713

Durango, Nick (Cowboy; Bodyguard)
Cherish the Night - Penelope Neri 1437

Durant, Aurora (Military Personnel; Time Traveller)
Somewhere in Time - Merline Lovelace 1228

Durant, Keely (Journalist)
Bad for Each Other - Billie Green 754

Durant, Mitch (Lawyer)
Kiss in the Dark - Meryl Sawyer 1730

Duval, Giddeon (Sea Captain)
Texas Gamble - Vivian Vaughn 1975

Duval, Gillie (Guttersnipe)
Stolen Dreams - Catherine Lyndell 1238

Dvorak, Harriet (Housewife)
Confession - Lori Herter 878

Dvorak, Stefan (Nobleman; Gypsy)
Gypsy Baron - Mary Daheim 451

Dylan, Josh (Financier; Businessman)
The Gilded Cage - Edith Layton 1169

Dysart, Hugo (Nobleman)
The Only Hope - Jan Constant 389

E

Eadyth of Hawk's Lair (Noblewoman; Beekeeper)
The Tarnished Lady - Sandra Hill 892

Eagle, Jesse (Singer)
Diamond - Sharon Sala 1714

Eagleton, Sibyl (Debutante)
A Scandalous Suggestion - Emily Hendrickson 857

Earl of Coltrane (Nobleman; Guardian)
A Spirited Affair - Lynn Kerstan 1060

Earl of Haukedon (Nobleman)
The Haunted Miss Hampshire - Kasey Michaels 1364

Earl of Wyndham (Nobleman)
A Touch of Forever - Janice Bennett 126

Eastman, Jack (Businessman)
Time After Time - Antoinette Stockenberg 1883

Easton, Judith (Widow(er); Gentlewoman)
Christmas Beau - Mary Balogh 55

Easton, Portia "Tia" (Noblewoman)
Devil's Bargain - Marlene Suson 1898

Eberhart, Ena (Dancer; Cook)
After All - Jill Marie Landis 1142

Edana, Bronwyn (Gentlewoman)
Priceless - Christina Dodd 540

Eddington, Joshua (Businessman; Lobbyist)
Iron and Lace - Nadine Miller 1388

Eden, Bonnie (Runaway; Servant)
A Fire in the Heart - Katherine Sutcliffe 1902

Edgemont, Dominic (Nobleman; Gypsy)
Gypsy Lord - Kat Martin 1276

Edwards, Felicia (Frontierswoman)
Sweet Savage Splendor - Lauren Wilde 2030

Edwards, Kristen (Store Owner)
Love's Quiet Corner - Laura Parrish 1511

Edwards, Meghan (Photographer)
Ashton's Secret - Liana Laverentz 1163

Edwin (Nobleman)
Talk of the Town - Irene Saunders 1724

Egan, Molly (Servant; Seamstress)
By My Heart Betrayed - Olga Bicos 140

Eglinton, Philip (Spirit)
Ghostly Enchantment - Angie Ray 1600

Eirik of Ravenshire (Nobleman)
The Tarnished Lady - Sandra Hill 892

Eirriel (Captive; Psychic)
Golden Temptress - Patricia Roenbuck 1685

Eithne (Witch; Handicapped)
Swan Witch - Betina Lindsey 1194

Eleanor (Royalty; Historical Figure)
The Dragon and the Jewel - Virginia Henley 869

Eleanor of Aquitane (Royalty; Historical Figure)
Beloved Enemy - Ellen Jones 1012

Elen of Teifi (Noblewoman)
Where Love Dwells - Elizabeth Stuart 1895

Elienor of Baume-les-Nonnes (Captive; Noblewoman)
Viking's Prize - Tanya Anne Crosby 435

Elijah (Lighthouse Keeper)
Savage Tides - Mary Mayer Holmes 917

Elin (Young Woman)
Devoted - Alice Borchardt 184

Eliot, Susan (Lawyer; Heiress)
Puzzle Mansion - Colleen Edwards 596

Elizabeth (Loyalist)
Traitor's Embrace - Christine Dorsey 553

Elizabeth (Noblewoman; Spinster)
The Duke's Daughter - Melinda McRae 1334

Elizabeth of Riveaux (Noblewoman; Widow(er))
The Fire and the Fury - Anita Mills 1393

Ellicott, Gillian (Noblewoman)
Fool of Hearts - Terri Lynn Wilhelm 2032

Elliot, Edwin (Nobleman)
Deck the Halls - Marian Devon 524

Elliot, Michael (Military Personnel; Nobleman)
Betrayed - Arnette Lamb 1133

Elliott, Jace (Guide)
Whispered Kisses - Janelle Taylor 1919

Elliott, Liam (Military Personnel)
Morning's Gate - Ann Victoria Roberts 1658

Elliott, Samantha (Young Woman)
Sweet Liar - Jude Deveraux 518

Elliott, Steven (Sailor)
Morning's Gate - Ann Victoria Roberts 1658

Ellison, Susan (Nurse)
This Time Forever - Kathleen Eagle 583

Elsbach, Stefan (Diplomat)
The Princess Royal - Virginia Coffman 374

Elyssa of Freyne (Widow(er); Noblewoman)
Autumn's Flame - Denise Domning 546

Emerson, Amanda (Writer; Rancher)
Wild Is the Night - Colleen Quinn 1580

Emerson, Grant (Gambler)
Riverboat Seduction - Caroline Bourne 192

Emerson, Isobel (Heiress; Socialite)
Love's Perfect Dream - Caroline Bourne 191

Emerson, Luke (Animal Lover)
Midnight Ecstasy - Rita Balkey 51

Emerson, Radcliffe (Archaeologist)
The Snake, the Crocodile, and the Dog - Elizabeth
   Peters 1519

Endicott, Karma (Accountant; Parent)
Merry Christmas, Mommy - Muriel Jensen 985

English, Sam (Detective; Police Officer)
Nowhere to Run - Pat Warren 1995

Entwhistle, Marjorie (Spinster; Postal Worker)
The Betrothal - Arnette Lamb 1134

Eric (Knight; Adoptee)
The Vow - Mary Spencer 1861

Eric of Dubhlain (Royalty; Warrior)
The Viking's Woman - Heather Graham 742

Erickson, Rand (Military Personnel)
Sioux Slave - Georgina Gentry 716

Erik (Warrior)
The Last Viking Queen - Janelle Taylor 1917

Erika of Gronwood (Noblewoman)
Surrender My Love - Johanna Lindsey 1209

Esme (Telepath)
Daughter of Destiny - Jackie Casto 327

Esther (Student)
Daniel and Esther - Patrick Raymond 1603

Etoile, Leda (Seamstress)
The Shadow and the Star - Laura Kinsale 1081

Evans, Cherokee (Miner)
Quicksilver Passion - Georgina Gentry 714

Evans, March (Abuse Victim; Housekeeper)
Desert Angel - Pamela K. Forrest 660

Everett, Julia Ames (Singer; Gentlewoman)
Golden Prospect - Shirley Parenteau 1495

Everly, Sierra (Vintner)
Red Velvet - Barbara Boswell 185

F

Fairburn (Heiress; Fiance(e))
Beloved Avenger - Joan Van Nuys 1970

Fairchild, Alana (Singer)
Midnight Rain - Elizabeth Turner 1964

Fairchild, Cara (Orphan; Gentlewoman)
Destiny's Will - Elizabeth Ann Michaels 1360

Fairchild, Katherine (Religious)
Heaven and Earth - Kathleen Eagle 581

Fairchild, Lorna (Gentlewoman)
Tiger Dance - Jillian Hunter 954

Fairdane, Rhys (Trader)
All's Fair - Anne Avery 37

Faire, Lucinda (Heiress)
An Angel for the Earl - Barbara Metzger 1351

Fairfax, Ana (Widow(er))
Homeplace - Dorothy Garlock 686

Fairfax, Penelope (Landowner; Psychic)
Lord of Enchantment - Suzanne Robinson 1683

Fairfax, Steven (Gunfighter)
Emma and the Outlaw - Linda Lael Miller 1379

Fairfield, Alexa (Plantation Owner; Heiress)
Island Star - Kit Gardner 684

Fairfield, Tia (Runaway; Thief)
Brave Land, Brave Love - Connie Mason 1288

Fairhaven, Anne (Noblewoman; Widow(er))
The Painted Veil - Susan Carroll 324

Fairmont, Meg (Gypsy)
Sweet Seduction - Patricia Pellicane 1515

Falcon (Kidnapper)
Broken Promise - Theresa Scott 1755

Falconi, Stephen (Accountant)
The Scarlet Thread - Evelyn Anthony 26

Fallon, Jacob (Military Personnel; Lawman)
Mountain Dawn - Kathleen Kane 1040

Fallon, Susannah (Widow(er); Rancher)
Renegade - Patricia Potter 1544

Falon, Damien (Nobleman)
Devil's Prize - Kat Martin 1275

Faraday, Jake (Lawman)
Heart Strings - Lydia Browne 237

Faring, James (Nobleman; Rake)
Angel's Devil - Suzanne Enoch 613

Faringdon, Emily (Spinster)
Scandal - Amanda Quick 1574

Farleigh, Leonore (Gentlewoman)
The Vampire Viscount - Karen Harbaugh 803

Farley, J. Monroe (Scholar)
Marrying Stone - Pamela Morsi 1428

Farnsworth, Grace (Governess; Imposter)
Madcap Miss - Joan Smith 1845

Farraday (Imposter)
The Reluctant Suitor - Sarah Eagle 587

Farraday, Amanda (Amnesiac)
Shattered Illusions - Linda Renee De Jong 487

Farraday, Brent (Doctor)
Shattered Illusions - Linda Renee De Jong 487

Farrall, Reba (Mine Owner)
Lover in the Rough - Elizabeth Lowell 1230

Farrell, Christine (Spouse)
The Farrell Marriage - Dee Holmes 916

Farrell, Matthew (Businessman; Worker)
Paradise - Judith McNaught 1332

Farrell, Rafe (Imposter; Detective)
Emerald Angel - Susan Sackett 1709

Farrell, Reid (Spy)
The Farrell Marriage - Dee Holmes 916

Farrell, Stephen (Gentleman)
Lady Maryann's Dilemma - Karla Hocker 903

Farrell, Travis (Military Personnel)
Dragonfire - Patricia Potter 1538

Farrell, Zeb (Consultant)
Swinging on a Star - Pamela Bauer 101

Farrington, Myles (Nobleman)
Crown of Dreams - Kimberly Cates 328

Farroux, Julie (Gentlewoman)
Terms of Surrender - Mollie Ashton 33

Farrow, Will (Doctor)
Surrender the Night - Colleen Shannon 1770

Farthingham, Frederica "Freddie" (Noblewoman)
Lady's Choice - Judith Nelson 1434

Faulconer, Susannah (Businesswoman; Computer
   Expert)
Hot Shot - Susan Elizabeth Phillips 1528

Faulkner, Caroline (Student; Divorced Person)
The Law of Love - Martha Schroeder 1734

Faulkner, Garrett (Sea Captain; Privateer)
Fortune's Bride - Judith E. French 666

Faulkner, Sarah (Writer; Spinster)
Fire on the Wind - Barbara Dawson Smith 1830

Faulkner, William Devereaux (Nobleman;
   Diplomat)
Forevermore - Maura Seger 1758

Faust, Elaine (Landowner; Equestrian)
The Mistress of Foxgrove - Lee Magner 1263

Fell, Tabitha (Governess)
Heart of the Falcon - Diane Wicker Davis 472

Fenemore, Rose (Writer; Scholar)
The Stormy Petrel - Mary Stewart 1880

Ferguson, Catriona (Bride)
Lavender Flame - Karen Stratford 1886

Fergusson, Chelsea (Noblewoman; Horse Trainer)
Sinful - Susan Johnson 1003

Fersten, Cary (Producer)
Hot Streak - Jill Barkin 84

Ffolkes, Alissa (Gentlewoman; Animal Trainer)
The Gallant Lord Ives - Emily Hendrickson 852

Fielding, Anthony (Rake; Landowner)
Liberty Rose - Stef Ann Holm 913

Fielding, Cameo (Frontierswoman)
More than Just a Night - Connie Rinehold 1642

Fielding, David Michael (Spy)
Island of Dreams - Patricia Potter 1539

Fielding, Erin (Student)
The Christmas Wish - Rexanne Becnel 110

Fielding, Mary (Noblewoman)
Far Horizons - Katherine Sinclair 1807

Fielding, Roderick (Nobleman; Military Personnel)
Sunshine and Shadow - Kathleen Harrington 816

Fielding, Samantha (Twin; Revolutionary)
The Scarlet Temptress - Sue Rich 1625

Fielding, Ventia (Noblewoman; Runaway)
Gretna Bride - Eva Rutland 1702

Fields, Dan (Lawman)
Love's Bounty - Alisa McBride 1299

Fierce Hawk, David (Lawyer; Lawman)
Lone Star Loving - Martha Hix 896

Fierro, Mando (Warrior)
Dance with the Devil - Pamela Litton 1215

Finney, Rick (Journalist)
Intimate Connections - Joanne Z. Adams 2

Fire Dancer (Indian; Royalty)
Dance with Fire - JoAnne Redd 1607

Firewalker (Indian)
Beloved Intruder - Joan Van Nuys 1971

Fiske, Melpomene "Pommy" (Heiress)
Best-Laid Plans - Vanessa Gray 752

Fitz (Animal)
A Loyal Companion - Barbara Metzger 1354

French, Danny (Musician; Activist)
Till the Stars Fall - Kathleen Gilles Seidel   1768

French, Krissa (Manager; Housewife)
Till the Stars Fall - Kathleen Gilles Seidel   1768

Fridrick, Janet (Aged Person)
I'll Be Seeing You - Kristine Rolofson   1696

Frobisher, Alisha (Plantation Owner; Activist)
Sweet Southern Caress - Wendy Garrett   696

Frome, Bentley (Nobleman; Imposter)
The Denville Diamond - Winifred Witton   2055

Frost, Kayne (Doctor)
The Bear Affair - Cynthia Powell   1546

Frost, Tara (Public Relations)
Guardian Angel - Patricia Wilson   2047

Frye, Christian (Relative)
A Woman Betrayed - Barbara Delinsky   503

Frye, Jeffrey (Spouse; Accountant)
A Woman Betrayed - Barbara Delinsky   503

Frye, Laura (Businesswoman; Spouse)
A Woman Betrayed - Barbara Delinsky   503

G

Gabriel, Christian (Saloon Keeper/Owner; Military Personnel)
Hot as Sin - Debra Dixon   532

Gabriel, Sylvia (Debutante; Sports Figure)
Miss Gabriel's Gambit - Rita Boucher   187

Galbraith, Catriona (Landowner)
Highland Rebel - Stephanie Bartlett   96

Gale, Nicholas (Vampire)
Prince of Dreams - Susan Krinard   1115

Gallager, Molly (Widow(er))
Wild Savage Heart - Pamela K. Forrest   661

Gallagher, Alina (Orphan; Accountant)
The Irish Rose - Jessica Wulf   2073

Gallagher, Chase (Lawman)
Temptation's Fire - Millie Criswell   429

Gallagher, Jack (Photographer)
Red - Erica Spindler   1862

Gallagher, Leandra (Single Parent)
The Stillman Curse - Peggy Morse   1424

Gallagher, Molly (Bride)
The Barefoot Bride - Joan Johnston   1004

Gallagher, Pack (Hero)
Midnight Blue - Dorothy Garlock   687

Gallagher, Rafe (Indian; Cowboy)
Forbidden Fires - Madeline Baker   43

Gallant, Travis Lord (Nobleman)
The Infamous Rake - Norma Lee Clark   361

Gallatin, Justis (Miner)
Beloved Woman - Deborah Smith   1838

Galloway, Rook (Fugitive)
Star-Crossed - Susan Krinard   1117

Gamble, Sam (Computer Expert; Businessman)
Hot Shot - Susan Elizabeth Phillips   1528

Gannon, Aaron (Hotel Owner; Immigrant)
Jenny's Dream - Victoria Morrow   1423

Garat, Max (Widow(er); Settler)
Tender Heart - Gwen Cleary   366

Gardner, Grant (Farmer)
Temptation - Catherine Hart   823

Gardner, Matt (Troubleshooter)
Beginnings - Laura Phillips   1522

Gareth (Nobleman; Knight)
Shadows and Lace - Teresa Medeiros   1342

Gareth of Wyckmore (Knight)
Desire - Amanda Quick   1568

Garner, Elizabeth (Thief; Businesswoman)
Desperado Passion - Patricia Pellicane   1514

Garnett, Margaret (Professor; Time Traveller)
Ashton's Bride - Judith O'Brien   1450

Garnier, Clay (Detective—Police)
Night's Immortal Touch - Cherlyn Jac   960

Garrett, Cam (Outlaw)
Hostage Heart - Lisa Hendrix   859

Garrett, Cody (Rescuer)
Bittersweet Promises - Trana Mae Simmons   1791

Garrett, Kelsey "Orchid Simpson" (Spinster)
Jesse's Renegade - Nancy Bush   260

Garrett, Lacey (Heiress; Rancher)
Western Winds - Theresa DiBenedetto   528

Garrett, Mark (Contractor; Single Parent)
All but Love - Ann Howard White   2013

Garrick, Alexa (Debutante)
Devil's Prize - Kat Martin   1275

Garrick, Sean (Widow(er); Businessman)
Autumn Leaves - Jill Metcalf   1347

Garrison, Alex (Teacher; Coach)
Touchdown for Love - Diane Gonzales Bertrand   130

Garrison, Doug (Businessman)
Hot Property - Elise Title   1949

Garrison, Sam (Mine Owner)
Montana Mistress - Thea Devine   521

Gase, Adam (Convict)
A Love So Wild - Evelyn Rogers   1688

Gaspard, Nicholas "Bear" (Indian)
Secrets of a Midnight Moon - Jane Bonander   181

Gaston de Thorne (Knight)
Rose Among Thorns - Catherine Archer   27

Gates, Phillip (Lawyer)
High Society - Diane Cory   399

Gatewood, James (Scholar; Nobleman)
Miss Grimsley's Oxford Career - Carla Kelly   1054

Gaverly, Golden (Orphan)
Tradewinds - Annee Cartier   326

Gavin (Spouse)
The Last Viking Queen - Janelle Taylor   1917

Gawain, Anthony (Television Personality)
Naughty Talk - Tiffany White   2014

Gellee de Vacheron, Isabella (Actress; Noblewoman)
Christmas Belle - Mary Balogh   56

Gerard, Samuel (Martial Arts Expert; Thief)
The Shadow and the Star - Laura Kinsale   1081

Gerard, Simone (Writer; Psychic)
Night Vision - Deborah Nicholas   1441

Gerrard, Matt (Journalist)
Angels in the Sand - Jan McDaniel   1306

Gervais, Leila (Doctor)
Captive Rose - Miriam Minger   1397

Gevaudan, Luke (Guide; Werewolf)
Prince of Wolves - Susan Krinard   1116

Ghant, Orrin (Businessman; Widow(er))
Eden Creek - Lisa Bingham   146

Ghost Dancer "Angelique" (Psychic; Religious)
Ghost Dancer - Fela Dawson Scott   1754

Gibson, Sam (Landowner)
Swept Away - Cay David   467

Gilbert, Darcy (Journalist; Abuse Victim)
At Risk - Jeanne Stephens   1875

Gilbert, Katherine (Fiance(e); Noblewoman)
The Lady and the Wolf - Julie Beard   105

Gilbraith, Sylvester (Nobleman; Heir)
Valentine - Jane Feather   632

Gilchrist, Luke (Businessman; Restauranteur)
Family Man - Jayne Ann Krentz   1107

Gilchrist, Roarke (Nobleman; Bastard Son)
Bold Breathless Nights - Penelope Neri   1436

Giles of Moray (Warrior; Nobleman)
The Fire and the Fury - Anita Mills   1393

Gillard, Hacon (Warrior; Knight)
Conqueror's Kiss - Hannah Howell   937

Glendower, Morgan (Doctor; Recluse)
Beneath a Harvest Moon - Catherine Wyatt   2074

Glenn, Morgan (Military Personnel)
The Firelands - Karen Harper   811

GlenRoss (Nobleman)
The Barbarous Scot - Dawn Lindsey   1197

Glentyre, Davina (Teacher)
Snare of Serpents - Victoria Holt   919

Goddard, Jack (Producer)
Lie and Say You Love Me - Robin St. Thomas   1867

Godfrey (Nobleman)
The Marriage Mart - Teresa DesJardien   510

Godfrey, Christina (Heiress)
A Heart in Peril - Emma Lange   1158

Godwin, Celine (Debutante; Fiance(e))
His Magic Touch - Stella Cameron   287

Godwinson, Fallon (Royalty)
Princess of Fire - Shannon Drake   567

Goforth, Griffin (Psychic)
Fire Lily - Deborah Camp   295

Gold, Odessa (Convict)
Odessa Gold - Linda Shaw   1776

Gold, Solange (Socialite)
Lies - Doris Parmett   1506

Goldie Mae (Young Woman)
Diamonds and Dreams - Rebecca Paisley   1480

Goldsborough, Elizabeth (Gentlewoman)
The Substitute Bridegroom - Charlotte Louise Dolan   545

Goodness (Angel)
A Season of Angels - Debbie Macomber   1254
Touched by Angels - Debbie Macomber   1256
The Trouble with Angels - Debbie Macomber   1257

Goodwin, Bliss (Castaway)
Miss Robinson Crusoe - Tracy Sinclair   1814

Gordon, Emily (Agent)
Maybe This Time - Kathleen Gilles Seidel 1766

Gordon, Lindsey (Noblewoman; Warrior)
Highland Heart - Ruth Langan 1155

Gordon, Theodora (Cartographer)
Cherish the Dream - Kathleen Harrington 815

Gorton, Emily (Doctor; Spinster)
Blazing Passion - Barbara Cummings 445

Gower, Alec (Musician; Nobleman)
Lady Barbara's Dilemma - Marjorie Farrell 623

Grabowski, Joseph (Police Officer)
Prescription for Death - Janet McGiffin 1310

Graham, Angelique (Noblewoman; Fiance(e))
Angel's Devil - Suzanne Enoch 613

Graham, Chase (Nobleman)
Wild Scottish Embrace - Rebecca Sinclair 1812

Graham, Elizabeth (Noblewoman; Captive)
Outlaw - Susan Johnson 1001

Graham, Elyse (Widow(er); Frontierswoman)
Passion's Gift - Jane Kidder 1064

Graham, Gilbert (Nobleman; Diplomat)
Marian's Christmas Wish - Carla Kelly 1052

Graham, Somerset (Nobleman)
The Duke's Daughter - Melinda McRae 1334

Graiston, Temric (Knight; Bastard Son)
Summer Storm - Denise Domning 547

Granger, Devlin "White Shadow" (Indian)
Wild Mountain Honey - Carol Finch 648

Granger, Victoria (Heiress; Activist)
Surrender the Dream - Debra Dier 531

Grania (Sorceress)
Heartspell - Blaine Anderson 15

Grant, C.J. (Detective—Private; Actress)
Partners in Time - Pamela Simpson 1802

Grant, Cameron (Loyalist)
Liberty's Lady - Caryn Cameron 280

Grant, Jason (Director; Heir)
The Cinderella Game - Jane Shore 1786

Grant, Jeff (Teacher; Writer)
Maybe This Time - Kathleen Gilles Seidel 1766

Grant, Maximilian (Sports Figure; Gambler)
Desert Fire - Evelyn Rogers 1686

Grant, Rachel (Teacher)
One Summer - Karen Robards 1653

Grant-Fortune, Christina (Banker; Heiress)
Fortune's Child - Pamela Simpson 1801

Gray, B.J. (Teacher)
Golden Swan - Judy Gill 725

Gray Cloud (Indian)
Thunder Mountain - Rachel Lee 1173

Gray Eyes (Indian; Shaman)
Comes the Rain - Beverly Bird 149

Graymist, Shaylah (Pilot; Military Personnel)
Lord of the Storm - Justine Davis 473

Grayson, Matt (Rancher)
Wish Me a Rainbow - Jessica Douglass 561

Grayson, Morgan (Rancher; Heir)
The Flaming - Pat Tracy 1955

Grayson, Nate (Political Figure)
Vivid - Beverly Jenkins 981

Grayson, Nellie (Spinster; Housekeeper)
Wishes - Jude Deveraux 520

Grayson, Sterling (Spy; Imposter)
Temptation's Tender Kiss - Colleen Faulkner 627

Grayson, Walker (Military Personnel)
Comanche Love Song - Cheryl Black 165

Grayum, Melody (Businesswoman; Wealthy)
Sweet Conquest - Marsha Bauer 100

Green, Jubal (Cowboy)
One Bright Morning - Alice Duncan 571

Greene, Joshua (Farmer)
Eternity - Jude Deveraux 512

Greenley, Camilla (Young Woman)
Shameless - Jennifer Blake 173

Greenwood, Lucas (Plantation Owner)
Cypress Moon - Myra Rowe 1699

Greetwell, Primula (Gentlewoman; Bride)
Fleeting Fancy - Rosemary Edghill 591

Gregg, Mary (Noblewoman)
The Notorious Rake - Mary Balogh 61

Gregory, Beaumont (Gambler)
No Man's Fortune - Kristie Knight 1092

Gregory, Bridey (Rancher)
Bridey's Mountain - Yvonne Adamson 3

Gregory, Heather (Counselor)
For Always - Bette Ford 656

Gregory, Morna (Singer)
Bridey's Mountain - Yvonne Adamson 3

Gregory, Tess "Amarylis" (Handicapped; Time Traveller)
Once in Every Life - Kristin Hannah 799

Grenville, Juliana (Widow(er))
The Rake's Redemption - Leslie Lynn 1240

Grenville, Shawnalese (Ward)
Through All Eternity - Brenna Braxton-Barshon 210

Gresham, Chloe (Heiress; Orphan)
Vixen - Jane Feather 636

Gresham, Wylie (Mine Owner; Businessman)
Rainbow's End - Rebecca Brandewyne 203

Grey, Arabella (Noblewoman)
The Spitfire - Bertrice Small 1825

Grey, Jacob (Lawman)
Silken Promises - Lisa Bingham 148

Grey, Jenna (Businesswoman)
The Invisible Groom - Barbara Bretton 212

Grey, Kassandra (Young Woman)
Dream Castle - Andrea Kane 1037

Grey, Lettie (Young Woman)
Silken Dreams - Lisa Bingham 147

Grey, Simon (Nobleman; Military Personnel)
Dunraven's Folly - Dawn Lindsey 1198

Grey, Townsend (Gentlewoman)
If This Be Magic - Ellen Tanner Marsh 1270

Griffin, Evan (Twin; Nobleman)
Mad Maria's Daughter - Patricia Rice 1616

Griffin, Gordon (Twin; Nobleman)
Mad Maria's Daughter - Patricia Rice 1616

Grimes, Ivy (Divorced Person)
Lovers and Friends - Claire Bocardo 176

Grimsley, Ellen (Feminist; Student)
Miss Grimsley's Oxford Career - Carla Kelly 1054

Grisham, Burke (Nobleman)
A Glimpse of Heaven - Barbara Dawson Smith 1831

Grissom, Buck (Lawman)
Moonlight and Mistletoe - Maggie Daniels 462

Groves, Trudi (Socialite)
High Society - Diane Cory 399

Guarneri, Margaret (Servant; Widow(er))
Lady in Black - Christina Dodd 537

Gunn, Christopher (Diplomat; Backwoodsman)
Silver Tears - Becky Lee Weyrich 2009

Gunther, Rose (Healer; Religious)
Highland Jewel - Lois Greiman 769

Guthrie, Susanna (Imposter; Plantation Owner)
Defiant Imposter - Miriam Minger 1398

Guy (Warrior; Landowner)
Castle of Dreams - Flora M. Speer 1853

H

Haardrad, Selig (Warrior; Settler)
Surrender My Love - Johanna Lindsey 1209

Hackett, Sam (Lawman)
Partners in Time - Pamela Simpson 1802

Hadley, Edward (Gentleman)
The Spanish Lady - Joan Smith 1846

Hadley, Laura (Captive)
Rebel's Captive - Amy Christopher 356

Hadley, Sarah (Widow(er); Rancher)
Sweet Texas Surrender - Victoria Thompson 1935

Haige, Gillian (Servant)
Only for Love - Elaine Barbieri 73

Hale, Abbie (Young Woman)
The Man Who Came for Christmas - Bethany Campbell 299

Hale, Marty (Businessman)
Everything - Muriel Jensen 984

Hall, Jakob (Businessman)
Home Fires - Susan Kay Law 1164

Hall, Susannah (Editor; Time Traveller)
A Wife in Time - Cathie Linz 1214

Hall, Tristan (Sea Captain)
Sweet Seduction - Patricia Pellicane 1515

Hallbrook, Colin (Nobleman)
Castles - Julie Garwood 700

Halliday, Caleb (Military Personnel)
Lily and the Major - Linda Lael Miller 1382

Halliday, Justin (Nobleman)
The Snow Angel - Mary Balogh 68

Halliday, Katie (Writer)
Wild Western Desire - Kathy Jones 1015

Halloran, Travis (Businessman)
Suspicion's Gate - Justine Davis 475

Halyard, Revan (Knight)
Highland Hearts - Sandra Dustin 578

Hamilton, Acadiana "Cade" (Plantation Owner; Southern Belle)
Bayou Dreams - Libby Sydes 1908

Hamilton, Braden (Nobleman; Privateer)
Wind Rose - Krista Janssen 977

Hamilton, Brand (Printer; Businessman)
Gold Is the Game - Rae Muir 1433

Hamilton, Elliot (Banker)
Camelot Jones - Mayo Lucas 1237

Hamilton, Kate (Actress)
Taboo - Elizabeth Gage 681

Hamilton, Kelly (Archaeologist; Psychic)
Hour of the Rose - Christina Skye 1820

Hamilton, Lainie (Health Care Professional)
Heart Song - Judi Lind 1189

Hamilton, Marc (Nobleman)
Devil's Bargain - Marlene Suson 1898

Hamilton, Patrick (Lawyer)
Secret Nights - Anita Mills 1395

Hamilton, Reid (Amnesiac)
Tender Lies - Kay McMahon 1328

Hamilton, Trevor (Nobleman; Sea Captain)
A Time for Roses - Elaine Coffman 373

Hampshire, Cassandra (Heiress)
The Haunted Miss Hampshire - Kasey
  Michaels 1364

Hampton, Alex (Detective)
Rebel Dreams - Patricia Rice 1620

Hampton, Alyson (Heiress; Psychic)
Moon Dreams - Patricia Rice 1617

Hampton, Anthony (Nobleman; Guardian)
Patience Is a Virtue - Judith Nelson 1435

Hampton, Judith Elizabeth (Young Woman;
  Midwife)
The Secret - Julie Garwood 707

Hampton, Melissa (Gentlewoman; Heiress)
Fortune Hunter - Deborah Simmons 1788

Hampton, Tristan (Military Personnel; Scout)
The Silver Link - Patricia Potter 1545

Handcock, Leah (Pioneer)
Deepwater - Pamela Jeckel 979

Hanford (Nobleman)
The Ill-Bred Bride - Rosemary Edghill 592

Hanlon, Megan (Actress)
The Past Is Another Country - Lois Battle 97

Hanover, Georgina (Gentlewoman; Fiance(e))
Paper Tiger - Patricia Rice 1619

Hansen, Hedy (Orphan)
The Snow Garden - Bethany Campbell 300

Hanson, Maggie (Resistance Fighter; Imposter)
Dangerous Charade - Madeline Harper 813

Haraldsson, Rorik (Warrior)
Lord of Hawkfell Island - Catherine Coulter 405

Harcourt, Emily (Runaway)
Midnight Enchantment - Jeanne E. Hansen 802

Harcourt, Kristiana (Noblewoman)
Deeper than Roses - Charlene Cross 437

Harden, Trace (Gambler)
The Seduction of Samantha Kincade - Maggie
  Osborne 1468

Hardin, Cy (Rancher; Businessman)
True Colors - Susan Kyle 1123

Harding, Cassandra "Cassie" (Young Woman)
Call Home the Heart - Rebecca George 718

Harding, Emma (Noblewoman)
The Blade and the Bath Miss - Gail Whitaker 2012

Harding, Felicia (Noblewoman; Debutante)
Felicia - Cathleen Clare 357

Harding, Patience (Loyalist; Spouse)
To Spite the Devil - Paula Jonas 1011

Hardy, Carolyn (Debutante)
Bath Charade - Amanda Scott 1742

Hardy, Mark (Rebel)
Seasons of the Heart - Marilyn Cunningham 449

Hargraves, Anne (Singer; Spy)
Dangerous Deceptions - Erin Yorke 2079

Hargreaves, Sara (Convict; Waiter/Waitress)
Flight to Yesterday - Velda Johnston 1010

Harken, Jens (Artisan; Servant)
November of the Heart - LaVyrle Spencer 1860

Harkner, Jake (Outlaw)
Outlaw Hearts - Rosanne Bittner 159

Harland, Emily (Noblewoman)
The Heart's Desire - Gayle Wilson 2045

Harlowe, Sunny (Bounty Hunter; Detective)
My Only Desire - Andrea Parnell 1508

Harmon, Cassie (Orphan; Debutante)
Flame in the Night - Jack McGowan 1311

Harmon, Robert (Orphan; Businessman)
Flame in the Night - Jack McGowan 1311

Harper, Caleb (Indian; Scout)
All My Heart Can Hold - Jessica Douglass 559

Harper, Libby (Divorced Person)
Operation Homefront - Marilyn Pappano 1494

Harper, Meg (Abuse Victim; Teenager)
The Way Home - Dallas Schulze 1739

Harper, Suzi (Critic; Vacationer)
Timely Matrimony - Kasey Michaels 1371

Harrell, David (Nobleman)
Light on the Mountain - Maura Seger 1762

Harrington, Jason "J.T." (Wealthy)
Jade - Jill Marie Landis 1144

Harris, Bob (Writer; Teacher)
The Promise of Summer - Lynn Bulock 251

Harris, Johnny (Convict)
One Summer - Karen Robards 1653

Harris, Rachel (Governess)
Promise Me Spring - Robin Lee Hatcher 831

Harrison, Bliss (Bounty Hunter)
Outlaw Seduction - Kathryn Hockett 905

Harrison, Catherine (Journalist)
Flirting with Danger - Carol Jerina 988

Harrison, Francesca "Francie" (Businesswoman)
Fortune Is a Woman - Elizabeth Adler 4

Harrison, Parker (Musician)
Serenade - Sandra Kitt 1086

Harrison, Virginia "Ginny" (Businesswoman)
Seasons - Constance O'Day-Flannery 1453

Harry (Nobleman)
The Somerville Farce - Michelle Kasey 1046

Hart, Justin (Nobleman; Rake)
Sabelle - Veronica Sattler 1722

Hart, Nicole (Writer; Waiter/Waitress)
Naughty Talk - Tiffany White 2014

Hart, Samuel (Recluse)
Small Treasures - Kathleen Kane 1041

Harte, Jessica (Scholar)
Virgin Fire - Elizabeth Chadwick 334

Harter, Christine (Student; Detective—Amateur)
Tug of Hearts - Julia Winfield 2050

Hartford, Miranda (Young Woman)
Love's Endless Flame - Betty Brooks 223

Hartford, Sybella (Gentlewoman)
Destiny's Dream - Joanna Jordan 1017

Hartman, Zoe (Actress)
First Loves - Jean Stone 1884

Hartwell, Maggie (Widow(er))
Winter's Flame - Maria Greene 756

Harvey, Kate (Nurse)
Legacy of the Rose - Kasey Michaels 1367

Hassan, Muley Abdul (Royalty)
The Eagle and the Dove - Jane Feather 630

Hastings, Adam (Military Personnel)
Follow the Heart - Anita Mills 1394

Hastings, Blake (Activist)
Caress - Rosanne Bittner 153

Hastings, Julia (Socialite)
Julia's Story - Catherine M. Rae 1584

Hastings, Maggie (Heiress)
Southern Nights - Marcia Martin 1280

Hastings, Sam (Architect; Political Figure)
Blessings of the Heart - Jane McBride Choate 352

Hatchard, Sam "Hatch" (Businessman)
Sweet Fortune - Jayne Ann Krentz 1112

Hathaway, Diana (Thief)
Cypress Moon - Myra Rowe 1699

Hathaway, Kate (Debutante)
The Heart Remembers - Barbara Hazard 842

Hatherill, Diana (Noblewoman)
The Willful Widow - Evelyn Richardson 1634

Hatter, Emmaline (Businesswoman)
The Enchantment - Kristin Hannah 796

Haukinge, Christian (Nobleman; Smuggler)
Kissed - Tanya Anne Crosby 432

Havering, Peregrine (Nobleman)
Meridon - Philippa Gregory 768

Haviland, Bronte (Administrator)
Once a Hero - Katherine Sutcliffe 1905

Haviland, Mary (Spinster; Noblewoman)
A Change of Heart - Candice Hern 874

Havyes, Nigel (Nobleman)
Moonlight Veil - Janis Laden 1128

Hawk (Indian; Warrior)
Comes the Rain - Beverly Bird 149

Hawk (Frontiersman; Indian)
Sweet Savage Splendor - Lauren Wilde 2030

Hawk, Ethan (Rancher; Prisoner)
Outlaw's Bride - Joan Johnston 1008

Hawk, Jackson (Lawyer; Indian)
Sleeping with the Enemy - Laurie Paige 1477

Hawke, John (Military Personnel; Rogue)
A Love for All Time - Sandra Davidson 470

Hawke, Matthew (Privateer)
Promise Me Forever - Cara Miles 1374

Kent, Adam (Nobleman)
The Secret Pearl - Mary Balogh   67

Kent, Alexander (Spy)
Traitor's Embrace - Christine Dorsey   553

Kent, Jamie (Photographer)
Whisper of Midnight - Patricia Simpson   1805

Kent, Sorrel (Young Woman)
The American Cousin - Dawn Lindsey   1196

Ker, Elsbeth (Laird)
The Abduction - Patricia Potter   1536

Kerns, Stephen (Tour Guide; Professor)
Roman Butterfly - Betty Dahlin   452

Kerr, Duncan (Nobleman; Outlaw)
The Border Lord - Arnette Lamb   1136

Kerr, Malcolm (Nobleman)
Border Bride - Arnette Lamb   1135

Kerrigan, Burke (Gunfighter)
Sweetwater Seduction - Joan Johnston   1009

Kerry, Sean (Kidnapper)
Wild Irish Heather - Ashland Price   1555

Kersaint, Lysette (Gentlewoman; Runaway)
Only in Your Arms - Lisa Kleypas   1088

Khalil (Ruler)
Sands of Time - Terri Valentine   1967

Khanauri, Mikahl (Royalty)
Silk and Shadows - Mary Jo Putney   1562

Kierney, Rianne (Musician)
Western Enchantress - Wendy Garrett   697

Kiley, Jake (Lawman)
Kiley's Storm - Suzanne Elizabeth   599

Killian, James Comanche (Foreman)
Lawless - Alexandra Thorne   1940

Killian, John (Outlaw)
When Lightning Strikes - Kristin Hannah   801

Killian, Noah (Military Personnel)
Angel of Fire - Jessica Douglass   560

Kilpatrick, Kip (Photojournalist)
The Heart Remembers - Lenore Carroll   319

Kilpatrick, Rourke (Lawyer)
Night Fever - Susan Kyle   1122

Kimball, Clare (Artist)
Divine Evil - Nora Roberts   1666

Kimberly, Carlinn (Nobleman; Guardian)
A Suspicious Affair - Barbara Metzger   1356

Kimbrough, Mark (Financier)
Blind Chance - Meryl Sawyer   1729

Kimimila (Indian)
Sioux Slave - Georgina Gentry   716

Kincade, Jennifer (Military Personnel; Nurse)
Of Love and Glory - Evelyn Kennedy   1057

Kincade, Samantha (Bounty Hunter; Imposter)
The Seduction of Samantha Kincade - Maggie Osborne   1468

Kincaid, Alec (Laird)
The Bride - Julie Garwood   699

Kincaid, Aurora (Captive)
Dakota Dawn - Dana Ransom   1589

Kincaid, Carlisle (Young Woman)
Midnight Fire - Linda Ladd   1126

Kincaid, Douglas (Businessman)
Legends - Deborah Smith   1839

Kincaid, Elly (Bride)
The Stolen Bride of Glengarra Castle - Anne Knoll   1095

Kincaid, Gray (Businessman)
Frostfire - Linda Ladd   1125

Kincaid, Jason (Twin; Revolutionary)
The Scarlet Temptress - Sue Rich   1625

Kincaid, Laura (Abuse Victim; Spinster)
Shelter From the Storm - Patricia Rice   1621

Kincaid, Luke (Rancher)
Sweet Hannah Rose - Lori Copeland   395

Kincaid, Matthew (Young Man)
The Emerald Tears of Foxfire Manor - Clara Wimberly   2048

Kincaid, Mitchell (Detective—Private; Stock Broker)
What the Lady Wants - Jennifer Crusie   442

Kincaid, Nathan (Convict; Nobleman)
No Sweeter Paradise - Penelope Neri   1440

Kincaid, Nick (Twin)
The Scarlet Temptress - Sue Rich   1625

Kincaid, Spence (Shipowner)
Surrender the Dream - Debra Dier   531

Kincaid, Steven (Rancher)
Scoundrel's Captive - JoAnn De Lazzari   488

Kincaid, Stone (Avenger)
Dragon Fire - Linda Ladd   1124

Kincaid, Travis (Lawman)
Sweet Fury - Catherine Hart   821

Kincannon, Lee (Hotel Owner; Military Personnel)
Riverbend - Mary McBride   1300

King, Alexander (Activist)
Scoundrel's Desire - JoAnn De Lazzari   489

King, Jason (Principal)
One Perfect Springtime - Constance Walker   1987

King, Nick (Businessman)
Maggy's Child - Karen Robards   1650

King, Savannah (Socialite)
Southern Secrets - Marcia Martin   1281

Kingman, Adrian (Businessman)
Dangerous Bequest - Lee Anderson   21

Kingsblood, Julianna (Noblewoman)
Moonshadow - Laura Parker   1504

Kingsblood, Maxwell (Nobleman)
For Love's Sake Only - Laura Parker   1502

Kingsland, Amber (Secretary; Single Parent)
A Song in the Wilderness - Lee Stafford   1868

Kingsley, Bart (Outlaw; Indian)
Gunman's Lady - Catherine Palmer   1485

Kingsley, Rosie (Teacher)
Gunman's Lady - Catherine Palmer   1485

Kingston, Andrea (Computer Expert; Troubleshooter)
Programmed for Danger - Karen G. McCullough   1305

Kingston, Claire (Producer)
The Right Direction - Candace Schuler   1735

Kingston, Fancy (Gentlewoman)
Heart of Fancy - Claudette Williams   2035

Kingston, Lyle (Manager)
Tattered Silk - Elaine Barbieri   75

Kinrade, Brianna (Noblewoman; Spy)
Unwilling Betrayer - Joan Van Nuys   1972

Kinross, Colin (Widow(er); Nobleman)
The Heiress Bride - Catherine Coulter   404

Kinsdale, Skye (Runaway)
A Pirate's Pleasure - Heather Graham   740

Kinsworth, Marcus (Nobleman)
An Uncommon Miss - Melissa Lynn Jones   1016

Kionee (Indian; Warrior)
Destiny Mine - Janelle Taylor   1913

Kiore (Sailor)
Sister of the Sun - Clare Coleman   376

Kirby, Athelstan (Military Personnel)
Winds of Eden - Justina Burgess   254

Kirk, Simon (Police Officer)
Terror by Design - Jane Edwards   598

Kirkcaldy, Frances Catherine (Young Woman)
The Secret - Julie Garwood   707

Kirkland, David (Miner)
In the Shadow of the Mountains - Rosanne Bittner   156

Kirkland, Dominica (Orphan)
Whisper My Name - Raine Cantrell   312

Kirkland, Irene (Indian)
In the Shadow of the Mountains - Rosanne Bittner   156

Kirkland, London (Grandparent)
Crossing Eden - Emma Gordon   735

Kirkpatrick, Isobel (Spouse)
The Heart and the Heather - Nancy Richards-Akers   1630

Kirkpatrick, Malcolm (Chieftain)
The Heart and the Heather - Nancy Richards-Akers   1630

Kitteridge, Ashton (Artist; Nobleman)
Sunswept - Leigh Bristol   218

Kitteridge, Ellen (Socialite)
Desperate Measures - Linda Cajio   273

Knight, Joseph (Filmmaker)
Taboo - Elizabeth Gage   681

Knight, Marty (Entertainer)
Knight and Day - Carole Buck   244

Knollis, Leander (Nobleman)
The Christmas Angel - Jo Beverley   132

Knowles, Marcus (Nobleman)
Lady Vengeance - Sarah Eagle   585

Knox, Jonathan (Sea Captain; Plantation Owner)
Captain's Captive - Christine Dorsey   549

Kolt (Psychic)
The Golden Conquest - Patricia Roenbuck   1684

Krikorian, Hannah (Widow(er))
Bleeding Hearts - Jane Haddam   774

Kuragin, Alexia (Royalty)
The Princess Royal - Virginia Coffman   374

Kutachna (Indian)
Sun Woman - Lindsay McKenna   1321

Kuzan-Lazaroff, Lisaveta (Royalty; Scholar)
Golden Paradise - Susan Johnson   1000

Kwan, Maylene (Architect)
Pearl Moon - Katherine Stone   1885

Kwani (Indian; Shaman)
Voice of the Eagle - Linda Lay Shuler   1787

Kyle, Alyssa (Handicapped; Captive)
Lord of Shadowhawk - Lindsay McKenna   1317

Kyle, Devlin (Military Personnel)
King of Swords - Lindsay McKenna   1316

L

La Marsh, Jordan (Artist; Widow(er))
The Crimson Roses of Fountain Court - Peggy
   Darty   465

La Mont, Travis (Journalist; Photographer)
Outlaw Seduction - Kathryn Hockett   905

Lacey, Alice (Noblewoman; Debutante)
The Desirable Duchess - Marion Chesney   347

Lacey, Arianne (Store Owner)
The Willow File - Lori Herter   882

Lacey, Sarah "Meridon" (Heiress—Lost)
Meridon - Philippa Gregory   768

Lachman, Alette (Artist; Landscaper)
Sweeter than Sin - Sara Orwig   1465

Lafitte, Jean (Pirate; Historical Figure)
Forever, for Love - Becky Lee Weyrich   2007

Laindon, Horatio Clement (Nobleman)
Had We Never Loved - Patricia Veryan   1979

Lamartine, Engelina (Gentlewoman)
The Loving - Sandra Canfield   305

Lamb, Anthony (Nobleman; Twin)
Seduced - Virginia Henley   873

Lamb, Antonia (Noblewoman; Twin)
Seduced - Virginia Henley   873

Lamb, Jillian (Debutante; Farmer)
A Spirited Affair - Lynn Kerstan   1060

Lambert, Arlene (Single Parent)
Bad Billy Culver - Judy Gill   724

Lambert, Charles (Nobleman; Art Dealer)
And Heaven Too - Julie Tetel   1923

Lambert, Mary Alexandra (Noblewoman; Captive)
Flames of Love - Colleen Faulkner   624

Lambert, Phillipa (Scholar; Gentlewoman)
The Viscount's Vixen - Joan Overfield   1473

Lamond, Beau (Horse Trainer)
The Mistress of Foxgrove - Lee Magner   1263

Lamont, Brett (Artisan)
Promise Me Anything - Meryl Sawyer   1732

Lampman, Peregrine (Gentleman)
Promise of Spring - Mary Balogh   62

Lancaster, Chase (Diplomat)
Midnight Fire - Linda Ladd   1126

Lancaster, Cort (Young Man)
Fire and Ice - DeLoras Scott   1750

Lancaster, Hayley (Businesswoman)
A Private Proposal - La Verne St. George   1863

Lancaster, James "Jamie" (Heir; Shipowner)
Defiant Heart - Nancy Moulton   1432

Lancaster, Viveca "Vivid" (Doctor)
Vivid - Beverly Jenkins   981

Lancer, Shane (Rancher)
Summer Rose - Bonnie K. Winn   2051

Landon, Jessica (Orphan)
Love's Sweet Bounty - Colleen Faulkner   625

Landry, Charles (Gentleman)
Woman Without a Past - Phyllis A. Whitney   2019

Landry, Jessica (Governess)
Comanche Flame - Madeline Baker   41

Landsford, Victoria (Bounty Hunter; Imposter)
Angel of Fire - Jessica Douglass   560

Lane, Hayden (Writer; Reincarnated Person)
Remembrance - Jude Deveraux   517

Lane, Jessica (Rancher)
Follow the Wind - Janelle Taylor   1914

Lane, Moriah (Convict; Abuse Victim)
Evergreen - Delia Parr   1510

Lang, David (Mine Owner)
Wishes on the Wind - Elaine Barbieri   77

Lang, Sunny (Heiress; Farmer)
Sunny - Linda Madl   1260

Lang, Trilby (Heiress)
Trilby - Diana Palmer   1492

Langdon, Alex (Journalist)
In Your Dreams - Lynn Bulock   250

Langdon, Elizabeth (Gentlewoman; Mine Owner)
Torchlight - Doreen Owens Malek   1266

Langdon, Joshua (Military Personnel; Spy)
Sapphire - Venita Helton   849

Lange, Angelina "Angel" (Artist)
A Woman Without Lies - Elizabeth Lowell   1236

Langford, Sam (Professor)
Moon Showers - Laura Phillips   1523

Langford, Violet (Gentlewoman; Imposter)
The Denville Diamond - Winifred Witton   2055

Langland, Christian (Nobleman; Handicapped)
Flowers From the Storm - Laura Kinsale   1077

Langolet, Emma (Heiress; Orphan)
To Love a Dark Lord - Anne Stuart   1891

Langston, Alan (Plantation Owner; Nobleman)
Carolina Dawn - Wendy Garrett   694

Langston, Charlotte (Noblewoman)
The Return - Diane Haeger   776

Langston, Edward (Military Personnel)
The Return - Diane Haeger   776

Lannier, Elina (Young Woman)
Creole Nights - Deborah Martin   1271

Lannigan, Jack (Spirit; Angel)
Second Chances - Constance O'Day-Flannery   1454

Laomede, Marissa (Warrior)
Crystal Fire - Kathleen Morgan   1412

Larabee, Nick (Cowboy)
Arizona Lovestorm - Wendy Garrett   693

LaRouche, Nevada (Businessman)
Honor - Lindsay Chase   336

Larren, Coil (Wanderer)
Far Star - Anne Avery   38

Larson, Davey (Orphan)
Spirit of the Season - Heather Graham   741

Larson, Eli (Lawman)
Outlaw Bride - Katherine Compton   381

LaRue, Eulalia Grace "Lollie" (Southern Belle)
Just a Kiss Away - Jill Barnett   89

Lassater, Will (Businessman)
The Forever Tree - Rosanne Bittner   155

Lassiter, Aurora (Healer; Witch)
Lion Heart - Amy J. Fetzer   640

Latham, Lili (Young Woman)
The Master's Bride - Suzannah Davis   481

Latham, Lorelei (Businesswoman; Captive)
Sweet Texas Magic - Evelyn Rogers   1689

Latham, Val (Nobleman; Rake)
The Contrary Corinthian - Emily Hendrickson   850

Lattimer, Hugo (Nobleman; Guardian)
Vixen - Jane Feather   636

Lattimore, Dante (Coach)
Hearts Afire - Monique Gilmore   727

Lattimore, Sydney (Gentlewoman)
An Affair of Interest - Barbara Metzger   1350

Laughton, Laurel Sinclair (Widow(er))
Legacy - Leigh Bristol   217

Laurence, Malcolm (Wealthy)
Secret in the Shadows - Marina Malcolm   1265

Laurent, Claire (Businesswoman)
French Silk - Sandra Brown   228

Laverty, Mariah (Heiress—Dispossessed;
   Handicapped)
Wild Mountain Honey - Carol Finch   648

Lawrence, Adam (Gardener)
Scarlet Scandals - Carol Budd   249

Lawrence, Joe "Sky Warrior" (Imposter; Diplomat)
Forever Ecstasy - Janelle Taylor   1915

Lawrence, Jonathan (Widow(er); Journalist)
Rosewood - Candace Camp   291

Lawrence, Victoria (Captive)
Capture My Heart - Bobbi Smith   1835

Lawson, Josh (Publisher)
Escapade - Susan Kyle   1121

Lawson, Katrina (Young Woman)
Surrender the Night - Colleen Shannon   1770

Lawson, Lily (Gentlewoman)
Then Came You - Lisa Kleypas   1090

Lawson, Wendall (Doctor)
Risk - Doris Parmett   1507

Layton, Jeff (Fiance(e))
Once upon Forever - Becky Lee Weyrich   2008

Layton, Phoebe (Noblewoman)
Reckless - Amanda Quick   1572

Lazo, Dallas (Parent)
A Man Without a Wife - Beverly Bird   150

Le Blanc, Armand (Fisherman)
Jessica's Song - Virginia Nielsen   1442

Le Clerc, Catherine (Widow(er))
King of the Pirates - Stef Ann Holm   912

Le Clerc, Cendrine (Dancer)
Gilded Dreams - Kristy Daniels   461

le Clerc, Lorilie (Healer)
The Raven and the Rose - Susan Wiggs   2027

Le Fontin, Brielle (Noblewoman)
A Love So Fierce - Joanna McGauran   1309

Leandra of Lyonesse (Noblewoman; Fiance(e))
A Tender Magic - Linda Madl   1262

LeClair of Ravenwood (Noblewoman)
The Lion's Angel - Libby Sydes   1909

LeClerc, Luc "Bear" (Trapper)
Autumn Ecstasy - Pamela K. Forrest   659

LeCoeur, Gabrielle (Bastard Daughter)
The Perfect Mistress - Betina M. Krahn   1104

LeCompte, Dominique (Plantation Owner)
South of the Line - Catherine Ennis   611

Lederer, Orchid (Writer; Actress)
Blue Orchids - Julia Fenton   637

Lederer, Valentina (Actress; Adoptee)
Blue Orchids - Julia Fenton   637

Lee, Becky Lynn (Model)
Red - Erica Spindler   1862

Lee, Elizabeth (Feminist)
Heaven on Earth - Michelle Brandon   205

Leighton, David (Nobleman; Rake)
Elizabeth's Rake - Emily Hendrickson   851

Leighton, Dawn (Orphan; Gentlewoman)
Lady Rogue - Kathryn Kramer   1106

Leighton, Deanna (Veterinarian)
On the Line - Anne Marie Duquette   576

Leighton, Jonathan (Spy)
Traitorous Hearts - Susan Kay Law   1165

Leighton, Theresa "Tess" (Saloon Keeper/Owner; Smuggler)
The Black Rose - Christina Skye   1818

Lennox, Richard (Nobleman)
Dreaming - Jill Barnett   87

Leonard, Keith (Producer)
Blue Orchids - Julia Fenton   637

Lesneven, Alwyn (Noblewoman)
Blood Red Roses - Katherine Deauville   493

Letty, Jessalyn (Horse Trainer)
Once in a Blue Moon - Penelope Williamson   2038

Lewis, Darcy (Nurse; Social Worker)
Harvest of Love - Nancy Sheehan   1780

Leyla (Healer)
Warrior's Lady - Madeline Baker   48

Leyton, Claire (Thief)
Deception - Ruth Langan   1153

Leyton, Linnea (Noblewoman)
The Rake and His Lady - Julie Caille   269

Liane (Psychic; Healer)
Heart's Lair - Kathleen Morgan   1416

Lianna (Noblewoman; Heiress)
The Lily and the Leopard - Susan Wiggs   2025

Lightfoot, Nicodemus "Nick" (Businessman)
The Golden Chance - Jayne Ann Krentz   1108

Lilliane of Orrick, Lady (Noblewoman)
My Gallant Enemy - Rexanne Becnel   112

Lind, Faith (Teacher)
Keeping Faith - Kathleen Kane   1039

Lindale, Regina (Noblewoman)
For Love's Sake Only - Laura Parker   1502

Lindell, Jan (Student; Archaeologist)
The Night Prowlers - Karen G. McCullough   1304

Linden, Arabella (Socialite)
The Destiny - Fayrene Preston   1552

Linder, Beth Ann (Young Woman; Outcast)
Angel Eyes - Suzannah Davis   478

Lindhurst, Phillipa (Noblewoman; Abuse Victim)
Summer Storm - Denise Domning   547

Lindley, Rowan (Nobleman)
Wild Jasmine - Bertrice Small   1827

Lindsay, Diana (Prostitute)
Dearly Beloved - Mary Jo Putney   1558

Lindsay, Jessica (Southern Belle)
Morning Song - Karen Robards   1651

Linness of Sauvage (Psychic; Imposter)
A Kiss in the Night - Jennifer Horsman   927

Linnett (Noblewoman)
The Eagle's Song - Marylyle Rogers   1693

Linton, Kate (Young Woman)
The Last Summer of Innocence - Linda Sole   1850

Linton, Rachel (Captive; Spinster)
Captive Kiss - Amy Christopher   355

Lionheart, Justin (Military Personnel)
The Garden Path - Kristie Knight   1091

Litchfield, Tempest (Lawyer)
Apache Wind - Carol Finch   643

Livingston, Tom (Spouse)
Dream Time - Paris Afton Bonds   182

Llewellen, Rhys (Sea Captain; Privateer)
Dangerous Desire - Ashley Snow   1849

Llewellyn, Jenna (Healer; Witch)
Carolina Dawn - Wendy Garrett   694

Llewellyn, Reagan (Revolutionary)
Temptation's Tender Kiss - Colleen Faulkner   627

Lloyd, Arienne (Southern Belle)
Sapphire - Venita Helton   849

Lloyd, Teglan (Heiress—Dispossessed; Imposter)
The Wild Winds - Catherine Palmer   1487

Llys (Religious; Orphan)
Chanting the Morning Star - Marylyle Rogers   1691

Lobo "Jess" (Gunfighter)
Lawless - Patricia Potter   1540

Locke, Rachel (Librarian)
In the Cards - Julie Meyers   1357

Locke, Shara (Scientist; Time Traveller)
Stolen Dreams - Marilyn Campbell   303

Locke, Wesley (Sea Captain)
Sweet Abandon - Sara Blayne   175

Lockhart, Dylon (Plantation Owner; Rake)
Love's Sweetest Secret - Gina Robins   1674

Lockhart, Trace (Businessman; Thief)
Rogue's Honor - DeLoras Scott   1752

Lockwood, Dillon (Heir)
Thief of My Heart - Rexanne Becnel   114

Lockwood, Jane (Spinster)
The Highwayman - Catherine Reynolds   1611

Lockwood, Leara James (Child-Care Giver)
Home Fires - Dixie Dubois   569

Lockwood, Nicki (Businesswoman)
Suspicion's Gate - Justine Davis   475

Logan, Brock (Businessman)
The Long Road Home - Pat Warren   1994

Logan, Daniel (Detective—Private)
Sweetwater - Sandra Chastain   346

Logan, Gamel (Knight)
Silver Flame - Hannah Howell   939

Logan, Ginny (Widow(er); Advertising)
Mrs. Perfect - Peggy Roberts   1670

Logan, Joshua (Archaeologist; Psychic)
Mountain Mystic - Debra Dixon   533

Logan, Katha (Businesswoman)
Mixed Signals - Joan Elliott Pickart   1532

Logan, Michele (Insurance Investigator)
Star-Crossed Lovers - Kay Hooper   924

Logan, Mike (Vintner)
Moments - Georgia Bockoven   178

Logan, Mitch (Writer)
The Unwitting Witness - Alma Blair   167

Logan, Trace (Businessman)
Honor's Promise - Sharon Sala   1715

Logan, Vince (Gunfighter; Rancher)
Thunder's Tender Touch - Carol Finch   647

Logan, Wolf Star (Warrior; Adoptee)
Yesterday's Shadows - Marianne Willman   2042

Lombard, Kane (Businessman; Widow(er))
After Midnight - Susan Kyle   1120

London, Gabe (Police Officer)
Charity's Angel - Dallas Schulze   1737

Lone Wolf (Indian; Warrior)
Cheyenne Dreams - Peggy Hanchar   790

Lonetree, Ellen (Nurse)
A Man Without a Wife - Beverly Bird   150

Lonetree, Wolf (Indian; Nobleman)
Only Mine - Elizabeth Lowell   1233

Longbaugh, Lacey (Orphan)
Cherokee Dawn - Genell Dellin   504

Longmore, Hattie (Divorced Person; Rancher)
Mountain Ecstasy - Linda Sandifer   1718

Longpre, Frank (Police Officer)
Whispers in Time - Becky Lee Weyrich   2011

Longren, Case (Rancher)
Always a Lady - Sharon Sala   1712

Longstreet, Case (Indian; Military Personnel)
Blossom - Constance Bennett   120

Longstreet, Tucker (Plantation Owner)
Carnal Innocence - Nora Roberts   1665

Lopez, Swift "Swift Antelope" (Gunfighter; Indian)
Comanche Heart - Catherine Anderson   17

Lord, Christian (Sea Captain)
Master of My Dreams - Danelle Harmon   809

Lord, Hunter (Producer)
Miss Robinson Crusoe - Tracy Sinclair   1814

Loren, Christy (Psychic)
Rainbow in the Mist - Phyllis A. Whitney   2017

Loring, Steve (Fugitive)
Terms of Love - Shirl Henke   868

Louvierre, Aimee (Southern Belle)
Delta Desire - Diane Gates Robinson   1678

Love (Radio Personality)
The Christmas Husband - Mary Anne Wilson   2046

MacKinnon, Nicholas (Businessman)
Angel in Marble - Elaine Coffman   368

MacKinnon, Ross (Nobleman; Rake)
Somewhere Along the Way - Elaine Coffman   372

MacKinnon, Tavis (Artisan)
Heaven Knows - Elaine Coffman   371

MacLaren, "Black Alexander" (Laird)
Highland Rogue - Casey Stuart   1892

MacLean, Robert (Warrior)
Lavender Flame - Karen Stratford   1886

MacLean, Rory (Privateer; Laird)
Moon Dreams - Patricia Rice   1617

MacLeod, Sebastian "Shadow Panther" (Indian; Heir)
Delta Desire - Diane Gates Robinson   1678

MacLinn, Meg (Heiress—Dispossessed; Noblewoman)
Highland Hearts - Scotney St. James   1864

MacNamara, Seagan (Nobleman)
Mistress of the Eagles - Elona Malterre   1267

MacNeill, Ian (Doctor)
A Deeper Magic - Jillian Hunter   953

MacPherson, Mary Kate (Noblewoman; Bride)
Border Bride - Amanda Scott   1744

MacQuade, Garret (Guide)
Only Forever - Kimberly Cates   330

MacRae, Skylar (Debutante)
Whispers of Love - Gina Robins   1677

MacRoth, Elgiva (Artisan; Kidnapper)
Legends - Deborah Smith   1839

Maddox, Tanner (Lawman)
Desperado Passion - Patricia Pellicane   1514

Madison, Zach (Rogue; Imposter)
Angel Eyes - Suzannah Davis   478

Madoc of Powys (Royalty)
A Moment in Time - Bertrice Small   1824

Maeve (Ruler; Warrior)
Fire Queen - Deborah Grambien   743

Maggie (Orphan)
Promised Sunrise - Robin Lee Hatcher   832

Maguire, Hunter (Farmer)
Spring Blossom - Jill Metcalf   1349

Mahoney, Sassy (Young Woman)
Wild Texas Blossom - Arlene Holliday   910

Maidenhall, Axia (Heiress; Imposter)
The Heiress - Jude Deveraux   513

Maintree, Suzanne (Socialite; Bride)
Golden Nights - Christine Monson   1404

Mainwaring, Forrest (Nobleman)
An Affair of Interest - Barbara Metzger   1350

Maitland, Chloe (Noblewoman; Heiress)
The Scoundrel's Bride - Emily Hendrickson   858

Maitland, Dominic (Spy; Handicapped)
The Heart's Desire - Gayle Wilson   2045

Maitland, Iain (Laird)
The Secret - Julie Garwood   707

Maitland, Reid (Political Figure)
Seasons - Lisa Gregory   766

Maitland, S.T. (Highwayman)
The Prince of Midnight - Laura Kinsale   1079

Maitland, Taryn (Noblewoman)
Knight's Desire - Judith Hill   890

Makena, Lani "Kapiolani" (Banker)
Once Burned, Twice as Hot - Patt Bucheister   243

Malkin, Randolf (Nobleman; Handicapped)
Move Heaven and Earth - Christina Dodd   538

Malloren, Arcenbryght (Nobleman; Rake)
Tempting Fortune - Jo Beverley   138

Malloren, Cynric (Nobleman; Military Personnel)
My Lady Notorious - Jo Beverley   136

Mallory, Pete (Pilot)
One Man's War - Lindsay McKenna   1318

Malloy, Zeke (Political Figure; Activist)
Scandalous - Sonia Simone   1796

Malone, Abby (Journalist)
Angels in the Light - Margot Dalton   456

Malone, Dalton (Renegade)
Seduced - Carla Simpson   1799

Malone, Kate (Bounty Hunter)
Love's Bounty - Alisa McBride   1299

Malone, Kate (Doctor)
Witch Dance - Peggy Webb   1998

Malone, Maureen (Writer)
Once in a Lifetime - Constance O'Day-Flannery   1452

Malone, Piper (Heiress—Dispossessed)
Thunder's Tender Touch - Carol Finch   647

Malone, Rachel (Heiress)
Undeniable - Francis Ray   1602

Malone, Shae (Writer)
Darling Deceiver - Lori Copeland   390

Maloney, Kate (Young Woman; Fiance(e))
Taming Kate - Eugenia Riley   1638

Malory, Amy (Noblewoman)
The Magic of You - Johanna Lindsey   1204

Malory, James (Sea Captain; Privateer)
Gentle Rogue - Johanna Lindsey   1201

Malotti, Louise (Inspector)
Dead Heat - Wendy Haley   784

Manchester, Deborah (Heiress)
Moonflower - Shirl Henke   862

Manchester, Royce (Plantation Owner)
Whisper to Me of Love - Shirlee Busbee   259

Mandell (Nobleman)
The Painted Veil - Susan Carroll   324

Mandrell, Colt (Rancher)
The Heart Remembers - Sandra Davidson   469

Mannering, Quinten (Archaeologist)
Passion's Golden Fire - Susan Sackett   1710

Mannering, Wyatt (Nobleman)
Touched by Magic - Patricia Rice   1623

Manning, Jon Edward Sebastian (Nobleman; Rake)
The Highwayman - Catherine Reynolds   1611

Manning, Rich (Engineer)
Marriage of Inconvenience - Debbie Macomber   1251

Mansard, Catherine (Heiress; Debutante)
An Impetuous Miss - Mary Chase Comstock   383

Mansfield, Arden (Nobleman; Adventurer)
The Dream Hunter - Laura Kinsale   1076

Mansfield, David (Businessman)
A Private Proposal - La Verne St. George   1863

Maples, Genevieve (Actress; Designer)
Dance of Deception - Suzannah Davis   479

Mapleton, Amelia (Debutante; Gentlewoman)
Amelia's Intrigue - Judith A. Lansdowne   1162

Mar (Prehistoric Human; Warrior)
Daughter of the Red Deer - Joan Wolf   2057

Mara (Adventurer)
Silversword - Lindsay Randall   1588

Marcassa, Mike (Immigrant)
Avenue of Dreams - Lucy Taylor   1921

Marchant, Gerard (Nobleman)
A Valentine's Day Fancy - Julie Caille   270

Marchant, Gervaise (Nobleman)
Dangerous Diversions - Margaret Evans Porter   1534

Marchwood, Dane (Nobleman)
Magic at Midnight - Sandra Heath   846

Marcus (Military Personnel)
Enchant the Heavens - Kathleen Morgan   1414

Marcus (Nobleman)
Mutual Consent - Gayle Buck   247

Marcus, Emily (Captive)
Texas Destiny - Dana Ransom   1593

Marcus, Niles (Explorer)
Seek the Wild Shore - Leslie O'Grady   1456

Marek, Ty (Writer)
The Snow Garden - Bethany Campbell   300

Margaret (Noblewoman)
The Vow - Mary Spencer   1861

Margaret of Blackthorne (Witch; Noblewoman)
Untamed - Elizabeth Lowell   1235

Markham, Lucy (Actress; Singer)
The Gilded Cage - Edith Layton   1169

Markham, Mirabelle "Mira" (Debutante)
The Dreadful Debutante - Marion Chesney   348

Markham, Selena (Southern Belle)
Moonwitch - Nicole Jordan   1018

Marleigh, Vivian (Handicapped; Heiress)
Speak Only Love - Deana James   970

Marley, Sylvie (Teenager; Werewolf)
The Werewolf's Kiss - Cheri Scotch   1740

Marlow, Leah (Young Woman; Captive)
The Sheikh's Revenge - Emma Darcy   464

Marlowe, Anna (Noblewoman; Spinster)
Heartless - Mary Balogh   59

Marlowe, Carol (Psychic; Detective)
Whispers in Time - Becky Lee Weyrich   2011

Marlowe, Garrick (Sea Captain)
The Taming of Amelia - Maura Seger   1764

Marlowe, Mary (Companion; Gentlewoman)
Christmas Escapade - Meg-Lynn Roberts   1661

Marone, Sophia (Designer; Worker)
Tattered Silk - Elaine Barbieri   75

Marsh, Delaney (Orphan)
Wings of a Dove - Elaine Barbieri   76

Marshall, Amelia (Spinster)
Weeping Angel - Stef Ann Holm   915

Marshall, Anne (Gentlewoman; Equestrian)
Heir to Vengeance - Roberta Eckert   590

Mont, Darcy (Spy; Nobleman)
Freedom Flame - Caryn Cameron 279

Montagne, Faith (Noblewoman)
Devil's Lady - Patricia Rice 1614

Montagne, Jocelyn (Noblewoman)
Bride of the Lion - Elizabeth Stuart 1894

Montague, Blase (Nobleman)
The Rake and the Redhead - Emily Hendrickson 856

Montague, Lily (Debutante)
Promise Me Forever - Cara Miles 1374

Montana, Cade (Rancher)
Gabrielle - Leta Tegler 1922

Montana, Lacey (Young Woman)
Lacey's Way - Madeline Baker 44

Montana, Lane (Businesswoman; Detective)
Crime of Passion - Kay Hooper 921

Montana, Roman (Bodyguard)
Heartstrings - Rebecca Paisley 1481

Montclair, Valentine (Gentleman)
Logic of the Heart - Patricia Veryan 1980

Montclaire, Ross (Nobleman; Rake)
Lady in Green - Barbara Metzger 1353

Monteigne, Tyler (Gambler)
Paper Roses - Patricia Rice 1618

Montera, Nick (Photographer)
Come Midnight - Suzanne Forster 663

Montfort, Lucian (Rake; Nobleman)
A Second Match - Emma Lange 1159

Montgomery, Blake (Gunfighter)
Forever Gold - Catherine Hart 819

Montgomery, Brandon (Publisher)
Wild Heather - Millie Criswell 430

Montgomery, Brice (Sea Captain; Nobleman)
When Midnight Comes - Robin Burcell 253

Montgomery, Cabot (Wealthy)
Almost Home - Debra Cowan 414

Montgomery, Carrie (Bride; Matchmaker)
Eternity - Jude Deveraux 512

Montgomery, Charles (Businessman)
Christmas Journey - Rexanne Becnel 109

Montgomery, Cord (Wagonmaster)
The Turquoise Trail - Susannah Leigh 1182

Montgomery, Cynthia (Teenager)
For Always - Bette Ford 656

Montgomery, Dalton (Businessman; Gambler)
Priceless - Mary Lynn Baxter 102

Montgomery, David (Nobleman)
Rebel Wildfire - Barbara Cummings 447

Montgomery, Dougless (Teacher)
A Knight in Shining Armor - Jude Deveraux 515

Montgomery, James (Scout)
Web of Loving Lies - Barbara Leigh 1177

Montgomery, Jamie (Nobleman; Knight)
The Heiress - Jude Deveraux 513

Montgomery, Jocelyn "Jace" (Businessman)
Wishes - Jude Deveraux 520

Montgomery, Judith (Spouse)
Christmas Journey - Rexanne Becne! 109

Montgomery, Juliana (Orphan)
Cherished - Jill Gregory 762

Montgomery, Julienne (Orphan)
Montana Mistress - Thea Devine 521

Montgomery, Kathleen (Loyalist; Plantation Owner)
Midnight Treasure - Katherine Kincaid 1067

Montgomery, Kay (Activist)
A Lifetime of Heaven - Nan Ryan 1705

Montgomery, Lacie (Teacher; Imposter)
Thief of My Heart - Rexanne Becnel 114

Montgomery, Quinn (Lawyer)
For Always - Bette Ford 656

Montgomery, Ransom (Pirate)
Lion Heart - Amy J. Fetzer 640

Montgomery, Ring (Military Personnel)
Mountain Laurel - Jude Deveraux 516

Montgomery, Tanner (Nobleman)
The Hawk and the Heather - Robin Leigh 1179

Montoya, Amado (Businessman; Vintner)
Moments - Georgia Bockoven 178

Montoya, Rafael (Rancher)
Comanche Flame - Genell Dellin 507

Montoya, Sterling (Cowboy)
Moonlight and Magic - Rebecca Paisley 1483

Montrose, Matt (Photojournalist)
All That Glitters - Ruth Langan 1150

Montrose, Thomas (Rake; Spy)
Promise Me Heaven - Connie Brockway 221

Moraga, Dory (Journalist; Lesbian)
The Sure Thing - Melissa Hartman 826

Morales, Kaylene (Teacher)
Touchdown for Love - Diane Gonzales Bertrand 130

Moran, Chad (Lawyer; Handicapped)
Family Reunion - Jill Metcalf 1348

Moran, Whip (Drifter)
Only Love - Elizabeth Lowell 1232

Moran, Willow (Southern Belle)
Only His - Elizabeth Lowell 1231

Morand, Celine (Widow(er))
The Heart's Legacy - Barbara Keller 1047

Morand, Gerard (Hero)
The Heart's Legacy - Barbara Keller 1047

Moreland, Adam (Drifter; Businessman)
Bouquet - Shirl Henke 860

Moreland, Adam (Heir; Worker)
Summer Has No Name - Shirl Henke 867

Moreland, Viscount (Nobleman; Spy)
Daring Illusion - Christina Cordaire 398

Morgan, Abigail (Captive; Fiance(e))
Hostage Heart - Lisa Hendrix 859

Morgan, Amos (Farmer)
Heirloom - Candace Camp 290

Morgan, Blake (Drifter; Guide)
Boston Renegade - June Lund Shiplett 1785

Morgan, Brier (Runaway)
A Wild Desire - Rebecca George 719

Morgan, Clare (Teacher; Spinster)
Thunder and Roses - Mary Jo Putney 1563

Morgan, Clay (Rancher)
Beloved Wife - Lynda Trent 1956

Morgan, Clint (Lawman)
Devil's Delight - DeLoras Scott 1749

Morgan, Dan (Imposter; Gunfighter)
Lover's Gold - Kat Martin 1277

Morgan, Erin (Researcher)
What Child Is This? - Rebecca York 2078

Morgan, Garret (Knight)
Beneath a Pale Moon - Victoria Morrow 1422

Morgan, Gentry (Indian; Spy)
The Schemers - Lois Wolfe 2059

Morgan, Gray (Hero)
River's Dream - Virginia Lynn 1243

Morgan, Jacob (Military Personnel; Doctor)
Kansas Kiss - Christine Dorsey 550

Morgan, Jessica (Rancher)
Scoundrel's Captive - JoAnn De Lazzari 488

Morgan, Justice (Gunfighter)
Morning Sky - Constance Bennett 121

Morgan, Lewis (Spy)
My Own True Love - Susan Sizemore 1816

Morgan, Libby (Publisher; Revolutionary)
Liberty's Lady - Caryn Cameron 280

Morgan, Mac (Businessman; Drifter)
Dreams and Wishes - Karren Radko 1583

Morgan, Margaret (Artist)
The Crimson Roses of Fountain Court - Peggy Darty 465

Morgan, Mariah (Heiress)
Defiant Heart - Nancy Moulton 1432

Morgan, Meredith "Merry" (Spy)
Freedom Flame - Caryn Cameron 279

Morgan, Moriah (Imposter)
Mistress of Sin - Sue Rich 1624

Morgan, Nicholas (Nobleman; Heir)
The Kissing Bough - Joan Smith 1844

Morgan, Owen (Hugo) (Businessman; Knight)
By All That Is Sacred - Laura Gilmour Bennett 127

Morgan, Rhys (Settler)
Northern Fire, Northern Star - Scotney St. James 1865

Morgan, Selene (Apothecary)
Bayou Passion - Jane Archer 29

Morgan, Slade (Drifter; Cowboy)
Scarlet Sunset, Silver Nights - Leigh Greenwood 759

Morgan, Tara (Travel Agent; Courier)
The Road to Forever - Frances Williams 2036

Morgana (Noblewoman)
Firebrand's Lady - Caryl Wilson 2043

Moria (Mythical Creature)
Swan Bride - Betina Lindsey 1192

Morisette, Jeanne (Spy)
Beyond the Sunrise - Mary Balogh 54

Morland, Shana (Witch)
A Touch of Magic - Carin Rafferty 1585

Morning Hawk, Nathan (Indian)
Wild Savage Heart - Pamela K. Forrest 661

Morning Light (Healer; Indian)
Texas Healer - Ruth Langan 1157

Morning Song (Orphan; Indian)
Orenda - Kate Cameron 282

Morning Star (Indian)
Forever Ecstasy - Janelle Taylor 1915

Morningstar, Matthew (Indian; Entertainer)
A Wilder Love - Laura Parker 1505

Morrell, Christian (Religious)
To Love and to Cherish - Patricia Gaffney 680

Morris, Brianna (Debutante; Ward)
The Captured Heart - Sheila O'Hallion 1458

Morrison, Tom (Patriot; Servant)
To Spite the Devil - Paula Jonas 1011

Morrow, Alexandra (Singer; Teacher)
Serenade - Sandra Kitt 1086

Morrow, Chad (Hero)
Deceptive Desires - Wanda Owen 1474

Morrow, Julian (Nobleman; Widow(er))
Touch Me with Fire - Nicole Jordan 1020

Mortimer, Anthony (Nobleman)
Lady Lucinde's Locket - Irene Saunders 1723

Mortimer-Hawkes, Regina (Captive; Noblewoman)
Wild Dawn - Cait Logan 1225

Morton, Delilah Smith (Widow(er); Rancher)
Delilah - Cait Logan 1223

Mountjoy, Damian (Nobleman; Outlaw)
Damsel in Distress - Shannon Drake 564

Mueller, Carson (Businesswoman)
Nevada Temptation - Gwen Cleary 364

Muhdula Ali "Muddy" (Mythical Creature)
Imagine - Jill Barnett 88

Muir, Dante (Nobleman; Amnesiac)
The Illusion of Love - Kasey Michaels 1366

Muldoon, Mattie (Businesswoman)
The Bonnie Blue - Joan Elliott Pickart 1531

Mulloney, Daniel (Journalist; Imposter)
Paper Tiger - Patricia Rice 1619

Mulvehey, Rosie (Farmer; Spouse)
The Wives of Bowie Stone - Maggie Osborne 1469

Munday, Jennie (Runaway)
The Texan and the Lady - Jodi Thomas 1932

Murdoch, Lucas "Doc" (Doctor; Cowboy)
Texas Temptation - Gina Robins 1676

Murphy, Danny (Writer)
Sungold - Jillian Dagg 450

Murphy, Patrick (Widow(er); Businessman)
For the Love of Laura - Karen Morrell 1419

Murray, Lucas (Businessman)
Love's Quiet Corner - Laura Parrish 1511

Myer, Melanie (Student; Lesbian)
Gardenias Where There Are None - Molleen Zanger 2081

Myles, Hilary (Artisan)
Love's Safe Harbor - Cindy T. Moss 1431

N

Nadeau, Phillipe (Singer)
Wish upon a Star - Karen Morrell 1420

Najero, Maya (Nurse)
The Moon Pool - Diana Stuart 1893

Nash, Adria (Heiress)
Treasures - Lisa Jackson 962

Navarro, Danica "Danni" (Widow(er); Store Owner)
Yankee's Caress - Terri Valentine 1969

Needham, Adrian (Director)
Hot Property - Elise Title 1949

Neill, Hillary (Accountant; Heiress)
Moon Showers - Laura Phillips 1523

Neillson, Robert (Businessman)
When Someday Comes - Faith E.W. Garner 691

Nesbitt, Benedict (Nobleman; Imposter)
Libby's London Merchant - Carla Kelly 1051

Nesbitt, Maggie (Seamstress; Designer)
Through the Years - Katherine Sinclair 1808

Neubauer, Anton (Farmer; Immigrant)
Rain Shadow - Cheryl St. John 1866

Neville, Liana (Heiress)
The Taming - Jude Deveraux 519

Neville, Sabrina (Widow(er); Imposter)
Romantic Masquerade - Lois Stewart 1878

Newberry, Marcie (Teacher; Landowner)
Somewhere Near Paradise - Marjorie Everitt 616

Newby, Nerissa (Spinster)
Road to Ruin - Margaret Evans Porter 1535

Newcomb, Kit (Young Woman)
Cherokee Bride - Patricia Werner 2003

Newman, Jared (Bounty Hunter)
Rugged Splendor - Robin Leigh 1180

Newman, Jeremy (Fiance(e))
Passions - Christiane Heggan 847

Newman, Samantha (Spinster)
Lord Carew's Bride - Mary Balogh 60

Newton, Bethany (Fugitive; Convict)
Far Horizons - Katherine Sinclair 1807

Niall (Royalty)
Heartspell - Blaine Anderson 15

Nic Lachlan, Brianna (Noblewoman)
Flame Across the Highlands - Katherine Vickery 1982

Nichola (Noblewoman)
The Prize - Julie Garwood 705

Nicholai, Nicholas (Businessman; Heir)
Red Velvet - Barbara Boswell 185

Nichols, Cole (Heir—Dispossessed; Sports Figure)
The Legacy - Patricia Simpson 1803

Nicholson, Chris (Widow(er); Teacher)
Love Game - Mallory Rush 1701

Nick (Inventor)
Shotgun Wedding - Barbara Caitlin 271

Nicola (Gentlewoman)
Counterfeit Heart - Anthea Malcolm 1264

Nicolet, Etienne (Trapper)
Windsong - Kelly Ferjutz 638

Night Wind (Indian; Warrior)
Night Wind's Woman - Shirl Henke 864

Nikki (Student—High School; Musician)
Sounds of Silence - Marilyn Levy 1185

Niniane, s (Royalty)
Born of the Sun - Joan Wolf 2056

Nix, John (Businessman)
Yesterday's Dream - Alice Sharpe 1775

Nolan, Callie (Governess)
Arizona Captive - LaRee Bryant 241

Nolan, Emma (Teacher)
A Margin in Time - Laura Hayden 837

Nolan, Riordan (Archaeologist)
The Turtledove's Secret - Laura Hastings 827

Nolenberg, Eliza (Worker; Guardian)
Heart Song - Barbara Hargis 804

Nolte, Victor (Gentleman)
With One Look - Jennifer Horsman 929

North, Bentley (Businesswoman)
Maverick's Lady - Linda Jenkins 982

Northcutt, Luke (Neighbor)
Country Kiss - Sharon Harlow 805

Northway, Kurt (Military Personnel; Single Parent)
Love Me Tonight - Nan Ryan 1706

O

Oakes, Simon (Lawman)
Delilah - Cait Logan 1223

Oakham, Harry (Spy)
The Doll's House - Evelyn Anthony 25

Oaks, Calla (Orphan; Spouse)
A Delicate Matter - Rebecca Forster 662

O'Bannion, Jennie "Fire Flower" (Fugitive)
Comanche Wind - Genell Dellin 508

O'Brien, Angelina (Southern Belle)
Angel Fire - Deborah Satinwood 1719

O'Brien, Annie Laurie (Teacher)
Annie and the Outlaw - Sharon Sala 1713

O'Brien, Carrie (Fugitive)
The Miss and the Maverick - DeLoras Scott 1751

O'Brien, Elayna (Young Woman)
A Whisper on the Wind - Madeline Baker 49

O'Brien, Fortune (Parent)
Atlanta - Sara Orwig 1462

O'Brien, Honor (Heiress—Lost)
Honor's Promise - Sharon Sala 1715

O'Carroll, Connor (Nobleman)
Heaven's Gate - Erin Yorke 2080

O'Carroll, Kathleen Lacey (Mail Order Bride)
The Bride Wore Spurs - Sharon Ihle 956

O'Connell, Gabriel William Danaher (Miner; Fugitive)
Outcast - Emily Carmichael 316

O'Connell, Kate (Religious)
Heaven's Embrace - Lynda Trent 1960

O'Connor, Adam (Investigator; Diver)
Eyes of Fire - Heather Graham Pozzessere 1549

O'Connor, Bobby (Spirit)
Once in a Lifetime - Constance O'Day-Flannery 1452

O'Connor, Katie (Companion; Imposter)
Unveiled - Colleen Quinn 1579

O'Connor, Meghan (Servant)
Wishes on the Wind - Elaine Barbieri 77

O'Connor, Roarke (Privateer)
The Black Angel - Cordia Byers 261

O'Dalaigh, Duvessa (Heroine)
Wolf's Embrace - Gail Link 1212

O'Day, Elinor (Debutante)
Lord Dearborn's Destiny - Brenda Hiatt 888

O'Devir, Deirdre (Stowaway)
Master of My Dreams - Danelle Harmon 809

O'Donald, Kathleen Anne Mary (Immigrant;
   Worker)
Kathleen O'Donald - Penny Hayes 839

O'Donnell, Alana (Heiress)
Captive of Desire - Ruth Langan 1151

O'Donnell, Arrah (Noblewoman; Pirate)
Mistress of the Eagles - Elona Malterre 1267

O'Donnell, Michael Ann (Thief; Businesswoman)
Gotta Have It - Faye Hughes 951

O'Donovan, Kate (Mail Order Bride; Captive)
The Lady and the Outlaw - Katherine Compton 380

O'Duine, Tearlach (Frontiersman; Trader)
Wild Conquest - Hannah Howell 941

O'Halloran, Tabor (Businessman)
Masque of Sapphire - Deana James 969

O'Hara, Meara (Journalist; Governess)
Island of Dreams - Patricia Potter 1539

O'Hara, Michael (Detective—Police)
Hot Property - Sherryl Woods 2067

O'Hara, Michael (Detective—Police; Police Officer)
Hot Secret - Sherryl Woods 2068

O'Hara, Sean (Sea Captain)
A Dangerous Longing - Veronica Sattler 1720

O'Keefe, Reagan (Orphan)
Mountain Rose - Norah Hess 886

O'Leary, Carrie (Journalist; Activist)
Spitfire - Sonya Birmingham 151

O'Lindon, Daisy (Model)
Hell Hath No Fury - Malcolm Macdonald 1244

Oliver, Belinda (Socialite)
Birthstone - Mollie Gregory 767

O'Malley, Dana (Bastard Daughter)
They Call Her Dana - Jennifer Wilde 2029

O'Malley, Fergus (Spirit)
Emily's Ghost - Antoinette Stockenberg 1882

O'Malley, Mary Katherine (Fiance(e))
Denver - Sara Orwig 1463

O'Malley, Shayna (Widow(er); Teacher)
Iron and Lace - Nadine Miller 1388

O'Mara, Kieran (Warrior)
Highland Fire - Ruth Langan 1154

O'Monoghan, Gelina (Warrior)
Lady of Conquest - Teresa Medeiros 1340

O'Neal, Brent (Gambler)
Riverboat Rogue - Jane Toombs 1952

O'Neal, Dancy (Orphan)
A Forever Kind of Love - Patricia Hagan 778

O'Neal, Faith (Governess)
South of the Line - Catherine Ennis 611

O'Neal, Fiona (Healer; Servant)
Moon Dancer - Judith E. French 669

O'Neil, Autumn (Administrator)
Midnight Kiss - Marcia Evanick 615

O'Neil, Jeff (Businessman)
Sweeter than Sin - Sara Orwig 1465

O'Neile, Summer (Mail Order Bride)
Dream Fever - Katherine Sutcliffe 1901

O'Neill, Dierdre (Gentlewoman)
Beloved Enemy - Maura Seger 1757

O'Neill, Garrett (Plantation Owner)
Freedom Angel - Robin LeAnne Wiete 2021

O'Neill, Hugh (Nobleman)
Emerald Enchantment - Patricia Grasso 748

O'Neill, Liam (Nobleman; Pirate)
The Game - Brenda Joyce 1027

Orchin, David (Doctor)
Lies - Doris Parmett 1506

O'Riley, Kathleen "Kate" Moira (Prospector)
Tomorrow's Dream - Peggy Hanchar 792

O'Riley, Lyla (Housekeeper)
Colorado Moonfire - Charlotte Hubbard 943

Ormsby, Andrew (Nobleman; Guardian)
The Captured Heart - Sheila O'Hallion 1458

O'Rourke, Amelia (Young Woman)
Wish Me a Rainbow - Jessica Douglass 561

O'Rourke, Bevan (Fiance(e))
Tender Lies - Kay McMahon 1328

O'Rourke, Darcey (Accountant)
Moonlight Enchantment - Carol Finch 645

O'Rourke, Deagan (Rancher)
Wishes - Lisa Jackson 963

O'Rourke, Josselyn (Religious; Mine Owner)
Rainbow's End - Rebecca Brandewyne 203

O'Rourke, Kathleen (Police Officer)
Badge of Love - Jane McBride Choate 351

O'Rourke, Mary Margaret (Mine Owner; Captive)
Calico - Raine Cantrell 309

O'Rourke, Megan (Con Artist; Captive)
Surrender My Heart - Lois Greiman 770

O'Rourke, Tiernan (Spirit; Nobleman)
Shadows on a Sunset Sea - Sabine Kells 1050

Osborn, Eliza (Debutante)
Miss Osborne Misbehaves - Marian Devon 526

Osborn, Meridee (Businesswoman)
Swinging on a Star - Pamela Bauer 101

Osborne, Rebecca (Widow(er))
When Morning Comes - Robin LeAnne Wiete 2022

Osborne, Richard (Boyfriend)
True Love - Diane E. Lock 1221

O'Shea, Ashleen (Religious; Heiress)
Only Forever - Kimberly Cates 330

O'Shea, Devon (Store Owner)
A Handful of Heaven - Kristin Hannah 797

O'Shea, Flannery (Scientist)
Flannery's Rainbow - Julie Kistler 1084

O'Shea, Hogan (Prospector)
Tomorrow's Dream - Peggy Hanchar 792

O'Shea, Mercy (Ward; Spouse)
Rogue's Mistress - Eugenia Riley 1637

O'Toole, Ronan (Guardian; Chieftain)
Wild Angel - Miriam Minger 1400

O'Toole, Susan (Paralegal)
A Matter of Compromise - Judith Yoder 2077

O'Toole, Triona (Orphan; Ward)
Wild Angel - Miriam Minger 1400

Owen (Religious)
Devoted - Alice Borchardt 184

Owen, Jessica (Scientist)
Jessica's Song - Virginia Nielsen 1442

Owen, John (Military Personnel; Farmer)
A Child's Promise - Deborah Bedford 117

Owens, Dara (Businesswoman)
Silver Mist - Theresa DiBenedetto 527

Oxenby, Jane (Noblewoman)
Scandalous - Pamela Caldwell 276

P

Pagan St. Cyr, Deveril (Plantation Owner)
The Ruby - Christina Skye 1821

Page, Alissa (Socialite)
First Loves - Jean Stone 1884

Paget, Alex (Nobleman)
Miss Wickham's Betrothal - Nancy Richards-
   Akers 1632

Paige, Margaret (Lawyer; Lesbian)
Up, Up and Away - Catherine Ennis 612

Paige, Norah (Gentlewoman; Orphan)
Sea of Dreams - Elizabeth DeLancey 497

Paletot, Serra (Orphan; Imposter)
Outlaw's Kiss - Terri Valentine 1966

Paley, Kate (Businesswoman)
Hot Property - Elise Title 1949

Palmer, Barbara (Lover; Historical Figure)
The Pleasure of Love - Jean Plaidy 1533

Palmer, Duncan (Sea Captain; Nobleman)
Midnight Lace - Elizabeth Kary 1045

Paloma (Slave)
Jewel of the Sea - Susan Wiggs 2024

Papandreou, Greta (Farmer)
The Past Is Another Country - Lois Battle 97

Paradise, Kate (Singer; Heiress)
Paradise in His Arms - Elizabeth Daniels 460

Parish, Lisa (Rancher)
A Promise Made - Catherine Lanigan 1161

Parker, Annie (Doctor)
The Touch of Fire - Linda Howard 935

Parker, Beauregard (Rancher)
The Irish Rose - Jessica Wulf 2073

Parker, Ginny (Mail Order Bride)
Eden Creek - Lisa Bingham 146

Parker, Luke (Gunfighter)
Wild Is the Night - Colleen Quinn 1580

Parker, Margaret (Spinster)
Temptation's Fire - Millie Criswell 429

Parker, Noa (Tour Guide)
Nightmare in Morocco - Loretta Jackson 964

Parkins, Mariah (Young Woman; Fiance(e))
Renegade Bride - Barbara Ankrum 23

Parks, Reynard (Detective)
Santana Rose - Olga Bicos 141

Parnell, Travis (Businessman; Rancher)
Virgin Fire - Elizabeth Chadwick   334

Parriah, Jake (Outlaw)
When Destiny Calls - Suzanne Elizabeth   600

Parrish, Rachel (Rancher)
Unspoken Vows - Connie Rinehold   1643

Parrish, Rafe (Heir; Rancher)
Western Winds - Theresa DiBenedetto   528

Parsons, John (Scientist)
The Stormy Petrel - Mary Stewart   1880

Patrick, James (Nobleman)
To Love a Dark Lord - Anne Stuart   1891

Paxton, Antonia (Widow(er); Noblewoman)
The Last Bachelor - Betina M. Krahn   1099

Paxton, Eugenia (Businesswoman; Imposter)
Night Storm - Catherine Coulter   407

Paxton, Jake (Drifter; Abuse Victim)
For The Love of Grace - Ginna Gray   750

Paxton, Ryan (Businessman; Saloon Keeper/Owner)
Highland Bride - Kathryn Kramer   1105

Paxton, Susanna (Southern Belle)
Song of the Bayou - Elinor Lynley   1239

Payne, Sabine (Archaeologist)
Passion's Golden Fire - Susan Sackett   1710

Paynter, Bliss (Noblewoman; Ward)
Nightrider - Sandra DuBay   568

Payton, Steven (Rancher; Heir)
Dangerous Charade - Madeline Harper   813

Peabody Emerson, Amelia (Archaeologist)
The Snake, the Crocodile, and the Dog - Elizabeth Peters   1519

Pearson, Carlie (Spouse)
Better than Before - Judith Duncan   572

Pearson, Derek (Farmer)
Better than Before - Judith Duncan   572

Pembroke, Allegra (Plantation Owner; Businesswoman)
A Taste of Heaven - Laura Simon   1795

Pendelton, Marcus (Nobleman)
Out of the Blue - Kasey Michaels   1369

Pendenning, Marisol (Widow(er); Noblewoman)
A Suspicious Affair - Barbara Metzger   1356

Penderton, Joslyn (Fiance(e))
The Reluctant Suitor - Sarah Eagle   587

Penhurst (Nobleman)
An Unlikely Attraction - Melinda McRae   1338

Pennington, Alexandra (Widow(er))
Winds of Glory - Gretchen Genet   711

Pennington, Claire (Gentlewoman)
The Jade Garden - Laurel Collins   378

Pennington, Rachel (Spinster)
Rachel - Lynda Trent   1961

Penrhys, Morgana (Teacher)
Light on the Mountain - Maura Seger   1762

Penrod, Ben (Rancher)
Brave Land, Brave Love - Connie Mason   1288

Penrod, Jane Millicent (Artist)
Changes of Heart - Elizabeth Bennett   122

Pentworthy, Megan (Gentlewoman)
Man of My Dreams - Johanna Lindsey   1205

Pepperell, Bethia (Heiress)
The Counterfeit Gentleman - Charlotte Louise Dolan   543

Percy, Len (Doctor)
Darkness at Cottonwood Hall - Madelyn Sanders   1717

Peregrine, Rogan (Landowner)
The Taming - Jude Deveraux   519

Peregrine, Zared (Noblewoman)
The Conquest - Jude Deveraux   511

Perrine, Noah (Administrator)
Suddenly - Barbara Delinsky   502

Perrivale, Simon (Nobleman; Fugitive)
The Captive - Victoria Holt   918

Peters, Alexandra (Artisan; Musician)
Possession - Lori Herter   881

Peters, Brock (Drifter)
Diamond in the Rough - Millie Criswell   426

Peters, Sara (Mountain Woman)
Sara's Family - Ann Justice   1033

Pfeiffer, Paige (Doctor)
Suddenly - Barbara Delinsky   502

Phillips, Amie (Activist)
Pure Instinct - Ellen Fletcher   653

Phillips, Dalton "Jack Flash" (Patriot; Horse Trainer)
Winds of Glory - Gretchen Genet   711

Phillips, Maura (Engineer)
Bits and Pieces - Merline Lovelace   1227

Picard, Devon (Activist)
The Schemers - Lois Wolfe   2059

Pickett, Tom (Farmer)
Pickett's Fence - Linda Shertzer   1783

Pierce, Allie (Orphan)
Wings of a Dove - Elaine Barbieri   76

Pierce, Cori (Entertainer)
Mississippi Mistress - Gina Robins   1675

Pierce, Justin (Doctor; Military Personnel)
The Falcon and the Swan - Diane Gates Robinson   1680

Pierce, Seneca (Indian; Surveyor)
Blue Mountain Magic - Garda Parker   1498

Pierson, Robert (Doctor)
The Moon Pool - Diana Stuart   1893

Pinkney, Adelaide (Farmer; Heiress)
Surrender a Dream - Jill Barnett   91

Pipestone, Ben (Cowboy; Indian)
Reason to Believe - Kathleen Eagle   582

Pipestone, Clara (Historian)
Reason to Believe - Kathleen Eagle   582

Planchet, Trevor (Television Personality)
Stolen Kisses - Sally Falcon   622

Polonsky, Elise Chatham (Noblewoman)
Sweet Ransom - Linda Madl   1261

Polwyche, Piers (Nobleman; Bridegroom)
Speak Only Love - Deana James   970

Pomeroy, Harriet (Archaeologist; Spinster)
Ravished - Amanda Quick   1571

Pope, Annie (Professor)
More than Friends - Barbara Delinsky   500

Pope, Sam (Lawyer)
More than Friends - Barbara Delinsky   500

Potter, Susannah (Heiress; Orphan)
The Ill-Bred Bride - Rosemary Edghill   592

Powell, Lucy (Debutante; Writer)
A Noble Deception - Sara Blayne   174

Powell, Sterling (Detective—Private; Widow(er))
Sterling's Reasons - Joey Light   1188

Powers, Lee (Architect)
Southern Storms - Marcia Martin   1282

Powers, Lisa (Captive)
Arizona Ecstasy - Rosanne Bittner   152

Powers, Logan (Bodyguard)
Arizona Captive - LaRee Bryant   241

Praed, Nathaniel (Spy)
Velvet - Jane Feather   633

Prentice, Cody (Plantation Owner)
The Thorn Trees - Marcella Thum   1946

Prentice, Suzanne (Widow(er); Saloon Hostess)
Fortune's Lady - Victoria Thompson   1933

Prentiss, Luke (Musician; Recluse)
Sing Me to Sleep - Mary-Ben Lorris   1226

Prentiss, Sara (Professor)
Let Me Count the Ways - Leigh Michaels   1372

Prescott, Aiden (Noblewoman)
A Heart So Innocent - Charlene Cross   438

Prescott, Ethan (Mountain Man; Doctor)
Dakota Dawn - Dana Ransom   1589

Prescott, Gideon (Pirate)
Passion's Ransom - Betina M. Krahn   1103

Prescott, Jared (Landowner)
Rachel - Lynda Trent   1961

Prescott, Laura (Fiance(e))
Across a Starlit Sea - Rebecca Brandewyne   198

Prescott, Logan (Contractor)
Undeniable - Francis Ray   1602

Prescott, Matt (Military Personnel; Scout)
Temptation's Price - Dallas Schulze   1738

Prescott, Myrtle (Noblewoman; Heiress)
Highland Ecstasy - Mary Burkhardt   256

Prescott, Robyn (Amnesiac; Model)
Once Innocent - Jessica Gregory   761

Prescott, Rori "Aurora" (Indian)
Arizona Caress - Bobbi Smith   1832

Prescott, Rory (Gentleman)
Dakota Destiny - Dana Ransom   1591

Prescott, Scott (Lawyer; Indian)
Dakota Desire - Dana Ransom   1590

Prescott, Seneca (Sea Captain)
Midnight Enchantment - Jeanne E. Hansen   802

Preston, Joanna (Noblewoman)
A Dove at Midnight - Rexanne Becnel   111

Preston, Kat (Noblewoman; Courtier)
Traitor's Kiss - Joy Tucker   1963

Prestwich, Meribe (Debutante)
The Black Widow - Charlotte Louise Dolan   542

Pretty Sky, Ysidora (Indian; Royalty)
Comanche Flame - Genell Dellin   507

Prewitt, Cindy (Prostitute)
The Brides - Gila Berkowitz   128

Price, Maggie (Businesswoman)
Charade - Christina Hamlett   788

Price, Phil (Filmmaker)
There Is a Season - Phyllis Houseman   930

Pride, Caitlin (Model; Rancher)
Lawless - Alexandra Thorne   1940

Pride, Patrick (Rancher)
Boundless - Alexandra Thorne   1939

Prindle, Charity (Widow(er))
Tempest - Catherine Hart   822

Pringle, Letty (Single Parent)
Ribbon in the Sky - Dorothy Garlock   689

Pritchard, Eulalie (Spinster)
Emerald Rain - Maggie Osborne   1467

Pritchard, Merissa (Gentlewoman)
The Captain's Dilemma - Gail Eastwood   588

Proctor, Constance (Widow(er))
Frontier Fire - Barbara Cummings   446

Profitt, Alexander (Journalist)
Gilded Dreams - Kristy Daniels   461

Pruitt, Victoria (Settler; Farmer)
Dearest Enemy - Stephanie Bartlett   94

Pulneshti, Sandor (Boarder)
In the Cards - Julie Meyers   1357

Purcell, David (Businessman)
Programmed for Danger - Karen G. McCullough   1305

Q

Quade, Brigham (Widow(er))
Yankee Wife - Linda Lael Miller   1387

Quade, Charlotte (Adventurer)
Taming Charlotte - Linda Lael Miller   1386

Quade, Josh (Wagonmaster)
Wildfire - Norah Hess   887

Quarternight, West (Spy; Guide)
The Legend of Love - Nan Ryan   1704

Quigley, Jack (Spirit)
Springtown - DeLoras Scott   1753

Quinlan, Spencer (Journalist)
Midnight Whispers - Jane Toombs   1950

Quinn, Catlin (Southern Belle)
Texas Temptation - Gina Robins   1676

Quinn, Chase (Magician)
The Invisible Groom - Barbara Bretton   212

Quinn, Daniel (Publisher; Widow(er))
His Chariot Awaits - Kasey Michaels   1365

Quinn, Emily (Fugitive; Imposter)
Hot as Sin - Debra Dixon   532

Quinn, Kate (Runaway; Abuse Victim)
Beyond All Reason - Judith Duncan   573

Quinn, Marissa (Young Woman)
The Night Orchid - Patricia Simpson   1804

Quinn, Michael (Police Officer)
Night Watcher - Tracey Tillis   1948

Quintaro, Luiz "Tonatiuh" (Military Personnel)
Sun God - Nan Ryan   1707

R

Radbourne, Elise (Noblewoman)
So Worthy My Love - Kathleen E. Woodiwiss   2062

Radbourne, Galen (Sorcerer)
A Certain Magic - Kathleen Morgan   1410

Radcliffe, Amelia (Spinster)
Everlasting - Lynda Trent   1958

Radcliffe, Electra (Designer)
Everlasting - Lynda Trent   1958

Raeburn, Jack (Rake; Nobleman)
A Change of Heart - Candice Hern   874

Rafferty, Cameron (Police Officer)
Divine Evil - Nora Roberts   1666

Rafferty, J.D. (Rancher)
Dark Paradise - Tami Hoag   898

Rafferty, Jack (Rancher)
Once in Every Life - Kristin Hannah   799

Rafferty, Quinn (Businessman)
My Darling Melissa - Linda Lael Miller   1383

Rain, Oliver (Businessman)
Wildest Hearts - Jayne Ann Krentz   1114

Rain Shadow (Adoptee; Entertainer)
Rain Shadow - Cheryl St. John   1866

Raincliff, Frederica (Widow(er); Noblewoman)
Mistress of Mischief - Susan Carroll   323

Raincrow, Jake (Indian; Psychic)
Silk and Stone - Deborah Smith   1842

Raine (Knight; Bastard Son)
Keeper of the Dream - Penelope Williamson   2037

Raines, Margie (Young Woman)
Summer of the Soldiers - Sandra Chastain   345

Rainsford, Gabriel (Nobleman)
Fallen Angel - Charlotte Louise Dolan   544

Raithby, Philippa (Debutante; Equestrian)
Unlikely Guardian - Carol Proctor   1556

Ralston, Kit (Military Personnel)
Bold Destiny - Jane Feather   628

Ramey, Anna (Widow(er))
Dark Journey - Sandra Canfield   304

Ramirez, Antonia (Rancher)
The Silver Link - Patricia Potter   1545

Ramlin, Sebastian (Gentleman)
Terms of Surrender - Mollie Ashton   33

Ramon "The Falcon" (Indian; Chieftain)
Apache Bride - JoAnne Redd   1606

Ramsay, Aurora (Gentlewoman; Steward)
The Love Knot - Elisabeth Fairchild   619

Ramsay, Quinn (Businessman)
California Man - Carole Dean   490

Ramsbottom, Belinda (Debutante)
Christmas Escapade - Meg-Lynn Roberts   1661

Ramsey, Elisa (Teacher)
Iguana Bay - Theresa Weir   1999

Ramsey, Gib (Military Personnel)
Ride the Tiger - Lindsay McKenna   1320

Ramsey, Jane (Gentlewoman; Spinster)
The Kissing Bough - Joan Smith   1844

Ramsey, Kate (Widow(er); Rancher)
Outback Legacy - Elizabeth Duke   570

Ramsey, Kyle (Sea Captain; Plantation Owner)
Moonwitch - Nicole Jordan   1018

Ramsey, Nick (Relative)
Outback Legacy - Elizabeth Duke   570

Ramsey, Nick (Cowboy)
To Love a Cowboy - Laura Phillips   1524

Ramsey, Price (Actor; Crime Suspect)
My Only Desire - Andrea Parnell   1508

Ramsey, Tess (Volunteer)
One Man's War - Lindsay McKenna   1318

Ramsey, Tyler (Orphan)
Outlaw's Kiss - Terri Valentine   1966

Rand, Elise (Gentlewoman)
Secret Nights - Anita Mills   1395

Rand, Fletcher (Nobleman)
Mrs. Drew Plays Her Hand - Carla Kelly   1056

Rand, Jake (Businessman; Imposter)
Indigo Blue - Catherine Anderson   19

Rand, Jonty (Imposter; Bastard Daughter)
Devil in Spurs - Norah Hess   883

Rand, Taber (Tour Guide)
Nightmare in Morocco - Loretta Jackson   964

Randal, Caitlin (Revolutionary)
Highland Fire - Elizabeth Thornton   1942

Randal, Iaian (Nobleman; Revolutionary)
Highland Fire - Elizabeth Thornton   1942

Randall, Brianna (Child)
Voyager - Diana Gabaldon   675

Randall, Cecily (Debutante; Noblewoman)
The Rake's Reward - Mary Kingsley   1074

Randall, Claire Beauchamp (Time Traveller; Doctor)
Dragonfly in Amber - Diana Gabaldon   673

Randall, Claire Beauchamp (Nurse; Time Traveller)
Outlander - Diana Gabaldon   674

Randall, Claire Beauchamp (Doctor; Time Traveller)
Voyager - Diana Gabaldon   675

Randall, Diana (Lawyer; Imposter)
Vanish with the Rose - Barbara Michaels   1359

Randall, Gilbert (Nobleman; Time Traveller)
Forever in Time - Janice Bennett   124

Randall, Jessica (Young Woman)
Silver Thunder - Joan Hohl   909

Randall, Joelle (Architect; Orphan)
Prince of Wolves - Susan Krinard   1116

Randall, Luke (Doctor)
Harvest of Love - Nancy Sheehan   1780

Randell, Hannah (Fugitive; Imposter)
Forever in Texas - Jodi Thomas   1930

Randol, Charles Alexander III (Businessman; Coach)
Forever After - Bette Ford   657

Randolph, Henry (Lawman)
Laurel - Leigh Greenwood   758

Randolph, Madison (Lawyer)
Fern - Leigh Greenwood   757

Randolph, Maggie (Widow(er); Waiter/Waitress)
For the Thrill - Janis Reams Hudson   949

Randolph, Miles (Villain)
Dream Time - Paris Afton Bonds   182

Randolph, Quint (Cowboy)
Nevada Nights - Georgina Gentry   713

Randolph, Rush (Businessman)
Jasmine and Silk - Sandra Chastain   341

Randolph, Sonya (Debutante; Animal Lover)
A Loyal Companion - Barbara Metzger   1354

Randsome, Julia (Feminist; Gentlewoman)
Storyville - Lois Battle   98

Ransford, Oliver (Gentleman)
Dangerous Masquerade - April Kihlstrom   1065

Ransom, Diana (Psychologist)
Prince of Dreams - Susan Krinard   1115

Ransom, Gat (Cowboy; Guide)
Waltz with the Lady - Betina Lindsey   1195

Ransom, Kane (Lawman; Imposter)
Wildfire - Virginia Brown   236

Ransom, William Alexander (Military Personnel)
Passion's Timeless Hour - Vivian Knight-Jenkins   1094

Ransome, Robert (Nobleman; Rake)
Heart of the Falcon - Diane Wicker Davis   472

Raouille, Gytha (Young Woman)
Beauty and the Beast - Hannah Howell   936

Rappaport, Leigh (Psychologist)
Come Midnight - Suzanne Forster   663

Raul (Spaceship Captain)
Daughter of Destiny - Jackie Casto   327

Raven, Helen (Artist)
All the Winters That Have Been - Evan Maxwell   1297

Raveneau, Nathan (Guardian; Pirate)
Barbados - Cynthia Wright   2070

Ravenna (Young Woman)
The Ground She Walks Upon - Meagan McKinney   1323

Ravenscroft, Tessa (Foundling; Witch)
Wildwitch - Kimberleigh Caitlin   272

Ravenville, Phineas (Nobleman; Rake)
Miss Drayton's Downfall - Patricia Oliver   1460

Rawdon, Cole (Bounty Hunter)
Cherished - Jill Gregory   762

Rawlings, Sara (Young Woman; Ward)
Love a Dark Rider - Shirlee Busbee   258

Raymond of Avrache (Nobleman; Imposter)
Castles in the Air - Christina Dodd   535

Rayner, Jonathan (Nobleman; Landlord)
The Duke's Mistress - Lois Stewart   1877

Raynor, Julian (Gentleman; Rake)
Dangerous to Love - Elizabeth Thornton   1941

Reade, John "Jack" (Bastard Son; Nobleman)
The Heart Remembers - Barbara Hazard   842

Reagor, Whit (Rancher)
Wild Texas Rose - Martha Hix   897

Reardon, Jessie (Businessman)
Midnight Lover - Barbara Bretton   214

Red Hawk (Indian)
Cherokee Bride - Patricia Werner   2003

Red Wolf (Indian; Warrior)
Sioux Splendor - Rosanne Bittner   161

Redding, Rhys (Prisoner; Blockade Runner)
Renegade - Patricia Potter   1544

Redfern, Harry (Nobleman)
The Last Summer of Innocence - Linda Sole   1850

Redman, Susannah (Spinster)
Nobody's Angel - Karen Robards   1652

Redruth, Andrew (Nobleman)
The Dark Towers of Trelochlen - Rachel Cosgrove Payes   1513

Reed, Dake (Military Personnel)
Until Tomorrow - Jill Marie Landis   1148

Reese, Leah (Young Woman)
Tarnished Hearts - Raine Cantrell   311

Reeves, Clint (Settler)
Montana Woman - Rosanne Bittner   157

Regrett, Mason (Rancher)
No Greater Love - Alison Irving   959

Remington, Adam (Nobleman; Indian)
Shadowed Vows - Sue Rich   1626

Renard, Blake (Military Personnel; Hunter)
Apache Legacy - Janis Reams Hudson   947

Renard, Gus (Indian)
Storm Dancers - Allison Hayes   838

Renaud, Tiffany (Debutante)
Deceptive Desires - Wanda Owen   1474

Renaudot, Lucien (Bastard Son)
Promise of Summer - Louisa Rawlings   1597

Rendel, Digory (Smuggler)
The Counterfeit Gentleman - Charlotte Louise Dolan   543

Renfrew, Mark Juan Carlos (Nobleman; Widow(er))
Deirdre and Don Juan - Jo Beverley   134

Renneau, Annalese (Companion; Noblewoman)
A Jewel So Rare - Elizabeth Ann Michaels   1361

Reno, Jake (Outlaw)
Desperado's Caress - Carla Simpson   1798

Renshaw, Simon (Lawyer)
A Deceitful Heart - Karla Hocker   901

Reynolds, Greg (Military Personnel)
Love Game - Mallory Rush   1701

Reynolds, Justin (Nobleman; Sea Captain)
Destiny's Will - Elizabeth Ann Michaels   1360

Reynolds, Reilly (Photographer)
Nevada Ecstasy - Lindsey Hanks   794

Rhea (Noblewoman)
Captive to a Dream - Susan Tanner   1911

Rhea (Mythical Creature)
Dawn on a Jade Sea - Jessica Bryan   240

Rhianna (Royalty)
Enchant the Heavens - Kathleen Morgan   1414

Rhiannon (Hunter)
Beyond the Starlit Frost - Rebecca Brandewyne   199

Rhiannon (Noblewoman)
The Viking's Woman - Heather Graham   742

Rhodare "Demon Dare" (Nobleman)
Dark Whispers - Marylyle Rogers   1692

Rhowenna (Royalty; Captive)
Swan Road - Rebecca Brandewyne   204

Rhy, Cleavis (Store Owner)
Garters - Pamela Morsi   1426

Rhyca (Young Woman; Abuse Victim)
Hearts Enslaved - Judith Hill   889

Rhys ap Griffith (Royalty)
The Eagle's Song - Marylyle Rogers   1693

Richard (Nobleman)
The Absentee Earl - Clarice Peters   1518

Richard of Kent (Nobleman)
Where Love Dwells - Elizabeth Stuart   1895

Richard of Kingsclere (Knight)
Emerald Fire - Laurie Grant   745

Richards, Georgette (Socialite; Heiress)
Scarlet Scandals - Carol Budd   249

Richards, Kimberly (Heiress)
Love Me Forever - Johanna Lindsey   1203

Richards, Matt (Religious)
Irresistible - Catherine Hart   820

Richards, Quint (Lawyer)
Rainbow's End - Kay Wilding   2031

Richmond, Oriel (Heiress)
Lady Defiant - Suzanne Robinson   1681

Richmond, Windsor (Healer; Martial Arts Expert)
Dragon Fire - Linda Ladd   1124

Rider, Jim (Rancher; Drifter)
Mountain Ecstasy - Linda Sandifer   1718

Rider, Will (Landlord)
Where the Heart Is - Robin Lee Hatcher   833

Ridgely, Alessandra (Noblewoman)
A Worthy Engagement - Eileen Winwood   2054

Ridley, Charles (Nobleman)
A Brilliant Alliance - Elizabeth Jackson   961

Riley, A.L. (Store Owner)
Into the Darkness - Barbara Michaels   1358

Ringling, Doug (Filmmaker)
More than You Dreamed - Kathleen Gilles Seidel   1767

Riordan, Annabel (Saloon Keeper/Owner)
Into the Storm - Maura Seger   1760

Riordan, Jenna (Southern Belle)
All My Heart Can Hold - Jessica Douglass   559

Riordan, Tony (Military Personnel)
A Soldier's Heart - Kathleen Korbel   1096

Rios, Sabella (Heiress; Rancher)
Because You're Mine - Nan Ryan   1703

Ritter, Beatrice (Spouse; Orphan)
In the Shadow of the Mountains - Rosanne Bittner   156

Rivers, Diane (Teacher)
Forever After - Bette Ford   657

Rivers, Josh (Guide)
Oregon Bride - Rosanne Bittner   158

Rivers, Sash (Fisherman)
Slow Dance - Donna Julian   1031

Rivers, Silena (Young Woman)
Silena - Terri Herrington   877

Riverton, Serena (Widow(er); Noblewoman)
Forbidden - Jo Beverley   135

Rivington, Maryann (Noblewoman; Debutante)
Lady Maryann's Dilemma - Karla Hocker   903

Roark, Pagan (Saloon Keeper/Owner)
Western Enchantress - Wendy Garrett   697

Roarke (Businessman)
Naked in Death - J.D. Robb   1656

Roarke, Gannon (Businessman)
Sweet Deception - Vanessa Hale   783

Robards, Carolyn (Divorced Person; Counselor)
A Christmas Love - Kathleen Creighton   416

Robards, Megan Thomas (Doctor)
Visions of Tomorrow - Katherine Sinclair   1809

Robbins, Cleopatra (Innkeeper)
Grand Passion - Jayne Ann Krentz   1109

Robbins, Jenny (Child-Care Giver)
As Sweet as Candy - Linda Varner   1973

Robbins, Jesse (Gunfighter)
A Fire in the Blood - Shirl Henke   861

Robbins, Monique (Businesswoman)
Breathless - Margie Walker   1988

Robelard, Drew (Military Personnel)
Sunburst - Suzanne Ellison   610

Robert (Nobleman)
A Proper Companion - Candice Hern   875

Robert (Nobleman; Widow(er))
The Waltzing Widow - Gayle Buck   248

Roberts, Amanda (Journalist)
Body and Soul - Sherryl Woods   2065
Hide and Seek - Sherryl Woods   2066
Stolen Moments - Sherryl Woods   2069

Roberts, Blade (Military Personnel; Indian)
Cherish the Dream - Kathleen Harrington   815

Roberts, David "Robbie" (Pirate)
Buccaneer's Bride - Jean Innes   958

Roberts, Lauren (Model)
American Star - Jackie Collins   377

Robinson, Elizabeth "Lizzie" (Gentlewoman)
Heaven Knows - Elaine Coffman   371

Rodene, Gavin (Doctor)
Dark Cries of Gray Oaks - Lee Karr   1043

Rogan, Serena "Brave Heart" (Abuse Victim; Activist)
Brave Heart - Lindsay McKenna   1315

Rogue, T.J. (Gunfighter)
Kiss of the Night Wind - Janelle Taylor   1916

Rolf de Valmont (Nobleman)
Tender Warrior - Linda Lang Bartell   93

Rolf of Dragonwyck (Nobleman)
The Quest - Juliana Garnett   692

Rolfe (Nobleman; Government Official)
Tender the Storm - Elizabeth Thornton   1944

Rolfe, Mike (Lawyer; Hotel Owner)
Flight to Yesterday - Velda Johnston   1010

Romanov, Juliana (Royalty; Gypsy)
Circle in the Water - Susan Wiggs   2023

Romney, Valerian (Crime Suspect)
Shadow Dance - Anne Stuart   1890

Roper, Jake (Cowboy)
A Lady of the West - Linda Howard   934

Rordan, Geoffrey (Nobleman; Hunter)
Flames of Love - Colleen Faulkner   624

Rosalynde (Noblewoman)
The Rose of Blacksword - Rexanne Becnel   113

Rose, Margaret (Healer)
A Deeper Magic - Jillian Hunter   953

Rose, Regina (Activist; Innkeeper)
My Wild Rose - Deborah Camp   297

Rose of Carlyle (Noblewoman)
Rose Among Thorns - Catherine Archer   27

Rosencrantz "Rosie" (Actress; Heiress—Lost)
The Greatest Lover in All England - Christina Dodd   536

Rosenstein, Billie (Businesswoman; Lesbian)
Keep to Me, Stranger - Sarah Aldridge   6

Rosewynn, Briana (Noblewoman)
A Lady in Disguise - Mellyora Ashley   32

Roshelle Marie of Reales (Noblewoman)
Awaken My Fire - Jennifer Horsman   926

Rosie (Saloon Keeper/Owner)
More Precious than Gold - Elaine Barbieri   72

Ross, Amanda Mary "Maria" (Rancher; Orphan)
Comanche Moon - Anita Mills   1391

Ross, Garland (Store Owner)
Shadow Whispers - Wendy Haley   785

Ross, Georgiana (Handicapped)
The Wings of the Morning - Thomas Tryon   1962

Ross, Lucas (Nobleman; Mountain Man)
Prince Charming - Julie Garwood   704

Rossi, Caitlin (Amnesiac)
Kiss of the Shadow Man - Maggie Shayne   1778

Rossi, Dylan (Architect)
Kiss of the Shadow Man - Maggie Shayne   1778

Rossignole, Anthea (Businesswoman; Lesbian)
Car Pool - Karin Kallmaker   1034

Rossiter, Judith (Widow(er))
The Christmas Angel - Jo Beverley   132

Rossiter, Morgan (Lawman)
Sweet Justice - Jan McKee   1312

Rossmara, Arran (Widow(er); Nobleman)
Fascination - Stella Cameron   286

Roswell, Rebecca (Businesswoman; Widow(er))
Over the Moon - Betty Cothran   401

Roth, Colby (Military Personnel)
Rebel's Captive - Amy Christopher   356

Rouillard, Gray (Businessman)
After the Night - Linda Howard   931

Rourke, Diana (Psychic; Heiress)
Allegheny Ecstasy - Caroline Bourne   190

Rourke, Duncan (Pirate; Patriot)
Pirates - Linda Lael Miller   1384

Rowe, Diana (Heiress)
For the Children - Elizabeth Krueger   1118

Rowe, Garrick (Frontiersman)
Nightrose - Dorothy Garlock   688

Rowena (Noblewoman)
Shadows and Lace - Teresa Medeiros   1342

Rowena of Benfield (Religious)
Winter's Heat - Denise Domning   548

Rowley, Marion (Nurse; Widow(er))
Sweet Illusion - Angela Carson   325

Royce (Nobleman)
The Prize - Julie Garwood   705

Royland, Clare (Landowner; Psychic)
Kingdom of Shadows - Barbara Erskine   614

Royland, Paul (Spouse)
Kingdom of Shadows - Barbara Erskine   614

Rozlynd (Healer; Sorceress)
Awakenings - Saranne Dawson   483

Ruadrik "Ruck" of Wolfscar (Nobleman; Knight)
For My Lady's Heart - Laura Kinsale   1078

Rubinoff, Theresa "Tess" (Royalty)
The Golden Barbarian - Iris Johansen   990

Rugger, Caressa (Widow(er); Noblewoman)
Caressa - Linda Lang Bartell   92

Ruiford, Alex (Nobleman; Widow(er))
Then Came You - Lisa Kleypas   1090

Rupert of Grantley, Marquess (Nobleman)
The Dreadful Debutante - Marion Chesney   348

Rurik (Nobleman; Warrior)
The Pagan's Prize - Miriam Minger   1399

Rurik (Nobleman)
The Valiant Heart - Anita Gordon   733

Rush, Sandy (Saleswoman)
Memory's Lamp - Marilyn Tracy   1954

Rushcliffe, Peter (Nobleman)
Lady Barbara's Dilemma - Marjorie Farrell   623

Russel, Alex (Businessman; Advertising)
Mrs. Perfect - Peggy Roberts   1670

Russell, Barrett (Villain)
A Promise Made - Catherine Lanigan   1161

Russell, Grace (Con Artist; Imposter)
Crooked Hearts - Patricia Gaffney   676

Russell, Harmony (Gentlewoman)
Tempt Me with Kisses - Phoebe Conn   387

Russell, Sienna (Fugitive)
The Passion Ruby - Eboni Snoe   1848

Rutherford, David (Nobleman; Sports Figure)
Miss Gabriel's Gambit - Rita Boucher   187

Rutherford, Norah (Widow(er); Artist)
Fire at Midnight - Barbara Dawson Smith   1829

Ruthland, Damon (Gentleman; Guardian)
Forever My Love - Constance O'Banyon   1448

Rutledge, Justin (Nobleman)
Best-Laid Plans - Vanessa Gray   752

Rutledge, Tate (Political Figure)
Mirror Image - Sandra Brown   229

Rutledge, Zane Grey (Adventurer; Time Traveller)
Somewhere in Time - Barbara Bretton   216

Ryan, Christopher "The Dandy" (Pirate)
Devil's Deception - Suzannah Davis   480

Ryan, Kayley (Rancher)
Sweet Obsession - Kathy Jones   1014

Rycliffe, Anthony "Tody" (Nobleman; Bastard Son)
The Greatest Lover in All England - Christina Dodd   536

Rycroft, Tyrone (Military Personnel)
Forever in Your Embrace - Kathleen E. Woodiwiss   2061

Ryder, Ben (Veterinarian)
As Sweet as Candy - Linda Varner   1973

Ryder, Jared (Nobleman; Imposter)
Deception - Amanda Quick   1567

Ryder, Samantha "Sam" (Young Woman; Artisan)
Silk and Stone - Deborah Smith   1842

Sayers, Reid (Hero)
Shameless - Jennifer Blake   173

Saylah "Tanu" (Shaman; Servant)
Sing to Me of Dreams - Kathryn Lynn Davis   477

Scaggs, Scarlet O'Hara (Runaway)
Moonlight and Mistletoe - Maggie Daniels   462

Scanlon, Cecelia (Young Woman)
Love Evergreen - Jenny Aiken   5

Scarborough, Emily (Ward; Debutante)
Once an Angel - Teresa Medeiros   1341

Scarborough, Sara (Scientist; Captive)
Sara's Surprise - Deborah Smith   1841

Schaeffer, Maggie (Investigator; Indian)
Sleeping with the Enemy - Laurie Paige   1477

Scott, Brianna (Feminist; Roommate)
King's Ransom - Diana Palmer   1489

Scott, Buck (Mountain Man; Trapper)
Come Spring - Jill Marie Landis   1143

Scott, Charity (Singer)
Gambler's Tempting Kisses - Charlotte Hubbard   944

Scott, Christopher (Fortune Hunter)
Unveiled - Colleen Quinn   1579

Scott, Jordan (Indian; Frontiersman)
Visions of the Heart - Emily Carmichael   317

Scott, Lincoln "Linc" (Gunfighter)
Wild Texas Promise - Victoria Thompson   1936

Scott, Vincent (Military Personnel)
Wilderness Flame - Barbara Cummings   448

Seanessy, Sean (Sea Captain)
Virgin Star - Jennifer Horsman   928

Sears, Robert (Privateer; Sea Captain)
Blazing Passion - Barbara Cummings   445

Seaton, Edward (Nobleman)
A Natural Attachment - Katherine Kingsley   1070

Seaton, Meredith (Southern Belle; Heiress)
Rainbow - Patricia Potter   1543

Sedgwick, Eve Marie (Widow(er); Castaway)
Swept Away - Julie Tetel   1925

Sedgwick, Galen (Nobleman)
The Last Lord - Melinda Pryce   1557

Selby, Melissa (Runaway)
A Gentleman's Desire - Mary Kingsley   1072

Selena "Agnes" (Amnesiac; Handicapped)
Waiting for the Moon - Kristin Hannah   800

Sellington, Amanda "Amy Smith" (Fugitive)
Home Fires - Susan Kay Law   1164

Selwyn, Crystal (Auditor)
Awakening Dreams - Vanessa Grant   746

Seneca (Royalty)
Midnight and Magnolias - Rebecca Paisley   1482

Serre, Adam (Nobleman; Indian)
Pure Sin - Susan Johnson   1002

Seton, Garrick (Nobleman; Architect)
Lady Rogue - Kathryn Kramer   1106

Seton, Jessica (Gentlewoman; Heiress)
Poetic Justice - Alicia Rasley   1596

Sevaric, Gwendolyn (Spinster; Noblewoman)
Gwen's Christmas Ghost - Lynn Kerstan   1059

Severin, Daniel (Mercenary)
The Raven and the Rose - Susan Wiggs   2027

Severn (Nobleman; Rake)
Fleeting Fancy - Rosemary Edghill   591

Severson, Eric (Businessman; Sailor)
Bittersweet - LaVyrle Spencer   1857

Seymour, Maxim (Nobleman; Fugitive)
So Worthy My Love - Kathleen E. Woodiwiss   2062

Seymour, Nick (Landowner)
Sweet Bargain - Kate Moore   1407

Seymour, Nikki (Young Woman)
After Midnight - Susan Kyle   1120

Shadow Hawk (Shaman; Indian)
The Spirit Path - Madeline Baker   47

Shaffer, Zach (Doctor)
At Risk - Jeanne Stephens   1875

Shahan, Meg (Spouse)
Wild Tory Rose - Linda Covington   413

Shalyn (Amnesiac)
Virgin Star - Jennifer Horsman   928

Shannon, Beau (Rancher)
An Angel in My Arms - Victoria Morrow   1421

Shannon, Laura Lee (Southern Belle)
Golden Bird - Jo Ann Algermissen   9

Shapiro, Ben (Public Relations)
Guardian Angel - Patricia Wilson   2047

Sharpe, Jordan (Military Personnel)
The Jade Garden - Laurel Collins   378

Sharpe, Mattie (Art Dealer)
Silver Linings - Jayne Ann Krentz   1111

Shaw, Hannah Whitby (Spouse)
The Vow - Lindsay Chase   337

Shaw, Isabel (Young Woman)
Sweet Bargain - Kate Moore   1407

Shaw, Reiver (Businessman)
The Vow - Lindsay Chase   337

Shaw, Samuel (Artist)
The Vow - Lindsay Chase   337

Sheffield, Amanda (Gentlewoman; Fiance(e))
Wind Rose - Krista Janssen   977

Sheffield, Braden (Nobleman)
Dream Castle - Andrea Kane   1037

Shelby, Jessica (Scientist)
The Heart Remembers - Lenore Carroll   319

Shelby, Trevor (Landowner; Military Personnel)
Tarnished Hearts - Raine Cantrell   311

Sheldon, Elizabeth (Spinster)
Harvest Song - Karen Lockwood   1222

Sheldon, Sabrina (Businesswoman)
A Loving Spirit - Annette Broadrick   220

Shelton, Nicole Bragg (Heiress; Noblewoman)
Scandalous Love - Brenda Joyce   1029

Shelton, Regina (Amnesiac; Noblewoman)
Secrets - Brenda Joyce   1030

Shepard, Cole (Pilot)
Pink Topaz - Jennifer Greene   755

Shepherd, Meg (Public Relations)
In Your Dreams - Lynn Bulock   250

Sherbrooke, Douglas (Nobleman; Bridegroom)
The Sherbrooke Bride - Catherine Coulter   409

Sherbrooke, Sinjin (Heiress)
The Heiress Bride - Catherine Coulter   404

Sheridan, Danielle (Saloon Hostess)
Phantom Lover - Millie Criswell   428

Sheridan, Deke (Hunter; Frontiersman)
Cheyenne Amber - Catherine Anderson   16

Sheridan, Philip (Lawyer)
Secret in the Shadows - Marina Malcolm   1265

Sheridan, Serena (Psychologist)
Lucky's Lady - Tami Hoag   899

Sheridan, Trevor (Financier)
Lions and Lace - Meagan McKinney   1324

Sherwin, Saranda (Con Artist; Socialite)
Princess of Thieves - Katherine O'Neal   1461

Sherwood, Addie (Teacher)
Where the Heart Is - Robin Lee Hatcher   833

Sherwood, Charissa (Noblewoman; Heiress)
Allegheny Captive - Caroline Bourne   189

Sherwood, Clover (Gentlewoman)
Kentucky Bride - Hannah Howell   938

Sherwood, Pandora (Psychic; Reincarnated Person)
Forever, for Love - Becky Lee Weyrich   2007

Shirley (Angel)
A Season of Angels - Debbie Macomber   1254
Touched by Angels - Debbie Macomber   1256
The Trouble with Angels - Debbie Macomber   1257

Shreve, Allison (Model; Vacationer)
Trust Me - Jeane Renick   1610

Silver, Jake (Rancher)
Rebel in Silk - Sandra Chastain   343

Silver Dawn (Captive; Indian)
Comanche Love Song - Cheryl Black   165

Silver Wolf, Bruce Marshal (Indian; Government Official)
Dream Warrior - Bobbi Smith   1836

Silverbrake, Dax (Pirate)
The Sky Pirate - Justine Davis   474

Simmons, Alison (Businesswoman; Guardian)
A Garland of Love - Alice Sharpe   1771

Simmons, Susannah (Businesswoman)
Rainy Day Kisses - Debbie Macomber   1253

Simms, India (Suffragette)
Waltz with the Lady - Betina Lindsey   1195

Simon, Katherine (Rancher)
For All the Right Reasons - Elaine Coffman   370

Simon the Loyal (Nobleman; Warrior)
Enchanted - Elizabeth Lowell   1229

Simonov, Natasha (Orphan; Ward)
A Time for Roses - Elaine Coffman   373

Simpson, Gary (Architect; Landowner)
The Night Prowlers - Karen G. McCullough   1304

Simpson, Loretta (Handicapped)
Comanche Moon - Catherine Anderson   18

Sinclair, Alec (Nobleman; Rake)
The Dream - Kit Gardner   683

Sinclair, Alexander "Alex" (Nobleman)
Highland Flame - Catherine Linden   1190

Sinclair, Brazo (Drifter)
Capture the Night - Geralyn Dawson   482

Sinclair, Catherine "Cat" (Noblewoman)
Promise Me Heaven - Connie Brockway   221

Sinclair, Clover (Animal Lover)
Midnight Ecstasy - Rita Balkey   51

Star (Captive)
Broken Promise - Theresa Scott 1755

Stark, Sam (Businessman; Computer Expert)
Trust Me - Jayne Ann Krentz 1113

Stark, Valentine "Val" (Rancher)
Stark Lightning - Elaine Rome 1697

Starkeeper (Captive)
Written in the Stars - Nan Ryan 1708

Staulet, Noel (Heir)
Love and Smoke - Jennifer Blake 172

Staulet, Riva (Socialite; Widow(er))
Love and Smoke - Jennifer Blake 172

Staynes, William (Nobleman; Bridegroom)
A Special License - Kathleen Elliott 604

Stearn, Maggie (Widow(er); Innkeeper)
Bittersweet - LaVyrle Spencer 1857

Stearns, Justin (Gentleman; Plantation Owner)
Surrender My Heart - Lois Greiman 770

Steed, Landon (Heir)
Elusive Caress - Rosalyn Alsobrook 10

Steel, Drake (Businessman)
Beyond the Savage Sea - JoAnn Wendt 2000

Steele, Alex (Military Personnel)
Once a Rebel - Micki Brown 226

Steele, Caroline (Plantation Owner)
Fortune's Bride - Judith E. French 666

Steele, Jackson Ledgeway (Detective; Cowboy)
Seasons of Gold - Stef Ann Holm 914

Steele, Jake (Outlaw; Bridegroom)
Mail Order Outlaw - Millie Criswell 427

Steele, Rachel (Widow(er))
Tender Victory - Susan Macias 1245

Stephanson, Laura (Orphan)
Veils of Silk - Mary Jo Putney 1565

Stephen (Nobleman; Historical Figure)
The Fatal Crown - Ellen Jones 1013

Stephens, Rebecca (Widow(er))
Country Kiss - Sharon Harlow 805

Sterling, Amanda (Noblewoman; Spy)
Love Not a Rebel - Heather Graham 738

Sterling, Erin (Activist)
Midnight Rose - Patricia Hagan 780

Sterling, Luke (Gunfighter)
Tempest - Catherine Hart 822

Sterling, Will (Settler)
A Durable Fire - Virginia Bernhard 129

Stern, Adam (Indian; Detective)
Love's Sweet Bounty - Colleen Faulkner 625

Stevens, Carla (Religious; Activist)
Blessings of the Heart - Jane McBride Choate 352

Stewart, Annabella (Noblewoman)
Somewhere Along the Way - Elaine Coffman 372

Stewart, Annie (Waiter/Waitress; Vacationer)
Wish upon a Star - Karen Morrell 1420

Stewart, Bethany Rose (Mountain Woman)
Dream Catcher - Thomasina Ring 1644

Stewart, January (Lawyer)
Temptation From the Past - Cindy Gerard 720

Stewart, Moonfeather "Leah" (Indian; Noblewoman)
Moonfeather - Judith E. French 670

Stewart, Rose (Immigrant; Worker)
Kathleen O'Donald - Penny Hayes 839

Stewart, Ruarke (Gambler)
Angel Hunter - Ana Leigh 1175

Stewart, Savannah (Artist; Spy)
Rebel Wildfire - Barbara Cummings 447

Stewart, Tavis (Nobleman)
The Spitfire - Bertrice Small 1825

Stillman, Todd (Doctor)
The Stillman Curse - Peggy Morse 1424

Stoane, Audrey (Servant; Businesswoman)
Elusive Caress - Rosalyn Alsobrook 10

Stockdale, Lila "Cat" (Socialite)
Blue Mountain Magic - Garda Parker 1498

Stockwell, Amy (Heiress; Businesswoman)
The Panther and the Rose - Mary Burkhardt 257

Stokehurst, Luke (Nobleman)
Midnight Angel - Lisa Kleypas 1087

Stone, Adam (Economist)
Sing Carols with the Angels - Mary Leask 1171

Stone, Andrew "Drew" (Rancher)
The Yankee - Kristin James 972

Stone, Bowie (Military Personnel; Convict)
The Wives of Bowie Stone - Maggie Osborne 1469

Stone, Ethan (Imposter; Thief)
Wild Sweet Ecstasy - Jo Goodman 731

Stone, Genny (Gentlewoman)
Storm Dancers - Allison Hayes 838

Stone, Griffin (Nobleman)
To Catch the Flame - Kimberly Cates 332

Stone, Jessamine (Young Woman)
Kissed - Tanya Anne Crosby 432

Stone, Jonathan (Gentleman)
Chase the Dawn - Kay McMahon 1327

Stone, Lawton (Lawman)
Promise Me Moonlight - Carol Finch 646

Stone, Mad Dog (Drifter; Handyman)
If You Believe - Kristin Hannah 798

Stone, Susan (Teacher; Spouse)
The Wives of Bowie Stone - Maggie Osborne 1469

Stone, Theadora (Historian)
June Love - Karla Hocker 902

Stone, Travis (Adoptee)
What Child Is This? - Rebecca York 2078

Storm, Annika (Captive; Young Woman)
Come Spring - Jill Marie Landis 1143

Storm, Daniella (Frontierswoman)
Kiley's Storm - Suzanne Elizabeth 599

Storm, Kase (Lawman; Indian)
Rose - Jill Marie Landis 1147

Storr (Scout)
Viking Rose - Ashland Price 1554

Stourbridge, Trixy (Governess)
The Somerville Farce - Michelle Kasey 1046

Stover, Carrie Sue (Runaway; Teacher)
Kiss of the Night Wind - Janelle Taylor 1916

Stowe, Deirdre (Noblewoman; Artist)
Deirdre and Don Juan - Jo Beverley 134

Strachan, Leigh (Noblewoman; Orphan)
The Prince of Midnight - Laura Kinsale 1079

Straffen, Meredith "Merrie" (Heiress; Noblewoman)
Caught in the Act - Betina M. Krahn 1098

Stratton, Jared (Rancher)
The Doubletree - Victoria Pade 1476

Streeter, Judd (Foreman)
The Passions of Chelsea Kane - Barbara Delinsky 501

Stryker, Blade "Swift Blade" (Scout; Indian)
Beyond the Horizon - Connie Mason 1287

Stryker, Caleb (Bounty Hunter; Guardian)
Cheyenne Surrender - Madeline Baker 40

Stryker, Grady "Thunder" (Widow(er); Indian)
A Promise of Thunder - Connie Mason 1290

Stuart, Cassandra (Matchmaker; Frontierswoman)
Angel - Johanna Lindsey 1199

Stuart, Elizabeth (Journalist; Divorced Person)
Still Waters - Tami Hoag 900

Stuart, Grant (Rancher)
A Man of Few Words - Thelma Zirkelbach 2082

Stuart, Ian (Architect)
Star-Crossed Lovers - Kay Hooper 924

Stuart, Jonathan (Spirit; Gentleman)
Shadow's Kiss - Joan Hohl 908

Styer, Frisco (Accountant)
Compromises - Joan Hohl 906

Sullivan, Amy (Rancher)
Sun God - Nan Ryan 1707

Sullivan, Breanna (Young Woman; Activist)
Scoundrel's Desire - JoAnn De Lazzari 489

Sullivan, China (Young Woman)
A Light for My Love - Alexis Harrington 814

Sullivan, Dru (Rancher)
Montana Mistress - Carol Finch 644

Sullivan, Frederick (Rake)
Dancing with Clara - Mary Balogh 57

Sullivan, Leanne (Dancer; Time Traveller)
Love's Timeless Dance - Vivian Knight-Jenkins 1093

Sullivan, Mae Belle (Heiress; Volunteer)
What the Lady Wants - Jennifer Crusie 442

Sullivan, Ward (Handicapped; Pilot)
Broken Wings - Doreen Roberts 1659

Summer (Young Woman)
Dark Renegade - Theresa Scott 1756

Summerfield, Gloria "Glory" (Southern Belle)
The Captain's Bride - Kat Martin 1273

Summerfield, Libby (Widow(er))
Rawhide and Lace - Margaret Brownley 238

Summerfield, Zachariah (Museum Curator; Adventurer)
Eden's Angel - Katherine Compton 379

Summers, Jon (Teenager; Psychic)
Wishes - Lisa Jackson 963

Summers, Julia (Writer)
Genuine Lies - Nora Roberts 1667

Thomas, Solomon (Businessman)
Breathless - Margie Walker   1988

Thomas, Toby (Widow(er))
Love and Other Surprises - Kathleen Creighton   417

Thompson, Barry (Lawman)
Colorado Moonfire - Charlotte Hubbard   943

Thompson, Maria (Nurse)
Prescription for Love - Anne Ladley   1130

Thompson, Max (Lawyer)
The Runaway Heart - Anne Ladley   1131

Thompson, Sharon (Single Parent; Artist)
Seasons - Lisa Gregory   766

Thompson, Travis (Rancher; Guardian)
Morning Comes Softly - Debbie Macomber   1252

Thork (Warrior)
The Reluctant Viking - Sandra Hill   891

Thorn, Katherine (Rancher)
Snow Angel - Susan Amarillas   14

Thorne, Becket (Military Personnel)
Surrender in Scarlet - Patricia Camden   278

Thorne, Byron (Steward)
Strange Encounter - Sally Wentworth   2002

Thorne, Godfrey (Thief)
Stolen Fire - Danette Chartier   335

Thorne, Grayson (Writer)
Born in Ice - Nora Roberts   1664

Thorne, Lucien (Pirate)
Beloved Avenger - Joan Van Nuys   1970

Thorne, Regan (Appraiser)
Pink Topaz - Jennifer Greene   755

Thornleigh, Isabel (Gentlewoman; Revolutionary)
A Dangerous Devotion - Barbara Kyle   1119

Thornquist, Letitia "Letty" (Librarian; Businesswoman)
Perfect Partners - Jayne Ann Krentz   1110

Thornton, Adam (Manager; Servant)
Defiant Imposter - Miriam Minger   1398

Thornton, Cassandra (Photographer)
The Golden Mountain - Annalise Sun   1897

Thornton, Elizabeth (Highwayman; Prisoner)
Midnight Raider - Shelly Thacker   1928

Thornton, Ian (Nobleman)
Almost Heaven - Judith McNaught   1329

Thornton, Matilda (Mail Order Bride)
Prairie Heat - Madeline Baker   46

Thornton, Phillip (Nobleman)
A Maddening Minx - Mary Kingsley   1073

Thornton, Robert (Businessman)
Baby Makes Five - Lacey Dancer   457

Thornton, Sunny (Young Woman)
Wild Texas Flame - Janis Reams Hudson   950

Thornton, Sybilla (Young Woman)
Pirate's Kiss - Diana Haviland   834

Thorpe, Phoebe (Gentlewoman; Governess)
The Contrary Corinthian - Emily Hendrickson   850

Thorsson, Wulf (Nobleman; Military Personnel)
Unwilling Betrayer - Joan Van Nuys   1972

Thorverton, Demetrius (Nobleman)
The Black Widow - Charlotte Louise Dolan   542

Throckmorton, Mariah (Spinster; Farmer)
If You Believe - Kristin Hannah   798

Thunder, Colt (Guide; Indian)
Savage Thunder - Johanna Lindsey   1208

Tiernan, Jacy (Teacher)
The Legacy - Linda Lael Miller   1381

Tiger, Nicolas (Privateer; Sea Captain)
Always and Forever - Gina Robins   1671

Timms, Maddy (Young Woman; Care Giver)
Flowers From the Storm - Laura Kinsale   1077

Tod (Boyfriend)
Heartbeat - Norma Fox Mazer   1298

Todd, Amanda (Publisher)
Escapade - Susan Kyle   1121

Todd, Christie (Student—High School)
Going Hollywood - Marion Schultz   1736

Todd, Rachel (Gentlewoman)
Jade Dawn - Susannah Leigh   1181

Tor (Warrior)
Keepers of the Misty Time - Patricia Rowe   1700

Torington, Robert (Nobleman; Rake)
Heart of Fancy - Claudette Williams   2035

Torres, Aaron (Military Personnel)
Paradise and More - Shirl Henke   865

Torres, Benjamin (Doctor)
Return to Paradise - Shirl Henke   866

Torrington, Victoria Elizabeth (Rancher)
Victoria's Ecstasy - Gwen Cleary   367

Toulon, Miriam (Doctor)
Return to Paradise - Shirl Henke   866

Towbridge, Sarah (Heiress; Gentlewoman)
The Illusion of Love - Kasey Michaels   1366

Towers, Kathryn (Gentlewoman)
The Bishop's Daughter - Susan Carroll   321

Townsend, Bell (Rake)
Falling Stars - Anita Mills   1392

Townsend, Emily (Companion; Noblewoman)
A Proper Companion - Candice Hern   875

Townsend, Garner (Military Personnel)
Love's Brazen Fire - Betina M. Krahn   1100

Townsend, Hope (Hotel Owner)
Dragonfire - Patricia Potter   1538

Townsend, Nate (Neighbor)
Rainy Day Kisses - Debbie Macomber   1253

Townsend, Reed (Contractor; Philanthropist)
Jade's Passion - Laura Taylor   1920

Townsend, Sarah (Housekeeper)
Bewitching Kisses - Rainy Kirkland   1083

Townsend, Sloan (Chieftain)
Captive of Desire - Ruth Langan   1151

Townsend, Victoria (Noblewoman)
Shadowed Vows - Sue Rich   1626

Traeth of Rhune (Warrior; Nobleman)
Swan Star - Betina Lindsey   1193

Traherne, Anna (Plantation Owner; Widow(er))
Green Eyes - Karen Robards   1649

Traherne, Joanna (Gentlewoman)
Visions of Tomorrow - Katherine Sinclair   1809

Traherne, Simon (Nobleman)
Scandal - Amanda Quick   1574

Trask, Morgan (Sea Captain)
Savannah Heat - Kat Martin   1278

Travis, Jim (Rancher; Widow(er))
Desert Angel - Pamela K. Forrest   660

Travis, John (Actor)
Aspen Gold - Janet Dailey   453

Travis, Rae "Rachel" (Engineer)
Terror by Design - Jane Edwards   598

Trayhern, Tristan "Tray" (Handicapped; Nobleman)
Lord of Shadowhawk - Lindsay McKenna   1317

Traynor, Clay (Police Officer; Farmer)
A Christmas Love - Kathleen Creighton   416

Tredair, Earl of (Nobleman)
The First Rebellion - Marion Chesney   349

Tredman, Harry (Nobleman)
A Handful of Dreams - Barbara Hazard   841

Trefarron, Payne (Twin)
The Bridegroom - Carol Jerina   987

Trefarron, Prescott (Twin; Fiance(e))
The Bridegroom - Carol Jerina   987

Tregaran, John (Young Man; Wealthy)
The Legacy of Tregaran - Mary Lide   1186

Tregarn, Alice (Young Woman)
The Legacy of Tregaran - Mary Lide   1186

Tregaron, Celia (Widow(er); Heiress)
Lady Vengeance - Sarah Eagle   585

Trehearne, Lily (Servant; Runaway)
Lily - Patricia Gaffney   677

Trelawny, McCady (Nobleman; Rake)
Once in a Blue Moon - Penelope Williamson   2038

Tremain, Brandon (Prisoner; Imposter)
Once a Hero - Katherine Sutcliffe   1905

Tremain, Lucien (Military Personnel)
Legacy of the Rose - Kasey Michaels   1367

Tremaine, Bryce (Sea Captain)
A Promise of Fire - Veronica Sattler   1721

Tremaine, Lily (Governess)
Night Shadow - Catherine Coulter   406

Tremaine, Lucien (Nobleman)
A Worthy Engagement - Eileen Winwood   2054

Tremayne, Aidan (Vampire; Artist)
Forever and the Night - Linda Lael Miller   1380

Tremayne, Ian (Hero)
Forbidden Fire - Heather Graham Pozzessere   1550

Tremayne, Jareth (Gambler; Nobleman)
Romantic Masquerade - Lois Stewart   1878

Tremayne, Kelsey (Plantation Owner)
Freedom Angel - Robin LeAnne Wiete   2021

Tremayne, Luke (Journalist)
A Song in the Wilderness - Lee Stafford   1868

Tremayne, Saber (Nobleman)
Diamonds and Dreams - Rebecca Paisley   1480

Trent, Ethan (Patriot)
Eden's Gate - Karen Harper   810

Trent, Jessica (Spinster)
Lord of Scoundrels - Loretta Chase   340

Trent, William (Military Personnel; Guardian)
Christmas Belles - Susan Carroll   322

Character Name Index

Volner, Currie (Sports Figure)
A Season to Remember - Lynda Stowe Landers   1141

Volsky, Alexei (Nobleman)
Falling Stars - Anita Mills   1392

Von Berg, Maximilian (Military Personnel; Spy)
Promises to Keep - Nina Beaumont   107

Von Hamel, Erica "Riki" (Heiress; Time Traveller)
Forever in Time - Janice Bennett   124

Vothers, Matt (Bridegroom)
The Vanishing Bridegroom - Alice Sharpe   1773

Voyager, Gallant (Space Explorer)
Stardust Dreams - Marilyn Campbell   302

W

Wade, Cameron (Military Personnel)
Ghost Dancer - Fela Dawson Scott   1754

Wade, Hartley (Nobleman)
Lord Carew's Bride - Mary Balogh   60

Wade, Katy (Businesswoman; Restauranteur)
Family Man - Jayne Ann Krentz   1107

Wade, Luke (Defendant)
White Lies and Alibis - Tracy Hughes   952

Wainwright, Desdemona (Caterer)
Trust Me - Jayne Ann Krentz   1113

Wainwright, Honor (Young Woman)
Emerald Angel - Susan Sackett   1709

Wainwright, Kallie (Imposter; Southern Belle)
Nightfire - Leona Karr   1044

Waite, Edmond (Nobleman; Rake)
The Notorious Rake - Mary Balogh   61

Wakefield, Alexander "Serad" (Nobleman; Pirate)
Capture My Heart - Bobbi Smith   1835

Wakefield, Danielle "Danni" (Gentlewoman)
Scandal's Darling - Anne Caldwell   275

Wakefield, Gideon (Heiress; Amnesiac)
Fool Me Once - Lori Copeland   391

Wakefield, Megan (Noblewoman; Thief)
Desire and Deceive - Cordia Byers   262

Walker, Ashlee (Recluse)
The Silver Witch - Sue Rich   1627

Walker, Blake (Rancher)
Stark Lightning - Elaine Rome   1697

Walker, Chance (Scientist; Adventurer)
Lover in the Rough - Elizabeth Lowell   1230

Walker, Eben (Blacksmith)
Playing with Fire - Victoria Thompson   1934

Walker, Freedom (Activist)
Stormswept - Katherine Kincaid   1068

Walker, Luke (Gunfighter; Foreman)
Cheyenne's Lady - Patricia Rice   1613

Walker, Remington (Detective—Private)
Liberty Blue - Robin Lee Hatcher   828

Walker, Susannah (Abuse Victim; Fugitive)
Dancing on Snowflakes - Jane Bonander   180

Wallace, Andrew (Spirit)
Reunited - Evelyn A. Crowe   441

Wallace, Neely (Assistant)
Forever and the Night - Linda Lael Miller   1380

Waller, Benton (Mechanic)
Sins of Summer - Dorothy Garlock   690

Walsh, Andrea (Parent; Spouse)
True Love - Diane E. Lock   1221

Walsh, Hunter (Outlaw; Spy)
Stolen Ecstasy - Hannah Howell   940

Walsh, Stuart (Spouse; Parent)
True Love - Diane E. Lock   1221

Walters, Samantha (Activist)
Caress - Rosanne Bittner   153

Waltham, Leonora (Noblewoman; Captive)
The Highlander - Ruth Langan   1156

Warby, Gerald (Nobleman)
The Desirable Duchess - Marion Chesney   347

Ward, Elizabeth (Noblewoman; Amnesiac)
Deceived - Mary Balogh   58

Ward, Jessica (Neighbor; Scientist)
The Legacy - Patricia Simpson   1803

Ward, Serena (Gentlewoman; Rebel)
Dangerous to Love - Elizabeth Thornton   1941

Wardieu, Rannulf (Warrior)
Warrior Bride - Tamara Leigh   1184

Ware, Chastity (Noblewoman; Highwayman)
My Lady Notorious - Jo Beverley   136

Ware, Grayson (Noblewoman; Actress)
Midnight Lace - Elizabeth Kary   1045

Warfield, Jessie (Gentlewoman; Child-Care Giver)
The Valentine Legacy - Catherine Coulter   410

Warfield, Justin (Nobleman; Rake)
A Heart So Innocent - Charlene Cross   438

Warfield, Max (Nobleman)
Mistress of Mischief - Susan Carroll   323

Warfield, Penn (Sea Captain)
The Warfield Bride - Bronwyn Williams   2034

Warne, Kate (Detective)
A Rose in the Shadows - Catherine Wyatt   2075

Warnecke, Luc (Relative)
Shameless - Suzanne Forster   664

Warner, Mary (Mail Order Bride; Librarian)
Morning Comes Softly - Debbie Macomber   1252

Warren, Glory (Young Woman; Witch)
Wild Glory - Andrea Parnell   1509

Warren, Jamie (Parent)
Marriage of Inconvenience - Debbie Macomber   1251

Warren, Margaret (Spinster)
Bodie Bride - Isabel Whitfield   2015

Warren, Rebecca Ann (Time Traveller; Nurse)
Passion's Timeless Hour - Vivian Knight-Jenkins   1094

Warrington, Graceanne (Widow(er); Noblewoman)
Father Christmas - Barbara Metzger   1352

Warrington, Leland (Nobleman)
Father Christmas - Barbara Metzger   1352

Warwick, Damien (Nobleman)
A Fire in the Heart - Katherine Sutcliffe   1902

Warwick, Miles Kemball (Mine Owner)
My Only Love - Katherine Sutcliffe   1904

Warwick, Robert (Nobleman)
Rosefire - Sandra Davidson   471

Washburn, Florence (Bride; Gentlewoman)
Married by Mistake - Melinda McRae   1337

Washington, Leona (Fiance(e); Outlaw)
Midnight Rose - Robin Lee Hatcher   830

Watson, Henry Lee (Bridegroom; Businessman)
Heaven Sent - Pamela Morsi   1427

Watson, Oliver (Advertising)
Daddy - Danielle Steel   1869

Waverly, Caroline (Musician)
Carnal Innocence - Nora Roberts   1665

Waverly, Chloe (Debutante; Ward)
Christmas Belles - Susan Carroll   322

Waverly, Fanny (Foundling)
The First Rebellion - Marion Chesney   349

Waverly, Frederica (Foundling)
Silken Bonds - Marion Chesney   350

Waverly, Victoria (Bride; Southern Belle)
A Lady of the West - Linda Howard   934

Waxton, Gavin (Landowner)
Sweet Deception - Colleen Faulkner   626

Waxton, Thomasina (Noblewoman; Actress)
Sweet Deception - Colleen Faulkner   626

Wayland, Janna (Mountain Woman)
Reckless Love - Elizabeth Lowell   1234

Weatherford, Lanie (Animal Lover)
Kiss of Bliss - Carolyn Monroe   1403

Weatherly, Jane (Friend; Suffragette)
A Distant Dawn - Katherine Sinclair   1806

Webb, Thaddeus (Detective—Private; Antiques Dealer)
Winter's Flame - Maria Greene   756

Webster, Laura Leigh (Heiress)
Whispered Kisses - Janelle Taylor   1919

Weiss, Aaron (Businessman)
Tattered Silk - Elaine Barbieri   75

Welland, Emily (Businesswoman)
California Man - Carole Dean   490

Wellesley, Eric (Farmer)
Mail-Order Temptress - Jane Kidder   1062

Wellesley, Geoffrey (Businessman)
Passion's Bargain - Jane Kidder   1063

Wellesley, Nathan (Lawman)
Passion's Gift - Jane Kidder   1064

Wellington, Cailie (Orphan)
A Deeper Hunger - Sabine Kells   1049

Wellington, Evelyn "E.A." (Businesswoman)
Rebel Dreams - Patricia Rice   1620

Wells, Cynthia Ann (Captive; Gentlewoman)
Sioux Splendor - Rosanne Bittner   161

Wells, David (Journalist)
Pretty Maids in a Row - Marilyn Campbell   301

Wells, Georgia (Widow(er); Seamstress)
No Greater Love - Katherine Kingsley   1071

Wells, Nicky (Television Personality)
Remember - Barbara Taylor Bradford   193

Wells, Shane (Police Officer)
Hold Back the Night - Sandra Steffen   1873

Wendon, Lucien (Nobleman)
The Spirited Bluestocking - Joan Overfield   1472

Willis, Tag (Saloon Keeper/Owner)
More Precious than Gold - Elaine Barbieri   72

Willoughby, Clarissa (Widow(er); Imposter)
Caprice - Laura Parker   1501

Willow (Teacher; Indian)
Song of the Warrior - Georgina Gentry   717

Wilmot, Jack (Sports Figure)
Passion's Fury - Rita Balkey   52

Wilson, Letitia (Frontierswoman)
Savage Promise - Cassie Edwards   593

Wilton, Emily (Gentlewoman)
The Much Maligned Lord - Barbara Reeves   1609

Wimberly, Rowanne (Debutante)
The Luck of the Devil - Barbara Metzger   1355

Winchester, Nash (Architect)
Garden of Fantasy - Karen Rose Smith   1847

Winchester, Sara (Noblewoman)
The Gift - Julie Garwood   702

Wind, Bethany (Government Official)
Chase the Wind - Janelle Taylor   1912

Windermere, Margaret "Daisy" (Widow(er);
Noblewoman)
The Inheritance - Joan Johnston   1005

Windrider (Chieftain; Indian)
Comanche Wind - Genell Dellin   508

Windsong (Indian; Widow(er))
Windsong - Kelly Ferjutz   638

Windsor, Aerial (Sports Figure)
Love's Windswept Embrace - Michalann Perry   1517

Windsor, Angela (Fugitive)
Beneath Passion's Skies - Bobbi Smith   1834

Windsor, Devlin (Landowner)
Love Across Time - Anne Meredith   1343

Windsor, Erin Shane (Mine Owner)
The Diamond Tiger - Ann Maxwell   1296

Windsor, Jessamyn (Southern Belle)
Once a Rebel - Micki Brown   226

Windsor, Nick (Prisoner)
Because of You - Micki Brown   225

Windsor, Sarah (Fugitive)
Beneath Passion's Skies - Bobbi Smith   1834

Winfield, Edwina (Child-Care Giver; Spinster)
No Greater Love - Danielle Steel   1870

Winfield, Nara (Heiress)
Traitor's Kiss - Jane Toombs   1953

Winford, Charles (Nobleman; Spy)
Queen of the May - Emily Hendrickson   855

Wingate, Cole (Prisoner)
Heartbreak Trail - Barbara Keller   1048

Wingate, Nerissa (Seamstress)
The Lady and the Rake - Carola Dunn   574

Wingfield, Olympia (Spinster)
Deception - Amanda Quick   1567

Wingrave, Emily (Gentlewoman)
The Dauntless Miss Wingrave - Amanda Scott   1746

Winslow, Andrea (Widow(er); Farmer)
Renegade's Kiss - Barbara Ankrum   24

Winslow, Barrett (Adventurer; Amnesiac)
The Ruby - Christina Skye   1821

Winslow, Glory (Young Woman)
Summer of the Soldiers - Sandra Chastain   345

Winslow, Jesse (Landowner; Farmer)
Renegade's Kiss - Barbara Ankrum   24

Winslow, Summer (Historian; Time Traveller)
A Love for All Time - Sandra Davidson   470

Winslowe, Ethan (Recluse; Wealthy)
Night of the Phantom - Anne Stuart   1888

Winstead, Kate (Noblewoman)
Falling Stars - Anita Mills   1392

Winston, Charlotte (Fiance(e); Gentlewoman)
Captain's Captive - Christine Dorsey   549

Winston, Dakota (Detective—Police)
Cowboy Cop - Rachel Lee   1172

Winston, Rosalind (Imposter; Gentlewoman)
Daring Illusion - Christina Cordaire   398

Winston, Rosalind (Debutante)
Lord Dearborn's Destiny - Brenda Hiatt   888

Winston, Royce (Journalist)
Kiss in the Dark - Meryl Sawyer   1730

Winter, Ardith (Noblewoman; Spinster)
The Last of the Winter Roses - Jeanne Savery   1726

Winter, Mason (Businessman)
A Marriage of Convenience - Georgia Bockoven   177

Winterhawke, John (Frontiersman)
The Bride Wore Spurs - Sharon Ihle   956

Winters, Hannah (Teacher; Rancher)
Boston Renegade - June Lund Shiplett   1785

Winters, Leah (Musician; Teacher)
Leah's Love Song - Susan E. Kirby   1082

Winters, Lorna (Young Woman)
Desert Bride - JoAnne Redd   1608

Winthrop, Adam (Shipowner; Castaway)
Swept Away - Julie Tetel   1925

Winthrop, Araminta (Journalist; Artist)
Desperado - Rebecca Brandewyne   200

Winthrop, Jack (Rancher)
Golden Bird - Jo Ann Algermissen   9

Winthrop, Knight (Nobleman; Rake)
Night Shadow - Catherine Coulter   406

Winthrop, Lauren (Art Dealer)
Midnight in Marrakesh - Meryl Sawyer   1731

Winthrop, Miranda (Heiress; Time Traveller)
The Door Ajar - Joan Overfield   1471

Winthrop, Paul (Writer)
Genuine Lies - Nora Roberts   1667

Witherton, Patience (Gentlewoman; Debutante)
Patience Is a Virtue - Judith Nelson   1435

Wochek, Ed (Widow(er); Businessman)
Loveknot - Marissa Carroll   320

Wolf (Slave)
Lord of the Storm - Justine Davis   473

Wolf, Indigo (Indian; Mine Owner)
Indigo Blue - Catherine Anderson   19

Wolf, Jack (Pilot)
Wolf and the Angel - Kathleen Creighton   419

Wolf, Jacob (Shipowner; Sea Captain)
Mississippi Mistress - Gina Robins   1675

Wolf, Michael (Indian; Time Traveller)
A Whisper on the Wind - Madeline Baker   49

Wolf, Nathan (Bounty Hunter)
Dancing on Snowflakes - Jane Bonander   180

Wolf Shadow (Shaman; Indian)
Moon Dancer - Judith E. French   669

Wolfe, Andrew (Doctor)
Walk in the Light - Charles Durham   577

Wolframson, Rorick (Explorer; Settler)
Gentle Warrior - Kathryn Hockett   904

Wolverton, Jim (Restauranteur)
Somewhere Near Paradise - Marjorie Everitt   616

Wolverton, Maxim (Nobleman)
A Merry Go-Round - Coral Hoyle   942

Wolverton, Pierce (Nobleman; Highwayman)
Midnight Raider - Shelly Thacker   1928

Wolveston, Alys (Noblewoman)
The Rose at Twilight - Amanda Scott   1748

Woodard, Frank (Zoo Keeper)
Warm Creature Comforts - Miriam Pace   1475

Woodbine, Rose (Heiress)
Bride of the Wind - Shannon Drake   563

Woodruff, Ivy (Gentlewoman)
Pirate's Angel - Marsha Bauer   99

Woodward, Kyle (Scientist)
The Night Orchid - Patricia Simpson   1804

Woolrich, Blythe (Businesswoman; Captive)
Passion's Ransom - Betina M. Krahn   1103

Worrall, Helena (Businesswoman; Lesbian)
Keep to Me, Stranger - Sarah Aldridge   6

Worth, Maddie "La Reina" (Singer)
Mountain Laurel - Jude Deveraux   516

Worth, Richard (Military Personnel)
Sweet Suspicions - Julie Tetel   1924

Worth, St. John (Nobleman)
The Last of the Winter Roses - Jeanne Savery   1726

Worth, Theodosia (Scientist; Researcher)
Heartstrings - Rebecca Paisley   1481

Worthington, Matt (Journalist; Editor)
Spitfire - Sonya Birmingham   151

Worthy, Asher (Businessman; Shipowner)
Sultry Nights - Charla Cameron   281

Wren, Grace (Noblewoman; Spinster)
Fascination - Stella Cameron   286

Wrotham, Christopher (Nobleman; Military
Personnel)
Lady Alex's Gamble - Evelyn Richardson   1633

Wulf of Rugen (Nobleman)
Captive to His Kiss - Paige Brantley   207

Wulfayne (Warrior)
Chanting the Dawn - Marylyle Rogers   1690

Wulfsun (Warrior)
Swan Bride - Betina Lindsey   1192

Wyatt, Chance (Cowboy)
The Tender Texan - Jodi Thomas   1931

Wyatt, Hank (Fugitive; Castaway)
Imagine - Jill Barnett   88

Wycherly, Guy (Nobleman; Military Personnel)
The American Cousin - Dawn Lindsey   1196

Wydner, Elizabeth (Psychic)
Elizabeth's Gift - Donna Davidson   468

Wylde, Quade (Trapper)
Wild Glory - Andrea Parnell   1509

Wyler, Miko (Designer)
The Runaway Heart - Anne Ladley   1131

Wyler, Tom (Detective—Police; Vacationer)
Embers - Antoinette Stockenberg   1881

Wylie, Kelly (Police Officer)
Deadly Masquerade - Tracey Tillis   1947

Wyndham, Angus (Laird)
The Lady and the Laird - Maura Seger   1761

Wyndham, Hale (Archaeologist)
Captive Treasure - Tena Carlyle   314

Wyndham, James (Nobleman; Equestrian)
The Valentine Legacy - Catherine Coulter   410

Wyndham, Marcus (Nobleman)
The Wyndham Legacy - Catherine Coulter   411

Wyndham, Marianna (Teacher)
Miss Wyndham's Escapade - Emily Hendrickson   854

Wyngate, Charity (Gentlewoman; Guardian)
The Arrogant Lord Alistair - Sheila Walsh   1989

Wynne, Kate (Lawyer)
Love on Trial - Wendy Martin   1285

Wynne of Gwernach (Noblewoman)
A Moment in Time - Bertrice Small   1824

Wynswich, Marian (Debutante)
Marian's Christmas Wish - Carla Kelly   1052

Y

Yarbro, Ian (Fiance(e))
The Legacy - Linda Lael Miller   1381

Yardley, Temperance (Settler)
A Durable Fire - Virginia Bernhard   129

Yeager, Tim (Sports Figure)
Spirit of the Season - Heather Graham   741

York, Calista (Trader)
All's Fair - Anne Avery   37

York, Jeremiah (Trapper)
Eagles of Destiny - Jory Sherman   1782

York, Steven (Businessman)
The Christmas Husband - Mary Anne Wilson   2046

Yost, Hannah (Orphan)
Wilderness Flame - Barbara Cummings   448

Young, Allison (Widow(er); Businesswoman)
Winter Heat - Mary Lynn Baxter   104

Youngblood, Clay (Military Personnel)
Shameless - Rosanne Bittner   160

Youngblood, Ryan (Plantation Owner)
Midnight Rose - Patricia Hagan   780

Youngthunder, Michael (Businessman; Indian)
Arrowpoint - Suzanne Ellison   607

Z

Zachary, Sam (Imposter; Lawman)
Wild Wyoming Love - Dana Ransom   1595

Zamora, Santiago (Gunfighter)
Rainbows and Rapture - Rebecca Paisley   1484

Zeller, Corey (Businessman)
This Fragile Heart - Jan McDaniel   1307

Zenkavna, Synnovea (Noblewoman)
Forever in Your Embrace - Kathleen E. Woodiwiss   2061

Zora (Royalty)
The Pagan's Prize - Miriam Minger   1399

Character Description Index

This index alphabetically lists descriptions of the major characters in featured titles. The descriptions may be occupations (astronaut, lawyer, etc.) or may describe personas (amnesiac, runaway, teenager, etc.). For each description, character names are listed alphabetically. Also provided are book titles, author names, and entry numbers.

ABUSE VICTIM

Cheney, Laura
Cheyenne Amber - Catherine Anderson 16

Evans, March
Desert Angel - Pamela K. Forrest 660

Forrest, Maggy
Maggy's Child - Karen Robards 1650

Gilbert, Darcy
At Risk - Jeanne Stephens 1875

Harper, Meg
The Way Home - Dallas Schulze 1739

Jackson, Carrie
Love So Wild - Elaine Crawford 415

Jensen, Lisa Jo
A Child's Promise - Deborah Bedford 117

Jones, Silver
Quicksilver Passion - Georgina Gentry 714

Kincaid, Laura
Shelter From the Storm - Patricia Rice 1621

Lane, Moriah
Evergreen - Delia Parr 1510

Lindhurst, Phillipa
Summer Storm - Denise Domning 547

MacGowan, Juliette
Shadow Dance - Anne Stuart 1890

Paxton, Jake
For The Love of Grace - Ginna Gray 750

Quinn, Kate
Beyond All Reason - Judith Duncan 573

Rhyca
Hearts Enslaved - Judith Hill 889

Rogan, Serena "Brave Heart"
Brave Heart - Lindsay McKenna 1315

Walker, Susannah
Dancing on Snowflakes - Jane Bonander 180

ACCIDENT VICTIM

McKendrick, Tyler
The Way Home - Dallas Schulze 1739

ACCOUNTANT

Dayny, Sara
My Own True Love - Susan Sizemore 1816

Endicott, Karma
Merry Christmas, Mommy - Muriel Jensen 985

Falconi, Stephen
The Scarlet Thread - Evelyn Anthony 26

Frye, Jeffrey
A Woman Betrayed - Barbara Delinsky 503

Gallagher, Alina
The Irish Rose - Jessica Wulf 2073

Holland, Jessica
The Dark Side of Paradise - Alma Blair 166

Matthias, Connie
White Light - Wendy Haley 786

Neill, Hillary
Moon Showers - Laura Phillips 1523

O'Rourke, Darcey
Moonlight Enchantment - Carol Finch 645

Styer, Frisco
Compromises - Joan Hohl 906

ACTIVIST

Brooks, Liberty
Scandalous - Sonia Simone 1796

Fleming, Melanie
Night Flower - Shirl Henke 863

Foster, Harriet
The Heart's Journey - Emily Bradshaw 197

French, Danny
Till the Stars Fall - Kathleen Gilles Seidel 1768

Frobisher, Alisha
Sweet Southern Caress - Wendy Garrett 696

Granger, Victoria
Surrender the Dream - Debra Dier 531

Hastings, Blake
Caress - Rosanne Bittner 153

Holt, Jacqueline
Masques of Betrayal - Andrea Kane 1038

King, Alexander
Scoundrel's Desire - JoAnn De Lazzari 489

Lowery, Samantha
Kansas Kiss - Christine Dorsey 550

Malloy, Zeke
Scandalous - Sonia Simone 1796

Merrifield, Lark
Vows Made in Wine - Susan Wiggs 2028

Montgomery, Kay
A Lifetime of Heaven - Nan Ryan 1705

O'Leary, Carrie
Spitfire - Sonya Birmingham 151

Phillips, Amie
Pure Instinct - Ellen Fletcher 653

Picard, Devon
The Schemers - Lois Wolfe 2059

Rogan, Serena "Brave Heart"
Brave Heart - Lindsay McKenna 1315

Rose, Regina
My Wild Rose - Deborah Camp 297

Sterling, Erin
Midnight Rose - Patricia Hagan 780

Stevens, Carla
Blessings of the Heart - Jane McBride Choate 352

Sullivan, Breanna
Scoundrel's Desire - JoAnn De Lazzari 489

Tate, Becky
Winds of Destiny - Victoria Thompson 1938

Van Hausen, Reba
Sweet Paradise - Terri Valentine 1968

Walker, Freedom
Stormswept - Katherine Kincaid 1068

Walters, Samantha
Caress - Rosanne Bittner 153

Wentworth, Naomi
A Nothing Town in Texas - Lass Small 1828

ACTOR

Angelo, Nick
American Star - Jackie Collins 377

Carrick, Nicholas
A Rose Without Thorns - Lucy Kidd 1061

Catherwood, Shreve
Acts of Love - Deana James 967
Acts of Passion - Deana James 968

Cooper, Wes
High Riding Heroes - Joey Light 1187

Cormick, Bryce Darcy
Dance of Deception - Suzannah Davis 479

Creighton, Elliot
Sweet Forever - Becky Lee Weyrich 2010

Dodge, Danny
Going Hollywood - Marion Schultz 1736

McDowell, Matthew
Eternity - Lori Herter 879

Ramsey, Price
My Only Desire - Andrea Parnell 1508

St. James, Matthew
Secret Sins - JoAnn Ross 1698

Tate, Dylan
Bad for Each Other - Billie Green 754

Travis, John
Aspen Gold - Janet Dailey 453

Vane, Robert
Curtain - Michael Corda 397

Wild, Ian
Wild Card - Nancy Hutchinson 955

ACTRESS

Benedict, Eve
Genuine Lies - Nora Roberts 1667

Billings, Katherine
Miss Billings Treads the Boards - Carla Kelly 1053

Blair-Coupland, Alison
The Brides of Eden - Clare Benedict 119

Bourne, Fancy
Fancy Lady - Peggy Hanchar 791

Cantrell, Kate
The Thorn Trees - Marcella Thum 1946

Carstairs, Augusta
A Tempting Miss - Janice Bennett 125

Cochran, Cherry
Stardust Dreams - Marilyn Campbell 302

Culhane, Lily
The Lily and the Hawk - Marlene Suson 1900

Deschamps, Clairisse
The Mock Marriage - Dorothy Mack 1247

Drake, Juliet
Heirloom - Candace Camp 290

Drummond, Miranda
Acts of Love - Deana James 967
Acts of Passion - Deana James 968

Drussard, Justine
Fallen Angel - Deborah Camp 294

Fontaine, Alice
The Sensation - Rebecca Flanders 651

Gellee de Vacheron, Isabella
Christmas Belle - Mary Balogh 56

Grant, C.J.
Partners in Time - Pamela Simpson 1802

Hamilton, Kate
Taboo - Elizabeth Gage 681

Hanlon, Megan
The Past Is Another Country - Lois Battle 97

Hartman, Zoe
First Loves - Jean Stone 1884

John, Melissa
The Brides - Gila Berkowitz 128

Kennedy, Mollene
Lost Treasure - Catriona Flynt 655

Lederer, Orchid
Blue Orchids - Julia Fenton 637

Lederer, Valentina
Blue Orchids - Julia Fenton 637

Lyle, Felicia
Curtain - Michael Corda 397

MacIntosh, Portia
Sweetwater - Sandra Chastain 346

Maples, Genevieve
Dance of Deception - Suzannah Davis 479

Markham, Lucy
The Gilded Cage - Edith Layton 1169

Masters, Kit
Aspen Gold - Janet Dailey 453

Maynard, Arabella Taylor
Silver Deceptions - Deborah Martin 1272

McCall, Persephone "Persey"
Lord Harlequin - Marian Devon 525

Rosencrantz "Rosie"
The Greatest Lover in All England - Christina Dodd 536

Sinclair, Eve
Taboo - Elizabeth Gage 681

Ware, Grayson
Midnight Lace - Elizabeth Kary 1045

Waxton, Thomasina
Sweet Deception - Colleen Faulkner 626

Wentworth, Nora O'Connell
Fortune's Tide - Maura Seger 1759

ADMINISTRATOR

Blue, Toinette
Body and Soul - Felicia Mason 1293

Clayborne, Thane
Midnight Kiss - Marcia Evanick 615

Haviland, Bronte
Once a Hero - Katherine Sutcliffe 1905

O'Neil, Autumn
Midnight Kiss - Marcia Evanick 615

Perrine, Noah
Suddenly - Barbara Delinsky 502

ADOPTEE

Carmichael, Delany
Desert Sunrise - Raine Cantrell 310

Copper-Headed Woman
Lady Legend - Deborah Camp 296

Crawford, Eva
All We Hold Dear - Kathryn Lynn Davis 476

Eric
The Vow - Mary Spencer 1861

Kane, Chelsea
The Passions of Chelsea Kane - Barbara Delinsky 501

Lederer, Valentina
Blue Orchids - Julia Fenton 637

Logan, Wolf Star
Yesterday's Shadows - Marianne Willman 2042

Maucelerc, Sophie
The Sorceress - Claire Delacroix 495

Rain Shadow
Rain Shadow - Cheryl St. John 1866

Smith, Serita
Intimate Connections - Joanne Z. Adams 2

Stone, Travis
What Child Is This? - Rebecca York 2078

ADVENTURER

Abbott, Hugh
Silver Linings - Jayne Ann Krentz 1111

Anthony, Fortune
No Man's Fortune - Kristie Knight 1092

Aratar
Silversword - Lindsay Randall 1588

Armando
Jewel of the Sea - Susan Wiggs 2024

Braddock, Kit
Brazen - Susan Johnson 998

Carlisle, Ross
Silk and Secrets - Mary Jo Putney 1561

de Tourneay, Roland
Secret Song - Catherine Coulter 408

Dennehy, Mary Schuyler "Skye"
Always in My Dreams - Jo Goodman 730

DeWinter, Michael
Desert Song - Constance O'Banyon 1447

Flynn, Lucas "Tiger"
Tilly and the Tiger - Marianne Willman 2041

Forester, Sam
Just a Kiss Away - Jill Barnett 89

Jackson, Hennessy "Hawk"
The Passion Ruby - Eboni Snoe 1848

Kane, Morgan
Shadow Play - Katherine Sutcliffe 1906

Mansfield, Arden
The Dream Hunter - Laura Kinsale 1076

Mara
Silversword - Lindsay Randall 1588

McAllister, Zane
At Long Last Love - Catherine Lanigan 1160

McLaren, Ruel
Tiger Prince - Iris Johansen 994

Quade, Charlotte
Taming Charlotte - Linda Lael Miller 1386

Rutledge, Zane Grey
Somewhere in Time - Barbara Bretton 216

Summerfield, Zachariah
Eden's Angel - Katherine Compton 379

Trevarren, Patrick
Taming Charlotte - Linda Lael Miller 1386

Walker, Chance
Lover in the Rough - Elizabeth Lowell 1230

Whitney-King, Tempest
Lightning Strikes Twice - Lacey Dancer 459

Winslow, Barrett
The Ruby - Christina Skye 1821

ADVERTISING

Cavanaugh, Jenny
Moments - Georgia Bockoven 178

Dorn, Zachary
Changes of Heart - Elizabeth Bennett 122

Logan, Ginny
Mrs. Perfect - Peggy Roberts 1670

Lynch, Nancy
Seasons - Constance O'Day-Flannery 1453

Russel, Alex
Mrs. Perfect - Peggy Roberts 1670

Watson, Oliver
Daddy - Danielle Steel 1869

AGED PERSON

Fridrick, Janet
I'll Be Seeing You - Kristine Rolofson   1696

Sandetti, Ray
I'll Be Seeing You - Kristine Rolofson   1696

AGENT

Cameron, Skye
The Promise of Summer - Lynn Bulock   251

Gordon, Emily
Maybe This Time - Kathleen Gilles Seidel   1766

Hawking, Robin
Traitor's Kiss - Joy Tucker   1963

Sloan, Nathan
Desert Bride - JoAnne Redd   1608

ALCOHOLIC

Slade, Morgan
Midnight Fire - Madeline Baker   45

ALIEN

Janella
Out of This World Marriage - Maggie Shayne   1779

AMBASSADOR

Kalisson, Rugar
Behind Closed Doors - Betina M. Krahn   1097

AMNESIAC

Addams
The Anonymous Miss Addams - Kasey
   Michaels   1362

Breckenridge, Fancy
Wild Texas Heart - Deana James   971

Cambridge, Aaron "Cain"
When Morning Comes - Robin LeAnne Wiete   2022

Daulton, Amanda
Amanda - Kay Hooper   920

de Vere, Meriel
Uncommon Vows - Mary Jo Putney   1564

Farraday, Amanda
Shattered Illusions - Linda Renee De Jong   487

Forrester, Elizabeth
California Temptress - Millie Criswell   424

Hamilton, Reid
Tender Lies - Kay McMahon   1328

Jardin, Remy
Masquerade - Janet Dailey   454

Jennings, Faith
Yesterday's Promise - DiAnna June   1032

MacAlpin, Megan
Highland Fire - Ruth Langan   1154

MacDougal, Lynn
Sing Carols with the Angels - Mary Leask   1171

McNair, Catriona
Bold Breathless Nights - Penelope Neri   1436

Muir, Dante
The Illusion of Love - Kasey Michaels   1366

Prescott, Robyn
Once Innocent - Jessica Gregory   761

Rossi, Caitlin
Kiss of the Shadow Man - Maggie Shayne   1778

St. John, Morgan "Tristan"
Lord of Enchantment - Suzanne Robinson   1683

Selena "Agnes"
Waiting for the Moon - Kristin Hannah   800

Shalyn
Virgin Star - Jennifer Horsman   928

Shelton, Regina
Secrets - Brenda Joyce   1030

Venado
Sweet Mountain Magic - Rosanne Bittner   162

Wakefield, Gideon
Fool Me Once - Lori Copeland   391

Ward, Elizabeth
Deceived - Mary Balogh   58

Winslow, Barrett
The Ruby - Christina Skye   1821

ANGEL

Angel, Cathy
An Angel's Touch - Heather Graham
   Pozzessere   1548

Angel, Don
An Angel's Touch - Heather Graham
   Pozzessere   1548

Goodness
A Season of Angels - Debbie Macomber   1254
Touched by Angels - Debbie Macomber   1256
The Trouble with Angels - Debbie Macomber   1257

Heese, Lauren
Second Chances - Constance O'Day-Flannery   1454

Lannigan, Jack
Second Chances - Constance O'Day-Flannery   1454

Mercy
A Season of Angels - Debbie Macomber   1254
Touched by Angels - Debbie Macomber   1256
The Trouble with Angels - Debbie Macomber   1257

Shirley
A Season of Angels - Debbie Macomber   1254
Touched by Angels - Debbie Macomber   1256
The Trouble with Angels - Debbie Macomber   1257

Tabitha
Heaven on Earth - Michelle Brandon   205

ANIMAL

Fitz
A Loyal Companion - Barbara Metzger   1354

Midnight Louie
Crystal Days - Carole Nelson Douglas   554
Crystal Nights - Carole Nelson Douglas   555

ANIMAL LOVER

Chastain, Cara
Southern Storms - Marcia Martin   1282

Corstairs, Sabelle "Isabelle"
Sabelle - Veronica Sattler   1722

Emerson, Luke
Midnight Ecstasy - Rita Balkey   51

Randolph, Sonya
A Loyal Companion - Barbara Metzger   1354

Sinclair, Clover
Midnight Ecstasy - Rita Balkey   51

Weatherford, Lanie
Kiss of Bliss - Carolyn Monroe   1403

ANIMAL TRAINER

Ffolkes, Alissa
The Gallant Lord Ives - Emily Hendrickson   852

Monroe, Abby
Beginnings - Laura Phillips   1522

ANTHROPOLOGIST

Bonham, Flora
Pure Sin - Susan Johnson   1002

ANTIQUES DEALER

Bowleigh, Zack
Timeless - Jasmine Cresswell   421

Conroy, Dora
Hidden Riches - Nora Roberts   1669

Delany, Robyn
Timeless - Jasmine Cresswell   421

Webb, Thaddeus
Winter's Flame - Maria Greene   756

APOTHECARY

Arnold, Althea
The Firelands - Karen Harper   811

Morgan, Selene
Bayou Passion - Jane Archer   29

APPRAISER

Connley, Yates
The Man Who Came for Christmas - Bethany
   Campbell   299

Crosse, Emilie
Somewhere in Time - Barbara Bretton   216

Thorne, Regan
Pink Topaz - Jennifer Greene   755

APPRENTICE

Dugan, Sara
Mad Hatter - Georgia Helm   848

ARCHAEOLOGIST

Bailey, Mike
A Love Beyond Time - Flora M. Speer   1855

Brasfield, Bethany
Emerald Nights - Virginia Brown   233

Broderick, Cliff
Memory's Lamp - Marilyn Tracy   1954

Collier, Lina
Golden Fires - Colleen Shannon   1769

Emerson, Radcliffe
The Snake, the Crocodile, and the Dog - Elizabeth
   Peters   1519

Hamilton, Kelly
Hour of the Rose - Christina Skye   1820

Lindell, Jan
The Night Prowlers - Karen G. McCullough   1304

Logan, Joshua
Mountain Mystic - Debra Dixon   533

Mannering, Quinten
Passion's Golden Fire - Susan Sackett   1710

Mitchell, Lilli
At Long Last Love - Catherine Lanigan   1160

Nolan, Riordan
The Turtledove's Secret - Laura Hastings   827

Payne, Sabine
Passion's Golden Fire - Susan Sackett   1710

Peabody Emerson, Amelia
The Snake, the Crocodile, and the Dog - Elizabeth
   Peters   1519

Pomeroy, Harriet
Ravished - Amanda Quick   1571

Whitmore, Katherine
A Quest of Dreams - Debra Dier   530

Wyndham, Hale
Captive Treasure - Tena Carlyle   314

ARCHITECT

Asche, Stephen
The Singing Stones - Phyllis A. Whitney   2018

Conroe, Gareth
Home Fires - Dixie Dubois   569

Frakes, Jackie
Painted Moon - Karin Kallmaker   1036

Frazier, Leah
Priceless - Mary Lynn Baxter   102

Hastings, Sam
Blessings of the Heart - Jane McBride Choate   352

Jefferson, Annie
Intimate Betrayal - Linda Barlow   85

Kane, Chelsea
The Passions of Chelsea Kane - Barbara
   Delinsky   501

Kwan, Maylene
Pearl Moon - Katherine Stone   1885

MacGregor-Smythe, Madaline
The Virgin Wife - Elizabeth August   36

Martin, Alex
Puzzle Mansion - Colleen Edwards   596

Powers, Lee
Southern Storms - Marcia Martin   1282

Randall, Joelle
Prince of Wolves - Susan Krinard   1116

Rossi, Dylan
Kiss of the Shadow Man - Maggie Shayne   1778

Seton, Garrick
Lady Rogue - Kathryn Kramer   1106

Simpson, Gary
The Night Prowlers - Karen G. McCullough   1304

Stuart, Ian
Star-Crossed Lovers - Kay Hooper   924

Terrell, Beth
Garden of Fantasy - Karen Rose Smith   1847

Whittaker, Paula
No Blueprint for Love - Audrey McConachie   1302

Winchester, Nash
Garden of Fantasy - Karen Rose Smith   1847

ART DEALER

Chaplin, Anne
In Spite of Themselves - Elizabeth Barnes   86

Fletcher, Miles
The Love Knot - Elisabeth Fairchild   619

Lambert, Charles
And Heaven Too - Julie Tetel   1923

MacKenzie, Joshua
Sapphire and Shadow - Marie Ferrarella   639

McAllister, Jim
Ride the Rainbow Home - Susan Aylworth   39

Sharpe, Mattie
Silver Linings - Jayne Ann Krentz   1111

Sweeney, Rogan
Born in Fire - Nora Roberts   1663

Winthrop, Lauren
Midnight in Marrakesh - Meryl Sawyer   1731

ARTISAN

Beaumont, Rafe
Winter Heat - Mary Lynn Baxter   104

Costhaler, Nick
Yes, Virginia - Peg Sutherland   1907

de Clerc, Ariana
Knight's Lady - Suzanne Barclay   83

Harken, Jens
November of the Heart - LaVyrle Spencer   1860

James, Cara
Until Tomorrow - Jill Marie Landis   1148

Lamont, Brett
Promise Me Anything - Meryl Sawyer   1732

MacKinnon, Tavis
Heaven Knows - Elaine Coffman   371

MacRoth, Elgiva
Legends - Deborah Smith   1839

Myles, Hilary
Love's Safe Harbor - Cindy T. Moss   1431

Peters, Alexandra
Possession - Lori Herter   881

Ryder, Samantha "Sam"
Silk and Stone - Deborah Smith   1842

ARTIST

Allen, Victor
Gretna Bride - Eva Rutland   1702

Allington, Ruth
Ask Me No Questions - Patricia Veryan   1978

Armstrong, Dana
The Silver Link - Carol Marsh   1268

Aveline
Tapestry - Maura Seger   1765

Beaumont, Leila
Captives of the Night - Loretta Chase   338

Beck, Leah
Painted Moon - Karin Kallmaker   1036

Brooks, Belinda
Sweet Deception - Vanessa Hale   783

Burnside, Talitha
A Talent for Trouble - Anne Barbour   82

Chandler, Sabrina
The House in the Trees - Georgette Livingston   1219

Clifford, Zoe
Morning's Gate - Ann Victoria Roberts   1658

Concannon, Margaret Mary "Maggie"
Born in Fire - Nora Roberts   1663

de Saint Vallier, Nardi
Bliss - Judy Cuevas   444

Downey, Leah
The Color of Love - Sandra Kitt   1085

Forsythe, Jessamyn
Seductive Caress - Carla Simpson   1800

Jennings, Sarah
A Tryst in Time - Eugenia Riley   1640

Kimball, Clare
Divine Evil - Nora Roberts   1666

Kitteridge, Ashton
Sunswept - Leigh Bristol   218

La Marsh, Jordan
The Crimson Roses of Fountain Court - Peggy
   Darty   465

Lachman, Alette
Sweeter than Sin - Sara Orwig   1465

Lange, Angelina "Angel"
A Woman Without Lies - Elizabeth Lowell   1236

Martin, Heather
Wild Heather - Millie Criswell   430

Meriweather, Hazel
Dreams of Paradise - Laura Simon   1793

Meyer, Renata
Arrowpoint - Suzanne Ellison   607

Mitchell, Carin
When Someday Comes - Faith E.W. Garner   691

Mixall, Cal
Golden Swan - Judy Gill   725

Morgan, Margaret
The Crimson Roses of Fountain Court - Peggy
   Darty   465

Penrod, Jane Millicent
Changes of Heart - Elizabeth Bennett   122

Raven, Helen
All the Winters That Have Been - Evan
   Maxwell   1297

Rutherford, Norah
Fire at Midnight - Barbara Dawson Smith   1829

St. George, Pamela
Facets - Barbara Delinsky   499

St. Peters, Ivan
Desire - Georgia Hampton   789

Sanders, Marianna
The Beloved Scoundrel - Iris Johansen   989

Shaw, Samuel
The Vow - Lindsay Chase   337

Stewart, Savannah
Rebel Wildfire - Barbara Cummings   447

Stowe, Deirdre
Deirdre and Don Juan - Jo Beverley   134

Thompson, Sharon
Seasons - Lisa Gregory   766

Tremayne, Aidan
Forever and the Night - Linda Lael Miller   1380

Weston, Carrie McKamey
The Long Road Home - Pat Warren   1994

Wheeler, Mitch
A Liberated Man - Diana Whitney   2016

Whitney, Johanna
Sapphire and Shadow - Marie Ferrarella   639

Winthrop, Araminta
Desperado - Rebecca Brandewyne   200

ASSISTANT

Wallace, Neely
Forever and the Night - Linda Lael Miller   1380

AUDITOR

Selwyn, Crystal
Awakening Dreams - Vanessa Grant   746

AVENGER

Barwick, Adam
Dream Catcher - Thomasina Ring   1644

Brandon, John Lee
The Redhead and the Preacher - Sandra Chastain   344

Coulter, Adam
Runaway Heart - Tena Carlyle   315

Kincaid, Stone
Dragon Fire - Linda Ladd   1124

BACHELOR

Crawford, Nick
The Sensation - Rebecca Flanders   651

BACKWOODSMAN

Gunn, Christopher
Silver Tears - Becky Lee Weyrich   2009

MacGregor, Ballard
Kentucky Bride - Hannah Howell   938

MacKenzie, Tyler
Forever in His Arms - Penelope Neri   1439

BACKWOODSWOMAN

Delaney, Jenny Lynn
Forever in His Arms - Penelope Neri   1439

BAKER

Huckabee, Florence
Lovers and Friends - Claire Bocardo   176

BANKER

Andreas, Jean Marc
Storm Winds - Iris Johansen   993

Blessing, Lucille "Lucy"
Wild Wyoming Love - Dana Ransom   1595

Carson, Hunter
Touch of Heaven - Michelle Brandon   206

Drake, Charlotte
Desert Fire - Evelyn Rogers   1686

Grant-Fortune, Christina
Fortune's Child - Pamela Simpson   1801

Hamilton, Elliot
Camelot Jones - Mayo Lucas   1237

Huntington, Charlotte
Swept Away - Cay David   467

Makena, Lani "Kapiolani"
Once Burned, Twice as Hot - Patt Bucheister   243

Wharton, Michael
Defiant Rose - Colleen Quinn   1578

BARBARIAN

Ly-San-Ter, Challen
Warrior's Woman - Johanna Lindsey   1211

BASTARD DAUGHTER

Bigod, Barbara
The Silver Mirror - Roberta Gellis   710

Ceidre
The Conqueror - Brenda Joyce   1023

Jasmine
The Falcon and the Flower - Virginia Henley   870

LeCoeur, Gabrielle
The Perfect Mistress - Betina M. Krahn   1104

O'Malley, Dana
They Call Her Dana - Jennifer Wilde   2029

Rand, Jonty
Devil in Spurs - Norah Hess   883

BASTARD SON

Black, James
Fortune's Mistress - Judith E. French   667

Campbell, Leander
Rogue's Reward - Jean R. Ewing   617

Ceawlin
Born of the Sun - Joan Wolf   2056

D'Aix, Sir Alphonse
The Silver Mirror - Roberta Gellis   710

Deverell, Jake
The Destiny - Fayrene Preston   1552

Gilchrist, Roarke
Bold Breathless Nights - Penelope Neri   1436

Graiston, Temric
Summer Storm - Denise Domning   547

Love, Hunter
The Passions of Chelsea Kane - Barbara Delinsky   501

Loxton, Hugh
Heart's Awakening - Paige Brantley   208

MacAmlaid, Gavin "Berenhard"
Captive to a Dream - Susan Tanner   1911

Raine
Keeper of the Dream - Penelope Williamson   2037

Reade, John "Jack"
The Heart Remembers - Barbara Hazard   842

Renaudot, Lucien
Promise of Summer - Louisa Rawlings   1597

Rycliffe, Anthony "Tody"
The Greatest Lover in All England - Christina Dodd   536

BEEKEEPER

Eadyth of Hawk's Lair
The Tarnished Lady - Sandra Hill   892

BIKER

Donner, Gabriel
Annie and the Outlaw - Sharon Sala   1713

Santiago, Gabriel
Moriah's Magic - Anne Ladley   1129

BLACKSMITH

Walker, Eben
Playing with Fire - Victoria Thompson   1934

BLOCKADE RUNNER

Carrington, Ty
Stormswept - Katherine Kincaid   1068

Courtland, Derek
White Rose - Linda Ladd   1127

Redding, Rhys
Renegade - Patricia Potter   1544

BOARDER

Pulneshti, Sandor
In the Cards - Julie Meyers   1357

BODYGUARD

Cain, Walker
Always in My Dreams - Jo Goodman   730

Cord
Pirate's Princess - Constance O'Banyon   1449

Durango, Nick
Cherish the Night - Penelope Neri   1437

Hunter
Wild Wind - Jane Archer   31

Montana, Roman
Heartstrings - Rebecca Paisley   1481

Powers, Logan
Arizona Captive - LaRee Bryant   241

BOOTLEGGER

Barnes, Seth
Julia's Story - Catherine M. Rae   1584

BOUNTY HUNTER

Branston, Craig
Nevada Flame - Rochelle Wayne   1997

Calloway, Nicholas
The Inheritance - Joan Johnston   1005

Devereaux, Creed
Renegade Bride - Barbara Ankrum   23

Durango, Charlie
Taming Kate - Eugenia Riley   1638

Harlowe, Sunny
My Only Desire - Andrea Parnell   1508

Harrison, Bliss
Outlaw Seduction - Kathryn Hockett   905

Kincade, Samantha
The Seduction of Samantha Kincade - Maggie Osborne   1468

Landsford, Victoria
Angel of Fire - Jessica Douglass   560

MacAllister, Cade
Forbidden Desires - Rebecca Sinclair   1811

Malone, Kate
Love's Bounty - Alisa McBride   1299

Maverick, Slade
Heartland - Rebecca Brandewyne   201

McCord, Jesse
Prairie Heat - Madeline Baker   46

McFarland, Cale
Sunny - Linda Madl   1260

McKnight, Tanner
When Lightning Strikes - Rexanne Becnel   115

Newman, Jared
Rugged Splendor - Robin Leigh   1180

Rawdon, Cole
Cherished - Jill Gregory   762

Stryker, Caleb
Cheyenne Surrender - Madeline Baker   40

Wolf, Nathan
Dancing on Snowflakes - Jane Bonander   180

BOYFRIEND

Osborne, Richard
True Love - Diane E. Lock   1221

Tod
Heartbeat - Norma Fox Mazer   1298

BRIDE

Ariane the Betrayed
Enchanted - Elizabeth Lowell   1229

Ashley, Linnea
A Special License - Kathleen Elliott   604

Brewster, Kate
The Vanishing Bridegroom - Alice Sharpe   1773

Bunch, Hannah
Heaven Sent - Pamela Morsi   1427

Cardew, Lilith
The Serpent Beguiled - Betina Lindsey   1191

Chambers, Alexandra
The Sherbrooke Bride - Catherine Coulter   409

Delawney, Rue
Hawke's Pride - Norah Hess   884

Devereux, Brigitte
Highland Belle - Patricia Grasso   749

Drayton, Cassandra
Miss Drayton's Downfall - Patricia Oliver   1460

Ferguson, Catriona
Lavender Flame - Karen Stratford   1886

Gallagher, Molly
The Barefoot Bride - Joan Johnston   1004

Greetwell, Primula
Fleeting Fancy - Rosemary Edghill   591

Hughes, Elizabeth
The Keepsake - Marylyle Rogers   1695

James, Kathleen
Pirate's Bride - Elizabeth August   35

Johanna
Saving Grace - Julie Garwood   706

Kincaid, Elly
The Stolen Bride of Glengarra Castle - Anne Knoll   1095

MacPherson, Mary Kate
Border Bride - Amanda Scott   1744

Maintree, Suzanne
Golden Nights - Christine Monson   1404

Montgomery, Carrie
Eternity - Jude Deveraux   512

St. James, Jordan
Bayou Bride - Bobbi Smith   1833

Van Allen, Alana
Lions and Lace - Meagan McKinney   1324

Washburn, Florence
Married by Mistake - Melinda McRae   1337

Waverly, Victoria
A Lady of the West - Linda Howard   934

BRIDEGROOM

Polwyche, Piers
Speak Only Love - Deana James   970

Sherbrooke, Douglas
The Sherbrooke Bride - Catherine Coulter   409

Staynes, William
A Special License - Kathleen Elliott   604

Steele, Jake
Mail Order Outlaw - Millie Criswell   427

Vothers, Matt
The Vanishing Bridegroom - Alice Sharpe   1773

Watson, Henry Lee
Heaven Sent - Pamela Morsi   1427

BUSINESSMAN

Adams, Richard
South of Paradise - Marcia Martin   1279

Anderson, Warren
The Magic of You - Johanna Lindsey   1204

Antonovic, Nick
The Marriage Bracelet - Rebecca Winters   2053

Austin, Stewart
Avenue of Dreams - Lucy Taylor   1921

Baron, Kohl
Nevada Temptation - Gwen Cleary   364

Bartlett, Shane
Matchmaker, Matchmaker - Donna Carlisle   313

Blackstone, Joel
Perfect Partners - Jayne Ann Krentz   1110

Brank, Stony
Love and Other Surprises - Kathleen Creighton   417

Breaker, Sinjin
Breathless - Stella Cameron   284

Bronson, Daniel
One and Only - Barbara Bretton   215

Brooks, Stephen
Dreams of Joy - Holly S. McClure   1301

Buchanan, Cole
Masquerade - Janet Dailey   454

Butler, Rhett
Scarlett - Alexandra Ripley   1647

Callan, J. Barrett V
A Margin in Time - Laura Hayden   837

Cameron, Buck
Pure Instinct - Ellen Fletcher   653

Campbell, Josh
The Dreamweavers: Bewitching Lady - Gail Douglas   557

Carlini, Joe
Desperate Measures - Linda Cajio   273

Carlyle, Matt
Intimate Betrayal - Linda Barlow   85

Channing, Derek
Charade - Christina Hamlett   788

Chanson, Alain
Changes of Heart - Elizabeth Bennett   122

Chekote, Kingfisher
Cherokee Nights - Genell Dellin   505

Chenault, Nick
Lucky - Sharon Sala   1716

Coulter, Sam
Pearl Moon - Katherine Stone   1885

Culver, Billy
Bad Billy Culver - Judy Gill   724

Dalton, Jeff
Tempest in Time - Eugenia Riley   1639

Daniels, Simon
Love's Safe Harbor - Cindy T. Moss   1431

De Groot, Wim Pieter
Garden of Dreams - Laura Simon   1794

Decker, Noah
Out of the Blue - Garda Parker   1499

Devereau, Dillon
Gambler's Tempting Kisses - Charlotte Hubbard   944

Deverell, Jake
The Destiny - Fayrene Preston   1552

Devos, Michael
Dangerous Odyssey - Jane Edwards   597

DiBarto, Jamie
On the Way to Heaven - Tina Wainscott   1986

Dixon, Owen
Mad Hatter - Georgia Helm   848

Donovan, Reid
Lady in Black - Christina Dodd   537

Drake, Reed
The Heart's Journey - Nancy Sheehan   1781

Dryden, John
Poetic Justice - Alicia Rasley   1596

Dunn, Andrew
Noelle - Diana Palmer   1491

Durand, Fontaine
Favors of the Rich - Sara Orwig   1464

Dylan, Josh
The Gilded Cage - Edith Layton   1169

Eastman, Jack
Time After Time - Antoinette Stockenberg   1883

Eddington, Joshua
Iron and Lace - Nadine Miller   1388

Farrell, Matthew
Paradise - Judith McNaught   1332

Fitzroy, Darcy
China Blossom - Margaret Moore   1408

Fletcher, Coop
Fancy Lady - Peggy Hanchar   791

Fortune, Max
Grand Passion - Jayne Ann Krentz   1109

Fortune, Winslow
Lost Treasure - Catriona Flynt   655

Foster, Nick
Riverboat Temptation - Gwen Cleary   365

Fowler, Marshall
The Silver Link - Carol Marsh   1268

Gamble, Sam
Hot Shot - Susan Elizabeth Phillips   1528

Garrick, Sean
Autumn Leaves - Jill Metcalf   1347

Garrison, Doug
Hot Property - Elise Title   1949

Ghant, Orrin
Eden Creek - Lisa Bingham   146

Gilchrist, Luke
Family Man - Jayne Ann Krentz   1107

Gresham, Wylie
Rainbow's End - Rebecca Brandewyne   203

Hale, Marty
Everything - Muriel Jensen   984

Hall, Jakob
Home Fires - Susan Kay Law   1164

Halloran, Travis
Suspicion's Gate - Justine Davis   475

Hamilton, Brand
Gold Is the Game - Rae Muir 1433

Hardin, Cy
True Colors - Susan Kyle 1123

Harmon, Robert
Flame in the Night - Jack McGowan 1311

Hatchard, Sam "Hatch"
Sweet Fortune - Jayne Ann Krentz 1112

Hawkins, Miles "Hawk"
A Woman Without Lies - Elizabeth Lowell 1236

Hollander, Blaise
Common Ground - Jeane Gilbert-Lewis 723

Hunter, Reid
Maverick's Lady - Linda Jenkins 982

Kane, Garrick
Sweet Harvest - Lisa Ann Verge 1977

Karazoc, Alex
Reap the Wind - Iris Johansen 992

Keane, Oliver
Island Star - Kit Gardner 684

Kendall, Scott
Once Innocent - Jessica Gregory 761

Kincaid, Douglas
Legends - Deborah Smith 1839

Kincaid, Gray
Frostfire - Linda Ladd 1125

King, Nick
Maggy's Child - Karen Robards 1650

Kingman, Adrian
Dangerous Bequest - Lee Anderson 21

LaRouche, Nevada
Honor - Lindsay Chase 336

Lassater, Will
The Forever Tree - Rosanne Bittner 155

Lightfoot, Nicodemus "Nick"
The Golden Chance - Jayne Ann Krentz 1108

Lockhart, Trace
Rogue's Honor - DeLoras Scott 1752

Logan, Brock
The Long Road Home - Pat Warren 1994

Logan, Trace
Honor's Promise - Sharon Sala 1715

Lombard, Kane
After Midnight - Susan Kyle 1120

MacCanna, Lucas
Compromises - Joan Hohl 906

MacKenzie, Connor
A World of Difference - Leona Blair 168

MacKenzie, Oliver
A Taste of Heaven - Laura Simon 1795

MacKinnon, Nicholas
Angel in Marble - Elaine Coffman 368

Mansfield, David
A Private Proposal - La Verne St. George 1863

Masardi, Reece
Kiss of Bliss - Carolyn Monroe 1403

Mayfield, Blake
Follow Your Heart - Lynda Trent 1959

McAllister, Mike
Tender Is the Touch - Ana Leigh 1176

McCrey, Tanner
Tall Cotton - Lori Copeland 396

McKeegan, Jack
Flannery's Rainbow - Julie Kistler 1084

McKenna, Ross
Fortune's Child - Pamela Simpson 1801

McKin, Lock
The Master's Bride - Suzannah Davis 481

Merlin, Richard
The Wizard of Seattle - Kay Hooper 925

Mitchell, Hayden
Rainbow in the Mist - Phyllis A. Whitney 2017

Monroe, Taylor
One Tough Cookie - Carole Dean 491

Montgomery, Charles
Christmas Journey - Rexanne Becnel 109

Montgomery, Dalton
Priceless - Mary Lynn Baxter 102

Montgomery, Jocelyn "Jace"
Wishes - Jude Deveraux 520

Montoya, Amado
Moments - Georgia Bockoven 178

Moreland, Adam
Bouquet - Shirl Henke 860

Morgan, Mac
Dreams and Wishes - Karren Radko 1583

Morgan, Owen (Hugo)
By All That Is Sacred - Laura Gilmour Bennett 127

Murphy, Patrick
For the Love of Laura - Karen Morrell 1419

Murray, Lucas
Love's Quiet Corner - Laura Parrish 1511

Neillson, Robert
When Someday Comes - Faith E.W. Garner 691

Nicholai, Nicholas
Red Velvet - Barbara Boswell 185

Nix, John
Yesterday's Dream - Alice Sharpe 1775

O'Halloran, Tabor
Masque of Sapphire - Deana James 969

O'Neil, Jeff
Sweeter than Sin - Sara Orwig 1465

Parnell, Travis
Virgin Fire - Elizabeth Chadwick 334

Paxton, Ryan
Highland Bride - Kathryn Kramer 1105

Purcell, David
Programmed for Danger - Karen G.
  McCullough 1305

Rafferty, Quinn
My Darling Melissa - Linda Lael Miller 1383

Rain, Oliver
Wildest Hearts - Jayne Ann Krentz 1114

Ramsay, Quinn
California Man - Carole Dean 490

Rand, Jake
Indigo Blue - Catherine Anderson 19

Randol, Charles Alexander III
Forever After - Bette Ford 657

Randolph, Rush
Jasmine and Silk - Sandra Chastain 341

Reardon, Jessie
Midnight Lover - Barbara Bretton 214

Roarke
Naked in Death - J.D. Robb 1656

Roarke, Gannon
Sweet Deception - Vanessa Hale 783

Rouillard, Gray
After the Night - Linda Howard 931

Russel, Alex
Mrs. Perfect - Peggy Roberts 1670

St. George, John
Facets - Barbara Delinsky 499

Savich, Alex
Promise Me Anything - Meryl Sawyer 1732

Severson, Eric
Bittersweet - LaVyrle Spencer 1857

Shaw, Reiver
The Vow - Lindsay Chase 337

Sinclair, Logan
Look Beyond the Dream - Noelle Berry McCue 1303

Sinclair, Trevor
To Love a Stranger - Blythe Bradley 194

Stark, Sam
Trust Me - Jayne Ann Krentz 1113

Steel, Drake
Beyond the Savage Sea - JoAnn Wendt 2000

Tanner, Royle
Wild Savage Love - Dana Ransom 1594

Taylor, Zachary
First Comes Marriage - Debbie Macomber 1249

Tenkiller, Tiana
Cherokee Sundown - Genell Dellin 506

Thayer, Nicholas
In Spite of Themselves - Elizabeth Barnes 86

Thomas, Solomon
Breathless - Margie Walker 1988

Thornton, Robert
Baby Makes Five - Lacey Dancer 457

Truesdale, Nate
Heart Song - Barbara Hargis 804

Tyler, Chase
Texas! Chase - Sandra Brown 230

Tyler, Lucky
Texas! Lucky - Sandra Brown 231

Valerius, Toshiro
The Panther and the Rose - Mary Burkhardt 257

Watson, Henry Lee
Heaven Sent - Pamela Morsi 1427

Weiss, Aaron
Tattered Silk - Elaine Barbieri 75

Wellesley, Geoffrey
Passion's Bargain - Jane Kidder 1063

Weston, Jake
Tin Angel - Kathy Lawrence 1166

Wheeler, Clint
The Dark Side of Paradise - Alma Blair 166

Whitlow, Cain
Renegade - Christine Flynn 654

Winter, Mason
A Marriage of Convenience - Georgia Bockoven 177

Wochek, Ed
Loveknot - Marissa Carroll 320

Worthy, Asher
Sultry Nights - Charla Cameron 281

York, Steven
The Christmas Husband - Mary Anne Wilson 2046

Youngthunder, Michael
Arrowpoint - Suzanne Ellison 607

Zeller, Corey
This Fragile Heart - Jan McDaniel 1307

BUSINESSWOMAN

Abbot, Joey
His Chariot Awaits - Kasey Michaels 1365

Armstrong, Kylie
Wedding Bell Blues - Alice Sharpe 1774

Arnette, Penny
This Fragile Heart - Jan McDaniel 1307

Ashley, Sarah
Come Be My Love - Patricia Watters 1996

Averil, Cassie
Matchmaker, Matchmaker - Donna Carlisle 313

Bancroft, Meredith
Paradise - Judith McNaught 1332

Barnaby, Jane
Tiger Prince - Iris Johansen 994

Becker, Leah
Almost Home - Debra Cowan 414

Benedict, Jessie
Sweet Fortune - Jayne Ann Krentz 1112

Bennett, Caroline
Midnight Lover - Barbara Bretton 214

Bennett, Ellie
Renegade - Christine Flynn 654

Bodman, Sarah
Up, Up and Away - Catherine Ennis 612

Brandon, Georgia
A World of Difference - Leona Blair 168

Brandon, Heather
Never on Sundae - Rita Rainville 1586

Brewster, Kate
The Vanishing Bridegroom - Alice Sharpe 1773

Brian, Jessica
In Every Port - Karin Kallmaker 1035

Briscoll, Nan
Dream Time - Paris Afton Bonds 182

Burns, Maddie
Sunswept - Leigh Bristol 218

Campbell, Christy
A Christmas Keepsake - Janice Bennett 123

Carey, Louise (Sancha)
By All That Is Sacred - Laura Gilmour Bennett 127

Carey, Megan
Night of the Phantom - Anne Stuart 1888

Carlisle, Shannon
Everything - Muriel Jensen 984

Carlyle, Samantha
Eyes of Fire - Heather Graham Pozzessere 1549

Carney, Rose
Defiant Rose - Colleen Quinn 1578

Castle, Jenny
Above Suspicion - Eleanor Woods 2064

Chandler, Nicki
Sight Unseen - Kathy Clark 359

Chandler, Victoria
Forever Yours - Francis Ray 1601

Chiari, Gabrielle
Night Fires - Sandra Marton 1286

Chisholm, Cimarron
Favors of the Rich - Sara Orwig 1464

Claiborne, Chelsey
If the Truth Be Told - Tracy Sinclair 1813

Clarke-Jargon, Deirdre
Wild Wind - Jane Archer 31

Clay, Victoria
High Riding Heroes - Joey Light 1187

Colangelo, Nina
Garden of Dreams - Laura Simon 1794

Consett, Evelyn
Tasmanian Devil - Valerie Parv 1512

Coppersmith, Liz
Time After Time - Antoinette Stockenberg 1883

Cotter, Tracey
Stand by Your Man - Kathy Clark 360

Cramer, Lillian "Lili"
The Firebirds - Beverly Byrne 264

Daniels, Whitney
Love's Brazen Fire - Betina M. Krahn 1100

Darian, Molly
Hot Streak - Jill Barkin 84

Dayne, Sariana
Shield's Lady - Amanda Glass 729

DeLord, Jessie
Stolen Kisses - Sally Falcon 622

Devlin Hardy, Faith
After the Night - Linda Howard 931

Drysdale, Zoe
Yesterday's Dream - Alice Sharpe 1775

Faulconer, Susannah
Hot Shot - Susan Elizabeth Phillips 1528

Fremont, Thalia
The Garden Path - Kristie Knight 1091

Frye, Laura
A Woman Betrayed - Barbara Delinsky 503

Garner, Elizabeth
Desperado Passion - Patricia Pellicane 1514

Grayum, Melody
Sweet Conquest - Marsha Bauer 100

Grey, Jenna
The Invisible Groom - Barbara Bretton 212

Harrison, Francesca "Francie"
Fortune Is a Woman - Elizabeth Adler 4

Harrison, Virginia "Ginny"
Seasons - Constance O'Day-Flannery 1453

Hatter, Emmaline
The Enchantment - Kristin Hannah 796

Huntington, Spencer
Slow Burn - Heather Graham Pozzessere 1551

Isabelle
One and Only - Barbara Bretton 215

Jefferson, Annie
Intimate Betrayal - Linda Barlow 85

Jordan, Ruby
The Reluctant Viking - Sandra Hill 891

Jourdaine, Anna
Thief of Hearts - Patricia Gaffney 679

Lancaster, Hayley
A Private Proposal - La Verne St. George 1863

Latham, Lorelei
Sweet Texas Magic - Evelyn Rogers 1689

Laurent, Claire
French Silk - Sandra Brown 228

Lockwood, Nicki
Suspicion's Gate - Justine Davis 475

Logan, Katha
Mixed Signals - Joan Elliott Pickart 1532

Lyncroft, Annie
Wildest Hearts - Jayne Ann Krentz 1114

MacKenzie, Elizabeth
A Time for Love - Constance O'Day-Flannery 1455

McKenzie, Kate
Brighter than Gold - Cynthia Wright 2071

McNeal, Kari
The Heart's Journey - Nancy Sheehan 1781

Merrill, Catherine "Cat"
In Every Port - Karin Kallmaker 1035

Miller, Laura
Beating the Odds - Deborah Gordon 734

Monroe, Melissa "Missy"
Tempest in Time - Eugenia Riley 1639

Montana, Lane
Crime of Passion - Kay Hooper 921

Mueller, Carson
Nevada Temptation - Gwen Cleary 364

Muldoon, Mattie
The Bonnie Blue - Joan Elliott Pickart 1531

North, Bentley
Maverick's Lady - Linda Jenkins 982

O'Donnell, Michael Ann
Gotta Have It - Faye Hughes 951

Osborn, Meridee
Swinging on a Star - Pamela Bauer 101

Owens, Dara
Silver Mist - Theresa DiBenedetto 527

Paley, Kate
Hot Property - Elise Title 1949

Paxton, Eugenia
Night Storm - Catherine Coulter 407

Pembroke, Allegra
A Taste of Heaven - Laura Simon 1795

Price, Maggie
Charade - Christina Hamlett 788

Robbins, Monique
Breathless - Margie Walker 1988

Rosenstein, Billie
Keep to Me, Stranger - Sarah Aldridge 6

Rossignole, Anthea
Car Pool - Karin Kallmaker 1034

Roswell, Rebecca
Over the Moon - Betty Cothran 401

St. George, Pamela
Facets - Barbara Delinsky 499

Sheldon, Sabrina
A Loving Spirit - Annette Broadrick 220

Simmons, Alison
A Garland of Love - Alice Sharpe 1771

Simmons, Susannah
Rainy Day Kisses - Debbie Macomber 1253

Sommers, Jessica
Wild Star - Nicole Jordan 1021

Sonnschein, Elke Von Braun
Boundless - Alexandra Thorne 1939

Sperry, Jade
Breath of Scandal - Sandra Brown 227

Stagnall, Leona
Endless Seduction - Rosalyn Alsobrook 11

Stoane, Audrey
Elusive Caress - Rosalyn Alsobrook 10

Stockwell, Amy
The Panther and the Rose - Mary Burkhardt 257

Taggart, Jessica
Tin Angel - Kathy Lawrence 1166

Talbot-Harrow, Judith
Masque of Sapphire - Deana James 969

Taylor, Christine
A Marriage of Convenience - Georgia Bockoven 177

Taylor, Megan
Passion's Bargain - Jane Kidder 1063

Tennison, Meredith Ashe "Kip"
True Colors - Susan Kyle 1123

Thornquist, Letitia "Letty"
Perfect Partners - Jayne Ann Krentz 1110

Character Description Index

CONVICT

Beaumont, Rafe
Winter Heat - Mary Lynn Baxter   104

Briscoll, Nan
Dream Time - Paris Afton Bonds   182

Corbett, Jack
Sweet Obsession - Kathy Jones   1014

Cutter, Jake
Rough Passage - Paula Detmer Riggs   1635

Fletcher, Robin
Wild Land, Wild Love - Connie Mason   1292

Gase, Adam
A Love So Wild - Evelyn Rogers   1688

Gold, Odessa
Odessa Gold - Linda Shaw   1776

Hargreaves, Sara
Flight to Yesterday - Velda Johnston   1010

Harris, Johnny
One Summer - Karen Robards   1653

Kincaid, Nathan
No Sweeter Paradise - Penelope Neri   1440

Lane, Moriah
Evergreen - Delia Parr   1510

Lowell, Jamie
The Fictitious Marquis - Alina Adams   1

McBride, Christian
Under the Desert Moon - Marsha Canham   308

McCord, Asher
Wild Texas Flame - Janis Reams Hudson   950

Newton, Bethany
Far Horizons - Katherine Sinclair   1807

Sinclair, Lucien
The Jacaranda Tree - Rebecca Brandewyne   202

Slaughter, Garrick
Miss Osborne Misbehaves - Marian Devon   526

Stone, Bowie
The Wives of Bowie Stone - Maggie Osborne   1469

COOK

Brownfield, Lily
Always a Lady - Sharon Sala   1712

de Lorgny, Ghislaine "Gilly"
A Rose at Midnight - Anne Stuart   1889

Devon, Mallory
Does Cupid Do Take-Out? - Kathryn E. Coulter   412

Eberhart, Ena
After All - Jill Marie Landis   1142

Huckabee, Florence
Lovers and Friends - Claire Bocardo   176

Keller, Lisette
Caress of Fire - Martha Hix   895

COUNSELOR

Gregory, Heather
For Always - Bette Ford   656

Robards, Carolyn
A Christmas Love - Kathleen Creighton   416

COURIER

Daniels, Doone
No Easy Task - Chloe Summers   1896

Morgan, Tara
The Road to Forever - Frances Williams   2036

COURT REPORTER

Jennings, Marilee
Dark Paradise - Tami Hoag   898

COURTIER

de Vere, Katherine
Gypsy Baron - Mary Daheim   451

Heron, Christopher "Christie"
The Lodestar - Pamela Belle   118

Preston, Kat
Traitor's Kiss - Joy Tucker   1963

COUSIN

Kate
Kate and the Soldier - Anne Barbour   79

Sallie
Shelter From the Storm - Patricia Rice   1621

COWBOY

Bass, Harmon
Temptation's Trail - Dana Ransom   1592

Boyer, Chance
Springtown - DeLoras Scott   1753

Buchanan, Noah
Outlaw Heart - Catherine Palmer   1486

Burnett, Jake
Sweet Lullaby - Lorraine Heath   843

Dalton, Drake
Bayou Passion - Jane Archer   29

Dillon, Alex
For the Thrill - Janis Reams Hudson   949

Durango, Nick
Cherish the Night - Penelope Neri   1437

Gallagher, Rafe
Forbidden Fires - Madeline Baker   43

Green, Jubal
One Bright Morning - Alice Duncan   571

Jones, Decker
A Nothing Town in Texas - Lass Small   1828

Larabee, Nick
Arizona Lovestorm - Wendy Garrett   693

Montoya, Sterling
Moonlight and Magic - Rebecca Paisley   1483

Morgan, Slade
Scarlet Sunset, Silver Nights - Leigh Greenwood   759

Murdoch, Lucas "Doc"
Texas Temptation - Gina Robins   1676

Pipestone, Ben
Reason to Believe - Kathleen Eagle   582

Ramsey, Nick
To Love a Cowboy - Laura Phillips   1524

Randolph, Quint
Nevada Nights - Georgina Gentry   713

Ransom, Gat
Waltz with the Lady - Betina Lindsey   1195

Roper, Jake
A Lady of the West - Linda Howard   934

Savage, Luke
The Miss and the Maverick - DeLoras Scott   1751

Sproull, Fern
Fern - Leigh Greenwood   757

Steele, Jackson Ledgeway
Seasons of Gold - Stef Ann Holm   914

Terrell, Haste
Journey's End - Mildred Riley   1641

Wyatt, Chance
The Tender Texan - Jodi Thomas   1931

CRIME SUSPECT

Benedict, Zach
Perfect - Judith McNaught   1333

Hawkinson, Nicholas
Ashton's Secret - Liana Laverentz   1163

Ramsey, Price
My Only Desire - Andrea Parnell   1508

Romney, Valerian
Shadow Dance - Anne Stuart   1890

CRIME VICTIM

Beaumont, Francis
Captives of the Night - Loretta Chase   338

Kaufman, Holly
Pretty Maids in a Row - Marilyn Campbell   301

CRIMINAL

Cade, Nicolas
Renegade Embrace - Virginia Brown   235

McGuire, Ethan
Silken Dreams - Lisa Bingham   147

McIntosh, Cord
Apache Wind - Carol Finch   643

Teran
The Knowing Crystal - Kathleen Morgan   1417

CRITIC

Harper, Suzi
Timely Matrimony - Kasey Michaels   1371

DANCER

Asquith, Courtney
Tonight and Forever - Caryl Wilson   2044

Chapin, Marianna
Country Dance - Margaret Westhaven   2005

de Barante, Rosalie
Dangerous Diversions - Margaret Evans Porter   1534

Domenici, Carlo
Pirouette - Madeline Hale   782

Eberhart, Ena
After All - Jill Marie Landis   1142

Le Clerc, Cendrine
Gilded Dreams - Kristy Daniels   461

Sullivan, Leanne
Love's Timeless Dance - Vivian Knight-Jenkins   1093

Varonne, Nicole
Pirouette - Madeline Hale   782

Wild, Ian
Wild Card - Nancy Hutchinson   955

DEBUTANTE

Acton, Eleanor
Rogue's Reward - Jean R. Ewing   617

Bragg, Lucy
The Fires of Paradise - Brenda Joyce   1026

Brightham, Betsy
Bringing Out Betsy - Sheila Rabe   1582

Bryn, Dilys
The Infamous Rake - Norma Lee Clark   361

Carlisle, Drewe
The Barbarous Scot - Dawn Lindsey   1197

Carr, Alison
Apache Bride - JoAnne Redd   1606

Carter, Candice
Darkest Heart - Brenda Joyce   1025

Carteret, Georgiana "Georgie"
Love's Gambit - Meg-Lynn Roberts   1662

Caulfield, Allegra
Moonlight Veil - Janis Laden   1128

Cheney, Emma
Miss Cheney's Charade - Emily Hendrickson   853

Chivenham, Eleanor
An Arranged Marriage - Jo Beverley   131

Corstairs, Sabelle "Isabelle"
Sabelle - Veronica Sattler   1722

Devane, Patricia
The Last Lord - Melinda Pryce   1557

Devane, Susan
The Last Lord - Melinda Pryce   1557

Dubay, Gabrielle
Midnight Rogue - Elaine Barbieri   70

Dundas, Caroline
A Deceitful Heart - Karla Hocker   901

Eagleton, Sibyl
A Scandalous Suggestion - Emily Hendrickson   857

Fitzgerald, Susannah "Butterfly"
Perchance to Dream - Maura Seger   1763

Gabriel, Sylvia
Miss Gabriel's Gambit - Rita Boucher   187

Garrick, Alexa
Devil's Prize - Kat Martin   1275

Godwin, Celine
His Magic Touch - Stella Cameron   287

Harding, Felicia
Felicia - Cathleen Clare   357

Hardy, Carolyn
Bath Charade - Amanda Scott   1742

Harmon, Cassie
Flame in the Night - Jack McGowan   1311

Hathaway, Kate
The Heart Remembers - Barbara Hazard   842

Helena
The Spanish Lady - Joan Smith   1846

Hillary
The Bedeviled Baron - Sarah Eagle   584

Hornsby, Letitia "Letty"
Dreaming - Jill Barnett   87

Lacey, Alice
The Desirable Duchess - Marion Chesney   347

Lamb, Jillian
A Spirited Affair - Lynn Kerstan   1060

MacAfee, Prudence "Angel"
The Passion of an Angel - Kasey Michaels   1370

MacRae, Skylar
Whispers of Love - Gina Robins   1677

Mansard, Catherine
An Impetuous Miss - Mary Chase Comstock   383

Mapleton, Amelia
Amelia's Intrigue - Judith A. Lansdowne   1162

Markham, Mirabelle "Mira"
The Dreadful Debutante - Marion Chesney   348

Melcombe, Rowena
The Halloween Husband - Sandra Heath   844

Montague, Lily
Promise Me Forever - Cara Miles   1374

Morris, Brianna
The Captured Heart - Sheila O'Hallion   1458

O'Day, Elinor
Lord Dearborn's Destiny - Brenda Hiatt   888

Osborn, Eliza
Miss Osborne Misbehaves - Marian Devon   526

Powell, Lucy
A Noble Deception - Sara Blayne   174

Prestwich, Meribe
The Black Widow - Charlotte Louise Dolan   542

Raithby, Philippa
Unlikely Guardian - Carol Proctor   1556

Ramsbottom, Belinda
Christmas Escapade - Meg-Lynn Roberts   1661

Randall, Cecily
The Rake's Reward - Mary Kingsley   1074

Randolph, Sonya
A Loyal Companion - Barbara Metzger   1354

Renaud, Tiffany
Deceptive Desires - Wanda Owen   1474

Rivington, Maryann
Lady Maryann's Dilemma - Karla Hocker   903

St. Helm, Rosamund
Wild Rose - Rebecca Ward   1990

St. James, Cassandra
Love Hear My Heart - Sonya T. Pelton   1516

Scarborough, Emily
Once an Angel - Teresa Medeiros   1341

Standing, Charity
Midnight Magic - Betina M. Krahn   1101

Stanton, Melanie
When Passion Calls - Cassie Edwards   594

Sutton, Lizzie
Two Corinthians - Carola Dunn   575

Talbot, Diana
Madcap Johnny - Jeanne Carmichael   318

Talbot-Harrow, Laura
Masque of Jade - Emma Merritt   1346

Thackery, Amethyst
The Thackery Jewels - Phyllis Taylor Pianka   1530

Thackery, Emerald
The Thackery Jewels - Phyllis Taylor Pianka   1530

Thackery, Topaz
The Thackery Jewels - Phyllis Taylor Pianka   1530

Trevarren, Annie
Princess Annie - Linda Lael Miller   1385

Waverly, Chloe
Christmas Belles - Susan Carroll   322

Wickham, Lucy
Miss Wickham's Betrothal - Nancy Richards-Akers   1632

Wilde, Katherine
A Traitorous Heart - Violet Hamilton   787

Wimberly, Rowanne
The Luck of the Devil - Barbara Metzger   1355

Winston, Rosalind
Lord Dearborn's Destiny - Brenda Hiatt   888

Witherton, Patience
Patience Is a Virtue - Judith Nelson   1435

Wynswich, Marian
Marian's Christmas Wish - Carla Kelly   1052

DEFENDANT

Wade, Luke
White Lies and Alibis - Tracy Hughes   952

DEMON

Monckton, Rex (Gaucelm)
By All That Is Sacred - Laura Gilmour Bennett   127

DENTIST

Dunbar, Celeste
Hearts Afire - Monique Gilmore   727

DESIGNER

Bonsseauc, Samara
Lies - Doris Parmett   1506

Childs, Sandy
The Cinderella Game - Jane Shore   1786

Donaldson, Jess
Unwilling Woman - Sue Peters   1520

Maples, Genevieve
Dance of Deception - Suzannah Davis   479

Marone, Sophia
Tattered Silk - Elaine Barbieri   75

Nesbitt, Maggie
Through the Years - Katherine Sinclair   1808

Radcliffe, Electra
Everlasting - Lynda Trent   1958

Wyler, Miko
The Runaway Heart - Anne Ladley   1131

DETECTIVE

Ames, Kenyon
A Perfect Gentleman - Arlene James   965

Banning, Dallas
Rebel in Silk - Sandra Chastain   343

Blood, Sebastian
San Francisco Surrender - Donna Fletcher   652

Brock, Sawyer
Sweet Justice - Mary Lynn Baxter   103

Burke, Devlin
Seductive Caress - Carla Simpson   1800

Cantrell, Holt
Deception's Sweet Kiss - Gina Robins   1672

Chase, Catherine
Betray the Night - Kay McMahon   1326

Clarebridge, Joy
Forever Joy - Lacey Dancer   458

Crocker, Daniel
Distant Thunder - Lisa Bingham   145

Dalton, Alec
A Rose in the Shadows - Catherine Wyatt   2075

Dane
The Case of the Mesmerizing Boss - Diana Palmer   1488

Donelli, Joe
Stolen Moments - Sherryl Woods 2069

English, Sam
Nowhere to Run - Pat Warren 1995

Farrell, Rafe
Emerald Angel - Susan Sackett 1709

Hampton, Alex
Rebel Dreams - Patricia Rice 1620

Harlowe, Sunny
My Only Desire - Andrea Parnell 1508

Hawkes, Stephen
Love's Magic Spell - Wendy Garrett 695

Hollister, Lane
Seduction's Raging Flame - Judith Steel 1871

MacKennoch
A Tempting Miss - Janice Bennett 125

Marlowe, Carol
Whispers in Time - Becky Lee Weyrich 2011

McCormick, Troy
Charade - Christina Hamlett 788

McKenzie, Matt
Passions - Christiane Heggan 847

Montana, Lane
Crime of Passion - Kay Hooper 921

Parks, Reynard
Santana Rose - Olga Bicos 141

Savage, T.J.
Betray the Night - Kay McMahon 1326

Steele, Jackson Ledgeway
Seasons of Gold - Stef Ann Holm 914

Stern, Adam
Love's Sweet Bounty - Colleen Faulkner 625

Tyson, Revel
Desperado's Caress - Carla Simpson 1798

Warne, Kate
A Rose in the Shadows - Catherine Wyatt 2075

DETECTIVE—AMATEUR

DeWitt, Molly
Hot Property - Sherryl Woods 2067
Hot Secret - Sherryl Woods 2068

Harter, Christine
Tug of Hearts - Julia Winfield 2050

DETECTIVE—HOMICIDE

Browning, Kendra
When Midnight Comes - Robin Burcell 253

Dallas, Eve
Naked in Death - J.D. Robb 1656

DETECTIVE—POLICE

Bramwell, Alex
The Door Ajar - Joan Overfield 1471

Calloway, Clint
Cowboy Cop - Rachel Lee 1172

Cross, Zachary
Trust Me - Jeane Renick 1610

Garnier, Clay
Night's Immortal Touch - Cherlyn Jac 960

Hollister, Dane
Dream Man - Linda Howard 933

O'Hara, Michael
Hot Property - Sherryl Woods 2067

Hot Secret - Sherryl Woods 2068

Winston, Dakota
Cowboy Cop - Rachel Lee 1172

Wyler, Tom
Embers - Antoinette Stockenberg 1881

DETECTIVE—PRIVATE

Callahan, Kane
Moonlight Enchantment - Carol Finch 645

Cassidy, Lane
Last Chance - Jill Marie Landis 1145

Delgado, David
Slow Burn - Heather Graham Pozzessere 1551

Dennigan, Matt
Mask of Night - Lois Wolfe 2058

Fleetwood, Sebastian
Dangerous - Amanda Quick 1566

Grant, C.J.
Partners in Time - Pamela Simpson 1802

Keane, Holden
Colorado Flame - Colleen Quinn 1577

Kincaid, Mitchell
What the Lady Wants - Jennifer Crusie 442

Logan, Daniel
Sweetwater - Sandra Chastain 346

MacKenzie, Hunter
No Easy Task - Chloe Summers 1896

Master, York
Fallen Angel - Deborah Camp 294

McAllister, Jace
The Stolen Heart - Kit Gardner 685

McCal, Jonah
Above Suspicion - Eleanor Woods 2064

McGowan, Shawn
Passion's Bold Fire - Rosalyn Alsobrook 12

Midnight Louie
Crystal Days - Carole Nelson Douglas 554
Crystal Nights - Carole Nelson Douglas 555

Powell, Sterling
Sterling's Reasons - Joey Light 1188

St. James, Holly
Ekahi - Georgette Livingston 1218

Surprise, Kyle
Sara's Surprise - Deborah Smith 1841

Terrell, Haste
Journey's End - Mildred Riley 1641

Walker, Remington
Liberty Blue - Robin Lee Hatcher 828

Webb, Thaddeus
Winter's Flame - Maria Greene 756

DIETICIAN

Daniels, Erin
Look Beyond the Dream - Noelle Berry McCue 1303

DIPLOMAT

ben Rashid, Ahmed
King's Ransom - Diana Palmer 1489

Bennett, Rosa
The Doll's House - Evelyn Anthony 25

de Montfort, David
Into the Storm - Maura Seger 1760

de Pontesse, Hugues
The Sorceress - Claire Delacroix 495

Donovan, Thomas Joseph
Masquerade in Moonlight - Kasey Michaels 1368

Elsbach, Stefan
The Princess Royal - Virginia Coffman 374

Faulkner, William Devereaux
Forevermore - Maura Seger 1758

Graham, Gilbert
Marian's Christmas Wish - Carla Kelly 1052

Gunn, Christopher
Silver Tears - Becky Lee Weyrich 2009

Lancaster, Chase
Midnight Fire - Linda Ladd 1126

Lawrence, Joe "Sky Warrior"
Forever Ecstasy - Janelle Taylor 1915

McDonald, Miriam
The Border Lord - Arnette Lamb 1136

DIRECTOR

Benedict, Zach
Perfect - Judith McNaught 1333

Bullard, Julie
Joy and Anger - Jennifer Blake 171

Catherwood, Shreve
Acts of Love - Deana James 967
Acts of Passion - Deana James 968

Grant, Jason
The Cinderella Game - Jane Shore 1786

Needham, Adrian
Hot Property - Elise Title 1949

Santana, Rafe
The Right Direction - Candace Schuler 1735

DIVER

O'Connor, Adam
Eyes of Fire - Heather Graham Pozzessere 1549

DIVORCED PERSON

Adams, John
Love Lesson - Marian Oaks 1445

Anderson, Ellen
Shifting Sands - Suzanne Ellison 609

Barnhart, Anne
Deadly Secret - Martha Johnson 997

Briggs, Cora
Wild Oats - Pamela Morsi 1430

Cannon, Christine
Maybe This Time - Barbara Bretton 213

Curran, Bess
Bygones - LaVyrle Spencer 1858

Curran, Michael
Bygones - LaVyrle Spencer 1858

Faulkner, Caroline
The Law of Love - Martha Schroeder 1734

Grimes, Ivy
Lovers and Friends - Claire Bocardo 176

Harper, Libby
Operation Homefront - Marilyn Pappano 1494

Longmore, Hattie
Mountain Ecstasy - Linda Sandifer 1718

MacKenzie, Chelsey
First Comes Baby - Kristin Morgan 1418

Matthias, Connie
White Light - Wendy Haley   786

McMurphy, Joe
Maybe This Time - Barbara Bretton   213

Robards, Carolyn
A Christmas Love - Kathleen Creighton   416

Smith, Chloe
No Illusion - Lynette Kent   1058

Stuart, Elizabeth
Still Waters - Tami Hoag   900

Talbot, Cornelia Lloyd
Colorado Temptation - Gwen Cleary   362

Turlow, Phoebe
Pirates - Linda Lael Miller   1384

Turner, Hannah
Tender Heart - Gwen Cleary   366

Whitaker, Carolyn
Love Lesson - Marian Oaks   1445

DOCTOR

Alden, Ryan
A Touch of Magic - Carin Rafferty   1585

Aragon, Daniel
Tempt Me with Kisses - Phoebe Conn   387

Banks, James
The Rainbow Promise - Lisa Gregory   765

Baron, Olivia
Outcast - Emily Carmichael   316

Bascom, Will
Highland Flame - Stephanie Bartlett   95

Beaumont, Adria
Chase the Dawn - Kay McMahon   1327

Blue Song, Katherine
Beloved Woman - Deborah Smith   1838

Bowcock, Elizabeth
Sagebrush Bride - Tanya Anne Crosby   434

Brigham, Gilbert
Private Paradise - Lucy Elliot   603

Browne, Chelsea
Sands of Time - Terri Valentine   1967

Caldwell, Hope
Beloved Intruder - Joan Van Nuys   1971

Caldwell, Lathe
Endless Seduction - Rosalyn Alsobrook   11

Calhoun, Rachel
Walk in the Light - Charles Durham   577

Cameron, Jesse
One Wore Blue - Heather Graham   739

Carrick, Ian
Waiting for the Moon - Kristin Hannah   800

Challoner, Luke
Sweet Illusion - Angela Carson   325

Chambers, Catherine
All but Love - Ann Howard White   2013

Clayborne, Thane
Midnight Kiss - Marcia Evanick   615

Colton, Spencer
Apache Heartsong - Janis Reams Hudson   946

Conway, Dan
Texas Healer - Ruth Langan   1157

Cook, Anthony
Libby's London Merchant - Carla Kelly   1051

Daniels, Drew
Just Desserts - Theresa Gladden   728

Danners, Zachary
Harvest Song - Karen Lockwood   1222

de Savin, Sebastien
Miracle - Deborah Smith   1840

Drake, Jonathan
A Delicate Matter - Rebecca Forster   662

Duffy, Thomas
Out of This World Marriage - Maggie Shayne   1779

Duncan, Terry
Wolf and the Angel - Kathleen Creighton   419

Farraday, Brent
Shattered Illusions - Linda Renee De Jong   487

Farrow, Will
Surrender the Night - Colleen Shannon   1770

Foster, Nathan
Merry Christmas, Mommy - Muriel Jensen   985

Frost, Kayne
The Bear Affair - Cynthia Powell   1546

Gervais, Leila
Captive Rose - Miriam Minger   1397

Glendower, Morgan
Beneath a Harvest Moon - Catherine Wyatt   2074

Gorton, Emily
Blazing Passion - Barbara Cummings   445

Herne
No Other Love - Flora M. Speer   1856

Hunter, Quinn
Till the Stars Fall - Kathleen Gilles Seidel   1768

Jacobs, Roan
The Loving - Sandra Canfield   305

Kendrick, Seth
The Barefoot Bride - Joan Johnston   1004

Kenneman, Aaron
Forever Ashley - Lori Copeland   392

Lancaster, Viveca "Vivid"
Vivid - Beverly Jenkins   981

Lawson, Wendall
Risk - Doris Parmett   1507

MacKenzie, Alexandra
Northern Fire, Northern Star - Scotney St. James   1865

MacKenzie, Caitlin
Just Desserts - Theresa Gladden   728

MacNeill, Ian
A Deeper Magic - Jillian Hunter   953

Malone, Kate
Witch Dance - Peggy Webb   1998

McCall, Darcy
Heart of the Wild - Donna Stephens   1874

McNamara, Jason
Prescription for Love - Anne Ladley   1130

Morgan, Jacob
Kansas Kiss - Christine Dorsey   550

Murdoch, Lucas "Doc"
Texas Temptation - Gina Robins   1676

Orchin, David
Lies - Doris Parmett   1506

Parker, Annie
The Touch of Fire - Linda Howard   935

Percy, Len
Darkness at Cottonwood Hall - Madelyn Sanders   1717

Pfeiffer, Paige
Suddenly - Barbara Delinsky   502

Pierce, Justin
The Falcon and the Swan - Diane Gates Robinson   1680

Pierson, Robert
The Moon Pool - Diana Stuart   1893

Prescott, Ethan
Dakota Dawn - Dana Ransom   1589

Randall, Claire Beauchamp
Dragonfly in Amber - Diana Gabaldon   673
Voyager - Diana Gabaldon   675

Randall, Luke
Harvest of Love - Nancy Sheehan   1780

Robards, Megan Thomas
Visions of Tomorrow - Katherine Sinclair   1809

Rodene, Gavin
Dark Cries of Gray Oaks - Lee Karr   1043

St. Clair, Maxene
Prescription for Death - Janet McGiffin   1310

Savitch, Ty
A Wild Yearning - Penelope Williamson   2039

Shaffer, Zach
At Risk - Jeanne Stephens   1875

Stillman, Todd
The Stillman Curse - Peggy Morse   1424

Torres, Benjamin
Return to Paradise - Shirl Henke   866

Toulon, Miriam
Return to Paradise - Shirl Henke   866

Vallerand, Philippe
Only with Your Love - Lisa Kleypas   1089

Wilkes, Tyler
Sweet Everlasting - Patricia Gaffney   678

Wolfe, Andrew
Walk in the Light - Charles Durham   577

DRIFTER

Beaumont, Will "Billy Ray"
In Sinful Harmony - Marilyn Pappano   1493

Booth, Gib
Meant to Be - Elizabeth DeLancey   496

Boyd, Harlan
Texas! Sage - Sandra Brown   232

Carradine, Jake
The Heart's Journey - Emily Bradshaw   197

Mayhew, Jeremy
Golden Fires - Colleen Shannon   1769

Moran, Whip
Only Love - Elizabeth Lowell   1232

Moreland, Adam
Bouquet - Shirl Henke   860

Morgan, Blake
Boston Renegade - June Lund Shiplett   1785

Morgan, Mac
Dreams and Wishes - Karren Radko   1583

Morgan, Slade
Scarlet Sunset, Silver Nights - Leigh Greenwood   759

Paxton, Jake
For The Love of Grace - Ginna Gray   750

Peters, Brock
Diamond in the Rough - Millie Criswell   426

Rider, Jim
Mountain Ecstasy - Linda Sandifer   1718

Sinclair, Brazo
Capture the Night - Geralyn Dawson   482

Stone, Mad Dog
If You Believe - Kristin Hannah   798

ECONOMIST

Stone, Adam
Sing Carols with the Angels - Mary Leask   1171

EDITOR

Banning, Dallas
Rebel in Silk - Sandra Chastain   343

D'Arcy, Monique
Something Borrowed, Something Blue - Jillian Karr   1042

Hall, Susannah
A Wife in Time - Cathie Linz   1214

Kelley, Cassandra
Out of the Blue - Kasey Michaels   1369

McShane, Liz
Rhapsody in Time - Judith O'Brien   1451

Worthington, Matt
Spitfire - Sonya Birmingham   151

ENGINEER

Boyd, Harlan
Texas! Sage - Sandra Brown   232

Burke, Dillon
Breath of Scandal - Sandra Brown   227

Manning, Rich
Marriage of Inconvenience - Debbie Macomber   1251

Phillips, Maura
Bits and Pieces - Merline Lovelace   1227

Travis, Rae "Rachel"
Terror by Design - Jane Edwards   598

ENTERTAINER

Avenil, Lily
Wyoming Wildfire - Anne Harmon   807

Buchanan, Diane
Written in the Stars - Nan Ryan   1708

Carmichael, Joy
Dreams of Joy - Holly S. McClure   1301

Carney, Rose
Defiant Rose - Colleen Quinn   1578

Cenred
The Amethyst Crown - Katherine Deauville   492

Costello, Kate "Leather"
Homeward Bound - Kathryn Attalla   34

Howard, Kelsey
Love and Laughter - Carole Buck   245

Knight, Marty
Knight and Day - Carole Buck   244

Miracle, Amy
Miracle - Deborah Smith   1840

Morningstar, Matthew
A Wilder Love - Laura Parker   1505

Pierce, Cori
Mississippi Mistress - Gina Robins   1675

Rain Shadow
Rain Shadow - Cheryl St. John   1866

EQUESTRIAN

Avenil, Lily
Wyoming Wildfire - Anne Harmon   807

Buchanan, Diane
Written in the Stars - Nan Ryan   1708

Faust, Elaine
The Mistress of Foxgrove - Lee Magner   1263

Marshall, Anne
Heir to Vengeance - Roberta Eckert   590

Raithby, Philippa
Unlikely Guardian - Carol Proctor   1556

Wyndham, James
The Valentine Legacy - Catherine Coulter   410

EXPLORER

Digby, Lorence
The Enchantment - Kristin Hannah   796

Dunraven, Adam
The Serpent Beguiled - Betina Lindsey   1191

Marcus, Niles
Seek the Wild Shore - Leslie O'Grady   1456

Troy
Wild Flower - Jill Marie Landis   1149

Wolframson, Rorick
Gentle Warrior - Kathryn Hockett   904

FARMER

Beaumont, Stephen
Dearest Enemy - Stephanie Bartlett   94

Beckham, Daniel
Daniel's Bride - Linda Lael Miller   1378

Bergendahl, Kristianna
Firefly - Stef Ann Holm   911

Bright, Maggie
One Bright Morning - Alice Duncan   571

Chalmers, Lily
Lily and the Major - Linda Lael Miller   1382

Colfax, Hattie
Courting Miss Hattie - Pamela Morsi   1425

Courtney, Helen
Love Me Tonight - Nan Ryan   1706

Creed, Montana
Surrender a Dream - Jill Barnett   91

Donelli, Joe
Body and Soul - Sherryl Woods   2065
Hide and Seek - Sherryl Woods   2066

Drake, Andrew
Sungold - Jillian Dagg   450

Flannery, Mitch
Love's Stolen Promise - Sylvie Sommerfield   1852

Gardner, Grant
Temptation - Catherine Hart   823

Greene, Joshua
Eternity - Jude Deveraux   512

Hosea, Michael
Redeeming Love - Francine Rivers   1648

Jamison, Owen
Homeplace - Dorothy Garlock   686

Lamb, Jillian
A Spirited Affair - Lynn Kerstan   1060

Lang, Sunny
Sunny - Linda Madl   1260

Lowery, Samantha
Kansas Kiss - Christine Dorsey   550

Maguire, Hunter
Spring Blossom - Jill Metcalf   1349

Mathieson, Matt
This Side of Heaven - Karen Robards   1654

McKenna, Jamie
Angelfire - Linda Lael Miller   1376

Morgan, Amos
Heirloom - Candace Camp   290

Mulvehey, Rosie
The Wives of Bowie Stone - Maggie Osborne   1469

Neubauer, Anton
Rain Shadow - Cheryl St. John   1866

Owen, John
A Child's Promise - Deborah Bedford   117

Papandreou, Greta
The Past Is Another Country - Lois Battle   97

Pearson, Derek
Better than Before - Judith Duncan   572

Pickett, Tom
Pickett's Fence - Linda Shertzer   1783

Pinkney, Adelaide
Surrender a Dream - Jill Barnett   91

Pruitt, Victoria
Dearest Enemy - Stephanie Bartlett   94

Sites, Amanda
Temptation - Catherine Hart   823

Throckmorton, Mariah
If You Believe - Kristin Hannah   798

Traynor, Clay
A Christmas Love - Kathleen Creighton   416

Tyler, Reed
Courting Miss Hattie - Pamela Morsi   1425

Wellesley, Eric
Mail-Order Temptress - Jane Kidder   1062

Williams, Rachel
Pickett's Fence - Linda Shertzer   1783

Winslow, Andrea
Renegade's Kiss - Barbara Ankrum   24

Winslow, Jesse
Renegade's Kiss - Barbara Ankrum   24

FBI AGENT

Demarkian, Gregor
Bleeding Hearts - Jane Haddam   774

Donay, Carl
Chance Encounter - Molly Rice   1612

West, Logan
Ekahi - Georgette Livingston   1218

FEMINIST

Castle, Antonia
Heart Strings - Lydia Browne   237

Cavanaugh, Kate
Storyville - Lois Battle   98

Grimsley, Ellen
Miss Grimsley's Oxford Career - Carla Kelly   1054

Lee, Elizabeth
Heaven on Earth - Michelle Brandon   205

McBride, Shiloh
Deception's Sweet Kiss - Gina Robins   1672

Randsome, Julia
Storyville - Lois Battle   98

Scott, Brianna
King's Ransom - Diana Palmer   1489

FIANCE(E)

Alton, Simon Hilliard
The Marriage Gamble - Sarah Eagle   586

Bliss, Chloe
The Bridegroom - Carol Jerina   987

Campbell, Malen
Lucky in Love - Rebecca Robbins   1657

Chauncey, Philipa
Charmed - Stella Cameron   285

Collins, Todd
Always a Lady - Sharon Sala   1712

Creighton, Elliot
Sweet Forever - Becky Lee Weyrich   2010

Dalton, Jeff
Tempest in Time - Eugenia Riley   1639

D'Arcy, Monique
Something Borrowed, Something Blue - Jillian
    Karr   1042

De Leroy, Michelle
Wild Magnolia - Betty Brooks   224

Delaney, Thorin
The Lady and the Outlaw - Katherine Compton   380

Denbeigh, Bernard
Ghostly Enchantment - Angie Ray   1600

Fairburn
Beloved Avenger - Joan Van Nuys   1970

Fontenot, Fabian
Tempest in Time - Eugenia Riley   1639

Gilbert, Katherine
The Lady and the Wolf - Julie Beard   105

Godwin, Celine
His Magic Touch - Stella Cameron   287

Graham, Angelique
Angel's Devil - Suzanne Enoch   613

Hanover, Georgina
Paper Tiger - Patricia Rice   1619

Ives, Richard
Something Borrowed, Something Blue - Jillian
    Karr   1042

Jamison, Cassandra
The Magic - Robin Lee Hatcher   829

Jordan, Liberty
Love's Sweetest Secret - Gina Robins   1674

Layton, Jeff
Once upon Forever - Becky Lee Weyrich   2008

Leandra of Lyonesse
A Tender Magic - Linda Madl   1262

Maloney, Kate
Taming Kate - Eugenia Riley   1638

Matlock, Silver
Rugged Splendor - Robin Leigh   1180

McCord, Judd
Wild Magnolia - Betty Brooks   224

McDonald, Fanny
Lucky in Love - Rebecca Robbins   1657

McGuire, Mariah Rose
Wild Texas Rose - Martha Hix   897

Monaghan, Heather
Wild Irish Heather - Ashland Price   1555

Morgan, Abigail
Hostage Heart - Lisa Hendrix   859

Newman, Jeremy
Passions - Christiane Heggan   847

O'Malley, Mary Katherine
Denver - Sara Orwig   1463

O'Rourke, Bevan
Tender Lies - Kay McMahon   1328

Parkins, Mariah
Renegade Bride - Barbara Ankrum   23

Penderton, Joslyn
The Reluctant Suitor - Sarah Eagle   587

Prescott, Laura
Across a Starlit Sea - Rebecca Brandewyne   198

Salazar, Diego
Midnight Rose - Robin Lee Hatcher   830

Sheffield, Amanda
Wind Rose - Krista Janssen   977

Talbot, Simon
Angel's Devil - Suzanne Enoch   613

Tarrant, Damara
The Marriage Gamble - Sarah Eagle   586

Trefarron, Prescott
The Bridegroom - Carol Jerina   987

Trowbridge, Genevieve
Dakota Desire - Dana Ransom   1590

Washington, Leona
Midnight Rose - Robin Lee Hatcher   830

Westbourne, Margaret
Ghostly Enchantment - Angie Ray   1600

Whitfield, Ashley
Magnificent Affair - Fayrene Preston   1553

Winston, Charlotte
Captain's Captive - Christine Dorsey   549

Yarbro, Ian
The Legacy - Linda Lael Miller   1381

FILMMAKER

Clark, Catlin
Special Effects - Jo Leigh   1178

Knight, Joseph
Taboo - Elizabeth Gage   681

McKeever, Luke
Special Effects - Jo Leigh   1178

Price, Phil
There Is a Season - Phyllis Houseman   930

Ringling, Doug
More than You Dreamed - Kathleen Gilles
    Seidel   1767

Snow, Gracie
Heaven, Texas - Susan Elizabeth Phillips   1527

FINANCIER

Barzan, Carlos
Midnight in Marrakesh - Meryl Sawyer   1731

Dylan, Josh
The Gilded Cage - Edith Layton   1169

Kimbrough, Mark
Blind Chance - Meryl Sawyer   1729

Mendoza, Robert
A Lasting Fire - Beverly Byrne   266

Sheridan, Trevor
Lions and Lace - Meagan McKinney   1324

FIRE FIGHTER

Valle, Derek
White Light - Wendy Haley   786

FISHERMAN

Adair, Duncan
Golden Prospect - Shirley Parenteau   1495

Le Blanc, Armand
Jessica's Song - Virginia Nielsen   1442

Rivers, Sash
Slow Dance - Donna Julian   1031

FOREMAN

Calder, Lance
The Savage - Nicole Jordan   1019

Cordell, Nathan
Follow the Wind - Janelle Taylor   1914

de Suela, Cade
Texas Lily - Patricia Rice   1622

Foster, Wade
Defiant - Patricia Potter   1537

Frazer, Duncan "Segundo"
Silver Thunder - Joan Hohl   909

Hollis, Zach
Desert Flame - Anne Harmon   806

Killian, James Comanche
Lawless - Alexandra Thorne   1940

Streeter, Judd
The Passions of Chelsea Kane - Barbara
    Delinsky   501

Tyake, Will
Meridon - Philippa Gregory   768

Walker, Luke
Cheyenne's Lady - Patricia Rice   1613

FORTUNE HUNTER

McIntock, Clive
Morning Song - Karen Robards   1651

Scott, Christopher
Unveiled - Colleen Quinn   1579

FOUNDLING

Ravenscroft, Tessa
Wildwitch - Kimberleigh Caitlin   272

Waverly, Fanny
The First Rebellion - Marion Chesney   349

Waverly, Frederica
Silken Bonds - Marion Chesney   350

FRIEND

Briggs, Luther
Runabout - Pamela Morsi   1429

McCormick, Flint
Bold Montana Bride - Karen Bale   50

McLaren, Ross
Deadly Secret - Martha Johnson   997

Weatherly, Jane
A Distant Dawn - Katherine Sinclair   1806

FRONTIERSMAN

Hawk
Sweet Savage Splendor - Lauren Wilde   2030

Martin, Cody
Christmas Miracle - Ruth Langan   1152

O'Duine, Tearlach
Wild Conquest - Hannah Howell   941

Rowe, Garrick
Nightrose - Dorothy Garlock   688

St. Claire, Eben
Rough and Tender - Selena MacPherson   1258

Scott, Jordan
Visions of the Heart - Emily Carmichael   317

Sheridan, Deke
Cheyenne Amber - Catherine Anderson   16

Winterhawke, John
The Bride Wore Spurs - Sharon Ihle   956

FRONTIERSWOMAN

Alexander, D'lise
Kentucky Bride - Norah Hess   885

Ballard, Liberty Anne
Temptation's Price - Dallas Schulze   1738

Becket, Faith Ann
Desert Sunrise - Raine Cantrell   310

Bliss, Abigail
When Lightning Strikes - Rexanne Becnel   115

Edwards, Felicia
Sweet Savage Splendor - Lauren Wilde   2030

Fielding, Cameo
More than Just a Night - Connie Rinehold   1642

Graham, Elyse
Passion's Gift - Jane Kidder   1064

Jacobson, Melissa
A Fire in the Blood - Shirl Henke   861

James, Cara
Until Tomorrow - Jill Marie Landis   1148

Kennedy, Storm
A Promise of Thunder - Connie Mason   1290

Lucton, Cassandra
Silver Shadows - Marianne Willman   2040

Maxwell, Maxie
Cactus Blossom - Emily Bradshaw   195

Mead, Colly "Spotted Woman"
Cheyenne Dreams - Peggy Hanchar   790

Smith, Shannon Connor
Only Love - Elizabeth Lowell   1232

Storm, Daniella
Kiley's Storm - Suzanne Elizabeth   599

Stuart, Cassandra
Angel - Johanna Lindsey   1199

Wilson, Letitia
Savage Promise - Cassie Edwards   593

FUGITIVE

Ashford, Henry
Unspoken Vows - Connie Rinehold   1643

Baker, Taylor
Prince Charming - Julie Garwood   704

Berenger, Rye
Love's Windswept Embrace - Michalann Perry   1517

Blue, Liberty "Libby"
Liberty Blue - Robin Lee Hatcher   828

Calhoun, McKenzie Kathryn "Macky"
The Redhead and the Preacher - Sandra
  Chastain   344

Chiari, Gabrielle
Night Fires - Sandra Marton   1286

Crockett, Casity
Forbidden Kiss - Gina Robins   1673

Dalton, Tyler
Outlaw Lover - Lindsey Hanks   795

Devlin, Elizabeth
Mississippi Flame - Cheryl Biggs   143

Drusus, Cailin
To Love Again - Bertrice Small   1826

Dryden, Claire
Atlanta - Sara Orwig   1462

Dugan, Bridget
Mountain Dawn - Kathleen Kane   1040

Forsythe, Jonathan
Lord Harlequin - Marian Devon   525

Foster, Wade
Defiant - Patricia Potter   1537

Galloway, Rook
Star-Crossed - Susan Krinard   1117

Loring, Steve
Terms of Love - Shirl Henke   868

McCain, Shadoe
Love's Perfect Dream - Caroline Bourne   191

McCay, Rafe
The Touch of Fire - Linda Howard   935

McClure, Brianna
The Black Angel - Cordia Byers   261

McGuire, Ethan
Silken Dreams - Lisa Bingham   147

Mills, Laura
Nevada Flame - Rochelle Wayne   1997

Newton, Bethany
Far Horizons - Katherine Sinclair   1807

O'Bannion, Jennie "Fire Flower"
Comanche Wind - Genell Dellin   508

O'Brien, Carrie
The Miss and the Maverick - DeLoras Scott   1751

O'Connell, Gabriel William Danaher
Outcast - Emily Carmichael   316

Perrivale, Simon
The Captive - Victoria Holt   918

Quinn, Emily
Hot as Sin - Debra Dixon   532

Randell, Hannah
Forever in Texas - Jodi Thomas   1930

Russell, Sienna
The Passion Ruby - Eboni Snoe   1848

Savage, Shoz
The Fires of Paradise - Brenda Joyce   1026

Sellington, Amanda "Amy Smith"
Home Fires - Susan Kay Law   1164

Seymour, Maxim
So Worthy My Love - Kathleen E. Woodiwiss   2062

Smith, Dayra
Far Star - Anne Avery   38

Sutcliffe, Miriam "Miri"
Visions of the Heart - Emily Carmichael   317

Valmont, Alexandre
The Captain's Dilemma - Gail Eastwood   588

Van Allen, Christal
Fair Is the Rose - Meagan McKinney   1322

Van Alstyne, Shanna
Bittersweet Promises - Trana Mae Simmons   1791

Walker, Susannah
Dancing on Snowflakes - Jane Bonander   180

Windsor, Angela
Beneath Passion's Skies - Bobbi Smith   1834

Windsor, Sarah
Beneath Passion's Skies - Bobbi Smith   1834

Wyatt, Hank
Imagine - Jill Barnett   88

GAMBLER

Beaumont, Jaine
Tempted by Fire - Thea Devine   523

Caine, Jared
Fortune's Lady - Victoria Thompson   1933

Cantrell, Grayson
Mississippi Flame - Cheryl Biggs   143

Cavanaugh, Matt
A Wild Desire - Rebecca George   719

Chandler, Sam
Nevada Ecstasy - Lindsey Hanks   794

Courtenay, Miles
The Lady and the Rake - Carola Dunn   574

Davenport, Judith
Virtue - Jane Feather   635

de Navarro, Durango
Rainbow's End - Rebecca Brandewyne   203

Devereau, Dillon
Gambler's Tempting Kisses - Charlotte Hubbard   944

Devereaux, Quinn
Rainbow - Patricia Potter   1543

Devlin, Garrett
Wild Star - Nicole Jordan   1021

Emerson, Grant
Riverboat Seduction - Caroline Bourne   192

Grant, Maximilian
Desert Fire - Evelyn Rogers   1686

Gregory, Beaumont
No Man's Fortune - Kristie Knight   1092

Harden, Trace
The Seduction of Samantha Kincade - Maggie
  Osborne   1468

Honeycutt, DeLacey
Hearts Are Wild - Teresa Hart   824

McCain, Shadoe
Love's Perfect Dream - Caroline Bourne   191

McFee, Fiona
Silken Promises - Lisa Bingham   148

McIntock, Clive
Morning Song - Karen Robards   1651

McLeod, Hector
Winds of Eden - Justina Burgess   254

Monteigne, Tyler
Paper Roses - Patricia Rice   1618

Montgomery, Dalton
Priceless - Mary Lynn Baxter   102

O'Neal, Brent
Riverboat Rogue - Jane Toombs   1952

Sites, Amanda
Temptation - Catherine Hart   823

Stewart, Ruarke
Angel Hunter - Ana Leigh   1175

Sutherland, Clay
Masque of Jade - Emma Merritt   1346

Tremayne, Jareth
Romantic Masquerade - Lois Stewart   1878

GARDENER

Lawrence, Adam
Scarlet Scandals - Carol Budd   249

GENIUS

Fletcher, Elias
Love and Laughter - Carole Buck   245

GENTLEMAN

Ballenrose
Ballenrose - Mallory Burgess   255

Banner, Gabriel
Reckless - Amanda Quick   1572

Blackthorne, Nicholas
A Rose at Midnight - Anne Stuart   1889

Blackwell, Saxon
Barefoot Bride - Rebecca Paisley   1478

Bouclair, Armand Kordell "Kord"
Southern Oaks - Brenna Braxton-Barshon   209

Braxton, Jared
Masque of Enchantment - Charlene Cross   439

Cavendish, Bart
Lady of the Moors - Mary Ellen Petty   1521

Charles
Counterfeit Heart - Anthea Malcolm   1264

Dalton, Richard
Thick as Thieves - Jennie Gallant   682

de Blanc, Rowan
Arrow to the Heart - Jennifer Blake   169

Diamond, Sylvester
Love Hear My Heart - Sonya T. Pelton   1516

Drummond, Daniel
Reckless Angel - Jane Feather   631

Duke, Henry
Country Dance - Margaret Westhaven   2005

Farrell, Stephen
Lady Maryann's Dilemma - Karla Hocker   903

Fitzroy, Darcy
China Blossom - Margaret Moore   1408

Flamenco, Rafael
Moonflower - Shirl Henke   862

Fletcher, Miles
The Love Knot - Elisabeth Fairchild   619

Fontenot, Fabian
Tempest in Time - Eugenia Riley   1639

Frazer, Jack
Christmas Belle - Mary Balogh   56

Hadley, Edward
The Spanish Lady - Joan Smith   1846

Hawkes, Gideon
Fireflower - Edith Layton   1168

Hawthorne, Adam
Enchantment - Coral Smith Saxe   1733

Hazelford, Charles
An Impetuous Miss - Mary Chase Comstock   383

Lampman, Peregrine
Promise of Spring - Mary Balogh   62

Landry, Charles
Woman Without a Past - Phyllis A. Whitney   2019

Lyndon-Fury, Napier
Hell Hath No Fury - Malcolm Macdonald   1244

Medland, Robert
A Scandalous Suggestion - Emily Hendrickson   857

Montclair, Valentine
Logic of the Heart - Patricia Veryan   1980

Nolte, Victor
With One Look - Jennifer Horsman   929

Prescott, Rory
Dakota Destiny - Dana Ransom   1591

Ramlin, Sebastian
Terms of Surrender - Mollie Ashton   33

Ransford, Oliver
Dangerous Masquerade - April Kihlstrom   1065

Raynor, Julian
Dangerous to Love - Elizabeth Thornton   1941

Ruthland, Damon
Forever My Love - Constance O'Banyon   1448

St. Ives, Julian
A Midsummer's Magic - Mary Chase Comstock   384

Slade, Cameron
A Jewel So Rare - Elizabeth Ann Michaels   1361

Standish, Pierre Claghorn
The Anonymous Miss Addams - Kasey
   Michaels   1362

Stearns, Justin
Surrender My Heart - Lois Greiman   770

Stone, Jonathan
Chase the Dawn - Kay McMahon   1327

Stuart, Jonathan
Shadow's Kiss - Joan Hohl   908

Talbot, Anthony
Amelia's Intrigue - Judith A. Lansdowne   1162

Tattershall, Peter
A Delicate Balance - Roberta Gellis   708

Vallerand, Max
Only in Your Arms - Lisa Kleypas   1088

GENTLEWOMAN

Addams
The Anonymous Miss Addams - Kasey
   Michaels   1362

Allen, Laurette
Renegade Embrace - Virginia Brown   235

Ashford, Libby
Blossom - Constance Bennett   120

Barnett, Lorna
November of the Heart - LaVyrle Spencer   1860

Bowen, Susannah
An Improper Widow - Kate Moore   1406

Bradford, Royal
Forever My Love - Constance O'Banyon   1448

Brasfield, Bethany
Emerald Nights - Virginia Brown   233

Brig, Susannah
A Rose Without Thorns - Lucy Kidd   1061

Carstairs, Augusta
A Tempting Miss - Janice Bennett   125

Carteret, Georgiana "Georgie"
Love's Gambit - Meg-Lynn Roberts   1662

Castlereagh, Katrine
Arrow to the Heart - Jennifer Blake   169

Chambers, Margaret "Maggie"
Bride's Leap - Joan Overfield   1470

Chandon, Claire
Eden's Gate - Karen Harper   810

Chapin, Marianna
Country Dance - Margaret Westhaven   2005

Cranleigh, Rosetta
The Captive - Victoria Holt   918

Curran, Lila
The Flames of Vengeance - Beverly Byrne   265

Darracott, Arabella
The Jacaranda Tree - Rebecca Brandewyne   202

de Clement, Juliette
Storm Winds - Iris Johansen   993

de la Rosa, Elena
Eagle Knight - Suzanne Ellison   608

Denning, Elinore
The Spirited Bluestocking - Joan Overfield   1472

Deschamps, Clairisse
The Mock Marriage - Dorothy Mack   1247

Devereaux, Zoe
Tender the Storm - Elizabeth Thornton   1944

Devereux, Claire
Velvet Is the Night - Elizabeth Thornton   1945

Devonshire, Olivia
My Only Love - Katherine Sutcliffe   1904

Donnelly, Amelia
Secret in the Shadows - Marina Malcolm   1265

Dorne, Rachel
An Uncommon Miss - Melissa Lynn Jones   1016

Dorring, Sophy
Seduction - Amanda Quick   1575

Douglas, Arabella
Sapphire Magic - Nina Beaumont   108

Drayton, Cassandra
Miss Drayton's Downfall - Patricia Oliver   1460

Easton, Judith
Christmas Beau - Mary Balogh   55

Edana, Bronwyn
Priceless - Christina Dodd   540

Everett, Julia Ames
Golden Prospect - Shirley Parenteau   1495

Fairchild, Cara
Destiny's Will - Elizabeth Ann Michaels   1360

Fairchild, Lorna
Tiger Dance - Jillian Hunter   954

Farleigh, Leonore
The Vampire Viscount - Karen Harbaugh   803

Farroux, Julie
Terms of Surrender - Mollie Ashton   33

Ffolkes, Alissa
The Gallant Lord Ives - Emily Hendrickson   852

Forrester, Elizabeth
California Temptress - Millie Criswell   424

Goldsborough, Elizabeth
The Substitute Bridegroom - Charlotte Louise
   Dolan   545

Greetwell, Primula
Fleeting Fancy - Rosemary Edghill   591

Grey, Townsend
If This Be Magic - Ellen Tanner Marsh   1270

Hampton, Melissa
Fortune Hunter - Deborah Simmons   1788

Hanover, Georgina
Paper Tiger - Patricia Rice   1619

Hartford, Sybella
Destiny's Dream - Joanna Jordan   1017

Landry, Jessica
Comanche Flame - Madeline Baker   41

Martin, Heather
Wild Heather - Millie Criswell   430

Nolan, Callie
Arizona Captive - LaRee Bryant   241

O'Hara, Meara
Island of Dreams - Patricia Potter   1539

O'Neal, Faith
South of the Line - Catherine Ennis   611

St. Erney, Jillian
An Alluring Lady - Meg-Lynn Roberts   1660

Stourbridge, Trixy
The Somerville Farce - Michelle Kasey   1046

Thorpe, Phoebe
The Contrary Corinthian - Emily Hendrickson   850

Tremaine, Lily
Night Shadow - Catherine Coulter   406

Westfall, Melinda
Lady of the Moors - Mary Ellen Petty   1521

White, Juliet
Highland Rogue - Arnette Lamb   1138

GOVERNMENT OFFICIAL

Aragon, Rick
Appointment with Love - Sheila Fyfe   672

Booker, Sandy
Appointment with Love - Sheila Fyfe   672

Breed, Navarro
Chase the Wind - Janelle Taylor   1912

Camden, Royd
Evergreen - Delia Parr   1510

Claiborne, Grant
Cherokee Bride - Teresa Warfield   1992

Dayne, Breverton
A Midsummer Night's Kiss - Cleo Chadwick   333

FitzHenry, Geoffrey
Autumn's Flame - Denise Domning   546

Hobart, Kyle
Badge of Love - Jane McBride Choate   351

Hunter, Morgan
Sweet Texas Fury - LaRee Bryant   242

Rolfe
Tender the Storm - Elizabeth Thornton   1944

St. James, Ross
Tiger Dance - Jillian Hunter   954

Silver Wolf, Bruce Marshal
Dream Warrior - Bobbi Smith   1836

Wind, Bethany
Chase the Wind - Janelle Taylor   1912

GRANDPARENT

Jordan, Steve
Over the Moon - Betty Cothran   401

Kirkland, London
Crossing Eden - Emma Gordon   735

GUARDIAN

ab Gruffydd, Wynne
Where Magic Dwells - Rexanne Becnel   116

Bragg, Nicolas
Dark Fires - Brenda Joyce   1024

Caldwell, Rait
Wild Western Desire - Kathy Jones   1015

Carrington, Gayhawke
Through All Eternity - Brenna Braxton-Barshon   210

Cavanagh, Miles
Dangerous Joy - Jo Beverley   133

Connors, Justin
Once an Angel - Teresa Medeiros   1341

D'Argent, Miles
Nightfire - Leona Karr   1044

Devereaux, Julian
Rogue's Mistress - Eugenia Riley   1637

Earl of Coltrane
A Spirited Affair - Lynn Kerstan   1060

FitzHenry, Geoffrey
Autumn's Flame - Denise Domning   546

Hampton, Anthony
Patience Is a Virtue - Judith Nelson   1435

Jack
The Dauntless Miss Wingrave - Amanda Scott   1746

Kimberly, Carlinn
A Suspicious Affair - Barbara Metzger   1356

Lattimer, Hugo
Vixen - Jane Feather   636

Lovelace, Evelyn
Unlikely Guardian - Carol Proctor   1556

McBain, Cord
Devil in Spurs - Norah Hess   883

Nolenberg, Eliza
Heart Song - Barbara Hargis   804

Ormsby, Andrew
The Captured Heart - Sheila O'Hallion   1458

O'Toole, Ronan
Wild Angel - Miriam Minger   1400

Raveneau, Nathan
Barbados - Cynthia Wright   2070

Ruthland, Damon
Forever My Love - Constance O'Banyon   1448

Savage, Adam
Seduced - Virginia Henley   873

Simmons, Alison
A Garland of Love - Alice Sharpe   1771

Stryker, Caleb
Cheyenne Surrender - Madeline Baker   40

Talbot, Banning
The Passion of an Angel - Kasey Michaels   1370

Talent, Simon
My Cousin Jane - Anne Barbour   81

Thompson, Travis
Morning Comes Softly - Debbie Macomber   1252

Trent, William
Christmas Belles - Susan Carroll   322

Wilder, Rachel
Heartland - Rebecca Brandewyne   201

Wyngate, Charity
The Arrogant Lord Alistair - Sheila Walsh   1989

GUIDE

Adair, Duncan
Golden Prospect - Shirley Parenteau   1495

Addison, March
Emerald Rain - Maggie Osborne   1467

Bass, Harmon
Temptation's Trail - Dana Ransom   1592

Black, Caleb
Only His - Elizabeth Lowell   1231

Costhaler, Nick
Yes, Virginia - Peg Sutherland   1907

Devlin, Hawk
Destiny's Dream - Joanna Jordan   1017

Doucet, Lucky
Lucky's Lady - Tami Hoag   899

Elliott, Jace
Whispered Kisses - Janelle Taylor   1919

Gevaudan, Luke
Prince of Wolves - Susan Krinard   1116

MacQuade, Garret
Only Forever - Kimberly Cates   330

Mayhew, Jeremy
Golden Fires - Colleen Shannon   1769

McCain, Devlin
A Quest of Dreams - Debra Dier   530

Morgan, Blake
Boston Renegade - June Lund Shiplett   1785

Quarternight, West
The Legend of Love - Nan Ryan   1704

Ransom, Gat
Waltz with the Lady - Betina Lindsey   1195

Rivers, Josh
Oregon Bride - Rosanne Bittner   158

Savitch, Ty
A Wild Yearning - Penelope Williamson   2039

Smith, Rafer
Golden Nights - Christine Monson   1404

Taylor, Trace
Emerald Nights - Virginia Brown   233

Thunder, Colt
Savage Thunder - Johanna Lindsey   1208

GUNFIGHTER

Angel
Angel - Johanna Lindsey   1199

Baron, Kohl
Nevada Temptation - Gwen Cleary   364

Black, Caleb
Only His - Elizabeth Lowell   1231

Breed, Navarro
Follow the Wind - Janelle Taylor   1914

Caldwell, Rait
Wild Western Desire - Kathy Jones   1015

Canton, Marsh
Notorious - Patricia Potter   1542

Cantrell, Grayson
Mississippi Flame - Cheryl Biggs   143

Carradine, Jake
The Heart's Journey - Emily Bradshaw   197

Cassidy, Lane
Last Chance - Jill Marie Landis   1145

Cheyenne, Jonnie
Cheyenne's Shadow - Deborah Camp   293

Dancer
Comanche Flame - Madeline Baker   41

Darnell, Jess
Heaven's Embrace - Lynda Trent   1960

Devlin, Garrett
Wild Star - Nicole Jordan   1021

Dunn, Jared
Noelle - Diana Palmer   1491

Snow Flower
Passion's Melody - Jane Toombs   1951

Somerset, Thorne
King of Swords - Lindsay McKenna   1316

Tamudj, Zhao
Dawn on a Jade Sea - Jessica Bryan   240

Teeka
Woman of the Mists - Lynn Armistead McKee   1314

Wheaton, Elizabeth
Many Fires - Kathleen Sage   1711

Wiggins, Carrie
Sweet Everlasting - Patricia Gaffney   678

HEALTH CARE PROFESSIONAL

Buchanan, Tibbie
Angel in Marble - Elaine Coffman   368

Connery, Kelly
A Man of Few Words - Thelma Zirkelbach   2082

Davis, Meredith
Time-Spun Treasure - Thomasina Ring   1646

Hamilton, Lainie
Heart Song - Judi Lind   1189

HEIR

Aragon y Bourbon, Luis Augustin
Desire - Phoebe Conn   386

Blackwell, Saxon
Barefoot Bride - Rebecca Paisley   1478

Burnett, Jake
Sweet Lullaby - Lorraine Heath   843

Chandler, Gordon
Ask Me No Questions - Patricia Veryan   1978

Clayton, Andrew
Secrets of Echo Moon - Jill Giencke   722

Creed, Montana
Surrender a Dream - Jill Barnett   91

Daniels, Rolfe
Traitor's Kiss - Jane Toombs   1953

Daventry, Nicholas
No Greater Love - Katherine Kingsley   1071

DeVaux, Lucien
An Unwilling Bride - Jo Beverley   139

Fortune, Max
Grand Passion - Jayne Ann Krentz   1109

Gilbraith, Sylvester
Valentine - Jane Feather   632

Grant, Jason
The Cinderella Game - Jane Shore   1786

Grayson, Morgan
The Flaming - Pat Tracy   1955

Kane, Dominic
Bayou Bride - Bobbi Smith   1833

Lancaster, James "Jamie"
Defiant Heart - Nancy Moulton   1432

Lockwood, Dillon
Thief of My Heart - Rexanne Becnel   114

MacFuaran, Calum
Fool of Hearts - Terri Lynn Wilhelm   2032

MacLeod, Sebastian "Shadow Panther"
Delta Desire - Diane Gates Robinson   1678

Martin, Alex
Puzzle Mansion - Colleen Edwards   596

Merritt, David
Kate and the Soldier - Anne Barbour   79

Moreland, Adam
Summer Has No Name - Shirl Henke   867

Morgan, Nicholas
The Kissing Bough - Joan Smith   1844

Nicholai, Nicholas
Red Velvet - Barbara Boswell   185

Parrish, Rafe
Western Winds - Theresa DiBenedetto   528

Payton, Steven
Dangerous Charade - Madeline Harper   813

Saitum, Thyer
Beauty and the Beast - Hannah Howell   936

Staulet, Noel
Love and Smoke - Jennifer Blake   172

Steed, Landon
Elusive Caress - Rosalyn Alsobrook   10

HEIR—DISPOSSESSED

Fox, Mark
Southern Nights - Marcia Martin   1280

Innes, Calum
Charmed - Stella Cameron   285

Nichols, Cole
The Legacy - Patricia Simpson   1803

St. Giles, James
His Magic Touch - Stella Cameron   287

HEIRESS

Abelard, Claudia
A Distant Dawn - Katherine Sinclair   1806

Alexander, Isabella
American Princess - Sheila O'Hallion   1457

Annalise
Lady in Green - Barbara Metzger   1353

Armstrong, Dana
The Silver Link - Carol Marsh   1268

Ashcroft, Stacia
An Impetuous Bride - Julie Caille   267

Bancroft, Meredith
Paradise - Judith McNaught   1332

Baron, Leigh
Secret Sins - JoAnn Ross   1698

Bennett, Caroline
Midnight Lover - Barbara Bretton   214

Bennington, Katherine
Travelin' Man - Lois Faye Dyer   579

Brandon, Georgia
A World of Difference - Leona Blair   168

Callot, Sabre
A Perfect Gentleman - Arlene James   965

Cameron, Elizabeth
Almost Heaven - Judith McNaught   1329

Caron, Candeliera
Always and Forever - Gina Robins   1671

Chambers, Margaret "Maggie"
Bride's Leap - Joan Overfield   1470

Champion, Jill
Dangerous Bequest - Lee Anderson   21

Clayborne, Mary Rose
For the Roses - Julie Garwood   701

Clayton, Cassandra
Terms of Love - Shirl Henke   868

Coleridge, Laine
Arizona Temptation - Garda Parker   1497

Corbin, Melissa
My Darling Melissa - Linda Lael Miller   1383

Dalton, Cassandra
Summer Rose - Bonnie K. Winn   2051

Danford, Clara
Dancing with Clara - Mary Balogh   57

Daniels, Amelia
The Taming of Amelia - Maura Seger   1764

Daulton, Amanda
Amanda - Kay Hooper   920

de Fortesque, Daria
Secret Song - Catherine Coulter   408

De Rojas, Estrellita
Eagles of Destiny - Jory Sherman   1782

Delangue, Anya
The Flaming - Pat Tracy   1955

Delgado, Comyn "Tess"
Highland Hearts - Sandra Dustin   578

Dennehy, Mary Schuyler "Skye"
Always in My Dreams - Jo Goodman   730

Denver, Eve
Thick as Thieves - Jennie Gallant   682

Dobias, Corey
Her Father's Daughter - Terri Herrington   876

Dorne, Rachel
An Uncommon Miss - Melissa Lynn Jones   1016

Eliot, Susan
Puzzle Mansion - Colleen Edwards   596

Emerson, Isobel
Love's Perfect Dream - Caroline Bourne   191

Fairburn
Beloved Avenger - Joan Van Nuys   1970

Faire, Lucinda
An Angel for the Earl - Barbara Metzger   1351

Fairfield, Alexa
Island Star - Kit Gardner   684

Fiske, Melpomene "Pommy"
Best-Laid Plans - Vanessa Gray   752

Flynn, Darcy
Shadow's Kiss - Joan Hohl   908

Fortune
Lady Fortune - Cordia Byers   263

Fox, Philadelphia "Phila"
The Golden Chance - Jayne Ann Krentz   1108

Foxe, Lindsay "Eden"
Beyond Eden - Catherine Coulter   402

Garrett, Lacey
Western Winds - Theresa DiBenedetto   528

Godfrey, Christina
A Heart in Peril - Emma Lange   1158

Granger, Victoria
Surrender the Dream - Debra Dier   531

Grant-Fortune, Christina
Fortune's Child - Pamela Simpson   1801

Gresham, Chloe
Vixen - Jane Feather   636

Hampshire, Cassandra
The Haunted Miss Hampshire - Kasey
   Michaels   1364

Hampton, Alyson
Moon Dreams - Patricia Rice   1617

Hampton, Melissa
Fortune Hunter - Deborah Simmons   1788

Hastings, Maggie
Southern Nights - Marcia Martin   1280

McVie, Andrew
Somewhere in Time - Barbara Bretton   216

Morand, Gerard
The Heart's Legacy - Barbara Keller   1047

Morgan, Gray
River's Dream - Virginia Lynn   1243

Morrow, Chad
Deceptive Desires - Wanda Owen   1474

Sayers, Reid
Shameless - Jennifer Blake   173

Tremayne, Ian
Forbidden Fire - Heather Graham Pozzessere   1550

HEROINE

Allison, Jennifer "Jenny"
Wildfire - Virginia Brown   236

O'Dalaigh, Duvessa
Wolf's Embrace - Gail Link   1212

HIGHWAYMAN

De Burgh, Isabeau "Beau"
To Catch the Flame - Kimberly Cates   332

de Lacy, Morgan
Devil's Lady - Patricia Rice   1614

de Wylde, Christopher
Nightrider - Sandra DuBay   568

Maitland, S.T.
The Prince of Midnight - Laura Kinsale   1079

St. Clair, Justin Tyler
Pirates and Promises - Anne Caldwell   274

Thornton, Elizabeth
Midnight Raider - Shelly Thacker   1928

Ware, Chastity
My Lady Notorious - Jo Beverley   136

Wolverton, Pierce
Midnight Raider - Shelly Thacker   1928

HISTORIAN

Crane, Peter
The Silver Link - Carol Marsh   1268

Dancy, Peter
Miss Cheney's Charade - Emily Hendrickson   853

Merin
No Other Love - Flora M. Speer   1856

Pipestone, Clara
Reason to Believe - Kathleen Eagle   582

Stone, Theadora
June Love - Karla Hocker   902

Van Bredin, Noelle
To Catch the Wind - Jasmine Cresswell   422

Winslow, Summer
A Love for All Time - Sandra Davidson   470

HISTORICAL FIGURE

Catherine of Braganza
The Pleasure of Love - Jean Plaidy   1533

Charles II
The Pleasure of Love - Jean Plaidy   1533

de Medici, Catherine
Courtesan - Diane Haeger   775

de Montfort, Simon
The Dragon and the Jewel - Virginia Henley   869

De Poitiers, Diane
Courtesan - Diane Haeger   775

Eleanor
The Dragon and the Jewel - Virginia Henley   869

Eleanor of Aquitane
Beloved Enemy - Ellen Jones   1012

Henri II
Courtesan - Diane Haeger   775

Henry of Anjou
Beloved Enemy - Ellen Jones   1012

Lafitte, Jean
Forever, for Love - Becky Lee Weyrich   2007

Maud
The Fatal Crown - Ellen Jones   1013

Palmer, Barbara
The Pleasure of Love - Jean Plaidy   1533

Stephen
The Fatal Crown - Ellen Jones   1013

HORSE TRAINER

Clements, Joseph
Horses of War - Duff Hart-Davis   825

Dunraven, Cat
Dunraven's Folly - Dawn Lindsey   1198

Fergusson, Chelsea
Sinful - Susan Johnson   1003

Lamond, Beau
The Mistress of Foxgrove - Lee Magner   1263

Letty, Jessalyn
Once in a Blue Moon - Penelope Williamson   2038

McDonald, Deborah
Ride the Wind - Krista Janssen   976

Phillips, Dalton "Jack Flash"
Winds of Glory - Gretchen Genet   711

St. John, Sinjin
Sinful - Susan Johnson   1003

Smith, Kelly
Tall Cotton - Lori Copeland   396

HOTEL OWNER

Coleridge, Laine
Arizona Temptation - Garda Parker   1497

Danvers, Zachary
Treasures - Lisa Jackson   962

Gannon, Aaron
Jenny's Dream - Victoria Morrow   1423

Kincannon, Lee
Riverbend - Mary McBride   1300

Mixall, Cal
Golden Swan - Judy Gill   725

Rolfe, Mike
Flight to Yesterday - Velda Johnston   1010

Sorrenson, Max
Penthouse Suite - Sandra Chastain   342

Townsend, Hope
Dragonfire - Patricia Potter   1538

Wilbourne, Matt
Heart Song - Judi Lind   1189

HOUSEHOLDER

Dana
By Love Enslaved - Phoebe Conn   385

HOUSEKEEPER

Annalise
Lady in Green - Barbara Metzger   1353

Evans, March
Desert Angel - Pamela K. Forrest   660

Grayson, Nellie
Wishes - Jude Deveraux   520

Howard, Felicity
Silver Caress - Charlotte Simms   1792

Maxwell, Katherine
Treasure of the Sun - Christina Dodd   541

McGuire, Callie
Cheyenne Surrender - Madeline Baker   40

O'Riley, Lyla
Colorado Moonfire - Charlotte Hubbard   943

Townsend, Sarah
Bewitching Kisses - Rainy Kirkland   1083

HOUSEWIFE

Barbera, Allyson (Allie)
Seasons - Constance O'Day-Flannery   1453

Dvorak, Harriet
Confession - Lori Herter   878

French, Krissa
Till the Stars Fall - Kathleen Gilles Seidel   1768

Maxwell, Teke
More than Friends - Barbara Delinsky   500

HUNTER

Cameron, Buck
Pure Instinct - Ellen Fletcher   653

Renard, Blake
Apache Legacy - Janis Reams Hudson   947

Rhiannon
Beyond the Starlit Frost - Rebecca Brandewyne   199

Rordan, Geoffrey
Flames of Love - Colleen Faulkner   624

Sheridan, Deke
Cheyenne Amber - Catherine Anderson   16

IMMIGRANT

Aaranson, Alec
Rhapsody in Time - Judith O'Brien   1451

Audi, Rosa
Rose - Jill Marie Landis   1147

Bydalek, Jenny
Jenny's Dream - Victoria Morrow   1423

Christie, Shannon
Far and Away - Sonja Massie   1294

Colangelo, Nina
Garden of Dreams - Laura Simon   1794

De Groot, Wim Pieter
Garden of Dreams - Laura Simon   1794

Donelly, Joseph
Far and Away - Sonja Massie   1294

Drury, Joanna
The Dreaming - Barbara Wood   2060

Dunay, Anna
Reach for the Dream - Sandra Bregman   211

Gannon, Aaron
Jenny's Dream - Victoria Morrow   1423

Character Description Index

Stolen Moments - Sherryl Woods   2069

Savage, Samantha
Outlaw Lover - Lindsey Hanks   795

Sawyer, Danny
Southern Secrets - Marcia Martin   1281

Spencer, Allyce "Lacey"
Morning Sky - Constance Bennett   121

Stafford, Eliza
Gold Is the Game - Rae Muir   1433

Stuart, Elizabeth
Still Waters - Tami Hoag   900

Tanner, Sydney
Reunited - Evelyn A. Crowe   441

Tremayne, Luke
A Song in the Wilderness - Lee Stafford   1868

Vance, Logan
Black-Eyed Susan - Deborah Camp   292

Vansomeren, Kathryn
Magic at Midnight - Sandra Heath   846

Wells, David
Pretty Maids in a Row - Marilyn Campbell   301

Winston, Royce
Kiss in the Dark - Meryl Sawyer   1730

Winthrop, Araminta
Desperado - Rebecca Brandewyne   200

Worthington, Matt
Spitfire - Sonya Birmingham   151

JUDGE

Colson, Kate
Sweet Justice - Mary Lynn Baxter   103

KIDNAPPER

de Mont St. Michel, Rolphe
Splendor - Charlene Cross   440

Falcon
Broken Promise - Theresa Scott   1755

Kerry, Sean
Wild Irish Heather - Ashland Price   1555

MacRoth, Elgiva
Legends - Deborah Smith   1839

KNIGHT

Ap Bleddyn, Davvyd
Wings of the Storm - Susan Sizemore   1817

Aric of Wycliffe
The Rose of Blacksword - Rexanne Becnel   113

Bartingham, Stephen
The Lady and the Wolf - Julie Beard   105

Bernay, Garrett
A Tender Magic - Linda Madl   1262

Blaise de Rouen
Firebrand's Lady - Caryl Wilson   2043

Bron
Swan Witch - Betina Lindsey   1194

Chamberlain, Paxton Gaillard
A Kiss in the Night - Jennifer Horsman   927

d'Ambroise, Eduard FitzRandewulf
In the Shadow of Midnight - Marsha Canham   306

de Borge, Simon
Daggers of Gold - Katherine Deauville   494

de Burgh, Falcon
The Falcon and the Flower - Virginia Henley   870

de Chaville, Warrick
Prisoner of My Desire - Johanna Lindsey   1207

de Lyon, Rey
Lyon's Prize - Virginia Lynn   1242

de Marche, Guy
My Cherished Enemy - Samantha James   973

de Mont St. Michel, Rolphe
Splendor - Charlene Cross   440

de Montfort, Simon
The Dragon and the Jewel - Virginia Henley   869

de Pontesse, Hugues
The Sorceress - Claire Delacroix   495

de St. Brieuc, Borgia
The Lion's Angel - Libby Sydes   1909

de Tourneay, Roland
Secret Song - Catherine Coulter   408

De Varennes, Gaston
Forever His - Shelly Thacker   1927

de Warenne, Guy
Captive Rose - Miriam Minger   1397

de Warenne, Rolfe "the Relentless"
The Conqueror - Brenda Joyce   1023

de Warenne, Stephen
Promise of the Rose - Brenda Joyce   1028

d'Lucy, Blaec
Once upon a Kiss - Tanya Anne Crosby   433

Dominic le Sabra
Untamed - Elizabeth Lowell   1235

Dunbarton, Adam
A Love So Fierce - Joanna McGauran   1309

Eric
The Vow - Mary Spencer   1861

Fitz Hugh, Ranulf
Defy Not the Heart - Johanna Lindsey   1200

Fitzmarc, Enguarrand "Rand"
The Lily and the Leopard - Susan Wiggs   2025

Fitzroy, Urien
A Warrior's Quest - Margaret Moore   1409

Fitzstephens, Weston "the Silver Wolf"
Angel of Fire - Tanya Anne Crosby   431

Fitzwarin, Cleve
Where Magic Dwells - Rexanne Becnel   116

Gareth
Shadows and Lace - Teresa Medeiros   1342

Gareth of Wyckmore
Desire - Amanda Quick   1568

Gaston de Thorne
Rose Among Thorns - Catherine Archer   27

Gillard, Hacon
Conqueror's Kiss - Hannah Howell   937

Graiston, Temric
Summer Storm - Denise Domning   547

Halyard, Revan
Highland Hearts - Sandra Dustin   578

Hubert de Thorne
Rose Among Thorns - Catherine Archer   27

Logan, Gamel
Silver Flame - Hannah Howell   939

MacAmlaid, Gavin "Berenhard"
Captive to a Dream - Susan Tanner   1911

McDonald, Jamie
Highland Heart - Ruth Langan   1155

Montgomery, Jamie
The Heiress - Jude Deveraux   513

Morgan, Garret
Beneath a Pale Moon - Victoria Morrow   1422

Morgan, Owen (Hugo)
By All That Is Sacred - Laura Gilmour Bennett   127

Raine
Keeper of the Dream - Penelope Williamson   2037

Richard of Kingsclere
Emerald Fire - Laurie Grant   745

Ruadrik "Ruck" of Wolfscar
For My Lady's Heart - Laura Kinsale   1078

Rylan
A Dove at Midnight - Rexanne Becnel   111

Saker, Adam
Beloved Deceiver - Laurie Grant   744

Thomas
Castle of the Heart - Flora M. Speer   1854

LAIRD

Campbell, Dillon
The Highlander - Ruth Langan   1156

Campbell, Niall
Child of the Mist - Kathleen Morgan   1411

Campbell, Simon
Lady of Lochabar - Jeanette Baker Ramirez   1587

Carre, Johnnie
Outlaw - Susan Johnson   1001

Douglas, Adam
Border Bride - Amanda Scott   1744

Forbes, Leith
Highland Jewel - Lois Greiman   769

Ker, Elsbeth
The Abduction - Patricia Potter   1536

Kincaid, Alec
The Bride - Julie Garwood   699

MacAlpin, Megan
Highland Fire - Ruth Langan   1154

MacArthur, Ian
Highland Belle - Patricia Grasso   749

MacDubb, Alexander
Reckless - Anna Jennet   983

MacDuncan, Malcolm
Lord of Fire - Emma Merritt   1345

MacGregor, Lachlan
Love Me Forever - Johanna Lindsey   1203

MacLaren, "Black Alexander"
Highland Rogue - Casey Stuart   1892

MacLean, Rory
Moon Dreams - Patricia Rice   1617

Maitland, Iain
The Secret - Julie Garwood   707

McBain, Gabriel
Saving Grace - Julie Garwood   706

McQueen, Drummond
Chieftain - Arnette Lamb   1137

Sinclair, Ian
Highland Ecstasy - Mary Burkhardt   256

Wyndham, Angus
The Lady and the Laird - Maura Seger   1761

LANDLORD

Rayner, Jonathan
The Duke's Mistress - Lois Stewart   1877

Rider, Will
Where the Heart Is - Robin Lee Hatcher   833

Taggert, Michael
Sweet Liar - Jude Deveraux   518

LANDOWNER

Austerleigh, Eliza
A Natural Attachment - Katherine Kingsley   1070

Brand, Joshua
The House in the Trees - Georgette Livingston   1219

Chandler, Jarrett
Across a Starlit Sea - Rebecca Brandewyne   198

Cortivas, Serita
Texas Gamble - Vivian Vaughn   1975

Davenport, Richard "Reggie"
The Rake and the Reformer - Mary Jo Putney   1560

de la Sol, Damian
Treasure of the Sun - Christina Dodd   541

Fairfax, Penelope
Lord of Enchantment - Suzanne Robinson   1683

Faust, Elaine
The Mistress of Foxgrove - Lee Magner   1263

Fielding, Anthony
Liberty Rose - Stef Ann Holm   913

Galbraith, Catriona
Highland Rebel - Stephanie Bartlett   96

Gibson, Sam
Swept Away - Cay David   467

Guy
Castle of Dreams - Flora M. Speer   1853

Hawkes, Gideon
Fireflower - Edith Layton   1168

Hutton, Lily Dawn
Slow Dance - Donna Julian   1031

Jackson, Martha "Blossom"
Rogue's Honor - DeLoras Scott   1752

Masters, Valsin
Mistress of Sin - Sue Rich   1624

McCabe, Clint
A Forever Kind of Love - Patricia Hagan   778

Meade, Sarah "S. J."
The Claim - Lucy Elliot   601

Newberry, Marcie
Somewhere Near Paradise - Marjorie Everitt   616

Peregrine, Rogan
The Taming - Jude Deveraux   519

Prescott, Jared
Rachel - Lynda Trent   1961

Royland, Clare
Kingdom of Shadows - Barbara Erskine   614

Seymour, Nick
Sweet Bargain - Kate Moore   1407

Shelby, Trevor
Tarnished Hearts - Raine Cantrell   311

Simpson, Gary
The Night Prowlers - Karen G. McCullough   1304

Swann, Dee
Angel Creek - Linda Howard   932

Waxton, Gavin
Sweet Deception - Colleen Faulkner   626

Wickliffe, Cassius "Cash"
Shelter From the Storm - Patricia Rice   1621

Windsor, Devlin
Love Across Time - Anne Meredith   1343

Winslow, Jesse
Renegade's Kiss - Barbara Ankrum   24

LANDSCAPER

Carber, Andrea
Just One More Secret - Alice Sharpe   1772

Lachman, Alette
Sweeter than Sin - Sara Orwig   1465

LAWMAN

Bass, Jack
Texas Destiny - Dana Ransom   1593

Beaumont, Ty
Wild Texas Blossom - Arlene Holliday   910

Berringer, Ross
Call Me Sin - Jan Hudson   945

Blade, Coleman "Cole"
Long Texas Nights - Lindsey Hanks   793

Cain, McCauley
Fair Is the Rose - Meagan McKinney   1322

Callan, J. Barrett V
A Margin in Time - Laura Hayden   837

Campbell, Noah
Forgiving - LaVyrle Spencer   1859

Cantrell, Ethan
Twice Blessed - Leigh Bristol   219

Culhane, Jay
Escape Not My Love - Elaine Coffman   369

d'Agounville, Renard
Tapestry - Maura Seger   1765

Darnell, Jess
Heaven's Embrace - Lynda Trent   1960

Dolan, Holt
Wild Colorado Passion - Judith Steel   1872

Fallon, Jacob
Mountain Dawn - Kathleen Kane   1040

Faraday, Jake
Heart Strings - Lydia Browne   237

Fields, Dan
Love's Bounty - Alisa McBride   1299

Fierce Hawk, David
Lone Star Loving - Martha Hix   896

Fletcher, Aaron
Cactus Blossom - Emily Bradshaw   195

Foster, Nate
Embers of the Heart - Rosanne Bittner   154

Gallagher, Chase
Temptation's Fire - Millie Criswell   429

Grey, Jacob
Silken Promises - Lisa Bingham   148

Grissom, Buck
Moonlight and Mistletoe - Maggie Daniels   462

Hackett, Sam
Partners in Time - Pamela Simpson   1802

Jarret, Carson
Silver Surrender - Vivian Vaughn   1974

Jones, Clementina "Clem"
Beneath a Texas Star - Emma Merritt   1344

Kearney, Jake
Kid Calhoun - Joan Johnston   1006

Kiley, Jake
Kiley's Storm - Suzanne Elizabeth   599

Kincaid, Travis
Sweet Fury - Catherine Hart   821

Larson, Eli
Outlaw Bride - Katherine Compton   381

Maddox, Tanner
Desperado Passion - Patricia Pellicane   1514

Masterson, Clint
Winds of Destiny - Victoria Thompson   1938

McAlester, Clay
Comanche Moon - Anita Mills   1391

McCormick, Austin
The Texan and the Lady - Jodi Thomas   1932

McQuaid, Sam
Scoundrel - Pamela Litton   1216

Morgan, Clint
Devil's Delight - DeLoras Scott   1749

Oakes, Simon
Delilah - Cait Logan   1223

Randolph, Henry
Laurel - Leigh Greenwood   758

Ransom, Kane
Wildfire - Virginia Brown   236

Rossiter, Morgan
Sweet Justice - Jan McKee   1312

Stone, Lawton
Promise Me Moonlight - Carol Finch   646

Storm, Kase
Rose - Jill Marie Landis   1147

Thompson, Barry
Colorado Moonfire - Charlotte Hubbard   943

Turlow, Jake
Oklahoma Angel - Phoebe Fitzjames   649

Wellesley, Nathan
Passion's Gift - Jane Kidder   1064

Zachary, Sam
Wild Wyoming Love - Dana Ransom   1595

LAWYER

Aragon, Rick
Appointment with Love - Sheila Fyfe   672

Bannon, Tom
Aspen Gold - Janet Dailey   453

Bennett, Tyler
Temptation's Wild Embrace - Rene J. Garrod   698

Black, Daisy
Forbidden - Susan Johnson   999

Brandon, Tony
A Matter of Compromise - Judith Yoder   2077

Briarcliff, Ross
The Willow File - Lori Herter   882

Cassidy, Robert
French Silk - Sandra Brown   228

Collins, Todd
Always a Lady - Sharon Sala   1712

Cooper, Meg
First Loves - Jean Stone   1884

Dane, Theodore
My Wild Rose - Deborah Camp   297

Davis, Honor
Honor - Lindsay Chase   336

Dunn, Jared
Noelle - Diana Palmer   1491

Durant, Mitch
Kiss in the Dark - Meryl Sawyer   1730

Eliot, Susan
Puzzle Mansion - Colleen Edwards   596

Fierce Hawk, David
Lone Star Loving - Martha Hix   896

Gates, Phillip
High Society - Diane Cory　399

Hamilton, Patrick
Secret Nights - Anita Mills　1395

Hawk, Jackson
Sleeping with the Enemy - Laurie Paige　1477

Hawthorne, Celina
Cherokee Nights - Genell Dellin　505

Hixon, Harrison
Sara's Family - Ann Justice　1033

Jones, Rhys
Once Burned, Twice as Hot - Patt Bucheister　243

Jordan, Kristen
White Lies and Alibis - Tracy Hughes　952

Kilpatrick, Rourke
Night Fever - Susan Kyle　1122

Litchfield, Tempest
Apache Wind - Carol Finch　643

MacAlister, Cole
California Temptress - Millie Criswell　424

MacDonald, Andrew
To Catch the Wind - Jasmine Cresswell　422

Mayview, Robinson III
Body and Soul - Felicia Mason　1293

McLelland, Walker
Amanda - Kay Hooper　920

Montgomery, Quinn
For Always - Bette Ford　656

Moran, Chad
Family Reunion - Jill Metcalf　1348

Paige, Margaret
Up, Up and Away - Catherine Ennis　612

Pope, Sam
More than Friends - Barbara Delinsky　500

Prescott, Scott
Dakota Desire - Dana Ransom　1590

Randall, Diana
Vanish with the Rose - Barbara Michaels　1359

Randolph, Madison
Fern - Leigh Greenwood　757

Renshaw, Simon
A Deceitful Heart - Karla Hocker　901

Richards, Quint
Rainbow's End - Kay Wilding　2031

Rolfe, Mike
Flight to Yesterday - Velda Johnston　1010

Sheridan, Philip
Secret in the Shadows - Marina Malcolm　1265

Sinclair, Ian
Almost a Whisper - Charlene Cross　436

Smith, Margaret Huntington
Imagine - Jill Barnett　88

Stewart, January
Temptation From the Past - Cindy Gerard　720

Thompson, Max
The Runaway Heart - Anne Ladley　1131

Wynne, Kate
Love on Trial - Wendy Martin　1285

LEADER

Alin
Daughter of the Red Deer - Joan Wolf　2057

MacDuff, Revas
Maiden of Inverness - Arnette Lamb　1139

LESBIAN

Beck, Leah
Painted Moon - Karin Kallmaker　1036

Bodman, Sarah
Up, Up and Away - Catherine Ennis　612

Frakes, Jackie
Painted Moon - Karin Kallmaker　1036

Houghton, Laura
Michaela - Sarah Aldridge　7

Julia
Michaela - Sarah Aldridge　7

Kennedy, Christine
The Sure Thing - Melissa Hartman　826

Moraga, Dory
The Sure Thing - Melissa Hartman　826

Myer, Melanie
Gardenias Where There Are None - Molleen Zanger　2081

Paige, Margaret
Up, Up and Away - Catherine Ennis　612

Rosenstein, Billie
Keep to Me, Stranger - Sarah Aldridge　6

Rossignole, Anthea
Car Pool - Karin Kallmaker　1034

Sumoto, Shay
Car Pool - Karin Kallmaker　1034

Worrall, Helena
Keep to Me, Stranger - Sarah Aldridge　6

LIBRARIAN

Holmes, Sarah
Secrets of Echo Moon - Jill Giencke　722

Hunter, Celine
In Sinful Harmony - Marilyn Pappano　1493

Locke, Rachel
In the Cards - Julie Meyers　1357

Thornquist, Letitia "Letty"
Perfect Partners - Jayne Ann Krentz　1110

Warner, Mary
Morning Comes Softly - Debbie Macomber　1252

LIGHTHOUSE KEEPER

Elijah
Savage Tides - Mary Mayer Holmes　917

LOBBYIST

Eddington, Joshua
Iron and Lace - Nadine Miller　1388

Kaufman, Holly
Pretty Maids in a Row - Marilyn Campbell　301

LOVER

Palmer, Barbara
The Pleasure of Love - Jean Plaidy　1533

LOYALIST

Elizabeth
Traitor's Embrace - Christine Dorsey　553

Grant, Cameron
Liberty's Lady - Caryn Cameron　280

Harding, Patience
To Spite the Devil - Paula Jonas　1011

Montgomery, Kathleen
Midnight Treasure - Katherine Kincaid　1067

LUMBERJACK

Flannigan, Tom
Fool Me Once - Lori Copeland　391

MADAM

Flynn, Darcy
Shadow's Kiss - Joan Hohl　908

MAGICIAN

Quinn, Chase
The Invisible Groom - Barbara Bretton　212

Smith, Chloe
No Illusion - Lynette Kent　1058

MAIDEN

Aaren
My Warrior's Heart - Betina M. Krahn　1102

Alanna
Viking Rose - Ashland Price　1554

Breanne
The Demon Prince - Kathleen Morgan　1413

MAIL ORDER BRIDE

Ashe, Glenna
The Doubletree - Victoria Pade　1476

Ballinger, Hannah
The Warfield Bride - Bronwyn Williams　2034

Becker, Ammity
Beloved Wife - Lynda Trent　1956

Bourne, Fancy
Fancy Lady - Peggy Hanchar　791

Crockett, Casity
Forbidden Kiss - Gina Robins　1673

Dunmore, Erin
Gifts of Love - Theresa Michaels　1373

Honeycutt, DeLacey
Hearts Are Wild - Teresa Hart　824

Lundgren, Kirsten
Mail-Order Temptress - Jane Kidder　1062

MacKenzie, Elizabeth
A Time for Love - Constance O'Day-Flannery　1455

Mayhew, Augusta
Savage Tides - Mary Mayer Holmes　917

McQuaid, Delia
A Wild Yearning - Penelope Williamson　2039

McQuire, Lydia
Yankee Wife - Linda Lael Miller　1387

O'Carroll, Kathleen Lacey
The Bride Wore Spurs - Sharon Ihle　956

O'Donovan, Kate
The Lady and the Outlaw - Katherine Compton　380

O'Neile, Summer
Dream Fever - Katherine Sutcliffe　1901

Parker, Ginny
Eden Creek - Lisa Bingham　146

Thornton, Matilda
Prairie Heat - Madeline Baker   46

Warner, Mary
Morning Comes Softly - Debbie Macomber   1252

MAINTENANCE WORKER

Doherty, Shannon
A Liberated Man - Diana Whitney   2016

McFee, Summer
Walking After Midnight - Karen Robards   1655

Weston, Kate
Penthouse Suite - Sandra Chastain   342

MANAGER

Berne, Taylor
The Bear Affair - Cynthia Powell   1546

Fletcher, Robin
Wild Land, Wild Love - Connie Mason   1292

French, Krissa
Till the Stars Fall - Kathleen Gilles Seidel   1768

Henslowe, Katie
Mask of Night - Lois Wolfe   2058

Kingston, Lyle
Tattered Silk - Elaine Barbieri   75

Thornton, Adam
Defiant Imposter - Miriam Minger   1398

MARTIAL ARTS EXPERT

Gerard, Samuel
The Shadow and the Star - Laura Kinsale   1081

Richmond, Windsor
Dragon Fire - Linda Ladd   1124

MATCHMAKER

Cummings, Cecelia
Cousin Cecelia - Joan Smith   1843

Montgomery, Carrie
Eternity - Jude Deveraux   512

Stuart, Cassandra
Angel - Johanna Lindsey   1199

MECHANIC

Braddock, Leslie
Common Ground - Jeane Gilbert-Lewis   723

Hilary
Heartbeat - Norma Fox Mazer   1298

Waller, Benton
Sins of Summer - Dorothy Garlock   690

MERCENARY

ap Powel, Griffith
Outrageous - Christina Dodd   539

Baron, Tamsyn "La Violette"
Violet - Jane Feather   634

De La Casas, Rodrigo "Rigo"
Return to Paradise - Shirl Henke   866

De Varennes, Gaston
Forever His - Shelly Thacker   1927

Fitz Hugh, Ranulf
Defy Not the Heart - Johanna Lindsey   1200

Fitzroy, Urien
A Warrior's Quest - Margaret Moore   1409

Hawkwind
Fire Queen - Kathleen Morgan   1415

McClellan, Cain
Someday Soon - Debbie Macomber   1255

Severin, Daniel
The Raven and the Rose - Susan Wiggs   2027

Valverde, Carlos
A Dangerous Devotion - Barbara Kyle   1119

MIDWIFE

Bennett, Victoria
Mountain Mystic - Debra Dixon   533

Hampton, Judith Elizabeth
The Secret - Julie Garwood   707

MILITARY PERSONNEL

Acton, Richard
Virtue's Reward - Jean R. Ewing   618

Antonius, Lucius
Somewhere in Time - Merline Lovelace   1228

Arundel, Harcourt "Harry"
The Bishop's Daughter - Susan Carroll   321

Aspar, Flavius
To Love Again - Bertrice Small   1826

Ballanger, Nicholas "Nick"
Cheyenne Sunrise - Constance O'Banyon   1446

Bariatinsky, Stefan
Golden Paradise - Susan Johnson   1000

Berg, Fernando "Nando"
Sapphire Magic - Nina Beaumont   108

Blake, Gabriel
Impetuous - Laura Parker   1503

Bonchard, Noel
Wicked Stranger - Louisa Rawlings   1599

Bouchard, Adam
Stranger in My Arms - Louisa Rawlings   1598

Breckinridge, Hunter
Once upon Forever - Becky Lee Weyrich   2008

Brownell, Eli
The Conquest - Lucy Elliot   602

Burke, Michael
Hour of the Rose - Christina Skye   1820

Cameron, Daniel
And One Wore Gray - Heather Graham   737

Cameron, Jesse
One Wore Blue - Heather Graham   739

Cardwell, Julian
Tangled - Mary Balogh   69

Clavell, Derek
This Fiery Splendor - Christine Monson   1405

Conover, Darius
A Loyal Companion - Barbara Metzger   1354

Cutter, Jake
Does Cupid Do Take-Out? - Kathryn E. Coulter   412

de Castillo, Rigo
Desperado - Rebecca Brandewyne   200

Deering, Charles
The Courtship of Peggy McCoy - Ray Sipherd   1815

Delverson, Carey
The Luck of the Devil - Barbara Metzger   1355

Dempster, Bramwell
The Bedeviled Baron - Sarah Eagle   584

Dolan, Mike
Ribbon in the Sky - Dorothy Garlock   689

Donovan, Callie
Point of Departure - Lindsay McKenna   1319

Drummond, Nick
Surrender to the Fury - Cara Miles   1375

Durant, Aurora
Somewhere in Time - Merline Lovelace   1228

Elliot, Michael
Betrayed - Arnette Lamb   1133

Elliott, Liam
Morning's Gate - Ann Victoria Roberts   1658

Erickson, Rand
Sioux Slave - Georgina Gentry   716

Fallon, Jacob
Mountain Dawn - Kathleen Kane   1040

Farrell, Travis
Dragonfire - Patricia Potter   1538

Fielding, Roderick
Sunshine and Shadow - Kathleen Harrington   816

Flannery, Mitch
Love's Stolen Promise - Sylvie Sommerfield   1852

Forrester, Cameron
Angel Fire - Deborah Satinwood   1719

Fraser, Jamie
Dragonfly in Amber - Diana Gabaldon   673
Outlander - Diana Gabaldon   674
Voyager - Diana Gabaldon   675

Gabriel, Christian
Hot as Sin - Debra Dixon   532

Glenn, Morgan
The Firelands - Karen Harper   811

Graymist, Shaylah
Lord of the Storm - Justine Davis   473

Grayson, Walker
Comanche Love Song - Cheryl Black   165

Grey, Simon
Dunraven's Folly - Dawn Lindsey   1198

Halliday, Caleb
Lily and the Major - Linda Lael Miller   1382

Hampton, Tristan
The Silver Link - Patricia Potter   1545

Hastings, Adam
Follow the Heart - Anita Mills   1394

Hawke, John
A Love for All Time - Sandra Davidson   470

Hayes, Guthrie
Caroline and the Raider - Linda Lael Miller   1377

Howe, John
The Prisoner - Cheryl Reavis   1604

Irons, Fletcher
Faith and Honor - Robin Maderich   1259

Jackson, Matt
Flame - Evelyn Rogers   1687

Jameson, John
The Persistent Earl - Gail Eastwood   589

Jefferson, Chase
Night Song - Beverly Jenkins   980

Johnson, Ashton
Ashton's Bride - Judith O'Brien   1450

Jones, Tucker
Lady Legend - Deborah Camp   296

Kendall, Scott
The Errant Earl - Marlene Suson   1899

Killian, Noah
Angel of Fire - Jessica Douglass   560

Kincade, Jennifer
Of Love and Glory - Evelyn Kennedy   1057

Kincannon, Lee
Riverbend - Mary McBride   1300

Kirby, Athelstan
Winds of Eden - Justina Burgess   254

Kyle, Devlin
King of Swords - Lindsay McKenna   1316

Langdon, Joshua
Sapphire - Venita Helton   849

Langston, Edward
The Return - Diane Haeger   776

Lionheart, Justin
The Garden Path - Kristie Knight   1091

Longstreet, Case
Blossom - Constance Bennett   120

MacKennoch
A Tempting Miss - Janice Bennett   125

MacKenzie, Tyler
Forever in His Arms - Penelope Neri   1439

Malloren, Cynric
My Lady Notorious - Jo Beverley   136

Marcus
Enchant the Heavens - Kathleen Morgan   1414

Marshall, Sloan
Dark Journey - Sandra Canfield   304

Mathieson, Joe
Operation Homefront - Marilyn Pappano   1494

Mauricius, Galen
Hearts Enslaved - Judith Hill   889

McCauley, Jeremy
And One Rode West - Heather Graham   736

McCoy, Gibson
Sun Woman - Lindsay McKenna   1321

McCoy, Peggy
The Courtship of Peggy McCoy - Ray Sipherd   1815

McCullough, Clint
Rebel Seduction - Jane Archer   30

McVie, Andrew
Somewhere in Time - Barbara Bretton   216

Merritt, David
Kate and the Soldier - Anne Barbour   79

Montgomery, Ring
Mountain Laurel - Jude Deveraux   516

Morgan, Jacob
Kansas Kiss - Christine Dorsey   550

Northway, Kurt
Love Me Tonight - Nan Ryan   1706

Owen, John
A Child's Promise - Deborah Bedford   117

Pierce, Justin
The Falcon and the Swan - Diane Gates
   Robinson   1680

Prescott, Matt
Temptation's Price - Dallas Schulze   1738

Quintaro, Luiz "Tonatiuh"
Sun God - Nan Ryan   1707

Ralston, Kit
Bold Destiny - Jane Feather   628

Ramsey, Gib
Ride the Tiger - Lindsay McKenna   1320

Ransom, William Alexander
Passion's Timeless Hour - Vivian Knight-
   Jenkins   1094

Reed, Dake
Until Tomorrow - Jill Marie Landis   1148

Renard, Blake
Apache Legacy - Janis Reams Hudson   947

Reynolds, Greg
Love Game - Mallory Rush   1701

Riordan, Tony
A Soldier's Heart - Kathleen Korbel   1096

Robelard, Drew
Sunburst - Suzanne Ellison   610

Roberts, Blade
Cherish the Dream - Kathleen Harrington   815

Roth, Colby
Rebel's Captive - Amy Christopher   356

Rycroft, Tyrone
Forever in Your Embrace - Kathleen E.
   Woodiwiss   2061

Ryerson, James
Many Fires - Kathleen Sage   1711

St. John, Darius
The Substitute Bridegroom - Charlotte Louise
   Dolan   545

St. John, Nicholas
Scandal's Lady - Mary Kingsley   1075

St. Simon, Julian
Violet - Jane Feather   634

Scott, Vincent
Wilderness Flame - Barbara Cummings   448

Sharpe, Jordan
The Jade Garden - Laurel Collins   378

Shelby, Trevor
Tarnished Hearts - Raine Cantrell   311

Sommerton, Ave
A Christmas Treasure - Jeanne Savery   1725

Steele, Alex
Once a Rebel - Micki Brown   226

Stone, Bowie
The Wives of Bowie Stone - Maggie Osborne   1469

Sutherland, Joseph
A Token of Jewels - Diane Cory   400

Tavistock, David
Tangled - Mary Balogh   69

Temple, Ethan
Unforgettable - Rosanne Bittner   163

Thorne, Becket
Surrender in Scarlet - Patricia Camden   278

Thorsson, Wulf
Unwilling Betrayer - Joan Van Nuys   1972

Torres, Aaron
Paradise and More - Shirl Henke   865

Townsend, Garner
Love's Brazen Fire - Betina M. Krahn   1100

Tremain, Lucien
Legacy of the Rose - Kasey Michaels   1367

Trent, William
Christmas Belles - Susan Carroll   322

Trevor, Evan
Dance with Fire - JoAnne Redd   1607

Tweksbury-Hampton, Henry
Miss Billings Treads the Boards - Carla Kelly   1053

Tyrell, Hunter
Flame Lily - Candace Camp   289

Valmont, Alexandre
The Captain's Dilemma - Gail Eastwood   588

Von Berg, Maximilian
Promises to Keep - Nina Beaumont   107

Wade, Cameron
Ghost Dancer - Fela Dawson Scott   1754

Whitlaw, Chase
Chase the Fire - Barbara Ankrum   22

Whitney, Rogan
Midnight Rogue - Elaine Barbieri   70

Worth, Richard
Sweet Suspicions - Julie Tetel   1924

Wrotham, Christopher
Lady Alex's Gamble - Evelyn Richardson   1633

Wycherly, Guy
The American Cousin - Dawn Lindsey   1196

Youngblood, Clay
Shameless - Rosanne Bittner   160

MINE OWNER

Alexander, Damon
Wild, Wicked Eden - Lynette Vinet   1985

Bennett, Hope
California Caress - Rebecca Sinclair   1810

Caine, Karissa
Passion's Bold Fire - Rosalyn Alsobrook   12

Dancer, Holly
Seasons of Gold - Stef Ann Holm   914

de Navarro, Durango
Rainbow's End - Rebecca Brandewyne   203

Farrall, Reba
Lover in the Rough - Elizabeth Lowell   1230

Flynn, Eden
Wild, Wicked Eden - Lynette Vinet   1985

Garrison, Sam
Montana Mistress - Thea Devine   521

Gresham, Wylie
Rainbow's End - Rebecca Brandewyne   203

Lang, David
Wishes on the Wind - Elaine Barbieri   77

Langdon, Elizabeth
Torchlight - Doreen Owens Malek   1266

McCullough, Jake
Silver Caress - Charlotte Simms   1792

O'Rourke, Josselyn
Rainbow's End - Rebecca Brandewyne   203

O'Rourke, Mary Margaret
Calico - Raine Cantrell   309

Warwick, Miles Kemball
My Only Love - Katherine Sutcliffe   1904

Windsor, Erin Shane
The Diamond Tiger - Ann Maxwell   1296

Wolf, Indigo
Indigo Blue - Catherine Anderson   19

MINER

Castillo, Tigre Dan "Dan Castle"
Denver - Sara Orwig   1463

Cramer, Tweed
Forbidden Kiss - Gina Robins   1673

Evans, Cherokee
Quicksilver Passion - Georgina Gentry   714

Gallatin, Justis
Beloved Woman - Deborah Smith   1838

Jameson, Sean
Torchlight - Doreen Owens Malek   1266

Kirkland, David
In the Shadow of the Mountains - Rosanne
   Bittner   156

Character Description Index entries

McCain, Shayler
Forbidden Kiss - Gina Robins   1673

McGowan, Shawn
Passion's Bold Fire - Rosalyn Alsobrook   12

McQuade, Eden "Silver"
Silver Mist - Theresa DiBenedetto   527

O'Connell, Gabriel William Danaher
Outcast - Emily Carmichael   316

St. John, Logan
Rawhide and Lace - Margaret Brownley   238

MINSTREL

Taliesin
Keeper of the Dream - Penelope Williamson   2037

MODEL

Bonsseauc, Samara
Lies - Doris Parmett   1506

Foxe, Lindsay "Eden"
Beyond Eden - Catherine Coulter   402

John, Melissa
The Brides - Gila Berkowitz   128

Lee, Becky Lynn
Red - Erica Spindler   1862

O'Lindon, Daisy
Hell Hath No Fury - Malcolm Macdonald   1244

Prescott, Robyn
Once Innocent - Jessica Gregory   761

Pride, Caitlin
Lawless - Alexandra Thorne   1940

Roberts, Lauren
American Star - Jackie Collins   377

Shreve, Allison
Trust Me - Jeane Renick   1610

Vargas, Lucy Ann
The Christmas Wish - Rexanne Becnel   110

MOUNTAIN MAN

Devlin, Kane
Kentucky Bride - Norah Hess   885

MacKenzie, Sage
Sweet Mountain Magic - Rosanne Bittner   162

McCain, Shayler
Forbidden Kiss - Gina Robins   1673

McNeil, Drake
More Precious than Gold - Elaine Barbieri   72

Prescott, Ethan
Dakota Dawn - Dana Ransom   1589

Ross, Lucas
Prince Charming - Julie Garwood   704

St. John, Logan
Rawhide and Lace - Margaret Brownley   238

Scott, Buck
Come Spring - Jill Marie Landis   1143

MOUNTAIN WOMAN

Crabb, Esme
Garters - Pamela Morsi   1426

Dani
Wild Flower - Jill Marie Landis   1149

Jones, Camelot
Camelot Jones - Mayo Lucas   1237

McBride, Keely "Chickadee"
Barefoot Bride - Rebecca Paisley   1478

McGee, Peachy
Midnight and Magnolias - Rebecca Paisley   1482

Peters, Sara
Sara's Family - Ann Justice   1033

Stewart, Bethany Rose
Dream Catcher - Thomasina Ring   1644

Wayland, Janna
Reckless Love - Elizabeth Lowell   1234

MURDERER

Barwick, Adam
Dream Catcher - Thomasina Ring   1644

Denton, Ace
Renegade Angel - Phoebe Fitzjames   650

Donovan, Cole
Allegheny Ecstasy - Caroline Bourne   190

MUSEUM CURATOR

Merriman, Joselyn
The Turtledove's Secret - Laura Hastings   827

Summerfield, Zachariah
Eden's Angel - Katherine Compton   379

MUSICIAN

Borders, J.D. "Jamey"
Moments in Time - Mariah Stewart   1879

Cochrane, Pete
The Dreamweavers: Sophisticated Lady - Gail Douglas   558

Costello, Kate "Leather"
Homeward Bound - Kathryn Attalla   34

Daniel
Daniel and Esther - Patrick Raymond   1603

Devereaux, Fable
Tears of Fire - Nelle McFather   1308

French, Danny
Till the Stars Fall - Kathleen Gilles Seidel   1768

Gower, Alec
Lady Barbara's Dilemma - Marjorie Farrell   623

Harrison, Parker
Serenade - Sandra Kitt   1086

Hebb, Roslin
Goodbye Forever - Sandra Field   642

Hunter, Quinn
Till the Stars Fall - Kathleen Gilles Seidel   1768

Kierney, Rianne
Western Enchantress - Wendy Garrett   697

Merribeth
Riverboat Rogue - Jane Toombs   1952

Nikki
Sounds of Silence - Marilyn Levy   1185

Peters, Alexandra
Possession - Lori Herter   881

Prentiss, Luke
Sing Me to Sleep - Mary-Ben Lorris   1226

Stanley, Barbara
Lady Barbara's Dilemma - Marjorie Farrell   623

Tate, Dylan
Bad for Each Other - Billie Green   754

Trevain, Jonquil Rose
Runaway Heart - Tena Carlyle   315

Waverly, Caroline
Carnal Innocence - Nora Roberts   1665

Will
Jewel of the Sea - Susan Wiggs   2024

Winters, Leah
Leah's Love Song - Susan E. Kirby   1082

MYTHICAL CREATURE

Arrah of Myr
Swan Star - Betina Lindsey   1193

Moria
Swan Bride - Betina Lindsey   1192

Muhdula Ali "Muddy"
Imagine - Jill Barnett   88

Rhea
Dawn on a Jade Sea - Jessica Bryan   240

Splendor
A Basket of Wishes - Rebecca Paisley   1479

NATURALIST

Corvin, Dane
All the Winters That Have Been - Evan Maxwell   1297

NEIGHBOR

Breckenridge, Locke
Colorado Temptation - Gwen Cleary   362

Northcutt, Luke
Country Kiss - Sharon Harlow   805

Townsend, Nate
Rainy Day Kisses - Debbie Macomber   1253

Ward, Jessica
The Legacy - Patricia Simpson   1803

NOBLEMAN

Acton, Richard
Virtue's Reward - Jean R. Ewing   618

Adam
Chanting the Morning Star - Marylyle Rogers   1691

Alaric of Anion
Princess of Fire - Shannon Drake   567

Alderney, Justin
The Halloween Husband - Sandra Heath   844

Aldric, John
A Heart in Peril - Emma Lange   1158

Alistair, Lord
The Arrogant Lord Alistair - Sheila Walsh   1989

Althson, Lyting
The Defiant Heart - Anita Gordon   732

Alton, Simon Hilliard
The Marriage Gamble - Sarah Eagle   586

Amberville, Jourdian
A Basket of Wishes - Rebecca Paisley   1479

Andreas, Lionello
The Wind Dancer - Iris Johansen   995

Archer, Stuart
June Love - Karla Hocker   902

Arden, Frances William
An Improper Widow - Kate Moore   1406

Arundel, Harcourt "Harry"
The Bishop's Daughter - Susan Carroll   321

Ashburne, Tom
Lost Love Found - Bertrice Small 1822

Ashford, Henry
Unspoken Vows - Connie Rinehold 1643

Ashford, Lucien
Unspoken Vows - Connie Rinehold 1643

Audley, Phillip
Forever After - Jill Gregory 763

Austen, Rane "Bulldog"
Midnight Magic - Betina M. Krahn 1101

Balo
Deeper than Roses - Charlene Cross 437

Barencourte, Clinton
Defiant Angel - Stephanie Stevens 1876

Barrington, Alexander
The Village Spinster - Laura Matthews 1295

Beauchamp, Edward
A Highly Respected Widow - Melinda McRae 1335

Beaumont, Max
Unwilling Woman - Sue Peters 1520

Berg, Fernando "Nando"
Sapphire Magic - Nina Beaumont 108

Bernay, Garrett
A Tender Magic - Linda Madl 1262

Beverley
Lady Sarah's Charade - Nancy Richards-Akers 1631

Black Wolf
Through a Dark Mist - Marsha Canham 307

Blackburne, Hadrian
Caprice - Laura Parker 1501

Blackthorne, Quinton
Skylark - Elane Osborn 1466

Blackwood, John
Dancing at Midnight - Julia Quinn 1581

Blakely, Morgan
Bride of the Unicorn - Kasey Michaels 1363

Blythe, Dominic
Road to Ruin - Margaret Evans Porter 1535

Bouchard, Christopher
Deceived - Mary Balogh 58

Bragg, Nicolas
Dark Fires - Brenda Joyce 1024

Brandelin, Gervase
Dearly Beloved - Mary Jo Putney 1558

Brandon
Moonfeather - Judith E. French 670

Brandt, Grayson
The Keepsake - Marylyle Rogers 1695

Braxton-Lowell, Hadrian
Scandalous Love - Brenda Joyce 1029

Brent, Anthony
A Dangerous Charade - Anne Barbour 78

Broderick, Miles
Maverick Heart - Joan Johnston 1007

Brougham, Jervis
Deck the Halls - Marian Devon 524

Burke, Michael
Hour of the Rose - Christina Skye 1820

Caine
Guardian Angel - Julie Garwood 703

Caine, Valerian
Gwen's Christmas Ghost - Lynn Kerstan 1059

Calloway, Nicholas
The Inheritance - Joan Johnston 1005

Cameron, Ian
Veils of Silk - Mary Jo Putney 1565

Campbell, Malen
Lucky in Love - Rebecca Robbins 1657

Cardwell, Burke
Bride of the Wilderness - Elizabeth Grayson 753

Cardwell, Julian
Tangled - Mary Balogh 69

Carey, Alex
The Abduction - Patricia Potter 1536

Carlington, Shannon
Felicia - Cathleen Clare 357

Carlisle, Devlyn
Come the Dawn - Christina Skye 1819

Carlisle, Ross
Silk and Secrets - Mary Jo Putney 1561

Carmichael, Phillip
A Noble Deception - Sara Blayne 174

Carr, Remington
The Last Bachelor - Betina M. Krahn 1099

Carradine, Nicholas
Tempted by Fire - Thea Devine 523

Carrick, Alec
Night Storm - Catherine Coulter 407

Carrington, Frederick
A Reformed Rake - Jeanne Savery 1727

Carrington, Gayhawke
Through All Eternity - Brenna Braxton-Barshon 210

Carrock, Alexander
The Marquis of Carabas - Elizabeth Brodnax 222

Carsley, Edward
Highland Fling - Amanda Scott 1747

Cartwright, Simon
Queen of Hearts - Michelle Martin 1283

Cavanagh, Miles
Dangerous Joy - Jo Beverley 133

Chamberlain, Paxton Gaillard
A Kiss in the Night - Jennifer Horsman 927

Charles, Ian
Bride's Leap - Joan Overfield 1470

Chase, Julian
Green Eyes - Karen Robards 1649

Chelmsford
A Talent for Trouble - Anne Barbour 82

Chesterfield, Blake
The Betrothal - Arnette Lamb 1134

Chilesworth, Anthony "Tony"
Lady's Choice - Judith Nelson 1434

Clavell, Derek
This Fiery Splendor - Christine Monson 1405

Cloud, Marcus Valerius
Mistress - Amanda Quick 1569

Colburne, Cam
Scarlet Angel - Elizabeth Thornton 1943

Colebrook, Lucas
Surrender - Amanda Quick 1576

Coleridge, Damien
Fire on the Wind - Barbara Dawson Smith 1830

Coleridge, Kit
Fire at Midnight - Barbara Dawson Smith 1829

Connelly, Ian
Nobody's Angel - Karen Robards 1652

Connor of Glenshiel
Falcon on the Wind - Shelly Thacker 1926

Corbett of Colchester
My Gallant Enemy - Rexanne Becnel 112

Corvin, Daniel
The Scandalous Schoolmistress - Rita Boucher 188

Craigie, Edward
Stolen Dreams - Catherine Lyndell 1238

Crandell, Blake
Hidden Touch - Virginia Brown 234

Creeghan, Bruce
Emerald Embrace - Shannon Drake 565

Cristobal, Danton Luis
King of the Pirates - Stef Ann Holm 912

d'Agenais, Achille
Scarlet Kisses - Patricia Camden 277

D'Aix, Sir Alphonse
The Silver Mirror - Roberta Gellis 710

Dakon
Prince of the Night - Jasmine Cresswell 420

d'Ambroise, Eduard FitzRandewulf
In the Shadow of Midnight - Marsha Canham 306

Dancy, Peter
Miss Cheney's Charade - Emily Hendrickson 853

Dane, Julian
Wild Rose - Rebecca Ward 1990

Danger, Harry
Silken Bonds - Marion Chesney 350

d'Anlou, Bret
Knight of Fire - Shannon Drake 566

Danvers, Nicholas
Susannah's Secret - Judy Christenberry 354

Darcy, Alexander
The Rake's Reward - Mary Kingsley 1074

Darkwell, Devon
Lily - Patricia Gaffney 677

Darnier
A Lady in Disguise - Mellyora Ashley 32

d'Aubigny, Garret
Knight's Desire - Judith Hill 890

Daventry, Nicholas
No Greater Love - Katherine Kingsley 1071

David
American Princess - Sheila O'Hallion 1457

Davies, Nicholas
Thunder and Roses - Mary Jo Putney 1563

Dayne, Breverton
A Midsummer Night's Kiss - Cleo Chadwick 333

de Allesandro, Dante
Caressa - Linda Lang Bartell 92

de Ath Ballister, Sebastian
Lord of Scoundrels - Loretta Chase 340

de Bron, Geoffrey
Desire of the Heart - Katherine Vickery 1981

de Burgh, Falcon
The Falcon and the Flower - Virginia Henley 870

de Chaville, Warrick
Prisoner of My Desire - Johanna Lindsey 1207

de Clairmont, Hugh
A Vow to Keep - Elizabeth Bonner 183

de Clare, Lucien
Autumn Rain - Anita Mills 1389

De Forrest, Brandon
Passion's Legacy - Jennifer West 2004

de Forte, Pierce
Bride of the Wind - Shannon Drake 563

de Fortenberry, Dienwald
Earth Song - Catherine Coulter 403

De Gautier, Lucien
Pagan Bride - Tamara Leigh 1183

de Gervais, Guy
Brazen Whispers - Jane Feather 629

Talbot, Banning
The Passion of an Angel - Kasey Michaels 1370

Talbot, Simon
Angel's Devil - Suzanne Enoch 613

Talent, Simon
My Cousin Jane - Anne Barbour 81

Tate, George Aubrey
Scandalous - Pamela Caldwell 276

Tavistock, David
Tangled - Mary Balogh 69

Tavistock, Jamie
Remembrance - Jude Deveraux 517

Tedric of Woodrose
Knight's Caress - Lynette Vinet 1983

Thomas
Castle of the Heart - Flora M. Speer 1854
Married by Mistake - Melinda McRae 1337

Thornton, Ian
Almost Heaven - Judith McNaught 1329

Thornton, Phillip
A Maddening Minx - Mary Kingsley 1073

Thorsson, Wulf
Unwilling Betrayer - Joan Van Nuys 1972

Thorverton, Demetrius
The Black Widow - Charlotte Louise Dolan 542

Torington, Robert
Heart of Fancy - Claudette Williams 2035

Traeth of Rhune
Swan Star - Betina Lindsey 1193

Traherne, Simon
Scandal - Amanda Quick 1574

Trayhern, Tristan "Tray"
Lord of Shadowhawk - Lindsay McKenna 1317

Tredair, Earl of
The First Rebellion - Marion Chesney 349

Tredman, Harry
A Handful of Dreams - Barbara Hazard 841

Trelawny, McCady
Once in a Blue Moon - Penelope Williamson 2038

Tremaine, Lucien
A Worthy Engagement - Eileen Winwood 2054

Tremayne, Jareth
Romantic Masquerade - Lois Stewart 1878

Tremayne, Saber
Diamonds and Dreams - Rebecca Paisley 1480

Trenton, Nicholas
Hidden Touch - Virginia Brown 234

Trevallyan, Niall
The Ground She Walks Upon - Meagan McKinney 1323

Trevaron, Rhys
The Constant Flame - Patricia Phillips 1525

Trevelyn, Graham
Love Forever After - Patricia Rice 1615

Trevelyn, Jos
Moonshadow - Laura Parker 1504

Trevor, Evan
Dance with Fire - JoAnne Redd 1607

Tristan
The Blade and the Bath Miss - Gail Whitaker 2012

Tweksbury-Hampton, Henry
Miss Billings Treads the Boards - Carla Kelly 1053

Valerius, Toshiro
The Panther and the Rose - Mary Burkhardt 257

Vashon
Till Dawn Tames the Night - Meagan McKinney 1325

Volsky, Alexei
Falling Stars - Anita Mills 1392

Wade, Hartley
Lord Carew's Bride - Mary Balogh 60

Waite, Edmond
The Notorious Rake - Mary Balogh 61

Wakefield, Alexander "Serad"
Capture My Heart - Bobbi Smith 1835

Warby, Gerald
The Desirable Duchess - Marion Chesney 347

Warfield, Justin
A Heart So Innocent - Charlene Cross 438

Warfield, Max
Mistress of Mischief - Susan Carroll 323

Warrington, Leland
Father Christmas - Barbara Metzger 1352

Warwick, Damien
A Fire in the Heart - Katherine Sutcliffe 1902

Warwick, Robert
Rosefire - Sandra Davidson 471

Wendon, Lucien
The Spirited Bluestocking - Joan Overfield 1472

Westbrook, Gideon
Ravished - Amanda Quick 1571

Westbury, William
The Bumblebroth - Patricia Wynn 2076

Weston, Geoffrey
Wildblossom - Cynthia Wright 2072

Whewett
Madcap Miss - Joan Smith 1845

Wicke, Lawrence
Diamond in the Rough - Suzanne Simmons 1790

Wickham
Cousin Cecelia - Joan Smith 1843

William of Blacklieth
Winter Roses - Anita Mills 1396

William of Miraval
Candle in the Window - Christina Dodd 534

Winford, Charles
Queen of the May - Emily Hendrickson 855

Winthrop, Knight
Night Shadow - Catherine Coulter 406

Wolverton, Maxim
A Merry Go-Round - Coral Hoyle 942

Wolverton, Pierce
Midnight Raider - Shelly Thacker 1928

Worth, St. John
The Last of the Winter Roses - Jeanne Savery 1726

Wrotham, Christopher
Lady Alex's Gamble - Evelyn Richardson 1633

Wulf of Rugen
Captive to His Kiss - Paige Brantley 207

Wycherly, Guy
The American Cousin - Dawn Lindsey 1196

Wyndham, James
The Valentine Legacy - Catherine Coulter 410

Wyndham, Marcus
The Wyndham Legacy - Catherine Coulter 411

NOBLEWOMAN

Acton, Eleanor
Rogue's Reward - Jean R. Ewing 617

Adamson, Samantha
Queen of Hearts - Michelle Martin 1283

Alessandra
A June Bride - Teresa DesJardien 509

Alice
Mystique - Amanda Quick 1570

Alyce
Dark Whispers - Marylyle Rogers 1692

Arabella of Woolford
Winter Roses - Anita Mills 1396

Ariane the Betrayed
Enchanted - Elizabeth Lowell 1229

Arianna
Castle of the Heart - Flora M. Speer 1854
Keeper of the Dream - Penelope Williamson 2037

Arianne
Rosefire - Sandra Davidson 471

Ashton, Elinor
Autumn Rain - Anita Mills 1389

Ashton, Elizabeth Anne
An Angel in My Arms - Victoria Morrow 1421

Aveline
Tapestry - Maura Seger 1765

Averham, Jane
Four in Hand - Margaret Westhaven 2006

Baker, Taylor
Prince Charming - Julie Garwood 704

Balfour, Marguerite
Masquerade in Moonlight - Kasey Michaels 1368

Ballinger, Augusta
Rendezvous - Amanda Quick 1573

Barclay, Jane
Dark Fires - Brenda Joyce 1024

Baron, Tamsyn "La Violette"
Violet - Jane Feather 634

Barrington, Catherine
Gypsy Lord - Kat Martin 1276

Basewell, Megan
The Crimson Crown - Edith Layton 1167

Batthyny, Eleanora
Scarlet Kisses - Patricia Camden 277

Baxter, Merideth
Sea of Dreams - Christine Dorsey 552

Bayard, Alessandra
Pagan Bride - Tamara Leigh 1183

Beauchamp, Dominique
Once upon a Kiss - Tanya Anne Crosby 433

Beaufort, Judith
And Heaven Too - Julie Tetel 1923

Becket, Eleanora "Nora"
Lady Gallant - Suzanne Robinson 1682

Belleme, Rowena
Prisoner of My Desire - Johanna Lindsey 1207

Belmont, Theodora
Valentine - Jane Feather 632

Berringer, Christina
Sunshine and Shadow - Kathleen Harrington 816

Bigod, Barbara
The Silver Mirror - Roberta Gellis 710

Blackburne, Jane
Impetuous - Laura Parker 1503

Blair-Coupland, Alison
The Brides of Eden - Clare Benedict 119

Blydon, Arabella "Belle"
Dancing at Midnight - Julia Quinn 1581

St. Clair, Nicholas
Angel of Midnight - Jo-Ann Power   1547

Steele, Jake
Mail Order Outlaw - Millie Criswell   427

Tait, Seth "Peach Brady"
Legacy - Leigh Bristol   217

Velazquez, Lee
Night Flower - Shirl Henke   863

Walsh, Hunter
Stolen Ecstasy - Hannah Howell   940

Washington, Leona
Midnight Rose - Robin Lee Hatcher   830

OVERSEER

James, Coleton
Always, My Love - Carla Simpson   1797

Spencer, Blake
Forever Paradise - Miranda North   1444

PACIFIST

Jorund
My Warrior's Heart - Betina M. Krahn   1102

PARALEGAL

O'Toole, Susan
A Matter of Compromise - Judith Yoder   2077

PARANORMAL INVESTIGATOR

Clement-Brooke, Sarah
Lady Sarah's Charade - Nancy Richards-Akers   1631

Merryweather, Prudence
Dangerous - Amanda Quick   1566

PARENT

Barnhart, Anne
Deadly Secret - Martha Johnson   997

Colton, Travis
Apache Magic - Janis Reams Hudson   948

Dryden, Claire
Atlanta - Sara Orwig   1462

Endicott, Karma
Merry Christmas, Mommy - Muriel Jensen   985

Howard, Maggie
Shotgun Wedding - Barbara Caitlin   271

Jensen, Lisa Jo
A Child's Promise - Deborah Bedford   117

Lazo, Dallas
A Man Without a Wife - Beverly Bird   150

MacKenzie, Chelsey
First Comes Baby - Kristin Morgan   1418

O'Brien, Fortune
Atlanta - Sara Orwig   1462

Summers, Kate
Wishes - Lisa Jackson   963

Taylor, Christine
A Marriage of Convenience - Georgia Bockoven   177

Truesdale, Nate
Heart Song - Barbara Hargis   804

Valle, Derek
White Light - Wendy Haley   786

Walsh, Andrea
True Love - Diane E. Lock   1221

Walsh, Stuart
True Love - Diane E. Lock   1221

Warren, Jamie
Marriage of Inconvenience - Debbie Macomber   1251

PATRIOT

Cameron, Eric
Love Not a Rebel - Heather Graham   738

Cameron, Phillip
Phantom Lover - Millie Criswell   428

Fortune, Daniel
Desire's Endless Kiss - Millie Criswell   425

Foxworth, Benjamin
Time-Spun Treasure - Thomasina Ring   1646

Jones, Elizabeth
Traitorous Hearts - Susan Kay Law   1165

Morrison, Tom
To Spite the Devil - Paula Jonas   1011

Phillips, Dalton "Jack Flash"
Winds of Glory - Gretchen Genet   711

Rourke, Duncan
Pirates - Linda Lael Miller   1384

Trent, Ethan
Eden's Gate - Karen Harper   810

PHILANTHROPIST

Townsend, Reed
Jade's Passion - Laura Taylor   1920

PHOTOGRAPHER

Branson, Cray
Sweet Paradise - Terri Valentine   1968

Coleridge, Damien
Fire on the Wind - Barbara Dawson Smith   1830

Edwards, Meghan
Ashton's Secret - Liana Laverentz   1163

Gallagher, Jack
Red - Erica Spindler   1862

Kent, Jamie
Whisper of Midnight - Patricia Simpson   1805

La Mont, Travis
Outlaw Seduction - Kathryn Hockett   905

Masterson, Kent
The Road to Forever - Frances Williams   2036

McKenna, Stone Man
A Handful of Heaven - Kristin Hannah   797

Monroe, Dan
One Tough Cookie - Carole Dean   491

Montera, Nick
Come Midnight - Suzanne Forster   663

Reynolds, Reilly
Nevada Ecstasy - Lindsey Hanks   794

Thornton, Cassandra
The Golden Mountain - Annalise Sun   1897

Whitaker, Allison Parish
Pearl Moon - Katherine Stone   1885

Whitaker, Karen
The Unwitting Witness - Alma Blair   167

Williams, Dee
To Love a Cowboy - Laura Phillips   1524

PHOTOJOURNALIST

Donovan, Clee
Remember - Barbara Taylor Bradford   193

Kilpatrick, Kip
The Heart Remembers - Lenore Carroll   319

Lowell, Jennifer
One Perfect Springtime - Constance Walker   1987

McKendrick, Ryder
Morning Rain - Leigh Riker   1636

Montrose, Matt
All That Glitters - Ruth Langan   1150

PILOT

Ballard, Ty
Point of Departure - Lindsay McKenna   1319

Cameron, Linc
Wings of Desire - Elizabeth Lambert   1140

Campbell, Jesse
Awakening Dreams - Vanessa Grant   746

Claxton, Califa
The Sky Pirate - Justine Davis   474

Decker, Noah
Out of the Blue - Garda Parker   1499

Graymist, Shaylah
Lord of the Storm - Justine Davis   473

Hollinger, Dan
Formula for Murder - S.R. Hawley   836

Jones, Cassie
Wings of Desire - Elizabeth Lambert   1140

Mallory, Pete
One Man's War - Lindsay McKenna   1318

McAllister, Jake
Bits and Pieces - Merline Lovelace   1227

McKendrick, Tyler
The Way Home - Dallas Schulze   1739

Saranoff, Columbia
Riverboat Temptation - Gwen Cleary   365

Shepard, Cole
Pink Topaz - Jennifer Greene   755

Sullivan, Ward
Broken Wings - Doreen Roberts   1659

Wilde, Majesty
Out of the Blue - Garda Parker   1499

Wolf, Jack
Wolf and the Angel - Kathleen Creighton   419

PIONEER

Handcock, Leah
Deepwater - Pamela Jeckel   979

Mills, Allyson
Unforgettable - Rosanne Bittner   163

PIRATE

Aquilera y Perez, Rafael
The Eagle and the Rose - Diane Gates Robinson   1679

Banner, Gabriel
Reckless - Amanda Quick   1572

Black, James
Fortune's Mistress - Judith E. French   667

Blackstone, Jack
Sea Fires - Christine Dorsey   551

Character Description Index

Bonnard, Jacques
To Love a Pirate - Virginia Nielsen   1443

Bristol, Ian "Hawk"
Pirate's Bride - Lynette Vinet   1984

Broderick, Gavin
Pirate's Kiss - Diana Haviland   834

Cameron, Roarke
The Heart's Disguise - Lisa Ann Verge   1976

Cameron, Roc "Silver Hawk"
A Pirate's Pleasure - Heather Graham   740

Cristobal, Danton Luis
King of the Pirates - Stef Ann Holm   912

de Forte, Pierce
Bride of the Wind - Shannon Drake   563

Diablo
Tempt the Devil - Connie Mason   1291

Jade "Pagan"
Guardian Angel - Julie Garwood   703

Jordan, Drake
Pirate's Angel - Marsha Bauer   99

Lafitte, Jean
Forever, for Love - Becky Lee Weyrich   2007

Montgomery, Ransom
Lion Heart - Amy J. Fetzer   640

O'Donnell, Arrah
Mistress of the Eagles - Elona Malterre   1267

O'Neill, Liam
The Game - Brenda Joyce   1027

Prescott, Gideon
Passion's Ransom - Betina M. Krahn   1103

Raveneau, Nathan
Barbados - Cynthia Wright   2070

Roberts, David "Robbie"
Buccaneer's Bride - Jean Innes   958

Rourke, Duncan
Pirates - Linda Lael Miller   1384

Ryan, Christopher "The Dandy"
Devil's Deception - Suzannah Davis   480

Silverbrake, Dax
The Sky Pirate - Justine Davis   474

Tate, Damien
The Magic - Robin Lee Hatcher   829

Thorne, Lucien
Beloved Avenger - Joan Van Nuys   1970

Vallerand, Justin "The Griffin"
Only with Your Love - Lisa Kleypas   1089

Vanderzee, Brom
Sweet Forever - Becky Lee Weyrich   2010

Vashon
Till Dawn Tames the Night - Meagan McKinney   1325

Wakefield, Alexander "Serad"
Capture My Heart - Bobbi Smith   1835

Whitney, Rogan
Midnight Rogue - Elaine Barbieri   70

PLANNER

Campbell, Reed
Shifting Sands - Suzanne Ellison   609

Foley, Jocelyn
Valentine Hearts and Flowers - Muriel Jensen   986

PLANTATION OWNER

Armitage, Sebastian
A Misbegotten Match - Rita Boucher   186

Ashford, Jonathan
Pirate's Bride - Elizabeth August   35

Barnett, Brandelene
Southern Oaks - Brenna Braxton-Barshon   209

Braddock, Leslie
Common Ground - Jeane Gilbert-Lewis   723

Butler, Scarlett
Scarlett - Alexandra Ripley   1647

Caden, Amanda
Jasmine and Silk - Sandra Chastain   341

Cameron, Christa
And One Rode West - Heather Graham   736

Cantrell, Caramarena
Sultry Nights - Charla Cameron   281

Carrington, Ty
Stormswept - Katherine Kincaid   1068

Courtland, Jonas
Bayou Dreams - Libby Sydes   1908

Crawford, Edwinna
Beyond the Savage Sea - JoAnn Wendt   2000

Daventry, Montrose
No Greater Love - Alison Irving   959

Donovan, Conner
Wild Tory Rose - Linda Covington   413

du Villier, Alexandre
Creole Fires - Kat Martin   1274

Dupre, Maria-Theresa
To Love a Pirate - Virginia Nielsen   1443

Fairfield, Alexa
Island Star - Kit Gardner   684

Fontaine, Damien
A Tryst in Time - Eugenia Riley   1640

Frobisher, Alisha
Sweet Southern Caress - Wendy Garrett   696

Greenwood, Lucas
Cypress Moon - Myra Rowe   1699

Guthrie, Susanna
Defiant Imposter - Miriam Minger   1398

Hamilton, Acadiana "Cade"
Bayou Dreams - Libby Sydes   1908

James, Coleton
Always, My Love - Carla Simpson   1797

Jordan, Drake
Pirate's Angel - Marsha Bauer   99

Jourdain, Nicholas
Song of the Bayou - Elinor Lynley   1239

Kane, Dominic
Bayou Bride - Bobbi Smith   1833

Knox, Jonathan
Captain's Captive - Christine Dorsey   549

Langston, Alan
Carolina Dawn - Wendy Garrett   694

LeCompte, Dominique
South of the Line - Catherine Ennis   611

Lockhart, Dylon
Love's Sweetest Secret - Gina Robins   1674

Longstreet, Tucker
Carnal Innocence - Nora Roberts   1665

MacKenzie, Oliver
A Taste of Heaven - Laura Simon   1795

Manchester, Royce
Whisper to Me of Love - Shirlee Busbee   259

Marston, Serena
The Eagle and the Rose - Diane Gates Robinson   1679

Montgomery, Kathleen
Midnight Treasure - Katherine Kincaid   1067

O'Neill, Garrett
Freedom Angel - Robin LeAnne Wiete   2021

Pagan St. Cyr, Deveril
The Ruby - Christina Skye   1821

Pembroke, Allegra
A Taste of Heaven - Laura Simon   1795

Prentice, Cody
The Thorn Trees - Marcella Thum   1946

Ramsey, Kyle
Moonwitch - Nicole Jordan   1018

St. James, Martise
Emerald Embrace - Shannon Drake   565

Spencer, Amanda
Always, My Love - Carla Simpson   1797

Stearns, Justin
Surrender My Heart - Lois Greiman   770

Steele, Caroline
Fortune's Bride - Judith E. French   666

Taggart, Cassandra
Southern Seduction - Thea Devine   522

Traherne, Anna
Green Eyes - Karen Robards   1649

Tremayne, Kelsey
Freedom Angel - Robin LeAnne Wiete   2021

Villard, Danielle "Dany"
Ride the Tiger - Lindsay McKenna   1320

Westmacott, Roger
The Thorn Trees - Marcella Thum   1946

Youngblood, Ryan
Midnight Rose - Patricia Hagan   780

POLICE OFFICER

Abella, Nicholas
Deadly Masquerade - Tracey Tillis   1947

Calhoun, Steve
Walking After Midnight - Karen Robards   1655

Connley, Yates
The Man Who Came for Christmas - Bethany Campbell   299

Cooper, Wes
High Riding Heroes - Joey Light   1187

Cutter, Jake
Rough Passage - Paula Detmer Riggs   1635

David
A Step Away - B.J. James   966

Davis, Dylan
Iguana Bay - Theresa Weir   1999

Donelli, Joe
Body and Soul - Sherryl Woods   2065
Hide and Seek - Sherryl Woods   2066
Stolen Moments - Sherryl Woods   2069

Donovan, Michael
A Loving Spirit - Annette Broadrick   220

English, Sam
Nowhere to Run - Pat Warren   1995

Ford, Kristen
When Destiny Calls - Suzanne Elizabeth   600

Fortier, Trey
Crime of Passion - Kay Hooper   921

Grabowski, Joseph
Prescription for Death - Janet McGiffin   1310

Horn, Jason
The Color of Love - Sandra Kitt   1085

Jantzen, Dan
Still Waters - Tami Hoag   900

Kelly, Jake
Sight Unseen - Kathy Clark   359

Kirk, Simon
Terror by Design - Jane Edwards   598

London, Gabe
Charity's Angel - Dallas Schulze   1737

Longpre, Frank
Whispers in Time - Becky Lee Weyrich   2011

MacDaniels, Joe
Sterling's Reasons - Joey Light   1188

McCormick, Troy
Charade - Christina Hamlett   788

O'Hara, Michael
Hot Secret - Sherryl Woods   2068

O'Rourke, Kathleen
Badge of Love - Jane McBride Choate   351

Quinn, Michael
Night Watcher - Tracey Tillis   1948

Rafferty, Cameron
Divine Evil - Nora Roberts   1666

Santini, Vince
Mixed Signals - Joan Elliott Pickart   1532

Skimmerhorn, Jed
Hidden Riches - Nora Roberts   1669

Taylor, S.C.
Beyond Eden - Catherine Coulter   402

Traynor, Clay
A Christmas Love - Kathleen Creighton   416

Wells, Shane
Hold Back the Night - Sandra Steffen   1873

Whitaker, Bob
Dead Heat - Wendy Haley   784

Wylie, Kelly
Deadly Masquerade - Tracey Tillis   1947

POLITICAL FIGURE

Alden, Arthur Lee
Emily's Ghost - Antoinette Stockenberg   1882

Colston, Sanford
Forever in Texas - Jodi Thomas   1930

Cromwell, Jon
Come Be My Love - Patricia Watters   1996

Grayson, Nate
Vivid - Beverly Jenkins   981

Hastings, Sam
Blessings of the Heart - Jane McBride Choate   352

Maitland, Reid
Seasons - Lisa Gregory   766

Malloy, Zeke
Scandalous - Sonia Simone   1796

Mayfield, Blake
Follow Your Heart - Lynda Trent   1959

Rutledge, Tate
Mirror Image - Sandra Brown   229

Westerbrooke, Dane
Masques of Betrayal - Andrea Kane   1038

POSTAL WORKER

Entwhistle, Marjorie
The Betrothal - Arnette Lamb   1134

PREHISTORIC HUMAN

Alin
Daughter of the Red Deer - Joan Wolf   2057

Atlan
Daughter of the Red Deer - Joan Wolf   2057

Mar
Daughter of the Red Deer - Joan Wolf   2057

PRINCIPAL

Cooper, Gil
The Christmas Wish - Rexanne Becnel   110

King, Jason
One Perfect Springtime - Constance Walker   1987

McCain, Michael J.
Shadows and Secrets - Carol Blake Gerrond   721

PRINTER

Hamilton, Brand
Gold Is the Game - Rae Muir   1433

McGann, Sophie
Wicked Company - Ciji Ware   1991

PRISONER

Ardane, Brace
Crystal Fire - Kathleen Morgan   1412

Black Horse, Cleve
This Time Forever - Kathleen Eagle   583

Hawk, Ethan
Outlaw's Bride - Joan Johnston   1008

Mironov, Katya
Horses of War - Duff Hart-Davis   825

Redding, Rhys
Renegade - Patricia Potter   1544

Thornton, Elizabeth
Midnight Raider - Shelly Thacker   1928

Tremain, Brandon
Once a Hero - Katherine Sutcliffe   1905

Windsor, Nick
Because of You - Micki Brown   225

Wingate, Cole
Heartbreak Trail - Barbara Keller   1048

PRIVATEER

Blackstone, Jared
Sea of Dreams - Christine Dorsey   552

Carre, Johnnie
Outlaw - Susan Johnson   1001

Chandler, Robert
The Black Hawk - Lynda Trent   1957

Courtland, Derek
White Rose - Linda Ladd   1127

Dryden, John
Poetic Justice - Alicia Rasley   1596

Du Prey, Ransom
Heart's Masquerade - Deborah Simmons   1789

Faulkner, Garrett
Fortune's Bride - Judith E. French   666

Hamilton, Braden
Wind Rose - Krista Janssen   977

Hawke, Matthew
Promise Me Forever - Cara Miles   1374

Helford, Ruark
The Pirate and the Pagan - Virginia Henley   872

Llewellen, Rhys
Dangerous Desire - Ashley Snow   1849

MacKenzie, Jeremy
Highland Whispers - Sharon Gillenwater   726

MacLean, Rory
Moon Dreams - Patricia Rice   1617

Malory, James
Gentle Rogue - Johanna Lindsey   1201

Merrick, Brendan Jay
Captain of My Heart - Danelle Harmon   808

O'Connor, Roarke
The Black Angel - Cordia Byers   261

St. Clair, Ransom
Highland Hearts - Scotney St. James   1864

Sears, Robert
Blazing Passion - Barbara Cummings   445

Sparhawk, Gabriel
Mariah's Prize - Miranda Jarrett   978

Tiger, Nicolas
Always and Forever - Gina Robins   1671

West, Jason
Fortune's Tide - Maura Seger   1759

PRODUCER

Fersten, Cary
Hot Streak - Jill Barkin   84

Goddard, Jack
Lie and Say You Love Me - Robin St. Thomas   1867

Jarman, Mark
The Brides of Eden - Clare Benedict   119

Kingston, Claire
The Right Direction - Candace Schuler   1735

Leonard, Keith
Blue Orchids - Julia Fenton   637

Lord, Hunter
Miss Robinson Crusoe - Tracy Sinclair   1814

PROFESSOR

Carroll, Peter
No Illusion - Lynette Kent   1058

Digby, Lorence
The Enchantment - Kristin Hannah   796

Foxx, Jack
A Garland of Love - Alice Sharpe   1771

Fratelli, Daniel
The Law of Love - Martha Schroeder   1734

Garnett, Margaret
Ashton's Bride - Judith O'Brien   1450

Julia
Michaela - Sarah Aldridge   7

Kerns, Stephen
Roman Butterfly - Betty Dahlin   452

Langford, Sam
Moon Showers - Laura Phillips   1523

Merrill, Adam
Let Me Count the Ways - Leigh Michaels   1372

Pope, Annie
More than Friends - Barbara Delinsky   500

Prentiss, Sara
Let Me Count the Ways - Leigh Michaels   1372

White, Roseleen
Until Forever - Johanna Lindsey   1210

PROSPECTOR

Adams, Jack
Brighter than Gold - Cynthia Wright   2071

Devlin, Hawk
Destiny's Dream - Joanna Jordan   1017

MacKinnon, Alex
For All the Right Reasons - Elaine Coffman   370

O'Riley, Kathleen "Kate" Moira
Tomorrow's Dream - Peggy Hanchar   792

O'Shea, Hogan
Tomorrow's Dream - Peggy Hanchar   792

PROSTITUTE

Bradshaw, Isabelle Fleur
The Secret Pearl - Mary Balogh   67

Cavanaugh, Kate
Storyville - Lois Battle   98

Drussard, Justine
Fallen Angel - Deborah Camp   294

Lindsay, Diana
Dearly Beloved - Mary Jo Putney   1558

Monk, Mary
Fireflower - Edith Layton   1168

Prewitt, Cindy
The Brides - Gila Berkowitz   128

Stafford, "Angel" Sarah
Redeeming Love - Francine Rivers   1648

Valentine, Russia
Rainbows and Rapture - Rebecca Paisley   1484

PSYCHIC

Arianna
Keeper of the Dream - Penelope Williamson   2037

Aylan
The Golden Conquest - Patricia Roenbuck   1684

Blackwood, Daniella "Dani"
Apache Magic - Janis Reams Hudson   948

Bradshaw, Joey
Forgotten Vows - Maggie Shayne   1777

Bruycker, John
White Light - Wendy Haley   786

Burnett, Lacy
Fortune's Mistress - Judith E. French   667

Chandler, Nicki
Sight Unseen - Kathy Clark   359

Channing, Amaris
Follow Your Heart - Lynda Trent   1959

Chassyn, Gryph
Shield's Lady - Amanda Glass   729

Eirriel
Golden Temptress - Patricia Roenbuck   1685

Fairfax, Penelope
Lord of Enchantment - Suzanne Robinson   1683

Gerard, Simone
Night Vision - Deborah Nicholas   1441

Ghost Dancer "Angelique"
Ghost Dancer - Fela Dawson Scott   1754

Goforth, Griffin
Fire Lily - Deborah Camp   295

Hamilton, Kelly
Hour of the Rose - Christina Skye   1820

Hampton, Alyson
Moon Dreams - Patricia Rice   1617

Keen, Marlie
Dream Man - Linda Howard   933

Kolt
The Golden Conquest - Patricia Roenbuck   1684

Liane
Heart's Lair - Kathleen Morgan   1416

Linness of Sauvage
A Kiss in the Night - Jennifer Horsman   927

Logan, Joshua
Mountain Mystic - Debra Dixon   533

Loren, Christy
Rainbow in the Mist - Phyllis A. Whitney   2017

Marlowe, Carol
Whispers in Time - Becky Lee Weyrich   2011

Meeker, Lily
Fire Lily - Deborah Camp   295

Raincrow, Jake
Silk and Stone - Deborah Smith   1842

Rourke, Diana
Allegheny Ecstasy - Caroline Bourne   190

Royland, Clare
Kingdom of Shadows - Barbara Erskine   614

Sherwood, Pandora
Forever, for Love - Becky Lee Weyrich   2007

Summers, Jon
Wishes - Lisa Jackson   963

Wydner, Elizabeth
Elizabeth's Gift - Donna Davidson   468

PSYCHOLOGIST

Day, Donna
Knight and Day - Carole Buck   244

McLeod, Lynn
The Singing Stones - Phyllis A. Whitney   2018

Ransom, Diana
Prince of Dreams - Susan Krinard   1115

Rappaport, Leigh
Come Midnight - Suzanne Forster   663

Sheridan, Serena
Lucky's Lady - Tami Hoag   899

PUBLIC RELATIONS

Frost, Tara
Guardian Angel - Patricia Wilson   2047

Shapiro, Ben
Guardian Angel - Patricia Wilson   2047

Shepherd, Meg
In Your Dreams - Lynn Bulock   250

Turner, Jodie
Sing Me to Sleep - Mary-Ben Lorris   1226

PUBLISHER

Alvar, Mark
Night Vision - Deborah Nicholas   1441

Blackwood, Mace
Princess of Thieves - Katherine O'Neal   1461

Ives, Richard
Something Borrowed, Something Blue - Jillian Karr   1042

Lawson, Josh
Escapade - Susan Kyle   1121

McLean, Alex
After Hours - Gail Douglas   556

Montgomery, Brandon
Wild Heather - Millie Criswell   430

Morgan, Libby
Liberty's Lady - Caryn Cameron   280

Quinn, Daniel
His Chariot Awaits - Kasey Michaels   1365

Todd, Amanda
Escapade - Susan Kyle   1121

Vance, Logan
Black-Eyed Susan - Deborah Camp   292

RADIO

Adair, Peyton
Heart Waves - Gloria Alvarez   13

Hertz, Riley
Deadly Secrets - S.R. Hawley   835

Meade, Marissa
Deadly Secrets - S.R. Hawley   835

Sloane, Cassidy
Heart Waves - Gloria Alvarez   13

RADIO PERSONALITY

Love
The Christmas Husband - Mary Anne Wilson   2046

RAILROAD WORKER

Barnaby, Jane
Tiger Prince - Iris Johansen   994

Matthews, Trey
Midnight Rain - Elizabeth Turner   1964

RAKE

Alderney, Justin
The Halloween Husband - Sandra Heath   844

Bedford, James Cortez
Ride the Wind - Krista Janssen   976

Blackburne, Hadrian
Caprice - Laura Parker   1501

Blackheath, Ian
The Raider's Bride - Kimberly Cates   331

Braddock, Kit
Brazen - Susan Johnson   998

Campbell, Leander
Rogue's Reward - Jean R. Ewing   617

Carlington, Shannon
Felicia - Cathleen Clare   357

Carrington, Frederick
A Reformed Rake - Jeanne Savery   1727

Coleridge, Kit
Fire at Midnight - Barbara Dawson Smith   1829

Courtenay, Miles
The Lady and the Rake - Carola Dunn   574

Davenport, Richard "Reggie"
The Rake and the Reformer - Mary Jo Putney   1560

Kincaid, Steven
Scoundrel's Captive - JoAnn De Lazzari   488

Lancer, Shane
Summer Rose - Bonnie K. Winn   2051

Lane, Jessica
Follow the Wind - Janelle Taylor   1914

Logan, Vince
Thunder's Tender Touch - Carol Finch   647

Longmore, Hattie
Mountain Ecstasy - Linda Sandifer   1718

Longren, Case
Always a Lady - Sharon Sala   1712

MacKenzie, Alec
A Gentle Taming - Adrienne Day   486

MacKinnon, Alex
For All the Right Reasons - Elaine Coffman   370

Mandrell, Colt
The Heart Remembers - Sandra Davidson   469

Masters, Hawke
Hawke's Pride - Norah Hess   884

Matthews, Shelby
Wildblossom - Cynthia Wright   2072

McCade, Jordan
A Time for Love - Constance O'Day-Flannery   1455

McCall, Mara Shannon
Midnight Blue - Dorothy Garlock   687

McCall, Tanner
Beyond All Reason - Judith Duncan   573

McClaren, Rogue
Love's Endless Flame - Betty Brooks   223

McCloud, Logan
Snow Angel - Susan Amarillas   14

McGarrett, Chase
Ice and Rapture - Connie Mason   1289

McKenzie, Katherine Molly
Wild Land, Wild Love - Connie Mason   1292

McLaughlin, Gil
Caress of Fire - Martha Hix   895

McLeod, Catriona
Highland Flame - Stephanie Bartlett   95

McLeod, Ian
Highland Rebel - Stephanie Bartlett   96

McRae, Joss
Hearts Are Wild - Teresa Hart   824

Merritt, Shane
Temptation's Flame - Garda Parker   1500

Meyrick, Billie
Arizona Lovestorm - Wendy Garrett   693

Montana, Cade
Gabrielle - Leta Tegler   1922

Montoya, Rafael
Comanche Flame - Genell Dellin   507

Morgan, Clay
Beloved Wife - Lynda Trent   1956

Morgan, Jessica
Scoundrel's Captive - JoAnn De Lazzari   488

Morton, Delilah Smith
Delilah - Cait Logan   1223

O'Rourke, Deagan
Wishes - Lisa Jackson   963

Parish, Lisa
A Promise Made - Catherine Lanigan   1161

Parker, Beauregard
The Irish Rose - Jessica Wulf   2073

Parnell, Travis
Virgin Fire - Elizabeth Chadwick   334

Parrish, Rachel
Unspoken Vows - Connie Rinehold   1643

Parrish, Rafe
Western Winds - Theresa DiBenedetto   528

Payton, Steven
Dangerous Charade - Madeline Harper   813

Penrod, Ben
Brave Land, Brave Love - Connie Mason   1288

Pride, Caitlin
Lawless - Alexandra Thorne   1940

Pride, Patrick
Boundless - Alexandra Thorne   1939

Rafferty, J.D.
Dark Paradise - Tami Hoag   898

Rafferty, Jack
Once in Every Life - Kristin Hannah   799

Ramirez, Antonia
The Silver Link - Patricia Potter   1545

Ramsey, Kate
Outback Legacy - Elizabeth Duke   570

Reagor, Whit
Wild Texas Rose - Martha Hix   897

Regrett, Mason
No Greater Love - Alison Irving   959

Rider, Jim
Mountain Ecstasy - Linda Sandifer   1718

Rios, Sabella
Because You're Mine - Nan Ryan   1703

Ross, Amanda Mary "Maria"
Comanche Moon - Anita Mills   1391

Ryan, Kayley
Sweet Obsession - Kathy Jones   1014

Sabre, Nicholas
Dream Fever - Katherine Sutcliffe   1901

Shannon, Beau
An Angel in My Arms - Victoria Morrow   1421

Silver, Jake
Rebel in Silk - Sandra Chastain   343

Simon, Katherine
For All the Right Reasons - Elaine Coffman   370

Stark, Valentine "Val"
Stark Lightning - Elaine Rome   1697

Stone, Andrew "Drew"
The Yankee - Kristin James   972

Stratton, Jared
The Doubletree - Victoria Pade   1476

Stuart, Grant
A Man of Few Words - Thelma Zirkelbach   2082

Sullivan, Amy
Sun God - Nan Ryan   1707

Sullivan, Dru
Montana Mistress - Carol Finch   644

Taggart, Kane
Forever Yours - Francis Ray   1601

Thompson, Travis
Morning Comes Softly - Debbie Macomber   1252

Thorn, Katherine
Snow Angel - Susan Amarillas   14

Torrington, Victoria Elizabeth
Victoria's Ecstasy - Gwen Cleary   367

Travis, Jim
Desert Angel - Pamela K. Forrest   660

Upton, Lydia
Sweet Texas Fury - LaRee Bryant   242

Vance, Thornton
Trilby - Diana Palmer   1492

Vaughn, J.D.
On the Line - Anne Marie Duquette   576

Walker, Blake
Stark Lightning - Elaine Rome   1697

Westbrook, Hugh
The Dreaming - Barbara Wood   2060

Weston, Summer
The Savage - Nicole Jordan   1019

White, Penelope
Scarlet Sunset, Silver Nights - Leigh Greenwood   759

Whitehall, Coleman
Lacy - Diana Palmer   1490

Whitfield, Kate
Devil's Delight - DeLoras Scott   1749

Whitten, Susan
Touch of Heaven - Michelle Brandon   206

Williams, Mary Jo
Defiant - Patricia Potter   1537

Winters, Hannah
Boston Renegade - June Lund Shiplett   1785

Winthrop, Jack
Golden Bird - Jo Ann Algermissen   9

REAL ESTATE AGENT

Johns, Marcie
Texas! Chase - Sandra Brown   230

REBEL

Hardy, Mark
Seasons of the Heart - Marilyn Cunningham   449

McBride, Caitlin
The Mist and the Magic - Susan Wiggs   2026

Ward, Serena
Dangerous to Love - Elizabeth Thornton   1941

RECLUSE

Fox, Caitland
Baby Makes Five - Lacey Dancer   457

Glendower, Morgan
Beneath a Harvest Moon - Catherine Wyatt   2074

Hart, Samuel
Small Treasures - Kathleen Kane   1041

Martin, Cody
Christmas Miracle - Ruth Langan   1152

Masters, Valsin
Mistress of Sin - Sue Rich   1624

Prentiss, Luke
Sing Me to Sleep - Mary-Ben Lorris   1226

Walker, Ashlee
The Silver Witch - Sue Rich   1627

Winslowe, Ethan
Night of the Phantom - Anne Stuart   1888

REFUGEE

Devereaux, Zoe
Tender the Storm - Elizabeth Thornton   1944

Wetherby, Caroline
This Side of Heaven - Karen Robards   1654

Canadys, Allora
Knight of Fire - Shannon Drake   566

Catherine of Braganza
The Pleasure of Love - Jean Plaidy   1533

Ceawlin
Born of the Sun - Joan Wolf   2056

Charles II
The Pleasure of Love - Jean Plaidy   1533

Crisdean, Alysa Malvern
The Last Viking Queen - Janelle Taylor   1917

Danagasta
Cherokee Bride - Teresa Warfield   1992

de Canti e Calda, Ashiana
Silver and Sapphires - Shelly Thacker   1929

de Marisco, Jasmine "Yasaman"
Wild Jasmine - Bertrice Small   1827

de Medici, Catherine
Courtesan - Diane Haeger   775

del Monteverde, Melanthe
For My Lady's Heart - Laura Kinsale   1078

Delvina, Ismal
Captives of the Night - Loretta Chase   338

Dorian
Across a Wine-Dark Sea - Jessica Bryan   239

Drummond, Margaret
Ravished Bride - Sheila O'Hallion   1459

Eleanor
The Dragon and the Jewel - Virginia Henley   869

Eleanor of Aquitane
Beloved Enemy - Ellen Jones   1012

Eric of Dubhlain
The Viking's Woman - Heather Graham   742

Fire Dancer
Dance with Fire - JoAnne Redd   1607

Godwinson, Fallon
Princess of Fire - Shannon Drake   567

Hassan, Muley Abdul
The Eagle and the Dove - Jane Feather   630

Henri II
Courtesan - Diane Haeger   775

Henry of Anjou
Beloved Enemy - Ellen Jones   1012

Iona
Princess of the Veil - Helen Mittermeyer   1401

Isabelle
One and Only - Barbara Bretton   215

Iskander
Beyond the Starlit Frost - Rebecca Brandewyne   199

Janacek, Titiana "Tanya"
Once a Princess - Johanna Lindsey   1206

Karic
Heart's Lair - Kathleen Morgan   1416

Khanauri, Mikahl
Silk and Shadows - Mary Jo Putney   1562

Kuragin, Alexia
The Princess Royal - Virginia Coffman   374

Kuzan-Lazaroff, Lisaveta
Golden Paradise - Susan Johnson   1000

Lucas
Beloved Bondage - Katherine Kincaid   1066

Madoc of Powys
A Moment in Time - Bertrice Small   1824

Marshall, Katherine Nicole "Nicky"
White Tiger - Olga Bicos   142

Mary
Promise of the Rose - Brenda Joyce   1028

Maud
The Fatal Crown - Ellen Jones   1013

Niall
Heartspell - Blaine Anderson   15

Niniane, s
Born of the Sun - Joan Wolf   2056

Pretty Sky, Ysidora
Comanche Flame - Genell Dellin   507

Rhianna
Enchant the Heavens - Kathleen Morgan   1414

Rhowenna
Swan Road - Rebecca Brandewyne   204

Rhys ap Griffith
The Eagle's Song - Marylyle Rogers   1693

Romanov, Juliana
Circle in the Water - Susan Wiggs   2023

Rubinoff, Theresa "Tess"
The Golden Barbarian - Iris Johansen   990

Sadiq, Zakr Tahnun
The Falcon's Mistress - Emma Darcy   463

St. James, Rafael
Princess Annie - Linda Lael Miller   1385

St. Leger, Olympia
Seize the Fire - Laura Kinsale   1080

Santiago, Tizoc
Eagle Knight - Suzanne Ellison   608

Seneca
Midnight and Magnolias - Rebecca Paisley   1482

Splendor
A Basket of Wishes - Rebecca Paisley   1479

Tepua
Daughter of the Reef - Clare Coleman   375

Zora
The Pagan's Prize - Miriam Minger   1399

RULER

Conn
Lady of Conquest - Teresa Medeiros   1340

Connal
Fire Queen - Deborah Grambien   743

Justan
Awakenings - Saranne Dawson   483

Khalil
Sands of Time - Terri Valentine   1967

Maeve
Fire Queen - Deborah Grambien   743

RUNAWAY

Amberly, Catherine "Cat"
Heart's Masquerade - Deborah Simmons   1789

Angelique
Sweet Abandon - Sara Blayne   175

Ashby, Henrietta "Harry"
Reckless Angel - Jane Feather   631

Blakemore, Marianne
Fortune's Lady - Robin LeAnne Wiete   2020

Boucher, Stone
Firefly - Stef Ann Holm   911

Bradshaw, Amanda
Springtown - DeLoras Scott   1753

Cameron, Thea
Rainbow's End - Kay Wilding   2031

Carlisle, Juliet
Silk and Secrets - Mary Jo Putney   1561

Chandler, Carolyn
Midnight Fire - Madeline Baker   45

Corbin, Melissa
My Darling Melissa - Linda Lael Miller   1383

Desmond, Sally
A Handful of Dreams - Barbara Hazard   841

Durango, Dallas
Nevada Nights - Georgina Gentry   713

Eden, Bonnie
A Fire in the Heart - Katherine Sutcliffe   1902

Fairfield, Tia
Brave Land, Brave Love - Connie Mason   1288

Fielding, Ventia
Gretna Bride - Eva Rutland   1702

Harcourt, Emily
Midnight Enchantment - Jeanne E. Hansen   802

Hebb, Roslin
Goodbye Forever - Sandra Field   642

Hollis, Elizabeth "Libby"
Ecstasy's Masquerade - Gwen Cleary   363

Hunter, Rosamund
The Snow Angel - Mary Balogh   68

Huxley, Sarah
Buccaneer's Bride - Jean Innes   958

Jones, Silver
Savannah Heat - Kat Martin   1278

Keller, Lisette
Caress of Fire - Martha Hix   895

Kersaint, Lysette
Only in Your Arms - Lisa Kleypas   1088

Kinsdale, Skye
A Pirate's Pleasure - Heather Graham   740

MacGowan, Juliette
Shadow Dance - Anne Stuart   1890

Morgan, Brier
A Wild Desire - Rebecca George   719

Munday, Jennie
The Texan and the Lady - Jodi Thomas   1932

Quinn, Kate
Beyond All Reason - Judith Duncan   573

St. James, Cassandra
Love Hear My Heart - Sonya T. Pelton   1516

Scaggs, Scarlet O'Hara
Moonlight and Mistletoe - Maggie Daniels   462

Selby, Melissa
A Gentleman's Desire - Mary Kingsley   1072

Sinclair, Phoebe
The Stolen Heart - Kit Gardner   685

Smythe, Sabrina "Bree"
Pirates and Promises - Anne Caldwell   274

Stafford, Bliss
Angelfire - Linda Lael Miller   1376

Stover, Carrie Sue
Kiss of the Night Wind - Janelle Taylor   1916

Trehearne, Lily
Lily - Patricia Gaffney   677

Valentine, Russia
Rainbows and Rapture - Rebecca Paisley   1484

Whitfield, Ashley
Magnificent Affair - Fayrene Preston   1553

SAILOR

Brody, John
Thief of Hearts - Patricia Gaffney   679

Daniels, Rolfe
Traitor's Kiss - Jane Toombs 1953

Elliott, Steven
Morning's Gate - Ann Victoria Roberts 1658

Joubet, Adriana
The Heart's Disguise - Lisa Ann Verge 1976

Kiore
Sister of the Sun - Clare Coleman 376

Severson, Eric
Bittersweet - LaVyrle Spencer 1857

Westing, Tom
Lisbon - Valerie Sherwood 1784

SALESWOMAN

Rush, Sandy
Memory's Lamp - Marilyn Tracy 1954

SALOON HOSTESS

Brent, Camilla
Forever After - Jill Gregory 763

Caine, Karissa
Passion's Bold Fire - Rosalyn Alsobrook 12

Douchand, Catherine
A Love So Wild - Evelyn Rogers 1688

Janacek, Titiana "Tanya"
Once a Princess - Johanna Lindsey 1206

McKenzie, Abby
Outlaw Heart - Samantha James 974

McLellan, Carrie
Gamblin' Man - Barbara Faith 621

Prentice, Suzanne
Fortune's Lady - Victoria Thompson 1933

Sheridan, Danielle
Phantom Lover - Millie Criswell 428

SALOON KEEPER/OWNER

Brody, Frank
Weeping Angel - Stef Ann Holm 915

Canton, Marsh
Notorious - Patricia Potter 1542

Craddock, Matthew
Gamblin' Man - Barbara Faith 621

Drake, Nicholas
The Naked Huntress - Shirley Parenteau 1496

Gabriel, Christian
Hot as Sin - Debra Dixon 532

Hillard, Catalina
Notorious - Patricia Potter 1542

Jackson, Martha "Blossom"
Rogue's Honor - DeLoras Scott 1752

Jones, Silver
Quicksilver Passion - Georgina Gentry 714

Leighton, Theresa "Tess"
The Black Rose - Christina Skye 1818

MacDonnell, Frances
The Wind Casts No Shadow - Roslynn Griffith 771

McCabe, Nick
A Lifetime of Heaven - Nan Ryan 1705

McCready, C.V.
Calico - Raine Cantrell 309

Paxton, Ryan
Highland Bride - Kathryn Kramer 1105

Riordan, Annabel
Into the Storm - Maura Seger 1760

Roark, Pagan
Western Enchantress - Wendy Garrett 697

Rosie
More Precious than Gold - Elaine Barbieri 72

Willis, Tag
More Precious than Gold - Elaine Barbieri 72

SCHOLAR

Denning, Elinore
The Spirited Bluestocking - Joan Overfield 1472

Farley, J. Monroe
Marrying Stone - Pamela Morsi 1428

Fenemore, Rose
The Stormy Petrel - Mary Stewart 1880

Gatewood, James
Miss Grimsley's Oxford Career - Carla Kelly 1054

Harte, Jessica
Virgin Fire - Elizabeth Chadwick 334

Kuzan-Lazaroff, Lisaveta
Golden Paradise - Susan Johnson 1000

Lambert, Phillipa
The Viscount's Vixen - Joan Overfield 1473

SCIENTIST

Adamson, Jared
Unlikely Eden - Anne Marie Winston 2052

Atley, Holt
White Tiger - Olga Bicos 142

Bayliss, Meredith
Unlikely Eden - Anne Marie Winston 2052

Chadwick, Miranda
Sea Fires - Christine Dorsey 551

Chambers, Jessica
Formula for Murder - S.R. Hawley 836

Cristie, Beth
There Is a Season - Phyllis Houseman 930

Fletcher, Elias
Love and Laughter - Carole Buck 245

Florian, Jane
Wings of the Storm - Susan Sizemore 1817

Hunter, Joshua
There Is a Season - Phyllis Houseman 930

Kendrick, Mercy
Thunder Mountain - Rachel Lee 1173

Kennedy, Christine
The Sure Thing - Melissa Hartman 826

Locke, Shara
Stolen Dreams - Marilyn Campbell 303

Mayne, George
Miss Wyndham's Escapade - Emily Hendrickson 854

McAllister, Lisa
Bits and Pieces - Merline Lovelace 1227

O'Shea, Flannery
Flannery's Rainbow - Julie Kistler 1084

Owen, Jessica
Jessica's Song - Virginia Nielsen 1442

Parsons, John
The Stormy Petrel - Mary Stewart 1880

Scarborough, Sara
Sara's Surprise - Deborah Smith 1841

Shelby, Jessica
The Heart Remembers - Lenore Carroll 319

Stanbridge, Jessica
Past Promises - Jill Marie Landis 1146

Sumoto, Shay
Car Pool - Karin Kallmaker 1034

Tate, Elijah
The Wild Winds - Catherine Palmer 1487

Walker, Chance
Lover in the Rough - Elizabeth Lowell 1230

Ward, Jessica
The Legacy - Patricia Simpson 1803

Woodward, Kyle
The Night Orchid - Patricia Simpson 1804

Worth, Theodosia
Heartstrings - Rebecca Paisley 1481

SCOUT

Carmichael, Delany
Desert Sunrise - Raine Cantrell 310

Cholla
Apache Caress - Georgina Gentry 712

Hampton, Tristan
The Silver Link - Patricia Potter 1545

Harper, Caleb
All My Heart Can Hold - Jessica Douglass 559

Jackson, Matt
Flame - Evelyn Rogers 1687

Jackson, Rio
Desire's Slave - Linda Hilton 893

Montgomery, James
Web of Loving Lies - Barbara Leigh 1177

Prescott, Matt
Temptation's Price - Dallas Schulze 1738

Storr
Viking Rose - Ashland Price 1554

Stryker, Blade "Swift Blade"
Beyond the Horizon - Connie Mason 1287

SEA CAPTAIN

Andrews, Derek
Only for Love - Elaine Barbieri 73

Barrett, Hugh
Sweet Southern Caress - Wendy Garrett 696

Barron, Matthew
Jade Dawn - Susannah Leigh 1181

Blackstone, Jack
Sea Fires - Christine Dorsey 551

Blackstone, Jared
Sea of Dreams - Christine Dorsey 552

Blackwell, Nicholas
The Captain's Bride - Kat Martin 1273

Broderick, Chance
Arizona Caress - Bobbi Smith 1832

Broderick, Gavin
Pirate's Kiss - Diana Haviland 834

Carrick, Alec
Night Storm - Catherine Coulter 407

Chastaine, Jake
A Light for My Love - Alexis Harrington 814

Donovan, Andrew
Allegheny Captive - Caroline Bourne 189

Drake, Sheridan
Seize the Fire - Laura Kinsale 1080

Duval, Giddeon
Texas Gamble - Vivian Vaughn 1975

Faulkner, Garrett
Fortune's Bride - Judith E. French   666

Hall, Tristan
Sweet Seduction - Patricia Pellicane   1515

Hamilton, Trevor
A Time for Roses - Elaine Coffman   373

Innes, Caleb
Paradise in His Arms - Elizabeth Daniels   460

Irons, Jonas
Midnight Treasure - Katherine Kincaid   1067

Iverson, Mast
Tradewinds - Annee Cartier   326

Knox, Jonathan
Captain's Captive - Christine Dorsey   549

Llewellen, Rhys
Dangerous Desire - Ashley Snow   1849

Locke, Wesley
Sweet Abandon - Sara Blayne   175

Lord, Christian
Master of My Dreams - Danelle Harmon   809

MacKenzie, Rob
Sea of Dreams - Elizabeth DeLancey   497

Malory, James
Gentle Rogue - Johanna Lindsey   1201

Marlowe, Garrick
The Taming of Amelia - Maura Seger   1764

McNair, Gideon
Gideon's Fall - Bronwyn Williams   2033

Montgomery, Brice
When Midnight Comes - Robin Burcell   253

O'Hara, Sean
A Dangerous Longing - Veronica Sattler   1720

Palmer, Duncan
Midnight Lace - Elizabeth Kary   1045

Prescott, Seneca
Midnight Enchantment - Jeanne E. Hansen   802

Ramsey, Kyle
Moonwitch - Nicole Jordan   1018

Reynolds, Justin
Destiny's Will - Elizabeth Ann Michaels   1360

Santador, Rafael "Rafe"
Wildwitch - Kimberleigh Caitlin   272

Seanessy, Sean
Virgin Star - Jennifer Horsman   928

Sears, Robert
Blazing Passion - Barbara Cummings   445

Sparhawk, Gabriel
Mariah's Prize - Miranda Jarrett   978

Spark, Daniel
Miss Whittier Makes a List - Carla Kelly   1055

Talbot, Adrian
Lightning - Patricia Potter   1541

Tate, Damien
The Magic - Robin Lee Hatcher   829

Tiger, Nicolas
Always and Forever - Gina Robins   1671

Trask, Morgan
Savannah Heat - Kat Martin   1278

Tremaine, Bryce
A Promise of Fire - Veronica Sattler   1721

Trevarren, Patrick
Taming Charlotte - Linda Lael Miller   1386

Vallerand, Justin "The Griffin"
Only with Your Love - Lisa Kleypas   1089

Vanderzee, Brom
Sweet Forever - Becky Lee Weyrich   2010

Warfield, Penn
The Warfield Bride - Bronwyn Williams   2034

West, Morgan
The Wings of Morning - Karen Harper   812

Weston, Drake
Stolen Fire - Danette Chartier   335

Wolf, Jacob
Mississippi Mistress - Gina Robins   1675

SEAMSTRESS

d'Autrecourt, Emily Rose
The Raider's Bride - Kimberly Cates   331

Egan, Molly
By My Heart Betrayed - Olga Bicos   140

Etoile, Leda
The Shadow and the Star - Laura Kinsale   1081

MacClure, Esmeralda
By My Heart Betrayed - Olga Bicos   140

Massie, Anna
Touch of Lace - Elizabeth DeLancey   498

Nesbitt, Maggie
Through the Years - Katherine Sinclair   1808

Sardanno, Chiara
Avenue of Dreams - Lucy Taylor   1921

Tabor, Lena
Private Paradise - Lucy Elliot   603

Wells, Georgia
No Greater Love - Katherine Kingsley   1071

Wingate, Nerissa
The Lady and the Rake - Carola Dunn   574

SECRETARY

Brooks, Liberty
Scandalous - Sonia Simone   1796

Delaney, Sydney
Tender Is the Touch - Ana Leigh   1176

Dugan, Sara
Mad Hatter - Georgia Helm   848

Kingsland, Amber
A Song in the Wilderness - Lee Stafford   1868

Meriwether, Tess
The Case of the Mesmerizing Boss - Diana
   Palmer   1488

SECRETARY—LEGAL

Brownfield, Lily
Always a Lady - Sharon Sala   1712

Cullen, Rebecca
Night Fever - Susan Kyle   1122

SECURITY OFFICER

De Arr, Tedra
Warrior's Woman - Johanna Lindsey   1211

McGuire, Slater
Forever Joy - Lacey Dancer   458

SERVANT

Asquith, Courtney
Tonight and Forever - Caryl Wilson   2044

Bouclair, Armand Kordell "Kord"
Southern Oaks - Brenna Braxton-Barshon   209

Chandon, Claire
Eden's Gate - Karen Harper   810

Connelly, Ian
Nobody's Angel - Karen Robards   1652

Courtney, Liberty Rose
Liberty Rose - Stef Ann Holm   913

Dunstan, Pleasance
Wild Conquest - Hannah Howell   941

Eden, Bonnie
A Fire in the Heart - Katherine Sutcliffe   1902

Egan, Molly
By My Heart Betrayed - Olga Bicos   140

Guarneri, Margaret
Lady in Black - Christina Dodd   537

Haige, Gillian
Only for Love - Elaine Barbieri   73

Harken, Jens
November of the Heart - LaVyrle Spencer   1860

Morrison, Tom
To Spite the Devil - Paula Jonas   1011

O'Connor, Meghan
Wishes on the Wind - Elaine Barbieri   77

O'Neal, Fiona
Moon Dancer - Judith E. French   669

St. Claire, Nicole
Creole Fires - Kat Martin   1274

St. James, Blaise
Touch Me with Fire - Nicole Jordan   1020

St. James, Jordan
Bayou Bride - Bobbi Smith   1833

Saylah "Tanu"
Sing to Me of Dreams - Kathryn Lynn Davis   477

Stoane, Audrey
Elusive Caress - Rosalyn Alsobrook   10

Taliesin
Keeper of the Dream - Penelope Williamson   2037

Templeton, Jenny
Renegade Angel - Phoebe Fitzjames   650

Thornton, Adam
Defiant Imposter - Miriam Minger   1398

Trehearne, Lily
Lily - Patricia Gaffney   677

SETTLER

Arlington, Thomas
Time-Spun Rapture - Thomasina Ring   1645

Branigan, Tucker
Promised Sunrise - Robin Lee Hatcher   832

Cavanaugh, Conn
Quiet Fires - Ginna Gray   751

Garat, Max
Tender Heart - Gwen Cleary   366

Haardrad, Selig
Surrender My Love - Johanna Lindsey   1209

MacKinder, Marybeth
Oregon Bride - Rosanne Bittner   158

Masters, Joline
Montana Woman - Rosanne Bittner   157

Meyer, Anne Marie
The Tender Texan - Jodi Thomas   1931

Mills, Allyson
Unforgettable - Rosanne Bittner   163

Morgan, Rhys
Northern Fire, Northern Star - Scotney St.
   James   1865

Lewis, Darcy
Harvest of Love - Nancy Sheehan   1780

SOCIALITE

Benedict, Laurel Frasier
Morning Rain - Leigh Riker   1636

Blackstone, Emma
Desire - Georgia Hampton   789

Blair, Layne Fielding
Lie and Say You Love Me - Robin St. Thomas   1867

Brassova, Annastatia
A Token of Jewels - Diane Cory   400

Brice, Claire Jameson
Risk - Doris Parmett   1507

Caulfield, Allison
Seduced - Carla Simpson   1799

Clay, Victoria
High Riding Heroes - Joey Light   1187

Day, Francesca
Fancy Pants - Susan Elizabeth Phillips   1526

Drummond, Julia
The Matchmaker - Kay Hooper   923

Emerson, Isobel
Love's Perfect Dream - Caroline Bourne   191

Fontaine, Celine
Forever His - Shelly Thacker   1927

Forrest, Maggy
Maggy's Child - Karen Robards   1650

Gold, Solange
Lies - Doris Parmett   1506

Groves, Trudi
High Society - Diane Cory   399

Hastings, Julia
Julia's Story - Catherine M. Rae   1584

Jardin, Remy
Masquerade - Janet Dailey   454

King, Savannah
Southern Secrets - Marcia Martin   1281

Kitteridge, Ellen
Desperate Measures - Linda Cajio   273

Linden, Arabella
The Destiny - Fayrene Preston   1552

Lowell, Lyris
The Naked Huntress - Shirley Parenteau   1496

Maintree, Suzanne
Golden Nights - Christine Monson   1404

Oliver, Belinda
Birthstone - Mollie Gregory   767

Page, Alissa
First Loves - Jean Stone   1884

Richards, Georgette
Scarlet Scandals - Carol Budd   249

Sherwin, Saranda
Princess of Thieves - Katherine O'Neal   1461

Staulet, Riva
Love and Smoke - Jennifer Blake   172

Stockdale, Lila "Cat"
Blue Mountain Magic - Garda Parker   1498

Templeton, Cassandra
Mail Order Outlaw - Millie Criswell   427

Van Allen, Alana
Lions and Lace - Meagan McKinney   1324

Vanderveer, Alexandra
Silk and Stone - Deborah Smith   1842

Weston, Carly
Nowhere to Run - Pat Warren   1995

Wilder, Samantha
Desire's Endless Kiss - Millie Criswell   425

SORCERER

Alyeka
The Enchanted Land - Saranne Dawson   484

Radbourne, Galen
A Certain Magic - Kathleen Morgan   1410

SORCERESS

Grania
Heartspell - Blaine Anderson   15

Rozlynd
Awakenings - Saranne Dawson   483

SOUTHERN BELLE

Bain, Serena
Wildfire - Norah Hess   887

Barnett, Brandelene
Southern Oaks - Brenna Braxton-Barshon   209

Bennett, Hope
California Caress - Rebecca Sinclair   1810

Brannigan, Shannon
Beyond the Horizon - Connie Mason   1287

Cantrell, Caramarena
Sultry Nights - Charla Cameron   281

Clayborn, Whitney
Love's Stolen Promise - Sylvie Sommerfield   1852

Collins, Faith
Golden Chances - Rebecca Hagan Lee   1174

Curtin, Elizabeth Montbleau
The Legend of Love - Nan Ryan   1704

Dade, Jessamine
Riverbend - Mary McBride   1300

Douglas, Amanda
The Prisoner - Cheryl Reavis   1604

du Pres, Genevieve
Desire's Slave - Linda Hilton   893

Dupre, Maria-Theresa
To Love a Pirate - Virginia Nielsen   1443

Fremont, Thalia
The Garden Path - Kristie Knight   1091

Hamilton, Acadiana "Cade"
Bayou Dreams - Libby Sydes   1908

LaRue, Eulalia Grace "Lollie"
Just a Kiss Away - Jill Barnett   89

Lindsay, Jessica
Morning Song - Karen Robards   1651

Lloyd, Arienne
Sapphire - Venita Helton   849

Louvierre, Aimee
Delta Desire - Diane Gates Robinson   1678

MacKay, Kiernan
One Wore Blue - Heather Graham   739

MacKenzie, Tyler
Frostfire - Linda Ladd   1125

Markham, Selena
Moonwitch - Nicole Jordan   1018

Moran, Willow
Only His - Elizabeth Lowell   1231

O'Brien, Angelina
Angel Fire - Deborah Satinwood   1719

Paxton, Susanna
Song of the Bayou - Elinor Lynley   1239

Quinn, Catlin
Texas Temptation - Gina Robins   1676

Riordan, Jenna
All My Heart Can Hold - Jessica Douglass   559

St. Claire, Gabrielle
Gabrielle - Leta Tegler   1922

Seaton, Meredith
Rainbow - Patricia Potter   1543

Shannon, Laura Lee
Golden Bird - Jo Ann Algermissen   9

Summerfield, Gloria "Glory"
The Captain's Bride - Kat Martin   1273

Trevor, Aimee
Surrender to the Fury - Cara Miles   1375

Wainwright, Kallie
Nightfire - Leona Karr   1044

Waverly, Victoria
A Lady of the West - Linda Howard   934

Whitmore, Lacey
Rebel Seduction - Jane Archer   30

Wickley, Delilah
Riverboat Seduction - Caroline Bourne   192

Windsor, Jessamyn
Once a Rebel - Micki Brown   226

SPACE EXPLORER

Voyager, Gallant
Stardust Dreams - Marilyn Campbell   302

SPACESHIP CAPTAIN

Aubin
Golden Temptress - Patricia Roenbuck   1685

Raul
Daughter of Destiny - Jackie Casto   327

SPINSTER

Aames, Libby
Libby's London Merchant - Carla Kelly   1051

Armitage, Elizabeth
An Unwilling Bride - Jo Beverley   139

Austerleigh, Eliza
A Natural Attachment - Katherine Kingsley   1070

Babcock, Elizabeth
Wicked Stranger - Louisa Rawlings   1599

Bunch, Hannah
Heaven Sent - Pamela Morsi   1427

Burbridge, Elizabeth
The Dream - Kit Gardner   683

Burns, Katy
Nightrose - Dorothy Garlock   688

Chambers, Brittany
A Promise of Fire - Veronica Sattler   1721

Clare
Desire - Amanda Quick   1568

Colfax, Hattie
Courting Miss Hattie - Pamela Morsi   1425

Daniels, Prudence
Diamond in the Rough - Millie Criswell   426

O'Shea, Mercy
Rogue's Mistress - Eugenia Riley   1637

Pearson, Carlie
Better than Before - Judith Duncan   572

Ritter, Beatrice
In the Shadow of the Mountains - Rosanne
   Bittner   156

Royland, Paul
Kingdom of Shadows - Barbara Erskine   614

Shahan, Meg
Wild Tory Rose - Linda Covington   413

Shaw, Hannah Whitby
The Vow - Lindsay Chase   337

Smythe, Devin
The Virgin Wife - Elizabeth August   36

Stone, Susan
The Wives of Bowie Stone - Maggie Osborne   1469

Talbot, Bethlyn
Pirate's Bride - Lynette Vinet   1984

Walsh, Andrea
True Love - Diane E. Lock   1221

Walsh, Stuart
True Love - Diane E. Lock   1221

Whitney, Johanna
Sapphire and Shadow - Marie Ferrarella   639

SPY

Abbott, Hugh
Silver Linings - Jayne Ann Krentz   1111

Asher, Faith Mary
Faith and Honor - Robin Maderich   1259

Becket, Eleanora "Nora"
Lady Gallant - Suzanne Robinson   1682

Bennett, Rosa
The Doll's House - Evelyn Anthony   25

Blackheath, Ian
The Raider's Bride - Kimberly Cates   331

Blake, Robert
Beyond the Sunrise - Mary Balogh   54

Blakely, Morgan
Bride of the Unicorn - Kasey Michaels   1363

Bradley, Lauren
Lightning - Patricia Potter   1541

Brant, Cord
Love and Triumph - Patricia Hagan   779

Cabot, Rand
Perchance to Dream - Maura Seger   1763

Caine
Guardian Angel - Julie Garwood   703

Carrington, Sinclair
Rendezvous - Serena Richards   1629

Charles, Ian
Bride's Leap - Joan Overfield   1470

Cormick, Bryce Darcy
Dance of Deception - Suzannah Davis   479

Darcy, Alexander
The Rake's Reward - Mary Kingsley   1074

d'Autrecourt, Emily Rose
The Raider's Bride - Kimberly Cates   331

de Beaucaire, Gabrielle
Velvet - Jane Feather   633

de Rivers, Christian
Lady Gallant - Suzanne Robinson   1682

de Vire, Elise
Beloved Deceiver - Laurie Grant   744

Delacroix, John
Beloved Enemy - Maura Seger   1757

Delaney, Cassandra
White Rose - Linda Ladd   1127

D'Epier, Jean Louis
Frontier Fire - Barbara Cummings   446

Doucet, Anne-Marie
The Conquest - Lucy Elliot   602

Drake, Barrett
Promise Me Today - Lori Copeland   394

Drayton, John
Madcap Johnny - Jeanne Carmichael   318

Farrell, Reid
The Farrell Marriage - Dee Holmes   916

Fielding, David Michael
Island of Dreams - Patricia Potter   1539

Fitzgerald, Susannah "Butterfly"
Perchance to Dream - Maura Seger   1763

Fitzstephen, Blade
Lady Defiant - Suzanne Robinson   1681

Fleming, Harry
Rendezvous - Amanda Quick   1573

Grayson, Sterling
Temptation's Tender Kiss - Colleen Faulkner   627

Hargraves, Anne
Dangerous Deceptions - Erin Yorke   2079

Hawkins, John Wesley
The Mist and the Magic - Susan Wiggs   2026

Holt, Jacqueline
Masques of Betrayal - Andrea Kane   1038

Irons, Forest
Scarlet Ribbons - Judith E. French   671

Janos, Magda
Petals in the Storm - Mary Jo Putney   1559

Jeffreys, Colin
Silver Deceptions - Deborah Martin   1272

Jones, Decker
A Nothing Town in Texas - Lass Small   1828

Kendall, Kegan
Passion's Melody - Jane Toombs   1951

Kendrick, Ian
Dangerous Deceptions - Erin Yorke   2079

Kent, Alexander
Traitor's Embrace - Christine Dorsey   553

Kinrade, Brianna
Unwilling Betrayer - Joan Van Nuys   1972

Langdon, Joshua
Sapphire - Venita Helton   849

Leighton, Jonathan
Traitorous Hearts - Susan Kay Law   1165

Lovet, Lucas
The Crimson Crown - Edith Layton   1167

MacDrumin, Maggie
Highland Fling - Amanda Scott   1747

MacKenzie, Slater
Kiss Me Forever - Bobbi Smith   1837

Maitland, Dominic
The Heart's Desire - Gayle Wilson   2045

Maury, Justine "Jess"
Dangerous Desire - Ashley Snow   1849

McAllister, Zach
More than Just a Night - Connie Rinehold   1642

McClure, Fox
Yankee's Caress - Terri Valentine   1969

McCullough, Clint
Rebel Seduction - Jane Archer   30

Mont, Darcy
Freedom Flame - Caryn Cameron   279

Montrose, Thomas
Promise Me Heaven - Connie Brockway   221

Moreland, Viscount
Daring Illusion - Christina Cordaire   398

Morgan, Gentry
The Schemers - Lois Wolfe   2059

Morgan, Lewis
My Own True Love - Susan Sizemore   1816

Morgan, Meredith "Merry"
Freedom Flame - Caryn Cameron   279

Morisette, Jeanne
Beyond the Sunrise - Mary Balogh   54

Oakham, Harry
The Doll's House - Evelyn Anthony   25

Praed, Nathaniel
Velvet - Jane Feather   633

Quarternight, West
The Legend of Love - Nan Ryan   1704

St. Claire, Gabrielle
Gabrielle - Leta Tegler   1922

St. John, Morgan "Tristan"
Lord of Enchantment - Suzanne Robinson   1683

Saker, Adam
Beloved Deceiver - Laurie Grant   744

Sterling, Amanda
Love Not a Rebel - Heather Graham   738

Stewart, Savannah
Rebel Wildfire - Barbara Cummings   447

Valcour, Ariane
The Falcon and the Swan - Diane Gates
   Robinson   1680

Varens, Isabelle
Rendezvous - Serena Richards   1629

Von Berg, Maximilian
Promises to Keep - Nina Beaumont   107

Walsh, Hunter
Stolen Ecstasy - Hannah Howell   940

Westcott, Ryan
Midnight in Marrakesh - Meryl Sawyer   1731

Whitbourne, Rafe
Petals in the Storm - Mary Jo Putney   1559

Winford, Charles
Queen of the May - Emily Hendrickson   855

STEP-PARENT

Corbin, Ysabel Belfort
Winter Bride - Iris Johansen   996

Flood-Warnecke, Jessie
Shameless - Suzanne Forster   664

STEWARD

Ramsay, Aurora
The Love Knot - Elisabeth Fairchild   619

Thorne, Byron
Strange Encounter - Sally Wentworth   2002

Weston, Alys "A.E."
The Rake and the Reformer - Mary Jo Putney   1560

STOCK BROKER

Balkan, Dane
Tasmanian Devil - Valerie Parv   1512

Character Description Index

Lamb, Antonia
Seduced - Virginia Henley 873

Trefarron, Payne
The Bridegroom - Carol Jerina 987

Trefarron, Prescott
The Bridegroom - Carol Jerina 987

Trenton, Alyssa
Hidden Touch - Virginia Brown 234

Trenton, Nicholas
Hidden Touch - Virginia Brown 234

UNDERTAKER

Sparrow, Jedwin
Wild Oats - Pamela Morsi 1430

VACATIONER

Campbell, Rorie
A Little Bit of Country - Debbie Macomber 1250

Channing, Nick
That Certain Yearning - Claudia Jameson 975

Cross, Zachary
Trust Me - Jeane Renick 1610

Delaney, Regan
Rough Passage - Paula Detmer Riggs 1635

Harper, Suzi
Timely Matrimony - Kasey Michaels 1371

MacKay, Ewen
The Stormy Petrel - Mary Stewart 1880

Masters, Carolyn
Shadows on a Sunset Sea - Sabine Kells 1050

Shreve, Allison
Trust Me - Jeane Renick 1610

Stewart, Annie
Wish upon a Star - Karen Morrell 1420

West, Diane
That Certain Yearning - Claudia Jameson 975

Wyler, Tom
Embers - Antoinette Stockenberg 1881

VAMPIRE

Beaumondier, Suzanne
Night's Immortal Touch - Cherlyn Jac 960

Dakon
Prince of the Night - Jasmine Cresswell 420

de Morrissey, David
Confession - Lori Herter 878
Eternity - Lori Herter 879
Obsession - Lori Herter 880
Possession - Lori Herter 881

Gale, Nicholas
Prince of Dreams - Susan Krinard 1115

St. Vire, Nicholas
The Vampire Viscount - Karen Harbaugh 803

Tremayne, Aidan
Forever and the Night - Linda Lael Miller 1380

Tresand
A Deeper Hunger - Sabine Kells 1049

Victoire, Darienne
Confession - Lori Herter 878
Eternity - Lori Herter 879
Obsession - Lori Herter 880
Possession - Lori Herter 881

VETERAN

Beaumont, Stephen
Dearest Enemy - Stephanie Bartlett 94

VETERINARIAN

Boyer, Rose
A Christmas Embrace - Ellen Tanner Marsh 1269

Brighton, Theo
Wedding Bell Blues - Alice Sharpe 1774

Davis, Brian
Love on Trial - Wendy Martin 1285

Hernandez, Manny
Stand by Your Man - Kathy Clark 360

Leighton, Deanna
On the Line - Anne Marie Duquette 576

Ryder, Ben
As Sweet as Candy - Linda Varner 1973

Sanchez, Sierra
Warm Creature Comforts - Miriam Pace 1475

VIGILANTE

Brownell, Zeke
The Claim - Lucy Elliot 601

VILLAIN

Chilton, James
The Prince of Midnight - Laura Kinsale 1079

Randolph, Miles
Dream Time - Paris Afton Bonds 182

Russell, Barrett
A Promise Made - Catherine Lanigan 1161

VINTNER

Beaumont, Marti
Bouquet - Shirl Henke 860
Summer Has No Name - Shirl Henke 867

Everly, Sierra
Red Velvet - Barbara Boswell 185

Karlson, Amanda
Sweet Harvest - Lisa Ann Verge 1977

Logan, Mike
Moments - Georgia Bockoven 178

Montoya, Amado
Moments - Georgia Bockoven 178

VOLUNTEER

Metcalf, Cecily
Fire and Rain - Kathleen Eagle 580

Ramsey, Tess
One Man's War - Lindsay McKenna 1318

Sullivan, Mae Belle
What the Lady Wants - Jennifer Crusie 442

WAGONMASTER

Austin, Cord
Orchids in Moonlight - Patricia Hagan 781

D'Arcy, Luc
Night Fire - Cait Logan 1224

Montgomery, Cord
The Turquoise Trail - Susannah Leigh 1182

Quade, Josh
Wildfire - Norah Hess 887

WAITER/WAITRESS

Channing, Amaris
Follow Your Heart - Lynda Trent 1959

Hargreaves, Sara
Flight to Yesterday - Velda Johnston 1010

Hart, Nicole
Naughty Talk - Tiffany White 2014

Randolph, Maggie
For the Thrill - Janis Reams Hudson 949

Stewart, Annie
Wish upon a Star - Karen Morrell 1420

WANDERER

Larren, Coil
Far Star - Anne Avery 38

Santiago, Gabriel
Moriah's Magic - Anne Ladley 1129

WARD

Barclay, Jane
Dark Fires - Brenda Joyce 1024

Campbell, Maura
Highland Rogue - Casey Stuart 1892

Grenville, Shawnalese
Through All Eternity - Brenna Braxton-Barshon 210

MacAfee, Prudence "Angel"
The Passion of an Angel - Kasey Michaels 1370

McGuire, Callie
Cheyenne Surrender - Madeline Baker 40

Monahan, Felicity
Dangerous Joy - Jo Beverley 133

Morris, Brianna
The Captured Heart - Sheila O'Hallion 1458

O'Shea, Mercy
Rogue's Mistress - Eugenia Riley 1637

O'Toole, Triona
Wild Angel - Miriam Minger 1400

Paynter, Bliss
Nightrider - Sandra DuBay 568

Rawlings, Sara
Love a Dark Rider - Shirlee Busbee 258

Scarborough, Emily
Once an Angel - Teresa Medeiros 1341

Simonov, Natasha
A Time for Roses - Elaine Coffman 373

Waverly, Chloe
Christmas Belles - Susan Carroll 322

WARRIOR

Aaren
My Warrior's Heart - Betina M. Krahn 1102

Adam
Chanting the Morning Star - Marylyle Rogers 1691

Alek
The Night Orchid - Patricia Simpson 1804

Alena
A Certain Magic - Kathleen Morgan 1410

Balmaine, Lizanne
Warrior Bride - Tamara Leigh 1184

Nolenberg, Eliza
Heart Song - Barbara Hargis   804

O'Donald, Kathleen Anne Mary
Kathleen O'Donald - Penny Hayes   839

Stewart, Rose
Kathleen O'Donald - Penny Hayes   839

WRITER

Abbot, Joey
His Chariot Awaits - Kasey Michaels   1365

Bliss, Abigail
When Lightning Strikes - Rexanne Becnel   115

Buchanan, Noah
Outlaw Heart - Catherine Palmer   1486

Burnett, Rory
Past Promises - Jill Marie Landis   1146

Cavanaugh, Moriah
Moriah's Magic - Anne Ladley   1129

Chelmsford
A Talent for Trouble - Anne Barbour   82

Corvin, Dane
All the Winters That Have Been - Evan
   Maxwell   1297

Costanza, Alaina "Lainie"
When Lightning Strikes - Kristin Hannah   801

Cox, Hillary
Facets - Barbara Delinsky   499

Davidson, Destiny
The Heart Remembers - Sandra Davidson   469

de Morrissey, David
Confession - Lori Herter   878
Eternity - Lori Herter   879
Obsession - Lori Herter   880
Possession - Lori Herter   881

Dean, Angelica
Breathless - Stella Cameron   284

Desmond, Willy
One Tough Cookie - Carole Dean   491

Emerson, Amanda
Wild Is the Night - Colleen Quinn   1580

Faulkner, Sarah
Fire on the Wind - Barbara Dawson Smith   1830

Fenemore, Rose
The Stormy Petrel - Mary Stewart   1880

Fleming, Harry
Rendezvous - Amanda Quick   1573

Gerard, Simone
Night Vision - Deborah Nicholas   1441

Grant, Jeff
Maybe This Time - Kathleen Gilles Seidel   1766

Halliday, Katie
Wild Western Desire - Kathy Jones   1015

Harris, Bob
The Promise of Summer - Lynn Bulock   251

Hart, Nicole
Naughty Talk - Tiffany White   2014

Holborn, James
A Christmas Keepsake - Janice Bennett   123

Hunt, Molly
Woman Without a Past - Phyllis A. Whitney   2019

James, Derek
Roses for Caroline - Lynn Bulock   252

Lane, Hayden
Remembrance - Jude Deveraux   517

Lederer, Orchid
Blue Orchids - Julia Fenton   637

Logan, Mitch
The Unwitting Witness - Alma Blair   167

MacKenzie, Alexa
Blind Chance - Meryl Sawyer   1729

Malone, Maureen
Once in a Lifetime - Constance O'Day-
   Flannery   1452

Malone, Shae
Darling Deceiver - Lori Copeland   390

Marek, Ty
The Snow Garden - Bethany Campbell   300

McCann, Jason
Mrs. Perfect - Peggy Roberts   1670

McDonald, Sarah
Wild Card - Nancy Hutchinson   955

McGann, Sophie
Wicked Company - Ciji Ware   1991

Mendoza, Andrew
The Firebirds - Beverly Byrne   264

Merrill, Adam
Let Me Count the Ways - Leigh Michaels   1372

Miracle, Amy
Miracle - Deborah Smith   1840

Murphy, Danny
Sungold - Jillian Dagg   450

Powell, Lucy
A Noble Deception - Sara Blayne   174

St. Claire, Maggie
The Spirit Path - Madeline Baker   47

St. James, Matthew
Secret Sins - JoAnn Ross   1698

Summers, Julia
Genuine Lies - Nora Roberts   1667

Thorne, Grayson
Born in Ice - Nora Roberts   1664

Vail, Hester
Passion's Fury - Rita Balkey   52

Wilde, Harry
Timely Matrimony - Kasey Michaels   1371

Winthrop, Paul
Genuine Lies - Nora Roberts   1667

YANKEE

McClure, Fox
Yankee's Caress - Terri Valentine   1969

Michaelson, Callie
And One Wore Gray - Heather Graham   737

YOUNG MAN

Banning, John
Bodie Bride - Isabel Whitfield   2015

Carroll, Eric
No Illusion - Lynette Kent   1058

Duran, Jared
The Golden Mountain - Annalise Sun   1897

Duran, King
The Golden Mountain - Annalise Sun   1897

Fitz William, Galen
Hidden Hearts - Marylyle Rogers   1694

Kincaid, Matthew
The Emerald Tears of Foxfire Manor - Clara
   Wimberly   2048

Lancaster, Cort
Fire and Ice - DeLoras Scott   1750

MacKenzie, Wade
Never on Sundae - Rita Rainville   1586

Taggart, Coltrane "Trane"
Southern Seduction - Thea Devine   522

Tregaran, John
The Legacy of Tregaran - Mary Lide   1186

YOUNG WOMAN

Amicia of Wryborn, Lady
Hidden Hearts - Marylyle Rogers   1694

Anderson, Rebecca
Sweet Lullaby - Lorraine Heath   843

Arnold, Althea
The Firelands - Karen Harper   811

Ashford, Sara
Crossing Eden - Emma Gordon   735

Ashley, Linnea
A Special License - Kathleen Elliott   604

Belmont, Ariana
A Dangerous Longing - Veronica Sattler   1720

Best, Meggie
Marrying Stone - Pamela Morsi   1428

Blue, Aubrey
Under the Desert Moon - Marsha Canham   308

Branson, Leonida
Wild Splendor - Cassie Edwards   595

Brennan, Shannon
Pirate's Wild Embrace - Linda Windsor   2049

Brixton, Angelica "Angel"
Cherish the Night - Penelope Neri   1437

Broderick, Maddie
Bold Montana Bride - Karen Bale   50

Brodie, Sine Catriona
Silver Flame - Hannah Howell   939

Bruder, Tulsy Mae
Runabout - Pamela Morsi   1429

Cadwalder, Melissa
Web of Loving Lies - Barbara Leigh   1177

Caine, Charity
Oklahoma Angel - Phoebe Fitzjames   649

Calwalder, Beth Ann
Web of Loving Lies - Barbara Leigh   1177

Carlyle, Genevieve "Jenny"
Odessa Gold - Linda Shaw   1776

Caslar, Jill
More than You Dreamed - Kathleen Gilles
   Seidel   1767

Chadwick, Flame
Flame - Evelyn Rogers   1687

Colton, Jessica
Apache Legacy - Janis Reams Hudson   947

Cribbage, Barbara
Mutual Consent - Gayle Buck   247

Davidson, Starr
Hold Back the Night - Sandra Steffen   1873

Delacour, Raven
Rough and Tender - Selena MacPherson   1258

Delaney, Jenny Lynn
Forever in His Arms - Penelope Neri   1439

Desmond, Sally
A Handful of Dreams - Barbara Hazard   841

Devon, Annalise
This Fiery Splendor - Christine Monson   1405

Author Index

This index alphabetically lists authors of books featured or mentioned in entries in the main section of this book. For each author, the titles of books written and entry numbers are shown. A bold entry number indicates a featured main entry under the title and author in question; lightface numbers refer to entries for other books that mention the title in question under the rubric "Other books you might like."

A

Adams, Alina
The Fictitious Marquis **1**

Adams, Joanne Z.
Intimate Connections **2**, 13, 193, 228, 402, 761, 996, 1058, 1319, 2014

Adamson, Mary Jo
Bridey's Mountain **3**

Adamson, Yvonne
Bridey's Mountain **3**, 155, 163, 164, 514, 621, 820

Adler, Elizabeth
Fortune Is a Woman **4**, 257, 264, 460, 605, 1081, 1870

Aiken, Jenny
Love Evergreen **5**, 1485, 1498, 2073

Aiken, Joan
A Cluster of Separate Sparks 166, 597, 964, 1220, 1880
The Five-Minute Marriage 62, 124, 137, 139, 275, 586, 855, 1362
If I Were You 222, 942
The Smile of a Stranger 1466

Aldridge, Sarah
All True Lovers 1057
Keep to Me, Stranger **6**, 612, 1034, 1035, 1036
The Latecomer 1035
Michaela **7**, 658, 826
Tottie: A Tale of the Sixties 1057

Alers, Rochelle
Holiday Cheer **8**

Alexander, Thelma
True Texas Love 1734

Algermissen, Jo Ann
Golden Bird **9**, 1647, 1797

Allen, Charlotte Vale
Pieces of Dreams 1737

Alsobrook, Rosalyn
Elusive Caress **10**, 603, 1150, 1169
Endless Seduction **11**, 794
Passion's Bold Fire **12**, 560, 730

Alter, Judy
Mattie 1865

Alvarez, Gloria
Heart Waves **13**, 622, 653, 2014

Amarillas, Susan
Snow Angel **14**

Anderson, Blaine
Destiny's Kiss 439
Heartspell **15**
Love's Sweet Captive 385, 772, 1340

Anderson, Catherine
Cheyenne Amber **16**, 20, 180, 660, 1096, 1391, 1510, 1866
Comanche Heart **17**, 41, 415, 1593, 1937
Comanche Magic 1391
Comanche Moon **18**, 1287, 1321, 1838, 1913, 2042
Coming Up Roses 20, 1096, 1510, 1745
Indigo Blue **19**, 909
Tall, Dark, and Dangerous **20**, 715, 2063
Three Weddings and a Kiss **2063**

Anderson, Lee
Dangerous Bequest **21**, 596, 836

Anderson, Susan
Shadow Dance 1111, 1286, 1875, 2065, 2069
Silversword **1588**

Ankrum, Barbara
Chase the Fire **22**, 935
Renegade Bride **23**, 1508, 1811, 1997
Renegade's Kiss **24**, 94, 217, 289, 1347

Anthony, Evelyn
The Doll's House **25**, 1310
Mission to Malaspiga 1220
A Place to Hide 2036
The Scarlet Thread **26**, 374, 1539
The Tamarind Seed 598, 1305

Archer, Catherine
Rose Among Thorns **27**, 973, 1909

Archer, Ellen
Under His Spell **28**, 90

Archer, Jane
Bayou Passion **29**, 1300, 1678
Rebel Seduction **30**, 1918
Wild Wind **31**

Armstrong, Lindsay
The Marrying Game 252

Arnston, Harrison
Trade-Off 720

Ashford, Jane
The Bluestocking 1054, 1472, 1473

Ashley, Mellyora
A Lady in Disguise **32**

Ashton, Mollie
Terms of Surrender **33**, 1061, 1629, 1760, 1943, 1945

Attalla, Kathryn
Homeward Bound **34**, 573, 1058

Auel, Jean M.
Clan of the Cave Bear 375, 376, 1313, 1700, 1755, 1756, 1787, 2057
The Mammoth Hunters 1755, 1756

August, Elizabeth
Pirate's Bride **35**, 1904
The Virgin Wife **36**, 194, 537, 1441, 2078

Austell, Diane
Lights Along the Shore 489, 541

Avery, Anne
All's Fair **37**, 473
Enchanted Crossings **42**
Far Star **38**

Aylworth, Susan
Ride the Rainbow Home **39**, 691

B

Baker, Madeline
Cheyenne Surrender **40**
Comanche Flame 17, **41**, 380, 717, 1215, 1233
Enchanted Crossings **42**, 144, 715, 907, 1779, 1954
Forbidden Fires **43**, 181, 659, 947, 1859, 1937
Lacey's Way **44**, 145, 559, 593, 594, 698, 1594
Midnight Fire **45**, 717

Prairie Heat 23, **46**, 380, 507, 1124, 1373, 1997
Secrets of the Heart **715**
The Spirit Path **47**, 469, 1173
Warrior's Lady **48**, 1410
A Whisper on the Wind 18, **49**, 505, 583, 607, 1455, 2042

Bakker, Kit
Julianne's Song 899, 1239, 1442

Bale, Karen
Bold Montana Bride **50**, 1427

Balkey, Rita
Midnight Ecstasy **51**
Passion's Fury **52**, 346, 1129, 1265, 1456, 1577, 1580, 1710

Ball, Donna
The Sensation **651**

Ball, Margaret
Stolen Dreams **1238**

Balogh, Mary
Angel Christmas **53**, 529, 760, 1256, 1330
Beyond the Sunrise **54**, 633, 634, 989, 1559, 1572, 1942, 2038
Christmas Beau **55**, 132, 139, 267, 322, 1056
Christmas Belle **56**, 64, 65, 382, 524, 525, 584, 1056, 1534, 1844
Dancing with Clara **57**, 620, 1158
Deceived **58**, 324, 373, 404, 1368, 1395, 1831
Heartless **59**
Lord Carew's Bride **60**
The Notorious Rake **61**, 338, 339, 340, 1609, 1891
Promise of Spring **62**, 586, 852, 903, 1052, 1070, 1170, 1197
A Regency Christmas II **63**
A Regency Christmas VI **64**, 382
A Regency Christmas VII 53, **65**
A Regency Valentine **66**, 922, 1170
The Secret Pearl **67**, 82, 1037, 1099, 1104
The Snow Angel **68**, 123, 131, 132, 186, 587, 1159, 1197, 1553, 1614, 1722, 1726
Tangled **69**

Barbieri, Elaine
Midnight Rogue **70**

Author Index

Z

Title Index

This index alphabetically lists all titles featured or mentioned in entries in the main section of this book. Each title is followed by the name of the main author and the entry number(s) of the entry or entries where the title wil be found. A bold entry number indicates that the title in question is a featured main entry; lightface numbers refer to entries for other books that mention the title in question under the rubric "Other books you might like."

Cotillion
Heyer, Georgette 348, 752

The Count of Monte Cristo
Dumas, Alexandre 1368

The Counterfeit Gentleman
Dolan, Charlotte Louise **543**, 617,
1283

Counterfeit Heart
Malcolm, Anthea **1264**, 1336, 1355,
1625, 1725

Counterfeit Lady
Vivian, Daisy 222, 1334, 1845

Counterpoint
Holland, Isabelle 918, 1043

A Countess Below Stairs
Ibbotson, Eva 400

Country Bride
Macomber, Debbie 251

Country Dance
Westhaven, Margaret **2005**, 2055

Country Kiss
Harlow, Sharon 678, **805**, 1222,
2034

Courtesan
Haeger, Diane **775**

Courting Catherine
Roberts, Nora 622, 1249, 1775,
1973

Courting Miss Hattie
Morsi, Pamela 290, 429, 561, 680,
683, 701, 798, 915, 1006, 1015,
1293, 1349, **1425**, 1469, 1482,
1484, 1718, 1938, 2006

The Court's Illusion
Jarman, Rosemary 1167

The Courtship of Peggy McCoy
Sipherd, Ray 176, 401, 1499, **1815**

Cousin Cecelia
Smith, Joan 903, 1616, **1843**, 1877,
2012

Cousin Kate
Heyer, Georgette 1037, 1065, 1890

A Cousinly Connexion
Simonson, Sheila 79, 80, 591, 1054,
1069, 1198, 1337, 1389, 1407,
1518, 1723, 1899, 1980

Cowboy Cop
Lee, Rachel 955, **1172**, 1477

*The Cowboy, the Baby, and the
Runaway Bride*
Longford, Lindsay 1255

Creole Fires
Martin, Kat 770, 1088, 1175, 1271,
1274

Creole Nights
Martin, Deborah 141, 481, 770,
1047, **1271**

Crescent City
Plain, Belva 1808

Crime of Passion
Hooper, Kay 249, 458, **921**, 1465,
2019, 2067, 2075

The Crimson Crown
Layton, Edith **1167**, 1396, 1682,
1854

The Crimson Roses of Fountain Court
Darty, Peggy **465**, 1640, 1717

Crocodile on the Sandbank
Peters, Elizabeth 249, 1054, 1146,
1265, 1304, 1571

Crooked Hearts
Gaffney, Patricia 430, **676**

Crossing Eden
Gordon, Emma **735**

Crossings
Steel, Danielle 923, 1636

Crown in Candlelight
Jarman, Rosemary 1167, 1825

Crown of Dreams
Cates, Kimberly **328**, 1941

Crown of Mist
Cates, Kimberly 631, 1892, 2001

A Cry in the Night
Clark, Mary Higgins 997

The Crying Child
Michaels, Barbara 2018

Crystal Days
Douglas, Carole Nelson 249, **554**

Crystal Fire
Morgan, Kathleen **1412**

Crystal Nights
Douglas, Carole Nelson **555**

Crystal Rapture
Edwards, Sarah 263, 1449, 1457,
1597, 2049

Crystal Singer
McCaffrey, Anne 729, 1211, 1412,
1684

Curious Wine
Forrest, Katherine V. 826, 1036

The Curse of the Pharaohs
Peters, Elizabeth 268, 1631

Curtain
Corda, Michael **397**, 681

Cutting Edge
Chance, Lisbeth 921, 1279

Cypress Moon
Rowe, Myra 332, **1699**, 1918

D

Daddy
Steel, Danielle 499, **1869**

The Daddy List
Mackenzie, Myrna 1255

Daddy-Long-Legs
Webster, Jean 460

Daggers of Gold
Deauville, Katherine 208, 306, **494**,
1345

Dakota Dawn
Ransom, Dana 638, 885, 893, 948,
1290, **1589**

Dakota Desire
Ransom, Dana **1590**

Dakota Destiny
Ransom, Dana 148, 676, 824, 905,
1591

Dakota Flame
Pelton, Sonya T. 152

Damsel in Distress
Drake, Shannon **564**, 1154, 1757

Dance of Deception
Davis, Suzannah **479**

Dance with Fire
Redd, JoAnne **1607**, 2030

Dance with the Devil
Litton, Pamela 296, 1157, **1215**,
1754

Dancer of Dreams
Matthews, Patricia 108

Dances with Wolves
Blake, Michael 47, 149, 282, 506,
580, 595, 638, 665, 1290

Dancing at Midnight
Quinn, Julia **1581**

Dancing in the Aisles
Blair, Kathryn 984

Dancing on Snowflakes
Bonander, Jane **180**, 571, 1142

Dancing with Clara
Balogh, Mary **57**, 620, 1158

Danger in Paradise
Faith, Barbara 1122, 2064

Dangerous
Quick, Amanda 138, 274, 1339,
1566, 1599, 1758

Dangerous Bequest
Anderson, Lee **21**, 596, 836

A Dangerous Charade
Barbour, Anne **78**

Dangerous Charade
Harper, Madeline **813**

Dangerous Deceptions
Yorke, Erin 730, 1800, 2075, **2079**

Dangerous Desire
Snow, Ashley 364, 627, 1180, 1675,
1849

A Dangerous Devotion
Kyle, Barbara **1119**, 2028

Dangerous Diversions
Porter, Margaret Evans 606, **1534**

Dangerous Flirtation
Fielding, Liz 119

Dangerous Illusions
Scott, Amanda 16, **1745**

Dangerous Joy
Beverley, Jo **133**

A Dangerous Longing
Sattler, Veronica 277, 278, 1317,
1720

Dangerous Masquerade
Kihlstrom, April 78, 398, **1065**,
1075, 1353, 1951

Dangerous Odyssey
Edwards, Jane 452, **597**, 964

A Dangerous Temptation
Kyle, Barbara 2028

Dangerous to Love
Thornton, Elizabeth **1941**

Danger's Kiss
Michels, Christine 898

Daniel and Esther
Raymond, Patrick **1603**

Daniel's Bride
Miller, Linda Lael 288, 344, 649,
1062, 1064, **1378**, 1956

The Daring
Hagan, Patricia 739, **777**

Daring Illusion
Cordaire, Christina **398**, 1075

Dark Cries of Gray Oaks
Karr, Lee 198, 439, 726, **1043**,
1513, 2018, 2048

Dark Fires
Joyce, Brenda 286, 411, 636, 873,
1024, 1288, 1637, 1818, 1889

Dark Illusion
Wilson, Patricia 119

Dark Inheritance
Salisbury, Carola 1358, 1513

Dark Journey
Canfield, Sandra **304**, 664, 774,
1226, 1777

Dark Moon, Lost Lady
Lee, Elsie 466, 919, 1043

Dark Moon Rising
James, Dana 672

Dark Paradise
Hoag, Tami 85, **898**, 920, 931, 933,
955, 1493, 1650

Dark Renegade
Scott, Theresa **1756**

The Dark Shore
Howatch, Susan 465

The Dark Side of Paradise
Blair, Alma **166**, 708, 1218, 1219,
1773, 1880

The Dark Towers of Trelochlen
Payes, Rachel Cosgrove **1513**, 1521

Dark Whispers
Rogers, Marylyle 183, 494, 926,
1028, 1037, **1692**

Darkest Heart
Joyce, Brenda 317, 482, 716, 948,
1025, 1461, 1704

Darkness at Cottonwood Hall
Sanders, Madelyn **1717**

Darkness Falls
Schneider, Joyce Anne 2050

Darkwater
Eden, Dorothy 466, 2048

K

Kansas Kiss
Dorsey, Christine   153, 197, 225, 226, **550**, 736, 737, 1300, 1680

Kate and the Soldier
Barbour, Anne   **79**, 591

Katherine
Seton, Anya   775, 1012, 1119, 1825

Kathleen O'Donald
Hayes, Penny   **839**

Keep to Me, Stranger
Aldridge, Sarah   **6**, 612, 1034, 1035, 1036

Keeper of the Dawn
Williamson, Penelope   1194

Keeper of the Dream
Williamson, Penelope   116, 476, 495, 694, 991, 1229, 1235, 1262, 1323, 1691, 1733, **2037**

Keeper of the Heart
Lindsey, Johanna   48, 302, **1202**

Keepers of the Misty Time
Rowe, Patricia   **1700**, 1756

Keeping Faith
Kane, Kathleen   **1039**, 1783, 1791

The Keepsake
Rogers, Marylyle   **1695**

Kentucky Bride
Hess, Norah   309, 478, 833, **885**, 938, 1361, 2022

Kentucky Bride
Howell, Hannah   **938**

Kid Calhoun
Johnston, Joan   877, **1006**, 1216, 1641

Kiley's Storm
Elizabeth, Suzanne   **599**

Killashandra
McCaffrey, Anne   302, 729, 1211, 1412, 1685

Kindred Spirits
Temple, Sarah   220

King of Hearts
Kingsley, Katherine   618, 856, 913, **1069**

King of Swords
McKenna, Lindsay   451, 1276, 1288, **1316**, 1559

The King of the Castle
Holt, Victoria   465, 466

King of the Pirates
Holm, Stef Ann   73, 326, **912**

King Solomon's Mines
Haggard, H. Rider   142

Kingdom of Shadows
Erskine, Barbara   484, **614**, 729, 1050, 1824, 2007

The King's Bed
Barnes, Margaret Campbell   118

King's Ransom
Palmer, Diana   464, **1489**

Kiss an Angel
Phillips, Susan Elizabeth   213, 442, 1113

Kiss in the Dark
Sawyer, Meryl   85, 933, **1730**, 1948

A Kiss in the Night
Horsman, Jennifer   **927**, 998

Kiss Me Forever
Smith, Bobbi   **1837**, 1918

Kiss of Bliss
Monroe, Carolyn   450, 823, **1403**, 1522

Kiss of the Night Wind
Taylor, Janelle   363, 693, 713, 719, 759, 1044, 1237, **1916**, 1950, 1952, 1965, 2020

Kiss of the Shadow Man
Shayne, Maggie   304, 920, 1226, **1778**, 1986

Kissed
Crosby, Tanya Anne   **432**

The Kissing Bough
Smith, Joan   382, 524, 1352, 1661, **1844**

Knight and Day
Buck, Carole   **244**, 728, 1488, 1610

A Knight in Shining Armor
Deveraux, Jude   123, 124, 126, 127, 305, 422, **515**, 614, 673, 674, 1093, 1094, 1097, 1105, 1192, 1210, 1449, 1455, 1483, 1645, 1646, 1802, 1805, 1817, 1824, 1911, 2007, 2010, 2062

Knight of Fire
Drake, Shannon   405, **566**, 1028, 1184, 1209, 1547, 1826

Knight's Caress
Vinet, Lynette   183, 440, 1184, **1983**

Knight's Desire
Hill, Judith   113, 287, **890**, 1459, 2061

Knight's Lady
Barclay, Suzanne   **83**, 1309

The Knowing Crystal
Morgan, Kathleen   327, 1117, **1417**, 1684, 1856

L

Lace
Conran, Shirley   1506, 1867

Lacey's Way
Baker, Madeline   **44**, 145, 559, 593, 594, 698, 1594

Lacy
Palmer, Diana   **1490**, 1738, 1850, 2073

The Ladies of Missalonghi
McCullough, Colleen   520, 798, 1243, 1504

Lady Alex's Gamble
Richardson, Evelyn   80, 619, 853, 874, 1596, **1633**

The Lady and the Laird
Seger, Maura   28, 1005, 1135, 1747, **1761**, 1887

The Lady and the Outlaw
Compton, Katherine   **380**

The Lady and the Rake
Dunn, Carola   **574**

The Lady and the Wolf
Beard, Julie   **105**

Lady Barbara's Dilemma
Farrell, Marjorie   620, **623**

Lady Defiant
Robinson, Suzanne   775, **1681**, 1963

Lady Diamond
Halldorson, Phyllis   835

Lady Elizabeth's Comet
Simonson, Sheila   187, 854, 857, 1051, 1054, 1355, 1519, 1567, 1571, 1573, 1596, 1631

Lady Fortescue Steps Out
Chesney, Marion   913, 1069

Lady Fortune
Byers, Cordia   140, **263**, 593, 594, 965, 1098, 1243, 1385, 1432, 1446, 1448, 1449, 1457, 1478, 1515, 1575, 1597, 1695, 1699, 1795, 2049

Lady Gallant
Robinson, Suzanne   107, 633, **1682**, 1827

Lady in Black
Dodd, Christina   36, 194, **537**, 723, 1348

A Lady in Disguise
Ashley, Mellyora   **32**

Lady in Green
Metzger, Barbara   78, 81, 398, 606, 850, 1075, 1159, 1283, **1353**, 1634

Lady Legend
Camp, Deborah   296, 415, 790, 1157, 1215, 1315, 1754

Lady Leprechaun
McRae, Melinda   **1336**

Lady Lu
Kidd, Elisabeth   1899

Lady Lucinde's Locket
Saunders, Irene   54, 248, 1355, **1723**, 1725

Lady Maryann's Dilemma
Hocker, Karla   269, 623, **903**, 1247

Lady of Conquest
Medeiros, Teresa   743, 773, 889, 1066, 1079, **1340**, 1345, 2056

Lady of Lochabar
Ramirez, Jeanette Baker   1272, **1587**, 2026

Lady of Quality
Heyer, Georgette   248, 389, 575, 1338, 1567, 1843, 1877

The Lady of the Labyrinth
Llewellyn, Carolyn   1220

Lady of the Moors
Petty, Mary Ellen   1513, **1521**

A Lady of the West
Howard, Linda   3, 72, 95, 154, 163, 311, 486, 512, 736, 778, **934**, 1392, 1468, 1486, 1492, 1544, 1593, 1622, 1642, 1922, 2040

Lady Pamela
Darcy, Clare   137, 787, 1241, 1338, 2055

Lady Rogue
Kramer, Kathryn   234, 339, 913, 1020, **1106**, 1179, 1847, 1876, 2012

Lady Sarah's Charade
Richards-Akers, Nancy   **1631**, 1846

The Lady Says No
Estrada, Rita Clay   1920

Lady Vengeance
Eagle, Sarah   324, **585**

Lady's Choice
Krentz, Jayne Ann   313, 1813

Lady's Choice
Nelson, Judith   383, 509, 1247, 1264, 1354, **1434**, 1742

Lament for a Lost Lover
Carr, Philippa   1168, 1533, 2001

Land of Enchantment
Palmer, Catherine   1968

The Last Bachelor
Krahn, Betina M.   704, 874, 1005, 1090, **1099**, 1900, 1938

Last Chance
Landis, Jill Marie   **1145**

The Last Lord
Pryce, Melinda   383, 961, 1530, **1557**

The Last of the Winter Roses
Savery, Jeanne   267, 683, 1159, 1353, 1420, 1634, **1726**, 1846, 1961

The Last Summer of Innocence
Sole, Linda   **1850**

The Last Viking Queen
Taylor, Janelle   **1917**

The Last Waltz
Zaroulis, Nancy   1809

A Lasting Fire
Byrne, Beverly   **266**, 866, 2024

The Latecomer
Aldridge, Sarah   1035

Laurel
Greenwood, Leigh   **758**

Lavender Flame
Stratford, Karen   497, 1459, 1617, **1886**, 2004, 2009

Lavender Lady
Dunn, Carola   852, 1198, 1407, 1989

The Law of Love
Schroeder, Martha   **1734**

Lawless
Potter, Patricia   656, 1491, **1540**

Lawless
Roberts, Nora   713

Title Index